ALTERNATE EDITION

D1782791

Fundamentals of
Corporate Finance

THE McGRAW-HILL/IRWIN SERIES IN FINANCE, INSURANCE AND REAL ESTATE

Consulting Editor Stephen A. Ross
Franco Modigliani Professor of Finance and Economics
Sloan School of Management, Massachusetts Institute of Technology

Financial Management

Adair
Excel Applications for Corporate Finance
First Edition

Benninga and Sarig
Corporate Finance: A Valuation Approach

Block and Hirt
Foundations of Financial Management
Eleventh Edition

Brealey, Myers, and Allen
Principles of Corporate Finance
Eighth Edition

Brealey, Myers, and Marcus
Fundamentals of Corporate Finance
Fourth Edition

Brooks
FinGame Online 4.0

Bruner
Case Studies in Finance: Managing for Corporate Value Creation
Fourth Edition

Chew
The New Corporate Finance: Where Theory Meets Practice
Third Edition

Chew and Gillan
Corporate Governance at the Crossroads: A Book of Readings
First Edition

DeMello
Cases in Finance
Second Edition

Grinblatt and Titman
Financial Markets and Corporate Strategy
Second Edition

Helfert
Techniques of Financial Analysis: A Guide to Value Creation
Eleventh Edition

Higgins
Analysis for Financial Management
Seventh Edition

Kester, Ruback, and Tufano
Case Problems in Finance
Twelfth Edition

Ross, Westerfield, and Jaffe
Corporate Finance
Seventh Edition

Ross, Westerfield, and Jordan
Essentials of Corporate Finance
Fourth Edition

Ross, Westerfield, and Jordan
Fundamentals of Corporate Finance
Seventh Edition

Smith
The Modern Theory of Corporate Finance
Second Edition

White
Financial Analysis with an Electronic Calculator
Fifth Edition

Investments

Bodie, Kane, and Marcus
Essentials of Investments
Fifth Edition

Bodie, Kane, and Marcus
Investments
Sixth Edition

Cohen, Zinbarg, and Zeikel
Investment Analysis and Portfolio Management
Fifth Edition

Corrado and Jordan
Fundamentals of Investments: Valuation and Management
Third Edition

Farrell
Portfolio Management: Theory and Applications
Second Edition

Hirt and Block
Fundamentals of Investment Management
Eighth Edition

Financial Institutions and Markets

Cornett and Saunders
Fundamentals of Financial Institutions Management

Rose and Hudgins
Bank Management and Financial Services
Sixth Edition

Rose and Marquis
Money and Capital Markets: Financial Institutions and Instruments in a Global Marketplace
Ninth Edition

Santomero and Babbel
Financial Markets, Instruments, and Institutions
Second Edition

Saunders and Cornett
Financial Institutions Management: A Risk Management Approach
Fifth Edition

Saunders and Cornett
Financial Markets and Institutions: A Modern Perspective
Second Edition

International Finance

Beim and Calomiris
Emerging Financial Markets

Eun and Resnick
International Financial Management
Third Edition

Kuemmerle
Case Studies in International Entrepreneurship: Managing and Financing Ventures in the Global Economy
First Edition

Levich
International Financial Markets: Prices and Policies
Second Edition

Real Estate

Brueggeman and Fisher
Real Estate Finance and Investments
Twelfth Edition

Corgel, Ling, and Smith
Real Estate Perspectives: An Introduction to Real Estate
Fourth Edition

Ling and Archer
Real Estate Principles: A Value Approach
First Edition

Financial Planning and Insurance

Allen, Melone, Rosenbloom, and Mahoney
Pension Planning: Pension, Profit-Sharing, and Other Deferred Compensation Plans
Ninth Edition

Crawford
Life and Health Insurance Law
Eighth Edition (LOMA)

Harrington and Niehaus
Risk Management and Insurance
Second Edition

Hirsch
Casualty Claim Practice
Sixth Edition

Kapoor, Dlabay, and Hughes
Focus on Personal Finance: An active approach to help you develop successful financial skills
First Edition

Kapoor, Dlabay, and Hughes
Personal Finance
Seventh Edition

Williams, Smith, and Young
Risk Management and Insurance
Eighth Edition

ALTERNATE EDITION

SEVENTH EDITION

Fundamentals of Corporate Finance

Stephen A. Ross
Massachusetts Institute of Technology

Randolph W. Westerfield
University of Southern California

Bradford D. Jordan
University of Kentucky

McGraw-Hill Irwin

Boston Burr Ridge, IL Dubuque, IA Madison, WI New York San Francisco St. Louis
Bangkok Bogotá Caracas Kuala Lumpur Lisbon London Madrid Mexico City
Milan Montreal New Delhi Santiago Seoul Singapore Sydney Taipei Toronto

The McGraw-Hill Companies

McGraw-Hill Irwin

FUNDAMENTALS OF CORPORATE FINANCE

Published by McGraw-Hill/Irwin, a business unit of The McGraw-Hill Companies, Inc., 1221 Avenue of the Americas, New York, NY, 10020.

This book is printed on acid-free paper.

1 2 3 4 5 6 7 8 9 0 VNH/VNH 0 9 8 7 6 5

ISBN 0-07-299159-3 (standard edition)
ISBN 0-07-299121-6 (alternate edition)
ISBN 0-07-299158-5 (annotated instructor's edition)

Publisher: *Stephen M. Patterson*
Senior sponsoring editor: *Michele Janicek*
Developmental editor: *Jennifer V. Rizzi*
Executive marketing manager: *Rhonda Seelinger*
Lead producer, Media technology: *Kai Chiang*
Senior project manager: *Christine A. Vaughan*
Senior production supervisor: *Rose Hepburn*
Director of design BR: *Keith J. McPherson*
Senior supplement producer: *Carol Loreth*
Media project manager: *Lynn M. Bluhm*
Developer, Media technology: *Brian Nacik*
Interior design: *Maureen McCutcheon*
Cover image: *Sharon Hoogstraten*
Typeface: *10/12 Times Roman*
Compositor: *Interactive Composition Corporation*
Printer: *Von Hoffmann Corporation*

Library of Congress Cataloging-in-Publication Data

Ross, Stephen A.
Fundamentals of corporate finance / Stephen A. Ross, Randolph W. Westerfield, Bradford D. Jordan.—7th ed.
p. cm.—(The McGraw-Hill/Irwin series in finance, insurance, and real estate)
Includes index.
ISBN 0-07-299159-3 (standard ed. : alk. paper)—ISBN 0-07-299121-6 (alternate ed. : alk. paper)
1. Corporations—Finance. I. Westerfield, Randolph. II. Jordan, Bradford D. III. Title.
IV. Series.
HG4026.R677 2006
658.15—dc22

2004059733

www.mhhe.com

To our families and friends with love and gratitude.

S.A.R. R.W.W. B.D.J.

About the Authors

Stephen A. Ross

Sloan School of Management, Franco Modigliani Professor of Finance and Economics, Massachusetts Institute of Technology

Stephen A. Ross is the Franco Modigliani Professor of Finance and Economics at the Sloan School of Management, Massachusetts Institute of Technology. One of the most widely published authors in finance and economics, Professor Ross is recognized for his work in developing the Arbitrage Pricing Theory and his substantial contributions to the discipline through his research in signaling, agency theory, option pricing, and the theory of the term structure of interest rates, among other topics. A past president of the American Finance Association, he currently serves as an associate editor of several academic and practitioner journals. He is a trustee of CalTech and a director of the College Retirement Equity Fund (CREF) and Freddie Mac. He is also the co-chairman of Roll and Ross Asset Management Corporation.

Randolph W. Westerfield

Marshall School of Business, University of Southern California

Randolph W. Westerfield is Dean Emeritus of the University of Southern California's Marshall School of Business and is the Charles B. Thornton Professor of Finance.

He came to USC from the Wharton School, University of Pennsylvania, where he was the chairman of the finance department and a member of the finance faculty for 20 years. He is a member of several public company boards of directors including Health Management Associates, Inc., William Lyons Homes, and the Nicholas Applegate growth fund. His areas of expertise include corporate financial policy, investment management, and stock market price behavior.

Bradford D. Jordan

Gatton College of Business and Economics, Professor of Finance and holder of the Richard W. and Janis H. Furst Endowed Chair in Finance, University of Kentucky

Bradford D. Jordan is Professor of Finance and holder of the Richard W. and Janis H. Furst Endowed Chair in Finance at the University of Kentucky. He has a long-standing interest in both applied and theoretical issues in corporate finance and has extensive experience teaching all levels of corporate finance and financial management policy. Professor Jordan has published numerous articles on issues such as cost of capital, capital structure, and the behavior of security prices. He is a past president of the Southern Finance Association, and he is coauthor (with Charles J. Corrado) of *Fundamentals of Investments: Valuation and Management,* 3e, a leading investments text, also published by McGraw-Hill/Irwin.

Preface from the Authors

When the three of us decided to write a book, we were united by one strongly held principle: Corporate finance should be developed in terms of a few integrated, powerful ideas. We believed that the subject was all too often presented as a collection of loosely related topics, unified primarily by virtue of being bound together in one book, and we thought there must be a better way.

One thing we knew for certain was that we didn't want to write a "me-too" book. So, with a lot of help, we took a hard look at what was truly important and useful. In doing so, we were led to eliminate topics of dubious relevance, downplay purely theoretical issues, and minimize the use of extensive and elaborate calculations to illustrate points that are either intuitively obvious or of limited practical use.

As a result of this process, three basic themes became our central focus in writing *Fundamentals of Corporate Finance:*

An Emphasis on Intuition

We always try to separate and explain the principles at work on a common sense, intuitive level before launching into any specifics. The underlying ideas are discussed first in very general terms and then by way of examples that illustrate in more concrete terms how a financial manager might proceed in a given situation.

A Unified Valuation Approach

We treat net present value (NPV) as the basic concept underlying corporate finance. Many texts stop well short of consistently integrating this important principle. The most basic and important notion, that NPV represents the excess of market value over cost, often is lost in an overly mechanical approach that emphasizes computation at the expense of comprehension. In contrast, every subject we cover is firmly rooted in valuation, and care is taken throughout to explain how particular decisions have valuation effects.

A Managerial Focus

Students shouldn't lose sight of the fact that financial management concerns management. We emphasize the role of the financial manager as decision maker, and we stress the need for managerial input and judgment. We consciously avoid "black box" approaches to finance, and, where appropriate, the approximate, pragmatic nature of financial analysis is made explicit, possible pitfalls are described, and limitations are discussed.

In retrospect, looking back to our 1991 first edition IPO, we had the same hopes and fears as any entrepreneurs. How would we be received in the market? At the time, we had no idea that just 14 years later, we would be working on a seventh edition. We certainly never dreamed that in those years we would work with friends and colleagues from around the world to create country-specific Australian, Canadian, and South African editions, an International edition, Chinese, French, Polish, and Spanish language editions, and an entirely separate book, *Essentials of Corporate Finance,* now in its fourth edition.

Today, as we prepare to once more enter the market, our goal is to stick with the basic principles that have brought us this far. However, based on an enormous amount of feedback we have received from you and your colleagues, we have made this edition and its package even *more flexible* than previous editions. We offer flexibility in coverage, by continuing to offer a variety of editions, and flexibility in pedagogy, by providing a wide variety of features in the book to help students to learn about corporate finance. We also provide flexibility in package options by offering the most extensive collection of teaching, learning, and technology aids of any corporate finance text. Whether you use just the textbook, or the book in conjunction with our other products, we believe you will find a combination with this edition that will meet your current as well as your changing needs.

Stephen A. Ross
Randolph W. Westerfield
Bradford D. Jordan

Coverage

This book was designed and developed explicitly for a first course in business or corporate finance, for both finance majors and non-majors alike. In terms of background or prerequisites, the book is nearly self-contained, assuming some familiarity with basic algebra and accounting concepts, while still reviewing important accounting principles very early on. The organization of this text has been developed to give instructors the flexibility they need.

Just to get an idea of the breadth of coverage in the seventh edition of *Fundamentals*, the following grid presents, for each chapter, some of the most significant new features as well as a few selected chapter highlights. Of course, in every chapter, opening vignettes, boxed features, in-chapter illustrated examples using real companies, and end-of-chapter material have been thoroughly updated as well.

Chapters	Selected Topics of Interest	Benefits to You
>> PART ONE Overview of Corporate Finance		
Chapter 1 Introduction to Corporate Finance	Goal of the firm and agency problems.	Stresses value creation as the most fundamental aspect of management and describes agency issues that can arise.
	Ethics, financial management, and executive compensation.	Brings in real-world issues concerning conflicts of interest and current controversies surrounding ethical conduct and management pay.
Chapter 2 Financial Statements, Taxes, and Cash Flow	*New mini-case:* Cash Flows and Financial Statements at Sunset Boards, Inc.	New case written for this edition reinforces key cash flow concepts in a small-business setting.
	Cash flow vs. earnings.	Clearly defines cash flow and spells out the differences between cash flow and earnings.
	Market values vs. book values.	Emphasizes the relevance of market values over book values.
>> PART TWO Financial Statements and Long-Term Financial Planning		
Chapter 3 Working with Financial Statements	*New section:* Expanded Du Pont analysis.	New section expands the basic Du Pont equation to better explore the interrelationships between operating and financial performance.
	New material: Du Pont analysis for real companies using data from S&P *Market Insight.*	New analysis shows students how to get and use real-world data, thereby applying key chapter ideas.
	Ratio and financial statement analysis using smaller firm data.	Uses firm data from *RMA* to show students how to actually get and evaluate financial statements benchmarks.

Coverage (continued)

Chapters	Selected Topics of Interest	Benefits to You
Chapter 4 Long-Term Financial Planning and Growth	*New mini-case:* Financial Planning at S&S Air, Inc.	New case written for this edition illustrates the importance of financial planning in a small firm.
	New material: Explanation of alternative formulas for sustainable and internal growth rates.	Explanation of growth rate formulas clears up a common misunderstanding about these formulas and the circumstances under which alternative formulas are correct.
	Thorough coverage of sustainable growth as a planning tool.	Provides a vehicle for examining the interrelationships between operations, financing, and growth.
>> PART THREE Valuation of Future Cash Flows		
Chapter 5 Introduction to Valuation: The Time Value of Money	First of two chapters on time value of money.	Relatively short chapter introduces just the basic ideas on time value of money to get students started on this traditionally difficult topic.
Chapter 6 Discounted Cash Flow Valuation	Second of two chapters on time value of money.	Covers more advanced time value topics with numerous examples, calculator tips, and Excel spreadsheet exhibits. Contains many real-world examples.
Chapter 7 Interest Rates and Bond Valuation	*New material:* "Clean" vs. "dirty" bond prices and accrued interest.	Clears up the pricing of bonds between coupon payment dates and also bond market quoting conventions.
	New material: NASD's new TRACE system and transparency in the corporate bond market.	Up-to-date discussion of new developments in fixed income with regard to price, volume, and transactions reporting.
	New material: "Make-whole" call provisions.	Up-to-date discussion of relatively new type of call provision that has become very common.
Chapter 8 Stock Valuation	*New mini-case:* Financing S&S Air's Expansion Plans with a Bond Issue.	New case written for this edition examines the debt issuance process for a small firm.
	Stock valuation	Thorough coverage of constant and non-constant growth models.
	NYSE and Nasdaq Market operations	Up-to-date description of major stock market operations
>> PART FOUR Capital Budgeting		
Chapter 9 Net Present Value and Other Investment Criteria	First of three chapters on capital budgeting.	Relatively short chapter introduces key ideas on an intuitive level to help students with this traditionally difficult topic.
	NPV, IRR, payback, discounted payback, and accounting rate of return.	Consistent, balanced examination of advantages and disadvantages of various criteria.

Chapters	Selected Topics of Interest	Benefits to You
Chapter 10 Making Capital Investment Decisions	Project cash flow.	Thorough coverage of project cash flows and the relevant numbers for a project analysis.
	Alternative cash flow definitions.	Emphasizes the equivalence of various formulas, thereby removing common misunderstandings.
	Special cases of DCF analysis.	Considers important applications of chapter tools.
Chapter 11 Project Analysis and Evaluation	*New mini-case:* Conch Republic Electronics.	New case written for this edition analyzes capital budgeting issues and complexities.
	Sources of value.	Stresses the need to understand the economic basis for value creation in a project.
	Scenario and sensitivity "what-if" analyses.	Illustrates how to actually apply and interpret these tools in a project analysis.
	Break-even analysis.	Covers cash, accounting, and financial break-even levels.
>> PART FIVE Risk and Return		
Chapter 12 Some Lessons from Capital Market History	*New section:* Geometric vs. arithmetic returns.	Discusses calculation and interpretation of geometric returns. Clarifies common misconceptions regarding appropriate use of arithmetic vs. geometric average returns.
	Capital market history.	Extensive coverage of historical returns, volatilities, and risk premiums.
	Market efficiency.	Efficient markets hypothesis discussed along with common misconceptions.
Chapter 13 Return, Risk, and the Security Market Line	Diversification, systematic and unsystematic risk.	Illustrates basics of risk and return in a straightforward fashion.
	Beta and the security market line.	Develops the security market line with an intuitive approach that bypasses much of the usual portfolio theory and statistics.
Chapter 14 Options and Corporate Finance	*New mini-case:* S&S Air's Convertible Bond.	New case written for this edition examines security issuance issues for a small firm.
	Stock options, employee stock options, and real options.	Discusses the basics of these important option types.
	Option-embedded securities.	Describes the different types of option found in corporate securities.
>> PART SIX Cost of Capital and Long-Term Financial Policy		
Chapter 15 Cost of Capital	*New discussion:* geometric vs. arithmetic growth rates.	Both approaches are used in practice. Clears up issues surrounding growth rate estimates.
	Cost of capital estimation.	Contains a complete, Web-based illustration of cost of capital for a real company.

Coverage (concluded)

Chapters	Selected Topics of Interest	Benefits to You
Chapter 16 Raising Capital	*New discussion:* Dutch auction IPOs.	Explains uniform price auctions using recent Google IPO as an example.
	New discussion: IPO "quiet periods."	Explains the SEC's quiet period rules.
	New discussion: rights vs. warrants.	Clarifies the option-like nature of rights prior to their expiration dates.
	IPO valuation.	Extensive, up-to-date discussion of IPOs, including the 1999–2000 period.
Chapter 17 Financial Leverage and Capital Structure Policy	Basics of financial leverage.	Illustrates effect of leverage on risk and return.
	Optimal capital structure.	Describes the basic trade-offs leading to an optimal capital structure.
	Financial distress and bankruptcy.	Briefly surveys the bankruptcy process.
Chapter 18 Dividends and Dividend Policy	*New mini-case:* Cost of Capital for Hubbard Computer, Inc.	New case written for this edition analyzes cost of capital estimation for a non-public firm.
	New material: Very recent survey evidence on dividend policy.	New survey results show the most important (and least important) factors considered by financial managers in setting dividend policy.
	New material: Effect of new tax laws.	Discusses implications of new, lower dividend, and capital gains rates.
	Dividends and dividend policy.	Describes dividend payments and the factors favoring higher and lower payout policies.
>> PART SEVEN Short-Term Financial Planning and Management		
Chapter 19 Short-Term Finance and Planning	Operating and cash cycles.	Stresses the importance of cash flow timing.
	Short-term financial planning.	Illustrates creation of cash budgets and potential need for financing.
Chapter 20 Cash and Liquidity Management	Float management.	Thorough coverage of float management and potential ethical issues.
	Cash collection and disbursement.	Examination of systems used by firms to handle cash inflows and outflows.
Chapter 21 Credit and Inventory Management	*New mini-case:* Piepkorn Manufacturing Working Capital Management.	New case written for this edition evaluates working capital issues for a small firm.
	Credit management	Analysis of credit policy and implementation.
	Inventory management	Brief overview of important inventory concepts.

Chapters	Selected Topics of Interest	Benefits to You
>> PART EIGHT Topics in Corporate Finance		
Chapter 22 International Corporate Finance	Foreign exchange.	Covers essentials of exchange rates and their determination.
	International capital budgeting.	Shows how to adapt basic DCF approach to handle exchange rates.
	Exchange rate and political risk.	Discusses hedging and issues surrounding sovereign risk.
>> ALTERNATE EDITION—Additional Chapters		
>> PART EIGHT Topics in Corporate Finance		
Chapter 23 Risk Management: An Introduction to Financial Engineering	Volatility and risk.	Illustrates need to manage risk and some of the most important types of risk.
	Hedging with forwards, options, and swaps.	Shows how many risks can be managed with financial derivatives.
Chapter 24 Option Valuation	Put-call parity and Black-Scholes.	Develops modern option valuation and factors influencing option values.
	Options and corporate finance.	Applies option valuation to a variety of corporate issues, including mergers and capital budgeting.
Chapter 25 Mergers and Acquisitions	*New material:* Alternatives to mergers and acquisitions.	Covers strategic alliances and joint ventures and why they are important alternatives.
	New material: Defensive tactics.	Expanded discussion of anti-takeover provisions.
	New section: Divestitures and restructurings.	Important actions such as equity carve-outs, spins-offs, and split-ups are examined.
	Mergers and acquisitions.	Develops essentials of M&A analysis, including financial, tax, and accounting issues.
Chapter 26 Leasing	*New material:* Synthetic leases	Discusses controversial practice of custom-tailored, "off-balance-sheet" financing.
	Leases and lease valuation.	Essentials of leasing, good and bad reasons for leasing, and NPV of leasing are examined.

In-Text Study Features

In addition to illustrating pertinent concepts and presenting up-to-date coverage, *Fundamentals of Corporate Finance* strives to present the material in a way that makes it coherent and easy to understand. To meet the varied needs of its intended audience, *Fundamentals of Corporate Finance* is rich in valuable learning tools and support.

CHAPTER-OPENING VIGNETTES

Vignettes drawn from real-world events introduce students to the chapter concepts. Questions about these vignettes are posed to the reader to ensure understanding of the concepts in the end-of-chapter material. For examples, see Chapter 5, page 124; Chapter 6, page 149.

PEDAGOGICAL USE OF COLOR

This learning tool continues to be an important feature of *Fundamentals of Corporate Finance*. In almost every chapter, color plays an extensive, nonschematic, and largely self-evident role. A guide to the functional use of color is found on the endsheets of both the Annotated Instructor's Edition (AIE) and student version. For examples of this technique, see Chapter 3, page 50; Chapter 9, page 270.

COMPUTERFIELD CORPORATION
Financial Statements

Income Statement		Balance Sheet			
Sales	$1,000	Assets	$500	Debt	$250
Costs	800			Equity	250
Net income	$ 200	Total	$500	Total	$500

IN THEIR OWN WORDS BOXES

This series of boxes are the popular articles updated from previous editions written by a distinguished scholar or practitioner on key topics in the text. Boxes include essays by Merton Miller on capital structure, Fischer Black on dividends, and Roger Ibbotson on capital market history. A complete list of "In Their Own Words" boxes appears on page xliv.

IN THEIR OWN WORDS . . .

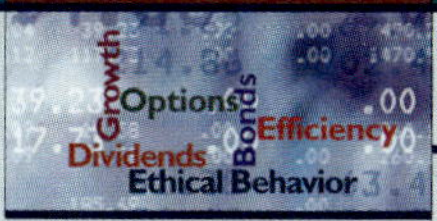

Clifford W. Smith Jr. on Market Incentives for Ethical Behavior

>> **Ethics is a topic** that has been receiving increased interest in the business community. Much of this discussion has been led by philosophers and has focused on moral principles. Rather than review these issues, I want to discuss a complementary (but often ignored) set of issues from an economist's viewpoint. Markets impose potentially substantial costs on individuals and institutions that engage in unethical behavior. These market forces thus provide important incentives that foster ethical behavior in the business community.

At its core, economics is the study of making choices. I thus want to examine ethical behavior simply as one choice facing an individual. Economic analysis suggests that in considering an action, you identify its expected costs and benefits. If the estimated benefits exceed the estimated costs, you take the action; if not, you don't. To focus this discussion, let's consider the following specific choice: Suppose you have a contract to deliver a product of a specified quality. Would you cheat by detection, thereby reducing any incentive to misstate the firm's financial condition.

Second, the higher the sanctions imposed if cheating is detected, the less likely an individual is to cheat. Hence, a business transaction that is expected to be repeated between the same parties faces a lower probability of cheating because the lost profits from the forgone stream of future sales provide powerful incentives for contract compliance. However, if continued corporate existence is more uncertain, so are the expected costs of forgone future sales. Therefore firms in financial difficulty are more likely to cheat than financially healthy firms. Firms thus have incentives to adopt financial policies that help credibly bond against cheating. For example, if product quality is difficult to assess prior to purchase, customers doubt a firm's claims about product quality. Where quality is more uncertain, customers are only willing to pay lower prices. Such firms thus have particularly strong incentives to adopt financial policies that imply a lower probability of insolvency.

others. Ethical standards also vary across markets. For example, a payment that if disclosed in the United States would be labeled a bribe might be viewed as a standard business practice in a third-world market. The costs imposed will be higher the greater the consensus that the behavior was unethical.

Establishing and maintaining a reputation for ethical behavior is a valuable corporate asset in the business community. This analysis suggests that a firm concerned about the ethical conduct of its employees should pay careful attention to potential conflicts among the firm's management, employees, customers, creditors, and shareholders. Consider Sears, the department store giant that was found to be charging customers for auto repairs of questionable necessity. In an effort to make the company more service oriented (in the way that competitors like Nordstrom are), Sears had initiated an across-the-board policy of commission sales. But what works in clothing and housewares does not always work the same way in the auto repair shop. A customer for a

WORK THE WEB

These boxes in the chapter material show students how to research financial issues using the Web and how to use the information they find to make business decisions. See examples in Chapter 3, page 77; Chapter 8, page 252.

WORK THE WEB

The U.S. Securities and Exchange Commission (SEC) requires that most public companies file regular reports, including annual and quarterly financial statements. The SEC has a public site named EDGAR that makes these free reports available at www.sec.gov. We went to "Search for Company Filings," "Companies & Other Filers," and entered "Sun Microsystems"

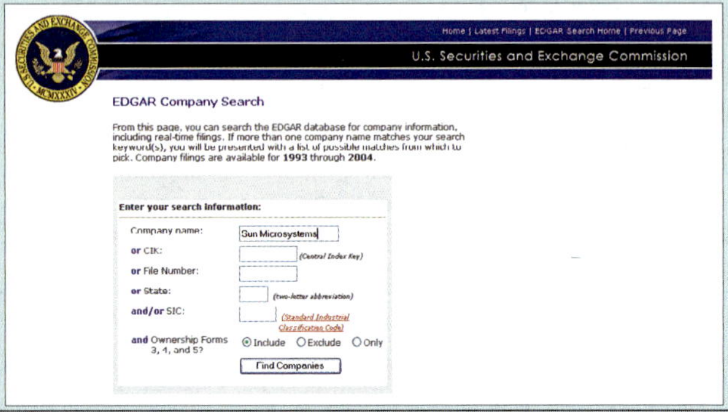

ENHANCED! REAL-WORLD EXAMPLES

Actual events are integrated throughout the text, tying chapter concepts to real life through illustration and reinforcing the relevance of the material. Some examples tie into the chapter opening vignette for added reinforcement. See example in Chapter 5, page 133.

SPREADSHEET STRATEGIES

This feature either introduces students to Excel or helps them brush up on their Excel spreadsheet skills, particularly as they relate to corporate finance. This feature appears in self-contained sections and shows students how to set up spreadsheets to analyze common financial problems—a vital part of every business student's education. For examples, see Chapter 6, page 156; Chapter 7, page 200.

SPREADSHEET STRATEGIES

Using a Spreadsheet for Time Value of Money Calculations

More and more, businesspeople from many different areas (and not just finance and accounting) rely on spreadsheets to do all the different types of calculations that come up in the real world. As a result, in this section, we will show you how to use a spreadsheet to handle the various time value of money problems we presented in this chapter. We will use Microsoft Excel™, but the commands are similar for other types of software. We assume you are already familiar with basic spreadsheet operations.

As we have seen, you can solve for any one of the following four potential unknowns: future value, present value, the discount rate, or the number of periods. With a spreadsheet, there is a separate formula for each. In Excel, these are as follows:

To Find	Enter This Formula
Future value	= FV (rate,nper,pmt,pv)
Present value	= PV (rate,nper,pmt,fv)
Discount rate	= RATE (nper,pmt,pv,fv)
Number of periods	= NPER (rate,pmt,pv,fv)

In these formulas, pv and fv are present and future value, nper is the number of periods, and rate is the discount, or interest, rate.

There are two things that are a little tricky here. First, unlike a financial calculator, the spreadsheet requires that the rate be entered as a decimal. Second, as with most financial calculators, you have to put a negative sign on either the present value or the future value to solve for the rate or the number of periods. For the same reason, if you solve for a present value, the answer will have a negative sign unless you input a negative future value. The same is true when you compute a future value.

To illustrate how you might use these formulas, we will go back to an example in the chapter. If you invest $25,000 at 12 percent per year, how long until you have $50,000? You might set up a spreadsheet like this:

	A	B	C	D	E	F	G	H
1								
2	Using a spreadsheet for time value of money calculations							
3								
4	If we invest $25,000 at 12 percent, how long until we have $50,000? We need to solve							
5	for the unknown number of periods, so we use the formula NPER(rate, pmt, pv, fv).							
6								
7	Present value (pv):	$25,000						
8	Future value (fv):	$50,000						
9	Rate (rate):	0.12						
10								
11	Periods:	**6.1162554**						
12								

CALCULATOR HINTS

These brief calculator tutorials have been added in selected chapters to help students learn or brush up on their financial calculator skills. These complement the just-mentioned Spreadsheet Strategies. For examples, see Chapter 5, page 129; Chapter 6, page 155.

You solve present value problems on a financial calculator just like you do future value problems. For the example we just examined (the present value of $1,000 to be received in three years at 15 percent), you would do the following:

Enter	3	15		1,000	
	N	I/Y	PMT	PV	FV
Solve for				−657.50	

Notice that the answer has a negative sign; as we discussed above, that's because it represents an outflow today in exchange for the $1,000 inflow later.

CONCEPT BUILDING

Chapter sections are intentionally kept short to promote a step-by-step, building block approach to learning. Each section is then followed by a series of short concept questions that highlight the key ideas just presented. Students use these questions to make sure they can identify and understand the most important concepts as they read. See Chapter 1, page 4; Chapter 3, page 52 for examples.

SUMMARY TABLES

These tables succinctly restate key principles, results, and equations. They appear whenever it is useful to emphasize and summarize a group of related concepts. For examples, see Chapter 2, page 32; Chapter 7, page 198.

LABELED EXAMPLES

Separate numbered and titled examples are extensively integrated into the chapters as indicated below. These examples provide detailed applications and illustrations of the text material in a step-by-step format. Each example is completely self-contained so students don't have to search for additional information. Based on our classroom testing, these examples are among the most useful learning aids because they provide both detail and explanation. See Chapter 2, page 22; Chapter 4, page 102.

EXAMPLE 2.1 >> Building the Balance Sheet

A firm has current assets of $100, net fixed assets of $500, short-term debt of $70, and long-term debt of $200. What does the balance sheet look like? What is shareholders' equity? What is net working capital?

In this case, total assets are $100 + 500 = $600 and total liabilities are $70 + 200 = $270, so shareholders' equity is the difference: $600 − 270 = $330. The balance sheet would thus look like:

Assets		Liabilities and Shareholders' Equity	
Current assets	$100	Current liabilities	$ 70
Net fixed assets	500	Long-term debt	200
		Shareholders' equity	330
Total assets	$600	Total liabilities and shareholders' equity	$600

Net working capital is the difference between current assets and current liabilities, or $100 − 70 = $30.

KEY TERMS

Key Terms are printed in bold type and defined within the text the first time they appear. They also appear in the margins with definitions for easy location and identification by the student. See Chapter 1, page 4; Chapter 3, page 49 for examples.

EXPLANATORY WEB LINKS

These Web links are provided in the margins of the text. They are specifically selected to accompany text material and provide students and instructors with a quick way to check for additional information using the Internet. See Chapter 5, page 126; Chapter 7, page 195.

Assets are normally listed on the balance sheet in order of decreasing liquidity, meaning that the most liquid assets are listed first. Current assets are relatively liquid and include cash and those assets that we expect to convert to cash over the next 12 months. Accounts receivable, for example, represents amounts not yet collected from customers on sales already made. Naturally, we hope these will convert to cash in the near future. Inventory is probably the least liquid of the current assets, at least for many businesses.

Fixed assets are, for the most part, relatively illiquid. These consist of tangible things

Annual and quarterly financial statements (and lots more) for most public U.S. corporations can be found in the EDGAR database at www.sec.gov.

KEY EQUATIONS

Called out in the text, key equations are identified by an equation number. The list in Appendix B shows the key equations by chapter, providing students with a convenient reference. For examples, see Chapter 5, page 126; Chapter 10, page 313.

HIGHLIGHTED CONCEPTS

Throughout the text, important ideas are pulled out and presented in a highlighted box—signaling to students that this material is particularly relevant and critical for their understanding. See Chapter 4, page 109; Chapter 7, page 205.

Terms of a Bond Corporate bonds usually have a face value (that is, a denomination) of $1,000. This is called the *principal value* and it is stated on the bond certificate. So, if a corporation wanted to borrow $1 million, 1,000 bonds would have to be sold. The par value (that is, initial accounting value) of a bond is almost always the same as the face value, and the terms are used interchangeably in practice.

Corporate bonds are usually in **registered form**. For example, the indenture might read as follows:

registered form
The form of bond issue in which the registrar of the company records ownership of each bond; payment is made directly to the owner of record.

Interest is payable semiannually on July 1 and January 1 of each year to the person in whose name the bond is registered at the close of business on June 15 or December 15, respectively.

This means that the company has a registrar who will record the ownership of each bond and record any changes in ownership. The company will pay the interest and principal by check mailed directly to the address of the owner of record. A corporate bond may be registered and have attached "coupons." To obtain an interest payment, the owner must separate a coupon from the bond certificate and send it to the company registrar (the paying agent).

CHAPTER SUMMARY AND CONCLUSIONS

Every chapter ends with a concise, but thorough, summary of the important ideas—helping students review the key points and providing closure to the chapter. See Chapter 1, page 17; Chapter 5, page 144.

CHAPTER REVIEW AND SELF-TEST PROBLEMS

Appearing after the Summary and Conclusion, each chapter includes a Chapter Review and Self-Test Problem section. These questions and answers allow students to test their abilities in solving key problems related to the chapter content and provide instant reinforcement. See Chapter 6, page 179; Chapter 10, page 321.

Chapter Review and Self-Test Problem

2.1 Cash Flow for Mara Corporation This problem will give you some practice working with financial statements and figuring cash flow. Based on the following information for Mara Corporation, prepare an income statement for 2005 and balance sheets for 2004 and 2005. Next, following our U.S. Corporation examples in the chapter, calculate cash flow from assets, cash flow to creditors, and cash flow to stockholders for Mara for 2005. Use a 35 percent tax rate throughout. You can check your answers against ours, found in the following section.

	2004	2005
Sales	$4,203	$4,507
Cost of goods sold	2,422	2,633
Depreciation	785	952
Interest	180	196
Dividends	225	250
Current assets	2,205	2,429
Net fixed assets	7,344	7,650
Current liabilities	1,003	1,255
Long-term debt	3,106	2,085

Answer to Chapter Review and Self-Test Problem

2.1 In preparing the balance sheets, remember that shareholders' equity is the residual. With this in mind, Mara's balance sheets are as follows:

Visit us at www.mhhe

CONCEPTS REVIEW AND CRITICAL THINKING QUESTIONS

This successful end-of-chapter section facilitates your students' knowledge of key principles, as well as intuitive understanding of the chapter concepts. A number of the questions relate to the chapter-opening vignette—reinforcing student critical-thinking skills and the learning of chapter material. For examples, see Chapter 1, page 18; Chapter 3, page 82.

Concepts Review and Critical Thinking Questions

1. **Liquidity** What does liquidity measure? Explain the trade-off a firm faces between high liquidity and low liquidity levels.
2. **Accounting and Cash Flows** Why is it that the revenue and cost figures shown on a standard income statement may not be representative of the actual cash inflows and outflows that occurred during a period?
3. **Book Values versus Market Values** In preparing a balance sheet, why do you think standard accounting practice focuses on historical cost rather than market value?
4. **Operating Cash Flow** In comparing accounting net income and operating cash flow, name two items you typically find in net income that are not in operating cash flow. Explain what each is and why it is excluded in operating cash flow.
5. **Book Values versus Market Values** Under standard accounting rules, it is possible for a company's liabilities to exceed its assets. When this occurs, the owners' equity is negative. Can this happen with market values? Why or why not?
6. **Cash Flow from Assets** Suppose a company's cash flow from assets was negative for a particular period. Is this necessarily a good sign or a bad sign?

END-OF-CHAPTER QUESTIONS AND PROBLEMS

We have found that many students learn better when they have plenty of opportunity to practice; therefore, we provide extensive end-of-chapter questions and problems. The end-of-chapter support greatly exceeds typical introductory textbooks. The questions and problems are segregated into three learning levels: Basic, Intermediate, and Challenge. All problems are fully annotated so that students and instructors can readily identify particular types. Answers to selected end-of-chapter material appear in Appendix C. Also, all problems are available in Homework Manager—see page xxv for details. See Chapter 6, page 182; Chapter 9, page 290.

www.mhhe.com/rwj

Questions and Problems

BASIC
(Questions 1–14)

1. **Interpreting Bond Yields** Is the yield to maturity on a bond the same thing as the required return? Is YTM the same thing as the coupon rate? Suppose today a 10 percent coupon bond sells at par. Two years from now, the required return on the same bond is 8 percent. What is the coupon rate on the bond now? The YTM?
2. **Interpreting Bond Yields** Suppose you buy a 7 percent coupon, 20-year bond today when it's first issued. If interest rates suddenly rise to 15 percent, what happens to the value of your bond? Why?
3. **Bond Prices** DTO, Inc., has 8 percent coupon bonds on the market that have 10 years left to maturity. The bonds make annual payments. If the YTM on these bonds is 6 percent, what is the current bond price?
4. **Bond Yields** Aragorn Co. has 9 percent coupon bonds on the market with nine years left to maturity. The bonds make annual payments. If the bond currently sells for $884.50, what is its YTM?
5. **Coupon Rates** Superstar Enterprises has bonds on the market making annual payments, with 16 years to maturity, and selling for $870. At this price, the bonds yield 6.8 percent. What must the coupon rate be on Superstar's bonds?
6. **Bond Prices** Borderline Co. issued 11-year bonds one year ago at a coupon rate of 8.2 percent. The bonds make semiannual payments. If the YTM on these bonds is 7.4 percent, what is the current bond price?

WHAT'S ON THE WEB?

These end-of-chapter activities show students how to use and learn from the vast amount of financial resources available on the Internet. See examples in Chapter 1, page 19; Chapter 4, page 121.

What's On the Web?

2.1. **Change in Net Working Capital** Find the most recent abbreviated balance sheets for General Dynamics at finance.yahoo.com. Enter the ticker symbol "GD," follow the "Research" link, and the "Financials" link. Using the two most recent balance sheets, calculate the change in net working capital. What does this number mean?

2.2. **Book Values versus Market Values** The home page for Coca-Cola Company can be found at www.coca-cola.com. Locate the most recent annual report, which contains a balance sheet for the company. What is the book value of equity for Coca-Cola? The market value of a company is the number of shares of stock outstanding times the price per share. This information can be found at finance.yahoo.com using the ticker symbol for Coca-Cola (KO). What is the market value of equity? Which number is more relevant for shareholders?

2.3. **Cash Flows to Stockholders and Creditors** Cooper Tire and Rubber Company provides financial information for investors on its web site at www.coopertires.com. Follow the "Investor Information" link and find the most recent annual report. Using the consolidated statements of cash flows, calculate the cash flow to stockholders and the cash flow to creditors.

Visit us at v

S&P MARKET INSIGHT PROBLEMS

Most chapters include two or three end-of-chapter problems that require the use of the Educational Version of *Market Insight*, Standard & Poor's powerful and well-known Compustat® database (free access packaged with each book). These problems provide an easy, online way for students to incorporate current, real-world data into their learning. See examples in Chapter 3, page 88; Chapter 4, page 120.

www.mhhe.com/edumarketinsight

S&P Problems

STANDARD & POOR'S

1. **Marginal and Average Tax Rates** Download the annual income statements for Sharper Image (SHRP). Looking back at Table 2.3, what is the marginal income tax rate for Sharper Image? Using the total income tax and the pretax income numbers calculate the average tax rate for Sharper Image. Is this number greater than 35 percent? Why or why not?
2. **Net Working Capital** Find the annual balance sheets for American Electric Power (AEP) and HJ Heinz (HNZ). Calculate the net working capital for each company. Is American Electric Power's net working capital negative? If so, does this indicate potential financial difficulty for the company? What about Heinz?
3. **Per Share Earnings and Dividends** Find the annual income statements for Harley Davidson (HDI), Hawaiian Electric Industries (HE) and Time Warner (TWX). What are the earnings per share (EPS Basic from operations) for each of these companies? What are the dividends per share for each company? Why do these companies pay out a different portion of income in the form of dividends?

NEW! **END-OF-PART CASES**

Located at the end of the book's first seven parts, these mini-cases focus on real-life company situations that embody important corporate finance topics. Each case presents a new scenario, data, and a dilemma. Several questions at the end of each case require students to analyze and focus on all of the material they learned from the chapters in that part. See examples in Chapter 2, page 47; Chapter 14, page 467.

PART ONE

>> MINI-CASE

Cash Flows and Financial Statements at Sunset Boards, Inc.

Sunset Boards is a small company that manufactures and sells surfboards in Malibu. Tad Marks, the founder of the company, is in charge of the design and sale of the surfboards, but his background is in surfing, not business. As a result, the company's financial records are not well maintained.

The initial investment in Sunset Boards was provided by Tad and his friends and family. Since the initial investment was relatively small, and the company has only made surfboards for its own store, the investors haven't required detailed financial statements from Tad. But, thanks to word of mouth among professional surfers, sales have picked up recently, and Tad is considering a major expansion. His plans include opening another surfboard store in Hawaii, as well as supplying his "sticks" (surfer lingo for boards) to other sellers.

Tad's expansion plans require a significant investment, which he plans to finance with a combination of additional funds from outsiders plus some money borrowed from banks. Naturally, the new investors and creditors require more organized and detailed financial statements than Tad has previously prepared. At the urging of his investors, Tad has hired financial analyst Christina Wolfe to evaluate the performance of the company over the past year.

After rooting through old bank statements, sales receipts, tax returns, and other records, Christina has assembled the following information:

	2004	2005
Cost of goods sold	$84,310	$106,450
Cash	12,165	18,380
Depreciation	23,800	26,900
Interest expense	5,180	5,930
Selling and administrative expenses	16,580	21,640
Accounts payable	21,500	24,350
Fixed assets	105,000	134,000
Sales	165,390	201,600
Accounts receivable	8,620	11,060
Notes payable	9,800	10,700
Long-term debt	53,000	61,000
Inventory	18,140	24,894
New equity	0	10,000

Sunset Boards currently pays out 30 percent of net income as dividends to Tad and the other original investors, and has a 20 percent tax rate. You are Christina's assistant, and she has asked you to prepare the following:

1. An income statement for 2004 and 2005.
2. A balance sheet for 2004 and 2005.
3. Operating cash flow for each year.
4. Cash flow from assets for 2005.
5. Cash flow to creditors for 2005.
6. Cash flow to stockholders for 2005.

Questions

1. How would you describe Sunset Boards' cash flows for 2005? Write up a brief discussion.
2. In light of your discussion in the previous question, what do you think about Tad's expansion plans?

Visit us at www.mhhe.com/rwj

Comprehensive Teaching and

This edition of *Fundamentals* has more options than ever in terms of the textbook, instructor supplements, student supplements, and multimedia products. Mix and match to create a package that is perfect for your course!

TEXTBOOK

As with the previous editions, we are offering two versions of this text, both of which are packaged with an exciting student CD-ROM (see description under "Student Supplements"),

- Standard Edition (22 Chapters)
- Alternate Edition (26 Chapters)

INSTRUCTOR SUPPLEMENTS

ANNOTATED INSTRUCTOR'S EDITION (AIE) ISBN 0072991585

All your teaching resources are tied together here! This handy resource contains extensive references to the Instructor's Manual regarding lecture tips, ethics notes, Internet references, international notes, and the availability of teaching PowerPoint slides. The lecture tips vary in content and purpose—providing an alternative perspective on a subject, suggesting important points to be stressed, giving further examples, or recommending other readings. The ethics notes present background on topics that motivate classroom discussion of finance-related ethical issues. Other annotations include notes for the Real-World Tips, Concept Questions, Self-Test Problems, End-of-Chapter Problems, Videos, and answers to the end-of-chapter problems.

INSTRUCTOR'S CD-ROM ISBN 0072991550

Keep all the supplements in one place! This CD contains all the necessary supplements—Instructor's Manual, Solutions Test Bank, Computerized Test Bank, and PowerPoint—all in one useful product in an electronic format.

- **Instructor's Manual**
  prepared by Cheri Etling, University of Tampa and Joseph Smolira, Belmont University
  A great place to find new lecture ideas! The IM has three main sections. The first section contains a chapter outline and other lecture materials designed for use with the Annotated Instructor's Edition. The annotated outline for each chapter includes lecture tips, real-world tips, ethics notes, suggested PowerPoint slides, and, when appropriate, a video synopsis. Detailed solutions for all end-of-chapter problems appear in section two. A print version of the Instructor's Manual (0072991542) is also available.

- **Test Bank**
  prepared by Kay Johnson, Penn State—Erie
  Great format for a better testing process! The Seventh Edition Test Bank has all new questions that closely link with the text material. Each chapter is divided into four parts. Part I contains questions that test the understanding of the key terms in the book. Part II includes questions patterned after the learning objectives, concept questions, chapter-opening vignettes, boxes, and highlighted phrases. Part III contains multiple-choice and true/false problems patterned after the end-of-chapter questions, in basic, intermediate, and challenge levels. Part IV provides essay questions to test problem-solving skills and more advanced understanding of concepts. Also included are ready-made quizzes to hand out in class.

- **Computerized Test Bank (Windows)**
  Create your own tests in a snap! These additional questions are found in a computerized test bank utilizing McGraw-Hill's EZ Test testing software to quickly create customized exams. This user-friendly program allows instructors to sort questions by format; edit existing questions or add new ones; and scramble questions for multiple versions of the same test.

- **PowerPoint Presentation System**
  prepared by Cheri Etling, University of Tampa
  Customize our content for your course! This presentation has been thoroughly revised to include more lecture-oriented slides, as well as exhibits and examples both from the book and from outside sources. Applicable slides have Web links that take you directly to specific Internet sites, or a spreadsheet link to show an example in Excel. You can also go to the Notes Page function for more tips in presenting the slides. If you already have PowerPoint installed on your PC, you have the ability to edit, print, or rearrange the complete presentation to meet your specific needs.

VIDEOS ISBN 0072991577

Current set of videos on hot topics! McGraw-Hill/Irwin produced a series of finance videos that are 10-minute case studies on topics such as Financial Markets, Careers, Rightsizing, Capital Budgeting, EVA (Economic Value Added), Mergers and Acquisitions, and International Finance.

STUDENT SUPPLEMENTS

SELF-STUDY SOFTWARE CD-ROM

FREE WITH A NEW TEXT!

Packaged free with every new copy of the book! This CD-ROM for students contains many features to help students learn corporate finance:

- **New! Self-Study Software**
  With the self-study program, students can test their knowledge of one chapter or a number of chapters by using questions written specifically for this text. There are at least 100 questions per chapter. Questions were prepared by Kay Johnson, Penn State—Erie.
- **New! Student Narrated PowerPoint**
  Created by Kay Johnson, Penn State—Erie, exclusively for students. Each chapter's slides follow the chapter topics and provide steps and explanations for how to solve those topics using real-life examples. Knowing that each student learns differently, a quick click on each slide and each slide will "talk through" its contents with you!
- **New! Interactive FinSims**
  Created by Eric Sandburg, Interactive Media, each module highlights a key concept of the book and simulates how to solve it, asking for the student to input certain variables. This hands-on approach guides students through difficult and important corporate finance topics.
- **Excel Templates**
  Corresponding to most end-of-chapter problems, each template allows the student to work through the problem using Excel, reinforcing each concept. Each end-of-chapter problem with a template is indicated by an Excel icon in the margin of the text. The templates may also be found on the book's online learning center (OLC) at www.mhhe.com/rwj.
- Links to this edition's *Online Learning Center (OLC), S&P Market Insight, Corporate Finance Online,* and *Finance Around the World.*

STANDARD & POOR'S EDUCATIONAL VERSION OF MARKET INSIGHT

McGraw-Hill/Irwin and the Institutional Market Services division of Standard & Poor's are pleased to announce an exclusive partnership that offers instructors and students FREE access to the educational version of Standard & Poor's Market Insight with each new textbook. The educational version of Market Insight is a rich online resource that provides six years of fundamental financial data for over 1000 companies in the database. S&P-specific problems can be found at the end of almost all chapters in this text and ask students to solve a problem by using research found on this site. For more details, please see the bound-in card inside the front cover of this text, or visit www.mhhe.com/edumarketinsight.

AVAILABLE FOR PURCHASE & PACKAGING

STUDENT PROBLEM MANUAL ISBN 0073027154

prepared by Thomas Eyssell, University of Missouri—St. Louis
Need additional reinforcement of the concepts? This valuable resource provides students with additional problems for practice. Each chapter begins with Concepts for Review, followed by Chapter Highlights. These re-emphasize the key terms and concepts in the chapter. A short Concept Test, averaging 10 questions and answers, appears next. Each chapter concludes with additional problems for the student to review. Answers to these problems appear at the end of the Student Problem Manual.

READY NOTES ISBN 0072991747

Improved listening and attention = improved retention! This innovative student supplement provides students with an inexpensive note-taking system that contains a reduced copy of every Instructor Powerpoint slide. With a copy of each slide in front of them, students can listen and record your comments about each point instead of hurriedly copying the slide into their notebooks. Ask your McGraw-Hill/Irwin representative about packaging options.

ONLINE SUPPORT AT www.mhhe.com/rwj

ONLINE LEARNING CENTER

The Online Learning Center (OLC) contains FREE access to additional Web-based study and teaching aids created for this text, such as:

- **Student Support**
  A great resource for those seeking additional practice, students can access self-grading quizzes, Excel template problems, electronic flashcards, more interactive modules, What's on the Web? questions, links to Corporate Finance Online questions, Finance Around the World problems, timely articles, and much more to help master the fundamentals of corporate finance!
- **Teaching Support**
  Along with having access to all of the same material your students can view on the book's OLC, you also have password protected access to the Instructor's Manual, solutions to end-of-chapter problems and Excel, Instructor's PowerPoint, Excel Template Solutions, Video clips, Video projects and questions, and teaching notes to Corporate Finance Online.

  As part of this OLC, instructors and students also have access to Corporate Finance Online, found on the opening page of the OLC. Corporate Finance Online is an exclusive web tool from McGraw-Hill/Irwin. The site provides over 54 exercises for 27 key corporate finance topics, allowing students to complete challenging exercises and discussion questions that draw on recent articles, company reports, government data, and other Web-based resources. For instructors, there are also password protected teaching notes to assist with classroom integration of the material.

McGRAW-HILL INVESTMENTS TRADER

Students receive free access to this web-based portfolio simulation with a hypothetical $100,000 brokerage account to buy and sell stocks and mutual funds. Students can use the real data found at this site in conjunction with the chapters on investments. They can also compete against students around the United States. This site is powered by Stock-Trak, the leading provider of investment simulation services to the academic community.

ADDITIONAL PACKAGE OPTIONS

Here are some options to enhance your teaching and your students' learning experience. For more details, please ask your campus representative, or contact us at www.mhhe.com!

McGRAW-HILL'S HOMEWORK MANAGER AND ONEPASS

Are you looking for a way to spend less time grading and to have more flexibility with the problems you assign as homework and tests? McGraw-Hill's Homework Manager is an exciting new package option developed for this text! Homework Manager is a Web-based tool for instructors and students for delivering, answering, and grading end-of-chapter problems and tests, and providing a limitless supply of self-graded practice for students.

All of the book's end-of-chapter Questions and Problems are loaded into Homework Manager, and instructors can choose to assign the exact problems as stated in the book, or algorithmic versions of them so each student has a unique set of variables for the problems. You create the assignments and control parameters such as do you want your students to receive hints, is this a graded assignment or practice, etc. The test bank is also available in Homework Manager, giving you the ability to use those questions for online tests. Both the problems and the tests are automatically graded and the results are stored in a private grade book, which is created when you set up your class. Detailed results let you see at a glance how each student does on an assignment or an individual problem—you can even see how many tries it took them to solve it. If you order this special package, students will receive a Homework Manager User's Guide and an access code packaged with their text.

There is also an enhanced version of McGraw-Hill's Homework Manager through the OnePass package option. If you order the text packaged with OnePass, your students will receive Homework Manager as described above, but with an integrated online text included. When students are in Homework Manager and need more help to solve a problem, there will be a link that takes them to the section of the text online that explains the concept they are struggling with. All of McGraw-Hill's media assets, such as videos, narrated lectures, and additional online quizzing, are also integrated at the appropriate places of the online text to provide students with a full learning experience. OnePass also gives students access to Powerweb for Corporate Finance—current events and articles pertaining to finance linked to appropriate chapters—all accessible with one access code. If you order this special package, students will receive the OnePass card packaged with their text, which gives them access to all of these products, as well as an online Homework Manager User's Guide.

McGraw-Hill's Homework Manager is powered by Brownstone.

THE WALL STREET JOURNAL SUBSCRIPTION

Your students can subscribe to *The Wall Street Journal* for 15 weeks at a specially priced rate of $20.00 in addition to the price of the text by ordering this special package. Students will receive a "How to Use the WSJ" handbook plus a subscription card shrink-wrapped with their new text. This subscription also gives students access to www.wsj.com.

BUSINESSWEEK SUBSCRIPTION

Your students can subscribe to *BusinessWeek* for a specially priced rate of $20.00 in addition to the price of the text. Students will receive a passcode card shrink-wrapped with their new text by ordering this special package. The card directs students to a Web site where they enter the code and then gain access to *BusinessWeek*'s registration page to enter address info and set up their print and online subscription for a 15-week period.

FINANCIAL TIMES SUBSCRIPTION

Your students can subscribe to the *Financial Times* for 15 weeks at a specially priced rate of $10 in addition to the price of the text by ordering this special package. Students will receive a subscription card shrink-wrapped with their new text to fill in and send to the *Financial Times* to start receiving their subscription. Instructors, once you order, make sure you contact your sales representative to receive a complimentary one-year subscription.

FINGAME ONLINE 4.0—JUST $15 WHEN BUNDLED WITH RWJ FUNDAMENTALS!

By LeRoy Brooks, John Carroll University

In this comprehensive simulation game, students control a hypothetical company over numerous periods of operation. The game is tied to the text by exercises found on the Online Learning Center (OLC). As students make major financial and operating decisions for their company, they will develop and enhance skills in financial management and financial accounting statement analysis.

PAGEOUT AT www.pageout.net

FREE to adopters, this Web page generation software is designed to help you create your own course Web site, without all of the hassle. In just a few minutes, even the most novice computer user can have a functioning course Web site.

Simply type your material into the template provided and PageOut instantly converts it to HTML—a universal Web language. Next, choose your favorite of three easy-to-navigate designs and your class Web homepage is created, complete with an online syllabus, lecture notes, and bookmarks. You can even include a separate instructor page and an assignment page.

PageOut offers enhanced point-and-click features, including a Syllabus Page that applies real-world links to original text material, an automatic grade book, and a discussion board where you and your students can exchange questions and post announcements. Ask your campus representative to show you a demo.

Acknowledgments

To borrow a phrase, writing an introductory finance textbook is easy—all you do is sit down at a word processor and open a vein. We never would have completed this book without the incredible amount of help and support we received from literally hundreds of our colleagues, students, editors, family members, and friends. We would like to thank, without implicating, all of you.

Clearly, our greatest debt is to our many colleagues (and their students) who, like us, wanted to try an alternative to what they were using and made the decision to change. Needless to say, without this support, we would not be publishing a seventh edition!

A great many of our colleagues read the drafts of our first and subsequent editions. The fact that this book has so little in common with our earliest drafts, along with the many changes and improvements we have made over the years, is a reflection of the value we placed on the many comments and suggestions that we received. To the following reviewers, then, we are grateful for their many contributions:

Ibrahim Affeneh
Robert Benecke
Gary Benesh
Scott Besley
Sanjai Bhaghat
Denis Boudreaux
William Brent
Ray Brooks
Charles C. Brown
Mary Chaffin
Raju Chenna
Barbara J. Childs
Charles M. Cox
Natalya Delcoure
Michael Dorigan
Michael Dunn
Alan Eastman
Adrian C. Edwards
Steve Engel
Cheri Etling
Thomas H. Eyssell
Michael Ferguson
Deborah Ann Ford
Jim Forjan
Micah Frankel
Jennifer R. Frazier
Devra Golbe
A. Steven Graham
Darryl E. J. Gurley
David Harraway
John M. Harris, Jr.
R. Stevenson Hawkey
Delvin D. Hawley
Robert C. Higgins
Karen Hogan
Steve Isberg
James Jackson
Pankaj Jain
James M. Johnson
Randy Jorgensen
Jarl G. Kallberg
Terry Keasler
David N. Ketcher
Jim Keys
Kee Kim
Robert Kleinman
David Kuipers
Morris A. Lamberson
John Lightstone
Jason Lin
Robert Lutz
Timothy Manuel
David G. Martin
Dubos J. Masson
John McDougald
Bob McElreath
Gordon Melms
Richard R. Mendenhall
Wayne Mikkelson
Lalatendu Misra
Karlyn Mitchell
Sunil Mohanty
Scott Moore
Michael J. Murray
Randy Nelson
Bulent Parker
Megan Partch
Samuel Penkar
Pamela P. Peterson
Robert Phillips
George A. Racette
Narendar V. Rao
Russ Ray
Ron Reiber
Thomas Rietz
Jay R. Ritter
Ricardo J. Rodriguez
Gary Sanger
Martha A. Schary
Robert Schwebach
Roger Severns
Dilip K. Shome
Neil W. Sicherman
Timothy Smaby
Vic Stanton
Charlene Sullivan
George S. Swales, Jr.

Philip Swensen
Philip Swicegood
John G. Thatcher
Harry Thiewes
A. Frank Thompson
Joseph Trefzger
Michael R. Vetsuypens
Joe Walker
James Washam
Alan Weatherford
Marsha Weber
Jill Wetmore
Mark White
Annie Wong
David J. Wright
Steve B. Wyatt
Michael Young
J. Kenton Zumwalt
Tom Zwirlein

Several of our most respected colleagues contributed original essays, which are entitled "In Their Own Words," and appear in selected chapters. To these individuals we extend a special thanks:

Edward I. Altman
New York University

Fischer Black

Robert C. Higgins
University of Washington

Roger Ibbotson
Yale University,
Ibbotson Associates

Michael C. Jensen
Harvard University

Robert C. Merton
Harvard University

Merton H. Miller

Jay R. Ritter
University of Florida

Richard Roll
University of California at
Los Angeles

Clifford W. Smith, Jr.
University of Rochester

Charles W. Smithson
Rutter Associates

Samuel C. Weaver
Lehigh University

We owe a special thanks to Cheryl Etling of the University of Tampa. Cheri worked on the many supplements that accompany this book, including the Instructor's Manual, PowerPoint Presentation System, and Ready Notes. Cheri also worked with us to develop the Annotated Instructor's Edition of the text which, along with Instructor's Manual, contains a wealth of teaching notes.

We also thank Joseph C. Smolira of Belmont University for his work on this edition. Joe worked closely with us to develop portions of the Instructor's Manual, along with the many vignettes and real-world examples we have added to this edition. We owe a special thank you to Thomas H. Eyssell of the University of Missouri. Tom has continued his exceptional work on our supplements by creating the Student Problem Manual for this edition. In addition, we would like to thank Kay Johnson, Penn State—Erie, for creating the self-study questions on the Self-Study CD-ROM, as well as revising, reorganizing, and expanding the very extensive testbank available with *Fundamentals,* as well as creating the Student PowerPoints. Also, thank you to Tom Test, for narrating the Student PowerPoints.

We would also like to thank Charles Bebrowsky, University of Kentucky; Dr. Steven D. Dolvin, Butler University; and Dr. Lei Wen, Buena Vista University for all of the help they provided in this edition.

The following University of Kentucky doctoral students did outstanding work on this edition of *Fundamentals:* Pankaj Maskara, Mark Pyks, and Qun Wu. To them fell the unenviable task of technical proofreading, and in particular, careful checking of each calculation throughout the text and Instructor's Manual.

Finally, in every phase of this project, we have been privileged to have had the complete and unwavering support of a great organization, McGraw-Hill/Irwin. We especially thank the McGraw-Hill/Irwin sales organization. The suggestions they provide, their professionalism in assisting potential adopters, and the service they provide to current adopters have been a major factor in our success.

We are deeply grateful to the select group of professionals who served as our development team on this edition: Michele Janicek, Senior Sponsoring Editor; Jennifer Rizzi, Development Editor; Rhonda Seelinger, Executive Marketing Manager; Christine Vaughan, Senior Project Manager; Keith McPherson, Design Director; and Rose Hepburn, Production Supervisor. Others at McGraw-Hill/Irwin, too numerous to list here, have improved the book in countless ways.

Throughout the development of this edition, we have taken great care to discover and eliminate errors. Our goal is to provide the best textbook available on the subject. To ensure that future editions are error free, we gladly offer $10 per arithmetic error to the first individual reporting it as a modest token of our appreciation. More than this, we would like to hear from instructors and students alike. Please write and tell us how to make this a better text. Forward your comments to: Dr. Brad Jordan, c/o Editorial—Finance, McGraw-Hill/Irwin, 1333 Burr Ridge Parkway, Burr Ridge, IL 60527 or visit us online at www.mhhe.com/rwj.

Stephen A. Ross
Randolph W. Westerfield
Bradford D. Jordan

Brief Contents

Contents

>> PART FIVE

Risk and Return

Chapter 21
Credit and Inventory Management 670

>> PART EIGHT
Topics in Corporate Finance

Chapter 22
International Corporate Finance 709

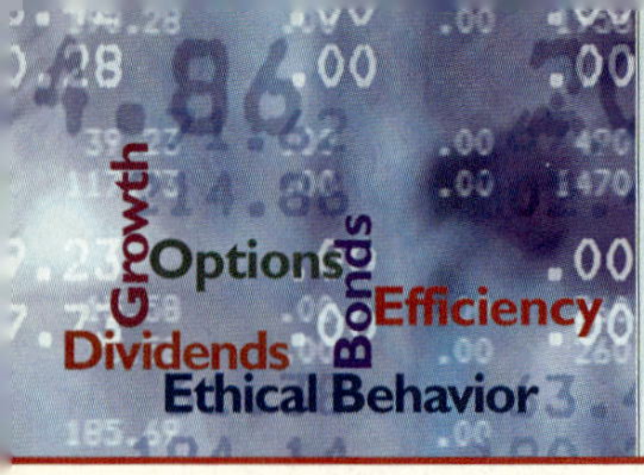

In Their Own Words Boxes

Chapter 1
Clifford W. Smith, Jr. *University of Rochester*
On Market Incentives for Ethical Behavior

Chapter 4
Robert C. Higgins *University of Washington*
On Sustainable Growth

Chapter 7
Edward I. Altman *New York University*
On Junk Bonds

Chapter 10
Samuel C. Weaver *Lehigh University*
On Capital Budgeting at Hershey Foods Corporation

Chapter 12
Roger Ibbotson *Yale University*
On Capital Market History
Richard Roll *University of California at Los Angeles*
On Market Efficiency

Chapter 14
Robert C. Merton *Harvard University*
On Applications of Option Analysis

Chapter 15
Samuel C. Weaver *Lehigh University*
On Cost of Capital and Hurdle Rates at Hershey Foods Corporation

Chapter 16
Jay R. Ritter *University of Florida*
On IPO Underpricing Around the World

Chapter 17
Merton H. Miller
On Capital Structure—M&M 30 Years Later

Chapter 18
Fischer Black
On Why Firms Pay Dividends

Chapter 23, Alternate Edition
Charles W. Smithson *Rutter Associates*
On Who Uses What

Chapter 25, Alternate Edition
Michael C. Jensen *Harvard University*
On Mergers and Acquisitions

1 Introduction to Corporate Finance

Apple Computer began as a two-man partnership in a garage. It grew rapidly and, by 1985, became a large publicly traded corporation with 60 million shares of stock and a total market value in excess of $1 billion. At that time, the firm's more visible cofounder, 30-year-old Steven Jobs, owned 7 million shares of Apple stock worth about $120 million.

Despite his stake in the company and his role in its founding and success, Jobs was forced to relinquish operating responsibilities in 1985 when Apple's financial performance turned sour, and he subsequently resigned altogether.

Of course, you can't keep a good entrepreneur down. Jobs formed Pixar Animation Studios, the company that is responsible for the animation in the hit movies *Monsters, Inc.*, and *Finding Nemo,* among others. Pixar went public in 1995, and, following an enthusiastic reception by the stock market, Jobs's 80 percent stake was valued at about $1.1 billion. Finally, just to show that what goes around comes around, in 1997, Apple's future was still in doubt, and the company, struggling for relevance in a "Wintel" world, decided to go the sequel route when it hired a new interim chief executive officer (CEO): Steven Jobs! How successful was he at his new (old) job? In January 2000, Apple's board of directors granted Jobs stock options worth $200 million and threw in $90 million for the purchase and care of a Gulfstream V jet. Board member Edgar Woolard stated, "This guy has saved the company." In 2004, following the introduction of products such as the highly acclaimed Apple iPod, *Business Week* named Jobs as a manager of the year.

Understanding Jobs's journey from garage-based entrepreneur to corporate executive to ex-employee and, finally, to CEO takes us into issues involving the corporate form of organization, corporate goals, and corporate control, all of which we discuss in this chapter.

To begin our study of modern corporate finance and financial management, we need to address two central issues. First, what is corporate finance and what is the role of the financial manager in the corporation? Second, what is the goal of financial management? To describe the financial management environment, we consider the corporate form of organization and discuss some conflicts that can arise within the corporation. We also take a brief look at financial markets in the United States.

Check out the companion web site for this text at www.mhhe.com/rwj.

1.1 CORPORATE FINANCE AND THE FINANCIAL MANAGER

In this section, we discuss where the financial manager fits in the corporation. We start by defining corporate finance and the financial manager's job.

What Is Corporate Finance?

Imagine that you were to start your own business. No matter what type you started, you would have to answer the following three questions in some form or another:

For job descriptions in finance and other areas, visit www.careers-in-business.com.

1. What long-term investments should you take on? That is, what lines of business will you be in and what sorts of buildings, machinery, and equipment will you need?
2. Where will you get the long-term financing to pay for your investment? Will you bring in other owners or will you borrow the money?
3. How will you manage your everyday financial activities such as collecting from customers and paying suppliers?

These are not the only questions by any means, but they are among the most important. Corporate finance, broadly speaking, is the study of ways to answer these three questions. Accordingly, we'll be looking at each of them in the chapters ahead.

The Financial Manager

For current issues facing CFOs, see www.cfo.com.

A striking feature of large corporations is that the owners (the stockholders) are usually not directly involved in making business decisions, particularly on a day-to-day basis. Instead, the corporation employs managers to represent the owners' interests and make decisions on their behalf. In a large corporation, the financial manager would be in charge of answering the three questions we raised in the preceding section.

The financial management function is usually associated with a top officer of the firm, such as a vice president of finance or some other chief financial officer (CFO). Figure 1.1 is a simplified organizational chart that highlights the finance activity in a large firm. As shown, the vice president of finance coordinates the activities of the treasurer and the controller. The controller's office handles cost and financial accounting, tax payments, and management information systems. The treasurer's office is responsible for managing the firm's cash and credit, its financial planning, and its capital expenditures. These treasury activities are all related to the three general questions raised earlier, and the chapters ahead deal primarily with these issues. Our study thus bears mostly on activities usually associated with the treasurer's office.

Financial Management Decisions

As the preceding discussion suggests, the financial manager must be concerned with three basic types of questions. We consider these in greater detail next.

Capital Budgeting The first question concerns the firm's long-term investments. The process of planning and managing a firm's long-term investments is called **capital budgeting**. In capital budgeting, the financial manager tries to identify investment opportunities that are worth more to the firm than they cost to acquire. Loosely speaking, this means that the value of the cash flow generated by an asset exceeds the cost of that asset.

capital budgeting
The process of planning and managing a firm's long-term investments.

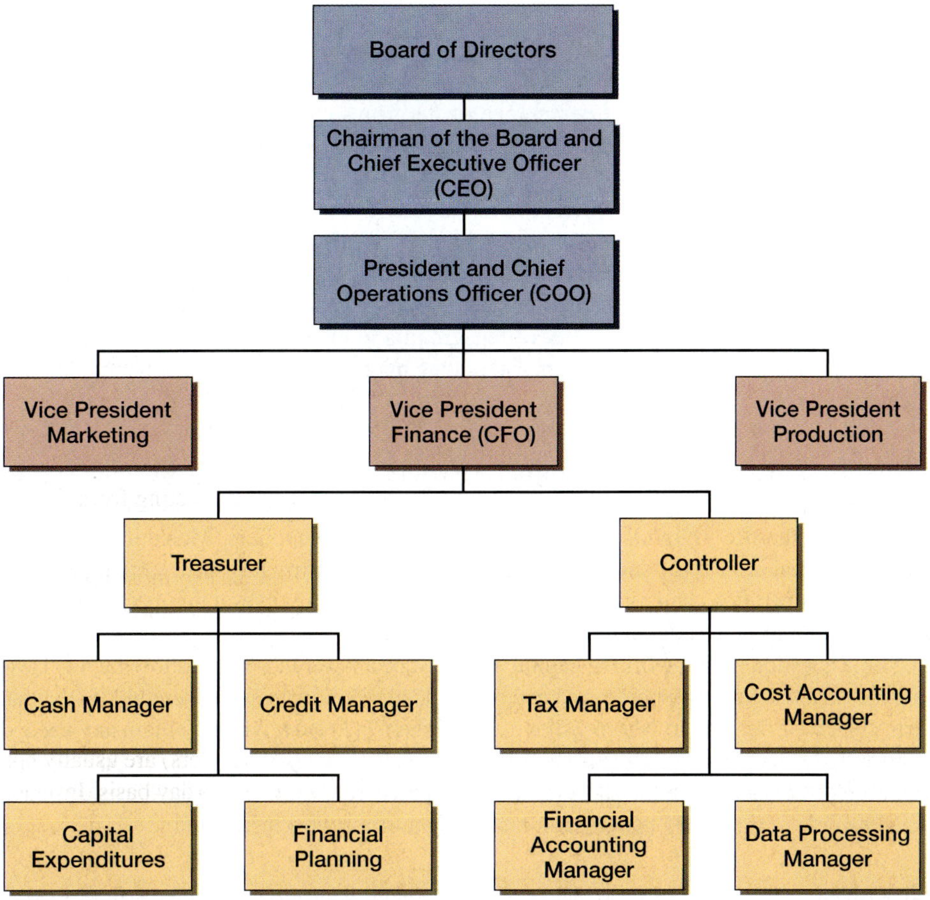

<< FIGURE 1.1

A Simplified Organizational Chart. The Exact Titles and Organization Differ from Company to Company.

The types of investment opportunities that would typically be considered depend in part on the nature of the firm's business. For example, for a large retailer such as Wal-Mart, deciding whether or not to open another store would be an important capital budgeting decision. Similarly, for a software company such as Oracle or Microsoft, the decision to develop and market a new spreadsheet would be a major capital budgeting decision. Some decisions, such as what type of computer system to purchase, might not depend so much on a particular line of business.

Regardless of the specific nature of an opportunity under consideration, financial managers must be concerned not only with how much cash they expect to receive, but also with when they expect to receive it and how likely they are to receive it. Evaluating the *size, timing,* and *risk* of future cash flows is the essence of capital budgeting. In fact, as we will see in the chapters ahead, whenever we evaluate a business decision, the size, timing, and risk of the cash flows will be, by far, the most important things we will consider.

Capital Structure The second question for the financial manager concerns ways in which the firm obtains and manages the long-term financing it needs to support its long-term investments. A firm's **capital structure** (or financial structure) is the specific mixture of long-term debt and equity the firm uses to finance its operations. The financial manager has two concerns in this area. First, how much should the firm borrow? That is, what

capital structure
The mixture of debt and equity maintained by a firm.

mixture of debt and equity is best? The mixture chosen will affect both the risk and the value of the firm. Second, what are the least expensive sources of funds for the firm?

If we picture the firm as a pie, then the firm's capital structure determines how that pie is sliced—in other words, what percentage of the firm's cash flow goes to creditors and what percentage goes to shareholders. Firms have a great deal of flexibility in choosing a financial structure. The question of whether one structure is better than any other for a particular firm is the heart of the capital structure issue.

In addition to deciding on the financing mix, the financial manager has to decide exactly how and where to raise the money. The expenses associated with raising long-term financing can be considerable, so different possibilities must be carefully evaluated. Also, corporations borrow money from a variety of lenders in a number of different, and sometimes exotic, ways. Choosing among lenders and among loan types is another job handled by the financial manager.

working capital
A firm's short-term assets and liabilities.

Working Capital Management The third question concerns **working capital** management. The term *working capital* refers to a firm's short-term assets, such as inventory, and its short-term liabilities, such as money owed to suppliers. Managing the firm's working capital is a day-to-day activity that ensures that the firm has sufficient resources to continue its operations and avoid costly interruptions. This involves a number of activities related to the firm's receipt and disbursement of cash.

Some questions about working capital that must be answered are the following: (1) How much cash and inventory should we keep on hand? (2) Should we sell on credit? If so, what terms will we offer, and to whom will we extend them? (3) How will we obtain any needed short-term financing? Will we purchase on credit or will we borrow in the short term and pay cash? If we borrow in the short term, how and where should we do it? These are just a small sample of the issues that arise in managing a firm's working capital.

Conclusion The three areas of corporate financial management we have described—capital budgeting, capital structure, and working capital management—are very broad categories. Each includes a rich variety of topics, and we have indicated only a few of the questions that arise in the different areas. The chapters ahead contain greater detail.

Concept Questions

1.1a What is the capital budgeting decision?

1.1b What do you call the specific mixture of long-term debt and equity that a firm chooses to use?

1.1c Into what category of financial management does cash management fall?

1.2 FORMS OF BUSINESS ORGANIZATION

Large firms in the United States, such as Ford and Microsoft, are almost all organized as corporations. We examine the three different legal forms of business organization—sole proprietorship, partnership, and corporation—to see why this is so. Each of the three forms has distinct advantages and disadvantages in terms of the life of the business, the ability of the business to raise cash, and taxes. A key observation is that, as a firm grows, the advantages of the corporate form may come to outweigh the disadvantages.

Sole Proprietorship

A **sole proprietorship** is a business owned by one person. This is the simplest type of business to start and is the least regulated form of organization. Depending on where you live, you might be able to start up a proprietorship by doing little more than getting a business license and opening your doors. For this reason, there are more proprietorships than any other type of business, and many businesses that later become large corporations start out as small proprietorships.

sole proprietorship
A business owned by a single individual.

The owner of a sole proprietorship keeps all the profits. That's the good news. The bad news is that the owner has *unlimited liability* for business debts. This means that creditors can look beyond business assets to the proprietor's personal assets for payment. Similarly, there is no distinction between personal and business income, so all business income is taxed as personal income.

For more information on forms of business organization, see the "Small Business" section at www.nolo.com.

The life of a sole proprietorship is limited to the owner's life span, and, it is important to note, the amount of equity that can be raised is limited to the amount of the proprietor's personal wealth. This limitation often means that the business is unable to exploit new opportunities because of insufficient capital. Ownership of a sole proprietorship may be difficult to transfer because this transfer requires the sale of the entire business to a new owner.

Partnership

A **partnership** is similar to a proprietorship, except that there are two or more owners (partners). In a *general partnership,* all the partners share in gains or losses, and all have unlimited liability for *all* partnership debts, not just some particular share. The way partnership gains (and losses) are divided is described in the *partnership agreement.* This agreement can be an informal oral agreement, such as "let's start a lawn mowing business," or a lengthy, formal written document.

partnership
A business formed by two or more individuals or entities.

In a *limited partnership,* one or more *general partners* will run the business and have unlimited liability, but there will be one or more *limited partners* who will not actively participate in the business. A limited partner's liability for business debts is limited to the amount that partner contributes to the partnership. This form of organization is common in real estate ventures, for example.

The advantages and disadvantages of a partnership are basically the same as those of a proprietorship. Partnerships based on a relatively informal agreement are easy and inexpensive to form. General partners have unlimited liability for partnership debts, and the partnership terminates when a general partner wishes to sell out or dies. All income is taxed as personal income to the partners, and the amount of equity that can be raised is limited to the partners' combined wealth. Ownership of a general partnership is not easily transferred, because a transfer requires that a new partnership be formed. A limited partner's interest can be sold without dissolving the partnership, but finding a buyer may be difficult.

Because a partner in a general partnership can be held responsible for all partnership debts, having a written agreement is very important. Failure to spell out the rights and duties of the partners frequently leads to misunderstandings later on. Also, if you are a limited partner, you must not become deeply involved in business decisions unless you are willing to assume the obligations of a general partner. The reason is that if things go badly, you may be deemed to be a general partner even though you say you are a limited partner.

Based on our discussion, the primary disadvantages of sole proprietorships and partnerships as forms of business organization are (1) unlimited liability for business debts on the part of the owners, (2) limited life of the business, and (3) difficulty of transferring ownership. These three disadvantages add up to a single, central problem: the ability of such businesses to grow can be seriously limited by an inability to raise cash for investment.

Corporation

corporation
A business created as a distinct legal entity composed of one or more individuals or entities.

The **corporation** is the most important form (in terms of size) of business organization in the United States. A corporation is a legal "person" separate and distinct from its owners, and it has many of the rights, duties, and privileges of an actual person. Corporations can borrow money and own property, can sue and be sued, and can enter into contracts. A corporation can even be a general partner or a limited partner in a partnership, and a corporation can own stock in another corporation.

Not surprisingly, starting a corporation is somewhat more complicated than starting the other forms of business organization. Forming a corporation involves preparing *articles of incorporation* (or a charter) and a set of *bylaws.* The articles of incorporation must contain a number of things, including the corporation's name, its intended life (which can be forever), its business purpose, and the number of shares that can be issued. This information must normally be supplied to the state in which the firm will be incorporated. For most legal purposes, the corporation is a "resident" of that state.

The bylaws are rules describing how the corporation regulates its own existence. For example, the bylaws describe how directors are elected. These bylaws may be a very simple statement of a few rules and procedures, or they may be quite extensive for a large corporation. The bylaws may be amended or extended from time to time by the stockholders.

In a large corporation, the stockholders and the managers are usually separate groups. The stockholders elect the board of directors, who then select the managers. Management is charged with running the corporation's affairs in the stockholders' interests. In principle, stockholders control the corporation because they elect the directors.

As a result of the separation of ownership and management, the corporate form has several advantages. Ownership (represented by shares of stock) can be readily transferred, and the life of the corporation is therefore not limited. The corporation borrows money in its own name. As a result, the stockholders in a corporation have limited liability for corporate debts. The most they can lose is what they have invested.

The relative ease of transferring ownership, the limited liability for business debts, and the unlimited life of the business are the reasons why the corporate form is superior when it comes to raising cash. If a corporation needs new equity, for example, it can sell new shares of stock and attract new investors. Apple Computer, which we discussed to open the chapter, is a case in point. Apple was a pioneer in the personal computer business. As demand for its products exploded, Apple had to convert to the corporate form of organization to raise the capital needed to fund growth and new product development. The number of owners can be huge; larger corporations have many thousands or even millions of stockholders. For example, in 2004, General Electric Corporation (better known as GE) had about 4 million stockholders and about 10 billion shares outstanding. In such cases, ownership can change continuously without affecting the continuity of the business.

The corporate form has a significant disadvantage. Because a corporation is a legal person, it must pay taxes. Moreover, money paid out to stockholders in the form of dividends is taxed again as income to those stockholders. This is *double taxation,* meaning that corporate profits are taxed twice: at the corporate level when they are earned and again at the personal level when they are paid out.[1]

Today, all 50 states have enacted laws allowing for the creation of a relatively new form of business organization, the limited liability company (LLC). The goal of this entity is to operate and be taxed like a partnership but retain limited liability for owners, so an LLC is essentially a hybrid of partnership and corporation. Although states have differing definitions

[1]An S corporation is a special type of small corporation that is essentially taxed like a partnership and thus avoids double taxation. In 2004, the maximum number of shareholders in an S corporation was 75.

for LLCs, the more important scorekeeper is the Internal Revenue Service (IRS). The IRS will consider an LLC a corporation, thereby subjecting it to double taxation, unless it meets certain specific criteria. In essence, an LLC cannot be too corporationlike, or it will be treated as one by the IRS. LLCs have become common. For example, Goldman, Sachs and Co., one of Wall Street's last remaining partnerships, decided to convert from a private partnership to an LLC (it later "went public," becoming a publicly held corporation). Large accounting firms and law firms by the score have converted to LLCs.

How hard is it to form an LLC? Visit www.llc.com to find out.

As the discussion in this section illustrates, the need of large businesses for outside investors and creditors is such that the corporate form will generally be the best for such firms. We focus on corporations in the chapters ahead because of the importance of the corporate form in the U.S. economy and world economies. Also, a few important financial management issues, such as dividend policy, are unique to corporations. However, businesses of all types and sizes need financial management, so the majority of the subjects we discuss bear on any form of business.

A Corporation by Another Name . . .

The corporate form of organization has many variations around the world. The exact laws and regulations differ from country to country, of course, but the essential features of public ownership and limited liability remain. These firms are often called *joint stock companies, public limited companies,* or *limited liability companies,* depending on the specific nature of the firm and the country of origin.

Table 1.1 gives the names of a few well-known international corporations, their country of origin, and a translation of the abbreviation that follows the company name.

Concept Questions

1.2a What are the three forms of business organization?

1.2b What are the primary advantages and disadvantages of sole proprietorships and partnerships?

1.2c What is the difference between a general and a limited partnership?

1.2d Why is the corporate form superior when it comes to raising cash?

TABLE 1.1 >> International Corporations

		Type of Company	
Company	**Country of Origin**	**In Original Language**	**Translated**
Bayerische Moterenwerke (BMW) AG	Germany	Aktiengesellschaft	Corporation
Dornier GmBH	Germany	Gesellschaft mit Beschraenkter Haftung	Limited liability company
Rolls-Royce PLC	United Kingdom	Public limited company	Public limited company
Shell UK Ltd.	United Kingdom	Limited	Corporation
Unilever NV	Netherlands	Naamloze Vennootschap	Joint stock company
Fiat SpA	Italy	Societa per Azioni	Joint stock company
Volvo AB	Sweden	Aktiebolag	Joint stock company
Peugeot SA	France	Société Anonyme	Joint stock company

1.3 THE GOAL OF FINANCIAL MANAGEMENT

Assuming that we restrict ourselves to for-profit businesses, the goal of financial management is to make money or add value for the owners. This goal is a little vague, of course, so we examine some different ways of formulating it in order to come up with a more precise definition. Such a definition is important because it leads to an objective basis for making and evaluating financial decisions.

Possible Goals

If we were to consider possible financial goals, we might come up with some ideas like the following:

Survive.

Avoid financial distress and bankruptcy.

Beat the competition.

Maximize sales or market share.

Minimize costs.

Maximize profits.

Maintain steady earnings growth.

These are only a few of the goals we could list. Furthermore, each of these possibilities presents problems as a goal for the financial manager.

For example, it's easy to increase market share or unit sales; all we have to do is lower our prices or relax our credit terms. Similarly, we can always cut costs simply by doing away with things such as research and development. We can avoid bankruptcy by never borrowing any money or never taking any risks, and so on. It's not clear that any of these actions are in the stockholders' best interests.

Profit maximization would probably be the most commonly cited goal, but even this is not a very precise objective. Do we mean profits this year? If so, then we should note that actions such as deferring maintenance, letting inventories run down, and taking other short-run cost-cutting measures will tend to increase profits now, but these activities aren't necessarily desirable.

The goal of maximizing profits may refer to some sort of "long-run" or "average" profits, but it's still unclear exactly what this means. First, do we mean something like accounting net income or earnings per share? As we will see in more detail in the next chapter, these accounting numbers may have little to do with what is good or bad for the firm. Second, what do we mean by the long run? As a famous economist once remarked, in the long run, we're all dead! More to the point, this goal doesn't tell us what the appropriate trade-off is between current and future profits.

The goals we've listed here are all different, but they do tend to fall into two classes. The first of these relates to profitability. The goals involving sales, market share, and cost control all relate, at least potentially, to different ways of earning or increasing profits. The goals in the second group, involving bankruptcy avoidance, stability, and safety, relate in some way to controlling risk. Unfortunately, these two types of goals are somewhat contradictory. The pursuit of profit normally involves some element of risk, so it isn't really possible to maximize both safety and profit. What we need, therefore, is a goal that encompasses both factors.

The Goal of Financial Management

The financial manager in a corporation makes decisions for the stockholders of the firm. Given this, instead of listing possible goals for the financial manager, we really need to answer a more fundamental question: From the stockholders' point of view, what is a good financial management decision?

If we assume that stockholders buy stock because they seek to gain financially, then the answer is obvious: Good decisions increase the value of the stock, and poor decisions decrease the value of the stock.

Given our observations, it follows that the financial manager acts in the shareholders' best interests by making decisions that increase the value of the stock. The appropriate goal for the financial manager can thus be stated quite easily:

The goal of financial management is to maximize the current value per share of the existing stock.

The goal of maximizing the value of the stock avoids the problems associated with the different goals we listed earlier. There is no ambiguity in the criterion, and there is no short-run versus long-run issue. We explicitly mean that our goal is to maximize the *current* stock value.

If this goal seems a little strong or one-dimensional to you, keep in mind that the stockholders in a firm are residual owners. By this we mean that they are only entitled to what is left after employees, suppliers, and creditors (and anyone else with a legitimate claim) are paid their due. If any of these groups go unpaid, the stockholders get nothing. So, if the stockholders are winning in the sense that the leftover, residual portion is growing, it must be true that everyone else is winning also.

Because the goal of financial management is to maximize the value of the stock, we need to learn how to identify those investments and financing arrangements that favorably impact the value of the stock. This is precisely what we will be studying. In fact, we could have defined corporate finance as the study of the relationship between business decisions and the value of the stock in the business.

A More General Goal

Given our goal as stated in the preceding section (maximize the value of the stock), an obvious question comes up: What is the appropriate goal when the firm has no traded stock? Corporations are certainly not the only type of business; and the stock in many corporations rarely changes hands, so it's difficult to say what the value per share is at any given time.

As long as we are dealing with for-profit businesses, only a slight modification is needed. The total value of the stock in a corporation is simply equal to the value of the owners' equity. Therefore, a more general way of stating our goal is as follows: maximize the market value of the existing owners' equity.

With this in mind, it doesn't matter whether the business is a proprietorship, a partnership, or a corporation. For each of these, good financial decisions increase the market value of the owners' equity and poor financial decisions decrease it. In fact, although we choose to focus on corporations in the chapters ahead, the principles we develop apply to all forms of business. Many of them even apply to the not-for-profit sector.

Finally, our goal does not imply that the financial manager should take illegal or unethical actions in the hope of increasing the value of the equity in the firm. What we mean is that the financial manager best serves the owners of the business by identifying goods and services that add value to the firm because they are desired and valued in the free marketplace.

Concept Questions

1.3a What is the goal of financial management?

1.3b What are some shortcomings of the goal of profit maximization?

1.3c Can you give a definition of corporate finance?

1.4 THE AGENCY PROBLEM AND CONTROL OF THE CORPORATION

We've seen that the financial manager acts in the best interests of the stockholders by taking actions that increase the value of the stock. However, we've also seen that in large corporations ownership can be spread over a huge number of stockholders. This dispersion of ownership arguably means that management effectively controls the firm. In this case, will management necessarily act in the best interests of the stockholders? Put another way, might not management pursue its own goals at the stockholders' expense? In the following pages, we briefly consider some of the arguments relating to this question.

Agency Relationships

The relationship between stockholders and management is called an *agency relationship*. Such a relationship exists whenever someone (the principal) hires another (the agent) to represent his/her interests. For example, you might hire someone (an agent) to sell a car that you own while you are away at school. In all such relationships, there is a possibility of conflict of interest between the principal and the agent. Such a conflict is called an **agency problem**.

agency problem
The possibility of conflict of interest between the stockholders and management of a firm.

Suppose that you hire someone to sell your car and that you agree to pay that person a flat fee when he/she sells the car. The agent's incentive in this case is to make the sale, not necessarily to get you the best price. If you offer a commission of, say, 10 percent of the sales price instead of a flat fee, then this problem might not exist. This example illustrates that the way in which an agent is compensated is one factor that affects agency problems.

Management Goals

To see how management and stockholder interests might differ, imagine that the firm is considering a new investment. The new investment is expected to favorably impact the share value, but it is also a relatively risky venture. The owners of the firm will wish to take the investment (because the stock value will rise), but management may not because there is the possibility that things will turn out badly and management jobs will be lost. If management does not take the investment, then the stockholders may lose a valuable opportunity. This is one example of an *agency cost.*

More generally, the term agency costs refers to the costs of the conflict of interest between stockholders and management. These costs can be indirect or direct. An indirect agency cost is a lost opportunity, such as the one we have just described.

IN THEIR OWN WORDS . . .

Clifford W. Smith Jr. on Market Incentives for Ethical Behavior

>> **Ethics is a topic** that has been receiving increased interest in the business community. Much of this discussion has been led by philosophers and has focused on moral principles. Rather than review these issues, I want to discuss a complementary (but often ignored) set of issues from an economist's viewpoint. Markets impose potentially substantial costs on individuals and institutions that engage in unethical behavior. These market forces thus provide important incentives that foster ethical behavior in the business community.

At its core, economics is the study of making choices. I thus want to examine ethical behavior simply as one choice facing an individual. Economic analysis suggests that in considering an action, you identify its expected costs and benefits. If the estimated benefits exceed the estimated costs, you take the action; if not, you don't. To focus this discussion, let's consider the following specific choice: Suppose you have a contract to deliver a product of a specified quality. Would you cheat by reducing quality to lower costs in an attempt to increase profits? Economics implies that the higher the expected costs of cheating, the more likely ethical actions will be chosen. This simple principle has several implications.

First, the higher the probability of detection, the less likely an individual is to cheat. This implication helps us understand numerous institutional arrangements for monitoring in the marketplace. For example, a company agrees to have its financial statements audited by an external public accounting firm. This periodic professional monitoring increases the probability of detection, thereby reducing any incentive to misstate the firm's financial condition.

Second, the higher the sanctions imposed if cheating is detected, the less likely an individual is to cheat. Hence, a business transaction that is expected to be repeated between the same parties faces a lower probability of cheating because the lost profits from the forgone stream of future sales provide powerful incentives for contract compliance. However, if continued corporate existence is more uncertain, so are the expected costs of forgone future sales. Therefore firms in financial difficulty are more likely to cheat than financially healthy firms. Firms thus have incentives to adopt financial policies that help credibly bond against cheating. For example, if product quality is difficult to assess prior to purchase, customers doubt a firm's claims about product quality. Where quality is more uncertain, customers are only willing to pay lower prices. Such firms thus have particularly strong incentives to adopt financial policies that imply a lower probability of insolvency.

Third, the expected costs are higher if information about cheating is rapidly and widely distributed to potential future customers. Thus information services like *Consumer Reports,* which monitor and report on product quality, help deter cheating. By lowering the costs for potential customers to monitor quality, such services raise the expected costs of cheating.

Finally, the costs imposed on a firm that is caught cheating depend on the market's assessment of the ethical breach. Some actions viewed as clear transgressions by some might be viewed as justifiable behavior by others. Ethical standards also vary across markets. For example, a payment that if disclosed in the United States would be labeled a bribe might be viewed as a standard business practice in a third-world market. The costs imposed will be higher the greater the consensus that the behavior was unethical.

Establishing and maintaining a reputation for ethical behavior is a valuable corporate asset in the business community. This analysis suggests that a firm concerned about the ethical conduct of its employees should pay careful attention to potential conflicts among the firm's management, employees, customers, creditors, and shareholders. Consider Sears, the department store giant that was found to be charging customers for auto repairs of questionable necessity. In an effort to make the company more service oriented (in the way that competitors like Nordstrom are), Sears had initiated an across-the-board policy of commission sales. But what works in clothing and housewares does not always work the same way in the auto repair shop. A customer for a man's suit might know as much as the salesperson about the product. But many auto repair customers know little about the inner workings of their cars and thus are more likely to rely on employee recommendations in deciding on purchases. Sears's compensation policy resulted in recommendations of unnecessary repairs to customers. Sears would not have had to deal with its repair shop problems and the consequent erosion of its reputation had it anticipated that its commission sales policy would encourage auto shop employees to cheat its customers.

Clifford W. Smith Jr. is the Epstein Professor of Finance at the University of Rochester's Simon School of Business Administration. He is an advisory editor of the *Journal of Financial Economics*. His research focuses on corporate financial policy and the structure of financial institutions.

Direct agency costs come in two forms. The first type is a corporate expenditure that benefits management but costs the stockholders. Perhaps the purchase of a luxurious and unneeded corporate jet would fall under this heading. The second type of direct agency cost is an expense that arises from the need to monitor management actions. Paying outside auditors to assess the accuracy of financial statement information could be one example.

It is sometimes argued that, left to themselves, managers would tend to maximize the amount of resources over which they have control or, more generally, corporate power or wealth. This goal could lead to an overemphasis on corporate size or growth. For example, cases in which management is accused of overpaying to buy up another company just to increase the size of the business or to demonstrate corporate power are not uncommon. Obviously, if overpayment does take place, such a purchase does not benefit the stockholders of the purchasing company.

Our discussion indicates that management may tend to overemphasize organizational survival to protect job security. Also, management may dislike outside interference, so independence and corporate self-sufficiency may be important goals.

Do Managers Act in the Stockholders' Interests?

Whether managers will, in fact, act in the best interests of stockholders depends on two factors. First, how closely are management goals aligned with stockholder goals? This question relates, at least in part, to the way managers are compensated. Second, can management be replaced if they do not pursue stockholder goals? This issue relates to control of the firm. As we will discuss, there are a number of reasons to think that, even in the largest firms, management has a significant incentive to act in the interests of stockholders.

Managerial Compensation Management will frequently have a significant economic incentive to increase share value for two reasons. First, managerial compensation, particularly at the top, is usually tied to financial performance in general and oftentimes to share value in particular. For example, managers are frequently given the option to buy stock at a bargain price. The more the stock is worth, the more valuable is this option. In fact, options are often used to motivate employees of all types, not just top management. For example, in 2001, Intel announced that it was issuing new stock options to 80,000 employees, thereby giving its workforce a significant stake in its stock price and better aligning employee and shareholder interests. Many other corporations, large and small, have adopted similar policies.

The second incentive managers have relates to job prospects. Better performers within the firm will tend to get promoted. More generally, those managers who are successful in pursuing stockholder goals will be in greater demand in the labor market and thus command higher salaries.

Business ethics are considered at www.business-ethics.com.

In fact, managers who are successful in pursuing stockholder goals can reap enormous rewards. For example, one of America's best paid executives in 2003 was Michael Dell, founder of Dell Computers; according to *Forbes* magazine, he made about $82 million. By way of comparison, Dell made less than Oprah Winfrey ($180 million) but more than Shaquille O'Neal ($30.5 million) and way more than the Olsen twins ($18 million). Over the period 1999–2003, Oracle CEO Larry Ellison was the highest paid executive, earning about $797 million. Michael Eisner, head of Disney, earned a not-so-Mickey-Mouse $715 million for the same period. Information on executive compensation, along with a ton of other information, can be easily found on the Web for almost any public company. Our nearby *Work the Web* box shows you how to get started.

WORK THE WEB

The Web is a great place to learn more about individual companies, and there are a slew of sites available to help you. Try pointing your web browser to finance.yahoo.com. Once you get there, you should see something like this on the page:

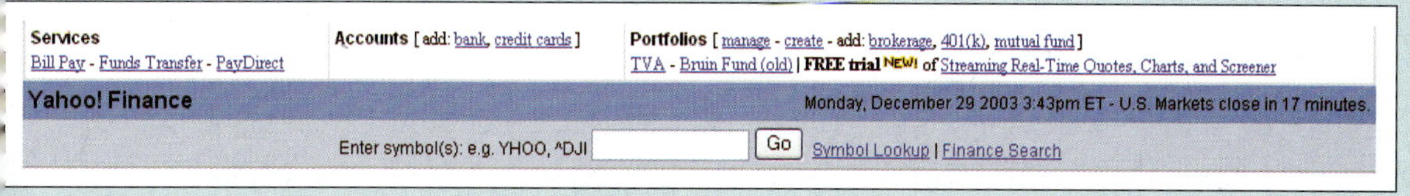

To look up a company, you must know its "ticker symbol" (or just ticker for short), which is a unique one-to-four-letter identifier. You can click on the "Symbol Lookup" link and type in the company's name to find the ticker. For example, we typed in "PZZA," which is the ticker for pizza-maker Papa John's. Here is a portion of what we got:

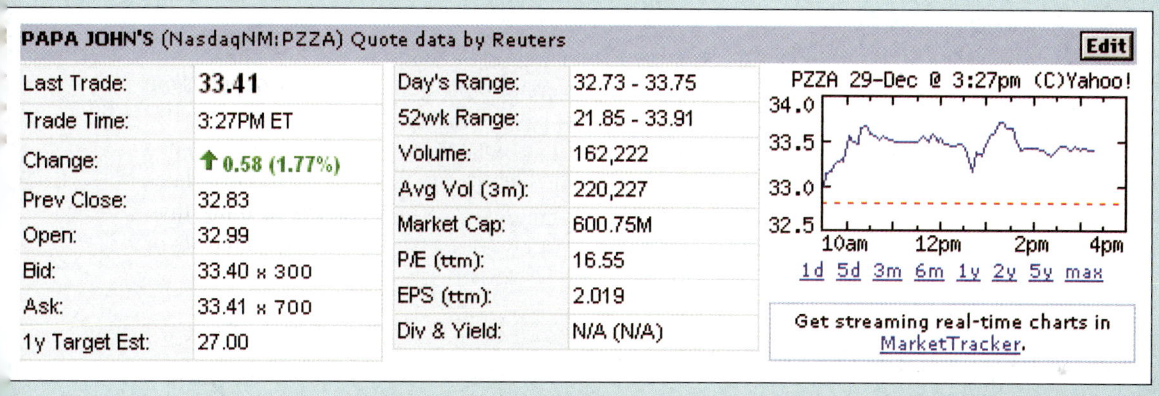

Last Trade:	33.41	Day's Range:	32.73 - 33.75
Trade Time:	3:27PM ET	52wk Range:	21.85 - 33.91
Change:	↑ 0.58 (1.77%)	Volume:	162,222
Prev Close:	32.83	Avg Vol (3m):	220,227
Open:	32.99	Market Cap:	600.75M
Bid:	33.40 x 300	P/E (ttm):	16.55
Ask:	33.41 x 700	EPS (ttm):	2.019
1y Target Est:	27.00	Div & Yield:	N/A (N/A)

There's a lot of information here and a lot of links for you to explore, so have at it. By the end of the term, we hope it all makes sense to you!

Control of the Firm Control of the firm ultimately rests with stockholders. They elect the board of directors, who, in turn, hire and fire management. The fact that stockholders control the corporation was made abundantly clear by Steven Jobs's experience at Apple, which we described to open the chapter. Even though he was a founder of the corporation and was largely responsible for its most successful products, there came a time when shareholders, through their elected directors, decided that Apple would be better off without him, so out he went.

An important mechanism by which unhappy stockholders can act to replace existing management is called a *proxy fight.* A proxy is the authority to vote someone else's stock. A proxy fight develops when a group solicits proxies in order to replace the existing board, and thereby replace existing management. For example, in early 2002, the proposed merger between Hewlett-Packard (HP) and Compaq triggered one of the most widely followed, bitterly contested, and expensive proxy fights in history, with an estimated price tag of well over $100 million. One group of shareholders, which included Walter B. Hewlett (a board member and heir to a cofounder of HP), opposed the merger and launched a proxy fight for control of HP. Another group, led by HP CEO Carly Fiorina supported the merger.

In a very close vote, Ms. Fiorina prevailed, the merger went through, and Mr. Hewlett resigned from the board.

Another way that management can be replaced is by takeover. Those firms that are poorly managed are more attractive as acquisitions than well-managed firms because a greater profit potential exists. Thus, avoiding a takeover by another firm gives management another incentive to act in the stockholders' interests. For example, in 2004 Comcast, the cable television giant, announced a surprise bid to buy Disney at a time when Disney's management was under close scrutiny for its performance. Not too surprisingly, Disney's management strongly opposed being acquired, and Comcast ultimately decided to withdraw, in part because of improvements in Disney's financial performance.

Conclusion The available theory and evidence are consistent with the view that stockholders control the firm and that stockholder wealth maximization is the relevant goal of the corporation. Even so, there will undoubtedly be times when management goals are pursued at the expense of the stockholders, at least temporarily.

Stakeholders

Our discussion thus far implies that management and stockholders are the only parties with an interest in the firm's decisions. This is an oversimplification, of course. Employees, customers, suppliers, and even the government all have a financial interest in the firm.

stakeholder
Someone other than a stockholder or creditor who potentially has a claim on the cash flows of the firm.

Taken together, these various groups are called **stakeholders** in the firm. In general, a stakeholder is someone other than a stockholder or creditor who potentially has a claim on the cash flows of the firm. Such groups will also attempt to exert control over the firm, perhaps to the detriment of the owners.

Concept Questions

1.4a What is an agency relationship?

1.4b What are agency problems and how do they come about? What are agency costs?

1.4c What incentives do managers in large corporations have to maximize share value?

1.5 FINANCIAL MARKETS AND THE CORPORATION

We've seen that the primary advantages of the corporate form of organization are that ownership can be transferred more quickly and easily than with other forms and that money can be raised more readily. Both of these advantages are significantly enhanced by the existence of financial markets, and financial markets play an extremely important role in corporate finance.

Cash Flows to and from the Firm

The interplay between the corporation and the financial markets is illustrated in Figure 1.2. The arrows in Figure 1.2 trace the passage of cash from the financial markets to the firm and from the firm back to the financial markets.

Suppose we start with the firm selling shares of stock and borrowing money to raise cash. Cash flows to the firm from the financial markets (A). The firm invests the cash in current and fixed assets (B). These assets generate some cash (C), some of which goes

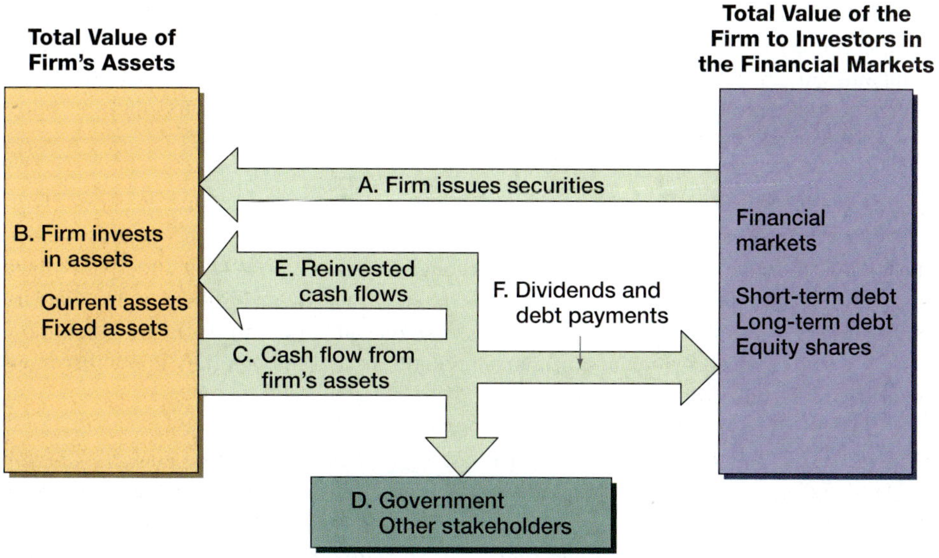

<< FIGURE 1.2

Cash Flows between the Firm and the Financial Markets

A. Firm issues securities to raise cash.
B. Firm invests in assets.
C. Firm's operations generate cash flow.
D. Cash is paid to government as taxes. Other stakeholders may receive cash.
E. Reinvested cash flows are plowed back into firm.
F. Cash is paid out to investors in the form of interest and dividends.

to pay corporate taxes (D). After taxes are paid, some of this cash flow is reinvested in the firm (E). The rest goes back to the financial markets as cash paid to creditors and shareholders (F).

A financial market, like any market, is just a way of bringing buyers and sellers together. In financial markets, it is debt and equity securities that are bought and sold. Financial markets differ in detail, however. The most important differences concern the types of securities that are traded, how trading is conducted, and who the buyers and sellers are. Some of these differences are discussed next.

Primary versus Secondary Markets

Financial markets function as both primary and secondary markets for debt and equity securities. The term *primary market* refers to the original sale of securities by governments and corporations. The *secondary markets* are those in which these securities are bought and sold after the original sale. Equities are, of course, issued solely by corporations. Debt securities are issued by both governments and corporations. In the discussion that follows, we focus on corporate securities only.

Primary Markets In a primary market transaction, the corporation is the seller, and the transaction raises money for the corporation. Corporations engage in two types of primary market transactions: public offerings and private placements. A public offering, as the name suggests, involves selling securities to the general public, whereas a private placement is a negotiated sale involving a specific buyer.

By law, public offerings of debt and equity must be registered with the Securities and Exchange Commission (SEC). Registration requires the firm to disclose a great deal of information before selling any securities. The accounting, legal, and selling costs of public offerings can be considerable.

To learn more about the SEC, visit www.sec.gov.

Partly to avoid the various regulatory requirements and the expense of public offerings, debt and equity are often sold privately to large financial institutions such as life insurance companies or mutual funds. Such private placements do not have to be registered with the SEC and do not require the involvement of underwriters (investment banks that specialize in selling securities to the public).

Secondary Markets A secondary market transaction involves one owner or creditor selling to another. It is therefore the secondary markets that provide the means for transferring ownership of corporate securities. Although a corporation is only directly involved in a primary market transaction (when it sells securities to raise cash), the secondary markets are still critical to large corporations. The reason is that investors are much more willing to purchase securities in a primary market transaction when they know that those securities can later be resold if desired.

Dealer versus Auction Markets There are two kinds of secondary markets: *auction* markets and *dealer* markets. Generally speaking, dealers buy and sell for themselves, at their own risk. A car dealer, for example, buys and sells automobiles. In contrast, brokers and agents match buyers and sellers, but they do not actually own the commodity that is bought or sold. A real estate agent, for example, does not normally buy and sell houses.

Dealer markets in stocks and long-term debt are called *over-the-counter* (OTC) markets. Most trading in debt securities takes place over the counter. The expression *over the counter* refers to days of old when securities were literally bought and sold at counters in offices around the country. Today, a significant fraction of the market for stocks and almost all of the market for long-term debt have no central location; the many dealers are connected electronically.

Auction markets differ from dealer markets in two ways. First, an auction market or exchange has a physical location (like Wall Street). Second, in a dealer market, most of the buying and selling is done by the dealer. The primary purpose of an auction market, on the other hand, is to match those who wish to sell with those who wish to buy. Dealers play a limited role.

Trading in Corporate Securities The equity shares of most of the large firms in the United States trade in organized auction markets. The largest such market is the New York Stock Exchange (NYSE), which accounts for more than 85 percent of all the shares traded in auction markets. Other auction exchanges include the American Stock Exchange (AMEX) and regional exchanges such as the Pacific Stock Exchange.

In addition to the stock exchanges, there is a large OTC market for stocks. In 1971, the National Association of Securities Dealers (NASD) made available to dealers and brokers an electronic quotation system called NASDAQ (which originally stood for NASD Automated Quotation system and is pronounced "naz-dak"). There are roughly two times as many companies on NASDAQ as there are on NYSE, but they tend to be much smaller in size and trade less actively. There are exceptions, of course. Both Microsoft and Intel trade OTC, for example. Nonetheless, the total value of NASDAQ stocks is much less than the total value of NYSE stocks.

To learn more about the exchanges, visit www.nyse.com and www.nasdaq.com.

There are many large and important financial markets outside the United States, of course, and U.S. corporations are increasingly looking to these markets to raise cash. The Tokyo Stock Exchange and the London Stock Exchange (TSE and LSE, respectively) are two well-known examples. The fact that OTC markets have no physical location means that national borders do not present a great barrier, and there is now a huge international

OTC debt market. Because of globalization, financial markets have reached the point where trading in many investments never stops; it just travels around the world.

Listing Stocks that trade on an organized exchange are said to be *listed* on that exchange. In order to be listed, firms must meet certain minimum criteria concerning, for example, asset size and number of shareholders. These criteria differ from one exchange to another.

NYSE has the most stringent requirements of the exchanges in the United States. For example, to be listed on NYSE, a company is expected to have a market value for its publicly held shares of at least $100 million. There are additional minimums on earnings, assets, and number of shares outstanding.

Concept Questions

1.5a What is a dealer market? How do dealer and auction markets differ?

1.5b What is the largest auction market in the United States?

1.5c What does *OTC* stand for? What is the large OTC market for stocks called?

SUMMARY AND CONCLUSIONS 1.6

This chapter introduced you to some of the basic ideas in corporate finance. In it, we saw that:

1. Corporate finance has three main areas of concern:
   a. Capital budgeting. What long-term investments should the firm take?
   b. Capital structure. Where will the firm get the long-term financing to pay for its investments? In other words, what mixture of debt and equity should we use to fund our operations?
   c. Working capital management. How should the firm manage its everyday financial activities?
2. The goal of financial management in a for-profit business is to make decisions that increase the value of the stock, or, more generally, increase the market value of the equity.
3. The corporate form of organization is superior to other forms when it comes to raising money and transferring ownership interests, but it has the significant disadvantage of double taxation.
4. There is the possibility of conflicts between stockholders and management in a large corporation. We called these conflicts agency problems and discussed how they might be controlled and reduced.
5. The advantages of the corporate form are enhanced by the existence of financial markets. Financial markets function as both primary and secondary markets for corporate securities and can be organized as either dealer or auction markets.

Of the topics we've discussed thus far, the most important is the goal of financial management: maximizing the value of the stock. Throughout the text, we will be analyzing many different financial decisions, but we will always ask the same question: How does the decision under consideration affect the value of the stock?

Visit us at www.mhhe.com/rwj

Concepts Review and Critical Thinking Questions

1. **The Financial Management Decision Process** What are the three types of financial management decisions? For each type of decision, give an example of a business transaction that would be relevant.
2. **Sole Proprietorships and Partnerships** What are the four primary disadvantages of the sole proprietorship and partnership forms of business organization? What benefits are there to these types of business organization as opposed to the corporate form?
3. **Corporations** What is the primary disadvantage of the corporate form of organization? Name at least two of the advantages of corporate organization.
4. **Corporate Finance Organization** In a large corporation, what are the two distinct groups that report to the chief financial officer? Which group is the focus of corporate finance?
5. **Goal of Financial Management** What goal should always motivate the actions of the firm's financial manager?
6. **Agency Problems** Who owns a corporation? Describe the process whereby the owners control the firm's management. What is the main reason that an agency relationship exists in the corporate form of organization? In this context, what kinds of problems can arise?
7. **Primary versus Secondary Markets** You've probably noticed coverage in the financial press of an initial public offering (IPO) of a company's securities. Is an IPO a primary-market transaction or a secondary-market transaction?
8. **Auction versus Dealer Markets** What does it mean when we say the New York Stock Exchange is an auction market? How are auction markets different from dealer markets? What kind of market is NASDAQ?
9. **Not-for-Profit Firm Goals** Suppose you were the financial manager of a not-for-profit business (a not-for-profit hospital, perhaps). What kinds of goals do you think would be appropriate?
10. **Goal of the Firm** Evaluate the following statement: Managers should not focus on the current stock value because doing so will lead to an overemphasis on short-term profits at the expense of long-term profits.
11. **Ethics and Firm Goals** Can our goal of maximizing the value of the stock conflict with other goals, such as avoiding unethical or illegal behavior? In particular, do you think subjects like customer and employee safety, the environment, and the general good of society fit in this framework, or are they essentially ignored? Try to think of some specific scenarios to illustrate your answer.
12. **International Firm Goal** Would our goal of maximizing the value of the stock be different if we were thinking about financial management in a foreign country? Why or why not?
13. **Agency Problems** Suppose you own stock in a company. The current price per share is $25. Another company has just announced that it wants to buy your company and will pay $35 per share to acquire all the outstanding stock. Your company's management immediately begins fighting off this hostile bid. Is management acting in the shareholders' best interests? Why or why not?
14. **Agency Problems and Corporate Ownership** Corporate ownership varies around the world. Historically, individuals have owned the majority of shares in public

Visit us at www.mhhe.com/rwj

corporations in the United States. In Germany and Japan, however, banks, other large financial institutions, and other companies own most of the stock in public corporations. Do you think agency problems are likely to be more or less severe in Germany and Japan than in the United States? Why? In recent years, large financial institutions such as mutual funds and pension funds have been becoming the dominant owners of stock in the United States, and these institutions are becoming more active in corporate affairs. What are thc implications of this trend for agency problems and corporate control?

15. **Executive Compensation** Critics have charged that compensation to top management in the United States is simply too high and should be cut back. For example, focusing on large corporations, Sanford Weill of Citigroup has been one of the best compensated CEOs in the United States, earning about $18 million in 2003 alone and $519 million over the 1999–2003 period. Are such amounts excessive? In answering, it might be helpful to recognize that superstar athletes such as Tiger Woods, top entertainers such as Tom Hanks and Oprah Winfrey, and many others at the top of their respective fields earn at least as much, if not a great deal more.

www.mhhe.com/edumarketinsight — S&P Problems

STANDARD & POOR'S

1. **Industry Comparison** On the Market Insight Home Page, follow the "Industry" link at the top of the page. You will be on the industry page. You can use the drop down menu to select different industries. Answer the following questions for these industries: Airlines, Automobile Manufacturers, Biotechnology, Computer Hardware, Homebuilding, Marine, Restaurants, Soft Drinks, and Wireless Telecommunications.
   a. How many companies are in each industry?
   b. What are the total sales for each industry?
   c. Do the industries with the largest total sales have the most companies in the industry? What does this tell you about competition in the various industries?

What's On the Web?

1.1 **Listing Requirements** This chapter discussed some of the listing requirements for the NYSE and NASDAQ. Find the complete listing requirements for the New York Stock Exchange at www.nyse.com and NASDAQ at www.nasdaq.com. Which exchange has more stringent listing requirements? Why don't the exchanges have the same listing requirements?

1.2 **Business Formation** As you may (or may not) know, many companies incorporate in Delaware for a variety of reasons. Visit Bizfilings at www.bizfilings.com to find out why. Which state has the highest fee for incorporation? For an LLC? While at the site, look at the FAQ section regarding corporations and LLCs.

2 Financial Statements, Taxes, and Cash Flow

In 2004, Cisco Systems, a manufacturer of computer networking equipment, announced it would take a charge of $567 million against earnings for the reporting period ending in January 2004. Cisco was not alone; many other companies were also forced to adjust their reported earnings. Performance wasn't the issue. Instead, a change in accounting rules forced companies to modify the way in which they handled the accounting for financial interests they had in other companies.

So, did stockholders in Cisco Systems lose $567 million as the result of an accounting rule change? Probably not. Understanding why ultimately leads us to the main subject of this chapter, that all-important substance known as *cash flow.*

In this chapter, we examine financial statements, taxes, and cash flow. Our emphasis is not on preparing financial statements. Instead, we recognize that financial statements are frequently a key source of information for financial decisions, so our goal is to briefly examine such statements and point out some of their more relevant features. We pay special attention to some of the practical details of cash flow.

As you read, pay particular attention to two important differences: (1) the difference between accounting value and market value, and (2) the difference between accounting income and cash flow. These distinctions will be important throughout the book.

THE BALANCE SHEET 2.1

The **balance sheet** is a snapshot of the firm. It is a convenient means of organizing and summarizing what a firm owns (its assets), what a firm owes (its liabilities), and the difference between the two (the firm's equity) at a given point in time. Figure 2.1 illustrates how the balance sheet is constructed. As shown, the left-hand side lists the assets of the firm, and the right-hand side lists the liabilities and equity.

balance sheet
Financial statement showing a firm's accounting value on a particular date.

Assets: The Left-Hand Side

Assets are classified as either *current* or *fixed.* A fixed asset is one that has a relatively long life. Fixed assets can be either *tangible,* such as a truck or a computer, or *intangible,* such as a trademark or patent. A current asset has a life of less than one year. This means that the asset will convert to cash within 12 months. For example, inventory would normally be purchased and sold within a year and is thus classified as a current asset. Obviously, cash itself is a current asset. Accounts receivable (money owed to the firm by its customers) is also a current asset.

Two excellent sites for company financial information are finance.yahoo.com and money.cnn.com.

Liabilities and Owners' Equity: The Right-Hand Side

The firm's liabilities are the first thing listed on the right-hand side of the balance sheet. These are classified as either *current* or *long-term.* Current liabilities, like current assets, have a life of less than one year (meaning they must be paid within the year) and are listed before long-term liabilities. Accounts payable (money the firm owes to its suppliers) is one example of a current liability.

A debt that is not due in the coming year is classified as a long-term liability. A loan that the firm will pay off in five years is one such long-term debt. Firms borrow in the long term from a variety of sources. We will tend to use the terms *bond* and *bondholders* generically to refer to long-term debt and long-term creditors, respectively.

Finally, by definition, the difference between the total value of the assets (current and fixed) and the total value of the liabilities (current and long-term) is the *shareholders' equity,* also called *common equity* or *owners' equity.* This feature of the balance sheet is intended to reflect the fact that, if the firm were to sell all of its assets and use the money to pay off its debts, then whatever residual value remained would belong to the shareholders.

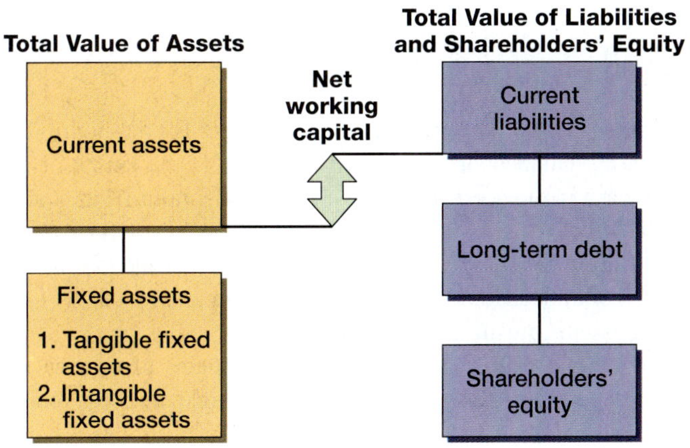

<< FIGURE 2.1
The Balance Sheet. Left Side: Total Value of Assets. Right Side: Total Value of Liabilities and Shareholders' Equity.

So, the balance sheet "balances" because the value of the left-hand side always equals the value of the right-hand side. That is, the value of the firm's assets is equal to the sum of its liabilities and shareholders' equity:[1]

$$\text{Assets} = \text{Liabilities} + \text{Shareholders' equity} \qquad \textbf{[2.1]}$$

This is the balance sheet identity, or equation, and it always holds because shareholders' equity is defined as the difference between assets and liabilities.

Net Working Capital

net working capital
Current assets less current liabilities.

As shown in Figure 2.1, the difference between a firm's current assets and its current liabilities is called **net working capital**. Net working capital is positive when current assets exceed current liabilities. Based on the definitions of current assets and current liabilities, this means that the cash that will become available over the next 12 months exceeds the cash that must be paid over that same period. For this reason, net working capital is usually positive in a healthy firm.

EXAMPLE 2.1 >> Building the Balance Sheet

A firm has current assets of $100, net fixed assets of $500, short-term debt of $70, and long-term debt of $200. What does the balance sheet look like? What is shareholders' equity? What is net working capital?

In this case, total assets are $100 + 500 = $600 and total liabilities are $70 + 200 = $270, so shareholders' equity is the difference: $600 − 270 = $330. The balance sheet would thus look like:

Assets		Liabilities and Shareholders' Equity	
Current assets	$100	Current liabilities	$ 70
Net fixed assets	500	Long-term debt	200
		Shareholders' equity	330
Total assets	$600	Total liabilities and shareholders' equity	$600

Net working capital is the difference between current assets and current liabilities, or $100 − 70 = $30.

Table 2.1 (next page) shows a simplified balance sheet for the fictitious U.S. Corporation. The assets on the balance sheet are listed in order of the length of time it takes for them to convert to cash in the normal course of business. Similarly, the liabilities are listed in the order in which they would normally be paid.

Disney has a good investor relations site at disney.go.com.

The structure of the assets for a particular firm reflects the line of business that the firm is in and also managerial decisions about how much cash and inventory to have and about credit policy, fixed asset acquisition, and so on.

The liabilities side of the balance sheet primarily reflects managerial decisions about capital structure and the use of short-term debt. For example, in 2005, total long-term debt

[1] The terms *owners' equity, shareholders' equity,* and *stockholders' equity* are used interchangeably to refer to the equity in a corporation. The term *net worth* is also used. Variations exist in addition to these.

<< TABLE 2.1

U.S. CORPORATION
2004 and 2005 Balance Sheets
($ in millions)

Assets	2004	2005	Liabilities and Owners' Equity	2004	2005
Current assets			Current liabilities		
Cash	$ 104	$ 160	Accounts payable	$ 232	$ 266
Accounts receivable	455	688	Notes payable	196	123
Inventory	553	555	Total	$ 428	$ 389
Total	$1,112	$1,403			
Fixed assets					
Net plant and equipment	$1,644	$1,709	Long-term debt	$ 408	$ 454
			Owners' equity		
			Common stock and paid-in surplus	600	640
			Retained earnings	1,320	1,629
			Total	$1,920	$2,269
Total assets	$2,756	$3,112	Total liabilities and owners' equity	$2,756	$3,112

for U.S. was $454 and total equity was $640 + 1,629 = $2,269, so total long-term financing was $454 + 2,269 = $2,723. (Note that, throughout, all figures are in millions of dollars.) Of this amount, $454/2,723 = 16.67% was long-term debt. This percentage reflects capital structure decisions made in the past by the management of U.S.

There are three particularly important things to keep in mind when examining a balance sheet: liquidity, debt versus equity, and market value versus book value.

Liquidity

Liquidity refers to the speed and ease with which an asset can be converted to cash. Gold is a relatively liquid asset; a custom manufacturing facility is not. Liquidity actually has two dimensions: ease of conversion versus loss of value. Any asset can be converted to cash quickly if we cut the price enough. A highly liquid asset is therefore one that can be quickly sold without significant loss of value. An illiquid asset is one that cannot be quickly converted to cash without a substantial price reduction.

Assets are normally listed on the balance sheet in order of decreasing liquidity, meaning that the most liquid assets are listed first. Current assets are relatively liquid and include cash and those assets that we expect to convert to cash over the next 12 months. Accounts receivable, for example, represents amounts not yet collected from customers on sales already made. Naturally, we hope these will convert to cash in the near future. Inventory is probably the least liquid of the current assets, at least for many businesses.

Annual and quarterly financial statements (and lots more) for most public U.S. corporations can be found in the EDGAR database at www.sec.gov.

Fixed assets are, for the most part, relatively illiquid. These consist of tangible things such as buildings and equipment that don't convert to cash at all in normal business activity (they are, of course, used in the business to generate cash). Intangible assets, such as a trademark, have no physical existence but can be very valuable. Like tangible fixed assets, they won't ordinarily convert to cash and are generally considered illiquid.

Liquidity is valuable. The more liquid a business is, the less likely it is to experience financial distress (that is, difficulty in paying debts or buying needed assets). Unfortunately, liquid assets are generally less profitable to hold. For example, cash holdings are the most liquid of all investments, but they sometimes earn no return at all—they just sit there. There is therefore a trade-off between the advantages of liquidity and forgone potential profits.

Debt versus Equity

To the extent that a firm borrows money, it usually gives first claim to the firm's cash flow to creditors. Equity holders are only entitled to the residual value, the portion left after creditors are paid. The value of this residual portion is the shareholders' equity in the firm, which is just the value of the firm's assets less the value of the firm's liabilities:

Shareholders' equity = Assets − Liabilities

This is true in an accounting sense because shareholders' equity is defined as this residual portion. More important, it is true in an economic sense: If the firm sells its assets and pays its debts, whatever cash is left belongs to the shareholders.

The use of debt in a firm's capital structure is called *financial leverage*. The more debt a firm has (as a percentage of assets), the greater is its degree of financial leverage. As we discuss in later chapters, debt acts like a lever in the sense that using it can greatly magnify both gains and losses. So, financial leverage increases the potential reward to shareholders, but it also increases the potential for financial distress and business failure.

Market Value versus Book Value

Generally Accepted Accounting Principles (GAAP)
The common set of standards and procedures by which audited financial statements are prepared.

The home page for the Financial Accounting Standards Board (FASB) is www.fasb.org.

The values shown on the balance sheet for the firm's assets are *book values* and generally are not what the assets are actually worth. Under **Generally Accepted Accounting Principles (GAAP)**, audited financial statements in the United States generally show assets at *historical cost*. In other words, assets are "carried on the books" at what the firm paid for them, no matter how long ago they were purchased or how much they are worth today.

For current assets, market value and book value might be somewhat similar because current assets are bought and converted into cash over a relatively short span of time. In other circumstances, the two values might differ quite a bit. Moreover, for fixed assets, it would be purely a coincidence if the actual market value of an asset (what the asset could be sold for) were equal to its book value. For example, a railroad might own enormous tracts of land purchased a century or more ago. What the railroad paid for that land could be hundreds or thousands of times less than what the land is worth today. The balance sheet would nonetheless show the historical cost.

The difference between market value and book value is important for understanding the impact of reported gains and losses. For example, to open the chapter, we discussed the huge charges against earnings taken by Cisco. What actually happened is that these charges were the result of accounting rule changes that led to reductions in the book value of certain types of assets. However, a change in accounting rules all by itself has no effect on what the assets in question are really worth. Instead, the market value of an asset depends on things like its riskiness and cash flows, neither of which have anything to do with accounting.

The balance sheet is potentially useful to many different parties. A supplier might look at the size of accounts payable to see how promptly the firm pays its bills. A potential creditor would examine the liquidity and degree of financial leverage. Managers within the firm can track things like the amount of cash and the amount of inventory that the firm keeps on hand. Uses such as these are discussed in more detail in Chapter 3.

Managers and investors will frequently be interested in knowing the value of the firm. This information is not on the balance sheet. The fact that balance sheet assets are listed at cost means that there is no necessary connection between the total assets shown and the value of the firm. Indeed, many of the most valuable assets that a firm might have—good management, a good reputation, talented employees—don't appear on the balance sheet at all.

Similarly, the shareholders' equity figure on the balance sheet and the true value of the stock need not be related. For financial managers, then, the accounting value of the stock is not an especially important concern; it is the market value that matters. Henceforth, whenever we speak of the value of an asset or the value of the firm, we will normally mean its *market value*. So, for example, when we say the goal of the financial manager is to increase the value of the stock, we mean the market value of the stock.

Market Value versus Book Value

EXAMPLE 2.2

The Klingon Corporation has fixed assets with a book value of $700 and an appraised market value of about $1,000. Net working capital is $400 on the books, but approximately $600 would be realized if all the current accounts were liquidated. Klingon has $500 in long-term debt, both book value and market value. What is the book value of the equity? What is the market value?

We can construct two simplified balance sheets, one in accounting (book value) terms and one in economic (market value) terms:

KLINGON CORPORATION
Balance Sheets
Market Value versus Book Value

Assets	Book	Market	Liabilities and Shareholders' Equity	Book	Market
Net working capital	$ 400	$ 600	Long-term debt	$ 500	$ 500
Net fixed assets	700	1,000	Shareholders' equity	600	1,100
	$1,100	$1,600		$1,100	$1,600

In this example, shareholders' equity is actually worth almost twice as much as what is shown on the books. The distinction between book and market values is important precisely because book values can be so different from true economic value.

Concept Questions

2.1a What is the balance sheet identity?

2.1b What is liquidity? Why is it important?

2.1c What do we mean by financial leverage?

2.1d Explain the difference between accounting value and market value. Which is more important to the financial manager? Why?

THE INCOME STATEMENT 2.2

The **income statement** measures performance over some period of time, usually a quarter or a year. The income statement equation is:

$$\text{Revenues} - \text{Expenses} = \text{Income} \qquad [2.2]$$

If you think of the balance sheet as a snapshot, then you can think of the income statement as a video recording covering the period between a before and an after picture. Table 2.2 gives a simplified income statement for U.S. Corporation.

TABLE 2.2 >>

U.S. CORPORATION
2005 Income Statement
($ in millions)

Net sales		$1,509
Cost of goods sold		750
Depreciation		65
Earnings before interest and taxes		$ 694
Interest paid		70
Taxable income		$ 624
Taxes		212
Net income		$ 412
Dividends	$103	
Addition to retained earnings	309	

income statement
Financial statement summarizing a firm's performance over a period of time.

The first thing reported on an income statement would usually be revenue and expenses from the firm's principal operations. Subsequent parts include, among other things, financing expenses such as interest paid. Taxes paid are reported separately. The last item is *net income* (the so-called bottom line). Net income is often expressed on a per-share basis and called *earnings per share (EPS).*

As indicated, U.S. paid cash dividends of $103. The difference between net income and cash dividends, $309, is the addition to retained earnings for the year. This amount is added to the cumulative retained earnings account on the balance sheet. If you'll look back at the two balance sheets for U.S. Corporation, you'll see that retained earnings did go up by this amount: $1,320 + 309 = $1,629.

EXAMPLE 2.3 >> Calculating Earnings and Dividends per Share

Suppose that U.S. had 200 million shares outstanding at the end of 2005. Based on the income statement in Table 2.2, what was EPS? What were dividends per share?

From the income statement, we see that U.S. had a net income of $412 million for the year. Total dividends were $103 million. Because 200 million shares were outstanding, we can calculate earnings per share, or EPS, and dividends per share as follows:

$$\begin{aligned}\text{Earnings per share} &= \text{Net income/Total shares outstanding}\\ &= \$412/200 = \$2.06 \text{ per share}\\ \text{Dividends per share} &= \text{Total dividends/Total shares outstanding}\\ &= \$103/200 = \$.515 \text{ per share}\end{aligned}$$

When looking at an income statement, the financial manager needs to keep three things in mind: GAAP, cash versus noncash items, and time and costs.

GAAP and the Income Statement

An income statement prepared using GAAP will show revenue when it accrues. This is not necessarily when the cash comes in. The general rule (the realization principle) is to recognize revenue when the earnings process is virtually complete and the value of an exchange of goods or services is known or can be reliably determined. In practice, this principle usually means that revenue is recognized at the time of sale, which need not be the same as the time of collection.

Expenses shown on the income statement are based on the matching principle. The basic idea here is to first determine revenues as described previously and then match those revenues with the costs associated with producing them. So, if we manufacture a product and then sell it on credit, the revenue is realized at the time of sale. The production and other costs associated with the sale of that product will likewise be recognized at that time. Once again, the actual cash outflows may have occurred at some very different time.

As a result of the way revenues and expenses are realized, the figures shown on the income statement may not be at all representative of the actual cash inflows and outflows that occurred during a particular period.

Noncash Items

A primary reason that accounting income differs from cash flow is that an income statement contains **noncash items**. The most important of these is *depreciation*. Suppose a firm purchases an asset for \$5,000 and pays in cash. Obviously, the firm has a \$5,000 cash outflow at the time of purchase. However, instead of deducting the \$5,000 as an expense, an accountant might depreciate the asset over a five-year period.

noncash items
Expenses charged against revenues that do not directly affect cash flow, such as depreciation.

If the depreciation is straight-line and the asset is written down to zero over that period, then \$5,000/5 = \$1,000 will be deducted each year as an expense.[2] The important thing to recognize is that this \$1,000 deduction isn't cash—it's an accounting number. The actual cash outflow occurred when the asset was purchased.

The depreciation deduction is simply another application of the matching principle in accounting. The revenues associated with an asset would generally occur over some length of time. So, the accountant seeks to match the expense of purchasing the asset with the benefits produced from owning it.

As we will see, for the financial manager, the actual timing of cash inflows and outflows is critical in coming up with a reasonable estimate of market value, so we need to learn how to separate the cash flows from the noncash accounting entries. In reality, the difference between cash flow and accounting income can be pretty dramatic. For example, auto manufacturer Ford Motor Company reported a net loss of \$793 million in the fourth quarter of 2003. Sounds bad, but Ford also reported *positive* cash flow of \$1.6 billion, a difference of over \$2 billion! The reason the difference is so huge is that Ford had particularly big noncash deductions related to a restructuring of its operations, among other things.

Time and Costs

It is often useful to think of the future as having two distinct parts: the short run and the long run. These are not precise time periods. The distinction has to do with whether costs are fixed or variable. In the long run, all business costs are variable. Given sufficient time, assets can be sold, debts can be paid, and so on.

If our time horizon is relatively short, however, some costs are effectively fixed—they must be paid no matter what (property taxes, for example). Other costs such as wages to laborers and payments to suppliers are still variable. As a result, even in the short run, the firm can vary its output level by varying expenditures in these areas.

The distinction between fixed and variable costs is important, at times, to the financial manager, but the way costs are reported on the income statement is not a good guide as to

[2]By "straight-line," we mean that the depreciation deduction is the same every year. By "written down to zero," we mean that the asset is assumed to have no value at the end of five years. Depreciation is discussed in more detail in Chapter 10.

WORK THE WEB

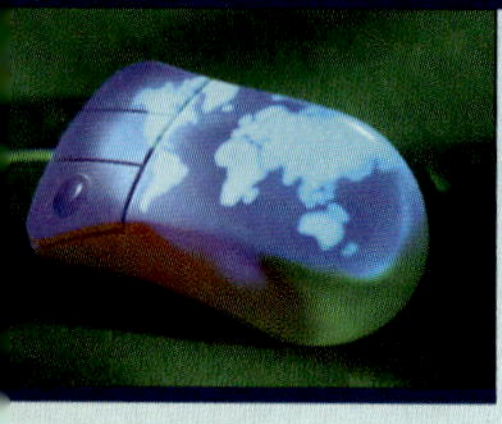

The U.S. Securities and Exchange Commission (SEC) requires that most public companies file regular reports, including annual and quarterly financial statements. The SEC has a public site named EDGAR that makes these free reports available at www.sec.gov. We went to "Search for Company Filings," "Companies & Other Filers," and entered "Sun Microsystems"

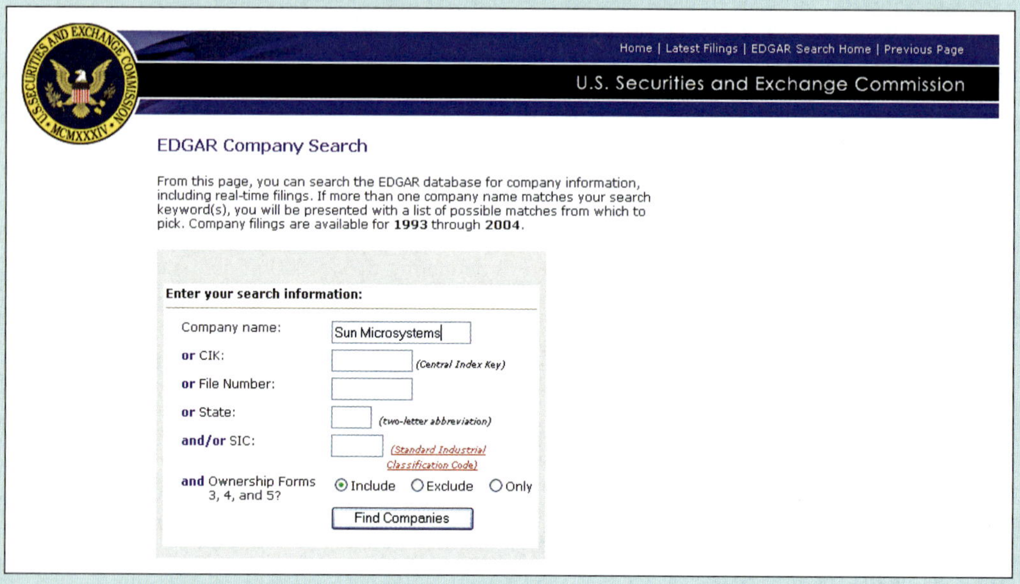

Home | Latest Filings | EDGAR Search Home | Previous Page

U.S. Securities and Exchange Commission

EDGAR Company Search

From this page, you can search the EDGAR database for company information, including real-time filings. If more than one company name matches your search keyword(s), you will be presented with a list of possible matches from which to pick. Company filings are available for **1993** through **2004**.

Enter your search information:

Company name: Sun Microsystems
or CIK: *(Central Index Key)*
or File Number:
or State: *(two-letter abbreviation)*
and/or SIC: *(Standard Industrial Classification Code)*
and Ownership Forms 3, 4, and 5? Include Exclude Only

Find Companies

Here is partial view of what we got:

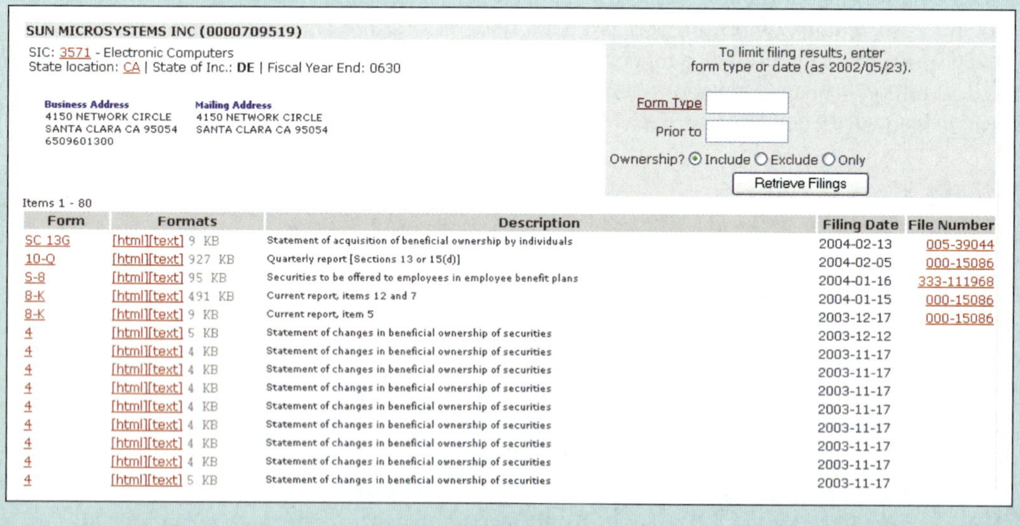

SUN MICROSYSTEMS INC (0000709519)
SIC: 3571 - Electronic Computers
State location: CA | State of Inc.: **DE** | Fiscal Year End: 0630

Business Address
4150 NETWORK CIRCLE
SANTA CLARA CA 95054
6509601300

Mailing Address
4150 NETWORK CIRCLE
SANTA CLARA CA 95054

To limit filing results, enter form type or date (as 2002/05/23).
Form Type
Prior to
Ownership? Include Exclude Only
Retrieve Filings

Items 1 - 80

Form	Formats	Description	Filing Date	File Number
SC 13G	[html][text] 9 KB	Statement of acquisition of beneficial ownership by individuals	2004-02-13	005-39044
10-Q	[html][text] 927 KB	Quarterly report [Sections 13 or 15(d)]	2004-02-05	000-15086
S-8	[html][text] 95 KB	Securities to be offered to employees in employee benefit plans	2004-01-16	333-111968
8-K	[html][text] 491 KB	Current report, items 12 and 7	2004-01-15	000-15086
8-K	[html][text] 9 KB	Current report, item 5	2003-12-17	000-15086
4	[html][text] 5 KB	Statement of changes in beneficial ownership of securities	2003-12-12	
4	[html][text] 4 KB	Statement of changes in beneficial ownership of securities	2003-11-17	
4	[html][text] 4 KB	Statement of changes in beneficial ownership of securities	2003-11-17	
4	[html][text] 4 KB	Statement of changes in beneficial ownership of securities	2003-11-17	
4	[html][text] 4 KB	Statement of changes in beneficial ownership of securities	2003-11-17	
4	[html][text] 4 KB	Statement of changes in beneficial ownership of securities	2003-11-17	
4	[html][text] 4 KB	Statement of changes in beneficial ownership of securities	2003-11-17	
4	[html][text] 4 KB	Statement of changes in beneficial ownership of securities	2003-11-17	
4	[html][text] 5 KB	Statement of changes in beneficial ownership of securities	2003-11-17	

As of the date of this search, EDGAR had 80 corporate filings by Sun Microsystems available for download. The two reports we look at the most are the 10-K, which is the annual report filed with the SEC, and the 10-Q. The 10-K includes the list of officers and their salaries, financial statements for the previous fiscal year, and an explanation by the company for the financial results. The 10-Q is a smaller report that includes the financial statements for the quarter.

which costs are which. The reason is that, in practice, accountants tend to classify costs as either product costs or period costs.

Product costs include such things as raw materials, direct labor expense, and manufacturing overhead. These are reported on the income statement as costs of goods sold, but they include both fixed and variable costs. Similarly, period costs are incurred during a particular time period and might be reported as selling, general, and administrative expenses. Once again, some of these period costs may be fixed and others may be variable. The company president's salary, for example, is a period cost and is probably fixed, at least in the short run.

The balance sheets and income statement we have been using thus far are hypothetical. Our nearby *Work the Web* box shows how to find actual balance sheets and income statements online for almost any company.

Concept Questions

2.2a What is the income statement equation?

2.2b What are the three things to keep in mind when looking at an income statement?

2.2c Why is accounting income not the same as cash flow? Give two reasons.

TAXES 2.3

Taxes can be one of the largest cash outflows that a firm experiences. For example, for the fiscal year 2003, Wal-Mart's earnings before taxes were about \$12.7 billion. Its tax bill, including all taxes paid worldwide, was a whopping \$4.5 billion, or about 35 percent of its pretax earnings. The size of the tax bill is determined through the tax code, an often amended set of rules. In this section, we examine corporate tax rates and how taxes are calculated.

If the various rules of taxation seem a little bizarre or convoluted to you, keep in mind that the tax code is the result of political, not economic, forces. As a result, there is no reason why it has to make economic sense.

Corporate Tax Rates

Corporate tax rates in effect for 2004 are shown in Table 2.3. A peculiar feature of taxation instituted by the Tax Reform Act of 1986 and expanded in the 1993 Omnibus Budget Reconciliation Act is that corporate tax rates are not strictly increasing. As shown, corporate tax rates rise from 15 percent to 39 percent, but they drop back to 34 percent on income over \$335,000. They then rise to 38 percent and subsequently fall to 35 percent.

According to the originators of the current tax rules, there are only four corporate rates: 15 percent, 25 percent, 34 percent, and 35 percent. The 38 and 39 percent brackets arise because of "surcharges" applied on top of the 34 and 35 percent rates. A tax is a tax is a tax, however, so there are really six corporate tax brackets, as we have shown.

Average versus Marginal Tax Rates

In making financial decisions, it is frequently important to distinguish between average and marginal tax rates. Your **average tax rate** is your tax bill divided by your taxable income, in other words, the percentage of your income that goes to pay taxes. Your

average tax rate
Total taxes paid divided by total taxable income.

TABLE 2.3 >>

Corporate Tax Rates

Taxable Income	Tax Rate
$ 0– 50,000	15%
50,001– 75,000	25
75,001– 100,000	34
100,001– 335,000	39
335,001–10,000,000	34
10,000,001–15,000,000	35
15,000,001–18,333,333	38
18,333,334+	35

marginal tax rate
Amount of tax payable on the next dollar earned.

marginal tax rate is the rate of the extra tax you would pay if you earned one more dollar. The percentage tax rates shown in Table 2.3 are all marginal rates. Put another way, the tax rates in Table 2.3 apply to the part of income in the indicated range only, not all income.

The difference between average and marginal tax rates can best be illustrated with a simple example. Suppose our corporation has a taxable income of $200,000. What is the tax bill? Using Table 2.3, we can figure our tax bill as:

$$
\begin{aligned}
.15(\$\ 50{,}000) &= \$\ 7{,}500 \\
.25(\$\ 75{,}000 - 50{,}000) &= 6{,}250 \\
.34(\$100{,}000 - 75{,}000) &= 8{,}500 \\
.39(\$200{,}000 - 100{,}000) &= \underline{39{,}000} \\
&\quad \$61{,}250
\end{aligned}
$$

The IRS has a great web site! (www.irs.gov)

Our total tax is thus $61,250.

In our example, what is the average tax rate? We had a taxable income of $200,000 and a tax bill of $61,250, so the average tax rate is $61,250/200,000 = 30.625%. What is the marginal tax rate? If we made one more dollar, the tax on that dollar would be 39 cents, so our marginal rate is 39 percent.

EXAMPLE 2.4 >> Deep in the Heart of Taxes

Algernon, Inc., has a taxable income of $85,000. What is its tax bill? What is its average tax rate? Its marginal tax rate?

From Table 2.3, we see that the tax rate applied to the first $50,000 is 15 percent; the rate applied to the next $25,000 is 25 percent, and the rate applied after that up to $100,000 is 34 percent. So Algernon must pay .15 × $50,000 + .25 × 25,000 + .34 × (85,000 − 75,000) = $17,150. The average tax rate is thus $17,150/85,000 = 20.18%. The marginal rate is 34 percent because Algernon's taxes would rise by 34 cents if it had another dollar in taxable income.

Table 2.4 summarizes some different taxable incomes, marginal tax rates, and average tax rates for corporations. Notice how the average and marginal tax rates come together at 35 percent.

With a *flat-rate* tax, there is only one tax rate, so the rate is the same for all income levels. With such a tax, the marginal tax rate is always the same as the average tax rate. As it stands now, corporate taxation in the United States is based on a modified flat-rate tax, which becomes a true flat rate for the highest incomes.

In looking at Table 2.4, notice that the more a corporation makes, the greater is the percentage of taxable income paid in taxes. Put another way, under current tax law, the

<< TABLE 2.4

Corporate Taxes and Tax Rates

(1) Taxable Income	(2) Marginal Tax Rate	(3) Total Tax	(3)/(1) Average Tax Rate
$ 45,000	15%	$ 6,750	15.00%
70,000	25	12,500	17.86
95,000	34	20,550	21.63
250,000	39	80,750	32.30
1,000,000	34	340,000	34.00
17,500,000	38	6,100,000	34.86
50,000,000	35	17,500,000	35.00
100,000,000	35	35,000,000	35.00

average tax rate never goes down, even though the marginal tax rate does. As illustrated, for corporations, average tax rates begin at 15 percent and rise to a maximum of 35 percent.

It will normally be the marginal tax rate that is relevant for financial decision making. The reason is that any new cash flows will be taxed at that marginal rate. Because financial decisions usually involve new cash flows or changes in existing ones, this rate will tell us the marginal effect of a decision on our tax bill.

There is one last thing to notice about the tax code as it affects corporations. It's easy to verify that the corporate tax bill is just a flat 35 percent of taxable income if our taxable income is more than $18.33 million. Also, for the many midsize corporations with taxable incomes in the range of $335,000 to $10,000,000, the tax rate is a flat 34 percent. Because we will normally be talking about large corporations, you can assume that the average and marginal tax rates are 35 percent unless we explicitly say otherwise.

Before moving on, we should note that the tax rates we have discussed in this section relate to federal taxes only. Overall tax rates can be higher once state, local, and any other taxes are considered.

Concept Questions

2.3a What is the difference between a marginal and an average tax rate?

2.3b Do the wealthiest corporations receive a tax break in terms of a lower tax rate? Explain.

CASH FLOW 2.4

At this point, we are ready to discuss perhaps one of the most important pieces of financial information that can be gleaned from financial statements: *cash flow*. By cash flow, we simply mean the difference between the number of dollars that came in and the number that went out. For example, if you were the owner of a business, you might be very interested in how much cash you actually took out of your business in a given year. How to determine this amount is one of the things we discuss next.

There is no standard financial statement that presents this information in the way that we wish. We will therefore discuss how to calculate cash flow for U.S. Corporation and point out how the result differs from that of standard financial statement calculations. There is a standard financial accounting statement called the *statement of cash flows,* but it is concerned with a somewhat different issue that should not be confused with what is discussed in this section. The accounting statement of cash flows is discussed in Chapter 3.

From the balance sheet identity, we know that the value of a firm's assets is equal to the value of its liabilities plus the value of its equity. Similarly, the cash flow from the firm's assets must equal the sum of the cash flow to creditors and the cash flow to stockholders (or owners):

$$\text{Cash flow from assets} = \text{Cash flow to creditors} + \text{Cash flow to stockholders} \qquad \textbf{[2.3]}$$

This is the cash flow identity. It says that the cash flow from the firm's assets is equal to the cash flow paid to suppliers of capital to the firm. What it reflects is the fact that a firm generates cash through its various activities, and that cash is either used to pay creditors or paid out to the owners of the firm. We discuss the various things that make up these cash flows next.

Cash Flow from Assets

cash flow from assets
The total of cash flow to creditors and cash flow to stockholders, consisting of the following: operating cash flow, capital spending, and change in net working capital.

Cash flow from assets involves three components: operating cash flow, capital spending, and change in net working capital. **Operating cash flow** refers to the cash flow that results from the firm's day-to-day activities of producing and selling. Expenses associated with the firm's financing of its assets are not included because they are not operating expenses.

As we discussed in Chapter 1, some portion of the firm's cash flow is reinvested in the firm. *Capital spending* refers to the net spending on fixed assets (purchases of fixed assets less sales of fixed assets). Finally, *change in net working capital* is measured as the net change in current assets relative to current liabilities for the period being examined and represents the amount spent on net working capital. The three components of cash flow are examined in more detail next.

operating cash flow
Cash generated from a firm's normal business activities.

Operating Cash Flow

To calculate operating cash flow (OCF), we want to calculate revenues minus costs, but we don't want to include depreciation because it's not a cash outflow, and we don't want to include interest because it's a financing expense. We do want to include taxes, because taxes are, unfortunately, paid in cash.

If we look at U.S. Corporation's income statement (Table 2.2), we see that earnings before interest and taxes (EBIT) are $694. This is almost what we want since it doesn't include interest paid. We need to make two adjustments. First, recall that depreciation is a noncash expense. To get cash flow, we first add back the $65 in depreciation because it wasn't a cash deduction. The other adjustment is to subtract the $212 in taxes because these were paid in cash. The result is operating cash flow:

U.S. CORPORATION 2005 Operating Cash Flow	
Earnings before interest and taxes	$694
+ Depreciation	65
− Taxes	212
Operating cash flow	$547

U.S. Corporation thus had a 2005 operating cash flow of $547.

Operating cash flow is an important number because it tells us, on a very basic level, whether or not a firm's cash inflows from its business operations are sufficient to cover its everyday cash outflows. For this reason, a negative operating cash flow is often a sign of trouble.

There is an unpleasant possibility of confusion when we speak of operating cash flow. In accounting practice, operating cash flow is often defined as net income plus depreciation. For U.S. Corporation, this would amount to $412 + 65 = $477.

The accounting definition of operating cash flow differs from ours in one important way: interest is deducted when net income is computed. Notice that the difference between the $547 operating cash flow we calculated and this $477 is $70, the amount of interest paid for the year. This definition of cash flow thus considers interest paid to be an operating expense. Our definition treats it properly as a financing expense. If there were no interest expense, the two definitions would be the same.

To finish our calculation of cash flow from assets for U.S. Corporation, we need to consider how much of the $547 operating cash flow was reinvested in the firm. We consider spending on fixed assets first.

Capital Spending Net capital spending is just money spent on fixed assets less money received from the sale of fixed assets. At the end of 2004, net fixed assets for U.S. Corporation (Table 2.1) were $1,644. During the year, U.S. wrote off (depreciated) $65 worth of fixed assets on the income statement. So, if the firm didn't purchase any new fixed assets, net fixed assets would have been $1,644 − 65 = $1,579 at year's end. The 2005 balance sheet shows $1,709 in net fixed assets, so U.S. must have spent a total of $1,709 − 1,579 = $130 on fixed assets during the year:

Ending net fixed assets	$1,709
− Beginning net fixed assets	1,644
+ Depreciation	65
Net capital spending	$ 130

This $130 is the net capital spending for 2005.

Could net capital spending be negative? The answer is yes. This would happen if the firm sold off more assets than it purchased. The *net* here refers to purchases of fixed assets net of any sales of fixed assets. You will often see capital spending called CAPEX, which is an acronym for capital expenditures. It usually means the same thing.

Change in Net Working Capital In addition to investing in fixed assets, a firm will also invest in current assets. For example, going back to the balance sheets in Table 2.1, we see that at the end of 2005, U.S. had current assets of $1,403. At the end of 2004, current assets were $1,112, so, during the year, U.S. invested $1,403 − 1,112 = $291 in current assets.

As the firm changes its investment in current assets, its current liabilities will usually change as well. To determine the change in net working capital, the easiest approach is just to take the difference between the beginning and ending net working capital (NWC) figures. Net working capital at the end of 2005 was $1,403 − 389 = $1,014. Similarly, at the end of 2004, net working capital was $1,112 − 428 = $684. So, given these figures, we have:

Ending NWC	$1,014
− Beginning NWC	684
Change in NWC	$ 330

Net working capital thus increased by $330. Put another way, U.S. Corporation had a net investment of $330 in NWC for the year. This change in NWC is often referred to as the "addition to" NWC.

Conclusion Given the figures we've come up with, we're ready to calculate cash flow from assets. The total cash flow from assets is given by operating cash flow less the amounts invested in fixed assets and net working capital. So, for U.S., we have:

U.S. CORPORATION 2005 Cash Flow from Assets	
Operating cash flow	$547
− Net capital spending	130
− Change in NWC	330
Cash flow from assets	$ 87

From the cash flow identity given earlier, we know that this $87 cash flow from assets equals the sum of the firm's cash flow to creditors and its cash flow to stockholders. We consider these next.

It wouldn't be at all unusual for a growing corporation to have a negative cash flow. As we see next, a negative cash flow means that the firm raised more money by borrowing and selling stock than it paid out to creditors and stockholders during the year.

free cash flow
Another name for cash flow from assets.

A Note on "Free" Cash Flow Cash flow from assets sometimes goes by a different name, **free cash flow**. Of course, there is no such thing as "free" cash (we wish!). Instead, the name refers to cash that the firm is free to distribute to creditors and stockholders because it is not needed for working capital or fixed asset investments. We will stick with "cash flow from assets" as our label for this important concept because, in practice, there is some variation in exactly how free cash flow is computed; different users calculate it in different ways. Nonetheless, whenever you hear the phrase "free cash flow," you should understand that what is being discussed is cash flow from assets or something quite similar.

Cash Flow to Creditors and Stockholders

cash flow to creditors
A firm's interest payments to creditors less net new borrowings.

cash flow to stockholders
Dividends paid out by a firm less net new equity raised.

The cash flows to creditors and stockholders represent the net payments to creditors and owners during the year. Their calculation is similar to that of cash flow from assets. **Cash flow to creditors** is interest paid less net new borrowing; **cash flow to stockholders** is dividends paid less net new equity raised.

Cash Flow to Creditors Looking at the income statement in Table 2.2, we see that U.S. paid $70 in interest to creditors. From the balance sheets in Table 2.1, we see that long-term debt rose by $454 − 408 = $46. So, U.S. Corporation paid out $70 in interest, but it borrowed an additional $46. Net cash flow to creditors is thus:

U.S. CORPORATION 2005 Cash Flow to Creditors	
Interest paid	$70
− Net new borrowing	46
Cash flow to creditors	$24

Cash flow to creditors is sometimes called *cash flow to bondholders;* we will use these terms interchangeably.

<< TABLE 2.5

Cash Flow Summary

I. The cash flow identity

Cash flow from assets = Cash flow to creditors (bondholders)
+ Cash flow to stockholders (owners)

II. Cash flow from assets

Cash flow from assets = Operating cash flow
− Net capital spending
− Change in net working capital (NWC)

where:

Operating cash flow = Earnings before interest and taxes (EBIT)
+ Depreciation − Taxes

Net capital spending = Ending net fixed assets − Beginning net fixed assets
+ Depreciation

Change in NWC = Ending NWC − Beginning NWC

III. Cash flow to creditors (bondholders)

Cash flow to creditors = Interest paid − Net new borrowing

IV. Cash flow to stockholders (owners)

Cash flow to stockholders = Dividends paid − Net new equity raised

Cash Flow to Stockholders From the income statement, we see that dividends paid to stockholders amounted to \$103. To get net new equity raised, we need to look at the common stock and paid-in surplus account. This account tells us how much stock the company has sold. During the year, this account rose by \$40, so \$40 in net new equity was raised. Given this, we have:

U.S. CORPORATION 2005 Cash Flow to Stockholders	
Dividends paid	\$103
− Net new equity raised	40
Cash flow to stockholders	\$ 63

The cash flow to stockholders for 2005 was thus \$63.

The last thing we need to do is to verify that the cash flow identity holds to be sure that we didn't make any mistakes. From the previous section, we know that cash flow from assets is \$87. Cash flow to creditors and stockholders is \$24 + 63 = \$87, so everything checks out. Table 2.5 contains a summary of the various cash flow calculations for future reference.

As our discussion indicates, it is essential that a firm keep an eye on its cash flow. The following serves as an excellent reminder of why doing so is a good idea, unless the firm's owners wish to end up in the "Po'" house.

QUOTH THE BANKER, "WATCH CASH FLOW"

Once upon a midnight dreary as I pondered weak and weary
Over many a quaint and curious volume of accounting lore,
Seeking gimmicks (without scruple) to squeeze through
  some new tax loophole,
Suddenly I heard a knock upon my door,
  Only this, and nothing more.

Then I felt a queasy tingling and I heard the cash a-jingling
As a fearsome banker entered whom I'd often seen before.
His face was money-green and in his eyes there could be seen
Dollar-signs that seemed to glitter as he reckoned up the score.
"Cash flow," the banker said, and nothing more.

I had always thought it fine to show a jet black bottom line.
But the banker sounded a resounding, "No.
Your receivables are high, mounting upward toward the sky;
Write-offs loom. What matters is cash flow."
He repeated, "Watch cash flow."

Then I tried to tell the story of our lovely inventory
Which, though large, is full of most delightful stuff.
But the banker saw its growth, and with a mighty oath
He waved his arms and shouted, "Stop! Enough!
Pay the interest, and don't give me any guff!"

Next I looked for noncash items which could add ad infinitum
To replace the ever-outward flow of cash,
But to keep my statement black I'd held depreciation back,
And my banker said that I'd done something rash.
He quivered, and his teeth began to gnash.

When I asked him for a loan, he responded, with a groan,
That the interest rate would be just prime plus eight,
And to guarantee my purity he'd insist on some security—
All my assets plus the scalp upon my pate.
Only this, a standard rate.

Though my bottom line is black, I am flat upon my back,
My cash flows out and customers pay slow.
The growth of my receivables is almost unbelievable:
The result is certain—unremitting woe!
And I hear the banker utter an ominous low mutter,
"Watch cash flow."

Herbert S. Bailey Jr.

Source: Reprinted from the January 13, 1975, issue of *Publishers Weekly*, published by R. R. Bowker, a Xerox company. Copyright © 1975 by the Xerox Corporation.

To which we can only add: "Amen."

An Example: Cash Flows for Dole Cola

This extended example covers the various cash flow calculations discussed in the chapter. It also illustrates a few variations that may arise.

Operating Cash Flow During the year, Dole Cola, Inc., had sales and cost of goods sold of \$600 and \$300, respectively. Depreciation was \$150 and interest paid was \$30. Taxes were calculated at a straight 34 percent. Dividends were \$30. (All figures are in millions of dollars.) What was operating cash flow for Dole? Why is this different from net income?

The easiest thing to do here is to go ahead and create an income statement. We can then pick up the numbers we need. Dole Cola's income statement is given here:

DOLE COLA **2005 Income Statement**		
Net sales		$600
Cost of goods sold		300
Depreciation		150
Earnings before interest and taxes		$150
Interest paid		30
Taxable income		$120
Taxes		41
Net income		$ 79
Dividends	$30	
Addition to retained earnings	49	

Net income for Dole was thus $79. We now have all the numbers we need. Referring back to the U.S. Corporation example and Table 2.5, we have:

DOLE COLA **2005 Operating Cash Flow**	
Earnings before interest and taxes	$150
+ Depreciation	150
− Taxes	41
Operating cash flow	$259

As this example illustrates, operating cash flow is not the same as net income, because depreciation and interest are subtracted out when net income is calculated. If you will recall our earlier discussion, we don't subtract these out in computing operating cash flow because depreciation is not a cash expense and interest paid is a financing expense, not an operating expense.

Net Capital Spending Suppose that beginning net fixed assets were $500 and ending net fixed assets were $750. What was the net capital spending for the year?

From the income statement for Dole, we know that depreciation for the year was $150. Net fixed assets rose by $250. Dole thus spent $250 along with an additional $150, for a total of $400.

Change in NWC and Cash Flow from Assets Suppose that Dole Cola started the year with $2,130 in current assets and $1,620 in current liabilities, and that the corresponding ending figures were $2,260 and $1,710. What was the change in NWC during the year? What was cash flow from assets? How does this compare to net income?

Net working capital started out as $2,130 − 1,620 = $510 and ended up at $2,260 − 1,710 = $550. The addition to NWC was thus $550 − 510 = $40. Putting together all the information for Dole, we have:

DOLE COLA **2005 Cash Flow from Assets**	
Operating cash flow	$259
− Net capital spending	400
− Change in NWC	40
Cash flow from assets	− $181

Dole had a cash flow from assets of −$181. Net income was positive at $79. Is the fact that cash flow from assets was negative a cause for alarm? Not necessarily. The cash flow here is negative primarily because of a large investment in fixed assets. If these are good investments, then the resulting negative cash flow is not a worry.

Cash Flow to Stockholders and Creditors We saw that Dole Cola had cash flow from assets of −$181. The fact that this is negative means that Dole raised more money in the form of new debt and equity than it paid out for the year. For example, suppose we know that Dole didn't sell any new equity for the year. What was cash flow to stockholders? To creditors?

Because it didn't raise any new equity, Dole's cash flow to stockholders is just equal to the cash dividend paid:

DOLE COLA 2005 Cash Flow to Stockholders	
Dividends paid	$30
− Net new equity raised	0
Cash flow to stockholders	$30

Now, from the cash flow identity, we know that the total cash paid to creditors and stockholders was −$181. Cash flow to stockholders is $30, so cash flow to creditors must be equal to −$181 − 30 = −$211:

$$\begin{aligned}\text{Cash flow to creditors} + \text{Cash flow to stockholders} &= -\$181\\ \text{Cash flow to creditors} + \$30 &= -\$181\\ \text{Cash flow to creditors} &= -\$211\end{aligned}$$

Because we know that cash flow to creditors is −$211 and interest paid is $30 (from the income statement), we can now determine net new borrowing. Dole must have borrowed $241 during the year to help finance the fixed asset expansion:

DOLE COLA 2005 Cash Flow to Creditors	
Interest paid	$ 30
− Net new borrowing	− 241
Cash flow to creditors	−$211

Concept Questions

2.4a What is the cash flow identity? Explain what it says.

2.4b What are the components of operating cash flow?

2.4c Why is interest paid not a component of operating cash flow?

SUMMARY AND CONCLUSIONS 2.5

This chapter has introduced you to some of the basics of financial statements, taxes, and cash flow. In it, we saw that:

1. The book values on an accounting balance sheet can be very different from market values. The goal of financial management is to maximize the market value of the stock, not its book value.
2. Net income as it is computed on the income statement is not cash flow. A primary reason is that depreciation, a noncash expense, is deducted when net income is computed.
3. Marginal and average tax rates can be different, and it is the marginal tax rate that is relevant for most financial decisions.
4. The marginal tax rate paid by the corporations with the largest incomes is 35 percent.
5. There is a cash flow identity much like the balance sheet identity. It says that cash flow from assets equals cash flow to creditors and stockholders.

The calculation of cash flow from financial statements isn't difficult. Care must be taken in handling noncash expenses, such as depreciation, and not to confuse operating costs with financing costs. Most of all, it is important not to confuse book values with market values, or accounting income with cash flow.

Chapter Review and Self-Test Problem

2.1 **Cash Flow for Mara Corporation** This problem will give you some practice working with financial statements and figuring cash flow. Based on the following information for Mara Corporation, prepare an income statement for 2005 and balance sheets for 2004 and 2005. Next, following our U.S. Corporation examples in the chapter, calculate cash flow from assets, cash flow to creditors, and cash flow to stockholders for Mara for 2005. Use a 35 percent tax rate throughout. You can check your answers against ours, found in the following section.

	2004	2005
Sales	$4,203	$4,507
Cost of goods sold	2,422	2,633
Depreciation	785	952
Interest	180	196
Dividends	225	250
Current assets	2,205	2,429
Net fixed assets	7,344	7,650
Current liabilities	1,003	1,255
Long-term debt	3,106	2,085

Answer to Chapter Review and Self-Test Problem

2.1 In preparing the balance sheets, remember that shareholders' equity is the residual. With this in mind, Mara's balance sheets are as follows:

Visit us at www.mhhe.com/rwj

MARA CORPORATION
2004 and 2005 Balance Sheets

	2004	2005		2004	2005
Current assets	$2,205	$ 2,429	Current liabilities	$1,003	$ 1,255
Net fixed assets	7,344	7,650	Long-term debt	3,106	2,085
			Equity	5,440	6,739
Total assets	$9,549	$10,079	Total liabilities and shareholders' equity	$9,549	$10,079

The income statement is straightforward:

MARA CORPORATION
2005 Income Statement

Sales		$4,507
Cost of goods sold		2,633
Depreciation		952
Earnings before interest and taxes		$ 922
Interest paid		196
Taxable income		$ 726
Taxes (35%)		254
Net income		$ 472
Dividends	$250	
Addition to retained earnings	222	

Notice that we've used an average 35 percent tax rate. Also notice that the addition to retained earnings is just net income less cash dividends.

We can now pick up the figures we need to get operating cash flow:

MARA CORPORATION
2005 Operating Cash Flow

Earnings before interest and taxes	$ 922
+ Depreciation	952
− Taxes	$ 254
Operating cash flow	$1,620

Next, we get the net capital spending for the year by looking at the change in fixed assets, remembering to account for depreciation:

Ending net fixed assets	$7,650
− Beginning net fixed assets	7,344
+ Depreciation	952
Net capital spending	$1,258

After calculating beginning and ending NWC, we take the difference to get the change in NWC:

Ending NWC	$1,174
− Beginning NWC	1,202
Change in NWC	−$ 28

We now combine operating cash flow, net capital spending, and the change in net working capital to get the total cash flow from assets:

MARA CORPORATION 2005 Cash Flow from Assets	
Operating cash flow	$1,620
– Net capital spending	1,258
– Change in NWC	–28
Cash flow from assets	$ 390

To get cash flow to creditors, notice that long-term borrowing decreased by $1,021 during the year and that interest paid was $196, so:

MARA CORPORATION 2005 Cash Flow to Creditors	
Interest paid	$ 196
– Net new borrowing	–1,021
Cash flow to creditors	$ 1,217

Finally, dividends paid were $250. To get net new equity raised, we have to do some extra calculating. Total equity was up by $6,739 − 5,440 = $1,299. Of this increase, $222 was from additions to retained earnings, so $1,077 in new equity was raised during the year. Cash flow to stockholders was thus:

MARA CORPORATION 2005 Cash Flow to Stockholders	
Dividends paid	$ 250
– Net new equity raised	1,077
Cash flow to stockholders	–$ 827

As a check, notice that cash flow from assets ($390) does equal cash flow to creditors plus cash flow to stockholders ($1,217 − 827 = $390).

Concepts Review and Critical Thinking Questions

1. **Liquidity** What does liquidity measure? Explain the trade-off a firm faces between high liquidity and low liquidity levels.
2. **Accounting and Cash Flows** Why is it that the revenue and cost figures shown on a standard income statement may not be representative of the actual cash inflows and outflows that occurred during a period?
3. **Book Values versus Market Values** In preparing a balance sheet, why do you think standard accounting practice focuses on historical cost rather than market value?
4. **Operating Cash Flow** In comparing accounting net income and operating cash flow, name two items you typically find in net income that are not in operating cash flow. Explain what each is and why it is excluded in operating cash flow.
5. **Book Values versus Market Values** Under standard accounting rules, it is possible for a company's liabilities to exceed its assets. When this occurs, the owners' equity is negative. Can this happen with market values? Why or why not?
6. **Cash Flow from Assets** Suppose a company's cash flow from assets was negative for a particular period. Is this necessarily a good sign or a bad sign?

7. **Operating Cash Flow** Suppose a company's operating cash flow was negative for several years running. Is this necessarily a good sign or a bad sign?
8. **Net Working Capital and Capital Spending** Could a company's change in NWC be negative in a given year? (Hint: Yes.) Explain how this might come about. What about net capital spending?
9. **Cash Flow to Stockholders and Creditors** Could a company's cash flow to stockholders be negative in a given year? (Hint: Yes.) Explain how this might come about. What about cash flow to creditors?
10. **Firm Values** Referring back to the Cisco example used at the beginning of the chapter, note that we suggested that Cisco's stockholders probably didn't suffer as a result of the reported loss. What do you think was the basis for our conclusion?

Questions and Problems

BASIC
(Questions 1–13)

1. **Building a Balance Sheet** Penguin Pucks, Inc., has current assets of $5,000, net fixed assets of $23,000, current liabilities of $4,300, and long-term debt of $13,000. What is the value of the shareholders' equity account for this firm? How much is net working capital?
2. **Building an Income Statement** Papa Roach Exterminators, Inc., has sales of $527,000, costs of $280,000, depreciation expense of $38,000, interest expense of $15,000, and a tax rate of 35 percent. What is the net income for this firm?
3. **Dividends and Retained Earnings** Suppose the firm in Problem 2 paid out $48,000 in cash dividends. What is the addition to retained earnings?
4. **Per-Share Earnings and Dividends** Suppose the firm in Problem 3 had 30,000 shares of common stock outstanding. What is the earnings per share, or EPS, figure? What is the dividends per share figure?
5. **Market Values and Book Values** Klingon Widgets, Inc., purchased new cloaking machinery three years ago for $7 million. The machinery can be sold to the Romulans today for $3.2 million. Klingon's current balance sheet shows net fixed assets of $4,000,000, current liabilities of $2,200,000, and net working capital of $900,000. If all the current assets were liquidated today, the company would receive $2.8 million cash. What is the book value of Klingon's assets today? What is the market value?
6. **Calculating Taxes** The Herrera Co. had $273,000 in 2005 taxable income. Using the rates from Table 2.3 in the chapter, calculate the company's 2005 income taxes.
7. **Tax Rates** In Problem 6, what is the average tax rate? What is the marginal tax rate?
8. **Calculating OCF** Ranney, Inc., has sales of $13,500, costs of $5,400, depreciation expense of $1,200, and interest expense of $680. If the tax rate is 35 percent, what is the operating cash flow, or OCF?
9. **Calculating Net Capital Spending** Gordon Driving School's 2004 balance sheet showed net fixed assets of $4.2 million, and the 2005 balance sheet showed net fixed assets of $4.7 million. The company's 2005 income statement showed a depreciation expense of $925,000. What was Gordon's net capital spending for 2005?
10. **Calculating Additions to NWC** The 2004 balance sheet of Rock 'N' Roll Records, Inc., showed current assets of $1,600 and current liabilities of $940. The 2005 balance sheet showed current assets of $1,720 and current liabilities of $1,180. What was the company's 2005 change in net working capital, or NWC?

11. **Cash Flow to Creditors** The 2004 balance sheet of Anna's Tennis Shop, Inc., showed long-term debt of $2.8 million, and the 2005 balance sheet showed long-term debt of $3.1 million. The 2005 income statement showed an interest expense of $340,000. What was the firm's cash flow to creditors during 2005?

12. **Cash Flow to Stockholders** The 2004 balance sheet of Anna's Tennis Shop, Inc., showed $820,000 in the common stock account and $6.8 million in the additional paid-in surplus account. The 2005 balance sheet showed $855,000 and $7.6 million in the same two accounts, respectively. If the company paid out $600,000 in cash dividends during 2005, what was the cash flow to stockholders for the year?

13. **Calculating Total Cash Flows** Given the information for Anna's Tennis Shop, Inc., in Problems 11 and 12, suppose you also know that the firm's net capital spending for 2005 was $760,000, and that the firm reduced its net working capital investment by $165,000. What was the firm's 2005 operating cash flow, or OCF?

INTERMEDIATE
(Questions 14–22)

14. **Calculating Total Cash Flows** Bedrock Gravel Corp. shows the following information on its 2005 income statement: sales = $145,000; costs = $86,000; other expenses = $4,900; depreciation expense = $7,000; interest expense = $15,000; taxes = $12,840; dividends = $8,700. In addition, you're told that the firm issued $6,450 in new equity during 2005, and redeemed $6,500 in outstanding long-term debt.
    a. What is the 2005 operating cash flow?
    b. What is the 2005 cash flow to creditors?
    c. What is the 2005 cash flow to stockholders?
    d. If net fixed assets increased by $5,000 during the year, what was the addition to NWC?

15. **Using Income Statements** Given the following information for Papa Joe Pizza Co., calculate the depreciation expense: sales = $29,000; costs = $13,000; addition to retained earnings = $4,500; dividends paid = $900; interest expense = $1,600; tax rate = 35 percent.

16. **Preparing a Balance Sheet** Prepare a 2005 balance sheet for Tim's Couch Corp. based on the following information: cash = $175,000; patents and copyrights = $720,000; accounts payable = $430,000; accounts receivable = $140,000; tangible net fixed assets = $2,900,000; inventory = $265,000; notes payable = $180,000; accumulated retained earnings = $1,240,000; long-term debt = $1,430,000.

17. **Residual Claims** Clapper's Clippers, Inc., is obligated to pay its creditors $3,500 during the year.
    a. What is the market value of the shareholders' equity if assets have a market value of $4,300?
    b. What if assets equal $3,200?

18. **Marginal versus Average Tax Rates** (Refer to Table 2.3.) Corporation Growth has $85,000 in taxable income, and Corporation Income has $8,500,000 in taxable income.
    a. What is the tax bill for each firm?
    b. Suppose both firms have identified a new project that will increase taxable income by $10,000. How much in additional taxes will each firm pay? Why is this amount the same?

19. **Net Income and OCF** During 2005, Raines Umbrella Corp. had sales of $850,000. Cost of goods sold, administrative and selling expenses, and depreciation expenses were $630,000, $120,000, and $130,000, respectively. In addition, the company had an interest expense of $85,000 and a tax rate of 35 percent. (Ignore any tax loss carry-back or carry-forward provisions.)

a. What is Raines's net income for 2005?
b. What is its operating cash flow?
c. Explain your results in (*a*) and (*b*).

20. Accounting Values versus Cash Flows In Problem 19, suppose Raines Umbrella Corp. paid out $30,000 in cash dividends. Is this possible? If spending on net fixed assets and net working capital was zero, and if no new stock was issued during the year, what do you know about the firm's long-term debt account?

21. Calculating Cash Flows Cusic Industries had the following operating results for 2005: sales = $12,800; cost of goods sold = $10,400; depreciation expense = $1,900; interest expense = $450; dividends paid = $500. At the beginning of the year, net fixed assets were $9,100, current assets were $3,200, and current liabilities were $1,800. At the end of the year, net fixed assets were $9,700, current assets were $3,850, and current liabilities were $2,100. The tax rate for 2005 was 34 percent.
a. What is net income for 2005?
b. What is the operating cash flow for 2005?
c. What is the cash flow from assets for 2005? Is this possible? Explain.
d. If no new debt was issued during the year, what is the cash flow to creditors? What is the cash flow to stockholders? Explain and interpret the positive and negative signs of your answers in (*a*) through (*d*).

22. Calculating Cash Flows Consider the following abbreviated financial statements for Parrothead Enterprises:

PARROTHEAD ENTERPRISES
2004 and 2005 Partial Balance Sheets

Assets	2004	2005	Liabilities and Owners' Equity	2004	2005
Current assets	$ 650	$ 705	Current liabilities	$ 265	$ 290
Net fixed assets	2,900	3,400	Long-term debt	1,500	1,720

PARROTHEAD ENTERPRISES
2005 Income Statement

Sales	$8,600
Costs	4,150
Depreciation	800
Interest paid	216

a. What is owners' equity for 2004 and 2005?
b. What is the change in net working capital for 2005?
c. In 2005, Parrothead Enterprises purchased $1,500 in new fixed assets. How much in fixed assets did Parrothead Enterprises sell? What is the cash flow from assets for the year? (The tax rate is 35 percent.)
d. During 2005, Parrothead Enterprises raised $300 in new long-term debt. How much long-term debt must Parrothead Enterprises have paid off during the year? What is the cash flow to creditors?

CHALLENGE
(Questions 23–26)

23. Net Fixed Assets and Depreciation On the balance sheet, the net fixed assets (NFA) account is equal to the gross fixed assets (FA) account, which records the acquisition cost of fixed assets, minus the accumulated depreciation (AD) account, which records the total depreciation taken by the firm against its fixed assets. Using the fact that NFA = FA − AD, show that the expression given in the chapter for net capital spending, $NFA_{end} - NFA_{beg} + D$ (where D is the depreciation expense during the year), is equivalent to $FA_{end} - FA_{beg}$.

24. Tax Rates Refer to the corporate marginal tax rate information in Table 2.3.
a. Why do you think the marginal tax rate jumps up from 34 percent to 39 percent at a taxable income of $100,001, and then falls back to a 34 percent marginal rate at a taxable income of $335,001?

b. Compute the average tax rate for a corporation with exactly $335,001 in taxable income. Does this confirm your explanation in part (*a*)? What is the average tax rate for a corporation with exactly $18,333,334? Is the same thing happening here?

c. The 39 percent and 38 percent tax rates both represent what is called a tax "bubble." Suppose the government wanted to lower the upper threshold of the 39 percent marginal tax bracket from $335,000 to $200,000. What would the new 39 percent bubble rate have to be?

Use the following information for Taco Swell, Inc., for Problems 25 and 26 (assume the tax rate is 34 percent):

	2004	2005
Sales	$4,018	$4,312
Depreciation	577	578
Cost of goods sold	1,382	1,569
Other expenses	328	274
Interest	269	309
Cash	2,107	2,155
Accounts receivable	2,789	3,142
Short-term notes payable	407	382
Long-term debt	7,056	8,232
Net fixed assets	17,669	18,091
Accounts payable	2,213	2,146
Inventory	4,959	5,096
Dividends	490	539

25. Financial Statements Draw up an income statement and balance sheet for this company for 2004 and 2005.

26. Calculating Cash Flow For 2005, calculate the cash flow from assets, cash flow to creditors, and cash flow to stockholders.

www.mhhe.com/edumarketinsight **S&P Problems**

STANDARD & POOR'S

1. Marginal and Average Tax Rates Download the annual income statements for Sharper Image (SHRP). Looking back at Table 2.3, what is the marginal income tax rate for Sharper Image? Using the total income tax and the pretax income numbers calculate the average tax rate for Sharper Image. Is this number greater than 35 percent? Why or why not?

2. Net Working Capital Find the annual balance sheets for American Electric Power (AEP) and HJ Heinz (HNZ). Calculate the net working capital for each company. Is American Electric Power's net working capital negative? If so, does this indicate potential financial difficulty for the company? What about Heinz?

3. Per Share Earnings and Dividends Find the annual income statements for Harley Davidson (HDI), Hawaiian Electric Industries (HE) and Time Warner (TWX). What are the earnings per share (EPS Basic from operations) for each of these companies? What are the dividends per share for each company? Why do these companies pay out a different portion of income in the form of dividends?

4. **Cash Flow Identity** Download the annual balance sheets and income statements for Landry's Seafood Restaurants (LNY). Using the most recent year calculate the cash flow identity for Landry Seafood. Explain your answer.

What's On the Web?

2.1. **Change in Net Working Capital** Find the most recent abbreviated balance sheets for General Dynamics at finance.yahoo.com. Enter the ticker symbol "GD," follow the "Research" link, and the "Financials" link. Using the two most recent balance sheets, calculate the change in net working capital. What does this number mean?

2.2. **Book Values versus Market Values** The home page for Coca-Cola Company can be found at www.coca-cola.com. Locate the most recent annual report, which contains a balance sheet for the company. What is the book value of equity for Coca-Cola? The market value of a company is the number of shares of stock outstanding times the price per share. This information can be found at finance.yahoo.com using the ticker symbol for Coca-Cola (KO). What is the market value of equity? Which number is more relevant for shareholders?

2.3. **Cash Flows to Stockholders and Creditors** Cooper Tire and Rubber Company provides financial information for investors on its web site at www.coopertires.com. Follow the "Investor Information" link and find the most recent annual report. Using the consolidated statements of cash flows, calculate the cash flow to stockholders and the cash flow to creditors.

2.4. **Average and Marginal Tax Rates** Find the most recent income statement for IBM at www.ibm.com. What is the marginal tax rate for IBM? What is the average tax rate for IBM? Is the average tax rate 35 percent? Why or why not?

>> MINI-CASE

Cash Flows and Financial Statements at Sunset Boards, Inc.

Sunset Boards is a small company that manufactures and sells surfboards in Malibu. Tad Marks, the founder of the company, is in charge of the design and sale of the surfboards, but his background is in surfing, not business. As a result, the company's financial records are not well maintained.

The initial investment in Sunset Boards was provided by Tad and his friends and family. Since the initial investment was relatively small, and the company has only made surfboards for its own store, the investors haven't required detailed financial statements from Tad. But, thanks to word of mouth among professional surfers, sales have picked up recently, and Tad is considering a major expansion. His plans include opening another surfboard store in Hawaii, as well as supplying his "sticks" (surfer lingo for boards) to other sellers.

Tad's expansion plans require a significant investment, which he plans to finance with a combination of additional funds from outsiders plus some money borrowed from banks. Naturally, the new investors and creditors require more organized and detailed financial statements than Tad has previously prepared. At the urging of his investors, Tad has hired financial analyst Christina Wolfe to evaluate the performance of the company over the past year.

After rooting through old bank statements, sales receipts, tax returns, and other records, Christina has assembled the following information:

	2004	2005
Cost of goods sold	$84,310	$106,450
Cash	12,165	18,380
Depreciation	23,800	26,900
Interest expense	5,180	5,930
Selling and administrative expenses	16,580	21,640
Accounts payable	21,500	24,350
Fixed assets	105,000	134,000
Sales	165,390	201,600
Accounts receivable	8,620	11,182
Notes payable	9,800	10,700
Long-term debt	53,000	61,000
Inventory	18,140	24,894
New equity	0	10,000

Sunset Boards currently pays out 30 percent of net income as dividends to Tad and the other original investors, and has a 20 percent tax rate. You are Christina's assistant, and she has asked you to prepare the following:

1. An income statement for 2004 and 2005.
2. A balance sheet for 2004 and 2005.
3. Operating cash flow for each year.
4. Cash flow from assets for 2005.
5. Cash flow to creditors for 2005.
6. Cash flow to stockholders for 2005.

Questions

1. How would you describe Sunset Boards' cash flows for 2005? Write up a brief discussion.
2. In light of your discussion in the previous question, what do you think about Tad's expansion plans?

PART TWO

Financial Statements and Long-Term Financial Planning

3 Working with Financial Statements

On February 24, 2004, the price of a share of common stock in Linux software distributor Red Hat, Inc., closed at about $17. At that price, *The Wall Street Journal* reported Red Hat had a price-earnings (PE) ratio of 130. That is, investors were willing to pay $130 for every dollar in income earned by Red Hat. At the same time, investors were willing to pay only $38, $29, and $17 for each dollar earned by Cisco, Tootsie Roll, and Kraft Foods, respectively. At the other extreme were eBay and Yahoo!, both relative newcomers to the stock market. Each had negative earnings for the previous year, yet eBay was priced at about $67 per share and Yahoo! at about $44 per share. Since they had negative earnings, their PE ratios would have been negative, so they were not reported. At that time, the typical stock in the S&P 500 index of large company stocks was trading at a PE of about 23, or about 23 times earnings, as they say on Wall Street.

Price-to-earnings comparisons are examples of the use of financial ratios. As we will see in this chapter, there are a wide variety of financial ratios, all designed to summarize specific aspects of a firm's financial position. In addition to discussing how to analyze financial statements and compute financial ratios, we will have quite a bit to say about who uses this information and why.

In chapter 2, we discussed some of the essential concepts of financial statements and cash flows. Part 2, this chapter and the next, continues where our earlier discussion left off. Our goal here is to expand your understanding of the uses (and abuses) of financial statement information.

Financial statement information will crop up in various places in the remainder of our book. Part 2 is not essential for understanding this material, but it will help give you an overall perspective on the role of financial statement information in corporate finance.

A good working knowledge of financial statements is desirable simply because such statements, and numbers derived from those statements, are the primary means of communicating financial information both within the firm and outside the firm. In short, much of the language of corporate finance is rooted in the ideas we discuss in this chapter.

Furthermore, as we shall see, there are many different ways of using financial statement information and many different types of users. This diversity reflects the fact that financial statement information plays an important part in many types of decisions.

In the best of all worlds, the financial manager has full market value information about all of the firm's assets. This will rarely (if ever) happen. So the reason we rely on accounting figures for much of our financial information is that we are almost always unable to obtain all (or even part) of the market information that we want. The only meaningful yardstick for evaluating business decisions is whether or not they create economic value (see Chapter 1). However, in many important situations, it will not be possible to make this judgment directly because we can't see the market value effects of decisions.

We recognize that accounting numbers are often just pale reflections of economic reality, but they are frequently the best available information. For privately held corporations, not-for-profit businesses, and smaller firms, for example, very little direct market value information exists at all. The accountant's reporting function is crucial in these circumstances.

Clearly, one important goal of the accountant is to report financial information to the user in a form useful for decision making. Ironically, the information frequently does not come to the user in such a form. In other words, financial statements don't come with a user's guide. This chapter and the next are first steps in filling this gap.

CASH FLOW AND FINANCIAL STATEMENTS: A CLOSER LOOK **3.1**

At the most fundamental level, firms do two different things: they generate cash and they spend it. Cash is generated by selling a product, an asset, or a security. Selling a security involves either borrowing or selling an equity interest (i.e., shares of stock) in the firm. Cash is spent in paying for materials and labor to produce a product and in purchasing assets. Payments to creditors and owners also require the spending of cash.

In Chapter 2, we saw that the cash activities of a firm could be summarized by a simple identity:

Cash flow from assets = Cash flow to creditors + Cash flow to owners

This cash flow identity summarizes the total cash result of all transactions a firm engages in during the year. In this section, we return to the subject of cash flows by taking a closer look at the cash events during the year that lead to these total figures.

Sources and Uses of Cash

Those activities that bring in cash are called **sources of cash**. Those activities that involve spending cash are called **uses** (or applications) **of cash**. What we need to do is to trace the changes in the firm's balance sheet to see how the firm obtained its cash and how the firm spent its cash during some time period.

sources of cash
A firm's activities that generate cash.

uses of cash
A firm's activities in which cash is spent. Also called applications of cash.

To get started, consider the balance sheets for the Prufrock Corporation in Table 3.1. Notice that we have calculated the change in each of the items on the balance sheets.

Looking over the balance sheets for Prufrock, we see that quite a few things changed during the year. For example, Prufrock increased its net fixed assets by $149 and its inventory by $29. (Note that, throughout, all figures are in millions of dollars.) Where did the money come from? To answer this and related questions, we need to first identify those changes that used up cash (uses) and those that brought cash in (sources).

A little common sense is useful here. A firm uses cash by either buying assets or making payments. So, loosely speaking, an increase in an asset account means the firm, on a net basis, bought some assets, a use of cash. If an asset account went down, then, on a net basis, the firm sold some assets. This would be a net source. Similarly, if a liability account goes down, then the firm has made a net payment, a use of cash.

Company financial information can be found many places on the Web, including www.financials.com, finance.yahoo.com, and moneycentral.msn.com.

Given this reasoning, there is a simple, albeit mechanical, definition you may find useful. An increase in a left-hand–side (asset) account or a decrease in a right-hand–side (liability or equity) account is a use of cash. Likewise, a decrease in an asset account or an increase in a liability (or equity) account is a source of cash.

TABLE 3.1 >>

PRUFROCK CORPORATION
2004 and 2005 Balance Sheets
($ in millions)

	2004	2005	Change
Assets			
Current assets			
Cash	$ 84	$ 98	+$ 14
Accounts receivable	165	188	+ 23
Inventory	393	422	+ 29
Total	$ 642	$ 708	+$ 66
Fixed assets			
Net plant and equipment	$2,731	$2,880	+$149
Total assets	$3,373	$3,588	+$215
Liabilities and Owners' Equity			
Current liabilities			
Accounts payable	$ 312	$ 344	+$ 32
Notes payable	231	196	− 35
Total	$ 543	$ 540	−$ 3
Long-term debt	$ 531	$ 457	−$ 74
Owners' equity			
Common stock and paid-in surplus	$ 500	$ 550	+$ 50
Retained earnings	1,799	2,041	+ 242
Total	$2,299	$2,591	+$292
Total liabilities and owners' equity	$3,373	$3,588	+$215

Looking again at Prufrock, we see that inventory rose by $29. This is a net use because Prufrock effectively paid out $29 to increase inventories. Accounts payable rose by $32. This is a source of cash because Prufrock effectively has borrowed an additional $32 payable by the end of the year. Notes payable, on the other hand, went down by $35, so Prufrock effectively paid off $35 worth of short-term debt—a use of cash.

Based on our discussion, we can summarize the sources and uses from the balance sheet as follows:

Sources of cash:	
Increase in accounts payable	$ 32
Increase in common stock	50
Increase in retained earnings	242
Total sources	$324
Uses of cash:	
Increase in accounts receivable	$ 23
Increase in inventory	29
Decrease in notes payable	35
Decrease in long-term debt	74
Net fixed asset acquisitions	149
Total uses	$310
Net addition to cash	$ 14

<< TABLE 3.2

PRUFROCK CORPORATION 2005 Income Statement ($ in millions)		
Sales		$2,311
Cost of goods sold		1,344
Depreciation		276
Earnings before interest and taxes		$ 691
Interest paid		141
Taxable income		$ 550
Taxes (34%)		187
Net income		$ 363
Dividends	$121	
Addition to retained earnings	242	

The net addition to cash is just the difference between sources and uses, and our $14 result here agrees with the $14 change shown on the balance sheet.

This simple statement tells us much of what happened during the year, but it doesn't tell the whole story. For example, the increase in retained earnings is net income (a source of funds) less dividends (a use of funds). It would be more enlightening to have these reported separately so we could see the breakdown. Also, we have only considered net fixed asset acquisitions. Total or gross spending would be more interesting to know.

To further trace the flow of cash through the firm during the year, we need an income statement. For Prufrock, the results for the year are shown in Table 3.2.

Notice here that the $242 addition to retained earnings we calculated from the balance sheet is just the difference between the net income of $363 and the dividends of $121.

The Statement of Cash Flows

statement of cash flows
A firm's financial statement that summarizes its sources and uses of cash over a specified period.

There is some flexibility in summarizing the sources and uses of cash in the form of a financial statement. However it is presented, the result is called the **statement of cash flows**. Historically, this statement was called the *statement of changes in financial position* and it was presented in terms of the changes in net working capital rather than cash flows. We will work with the newer cash format.

We present a particular format for this statement in Table 3.3. The basic idea is to group all the changes into three categories: operating activities, financing activities, and investment activities. The exact form differs in detail from one preparer to the next.

Don't be surprised if you come across different arrangements. The types of information presented will be very similar; the exact order can differ. The key thing to remember in this case is that we started out with $84 in cash and ended up with $98, for a net increase of $14. We're just trying to see what events led to this change.

Going back to Chapter 2, we note that there is a slight conceptual problem here. Interest paid should really go under financing activities, but unfortunately that's not the way the accounting is handled. The reason, you may recall, is that interest is deducted as an expense when net income is computed. Also, notice that the net purchase of fixed assets was $149. Because Prufrock wrote off $276 worth of assets (the depreciation), it must have actually spent a total of $149 + 276 = $425 on fixed assets.

Once we have this statement, it might seem appropriate to express the change in cash on a per-share basis, much as we did for net income. Ironically, despite the interest we might

TABLE 3.3 >>

PRUFROCK CORPORATION 2005 Statement of Cash Flows ($ in millions)	
Cash, beginning of year	$ 84
Operating activity	
Net income	$363
Plus:	
Depreciation	276
Increase in accounts payable	32
Less:	
Increase in accounts receivable	− 23
Increase in inventory	− 29
Net cash from operating activity	$619
Investment activity	
Fixed asset acquisitions	−$425
Net cash from investment activity	−$425
Financing activity	
Decrease in notes payable	−$ 35
Decrease in long-term debt	− 74
Dividends paid	− 121
Increase in common stock	50
Net cash from financing activity	−$180
Net increase in cash	$ 14
Cash, end of year	$ 98

have in some measure of cash flow per share, standard accounting practice expressly prohibits reporting this information. The reason is that accountants feel that cash flow (or some component of cash flow) is not an alternative to accounting income, so only earnings per share are to be reported.

As shown in Table 3.4, it is sometimes useful to present the same information a bit differently. We will call this the "sources and uses of cash" statement. There is no such statement in financial accounting, but this arrangement resembles one used many years ago. As we will discuss, this form can come in handy, but we emphasize again that it is not the way this information is normally presented.

Now that we have the various cash pieces in place, we can get a good idea of what happened during the year. Prufrock's major cash outlays were fixed asset acquisitions and cash dividends. It paid for these activities primarily with cash generated from operations.

Prufrock also retired some long-term debt and increased current assets. Finally, current liabilities were not greatly changed, and a relatively small amount of new equity was sold. Altogether, this short sketch captures Prufrock's major sources and uses of cash for the year.

Concept Questions

3.1a What is a source of cash? Give three examples.

3.1b What is a use, or application, of cash? Give three examples.

<< TABLE 3.4

PRUFROCK CORPORATION 2005 Sources and Uses of Cash ($ in millions)	
Cash, beginning of year	$ 84
Sources of cash	
Operations:	
Net income	$363
Depreciation	276
	$639
Working capital:	
Increase in accounts payable	$ 32
Long-term financing:	
Increase in common stock	50
Total sources of cash	$721
Uses of cash	
Working capital:	
Increase in accounts receivable	$ 23
Increase in inventory	29
Decrease in notes payable	35
Long-term financing:	
Decrease in long-term debt	74
Fixed asset acquisitions	425
Dividends paid	121
Total uses of cash	$707
Net addition to cash	$ 14
Cash, end of year	$ 98

STANDARDIZED FINANCIAL STATEMENTS

3.2

The next thing we might want to do with Prufrock's financial statements is to compare them to those of other, similar, companies. We would immediately have a problem, however. It's almost impossible to directly compare the financial statements for two companies because of differences in size.

For example, Ford and GM are obviously serious rivals in the auto market, but GM is much larger (in terms of assets), so it is difficult to compare them directly. For that matter, it's difficult to even compare financial statements from different points in time for the same company if the company's size has changed. The size problem is compounded if we try to compare GM and, say, Toyota. If Toyota's financial statements are denominated in yen, then we have a size *and* a currency difference.

To start making comparisons, one obvious thing we might try to do is to somehow standardize the financial statements. One very common and useful way of doing this is to work with percentages instead of total dollars. In this section, we describe two different ways of standardizing financial statements along these lines.

Common-Size Statements

To get started, a useful way of standardizing financial statements is to express each item on the balance sheet as a percentage of assets and to express each item on the income

TABLE 3.5 >>

PRUFROCK CORPORATION
Common-Size Balance Sheets 2004 and 2005

	2004	2005	Change
Assets			
Current assets			
Cash	2.5%	2.7%	+ .2%
Accounts receivable	4.9	5.2	+ .3
Inventory	11.7	11.8	+ .1
Total	19.1	19.7	+ .6
Fixed assets			
Net plant and equipment	80.9	80.3	− .6
Total assets	100.0%	100.0%	0.0
Liabilities and Owners' Equity			
Current liabilities			
Accounts payable	9.2%	9.6%	+ .4%
Notes payable	6.8	5.5	−1.3
Total	16.0	15.1	− .9
Long-term debt	15.7	12.7	−3.0
Owners' equity			
Common stock and paid-in surplus	14.8	15.3	+ .5
Retained earnings	53.3	56.9	+3.6
Total	68.1	72.2	+4.1
Total liabilities and owners' equity	100.0%	100.0%	0.0

common-size statement
A standardized financial statement presenting all items in percentage terms. Balance sheet items are shown as a percentage of assets and income statement items as a percentage of sales.

statement as a percentage of sales. The resulting financial statements are called **common-size statements**. We consider these next.

Common-Size Balance Sheets One way, though not the only way, to construct a common-size balance sheet is to express each item as a percentage of total assets. Prufrock's 2004 and 2005 common-size balance sheets are shown in Table 3.5.

Notice that some of the totals don't check exactly because of rounding errors. Also notice that the total change has to be zero because the beginning and ending numbers must add up to 100 percent.

In this form, financial statements are relatively easy to read and compare. For example, just looking at the two balance sheets for Prufrock, we see that current assets were 19.7 percent of total assets in 2005, up from 19.1 percent in 2004. Current liabilities declined from 16.0 percent to 15.1 percent of total liabilities and equity over that same time. Similarly, total equity rose from 68.1 percent of total liabilities and equity to 72.2 percent.

Overall, Prufrock's liquidity, as measured by current assets compared to current liabilities, increased over the year. Simultaneously, Prufrock's indebtedness diminished as a percentage of total assets. We might be tempted to conclude that the balance sheet has grown "stronger." We will say more about this later.

Common-Size Income Statements A useful way of standardizing the income statement is to express each item as a percentage of total sales, as illustrated for Prufrock in Table 3.6.

<< TABLE 3.6

PRUFROCK CORPORATION Common-Size Income Statement 2005		
Sales		100.0%
Cost of goods sold		58.2
Depreciation		11.9
Earnings before interest and taxes		29.9
Interest paid		6.1
Taxable income		23.8
Taxes (34%)		8.1
Net income		15.7%
Dividends	5.2%	
Addition to retained earnings	10.5	

This income statement tells us what happens to each dollar in sales. For Prufrock, interest expense eats up \$.061 out of every sales dollar and taxes take another \$.081. When all is said and done, \$.157 of each dollar flows through to the bottom line (net income), and that amount is split into \$.105 retained in the business and \$.052 paid out in dividends.

These percentages are very useful in comparisons. For example, a very relevant figure is the cost percentage. For Prufrock, \$.582 of each \$1 in sales goes to pay for goods sold. It would be interesting to compute the same percentage for Prufrock's main competitors to see how Prufrock stacks up in terms of cost control.

Common-Size Statements of Cash Flows Although we have not presented it here, it is also possible and useful to prepare a common-size statement of cash flows. Unfortunately, with the current statement of cash flows, there is no obvious denominator such as total assets or total sales. However, if the information is arranged in a way similar to that in Table 3.4, then each item can be expressed as a percentage of total sources (or total uses). The results can then be interpreted as the percentage of total sources of cash supplied or as the percentage of total uses of cash for a particular item.

Common–Base Year Financial Statements: Trend Analysis

Imagine we were given balance sheets for the last 10 years for some company and we were trying to investigate trends in the firm's pattern of operations. Does the firm use more or less debt? Has the firm grown more or less liquid? A useful way of standardizing financial statements in this case is to choose a base year and then express each item relative to the base amount. We will call the resulting statements **common–base year statements**.

For example, from 2004 to 2005, Prufrock's inventory rose from \$393 to \$422. If we pick 2004 as our base year, then we would set inventory equal to 1.00 for that year. For the next year, we would calculate inventory relative to the base year as \$422/393 = 1.07. In this case, we could say inventory grew by about 7 percent during the year. If we had multiple years, we would just divide the inventory figure for each one by \$393. The resulting series is very easy to plot, and it is then very easy to compare two or more different companies. Table 3.7 summarizes these calculations for the asset side of the balance sheet.

common–base year statement
A standardized financial statement presenting all items relative to a certain base-year amount.

TABLE 3.7 >>

PRUFROCK CORPORATION
Summary of Standardized Balance Sheets
(Asset side only)

	Assets ($ in millions)		Common-Size Assets		Common-Base Year Assets	Combined Common-Size and Base-Year Assets
	2004	2005	2004	2005	2005	2005
Current assets						
Cash	$ 84	$ 98	2.5%	2.7%	1.17	1.08
Accounts receivable	165	188	4.9	5.2	1.14	1.06
Inventory	393	422	11.7	11.8	1.07	1.01
Total current assets	$ 642	$ 708	19.1	19.7	1.10	1.03
Fixed assets						
Net plant and equipment	$2,731	$2,880	80.9	80.3	1.05	0.99
Total assets	$3,373	$3,588	100.0%	100.0%	1.06	1.00

NOTE: The common-size numbers are calculated by dividing each item by total assets for that year. For example, the 2004 common-size cash amount is $84/3,373 = 2.5%. The common–base year numbers are calculated by dividing each 2005 item by the base-year (2004) dollar amount. The common-base cash is thus $98/84 = 1.17, representing a 17 percent increase. The combined common-size and base-year figures are calculated by dividing each common-size amount by the base-year (2004) common-size amount. The cash figure is therefore 2.7%/2.5% = 1.08, representing an 8 percent increase in cash holdings as a percentage of total assets. Columns may not total precisely due to rounding.

Combined Common-Size and Base-Year Analysis

The trend analysis we have been discussing can be combined with the common-size analysis discussed earlier. The reason for doing this is that as total assets grow, most of the other accounts must grow as well. By first forming the common-size statements, we eliminate the effect of this overall growth.

For example, looking at Table 3.7, we see that Prufrock's accounts receivable were $165, or 4.9 percent of total assets, in 2004. In 2005, they had risen to $188, which was 5.2 percent of total assets. If we do our analysis in terms of dollars, then the 2005 figure would be $188/165 = 1.14, representing a 14 percent increase in receivables. However, if we work with the common-size statements, then the 2005 figure would be 5.2%/4.9% = 1.06. This tells us accounts receivable, as a percentage of total assets, grew by 6 percent. Roughly speaking, what we see is that of the 14 percent total increase, about 8 percent (14% − 6%) is attributable simply to growth in total assets.

Concept Questions

3.2a Why is it often necessary to standardize financial statements?

3.2b Name two types of standardized statements and describe how each is formed.

3.3 RATIO ANALYSIS

Another way of avoiding the problems involved in comparing companies of different sizes is to calculate and compare **financial ratios**. Such ratios are ways of comparing and investigating the relationships between different pieces of financial information. Using ratios eliminates the size problem because the size effectively divides out. We're then left with percentages, multiples, or time periods.

financial ratios
Relationships determined from a firm's financial information and used for comparison purposes.

There is a problem in discussing financial ratios. Because a ratio is simply one number divided by another, and because there is a substantial quantity of accounting numbers out there, there is a huge number of possible ratios we could examine. Everybody has a favorite. We will restrict ourselves to a representative sampling.

In this section, we only want to introduce you to some commonly used financial ratios. These are not necessarily the ones we think are the best. In fact, some of them may strike you as illogical or not as useful as some alternatives. If they do, don't be concerned. As a financial analyst, you can always decide how to compute your own ratios.

What you do need to worry about is the fact that different people and different sources seldom compute these ratios in exactly the same way, and this leads to much confusion. The specific definitions we use here may or may not be the same as ones you have seen or will see elsewhere. If you are ever using ratios as a tool for analysis, you should be careful to document how you calculate each one, and, if you are comparing your numbers to numbers from another source, be sure you know how those numbers are computed.

We will defer much of our discussion of how ratios are used and some problems that come up with using them until later in the chapter. For now, for each of the ratios we discuss, we consider several questions that come to mind:

1. How is it computed?
2. What is it intended to measure, and why might we be interested?
3. What is the unit of measurement?
4. What might a high or low value be telling us? How might such values be misleading?
5. How could this measure be improved?

Financial ratios are traditionally grouped into the following categories:

1. Short-term solvency, or liquidity, ratios
2. Long-term solvency, or financial leverage, ratios
3. Asset management, or turnover, ratios
4. Profitability ratios
5. Market value ratios

We will consider each of these in turn. In calculating these numbers for Prufrock, we will use the ending balance sheet (2005) figures unless we explicitly say otherwise. Also notice that the various ratios are color keyed to indicate which numbers come from the income statement and which come from the balance sheet.

Short-Term Solvency, or Liquidity, Measures

As the name suggests, short-term solvency ratios as a group are intended to provide information about a firm's liquidity, and these ratios are sometimes called *liquidity measures.* The primary concern is the firm's ability to pay its bills over the short run without undue stress. Consequently, these ratios focus on current assets and current liabilities.

For obvious reasons, liquidity ratios are particularly interesting to short-term creditors. Because financial managers are constantly working with banks and other short-term lenders, an understanding of these ratios is essential.

One advantage of looking at current assets and liabilities is that their book values and market values are likely to be similar. Often (though not always), these assets and liabilities just don't live long enough for the two to get seriously out of step. On the other hand,

Go to www.investor.reuters.com and follow the "Ratio" link to examine comparative ratios for a huge number of companies.

like any type of near-cash, current assets and liabilities can and do change fairly rapidly, so today's amounts may not be a reliable guide to the future.

Current Ratio One of the best known and most widely used ratios is the *current ratio*. As you might guess, the current ratio is defined as:

$$\text{Current ratio} = \frac{\text{Current assets}}{\text{Current liabilities}} \qquad [3.1]$$

For Prufrock, the 2005 current ratio is:

$$\text{Current ratio} = \frac{\$708}{\$540} = 1.31 \text{ times}$$

Because current assets and liabilities are, in principle, converted to cash over the following 12 months, the current ratio is a measure of short-term liquidity. The unit of measurement is either dollars or times. So, we could say Prufrock has $1.31 in current assets for every $1 in current liabilities, or we could say that Prufrock has its current liabilities covered 1.31 times over.

To a creditor, particularly a short-term creditor such as a supplier, the higher the current ratio, the better. To the firm, a high current ratio indicates liquidity, but it also may indicate an inefficient use of cash and other short-term assets. Absent some extraordinary circumstances, we would expect to see a current ratio of at least 1, because a current ratio of less than 1 would mean that net working capital (current assets less current liabilities) is negative. This would be unusual in a healthy firm, at least for most types of businesses.

The current ratio, like any ratio, is affected by various types of transactions. For example, suppose the firm borrows over the long term to raise money. The short-run effect would be an increase in cash from the issue proceeds and an increase in long-term debt. Current liabilities would not be affected, so the current ratio would rise.

Finally, note that an apparently low current ratio may not be a bad sign for a company with a large reserve of untapped borrowing power.

EXAMPLE 3.1 >> Current Events

Suppose a firm pays off some of its suppliers and short-term creditors. What happens to the current ratio? Suppose a firm buys some inventory. What happens in this case? What happens if a firm sells some merchandise?

The first case is a trick question. What happens is that the current ratio moves away from 1. If it is greater than 1 (the usual case), it will get bigger, but if it is less than 1, it will get smaller. To see this, suppose the firm has $4 in current assets and $2 in current liabilities for a current ratio of 2. If we use $1 in cash to reduce current liabilities, then the new current ratio is ($4 − 1)/($2 − 1) = 3. If we reverse the original situation to $2 in current assets and $4 in current liabilities, then the change will cause the current ratio to fall to 1/3 from 1/2.

The second case is not quite as tricky. Nothing happens to the current ratio because cash goes down while inventory goes up—total current assets are unaffected.

In the third case, the current ratio will usually rise because inventory is normally shown at cost and the sale will normally be at something greater than cost (the difference is the markup). The increase in either cash or receivables is therefore greater than the decrease in inventory. This increases current assets, and the current ratio rises.

The Quick (or Acid-Test) Ratio Inventory is often the least liquid current asset. It's also the one for which the book values are least reliable as measures of market value, because the quality of the inventory isn't considered. Some of the inventory may later turn out to be damaged, obsolete, or lost.

More to the point, relatively large inventories are often a sign of short-term trouble. The firm may have overestimated sales and overbought or overproduced as a result. In this case, the firm may have a substantial portion of its liquidity tied up in slow-moving inventory.

To further evaluate liquidity, the *quick,* or *acid-test, ratio* is computed just like the current ratio, except inventory is omitted:

$$\text{Quick ratio} = \frac{\text{Current assets} - \text{Inventory}}{\text{Current liabilities}} \qquad [3.2]$$

Notice that using cash to buy inventory does not affect the current ratio, but it reduces the quick ratio. Again, the idea is that inventory is relatively illiquid compared to cash.

For Prufrock, this ratio in 2005 was:

$$\text{Quick ratio} = \frac{\$708 - 422}{\$540} = .53 \text{ times}$$

The quick ratio here tells a somewhat different story than the current ratio, because inventory accounts for more than half of Prufrock's current assets. To exaggerate the point, if this inventory consisted of, say, unsold nuclear power plants, then this would be a cause for concern.

To give an example of current versus quick ratios, based on recent financial statements, Wal-Mart and Manpower Inc. had current ratios of .92 and 1.72, respectively. However, Manpower carries no inventory to speak of, whereas Wal-Mart's current assets are virtually all inventory. As a result, Wal-Mart's quick ratio was only .17, whereas Manpower's was 1.62, virtually the same as its current ratio.

Edward Lowe Peerspectives (peerspectives.org) provides educational information aimed at smaller, newer companies. Follow the "Acquiring and Managing Finances" link to read about financial statements.

Other Liquidity Ratios We briefly mention three other measures of liquidity. A very short-term creditor might be interested in the *cash ratio:*

$$\text{Cash ratio} = \frac{\text{Cash}}{\text{Current liabilities}} \qquad [3.3]$$

You can verify that for 2005 this works out to be .18 times for Prufrock.

Because net working capital, or NWC, is frequently viewed as the amount of short-term liquidity a firm has, we can consider the ratio of *NWC to total assets:*

$$\text{Net working capital to total assets} = \frac{\text{Net working capital}}{\text{Total assets}} \qquad [3.4]$$

A relatively low value might indicate relatively low levels of liquidity. Here, this ratio works out to be ($708 − 540)/$3,588 = 4.7%.

Finally, imagine that Prufrock was facing a strike and cash inflows began to dry up. How long could the business keep running? One answer is given by the *interval measure:*

$$\text{Interval measure} = \frac{\text{Current assets}}{\text{Average daily operating costs}} \qquad [3.5]$$

Total costs for the year, excluding depreciation and interest, were \$1,344. The average daily cost was \$1,344/365 = \$3.68 per day.[1] The interval measure is thus \$708/\$3.68 = 192 days. Based on this, Prufrock could hang on for six months or so.[2]

The interval measure (or something very similar) is also useful for newly founded or start-up companies that often have little in the way of revenues. For such companies, the interval measure indicates how long the company can operate until it needs another round of financing. The average daily operating cost for start-up companies is often called the burn rate, meaning the rate at which cash is burned in the race to become profitable.

Long-Term Solvency Measures

Long-term solvency ratios are intended to address the firm's long-run ability to meet its obligations, or, more generally, its financial leverage. These are sometimes called *financial leverage ratios* or just *leverage ratios*. We consider three commonly used measures and some variations.

Total Debt Ratio The *total debt ratio* takes into account all debts of all maturities to all creditors. It can be defined in several ways, the easiest of which is:

The online Women's Business Center has more information on financial statements, ratios, and small business topics (www.onlinewbc.gov).

$$\text{Total debt ratio} = \frac{\text{Total assets} - \text{Total equity}}{\text{Total assets}} = \frac{\$3{,}588 - 2{,}591}{\$3{,}588} = .28 \text{ times} \quad [3.6]$$

In this case, an analyst might say that Prufrock uses 28 percent debt.[3] Whether this is high or low or whether it even makes any difference depends on whether or not capital structure matters, a subject we discuss in Part 6.

Prufrock has \$.28 in debt for every \$1 in assets. Therefore, there is \$.72 in equity (\$1 − .28) for every \$.28 in debt. With this in mind, we can define two useful variations on the total debt ratio, the *debt-equity ratio* and the *equity multiplier:*

$$\begin{aligned}\text{Debt-equity ratio} &= \text{Total debt}/\text{Total equity} \\ &= \$.28/\$.72 = .39 \text{ times} \quad [3.7]\end{aligned}$$

$$\begin{aligned}\text{Equity multiplier} &= \text{Total assets}/\text{Total equity} \\ &= \$1/\$.72 = 1.39 \text{ times} \quad [3.8]\end{aligned}$$

The fact that the equity multiplier is 1 plus the debt-equity ratio is not a coincidence:

$$\begin{aligned}\text{Equity multiplier} &= \text{Total assets}/\text{Total equity} = \$1/\$.72 = 1.39 \\ &= (\text{Total equity} + \text{Total debt})/\text{Total equity} \\ &= 1 + \text{Debt-equity ratio} = 1.39 \text{ times}\end{aligned}$$

[1] For many of these ratios that involve average daily amounts, a 360-day year is often used in practice. This so-called banker's year has exactly four quarters of 90 days each and was computationally convenient in the days before pocket calculators. We'll use 365 days.

[2] Sometimes depreciation and/or interest is included in calculating average daily costs. Depreciation isn't a cash expense, so its inclusion doesn't make a lot of sense. Interest is a financing cost, so we excluded it by definition (we only looked at operating costs). We could, of course, define a different ratio that included interest expense.

[3] Total equity here includes preferred stock (discussed in Chapter 8 and elsewhere), if there is any. An equivalent numerator in this ratio would be Current liabilities + Long-term debt.

The thing to notice here is that given any one of these three ratios, you can immediately calculate the other two, so they all say exactly the same thing.

Ratios used to analyze technology firms can be found at www.chalfin.com under the "Publications" link.

A Brief Digression: Total Capitalization versus Total Assets Frequently, financial analysts are more concerned with the firm's long-term debt than its short-term debt, because the short-term debt will constantly be changing. Also, a firm's accounts payable may be more of a reflection of trade practice than debt management policy. For these reasons, the *long-term debt ratio* is often calculated as:

$$\text{Long-term debt ratio} = \frac{\text{Long-term debt}}{\text{Long-term debt} + \text{Total equity}} \tag{3.9}$$

$$= \frac{\$457}{\$457 + 2{,}591} = \frac{\$457}{\$3{,}048} = .15 \text{ times}$$

The $3,048 in total long-term debt and equity is sometimes called the firm's *total capitalization,* and the financial manager will frequently focus on this quantity rather than on total assets.

To complicate matters, different people (and different books) mean different things by the term *debt ratio.* Some mean a ratio of total debt, and some mean a ratio of long-term debt only, and, unfortunately, a substantial number are simply vague about which one they mean.

This is a source of confusion, so we choose to give two separate names to the two measures. The same problem comes up in discussing the debt-equity ratio. Financial analysts frequently calculate this ratio using only long-term debt.

Times Interest Earned Another common measure of long-term solvency is the *times interest earned* (TIE) *ratio.* Once again, there are several possible (and common) definitions, but we'll stick with the most traditional:

$$\text{Times interest earned ratio} = \frac{\text{EBIT}}{\text{Interest}} \tag{3.10}$$

$$= \frac{\$691}{\$141} = 4.9 \text{ times}$$

As the name suggests, this ratio measures how well a company has its interest obligations covered, and it is often called the interest coverage ratio. For Prufrock, the interest bill is covered 4.9 times over.

Cash Coverage A problem with the TIE ratio is that it is based on EBIT, which is not really a measure of cash available to pay interest. The reason is that depreciation, a noncash expense, has been deducted out. Because interest is most definitely a cash outflow (to creditors), one way to define the *cash coverage ratio* is:

$$\text{Cash coverage ratio} = \frac{\text{EBIT} + \text{Depreciation}}{\text{Interest}} \tag{3.11}$$

$$= \frac{\$691 + 276}{\$141} = \frac{\$967}{\$141} = 6.9 \text{ times}$$

The numerator here, EBIT plus depreciation, is often abbreviated EBITD (earnings before interest, taxes, and depreciation—say "ebbit-dee"). It is a basic measure of the firm's ability to generate cash from operations, and it is frequently used as a measure of cash flow available to meet financial obligations.

A common variation on EBITD is earnings before interest, taxes, depreciation, and amortization (EBITDA, say "ebbit-dah"). Here amortization refers to a noncash deduction very similar conceptually to depreciation, except it applies to an intangible asset (such as a patent) rather than a tangible asset (such as machine). Note that the word *amortization* here does not refer to the repayment of debt, a subject we discuss in a later chapter.

Asset Management, or Turnover, Measures

We next turn our attention to the efficiency with which Prufrock uses its assets. The measures in this section are sometimes called *asset utilization ratios*. The specific ratios we discuss can all be interpreted as measures of turnover. What they are intended to describe is how efficiently or intensively a firm uses its assets to generate sales. We first look at two important current assets, inventory and receivables.

Inventory Turnover and Days' Sales in Inventory During the year, Prufrock had a cost of goods sold of $1,344. Inventory at the end of the year was $422. With these numbers, *inventory turnover* can be calculated as:

$$\begin{aligned} \text{Inventory turnover} &= \frac{\text{Cost of goods sold}}{\text{Inventory}} \\ &= \frac{\$1{,}344}{\$422} = 3.2 \text{ times} \end{aligned} \quad [3.12]$$

In a sense, Prufrock sold off or turned over the entire inventory 3.2 times.[4] As long as we are not running out of stock and thereby forgoing sales, the higher this ratio is, the more efficiently we are managing inventory.

If we know that we turned our inventory over 3.2 times during the year, then we can immediately figure out how long it took us to turn it over on average. The result is the average *days' sales in inventory:*

$$\begin{aligned} \text{Days' sales in inventory} &= \frac{365 \text{ days}}{\text{Inventory turnover}} \\ &= \frac{365 \text{ days}}{3.2} = 114 \text{ days} \end{aligned} \quad [3.13]$$

This tells us that, roughly speaking, inventory sits 114 days on average before it is sold. Alternatively, assuming we have used the most recent inventory and cost figures, it will take about 114 days to work off our current inventory.

For example, in December 2003, Ford had an 84-day supply of cars and trucks, more than the 60-day supply considered normal. This means that, at the then-current rate of sales, it would have taken Ford 84 days to deplete the available supply, or, equivalently, that Ford had 84 days of vehicle sales in inventory. Of course, for any manufacturer, this varies from vehicle to vehicle. Hot-sellers, such as BMW's MINI Cooper were in short supply, whereas the slow-selling (understandably!) Pontiac Aztek was in significant oversupply. This type of information is useful to auto manufacturers in planning future marketing and production decisions.

[4]Notice that we used cost of goods sold in the top of this ratio. For some purposes, it might be more useful to use sales instead of costs. For example, if we wanted to know the amount of sales generated per dollar of inventory, then we could just replace the cost of goods sold with sales.

It might make more sense to use the average inventory in calculating turnover. Inventory turnover would then be $1,344/[($393 + 422)/2] = 3.3 times.[5] It really depends on the purpose of the calculation. If we are interested in how long it will take us to sell our current inventory, then using the ending figure (as we did initially) is probably better.

In many of the ratios we discuss in the following pages, average figures could just as well be used. Again, it really depends on whether we are worried about the past, in which case averages are appropriate, or the future, in which case ending figures might be better. Also, using ending figures is very common in reporting industry averages; so, for comparison purposes, ending figures should be used in such cases. In any event, using ending figures is definitely less work, so we'll continue to use them.

Receivables Turnover and Days' Sales in Receivables Our inventory measures give some indication of how fast we can sell product. We now look at how fast we collect on those sales. The *receivables turnover* is defined in the same way as inventory turnover:

$$\text{Receivables turnover} = \frac{\text{Sales}}{\text{Accounts receivable}} = \frac{\$2{,}311}{\$188} = 12.3 \text{ times} \qquad [3.14]$$

Loosely speaking, Prufrock collected its outstanding credit accounts and reloaned the money 12.3 times during the year.[6]

This ratio makes more sense if we convert it to days, so the *days' sales in receivables* is:

$$\text{Days' sales in receivables} = \frac{365 \text{ days}}{\text{Receivables turnover}} = \frac{365}{12.3} = 30 \text{ days} \qquad [3.15]$$

Therefore, on average, Prufrock collects on its credit sales in 30 days. For obvious reasons, this ratio is very frequently called the *average collection period* (ACP).

Also note that if we are using the most recent figures, we could also say that we have 30 days' worth of sales currently uncollected. We will learn more about this subject when we study credit policy in a later chapter.

Payables Turnover << **EXAMPLE 3.2**

Here is a variation on the receivables collection period. How long, on average, does it take for Prufrock Corporation to pay its bills? To answer, we need to calculate the accounts payable turnover rate using cost of goods sold. We will assume that Prufrock purchases everything on credit.

The cost of goods sold is $1,344, and accounts payable are $344. The turnover is therefore $1,344/$344 = 3.9 times. So payables turned over about every 365/3.9 = 94 days. On average, then, Prufrock takes 94 days to pay. As a potential creditor, we might take note of this fact.

---

[5] Notice that we calculated the average as (Beginning value + Ending value)/2.

[6] Here we have implicitly assumed that all sales are credit sales. If they were not, then we would simply use total credit sales in these calculations, not total sales.

Asset Turnover Ratios Moving away from specific accounts like inventory or receivables, we can consider several "big picture" ratios. For example, *NWC turnover* is:

$$\text{NWC turnover} = \frac{\text{Sales}}{\text{NWC}} = \frac{\$2{,}311}{\$708 - 540} = 13.8 \text{ times} \tag{3.16}$$

This ratio measures how much "work" we get out of our working capital. Once again, assuming we aren't missing out on sales, a high value is preferred (why?).

Similarly, *fixed asset turnover* is:

PricewaterhouseCoopers has a useful utility for extracting EDGAR data. Try it at edgarscan.pwcglobal.com.

$$\text{Fixed asset turnover} = \frac{\text{Sales}}{\text{Net fixed assets}} = \frac{\$2{,}311}{\$2{,}880} = .80 \text{ times} \tag{3.17}$$

With this ratio, it probably makes more sense to say that, for every dollar in fixed assets, Prufrock generated $.80 in sales.

Our final asset management ratio, the *total asset turnover*, comes up quite a bit. We will see it later in this chapter and in the next chapter. As the name suggests, the total asset turnover is:

$$\text{Total asset turnover} = \frac{\text{Sales}}{\text{Total assets}} = \frac{\$2{,}311}{\$3{,}588} = .64 \text{ times} \tag{3.18}$$

In other words, for every dollar in assets, Prufrock generated $.64 in sales.

To give an example of fixed and total asset turnover, based on recent financial statements, Delta Airlines had a total asset turnover of .54, as compared to .85 for IBM. However, the much higher investment in fixed assets in an airline is reflected in Delta's fixed asset turnover of .64, as compared to IBM's 1.50.

EXAMPLE 3.3 >> More Turnover

Suppose you find that a particular company generates $.40 in sales for every dollar in total assets. How often does this company turn over its total assets?

The total asset turnover here is .40 times per year. It takes 1/.40 = 2.5 years to turn total assets over completely.

Profitability Measures

The three measures we discuss in this section are probably the best known and most widely used of all financial ratios. In one form or another, they are intended to measure how efficiently the firm uses its assets and how efficiently the firm manages its operations. The focus in this group is on the bottom line, net income.

Profit Margin Companies pay a great deal of attention to their *profit margin:*

$$\text{Profit margin} = \frac{\text{Net income}}{\text{Sales}} \tag{3.19}$$

$$= \frac{\$363}{\$2,311} = 15.7\%$$

This tells us that Prufrock, in an accounting sense, generates a little less than 16 cents in profit for every dollar in sales.

All other things being equal, a relatively high profit margin is obviously desirable. This situation corresponds to low expense ratios relative to sales. However, we hasten to add that other things are often not equal.

For example, lowering our sales price will usually increase unit volume, but will normally cause profit margins to shrink. Total profit (or, more important, operating cash flow) may go up or down; so the fact that margins are smaller isn't necessarily bad. After all, isn't it possible that, as the saying goes, "Our prices are so low that we lose money on everything we sell, but we make it up in volume"?[7]

Return on Assets *Return on assets* (ROA) is a measure of profit per dollar of assets. It can be defined several ways, but the most common is:

$$\text{Return on assets} = \frac{\text{Net income}}{\text{Total assets}} \tag{3.20}$$

$$= \frac{\$363}{\$3,588} = 10.12\%$$

Return on Equity *Return on equity* (ROE) is a measure of how the stockholders fared during the year. Because benefiting shareholders is our goal, ROE is, in an accounting sense, the true bottom-line measure of performance. ROE is usually measured as:

$$\text{Return on equity} = \frac{\text{Net income}}{\text{Total equity}} \tag{3.21}$$

$$= \frac{\$363}{\$2,591} = 14\%$$

For every dollar in equity, therefore, Prufrock generated 14 cents in profit, but, again, this is only correct in accounting terms.

Because ROA and ROE are such commonly cited numbers, we stress that it is important to remember they are accounting rates of return. For this reason, these measures should properly be called *return on book assets* and *return on book equity.* In fact, ROE is sometimes called *return on net worth.* Whatever it's called, it would be inappropriate to compare the result to, for example, an interest rate observed in the financial markets. We will have more to say about accounting rates of return in later chapters.

The fact that ROE exceeds ROA reflects Prufrock's use of financial leverage. We will examine the relationship between these two measures in more detail next.

---

[7] No, it's not.

EXAMPLE 3.4 >> ROE and ROA

Because ROE and ROA are usually intended to measure performance over a prior period, it makes a certain amount of sense to base them on average equity and average assets, respectively. For Prufrock, how would you calculate these?

We first need to calculate average assets and average equity:

$$\text{Average assets} = (\$3{,}373 + 3{,}588)/2 = \$3{,}481$$
$$\text{Average equity} = (\$2{,}299 + 2{,}591)/2 = \$2{,}445$$

With these averages, we can recalculate ROA and ROE as follows:

$$\text{ROA} = \frac{\$363}{\$3{,}481} = 10.43\%$$

$$\text{ROE} = \frac{\$363}{\$2{,}445} = 14.85\%$$

These are slightly higher than our previous calculations because assets grew during the year, with the result that the average is below the ending value.

Market Value Measures

Our final group of measures is based, in part, on information not necessarily contained in financial statements—the market price per share of the stock. Obviously, these measures can only be calculated directly for publicly traded companies.

We assume that Prufrock has 33 million shares outstanding and the stock sold for $88 per share at the end of the year. If we recall that Prufrock's net income was $363 million, then we can calculate that its earnings per share were:

$$\text{EPS} = \frac{\text{Net income}}{\text{Shares outstanding}} = \frac{\$363}{33} = \$11$$

Price-Earnings Ratio The first of our market value measures, the *price-earnings* (PE) *ratio* (or multiple), is defined as:

$$\text{PE ratio} = \frac{\text{Price per share}}{\text{Earnings per share}} = \frac{\$88}{\$11} = 8 \text{ times} \qquad [3.22]$$

In the vernacular, we would say that Prufrock shares sell for eight times earnings, or we might say that Prufrock shares have or "carry" a PE multiple of 8.

PE ratios vary substantially across companies, but, in 2004, a typical large company in the United States had a PE in the low 20s. This is on the high side by historical standards, but not dramatically so. A low point for PEs was about 5 in 1974. PEs also vary across countries. For example, Japanese PEs have historically been much higher than those of their U.S. counterparts.

Because the PE ratio measures how much investors are willing to pay per dollar of current earnings, higher PEs are often taken to mean the firm has significant prospects for future growth. Of course, if a firm had no or almost no earnings, its PE would probably be quite large; so, as always, care is needed in interpreting this ratio.

Market-to-Book Ratio A second commonly quoted market value measure is the *market-to-book ratio:*

$$\text{Market-to-book ratio} = \frac{\text{Market value per share}}{\text{Book value per share}} = \frac{\$88}{(\$2{,}591/33)} = \frac{\$88}{\$78.5} = 1.12 \text{ times} \quad [3.23]$$

Notice that book value per share is total equity (not just common stock) divided by the number of shares outstanding.

Because book value per share is an accounting number, it reflects historical costs. In a loose sense, the market-to-book ratio therefore compares the market value of the firm's investments to their cost. A value less than 1 could mean that the firm has not been successful overall in creating value for its stockholders.

Market-to-book ratios in recent years appear high relative to past values. For example, for the 30 blue-chip companies that make up the widely followed Dow-Jones Industrial Average, the historical norm is about 1.7; however, the market-to-book ratio for this group has recently been twice this size.

TABLE 3.8 >> **Common Financial Ratios**

I. Short-term solvency, or liquidity, ratios	II. Long-term solvency, or financial leverage, ratios
$\text{Current ratio} = \frac{\text{Current assets}}{\text{Current liabilities}}$	$\text{Total debt ratio} = \frac{\text{Total assets} - \text{Total equity}}{\text{Total assets}}$
$\text{Quick ratio} = \frac{\text{Current assets} - \text{Inventory}}{\text{Current liabilities}}$	Debt-equity ratio = Total debt/Total equity Equity multiplier = Total assets/Total equity
$\text{Cash ratio} = \frac{\text{Cash}}{\text{Current liabilities}}$	$\text{Long-term debt ratio} = \frac{\text{Long-term debt}}{\text{Long-term debt} + \text{Total equity}}$
$\text{Net working capital to total assets} = \frac{\text{Net working capital}}{\text{Total assets}}$	$\text{Times interest earned ratio} = \frac{\text{EBIT}}{\text{Interest}}$
$\text{Interval measure} = \frac{\text{Current assets}}{\text{Average daily operating costs}}$	$\text{Cash coverage ratio} = \frac{\text{EBIT} + \text{Depreciation}}{\text{Interest}}$
III. Asset utilization, or turnover, ratios	**IV. Profitability ratios**
$\text{Inventory turnover} = \frac{\text{Cost of goods sold}}{\text{Inventory}}$	$\text{Profit margin} = \frac{\text{Net income}}{\text{Sales}}$
$\text{Days' sales in inventory} = \frac{365 \text{ days}}{\text{Inventory turnover}}$	$\text{Return on assets (ROA)} = \frac{\text{Net income}}{\text{Total assets}}$
$\text{Receivables turnover} = \frac{\text{Sales}}{\text{Accounts receivable}}$	$\text{Return on equity (ROE)} = \frac{\text{Net income}}{\text{Total equity}}$
$\text{Days' sales in receivables} = \frac{365 \text{ days}}{\text{Receivables turnover}}$	$\text{ROE} = \frac{\text{Net income}}{\text{Sales}} \times \frac{\text{Sales}}{\text{Assets}} \times \frac{\text{Assets}}{\text{Equity}}$
$\text{NWC turnover} = \frac{\text{Sales}}{\text{NWC}}$	**V. Market value ratios**
$\text{Fixed asset turnover} = \frac{\text{Sales}}{\text{Net fixed assets}}$	$\text{Price-earnings ratio} = \frac{\text{Price per share}}{\text{Earnings per share}}$
$\text{Total asset turnover} = \frac{\text{Sales}}{\text{Total assets}}$	$\text{Market-to-book ratio} = \frac{\text{Market value per share}}{\text{Book value per share}}$

Conclusion

This completes our definitions of some common ratios. We could tell you about more of them, but these are enough for now. We'll leave it here and go on to discuss some ways of using these ratios instead of just how to calculate them. Table 3.8 summarizes the ratios we've discussed.

Concept Questions

3.3a What are the five groups of ratios? Give two or three examples of each kind.

3.3b Turnover ratios all have one of two figures as the numerator. What are these two figures? What do these ratios measure? How do you interpret the results?

3.3c Profitability ratios all have the same figure in the numerator. What is it? What do these ratios measure? How do you interpret the results?

3.3d Given the total debt ratio, what other two ratios can be computed? Explain how.

3.4 THE DU PONT IDENTITY

As we mentioned in discussing ROA and ROE, the difference between these two profitability measures is a reflection of the use of debt financing, or financial leverage. We illustrate the relationship between these measures in this section by investigating a famous way of decomposing ROE into its component parts.

A Closer Look at ROE

To begin, let's recall the definition of ROE:

$$\text{Return on equity} = \frac{\text{Net income}}{\text{Total equity}}$$

If we were so inclined, we could multiply this ratio by Assets/Assets without changing anything:

$$\begin{aligned}\text{Return on equity} &= \frac{\text{Net income}}{\text{Total equity}} = \frac{\text{Net income}}{\text{Total equity}} \times \frac{\text{Assets}}{\text{Assets}} \\ &= \frac{\text{Net income}}{\text{Assets}} \times \frac{\text{Assets}}{\text{Total equity}}\end{aligned}$$

Notice that we have expressed the ROE as the product of two other ratios—ROA and the equity multiplier:

$$\text{ROE} = \text{ROA} \times \text{Equity multiplier} = \text{ROA} \times (1 + \text{Debt-equity ratio})$$

Looking back at Prufrock, for example, we see that the debt-equity ratio was .39 and ROA was 10.12 percent. Our work here implies that Prufrock's ROE, as we previously calculated, is:

$$\text{ROE} = 10.12\% \times 1.39 = 14\%$$

The difference between ROE and ROA can be substantial, particularly for certain businesses. For example, BankAmerica has an ROA of only 1.23 percent, which is actually fairly typical for a bank. However, banks tend to borrow a lot of money, and, as a result, have relatively large equity multipliers. For BankAmerica, ROE is about 16 percent, implying an equity multiplier of 13.

We can further decompose ROE by multiplying the top and bottom by total sales:

$$\text{ROE} = \frac{\text{Sales}}{\text{Sales}} \times \frac{\text{Net income}}{\text{Assets}} \times \frac{\text{Assets}}{\text{Total equity}}$$

If we rearrange things a bit, ROE is:

$$\text{ROE} = \underbrace{\frac{\text{Net income}}{\text{Sales}} \times \frac{\text{Sales}}{\text{Assets}}}_{\text{Return on assets}} \times \frac{\text{Assets}}{\text{Total equity}} \qquad [3.24]$$

$$= \text{Profit margin} \times \text{Total asset turnover} \times \text{Equity multiplier}$$

What we have now done is to partition ROA into its two component parts, profit margin and total asset turnover. The last expression of the preceding equation is called the **Du Pont identity**, after the Du Pont Corporation, which popularized its use.

Du Pont identity
Popular expression breaking ROE into three parts: operating efficiency, asset use efficiency, and financial leverage.

We can check this relationship for Prufrock by noting that the profit margin was 15.7 percent and the total asset turnover was .64. ROE should thus be:

$$\begin{aligned} \text{ROE} &= \text{Profit margin} \times \text{Total asset turnover} \times \text{Equity multiplier} \\ &= 15.7\% \times .64 \times 1.39 \\ &= 14\% \end{aligned}$$

This 14 percent ROE is exactly what we had before.

The Du Pont identity tells us that ROE is affected by three things:

1. Operating efficiency (as measured by profit margin)
2. Asset use efficiency (as measured by total asset turnover)
3. Financial leverage (as measured by the equity multiplier)

Weakness in either operating or asset use efficiency (or both) will show up in a diminished return on assets, which will translate into a lower ROE.

Considering the Du Pont identity, it appears that the ROE could be leveraged up by increasing the amount of debt in the firm. However, notice that increasing debt also increases interest expense, which reduces profit margins, which acts to reduce ROE. So, ROE could go up or down, depending. More important, the use of debt financing has a number of other effects, and, as we discuss at some length in Part 6, the amount of leverage a firm uses is governed by its capital structure policy.

The decomposition of ROE we've discussed in this section is a convenient way of systematically approaching financial statement analysis. If ROE is unsatisfactory by some measure, then the Du Pont identity tells you where to start looking for the reasons.

General Motors provides a good example of how Du Pont analysis can be very useful and also illustrates why care must be taken in interpreting ROE values. In 1989, GM had an ROE of 12.1 percent. By 1993, its ROE had improved to 44.1 percent, a dramatic improvement. On closer inspection, however, we find that, over the same period, GM's profit margin had declined from 3.4 to 1.8 percent, and ROA had declined from 2.4 to 1.3 percent. The decline in ROA was moderated only slightly by an increase in total asset turnover from .71 to .73 over the period.

Given this information, how is it possible for GM's ROE to have climbed so sharply? From our understanding of the Du Pont identity, it must be the case that GM's equity multiplier increased substantially. In fact, what happened was that GM's book equity value was almost wiped out overnight in 1992 by changes in the accounting treatment of pension liabilities. If a company's equity value declines sharply, its equity multiplier rises. In GM's case, the multiplier went from 4.95 in 1989 to 33.62 in 1993. In sum, the dramatic "improvement" in GM's ROE was almost entirely due to an accounting change that affected the equity multiplier and doesn't really represent an improvement in financial performance at all.

An Expanded Du Pont Analysis

So far, we've seen how the Du Pont equation lets us break down ROE into its basic three components: profit margin, total asset turnover, and financial leverage. We now extend this analysis to take a closer look at how key parts of a firm's operations feed into ROE. To get going, we went to the *S&P Market Insight* Web page (www.mhhe.com/edumarketinsight) and pulled abbreviated financial statements for food products giant General Mills. What we found is summarized in Table 3.9.

Using the information in Table 3.9, Figure 3.1 shows how we can construct an expanded Du Pont analysis for General Mills and present that analysis in chart form. The advantage of the extended Du Pont chart is that it lets us examine several ratios at once, thereby getting a better overall picture of a company's performance and also allowing us to determine possible items to improve.

Looking at the left-hand side of our Du Pont chart in Figure 3.1, we see items related to profitability. As always, profit margin is calculated as net income divided by sales. But, as our chart emphasizes, net income depends on sales and a variety of costs, such as cost of goods sold (CoGS) and selling, general, and administrative expenses (SG&A expense). General Mills can increase its ROE by increasing sales and also by reducing one or more of these costs. In other words, if we want to improve profitability, our chart clearly shows us the areas on which we should focus.

Turning to the right-hand side of Figure 3.1, we have an analysis of the key factors underlying total asset turnover. Thus, for example, we see that reducing inventory holdings through more efficient management reduces current assets, which reduces total assets, which then improves total asset turnover.

TABLE 3.9 >>

FINANCIAL STATEMENTS FOR GENERAL MILLS
12 months ending November 30, 2003
(All numbers are in millions)

Income Statement		Balance Sheet			
Sales	$10,769	Current assets		Current liabilities	
CoGS	5,946	Cash	$ 695	Accounts payable	$ 1,296
Gross profit	$ 4,823	Accounts receivable	1,196	Notes payable	1,202
SG&A expense	2,419	Inventory	1,707	Other	637
Depreciation	374	Total	$ 3,598	Total	$ 3,135
EBIT	$ 2,030				
Interest	526	Fixed assets	$15,181	Total long-term debt	$10,901
EBT	$ 1,504				
Taxes	504			Total equity	$ 4,743
Net income	$ 1,000	Total assets	$18,779	Total liabilities and equity	$18,779

FIGURE 3.1 >> Extended Du Pont Chart for General Mills

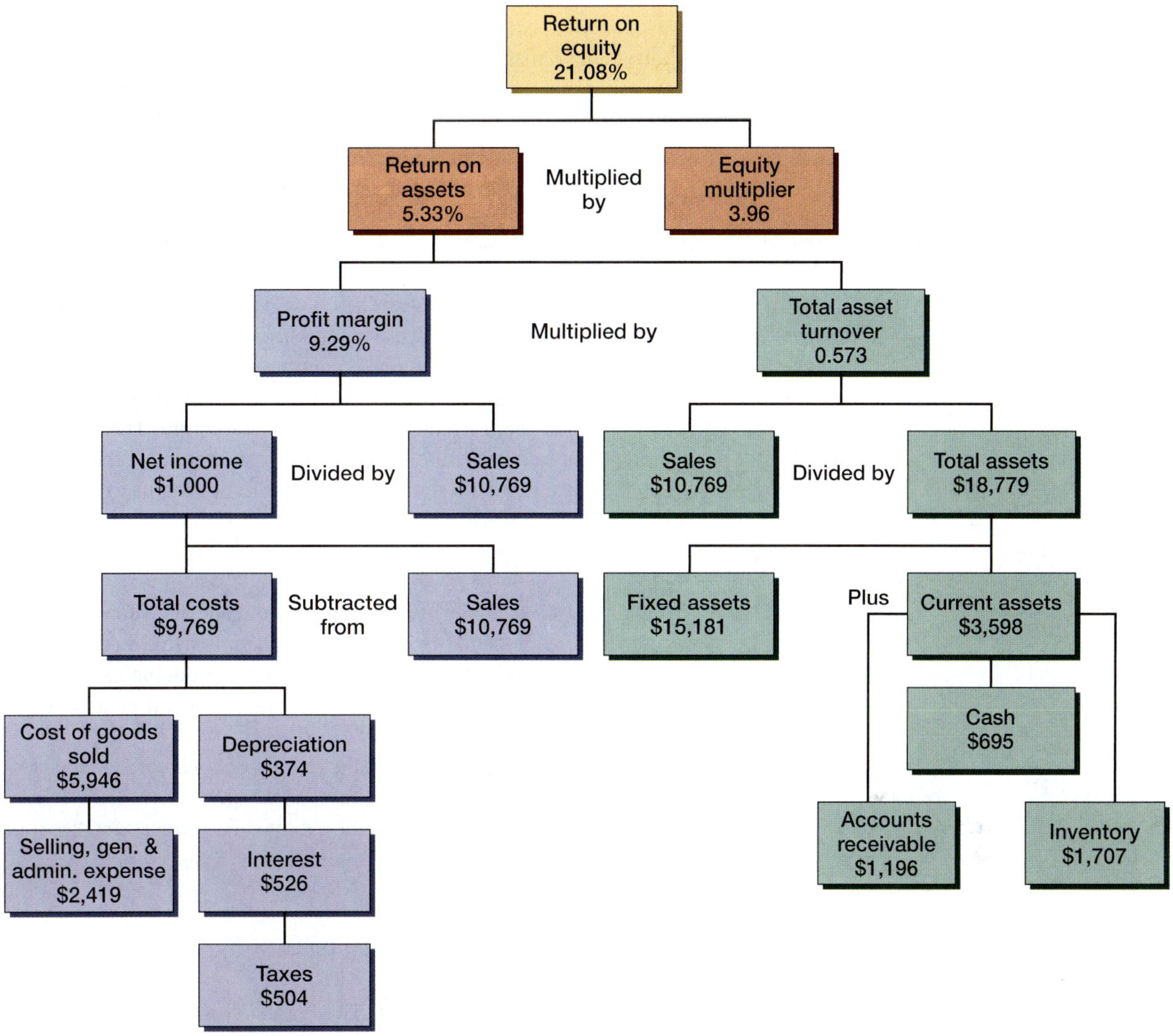

Concept Questions

3.4a Return on assets, or ROA, can be expressed as the product of two ratios. Which two?

3.4b Return on equity, or ROE, can be expressed as the product of three ratios. Which three?

USING FINANCIAL STATEMENT INFORMATION 3.5

Our last task in this chapter is to discuss in more detail some practical aspects of financial statement analysis. In particular, we will look at reasons for doing financial statement analysis, how to go about getting benchmark information, and some of the problems that come up in the process.

Why Evaluate Financial Statements?

As we have discussed, the primary reason for looking at accounting information is that we don't have, and can't reasonably expect to get, market value information. It is important to emphasize that, whenever we have market information, we will use it instead of accounting data. Also, if there is a conflict between accounting and market data, market data should be given precedence.

Financial statement analysis is essentially an application of "management by exception." In many cases, such analysis will boil down to comparing ratios for one business with some kind of average or representative ratios. Those ratios that seem to differ the most from the averages are tagged for further study.

Internal Uses Financial statement information has a variety of uses within a firm. Among the most important of these is performance evaluation. For example, managers are frequently evaluated and compensated on the basis of accounting measures of performance such as profit margin and return on equity. Also, firms with multiple divisions frequently compare the performance of those divisions using financial statement information.

Another important internal use that we will explore in the next chapter is planning for the future. As we will see, historical financial statement information is very useful for generating projections about the future and for checking the realism of assumptions made in those projections.

External Uses Financial statements are useful to parties outside the firm, including short-term and long-term creditors and potential investors. For example, we would find such information quite useful in deciding whether or not to grant credit to a new customer.

We would also use this information to evaluate suppliers, and suppliers would use our statements before deciding to extend credit to us. Large customers use this information to decide if we are likely to be around in the future. Credit-rating agencies rely on financial statements in assessing a firm's overall creditworthiness. The common theme here is that financial statements are a prime source of information about a firm's financial health.

We would also find such information useful in evaluating our main competitors. We might be thinking of launching a new product. A prime concern would be whether the competition would jump in shortly thereafter. In this case, we would be interested in learning about our competitors' financial strength to see if they could afford the necessary development.

Finally, we might be thinking of acquiring another firm. Financial statement information would be essential in identifying potential targets and deciding what to offer.

Choosing a Benchmark

Given that we want to evaluate a division or a firm based on its financial statements, a basic problem immediately comes up. How do we choose a benchmark, or a standard of comparison? We describe some ways of getting started in this section.

Time-Trend Analysis One standard we could use is history. Suppose we found that the current ratio for a particular firm is 2.4 based on the most recent financial statement information. Looking back over the last 10 years, we might find that this ratio had declined fairly steadily over that period.

Based on this, we might wonder if the liquidity position of the firm has deteriorated. It could be, of course, that the firm has made changes that allow it to more efficiently use its current assets, that the nature of the firm's business has changed, or that business practices have changed. If we investigate, we might find any of these possible explanations behind the decline. This is an example of what we mean by management by exception—a deteriorating time trend may not be bad, but it does merit investigation.

Peer Group Analysis The second means of establishing a benchmark is to identify firms similar in the sense that they compete in the same markets, have similar assets, and operate in similar ways. In other words, we need to identify a *peer group*. There are obvious problems with doing this since no two companies are identical. Ultimately, the choice of which companies to use as a basis for comparison is subjective.

One common way of identifying potential peers is based on **Standard Industrial Classification (SIC) codes**. These are four-digit codes established by the U.S. government for statistical reporting purposes. Firms with the same SIC code are frequently assumed to be similar.

Standard Industrial Classification (SIC) code
A U.S. government code used to classify a firm by its type of business operations.

The first digit in an SIC code establishes the general type of business. For example, firms engaged in finance, insurance, and real estate have SIC codes beginning with 6. Each additional digit narrows down the industry. So, companies with SIC codes beginning with 60 are mostly banks and banklike businesses, those with codes beginning with 602 are mostly commercial banks, and SIC code 6025 is assigned to national banks that are members of the Federal Reserve system. Table 3.10 is a list of selected two-digit codes (the first two digits of the four-digit SIC codes) and the industries they represent.

SIC codes are far from perfect. For example, suppose you were examining financial statements for Wal-Mart, the largest retailer in the United States. The relevant SIC code is 5310, Department Stores. In a quick scan of the nearest financial database, you would find about 20 large, publicly owned corporations with this same SIC code, but you might not be too comfortable with some of them. Target would seem to be a reasonable peer, but

<< TABLE 3.10

Selected Two-Digit SIC Codes

Agriculture, Forestry, and Fishing	Wholesale Trade
01 Agriculture production—crops	50 Wholesale trade—durable goods
08 Forestry	51 Wholesale trade—nondurable goods
09 Fishing, hunting, and trapping	
Mining	**Retail Trade**
10 Metal mining	54 Food stores
12 Bituminous coal and lignite mining	55 Automobile dealers and gas stations
13 Oil and gas extraction	58 Eating and drinking places
Construction	**Finance, Insurance, and Real Estate**
15 Building construction	60 Banking
16 Construction other than building	63 Insurance
17 Construction—special trade contractors	65 Real estate
Manufacturing	**Services**
28 Chemicals and allied products	78 Motion pictures
29 Petroleum refining and related industries	80 Health services
35 Machinery, except electrical	82 Educational services
37 Transportation equipment	
Transportation, Communication, Electric, Gas, and Sanitary Service	
40 Railroad transportation	
45 Transportation by air	
49 Electric, gas, and sanitary services	

Neiman-Marcus also carries the same industry code. Are Wal-Mart and Neiman-Marcus really comparable?

As this example illustrates, it is probably not appropriate to blindly use SIC code–based averages. Instead, analysts often identify a set of primary competitors and then compute a set of averages based on just this group. Also, we may be more concerned with a group of the top firms in an industry, not the average firm. Such a group is called an *aspirant group,* because we aspire to be like its members. In this case, a financial statement analysis reveals how far we have to go.

Learn more about NAICS at www.naics.com.

Beginning in 1997, a new industry classification system was initiated. Specifically, the North American Industry Classification System (NAICS, pronounced "nakes") is intended to replace the older SIC codes, and it will eventually. Currently, however, SIC codes are still widely used.

With these caveats about SIC codes in mind, we can now take a look at a specific industry. Suppose we are in the retail hardware business. Table 3.11 contains some condensed common-size financial statements for this industry from the Risk Management Association (RMA, formerly known as Robert Morris Associates), one of many sources of such information. Table 3.12 contains selected ratios from the same source.

There is a large amount of information here, most of which is self-explanatory. On the right in Table 3.11, we have current information reported for different groups based on sales. Within each sales group, common-size information is reported. For example, firms with sales in the $10 million to $25 million range have cash and equivalents equal to 5 percent of total assets. There are 31 companies in this group, out of 309 in all.

On the left, we have three years' worth of summary historical information for the entire group. For example, operating profit rose from 1.9 percent of sales to 2.5 percent over that time.

Table 3.12 contains some selected ratios, again reported by sales groups on the right and time period on the left. To see how we might use this information, suppose our firm has a current ratio of 2. Based on these ratios, is this value unusual?

Looking at the current ratio for the overall group for the most recent year (third column from the left in Table 3.12), we see that three numbers are reported. The one in the middle, 2.2, is the median, meaning that half of the 309 firms had current ratios that were lower and half had bigger current ratios. The other two numbers are the upper and lower quartiles. So, 25 percent of the firms had a current ratio larger than 3.7 and 25 percent had a current ratio smaller than 1.5. Our value of 2 falls comfortably within these bounds, so it doesn't appear too unusual. This comparison illustrates how knowledge of the range of ratios is important in addition to knowledge of the average. Notice how stable the current ratio has been for the last three years.

EXAMPLE 3.5 >> More Ratios

Take a look at the most recent numbers reported for Sales/Receivables and EBIT/Interest in Table 3.12. What are the overall median values? What are these ratios?

If you look back at our discussion, you will see that these are the receivables turnover and the times interest earned, or TIE, ratios. The median value for receivables turnover for the entire group is 26.5 times. So, the days in receivables would be 365/26.5 = 14, which is the bold-faced number reported. The median for the TIE is 2.8 times. The number in parentheses indicates that the calculation is meaningful for, and therefore based on, only 269 of the 309 companies. In this case, the reason is that only 269 companies paid any significant amount of interest.

TABLE 3.11 >> Selected Financial Statement Information

Retail—Hardware Stores SIC# 5072, 5251 (NAICS 444130)									
Comparative Historical Data				**Current Data Sorted by Sales**					
			Type of Statement						
9	11	17	Unqualified	1	1	2	1	4	8
38	42	54	Reviewed		8	10	16	14	6
88	85	110	Compiled	19	48	18	17	5	3
44	34	52	Tax Returns	10	30	5	1	5	1
67	57	76	Other	14	25	13	11	3	10
				58 (4/1-9/30/02)			**251 (10/1/02-3/31/03)**		
4/1/00-3/31/01 ALL	**4/1/01-3/31/02 ALL**	**4/1/02-3/31/03 ALL**		**0-1 MM**	**1-3 MM**	**3-5 MM**	**5-10 MM**	**10-25 MM**	**25MM & OVER**
246	229	309	**NUMBER OF STATEMENTS**	44	112	48	46	31	28
			ASSETS						
5.9%	6.1%	6.0%	Cash & Equivalents	5.3%	7.1%	7.4%	5.0%	5.0%	3.5%
12.2	13.3	13.8	Trade Receivables (net)	7.4	11.6	15.3	19.9	20.4	13.5
52.0	48.9	50.5	Inventory	62.4	50.1	47.8	47.3	44.5	50.4
1.3	1.3	1.8	All Other Current	1.8	1.7	1.7	2.1	.7	2.7
71.4	69.6	72.2	Total Current	76.8	70.4	72.2	74.2	70.5	70.1
17.3	17.8	17.0	Fixed Assets (net)	14.7	17.4	16.4	16.0	18.3	20.2
1.9	3.1	1.7	Intangibles (net)	1.1	1.6	1.5	2.0	.5	3.5
9.4	9.5	9.2	All Other Non-Current	7.3	10.5	9.9	7.8	10.7	6.2
100.0	100.0	100.0	Total	100.0	100.0	100.0	100.0	100.0	100.0
			LIABILITIES						
8.7	8.0	11.3	Notes Payable-Short Term	11.1	10.1	8.0	13.3	11.1	18.5
3.7	3.8	3.5	Cur. Mat.-L/T/D	2.9	3.6	3.5	5.2	2.6	2.0
15.7	15.6	15.5	Trade Payables	13.2	14.6	15.8	19.4	15.4	15.3
.2	.2	.2	Income Taxes Payable	.0	.5	.1	.2	.3	.1
7.1	8.1	7.0	All Other Current	7.8	7.3	5.8	6.0	7.1	8.2
35.3	35.6	37.4	Total Current	35.0	36.0	33.3	44.1	36.5	44.1
19.1	20.6	19.0	Long Term Debt	29.0	20.6	17.9	13.6	13.7	13.9
.1	.1	.1	Deferred Taxes	.1	.0	.0	.1	.3	.2
4.8	6.3	5.0	All Other Non-Current	8.9	4.8	5.4	1.3	3.5	6.4
40.6	37.4	38.5	Net Worth	27.0	38.6	43.3	40.9	46.0	35.5
100.0	100.0	100.0	Total Liabilities & Net Worth	100.0	100.0	100.0	100.0	100.0	100.0
			INCOME DATA						
100.0	100.0	100.0	Net Sales	100.0	100.0	100.0	100.0	100.0	100.0
35.0	35.3	35.7	Gross Profit	39.8	37.3	36.4	32.9	29.9	32.3
33.1	33.1	33.1	Operating Expenses	38.3	34.7	33.6	30.1	27.9	29.0
1.9	2.2	2.5	Operating Profit	1.5	2.7	2.8	2.8	2.0	3.4
.1	.4	.2	All Other Expenses (net)	.6	.2	.1	.2	−.3	.7
1.8	1.8	2.3	Profit Before Taxes	.9	2.5	2.7	2.6	2.3	2.7

MM = $ million.

Interpretation of Statement Studies Figures: RMA cautions that the studies be regarded only as a general guideline and not as an absolute industry norm. This is due to limited samples within categories, the categorization of companies by their primary Standard Industrial Classification (SIC) number only, and different methods of operations by companies within the same industry. For these reasons, RMA recommends that the figures be used only as general guidelines in addition to other methods of financial analysis.

TABLE 3.12 >> Selected Ratios

Retail—Hardware Stores SIC# 5072, 5251 (NAICS 444130)									
Comparative Historical Data				Current Data Sorted by Sales					
			Type of Statement						
9	11	17	Unqualified	1	1	2	1	4	8
38	42	54	Reviewed		8	10	16	14	6
88	85	110	Compiled	19	48	18	17	5	3
44	34	52	Tax Returns	10	30	5	1	5	1
67	57	76	Other	14	25	13	11	3	10
				58 (4/1-9/30/02)		251 (10/1/02-3/31/03)			
4/1/00-3/31/01 ALL	**4/1/01-3/31/02 ALL**	**4/1/02-3/31/03 ALL**	**NUMBER OF STATEMENTS**	**0-1 MM**	**1-3 MM**	**3-5 MM**	**5-10 MM**	**10-25 MM**	**25MM & OVER**
246	229	309		44	112	48	46	31	28
			RATIOS						
3.8%	3.7%	3.7%		6.6%	4.0%	3.4%	2.6%	2.8%	2.4%
2.1	2.2	2.2	Current	2.5	2.5	2.6	1.8	1.7	1.8
1.5	1.4	1.5		1.4	1.5	1.5	1.8	1.5	1.3
1.0	1.0	1.1		.9	1.1	1.2	1.0	1.1	.7
.5	.5	(308) .5	Quick	.4	.5	(47) .6	.5	.7	.5
.3	.2	.2		.2	.2	.3	.2	.4	.2
8 43.2	**7** 49.8	**7** 49.8		**4** 91.2	**8** 48.6	**6** 65.0	**11** 33.2	**11** 34.6	**5** 68.4
14 26.7	**15** 24.5	**14** 26.5	Sales/ Receivables	**11** 32.1	**12** 29.3	**15** 25.0	**20** 18.4	**26** 14.0	**15** 24.5
25 14.6	**27** 13.4	**29** 12.4		**20** 18.4	**25** 14.6	**34** 10.8	**43** 8.4	**39** 9.4	**38** 9.7
88 4.2	**81** 4.5	**85** 4.3		**137** 2.7	**93** 3.9	**78** 4.7	**70** 5.2	**57** 6.4	**81** 4.5
120 3.0	**121** 3.0	**120** 3.0	Cost of Sales/ Inventory	**179** 2.0	**121** 3.0	**114** 3.2	**108** 3.4	**83** 4.4	**104** 3.5
178 2.0	**163** 2.2	**171** 2.1		**262** 1.4	**172** 2.1	**167** 2.2	**161** 2.3	**120** 3.0	**149** 2.5
17 21.3	**18** 20.0	**17** 21.3		**0** UND	**17** 22.0	**17** 22.0	**22** 16.3	**15** 23.8	**18** 19.8
29 12.8	**29** 12.7	**30** 12.3	Cost of Sales/ Payables	**25** 14.3	**30** 12.3	**29** 12.7	**34** 10.6	**22** 16.4	**30** 12.1
48 7.7	**46** 7.9	**50** 7.4		**68** 5.4	**43** 8.5	**53** 6.9	**59** 6.2	**41** 8.8	**44** 8.3
4.2	4.4	4.2		2.6	4.1	4.4	5.4	5.7	5.7
6.4	6.7	7.0	Sales/ Working Capital	4.0	6.5	6.8	9.1	7.0	10.2
11.8	12.9	12.3		10.5	11.2	10.2	14.9	12.4	16.4
5.0	4.8	8.1		7.7	7.8	8.4	15.1	9.5	8.3
(225) 2.1	(213) 2.1	(269) 2.8	EBIT/Interest	(36) 2.4	(93) 2.5	(43) 4.0	(43) 3.2	(27) 4.1	(27) 3.2
.7	1.1	1.1		−.7	1.2	1.4	1.0	1.6	1.1
3.8	4.5	5.5	Net Profit + Depr.,		5.2	12.4	2.6	6.1	13.4
(58) 1.7	(53) 2.0	(73) 2.4	Dep., Amort./Cur.		(21) 1.9	(10) 2.0	(15) .6	(14) 2.8	(11) 5.3
.7	1.1	.5	Mat. L/T/D		.7	.1	.0	1.3	.5
.1	.2	.2		.0	.2	.1	.1	.1	.3
.4	.4	.4	Fixed/Worth	.4	.4	.4	.3	.3	.6
1.1	1.1	1.0		8.1	1.1	.9	.7	.8	1.2
.7	.6	.7		.8	.6	.7	.6	.6	1.2
1.6	1.7	1.5	Debt/Worth	2.8	1.6	1.4	1.7	1.0	2.2
3.8	4.8	3.7		NM	4.2	2.9	2.9	1.9	3.6
27.7	27.6	29.2	% Profit Before	46.5	25.3	28.4	31.0	17.6	40.4
(224) 9.9	(203) 10.4	(277) 11.9	Taxes/Tangible	(33) 12.3	(98) 11.5	(45) 15.0	(45) 10.9	(30) 9.6	(26) 23.7
.1	1.6	2.2	Net Worth	.4	.9	3.3	1.8	.3	2.5
9.4	9.1	11.5	% Profit	10.6	10.5	12.4	12.7	9.2	11.3
3.6	3.2	4.7	Before Taxes/	4.9	4.6	4.7	5.4	5.2	4.9
−1.2	.2	.2	Total Assets	−6.0	.2	1.5	.5	.2	.4
49.2	40.5	41.1		97.7	42.1	42.7	40.3	55.4	29.1
21.0	20.4	19.6	Sales/Net Fixed Assets	21.2	23.1	18.6	20.1	17.6	14.3
9.4	8.7	9.2		7.1	9.4	9.6	12.2	7.6	9.1
3.1	3.0	3.1		2.8	3.0	3.2	3.2	3.0	3.3
2.3	2.4	2.4	Sales/ Total Assets	2.0	2.5	2.4	2.5	2.4	2.3
1.8	1.8	1.8		1.1	1.9	1.8	1.7	2.2	1.9
.7	.7	.7		.8	.7	.7	.7	.8	.8
(222) 1.1	(200) 1.2	(266) 1.2	% Depr., Dep., Amort./Sales	(31) 1.2	(102) 1.5	(41) 1.2	(40) 1.0	(29) 1.1	(23) 1.2
2.0	2.2	2.0		2.4	2.5	1.6	1.3	1.8	1.7
2.9	2.0	2.3	% Officers',	3.7	2.7	2.0	2.1	1.3	
(132) 4.6	(136) 4.0	(168) 4.0	Directors', Owners'	(21) 5.3	(75) 4.5	(32) 3.8	(22) 3.0	(14) 2.0	
7.0	6.1	7.0	Comp/Sales	11.6	7.1	6.7	6.2	3.3	
2771100M	**2517327M**	**3762671M**	Net Sales ($)	**27586M**	**204026M**	**188955M**	**328481M**	**469173M**	**2544450M**
990644M	**1153657M**	**1607310M**	Total Assets ($)	**18552M**	**93100M**	**86254M**	**158179M**	**191739M**	**1059486M**

M = $ thousand; MM = $ million.

There are many sources of ratio information in addition to the one we examine here. Our nearby *Work the Web* box shows how to get this information for just about any company, along with some very useful benchmarking information. Be sure to look it over and then benchmark your favorite company.

Problems with Financial Statement Analysis

We close out our chapter on financial statements by discussing some additional problems that can arise in using financial statements. In one way or another, the basic problem with financial statement analysis is that there is no underlying theory to help us identify which quantities to look at and to guide us in establishing benchmarks.

As we discuss in other chapters, there are many cases in which financial theory and economic logic provide guidance in making judgments about value and risk. Very little such help exists with financial statements. This is why we can't say which ratios matter the most and what a high or low value might be.

One particularly severe problem is that many firms are conglomerates, owning more-or-less unrelated lines of business. The consolidated financial statements for such firms don't really fit any neat industry category. Going back to department stores, for example, Sears

WORK THE WEB

As we discussed in this chapter, ratios are an important tool for examining a company's performance. Gathering the necessary financial statements to calculate ratios can be tedious and time consuming. Fortunately, many sites on the Web provide this information for free. One of the best is www.investor.reuters.com. We went there, entered a ticker symbol ("TXN" for Texas Instruments), and selected the "Ratios" and "Financial Condition" links. Here is an abbreviated look at the results:

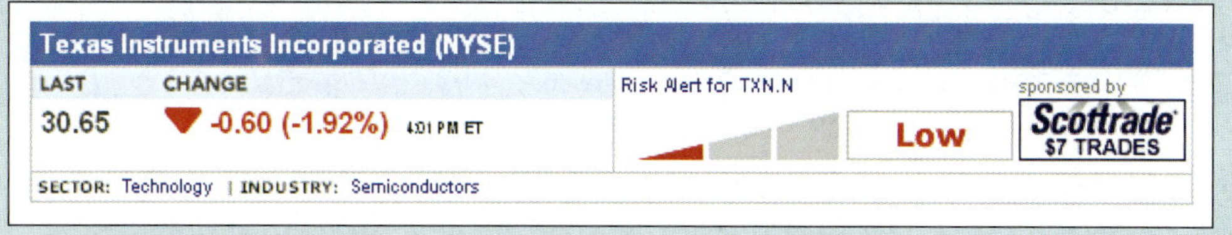

Financial Strength	Company	Industry	Sector	S&P 500
Quick Ratio (MRQ)	2.63	3.40	2.56	1.30
Current Ratio (MRQ)	3.50	4.14	3.02	1.81
LT Debt to Equity (MRQ)	0.03	0.13	0.23	0.72
Total Debt to Equity (MRQ)	0.07	0.15	0.28	0.89
Interest Coverage (TTM)	24.21	6.78	9.17	13.49

Most of the information is self-explanatory. Interest Coverage ratio is the same as the Times Interest Earned ratio discussed in the text. The abbreviation MRQ refers to results from the most recent quarterly financial statements, and TTM refers to results covering the previous ("trailing") 12 months. This site also provides a comparison to the industry, business sector, and S&P 500 average for the ratios. Other ratios available on the site have five-year averages calculated. Have a look!

has had an SIC code of 6710 (Holding Offices) because of its diverse financial and retailing operations. More generally, the kind of peer group analysis we have been describing is going to work best when the firms are strictly in the same line of business, the industry is competitive, and there is only one way of operating.

Another problem that is becoming increasingly common is that major competitors and natural peer group members in an industry may be scattered around the globe. The automobile industry is an obvious example. The problem here is that financial statements from outside the United States do not necessarily conform at all to GAAP. The existence of different standards and procedures makes it very difficult to compare financial statements across national borders.

Even companies that are clearly in the same line of business may not be comparable. For example, electric utilities engaged primarily in power generation are all classified in the same group (SIC 4911). This group is often thought to be relatively homogeneous. However, most utilities operate as regulated monopolies, so they don't compete very much with each other, at least not historically. Many have stockholders, and many are organized as cooperatives with no stockholders. There are several different ways of generating power, ranging from hydroelectric to nuclear, so the operating activities of these utilities can differ quite a bit. Finally, profitability is strongly affected by regulatory environment, so utilities in different locations can be very similar but show very different profits.

Several other general problems frequently crop up. First, different firms use different accounting procedures—for inventory, for example. This makes it difficult to compare statements. Second, different firms end their fiscal years at different times. For firms in seasonal businesses (such as a retailer with a large Christmas season), this can lead to difficulties in comparing balance sheets because of fluctuations in accounts during the year. Finally, for any particular firm, unusual or transient events, such as a one-time profit from an asset sale, may affect financial performance. In comparing firms, such events can give misleading signals.

Concept Questions

3.5a What are some uses for financial statement analysis?

3.5b What are SIC codes and how might they be useful?

3.5c Why do we say that financial statement analysis is management by exception?

3.5d What are some of the problems that can come up with financial statement analysis?

3.6 SUMMARY AND CONCLUSIONS

This chapter has discussed aspects of financial statement analysis:

1. Sources and uses of cash. We discussed how to identify the ways in which businesses obtain and use cash, and we described how to trace the flow of cash through the business over the course of the year. We briefly looked at the statement of cash flows.
2. Standardized financial statements. We explained that differences in size make it difficult to compare financial statements, and we discussed how to form common-size and common–base period statements to make comparisons easier.

3. Ratio analysis. Evaluating ratios of accounting numbers is another way of comparing financial statement information. We therefore defined and discussed a number of the most commonly reported and used financial ratios. We also discussed the famous Du Pont identity as a way of analyzing financial performance.
4. Using financial statements. We described how to establish benchmarks for comparison purposes and discussed some of the types of information that are available. We then examined some of the potential problems that can arise.

After you have studied this chapter, we hope that you will have some perspective on the uses and abuses of financial statements. You should also find that your vocabulary of business and financial terms has grown substantially.

Chapter Review and Self-Test Problems

3.1 Sources and Uses of Cash Consider the following balance sheets for the Philippe Corporation. Calculate the changes in the various accounts and, where applicable, identify the change as a source or use of cash. What were the major sources and uses of cash? Did the company become more or less liquid during the year? What happened to cash during the year?

PHILIPPE CORPORATION
2004 and 2005 Balance Sheets
($ in millions)

	2004	2005
Assets		
Current assets		
Cash	$ 210	$ 215
Accounts receivable	355	310
Inventory	507	328
Total	$1,072	$ 853
Fixed assets		
Net plant and equipment	$6,085	$6,527
Total assets	$7,157	$7,380
Liabilities and Owners' Equity		
Current liabilities		
Accounts payable	$ 207	$ 298
Notes payable	1,715	1,427
Total	$1,922	$1,725
Long-term debt	$1,987	$2,308
Owners' equity		
Common stock and paid-in surplus	$1,000	$1,000
Retained earnings	2,248	2,347
Total	$3,248	$3,347
Total liabilities and owners' equity	$7,157	$7,380

3.2 Common-Size Statements Below is the most recent income statement for Philippe. Prepare a common-size income statement based on this information. How do you interpret the standardized net income? What percentage of sales goes to cost of goods sold?

PHILIPPE CORPORATION 2005 Income Statement ($ in millions)		
Sales		$4,053
Cost of goods sold		2,780
Depreciation		550
Earnings before interest and taxes		$ 723
Interest paid		502
Taxable income		$ 221
Taxes (34%)		75
Net income		$ 146
Dividends	$47	
Addition to retained earnings	99	

3.3 Financial Ratios Based on the balance sheets and income statement in the previous two problems, calculate the following ratios for 2005:

Current ratio	______
Quick ratio	______
Cash ratio	______
Inventory turnover	______
Receivables turnover	______
Days' sales in inventory	______
Days' sales in receivables	______
Total debt ratio	______
Long-term debt ratio	______
Times interest earned ratio	______
Cash coverage ratio	______

3.4 ROE and the Du Pont Identity Calculate the 2005 ROE for the Philippe Corporation and then break down your answer into its component parts using the Du Pont identity.

Answers to Chapter Review and Self-Test Problems

3.1 We've filled in the answers in the following table. Remember, increases in assets and decreases in liabilities indicate that we spent some cash. Decreases in assets and increases in liabilities are ways of getting cash.

Philippe used its cash primarily to purchase fixed assets and to pay off short-term debt. The major sources of cash to do this were additional long-term borrowing, reductions in current assets, and additions to retained earnings.

PHILIPPE CORPORATION 2004 and 2005 Balance Sheets ($ in millions)				
	2004	**2005**	**Change**	**Source or Use of Cash**
Assets				
Current assets				
Cash	$ 210	$ 215	+$ 5	
Accounts receivable	355	310	− 45	Source
Inventory	507	328	− 179	Source
Total	$1,072	$ 853	−$219	
Fixed assets				
Net plant and equipment	$6,085	$6,527	+$442	Use
Total assets	$7,157	$7,380	+$223	
Liabilities and Owners' Equity				
Current liabilities				
Accounts payable	$ 207	$ 298	+$ 91	Source
Notes payable	1,715	1,427	− 288	Use
Total	$1,922	$1,725	−$197	
Long-term debt	$1,987	$2,308	+$321	Source
Owners' equity				
Common stock and paid-in surplus	$1,000	$1,000	+$ 0	—
Retained earnings	2,248	2,347	+ 99	Source
Total	$3,248	$3,347	+$ 99	
Total liabilities and owners' equity	$7,157	$7,380	+$223	

The current ratio went from $1,072/1,922 = .56 to $853/1,725 = .49, so the firm's liquidity appears to have declined somewhat. Overall, however, the amount of cash on hand increased by $5.

3.2 We've calculated the common-size income statement below. Remember that we simply divide each item by total sales.

PHILIPPE CORPORATION 2004 Common-Size Income Statement		
Sales		100.0%
Cost of goods sold		68.6
Depreciation		13.6
Earnings before interest and taxes		17.8
Interest paid		12.3
Taxable income		5.5
Taxes (34%)		1.9
Net income		3.6%
Dividends	1.2%	
Addition to retained earnings	2.4%	

Net income is 3.6 percent of sales. Because this is the percentage of each sales dollar that makes its way to the bottom line, the standardized net income is the firm's profit margin. Cost of goods sold is 68.6 percent of sales.

3.3 We've calculated the following ratios based on the ending figures. If you don't remember a definition, refer back to Table 3.8.

Current ratio	$853/$1,725	= .49 times
Quick ratio	$525/$1,725	= .30 times
Cash ratio	$215/$1,725	= .12 times
Inventory turnover	$2,780/$328	= 8.48 times
Receivables turnover	$4,053/$310	= 13.07 times
Days' sales in inventory	365/8.48	= 43.06 days
Days' sales in receivables	365/13.07	= 27.92 days
Total debt ratio	$4,033/$7,380	= 54.6%
Long-term debt ratio	$2,308/$5,655	= 40.8%
Times interest earned ratio	$723/$502	= 1.44 times
Cash coverage ratio	$1,273/$502	= 2.54 times

3.4 The return on equity is the ratio of net income to total equity. For Philippe, this is \$146/\$3,347 = 4.4%, which is not outstanding.

Given the Du Pont identity, ROE can be written as:

$$\begin{aligned} \text{ROE} &= \text{Profit margin} \times \text{Total asset turnover} \times \text{Equity multiplier} \\ &= \$146/\$4{,}053 \times \$4{,}053/\$7{,}380 \times \$7{,}380/\$3{,}347 \\ &= 3.6\% \times .549 \times 2.20 \\ &= 4.4\% \end{aligned}$$

Notice that return on assets, ROA, is 3.6% × .549 = 1.98%.

Concepts Review and Critical Thinking Questions

1. **Current Ratio** What effect would the following actions have on a firm's current ratio? Assume that net working capital is positive.
   a. Inventory is purchased.
   b. A supplier is paid.
   c. A short-term bank loan is repaid.
   d. A long-term debt is paid off early.
   e. A customer pays off a credit account.
   f. Inventory is sold at cost.
   g. Inventory is sold for a profit.
2. **Current Ratio and Quick Ratio** In recent years, Dixie Co. has greatly increased its current ratio. At the same time, the quick ratio has fallen. What has happened? Has the liquidity of the company improved?
3. **Current Ratio** Explain what it means for a firm to have a current ratio equal to .50. Would the firm be better off if the current ratio were 1.50? What if it were 15.0? Explain your answers.
4. **Financial Ratios** Fully explain the kind of information the following financial ratios provide about a firm:
   a. Quick ratio
   b. Cash ratio

c. Total asset turnover
d. Equity multiplier
e. Long-term debt ratio
f. Times interest earned ratio
g. Profit margin
h. Return on assets
i. Return on equity
j. Price-earnings ratio

5. **Standardized Financial Statements** What types of information do common-size financial statements reveal about the firm? What is the best use for these common-size statements? What purpose do common–base year statements have? When would you use them?
6. **Peer Group Analysis** Explain what peer group analysis means. As a financial manager, how could you use the results of peer group analysis to evaluate the performance of your firm? How is a peer group different from an aspirant group?
7. **Du Pont Identity** Why is the Du Pont identity a valuable tool for analyzing the performance of a firm? Discuss the types of information it reveals as compared to ROE considered by itself.
8. **Industry-Specific Ratios** Specialized ratios are sometimes used in specific industries. For example, the so-called book-to-bill ratio is closely watched for semiconductor manufacturers. A ratio of .93 indicates that for every $100 worth of chips shipped over some period, only $93 worth of new orders was received. In October 2003, the semiconductor equipment industry's book-to-bill ratio reached 1.01, compared to .96 during the month of September. The ratio had last been above 1.0 fourteen months previously during August 2002 when it was at 1.02. The book-to-bill ratio reached a low of .78 during October 2002. The three-month average of world-wide bookings in October 2003 was $871.1 million, an increase of 12 percent over September, while the three-month average billings were $873.4 million, an 8 percent increase from September. What is this ratio intended to measure? Why do you think it is so closely followed?
9. **Industry-Specific Ratios** So-called "same-store sales" are a very important measure for companies as diverse as McDonald's and Sears. As the name suggests, examining same-store sales means comparing revenues from the same stores or restaurants at two different points in time. Why might companies focus on same-store sales rather than total sales?
10. **Industry-Specific Ratios** There are many ways of using standardized financial information beyond those discussed in this chapter. The usual goal is to put firms on an equal footing for comparison purposes. For example, for auto manufacturers, it is common to express sales, costs, and profits on a per-car basis. For each of the following industries, give an example of an actual company and discuss one or more potentially useful means of standardizing financial information:

a. Public utilities
b. Large retailers
c. Airlines
d. On-line services
e. Hospitals
f. College textbook publishers

Visit us at www.mhhe.com/rwj

Questions and Problems

BASIC
(Questions 1–17)

1. **Calculating Liquidity Ratios** SDJ, Inc., has net working capital of $1,320, current liabilities of $4,460, and inventory of $1,875. What is the current ratio? What is the quick ratio?
2. **Calculating Profitability Ratios** Timber Line, Inc. has sales of $29 million, total assets of $37 million, and total debt of $13 million. If the profit margin is 9 percent, what is net income? What is ROA? What is ROE?
3. **Calculating the Average Collection Period** Bonds Lumber Yard has a current accounts receivable balance of $421,865. Credit sales for the year just ended were $2,873,150. What is the receivables turnover? The days' sales in receivables? How long did it take on average for credit customers to pay off their accounts during the past year?
4. **Calculating Inventory Turnover** The Sosa Cork Corporation has ending inventory of $386,500, and cost of goods sold for the year just ended was $2,532,095. What is the inventory turnover? The days' sales in inventory? How long on average did a unit of inventory sit on the shelf before it was sold?
5. **Calculating Leverage Ratios** Kid Pet Rocks, Inc., has a total debt ratio of .44. What is its debt-equity ratio? What is its equity multiplier?
6. **Calculating Market Value Ratios** Bellevue Corp. had additions to retained earnings for the year just ended of $310,000. The firm paid out $160,000 in cash dividends, and it has ending total equity of $6.5 million. If Bellevue currently has 180,000 shares of common stock outstanding, what are earnings per share? Dividends per share? Book value per share? If the stock currently sells for $78 per share, what is the market-to-book ratio? The price-earnings ratio?
7. **Du Pont Identity** If Roten Rooters, Inc., has an equity multiplier of 1.75, total asset turnover of 1.30, and a profit margin of 8.5 percent, what is its ROE?
8. **Du Pont Identity** Forester Fire Prevention Corp. has a profit margin of 9.20 percent, total asset turnover of 1.63, and ROE of 18.67 percent. What is this firm's debt-equity ratio?
9. **Sources and Uses of Cash** Based only on the following information for Sweeney Corp., did cash go up or down? By how much? Classify each event as a source or use of cash.

Increase in inventory	$600
Increase in accounts payable	330
Decrease in notes payable	790
Increase in accounts receivable	950

10. **Calculating Average Payables Period** For 2005, BDJ, Inc., had a cost of goods sold of $13,168. At the end of the year, the accounts payable balance was $2,965. How long on average did it take the company to pay off its suppliers during the year? What might a large value for this ratio imply?
11. **Cash Flow and Capital Spending** For the year just ended, Dolvin Frozen Yogurt shows an increase in its net fixed assets account of $580. The company took $165 in depreciation expense for the year. How much did Dolvin spend on new fixed assets? Is this a source or use of cash?

12. **Equity Multiplier and Return on Equity** Thomsen Fried Chicken Company has a debt-equity ratio of 1.40. Return on assets is 8.7 percent, and total equity is \$520,000. What is the equity multiplier? Return on equity? Net income?

Just Dew It Corporation reports the following balance sheet information for 2004 and 2005. Use this information to work Problems 13 through 17.

JUST DEW IT CORPORATION
2004 and 2005 Balance Sheets

Assets			Liabilities and Owners' Equity		
	2004	**2005**		**2004**	**2005**
Current assets			Current liabilities		
Cash	\$ 10,168	\$ 10,683	Accounts payable	\$ 73,185	\$ 59,309
Accounts receivable	27,145	28,613	Notes payable	39,125	48,168
Inventory	59,324	64,853	Total	\$112,310	\$107,477
Total	\$ 96,637	\$104,149	Long-term debt	\$ 50,000	\$ 62,000
Fixed assets			Owners' equity		
Net plant and equipment	\$304,165	\$347,168	Common stock and paid-in surplus	\$ 80,000	\$ 80,000
			Retained earnings	158,492	201,840
			Total	\$238,492	\$281,840
Total assets	\$400,802	\$451,317	Total liabilities and owners' equity	\$400,802	\$451,317

13. **Preparing Standardized Financial Statements** Prepare the 2004 and 2005 common-size balance sheets for Just Dew It.
14. **Preparing Standardized Financial Statements** Prepare the 2005 common–base year balance sheet for Just Dew It.
15. **Preparing Standardized Financial Statements** Prepare the 2005 combined common-size, common–base year balance sheet for Just Dew It.
16. **Sources and Uses of Cash** For each account on this company's balance sheet, show the change in the account during 2005 and note whether this change was a source or use of cash. Do your numbers add up and make sense? Explain your answer for total assets as compared to your answer for total liabilities and owners' equity.
17. **Calculating Financial Ratios** Based on the balance sheets given for Just Dew It, calculate the following financial ratios for each year:
    a. Current ratio
    b. Quick ratio
    c. Cash ratio
    d. NWC to total assets ratio
    e. Debt-equity ratio and equity multiplier
    f. Total debt ratio and long-term debt ratio

INTERMEDIATE
(Questions 18–30)

18. **Using the Du Pont Identity** Y3K, Inc., has sales of \$2,700, total assets of \$1,185, and a debt-equity ratio of 1.00. If its return on equity is 16 percent, what is its net income?
19. **Days' Sales in Receivables** A company has net income of \$173,000, a profit margin of 8.6 percent, and an accounts receivable balance of \$143,200. Assuming 75 percent of sales are on credit, what is the company's days' sales in receivables?
20. **Ratios and Fixed Assets** The Le Bleu Company has a long-term debt ratio of 0.70 and a current ratio of 1.20. Current liabilities are \$850, sales are \$4,310, profit

margin is 9.5 percent, and ROE is 21.5 percent. What is the amount of the firm's net fixed assets?

21. **Profit Margin** In response to complaints about high prices, a grocery chain runs the following advertising campaign: "If you pay your child $1 to go buy $50 worth of groceries, then your child makes twice as much on the trip as we do." You've collected the following information from the grocery chain's financial statements:

(millions)	
Sales	$770.0
Net income	7.7
Total assets	196.0
Total debt	130.0

Evaluate the grocery chain's claim. What is the basis for the statement? Is this claim misleading? Why or why not?

22. **Return on Equity** Firm A and Firm B have debt/total asset ratios of 60% and 40% and returns on total assets of 20% and 30%, respectively. Which firm has a greater return on equity?

23. **Calculating the Cash Coverage Ratio** Titan Inc.'s net income for the most recent year was $7,850. The tax rate was 34 percent. The firm paid $2,108 in total interest expense and deducted $1,687 in depreciation expense. What was Titan's cash coverage ratio for the year?

24. **Cost of Goods Sold** Guthrie Corp. has current liabilities of $340,000, a quick ratio of 1.8, inventory turnover of 4.2, and a current ratio of 3.3. What is the cost of goods sold for the company?

25. **Ratios and Foreign Companies** Prince Albert Canning PLC had a net loss of £13,156 on sales of £147,318 (both in thousands of pounds). What was the company's profit margin? Does the fact that these figures are quoted in a foreign currency make any difference? Why? In dollars, sales were $267,661. What was the net loss in dollars?

Some recent financial statements for Smolira Golf Corp. follow. Use this information to work Problems 26 through 30.

SMOLIRA GOLF CORP.
2004 and 2005 Balance Sheets

Assets	2004	2005	Liabilities and Owners' Equity	2004	2005
Current assets			Current liabilities		
Cash	$ 815	$ 906	Accounts payable	$ 983	$ 1,292
Accounts receivable	2,405	2,510	Notes Payable	720	840
Inventory	4,608	4,906	Other	105	188
Total	$ 7,828	$ 8,322	Total	$ 1,808	$ 2,320
Fixed assets			Long-Term debt	$ 4,817	$ 4,960
Net plant and equipment	$15,164	$19,167	Owners' equity		
			Common stock and paid-in surplus	$10,000	$10,000
			Retained earnings	6,367	10,209
			Total	$16,367	$20,209
Total assets	$22,992	$27,489	Total	$22,992	$27,489

SMOLIRA GOLF CORP. 2005 Income Statement		
Sales		$33,500
Cost of goods sold		18,970
Depreciation		1,980
Earnings before interest and taxes		$12,550
Interest paid		486
Taxable income		$12,064
Taxes (35%)		4,222
Net income		$ 7,842
Dividends	$4,000	
Addition to retained earnings	3,842	

26. **Calculating Financial Ratios** Find the following financial ratios for Smolira Golf Corp. (use year-end figures rather than average values where appropriate):

Short-term solvency ratios

a. Current ratio ____________________

b. Quick ratio ____________________

c. Cash ratio ____________________

Asset utilization ratios

d. Total asset turnover ____________________

e. Inventory turnover ____________________

f. Receivables turnover ____________________

Long-term solvency ratios

g. Total debt ratio ____________________

h. Debt-equity ratio ____________________

i. Equity multiplier ____________________

j. Times interest earned ratio ____________________

k. Cash coverage ratio ____________________

Profitability ratios

l. Profit margin ____________________

m. Return on assets ____________________

n. Return on equity ____________________

27. **Du Pont Identity** Construct the Du Pont identity for Smolira Golf Corp.
28. **Calculating the Interval Measure** For how many days could Smolira Golf Corp. continue to operate if its cash inflows were suddenly suspended?
29. **Statement of Cash Flows** Prepare the 2005 statement of cash flows for Smolira Golf Corp.
30. **Market Value Ratios** Smolira Golf Corp. has 2,500 shares of common stock outstanding, and the market price for a share of stock at the end of 2005 was $67. What is the price-earnings ratio? What are the dividends per share? What is the market-to-book ratio at the end of 2005?

S&P Problems

www.mhhe.com/edumarketinsight

1. **Equity Multiplier** Use the balance sheets for Amazon.com (AMZN), Bethlehem Steel (BS), American Electric Power (AEP), and Pfizer (PFE) to calculate the equity multiplier for each company over the most recent two years. Comment on any similarities or differences between the companies and explain how these might affect the equity multiplier.
2. **Inventory Turnover** Use the financial statements for Dell Computer Corporation (DELL) and Boeing Company (BA) to calculate the inventory turnover for each company over the past three years. Is there a difference in inventory turnover between the two companies? Is there a reason the inventory turnover is lower for Boeing? What does this tell you about comparing ratios across industries?
3. **SIC Codes** Find the SIC codes for Papa Johns' International (PZZA) and Darden Restaurants (DRI) on each company's home page. What is the SIC code for each of these companies? What does the business description say for each company? Are these companies comparable? What does this tell you about comparing ratios for companies based on SIC codes?
4. **Calculating the Du Pont Identity** Find the annual income statements and balance sheets for Dow Chemical (DOW) and Gateway (GTW). Calculate the Du Pont identity for each company for the most recent three years. Comment on the changes in each component of the Du Pont identity for each company over this period and compare the components between the two companies. Are the results what you expected? Why or why not?
5. **Ratio Analysis** Look under "Valuation" and download the "Profitability" spreadsheet for Southwest Airlines (LUV) and Continental Airlines (CAL). Find the ROA (Net ROA), ROE (Net ROE), PE ratio (P/E-High and P/E-low), and the market-to-book ratio (Price/Book-high and Price/Book-low) for each company. Since stock prices change daily, PE and market-to-book ratios are often reported as the highest and lowest values over the year, as is done in this instance. Look at these ratios for both companies over the past five years. Do you notice any trends in these ratios? Which company appears to be operating at a more efficient level based on these four ratios? If you were going to invest in an airline, which one (if either) of these companies would you choose based on this information? Why?

What's On the Web?

3.1 **Du Pont Identity** You can find financial statements for Walt Disney Company on the "Investor" link at Disney's home page, disney.go.com. For the three most recent years, calculate the Du Pont identity for Disney. How has ROE changed over this period? How have changes in each component of the Du Pont identity affected ROE over this period?

3.2 **Ratio Analysis** You want to examine the financial ratios for Dell Computer Corporation. Go to www.investors.reuters.com and type in the ticker symbol for the company (DELL). Next, go to the comparison link. You should find financial ratios for Dell and the industry, sector, and S&P 500 averages for each ratio.

- **a.** What do TTM and MRQ mean?
- **b.** How do Dell's recent profitability ratios compare to their values over the past five years? To the industry averages? To the sector averages? To the S&P 500

averages? Which is the better comparison group for Dell: the industry, sector, or S&P 500 averages? Why?

c. In what areas does Dell seem to outperform its competitors based on the financial ratios? Where does Dell seem to lag behind its competitors?

d. Dell's inventory turnover ratio is much larger than that for all comparison groups. Why do you think this is?

3.3. Sources and Uses of Cash Find the two most recent balance sheets for 3M at the "Investor Relations" link on the web site www.mmm.com. For each account in the balance sheet, show the change during the most recent year and note whether this was a source or use of cash. Do your numbers add up and make sense? Explain your answer for total assets as compared to your answer for total liabilities and owners' equity.

3.4. Asset Utilization Ratios Find the most recent financial statements for Wal-Mart at www.walmart.com and Boeing at www.boeing.com. Calculate the asset utilization ratio for these two companies. What does this ratio measure? Is the ratio similar for both companies? Why or why not?

4 Long-Term Financial Planning and Growth

In 2003, The Walking Company filed for bankruptcy. The company, which retails specialty shoes under the Dansko, Ecco, Merrill, and other well-known brand names, was a victim of its own success. It had grown rapidly from 20 stores to more than 100 stores in 2003 with about $65 million in sales. Unfortunately, following real estate and merchandising missteps, the company stumbled and ran out of cash. It emerged from bankruptcy in early 2004 when it was purchased by the parent company of Big Dog Sportswear for about $19 million.

The case of The Walking Company is not a unique one. Often firms that grow at a phenomenal pace run into cash flow problems and, subsequently, financial difficulties. In other words, it is literally possible to "grow broke." This chapter emphasizes the importance of planning for the future and discusses tools firms use to think about, and manage, growth.

A lack of effective long-range planning is a commonly cited reason for financial distress and failure. As we will develop in this chapter, long-range planning is a means of systematically thinking about the future and anticipating possible problems before they arrive. There are no magic mirrors, of course, so the best we can hope for is a logical and organized procedure for exploring the unknown. As one member of GM's board was heard to say, "Planning is a process that at best helps the firm avoid stumbling into the future backwards."

Financial planning establishes guidelines for change and growth in a firm. It normally focuses on the big picture. This means it is concerned with the major elements of a firm's financial and investment policies without examining the individual components of those policies in detail.

Our primary goals in this chapter are to discuss financial planning and to illustrate the interrelatedness of the various investment and financing decisions a firm makes. In the chapters ahead, we will examine in much more detail how these decisions are made.

We first describe what is usually meant by financial planning. For the most part, we talk about long-term planning. Short-term financial planning is discussed in a later chapter. We examine what the firm can accomplish by developing a long-term financial plan. To do this, we develop a simple, but very useful, long-range planning technique: the percentage of sales approach. We describe how to apply this approach in some simple cases, and we discuss some extensions.

To develop an explicit financial plan, management must establish certain elements of the firm's financial policy. These basic policy elements of financial planning are:

1. The firm's needed investment in new assets. This will arise from the investment opportunities the firm chooses to undertake, and it is the result of the firm's capital budgeting decisions.
2. The degree of financial leverage the firm chooses to employ. This will determine the amount of borrowing the firm will use to finance its investments in real assets. This is the firm's capital structure policy.
3. The amount of cash the firm thinks is necessary and appropriate to pay shareholders. This is the firm's dividend policy.
4. The amount of liquidity and working capital the firm needs on an ongoing basis. This is the firm's net working capital decision.

As we will see, the decisions a firm makes in these four areas will directly affect its future profitability, need for external financing, and opportunities for growth.

A key lesson to be learned from this chapter is that the firm's investment and financing policies interact and thus cannot truly be considered in isolation from one another. The types and amounts of assets the firm plans on purchasing must be considered along with the firm's ability to raise the capital necessary to fund those investments. Many business students are aware of the classic three *P*s (or even four *P*s) of marketing. Not to be outdone, financial planners have no fewer than six *P*s: *P*roper *P*rior *P*lanning *P*revents *P*oor *P*erformance.

Financial planning forces the corporation to think about goals. A goal frequently espoused by corporations is growth, and almost all firms use an explicit, companywide growth rate as a major component of their long-run financial planning. For example, in 2004, home-improvement retailer Lowe's projected that sales for 2005 would increase 17 percent, with same store sales increasing 5 to 6 percent. It also projected a further sales increase of 17 percent for 2006. The company said that EPS would grow at about 14 percent over this period.

There are direct connections between the growth a company can achieve and its financial policy. In the following sections, we show how financial planning models can be used to better understand how growth is achieved. We also show how such models can be used to establish the limits on possible growth.

WHAT IS FINANCIAL PLANNING? 4.1

Financial planning formulates the way in which financial goals are to be achieved. A financial plan is thus a statement of what is to be done in the future. Most decisions have long lead times, which means they take a long time to implement. In an uncertain world, this requires that decisions be made far in advance of their implementation. If a firm wants to build a factory in 2006, for example, it might have to begin lining up contractors and financing in 2004, or even earlier.

Growth as a Financial Management Goal

Because the subject of growth will be discussed in various places in this chapter, we need to start out with an important warning: Growth, by itself, is not an appropriate goal for the financial manager. Clothing retailer J. Peterman Co., whose quirky catalogs were made famous on the TV show "Seinfeld," learned this lesson the hard way. Despite its strong brand name and years of explosive revenue growth, the company filed for bankruptcy in 1999, the victim of an overly ambitious, growth-oriented, expansion plan.

Amazon.com, the big online retailer, is another example. At one time, Amazon's motto seemed to be "growth at any cost." Unfortunately, what really grew rapidly for the company were losses. Amazon refocused its business, explicitly sacrificing growth in the hope of achieving profitability. The plan seems to be working as Amazon.com turned a profit for the first time in the third quarter of 2003.

You can find growth rates under the research links at www.investor.reuters.com and finance.yahoo.com.

As we discussed in Chapter 1, the appropriate goal is increasing the market value of the owners' equity. Of course, if a firm is successful in doing this, then growth will usually result. Growth may thus be a desirable consequence of good decision making, but it is not an end unto itself. We discuss growth simply because growth rates are so commonly used in the planning process. As we will see, growth is a convenient means of summarizing various aspects of a firm's financial and investment policies. Also, if we think of growth as growth in the market value of the equity in the firm, then goals of growth and increasing the market value of the equity in the firm are not all that different.

Dimensions of Financial Planning

It is often useful for planning purposes to think of the future as having a short run and a long run. The short run, in practice, is usually the coming 12 months. We focus our attention on financial planning over the long run, which is usually taken to be the coming two to five years. This time period is called the **planning horizon**, and it is the first dimension of the planning process that must be established.

planning horizon
The long-range time period on which the financial planning process focuses, usually the next two to five years.

In drawing up a financial plan, all of the individual projects and investments the firm will undertake are combined to determine the total needed investment. In effect, the smaller investment proposals of each operational unit are added up, and the sum is treated as one big project. This process is called **aggregation**. The level of aggregation is the second dimension of the planning process that needs to be determined.

aggregation
The process by which smaller investment proposals of each of a firm's operational units are added up and treated as one big project.

Once the planning horizon and level of aggregation are established, a financial plan requires inputs in the form of alternative sets of assumptions about important variables. For example, suppose a company has two separate divisions: one for consumer products and one for gas turbine engines. The financial planning process might require each division to prepare three alternative business plans for the next three years:

1. **A worst case.** This plan would require making relatively pessimistic assumptions about the company's products and the state of the economy. This kind of disaster planning would emphasize a division's ability to withstand significant economic adversity, and it would require details concerning cost cutting, and even divestiture and liquidation. For example, sales were sluggish in the PC market in 2004. That left big manufacturers like Hewlett-Packard, Dell, and Gateway locked in a price war, fighting for market share at a time when revenues were stagnant.
2. **A normal case.** This plan would require making the most likely assumptions about the company and the economy.
3. **A best case.** Each division would be required to work out a case based on optimistic assumptions. It could involve new products and expansion and would then detail the financing needed to fund the expansion.

In this example, business activities are aggregated along divisional lines and the planning horizon is three years. This type of planning, which considers all possible events, is particularly important for cyclical businesses (businesses with sales that are strongly affected by the overall state of the economy or business cycles).

What Can Planning Accomplish?

Because the company is likely to spend a lot of time examining the different scenarios that will become the basis for the company's financial plan, it seems reasonable to ask what the planning process will accomplish.

Examining Interactions As we discuss in greater detail in the following pages, the financial plan must make explicit the linkages between investment proposals for the different operating activities of the firm and the financing choices available to the firm. In other words, if the firm is planning on expanding and undertaking new investments and projects, where will the financing be obtained to pay for this activity?

Exploring Options The financial plan provides the opportunity for the firm to develop, analyze, and compare many different scenarios in a consistent way. Various investment and financing options can be explored, and their impact on the firm's shareholders can be evaluated. Questions concerning the firm's future lines of business and questions of what financing arrangements are optimal are addressed. Options such as marketing new products or closing plants might be evaluated.

Avoiding Surprises Financial planning should identify what may happen to the firm if different events take place. In particular, it should address what actions the firm will take if things go seriously wrong, or, more generally, if assumptions made today about the future are seriously in error. As physicist Niels Bohr once observed, "Prediction is very difficult, particularly when it concerns the future." Thus, one of the purposes of financial planning is to avoid surprises and develop contingency plans.

For example, in December 2003, Motorola announced that its mobile phone sales fell 3 percent, compared with its prior target growth of 5 percent. The fall in sales did not occur because of a lack of demand; rather, Motorola experienced a shortage of parts. Apparently, Motorola found itself unable to meet orders when demand accelerated. Thus, a lack of planning for sales growth can be a problem for even the biggest companies.

Ensuring Feasibility and Internal Consistency Beyond a general goal of creating value, a firm will normally have many specific goals. Such goals might be couched in terms of market share, return on equity, financial leverage, and so on. At times, the linkages between different goals and different aspects of a firm's business are difficult to see. Not only does a financial plan make explicit these linkages, but it also imposes a unified structure for reconciling differing goals and objectives. In other words, financial planning is a way of verifying that the goals and plans made with regard to specific areas of a firm's operations are feasible and internally consistent. Conflicting goals will often exist. To generate a coherent plan, goals and objectives will therefore have to be modified, and priorities will have to be established.

For example, one goal a firm might have is 12 percent growth in unit sales per year. Another goal might be to reduce the firm's total debt ratio from 40 to 20 percent. Are these two goals compatible? Can they be accomplished simultaneously? Maybe yes, maybe no. As we will discuss, financial planning is a way of finding out just what is possible, and, by implication, what is not possible.

Conclusion Probably the most important result of the planning process is that it forces management to think about goals and to establish priorities. In fact, conventional business wisdom holds that financial plans don't work, but financial planning does. The future is inherently unknown. What we can do is establish the direction in which we want to travel and take some educated guesses at what we will find along the way. If we do a good job, then we won't be caught off guard when the future rolls around.

Concept Questions

4.1a What are the two dimensions of the financial planning process?

4.1b Why should firms draw up financial plans?

4.2 FINANCIAL PLANNING MODELS: A FIRST LOOK

Just as companies differ in size and products, the financial planning process will differ from firm to firm. In this section, we discuss some common elements in financial plans and develop a basic model to illustrate these elements. What follows is just a quick overview; later sections will take up the various topics in more detail.

A Financial Planning Model: The Ingredients

Most financial planning models require the user to specify some assumptions about the future. Based on those assumptions, the model generates predicted values for a large number of other variables. Models can vary quite a bit in terms of their complexity, but almost all will have the elements that we discuss next.

Sales Forecast Almost all financial plans require an externally supplied sales forecast. In our models that follow, for example, the sales forecast will be the "driver," meaning that the user of the planning model will supply this value, and most other values will be calculated based on it. This arrangement is common for many types of business; planning will focus on projected future sales and the assets and financing needed to support those sales.

Frequently, the sales forecast will be given as the growth rate in sales rather than as an explicit sales figure. These two approaches are essentially the same because we can calculate projected sales once we know the growth rate. Perfect sales forecasts are not possible, of course, because sales depend on the uncertain future state of the economy. To help a firm come up with its projections, some businesses specialize in macroeconomic and industry projections.

As we discussed previously, we frequently will be interested in evaluating alternative scenarios, so it isn't necessarily crucial that the sales forecast be accurate. In such cases, our goal is to examine the interplay between investment and financing needs at different possible sales levels, not to pinpoint what we expect to happen.

Spreadsheets to use for *pro forma* statements can be obtained at www.jaxworks.com.

Pro Forma Statements A financial plan will have a forecasted balance sheet, income statement, and statement of cash flows. These are called *pro forma statements,* or *pro formas* for short. The phrase *pro forma* literally means "as a matter of form." In our case, this means the financial statements are the form we use to summarize the different events projected for the future. At a minimum, a financial planning model will generate these statements based on projections of key items such as sales.

In the planning models we will describe, the pro formas are the output from the financial planning model. The user will supply a sales figure, and the model will generate the resulting income statement and balance sheet.

Asset Requirements The plan will describe projected capital spending. At a minimum, the projected balance sheet will contain changes in total fixed assets and net working capital. These changes are effectively the firm's total capital budget. Proposed capital spending in different areas must thus be reconciled with the overall increases contained in the long-range plan.

Financial Requirements The plan will include a section on the necessary financing arrangements. This part of the plan should discuss dividend policy and debt policy. Sometimes firms will expect to raise cash by selling new shares of stock or by borrowing. In this case, the plan will have to consider what kinds of securities have to be sold and what methods of issuance are most appropriate. These are subjects we consider in Part 6 of our book, where we discuss long-term financing, capital structure, and dividend policy.

The Plug After the firm has a sales forecast and an estimate of the required spending on assets, some amount of new financing will often be necessary because projected total assets will exceed projected total liabilities and equity. In other words, the balance sheet will no longer balance.

Because new financing may be necessary to cover all of the projected capital spending, a financial "plug" variable must be selected. The plug is the designated source or sources of external financing needed to deal with any shortfall (or surplus) in financing and thereby bring the balance sheet into balance.

For example, a firm with a great number of investment opportunities and limited cash flow may have to raise new equity. Other firms with few growth opportunities and ample cash flow will have a surplus and thus might pay an extra dividend. In the first case, external equity is the plug variable. In the second, the dividend is used.

Economic Assumptions The plan will have to state explicitly the economic environment in which the firm expects to reside over the life of the plan. Among the more important economic assumptions that will have to be made are the level of interest rates and the firm's tax rate.

A Simple Financial Planning Model

We can begin our discussion of long-term planning models with a relatively simple example. The Computerfield Corporation's financial statements from the most recent year are as follows:

COMPUTERFIELD CORPORATION
Financial Statements

Income Statement		Balance Sheet			
Sales	$1,000	Assets	$500	Debt	$250
Costs	800			Equity	250
Net income	$ 200	Total	$500	Total	$500

Unless otherwise stated, the financial planners at Computerfield assume that all variables are tied directly to sales and current relationships are optimal. This means that all items will grow at exactly the same rate as sales. This is obviously oversimplified; we use this assumption only to make a point.

Suppose sales increase by 20 percent, rising from $1,000 to $1,200. Planners would then also forecast a 20 percent increase in costs, from $800 to $800 × 1.2 = $960. The pro forma income statement would thus be:

Pro Forma Income Statement	
Sales	$1,200
Costs	960
Net income	$ 240

The assumption that all variables will grow by 20 percent will enable us to easily construct the pro forma balance sheet as well:

Pro Forma Balance Sheet			
Assets	$600 (+100)	Debt	$300 (+ 50)
		Equity	300 (+ 50)
Total	$600 (+100)	Total	$600 (+100)

Planware provides insight into cash flow forecasting in its "White Papers" Section (www.planware.org).

Notice we have simply increased every item by 20 percent. The numbers in parentheses are the dollar changes for the different items.

Now we have to reconcile these two pro formas. How, for example, can net income be equal to $240 and equity increase by only $50? The answer is that Computerfield must have paid out the difference of $240 − 50 = $190, possibly as a cash dividend. In this case, dividends are the plug variable.

Suppose Computerfield does not pay out the $190. In this case, the addition to retained earnings is the full $240. Computerfield's equity will thus grow to $250 (the starting amount) plus $240 (net income), or $490, and debt must be retired to keep total assets equal to $600.

With $600 in total assets and $490 in equity, debt will have to be $600 − 490 = $110. Since we started with $250 in debt, Computerfield will have to retire $250 − 110 = $140 in debt. The resulting pro forma balance sheet would look like this:

Pro Forma Balance Sheet			
Assets	$600 (+100)	Debt	$110 (−140)
		Equity	490 (+240)
Total	$600 (+100)	Total	$600 (+100)

In this case, debt is the plug variable used to balance out projected total assets and liabilities.

This example shows the interaction between sales growth and financial policy. As sales increase, so do total assets. This occurs because the firm must invest in net working capital and fixed assets to support higher sales levels. Because assets are growing, total liabilities and equity, the right-hand side of the balance sheet, will grow as well.

The thing to notice from our simple example is that the way the liabilities and owners' equity change depends on the firm's financing policy and its dividend policy. The growth in assets requires that the firm decide on how to finance that growth. This is strictly a managerial decision. Note that, in our example, the firm needed no outside funds. This won't usually be the case, so we explore a more detailed situation in the next section.

Concept Questions

4.2a What are the basic components of a financial plan?

4.2b Why is it necessary to designate a plug in a financial planning model?

4.3 THE PERCENTAGE OF SALES APPROACH

In the previous section, we described a simple planning model in which every item increased at the same rate as sales. This may be a reasonable assumption for some elements. For others, such as long-term borrowing, it probably is not, because the amount of long-term borrowing is something set by management, and it does not necessarily relate directly to the level of sales.

In this section, we describe an extended version of our simple model. The basic idea is to separate the income statement and balance sheet accounts into two groups, those that do vary directly with sales and those that do not. Given a sales forecast, we will then be able to calculate how much financing the firm will need to support the predicted sales level.

The financial planning model we describe next is based on the **percentage of sales approach**. Our goal here is to develop a quick and practical way of generating pro forma statements. We defer discussion of some "bells and whistles" to a later section.

percentage of sales approach
A financial planning method in which accounts are varied depending on a firm's predicted sales level.

The Income Statement

We start out with the most recent income statement for the Rosengarten Corporation, as shown in Table 4.1. Notice we have still simplified things by including costs, depreciation, and interest in a single cost figure.

Rosengarten has projected a 25 percent increase in sales for the coming year, so we are anticipating sales of $1,000 × 1.25 = $1,250. To generate a pro forma income statement, we assume that total costs will continue to run at $800/1,000 = 80% of sales. With this assumption, Rosengarten's pro forma income statement is as shown in Table 4.2. The effect here of assuming that costs are a constant percentage of sales is to assume that the profit margin is constant. To check this, notice that the profit margin was $132/1,000 = 13.2%. In our pro forma, the profit margin is $165/1,250 = 13.2%; so it is unchanged.

TABLE 4.1

ROSENGARTEN CORPORATION
Income Statement

Sales		$1,000
Costs		800
Taxable income		$ 200
Taxes (34%)		68
Net income		$ 132
Dividends	$44	
Addition to retained earnings	88	

TABLE 4.2 >>

ROSENGARTEN CORPORATION Pro Forma Income Statement	
Sales (projected)	$1,250
Costs (80% of sales)	1,000
Taxable income	$ 250
Taxes (34%)	85
Net income	$ 165

dividend payout ratio
The amount of cash paid out to shareholders divided by net income.

Next, we need to project the dividend payment. This amount is up to Rosengarten's management. We will assume Rosengarten has a policy of paying out a constant fraction of net income in the form of a cash dividend. For the most recent year, the **dividend payout ratio** was:

$$\begin{aligned}\text{Dividend payout ratio} &= \text{Cash dividends/Net income} \\ &= \$44/132 = 33\ 1/3\%\end{aligned} \quad [4.1]$$

We can also calculate the ratio of the addition to retained earnings to net income as:

$$\text{Addition to retained earnings/Net income} = \$88/132 = 66\ 2/3\%$$

retention ratio
The addition to retained earnings divided by net income. Also called the plowback ratio.

This ratio is called the **retention ratio** or **plowback ratio**, and it is equal to 1 minus the dividend payout ratio because everything not paid out is retained. Assuming that the payout ratio is constant, the projected dividends and addition to retained earnings will be:

Projected dividends paid to shareholders	= $165 × 1/3 =	$ 55
Projected addition to retained earnings	= $165 × 2/3 =	110
		$165

The Balance Sheet

To generate a pro forma balance sheet, we start with the most recent statement, as shown in Table 4.3.

On our balance sheet, we assume that some of the items vary directly with sales and others do not. For those items that do vary with sales, we express each as a percentage of sales for the year just completed. When an item does not vary directly with sales, we write "n/a" for "not applicable."

For example, on the asset side, inventory is equal to 60 percent of sales ($600/1,000) for the year just ended. We assume this percentage applies to the coming year, so for each $1 increase in sales, inventory will rise by $.60. More generally, the ratio of total assets to sales for the year just ended is $3,000/1,000 = 3, or 300%.

capital intensity ratio
A firm's total assets divided by its sales, or the amount of assets needed to generate $1 in sales.

This ratio of total assets to sales is sometimes called the **capital intensity ratio**. It tells us the amount of assets needed to generate $1 in sales; so the higher the ratio is, the more capital intensive is the firm. Notice also that this ratio is just the reciprocal of the total asset turnover ratio we defined in the last chapter.

For Rosengarten, assuming that this ratio is constant, it takes $3 in total assets to generate $1 in sales (apparently Rosengarten is in a relatively capital intensive business). Therefore, if sales are to increase by $100, then Rosengarten will have to increase total assets by three times this amount, or $300.

On the liability side of the balance sheet, we show accounts payable varying with sales. The reason is that we expect to place more orders with our suppliers as sales volume

TABLE 4.3 >>

ROSENGARTEN CORPORATION
Balance Sheet

Assets	$	Percentage of Sales	Liabilities and Owners' Equity	$	Percentage of Sales
Current assets			Current liabilities		
Cash	$ 160	16%	Accounts payable	$ 300	30%
Accounts receivable	440	44	Notes payable	100	n/a
Inventory	600	60	Total	$ 400	n/a
Total	$1,200	120	Long-term debt	$ 800	n/a
Fixed assets			Owners' equity		
Net plant and equipment	$1,800	180	Common stock and paid-in surplus	$ 800	n/a
			Retained earnings	1,000	n/a
			Total	$1,800	n/a
Total assets	$3,000	300%	Total liabilities and owners' equity	$3,000	n/a

increases, so payables will change "spontaneously" with sales. Notes payable, on the other hand, represents short-term debt such as bank borrowing. This will not vary unless we take specific actions to change the amount, so we mark this item as "n/a."

Similarly, we use "n/a" for long-term debt because it won't automatically change with sales. The same is true for common stock and paid-in surplus. The last item on the right-hand side, retained earnings, will vary with sales, but it won't be a simple percentage of sales. Instead, we will explicitly calculate the change in retained earnings based on our projected net income and dividends.

We can now construct a partial pro forma balance sheet for Rosengarten. We do this by using the percentages we have just calculated wherever possible to calculate the projected amounts. For example, net fixed assets are 180 percent of sales; so, with a new sales level of \$1,250, the net fixed asset amount will be $1.80 \times \$1{,}250 = \$2{,}250$, representing an increase of $\$2{,}250 - 1{,}800 = \$450$ in plant and equipment. It is important to note that for those items that don't vary directly with sales, we initially assume no change and simply write in the original amounts. The result is shown in Table 4.4. Notice that the change in retained earnings is equal to the \$110 addition to retained earnings we calculated earlier.

Inspecting our pro forma balance sheet, we notice that assets are projected to increase by \$750. However, without additional financing, liabilities and equity will only increase by \$185, leaving a shortfall of $\$750 - 185 = \$565$. We label this amount *external financing needed* (EFN).

A Particular Scenario

Our financial planning model now reminds us of one of those good news–bad news jokes. The good news is we're projecting a 25 percent increase in sales. The bad news is this isn't going to happen unless Rosengarten can somehow raise \$565 in new financing.

This is a good example of how the planning process can point out problems and potential conflicts. If, for example, Rosengarten has a goal of not borrowing any additional funds and not selling any new equity, then a 25 percent increase in sales is probably not feasible.

TABLE 4.4 >>

ROSENGARTEN CORPORATION
Partial Pro Forma Balance Sheet

Assets	Present Year	Change from Previous Year	Liabilities and Owners' Equity	Present Year	Change from Previous Year
Current assets			Current liabilities		
Cash	$ 200	$ 40	Accounts payable	$ 375	$ 75
Accounts receivable	550	110	Notes payable	100	0
Inventory	750	150	Total	$ 475	$ 75
Total	$1,500	$300	Long-term debt	$ 800	$ 0
Fixed assets					
Net plant and equipment	$2,250	$450	Owners' equity		
			Common stock and paid-in surplus	$ 800	$ 0
			Retained earnings	1,110	110
			Total	$1,910	$110
Total assets	$3,750	$750	Total liabilities and owners' equity	$3,185	$185
			External financing needed	$ 565	$565

If we take the need for $565 in new financing as given, we know that Rosengarten has three possible sources: short-term borrowing, long-term borrowing, and new equity. The choice of some combination among these three is up to management; we will illustrate only one of the many possibilities.

Suppose Rosengarten decides to borrow the needed funds. In this case, the firm might choose to borrow some over the short term and some over the long term. For example, current assets increased by $300 whereas current liabilities rose by only $75. Rosengarten could borrow $300 − 75 = $225 in short-term notes payable and leave total net working capital unchanged. With $565 needed, the remaining $565 − 225 = $340 would have to come from long-term debt. Table 4.5 shows the completed pro forma balance sheet for Rosengarten.

We have used a combination of short- and long-term debt as the plug here, but we emphasize that this is just one possible strategy; it is not necessarily the best one by any means. There are many other scenarios we could (and should) investigate. The various ratios we discussed in Chapter 3 come in very handy here. For example, with the scenario we have just examined, we would surely want to examine the current ratio and the total debt ratio to see if we were comfortable with the new projected debt levels.

Now that we have finished our balance sheet, we have all of the projected sources and uses of cash. We could finish off our pro formas by drawing up the projected statement of cash flows along the lines discussed in Chapter 3. We will leave this as an exercise and instead investigate an important alternative scenario.

An Alternative Scenario

The assumption that assets are a fixed percentage of sales is convenient, but it may not be suitable in many cases. In particular, note that we effectively assumed that Rosengarten was using its fixed assets at 100 percent of capacity, because any increase in sales led to an

TABLE 4.5 >>

ROSENGARTEN CORPORATION
Pro Forma Balance Sheet

Assets	Present Year	Change from Previous Year	Liabilities and Owners' Equity	Present Year	Change from Previous Year
Current assets			Current liabilities		
Cash	$ 200	$ 40	Accounts payable	$ 375	$ 75
Accounts receivable	550	110	Notes payable	325	225
Inventory	750	150	Total	$ 700	$300
Total	$1,500	$300	Long-term debt	$1,140	$340
Fixed assets					
Net plant and equipment	$2,250	$450	Owners' equity		
			Common stock and paid-in surplus	$ 800	$ 0
			Retained earnings	1,110	110
			Total	$1,910	$110
Total assets	$3,750	$750	Total liabilities and owners' equity	$3,750	$750

increase in fixed assets. For most businesses, there would be some slack or excess capacity, and production could be increased by, perhaps, running an extra shift.

For example, in early 2004, both Ford and GM announced plans to increase production in Venezuela. The increased production was to accommodate increased sales in that country. In Ford's case, the company planned no additional capital expenditures; in other words, the company did not plan to increase production facilities. GM's announcement of increased production came with an announcement that the company would invest in production facilities. Apparently, Ford had the capacity to expand production without significantly adding to fixed costs, while GM did not.

In another example also in early 2004, Simmons announced it was closing its mattress factory in Ohio. The company stated it would increase mattress production at other plants to compensate for the closing. Evidently, Simmons had significant excess capacity in its production facilities.

If we assume that Rosengarten is only operating at 70 percent of capacity, then the need for external funds will be quite different. When we say "70 percent of capacity," we mean that the current sales level is 70 percent of the full-capacity sales level:

$$\text{Current sales} = \$1{,}000 = .70 \times \text{Full-capacity sales}$$

$$\text{Full-capacity sales} = \$1{,}000/.70 = \$1{,}429$$

This tells us that sales could increase by almost 43 percent—from $1,000 to $1,429—before any new fixed assets would be needed.

In our previous scenario, we assumed it would be necessary to add $450 in net fixed assets. In the current scenario, no spending on net fixed assets is needed, because sales are projected to rise only to $1,250, which is substantially less than the $1,429 full-capacity level.

As a result, our original estimate of $565 in external funds needed is too high. We estimated that $450 in net new fixed assets would be needed. Instead, no spending on new net fixed assets is necessary. Thus, if we are currently operating at 70 percent capacity, then we need only $565 − 450 = $115 in external funds. The excess capacity thus makes a considerable difference in our projections.

EXAMPLE 4.1 >> **EFN and Capacity Usage**

Suppose Rosengarten were operating at 90 percent capacity. What would sales be at full capacity? What is the capital intensity ratio at full capacity? What is EFN in this case?

Full-capacity sales would be $1,000/.90 = $1,111. From Table 4.3, we know that fixed assets are $1,800. At full capacity, the ratio of fixed assets to sales is thus:

Fixed assets/Full-capacity sales = $1,800/1,111 = 1.62

This tells us that Rosengarten needs $1.62 in fixed assets for every $1 in sales once it reaches full capacity. At the projected sales level of $1,250, then, it needs $1,250 × 1.62 = $2,025 in fixed assets. Compared to the $2,250 we originally projected, this is $225 less, so EFN is $565 − 225 = $340.

Current assets would still be $1,500, so total assets would be $1,500 + 2,025 = $3,525. The capital intensity ratio would thus be $3,525/1,250 = 2.82, less than our original value of 3 because of the excess capacity.

These alternative scenarios illustrate that it is inappropriate to blindly manipulate financial statement information in the planning process. The results depend critically on the assumptions made about the relationships between sales and asset needs. We return to this point a little later.

One thing should be clear by now. Projected growth rates play an important role in the planning process. They are also important to outside analysts and potential investors. Our nearby *Work the Web* box shows you how to obtain growth rate estimates for real companies.

Concept Questions

4.3a What is the basic idea behind the percentage of sales approach?

4.3b Unless it is modified, what does the percentage of sales approach assume about fixed asset capacity usage?

4.4 EXTERNAL FINANCING AND GROWTH

External financing needed and growth are obviously related. All other things staying the same, the higher the rate of growth in sales or assets, the greater will be the need for external financing. In the previous section, we took a growth rate as given, and then we determined the amount of external financing needed to support that growth. In this section, we turn things around a bit. We will take the firm's financial policy as given and then examine the relationship between that financial policy and the firm's ability to finance new investments and thereby grow.

Once again, we emphasize that we are focusing on growth not because growth is an appropriate goal; instead, for our purposes, growth is simply a convenient means of

WORK THE WEB

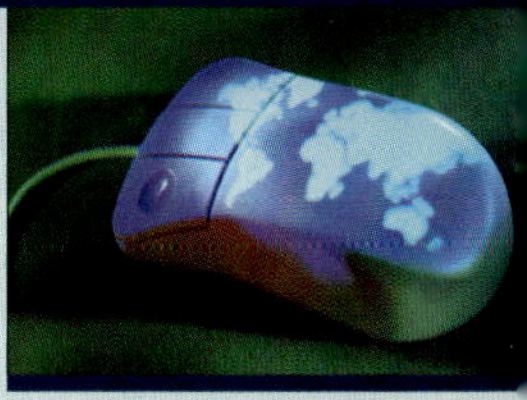

Calculating company growth rates can involve detailed research, and a major part of a stock analyst's job is to provide estimates of them. One place to find earnings and sales growth rates on the Web is Yahoo! Finance at finance.yahoo.com. Here, we pulled up a quote for Minnesota Mining & Manufacturing (MMM, or 3M as it is known) and followed the "Analyst Estimates" link. Below you will see an abbreviated look at the results.

Earnings Est	Current Qtr	Next Qtr	Current Year	Next Year
Avg. Estimate	0.87	0.91	3.61	4.04
No. of Analysts	13	10	16	13
Low Estimate	0.86	0.89	3.50	3.90
High Estimate	0.88	0.94	3.70	4.20
Year Ago EPS	0.71	0.78	3.09	3.61

Next Earnings Date: 19-Apr-04 - Set a Reminder

Revenue Est	Current Qtr	Next Qtr	Current Year	Next Year
Avg. Estimate	4.82B	5.05B	20.12B	21.48B
No. of Analysts	3	3	7	7
Low Estimate	4.76B	4.99B	19.65B	20.74B
High Estimate	4.88B	5.12B	20.31B	22.39B
Year Ago Sales	4.32B	4.58B	N/A	20.12B
Sales Growth (year/est)	11.7%	10.2%	N/A	6.8%

As shown, analysts expect, on average, revenue (sales) of $20.12 billion in 2004, growing to $21.48 billion in 2005, an increase of 6.8 percent. We also have the following table comparing MMM to some benchmarks:

Growth Est	MMM	Industry	Sector	S&P 500
Current Qtr.	22.5%	8.0%	19.0%	15.5%
Next Qtr.	16.7%	7.1%	18.3%	13.0%
This Year	16.8%	8.0%	18.2%	14.2%
Next Year	11.9%	14.6%	18.2%	12.1%
Past 5 Years (per annum)	8.7%	N/A	N/A	N/A
Next 5 Years (per annum)	11.5%	10.81%	11.67%	10.67%
Price/Earnings (avg. for comparison categories)	22.8	19.96	20.19	17.98
PEG Ratio (avg. for comparison categories)	1.98	1.85	1.73	1.69

As you can see, the estimated earnings growth rate for MMM is slightly higher than the industry and S&P 500 over the next five years. What does this mean for MMM stock? We'll get to that in a later chapter. Here is an assignment for you: What's a PEG ratio? Locate a financial glossary on the Web (there are lots of them) to find out.

examining the interactions between investment and financing decisions. In effect, we assume that the use of growth as a basis for planning is just a reflection of the very high level of aggregation used in the planning process.

EFN and Growth

The first thing we need to do is establish the relationship between EFN and growth. To do this, we introduce the simplified income statement and balance sheet for the Hoffman Company in Table 4.6. Notice we have simplified the balance sheet by combining short-term and long-term debt into a single total debt figure. Effectively, we are assuming that none of the current liabilities vary spontaneously with sales. This assumption isn't as restrictive as it sounds. If any current liabilities (such as accounts payable) vary with sales, we can assume that any such accounts have been netted out in current assets. Also, we continue to combine depreciation, interest, and costs on the income statement.

Suppose the Hoffman Company is forecasting next year's sales level at \$600, a \$100 increase. Notice that the percentage increase in sales is \$100/500 = 20%. Using the percentage of sales approach and the figures in Table 4.6, we can prepare a pro forma income statement and balance sheet as in Table 4.7. As Table 4.7 illustrates, at a 20 percent growth rate, Hoffman needs \$100 in new assets (assuming full capacity). The projected addition to retained earnings is \$52.8, so the external financing needed, EFN, is \$100 − 52.8 = \$47.2.

Notice that the debt-equity ratio for Hoffman was originally (from Table 4.6) equal to \$250/250 = 1.0. We will assume that the Hoffman Company does not wish to sell new equity. In this case, the \$47.2 in EFN will have to be borrowed. What will the new debt-equity ratio be? From Table 4.7, we know that total owners' equity is projected at \$302.8. The new total debt will be the original \$250 plus \$47.2 in new borrowing, or \$297.2 total. The debt-equity ratio thus falls slightly from 1.0 to \$297.2/302.8 = .98.

Table 4.8 shows EFN for several different growth rates. The projected addition to retained earnings and the projected debt-equity ratio for each scenario are also given (you should probably calculate a few of these for practice). In determining the debt-equity

TABLE 4.6 >>

HOFFMAN COMPANY
Income Statement and Balance Sheet

Income Statement

Sales		\$500
Costs		400
Taxable income		\$100
Taxes (34%)		34
Net income		\$ 66
Dividends	\$22	
Addition to retained earnings	44	

Balance Sheet

Assets	\$	Percentage of Sales	Liabilities and Owners' Equity	\$	Percentage of Sales
Current assets	\$200	40%	Total debt	\$250	n/a
Net fixed assets	300	60	Owners' equity	250	n/a
Total assets	\$500	100%	Total liabilities and owners' equity	\$500	n/a

TABLE 4.7 >>

HOFFMAN COMPANY
Pro Forma Income Statement and Balance Sheet

Income Statement

Sales (projected)		$600.0
Costs (80% of sales)		480.0
Taxable income		$120.0
Taxes (34%)		40.8
Net income		$ 79.2
Dividends	$26.4	
Addition to retained earnings	52.8	

Balance Sheet

Assets			Liabilities and Owners' Equity		
	$	Percentage of Sales		$	Percentage of Sales
Current assets	$240.0	40%	Total debt	$250.0	n/a
Net fixed assets	360.0	60	Owners' equity	302.8	n/a
Total assets	$600.0	100%	Total liabilities and owners' equity	$552.8	n/a
			External financing needed	$ 47.2	n/a

ratios, we assumed that any needed funds were borrowed, and we also assumed any surplus funds were used to pay off debt. Thus, for the zero growth case, the debt falls by $44, from $250 to $206. In Table 4.8, notice that the increase in assets required is simply equal to the original assets of $500 multiplied by the growth rate. Similarly, the addition to retained earnings is equal to the original $44 plus $44 times the growth rate.

Table 4.8 shows that for relatively low growth rates, Hoffman will run a surplus, and its debt-equity ratio will decline. Once the growth rate increases to about 10 percent, however, the surplus becomes a deficit. Furthermore, as the growth rate exceeds approximately 20 percent, the debt-equity ratio passes its original value of 1.0.

Figure 4.1 illustrates the connection between growth in sales and external financing needed in more detail by plotting asset needs and additions to retained earnings from Table 4.8 against the growth rates. As shown, the need for new assets grows at a much faster rate than the addition to retained earnings, so the internal financing provided by the addition to retained earnings rapidly disappears.

As this discussion shows, whether a firm runs a cash surplus or deficit depends on growth. Microsoft is a good example. Its revenue growth in the 1990s was amazing,

<< TABLE 4.8

Growth and Projected EFN for the Hoffman Company

Projected Sales Growth	Increase in Assets Required	Addition to Retained Earnings	External Financing Needed, EFN	Projected Debt-Equity Ratio
0%	$ 0	$44.0	−$44.0	.70
5	25	46.2	− 21.2	.77
10	50	48.4	1.6	.84
15	75	50.6	24.4	.91
20	100	52.8	47.2	.98
25	125	55.0	70.0	1.05

FIGURE 4.1 >>

Growth and Related Financing Needed for the Hoffman Company

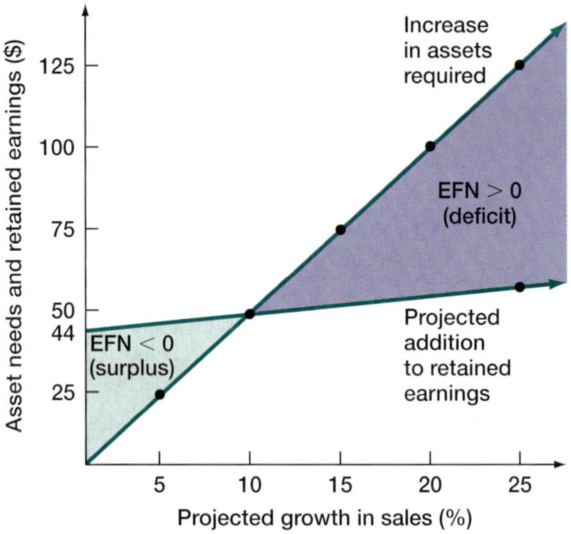

averaging well over 30 percent per year for the decade. Growth slowed down noticeably over the 2000–2004 period, but nonetheless, Microsoft's combination of growth and substantial profit margins led to enormous cash surpluses. In part because Microsoft paid few or no dividends, the cash really piled up; in 2004, Microsoft's cash horde exceeded $50 billion.

Financial Policy and Growth

Based on our discussion just preceding, we see that there is a direct link between growth and external financing. In this section, we discuss two growth rates that are particularly useful in long-range planning.

internal growth rate
The maximum growth rate a firm can achieve without external financing of any kind.

The Internal Growth Rate The first growth rate of interest is the maximum growth rate that can be achieved with no external financing of any kind. We will call this the **internal growth rate** because this is the rate the firm can maintain with internal financing only. In Figure 4.1, this internal growth rate is represented by the point where the two lines cross. At this point, the required increase in assets is exactly equal to the addition to retained earnings, and EFN is therefore zero. We have seen that this happens when the growth rate is slightly less than 10 percent. With a little algebra (see Problem 32 at the end of the chapter), we can define this growth rate more precisely as:

$$\text{Internal growth rate} = \frac{\text{ROA} \times b}{1 - \text{ROA} \times b} \qquad [4.2]$$

where ROA is the return on assets we discussed in Chapter 3, and b is the plowback, or retention, ratio defined earlier in this chapter.

For the Hoffman Company, net income was $66 and total assets were $500. ROA is thus $66/500 = 13.2%. Of the $66 net income, $44 was retained, so the plowback ratio, b, is $44/66 = 2/3. With these numbers, we can calculate the internal growth rate as:

$$\begin{aligned}\text{Internal growth rate} &= \frac{\text{ROA} \times b}{1 - \text{ROA} \times b} \\ &= \frac{.132 \times (2/3)}{1 - .132 \times (2/3)} \\ &= 9.65\%\end{aligned}$$

Thus, the Hoffman Company can expand at a maximum rate of 9.65 percent per year without external financing.

The Sustainable Growth Rate We have seen that if the Hoffman Company wishes to grow more rapidly than at a rate of 9.65 percent per year, then external financing must be arranged. The second growth rate of interest is the maximum growth rate a firm can achieve with no external *equity* financing while it maintains a constant debt-equity ratio. This rate is commonly called the **sustainable growth rate** because it is the maximum rate of growth a firm can maintain without increasing its financial leverage.

sustainable growth rate
The maximum growth rate a firm can achieve without external equity financing while maintaining a constant debt-equity ratio.

There are various reasons why a firm might wish to avoid equity sales. For example, as we discuss in Chapter 15, new equity sales can be very expensive. Alternatively, the current owners may not wish to bring in new owners or contribute additional equity. Why a firm might view a particular debt-equity ratio as optimal is discussed in Chapters 14 and 16; for now, we will take it as given.

Based on Table 4.8, the sustainable growth rate for Hoffman is approximately 20 percent because the debt-equity ratio is near 1.0 at that growth rate. The precise value can be calculated as (see Problem 32 at the end of the chapter):

$$\text{Sustainable growth rate} = \frac{\text{ROE} \times b}{1 - \text{ROE} \times b} \qquad [4.3]$$

This is identical to the internal growth rate except that ROE, return on equity, is used instead of ROA.

For the Hoffman Company, net income was \$66 and total equity was \$250; ROE is thus \$66/250 = 26.4 percent. The plowback ratio, b, is still 2/3, so we can calculate the sustainable growth rate as:

$$\begin{aligned}\text{Sustainable growth rate} &= \frac{\text{ROE} \times b}{1 - \text{ROE} \times b}\\ &= \frac{.264 \times (2/3)}{1 - .264 \times (2/3)}\\ &= 21.36\%\end{aligned}$$

Thus, the Hoffman Company can expand at a maximum rate of 21.36 percent per year without external equity financing.

Sustainable Growth

EXAMPLE 4.2

Suppose Hoffman grows at exactly the sustainable growth rate of 21.36 percent. What will the pro forma statements look like?

At a 21.36 percent growth rate, sales will rise from \$500 to \$606.8. The pro forma income statement will look like this:

HOFFMAN COMPANY Pro Forma Income Statement		
Sales (projected)		\$606.8
Costs (80% of sales)		485.4
Taxable income		\$121.4
Taxes (34%)		41.3
Net income		\$ 80.1
Dividends	\$26.7	
Addition to retained earnings	53.4	

continued

We construct the balance sheet just as we did before. Notice, in this case, that owners' equity will rise from $250 to $303.4 because the addition to retained earnings is $53.4.

HOFFMAN COMPANY
Pro Forma Balance Sheet

Assets			Liabilities and Owners' Equity		
	$	Percentage of Sales		$	Percentage of Sales
Current assets	$242.7	40%	Total debt	$250.0	n/a
Net fixed assets	364.1	60	Owners' equity	303.4	n/a
Total assets	$606.8	100%	Total liabilities and owners' equity	$553.4	n/a
			External financing needed	$ 53.4	n/a

As illustrated, EFN is $53.4. If Hoffman borrows this amount, then total debt will rise to $303.4, and the debt-equity ratio will be exactly 1.0, which verifies our earlier calculation. At any other growth rate, something would have to change.

Determinants of Growth In the last chapter, we saw that the return on equity, ROE, could be decomposed into its various components using the Du Pont identity. Because ROE appears so prominently in the determination of the sustainable growth rate, it is obvious that the factors important in determining ROE are also important determinants of growth.

From Chapter 3, we know that ROE can be written as the product of three factors:

$$\text{ROE} = \text{Profit margin} \times \text{Total asset turnover} \times \text{Equity multiplier}$$

If we examine our expression for the sustainable growth rate, we see that anything that increases ROE will increase the sustainable growth rate by making the top bigger and the bottom smaller. Increasing the plowback ratio will have the same effect.

Putting it all together, what we have is that a firm's ability to sustain growth depends explicitly on the following four factors:

1. **Profit margin.** An increase in profit margin will increase the firm's ability to generate funds internally and thereby increase its sustainable growth.
2. **Dividend policy.** A decrease in the percentage of net income paid out as dividends will increase the retention ratio. This increases internally generated equity and thus increases sustainable growth.
3. **Financial policy.** An increase in the debt-equity ratio increases the firm's financial leverage. Because this makes additional debt financing available, it increases the sustainable growth rate.
4. **Total asset turnover.** An increase in the firm's total asset turnover increases the sales generated for each dollar in assets. This decreases the firm's need for new assets as sales grow and thereby increases the sustainable growth rate. Notice that increasing total asset turnover is the same thing as decreasing capital intensity.

The sustainable growth rate is a very useful planning number. What it illustrates is the explicit relationship between the firm's four major areas of concern: its operating efficiency as measured by profit margin, its asset use efficiency as measured by total asset turnover, its dividend policy as measured by the retention ratio, and its financial policy as measured by the debt-equity ratio.

Given values for all four of these, there is only one growth rate that can be achieved. This is an important point, so it bears restating:

If a firm does not wish to sell new equity and its profit margin, dividend policy, financial policy, and total asset turnover (or capital intensity) are all fixed, then there is only one possible growth rate.

As we described early in this chapter, one of the primary benefits of financial planning is that it ensures internal consistency among the firm's various goals. The concept of the sustainable growth rate captures this element nicely. Also, we now see how a financial planning model can be used to test the feasibility of a planned growth rate. If sales are to grow at a rate higher than the sustainable growth rate, the firm must increase profit margins, increase total asset turnover, increase financial leverage, increase earnings retention, or sell new shares.

The two growth rates, internal and sustainable, are summarized in Table 4.9.

A Note on Sustainable Growth Rate Calculations

Very commonly, the sustainable growth rate is calculated using just the numerator in our expression, ROE $\times$ b. This causes some confusion, which we can clear up here. The issue has to do with how ROE is computed. Recall that ROE is calculated as net income divided by total equity. If total equity is taken from an ending balance sheet (as we have done consistently, and is commonly done in practice), then our formula is the right one. However, if total equity is from the beginning of the period, then the simpler formula is the correct one.

In principle, you'll get exactly the same sustainable growth rate regardless of which way you calculate it (as long you match up the ROE calculation with the right formula). In reality, you may see some differences because of accounting-related complications. By the way, if you use the average of beginning and ending equity (as some advocate), yet another formula is needed. Also, all of our comments here apply to the internal growth rate as well.

<< TABLE 4.9

Summary of Internal and Sustainable Growth Rates

I. Internal Growth Rate

$$\textit{Internal growth rate} = \frac{\text{ROA} \times b}{1 - \text{ROA} \times b}$$

where

ROA = Return on assets = Net income/Total assets

b = Plowback (retention) ratio

= Addition to retained earnings/Net income

The internal growth rate is the maximum growth rate than can be achieved with no external financing of any kind.

II. Sustainable Growth Rate

$$\textit{Sustainable growth rate} = \frac{\text{ROE} \times b}{1 - \text{ROE} \times b}$$

where

ROE = Return on equity = Net income/Total equity

b = Plowback (retention) ratio

= Addition to retained earnings/Net income

The sustainable growth rate is the maximum growth rate than can be achieved with no external equity financing while maintaining a constant debt-equity ratio.

IN THEIR OWN WORDS . . .

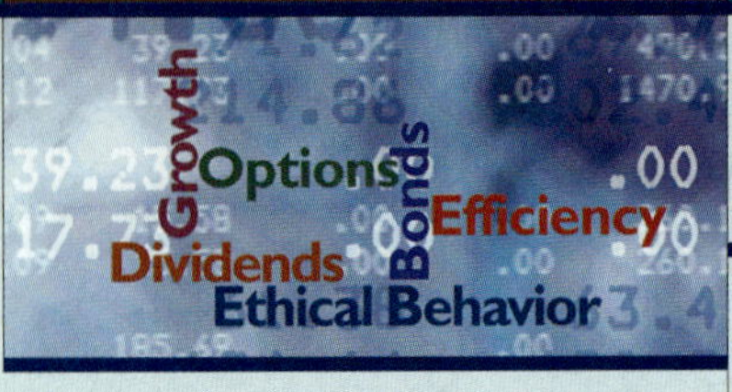

Robert C. Higgins on Sustainable Growth

Most financial officers know intuitively that it takes money to make money. Rapid sales growth requires increased assets in the form of accounts receivable, inventory, and fixed plant, which, in turn, require money to pay for assets. They also know that if their company does not have the money when needed, it can literally "grow broke." The sustainable growth equation states these intuitive truths explicitly.

Sustainable growth is often used by bankers and other external analysts to assess a company's creditworthiness. They are aided in this exercise by several sophisticated computer software packages that provide detailed analyses of the company's past financial performance, including its annual sustainable growth rate.

Bankers use this information in several ways. Quick comparison of a company's actual growth rate to its sustainable rate tells the banker what issues will be at the top of management's financial agenda. If actual growth consistently exceeds sustainable growth, management's problem will be where to get the cash to finance growth. The banker thus can anticipate interest in loan products. Conversely, if sustainable growth consistently exceeds actual, the banker had best be prepared to talk about investment products, because management's problem will be what to do with all the cash that keeps piling up in the till.

Bankers also find the sustainable growth equation useful for explaining to financially inexperienced small business owners and overly optimistic entrepreneurs that, for the long-run viability of their business, it is necessary to keep growth and profitability in proper balance.

Finally, comparison of actual to sustainable growth rates helps a banker understand why a loan applicant needs money and for how long the need might continue. In one instance, a loan applicant requested $100,000 to pay off several insistent suppliers and promised to repay in a few months when he collected some accounts receivable that were coming due. A sustainable growth analysis revealed that the firm had been growing at four to six times its sustainable growth rate and that this pattern was likely to continue in the foreseeable future. This alerted the banker to the fact that impatient suppliers were only a symptom of the much more fundamental disease of overly rapid growth, and that a $100,000 loan would likely prove to be only the down payment on a much larger, multiyear commitment.

Robert C. Higgins is Professor of Finance at the University of Washington. He pioneered the use of sustainable growth as a tool for financial analysis.

EXAMPLE 4.3 >> Profit Margins and Sustainable Growth

The Sandar Co. has a debt-equity ratio of .5, a profit margin of 3 percent, a dividend payout ratio of 40 percent, and a capital intensity ratio of 1. What is its sustainable growth rate? If Sandar desired a 10 percent sustainable growth rate and planned to achieve this goal by improving profit margins, what would you think?

ROE is $.03 \times 1 \times 1.5 = 4.5$ percent. The retention ratio is $1 - .40 = .60$. Sustainable growth is thus $.045(.60)/[1 - .045(.60)] = 2.77$ percent.

For the company to achieve a 10 percent growth rate, the profit margin will have to rise. To see this, assume that sustainable growth is equal to 10 percent and then solve for profit margin, PM:

$$.10 = \text{PM}(1.5)(.6)/[1 - \text{PM}(1.5)(.6)]$$
$$\text{PM} = .1/.99 = 10.1\%$$

For the plan to succeed, the necessary increase in profit margin is substantial, from 3 percent to about 10 percent. This may not be feasible.

Concept Questions

4.4a What are the determinants of growth?

4.4b How is a firm's sustainable growth related to its accounting return on equity (ROE)?

SOME CAVEATS REGARDING FINANCIAL PLANNING MODELS 4.5

Financial planning models do not always ask the right questions. A primary reason is that they tend to rely on accounting relationships and not financial relationships. In particular, the three basic elements of firm value tend to get left out, namely, cash flow size, risk, and timing.

Because of this, financial planning models sometimes do not produce output that gives the user many meaningful clues about what strategies will lead to increases in value. Instead, they divert the user's attention to questions concerning the association of, say, the debt-equity ratio and firm growth.

The financial model we used for the Hoffman Company was simple—in fact, too simple. Our model, like many in use today, is really an accounting statement generator at heart. Such models are useful for pointing out inconsistencies and reminding us of financial needs, but they offer very little guidance concerning what to do about these problems.

In closing our discussion, we should add that financial planning is an iterative process. Plans are created, examined, and modified over and over. The final plan will be a result negotiated between all the different parties to the process. In fact, long-term financial planning in most corporations relies on what might be called the Procrustes approach.[1] Upper-level management has a goal in mind, and it is up to the planning staff to rework and to ultimately deliver a feasible plan that meets that goal.

The final plan will therefore implicitly contain different goals in different areas and also satisfy many constraints. For this reason, such a plan need not be a dispassionate assessment of what we think the future will bring; it may instead be a means of reconciling the planned activities of different groups and a way of setting common goals for the future.

Concept Questions

4.5a What are some important elements that are often missing in financial planning models?

4.5b Why do we say planning is an iterative process?

SUMMARY AND CONCLUSIONS 4.6

Financial planning forces the firm to think about the future. We have examined a number of features of the planning process. We described what financial planning can accomplish and the components of a financial model. We went on to develop the relationship between

[1] In Greek mythology, Procrustes is a giant who seizes travelers and ties them to an iron bed. He stretches them or cuts off their legs as needed to make them fit the bed.

growth and financing needs, and we discussed how a financial planning model is useful in exploring that relationship.

Corporate financial planning should not become a purely mechanical activity. If it does, it will probably focus on the wrong things. In particular, plans all too often are formulated in terms of a growth target with no explicit linkage to value creation, and they frequently are overly concerned with accounting statements. Nevertheless, the alternative to financial planning is stumbling into the future. Perhaps the immortal Yogi Berra (the baseball catcher, not the cartoon character) put it best when he said, "Ya gotta watch out if you don't know where you're goin'. You just might not get there."[2]

Chapter Review and Self-Test Problems

4.1 Calculating EFN Based on the following information for the Skandia Mining Company, what is EFN if sales are predicted to grow by 10 percent? Use the percentage of sales approach and assume the company is operating at full capacity. The payout ratio is constant.

SKANDIA MINING COMPANY
Financial Statements

Income Statement		Balance Sheet: Assets		Liabilities and Owners' Equity	
Sales	$4,250.0	Current assets	$ 900.0	Current liabilities	$ 500.0
Costs	3,875.0	Net fixed assets	2,200.0	Long-term debt	1,800.0
Taxable income	$ 375.0	Total	$3,100.0	Owners' equity	800.0
Taxes (34%)	127.5			Total liabilities and owners' equity	$3,100.0
Net income	$ 247.5				
Dividends	$ 82.6				
Addition to retained earnings	164.9				

4.2 EFN and Capacity Use Based on the information in Problem 4.1, what is EFN, assuming 60 percent capacity usage for net fixed assets? Assuming 95 percent capacity?

4.3 Sustainable Growth Based on the information in Problem 4.1, what growth rate can Skandia maintain if no external financing is used? What is the sustainable growth rate?

Answers to Chapter Review and Self-Test Problems

4.1 We can calculate EFN by preparing the pro forma statements using the percentage of sales approach. Note that sales are forecasted to be $\$4,250 \times 1.10 = \$4,675$.

[2]We're not *exactly* sure what this means either, but we like the sound of it.

SKANDIA MINING COMPANY
Pro Forma Financial Statements

Income Statement

Sales	$4,675.0	Forecast
Costs	4,262.7	91.18% of sales
Taxable income	$ 412.3	
Taxes (34%)	140.2	
Net income	$ 272.1	
Dividends	$ 90.8	33.37% of net income
Addition to retained earnings	181.3	

Balance Sheet

Assets			Liabilities and Owners' Equity		
Current assets	$ 990.0	21.18%	Current liabilities	$ 550	11.76%
Net fixed assets	2,420.0	51.76%	Long-term debt	1,800.0	n/a
Total assets	$3,410.0	72.94%	Owners' equity	981.3	n/a
			Total liabilities and owners' equity	$3,331.3	n/a
			EFN	$ 78.7	n/a

4.2 Full-capacity sales are equal to current sales divided by the capacity utilization. At 60 percent of capacity:

$$\$4{,}250 = .60 \times \text{Full-capacity sales}$$
$$\$7{,}083 = \text{Full-capacity sales}$$

With a sales level of $4,675, no net new fixed assets will be needed, so our earlier estimate is too high. We estimated an increase in fixed assets of $2,420 − 2,200 = $220. The new EFN will thus be $78.7 − 220 = −$141.3, a surplus. No external financing is needed in this case.

At 95 percent capacity, full-capacity sales are $4,474. The ratio of fixed assets to full-capacity sales is thus $2,200/4,474 = 49.17%. At a sales level of $4,675, we will thus need $4,675 × .4917 = $2,298.7 in net fixed assets, an increase of $98.7. This is $220 − 98.7= $121.3 less than we originally predicted, so the EFN is now $78.7 − 121.3 = −$42.6, a surplus. No additional financing is needed.

4.3 Skandia retains $b = 1 - .3337 = 66.63\%$ of net income. Return on assets is $247.5/3,100 = 7.98%. The internal growth rate is:

$$\frac{\text{ROA} \times b}{1 - \text{ROA} \times b} = \frac{.0798 \times .6663}{1 - .0798 \times .6663}$$
$$= 5.62\%$$

Return on equity for Skandia is $247.5/800 = 30.94%, so we can calculate the sustainable growth rate as:

$$\frac{\text{ROE} \times b}{1 - \text{ROE} \times b} = \frac{.3094 \times .6663}{1 - .3094 \times .6663}$$
$$= 25.97\%$$

Concepts Review and Critical Thinking Questions

1. **Sales Forecast** Why do you think most long-term financial planning begins with sales forecasts? Put differently, why are future sales the key input?
2. **Sustainable Growth** In the chapter, we used Rosengarten Corporation to demonstrate how to calculate EFN. The ROE for Rosengarten is about 7.3 percent, and the plowback ratio is about 67 percent. If you calculate the sustainable growth rate for Rosengarten, you will find it is only 5.14 percent. In our calculation for EFN, we used a growth rate of 25 percent. Is this possible? (Hint: Yes. How?)
3. **External Financing Needed** Testaburger, Inc., uses no external financing and maintains a positive retention ratio. When sales grow by 15 percent, the firm has a negative projected EFN. What does this tell you about the firm's internal growth rate? How about the sustainable growth rate? At this same level of sales growth, what will happen to the projected EFN if the retention ratio is increased? What if the retention ratio is decreased? What happens to the projected EFN if the firm pays out all of its earnings in the form of dividends?
4. **EFN and Growth Rates** Broslofski Co. maintains a positive retention ratio and keeps its debt-equity ratio constant every year. When sales grow by 20 percent, the firm has a negative projected EFN. What does this tell you about the firm's sustainable growth rate? Do you know, with certainty, if the internal growth rate is greater than or less than 20 percent? Why? What happens to the projected EFN if the retention ratio is increased? What if the retention ratio is decreased? What if the retention ratio is zero?

   Use the following information to answer the next six questions: A small business called The Grandmother Calendar Company began selling personalized photo calendar kits. The kits were a hit, and sales soon sharply exceeded forecasts. The rush of orders created a huge backlog, so the company leased more space and expanded capacity, but it still could not keep up with demand. Equipment failed from overuse and quality suffered. Working capital was drained to expand production, and, at the same time, payments from customers were often delayed until the product was shipped. Unable to deliver on orders, the company became so strapped for cash that employee paychecks began to bounce. Finally, out of cash, the company ceased operations entirely three years later.

5. **Product Sales** Do you think the company would have suffered the same fate if its product had been less popular? Why or why not?
6. **Cash Flow** The Grandmother Calendar Company clearly had a cash flow problem. In the context of the cash flow analysis we developed in Chapter 2, what was the impact of customers' not paying until orders were shipped?
7. **Product Pricing** The firm actually priced its product to be about 20 percent less than that of competitors, even though the Grandmother calendar was more detailed. In retrospect, was this a wise choice?
8. **Corporate Borrowing** If the firm was so successful at selling, why wouldn't a bank or some other lender step in and provide it with the cash it needed to continue?
9. **Cash Flow** Which is the biggest culprit here: too many orders, too little cash, or too little production capacity?
10. **Cash Flow** What are some of the actions that a small company like The Grandmother Calendar Company can take if it finds itself in a situation in which growth in sales outstrips production capacity and available financial resources? What other

options (besides expansion of capacity) are available to a company when orders exceed capacity?

Questions and Problems

BASIC
(Questions 1–15)

1. **Pro Forma Statements** Consider the following simplified financial statements for the Fisk Corporation (assuming no income taxes):

Income Statement		**Balance Sheet**			
Sales	$16,000	Assets	$8,900	Debt	$5,100
Costs	12,500			Equity	3,800
Net income	$ 3,500	Total	$8,900	Total	$8,900

Fisk has predicted a sales increase of 10 percent. It has predicted that every item on the balance sheet will increase by 10 percent as well. Create the pro forma statements and reconcile them. What is the plug variable here?

2. **Pro Forma Statements and EFN** In the previous question, assume Fisk pays out half of net income in the form of a cash dividend. Costs and assets vary with sales, but debt and equity do not. Prepare the pro forma statements and determine the external financing needed.

3. **Calculating EFN** The most recent financial statements for Bradley's Bagels, Inc., are shown here (assuming no income taxes):

Income Statement		**Balance Sheet**			
Sales	$4,400	Assets	$13,400	Debt	$ 9,100
Costs	2,685			Equity	4,300
Net income	$1,715	Total	$13,400	Total	$13,400

Assets and costs are proportional to sales. Debt and equity are not. No dividends are paid. Next year's sales are projected to be $5,192. What is the external financing needed?

4. **EFN** The most recent financial statements for McGillicudy, Inc., are shown here:

Income Statement		**Balance Sheet**			
Sales	$19,200	Assets	$93,000	Debt	$20,400
Costs	15,550			Equity	72,600
Taxable income	$ 3,650	Total	$93,000	Total	$93,000
Taxes (34%)	1,241				
Net income	$ 2,409				

Assets and costs are proportional to sales. Debt and equity are not. A dividend of $963.60 was paid, and McGillicudy wishes to maintain a constant payout ratio. Next year's sales are projected to be $23,040. What is the external financing needed?

5. **EFN** The most recent financial statements for 2 Doors Down, Inc., are shown here:

Income Statement		Balance Sheet			
Sales	$3,600	Current assets	$4,500	Current liabilities	$ 920
Costs	2,900	Fixed assets	3,900	Long-term debt	1,840
Taxable income	$ 700			Equity	5,640
Taxes (34%)	238	Total	$8,400	Total	$8,400
Net income	$ 462				

Assets, costs, and current liabilities are proportional to sales. Long-term debt and equity are not. 2 Doors Down maintains a constant 50 percent dividend payout ratio. Like every other firm in its industry, next year's sales are projected to increase by exactly 15%. What is the external financing needed?

6. **Calculating Internal Growth** The most recent financial statements for Panama Co. are shown here:

Income Statement		Balance Sheet			
Sales	$10,400	Current assets	$11,000	Debt	$22,000
Costs	6,820	Fixed assets	27,000	Equity	16,000
Taxable income	$ 3,580	Total	$38,000	Total	$38,000
Taxes (35%)	1,253				
Net income	$ 2,327				

Assets and costs are proportional to sales. Debt and equity are not. Panama maintains a constant 20 percent dividend payout ratio. No external equity financing is possible. What is the internal growth rate?

7. **Calculating Sustainable Growth** For the company in the previous problem, what is the sustainable growth rate?

8. **Sales and Growth** The most recent financial statements for Fontenot Co. are shown here:

Income Statement		Balance Sheet			
Sales	$54,000	Current assets	$ 26,000	Long-term debt	$ 58,000
Costs	34,800	Fixed assets	105,000	Equity	73,000
Taxable income	$19,200	Total	$131,000	Total	$131,000
Taxes (34%)	6,528				
Net income	$12,672				

Assets and costs are proportional to sales. The company maintains a constant 30 percent dividend payout ratio and a constant debt-equity ratio. What is the maximum increase in sales that can be sustained assuming no new equity is issued?

9. **Calculating Retained Earnings from Pro Forma Income** Consider the following income statement for the Heir Jordan Corporation:

HEIR JORDAN CORPORATION Income Statement		
Sales		$29,000
Costs		11,200
Taxable income		$17,800
Taxes (34%)		6,052
Net income		$11,748
Dividends	$4,935	
Addition to retained earnings	6,813	

A 20 percent growth rate in sales is projected. Prepare a pro forma income statement assuming costs vary with sales and the dividend payout ratio is constant. What is the projected addition to retained earnings?

10. **Applying Percentage of Sales** The balance sheet for the Heir Jordan Corporation follows. Based on this information and the income statement in the previous problem, supply the missing information using the percentage of sales approach. Assume that accounts payable vary with sales, whereas notes payable do not. Put "n/a" where needed.

HEIR JORDAN CORPORATION
Balance Sheet

Assets	$	Percentage of Sales	Liabilities and Owners' Equity	$	Percentage of Sales
Current assets			Current liabilities		
Cash	$ 3,525	______	Accounts payable	$ 3,000	______
Accounts receivable	7,500	______	Notes payable	7,500	______
Inventory	6,000	______	Total	$10,500	______
Total	$17,025	______	Long-term debt	$19,500	______
Fixed assets			Owners' equity		
Net plant and equipment	$30,000	______	Common stock and paid-in surplus	$15,000	______
			Retained earnings	2,025	______
Total assets	$47,025	______	Total	$17,025	______
			Total liabilities and owners' equity	$47,025	______

11. **EFN and Sales** From the previous two questions, prepare a pro forma balance sheet showing EFN, assuming a 15 percent increase in sales, no new external debt or equity financing, and a constant payout ratio.
12. **Internal Growth** If Highfield Hobby Shop has a 10 percent ROA and a 20 percent payout ratio, what is its internal growth rate?
13. **Sustainable Growth** If the Layla Corp. has a 19 percent ROE and a 25 percent payout ratio, what is its sustainable growth rate?

14. **Sustainable Growth** Based on the following information, calculate the sustainable growth rate for Kaleb's Kickboxing:

    Profit margin = 8.9%
    Capital intensity ratio = .55
    Debt-equity ratio = .60
    Net income = $29,000
    Dividends = $15,000

    What is the ROE here?

15. **Sustainable Growth** Assuming the following ratios are constant, what is the sustainable growth rate?

    Total asset turnover = 1.40
    Profit margin = 7.6%
    Equity multiplier = 1.50
    Payout ratio = 40%

INTERMEDIATE
(Questions 16–27)

16. **Full-Capacity Sales** Thorpe Mfg., Inc., is currently operating at only 85 percent of fixed asset capacity. Current sales are $510,000. How fast can sales grow before any new fixed assets are needed?

17. **Fixed Assets and Capacity Usage** For the company in the previous problem, suppose fixed assets are $415,000 and sales are projected to grow to $680,000. How much in new fixed assets are required to support this growth in sales?

18. **Growth and Profit Margin** Top Hat Co. wishes to maintain a growth rate of 8 percent a year, a debt-equity ratio of .40, and a dividend payout ratio of 50 percent. The ratio of total assets to sales is constant at 1.30. What profit margin must the firm achieve?

19. **Growth and Debt-Equity Ratio** A firm wishes to maintain a growth rate of 11 percent and a dividend payout ratio of 60 percent. The ratio of total assets to sales is constant at .9, and profit margin is 9.5 percent. If the firm also wishes to maintain a constant debt-equity ratio, what must it be?

20. **Growth and Assets** A firm wishes to maintain an internal growth rate of 9 percent and a dividend payout ratio of 30 percent. The current profit margin is 8 percent and the firm uses no external financing sources. What must total asset turnover be?

21. **Sustainable Growth** Based on the following information, calculate the sustainable growth rate for Hendrix Guitars, Inc.:

    Profit margin = 6.4%
    Total asset turnover = 1.80
    Total debt ratio = .60
    Payout ratio = 60%

    What is the ROA here?

22. **Sustainable Growth and Outside Financing** You've collected the following information about Bad Company, Inc.:

    Sales = $140,000
    Net income = $21,000
    Dividends = $12,000
    Total debt = $85,000
    Total equity = $49,000

What is the sustainable growth rate for Bad Company, Inc.? If it does grow at this rate, how much new borrowing will take place in the coming year, assuming a constant debt-equity ratio? What growth rate could be supported with no outside financing at all?

23. **Sustainable Growth Rate** No Return, Inc., had equity of $165,000 at the beginning of the year. At the end of the year, the company had total assets of $250,000. During the year the company sold no new equity. Net income for the year was $80,000 and dividends were $49,000. What is the sustainable growth rate for the company? What is the sustainable growth rate if you use the formula ROE $\times$ b and beginning of period equity? What is the sustainable growth rate if you use end of period equity in this formula? Is this number too high or too low? Why?
24. **Internal Growth Rates** Calculate the internal growth rate for the company in the previous problem. Now calculate the internal growth rate using ROA $\times$ b for both beginning of period and end of period total assets. What do you observe?
25. **Calculating EFN** The most recent financial statements for Moose Tours, Inc., follow. Sales for 2005 are projected to grow by 20 percent. Interest expense will remain constant; the tax rate and the dividend payout rate will also remain constant. Costs, other expenses, current assets, and accounts payable increase spontaneously with sales. If the firm is operating at full capacity and no new debt or equity is issued, what is the external financing needed to support the 20 percent growth rate in sales?

MOOSE TOURS, INC.
2004 Income Statement

Sales		$905,000
Costs		710,000
Other expenses		12,000
Earnings before interest and taxes		$183,000
Interest paid		19,700
Taxable income		$163,300
Taxes (35%)		57,155
Net income		$106,145
Dividends	$42,458	
Addition to retained earnings	63,687	

MOOSE TOURS, INC.
Balance Sheet as of December 31, 2004

Assets		Liabilities and Owners' Equity	
Current assets		Current liabilities	
Cash	$ 25,000	Accounts payable	$ 65,000
Accounts receivable	43,000	Notes payable	9,000
Inventory	76,000	Total	$ 74,000
Total	$144,000	Long-term debt	$156,000
Fixed assets		Owners' equity	
Net plant and equipment	$364,000	Common stock and paid-in surplus	$ 21,000
		Retained earnings	257,000
		Total	$278,000
Total assets	$508,000	Total liabilities and owners' equity	$508,000

26. **Capacity Usage and Growth** In the previous problem, suppose the firm was operating at only 80 percent capacity in 2004. What is EFN now?

27. **Calculating EFN** In Problem 25, suppose the firm wishes to keep its debt-equity ratio constant. What is EFN now?

CHALLENGE
(Questions 28–32)

28. **EFN and Internal Growth** Redo Problem 25 using sales growth rates of 15 and 25 percent in addition to 20 percent. Illustrate graphically the relationship between EFN and the growth rate, and use this graph to determine the relationship between them. At what growth rate is the EFN equal to zero? Why is this internal growth rate different from that found by using the equation in the text?

29. **EFN and Sustainable Growth** Redo Problem 27 using sales growth rates of 30 and 35 percent in addition to 20 percent. Illustrate graphically the relationship between EFN and the growth rate, and use this graph to determine the relationship between them. At what growth rate is the EFN equal to zero? Why is this sustainable growth rate different from that found by using the equation in the text?

30. **Constraints on Growth** Bulla Recording, Inc., wishes to maintain a growth rate of 14 percent per year and a debt-equity ratio of .30. Profit margin is 6.2 percent, and the ratio of total assets to sales is constant at 1.55. Is this growth rate possible? To answer, determine what the dividend payout ratio must be. How do you interpret the result?

31. **EFN** Define the following:

    S = Previous year's sales
    A = Total assets
    D = Total debt
    E = Total equity
    g = Projected growth in sales
    PM = Profit margin
    b = Retention (plowback) ratio

    Show that EFN can be written as:

    $$\text{EFN} = -\text{PM(S)}b + (\text{A} - \text{PM(S)}b) \times g$$

    Hint: Asset needs will equal A × g. The addition to retained earnings will equal PM(S)b × (1 + g).

32. **Growth Rates** Based on the result in Problem 31, show that the internal and sustainable growth rates are as given in the chapter. Hint: For the internal growth rate, set EFN equal to zero and solve for g.

33. **Sustainable Growth Rate** In the chapter, we discussed the two versions of the sustainable growth rate formula. Derive the formula ROE × b from the formula given in the chapter, where ROE is based on beginning of period equity. Also, derive the formula ROA × b from the internal growth rate formula.

S&P Problems

www.mhhe.com/edumarketinsight

STANDARD &POOR'S

1. **Calculating EFN** Find the income statements and balance sheets for Huffy Corporation (HUF), the bicycle manufacturer. Assuming sales grow by 10 percent, what is the EFN for Huffy next year? Assume non-operating income/expense and special items will be zero next year. Assets, costs, and current liabilities are

proportional to sales. Long-term debt and equity are not. Huffy will have the same tax rate next year as it does in the current year.

2. **Internal and Sustainable Growth Rates** Look up the financial statements for Emerson Electric (EMR) and Wal-Mart (WMT). For each company, calculate the internal growth rate and sustainable growth rate over the past two years. Are the growth rates the same for each company for the two years? Why or why not?

What's On the Web?

4.1 Growth Rates Go to finance.yahoo.com and enter the ticker symbol "IP" for International Paper. When you get the quote, follow the "Analyst Estimates" link. What is the projected sales growth for International Paper for next year? What is the projected earnings growth rate for next year? For the next five years? How do these earnings growth projections compare to the industry, sector, and S&P 500 index?

4.2 Applying Percentage of Sales Locate the most recent annual financial statements for Du Pont at www.dupont.com under the "Investor Center" link. Locate the annual report. Using the growth in sales for the most recent year as the projected sales growth for next year, construct a pro forma income statement and balance sheet.

4.3 Growth Rates You can find the home page for Caterpillar, Inc., at www.caterpillar.com. Go to the Web page, select "About Cat," and find the most recent annual report. Using the information from the financial statements, what is the internal growth rate for Caterpillar? What is the sustainable growth rate?

Visit us at www.mhhe.com/rwj

>> MINI-CASE

Ratios and Financial Planning at S&S Air, Inc.

Chris Guthrie was recently hired by S&S Air, Inc., to assist the company with its financial planning, and to evaluate the company's performance. Chris graduated from college five years ago with a finance degree. He has been employed in the finance department of a Fortune 500 company since then.

S&S Air was founded 10 years ago by friends Mark Sexton and Todd Story. The company has manufactured and sold light airplanes over this period, and the company's products have received high reviews for safety and reliability. The company has a niche market in that it sells primarily to individuals who own and fly their own airplanes. The company has two models, the Birdie, which sells for $53,000, and the Eagle, which sells for $78,000.

While the company manufactures aircraft, its operations are different from commercial aircraft companies. S&S Air builds aircraft to order. By using prefabricated parts, the company is able to complete the manufacture of an airplane in only five weeks. The company also receives a deposit on each order, as well as another partial payment before the order is complete. In contrast, a commercial airplane may take one and one-half to two years to manufacture once the order is placed.

Mark and Todd have provided the following financial statements. Chris has gathered the industry ratios for the light airplane manufacturing industry.

S&S Air, Inc.
2004 Income Statement

Sales		$12,870,000
Cost of goods sold		9,070,000
Other expenses		1,538,000
Depreciation		420,000
EBIT		$ 1,842,000
Interest		231,500
Taxable income		$ 1,610,500
Taxes (40%)		644,200
Net income		$ 966,300
Dividends	$289,890	
Add. to retained earnings	676,410	

S&S Air, Inc.
2004 Balance Sheet

Assets		Liabilities & Equity	
Current assets		Current liabilities	
Cash	$ 234,000	Accounts payable	$ 497,000
Accounts receivable	421,000	Notes payable	1,006,000
Inventory	472,000	Total current liabilities	$1,503,000
Total current assets	$1,127,000		
		Long-term debt	$2,595,000
Fixed assets			
Net plant and equipment	$7,228,000	Shareholder equity	
		Common stock	$ 100,000
		Retained earnings	4,157,000
		Total equity	$4,257,000
Total assets	$8,355,000	Total liabilities & equity	$8,355,000

Light Airplane Industry Ratios			
	Lower Quartile	Median	Upper Quartile
Current ratio	0.50	1.43	1.89
Quick ratio	0.21	0.38	0.62
Cash ratio	0.08	0.21	0.39
Total asset turnover	0.68	0.85	1.38
Inventory turnover	4.89	6.15	10.89
Receivables turnover	6.27	9.82	14.11
Total debt ratio	0.44	0.52	0.61
Debt-equity ratio	0.79	1.08	1.56
Equity multiplier	1.79	2.08	2.56
Times interest earned	5.18	8.06	9.83
Cash coverage ratio	5.84	8.43	10.27
Profit margin	4.05%	6.98%	9.87%
Return on assets	6.05%	10.53%	13.21%
Return on equity	9.93%	16.54%	26.15%

Questions

1. Calculate the following ratios for S&S Air: current ratio, quick ratio, cash ratio, total asset turnover, inventory turnover, receivables turnover, total debt ratio, debt-equity ratio, equity multiplier, times interest earned, cash coverage, profit margin, return on assets, and return on equity.
2. Mark and Todd agree that a ratio analysis can provide a measure of the company's performance. They have chosen Boeing as an aspirant company. Would you choose Boeing as an aspirant company? Why or why not?
3. Compare the performance of S&S Air to the industry. For each ratio, comment on why it might be viewed as positive or negative relative to the industry. Suppose you create an inventory ratio calculated by inventory divided by current liabilities. How do you think S&S Air's ratio would compare to the industry average?
4. Calculate the internal growth rate and sustainable growth rate for S&S Air. What do these numbers mean?
5. S&S Air is planning for a growth rate of 20 percent next year. Calculate EFN assuming the company is operating at full capacity.
6. Most assets can be increased as a percentage of sales. For instance, cash can be increased by any amount. Fixed assets often must be increased in specific amounts since it is usually impossible or impractical to buy part of a new plant or machine. So, assume S&S Air cannot increase fixed assets as a percentage of sales. Instead, whenever the company needs to purchase new manufacturing equipment, it must purchase in the amount of $3,000,000. Calculate the new EFN with this assumption. What does this imply about capacity utilization for the company next year?

PART THREE

Valuation of Future Cash Flows

5

Introduction to Valuation: The Time Value of Money

On December 2, 1982, General Motors Acceptance Corporation (GMAC), a subsidiary of General Motors, offered some securities for sale to the public. Under the terms of the deal, GMAC promised to repay the owner of one of these securities $10,000 on December 1, 2012, but investors would receive nothing until then. Investors paid GMAC $500 for each of these securities, so they gave up $500 on December 2, 1982, for the promise of a $10,000 payment 30 years later. Such a security, for which you pay some amount today in exchange for a promised lump sum to be received at a future date, is about the simplest possible type.

Is giving up $500 in exchange for $10,000 in 30 years a good deal? On the plus side, you get back $20 for every $1 you put up. That probably sounds good, but, on the down side, you have to wait 30 years to get it. What you need to know is how to analyze this trade-off; this chapter gives you the tools you need.

One of the basic problems faced by the financial manager is how to determine the value today of cash flows expected in the future. For example, the jackpot in a PowerBall™ lottery drawing was $110 million. Does this mean the winning ticket was worth $110 million? The answer is no because the jackpot was actually going to pay out over a 20-year period at a rate of $5.5 million per year. How much was the ticket worth then? The answer depends on the time value of money, the subject of this chapter.

In the most general sense, the phrase *time value of money* refers to the fact that a dollar in hand today is worth more than a dollar promised at some time in the future. On a practical level, one reason for this is that you could earn interest while you waited; so a dollar today would grow to more than a dollar later. The trade-off between money now and money later thus depends on, among other things, the rate you can earn by investing. Our goal in this chapter is to explicitly evaluate this trade-off between dollars today and dollars at some future time.

A thorough understanding of the material in this chapter is critical to understanding material in subsequent chapters, so you should study it with particular care. We will present a number of examples in this chapter. In many problems, your answer may differ from ours slightly. This can happen because of rounding and is not a cause for concern.

FUTURE VALUE AND COMPOUNDING 5.1

The first thing we will study is future value. **Future value (FV)** refers to the amount of money an investment will grow to over some period of time at some given interest rate. Put another way, future value is the cash value of an investment at some time in the future. We start out by considering the simplest case, a single-period investment.

future value (FV)
The amount an investment is worth after one or more periods.

Investing for a Single Period

Suppose you invest \$100 in a savings account that pays 10 percent interest per year. How much will you have in one year? You will have \$110. This \$110 is equal to your original *principal* of \$100 plus \$10 in interest that you earn. We say that \$110 is the future value of \$100 invested for one year at 10 percent, and we simply mean that \$100 today is worth \$110 in one year, given that 10 percent is the interest rate.

In general, if you invest for one period at an interest rate of r, your investment will grow to $(1 + r)$ per dollar invested. In our example, r is 10 percent, so your investment grows to $1 + .10 = 1.1$ dollars per dollar invested. You invested \$100 in this case, so you ended up with $\$100 \times 1.10 = \$110$.

Investing for More Than One Period

Going back to our \$100 investment, what will you have after two years, assuming the interest rate doesn't change? If you leave the entire \$110 in the bank, you will earn $\$110 \times .10 = \$11$ in interest during the second year, so you will have a total of $\$110 + 11 = \$121$. This \$121 is the future value of \$100 in two years at 10 percent. Another way of looking at it is that one year from now you are effectively investing \$110 at 10 percent for a year. This is a single-period problem, so you'll end up with \$1.10 for every dollar invested, or $\$110 \times 1.1 = \$121$ total.

This \$121 has four parts. The first part is the \$100 original principal. The second part is the \$10 in interest you earned in the first year, and the third part is another \$10 you earn in the second year, for a total of \$120. The last \$1 you end up with (the fourth part) is interest you earn in the second year on the interest paid in the first year: $\$10 \times .10 = \$1$.

This process of leaving your money and any accumulated interest in an investment for more than one period, thereby *reinvesting* the interest, is called **compounding**. Compounding the interest means earning **interest on interest**, so we call the result **compound interest**. With **simple interest**, the interest is not reinvested, so interest is earned each period only on the original principal.

compounding
The process of accumulating interest on an investment over time to earn more interest.

interest on interest
Interest earned on the reinvestment of previous interest payments.

Interest on Interest

<< **EXAMPLE 5.1**

Suppose you locate a two-year investment that pays 14 percent per year. If you invest \$325, how much will you have at the end of the two years? How much of this is simple interest? How much is compound interest?

At the end of the first year, you will have $\$325 \times (1 + .14) = \$370.50$. If you reinvest this entire amount, and thereby compound the interest, you will have $\$370.50 \times 1.14 = \$422.37$ at the end of the second year. The total interest you earn is thus $\$422.37 - 325 = \$97.37$. Your \$325 original principal earns $\$325 \times .14 = \$45.50$ in interest each year, for a two-year total of \$91 in simple interest. The remaining $\$97.37 - 91 = \$6.37$ results from compounding. You can check this by noting that the interest earned in the first year is \$45.50. The interest on interest earned in the second year thus amounts to $\$45.50 \times .14 = \$6.37$, as we calculated.

compound interest
Interest earned on both the initial principal and the interest reinvested from prior periods.

simple interest
Interest earned only on the original principal amount invested.

We now take a closer look at how we calculated the \$121 future value. We multiplied \$110 by 1.1 to get \$121. The \$110, however, was \$100 also multiplied by 1.1. In other words:

$$
\begin{aligned}
\$121 &= \$110 \times 1.1 \\
&= (\$100 \times 1.1) \times 1.1 \\
&= \$100 \times (1.1 \times 1.1) \\
&= \$100 \times 1.1^2 \\
&= \$100 \times 1.21
\end{aligned}
$$

At the risk of belaboring the obvious, let's ask: How much would our \$100 grow to after three years? Once again, in two years, we'll be investing \$121 for one period at 10 percent. We'll end up with \$1.10 for every dollar we invest, or \$121 × 1.1 = \$133.10 total. This \$133.10 is thus:

For a discussion of time value concepts (and lots more) see www.financeprofessor.com.

$$
\begin{aligned}
\$133.10 &= \$121 \times 1.1 \\
&= (\$110 \times 1.1) \times 1.1 \\
&= (\$100 \times 1.1) \times 1.1 \times 1.1 \\
&= \$100 \times (1.1 \times 1.1 \times 1.1) \\
&= \$100 \times 1.1^3 \\
&= \$100 \times 1.331
\end{aligned}
$$

You're probably noticing a pattern to these calculations, so we can now go ahead and state the general result. As our examples suggest, the future value of \$1 invested for t periods at a rate of r per period is:

$$\text{Future value} = \$1 \times (1 + r)^t \qquad \textbf{[5.1]}$$

The expression $(1 + r)^t$ is sometimes called the *future value interest factor* (or just *future value factor*) for \$1 invested at r percent for t periods and can be abbreviated as FVIF(r, t).

In our example, what would your \$100 be worth after five years? We can first compute the relevant future value factor as:

$$(1 + r)^t = (1 + .10)^5 = 1.1^5 = 1.6105$$

Your \$100 will thus grow to:

$$\$100 \times 1.6105 = \$161.05$$

The growth of your \$100 each year is illustrated in Table 5.1. As shown, the interest earned in each year is equal to the beginning amount multiplied by the interest rate of 10 percent.

In Table 5.1, notice the total interest you earn is \$61.05. Over the five-year span of this investment, the simple interest is \$100 × .10 = \$10 per year, so you accumulate \$50 this way. The other \$11.05 is from compounding.

A brief introduction to key financial concepts is available at www.teachmefinance.com.

Figure 5.1 illustrates the growth of the compound interest in Table 5.1. Notice how the simple interest is constant each year, but the amount of compound interest you earn gets bigger every year. The amount of the compound interest keeps increasing because more and more interest builds up and there is thus more to compound.

Future values depend critically on the assumed interest rate, particularly for long-lived investments. Figure 5.2 illustrates this relationship by plotting the growth of \$1 for different rates and lengths of time. Notice the future value of \$1 after 10 years is about \$6.20 at a 20 percent rate, but it is only about \$2.60 at 10 percent. In this case, doubling the interest rate more than doubles the future value.

<< TABLE 5.1

Future Value of $100 at 10 Percent

Year	Beginning Amount	Simple Interest	Compound Interest	Total Interest Earned	Ending Amount
1	$100.00	$10	$ 0.00	$10.00	$110.00
2	110.00	10	1.00	11.00	121.00
3	121.00	10	2.10	12.10	133.10
4	133.10	10	3.31	13.31	146.41
5	146.41	10	4.64	14.64	161.05
		Total $50 simple interest	Total $11.05 compound interest	Total $61.05 interest	

<< FIGURE 5.1

Future Value, Simple Interest, and Compound Interest

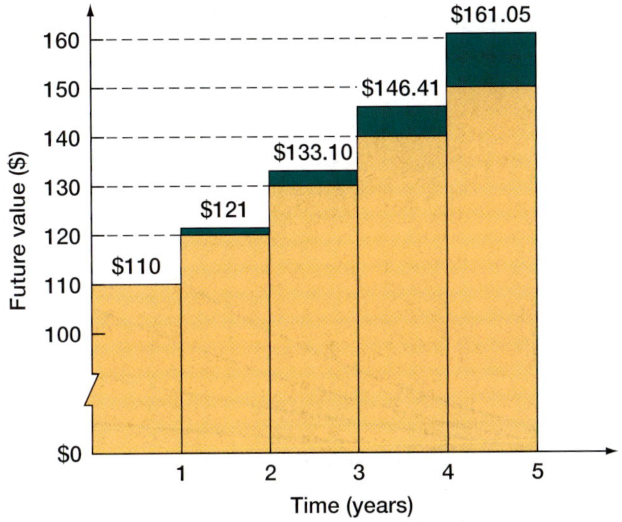

Growth of $100 original amount at 10% per year. Green shaded area represents the portion of the total that results from compounding of interest.

To solve future value problems, we need to come up with the relevant future value factors. There are several different ways of doing this. In our example, we could have multiplied 1.1 by itself five times. This would work just fine, but it would get to be very tedious for, say, a 30-year investment.

Fortunately, there are several easier ways to get future value factors. Most calculators have a key labeled "y^x." You can usually just enter 1.1, press this key, enter 5, and press the "=" key to get the answer. This is an easy way to calculate future value factors because it's quick and accurate.

Alternatively, you can use a table that contains future value factors for some common interest rates and time periods. Table 5.2 contains some of these factors. Table A.1 in the appendix at the end of the book contains a much larger set. To use the table, find the column that corresponds to 10 percent. Then, look down the rows until you come to five periods. You should find the factor that we calculated, 1.6105.

Tables such as 5.2 are not as common as they once were because they predate inexpensive calculators and are only available for a relatively small number of rates. Interest rates are often quoted to three or four decimal places, so the tables needed to deal with these accurately would be quite large. As a result, the real world has moved away from using them. We will emphasize the use of a calculator in this chapter.

TABLE 5.2 >>

Future Value Interest Factors

	Interest Rate			
Number of Periods	**5%**	**10%**	**15%**	**20%**
1	1.0500	1.1000	1.1500	1.2000
2	1.1025	1.2100	1.3225	1.4400
3	1.1576	1.3310	1.5209	1.7280
4	1.2155	1.4641	1.7490	2.0736
5	1.2763	1.6105	2.0114	2.4883

FIGURE 5.2 >>

Future Value of $1 for Different Periods and Rates

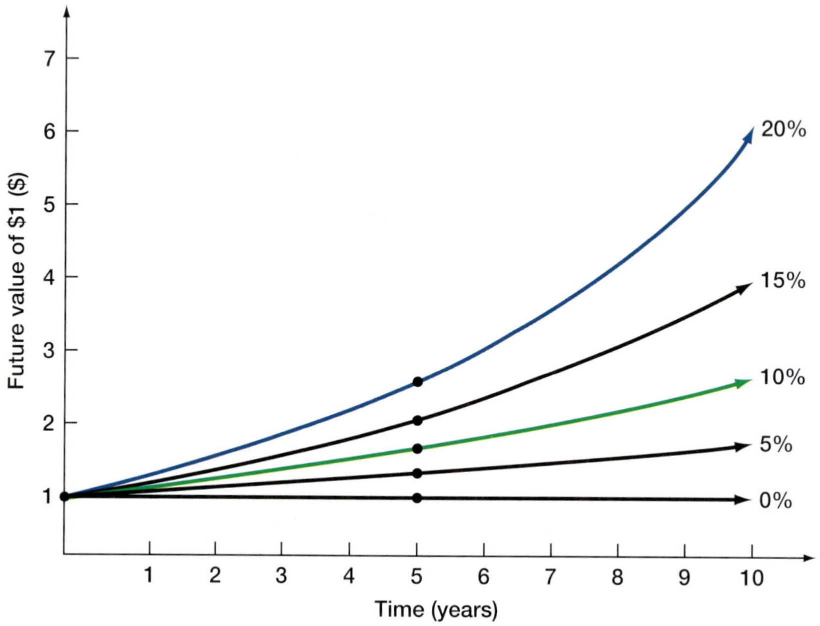

These tables still serve a useful purpose. To make sure you are doing the calculations correctly, pick a factor from the table and then calculate it yourself to see that you get the same answer. There are plenty of numbers to choose from.

EXAMPLE 5.2 >> Compound Interest

You've located an investment that pays 12 percent. That rate sounds good to you, so you invest $400. How much will you have in three years? How much will you have in seven years? At the end of seven years, how much interest will you have earned? How much of that interest results from compounding?

Based on our discussion, we can calculate the future value factor for 12 percent and three years as:

$$(1 + r)^t = 1.12^3 = 1.4049$$

Your $400 thus grows to:

$$\$400 \times 1.4049 = \$561.97$$

continued

After seven years, you will have:

$\$400 \times 1.12^7 = \$400 \times 2.2107 = \$884.27$

Thus, you will more than double your money over seven years.

Because you invested \$400, the interest in the \$884.27 future value is \$884.27 − 400 = \$484.27. At 12 percent, your \$400 investment earns \$400 × .12 = \$48 in simple interest every year. Over seven years, the simple interest thus totals 7 × \$48 = \$336. The other \$484.27 − 336 = \$148.27 is from compounding.

The effect of compounding is not great over short time periods, but it really starts to add up as the horizon grows. To take an extreme case, suppose one of your more frugal ancestors had invested \$5 for you at a 6 percent interest rate 200 years ago. How much would you have today? The future value factor is a substantial 1.06^{200} = 115,125.90 (you won't find this one in a table), so you would have \$5 × 115,125.91 = \$575,629.52 today. Notice that the simple interest is just \$5 × .06 = \$.30 per year. After 200 years, this amounts to \$60. The rest is from reinvesting. Such is the power of compound interest!

How Much for That Island?

<< EXAMPLE 5.3

To further illustrate the effect of compounding for long horizons, consider the case of Peter Minuit and the American Indians. In 1626, Minuit bought all of Manhattan Island for about \$24 in goods and trinkets. This sounds cheap, but the Indians may have gotten the better end of the deal. To see why, suppose the Indians had sold the goods and invested the \$24 at 10 percent. How much would it be worth today?

Roughly 377 years have passed since the transaction. At 10 percent, \$24 will grow by quite a bit over that time. How much? The future value factor is approximately:

$(1 + r)^t = 1.1^{377} \approx 4{,}000{,}000{,}000{,}000{,}000$

That is, 4 followed by 15 zeroes. The future value is thus on the order of \$24 × 4 = \$96 *quadrillion* (give or take a few hundreds of trillions).

Well, \$96 quadrillion is a lot of money. How much? If you had it, you could buy the United States. All of it. Cash. With money left over to buy Canada, Mexico, and the rest of the world, for that matter.

This example is something of an exaggeration, of course. In 1626, it would not have been easy to locate an investment that would pay 10 percent every year without fail for the next 377 years.

Using a Financial Calculator

Although there are the various ways of calculating future values we have described so far, many of you will decide that a financial calculator is the way to go. If you are planning on using one, you should read this extended hint; otherwise, skip it.

A financial calculator is simply an ordinary calculator with a few extra features. In particular, it knows some of the most commonly used financial formulas, so it can directly compute things like future values.

continued

Financial calculators have the advantage that they handle a lot of the computation, but that is really all. In other words, you still have to understand the problem; the calculator just does some of the arithmetic. In fact, there is an old joke (somewhat modified) that goes like this: Anyone can make a mistake on a time value of money problem, but to really screw one up takes a financial calculator! We therefore have two goals for this section. First, we'll discuss how to compute future values. After that, we'll show you how to avoid the most common mistakes people make when they start using financial calculators.

How to Calculate Future Values with a Financial Calculator

Examining a typical financial calculator, you will find five keys of particular interest. They usually look like this:

N	I/Y	PMT	PV	FV

For now, we need to focus on four of these. The keys labeled **PV** and **FV** are just what you would guess, present value and future value. The key labeled **N** refers to the *n*umber of periods, which is what we have been calling t. Finally, **I/Y** stands for the *i*nterest rate, which we have called r.[1]

If we have the financial calculator set up right (see our next section), then calculating a future value is very simple. Take a look back at our question involving the future value of $100 at 10 percent for five years. We have seen that the answer is $161.05. The exact keystrokes will differ depending on what type of calculator you use, but here is basically all you do:

1. Enter −100. Press the **PV** key. (The negative sign is explained below.)
2. Enter 10. Press the **I/Y** key. (Notice that we entered 10, not .10; see below.)
3. Enter 5. Press the **N** key.

Now we have entered all of the relevant information. To solve for the future value, we need to ask the calculator what the FV is. Depending on your calculator, you either press the button labeled "CPT" (for compute) and then press **FV**, or else you just press **FV**. Either way, you should get 161.05. If you don't (and you probably won't if this is the first time you have used a financial calculator!), we will offer some help in our next section.

Before we explain the kinds of problems that you are likely to run into, we want to establish a standard format for showing you how to use a financial calculator. Using the example we just looked at, in the future, we will illustrate such problems like this:

Enter	5	10		−100	
	N	I/Y	PMT	PV	FV
Solve for					161.05

Here is an important tip: Appendix D (which can be found on our Web site) contains some more detailed instructions for the most common types of financial calculators. See if yours is included, and, if it is, follow the instructions there if you need help. Of course, if all else fails, you can read the manual that came with the calculator.

How to Get the Wrong Answer Using a Financial Calculator

There are a couple of common (and frustrating) problems that cause a lot of trouble with financial calculators. In this section, we provide some important *dos* and *don'ts*. If you just can't seem to get a problem to work out, you should refer back to this section.

continued

---

[1]The reason financial calculators use N and I/Y is that the most common use for these calculators is determining loan payments. In this context, N is the number of payments and I/Y is the interest rate on the loan. But, as we will see, there are many other uses of financial calculators that don't involve loan payments and interest rates.

There are two categories we examine, three things you need to do only once and three things you need to do every time you work a problem. The things you need to do just once deal with the following calculator settings:

1. *Make sure your calculator is set to display a large number of decimal places.* Most financial calculators only display two decimal places; this causes problems because we frequently work with numbers—like interest rates—that are very small.
2. *Make sure your calculator is set to assume only one payment per period or per year.* Most financial calculators assume monthly payments (12 per year) unless you say otherwise.
3. *Make sure your calculator is in "end" mode.* This is usually the default, but you can accidently change to "begin" mode.

If you don't know how to set these three things, see Appendix D on our Web site or your calculator's operating manual. There are also three things you need to do *every time you work a problem:*

1. *Before you start, completely clear out the calculator.* This is very important. Failure to do this is the number one reason for wrong answers; you simply must get in the habit of clearing the calculator every time you start a problem. How you do this depends on the calculator (see Appendix D on our Web site), but you must do more than just clear the display. For example, on a Texas Instruments BA II Plus you must press **2nd** then **CLR TVM** for *clear time value of money.* There is a similar command on your calculator. Learn it!

   Note that turning the calculator off and back on won't do it. Most financial calculators remember everything you enter, even after you turn them off. In other words, they remember all your mistakes unless you explicitly clear them out. Also, if you are in the middle of a problem and make a mistake, *clear it out and start over.* Better to be safe than sorry.
2. *Put a negative sign on cash outflows.* Most financial calculators require you to put a negative sign on cash outflows and a positive sign on cash inflows. As a practical matter, this usually just means that you should enter the present value amount with a negative sign (because normally the present value represents the amount you give up today in exchange for cash inflows later). By the same token, when you solve for a present value, you shouldn't be surprised to see a negative sign.
3. *Enter the rate correctly.* Financial calculators assume that rates are quoted in percent, so if the rate is .08 (or 8 percent), you should enter 8, not .08.

If you follow these guidelines (especially the one about clearing out the calculator), you should have no problem using a financial calculator to work almost all of the problems in this and the next few chapters. We'll provide some additional examples and guidance where appropriate.

A Note on Compound Growth

If you are considering depositing money in an interest-bearing account, then the interest rate on that account is just the rate at which your money grows, assuming you don't remove any of it. If that rate is 10 percent, then each year you simply have 10 percent more money than you had the year before. In this case, the interest rate is just an example of a compound growth rate.

The way we calculated future values is actually quite general and lets you answer some other types of questions related to growth. For example, your company currently has 10,000 employees. You've estimated that the number of employees grows by 3 percent per year. How many employees will there be in five years? Here, we start with 10,000 people instead of dollars, and we don't think of the growth rate as an interest rate, but the calculation is exactly the same:

$$10{,}000 \times 1.03^5 = 10{,}000 \times 1.1593 = 11{,}593 \text{ employees}$$

There will be about 1,593 net new hires over the coming five years.

To give another example, according to Value Line (a leading supplier of business information for investors), Wal-Mart's 2003 sales were about \$258 billion. Suppose sales are projected to increase at a rate of 15 percent per year. What will Wal-Mart's sales be in the year 2008 if this is correct? Verify for yourself that the answer is about \$519 billion, just over twice as large.

EXAMPLE 5.4 >> Dividend Growth

The TICO Corporation currently pays a cash dividend of \$5 per share. You believe the dividend will be increased by 4 percent each year indefinitely. How big will the dividend be in eight years?

Here we have a cash dividend growing because it is being increased by management, but, once again, the calculation is the same:

$$\text{Future value} = \$5 \times 1.04^8 = \$5 \times 1.3686 = \$6.84$$

The dividend will grow by \$1.84 over that period. Dividend growth is a subject we will return to in a later chapter.

Concept Questions

5.1a What do we mean by the future value of an investment?

5.1b What does it mean to compound interest? How does compound interest differ from simple interest?

5.1c In general, what is the future value of \$1 invested at *r* per period for *t* periods?

5.2 PRESENT VALUE AND DISCOUNTING

When we discuss future value, we are thinking of questions like, What will my \$2,000 investment grow to if it earns a 6.5 percent return every year for the next six years? The answer to this question is what we call the future value of \$2,000 invested at 6.5 percent for six years (verify that the answer is about \$2,918).

There is another type of question that comes up even more often in financial management that is obviously related to future value. Suppose you need to have \$10,000 in 10 years, and you can earn 6.5 percent on your money. How much do you have to invest today to reach your goal? You can verify that the answer is \$5,327.26. How do we know this? Read on.

The Single-Period Case

present value (PV) The current value of future cash flows discounted at the appropriate discount rate.

We've seen that the future value of \$1 invested for one year at 10 percent is \$1.10. We now ask a slightly different question: How much do we have to invest today at 10 percent to get \$1 in one year? In other words, we know the future value here is \$1, but what is the **present value (PV)**? The answer isn't too hard to figure out. Whatever we invest today will be 1.1 times bigger at the end of the year. Because we need \$1 at the end of the year:

$$\text{Present value} \times 1.1 = \$1$$

Or, solving for the present value:

$$\text{Present value} = \$1/1.1 = \$.909$$

In this case, the present value is the answer to the following question: What amount, invested today, will grow to \$1 in one year if the interest rate is 10 percent? Present value is thus just the reverse of future value. Instead of compounding the money forward into the future, we **discount** it back to the present.

discount
Calculate the present value of some future amount.

Single-Period PV

EXAMPLE 5.5

Suppose you need \$400 to buy textbooks next year. You can earn 7 percent on your money. How much do you have to put up today?

We need to know the PV of \$400 in one year at 7 percent. Proceeding as in the previous example:

$$\text{Present value} \times 1.07 = \$400$$

We can now solve for the present value:

$$\text{Present value} = \$400 \times (1/1.07) = \$373.83$$

Thus, \$373.83 is the present value. Again, this just means that investing this amount for one year at 7 percent will result in your having a future value of \$400.

From our examples, the present value of \$1 to be received in one period is generally given as:

$$\text{PV} = \$1 \times [1/(1 + r)] = \$1/(1 + r)$$

We next examine how to get the present value of an amount to be paid in two or more periods into the future.

Present Values for Multiple Periods

Suppose you need to have \$1,000 in two years. If you can earn 7 percent, how much do you have to invest to make sure that you have the \$1,000 when you need it? In other words, what is the present value of \$1,000 in two years if the relevant rate is 7 percent?

Based on your knowledge of future values, you know the amount invested must grow to \$1,000 over the two years. In other words, it must be the case that:

$$\begin{aligned} \$1{,}000 &= \text{PV} \times 1.07 \times 1.07 \\ &= \text{PV} \times 1.07^2 \\ &= \text{PV} \times 1.1449 \end{aligned}$$

Given this, we can solve for the present value:

$$\text{Present value} = \$1{,}000/1.1449 = \$873.44$$

Therefore, \$873.44 is the amount you must invest in order to achieve your goal.

Saving Up

EXAMPLE 5.6

You would like to buy a new automobile. You have \$50,000 or so, but the car costs \$68,500. If you can earn 9 percent, how much do you have to invest today to buy the car in two years? Do you have enough? Assume the price will stay the same.

What we need to know is the present value of \$68,500 to be paid in two years, assuming a 9 percent rate. Based on our discussion, this is:

$$\text{PV} = \$68{,}500/1.09^2 = \$68{,}500/1.1881 = \$57{,}655.08$$

You're still about \$7,655 short, even if you're willing to wait two years.

As you have probably recognized by now, calculating present values is quite similar to calculating future values, and the general result looks much the same. The present value of \$1 to be received *t* periods into the future at a discount rate of *r* is:

$$PV = \$1 \times [1/(1+r)^t] = \$1/(1+r)^t \quad [5.2]$$

discount rate The rate used to calculate the present value of future cash flows.

discounted cash flow (DCF) valuation Calculating the present value of a future cash flow to determine its value today.

The quantity in brackets, $1/(1+r)^t$, goes by several different names. Because it's used to discount a future cash flow, it is often called a *discount factor*. With this name, it is not surprising that the rate used in the calculation is often called the **discount rate**. We will tend to call it this in talking about present values. The quantity in brackets is also called the *present value interest factor* (or just *present value factor*) for \$1 at *r* percent for *t* periods and is sometimes abbreviated as PVIF(*r*, *t*). Finally, calculating the present value of a future cash flow to determine its worth today is commonly called **discounted cash flow (DCF) valuation**.

To illustrate, suppose you need \$1,000 in three years. You can earn 15 percent on your money. How much do you have to invest today? To find out, we have to determine the present value of \$1,000 in three years at 15 percent. We do this by discounting \$1,000 back three periods at 15 percent. With these numbers, the discount factor is:

$$1/(1+.15)^3 = 1/1.5209 = .6575$$

The amount you must invest is thus:

$$\$1{,}000 \times .6575 = \$657.50$$

We say that \$657.50 is the present or discounted value of \$1,000 to be received in three years at 15 percent.

There are tables for present value factors just as there are tables for future value factors, and you use them in the same way (if you use them at all). Table 5.3 contains a small set. A much larger set can be found in Table A.2 in the book's appendix.

In Table 5.3, the discount factor we just calculated (.6575) can be found by looking down the column labeled "15%" until you come to the third row.

CALCULATOR HINTS

You solve present value problems on a financial calculator just like you do future value problems. For the example we just examined (the present value of \$1,000 to be received in three years at 15 percent), you would do the following:

Enter	3	15			1,000
	N	I/Y	PMT	PV	FV
Solve for				−657.50	

Notice that the answer has a negative sign; as we discussed above, that's because it represents an outflow today in exchange for the \$1,000 inflow later.

EXAMPLE 5.7

Deceptive Advertising?

Businesses sometimes advertise that you should "Come try our product. If you do, we'll give you $100 just for coming by!" If you read the fine print, what you find out is that they will give you a savings certificate that will pay you $100 in 25 years or so. If the going interest rate on such certificates is 10 percent per year, how much are they really giving you today?

What you're actually getting is the present value of $100 to be paid in 25 years. If the discount rate is 10 percent per year, then the discount factor is:

$$1/1.1^{25} = 1/10.8347 = .0923$$

This tells you that a dollar in 25 years is worth a little more than nine cents today, assuming a 10 percent discount rate. Given this, the promotion is actually paying you about $.0923 \times \$100 = \$9.23$. Maybe this is enough to draw customers, but it's not $100.

As the length of time until payment grows, present values decline. As Example 5.7 illustrates, present values tend to become small as the time horizon grows. If you look out far enough, they will always get close to zero. Also, for a given length of time, the higher the

TABLE 5.3

Present Value Interest Factors

	Interest Rate			
Number of Periods	**5%**	**10%**	**15%**	**20%**
1	.9524	.9091	.8696	.8333
2	.9070	.8264	.7561	.6944
3	.8638	.7513	.6575	.5787
4	.8227	.6830	.5718	.4823
5	.7835	.6209	.4972	.4019

FIGURE 5.3

Present Value of $1 for Different Periods and Rates

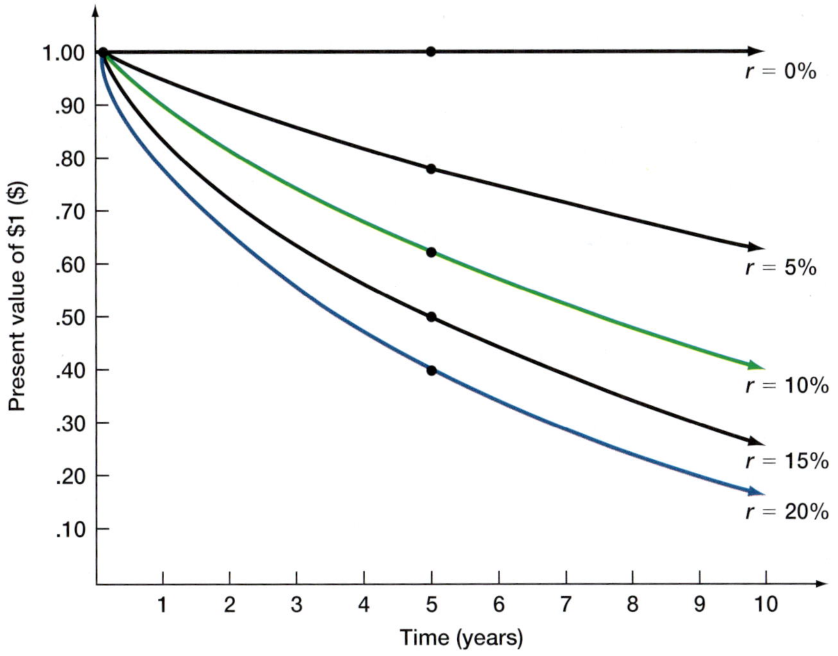

discount rate is, the lower is the present value. Put another way, present values and discount rates are inversely related. Increasing the discount rate decreases the PV and vice versa.

The relationship between time, discount rates, and present values is illustrated in Figure 5.3. Notice that by the time we get to 10 years, the present values are all substantially smaller than the future amounts.

Concept Questions

5.2a What do we mean by the present value of an investment?

5.2b The process of discounting a future amount back to the present is the opposite of doing what?

5.2c What do we mean by discounted cash flow, or DCF, valuation?

5.2d In general, what is the present value of $1 to be received in *t* periods, assuming a discount rate of *r* per period?

5.3 MORE ON PRESENT AND FUTURE VALUES

If you look back at the expressions we came up with for present and future values, you will see there is a very simple relationship between the two. We explore this relationship and some related issues in this section.

Present versus Future Value

What we called the present value factor is just the reciprocal of (that is, 1 divided by) the future value factor:

$$\text{Future value factor} = (1 + r)^t$$
$$\text{Present value factor} = 1/(1 + r)^t$$

In fact, the easy way to calculate a present value factor on many calculators is to first calculate the future value factor and then press the "$1/x$" key to flip it over.

If we let FV_t stand for the future value after t periods, then the relationship between future value and present value can be written very simply as one of the following:

$$\text{PV} \times (1 + r)^t = \text{FV}_t$$
$$\text{PV} = \text{FV}_t/(1 + r)^t = \text{FV}_t \times [1/(1 + r)^t] \qquad [5.3]$$

This last result we will call the *basic present value equation*. We will use it throughout the text. There are a number of variations that come up, but this simple equation underlies many of the most important ideas in corporate finance.

EXAMPLE 5.8 >> Evaluating Investments

To give you an idea of how we will be using present and future values, consider the following simple investment. Your company proposes to buy an asset for $335. This investment is very safe. You would sell off the asset in three years for $400. You know you could invest the $335 elsewhere at 10 percent with very little risk. What do you think of the proposed investment?

continued

This is not a good investment. Why not? Because you can invest the \$335 elsewhere at 10 percent. If you do, after three years it will grow to:

$$\begin{aligned}\$335 \times (1 + r)^t &= \$335 \times 1.1^3 \\ &= \$335 \times 1.331 \\ &= \$445.89\end{aligned}$$

Because the proposed investment only pays out \$400, it is not as good as other alternatives we have. Another way of seeing the same thing is to notice that the present value of \$400 in three years at 10 percent is:

$$\$400 \times [1/(1 + r)^t] = \$400/1.1^3 = \$400/1.331 = \$300.53$$

This tells us that we only have to invest about \$300 to get \$400 in three years, not \$335. We will return to this type of analysis later on.

Determining the Discount Rate

For a downloadable, Windows-based financial calculator, go to www.calculator.org.

It will turn out that we will frequently need to determine what discount rate is implicit in an investment. We can do this by looking at the basic present value equation:

$$PV = FV_t/(1 + r)^t$$

There are only four parts to this equation: the present value (PV), the future value (FV_t), the discount rate (r), and the life of the investment (t). Given any three of these, we can always find the fourth.

Finding *r* for a Single-Period Investment

EXAMPLE 5.9

You are considering a one-year investment. If you put up \$1,250, you will get back \$1,350. What rate is this investment paying?

First, in this single-period case, the answer is fairly obvious. You are getting a total of \$100 in addition to your \$1,250. The implicit rate on this investment is thus \$100/1,250 = 8 percent.

More formally, from the basic present value equation, the present value (the amount you must put up today) is \$1,250. The future value (what the present value grows to) is \$1,350. The time involved is one period, so we have:

$$\begin{aligned}\$1{,}250 &= \$1{,}350/(1 + r)^1 \\ 1 + r &= \$1{,}350/1{,}250 = 1.08 \\ r &= 8\%\end{aligned}$$

In this simple case, of course, there was no need to go through this calculation, but, as we describe next, it gets a little harder when there is more than one period.

To illustrate what happens with multiple periods, let's say that we are offered an investment that costs us \$100 and will double our money in eight years. To compare this to other investments, we would like to know what discount rate is implicit in these numbers. This discount rate is called the *rate of return,* or sometimes just *return,* on the investment. In this case, we have a present value of \$100, a future value of \$200 (double our money), and an eight-year life. To calculate the return, we can write the basic present value equation as:

$$\text{PV} = \text{FV}_t/(1 + r)^t$$
$$\$100 = \$200/(1 + r)^8$$

It could also be written as:

$$(1 + r)^8 = \$200/100 = 2$$

We now need to solve for r. There are three ways we could do it:

1. Use a financial calculator.
2. Solve the equation for $1 + r$ by taking the eighth root of both sides. Because this is the same thing as raising both sides to the power of ⅛ or .125, this is actually easy to do with the "y^x" key on a calculator. Just enter 2, then press "y^x," enter .125, and press the "=" key. The eighth root should be about 1.09, which implies that r is 9 percent.
3. Use a future value table. The future value factor after eight years is equal to 2. If you look across the row corresponding to eight periods in Table A.1, you will see that a future value factor of 2 corresponds to the 9 percent column, again implying that the return here is 9 percent.

Actually, in this particular example, there is a useful "back of the envelope" means of solving for r—the Rule of 72. For reasonable rates of return, the time it takes to double your money is given approximately by $72/r\%$. In our example, this means that $72/r\% = 8$ years, implying that r is 9 percent, as we calculated. This rule is fairly accurate for discount rates in the 5 percent to 20 percent range.

EXAMPLE 5.10 >> Baseball Collectibles as Investments

In 2001, when Barry Bonds was chasing baseball's single-season home run record, there was much speculation as to what might be the value of the final home run ball of the season. On October 7, Bonds hit his 73rd, and last, home run of the season. In 2003, after a lengthy legal battle over ownership of the ball, it sold for $450,000. "Experts" on such collectibles said that no matter what the ball sold for, it was sure to double in value over the next 10 years.

So, would the home run ball have been a good investment? By the Rule of 72, you already know the experts were predicting that the ball would double in value in 10 years, so the return predicted would be about 72/10 = 7.2 percent per year, which is only so-so.

At one time at least, a rule of thumb in the rarified world of fine art collecting was "your money back in 5 years, double your money in 10 years." Given this, let's see how an investment stacked up. In 1998, the Alberto Giacometti bronze statue *Homme qui Marche III* sold for $2,972,500. Five years later, the statue was sold again, walking out the door at a price of $4,039,500. So how did the seller do?

Why does the Rule of 72 work? See www.datachimp.com.

The rule of thumb has us doubling our money in 10 years, so, from the Rule of 72, we have that 7.2 percent per year was the norm. The statue was resold in almost exactly 5 years. The present value is $2,972,500, and the future value is $4,039,500. We need to solve for the unknown rate, r, as follows:

$$\$2{,}972{,}500 = \$4{,}039{,}500/(1 + r)^5$$
$$(1 + r)^5 = 1.3590$$

Solving for r, we find the seller earned about 6.33 percent per year, less than the 7.2 percent rule of thumb. At least the seller made his money back.

What about other collectibles? To a philatelist (a stamp collector to you and us), one of the most prized stamps is the 1918 24-cent inverted Jenny C3a. The stamp is a collectible because it has a picture of an upside-down biplane. One of these stamps sold at auction for \$120,000 in 2002. At what rate did its value grow? Verify for yourself that the answer is about 16.9 percent, assuming an 84-year period.

Perhaps the most desired coin for numismatics (coin collectors) is the 1933 \$20 gold double eagle. Outside of the U.S. Mint and the Smithsonian, only one of these coins is in circulation. In 2002, the coin sold at auction for \$7,590,020. See if you agree that this collectible gained about 20.5 percent per year.

A slightly more extreme example involves money bequeathed by Benjamin Franklin, who died on April 17, 1790. In his will, he gave 1,000 pounds sterling to Massachusetts and the city of Boston. He gave a like amount to Pennsylvania and the city of Philadelphia. The money had been paid to Franklin when he held political office, but he believed that politicians should not be paid for their service (it appears that this view is not widely shared by modern-day politicians).

Franklin originally specified that the money should be paid out 100 years after his death and used to train young people. Later, however, after some legal wrangling, it was agreed that the money would be paid out in 1990, 200 years after Franklin's death. By that time, the Pennsylvania bequest had grown to about \$2 million; the Massachusetts bequest had grown to \$4.5 million. The money was used to fund the Franklin Institutes in Boston and Philadelphia. Assuming that 1,000 pounds sterling was equivalent to \$1,000, what rate of return did the two states earn (the dollar did not become the official U.S. currency until 1792)?

For Pennsylvania, the future value is \$2 million and the present value is \$1,000. There are 200 years involved, so we need to solve for r in the following:

$$\$1{,}000 = \$2\text{ million}/(1 + r)^{200}$$
$$(1 + r)^{200} = 2{,}000$$

Solving for r, we see that the Pennsylvania money grew at about 3.87 percent per year. The Massachusetts money did better; verify that the rate of return in this case was 4.3 percent. Small differences in returns can add up!

We can illustrate how to calculate unknown rates using a financial calculator using these numbers. For Pennsylvania, you would do the following:

	N	I/Y	PMT	PV	FV
Enter	200			−1,000	2,000,000
Solve for		3.87			

As in our previous examples, notice the minus sign on the present value, representing Franklin's outlay made many years ago. What do you change to work the problem for Massachusetts?

EXAMPLE 5.11 >> Saving for College

You estimate that you will need about \$80,000 to send your child to college in eight years. You have about \$35,000 now. If you can earn 20 percent per year, will you make it? At what rate will you just reach your goal?

If you can earn 20 percent, the future value of your \$35,000 in eight years will be:

$$FV = \$35{,}000 \times 1.20^8 = \$35{,}000 \times 4.2998 = \$150{,}493.59$$

So, you will make it easily. The minimum rate is the unknown r in the following:

$$FV = \$35{,}000 \times (1 + r)^8 = \$80{,}000$$
$$(1 + r)^8 = \$80{,}000/35{,}000 = 2.2857$$

Therefore, the future value factor is 2.2857. Looking at the row in Table A.1 that corresponds to eight periods, we see that our future value factor is roughly halfway between the ones shown for 10 percent (2.1436) and 12 percent (2.4760), so you will just reach your goal if you earn approximately 11 percent. To get the exact answer, we could use a financial calculator or we could solve for r:

$$(1 + r)^8 = \$80{,}000/35{,}000 = 2.2857$$
$$1 + r = 2.2857^{(1/8)} = 2.2857^{.125} = 1.1089$$
$$r = 10.89\%$$

EXAMPLE 5.12 >> Only 18,262.5 Days to Retirement

You would like to retire in 50 years as a millionaire. If you have \$10,000 today, what rate of return do you need to earn to achieve your goal?

The future value is \$1,000,000. The present value is \$10,000, and there are 50 years until payment. We need to calculate the unknown discount rate in the following:

$$\$10{,}000 = \$1{,}000{,}000/(1 + r)^{50}$$
$$(1 + r)^{50} = 100$$

The future value factor is thus 100. You can verify that the implicit rate is about 9.65 percent.

How much do you need at retirement? Check out the "Money/Retirement" link at www.about.com.

Not taking the time value of money into account when computing growth rates or rates of return often leads to some misleading numbers in the real world. For example, the most loved (and hated) team in baseball, the New York Yankees, had the highest payroll during the 1988 season, about \$19 million. In 2004, the Yankees again had the highest payroll, a staggering \$183 million, an increase of almost 900 percent! If history is any guide, we can get a rough idea of the future growth in baseball payrolls. See if you don't agree that this represents an annual increase of 15.2 percent, a substantial growth rate, but much less than the gaudy 900 percent.

How about classic maps? A few years ago, the first map of America, printed in Rome in 1507, was valued at about \$135,000, 69 percent more than the \$80,000 it was worth 10 years earlier. Your return on investment if you were the proud owner of the map over those 10 years? Verify that it's about 5.4 percent per year, far worse than the 69 percent reported increase in price.

Whether it's maps or baseball payrolls, it's easy to be misled when returns are quoted without considering the time value of money. However, it's not just the uninitiated who are guilty of this slight form of deception. The title of a feature article in a leading business magazine predicted the Dow Jones Industrial Average would soar to a 70 percent gain over the coming five years. Do you think it meant a 70 percent return per year on your money? Think again!

Finding the Number of Periods

Suppose we are interested in purchasing an asset that costs \$50,000. We currently have \$25,000. If we can earn 12 percent on this \$25,000, how long until we have the \$50,000? Finding the answer involves solving for the last variable in the basic present value equation, the number of periods. You already know how to get an approximate answer to this particular problem. Notice that we need to double our money. From the Rule of 72, this will take about $72/12 = 6$ years at 12 percent.

To come up with the exact answer, we can again manipulate the basic present value equation. The present value is \$25,000, and the future value is \$50,000. With a 12 percent discount rate, the basic equation takes one of the following forms:

$$\$25{,}000 = \$50{,}000/1.12^t$$
$$\$50{,}000/25{,}000 = 1.12^t = 2$$

We thus have a future value factor of 2 for a 12 percent rate. We now need to solve for t. If you look down the column in Table A.1 that corresponds to 12 percent, you will see that a future value factor of 1.9738 occurs at six periods. It will thus take about six years, as we calculated. To get the exact answer, we have to explicitly solve for t (or use a financial calculator). If you do this, you will see that the answer is 6.1163 years, so our approximation was quite close in this case.

If you do use a financial calculator, here are the relevant entries:

	N	I/Y	PMT	PV	FV
Enter		12		−25,000	50,000
Solve for	6.1163				

Waiting for Godot

<< **EXAMPLE 5.13**

You've been saving up to buy the Godot Company. The total cost will be \$10 million. You currently have about \$2.3 million. If you can earn 5 percent on your money, how long will you have to wait? At 16 percent, how long must you wait?

At 5 percent, you'll have to wait a long time. From the basic present value equation:

$$\$2.3 \text{ million} = \$10 \text{ million}/1.05^t$$
$$1.05^t = 4.35$$
$$t = 30 \text{ years}$$

At 16 percent, things are a little better. Verify for yourself that it will take about 10 years.

SPREADSHEET STRATEGIES

Using a Spreadsheet for Time Value of Money Calculations

More and more, businesspeople from many different areas (and not just finance and accounting) rely on spreadsheets to do all the different types of calculations that come up in the real world. As a result, in this section, we will show you how to use a spreadsheet to handle the various time value of money problems we presented in this chapter. We will use Microsoft Excel™, but the commands are similar for other types of software. We assume you are already familiar with basic spreadsheet operations.

As we have seen, you can solve for any one of the following four potential unknowns: future value, present value, the discount rate, or the number of periods. With a spreadsheet, there is a separate formula for each. In Excel, these are as follows:

To Find	Enter This Formula
Future value	= FV (rate,nper,pmt,pv)
Present value	= PV (rate,nper,pmt,fv)
Discount rate	= RATE (nper,pmt,pv,fv)
Number of periods	= NPER (rate,pmt,pv,fv)

In these formulas, pv and fv are present and future value, nper is the number of periods, and rate is the discount, or interest, rate.

There are two things that are a little tricky here. First, unlike a financial calculator, the spreadsheet requires that the rate be entered as a decimal. Second, as with most financial calculators, you have to put a negative sign on either the present value or the future value to solve for the rate or the number of periods. For the same reason, if you solve for a present value, the answer will have a negative sign unless you input a negative future value. The same is true when you compute a future value.

To illustrate how you might use these formulas, we will go back to an example in the chapter. If you invest $25,000 at 12 percent per year, how long until you have $50,000? You might set up a spreadsheet like this:

	A	B	C	D	E	F	G	H
1								
2	**Using a spreadsheet for time value of money calculations**							
3								
4	If we invest $25,000 at 12 percent, how long until we have $50,000? We need to solve							
5	for the unknown number of periods, so we use the formula NPER(rate, pmt, pv, fv).							
6								
7	Present value (pv):	$25,000						
8	Future value (fv):	$50,000						
9	Rate (rate):	0.12						
10								
11	Periods:	**6.1162554**						
12								
13	The formula entered in cell B11 is =NPER(B9,0,-B7,B8); notice that pmt is zero and that pv							
14	has a negative sign on it. Also notice that rate is entered as a decimal, not a percentage.							

Learn more about using Excel for time value and other calculations at www.studyfinance.com.

U.S. EE Savings Bonds are a familiar investment for many. A U.S. EE Savings Bond is much like the GMAC Security we described at the start of the chapter. You purchase them for half of their $100 face value. In other words, you pay $50 today and get $100 at some point in the future when the bond "matures." You receive no interest in between, and the interest rate is adjusted every six months, so the length of time until your $50 grows to $100 depends on future interest rates. However, at worst, the bonds are guaranteed to be worth $100 at the end of 17 years, so this is the longest you would ever have to wait. If you do have to wait the full 17 years, what rate do you earn?

Because this investment is doubling in value in 17 years, the Rule of 72 tells you the answer right away: $72/17 = 4.24\%$. Remember, this is the minimum guaranteed return, so

WORK THE WEB

How important is the time value of money? A recent search on one Web search engine returned over 84,000 hits! Although you must understand the calculations behind the time value of money, the advent of financial calculators and spreadsheets has eliminated the need for tedious calculations. In fact, many Web sites offer time value of money calculators. The following is one example from www.investopedia.com. You have \$10,000 today and will invest it at 9.5 percent for 30 years. How much will it be worth at that time? With the Investopedia calculator, you simply enter the values and hit Calculate. The results look like this:

Interest Rate Per Time Period:	9.5 %
Number of Time Periods:	30
Present Value:	10000
	Calculate
Future Value:	**\$152,203.13**

Who said time value of money calculations are hard?

you might do better. This example finishes our introduction to basic time value concepts. Table 5.4 summarizes present and future value calculations for future reference. As our nearby *Work the Web* box shows, online calculators are widely available to handle these calculations, but it is still important to know what is really going on.

<< TABLE 5.4

Summary of Time Value Calculations

I. Symbols:

PV = Present value, what future cash flows are worth today

FV_t = Future value, what cash flows are worth in the future

r = Interest rate, rate of return, or discount rate per period—typically, but not always, one year

t = Number of periods—typically, but not always, the number of years

C = Cash amount

II. Future Value of C Invested at *r* Percent for *t* Periods:

$FV_t = C \times (1 + r)^t$

The term $(1 + r)^t$ is called the *future value factor.*

III. Present Value of C to Be Received in *t* Periods at *r* Percent per Period:

$PV = C/(1 + r)^t$

The term $1/(1 + r)^t$ is called the *present value factor.*

IV. The Basic Present Value Equation Giving the Relationship between Present and Future Value is:

$PV = FV_t/(1 + r)^t$

Concept Questions

5.3a What is the basic present value equation?

5.3b What is the Rule of 72?

5.4 SUMMARY AND CONCLUSIONS

This chapter has introduced you to the basic principles of present value and discounted cash flow valuation. In it, we explained a number of things about the time value of money, including:

1. For a given rate of return, the value at some point in the future of an investment made today can be determined by calculating the future value of that investment.
2. The current worth of a future cash flow or series of cash flows can be determined for a given rate of return by calculating the present value of the cash flow(s) involved.
3. The relationship between present value (PV) and future value (FV) for a given rate r and time t is given by the basic present value equation:

   $$PV = FV_t/(1 + r)^t$$

   As we have shown, it is possible to find any one of the four components (PV, FV_t, r, or t) given the other three.

The principles developed in this chapter will figure prominently in the chapters to come. The reason for this is that most investments, whether they involve real assets or financial assets, can be analyzed using the discounted cash flow (DCF) approach. As a result, the DCF approach is broadly applicable and widely used in practice. Before going on, therefore, you might want to do some of the problems that follow.

Visit us at www.mhhe.com/rwj

Chapter Review and Self-Test Problems

5.1 Calculating Future Values Assume you deposit $10,000 today in an account that pays 6 percent interest. How much will you have in five years?

5.2 Calculating Present Values Suppose you have just celebrated your 19th birthday. A rich uncle has set up a trust fund for you that will pay you $150,000 when you turn 30. If the relevant discount rate is 9 percent, how much is this fund worth today?

5.3 Calculating Rates of Return You've been offered an investment that will double your money in 10 years. What rate of return are you being offered? Check your answer using the Rule of 72.

5.4 Calculating the Number of Periods You've been offered an investment that will pay you 9 percent per year. If you invest $15,000, how long until you have $30,000? How long until you have $45,000?

Answers to Chapter Review and Self-Test Problems

5.1 We need to calculate the future value of $10,000 at 6 percent for five years. The future value factor is:

$$1.06^5 = 1.3382$$

The future value is thus $10,000 × 1.3382 = $13,382.26.

5.2 We need the present value of \$150,000 to be paid in 11 years at 9 percent. The discount factor is:

$$1/1.09^{11} = 1/2.5804 = .3875$$

The present value is thus about \$58,130.

5.3 Suppose you invest, say, \$1,000. You will have \$2,000 in 10 years with this investment. So, \$1,000 is the amount you have today, or the present value, and \$2,000 is the amount you will have in 10 years, or the future value. From the basic present value equation, we have:

$$\$2{,}000 = \$1{,}000 \times (1 + r)^{10}$$
$$2 = (1 + r)^{10}$$

From here, we need to solve for r, the unknown rate. As shown in the chapter, there are several different ways to do this. We will take the 10th root of 2 (by raising 2 to the power of 1/10):

$$2^{(1/10)} = 1 + r$$
$$1.0718 = 1 + r$$
$$r = 7.18\%$$

Using the Rule of 72, we have $72/t = r\%$, or $72/10 = 7.2\%$, so our answer looks good (remember that the Rule of 72 is only an approximation).

5.4 The basic equation is:

$$\$30{,}000 = \$15{,}000 \times (1 + .09)^t$$
$$2 = (1 + .09)^t$$

If we solve for t, we get that $t = 8.04$ years. Using the Rule of 72, we get $72/9 = 8$ years, so, once again, our answer looks good. To get \$45,000, verify for yourself that you will have to wait 12.75 years.

Concepts Review and Critical Thinking Questions

1. **Present Value** The basic present value equation has four parts. What are they?
2. **Compounding** What is compounding? What is discounting?
3. **Compounding and Period** As you increase the length of time involved, what happens to future values? What happens to present values?
4. **Compounding and Interest Rates** What happens to a future value if you increase the rate r? What happens to a present value?
5. **Ethical Considerations** Take a look back at Example 5.7. Is it deceptive advertising? Is it unethical to advertise a future value like this without a disclaimer?

To answer the next five questions, refer to the GMAC security we discussed to open the chapter.

6. **Time Value of Money** Why would GMAC be willing to accept such a small amount today (\$500) in exchange for a promise to repay 20 times that amount (\$10,000) in the future?
7. **Call Provisions** GMAC has the right to buy back the securities anytime it wishes by paying \$10,000 (this is a term of this particular deal). What impact does this feature have on the desirability of this security as an investment?
8. **Time Value of Money** Would you be willing to pay \$500 today in exchange for \$10,000 in 30 years? What would be the key considerations in answering yes or no? Would your answer depend on who is making the promise to repay?

9. **Investment Comparison** Suppose that when GMAC offered the security for $500, the U.S. Treasury had offered an essentially identical security. Do you think it would have had a higher or lower price? Why?

10. **Length of Investment** The GMAC security is bought and sold on the New York Stock Exchange. If you looked at the price today, do you think the price would exceed the $500 original price? Why? If you looked in the year 2008, do you think the price would be higher or lower than today's price? Why?

Questions and Problems

BASIC
(Questions 1–15)

1. **Simple Interest versus Compound Interest** First City Bank pays 7 percent simple interest on its savings account balances, whereas Second City Bank pays 7 percent interest compounded annually. If you made a $5,000 deposit in each bank, how much more money would you earn from your Second City Bank account at the end of 10 years?

2. **Calculating Future Values** For each of the following, compute the future value:

Present Value	Years	Interest Rate	Future Value
$ 2,250	19	10%	
9,310	13	8	
76,355	4	22	
183,796	8	7	

3. **Calculating Present Values** For each of the following, compute the present value:

Present Value	Years	Interest Rate	Future Value
	6	5%	$ 15,451
	9	11	51,557
	23	16	886,073
	18	19	550,164

4. **Calculating Interest Rates** Solve for the unknown interest rate in each of the following:

Present Value	Years	Interest Rate	Future Value
$ 265	2		$ 307
360	9		896
39,000	15		162,181
46,523	30		483,500

5. **Calculating the Number of Periods** Solve for the unknown number of years in each of the following:

Present Value	Years	Interest Rate	Future Value
$ 625		8%	$ 1,284
810		7	4,341
18,400		21	402,662
21,500		29	173,439

6. **Calculating Interest Rates** Assume the total cost of a college education will be $250,000 when your child enters college in 18 years. You presently have $43,000 to invest. What annual rate of interest must you earn on your investment to cover the cost of your child's college education?
7. **Calculating the Number of Periods** At 7 percent interest, how long does it take to double your money? To quadruple it?
8. **Calculating Interest Rates** In 2003, the automobile industry announced the average vehicle selling price in the United States was $28,835. Five years earlier, the average price was $21,608. What was the annual increase in vehicle selling price?
9. **Calculating the Number of Periods** You're trying to save to buy a new $150,000 Ferrari. You have $40,000 today that can be invested at your bank. The bank pays 5.5 percent annual interest on its accounts. How long will it be before you have enough to buy the car?
10. **Calculating Present Values** Imprudential, Inc., has an unfunded pension liability of $800 million that must be paid in 20 years. To assess the value of the firm's stock, financial analysts want to discount this liability back to the present. If the relevant discount rate is 9.5 percent, what is the present value of this liability?
11. **Calculating Present Values** You have just received notification that you have won the $1 million first prize in the Centennial Lottery. However, the prize will be awarded on your 100th birthday (assuming you're around to collect), 80 years from now. What is the present value of your windfall if the appropriate discount rate is 10 percent?
12. **Calculating Future Values** Your coin collection contains fifty 1952 silver dollars. If your grandparents purchased them for their face value when they were new, how much will your collection be worth when you retire in 2054, assuming they appreciate at a 5 percent annual rate?
13. **Calculating Interest Rates and Future Values** In 1895, the first U.S. Open Golf Championship was held. The winner's prize money was $150. In 2003, the winner's check was $1,080,000. What was the percentage increase in the winner's check over this period? If the winner's prize increases at the same rate, what will it be in 2040?
14. **Calculating Present Values** The first comic book featuring Superman was sold in 1938. In 2003, the estimated price for this comic book in good condition was about $350,000. This represented a return of 26.09 percent per year. For this to be true, what must the comic book have sold for when new?
15. **Calculating Rates of Return** Although appealing to more refined tastes, art as a collectible has not always performed so profitably. During 2003, Sothebys sold the Edgar Degas bronze sculpture *Petit Danseuse de Quartorze Ans* at auction for a price of $10,311,500. Unfortunately for the previous owner, he had purchased it in 1999 at a price of $12,377,500. What was his annual rate of return on this sculpture?

INTERMEDIATE
(Questions 16–20)

16. **Calculating Rates of Return** Referring to the GMAC security we discussed at the very beginning of the chapter:
    a. Based upon the $500 price, what rate was GMAC paying to borrow money?
    b. Suppose that, on December 1, 2004, this security's price was $6,700. If an investor had purchased it for $500 at the offering and sold it on this day, what annual rate of return would she have earned?
    c. If an investor had purchased the security at market on December 1, 2004, and held it until it matured, what annual rate of return would she have earned?

17. Calculating Present Values Suppose you are still committed to owning a $150,000 Ferrari (see Question 9). If you believe your mutual fund can achieve an 11 percent annual rate of return and you want to buy the car in 10 years on the day you turn 30, how much must you invest today?

18. Calculating Future Values You have just made your first $2,000 contribution to your individual retirement account. Assuming you earn a 10 percent rate of return and make no additional contributions, what will your account be worth when you retire in 45 years? What if you wait 10 years before contributing? (Does this suggest an investment strategy?)

19. Calculating Future Values You are scheduled to receive $30,000 in two years. When you receive it, you will invest it for six more years at 6.5 percent per year. How much will you have in eight years?

20. Calculating the Number of Periods You expect to receive $10,000 at graduation in two years. You plan on investing it at 10 percent until you have $120,000. How long will you wait from now?

S&P Problems

www.mhhe.com/edumarketinsight

STANDARD &POOR'S

1. Calculating Future Values Find the monthly adjusted prices for McCormick & Co. (MKC). If the stock appreciates 11 percent per year, what stock price do you expect to see in five years? In 10 years? Ignore dividends in your calculations.

2. Calculating Interest Rates Find the monthly adjusted prices for J C Penney Co. (JCP). What is the average annual return over the past four years?

3. Calculating the Number of Periods Find the monthly adjusted stock prices for Southwest Airlines (LUV). You find an analyst who projects the stock price will increase 12 percent per year for the foreseeable future. Based on the most recent monthly stock price, if the projection holds true, when will the stock price reach $150? When will it reach $200?

What's On the Web?

5.1 Calculating Future Values Go to www.dinkytown.net and follow the "Savings Calculator" link. If you currently have $10,000 and invest this money at 9 percent, how much will you have in 30 years? Assume you will not make any additional contributions. How much will you have if you can earn 11 percent?

5.2 Calculating the Number of Periods Go to www.dinkytown.net and follow the "Cool Million" link. You want to be a millionaire. You can earn 11.5 percent per year. Using your current age, at what age will you become a millionaire if you have $25,000 to invest, assuming you make no other deposits (ignore inflation)?

5.3 Future Values and Taxes Taxes can greatly affect the future value of your investment. The Financial Calculators Web site at www.fincalc.com has a financial calculator that adjusts your return for taxes. Suppose you have $50,000 to invest today. If you can earn a 12 percent return and no additional annual savings, how much will you have in 20 years? (Enter 0 percent as the tax rate.) Now, assume that your marginal tax rate is 27.5 percent. How much will you have at this tax rate?

Visit us at www.mhhe.com/rwj

6 Discounted Cash Flow Valuation

The signing of big-name athletes is often accompanied by great fanfare, but the numbers can be misleading. For example, in early 2004, catcher Ivan "Pudge" Rodriguez left the world champion Florida Marlins to sign with the Detroit Tigers, a team that set the American League record for most losses in a season the previous year. Pudge's four-year contract was widely reported as being worth $40 million. Not bad, especially for someone who makes a living using the "tools of ignorance" (jock jargon for a catcher's equipment). But not as good as Peyton Manning's NFL record contract with the Indianapolis Colts; its stated value was about $126 million!

A closer look at the numbers shows that both Pudge and Peyton did pretty well, but nothing like the quoted figures. Using Peyton's contract as an example, while the value was reported to be $126 million, it was actually payable over nine years. It consisted of a $34.04 million signing bonus plus $92 million in salary and future bonuses. The salary was to be distributed as $535,000 in 2004, $665,000 in 2005, $10 million in 2006, $11 million in 2007, $11.5 million in 2008, $14 million in 2009, $15.8 million in 2010, and $14 million in both 2011 and 2012. Since the payments were spread out over time, we must consider the time value of money, which means neither player received the quoted amounts. How much did they really get? This chapter gives you the "tools of knowledge" to answer that question.

In our previous chapter, we covered the basics of discounted cash flow valuation. However, so far, we have only dealt with single cash flows. In reality, most investments have multiple cash flows. For example, if Sears is thinking of opening a new department store, there will be a large cash outlay in the beginning and then cash inflows for many years. In this chapter, we begin to explore how to value such investments.

When you finish this chapter, you should have some very practical skills. For example, you will know how to calculate your own car payments or student loan payments. You will also be able to determine how long it will take to pay off a credit card if you make the minimum payment each month (a practice we do not recommend). We will show you how to compare interest rates to determine which are the highest and which are the lowest, and we will also show you how interest rates can be quoted in different, and at times deceptive, ways.

FIGURE 6.1 >>

Drawing and Using a Time Line

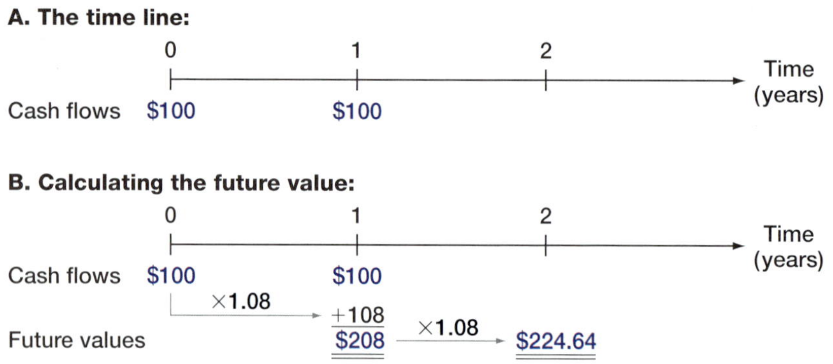

6.1 FUTURE AND PRESENT VALUES OF MULTIPLE CASH FLOWS

Thus far, we have restricted our attention to either the future value of a lump-sum present amount or the present value of some single future cash flow. In this section, we begin to study ways to value multiple cash flows. We start with future value.

Future Value with Multiple Cash Flows

Suppose you deposit $100 today in an account paying 8 percent. In one year, you will deposit another $100. How much will you have in two years? This particular problem is relatively easy. At the end of the first year, you will have $108 plus the second $100 you deposit, for a total of $208. You leave this $208 on deposit at 8 percent for another year. At the end of this second year, it is worth:

$$\$208 \times 1.08 = \$224.64$$

Figure 6.1 is a *time line* that illustrates the process of calculating the future value of these two $100 deposits. Figures such as this one are very useful for solving complicated problems. Almost anytime you are having trouble with a present or future value problem, drawing a time line will help you to see what is happening.

In the first part of Figure 6.1, we show the cash flows on the time line. The most important thing is that we write them down where they actually occur. Here, the first cash flow occurs today, which we label as Time 0. We therefore put $100 at Time 0 on the time line. The second $100 cash flow occurs one year from today, so we write it down at the point labeled as Time 1. In the second part of Figure 6.1, we calculate the future values one period at a time to come up with the final $224.64.

EXAMPLE 6.1 >> Saving Up Revisited

You think you will be able to deposit $4,000 at the end of each of the next three years in a bank account paying 8 percent interest. You currently have $7,000 in the account. How much will you have in three years? In four years?

At the end of the first year, you will have:

$$\$7{,}000 \times 1.08 + 4{,}000 = \$11{,}560$$

At the end of the second year, you will have:

$$\$11{,}560 \times 1.08 + 4{,}000 = \$16{,}484.80$$

continued

Repeating this for the third year gives:

$$\$16{,}484.80 \times 1.08 + 4{,}000 = \$21{,}803.58$$

Therefore, you will have $21,803.58 in three years. If you leave this on deposit for one more year (and don't add to it), at the end of the fourth year, you'll have:

$$\$21{,}803.58 \times 1.08 = \$23{,}547.87$$

When we calculated the future value of the two $100 deposits, we simply calculated the balance as of the beginning of each year and then rolled that amount forward to the next year. We could have done it another, quicker way. The first $100 is on deposit for two years at 8 percent, so its future value is:

$$\$100 \times 1.08^2 = \$100 \times 1.1664 = \$116.64$$

The second $100 is on deposit for one year at 8 percent, and its future value is thus:

$$\$100 \times 1.08 = \$108$$

The total future value, as we previously calculated, is equal to the sum of these two future values:

$$\$116.64 + 108 = \$224.64$$

Based on this example, there are two ways to calculate future values for multiple cash flows: (1) compound the accumulated balance forward one year at a time or (2) calculate the future value of each cash flow first and then add them up. Both give the same answer, so you can do it either way.

To illustrate the two different ways of calculating future values, consider the future value of $2,000 invested at the end of each of the next five years. The current balance is zero, and the rate is 10 percent. We first draw a time line, as shown in Figure 6.2.

On the time line, notice that nothing happens until the end of the first year, when we make the first $2,000 investment. This first $2,000 earns interest for the next four (not five) years. Also notice that the last $2,000 is invested at the end of the fifth year, so it earns no interest at all.

Figure 6.3 illustrates the calculations involved if we compound the investment one period at a time. As illustrated, the future value is $12,210.20.

FIGURE 6.2 >> Time Line for $2,000 per Year for Five Years

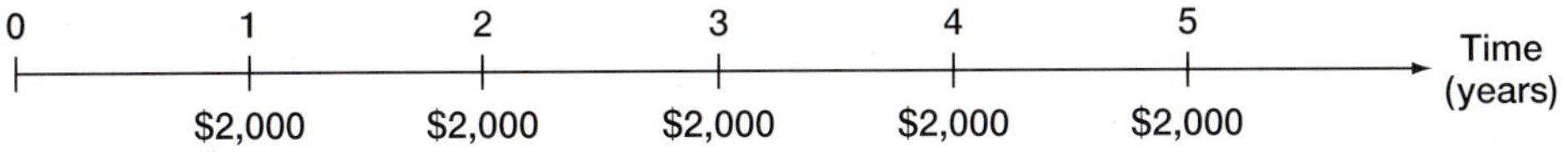

FIGURE 6.3 >> Future Value Calculated by Compounding Forward One Period at a Time

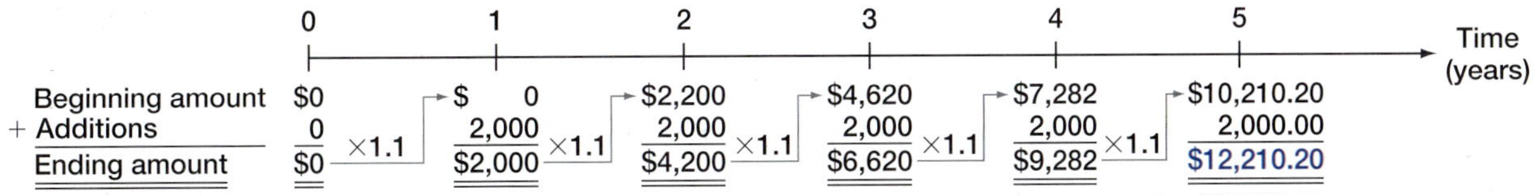

FIGURE 6.4 >>

Future Value Calculated by Compounding Each Cash Flow Separately

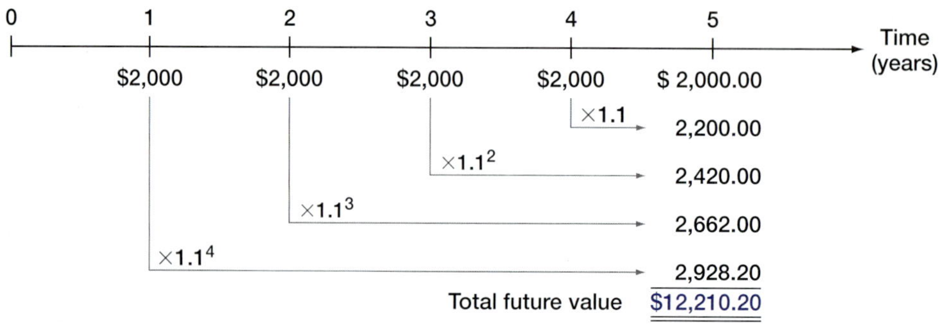

Figure 6.4 goes through the same calculations, but the second technique is used. Naturally, the answer is the same.

EXAMPLE 6.2 >> Saving Up Once Again

If you deposit $100 in one year, $200 in two years, and $300 in three years, how much will you have in three years? How much of this is interest? How much will you have in five years if you don't add additional amounts? Assume a 7 percent interest rate throughout.

We will calculate the future value of each amount in three years. Notice that the $100 earns interest for two years, and the $200 earns interest for one year. The final $300 earns no interest. The future values are thus:

$$\begin{aligned} \$100 \times 1.07^2 &= \$114.49 \\ \$200 \times 1.07 &= 214.00 \\ + \$300 &= \underline{300.00} \\ \text{Total future value} &= \underline{\underline{\$628.49}} \end{aligned}$$

The total future value is thus $628.49. The total interest is:

$$\$628.49 - (100 + 200 + 300) = \$28.49$$

How much will you have in five years? We know that you will have $628.49 in three years. If you leave that in for two more years, it will grow to:

$$\$628.49 \times 1.07^2 = \$628.49 \times 1.1449 = \$719.56$$

Notice that we could have calculated the future value of each amount separately. Once again, be careful about the lengths of time. As we previously calculated, the first $100 earns interest for only four years, the second deposit earns three years' interest, and the last earns two years' interest:

$$\begin{aligned} \$100 \times 1.07^4 = \$100 \times 1.3108 &= \$131.08 \\ \$200 \times 1.07^3 = \$200 \times 1.2250 &= 245.01 \\ + \$300 \times 1.07^2 = \$300 \times 1.1449 &= \underline{343.47} \\ \text{Total future value} &= \underline{\underline{\$719.56}} \end{aligned}$$

Present Value with Multiple Cash Flows

It will turn out that we will very often need to determine the present value of a series of future cash flows. As with future values, there are two ways we can do it. We can either discount back one period at a time, or we can just calculate the present values individually and add them up.

Suppose you need $1,000 in one year and $2,000 more in two years. If you can earn 9 percent on your money, how much do you have to put up today to exactly cover these amounts in the future? In other words, what is the present value of the two cash flows at 9 percent?

The present value of $2,000 in two years at 9 percent is:

$$\$2{,}000/1.09^2 = \$1{,}683.36$$

The present value of $1,000 in one year is:

$$\$1{,}000/1.09 = \$917.43$$

Therefore, the total present value is:

$$\$1{,}683.36 + 917.43 = \$2{,}600.79$$

To see why $2,600.79 is the right answer, we can check to see that after the $2,000 is paid out in two years, there is no money left. If we invest $2,600.79 for one year at 9 percent, we will have:

$$\$2{,}600.79 \times 1.09 = \$2{,}834.86$$

We take out $1,000, leaving $1,834.86. This amount earns 9 percent for another year, leaving us with:

$$\$1{,}834.86 \times 1.09 = \$2{,}000$$

This is just as we planned. As this example illustrates, the present value of a series of future cash flows is simply the amount that you would need today in order to exactly duplicate those future cash flows (for a given discount rate).

An alternative way of calculating present values for multiple future cash flows is to discount back to the present, one period at a time. To illustrate, suppose we had an investment that was going to pay $1,000 at the end of every year for the next five years. To find the present value, we could discount each $1,000 back to the present separately and then add them up. Figure 6.5 illustrates this approach for a 6 percent discount rate; as shown, the answer is $4,212.37 (ignoring a small rounding error).

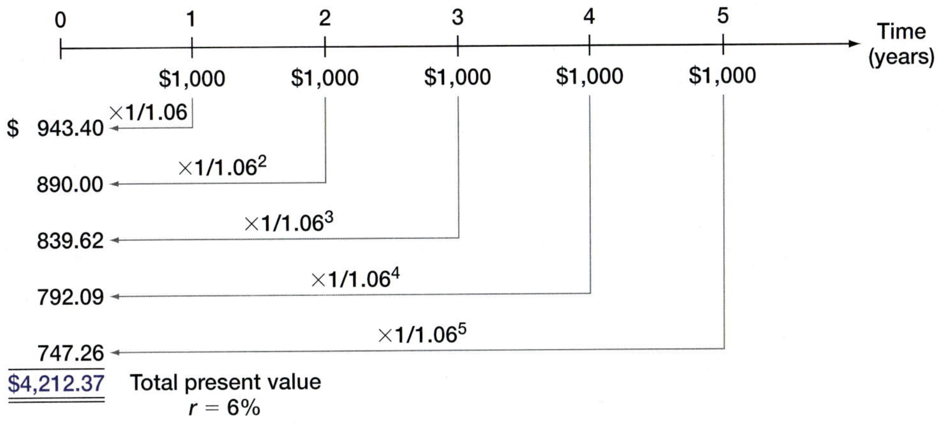

FIGURE 6.5

Present Value Calculated by Discounting Each Cash Flow Separately

FIGURE 6.6 >> **Present Value Calculated by Discounting Back One Period at a Time**

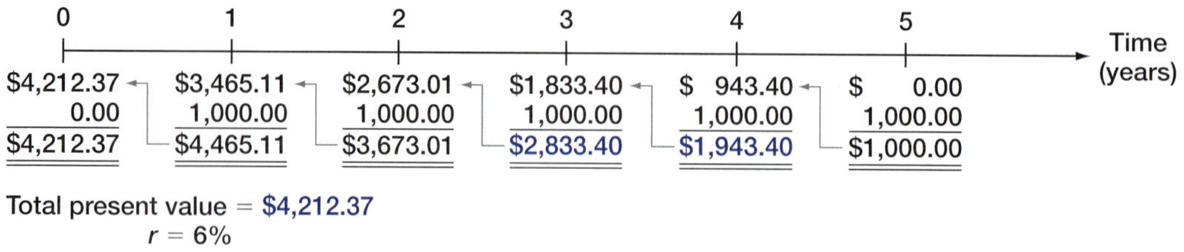

Alternatively, we could discount the last cash flow back one period and add it to the next-to-the-last cash flow:

($1,000/1.06) + 1,000 = $943.40 + 1,000 = $1,943.40

We could then discount this amount back one period and add it to the Year 3 cash flow:

($1,943.40/1.06) + 1,000 = $1,833.40 + 1,000 = $2,833.40

This process could be repeated as necessary. Figure 6.6 illustrates this approach and the remaining calculations.

EXAMPLE 6.3 >> How Much Is It Worth?

You are offered an investment that will pay you $200 in one year, $400 the next year, $600 the next year, and $800 at the end of the fourth year. You can earn 12 percent on very similar investments. What is the most you should pay for this one?

We need to calculate the present value of these cash flows at 12 percent. Taking them one at a time gives:

$$
\begin{aligned}
\$200 \times 1/1.12^1 &= \$200/1.1200 = \$\ \ 178.57 \\
\$400 \times 1/1.12^2 &= \$400/1.2544 = \quad 318.88 \\
\$600 \times 1/1.12^3 &= \$600/1.4049 = \quad 427.07 \\
+\ \$800 \times 1/1.12^4 &= \$800/1.5735 = \quad \underline{508.41} \\
\text{Total present value} &= \$1{,}432.93
\end{aligned}
$$

If you can earn 12 percent on your money, then you can duplicate this investment's cash flows for $1,432.93, so this is the most you should be willing to pay.

EXAMPLE 6.4 >> How Much Is It Worth? Part 2

You are offered an investment that will make three $5,000 payments. The first payment will occur four years from today. The second will occur in five years, and the third will follow in six years. If you can earn 11 percent, what is the most this investment is worth today? What is the future value of the cash flows?

We will answer the questions in reverse order to illustrate a point. The future value of the cash flows in six years is:

$$
\begin{aligned}
(\$5{,}000 \times 1.11^2) + (5{,}000 \times 1.11) + 5{,}000 &= \$6{,}160.50 + 5{,}550 + 5{,}000 \\
&= \$16{,}710.50
\end{aligned}
$$

continued

The present value must be:

$$\$16{,}710.50/1.11^6 = \$8{,}934.12$$

Let's check this. Taking them one at a time, the PVs of the cash flows are:

$$\begin{aligned} \$5{,}000 \times 1/1.11^6 &= \$5{,}000/1.8704 = \$2{,}673.20 \\ \$5{,}000 \times 1/1.11^5 &= \$5{,}000/1.6851 = 2{,}967.26 \\ + \$5{,}000 \times 1/1.11^4 &= \$5{,}000/1.5181 = \underline{3{,}293.65} \\ \text{Total present value} &= \underline{\underline{\$8{,}934.12}} \end{aligned}$$

This is as we previously calculated. The point we want to make is that we can calculate present and future values in any order and convert between them using whatever way seems most convenient. The answers will always be the same as long as we stick with the same discount rate and are careful to keep track of the right number of periods.

How to Calculate Present Values with Multiple Future Cash Flows Using a Financial Calculator

To calculate the present value of multiple cash flows with a financial calculator, we will simply discount the individual cash flows one at a time using the same technique we used in our previous chapter, so this is not really new. There is a shortcut, however, that we can show you. We will use the numbers in Example 6.3 to illustrate.

To begin, of course we first remember to clear out the calculator! Next, from Example 6.3, the first cash flow is $200 to be received in one year and the discount rate is 12 percent, so we do the following:

Enter	1	12			200
	N	I/Y	PMT	PV	FV
Solve for				−178.57	

Now you can write down this answer to save it, but that's inefficient. All calculators have a memory where you can store numbers. Why not just save it there? Doing so cuts way down on mistakes because you don't have to write down and/or rekey numbers, and it's much faster.

Next we value the second cash flow. We need to change N to 2 and FV to 400. As long as we haven't changed anything else, we don't have to reenter I/Y or clear out the calculator, so we have:

Enter	2				400
	N	I/Y	PMT	PV	FV
Solve for				−318.88	

You save this number by adding it to the one you saved in our first calculation, and so on for the remaining two calculations.

As we will see in a later chapter, some financial calculators will let you enter all of the future cash flows at once, but we'll discuss that subject when we get to it.

SPREADSHEET STRATEGIES

How to Calculate Present Values with Multiple Future Cash Flows Using a Spreadsheet

Just as we did in our previous chapter, we can set up a basic spreadsheet to calculate the present values of the individual cash flows as follows. Notice that we have simply calculated the present values one at a time and added them up:

	A	B	C	D	E
1					
2	**Using a spreadsheet to value multiple future cash flows**				
3					
4	What is the present value of $200 in one year, $400 the next year, $600 the next year, and				
5	$800 the last year if the discount rate is 12 percent?				
6					
7	Rate:	0.12			
8					
9	Year	Cash flows	Present values	Formula used	
10	1	$200	$178.57	=PV($B$7,A10,0,−B10)	
11	2	$400	$318.88	=PV($B$7,A11,0,−B11)	
12	3	$600	$427.07	=PV($B$7,A12,0,−B12)	
13	4	$800	$508.41	=PV($B$7,A13,0,−B13)	
14					
15		Total PV:	**$1,432.93**	=SUM(C10:C13)	
16					
17	Notice the negative signs inserted in the PV formulas. These just make the present values have				
18	positive signs. Also, the discount rate in cell B7 is entered as $B$7 (an "absolute" reference)				
19	because it is used over and over. We could have just entered ".12" instead, but our approach is more				
20	flexible.				
21					
22					

A Note on Cash Flow Timing

In working present and future value problems, cash flow timing is critically important. In almost all such calculations, it is implicitly assumed that the cash flows occur at the *end* of each period. In fact, all the formulas we have discussed, all the numbers in a standard present value or future value table, and, very importantly, all the preset (or default) settings on a financial calculator assume that cash flows occur at the end of each period. Unless you are very explicitly told otherwise, you should always assume that this is what is meant.

As a quick illustration of this point, suppose you are told that a three-year investment has a first-year cash flow of $100, a second-year cash flow of $200, and a third-year cash flow of $300. You are asked to draw a time line. Without further information, you should always assume that the time line looks like this:

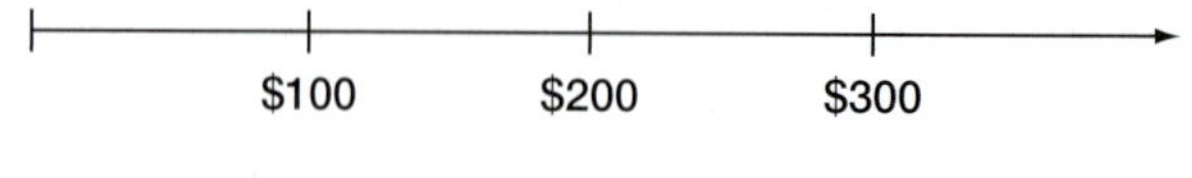

On our time line, notice how the first cash flow occurs at the end of the first period, the second at the end of the second period, and the third at the end of the third period.

We close this section by answering the question we posed concerning Peyton Manning's NFL contract at the beginning of the chapter. Recall that the contract called for a signing bonus of \$34.04 million to be paid by the end of the year, plus a salary of \$92 million, to be distributed as \$535,000 in 2004, \$665,000 in 2005, \$10 million in 2006, \$11 million in 2007, \$11.5 million in 2008, \$14 million in 2009, \$15.8 million in 2010, and \$14 million in both 2011 and 2012. If 12 percent is the appropriate interest rate, what kind of deal did the Colts' quarterback lasso?

To find the answer, we can calculate the present value by discounting each year's salary back to the present as follows (notice we combined the salary and signing bonus in 2004):

Year 1: $\$34{,}575{,}000 \times 1/1.12^1 = \$30{,}870{,}535.71$

Year 2: $\$665{,}000 \times 1/1.12^2 = \$530{,}133.93$

Year 3: $\$10{,}000{,}000 \times 1/1.12^3 = \$7{,}117{,}802.48$

. . .

. . .

. . .

Year 9: $\$14{,}000{,}000 \times 1/1.12^9 = \$5{,}048{,}540.35$

If you fill in the missing rows and then add (do it for practice), you will see that Manning's contract had a present value of about \$77 million, less than 2/3 of the \$126 million stated value.

Concept Questions

6.1a Describe how to calculate the future value of a series of cash flows.

6.1b Describe how to calculate the present value of a series of cash flows.

6.1c Unless we are explicitly told otherwise, what do we always assume about the timing of cash flows in present and future value problems?

VALUING LEVEL CASH FLOWS: ANNUITIES AND PERPETUITIES

6.2

We will frequently encounter situations in which we have multiple cash flows that are all the same amount. For example, a very common type of loan repayment plan calls for the borrower to repay the loan by making a series of equal payments over some length of time. Almost all consumer loans (such as car loans) and home mortgages feature equal payments, usually made each month.

More generally, a series of constant or level cash flows that occur at the end of each period for some fixed number of periods is called an ordinary **annuity**; or, more correctly, the cash flows are said to be in ordinary annuity form. Annuities appear very frequently in financial arrangements, and there are some useful shortcuts for determining their values. We consider these next.

annuity
A level stream of cash flows for a fixed period of time.

Present Value for Annuity Cash Flows

Suppose we were examining an asset that promised to pay \$500 at the end of each of the next three years. The cash flows from this asset are in the form of a three-year, \$500 annuity. If we wanted to earn 10 percent on our money, how much would we offer for this annuity?

From the previous section, we know that we can discount each of these \$500 payments back to the present at 10 percent to determine the total present value:

$$\begin{aligned}\text{Present value} &= (\$500/1.1^1) + (500/1.1^2) + (500/1.1^3)\\ &= (\$500/1.1) + (500/1.21) + (500/1.331)\\ &= \$454.55 + 413.22 + 375.66\\ &= \$1{,}243.43\end{aligned}$$

This approach works just fine. However, we will often encounter situations in which the number of cash flows is quite large. For example, a typical home mortgage calls for monthly payments over 30 years, for a total of 360 payments. If we were trying to determine the present value of those payments, it would be useful to have a shortcut.

Because the cash flows of an annuity are all the same, we can come up with a very useful variation on the basic present value equation. It turns out that the present value of an annuity of C dollars per period for t periods when the rate of return or interest rate is r is given by:

$$\begin{aligned}\text{Annuity present value} &= C \times \left(\frac{1 - \text{Present value factor}}{r}\right)\\ &= C \times \left\{\frac{1 - [1/(1 + r)^t]}{r}\right\}\end{aligned} \qquad \textbf{[6.1]}$$

The term in parentheses on the first line is sometimes called the present value interest factor for annuities and abbreviated PVIFA(r, t).

The expression for the annuity present value may look a little complicated, but it isn't difficult to use. Notice that the term in square brackets on the second line, $1/(1 + r)^t$, is the same present value factor we've been calculating. In our example from the beginning of this section, the interest rate is 10 percent and there are three years involved. The usual present value factor is thus:

$$\text{Present value factor} = 1/1.1^3 = 1/1.331 = .75131$$

To calculate the annuity present value factor, we just plug this in:

$$\begin{aligned}\text{Annuity present value factor} &= (1 - \text{Present value factor})/r\\ &= (1 - .75131)/.10\\ &= .248685/.10 = 2.48685\end{aligned}$$

Just as we calculated before, the present value of our \$500 annuity is then:

$$\text{Annuity present value} = \$500 \times 2.48685 = \$1{,}243.43$$

EXAMPLE 6.5 >> **How Much Can You Afford?**

After carefully going over your budget, you have determined you can afford to pay \$632 per month toward a new sports car. You call up your local bank and find out that the going rate is 1 percent per month for 48 months. How much can you borrow?

To determine how much you can borrow, we need to calculate the present value of \$632 per month for 48 months at 1 percent per month. The loan payments are in ordinary annuity form, so the annuity present value factor is:

$$\begin{aligned}\text{Annuity PV factor} &= (1 - \text{Present value factor})/r\\ &= [1 - (1/1.01^{48})]/.01\\ &= (1 - .6203)/.01 = 37.9740\end{aligned}$$

continued

With this factor, we can calculate the present value of the 48 payments of $632 each as:

Present value = $632 × 37.9740 = $24,000

Therefore, $24,000 is what you can afford to borrow and repay.

Annuity Tables Just as there are tables for ordinary present value factors, there are tables for annuity factors as well. Table 6.1 contains a few such factors; Table A.3 in the appendix to the book contains a larger set. To find the annuity present value factor we calculated just before Example 6.5, look for the row corresponding to three periods and then find the column for 10 percent. The number you see at that intersection should be 2.4869 (rounded to four decimal places), as we calculated. Once again, try calculating a few of these factors yourself and compare your answers to the ones in the table to make sure you know how to do it. If you are using a financial calculator, just enter $1 as the payment and calculate the present value; the result should be the annuity present value factor.

<< TABLE 6.1

Annuity Present Value Interest Factors

	Interest Rate			
Number of Periods	**5%**	**10%**	**15%**	**20%**
1	.9524	.9091	.8696	.8333
2	1.8594	1.7355	1.6257	1.5278
3	2.7232	2.4869	2.2832	2.1065
4	3.5460	3.1699	2.8550	2.5887
5	4.3295	3.7908	3.3522	2.9906

Annuity Present Values

To find annuity present values with a financial calculator, we need to use the **PMT** key (you were probably wondering what it was for). Compared to finding the present value of a single amount, there are two important differences. First, we enter the annuity cash flow using the **PMT** key, and, second, we don't enter anything for the future value, **FV**. So, for example, the problem we have been examining is a three-year, $500 annuity. If the discount rate is 10 percent, we need to do the following (after clearing out the calculator!):

Enter	3	10	500		
	N	**I/Y**	**PMT**	**PV**	**FV**
Solve for				−1,243.43	

As usual, we get a negative sign on the PV.

SPREADSHEET STRATEGIES

Annuity Present Values

Using a spreadsheet to find annuity present values goes like this:

	A	B	C	D	E	F	G
1							
2	**Using a spreadsheet to find annuity present values**						
3							
4	What is the present value of $500 per year for 3 years if the discount rate is 10 percent?						
5	We need to solve for the unknown present value, so we use the formula PV(rate, nper, pmt, fv).						
6							
7	Payment amount per period:	$500					
8	Number of payments:	3					
9	Discount rate:	0.1					
10							
11	Annuity present value:	**$1,243.43**					
12							
13	The formula entered in cell B11 is =PV(B9,B8,-B7,0); notice that fv is zero and that						
14	pmt has a negative sign on it. Also notice that rate is entered as a decimal, not a percentage.						
15							
16							
17							

Finding the Payment Suppose you wish to start up a new business that specializes in the latest of health food trends, frozen yak milk. To produce and market your product, the Yakkee Doodle Dandy, you need to borrow $100,000. Because it strikes you as unlikely that this particular fad will be long-lived, you propose to pay off the loan quickly by making five equal annual payments. If the interest rate is 18 percent, what will the payment be?

In this case, we know the present value is $100,000. The interest rate is 18 percent, and there are five years. The payments are all equal, so we need to find the relevant annuity factor and solve for the unknown cash flow:

$$\begin{aligned}
\text{Annuity present value} = \$100{,}000 &= C \times [(1 - \text{Present value factor})/r] \\
&= C \times \{[1 - (1/1.18^5)]/.18\} \\
&= C \times [(1 - .4371)/.18] \\
&= C \times 3.1272 \\
C &= \$100{,}000/3.1272 = \$31{,}978
\end{aligned}$$

Therefore, you'll make five payments of just under $32,000 each.

CALCULATOR HINTS

Annuity Payments

Finding annuity payments is easy with a financial calculator. In our example just above, the PV is $100,000, the interest rate is 18 percent, and there are five years. We find the payment as follows:

	N	I/Y	PMT	PV	FV
Enter	5	18		100,000	
Solve for			−31,978		

Here we get a negative sign on the payment because the payment is an outflow for us.

SPREADSHEET STRATEGIES

Annuity Payments

Using a spreadsheet to work the same problem goes like this:

	A	B	C	D	E	F	G
1							
2	**Using a spreadsheet to find annuity payments**						
3							
4	What is the annuity payment if the present value is $100,000, the interest rate is 18 percent, and						
5	there are 5 periods? We need to solve for the unknown payment in an annuity, so we use the						
6	formula PMT(rate, nper, pv, fv).						
7							
8	Annuity present value:	$100,000					
9	Number of payments:	5					
10	Discount rate:	0.18					
11							
12	Annuity payment:	**$31,977.78**					
13							
14	The formula entered in cell B12 is =PMT(B10, B9, -B8,0); notice that fv is zero and that the payment						
15	has a negative sign because it is an outflow to us.						
16							

EXAMPLE 6.6

Finding the Number of Payments

You ran a little short on your spring break vacation, so you put $1,000 on your credit card. You can only afford to make the minimum payment of $20 per month. The interest rate on the credit card is 1.5 percent per month. How long will you need to pay off the $1,000?

What we have here is an annuity of $20 per month at 1.5 percent per month for some unknown length of time. The present value is $1,000 (the amount you owe today). We need to do a little algebra (or else use a financial calculator):

$$\$1000 = \$20 \times [(1 - \text{Present value factor})/.015]$$
$$(\$1{,}000/20) \times .015 = 1 - \text{Present value factor}$$
$$\text{Present value factor} = .25 = 1/(1 + r)^t$$
$$1.015^t = 1/.25 = 4$$

At this point, the problem boils down to asking the question, How long does it take for your money to quadruple at 1.5 percent per month? Based on our previous chapter, the answer is about 93 months:

$$1.015^{93} = 3.99 \approx 4$$

It will take you about 93/12 = 7.75 years to pay off the $1,000 at this rate. If you use a financial calculator for problems like this one, you should be aware that some automatically round up to the next whole period.

CALCULATOR HINTS

Finding the Number of Payments

To solve this one on a financial calculator, do the following:

Enter		1.5	−20	1,000	
	N	I/Y	PMT	PV	FV
Solve for	93.11				

Notice that we put a negative sign on the payment you must make, and we have solved for the number of months. You still have to divide by 12 to get our answer. Also, some financial calculators won't report a fractional value for N; they automatically (without telling you) round up to the next whole period (not to the nearest value). With a spreadsheet, use the function =NPER(rate,pmt,pv,fv); be sure to put in a zero for fv and to enter −20 as the payment.

Finding the Rate The last question we might want to ask concerns the interest rate implicit in an annuity. For example, an insurance company offers to pay you $1,000 per year for 10 years if you will pay $6,710 up front. What rate is implicit in this 10-year annuity?

In this case, we know the present value ($6,710), we know the cash flows ($1,000 per year), and we know the life of the investment (10 years). What we don't know is the discount rate:

$$\$6{,}710 = \$1{,}000 \times [(1 - \text{Present value factor})/r]$$
$$\$6{,}710/1{,}000 = 6.71 = \{1 - [1/(1 + r)^{10}]\}/r$$

So, the annuity factor for 10 periods is equal to 6.71, and we need to solve this equation for the unknown value of r. Unfortunately, this is mathematically impossible to do directly. The only way to do it is to use a table or trial and error to find a value for r.

If you look across the row corresponding to 10 periods in Table A.3, you will see a factor of 6.7101 for 8 percent, so we see right away that the insurance company is offering just about 8 percent. Alternatively, we could just start trying different values until we got very close to the answer. Using this trial-and-error approach can be a little tedious, but, fortunately, machines are good at that sort of thing.[1]

To illustrate how to find the answer by trial and error, suppose a relative of yours wants to borrow $3,000. She offers to repay you $1,000 every year for four years. What interest rate are you being offered?

The cash flows here have the form of a four-year, $1,000 annuity. The present value is $3,000. We need to find the discount rate, r. Our goal in doing so is primarily to give you a feel for the relationship between annuity values and discount rates.

We need to start somewhere, and 10 percent is probably as good a place as any to begin. At 10 percent, the annuity factor is:

$$\text{Annuity present value factor} = [1 - (1/1.10^4)]/.10 = 3.1699$$

[1]Financial calculators rely on trial and error to find the answer. That's why they sometimes appear to be "thinking" before coming up with the answer. Actually, it is possible to directly solve for r if there are fewer than five periods, but it's usually not worth the trouble.

The present value of the cash flows at 10 percent is thus:

$$\text{Present value} = \$1{,}000 \times 3.1699 = \$3{,}169.90$$

You can see that we're already in the right ballpark.

Is 10 percent too high or too low? Recall that present values and discount rates move in opposite directions: increasing the discount rate lowers the PV and vice versa. Our present value here is too high, so the discount rate is too low. If we try 12 percent:

$$\text{Present value} = \$1{,}000 \times \{[1 - (1/1.12^4)]/.12\} = \$3{,}037.35$$

Now we're almost there. We are still a little low on the discount rate (because the PV is a little high), so we'll try 13 percent:

$$\text{Present value} = \$1{,}000 \times \{[1 - (1/1.13^4)]/.13\} = \$2{,}974.47$$

This is less than $3,000, so we now know that the answer is between 12 percent and 13 percent, and it looks to be about 12.5 percent. For practice, work at it for a while longer and see if you find that the answer is about 12.59 percent.

To illustrate a situation in which finding the unknown rate can be very useful, let us consider that the Tri-State Megabucks lottery in Maine, Vermont, and New Hampshire offers you a choice of how to take your winnings (most lotteries do this). In a recent drawing, participants were offered the option of receiving a lump-sum payment of $250,000 or an annuity of $500,000 to be received in equal installments over a 25-year period. (At the time, the lump-sum payment was always half the annuity option.) Which option was better?

To answer, suppose you were to compare $250,000 today to an annuity of $500,000/25 = $20,000 per year for 25 years. At what rate do these have the same value? This is the same problem we've been looking at; we need to find the unknown rate, *r*, for a present value of $250,000, a $20,000 payment, and a 25-year period. If you grind through the calculations (or get a little machine assistance), you should find that the unknown rate is about 6.24 percent. You should take the annuity option if that rate is attractive relative to other investments available to you. Notice that we have ignored taxes in this example, and taxes can significantly affect our conclusion. Be sure to consult your tax adviser anytime you win the lottery.

CALCULATOR HINTS

Finding the Rate

Alternatively, you could use a financial calculator to do the following:

Enter	4		1,000	−3,000	
	N	**I/Y**	**PMT**	**PV**	**FV**
Solve for		12.59			

Notice that we put a negative sign on the present value (why?). With a spreadsheet, use the function =RATE(nper,pmt,pv,fv); be sure to put in a zero for fv and to enter 1,000 as the payment and −3,000 as the pv.

Future Value for Annuities

On occasion, it's also handy to know a shortcut for calculating the future value of an annuity. As you might guess, there are future value factors for annuities as well as present value factors. In general, the future value factor for an annuity is given by:

$$\text{Annuity FV factor} = (\text{Future value factor} - 1)/r$$
$$= [(1 + r)^t - 1]/r \qquad \textbf{[6.2]}$$

To see how we use annuity future value factors, suppose you plan to contribute \$2,000 every year to a retirement account paying 8 percent. If you retire in 30 years, how much will you have?

The number of years here, t, is 30, and the interest rate, r, is 8 percent, so we can calculate the annuity future value factor as:

$$\text{Annuity FV factor} = (\text{Future value factor} - 1)/r$$
$$= (1.08^{30} - 1)/.08$$
$$= (10.0627 - 1)/.08$$
$$= 113.2832$$

The future value of this 30-year, \$2,000 annuity is thus:

$$\text{Annuity future value} = \$2{,}000 \times 113.28$$
$$= \$226{,}566$$

Sometimes we need to find the unknown rate, r, in the context of an annuity future value. For example, if you had invested \$100 per month in stocks over the 25-year period ended December 1978, your investment would have grown to \$76,374. This period had the *worst* stretch of stock returns of any 25-year period between 1925 and 2005. How bad was it?

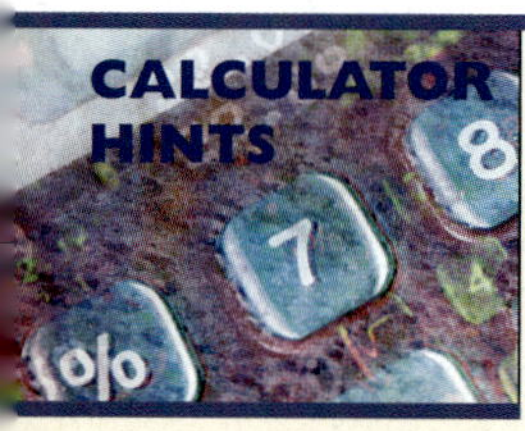

Future Values of Annuities

Of course, you could solve this problem using a financial calculator by doing the following:

Enter	30	8	−2,000		
	N	**I/Y**	**PMT**	**PV**	**FV**
Solve for					226,566

Notice that we put a negative sign on the payment (why?). With a spreadsheet, use the function =FV(rate,nper,pmt,pv); be sure to put in a zero for pv and to enter −2,000 as the payment.

Here we have the cash flows (\$100 per month), the *future* value (\$76,374), and the time period (25 years, or 300 months). We need to find the implicit rate, r:

$$\$76{,}374 = \$100 \times [(\text{Future value factor} - 1)/r]$$
$$763.74 = [(1 + r)^{300} - 1]/r$$

Because this is the worst period, let's try 1 percent:

$$\text{Annuity future value factor} = (1.01^{300} - 1)/.01 = 1{,}878.85$$

We see that 1 percent is too high. From here, it's trial and error. See if you agree that r is about .55 percent per month. As you will see later in the chapter, this works out to be about 6.8 percent per year.

A Note on Annuities Due

So far, we have only discussed ordinary annuities. These are the most important, but there is a variation that is fairly common. Remember that with an ordinary annuity, the cash flows occur at the end of each period. When you take out a loan with monthly payments, for example, the first loan payment normally occurs one month after you get the loan. However, when you lease an apartment, the first lease payment is usually due immediately. The second payment is due at the beginning of the second month, and so on. A lease is an example of an **annuity due**. An annuity due is an annuity for which the cash flows occur at the beginning of each period. Almost any type of arrangement in which we have to prepay the same amount each period is an annuity due.

annuity due
An annuity for which the cash flows occur at the beginning of the period.

There are several different ways to calculate the value of an annuity due. With a financial calculator, you simply switch it into "due" or "beginning" mode. It is very important to remember to switch it back when you are done! Another way to calculate the present value of an annuity due can be illustrated with a time line. Suppose an annuity due has five payments of $400 each, and the relevant discount rate is 10 percent. The time line looks like this:

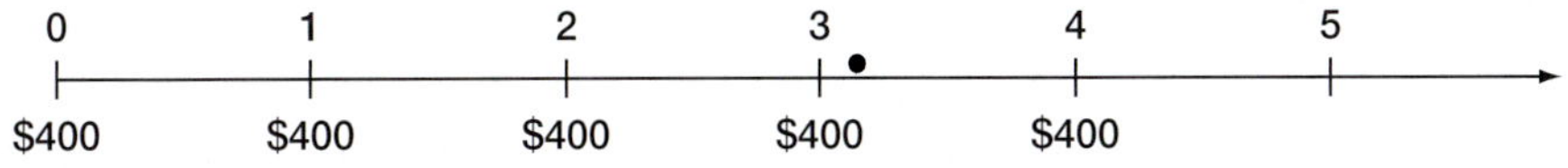

Notice how the cash flows here are the same as those for a *four*-year ordinary annuity, except that there is an extra $400 at Time 0. For practice, check to see that the value of a four-year ordinary annuity at 10 percent is $1,267.95. If we add on the extra $400, we get $1,667.95, which is the present value of this annuity due.

Time value applications abound on the Web. See, for example, www.collegeboard.com, www.1stmortgagedirectory.com, and personal.fidelity.com.

There is an even easier way to calculate the present or future value of an annuity due. If we assume cash flows occur at the end of each period when they really occur at the beginning, then we discount each one by one period too many. We could fix this by simply multiplying our answer by $(1 + r)$, where r is the discount rate. In fact, the relationship between the value of an annuity due and an ordinary annuity is just:

$$\text{Annuity due value} = \text{Ordinary annuity value} \times (1 + r) \qquad [6.3]$$

This works for both present and future values, so calculating the value of an annuity due involves two steps: (1) calculate the present or future value as though it were an ordinary annuity, and (2) multiply your answer by $(1 + r)$.

Perpetuities

We've seen that a series of level cash flows can be valued by treating those cash flows as an annuity. An important special case of an annuity arises when the level stream of cash flows continues forever. Such an asset is called a **perpetuity** because the cash flows are perpetual. Perpetuities are also called **consols**, particularly in Canada and the United Kingdom. See Example 6.7 for an important example of a perpetuity.

perpetuity
An annuity in which the cash flows continue forever.

consol
A type of perpetuity.

Because a perpetuity has an infinite number of cash flows, we obviously can't compute its value by discounting each one. Fortunately, valuing a perpetuity turns out to be the easiest possible case. The present value of a perpetuity is simply:

$$\text{PV for a perpetuity} = C/r \qquad [6.4]$$

For example, an investment offers a perpetual cash flow of $500 every year. The return you require on such an investment is 8 percent. What is the value of this investment? The value of this perpetuity is:

$$\text{Perpetuity PV} = C/r = \$500/.08 = \$6{,}250$$

This concludes our discussion of valuing investments with multiple cash flows. For future reference, Table 6.2 contains a summary of the annuity and perpetuity basic calculations we described. By now, you probably think that you'll just use online calculators to handle annuity problems. Before you do, see our nearby *Work the Web* box!

EXAMPLE 6.7 >> Preferred Stock

Preferred stock (or preference stock) is an important example of a perpetuity. When a corporation sells preferred stock, the buyer is promised a fixed cash dividend every period (usually every quarter) forever. This dividend must be paid before any dividend can be paid to regular stockholders, hence the term *preferred.*

Suppose the Fellini Co. wants to sell preferred stock at $100 per share. A very similar issue of preferred stock already outstanding has a price of $40 per share and offers a dividend of $1 every quarter. What dividend will Fellini have to offer if the preferred stock is going to sell?

The issue that is already out has a present value of $40 and a cash flow of $1 every quarter forever. Because this is a perpetuity:

$$\text{Present value} = \$40 = \$1 \times (1/r)$$
$$r = 2.5\%$$

To be competitive, the new Fellini issue will also have to offer 2.5 percent *per quarter;* so, if the present value is to be $100, the dividend must be such that:

$$\text{Present value} = \$100 = C \times (1/.025)$$
$$C = \$2.50 \text{ (per quarter)}$$

WORK THE WEB

As we discussed in the previous chapter, many Web sites have financial calculators. One of these sites is MoneyChimp, which is located at www.moneychimp.com. Suppose you are lucky enough to have $2,000,000. You think that you will be able to earn a 9 percent return. How much can you withdraw each year for the next 30 years? Here is what MoneyChimp says:

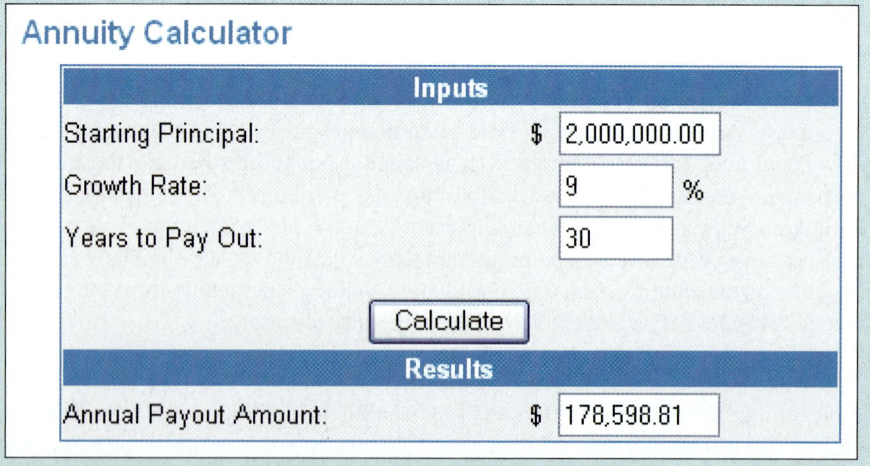

According to the MoneyChimp calculator, the answer is $178,598.81. How important is it to understand what you are doing? Calculate this one for yourself, and you should get $194,672.70. Which one is right? You are, of course! What's going on is that MoneyChimp assumes (but does not tell you) that the annuity is in the form of an annuity due, not an ordinary annuity. Recall that with an annuity due, the payments occur at the beginning of the period rather than the end of the period. The moral of the story is clear: *caveat calculator.*

<< TABLE 6.2

Summary of Annuity and Perpetuity Calculations

I. Symbols:

PV = Present value, what future cash flows are worth today

FV_t = Future value, what cash flows are worth in the future

r = Interest rate, rate of return, or discount rate per period—typically, but not always, one year

t = Number of periods—typically, but not always, the number of years

C = Cash amount

II. Future Value of *C* per Period for *t* Periods at *r* Percent per Period:

$FV_t = C \times \{[(1 + r)^t - 1]/r\}$

A series of identical cash flows is called an *annuity,* and the term $[(1 + r)^t - 1]/r$ is called the *annuity future value factor.*

III. Present Value of *C* per Period for *t* Periods at *r* Percent per Period:

$PV = C \times \{1 - [1/(1 + r)^t]\}/r$

The term $\{1 - [1/(1 + r)^t]\}/r$ is called the *annuity present value factor.*

IV. Present Value of a Perpetuity of *C* per Period:

$PV = C/r$

A *perpetuity* has the same cash flow every year forever.

Concept Questions

6.2a In general, what is the present value of an annuity of *C* dollars per period at a discount rate of *r* per period? The future value?

6.2b In general, what is the present value of a perpetuity?

COMPARING RATES: THE EFFECT OF COMPOUNDING

6.3

The last issue we need to discuss has to do with the way interest rates are quoted. This subject causes a fair amount of confusion because rates are quoted in many different ways. Sometimes the way a rate is quoted is the result of tradition, and sometimes it's the result of legislation. Unfortunately, at times, rates are quoted in deliberately deceptive ways to mislead borrowers and investors. We will discuss these topics in this section.

Effective Annual Rates and Compounding

If a rate is quoted as 10 percent compounded semiannually, this means the investment actually pays 5 percent every six months. A natural question then arises: Is 5 percent every six months the same thing as 10 percent per year? It's easy to see that it is not. If you invest \$1 at 10 percent per year, you will have \$1.10 at the end of the year. If you invest at 5 percent every six months, then you'll have the future value of \$1 at 5 percent for two periods, or:

$$\$1 \times 1.05^2 = \$1.1025$$

This is \$.0025 more. The reason is very simple. What has occurred is that your account was credited with $\$1 \times .05 = 5$ cents in interest after six months. In the following six months, you earned 5 percent on that nickel, for an extra $5 \times .05 = .25$ cents.

As our example illustrates, 10 percent compounded semiannually is actually equivalent to 10.25 percent per year. Put another way, we would be indifferent between 10 percent compounded semiannually and 10.25 percent compounded annually. Anytime we have compounding during the year, we need to be concerned about what the rate really is.

stated interest rate
The interest rate expressed in terms of the interest payment made each period. Also, quoted interest rate.

In our example, the 10 percent is called a **stated**, or **quoted**, **interest rate**. Other names are used as well. The 10.25 percent, which is actually the rate that you will earn, is called the **effective annual rate (EAR)**. To compare different investments or interest rates, we will always need to convert to effective rates. Some general procedures for doing this are discussed next.

effective annual rate (EAR)
The interest rate expressed as if it were compounded once per year.

Calculating and Comparing Effective Annual Rates

To see why it is important to work only with effective rates, suppose you've shopped around and come up with the following three rates:

Bank A: 15 percent compounded daily
Bank B: 15.5 percent compounded quarterly
Bank C: 16 percent compounded annually

Which of these is the best if you are thinking of opening a savings account? Which of these is best if they represent loan rates?

To begin, Bank C is offering 16 percent per year. Because there is no compounding during the year, this is the effective rate. Bank B is actually paying $.155/4 = .03875$ or 3.875 percent per quarter. At this rate, an investment of \$1 for four quarters would grow to:

$$\$1 \times 1.03875^4 = \$1.1642$$

The EAR, therefore, is 16.42 percent. For a saver, this is much better than the 16 percent rate Bank C is offering; for a borrower, it's worse.

Bank A is compounding every day. This may seem a little extreme, but it is very common to calculate interest daily. In this case, the daily interest rate is actually:

$$.15/365 = .000411$$

This is .0411 percent per day. At this rate, an investment of \$1 for 365 periods would grow to:

$$\$1 \times 1.000411^{365} = \$1.1618$$

The EAR is 16.18 percent. This is not as good as Bank B's 16.42 percent for a saver, and not as good as Bank C's 16 percent for a borrower.

This example illustrates two things. First, the highest quoted rate is not necessarily the best. Second, compounding during the year can lead to a significant difference between the quoted rate and the effective rate. Remember that the effective rate is what you get or what you pay.

If you look at our examples, you see that we computed the EARs in three steps. We first divided the quoted rate by the number of times that the interest is compounded. We then added 1 to the result and raised it to the power of the number of times the interest is compounded. Finally, we subtracted the 1. If we let m be the number of times the interest is compounded during the year, these steps can be summarized simply as:

$$\text{EAR} = [1 + (\text{Quoted rate}/m)]^m - 1 \qquad [6.5]$$

For example, suppose you are offered 12 percent compounded monthly. In this case, the interest is compounded 12 times a year; so *m* is 12. You can calculate the effective rate as:

$$\begin{aligned} \text{EAR} &= [1 + (\text{Quoted rate}/m)]^m - 1 \\ &= [1 + (.12/12)]^{12} - 1 \\ &= 1.01^{12} - 1 \\ &= 1.126825 - 1 \\ &= 12.6825\% \end{aligned}$$

What's the EAR?

EXAMPLE 6.8

A bank is offering 12 percent compounded quarterly. If you put $100 in an account, how much will you have at the end of one year? What's the EAR? How much will you have at the end of two years?

The bank is effectively offering 12%/4 = 3% every quarter. If you invest $100 for four periods at 3 percent per period, the future value is:

$$\begin{aligned} \text{Future value} &= \$100 \times 1.03^4 \\ &= \$100 \times 1.1255 \\ &= \$112.55 \end{aligned}$$

The EAR is 12.55 percent: $100 × (1 + .1255) = $112.55.

We can determine what you would have at the end of two years in two different ways. One way is to recognize that two years is the same as eight quarters. At 3 percent per quarter, after eight quarters, you would have:

$$\$100 \times 1.03^8 = \$100 \times 1.2668 = \$126.68$$

Alternatively, we could determine the value after two years by using an EAR of 12.55 percent; so after two years you would have:

$$\$100 \times 1.1255^2 = \$100 \times 1.2688 = \$126.68$$

Thus, the two calculations produce the same answer. This illustrates an important point. Anytime we do a present or future value calculation, the rate we use must be an actual or effective rate. In this case, the actual rate is 3 percent per quarter. The effective annual rate is 12.55 percent. It doesn't matter which one we use once we know the EAR.

Quoting a Rate

EXAMPLE 6.9

Now that you know how to convert a quoted rate to an EAR, consider going the other way. As a lender, you know you want to actually earn 18 percent on a particular loan. You want to quote a rate that features monthly compounding. What rate do you quote?

In this case, we know the EAR is 18 percent and we know this is the result of monthly compounding. Let *q* stand for the quoted rate. We thus have:

$$\begin{aligned} \text{EAR} &= [1 + (\text{Quoted rate}/m)]^m - 1 \\ .18 &= [1 + (q/12)]^{12} - 1 \\ 1.18 &= [1 + (q/12)]^{12} \end{aligned}$$

continued

We need to solve this equation for the quoted rate. This calculation is the same as the ones we did to find an unknown interest rate in Chapter 5:

$$1.18^{(1/12)} = 1 + (q/12)$$
$$1.18^{.08333} = 1 + (q/12)$$
$$1.0139 = 1 + (q/12)$$
$$q = .0139 \times 12$$
$$= 16.68\%$$

Therefore, the rate you would quote is 16.68 percent, compounded monthly.

EARs and APRs

annual percentage rate (APR)
The interest rate charged per period multiplied by the number of periods per year.

Sometimes it's not altogether clear whether or not a rate is an effective annual rate. A case in point concerns what is called the **annual percentage rate (APR)** on a loan. Truth-in-lending laws in the United States require that lenders disclose an APR on virtually all consumer loans. This rate must be displayed on a loan document in a prominent and unambiguous way.

Given that an APR must be calculated and displayed, an obvious question arises: Is an APR an effective annual rate? Put another way, if a bank quotes a car loan at 12 percent APR, is the consumer actually paying 12 percent interest? Surprisingly, the answer is no. There is some confusion over this point, which we discuss next.

The confusion over APRs arises because lenders are required by law to compute the APR in a particular way. By law, the APR is simply equal to the interest rate per period multiplied by the number of periods in a year. For example, if a bank is charging 1.2 percent per month on car loans, then the APR that must be reported is $1.2\% \times 12 = 14.4\%$. So, an APR is in fact a quoted, or stated, rate in the sense we've been discussing. For example, an APR of 12 percent on a loan calling for monthly payments is really 1 percent per month. The EAR on such a loan is thus:

$$\text{EAR} = [1 + (\text{APR}/12)]^{12} - 1$$
$$= 1.01^{12} - 1 = 12.6825\%$$

EXAMPLE 6.10 >> What Rate Are You Paying?

Depending on the issuer, a typical credit card agreement quotes an interest rate of 18 percent APR. Monthly payments are required. What is the actual interest rate you pay on such a credit card?

Based on our discussion, an APR of 18 percent with monthly payments is really $.18/12 = .015$ or 1.5 percent per month. The EAR is thus:

$$\text{EAR} = [1 + (.18/12)]^{12} - 1$$
$$= 1.015^{12} - 1$$
$$= 1.1956 - 1$$
$$= 19.56\%$$

This is the rate you actually pay.

The difference between an APR and an EAR probably won't be all that great, but it is somewhat ironic that truth-in-lending laws sometimes require lenders to be *un*truthful about the actual rate on a loan.

<< TABLE 6.3

Compounding Frequency and Effective Annual Rates

Compounding Period	Number of Times Compounded	Effective Annual Rate
Year	1	10.00000%
Quarter	4	10.38129
Month	12	10.47131
Week	52	10.50648
Day	365	10.51558
Hour	8,760	10.51703
Minute	525,600	10.51709

There are also truth-in-saving laws that require banks and other borrowers to quote an "annual percentage yield," or APY, on things like savings accounts. To make things a little confusing, an APY is an EAR. As a result, by law, the rates quoted to borrowers (APRs) and those quoted to savers (APYs) are not computed the same way.

Taking It to the Limit: A Note on Continuous Compounding

If you made a deposit in a savings account, how often could your money be compounded during the year? If you think about it, there isn't really any upper limit. We've seen that daily compounding, for example, isn't a problem. There is no reason to stop here, however. We could compound every hour or minute or second. How high would the EAR get in this case? Table 6.3 illustrates the EARs that result as 10 percent is compounded at shorter and shorter intervals. Notice that the EARs do keep getting larger, but the differences get very small.

As the numbers in Table 6.3 seem to suggest, there is an upper limit to the EAR. If we let q stand for the quoted rate, then, as the number of times the interest is compounded gets extremely large, the EAR approaches:

$$\text{EAR} = e^q - 1 \qquad [6.6]$$

where e is the number 2.71828 (look for a key labeled "e^x" on your calculator). For example, with our 10 percent rate, the highest possible EAR is:

$$\begin{aligned}\text{EAR} &= e^q - 1\\ &= 2.71828^{.10} - 1\\ &= 1.1051709 - 1\\ &= 10.51709\%\end{aligned}$$

In this case, we say that the money is continuously, or instantaneously, compounded. What is happening is that interest is being credited the instant it is earned, so the amount of interest grows continuously.

<< EXAMPLE 6.11

What's the Law?

At one time, commercial banks and savings and loan associations (S&Ls) were restricted in the interest rates they could offer on savings accounts. Under what was known as Regulation Q, S&Ls were allowed to pay at most 5.5 percent and banks were not allowed to pay more than 5.25 percent (the idea was to give the S&Ls a competitive advantage; it didn't work). The law did not say how often these rates could be compounded, however. Under Regulation Q, then, what were the maximum allowed interest rates?

continued

The maximum allowed rates occurred with continuous, or instantaneous, compounding. For the commercial banks, 5.25 percent compounded continuously would be:

$$\begin{aligned}\text{EAR} &= e^{.0525} - 1\\ &= 2.71828^{.0525} - 1\\ &= 1.0539026 - 1\\ &= 5.39026\%\end{aligned}$$

This is what banks could actually pay. Check for yourself to see that S&Ls could effectively pay 5.65406 percent.

Concept Questions

6.3a If an interest rate is given as 12 percent compounded daily, what do we call this rate?

6.3b What is an APR? What is an EAR? Are they the same thing?

6.3c In general, what is the relationship between a stated interest rate and an effective interest rate? Which is more relevant for financial decisions?

6.3d What does continuous compounding mean?

6.4 LOAN TYPES AND LOAN AMORTIZATION

Whenever a lender extends a loan, some provision will be made for repayment of the principal (the original loan amount). A loan might be repaid in equal installments, for example, or it might be repaid in a single lump sum. Because the way that the principal and interest are paid is up to the parties involved, there is actually an unlimited number of possibilities.

In this section, we describe a few forms of repayment that come up quite often, and more complicated forms can usually be built up from these. The three basic types of loans are pure discount loans, interest-only loans, and amortized loans. Working with these loans is a very straightforward application of the present value principles that we have already developed.

Pure Discount Loans

The *pure discount loan* is the simplest form of loan. With such a loan, the borrower receives money today and repays a single lump sum at some time in the future. A one-year, 10 percent pure discount loan, for example, would require the borrower to repay $1.10 in one year for every dollar borrowed today.

Because a pure discount loan is so simple, we already know how to value one. Suppose a borrower was able to repay $25,000 in five years. If we, acting as the lender, wanted a 12 percent interest rate on the loan, how much would we be willing to lend? Put another way, what value would we assign today to that $25,000 to be repaid in five years? Based on our work in Chapter 5, we know the answer is just the present value of $25,000 at 12 percent for five years:

$$\begin{aligned}\text{Present value} &= \$25{,}000/1.12^5\\ &= \$25{,}000/1.7623\\ &= \$14{,}186\end{aligned}$$

Pure discount loans are very common when the loan term is short, say, a year or less. In recent years, they have become increasingly common for much longer periods.

Treasury Bills « **EXAMPLE 6.12**

When the U.S. government borrows money on a short-term basis (a year or less), it does so by selling what are called *Treasury bills,* or *T-bills* for short. A T-bill is a promise by the government to repay a fixed amount at some time in the future, for example, 3 months or 12 months.

Treasury bills are pure discount loans. If a T-bill promises to repay $10,000 in 12 months, and the market interest rate is 7 percent, how much will the bill sell for in the market?

Because the going rate is 7 percent, the T-bill will sell for the present value of $10,000 to be repaid in one year at 7 percent, or:

Present value = $10,000/1.07 = $9,345.79

Interest-Only Loans

A second type of loan repayment plan calls for the borrower to pay interest each period and to repay the entire principal (the original loan amount) at some point in the future. Loans with such a repayment plan are called *interest-only loans.* Notice that if there is just one period, a pure discount loan and an interest-only loan are the same thing.

For example, with a three-year, 10 percent, interest-only loan of $1,000, the borrower would pay $1,000 × .10 = $100 in interest at the end of the first and second years. At the end of the third year, the borrower would return the $1,000 along with another $100 in interest for that year. Similarly, a 50-year interest-only loan would call for the borrower to pay interest every year for the next 50 years and then repay the principal. In the extreme, the borrower pays the interest every period forever and never repays any principal. As we discussed earlier in the chapter, the result is a perpetuity.

Most corporate bonds have the general form of an interest-only loan. Because we will be considering bonds in some detail in the next chapter, we will defer a further discussion of them for now.

Amortized Loans

With a pure discount or interest-only loan, the principal is repaid all at once. An alternative is an *amortized loan,* with which the lender may require the borrower to repay parts of the loan amount over time. The process of providing for a loan to be paid off by making regular principal reductions is called *amortizing* the loan.

A simple way of amortizing a loan is to have the borrower pay the interest each period plus some fixed amount. This approach is common with medium-term business loans. For example, suppose a business takes out a $5,000, five-year loan at 9 percent. The loan agreement calls for the borrower to pay the interest on the loan balance each year and to reduce the loan balance each year by $1,000. Because the loan amount declines by $1,000 each year, it is fully paid in five years.

In the case we are considering, notice that the total payment will decline each year. The reason is that the loan balance goes down, resulting in a lower interest charge each year, whereas the $1,000 principal reduction is constant. For example, the interest in the first year will be $5,000 × .09 = $450. The total payment will be $1,000 + 450 = $1,450. In the second year, the loan balance is \$4,000, so the interest is \$4,000 × .09 = \$360, and the total payment is \$1,360. We can calculate the total payment in each of the remaining years by preparing a simple *amortization schedule* as follows:

Year	Beginning Balance	Total Payment	Interest Paid	Principal Paid	Ending Balance
1	\$5,000	\$1,450	\$ 450	\$1,000	\$4,000
2	4,000	1,360	360	1,000	3,000
3	3,000	1,270	270	1,000	2,000
4	2,000	1,180	180	1,000	1,000
5	1,000	1,090	90	1,000	0
Totals		\$6,350	\$1,350	\$5,000	

Notice that in each year, the interest paid is given by the beginning balance multiplied by the interest rate. Also notice that the beginning balance is given by the ending balance from the previous year.

Probably the most common way of amortizing a loan is to have the borrower make a single, fixed payment every period. Almost all consumer loans (such as car loans) and mortgages work this way. For example, suppose our five-year, 9 percent, \$5,000 loan was amortized this way. How would the amortization schedule look?

We first need to determine the payment. From our discussion earlier in the chapter, we know that this loan's cash flows are in the form of an ordinary annuity. In this case, we can solve for the payment as follows:

$$\begin{aligned}\$5{,}000 &= C \times \{[1 - (1/1.09^5)]/.09\}\\ &= C \times [(1 - .6499)/.09]\end{aligned}$$

This gives us:

$$\begin{aligned}C &= \$5{,}000/3.8897\\ &= \$1{,}285.46\end{aligned}$$

The borrower will therefore make five equal payments of \$1,285.46. Will this pay off the loan? We will check by filling in an amortization schedule.

In our previous example, we knew the principal reduction each year. We then calculated the interest owed to get the total payment. In this example, we know the total payment. We will thus calculate the interest and then subtract it from the total payment to calculate the principal portion in each payment.

In the first year, the interest is \$450, as we calculated before. Because the total payment is \$1,285.46, the principal paid in the first year must be:

$$\text{Principal paid} = \$1{,}285.46 - 450 = \$835.46$$

The ending loan balance is thus:

$$\text{Ending balance} = \$5{,}000 - 835.46 = \$4{,}164.54$$

The interest in the second year is \$4,164.54 × .09 = \$374.81, and the loan balance declines by \$1,285.46 − 374.81 = \$910.65. We can summarize all of the relevant calculations in the following schedule:

Year	Beginning Balance	Total Payment	Interest Paid	Principal Paid	Ending Balance
1	$5,000.00	$1,285.46	$ 450.00	$ 835.46	$4,164.54
2	4,164.54	1,285.46	374.81	910.65	3,253.88
3	3,253.88	1,285.46	292.85	992.61	2,261.27
4	2,261.27	1,285.46	203.51	1,081.95	1,179.32
5	1,179.32	1,285.46	106.14	1,179.32	0.00
Totals		$6,427.30	$1,427.31	$5,000.00	

Because the loan balance declines to zero, the five equal payments do pay off the loan. Notice that the interest paid declines each period. This isn't surprising because the loan balance is going down. Given that the total payment is fixed, the principal paid must be rising each period.

If you compare the two loan amortizations in this section, you will see that the total interest is greater for the equal total payment case, $1,427.31 versus $1,350. The reason for

WORK THE WEB

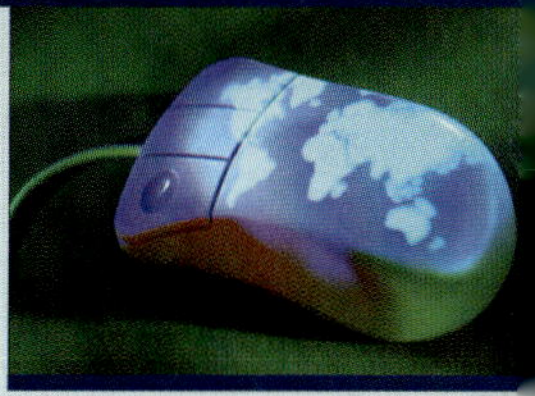

Preparing an amortization table is one of the more tedious time value of money applications. Using a spreadsheet makes it relatively easy, but there are also Web sites available that will prepare an amortization very quickly and simply. One such site is www.bankrate.com. This site has a mortgage calculator for home loans, but the same calculations apply to most other types of loans such as car loans and student loans. Suppose you graduate with a student loan of $20,000 and will repay the loan over the next 10 years at 6.25 percent. What are your monthly payments? Using the calculator we get:

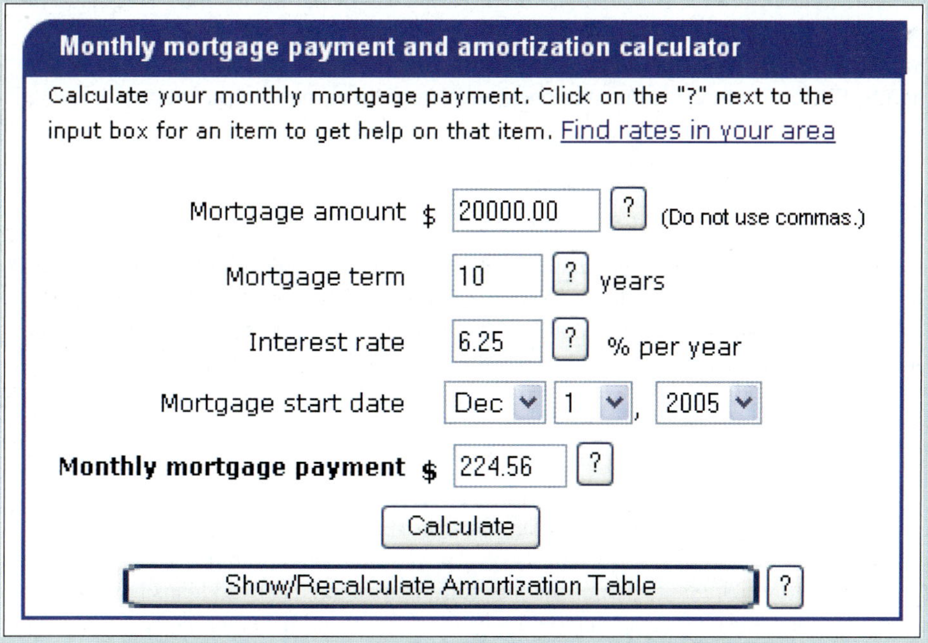

Try this example yourself and hit the "Show/Recalculate Amortization Table" button. You will find that your first payment will consist of $120.39 in principal and $104.17 in interest. Over the life of the loan you will pay a total of $6,947.22 in interest.

this is that the loan is repaid more slowly early on, so the interest is somewhat higher. This doesn't mean that one loan is better than the other; it simply means that one is effectively paid off faster than the other. For example, the principal reduction in the first year is \$835.46 in the equal total payment case as compared to \$1,000 in the first case. Many Web sites offer loan amortization schedules. See our nearby *Work the Web* box for an example.

EXAMPLE 6.13 >> Partial Amortization, or "Bite the Bullet"

A common arrangement in real estate lending might call for a 5-year loan with, say, a 15-year amortization. What this means is that the borrower makes a payment every month of a fixed amount based on a 15-year amortization. However, after 60 months, the borrower makes a single, much larger payment called a "balloon" or "bullet" to pay off the loan. Because the monthly payments don't fully pay off the loan, the loan is said to be partially amortized.

Suppose we have a \$100,000 commercial mortgage with a 12 percent APR and a 20-year (240-month) amortization. Further suppose the mortgage has a five-year balloon. What will the monthly payment be? How big will the balloon payment be?

The monthly payment can be calculated based on an ordinary annuity with a present value of \$100,000. There are 240 payments, and the interest rate is 1 percent per month. The payment is:

$$
\begin{aligned}
\$100{,}000 &= C \times [1 - (1/1.01^{240})/.01] \\
&= C \times 90.8194 \\
C &= \$1{,}101.09
\end{aligned}
$$

Now, there is an easy way and a hard way to determine the balloon payment. The hard way is to actually amortize the loan for 60 months to see what the balance is at that time. The easy way is to recognize that after 60 months, we have a 240 − 60 = 180-month loan. The payment is still \$1,101.09 per month, and the interest rate is still 1 percent per month. The loan balance is thus the present value of the remaining payments:

$$
\begin{aligned}
\text{Loan balance} &= \$1{,}101.09 \times [1 - (1/1.01^{180})/.01] \\
&= \$1{,}101.09 \times 83.3217 \\
&= \$91{,}744.69
\end{aligned}
$$

The balloon payment is a substantial \$91,744. Why is it so large? To get an idea, consider the first payment on the mortgage. The interest in the first month is \$100,000 × .01 = \$1,000. Your payment is \$1,101.09, so the loan balance declines by only \$101.09. Because the loan balance declines so slowly, the cumulative "pay down" over five years is not great.

We will close out this chapter with an example that may be of particular relevance. Federal Stafford loans are an important source of financing for many college students, helping to cover the cost of tuition, books, new cars, condominiums, and many other things. Sometimes students do not seem to fully realize that Stafford loans have a serious drawback: they must be repaid in monthly installments, usually beginning six months after the student leaves school.

Some Stafford loans are subsidized, meaning that the interest does not begin to accrue until repayment begins (this is a good thing). If you are a dependent undergraduate student under this particular option, the total debt you can run up is, at most, \$23,000. The maximum interest rate is 8.25 percent, or 8.25/12 = 0.6875 percent per month. Under the "standard repayment plan," the loans are amortized over 10 years (subject to a minimum payment of $50).

Suppose you max out borrowing under this program and also get stuck paying the maximum interest rate. Beginning six months after you graduate (or otherwise depart the ivory tower), what will your monthly payment be? How much will you owe after making payments for four years?

Given our earlier discussions, see if you don't agree that your monthly payment assuming a $23,000 total loan is $282.10 per month. Also, as explained in Example 6.13, after making payments for four years, you still owe the present value of the remaining payments. There are 120 payments in all. After you make 48 of them (the first four years), you have 72 to go. By now, it should be easy for you to verify that the present value of $282.10 per month for 72 months at 0.6875 percent per month is just under $16,000, so you still have a long way to go.

SPREADSHEET STRATEGIES

Loan Amortization Using a Spreadsheet

Loan amortization is a very common spreadsheet application. To illustrate, we will set up the problem that we examined earlier, a five-year, $5,000, 9 percent loan with constant payments. Our spreadsheet looks like this:

	A	B	C	D	E	F	G	H
1								
2				**Using a spreadsheet to amortize a loan**				
3								
4			Loan amount:	$5,000				
5			Interest rate:	0.09				
6			Loan term:	5				
7			Loan payment:	**$1,285.46**				
8				Note: payment is calculated using PMT(rate,nper,-pv,fv)				
9		*Amortization table:*						
10								
11		Year	Beginning	Total	Interest	Principal	Ending	
12			Balance	Payment	Paid	Paid	Balance	
13		1	$5,000.00	$1,285.46	$450.00	$835.46	$4,164.54	
14		2	4,164.54	1,285.46	374.81	910.65	3,253.88	
15		3	3,253.88	1,285.46	292.85	992.61	2,261.27	
16		4	2,261.27	1,285.46	203.51	1,081.95	1,179.32	
17		5	1,179.32	1,285.46	106.14	1,179.32	0.00	
18		Totals		6,427.31	1,427.31	5,000.00		
19								
20		*Formulas in the amortization table:*						
21								
22		Year	Beginning	Total	Interest	Principal	Ending	
23			Balance	Payment	Paid	Paid	Balance	
24		1	=+D4	=$D$7	=+$D$5*C13	=+D13-E13	=+C13-F13	
25		2	=+G13	=$D$7	=+$D$5*C14	=+D14-E14	=+C14-F14	
26		3	=+G14	=$D$7	=+$D$5*C15	=+D15-E15	=+C15-F15	
27		4	=+G15	=$D$7	=+$D$5*C16	=+D16-E16	=+C16-F16	
28		5	=+G16	=$D$7	=+$D$5*C17	=+D17-E17	=+C17-F17	
29								
30		Note: totals in the amortization table are calculated using the SUM formula.						
31								

Of course, it is possible to rack up much larger debts. According to a 2001 article in *Medical Economics,* two married MDs, fresh out of med school, had a combined education debt of \$544,000! Ouch! Is there a finance doctor in the house? The *smaller* of the two loans had a balance of \$234,000, and the payments on just this portion were \$1,750 per month. The interest rate was 7 percent. The article says it will take 22 years just to pay off the loan. Is that right?

In this case, we have an ordinary annuity of \$1,750 per month for some unknown number of months. The interest rate is $7/12 = .5833$ percent per month, and the present value is \$234,000. See if you agree that it will take about 260 months, or just under 22 years, to pay off the loan. Maybe MD really stands for "mucho debt!"

Concept Questions

6.4a What is a pure discount loan? An interest-only loan?

6.4b What does it mean to amortize a loan?

6.4c What is a balloon payment? How do you determine its value?

Visit us at www.mhhe.com/rwj

6.5 SUMMARY AND CONCLUSIONS

This chapter rounds out your understanding of fundamental concepts related to the time value of money and discounted cash flow valuation. Several important topics were covered, including:

1. There are two ways of calculating present and future values when there are multiple cash flows. Both approaches are straightforward extensions of our earlier analysis of single cash flows.
2. A series of constant cash flows that arrive or are paid at the end of each period is called an ordinary annuity, and we described some useful shortcuts for determining the present and future values of annuities.
3. Interest rates can be quoted in a variety of ways. For financial decisions, it is important that any rates being compared be first converted to effective rates. The relationship between a quoted rate, such as an annual percentage rate (APR), and an effective annual rate (EAR) is given by:

   $$\text{EAR} = [1 + (\text{Quoted rate}/m)]^m - 1$$

   where m is the number of times during the year the money is compounded or, equivalently, the number of payments during the year.
4. Many loans are annuities. The process of providing for a loan to be paid off gradually is called amortizing the loan, and we discussed how amortization schedules are prepared and interpreted.

The principles developed in this chapter will figure prominently in the chapters to come. The reason for this is that most investments, whether they involve real assets or financial assets, can be analyzed using the discounted cash flow (DCF) approach. As a result, the DCF approach is broadly applicable and widely used in practice. For example, the next two chapters show how to value bonds and stocks using an extension of the techniques presented in this chapter. Before going on, therefore, you might want to do some of the problems that follow.

Chapter Review and Self-Test Problems

6.1 **Present Values with Multiple Cash Flows** A first-round draft choice quarterback has been signed to a three-year, \$25 million contract. The details provide for an immediate cash bonus of \$2 million. The player is to receive \$5 million in salary at the end of the first year, \$8 million the next, and \$10 million at the end of the last year. Assuming a 15 percent discount rate, is this package worth \$25 million? How much is it worth?

6.2 **Future Value with Multiple Cash Flows** You plan to make a series of deposits in an individual retirement account. You will deposit \$1,000 today, \$2,000 in two years, and \$2,000 in five years. If you withdraw \$1,500 in three years and \$1,000 in seven years, assuming no withdrawal penalties, how much will you have after eight years if the interest rate is 7 percent? What is the present value of these cash flows?

6.3 **Annuity Present Value** You are looking into an investment that will pay you \$12,000 per year for the next 10 years. If you require a 15 percent return, what is the most you would pay for this investment?

6.4 **APR versus EAR** The going rate on student loans is quoted as 8 percent APR. The terms of the loans call for monthly payments. What is the effective annual rate (EAR) on such a student loan?

6.5 **It's the Principal That Matters** Suppose you borrow \$10,000. You are going to repay the loan by making equal annual payments for five years. The interest rate on the loan is 14 percent per year. Prepare an amortization schedule for the loan. How much interest will you pay over the life of the loan?

6.6 **Just a Little Bit Each Month** You've recently finished your MBA at the Darnit School. Naturally, you must purchase a new BMW immediately. The car costs about \$21,000. The bank quotes an interest rate of 15 percent APR for a 72-month loan with a 10 percent down payment. You plan on trading the car in for a new one in two years. What will your monthly payment be? What is the effective interest rate on the loan? What will the loan balance be when you trade the car in?

Visit us at www.mhhe.com/rwj

Answers to Chapter Review and Self-Test Problems

6.1 Obviously, the package is not worth \$25 million because the payments are spread out over three years. The bonus is paid today, so it's worth \$2 million. The present values for the three subsequent salary payments are:

$$(\$5/1.15) + (8/1.15^2) + (10/1.15^3) = (\$5/1.15) + (8/1.32) + (10/1.52)$$
$$= \$16.9721 \text{ million}$$

The package is worth a total of \$18.9721 million.

6.2 We will calculate the future values for each of the cash flows separately and then add them up. Notice that we treat the withdrawals as negative cash flows:

$\$1{,}000 \times 1.07^8 =$	$\$1{,}000 \times 1.7812 =$	\$ 1,718.19
$\$2{,}000 \times 1.07^6 =$	$\$2{,}000 \times 1.5007 =$	3,001.46
$-\$1{,}500 \times 1.07^5 =$	$-\$1{,}500 \times 1.4026 =$	−2,103.83
$\$2{,}000 \times 1.07^3 =$	$\$2{,}000 \times 1.2250 =$	2,450.09
$-\$1{,}000 \times 1.07^1 =$	$-\$1{,}000 \times 1.0700 =$	−1,070.00
Total future value	=	\$ 3,995.91

This value includes a small rounding error.

To calculate the present value, we could discount each cash flow back to the present or we could discount back a single year at a time. However, because we already know that the future value in eight years is \$3,995.91, the easy way to get the PV is just to discount this amount back eight years:

$$\text{Present value} = \$3{,}995.91/1.07^8$$
$$= \$3{,}995.91/1.7182$$
$$= \$2{,}325.64$$

We again ignore a small rounding error. For practice, you can verify that this is what you get if you discount each cash flow back separately.

6.3 The most you would be willing to pay is the present value of \$12,000 per year for 10 years at a 15 percent discount rate. The cash flows here are in ordinary annuity form, so the relevant present value factor is:

$$\text{Annuity present value factor} = (1 - \text{Present value factor})/r$$
$$= [1 - (1/1.15^{10})]/.15$$
$$= (1 - .2472)/.15$$
$$= 5.0188$$

The present value of the 10 cash flows is thus:

$$\text{Present value} = \$12{,}000 \times 5.0188$$
$$= \$60{,}225$$

This is the most you would pay.

6.4 A rate of 8 percent APR with monthly payments is actually 8%/12 = .67% per month. The EAR is thus:

$$\text{EAR} = [1 + (.08/12)]^{12} - 1 = 8.30\%$$

6.5 We first need to calculate the annual payment. With a present value of \$10,000, an interest rate of 14 percent, and a term of five years, the payment can be determined from:

$$\$10{,}000 = \text{Payment} \times \{[1 - (1/1.14^5)]/.14\}$$
$$= \text{Payment} \times 3.4331$$

Therefore, the payment is \$10,000/3.4331 = \$2,912.84 (actually, it's \$2,912.8355; this will create some small rounding errors in the following schedule). We can now prepare the amortization schedule as follows:

Year	Beginning Balance	Total Payment	Interest Paid	Principal Paid	Ending Balance
1	\$10,000.00	\$2,912.84	\$1,400.00	\$1,512.84	\$8,487.16
2	8,487.16	2,912.84	1,188.20	1,724.63	6,762.53
3	6,762.53	2,912.84	946.75	1,966.08	4,796.45
4	4,796.45	2,912.84	671.50	2,241.33	2,555.12
5	2,555.12	2,912.84	357.72	2,555.12	0.00
Totals		\$14,564.17	\$4,564.17	\$10,000.00	

6.6 The cash flows on the car loan are in annuity form, so we only need to find the payment. The interest rate is 15%/12 = 1.25% per month, and there are 72 months.

The first thing we need is the annuity factor for 72 periods at 1.25 percent per period:

$$\begin{aligned}\text{Annuity present value factor} &= (1 - \text{Present value factor})/r \\ &= [1 - (1/1.0125^{72})]/.0125 \\ &= [1 - (1/2.4459)]/.0125 \\ &= (1 - .4088)/.0125 \\ &= 47.2925\end{aligned}$$

The present value is the amount we finance. With a 10 percent down payment, we will be borrowing 90 percent of \$21,000, or \$18,900. So, to find the payment, we need to solve for C in the following:

$$\begin{aligned}\$18{,}900 &= C \times \text{Annuity present value factor} \\ &= C \times 47.2925\end{aligned}$$

Rearranging things a bit, we have:

$$\begin{aligned}C &= \$18{,}900 \times (1/47.2925) \\ &= \$18{,}900 \times .02115 \\ &= \$399.64\end{aligned}$$

Your payment is just under \$400 per month.

The actual interest rate on this loan is 1.25 percent per month. Based on our work in the chapter, we can calculate the effective annual rate as:

$$\text{EAR} = (1.0125)^{12} - 1 = 16.08\%$$

The effective rate is about one point higher than the quoted rate.

To determine the loan balance in two years, we could amortize the loan to see what the balance is at that time. This would be fairly tedious to do by hand. Using the information already determined in this problem, we can instead simply calculate the present value of the remaining payments. After two years, we have made 24 payments, so there are 72 − 24 = 48 payments left. What is the present value of 48 monthly payments of \$399.64 at 1.25 percent per month? The relevant annuity factor is:

$$\begin{aligned}\text{Annuity present value factor} &= (1 - \text{Present value factor})/r \\ &= [1 - (1/1.0125^{48})]/.0125 \\ &= [1 - (1/1.8154)]/.0125 \\ &= (1 - .5509)/.0125 \\ &= 35.9315\end{aligned}$$

The present value is thus:

$$\text{Present value} = \$399.64 \times 35.9315 = \$14{,}359.66$$

You will owe about \$14,360 on the loan in two years.

Concepts Review and Critical Thinking Questions

1. **Annuity Factors** There are four pieces to an annuity present value. What are they?
2. **Annuity Period** As you increase the length of time involved, what happens to the present value of an annuity? What happens to the future value?

3. **Interest Rates** What happens to the future value of an annuity if you increase the rate r? What happens to the present value?
4. **Present Value** What do you think about the Tri-State Megabucks lottery discussed in the chapter advertising a $500,000 prize when the lump-sum option is $250,000? Is it deceptive advertising?
5. **Present Value** If you were an athlete negotiating a contract, would you want a big signing bonus payable immediately and smaller payments in the future, or vice versa? How about looking at it from the team's perspective?
6. **Present Value** Suppose two athletes sign 10-year contracts for $80 million. In one case, we're told that the $80 million will be paid in 10 equal installments. In the other case, we're told that the $80 million will be paid in 10 installments, but the installments will increase by 5 percent per year. Who got the better deal?
7. **APR and EAR** Should lending laws be changed to require lenders to report EARs instead of APRs? Why or why not?
8. **Time Value** On subsidized Stafford loans, a common source of financial aid for college students, interest does not begin to accrue until repayment begins. Who receives a bigger subsidy, a freshman or a senior? Explain.
9. **Time Value** In words, how would you go about valuing the subsidy on a subsidized Stafford loan?
10. **Time Value** Eligibility for a subsidized Stafford loan is based on current financial need. However, both subsidized and unsubsidized Stafford loans are repaid out of future income. Given this, do you see a possible objection to having two types?

Questions and Problems

BASIC
(Questions 1–28)

1. **Present Value and Multiple Cash Flows** Conoly Co. has identified an investment project with the following cash flows. If the discount rate is 10 percent, what is the present value of these cash flows? What is the present value at 18 percent? At 24 percent?

Year	Cash Flow
1	$1,200
2	600
3	855
4	1,480

2. **Present Value and Multiple Cash Flows** Investment X offers to pay you $4,000 per year for nine years, whereas Investment Y offers to pay you $6,000 per year for five years. Which of these cash flow streams has the higher present value if the discount rate is 5 percent? If the discount rate is 22 percent?
3. **Future Value and Multiple Cash Flows** Rasputin, Inc., has identified an investment project with the following cash flows. If the discount rate is 8 percent, what is the future value of these cash flows in Year 4? What is the future value at a discount rate of 11 percent? At 24 percent?

Year	Cash Flow
1	$ 800
2	900
3	1,000
4	1,100

4. **Calculating Annuity Present Value** An investment offers $3,600 per year for 15 years, with the first payment occurring one year from now. If the required return is 10 percent, what is the value of the investment? What would the value be if the payments occurred for 40 years? For 75 years? Forever?
5. **Calculating Annuity Cash Flows** If you put up $28,000 today in exchange for a 7.65 percent, 14-year annuity, what will the annual cash flow be?
6. **Calculating Annuity Values** Your company will generate $80,000 in annual revenue each year for the next eight years from a new information database. If the appropriate interest rate is 8.2 percent, what is the present value of the savings?
7. **Calculating Annuity Values** If you deposit $2,000 at the end of each of the next 20 years into an account paying 10.5 percent interest, how much money will you have in the account in 20 years? How much will you have if you make deposits for 40 years?
8. **Calculating Annuity Values** You want to have $80,000 in your savings account 10 years from now, and you're prepared to make equal annual deposits into the account at the end of each year. If the account pays 5.8 percent interest, what amount must you deposit each year?
9. **Calculating Annuity Values** Dinero Bank offers you a $40,000, seven-year term loan at 9 percent annual interest. What will your annual loan payment be?
10. **Calculating Perpetuity Values** The Perpetual Life Insurance Co. is trying to sell you an investment policy that will pay you and your heirs $15,000 per year forever. If the required return on this investment is 8 percent, how much will you pay for the policy?
11. **Calculating Perpetuity Values** In the previous problem, suppose the Perpetual Life Insurance Co. told you the policy costs $195,000. At what interest rate would this be a fair deal?
12. **Calculating EAR** Find the EAR in each of the following cases:

Stated Rate (APR)	Number of Times Compounded	Effective Rate (EAR)
11%	Quarterly	
7	Monthly	
9	Daily	
17	Infinite	

13. **Calculating APR** Find the APR, or stated rate, in each of the following cases:

Stated Rate (APR)	Number of Times Compounded	Effective Rate (EAR)
	Semiannually	8.1%
	Monthly	7.6
	Weekly	16.8
	Infinite	26.2

14. **Calculating EAR** First National Bank charges 12.2 percent compounded monthly on its business loans. First United Bank charges 12.4 percent compounded semiannually. As a potential borrower, which bank would you go to for a new loan?
15. **Calculating APR** Copeland Credit Corp. wants to earn an effective annual return on its consumer loans of 17 percent per year. The bank uses daily compounding on its

loans. What interest rate is the bank required by law to report to potential borrowers? Explain why this rate is misleading to an uninformed borrower.

16. **Calculating Future Values** What is the future value of $800 in 20 years assuming an interest rate of 10.4 percent compounded semiannually?
17. **Calculating Future Values** Calvani Credit Bank is offering 7.1 percent compounded daily on its savings accounts. If you deposit $6,000 today, how much will you have in the account in 5 years? In 10 years? In 20 years?
18. **Calculating Present Values** An investment will pay you $24,000 in six years. If the appropriate discount rate is 11 percent compounded daily, what is the present value?
19. **EAR versus APR** Big Dom's Pawn Shop charges an interest rate of 30 percent per month on loans to its customers. Like all lenders, Big Dom must report an APR to consumers. What rate should the shop report? What is the effective annual rate?
20. **Calculating Loan Payments** You want to buy a new sports coupe for $56,850, and the finance office at the dealership has quoted you an 8.2 percent APR loan for 60 months to buy the car. What will your monthly payments be? What is the effective annual rate on this loan?
21. **Calculating Number of Periods** One of your customers is delinquent on his accounts payable balance. You've mutually agreed to a repayment schedule of $500 per month. You will charge .9 percent per month interest on the overdue balance. If the current balance is $16,500, how long will it take for the account to be paid off?
22. **Calculating EAR** Friendly's Quick Loans, Inc., offers you "three for four or I knock on your door." This means you get $3 today and repay $4 when you get your paycheck in one week (or else). What's the effective annual return Friendly's earns on this lending business? If you were brave enough to ask, what APR would Friendly's say you were paying?
23. **Valuing Perpetuities** Maybepay Life Insurance Co. is selling a perpetuity contract that pays $1,150 monthly. The contract currently sells for $58,000. What is the monthly return on this investment vehicle? What is the APR? The effective annual return?
24. **Calculating Annuity Future Values** You are to make monthly deposits of $150 into a retirement account that pays 11 percent interest compounded monthly. If your first deposit will be made one month from now, how large will your retirement account be in 20 years?
25. **Calculating Annuity Future Values** In the previous problem, suppose you make $1,800 annual deposits into the same retirement account. How large will your account balance be in 20 years?
26. **Calculating Annuity Present Values** Beginning three months from now, you want to be able to withdraw $1,200 each quarter from your bank account to cover college expenses over the next four years. If the account pays 0.50 percent interest per quarter, how much do you need to have in your bank account today to meet your expense needs over the next four years?
27. **Discounted Cash Flow Analysis** If the appropriate discount rate for the following cash flows is 13 percent compounded quarterly, what is the present value of the cash flows?

Year	Cash Flow
1	$ 900
2	750
3	0
4	1,140

28. **Discounted Cash Flow Analysis** If the appropriate discount rate for the following cash flows is 9.75 percent per year, what is the present value of the cash flows?

Year	Cash Flow
1	$2,800
2	0
3	8,100
4	1,940

INTERMEDIATE
(Questions 29–56)

29. **Simple Interest versus Compound Interest** First Simple Bank pays 8 percent simple interest on its investment accounts. If First Complex Bank pays interest on its accounts compounded annually, what rate should the bank set if it wants to match First Simple Bank over an investment horizon of 10 years?
30. **Calculating EAR** You are looking at an investment that has an effective annual rate of 16 percent. What is the effective semiannual return? The effective quarterly return? The effective monthly return?
31. **Calculating Interest Expense** You receive a credit card application from Shady Banks Savings and Loan offering an introductory rate of 1.90 percent per year, compounded monthly for the first six months, increasing thereafter to 16 percent compounded monthly. Assuming you transfer the $4,000 balance from your existing credit card and make no subsequent payments, how much interest will you owe at the end of the first year?
32. **Calculating Annuities** You are planning to save for retirement over the next 30 years. To do this, you will invest $700 a month in a stock account and $300 a month in a bond account. The return of the stock account is expected to be 11 percent, and the bond account will pay 7 percent. When you retire, you will combine your money into an account with a 9 percent return. How much can you withdraw each month from your account assuming a 25-year withdrawal period?
33. **Calculating Future Values** You have an investment that will pay you 1.16 percent per month. How much will you have per dollar invested in one year? In two years?
34. **Calculating Annuity Payments** You want to be a millionaire when you retire in 40 years. How much do you have to save each month if you can earn a 10 percent annual return? How much do you have to save if you wait 10 years before you begin your deposits? 20 years?
35. **Calculating Rates of Return** Suppose an investment offers to triple your money in 12 months (don't believe it). What rate of return per quarter are you being offered?
36. **Comparing Cash Flow Streams** You've just joined the investment banking firm of Dewey, Cheatum, and Howe. They've offered you two different salary arrangements. You can have $80,000 per year for the next two years, or you can have $60,000 per year for the next two years, along with a $35,000 signing bonus today. The bonus is paid immediately, and the salary is paid at the end of each year. If the interest rate is 10 percent compounded monthly, which do you prefer?
37. **Calculating Present Value of Annuities** Peter Piper wants to sell you an investment contract that pays equal $10,000 amounts at the end of each of the next 20 years. If you require a return of 0.7 percent per month on this investment, how much will you pay for the contract today?
38. **Calculating Rates of Return** You're trying to choose between two different investments, both of which have up-front costs of $50,000. Investment G returns $85,000 in five years. Investment H returns $175,000 in 11 years. Which of these investments has the higher return?

39. **Present Value and Interest Rates** What is the relationship between the value of an annuity and the level of interest rates? Suppose you just bought a 10-year annuity of $5,000 per year at the current interest rate of 10 percent per year. What happens to the value of your investment if interest rates suddenly drop to 5 percent? What if interest rates suddenly rise to 15 percent?
40. **Calculating the Number of Payments** You're prepared to make monthly payments of $125, beginning at the end of this month, into an account that pays 10 percent interest compounded monthly. How many payments will you have made when your account balance reaches $20,000?
41. **Calculating Annuity Present Values** You want to borrow $45,000 from your local bank to buy a new sailboat. You can afford to make monthly payments of $950, but no more. Assuming monthly compounding, what is the highest rate you can afford on a 60-month APR loan?
42. **Calculating Loan Payments** You need a 30-year, fixed-rate mortgage to buy a new home for $200,000. Your mortgage bank will lend you the money at a 6.8 percent APR for this 360-month loan. However, you can only afford monthly payments of $1,000, so you offer to pay off any remaining loan balance at the end of the loan in the form of a single balloon payment. How large will this balloon payment have to be for you to keep your monthly payments at $1,000?
43. **Present and Future Values** The present value of the following cash flow stream is $5,979 when discounted at 10 percent annually. What is the value of the missing cash flow?

Year	Cash Flow
1	$1,000
2	?
3	2,000
4	2,000

44. **Calculating Present Values** You just won the TVM Lottery. You will receive $1 million today plus another 10 annual payments that increase by $400,000 per year. Thus, in one year you receive $1.4 million. In two years, you get $1.8 million, and so on. If the appropriate interest rate is 10 percent, what is the present value of your winnings?
45. **EAR versus APR** You have just purchased a new warehouse. To finance the purchase, you've arranged for a 30-year mortgage loan for 80 percent of the $1,600,000 purchase price. The monthly payment on this loan will be $10,000. What is the APR on this loan? The EAR?
46. **Present Value and Break-Even Interest** Consider a firm with a contract to sell an asset for $115,000 three years from now. The asset costs $72,000 to produce today. Given a relevant discount rate on this asset of 13 percent per year, will the firm make a profit on this asset? At what rate does the firm just break even?
47. **Present Value and Multiple Cash Flows** What is the present value of $2,000 per year, at a discount rate of 12 percent, if the first payment is received 9 years from now and the last payment is received 25 years from now?
48. **Variable Interest Rates** A 15-year annuity pays $1,500 per month, and payments are made at the end of each month. If the interest rate is 15 percent compounded monthly for the first seven years, and 12 percent compounded monthly thereafter, what is the present value of the annuity?

49. Comparing Cash Flow Streams You have your choice of two investment accounts. Investment A is a 15-year annuity that features end-of-month $1,000 payments and has an interest rate of 10.5 percent compounded monthly. Investment B is a 9 percent continuously compounded lump-sum investment, also good for 15 years. How much money would you need to invest in B today for it to be worth as much as Investment A 15 years from now?

50. Calculating Present Value of a Perpetuity Given an interest rate of 6.5 percent per year, what is the value at date $t = 7$ of a perpetual stream of $3,000 payments that begin at date $t = 15$?

51. Calculating EAR A local finance company quotes a 14 percent interest rate on one-year loans. So, if you borrow $20,000, the interest for the year will be $2,800. Because you must repay a total of $22,800 in one year, the finance company requires you to pay $22,800/12, or $1,900, per month over the next 12 months. Is this a 14 percent loan? What rate would legally have to be quoted? What is the effective annual rate?

52. Calculating Present Values A 5-year annuity of ten $6,000 semiannual payments will begin 9 years from now, with the first payment coming 9.5 years from now. If the discount rate is 12 percent compounded monthly, what is the value of this annuity five years from now? What is the value three years from now? What is the current value of the annuity?

53. Calculating Annuities Due As discussed in the text, an ordinary annuity assumes equal payments at the end of each period over the life of the annuity. An *annuity due* is the same thing except the payments occur at the beginning of each period instead. Thus, a three-year annual annuity due would have periodic payment cash flows occurring at Years 0, 1, and 2, whereas a three-year annual ordinary annuity would have periodic payment cash flows occurring at Years 1, 2, and 3.

a. At a 9.5 percent annual discount rate, find the present value of a six-year ordinary annuity contract of $525 payments.

b. Find the present value of the same contract if it is an annuity due.

54. Calculating Annuities Due You want to buy a new sports car from Muscle Motors for $56,000. The contract is in the form of a 48-month annuity due at an 8.15 percent APR. What will your monthly payment be?

55. Amortization with Equal Payments Prepare an amortization schedule for a five-year loan of $30,000. The interest rate is 10 percent per year, and the loan calls for equal annual payments. How much interest is paid in the third year? How much total interest is paid over the life of the loan?

56. Amortization with Equal Principal Payments Rework Problem 55 assuming that the loan agreement calls for a principal reduction of $6,000 every year instead of equal annual payments.

CHALLENGE (Questions 57–75)

57. Calculating Annuity Values Bilbo Baggins wants to save money to meet three objectives. First, he would like to be able to retire 30 years from now with retirement income of $25,000 per month for 20 years, with the first payment received 30 years and 1 month from now. Second, he would like to purchase a cabin in Rivendell in 10 years at an estimated cost of $350,000. Third, after he passes on at the end of the 20 years of withdrawals, he would like to leave an inheritance of $750,000 to his nephew Frodo. He can afford to save $2,100 per month for the next 10 years. If he can earn an 11 percent EAR before he retires and an 8 percent EAR after he retires, how much will he have to save each month in years 11 through 30?

58. **Calculating Annuity Values** After deciding to buy a new car, you can either lease the car or purchase it on a 3-year loan. The car you wish to buy costs \$35,000. The dealer has a special leasing arrangement where you pay \$1 today and \$450 per month for the next three years. If you purchase the car, you will pay it off in monthly payments over the next three years at an 8% APR. You believe that you will be able to sell the car for \$23,000 in three years. Should you buy or lease the car? What break-even resale price in three years would make you indifferent between buying and leasing?

59. **Calculating Annuity Values** An All-Pro defensive lineman is in contract negotiations. The team has offered the following salary structure:

Time	Salary
0	\$8,000,000
1	\$4,000,000
2	\$4,800,000
3	\$5,700,000
4	\$6,400,000
5	\$7,000,000
6	\$7,500,000

All salaries are to be paid in a lump sum. The player has asked you as his agent to renegotiate the terms. He wants a \$9 million signing bonus payable today and a contract value increase of \$750,000. He also wants an equal salary paid every three months, with the first paycheck three months from now. If the interest rate is 4.5 percent compounded daily, what is the amount of his quarterly check? Assume 365 days in a year.

60. **Discount Interest Loans** This question illustrates what is known as *discount interest.* Imagine you are discussing a loan with a somewhat unscrupulous lender. You want to borrow \$20,000 for one year. The interest rate is 12 percent. You and the lender agree that the interest on the loan will be $.12 \times \$20{,}000 = \$2{,}400$. So the lender deducts this interest amount from the loan up front and gives you \$17,600. In this case, we say that the discount is \$2,400. What's wrong here?

61. **Calculating Annuity Values** You are serving on a jury. A plaintiff is suing the city for injuries sustained after a freak street sweeper accident. In the trial, doctors testified that it will be five years before the plaintiff is able to return to work. The jury has already decided in favor of the plaintiff. You are the foreperson of the jury and propose that the jury give the plaintiff an award to cover the following: 1) The present value of two years' back pay. The plaintiff's annual salary for the last two years would have been \$40,000 and \$43,000, respectively. 2) The present value of five years' future salary. You assume the salary will be \$45,000 per year. 3) \$100,000 for pain and suffering. 4) \$20,000 for court costs. Assume that the salary payments are equal amounts paid at the end of each month. If the interest rate you choose is a 9% EAR, what is the size of the settlement? If you were the plaintiff, would you like to see a higher or lower interest rate?

62. **Calculating EAR with Points** You are looking at a one-year loan of \$10,000. The interest rate is quoted as 10 percent plus three points. A *point* on a loan is simply 1 percent (one percentage point) of the loan amount. Quotes similar to this one are very common with home mortgages. The interest rate quotation in this example requires the borrower to pay three points to the lender up front and repay the loan later with 10 percent interest. What rate would you actually be paying here?

63. Calculating EAR with Points The interest rate on a one-year loan is quoted as 13 percent plus two points (see the previous problem). What is the EAR? Is your answer affected by the loan amount?

64. EAR versus APR There are two banks in the area that offer 30-year, $200,000 mortgages at 7.5 percent and charge a $1,500 loan application fee. However, the application fee charged by Insecurity Bank and Trust is refundable if the loan application is denied, whereas that charged by I. M. Greedy and Sons Mortgage Bank is not. The current disclosure law requires that any fees that will be refunded if the applicant is rejected be included in calculating the APR, but this is not required with nonrefundable fees (presumably because refundable fees are part of the loan rather than a fee). What are the EARs on these two loans? What are the APRs?

65. Calculating EAR with Add-On Interest This problem illustrates a deceptive way of quoting interest rates called *add-on interest.* Imagine that you see an advertisement for Crazy Judy's Stereo City that reads something like this: "$1,000 Instant Credit! 15% Simple Interest! Three Years to Pay! Low, Low Monthly Payments!" You're not exactly sure what all this means and somebody has spilled ink over the APR on the loan contract, so you ask the manager for clarification.

Judy explains that if you borrow $1,000 for three years at 15 percent interest, in three years you will owe:

$$\$1{,}000 \times 1.15^3 = \$1{,}000 \times 1.52088 = \$1{,}520.88.$$

Now, Judy recognizes that coming up with $1,520.88 all at once might be a strain, so she lets you make "low, low monthly payments" of $1,520.88/36 = $42.25 per month, even though this is extra bookkeeping work for her.

Is this a 15 percent loan? Why or why not? What is the APR on this loan? What is the EAR? Why do you think this is called add-on interest?

66. Calculating Annuity Payments This is a classic retirement problem. A time line will help in solving it. Your friend is celebrating her 35th birthday today and wants to start saving for her anticipated retirement at age 65. She wants to be able to withdraw $90,000 from her savings account on each birthday for 15 years following her retirement; the first withdrawal will be on her 66th birthday. Your friend intends to invest her money in the local credit union, which offers 8 percent interest per year. She wants to make equal annual payments on each birthday into the account established at the credit union for her retirement fund.

a. If she starts making these deposits on her 36th birthday and continues to make deposits until she is 65 (the last deposit will be on her 65th birthday), what amount must she deposit annually to be able to make the desired withdrawals at retirement?

b. Suppose your friend has just inherited a large sum of money. Rather than making equal annual payments, she has decided to make one lump-sum payment on her 35th birthday to cover her retirement needs. What amount does she have to deposit?

c. Suppose your friend's employer will contribute $1,500 to the account every year as part of the company's profit-sharing plan. In addition, your friend expects a $25,000 distribution from a family trust fund on her 55th birthday, which she will also put into the retirement account. What amount must she deposit annually now to be able to make the desired withdrawals at retirement?

67. Calculating the Number of Periods Your Christmas ski vacation was great, but it unfortunately ran a bit over budget. All is not lost, because you just received an offer in the mail to transfer your $10,000 balance from your current credit card, which charges an annual rate of 19.2 percent, to a new credit card charging a rate of 9.2 percent. How much faster could you pay the loan off by making your planned monthly payments of $200 with the new card? What if there was a 2 percent fee charged on any balances transferred?

68. Future Value and Multiple Cash Flows An insurance company is offering a new policy to its customers. Typically, the policy is bought by a parent or grandparent for a child at the child's birth. The details of the policy are as follows: The purchaser (say, the parent) makes the following six payments to the insurance company:

First birthday:	$750
Second birthday:	$750
Third birthday:	$850
Fourth birthday:	$850
Fifth birthday:	$950
Sixth birthday:	$950

After the child's sixth birthday, no more payments are made. When the child reaches age 65, he or she receives $250,000. If the relevant interest rate is 11 percent for the first six years and 7 percent for all subsequent years, is the policy worth buying?

69. Calculating a Balloon Payment You have just arranged for a $250,000 mortgage to finance the purchase of a large tract of land. The mortgage has an 8.5 percent APR, and it calls for monthly payments over the next 30 years. However, the loan has an eight-year balloon payment, meaning that the loan must be paid off then. How big will the balloon payment be?

70. Calculating Interest Rates A financial planning service offers a college savings program. The plan calls for you to make six annual payments of $8,000 each, with the first payment occurring today, your child's 12th birthday. Beginning on your child's 18th birthday, the plan will provide $20,000 per year for four years. What return is this investment offering?

71. Break-Even Investment Returns Your financial planner offers you two different investment plans. Plan X is a $10,000 annual perpetuity. Plan Y is a 10-year, $22,000 annual annuity. Both plans will make their first payment one year from today. At what discount rate would you be indifferent between these two plans?

72. Perpetual Cash Flows What is the value of an investment that pays $6,700 every *other* year forever, if the first payment occurs one year from today and the discount rate is 13 percent compounded daily? What is the value today if the first payment occurs four years from today?

73. Ordinary Annuities and Annuities Due As discussed in the text, an annuity due is identical to an ordinary annuity except that the periodic payments occur at the beginning of each period and not at the end of the period (see Question 53). Show that the relationship between the value of an ordinary annuity and the value of an otherwise equivalent annuity due is:

$$\text{Annuity due value} = \text{Ordinary annuity value} \times (1 + r)$$

Show this for both present and future values.

74. Calculating Annuities Due A 10-year annual annuity due with the first payment occurring at date $t = 7$ has a current value of $75,000. If the discount rate is 10 percent per year, what is the annuity payment amount?

75. Calculating EAR A check-cashing store is in the business of making personal loans to walk-up customers. The store makes only one-week loans at 10 percent interest per week.

a. What APR must the store report to its customers? What is the EAR that the customers are actually paying?

b. Now suppose the store makes one-week loans at 10 percent discount interest per week (see Question 60). What's the APR now? The EAR?

c. The check-cashing store also makes one-month add-on interest loans at 9 percent discount interest per week. Thus, if you borrow \$100 for one month (four weeks), the interest will be $(\$100 \times 1.09^4) - 100 = \$41.16$. Because this is discount interest, your net loan proceeds today will be \$58.84. You must then repay the store \$100 at the end of the month. To help you out, though, the store lets you pay off this \$100 in installments of \$25 per week. What is the APR of this loan? What is the EAR?

What's On the Web?

6.1 Annuity Future Value The St. Louis Federal Reserve Board has files listing historical interest rates on their Web site www.stls.frb.org. Find the link for "FRED II," then "Interest Rates." You will find listings for Moody's Seasoned Aaa Corporate Bond Yield and Moody's Seasoned Baa Corporate Bond Yield. (These rates are discussed in the next chapter.) If you invest \$2,000 per year for the next 40 years at the most recent Aaa yield, how much will you have? What if you invest the same amount at the Baa yield?

6.2 Loan Payments Finding the time necessary until you pay off a loan is simple if you make equal payments each month. However, when paying off credit cards many individuals only make the minimum monthly payment, which is generally \$10 or 2 percent to 3 percent of the balance, whichever is greater. You can find a credit card calculator at www.fincalc.com. You currently owe \$10,000 on a credit card with a 17 percent interest rate and a minimum payment of \$10 or 2 percent of your balance, whichever is greater. How soon will you pay off this debt if you make the minimum payment each month? How much total interest will you pay?

6.3 Annuity Payments Go to www.fcfcorp.com/onlinecalc.htm. Use the calculator to solve this problem. If you have \$1,500,000 when you retire and want to withdraw an equal amount for the next 30 years, how much can you withdraw each year if you earn 7 percent? What if you earn 9 percent?

6.4 Annuity Payments The St. Louis Federal Reserve Board has files listing historical interest rates on their Web site www.stls.frb.org. Find the link for "FRED II," then "Interest Rates." You will find a listing for the Bank Prime Loan Rate. The file lists the monthly prime rate since January 1949 (1949.01). What is the most recent prime rate? What is the highest prime rate over this period? If you bought a house for \$150,000 at the current prime rate on a 30-year mortgage with monthly payments, how much are your payments? If you had purchased the house at the same price when the prime rate was its highest, what would your monthly payments have been?

6.5 Loan Amortization You can find a calculator that will prepare a loan amortization table at www.hsh.com. You want to buy a home for \$200,000 on a 30-year mortgage with monthly payments at the rate quoted on the site. What percentage of your first month's payment is principal? What percentage of your last month's payment is principal? What is the total interest paid on the loan?

7 Interest Rates and Bond Valuation

In its most basic form, a bond is a pretty simple financial instrument. You loan a company some money, say $10,000. The company pays you interest on regular basis, and it repays the original loan amount of $10,000 at some point in the future. But bonds also can have unusual characteristics. For example, in 2002, Berkshire Hathaway, the company run by legendary investor Warren Buffett, issued some bonds with a surprising feature. Basically, bond buyers were required to *make* interest payments to Berkshire Hathaway for the privilege of owning the bonds, and the interest payments had to be made up front! Furthermore, if you paid $10,663.63 for one of these bonds, Berkshire Hathaway promised to pay you $10,000 in five years. Does this sound like a good deal? Investors must have thought it did; they bought $400 million worth!

This chapter takes what we have learned about the time value of money and shows how it can be used to value one of the most common of all financial assets, a bond. It then discusses bond features, bond types, and the operation of the bond market. What we will see is that bond prices depend critically on interest rates, so we will go on to discuss some very fundamental issues regarding interest rates. Clearly, interest rates are important to everybody because they underlie what businesses of all types—small and large—must pay to borrow money.

Our goal in this chapter is to introduce you to bonds. We begin by showing how the techniques we developed in Chapters 5 and 6 can be applied to bond valuation. From there, we go on to discuss bond features and how bonds are bought and sold. One important thing we learn is that bond values depend, in large part, on interest rates. We therefore close out the chapter with an examination of interest rates and their behavior.

BONDS AND BOND VALUATION

7.1

When a corporation (or government) wishes to borrow money from the public on a long-term basis, it usually does so by issuing or selling debt securities that are generically called bonds. In this section, we describe the various features of corporate bonds and some of the terminology associated with bonds. We then discuss the cash flows associated with a bond and how bonds can be valued using our discounted cash flow procedure.

Bond Features and Prices

As we mentioned in our previous chapter, a bond is normally an interest-only loan, meaning that the borrower will pay the interest every period, but none of the principal will be repaid until the end of the loan. For example, suppose the Beck Corporation wants to borrow \$1,000 for 30 years. The interest rate on similar debt issued by similar corporations is 12 percent. Beck will thus pay $.12 \times \$1{,}000 = \$120$ in interest every year for 30 years. At the end of 30 years, Beck will repay the \$1,000. As this example suggests, a bond is a fairly simple financing arrangement. There is, however, a rich jargon associated with bonds, so we will use this example to define some of the more important terms.

In our example, the \$120 regular interest payments that Beck promises to make are called the bond's **coupons**. Because the coupon is constant and paid every year, the type of bond we are describing is sometimes called a *level coupon bond.* The amount that will be repaid at the end of the loan is called the bond's **face value**, or **par value**. As in our example, this par value is usually \$1,000 for corporate bonds, and a bond that sells for its par value is called a *par value bond.* Government bonds frequently have much larger face, or par, values. Finally, the annual coupon divided by the face value is called the **coupon rate** on the bond; in this case, because $\$120/1{,}000 = 12\%$, the bond has a 12 percent coupon rate.

The number of years until the face value is paid is called the bond's time to **maturity**. A corporate bond will frequently have a maturity of 30 years when it is originally issued, but this varies. Once the bond has been issued, the number of years to maturity declines as time goes by.

coupon
The stated interest payment made on a bond.

face value
The principal amount of a bond that is repaid at the end of the term. Also, par value.

coupon rate
The annual coupon divided by the face value of a bond.

maturity
Specified date on which the principal amount of a bond is paid.

Bond Values and Yields

As time passes, interest rates change in the marketplace. The cash flows from a bond, however, stay the same. As a result, the value of the bond will fluctuate. When interest rates rise, the present value of the bond's remaining cash flows declines, and the bond is worth less. When interest rates fall, the bond is worth more.

To determine the value of a bond at a particular point in time, we need to know the number of periods remaining until maturity, the face value, the coupon, and the market interest rate for bonds with similar features. This interest rate required in the market on a bond is called the bond's **yield to maturity (YTM)**. This rate is sometimes called the bond's *yield* for short. Given all this information, we can calculate the present value of the cash flows as an estimate of the bond's current market value.

For example, suppose the Xanth (pronounced "zanth") Co. were to issue a bond with 10 years to maturity. The Xanth bond has an annual coupon of \$80. Similar bonds have a yield to maturity of 8 percent. Based on our preceding discussion, the Xanth bond will pay \$80 per year for the next 10 years in coupon interest. In 10 years, Xanth will pay \$1,000 to the owner of the bond. The cash flows from the bond are shown in Figure 7.1. What would this bond sell for?

yield to maturity (YTM)
The rate required in the market on a bond.

FIGURE 7.1 >> **Cash Flows for Xanth Co. Bond**

Cash flows

Year	0	1	2	3	4	5	6	7	8	9	10
Coupon		$80	$80	$80	$80	$80	$80	$80	$80	$80	$ 80
Face value											1,000
		$80	$80	$80	$80	$80	$80	$80	$80	$80	$1,080

As shown, the Xanth bond has an annual coupon of $80 and a face, or par, value of $1,000 paid at maturity in 10 years.

As illustrated in Figure 7.1, the Xanth bond's cash flows have an annuity component (the coupons) and a lump sum (the face value paid at maturity). We thus estimate the market value of the bond by calculating the present value of these two components separately and adding the results together. First, at the going rate of 8 percent, the present value of the $1,000 paid in 10 years is:

$$\text{Present value} = \$1{,}000/1.08^{10} = \$1{,}000/2.1589 = \$463.19$$

Second, the bond offers $80 per year for 10 years; the present value of this annuity stream is:

$$\begin{aligned}\text{Annuity present value} &= \$80 \times (1 - 1/1.08^{10})/.08\\ &= \$80 \times (1 - 1/2.1589)/.08\\ &= \$80 \times 6.7101\\ &= \$536.81\end{aligned}$$

We can now add the values for the two parts together to get the bond's value:

$$\text{Total bond value} = \$463.19 + 536.81 = \$1{,}000$$

This bond sells for exactly its face value. This is not a coincidence. The going interest rate in the market is 8 percent. Considered as an interest-only loan, what interest rate does this bond have? With an $80 coupon, this bond pays exactly 8 percent interest only when it sells for $1,000.

To illustrate what happens as interest rates change, suppose that a year has gone by. The Xanth bond now has nine years to maturity. If the interest rate in the market has risen to 10 percent, what will the bond be worth? To find out, we repeat the present value calculations with 9 years instead of 10, and a 10 percent yield instead of an 8 percent yield. First, the present value of the $1,000 paid in nine years at 10 percent is:

$$\text{Present value} = \$1{,}000/1.10^{9} = \$1{,}000/2.3579 = \$424.10$$

Second, the bond now offers $80 per year for nine years; the present value of this annuity stream at 10 percent is:

$$\begin{aligned}\text{Annuity present value} &= \$80 \times (1 - 1/1.10^{9})/.10\\ &= \$80 \times (1 - 1/2.3579)/.10\\ &= \$80 \times 5.7590\\ &= \$460.72\end{aligned}$$

We can now add the values for the two parts together to get the bond's value:

$$\text{Total bond value} = \$424.10 + 460.72 = \$884.82$$

Therefore, the bond should sell for about \$885. In the vernacular, we say that this bond, with its 8 percent coupon, is priced to yield 10 percent at \$885.

The Xanth Co. bond now sells for less than its \$1,000 face value. Why? The market interest rate is 10 percent. Considered as an interest-only loan of \$1,000, this bond only pays 8 percent, its coupon rate. Because this bond pays less than the going rate, investors are willing to lend only something less than the \$1,000 promised repayment. Because the bond sells for less than face value, it is said to be a *discount bond.*

A good bond site to visit is bonds.yahoo.com, which has loads of useful information.

The only way to get the interest rate up to 10 percent is to lower the price to less than \$1,000 so that the purchaser, in effect, has a built-in gain. For the Xanth bond, the price of \$885 is \$115 less than the face value, so an investor who purchased and kept the bond would get \$80 per year and would have a \$115 gain at maturity as well. This gain compensates the lender for the below-market coupon rate.

Another way to see why the bond is discounted by \$115 is to note that the \$80 coupon is \$20 below the coupon on a newly issued par value bond, based on current market conditions. The bond would be worth \$1,000 only if it had a coupon of \$100 per year. In a sense, an investor who buys and keeps the bond gives up \$20 per year for nine years. At 10 percent, this annuity stream is worth:

$$\begin{aligned}\text{Annuity present value} &= \$20 \times (1 - 1/1.10^9)/.10 \\ &= \$20 \times 5.7590 \\ &= \$115.18\end{aligned}$$

This is just the amount of the discount.

What would the Xanth bond sell for if interest rates had dropped by 2 percent instead of rising by 2 percent? As you might guess, the bond would sell for more than \$1,000. Such a bond is said to sell at a *premium* and is called a *premium bond.*

On-line bond calculators are available at personal.fidelity.com; interest rate information is available at money.cnn.com/markets/bondcenter and www.bankrate.com.

This case is just the opposite of that of a discount bond. The Xanth bond now has a coupon rate of 8 percent when the market rate is only 6 percent. Investors are willing to pay a premium to get this extra coupon amount. In this case, the relevant discount rate is 6 percent, and there are nine years remaining. The present value of the \$1,000 face amount is:

$$\text{Present value} = \$1{,}000/1.06^9 = \$1{,}000/1.6895 = \$591.89$$

The present value of the coupon stream is:

$$\begin{aligned}\text{Annuity present value} &= \$80 \times (1 - 1/1.06^9)/.06 \\ &= \$80 \times (1 - 1/1.6895)/.06 \\ &= \$80 \times 6.8017 \\ &= \$544.14\end{aligned}$$

We can now add the values for the two parts together to get the bond's value:

$$\text{Total bond value} = \$591.89 + 544.14 = \$1{,}136.03$$

Total bond value is therefore about \$136 in excess of par value. Once again, we can verify this amount by noting that the coupon is now \$20 too high, based on current market conditions. The present value of \$20 per year for nine years at 6 percent is:

$$\begin{aligned}\text{Annuity present value} &= \$20 \times (1 - 1/1.06^9)/.06 \\ &= \$20 \times 6.8017 \\ &= \$136.03\end{aligned}$$

This is just as we calculated.

Based on our examples, we can now write the general expression for the value of a bond. If a bond has (1) a face value of F paid at maturity, (2) a coupon of C paid per period, (3) t periods to maturity, and (4) a yield of r per period, its value is:

$$\text{Bond value} = C \times [1 - 1/(1 + r)^t]/r \quad + \quad F/(1 + r)^t$$

$$\text{Bond value} = \begin{matrix}\text{Present value}\\ \text{of the coupons}\end{matrix} + \begin{matrix}\text{Present value}\\ \text{of the face amount}\end{matrix} \qquad [7.1]$$

EXAMPLE 7.1 >> Semiannual Coupons

In practice, bonds issued in the United States usually make coupon payments twice a year. So, if an ordinary bond has a coupon rate of 14 percent, then the owner will get a total of $140 per year, but this $140 will come in two payments of $70 each. Suppose we are examining such a bond. The yield to maturity is quoted at 16 percent.

Bond yields are quoted like APRs; the quoted rate is equal to the actual rate per period multiplied by the number of periods. In this case, with a 16 percent quoted yield and semiannual payments, the true yield is 8 percent per six months. The bond matures in seven years. What is the bond's price? What is the effective annual yield on this bond?

Based on our discussion, we know the bond will sell at a discount because it has a coupon rate of 7 percent every six months when the market requires 8 percent every six months. So, if our answer exceeds $1,000, we know that we have made a mistake.

To get the exact price, we first calculate the present value of the bond's face value of $1,000 paid in seven years. This seven-year period has 14 periods of six months each. At 8 percent per period, the value is:

$$\text{Present value} = \$1{,}000/1.08^{14} = \$1{,}000/2.9372 = \$340.46$$

The coupons can be viewed as a 14-period annuity of $70 per period. At an 8 percent discount rate, the present value of such an annuity is:

$$\begin{aligned}\text{Annuity present value} &= \$70 \times (1 - 1/1.08^{14})/.08\\ &= \$70 \times (1 - .3405)/.08\\ &= \$70 \times 8.2442\\ &= \$577.10\end{aligned}$$

The total present value gives us what the bond should sell for:

$$\text{Total present value} = \$340.46 + 577.10 = \$917.56$$

To calculate the effective yield on this bond, note that 8 percent every six months is equivalent to:

$$\text{Effective annual rate} = (1 + .08)^2 - 1 = 16.64\%$$

The effective yield, therefore, is 16.64 percent.

Follow the "Investing Bonds" link at investorguide.com to learn more about bonds.

As we have illustrated in this section, bond prices and interest rates always move in opposite directions. When interest rates rise, a bond's value, like any other present value, will decline. Similarly, when interest rates fall, bond values rise. Even if we are considering a bond that is riskless in the sense that the borrower is certain to make all the payments, there is still risk in owning a bond. We discuss this next.

Interest Rate Risk

The risk that arises for bond owners from fluctuating interest rates is called *interest rate risk*. How much interest rate risk a bond has depends on how sensitive its price is to interest rate changes. This sensitivity directly depends on two things: the time to maturity and the coupon rate. As we will see momentarily, you should keep the following in mind when looking at a bond:

1. All other things being equal, the longer the time to maturity, the greater the interest rate risk.
2. All other things being equal, the lower the coupon rate, the greater the interest rate risk.

We illustrate the first of these two points in Figure 7.2. As shown, we compute and plot prices under different interest rate scenarios for 10 percent coupon bonds with maturities of 1 year and 30 years. Notice how the slope of the line connecting the prices is much steeper for the 30-year maturity than it is for the 1-year maturity. This steepness tells us that a relatively small change in interest rates will lead to a substantial change in the bond's value. In comparison, the one-year bond's price is relatively insensitive to interest rate changes.

Intuitively, we can see that the reason that longer-term bonds have greater interest rate sensitivity is that a large portion of a bond's value comes from the $1,000 face amount. The present value of this amount isn't greatly affected by a small change in interest rates if the amount is to be received in one year. Even a small change in the interest rate, however,

<< FIGURE 7.2

Interest Rate Risk and Time to Maturity

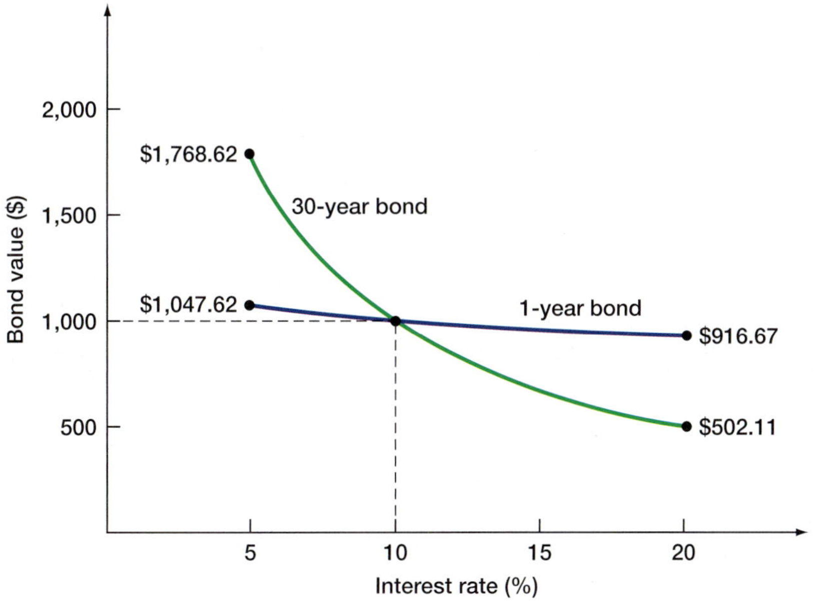

Value of a Bond with a 10 Percent Coupon Rate for Different Interest Rates and Maturities

	Time to Maturity	
Interest Rate	1 Year	30 Years
5%	$1,047.62	$1,768.62
10	1,000.00	1,000.00
15	956.52	671.70
20	916.67	502.11

once it is compounded for 30 years, can have a significant effect on the present value. As a result, the present value of the face amount will be much more volatile with a longer-term bond.

The other thing to know about interest rate risk is that, like most things in finance and economics, it increases at a decreasing rate. In other words, if we compared a 10-year bond to a 1-year bond, we would see that the 10-year bond has much greater interest rate risk. However, if you were to compare a 20-year bond to a 30-year bond, you would find that the 30-year bond has somewhat greater interest rate risk because it has a longer maturity, but the difference in the risk would be fairly small.

The reason that bonds with lower coupons have greater interest rate risk is essentially the same. As we discussed earlier, the value of a bond depends on the present value of its coupons and the present value of the face amount. If two bonds with different coupon rates have the same maturity, then the value of the one with the lower coupon is proportionately more dependent on the face amount to be received at maturity. As a result, all other things being equal, its value will fluctuate more as interest rates change. Put another way, the bond with the higher coupon has a larger cash flow early in its life, so its value is less sensitive to changes in the discount rate.

Bonds are rarely issued with maturities longer than 30 years. However, low interest rates in recent years have led to the issuance of much longer-term issues. In the 1990s, Walt Disney issued "Sleeping Beauty" bonds with a 100-year maturity. Similarly, BellSouth, Coca-Cola, and Dutch banking giant ABN AMRO all issued bonds with 100 year maturities. These companies evidently wanted to lock in the historical low interest rates for a *long* time. The current record holder for corporations looks to be Republic National Bank, which sold bonds with 1,000 years to maturity. Before these fairly recent issues, it appears the last time 100-year bonds were issued was in May 1954, by the Chicago and Eastern Railroad. Just in case you are wondering when the next 100-year bonds will be issued, you might have a long wait. The IRS has warned companies about such long-term issues and threatened to disallow the interest payment deduction on these bonds.

We can illustrate the effect of interest rate risk using the 100-year BellSouth issue and one other BellSouth issue. The following table provides some basic information on the two issues, along with their prices on December 31, 1995, July 31, 1996, and April 8, 2004.

Maturity	Coupon Rate	Price on 12/31/95	Price on 7/31/96	Percentage Change in Price 1995–96	Price on 4/08/04	Percentage Change in Price 1996–04
2095	7.00%	$1,000.00	$800.00	−20.0%	$1,092.80	+36.6 %
2033	7.50	1,040.00	960.00	− 7.7	$1,035.00	+ 7.81

Several things emerge from this table. First, interest rates apparently rose between December 31, 1995, and July 31, 1996 (why?). After that, however, they fell (why?). Second, the longer-term bond's price first lost 20 percent and then gained 36.6 percent. These swings are much greater than those on the shorter-lived issue, which illustrates that longer-term bonds have greater interest rate risk.

Finding the Yield to Maturity: More Trial and Error

Frequently, we will know a bond's price, coupon rate, and maturity date, but not its yield to maturity. For example, suppose we are interested in a six-year, 8 percent coupon bond. A broker quotes a price of $955.14. What is the yield on this bond?

We've seen that the price of a bond can be written as the sum of its annuity and lump-sum components. Knowing that there is an \$80 coupon for six years and a \$1,000 face value, we can say that the price is:

$$\$955.14 = \$80 \times [1 - 1/(1 + r)^6]/r + 1{,}000/(1 + r)^6$$

where r is the unknown discount rate, or yield to maturity. We have one equation here and one unknown, but we cannot solve it for r explicitly. The only way to find the answer is to use trial and error.

This problem is essentially identical to the one we examined in the last chapter when we tried to find the unknown interest rate on an annuity. However, finding the rate (or yield) on a bond is even more complicated because of the \$1,000 face amount.

We can speed up the trial-and-error process by using what we know about bond prices and yields. In this case, the bond has an \$80 coupon and is selling at a discount. We thus know that the yield is greater than 8 percent. If we compute the price at 10 percent:

$$\begin{aligned}\text{Bond value} &= \$80 \times (1 - 1/1.10^6)/.10 + 1{,}000/1.10^6 \\ &= \$80 \times 4.3553 + 1{,}000/1.7716 \\ &= \$912.89\end{aligned}$$

At 10 percent, the value we calculate is lower than the actual price, so 10 percent is too high. The true yield must be somewhere between 8 and 10 percent. At this point, it's "plug and chug" to find the answer. You would probably want to try 9 percent next. If you did, you would see that this is in fact the bond's yield to maturity.

Current market rates are available at www.bankrate.com.

A bond's yield to maturity should not be confused with its **current yield**, which is simply a bond's annual coupon divided by its price. In the example we just worked, the bond's annual coupon was \$80, and its price was \$955.14. Given these numbers, we see that the current yield is \$80/955.14 = 8.38 percent, which is less than the yield to maturity of 9 percent. The reason the current yield is too low is that it only considers the coupon portion of your return; it doesn't consider the built-in gain from the price discount. For a premium bond, the reverse is true, meaning that current yield would be higher because it ignores the built-in loss.

current yield
A bond's annual coupon divided by its price.

Our discussion of bond valuation is summarized in Table 7.1.

EXAMPLE 7.2

Current Events

A bond has a quoted price of \$1,080.42. It has a face value of \$1,000, a semiannual coupon of \$30, and a maturity of five years. What is its current yield? What is its yield to maturity? Which is bigger? Why?

Notice that this bond makes semiannual payments of \$30, so the annual payment is \$60. The current yield is thus \$60/1,080.42 = 5.55 percent. To calculate the yield to maturity, refer back to Example 7.1. Now, in this case, the bond pays \$30 every six months and it has 10 six-month periods until maturity. So, we need to find r as follows:

$$\$1{,}080.42 = \$30 \times [1 - 1/(1 + r)^{10}]/r + 1{,}000/(1 + r)^{10}$$

After some trial and error, we find that r is equal to 2.1 percent. But, the tricky part is that this 2.1 percent is the yield *per six months.* We have to double it to get the yield to maturity, so the yield to maturity is 4.2 percent, which is less than the current yield. The reason is that the current yield ignores the built-in loss of the premium between now and maturity.

TABLE 7.1 >>

Summary of Bond Valuation

I. Finding the Value of a Bond

Bond value $= C \times [1 - 1/(1 + r)^t]/r + F/(1 + r)^t$

where

C = Coupon paid each period

r = Rate per period

t = Number of periods

F = Bond's face value

II. Finding the Yield on a Bond

Given a bond value, coupon, time to maturity, and face value, it is possible to find the implicit discount rate, or yield to maturity, by trial and error only. To do this, try different discount rates until the calculated bond value equals the given value (or let a financial calculator do it for you). Remember that increasing the rate *decreases* the bond value.

EXAMPLE 7.3 >> Bond Yields

You're looking at two bonds identical in every way except for their coupons and, of course, their prices. Both have 12 years to maturity. The first bond has a 10 percent coupon rate and sells for $935.08. The second has a 12 percent coupon rate. What do you think it would sell for?

Because the two bonds are very similar, they will be priced to yield about the same rate. We first need to calculate the yield on the 10 percent coupon bond. Proceeding as before, we know that the yield must be greater than 10 percent because the bond is selling at a discount. The bond has a fairly long maturity of 12 years. We've seen that long-term bond prices are relatively sensitive to interest rate changes, so the yield is probably close to 10 percent. A little trial and error reveals that the yield is actually 11 percent:

$$
\begin{aligned}
\text{Bond value} &= \$100 \times (1 - 1/1.11^{12})/.11 + 1{,}000/1.11^{12} \\
&= \$100 \times 6.4924 + 1{,}000/3.4985 \\
&= \$649.24 + 285.84 \\
&= \$935.08
\end{aligned}
$$

With an 11 percent yield, the second bond will sell at a premium because of its $120 coupon. Its value is:

$$
\begin{aligned}
\text{Bond value} &= \$120 \times (1 - 1/1.11^{12})/.11 + 1{,}000/1.11^{12} \\
&= \$120 \times 6.4924 + 1{,}000/3.4985 \\
&= \$779.08 + 285.84 \\
&= \$1{,}064.92
\end{aligned}
$$

How to Calculate Bond Prices and Yields Using a Financial Calculator

Many financial calculators have fairly sophisticated built-in bond valuation routines. However, these vary quite a lot in implementation, and not all financial calculators have them. As a result, we will illustrate a simple way to handle bond problems that will work on just about any financial calculator.

continued

To begin, of course, we first remember to clear out the calculator! Next, for Example 7.3, we have two bonds to consider, both with 12 years to maturity. The first one sells for \$935.08 and has a 10 percent coupon rate. To find its yield, we can do the following:

Enter	12		100	−935.08	1,000
	N	I/Y	PMT	PV	FV
Solve for		11			

Notice that here we have entered both a future value of \$1,000, representing the bond's face value, and a payment of 10 percent of \$1,000, or \$100, per year, representing the bond's annual coupon. Also notice that we have a negative sign on the bond's price, which we have entered as the present value.

For the second bond, we now know that the relevant yield is 11 percent. It has a 12 percent coupon and 12 years to maturity, so what's the price? To answer, we just enter the relevant values and solve for the present value of the bond's cash flows:

Enter	12	11	120		1,000
	N	I/Y	PMT	PV	FV
Solve for				−1,064.92	

There is an important detail that comes up here. Suppose we have a bond with a price of \$902.29, 10 years to maturity, and a coupon rate of 6 percent. As we mentioned earlier, most bonds actually make semiannual payments. Assuming that this is the case for the bond here, what's the bond's yield? To answer, we need to enter the relevant numbers like this:

Enter	20		30	−902.29	1,000
	N	I/Y	PMT	PV	FV
Solve for		3.7			

Notice that we entered \$30 as the payment because the bond actually makes payments of \$30 every six months. Similarly, we entered 20 for N because there are actually 20 six-month periods. When we solve for the yield, we get 3.7 percent, but the tricky thing to remember is that this is the yield *per six months,* so we have to double it to get the right answer: $2 \times 3.7 = 7.4$ percent, which would be the bond's reported yield.

SPREADSHEET STRATEGIES

How to Calculate Bond Prices and Yields Using a Spreadsheet

Most spreadsheets have fairly elaborate routines available for calculating bond values and yields; many of these routines involve details that we have not discussed. However, setting up a simple spreadsheet to calculate prices or yields is straightforward, as our next two spreadsheets show:

continued

	A	B	C	D	E	F	G	H
1								
2	**Using a spreadsheet to calculate bond values**							
3								
4	Suppose we have a bond with 22 years to maturity, a coupon rate of 8 percent, and a yield to							
5	maturity of 9 percent. If the bond makes semiannual payments, what is its price today?							
6								
7	Settlement date:	1/1/00						
8	Maturity date:	1/1/22						
9	Annual coupon rate:	.08						
10	Yield to maturity:	.09						
11	Face value (% of par):	100						
12	Coupons per year:	2						
13	Bond price (% of par):	**90.49**						
14								
15	The formula entered in cell B13 is =PRICE(B7,B8,B9,B10,B11,B12); notice that face value and bond							
16	price are given as a percentage of face value.							

	A	B	C	D	E	F	G	H
1								
2	**Using a spreadsheet to calculate bond yields**							
3								
4	Suppose we have a bond with 22 years to maturity, a coupon rate of 8 percent, and a price of							
5	$960.17. If the bond makes semiannual payments, what is its yield to maturity?							
6								
7	Settlement date:	1/1/00						
8	Maturity date:	1/1/22						
9	Annual coupon rate:	.08						
10	Bond price (% of par):	96.017						
11	Face value (% of par):	100						
12	Coupons per year:	2						
13	Yield to maturity:	**.084**						
14								
15	The formula entered in cell B13 is =YIELD(B7,B8,B9,B10,B11,B12); notice that face value and bond							
16	price are entered as a percentage of face value.							
17								

In our spreadsheets, notice that we had to enter two dates, a settlement date and a maturity date. The settlement date is just the date you actually pay for the bond, and the maturity date is the day the bond actually matures. In most of our problems, we don't explicitly have these dates, so we have to make them up. For example, since our bond has 22 years to maturity, we just picked 1/1/2000 (January 1, 2000) as the settlement date and 1/1/2022 (January 1, 2022) as the maturity date. Any two dates would do as long as they are exactly 22 years apart, but these are particularly easy to work with. Finally, notice that we had to enter the coupon rate and yield to maturity in annual terms and then explicitly provide the number of coupon payments per year.

Concept Questions

7.1a What are the cash flows associated with a bond?

7.1b What is the general expression for the value of a bond?

7.1c Is it true that the only risk associated with owning a bond is that the issuer will not make all the payments? Explain.

MORE ON BOND FEATURES 7.2

In this section, we continue our discussion of corporate debt by describing in some detail the basic terms and features that make up a typical long-term corporate bond. We discuss additional issues associated with long-term debt in subsequent sections.

Securities issued by corporations may be classified roughly as *equity securities* and *debt securities*. At the crudest level, a debt represents something that must be repaid; it is the result of borrowing money. When corporations borrow, they generally promise to make regularly scheduled interest payments and to repay the original amount borrowed (that is, the principal). The person or firm making the loan is called the *creditor*, or *lender*. The corporation borrowing the money is called the *debtor*, or *borrower*.

From a financial point of view, the main differences between debt and equity are the following:

1. Debt is not an ownership interest in the firm. Creditors generally do not have voting power.
2. The corporation's payment of interest on debt is considered a cost of doing business and is fully tax deductible. Dividends paid to stockholders are *not* tax deductible.
3. Unpaid debt is a liability of the firm. If it is not paid, the creditors can legally claim the assets of the firm. This action can result in liquidation or reorganization, two of the possible consequences of bankruptcy. Thus, one of the costs of issuing debt is the possibility of financial failure. This possibility does not arise when equity is issued.

Information for bond investors can be found at www.investinginbonds.com.

Is It Debt or Equity?

Sometimes it is not clear if a particular security is debt or equity. For example, suppose a corporation issues a perpetual bond with interest payable solely from corporate income if and only if earned. Whether or not this is really a debt is hard to say and is primarily a legal and semantic issue. Courts and taxing authorities would have the final say.

Corporations are very adept at creating exotic, hybrid securities that have many features of equity but are treated as debt. Obviously, the distinction between debt and equity is very important for tax purposes. So, one reason that corporations try to create a debt security that is really equity is to obtain the tax benefits of debt and the bankruptcy benefits of equity.

As a general rule, equity represents an ownership interest, and it is a residual claim. This means that equity holders are paid after debt holders. As a result of this, the risks and benefits associated with owning debt and equity are different. To give just one example, note that the maximum reward for owning a debt security is ultimately fixed by the amount of the loan, whereas there is no upper limit to the potential reward from owning an equity interest.

Long-Term Debt: The Basics

Ultimately, all long-term debt securities are promises made by the issuing firm to pay principal when due and to make timely interest payments on the unpaid balance. Beyond this, there are a number of features that distinguish these securities from one another. We discuss some of these features next.

The maturity of a long-term debt instrument is the length of time the debt remains outstanding with some unpaid balance. Debt securities can be short-term (with maturities of one year or less) or long-term (with maturities of more than one year).[1] Short-term debt is sometimes referred to as *unfunded debt.*[2]

Debt securities are typically called *notes, debentures,* or *bonds.* Strictly speaking, a bond is a secured debt. However, in common usage, the word *bond* refers to all kinds of secured and unsecured debt. We will therefore continue to use the term generically to refer to long-term debt. Also, usually, the only difference between a note and a bond is the original maturity. Issues with an original maturity of 10 years or less are often called notes. Longer-term issues are called bonds.

The two major forms of long-term debt are public issue and privately placed. We concentrate on public-issue bonds. Most of what we say about them holds true for private-issue, long-term debt as well. The main difference between public-issue and privately placed debt is that the latter is directly placed with a lender and not offered to the public. Because this is a private transaction, the specific terms are up to the parties involved.

Information on individual bonds can be found at www.nasdbondinfo.com and www.bondresources.com.

There are many other dimensions to long-term debt, including such things as security, call features, sinking funds, ratings, and protective covenants. The following table illustrates these features for a bond issued by Pacific Gas and Electric Company. If some of these terms are unfamiliar, have no fear. We will discuss them all presently.

Features of a Pacific Gas and Electric Company Bond

Term		**Explanation**
Amount of issue	$300 million	The company issued $300 million worth of bonds.
Date of issue	03/18/2004	The bonds were sold on 03/18/2004.
Maturity	03/01/2034	The bonds mature on 03/01/2034.
Face value	$1,000	The denomination of the bonds is $1,000.
Annual coupon	6.05	Each bondholder will receive $60.50 per bond per year (6.05% of face value).
Offer price	99.512	The offer price will be 99.512% of the $1,000 face value, or $995.12, per bond.
Coupon payment dates	3/1, 9/1	Coupons of $60.50/2 = $30.25 will be paid on these dates.
Security	Mortgage	The bonds are secured with the first claim on all property owned by the company.
Sinking fund	None	The bonds have no sinking fund.
Call provision	At any time	The bonds do not have a deferred call.
Call price	Treasury rate plus 0.25%.	The bonds have a "make whole" call provision.
Rating	Moody's Baa2 S&P BBB	The bonds are at the lower end of the investment grade rating.

Many of these features will be detailed in the bond indenture, so we discuss this first.

[1]There is no universally agreed-upon distinction between short-term and long-term debt. In addition, people often refer to intermediate-term debt, which has a maturity of more than 1 year and less than 3 to 5, or even 10, years.

[2]The word *funding* is part of the jargon of finance. It generally refers to the long term. Thus, a firm planning to "fund" its debt requirements may be replacing short-term debt with long-term debt.

The Indenture

The **indenture** is the written agreement between the corporation (the borrower) and its creditors. It is sometimes referred to as the *deed of trust.*[3] Usually, a trustee (a bank, perhaps) is appointed by the corporation to represent the bondholders. The trust company must (1) make sure the terms of the indenture are obeyed, (2) manage the sinking fund (described in the following pages), and (3) represent the bondholders in default, that is, if the company defaults on its payments to them.

indenture
The written agreement between the corporation and the lender detailing the terms of the debt issue.

The bond indenture is a legal document. It can run several hundred pages and generally makes for very tedious reading. It is an important document, however, because it generally includes the following provisions:

1. The basic terms of the bonds
2. The total amount of bonds issued
3. A description of property used as security
4. The repayment arrangements
5. The call provisions
6. Details of the protective covenants

We discuss these features next.

Terms of a Bond

Terms of a Bond Corporate bonds usually have a face value (that is, a denomination) of $1,000. This is called the *principal value* and it is stated on the bond certificate. So, if a corporation wanted to borrow $1 million, 1,000 bonds would have to be sold. The par value (that is, initial accounting value) of a bond is almost always the same as the face value, and the terms are used interchangeably in practice.

Corporate bonds are usually in **registered form**. For example, the indenture might read as follows:

registered form
The form of bond issue in which the registrar of the company records ownership of each bond; payment is made directly to the owner of record.

> **Interest is payable semiannually on July 1 and January 1 of each year to the person in whose name the bond is registered at the close of business on June 15 or December 15, respectively.**

This means that the company has a registrar who will record the ownership of each bond and record any changes in ownership. The company will pay the interest and principal by check mailed directly to the address of the owner of record. A corporate bond may be registered and have attached "coupons." To obtain an interest payment, the owner must separate a coupon from the bond certificate and send it to the company registrar (the paying agent).

Alternatively, the bond could be in **bearer form**. This means that the certificate is the basic evidence of ownership, and the corporation will "pay the bearer." Ownership is not otherwise recorded, and, as with a registered bond with attached coupons, the holder of the bond certificate detaches the coupons and sends them to the company to receive payment.

bearer form
The form of bond issue in which the bond is issued without record of the owner's name; payment is made to whoever holds the bond.

There are two drawbacks to bearer bonds. First, they are difficult to recover if they are lost or stolen. Second, because the company does not know who owns its bonds, it cannot notify bondholders of important events. Bearer bonds were once the dominant type, but they are now much less common (in the United States) than registered bonds.

[3]The words *loan agreement* or *loan contract* are usually used for privately placed debt and term loans.

Security Debt securities are classified according to the collateral and mortgages used to protect the bondholder.

Collateral is a general term that frequently means securities (for example, bonds and stocks) that are pledged as security for payment of debt. For example, collateral trust bonds often involve a pledge of common stock held by the corporation. However, the term *collateral* is commonly used to refer to any asset pledged on a debt.

Mortgage securities are secured by a mortgage on the real property of the borrower. The property involved is usually real estate, for example, land or buildings. The Pacific Gas and Electric bond examined in the table is an example. The legal document that describes the mortgage is called a *mortgage trust indenture* or *trust deed.*

Sometimes mortgages are on specific property, for example, a railroad car. More often, blanket mortgages are used. A blanket mortgage pledges all the real property owned by the company.[4]

debenture
An unsecured debt, usually with a maturity of 10 years or more.

note
An unsecured debt, usually with a maturity under 10 years.

Bonds frequently represent unsecured obligations of the company. A **debenture** is an unsecured bond, for which no specific pledge of property is made. The term **note** is generally used for such instruments if the maturity of the unsecured bond is less than 10 or so years when the bond is originally issued. Debenture holders only have a claim on property not otherwise pledged, in other words, the property that remains after mortgages and collateral trusts are taken into account.

The terminology that we use here and elsewhere in this chapter is standard in the United States. Outside the United States, these same terms can have different meanings. For example, bonds issued by the British government ("gilts") are called treasury "stock." Also, in the United Kingdom, a debenture is a *secured* obligation.

At the current time, public bonds issued in the United States by industrial and financial companies are typically debentures. However, most utility and railroad bonds are secured by a pledge of assets.

The Bond Market Association Web site is www.bondmarkets.com.

Seniority In general terms, *seniority* indicates preference in position over other lenders, and debts are sometimes labeled as *senior* or *junior* to indicate seniority. Some debt is *subordinated,* as in, for example, a subordinated debenture.

In the event of default, holders of subordinated debt must give preference to other specified creditors. Usually, this means that the subordinated lenders will be paid off only after the specified creditors have been compensated. However, debt cannot be subordinated to equity.

Repayment Bonds can be repaid at maturity, at which time the bondholder will receive the stated, or face, value of the bond, or they may be repaid in part or in entirety before maturity. Early repayment in some form is more typical and is often handled through a sinking fund.

sinking fund
An account managed by the bond trustee for early bond redemption.

A **sinking fund** is an account managed by the bond trustee for the purpose of repaying the bonds. The company makes annual payments to the trustee, who then uses the funds to retire a portion of the debt. The trustee does this by either buying up some of the bonds in the market or calling in a fraction of the outstanding bonds. This second option is discussed in the next section.

There are many different kinds of sinking fund arrangements, and the details would be spelled out in the indenture. For example:

1. Some sinking funds start about 10 years after the initial issuance.
2. Some sinking funds establish equal payments over the life of the bond.

[4]Real property includes land and things "affixed thereto." It does not include cash or inventories.

3. Some high-quality bond issues establish payments to the sinking fund that are not sufficient to redeem the entire issue. As a consequence, there is the possibility of a large "balloon payment" at maturity.

The Call Provision A **call provision** allows the company to repurchase or "call" part or all of the bond issue at stated prices over a specific period. Corporate bonds are usually callable.

Generally, the call price is above the bond's stated value (that is, the par value). The difference between the call price and the stated value is the **call premium**. The amount of the call premium may become smaller over time. One arrangement is to initially set the call premium equal to the annual coupon payment and then make it decline to zero as the call date moves closer to the time of maturity.

Call provisions are often not operative during the first part of a bond's life. This makes the call provision less of a worry for bondholders in the bond's early years. For example, a company might be prohibited from calling its bonds for the first 10 years. This is a **deferred call provision**. During this period of prohibition, the bond is said to be **call protected**.

In just the last few years, a new type of call provision, a "make-whole" call, has become very widespread in the corporate bond market. With such a feature, bondholders receive approximately what the bonds are worth if they are called. Because when bondholders don't suffer a loss in the event of a call, they are "made whole."

To determine the make-whole call price, we calculate the present value of the remaining interest and principal payments at a rate specified in the indenture. For example, looking at our Pacific Gas and Electric issue, we see that the discount rate is "Treasury rate plus 0.25%." What this means is that we determine the discount rate by first finding a U.S. Treasury issue with the same maturity. We calculate the yield to maturity on the Treasury issue and then add on an additional 0.25 percent to get the discount rate we use.

Notice that, with a make-whole call provision, the call price is higher when interest rates are lower and vice versa (why?). Also notice that, as is common with a make-whole call, the Pacific Gas and Electric issue does not have a deferred call feature. Why might investors not be too concerned about the absence of this feature?

call provision
An agreement giving the corporation the option to repurchase the bond at a specified price prior to maturity.

call premium
The amount by which the call price exceeds the par value of the bond.

deferred call provision
A call provision prohibiting the company from redeeming the bond prior to a certain date.

call protected bond
A bond that, during a certain period, cannot be redeemed by the issuer.

protective covenant
A part of the indenture limiting certain actions that might be taken during the term of the loan, usually to protect the lender's interest.

Protective Covenants A **protective covenant** is that part of the indenture or loan agreement that limits certain actions a company might otherwise wish to take during the term of the loan. Protective covenants can be classified into two types: negative covenants and positive (or affirmative) covenants.

A *negative covenant* is a "thou shalt not" type of covenant. It limits or prohibits actions that the company might take. Here are some typical examples:

1. The firm must limit the amount of dividends it pays according to some formula.
2. The firm cannot pledge any assets to other lenders.
3. The firm cannot merge with another firm.
4. The firm cannot sell or lease any major assets without approval by the lender.
5. The firm cannot issue additional long-term debt.

A *positive covenant* is a "thou shalt" type of covenant. It specifies an action that the company agrees to take or a condition the company must abide by. Here are some examples:

1. The company must maintain its working capital at or above some specified minimum level.
2. The company must periodically furnish audited financial statements to the lender.
3. The firm must maintain any collateral or security in good condition.

Want detailed information on the amount and terms of the debt issued by a particular firm? Check out their latest financial statements by searching SEC filings at www.sec.gov.

This is only a partial list of covenants; a particular indenture may feature many different ones.

Concept Questions

7.2a What are the distinguishing features of debt as compared to equity?

7.2b What is the indenture? What are protective covenants? Give some examples.

7.2c What is a sinking fund?

7.3 BOND RATINGS

Firms frequently pay to have their debt rated. The two leading bond-rating firms are Moody's and Standard & Poor's (S&P). The debt ratings are an assessment of the creditworthiness of the corporate issuer. The definitions of creditworthiness used by Moody's and S&P are based on how likely the firm is to default and the protection creditors have in the event of a default.

It is important to recognize that bond ratings are concerned *only* with the possibility of default. Earlier, we discussed interest rate risk, which we defined as the risk of a change in the value of a bond resulting from a change in interest rates. Bond ratings do not address this issue. As a result, the price of a highly rated bond can still be quite volatile.

Bond ratings are constructed from information supplied by the corporation. The rating classes and some information concerning them are shown in the following table.

	Investment-Quality Bond Ratings				Low-Quality, Speculative, and/or "Junk" Bond Ratings					
	High Grade		Medium Grade		Low Grade		Very Low Grade			
Standard & Poor's	**AAA**	**AA**	**A**	**BBB**	**BB**	**B**	**CCC**	**CC**	**C**	**D**
Moody's	**Aaa**	**Aa**	**A**	**Baa**	**Ba**	**B**	**Caa**	**Ca**	**C**	**D**

Moody's	**S&P**	
Aaa	AAA	Debt rated Aaa and AAA has the highest rating. Capacity to pay interest and principal is extremely strong.
Aa	AA	Debt rated Aa and AA has a very strong capacity to pay interest and repay principal. Together with the highest rating, this group comprises the high-grade bond class.
A	A	Debt rated A has a strong capacity to pay interest and repay principal, although it is somewhat more susceptible to the adverse effects of changes in circumstances and economic conditions than debt in high-rated categories.
Baa	BBB	Debt rated Baa and BBB is regarded as having an adequate capacity to pay interest and repay principal. Whereas it normally exhibits adequate protection parameters, adverse economic conditions or changing circumstances are more likely to lead to a weakened capacity to pay interest and repay principal for debt in this category than in higher-rated categories. These bonds are medium-grade obligations.
Ba; B Caa Ca	BB; B CCC CC	Debt rated in these categories is regarded, on balance, as predominantly speculative with respect to capacity to pay interest and repay principal in accordance with the terms of the obligation. BB and Ba indicate the lowest degree of speculation, and CC and Ca the highest degree of speculation. Although such debt is likely to have some quality and protective characteristics, these are outweighed by large uncertainties or major risk exposures to adverse conditions. Some issues may be in default.
C	C	This rating is reserved for income bonds on which no interest is being paid.
D	D	Debt rated D is in default, and payment of interest and/or repayment of principal is in arrears.

NOTE: At times, both Moody's and S&P use adjustments (called notches) to these ratings. S&P uses plus and minus signs: A+ is the strongest A rating and A− the weakest. Moody's uses a 1, 2, or 3 designation, with 1 being the highest.

The highest rating a firm's debt can have is AAA or Aaa, and such debt is judged to be the best quality and to have the lowest degree of risk. For example, the 100-year BellSouth issue we discussed earlier was rated AAA. This rating is not awarded very often; AA or Aa ratings indicate very good quality debt and are much more common. The lowest rating is D, for debt that is in default.

Want to know what criteria are commonly used to rate corporate and municipal bonds? Go to www.standardandpoors.com, www.moodys.com, or www.fitchinv.com.

A large part of corporate borrowing takes the form of low-grade, or "junk," bonds. If these low-grade corporate bonds are rated at all, they are rated below investment grade by the major rating agencies. Investment-grade bonds are bonds rated at least BBB by S&P or Baa by Moody's.

Rating agencies don't always agree. For example, some bonds are known as "crossover" or "5B" bonds. The reason is that they are rated triple-B (or Baa) by one rating agency and double-B (or Ba) by another, a "split rating." For example, in March 2004, Rogers Communication sold an issue of 10-year notes rated BBB– by S&P and Ba2 by Moody's.

A bond's credit rating can change as the issuer's financial strength improves or deteriorates. For example, in 2004, S&P downgraded Sun Microsystems' long-term debt from BBB to BB+, pushing it from investment grade into junk bond status. Bonds that drop into junk territory like this are called fallen angels. Why was Sun Microsystems downgraded? A lot of reasons, but S&P was particularly concerned with weak and inconsistent profitability and the belief that Sun would be challenged to profitably expand its market presence.

Credit ratings are important because defaults really do occur, and, when they do, investors can lose heavily. For example, in 2000, AmeriServe Food Distribution, Inc., which supplied restaurants such as Burger King with everything from burgers to giveaway toys, defaulted on $200 million in junk bonds. After the default, the bonds traded at just 18 cents on the dollar, leaving investors with a loss of more than $160 million.

Even worse in AmeriServe's case, the bonds had been issued only four months earlier, thereby making AmeriServe an NCAA champion. While that might be a good thing for a college basketball team such as the University of Kentucky Wildcats, in the bond market it means "No Coupon At All," and it's not a good thing for investors.

If you're nervous about the level of debt piled up by the U.S. government, *don't* go to www.publicdebt.treas.gov, or to www.brillig.com/debt_clock! Learn all about government bonds at www.ny.frb.org.

Concept Questions

7.3a What is a junk bond?

7.3b What does a bond rating say about the risk of fluctuations in a bond's value resulting from interest rate changes?

SOME DIFFERENT TYPES OF BONDS 7.4

Thus far, we have considered only "plain vanilla" corporate bonds. In this section, we briefly look at bonds issued by governments and also at bonds with unusual features.

Government Bonds

The biggest borrower in the world—by a wide margin—is everybody's favorite family member, Uncle Sam. In 2004, the total debt of the U.S. government was $7.1 *trillion,* or about $24,000 per citizen (and growing!). When the government wishes to borrow money for more than one year, it sells what are known as Treasury notes and bonds to the public (in fact, it does so every month). Currently, outstanding Treasury notes and bonds have original maturities ranging from 2 to 30 years.

Most U.S. Treasury issues are just ordinary coupon bonds. Some older issues are callable, and a very few have some unusual features. There are two important things to keep in mind, however. First, U.S. Treasury issues, unlike essentially all other bonds, have no default risk because (we hope) the Treasury can always come up with the money to make the payments. Second, Treasury issues are exempt from state income taxes (though not federal income taxes). In other words, the coupons you receive on a Treasury note or bond are only taxed at the federal level.

State and local governments also borrow money by selling notes and bonds. Such issues are called *municipal* notes and bonds, or just "munis." Unlike Treasury issues, munis have varying degrees of default risk, and, in fact, they are rated much like corporate issues. Also, they are almost always callable. The most intriguing thing about munis is that their coupons are exempt from federal income taxes (though not necessarily state income taxes), which makes them very attractive to high-income, high–tax bracket investors.

Because of the enormous tax break they receive, the yields on municipal bonds are much lower than the yields on taxable bonds. For example, in April 2004, long-term Aa-rated corporate bonds were yielding about 5.91 percent. At the same time, long-term Aa munis were yielding about 4.24 percent. Suppose an investor was in a 30 percent tax bracket. All else being the same, would this investor prefer a Aa corporate bond or a Aa municipal bond?

Another good bond market site is money.cnn.com.

To answer, we need to compare the *aftertax* yields on the two bonds. Ignoring state and local taxes, the muni pays 4.24 percent on both a pretax and an aftertax basis. The corporate issue pays 5.91 percent before taxes, but it only pays $5.91 \times (1 - .30) = .041$, or 4.1 percent, once we account for the 30 percent tax bite. Given this, the muni has a better yield.

EXAMPLE 7.4 >> Taxable versus Municipal Bonds

Suppose taxable bonds are currently yielding 8 percent, while at the same time, munis of comparable risk and maturity are yielding 6 percent. Which is more attractive to an investor in a 40 percent bracket? What is the break-even tax rate? How do you interpret this rate?

For an investor in a 40 percent tax bracket, a taxable bond yields $8 \times (1 - .40) = 4.8$ percent after taxes, so the muni is much more attractive. The break-even tax rate is the tax rate at which an investor would be indifferent between a taxable and a nontaxable issue. If we let t^* stand for the break-even tax rate, then we can solve for it as follows:

$$
\begin{aligned}
.08 \times (1 - t^*) &= .06 \\
1 - t^* &= .06/.08 = .75 \\
t^* &= .25
\end{aligned}
$$

Thus, an investor in a 25 percent tax bracket would make 6 percent after taxes from either bond.

Zero Coupon Bonds

zero coupon bond
A bond that makes no coupon payments, thus initially priced at a deep discount.

A bond that pays no coupons at all must be offered at a price that is much lower than its stated value. Such bonds are called **zero coupon bonds**, or just *zeroes*.[5]

[5] A bond issued with a very low coupon rate (as opposed to a zero coupon rate) is an original-issue discount (OID) bond.

Year	Beginning Value	Ending Value	Implicit Interest Expense	Straight-Line Interest Expense
1	$497	$ 572	$ 75	$100.60
2	572	658	86	100.60
3	658	756	98	100.60
4	756	870	114	100.60
5	870	1,000	130	100.60
Total			$503	$503.00

<< TABLE 7.2

Interest Expense for EIN's Zeroes

Suppose the Eight-Inch Nails (EIN) Company issues a $1,000–face value, five-year zero coupon bond. The initial price is set at $497. It is straightforward to verify that, at this price, the bond yields 15 percent to maturity. The total interest paid over the life of the bond is $\$1,000 - 497 = \$503$.

For tax purposes, the issuer of a zero coupon bond deducts interest every year even though no interest is actually paid. Similarly, the owner must pay taxes on interest accrued every year, even though no interest is actually received.

The way in which the yearly interest on a zero coupon bond is calculated is governed by tax law. Before 1982, corporations could calculate the interest deduction on a straight-line basis. For EIN, the annual interest deduction would have been $\$503/5 = \$100.60$ per year.

Under current tax law, the implicit interest is determined by amortizing the loan. We do this by first calculating the bond's value at the beginning of each year. For example, after one year, the bond will have four years until maturity, so it will be worth $\$1,000/1.15^4 = \$572$; the value in two years will be $\$1,000/1.15^3 = \$658$; and so on. The implicit interest each year is simply the change in the bond's value for the year. The values and interest expenses for the EIN bond are listed in Table 7.2.

Notice that under the old rules, zero coupon bonds were more attractive because the deductions for interest expense were larger in the early years (compare the implicit interest expense with the straight-line expense).

Under current tax law, EIN could deduct $75 in interest paid the first year and the owner of the bond would pay taxes on $75 in taxable income (even though no interest was actually received). This second tax feature makes taxable zero coupon bonds less attractive to individuals. However, they are still a very attractive investment for tax-exempt investors with long-term dollar-denominated liabilities, such as pension funds, because the future dollar value is known with relative certainty.

Some bonds are zero coupon bonds for only part of their lives. For example, General Motors has a debenture outstanding that matures on March 15, 2036. For the first 20 years of its life, no coupon payments will be made, but, after 20 years, it begins paying coupons at a rate of 7.75 percent per year, payable semiannually.

Floating-Rate Bonds

The conventional bonds we have talked about in this chapter have fixed-dollar obligations because the coupon rate is set as a fixed percentage of the par value. Similarly, the principal is set equal to the par value. Under these circumstances, the coupon payment and principal are completely fixed.

With *floating-rate bonds (floaters),* the coupon payments are adjustable. The adjustments are tied to an interest rate index such as the Treasury bill interest rate or the 30-year Treasury bond rate. The EE Savings Bonds we mentioned back in Chapter 5 are a good example of a floater. For EE bonds purchased after May 1, 1997, the interest rate is adjusted every six months. The rate that the bonds earn for a particular six-month period is determined by taking 90 percent of the average yield on ordinary five-year Treasury notes over the previous six months.

The value of a floating-rate bond depends on exactly how the coupon payment adjustments are defined. In most cases, the coupon adjusts with a lag to some base rate. For example, suppose a coupon rate adjustment is made on June 1. The adjustment might be based on the simple average of Treasury bond yields during the previous three months. In addition, the majority of floaters have the following features:

1. The holder has the right to redeem his/her note at par on the coupon payment date after some specified amount of time. This is called a *put* provision, and it is discussed in the following section.
2. The coupon rate has a floor and a ceiling, meaning that the coupon is subject to a minimum and a maximum. In this case, the coupon rate is said to be "capped," and the upper and lower rates are sometimes called the *collar.*

Official information on U.S. inflation-indexed bonds is at www.publicdebt.treas.gov/gsr/gsrlist.htm.

A particularly interesting type of floating-rate bond is an *inflation-linked* bond. Such bonds have coupons that are adjusted according to the rate of inflation (the principal amount may be adjusted as well). The U.S. Treasury began issuing such bonds in January of 1997. The issues are sometimes called "TIPS," or Treasury Inflation Protection Securities. Other countries, including Canada, Israel, and Britain, have issued similar securities.

Other Types of Bonds

Many bonds have unusual or exotic features. So-called catastrophe, or cat, bonds provide an interesting example. In 2002, Syndicate 33, a member of Lloyd's of London, announced the placement of $33 million in "act of God" bonds. The way these bonds work is that Syndicate 33 will pay interest and principal in the usual way unless an earthquake occurs in California or the New Madrid seismic region. If this happens, interest and principal payments on the bonds can be suspended. A similar bond was issued by Swiss Reinsurance in 2003. These cat bonds covered a North Atlantic hurricane, a California earthquake, a European windstorm, and a Japanese earthquake.

Most cat bonds are issued by insurance companies to cover extraordinary losses, but they can also be issued by other companies. In what is believed to be the largest cat bond issued by a nonfinancial issuer, the French power company Electricité de France issued $242 million cat bonds in 2003 that were linked to wind speed in France. By the way, just in case you think cat bonds are unimportant, S&P estimated that more than $2 billion worth of them were issued in 2003.

An extra feature also explains why the Berkshire Hathaway bond we described at the beginning of the chapter actually had what amounts to a negative coupon rate. The buyers of these bonds also received the right to purchase shares of stock in Berkshire at a fixed price per share over the subsequent five years. Such a right, which is called a warrant, would be very valuable if the stock price climbed substantially (a later chapter discusses this subject in greater depth).

As these examples illustrate, bond features are really only limited by the imaginations of the parties involved. Unfortunately, there are far too many variations for us to cover in detail here. We therefore close out this discussion by mentioning only a few of the more common types.

Income bonds are similar to conventional bonds, except that coupon payments are dependent on company income. Specifically, coupons are paid to bondholders only if the

IN THEIR OWN WORDS . . .

Edward I. Altman on Junk Bonds

>> **One of the** most important developments in corporate finance over the last 20 years has been the reemergence of publicly owned and traded low-rated corporate debt. Originally offered to the public in the early 1900s to help finance some of our emerging growth industries, these high-yield, high-risk bonds virtually disappeared after the rash of bond defaults during the Depression. Recently, however, the junk bond market has been catapulted from being an insignificant element in the corporate fixed-income market to being one of the fastest-growing and most controversial types of financing mechanisms.

The term *junk* emanates from the dominant type of low-rated bond issues outstanding prior to 1977 when the "market" consisted almost exclusively of original-issue investment-grade bonds that fell from their lofty status to a higher–default risk, speculative-grade level. These so-called fallen angels amounted to about $8.5 billion in 1977. At the end of 1998, fallen angels comprised about 10 percent of the $450 billion publicly owned junk bond market.

Beginning in 1977, issuers began to go directly to the public to raise capital for growth purposes. Early users of junk bonds were energy-related firms, cable TV companies, airlines, and assorted other industrial companies. The emerging growth company rationale coupled with relatively high returns to early investors helped legitimize this sector.

By far the most important and controversial aspect of junk bond financing was its role in the corporate restructuring movement from 1985 to 1989. High-leverage transactions and acquisitions, such as leveraged buyouts (LBOs), which occur when a firm is taken private, and leveraged recapitalizations (debt-for-equity swaps), transformed the face of corporate America, leading to a heated debate as to the economic and social consequences of firms' being transformed with debt-equity ratios of at least 6:1.

These transactions involved increasingly large companies, and the multibillion-dollar takeover became fairly common, finally capped by the huge $25+ billion RJR Nabisco LBO in 1989. LBOs were typically financed with about 60 percent senior bank and insurance company debt, about 25–30 percent subordinated public debt (junk bonds), and 10–15 percent equity. The junk bond segment is sometimes referred to as "mezzanine" financing because it lies between the "balcony" senior debt and the "basement" equity.

These restructurings resulted in huge fees to advisors and underwriters and huge premiums to the old shareholders who were bought out, and they continued as long as the market was willing to buy these new debt offerings at what appeared to be a favorable risk-return trade-off. The bottom fell out of the market in the last six months of 1989 due to a number of factors including a marked increase in defaults, government regulation against S&Ls' holding junk bonds, and a recession.

The default rate rose dramatically to 4 percent in 1989 and then skyrocketed in 1990 and 1991 to 10.1 percent and 10.3 percent, respectively, with about $19 billion of defaults in 1991. By the end of 1990, the pendulum of growth in new junk bond issues and returns to investors swung dramatically downward as prices plummeted and the new-issue market all but dried up. The year 1991 was a pivotal year in that, despite record defaults, bond prices and new issues rebounded strongly as the prospects for the future brightened.

In the early 1990s, the financial market was questioning the very survival of the junk bond market. The answer was a resounding "yes," as the amount of new issues soared to record annual levels of $40 billion in 1992 and almost $60 billion in 1993, and in 1997 reached an impressive $119 billion. Coupled with plummeting default rates (under 2.0 percent each year in the 1993–97 period) and attractive returns in these years, the risk-return characteristics have been extremely favorable.

The junk bond market in the late 1990s was a quieter one compared to that of the 1980s, but, in terms of growth and returns, it was healthier than ever before. While the low default rates in 1992–98 helped to fuel new investment funds and new issues, the market experienced its ups and downs in subsequent years. Indeed, default rates started to rise in 1999 and accelerated in 2000 and 2001. The latter year saw defaults reach record levels as the economy slipped into a recession and investors suffered from the excesses of lending in the late 1990s. Despite these highly volatile events and problems with liquidity, we are convinced that high-yield bonds will be a major source of corporate debt financing and a legitimate asset class for investors.

Edward I. Altman is Max L. Heine Professor of Finance and vice director of the Salomon Center at the Stern School of Business of New York University. He is widely recognized as one of the world's experts on bankruptcy and credit analysis as well as the high-yield, or junk bond, market.

firm's income is sufficient. This would appear to be an attractive feature, but income bonds are not very common.

A *convertible bond* can be swapped for a fixed number of shares of stock anytime before maturity at the holder's option. Convertibles are relatively common, but the number has been decreasing in recent years.

A *put bond* allows the *holder* to force the issuer to buy the bond back at a stated price. For example, International Paper Co. has bonds outstanding that allow the holder to force International Paper to buy the bonds back at 100 percent of face value given that certain "risk" events happen. One such event is a change in credit rating from investment grade to lower than investment grade by Moody's or S&P. The put feature is therefore just the reverse of the call provision.

A given bond may have many unusual features. Two of the most recent exotic bonds are CoCo bonds, which have a coupon payment, and NoNo bonds, which are zero coupon bonds. CoCo and NoNo bonds are contingent convertible, putable, callable, subordinated bonds. The contingent convertible clause is similar to the normal conversion feature, except the contingent feature must be met. For example, a contingent feature may require that the company stock trade at 110 percent of the conversion price for 20 out of the most recent 30 days. Valuing a bond of this sort can be quite complex, and the yield to maturity calculation is often meaningless. For example, in 2004, a NoNo issued by Merrill Lynch was selling at a price of $1,052.07, with a yield to maturity of negative 18.36 percent. At the same time, a NoNo issued by Countrywide Financial was selling for $1,412.50, which implied a yield to maturity of negative 28.59 percent!

Concept Questions

7.4a Why might an income bond be attractive to a corporation with volatile cash flows? Can you think of a reason why income bonds are not more popular?

7.4b What do you think would be the effect of a put feature on a bond's coupon? How about a convertibility feature? Why?

7.5 BOND MARKETS

Bonds are bought and sold in enormous quantities every day. You may be surprised to learn that the trading volume in bonds on a typical day is many, many times larger than the trading volume in stocks (by trading volume, we simply mean the amount of money that changes hands). Here is a finance trivia question: What is the largest securities market in the world? Most people would guess the New York Stock Exchange. In fact, the largest securities market in the world in terms of trading volume is the U.S. Treasury market.

How Bonds Are Bought and Sold

As we mentioned all the way back in Chapter 1, most trading in bonds takes place over the counter, or OTC. Recall that this means that there is no particular place where buying and selling occur. Instead, dealers around the country (and around the world) stand ready to buy and sell. The various dealers are connected electronically.

One reason the bond markets are so big is that the number of bond issues far exceeds the number of stock issues. There are two reasons for this. First, a corporation would typically have only one common stock issue outstanding (there are exceptions to this that we discuss in our next chapter). However, a single large corporation could easily have a dozen or more

WORK THE WEB

Bond quotes have become more available with the rise of the Internet. One site where you can find current bond prices is www.nasdbondinfo.com. We went to the Web site and searched for bonds issued by Chevron-Texaco. Here is a look at one of the bonds we found:

Issue: CVX.GP TEXACO CAPITAL INC. 7.50 03/01/2043 — Time and Sales | Descriptive Data

In Portfolio	Rating Moody's/S&P	Last Sale Date	Last Sale Price	Last Sale Yield	Most Recent Date	Most Recent Price	Most Recent Yield
☐	Aa3 / AA	04/01/2004	113.75	5.52289	04/01/2004	113.75	5.52289

The bond has a coupon rate of 7.50 percent, and matures on March 1, 2043. The last sale on this bond was at a price of 113.75 percent of par, which gives a yield to maturity of about 5.52 percent. After finding the quotes, we followed the Descriptive Data link for this bond. The detailed information for this bond is:

Detailed Bond Information

Symbol: CVX.GP
Issue: CVX 7.500 03/01/43 '13
Cusip: 881685BD2
Bond Type: DEBENTURE
Moody's/S&P Rating Aa3 / AA
Payment Frequency: Semiannually
Industry: FINANCIAL
Industry Subsector: Financial - Other
Coupon Type: Fixed:Plain Vanilla Fixed Coupon
Callable: Y
Other Features:

Call Schedule

Call Date	Call Price
03/01/2013	102.717
03/01/2014	102.536
03/01/2015	102.354
03/01/2016	102.173
03/01/2017	101.992
03/01/2018	101.811
03/01/2019	101.63
03/01/2020	101.449
03/01/2021	101.268
03/01/2022	101.087

Composite Trade Information

Last Sale							Most Recent			Net Change
Date	Price	Yield	High Price	Low Price	High Yield	Low Yield	Date	Price	Yield	Price
04/01/2004	113.75	5.52289	113.75	113.75	5.52289	5.52289	04/01/2004	113.75	5.52289	-2.75

Not only does the site provide the most recent price and yield information, but it also provides important information about the bond. For instance, the fixed rate coupon is paid semiannually, and the bond is callable beginning March 1, 2013. The initial call price is 102.717 percent of par, and declines each year. The bond also has a credit rating of Aa3 from Moody's and AA from S&P.

note and bond issues outstanding. Beyond this, federal, state, and local borrowing is simply enormous. For example, even a small city would usually have a wide variety of notes and bonds outstanding, representing money borrowed to pay for things like roads, sewers, and schools. When you think about how many small cities there are in the United States, you begin to get the picture!

Because the bond market is almost entirely OTC, it has historically had little or no *transparency.* A financial market is transparent if it is possible to easily observe its prices and trading volume. On the New York Stock Exchange, for example, it is possible to see the price and quantity for every single transaction. In contrast, in the bond market, it is often not possible to observe either. Transactions are privately negotiated between parties, and there is little or no centralized reporting of transactions.

Although the total volume of trading in bonds far exceeds that in stocks, only a very small fraction of the total bond issues that exist actually trade on a given day. This fact, combined with the lack of transparency in the bond market, means that getting up-to-date prices on individual bonds can be difficult or impossible, particularly for smaller corporate or municipal issues. Instead, a variety of sources of estimated prices exist and are very commonly used.

Bond Price Reporting

In 2002, transparency in the corporate bond market began to improve dramatically. Under new regulations, corporate bond dealers are now required to report trade information through what is known as the Transactions Report and Compliance Engine (TRACE). As this is written, transaction prices are now reported on more than 4,000 bonds, amounting to approximately 75 percent of the investment grade market. More bonds will be added over time. Our nearby *Work the Web* box shows you how to get TRACE information.

To learn more about TRACE, visit www.nasd.com and select Market Systems.

As shown in Figure 7.3, *The Wall Street Journal* now provides a daily snapshot of the data from TRACE by reporting the 40 most active issues. The information reported is largely self-explanatory. The EST Spread is the estimated yield spread over a particular Treasury issue (a yield spread is just the difference in yields). The spread is reported in basis points, where 1 basis point is equal to .01 percent. The selected Treasury issue's maturity is given under UST, which is a standard abbreviation in the bond markets for U.S. Treasury. A "hot run" Treasury is the most recently issued of a particular maturity, better known as an on-the-run issue. Finally, the reported volume is the face value of bonds traded.

The Federal Reserve Bank of St. Louis maintains dozens of on-line files containing macroeconomic data as well as rates on U.S. Treasury issues. Go to www.stls.frb.org/fred/files.

As we mentioned before, the U.S. Treasury market is the largest securities market in the world. As with bond markets in general, it is an OTC market, so there is limited transparency. However, unlike the situation with bond markets in general, trading in Treasury issues, particularly recently issued ones, is very heavy. Each day, representative prices for outstanding Treasury issues are reported.

Figure 7.4 shows a portion of the daily Treasury note and bond listings from *The Wall Street Journal.* The entry that begins "8.000 Nov 21" is highlighted. Reading from left to right, the 8.000 is the bond's coupon rate, and the "Nov 21" tells us that the bond's maturity is November of 2021. Treasury bonds all make semiannual payments and have a face value of $1,000, so this bond will pay $40 per six months until it matures.

bid price
The price a dealer is willing to pay for a security.

asked price
The price a dealer is willing to take for a security.

bid-ask spread
The difference between the bid price and the asked price.

The next two pieces of information are the **bid** and **asked prices.** In general, in any OTC or dealer market, the bid price represents what a dealer is willing to pay for a security, and the asked price (or just "ask" price) is what a dealer is willing to take for it. The difference between the two prices is called the **bid-ask spread** (or just "spread"), and it represents the dealer's profit.

For historical reasons, Treasury prices are quoted in 32nds. Thus, the bid price on the 8.000 Nov 21 bond, 132:23, actually translates into 132 23/32, or 132.71875 percent of face value. With a $1,000 face value, this represents $1,327.1875. Because prices are quoted in 32nds, the smallest possible price change is 1/32. This is called the "tick" size.

The next number quoted is the change in the asked price from the previous day, measured in ticks (i.e., in 32nds), so this issue's asked price fell by 12/32 of 1 percent, or

Corporate Bonds

Wednesday, April 21, 2004

Forty most active fixed-coupon corporate bonds

COMPANY (TICKER)	COUPON	MATURITY	LAST PRICE	LAST YIELD	*EST SPREAD	UST†	EST $ VOL (000's)
Ford Motor Credit (F)	7.000	Oct 01, 2013	102.767	6.600	217	10	629,917
Ford Motor (F)	7.450	Jul 16, 2031	97.139	7.701	247	30	318,419
General Motors (GM)	8.375	Jul 15, 2033	108.987	7.603	237	30	187,192
Wal-Mart Stores (WMT)	4.125	Feb 15, 2011	96.725	4.692	26	10	130,505
Ford Motor Credit (F)	6.500	Jan 25, 2007	106.035	4.150	153	3	101,444
Morgan Stanley (MWD)	4.750	Apr 14, 2014	94.308	5.501	107	10	101,434
Ford Motor Credit (F)	7.375	Oct 28, 2009	107.245	5.818	231	5	100,285
AT&T Wireless Services (AWE)	8.750	Mar 01, 2031	123.152	6.852	162	30	92,152
General Electric Capital (GE)	3.125	Apr 01, 2009	96.465	3.920	41	5	79,690
Wyeth (WYE)	5.500	Feb 01, 2014	100.499	5.431	100	10	76,765
Ford Motor Credit (F)	7.500	Mar 15, 2005	104.458	2.381	21	2	74,323
Kellogg (K)	6.600	Apr 01, 2011	111.518	4.637	20	10	72,585
General Motors Acceptance (GMAC)	6.875	Sep 15, 2011	105.254	5.983	155	10	68,951
General Electric (GE)	5.000	Feb 01, 2013	100.267	4.961	54	10	67,474
Citigroup (C)	5.625	Aug 27, 2012	105.091	4.873	44	10	65,470
Pacific Gas and Electric (PCG)	6.050	Mar 01, 2034	95.351	6.401	117	30	61,166
Time Warner (TWX)	7.700	May 01, 2032	112.430	6.710	148	30	57,969
Goldman Sachs Group (GS)	3.875	Jan 15, 2009	98.929	4.126	62	5	55,285
Ford Motor Credit (F)	5.625	Oct 01, 2008	101.366	5.274	176	5	54,733
Verizon New York (VZ)	6.875	Apr 01, 2012	109.956	5.319	89	10	53,356
Lehman Brothers Holdings (LEH)	4.800	Mar 13, 2014	95.967	5.329	90	10	52,785
Goldman Sachs Group (GS)	5.150	Jan 15, 2014	98.024	5.413	99	10	51,451
Prudential Financial (PRU)	4.750	Apr 01, 2014	95.472	5.343	89	10	51,437
General Electric Capital (GE)	4.250	Dec 01, 2010	98.476	4.519	101	5	51,389
Ford Motor (F)	6.625	Oct 01, 2028	89.328	7.591	236	30	51,336
Sprint Capital (FON)	8.750	Mar 15, 2032	120.095	7.086	186	30	47,540
Time Warner (TWX)	6.875	May 01, 2012	110.449	5.260	83	10	47,054
Sprint Capital (FON)	6.000	Jan 15, 2007	106.771	3.371	75	3	43,822
Sprint Capital (FON)	6.875	Nov 15, 2028	99.205	6.942	171	30	43,735
DaimlerChrysler North America Holding (DCX)	4.750	Jan 15, 2008	101.642	4.266	77	5	43,290
Wal-Mart Stores (WMT)	6.875	Aug 10, 2009	113.153	4.083	58	5	42,832
Tyson Foods (TSN)	8.250	Oct 01, 2011	116.762	5.473	105	10	42,500
Conoco Global Funding (COP)	6.350	Oct 15, 2011	110.585	4.656	22	10	41,843
Motorola (MOT)	7.625	Nov 15, 2010	113.831	5.114	160	5	41,539
General Motors Acceptance (GMAC)	5.850	Jan 14, 2009	103.575	4.988	148	5	41,109
Telefonica Europe (TELEFO)	7.750	Sep 15, 2010	116.873	4.663	116	5	40,795
SBC Communications (SBC)	5.750	May 02, 2006	106.151	2.599	44	2	40,314
Ford Motor Credit (F)	7.875	Jun 15, 2010	109.550	5.990	247	5	39,393
National Rural Utilities Cooperative Finance (NRUC)	4.750	Mar 01, 2014	96.923	5.151	73	10	39,000
CIT Group (CIT)	7.750	Apr 02, 2012	116.350	5.207	77	10	38,642
Time Warner (TWX)	7.625	Apr 15, 2031	111.198	6.720	149	30	36,707

Volume represents total volume for each issue; price/yield data are for trades of $1 million and greater. * Estimated spreads, in basis points (100 basis points is one percentage point), over the 2, 3, 5, 10 or 30-year hot run Treasury note/bond. 2-year: 1.500 03/06; 3-year: 2.250 02/07; 5-year: 3.125 04/09; 10-year: 4.000 02/14; 30-year: 5.375 02/31. †Comparable U.S. Treasury issue.

Source: MarketAxess Corporate BondTicker

SOURCE: Reprinted by permission of *The Wall Street Journal*, via Copyright Clearance Center © 2004 Dow Jones and Company, Inc., April 22, 2004. All Rights Reserved Worldwide.

<< FIGURE 7.3

Sample *Wall Street Journal* Bond Quotation

.375 percent, of face value from the previous day. Finally, the last number reported is the yield to maturity, based on the asked price. Notice that this is a premium bond because it sells for more than its face value. Not surprisingly, its yield to maturity (5.14 percent) is less than its coupon rate (8 percent).

Some of the maturity dates in Figure 7.4 have an "n" after them. This just means that these issues are notes rather than bonds. The bonds with an "i" after them are the inflation-linked bonds, or TIPS, which we discussed in a previous section.

The very last ordinary bond listed, the 5.375 Feb 31, is often called the "bellwether" bond. This bond's yield is the one that is usually reported in the evening news. So, for example, when you hear that long-term interest rates rose, what is really being said is that the yield on this bond went up (and its price went down). As of 2004, the Treasury was no longer selling 30-year bonds, leaving the 10-year note as the longest maturity issue currently sold. As a result, the most recently issued 10-year note assumed bellwether status.

Current and historical Treasury yield information is available at www.publicdebt.treas.gov/of/ofaucrt.htm.

If you examine the yields on the various issues in Figure 7.4, you will clearly see that they vary by maturity. Why this occurs and what it might mean is one of the things we discuss in our next section.

FIGURE 7.4 >>

Sample *Wall Street Journal* U.S. Treasury Note and Bond Prices

Treasury Bonds, Notes and Bills

April 20, 2004

Explanatory Notes

Representative Over-the-Counter quotation based on transactions of $1 million or more. Treasury bond, note and bill quotes are as of mid-afternoon. Colons in bid-and-asked quotes represent 32nds; 101:01 means 101 1/32. Net changes in 32nds. n-Treasury note. i-Inflation-Indexed issue. Treasury bill quotes in hundredths, quoted on terms of a rate of discount. Days to maturity calculated from settlement date. All yields are to maturity and based on the asked quote. Latest 13-week and 26-week bills are boldfaced. For bonds callable prior to maturity, yields are computed to the earliest call date for issues quoted above par and to the maturity date for issues below par. *When issued.

Source: eSpeed/Cantor Fitzgerald

U.S. Treasury strips as of 3 p.m. Eastern time, also based on transactions of $1 million or more. Colons in bid and asked quotes represent 32nds; 99:01 means 99 1/32. Net changes in 32nds. Yields calculated on the asked quotation. ci-stripped coupon interest. bp-Treasury bond, stripped principal. np-Treasury note, stripped principal. For bonds callable prior to maturity, yields are computed to the earliest call date for issues quoted above par and to the maturity date for issues below par.

Source: Bear, Stearns & Co. via Street Software Technology Inc.

Government Bonds & Notes

RATE	MATURITY MO/YR	BID	ASKED	CHG	ASK YLD
3.375	Apr 04n	100:01	100:02	...	0.83
5.250	May 04n	100:08	100:09	...	0.73
7.250	May 04n	100:12	100:13	−1	0.82
12.375	May 04	100:23	100:24	−1	0.72
3.250	May 04n	100:07	100:08	...	0.81
2.875	Jun 04n	100:11	100:12	...	0.91
2.250	Jul 04n	100:10	100:11	...	0.95
2.125	Aug 04n	100:12	100:13	...	0.99
6.000	Aug 04n	101:17	101:18	−1	1.02
7.250	Aug 04n	101:30	101:31	−1	0.99
13.750	Aug 04	103:29	103:30	−1	1.31
1.875	Sep 04n	100:10	100:11	−1	1.06
2.125	Oct 04n	100:15	100:16	−1	1.17
5.875	Nov 04n	102:19	102:20	−1	1.18
7.875	Nov 04n	103:23	103:24	−1	1.20
11.625	Nov 04	105:25	105:26	−2	1.25
2.000	Nov 04n	100:14	100:15	−1	1.22
1.750	Dec 04n	100:10	100:11	−1	1.23
1.625	Jan 05n	100:08	100:09	...	1.26
7.500	Feb 05n	105:00	105:00	−2	1.32
1.500	Feb 05n	100:04	100:05	...	1.32
1.625	Mar 05n	100:07	100:08	...	1.36
1.625	Apr 05n	100:06	100:07	−1	1.41
6.500	May 05n	105:09	105:10	−2	1.44
6.750	May 05n	105:17	105:18	−1	1.46
12.000	May 05	111:03	111:04	...	1.43
1.250	May 05n	99:24	99:25	...	1.45
1.125	Jun 05n	99:16	99:17	−1	1.51
1.500	Jul 05n	99:27	99:28	−2	1.59
6.500	Aug 05n	106:09	106:10	−3	1.63
10.750	Aug 05	111:26	111:27	−2	1.63
2.000	Aug 05n	100:13	100:14	−2	1.66
1.625	Sep 05n	99:27	99:28	−2	1.70
1.625	Oct 05n	99:23	99:24	−2	1.78
5.750	Nov 05n	106:00	106:01	−3	1.81
5.875	Nov 05n	106:06	106:07	−3	1.82
1.875	Nov 05n	100:00	100:01	−2	1.84
1.875	Dec 05n	99:28	99:29	−3	1.92
1.875	Jan 06n	99:25	99:26	−3	1.97
5.625	Feb 06n	106:15	106:16	−3	1.96
9.375	Feb 06	113:04	113:05	−4	1.97
1.625	Feb 06n	99:08	99:09	−2	2.02
1.500	**Mar 06n**	**98:28**	**98:29**	**−3**	**2.07**
2.000	May 06n	99:22	99:23	−3	2.13
4.625	May 06n	105:00	105:00	−3	2.14
6.875	May 06n	109:16	109:17	−3	2.13
7.000	Jul 06n	110:09	110:10	−4	2.24
2.375	Aug 06n	100:05	100:06	−3	2.29
6.500	Oct 06n	109:26	109:27	−5	2.39

RATE	MATURITY MO/YR	BID	ASKED	CHG	ASK YLD
2.625	Nov 06n	100:14	100:15	−4	2.44
3.500	Nov 06n	102:20	102:21	−4	2.43
3.375	Jan 07i	108:27	108:28	−5	0.12
2.250	Feb 07n	99:05	99:06	−5	2.54
6.250	Feb 07n	110:00	110:00	−5	2.54
6.625	May 07n	111:17	111:18	−6	2.67
4.375	May 07n	104:30	104:31	−5	2.68
3.250	Aug 07n	101:14	101:15	−6	2.78
6.125	Aug 07n	110:15	110:16	−6	2.78
3.000	Nov 07n	100:13	100:14	−5	2.87
3.625	Jan 08i	111:10	111:11	−5	0.55
3.000	Feb 08n	99:30	99:31	−6	3.00
5.500	Feb 08n	109:00	109:00	−6	2.98
2.625	May 08n	98:03	98:04	−5	3.12
5.625	May 08n	109:16	109:17	−6	3.11
3.250	Aug 08n	100:03	100:04	−6	3.21
3.125	Sep 08n	99:12	99:13	−6	3.27
3.125	Oct 08n	99:08	99:09	−6	3.29
3.375	Nov 08n	100:07	100:08	−5	3.32
4.750	Nov 08n	106:02	106:03	−7	3.30
3.375	Dec 08n	100:02	100:03	−6	3.35
3.250	Jan 09n	99:12	99:13	−6	3.38
3.875	Jan 09i	113:22	113:23	−6	0.91
3.000	Feb 09n	98:06	98:07	−5	3.40
2.625	Mar 09n	96:14	96:15	−6	3.41
3.125	**Apr 09n**	**98:16**	**98:17**	**−6**	**3.44**
5.500	May 09n	109:19	109:20	−7	3.41
9.125	May 09	100:15	100:16	−2	1.25
6.000	Aug 09n	111:27	111:28	−8	3.53
10.375	Nov 09	105:00	105:00	−1	1.47
4.250	Jan 10i	116:29	116:30	−9	1.19
6.500	Feb 10n	114:22	114:23	−8	3.67
11.750	Feb 10	108:06	108:07	−3	1.60
10.000	May 10	108:23	108:24	−3	1.67
5.750	Aug 10n	110:27	110:28	−8	3.80
12.750	Nov 10	116:16	116:17	−2	1.97
3.500	Jan 11i	113:06	113:07	−11	1.43
5.000	Feb 11n	106:10	106:11	−8	3.93
13.875	May 11	123:16	123:17	−4	2.16
5.000	Aug 11n	106:00	106:00	−8	4.04
14.000	Nov 11	128:23	128:24	−6	2.38
3.375	Jan 12i	112:30	112:31	−12	1.59
4.875	Feb 12n	104:26	104:27	−8	4.14
3.000	Jul 12i	110:04	110:05	−11	1.67
4.375	Aug 12n	101:00	101:01	−8	4.22
4.000	Nov 12n	98:05	98:06	−8	4.25
10.375	Nov 12	125:01	125:02	−7	2.92
3.875	Feb 13n	96:29	96:30	−8	4.29
3.625	May 13n	95:05	95:06	−8	4.27
1.875	Jul 13i	100:14	100:15	−13	1.82

RATE	MATURITY MO/YR	BID	ASKED	CHG	ASK YLD
4.250	Aug 13n	99:02	99:03	−9	4.37
12.000	Aug 13	135:08	135:09	−12	3.19
4.250	Nov 13n	98:26	98:27	−8	4.40
2.000	Jan 14i	101:01	101:02	−13	1.88
4.000	**Feb 14n**	**96:25**	**96:26**	**−8**	**4.40**
13.250	May 14	145:10	145:11	−8	3.42
12.500	Aug 14	143:04	143:05	−8	3.52
11.750	Nov 14	140:28	140:29	−8	3.58
11.250	Feb 15	157:09	157:10	−13	4.50
10.625	Aug 15	153:01	153:02	−13	4.57
9.875	Nov 15	146:20	146:21	−12	4.62
9.250	Feb 16	141:05	141:06	−12	4.67
7.250	May 16	122:26	122:27	−11	4.74
7.500	Nov 16	125:09	125:10	−12	4.79
8.750	May 17	137:27	137:28	−13	4.81
8.875	Aug 17	139:08	139:09	−13	4.84
9.125	May 18	142:20	142:21	−12	4.89
9.000	Nov 18	141:25	141:26	−14	4.94
8.875	Feb 19	140:18	140:19	−13	4.97
8.125	Aug 19	132:28	132:29	−10	5.02
8.500	Feb 20	137:10	137:11	−12	5.04
8.750	May 20	140:12	140:13	−13	5.05
8.750	Aug 20	140:20	140:21	−12	5.06
7.875	Feb 21	130:28	130:29	−11	5.11
8.125	May 21	133:30	133:31	−12	5.12
8.125	Aug 21	134:02	134:03	−12	5.13
8.000	Nov 21	132:23	132:24	−12	5.14
7.250	Aug 22	124:02	124:03	−11	5.19
7.625	Nov 22	128:22	128:23	−12	5.20
7.125	Feb 23	122:21	122:22	−12	5.22
6.250	Aug 23	111:30	111:31	−12	5.25
7.500	Nov 24	128:06	128:07	−12	5.24
7.625	Feb 25	129:25	129:26	−13	5.25
6.875	Aug 25	120:10	120:11	−11	5.27
6.000	Feb 26	109:00	109:01	−10	5.30
6.750	Aug 26	118:29	118:30	−12	5.29
6.500	Nov 26	115:21	115:22	−12	5.30
6.625	Feb 27	117:12	117:13	−11	5.30
6.375	Aug 27	114:05	114:06	−10	5.31
6.125	Nov 27	110:26	110:27	−10	5.31
3.625	Apr 28i	124:00	124:01	−23	2.31
5.500	Aug 28	102:13	102:14	−9	5.32
5.250	Nov 28	99:01	99:02	−10	5.32
5.250	Feb 29	99:04	99:05	−7	5.31
3.875	Apr 29i	129:21	129:22	−24	2.30
6.125	Aug 29	111:09	111:10	−11	5.31
6.250	May 30	113:07	113:08	−12	5.30
5.375	**Feb 31**	**102:06**	**102:07**	**−11**	**5.22**
3.375	Apr 32i	123:24	123:25	−26	2.23

EXAMPLE 7.5 >> Treasury Quotes

Locate the Treasury note in Figure 7.4 maturing in April 2009. What is its coupon rate? What is its bid price? What was the *previous day's* asked price?

The note listed as 3.125 Apr 09 is the one we seek. Its coupon rate is 3.125, or 3.125 percent of face value. The bid price is 98:16, or 98.50 percent of face value. The ask price is 98:17, which is down by 6 ticks from the previous day. This means that the ask price on the previous day was equal to $98\frac{17}{32} + 6/32 = 98\frac{23}{32} = 98{:}23$.

A Note on Bond Price Quotes

If you buy a bond between coupon payment dates, the price you pay is usually more than the price you are quoted. The reason is that standard convention in the bond market is to quote prices net of "accrued interest," meaning that accrued interest is deducted to arrive at the quoted price. This quoted price is called the **clean price**. The price you actually pay, however, includes the accrued interest. This price is the **dirty price**, also known as the "full" or "invoice" price.

clean price
The price of a bond net of accrued interest; this is the price that is typically quoted.

dirty price
The price of a bond including accrued interest, also known as the *full* or *invoice price*. This is the price the buyer actually pays.

An example is the easiest way to understand these issues. Suppose you buy a bond with a 12 percent annual coupon, payable semiannually. You actually pay $1,080 for this bond, so $1,080 is the dirty, or invoice, price. Further, on the day you buy it, the next coupon is due in four months, so you are between coupon dates. Notice that the next coupon will be $60.

The accrued interest on a bond is calculated by taking the fraction of the coupon period that has passed, in this case two months out of six, and multiplying this fraction by the next coupon, $60. So, the accrued interest in this example is $2/6 \times \$60 = \$20$. The bond's quoted price (i.e., its clean price) would be $\$1{,}080 - \$20 = \$1{,}060$.[6]

Concept Questions

7.5a Why do we say bond markets may have little or no transparency?

7.5b In general, what are bid and ask prices?

7.5c What is the difference between a bond's clean price and dirty price?

INFLATION AND INTEREST RATES 7.6

So far, we haven't considered the role of inflation in our various discussions of interest rates, yields, and returns. Because this is an important consideration, we consider the impact of inflation next.

Real versus Nominal Rates

In examining interest rates, or any other financial market rates such as discount rates, bond yields, rates of return, and required returns, it is often necessary to distinguish between **real rates** and **nominal rates**. Nominal rates are called "nominal" because they have not been adjusted for inflation. Real rates are rates that have been adjusted for inflation.

real rates
Interest rates or rates of return that have been adjusted for inflation.

nominal rates
Interest rates or rates of return that have not been adjusted for inflation.

To see the effect of inflation, suppose prices are currently rising by 5 percent per year. In other words, the rate of inflation is 5 percent. An investment is available that will be worth $115.50 in one year. It costs $100 today. Notice that with a present value of $100 and a future value in one year of $115.50, this investment has a 15.5 percent rate of return. In calculating this 15.5 percent return, we did not consider the effect of inflation, however, so this is the nominal return.

[6]The way accrued interest is calculated actually depends on the type of bond being quoted, for example, Treasury or corporate. The difference has to do with exactly how the fractional coupon period is calculated. In our example above, we implicitly treated the months as having exactly the same length (i.e., 30 days each, 360 days in a year), which is consistent with the way corporate bonds are quoted. In contrast, for Treasury bonds, actual day counts are used.

What is the impact of inflation here? To answer, suppose pizzas cost \$5 apiece at the beginning of the year. With \$100, we can buy 20 pizzas. Because the inflation rate is 5 percent, pizzas will cost 5 percent more, or \$5.25, at the end of the year. If we take the investment, how many pizzas can we buy at the end of the year? Measured in pizzas, what is the rate of return on this investment?

Our \$115.50 from the investment will buy us \$115.50/5.25 = 22 pizzas. This is up from 20 pizzas, so our pizza rate of return is 10 percent. What this illustrates is that even though the nominal return on our investment is 15.5 percent, our buying power goes up by only 10 percent because of inflation. Put another way, we are really only 10 percent richer. In this case, we say that the real return is 10 percent.

Alternatively, we can say that with 5 percent inflation, each of the \$115.50 nominal dollars we get is worth 5 percent less in real terms, so the real dollar value of our investment in a year is:

$$\$115.50/1.05 = \$110$$

What we have done is to *deflate* the \$115.50 by 5 percent. Because we give up \$100 in current buying power to get the equivalent of \$110, our real return is again 10 percent. Because we have removed the effect of future inflation here, this \$110 is said to be measured in current dollars.

The difference between nominal and real rates is important and bears repeating:

The nominal rate on an investment is the percentage change in the number of dollars you have.
The real rate on an investment is the percentage change in how much you can buy with your dollars, in other words, the percentage change in your buying power.

The Fisher Effect

Fisher effect
The relationship between nominal returns, real returns, and inflation.

Our discussion of real and nominal returns illustrates a relationship often called the **Fisher effect** (after the great economist Irving Fisher). Because investors are ultimately concerned with what they can buy with their money, they require compensation for inflation. Let R stand for the nominal rate and r stand for the real rate. The Fisher effect tells us that the relationship between nominal rates, real rates, and inflation can be written as:

$$1 + R = (1 + r) \times (1 + h) \qquad [7.2]$$

where h is the inflation rate.

In the preceding example, the nominal rate was 15.50 percent and the inflation rate was 5 percent. What was the real rate? We can determine it by plugging in these numbers:

$$\begin{aligned} 1 + .1550 &= (1 + r) \times (1 + .05) \\ 1 + r &= 1.1550/1.05 = 1.10 \\ r &= 10\% \end{aligned}$$

This real rate is the same as we had before. If we take another look at the Fisher effect, we can rearrange things a little as follows:

$$\begin{aligned} 1 + R &= (1 + r) \times (1 + h) \\ R &= r + h + r \times h \end{aligned} \qquad [7.3]$$

What this tells us is that the nominal rate has three components. First, there is the real rate on the investment, r. Next, there is the compensation for the decrease in the value of the money originally invested because of inflation, h. The third component represents compensation for the fact that the dollars earned on the investment are also worth less because of the inflation.

This third component is usually small, so it is often dropped. The nominal rate is then approximately equal to the real rate plus the inflation rate:

$$R \approx r + h \qquad [7.4]$$

The Fisher Effect

<< EXAMPLE 7.6

If investors require a 10 percent real rate of return, and the inflation rate is 8 percent, what must be the approximate nominal rate? The exact nominal rate?

First of all, the nominal rate is approximately equal to the sum of the real rate and the inflation rate: 10% + 8% = 18%. From the Fisher effect, we have:

$$\begin{aligned} 1 + R &= (1 + r) \times (1 + h) \\ &= 1.10 \times 1.08 \\ &= 1.1880 \end{aligned}$$

Therefore, the nominal rate will actually be closer to 19 percent.

It is important to note that financial rates, such as interest rates, discount rates, and rates of return, are almost always quoted in nominal terms. To remind you of this, we will henceforth use the symbol R instead of r in most of our discussions about such rates.

Concept Questions

7.6a What is the difference between a nominal and a real return? Which is more important to a typical investor?

7.6b What is the Fisher effect?

DETERMINANTS OF BOND YIELDS 7.7

We are now in a position to discuss the determinants of a bond's yield. As we will see, the yield on any particular bond is a reflection of a variety of factors, some common to all bonds and some specific to the issue under consideration.

The Term Structure of Interest Rates

At any point in time, short-term and long-term interest rates will generally be different. Sometimes short-term rates are higher, sometimes lower. Figure 7.5 gives us a long-range perspective on this by showing almost two centuries of short- and long-term interest rates. As shown, through time, the difference between short- and long-term rates has ranged from essentially zero to up to several percentage points, both positive and negative.

The relationship between short- and long-term interest rates is known as the **term structure of interest rates**. To be a little more precise, the term structure of interest rates

FIGURE 7.5 >> **U.S. Interest Rates: 1800–2004**

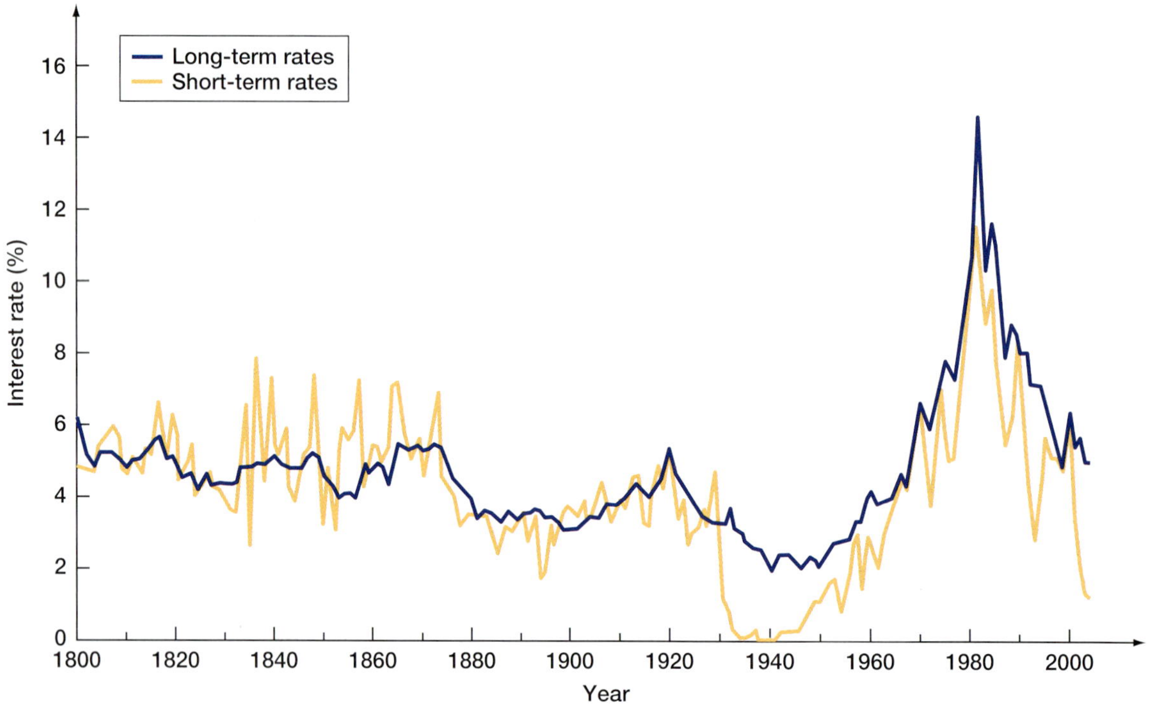

SOURCE: Jeremy J. Siegel, *Stocks for the Long Run,* 3rd edition, © McGraw-Hill, 2004, updated by the authors.

term structure of interest rates
The relationship between nominal interest rates on default-free, pure discount securities and time to maturity; that is, the pure time value of money.

tells us what *nominal* interest rates are on *default-free, pure discount* bonds of all maturities. These rates are, in essence, "pure" interest rates because they involve no risk of default and a single, lump-sum future payment. In other words, the term structure tells us the pure time value of money for different lengths of time.

When long-term rates are higher than short-term rates, we say that the term structure is upward sloping, and, when short-term rates are higher, we say it is downward sloping. The term structure can also be "humped." When this occurs, it is usually because rates increase at first, but then begin to decline as we look at longer- and longer-term rates. The most common shape of the term structure, particularly in modern times, is upward sloping, but the degree of steepness has varied quite a bit.

What determines the shape of the term structure? There are three basic components. The first two are the ones we discussed in our previous section, the real rate of interest and the rate of inflation. The real rate of interest is the compensation investors demand for forgoing the use of their money. You can think of it as the pure time value of money after adjusting for the effects of inflation.

The real rate of interest is the basic component underlying every interest rate, regardless of the time to maturity. When the real rate is high, all interest rates will tend to be higher, and vice versa. Thus, the real rate doesn't really determine the shape of the term structure; instead, it mostly influences the overall level of interest rates.

In contrast, the prospect of future inflation very strongly influences the shape of the term structure. Investors thinking about loaning money for various lengths of time recognize that future inflation erodes the value of the dollars that will be returned. As a result, investors demand compensation for this loss in the form of higher nominal rates. This extra compensation is called the **inflation premium**.

inflation premium
The portion of a nominal interest rate that represents compensation for expected future inflation.

If investors believe that the rate of inflation will be higher in the future, then long-term nominal interest rates will tend to be higher than short-term rates. Thus, an upward-sloping term structure may be a reflection of anticipated increases in inflation. Similarly, a downward-sloping term structure probably reflects the belief that inflation will be falling in the future.

You can actually see the inflation premium in U.S. Treasury yields. Look back at Figure 7.4 and recall that the entries with an "i" after them are Treasury Inflation Protection Securities (TIPS). If you compare the yields on a TIPS to a regular note or bond with a similar maturity, the difference in the yields is the inflation premium. For the issues in Figure 7.4, check that the spread is about 2 to 3 percent, meaning that investors demand an extra 2 or 3 percent in yield as compensation for potential future inflation.

The third, and last, component of the term structure has to do with interest rate risk. As we discussed earlier in the chapter, longer-term bonds have much greater risk of loss resulting from changes in interest rates than do shorter-term bonds. Investors recognize this risk, and they demand extra compensation in the form of higher rates for bearing it. This extra compensation is called the **interest rate risk premium**. The longer is the term to maturity, the greater is the interest rate risk, so the interest rate risk premium increases with maturity. However, as we discussed earlier, interest rate risk increases at a decreasing rate, so the interest rate risk premium does as well.[7]

interest rate risk premium
The compensation investors demand for bearing interest rate risk.

Putting the pieces together, we see that the term structure reflects the combined effect of the real rate of interest, the inflation premium, and the interest rate risk premium. Figure 7.6 shows how these can interact to produce an upward-sloping term structure (in the top part of Figure 7.6) or a downward-sloping term structure (in the bottom part).

In the top part of Figure 7.6, notice how the rate of inflation is expected to rise gradually. At the same time, the interest rate risk premium increases at a decreasing rate, so the combined effect is to produce a pronounced upward-sloping term structure. In the bottom part of Figure 7.6, the rate of inflation is expected to fall in the future, and the expected decline is enough to offset the interest rate risk premium and produce a downward-sloping term structure. Notice that if the rate of inflation was expected to decline by only a small amount, we could still get an upward-sloping term structure because of the interest rate risk premium.

We assumed in drawing Figure 7.6 that the real rate would remain the same. Actually, expected future real rates could be larger or smaller than the current real rate. Also, for simplicity, we used straight lines to show expected future inflation rates as rising or declining, but they do not necessarily have to look like this. They could, for example, rise and then fall, leading to a humped yield curve.

Bond Yields and the Yield Curve: Putting It All Together

Going back to Figure 7.4, recall that we saw that the yields on Treasury notes and bonds of different maturities are not the same. Each day, in addition to the Treasury prices and yields shown in Figure 7.4, *The Wall Street Journal* provides a plot of Treasury yields relative to maturity. This plot is called the **Treasury yield curve** (or just the yield curve). Figure 7.7 shows the yield curve drawn from the yields in Figure 7.4.

[7] In days of old, the interest rate risk premium was called a "liquidity" premium. Today, the term *liquidity premium* has an altogether different meaning, which we explore in our next section. Also, the interest rate risk premium is sometimes called a maturity risk premium. Our terminology is consistent with the modern view of the term structure.

FIGURE 7.6 >>

The Term Structure of Interest Rates

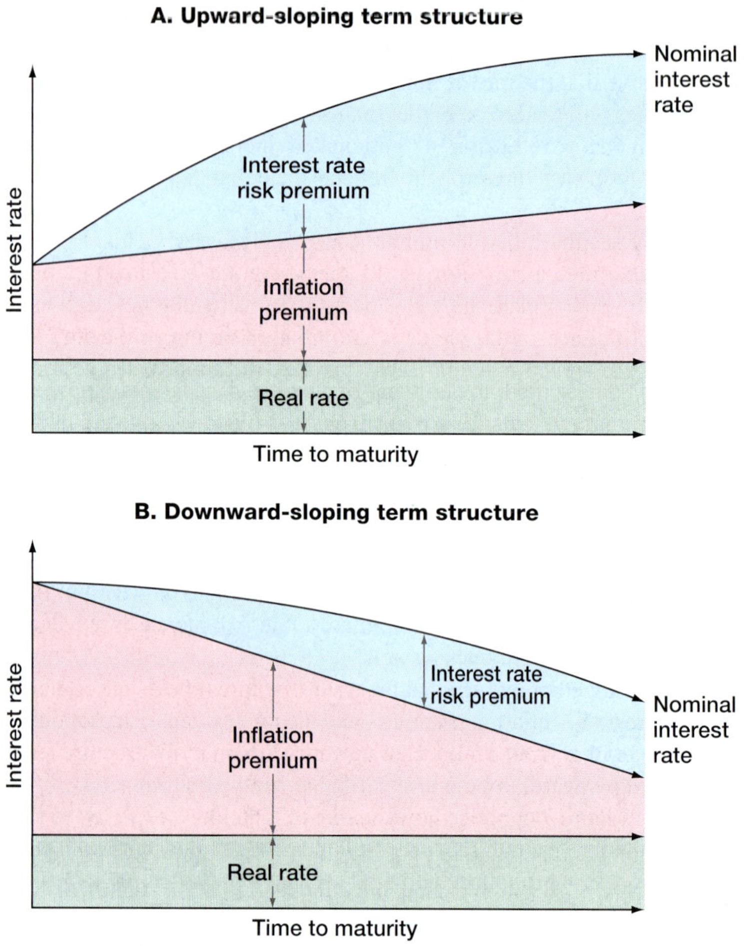

Treasury yield curve
A plot of the yields on Treasury notes and bonds relative to maturity.

On-line yield curve information is available at www.bloomberg.com/markets.

default risk premium
The portion of a nominal interest rate or bond yield that represents compensation for the possibility of default.

As you probably now suspect, the shape of the yield curve is a reflection of the term structure of interest rates. In fact, the Treasury yield curve and the term structure of interest rates are almost the same thing. The only difference is that the term structure is based on pure discount bonds, whereas the yield curve is based on coupon bond yields. As a result, Treasury yields depend on the three components that underlie the term structure—the real rate, expected future inflation, and the interest rate risk premium.

Treasury notes and bonds have three important features that we need to remind you of: they are default-free, they are taxable, and they are highly liquid. This is not true of bonds in general, so we need to examine what additional factors come into play when we look at bonds issued by corporations or municipalities.

The first thing to consider is credit risk, that is, the possibility of default. Investors recognize that issuers other than the Treasury may or may not make all the promised payments on a bond, so they demand a higher yield as compensation for this risk. This extra compensation is called the **default risk premium**. Earlier in the chapter, we saw how bonds were rated based on their credit risk. What you will find if you start looking at bonds of different ratings is that lower-rated bonds have higher yields.

An important thing to recognize about a bond's yield is that it is calculated assuming that all the promised payments will be made. As a result, it is really a promised yield, and it may or may not be what you will earn. In particular, if the issuer defaults, your actual yield will be lower, probably much lower. This fact is particularly important when it comes

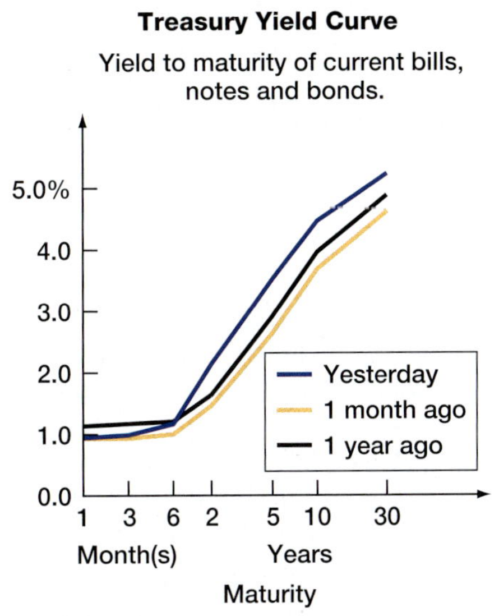

SOURCE: Reprinted by permission of *The Wall Street Journal,* via Copyright Clearance Center © 2004 by Dow Jones & Company, Inc., 2004. All Rights Reserved Worldwide.

<< FIGURE 7.7

The Treasury Yield Curve: April, 2004

to junk bonds. Thanks to a clever bit of marketing, such bonds are now commonly called high-yield bonds, which has a much nicer ring to it; but now you recognize that these are really high *promised* yield bonds.

Next, recall that we discussed earlier how municipal bonds are free from most taxes and, as a result, have much lower yields than taxable bonds. Investors demand the extra yield on a taxable bond as compensation for the unfavorable tax treatment. This extra compensation is the **taxability premium**.

taxability premium
The portion of a nominal interest rate or bond yield that represents compensation for unfavorable tax status.

Finally, bonds have varying degrees of liquidity. As we discussed earlier, there is an enormous number of bond issues, most of which do not trade on a regular basis. As a result, if you wanted to sell quickly, you would probably not get as good a price as you could otherwise. Investors prefer liquid assets to illiquid ones, so they demand a **liquidity premium** on top of all the other premiums we have discussed. As a result, all else being the same, less liquid bonds will have higher yields than more liquid bonds.

liquidity premium
The portion of a nominal interest rate or bond yield that represents compensation for lack of liquidity.

Conclusion

If we combine all of the things we have discussed regarding bond yields, we find that bond yields represent the combined effect of no fewer than six things. The first is the real rate of interest. On top of the real rate are five premiums representing compensation for (1) expected future inflation, (2) interest rate risk, (3) default risk, (4) taxability, and (5) lack of liquidity. As a result, determining the appropriate yield on a bond requires careful analysis of each of these effects.

Concept Questions

7.7a What is the term structure of interest rates? What determines its shape?

7.7b What is the Treasury yield curve?

7.7c What are the six components that make up a bond's yield?

7.8 SUMMARY AND CONCLUSIONS

This chapter has explored bonds, bond yields, and interest rates. We saw that:

1. Determining bond prices and yields is an application of basic discounted cash flow principles.
2. Bond values move in the direction opposite that of interest rates, leading to potential gains or losses for bond investors.
3. Bonds have a variety of features spelled out in a document called the indenture.
4. Bonds are rated based on their default risk. Some bonds, such as Treasury bonds, have no risk of default, whereas so-called junk bonds have substantial default risk.
5. A wide variety of bonds exist, many of which contain exotic or unusual features.
6. Almost all bond trading is OTC, with little or no market transparency in many cases. As a result, bond price and volume information can be difficult to find for some types of bonds.
7. Bond yields and interest rates reflect the effect of six different things: the real interest rate and five premiums that investors demand as compensation for inflation, interest rate risk, default risk, taxability, and lack of liquidity.

In closing, we note that bonds are a vital source of financing to governments and corporations of all types. Bond prices and yields are a rich subject, and our one chapter, necessarily, touches on only the most important concepts and ideas. There is a great deal more we could say, but, instead, we will move on to stocks in our next chapter.

Chapter Review and Self-Test Problems

7.1 **Bond Values** A Microgates Industries bond has a 10 percent coupon rate and a $1,000 face value. Interest is paid semiannually, and the bond has 20 years to maturity. If investors require a 12 percent yield, what is the bond's value? What is the effective annual yield on the bond?

7.2 **Bond Yields** A Macrohard Corp. bond carries an 8 percent coupon, paid semiannually. The par value is $1,000, and the bond matures in six years. If the bond currently sells for $911.37, what is its yield to maturity? What is the effective annual yield?

Answers to Chapter Review and Self-Test Problems

7.1 Because the bond has a 10 percent coupon yield and investors require a 12 percent return, we know that the bond must sell at a discount. Notice that, because the bond pays interest semiannually, the coupons amount to $100/2 = $50 every six months. The required yield is 12%/2 = 6% every six months. Finally, the bond matures in 20 years, so there are a total of 40 six-month periods.

The bond's value is thus equal to the present value of $50 every six months for the next 40 six-month periods plus the present value of the $1,000 face amount:

$$\begin{aligned}\text{Bond value} &= \$50 \times [(1 - 1/1.06^{40})/.06] + 1{,}000/1.06^{40} \\ &= \$50 \times 15.04630 + 1{,}000/10.2857 \\ &= \$849.54\end{aligned}$$

Notice that we discounted the \$1,000 back 40 periods at 6 percent per period, rather than 20 years at 12 percent. The reason is that the effective annual yield on the bond is $1.06^2 - 1 = 12.36\%$, not 12 percent. We thus could have used 12.36 percent per year for 20 years when we calculated the present value of the \$1,000 face amount, and the answer would have been the same.

7.2 The present value of the bond's cash flows is its current price, \$911.37. The coupon is \$40 every six months for 12 periods. The face value is \$1,000. So the bond's yield is the unknown discount rate in the following:

$$\$911.37 = \$40 \times [1 - 1/(1 + r)^{12}]/r + 1{,}000/(1 + r)^{12}$$

The bond sells at a discount. Because the coupon rate is 8 percent, the yield must be something in excess of that.

If we were to solve this by trial and error, we might try 12 percent (or 6 percent per six months):

$$\begin{aligned}\text{Bond value} &= \$40 \times (1 - 1/1.06^{12})/.06 + 1{,}000/1.06^{12}\\ &= \$832.32\end{aligned}$$

This is less than the actual value, so our discount rate is too high. We now know that the yield is somewhere between 8 and 12 percent. With further trial and error (or a little machine assistance), the yield works out to be 10 percent, or 5 percent every six months.

By convention, the bond's yield to maturity would be quoted as $2 \times 5\% = 10\%$. The effective yield is thus $1.05^2 - 1 = 10.25\%$.

Concepts Review and Critical Thinking Questions

1. **Treasury Bonds** Is it true that a U.S. Treasury security is risk-free?
2. **Interest Rate Risk** Which has greater interest rate risk, a 30-year Treasury bond or a 30-year BB corporate bond?
3. **Treasury Pricing** With regard to bid and ask prices on a Treasury bond, is it possible for the bid price to be higher? Why or why not?
4. **Yield to Maturity** Treasury bid and ask quotes are sometimes given in terms of yields, so there would be a bid yield and an ask yield. Which do you think would be larger? Explain.
5. **Call Provisions** A company is contemplating a long-term bond issue. It is debating whether or not to include a call provision. What are the benefits to the company from including a call provision? What are the costs? How do these answers change for a put provision?
6. **Coupon Rate** How does a bond issuer decide on the appropriate coupon rate to set on its bonds? Explain the difference between the coupon rate and the required return on a bond.
7. **Real and Nominal Returns** Are there any circumstances under which an investor might be more concerned about the nominal return on an investment than the real return?
8. **Bond Ratings** Companies pay rating agencies such as Moody's and S&P to rate their bonds, and the costs can be substantial. However, companies are not required to have their bonds rated in the first place; doing so is strictly voluntary. Why do you think they do it?

9. **Bond Ratings** U.S. Treasury bonds are not rated. Why? Often, junk bonds are not rated. Why?
10. **Term Structure** What is the difference between the term structure of interest rates and the yield curve?
11. **Crossover Bonds** Looking back at the crossover bonds we discussed in the chapter, why do you think split ratings such as these occur?
12. **Municipal Bonds** Why is it that municipal bonds are not taxed at the federal level, but are taxable across state lines? Why is it that U.S. Treasury bonds are not taxable at the state level? (You may need to dust off the history books for this one.)
13. **Bond Market** What are the implications for bond investors of the lack of transparency in the bond market?
14. **Treasury Market** All Treasury bonds are relatively liquid, but some are more liquid than others. Take a look back at Figure 7.4. Which issues appear to be the most liquid? The least liquid?
15. **Rating Agencies** A controversy erupted regarding bond-rating agencies when some agencies began to provide unsolicited bond ratings. Why do you think this is controversial?
16. **Bonds as Equity** The 100-year bonds we discussed in the chapter have something in common with junk bonds. Critics charge that, in both cases, the issuers are really selling equity in disguise. What are the issues here? Why would a company want to sell "equity in disguise"?

Questions and Problems

BASIC
(Questions 1–14)

1. **Interpreting Bond Yields** Is the yield to maturity on a bond the same thing as the required return? Is YTM the same thing as the coupon rate? Suppose today a 10 percent coupon bond sells at par. Two years from now, the required return on the same bond is 8 percent. What is the coupon rate on the bond now? The YTM?
2. **Interpreting Bond Yields** Suppose you buy a 7 percent coupon, 20-year bond today when it's first issued. If interest rates suddenly rise to 15 percent, what happens to the value of your bond? Why?
3. **Bond Prices** DTO, Inc., has 8 percent coupon bonds on the market that have 10 years left to maturity. The bonds make annual payments. If the YTM on these bonds is 6 percent, what is the current bond price?
4. **Bond Yields** Aragorn Co. has 9 percent coupon bonds on the market with nine years left to maturity. The bonds make annual payments. If the bond currently sells for $884.50, what is its YTM?
5. **Coupon Rates** Superstar Enterprises has bonds on the market making annual payments, with 16 years to maturity, and selling for $870. At this price, the bonds yield 6.8 percent. What must the coupon rate be on Superstar's bonds?
6. **Bond Prices** Borderline Co. issued 11-year bonds one year ago at a coupon rate of 8.2 percent. The bonds make semiannual payments. If the YTM on these bonds is 7.4 percent, what is the current bond price?
7. **Bond Yields** Raines Umbrella Corp. issued 12-year bonds 2 years ago at a coupon rate of 8.6 percent. The bonds make semiannual payments. If these bonds currently sell for 97 percent of par value, what is the YTM?

8. **Coupon Rates** Rhiannon Corporation has bonds on the market with 14.5 years to maturity, a YTM of 7.5 percent, and a current price of $1,145. The bonds make semiannual payments. What must the coupon rate be on these bonds?
9. **Calculating Real Rates of Return** If Treasury bills are currently paying 6 percent and the inflation rate is 4.5 percent, what is the approximate real rate of interest? The exact real rate?
10. **Inflation and Nominal Returns** Suppose the real rate is 4 percent and the inflation rate is 2.5 percent. What rate would you expect to see on a Treasury bill?
11. **Nominal and Real Returns** An investment offers a 15 percent total return over the coming year. Alan Wingspan thinks the total real return on this investment will be only 9 percent. What does Alan believe the inflation rate will be over the next year?
12. **Nominal versus Real Returns** Say you own an asset that had a total return last year of 13.4 percent. If the inflation rate last year was 4.5 percent, what was your real return?
13. **Using Treasury Quotes** Locate the Treasury issue in Figure 7.4 maturing in November 2027. Is this a note or a bond? What is its coupon rate? What is its bid price? What was the *previous day's* asked price?
14. **Using Treasury Quotes** Locate the Treasury bond in Figure 7.4 maturing in November 2024. Is this a premium or a discount bond? What is its current yield? What is its yield to maturity? What is the bid-ask spread?

INTERMEDIATE
(Questions 15–27)

15. **Bond Price Movements** Bond X is a premium bond making annual payments. The bond pays an 8 percent coupon, has a YTM of 6 percent, and has 13 years to maturity. Bond Y is a discount bond making annual payments. This bond pays a 6 percent coupon, has a YTM of 8 percent, and also has 13 years to maturity. If interest rates remain unchanged, what do you expect the price of these bonds to be one year from now? In three years? In eight years? In 12 years? In 13 years? What's going on here? Illustrate your answers by graphing bond prices versus time to maturity.
16. **Interest Rate Risk** Both Bond Sam and Bond Dave have 10 percent coupons, make semiannual payments, and are priced at par value. Bond Sam has 2 years to maturity, whereas Bond Dave has 15 years to maturity. If interest rates suddenly rise by 2 percent, what is the percentage change in the price of Bond Sam? Of Bond Dave? If rates were to suddenly fall by 2 percent instead, what would the percentage change in the price of Bond Sam be then? Of Bond Dave? Illustrate your answers by graphing bond prices versus YTM. What does this problem tell you about the interest rate risk of longer-term bonds?
17. **Interest Rate Risk** Bond J is a 5 percent coupon bond. Bond K is an 11 percent coupon bond. Both bonds have 8 years to maturity, make semiannual payments, and have a YTM of 7 percent. If interest rates suddenly rise by 2 percent, what is the percentage price change of these bonds? What if rates suddenly fall by 2 percent instead? What does this problem tell you about the interest rate risk of lower-coupon bonds?
18. **Bond Yields** Stealers Wheel Software has 8.4 percent coupon bonds on the market with 9 years to maturity. The bonds make semiannual payments and currently sell for 104 percent of par. What is the current yield on the bonds? The YTM? The effective annual yield?
19. **Bond Yields** Petty Co. wants to issue new 20-year bonds for some much-needed expansion projects. The company currently has 8 percent coupon bonds on the market

that sell for $1,095, make semiannual payments, and mature in 20 years. What coupon rate should the company set on its new bonds if it wants them to sell at par?

20. **Accrued Interest** You purchase a bond with a quoted price of $1,140. The bond has a coupon rate of 7.2 percent, and there are 5 months to the next semiannual coupon date. What is the clean price of the bond?

21. **Accrued Interest** You purchase a bond with a coupon rate of 6.5 percent, and a clean price of $865. If the next semiannual coupon payment is due in three months, what is the invoice price?

22. **Finding the Bond Maturity** Jude Corp. has 11 percent coupon bonds making annual payments with a YTM of 8.5 percent. The current yield on these bonds is 9.06 percent. How many years do these bonds have left until they mature?

23. **Using Bond Quotes** Suppose the following bond quotes for IOU Corporation appear in the financial page of today's newspaper. Assume the bond has a face value of $1,000 and the current date is April 15, 2005. What is the yield to maturity of the bond? What is the current yield? What is the yield to maturity on a comparable U.S. Treasury issue?

Company (Ticker)	Coupon	Maturity	Last Price	Last Yield	EST Spread	UST	EST Vol (000S)
IOU (IOU)	7.375	Apr 15, 2015	769.355	??	468	10	1,827

24. **Bond Prices versus Yields**
    a. What is the relationship between the price of a bond and its YTM?
    b. Explain why some bonds sell at a premium over par value while other bonds sell at a discount. What do you know about the relationship between the coupon rate and the YTM for premium bonds? What about for discount bonds? For bonds selling at par value?
    c. What is the relationship between the current yield and YTM for premium bonds? For discount bonds? For bonds selling at par value?

25. **Interest on Zeroes** HSD Corporation needs to raise funds to finance a plant expansion, and it has decided to issue 20-year zero coupon bonds to raise the money. The required return on the bonds will be 8 percent.
    a. What will these bonds sell for at issuance?
    b. Using the IRS amortization rule, what interest deduction can HSD Corporation take on these bonds in the first year? In the last year?
    c. Repeat part (*b*) using the straight-line method for the interest deduction.
    d. Based on your answers in (*b*) and (*c*), which interest deduction method would HSD Corporation prefer? Why?

26. **Zero Coupon Bonds** Suppose your company needs to raise $15 million and you want to issue 30-year bonds for this purpose. Assume the required return on your bond issue will be 7 percent, and you're evaluating two issue alternatives: a 7 percent annual coupon bond and a zero coupon bond. Your company's tax rate is 35 percent.
    a. How many of the coupon bonds would you need to issue to raise the $15 million? How many of the zeroes would you need to issue?
    b. In 30 years, what will your company's repayment be if you issue the coupon bonds? What if you issue the zeroes?

c. Based on your answers in (*a*) and (*b*), why would you ever want to issue the zeroes? To answer, calculate the firm's aftertax cash outflows for the first year under the two different scenarios. Assume the IRS amortization rules apply for the zero coupon bonds.

27. Finding the Maturity You've just found a 10 percent coupon bond on the market that sells for par value. What is the maturity on this bond?

CHALLENGE (Questions 28–32)

28. Components of Bond Returns Bond P is a premium bond with a 10 percent coupon. Bond D is a 6 percent coupon bond currently selling at a discount. Both bonds make annual payments, have a YTM of 8 percent, and have five years to maturity. What is the current yield for Bond P? For Bond D? If interest rates remain unchanged, what is the expected capital gains yield over the next year for Bond P? For Bond D? Explain your answers and the interrelationship among the various types of yields.

29. Holding Period Yield The YTM on a bond is the interest rate you earn on your investment if interest rates don't change. If you actually sell the bond before it matures, your realized return is known as the holding period yield (HPY).

a. Suppose that today you buy an 8 percent annual coupon bond for $1,150. The bond has 10 years to maturity. What rate of return do you expect to earn on your investment?

b. Two years from now, the YTM on your bond has declined by 1 percent, and you decide to sell. What price will your bond sell for? What is the HPY on your investment? Compare this yield to the YTM when you first bought the bond. Why are they different?

30. Valuing Bonds The Mallory Corporation has two different bonds currently outstanding. Bond M has a face value of $20,000 and matures in 20 years. The bond makes no payments for the first six years, then pays $1,200 every six months over the subsequent eight years, and finally pays $1,500 every six months over the last six years. Bond N also has a face value of $20,000 and a maturity of 20 years; it makes no coupon payments over the life of the bond. If the required return on both these bonds is 10 percent compounded semiannually, what is the current price of Bond M? Of Bond N?

31. Valuing the Call Feature Consider the prices in the following three Treasury issues as of February 24, 2005:

6.500	May 11n	106:10	106:12	−13	5.28
8.250	May 11	103:14	103:16	− 3	5.24
12.000	May 11	134:25	134:31	−15	5.32

The bond in the middle is callable in February 2006. What is the implied value of the call feature? (Hint: Is there a way to combine the two noncallable issues to create an issue that has the same coupon as the callable bond?)

32. Treasury Bonds The following Treasury bond quote appeared in *The Wall Street Journal* on May 11, 2004:

9.125	May 09	100:03	100:04	. . .	−2.15

Why would anyone buy this Treasury bond with a negative yield to maturity? How is this possible?

S&P Problem

www.mhhe.com/edumarketinsight

STANDARD & POOR'S

1. **Bond Ratings** Look up Coca-Cola (KO), Gateway (GTW), AT&T (T), and Navistar International (NAV). For each company, follow the "Financial Highlights" link and find the bond rating. Which companies have an investment grade rating? Which companies are rated below investment grade? Are any unrated? When you find the credit rating for one of the companies, click on the "S&P Issuer Credit Rating" link. What are the three considerations listed that Standard & Poor's uses to issue a credit rating?

What's On the Web?

7.1 **Bond Quotes** You can find current bond prices at www.bondsonline.com. You want to find the bond prices and yields for bonds issued by Georgia Pacific. To find these bonds at the site, click the "Bond Search" link, then the "Corporate" link. Type "Georgia Pacific" in the issue block, select "All" on the pull-down menu, and hit "Find Bonds." What is the shortest maturity bond issued by Georgia Pacific that is being offered for sale? What is the longest maturity bond? What are the credit ratings for Georgia Pacific's bonds? Do all of the bonds have the same credit rating? Why do you think this is?

7.2 **Yield Curves** You can find information regarding the most current bond yields at www.money.cnn.com. Follow the "Bonds & Rates" link and the "Latest Rates" link. Graph the yield curve for U.S. Treasury bonds. What is the general shape of the yield curve? What does this imply about the expected future inflation? Now graph the yield curve for AAA, AA and A rated corporate bonds. Is the corporate yield curve the same shape as the Treasury yield curve? Why or why not?

7.3 **Default Premiums** The St. Louis Federal Reserve Board has files listing historical interest rates on their Web site www.stls.frb.org. Find the link for "FRED II" data, then "Interest Rates." You will find listings for Moody's Seasoned Aaa Corporate Bond Yield and Moody's Seasoned Baa Corporate Bond Yield. A default premium can be calculated as the difference between the Aaa bond yield and the Baa bond yield. Calculate the default premium using these two bond indices for the most recent 36 months. Is the default premium the same for every month? Why do you think this is?

8 Stock Valuation

When the stock market closed on April 13, 2004, the common stock of McGraw-Hill, publisher of fine-quality college textbooks, was going for $76.17 per share. On that same day, Bank of America, one of the largest banks in the United States, closed at $78.50, while eBay, the online auction company, closed at $74.68. Since the stock prices of these three companies were so similar, you might expect that the three companies would be offering similar dividends to their stockholders, but you would be wrong. In fact, Bank of America's annual dividend was $3.20 per share, McGraw-Hill's was $1.20 per share, and eBay was paying no dividends at all!

As we will see in this chapter, the dividends currently being paid are one of the primary factors we look at when attempting to value common stocks. However, it is obvious from looking at eBay that current dividends are not the end of the story, so this chapter explores dividends, stock values, and the connection between the two.

In our previous chapter, we introduced you to bonds and bond valuation. In this chapter, we turn to the other major source of financing for corporations, common and preferred stock. We first describe the cash flows associated with a share of stock and then go on to develop a very famous result, the dividend growth model. From there, we move on to examine various important features of common and preferred stock, focusing on shareholder rights. We close out the chapter with a discussion of how shares of stock are traded and how stock prices and other important information are reported in the financial press.

8.1 COMMON STOCK VALUATION

A share of common stock is more difficult to value in practice than a bond, for at least three reasons. First, with common stock, not even the promised cash flows are known in advance. Second, the life of the investment is essentially forever, since common stock has no maturity. Third, there is no way to easily observe the rate of return that the market requires. Nonetheless, as we will see, there are cases in which we can come up with the present value of the future cash flows for a share of stock and thus determine its value.

Cash Flows

Imagine that you are considering buying a share of stock today. You plan to sell the stock in one year. You somehow know that the stock will be worth \$70 at that time. You predict that the stock will also pay a \$10 per share dividend at the end of the year. If you require a 25 percent return on your investment, what is the most you would pay for the stock? In other words, what is the present value of the \$10 dividend along with the \$70 ending value at 25 percent?

If you buy the stock today and sell it at the end of the year, you will have a total of \$80 in cash. At 25 percent:

$$\text{Present value} = (\$10 + 70)/1.25 = \$64$$

Therefore, \$64 is the value you would assign to the stock today.

More generally, let P_0 be the current price of the stock, and assign P_1 to be the price in one period. If D_1 is the cash dividend paid at the end of the period, then:

$$P_0 = (D_1 + P_1)/(1 + R) \qquad [8.1]$$

where R is the required return in the market on this investment.

Notice that we really haven't said much so far. If we wanted to determine the value of a share of stock today (P_0), we would first have to come up with the value in one year (P_1). This is even harder to do, so we've only made the problem more complicated.

What is the price in one period, P_1? We don't know in general. Instead, suppose we somehow knew the price in two periods, P_2. Given a predicted dividend in two periods, D_2, the stock price in one period would be:

$$P_1 = (D_2 + P_2)/(1 + R)$$

If we were to substitute this expression for P_1 into our expression for P_0, we would have:

$$P_0 = \frac{D_1 + P_1}{1 + R} = \frac{D_1 + \dfrac{D_2 + P_2}{1 + R}}{1 + R}$$

$$= \frac{D_1}{(1 + R)^1} + \frac{D_2}{(1 + R)^2} + \frac{P_2}{(1 + R)^2}$$

Now we need to get a price in two periods. We don't know this either, so we can procrastinate again and write:

$$P_2 = (D_3 + P_3)/(1 + R)$$

If we substitute this back in for P_2, we have:

$$P_0 = \frac{D_1}{(1+R)^1} + \frac{D_2}{(1+R)^2} + \frac{P_2}{(1+R)^2}$$

$$= \frac{D_1}{(1+R)^1} + \frac{D_2}{(1+R)^2} = \frac{\frac{D_3 + P_3}{1+R}}{(1+R)^2}$$

$$= \frac{D_1}{(1+R)^1} + \frac{D_2}{(1+R)^2} + \frac{D_3}{(1+R)^3} + \frac{P_3}{(1+R)^3}$$

You should start to notice that we can push the problem of coming up with the stock price off into the future forever. It is important to note that no matter what the stock price is, the present value is essentially zero if we push the sale of the stock far enough away.[1] What we are eventually left with is the result that the current price of the stock can be written as the present value of the dividends beginning in one period and extending out forever:

$$P_0 = \frac{D_1}{(1+R)^1} + \frac{D_2}{(1+R)^2} + \frac{D_3}{(1+R)^3} + \frac{D_4}{(1+R)^4} + \frac{D_5}{(1+R)^5} + \cdots$$

We have illustrated here that the price of the stock today is equal to the present value of all of the future dividends. How many future dividends are there? In principle, there can be an infinite number. This means that we still can't compute a value for the stock because we would have to forecast an infinite number of dividends and then discount them all. In the next section, we consider some special cases in which we can get around this problem.

EXAMPLE 8.1

Growth Stocks

You might be wondering about shares of stock in companies such as Yahoo! that currently pay no dividends. Small, growing companies frequently plow back everything and thus pay no dividends. Are such shares worth nothing? It depends. When we say that the value of the stock is equal to the present value of the future dividends, we don't rule out the possibility that some number of those dividends are zero. They just can't *all* be zero.

Imagine a company that has a provision in its corporate charter that prohibits the paying of dividends now or ever. The corporation never borrows any money, never pays out any money to stockholders in any form whatsoever, and never sells any assets. Such a corporation couldn't really exist because the IRS wouldn't like it; and the stockholders could always vote to amend the charter if they wanted to. If it did exist, however, what would the stock be worth?

The stock is worth absolutely nothing. Such a company is a financial "black hole." Money goes in, but nothing valuable ever comes out. Because nobody would ever get any return on this investment, the investment has no value. This example is a little absurd, but it illustrates that when we speak of companies that don't pay dividends, what we really mean is that they are not *currently* paying dividends.

[1]The only assumption we make about the stock price is that it is a finite number no matter how far away we push it. It can be extremely large, just not infinitely so. Because no one has ever observed an infinite stock price, this assumption is plausible.

Some Special Cases

There are a few very useful special circumstances under which we can come up with a value for the stock. What we have to do is make some simplifying assumptions about the pattern of future dividends. The three cases we consider are the following: (1) the dividend has a zero growth rate, (2) the dividend grows at a constant rate, and (3) the dividend grows at a constant rate after some length of time. We consider each of these separately.

Zero Growth The case of zero growth is one we've already seen. A share of common stock in a company with a constant dividend is much like a share of preferred stock. From Chapter 6 (Example 6.7), we know that the dividend on a share of preferred stock has zero growth and thus is constant through time. For a zero growth share of common stock, this implies that:

$$D_1 = D_2 = D_3 = D = \text{constant}$$

So, the value of the stock is:

$$P_0 = \frac{D}{(1+R)^1} + \frac{D}{(1+R)^2} + \frac{D}{(1+R)^3} + \frac{D}{(1+R)^4} + \frac{D}{(1+R)^5} + \cdots$$

Because the dividend is always the same, the stock can be viewed as an ordinary perpetuity with a cash flow equal to D every period. The per-share value is thus given by:

$$P_0 = D/R \qquad [8.2]$$

where R is the required return.

For example, suppose the Paradise Prototyping Company has a policy of paying a \$10 per share dividend every year. If this policy is to be continued indefinitely, what is the value of a share of stock if the required return is 20 percent? The stock in this case amounts to an ordinary perpetuity, so the stock is worth \$10/.20 = \$50 per share.

Constant Growth Suppose we know that the dividend for some company always grows at a steady rate. Call this growth rate g. If we let D_0 be the dividend just paid, then the next dividend, D_1, is:

$$D_1 = D_0 \times (1 + g)$$

The dividend in two periods is:

$$\begin{aligned} D_2 &= D_1 \times (1 + g) \\ &= [D_0 \times (1 + g)] \times (1 + g) \\ &= D_0 \times (1 + g)^2 \end{aligned}$$

We could repeat this process to come up with the dividend at any point in the future. In general, from our discussion of compound growth in Chapter 6, we know that the dividend t periods into the future, D_t, is given by:

$$D_t = D_0 \times (1 + g)^t$$

An asset with cash flows that grow at a constant rate forever is called a *growing perpetuity*. As we will see momentarily, there is a simple expression for determining the value of such an asset.

The assumption of steady dividend growth might strike you as peculiar. Why would the dividend grow at a constant rate? The reason is that, for many companies, steady growth in dividends is an explicit goal. For example, in 2004, Procter & Gamble, the

Cincinnati-based maker of personal care and household products, increased its dividend by 9.6 percent to $1.00 per share; this increase was notable because it was the 48th in a row. The subject of dividend growth falls under the general heading of dividend policy, so we will defer further discussion of it to a later chapter.

Dividend Growth

EXAMPLE 8.2

The Hedless Corporation has just paid a dividend of $3 per share. The dividend of this company grows at a steady rate of 8 percent per year. Based on this information, what will the dividend be in five years?

Here we have a $3 current amount that grows at 8 percent per year for five years. The future amount is thus:

$$\$3 \times 1.08^5 = \$3 \times 1.4693 = \$4.41$$

The dividend will therefore increase by $1.41 over the coming five years.

If the dividend grows at a steady rate, then we have replaced the problem of forecasting an infinite number of future dividends with the problem of coming up with a single growth rate, a considerable simplification. In this case, if we take D_0 to be the dividend just paid and g to be the constant growth rate, the value of a share of stock can be written as:

See the dividend discount model in action at www.dividenddiscountmodel.com.

$$P_0 = \frac{D_1}{(1+R)^1} + \frac{D_2}{(1+R)^2} + \frac{D_3}{(1+R)^3} + \cdots$$

$$= \frac{D_0(1+g)^1}{(1+R)^1} + \frac{D_0(1+g)^2}{(1+R)^2} + \frac{D_0(1+g)^3}{(1+R)^3} + \cdots$$

As long as the growth rate, g, is less than the discount rate, r, the present value of this series of cash flows can be written very simply as:

$$P_0 = \frac{D_0 \times (1+g)}{R-g} = \frac{D_1}{R-g} \qquad [8.3]$$

This elegant result goes by a lot of different names. We will call it the **dividend growth model**. By any name, it is very easy to use. To illustrate, suppose D_0 is $2.30, R is 13 percent, and g is 5 percent. The price per share in this case is:

dividend growth model
A model that determines the current price of a stock as its dividend next period divided by the discount rate less the dividend growth rate.

$$\begin{aligned} P_0 &= D_0 \times (1+g)/(R-g) \\ &= \$2.30 \times 1.05/(.13 - .05) \\ &= \$2.415/.08 \\ &= \$30.19 \end{aligned}$$

We can actually use the dividend growth model to get the stock price at any point in time, not just today. In general, the price of the stock as of time t is:

$$P_t = \frac{D_t \times (1+g)}{R-g} = \frac{D_{t+1}}{R-g} \qquad [8.4]$$

In our example, suppose we are interested in the price of the stock in five years, P_5. We first need the dividend at Time 5, D_5. Because the dividend just paid is $2.30 and the growth rate is 5 percent per year, D_5 is:

$$D_5 = \$2.30 \times 1.05^5 = \$2.30 \times 1.2763 = \$2.935$$

From the dividend growth model, we get the price of the stock in five years:

$$P_5 = \frac{D_5 \times (1 + g)}{R - g} = \frac{\$2.935 \times 1.05}{.13 - .05} = \frac{\$3.0822}{.08} = \$38.53$$

EXAMPLE 8.3 >> Gordon Growth Company

The next dividend for the Gordon Growth Company will be \$4 per share. Investors require a 16 percent return on companies such as Gordon. Gordon's dividend increases by 6 percent every year. Based on the dividend growth model, what is the value of Gordon's stock today? What is the value in four years?

The only tricky thing here is that the next dividend, D_1, is given as \$4, so we won't multiply this by $(1 + g)$. With this in mind, the price per share is given by:

$$\begin{aligned} P_0 &= D_1/(R - g) \\ &= \$4/(.16 - .06) \\ &= \$4/.10 \\ &= \$40 \end{aligned}$$

Because we already have the dividend in one year, we know that the dividend in four years is equal to $D_1 \times (1 + g)^3 = \$4 \times 1.06^3 = \$4.764$. The price in four years is therefore:

$$\begin{aligned} P_4 &= D_4 \times (1 + g)/(R - g) \\ &= \$4.764 \times 1.06/(.16 - .06) \\ &= \$5.05/.10 \\ &= \$50.50 \end{aligned}$$

Notice in this example that P_4 is equal to $P_0 \times (1 + g)^4$.

$$P_4 = \$50.50 = \$40 \times 1.06^4 = P_0 \times (1 + g)^4$$

To see why this is so, notice first that:

$$P_4 = D_5/(R - g)$$

However, D_5 is just equal to $D_1 \times (1 + g)^4$, so we can write P_4 as:

$$\begin{aligned} P_4 &= D_1 \times (1 + g)^4/(R - g) \\ &= [D_1/(R - g)] \times (1 + g)^4 \\ &= P_0 \times (1 + g)^4 \end{aligned}$$

This last example illustrates that the dividend growth model makes the implicit assumption that the stock price will grow at the same constant rate as the dividend. This really isn't too surprising. What it tells us is that if the cash flows on an investment grow at a constant rate through time, so does the value of that investment.

You might wonder what would happen with the dividend growth model if the growth rate, g, were greater than the discount rate, R. It looks like we would get a negative stock price because $R - g$ would be less than zero. This is not what would happen.

Instead, if the constant growth rate exceeds the discount rate, then the stock price is infinitely large. Why? If the growth rate is bigger than the discount rate, then the present value of the dividends keeps on getting bigger and bigger. Essentially, the same is true if the growth rate and the discount rate are equal. In both cases, the simplification that allows us to replace the infinite stream of dividends with the dividend growth model is "illegal," so the answers we get from the dividend growth model are nonsense unless the growth rate is less than the discount rate.

Finally, the expression we came up with for the constant growth case will work for any growing perpetuity, not just dividends on common stock. If C_1 is the next cash flow on a growing perpetuity, then the present value of the cash flows is given by:

$$\text{Present value} = C_1/(R - g) = C_0(1 + g)/(R - g)$$

Notice that this expression looks like the result for an ordinary perpetuity except that we have $R - g$ on the bottom instead of just R.

Nonconstant Growth The last case we consider is nonconstant growth. The main reason to consider this case is to allow for "supernormal" growth rates over some finite length of time. As we discussed earlier, the growth rate cannot exceed the required return indefinitely, but it certainly could do so for some number of years. To avoid the problem of having to forecast and discount an infinite number of dividends, we will require that the dividends start growing at a constant rate sometime in the future.

For a simple example of nonconstant growth, consider the case of a company that is currently not paying dividends. You predict that, in five years, the company will pay a dividend for the first time. The dividend will be \$.50 per share. You expect that this dividend will then grow at a rate of 10 percent per year indefinitely. The required return on companies such as this one is 20 percent. What is the price of the stock today?

To see what the stock is worth today, we first find out what it will be worth once dividends are paid. We can then calculate the present value of that future price to get today's price. The first dividend will be paid in five years, and the dividend will grow steadily from then on. Using the dividend growth model, we can say that the price in four years will be:

$$\begin{aligned} P_4 &= D_4 \times (1 + g)/(R - g) \\ &= D_5/(R - g) \\ &= \$.50/(.20 - .10) \\ &= \$5 \end{aligned}$$

If the stock will be worth \$5 in four years, then we can get the current value by discounting this price back four years at 20 percent:

$$P_0 = \$5/1.20^4 = \$5/2.0736 = \$2.41$$

The stock is therefore worth \$2.41 today.

The problem of nonconstant growth is only slightly more complicated if the dividends are not zero for the first several years. For example, suppose that you have come up with the following dividend forecasts for the next three years:

Year	Expected Dividend
1	\$1.00
2	\$2.00
3	\$2.50

After the third year, the dividend will grow at a constant rate of 5 percent per year. The required return is 10 percent. What is the value of the stock today?

In dealing with nonconstant growth, a time line can be very helpful. Figure 8.1 illustrates one for this problem. The important thing to notice is when constant growth starts. As

FIGURE 8.1 >>

Nonconstant Growth

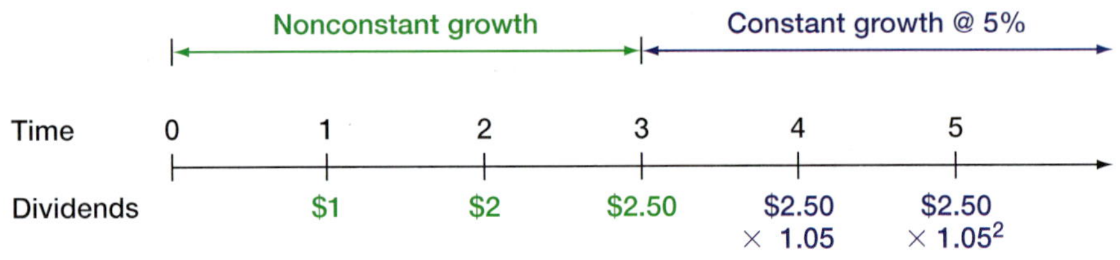

we've shown, for this problem, constant growth starts at Time 3. This means that we can use our constant growth model to determine the stock price at Time 3, P_3. By far the most common mistake in this situation is to incorrectly identify the start of the constant growth phase and, as a result, calculate the future stock price at the wrong time.

As always, the value of the stock is the present value of all the future dividends. To calculate this present value, we first have to compute the present value of the stock price three years down the road, just as we did before. We then have to add in the present value of the dividends that will be paid between now and then. So, the price in three years is:

$$\begin{aligned} P_3 &= D_3 \times (1 + g)/(R - g) \\ &= \$2.50 \times 1.05/(.10 - .05) \\ &= \$52.50 \end{aligned}$$

We can now calculate the total value of the stock as the present value of the first three dividends plus the present value of the price at Time 3, P_3:

$$\begin{aligned} P_0 &= \frac{D_1}{(1 + R)^1} + \frac{D_2}{(1 + R)^2} + \frac{D_3}{(1 + R)^3} + \frac{P_3}{(1 + R)^3} \\ &= \frac{\$1}{1.10} + \frac{2}{1.10^2} + \frac{2.50}{1.10^3} + \frac{52.50}{1.10^3} \\ &= \$.91 + 1.65 + 1.88 + 39.44 \\ &= \$43.88 \end{aligned}$$

The value of the stock today is thus $43.88.

EXAMPLE 8.4 >> Supernormal Growth

Chain Reaction, Inc., has been growing at a phenomenal rate of 30 percent per year because of its rapid expansion and explosive sales. You believe that this growth rate will last for three more years and that the rate will then drop to 10 percent per year. If the growth rate then remains at 10 percent indefinitely, what is the total value of the stock? Total dividends just paid were $5 million, and the required return is 20 percent.

Chain Reaction's situation is an example of supernormal growth. It is unlikely that a 30 percent growth rate can be sustained for any extended length of time. To value the equity in this company, we first need to calculate the total dividends over the supernormal growth period:

Year	Total Dividends (in millions)
1	$5.00 × 1.3 = $ 6.500
2	6.50 × 1.3 = 8.450
3	8.45 × 1.3 = 10.985

The price at Time 3 can be calculated as:

$$P_3 = D_3 \times (1 + g)/(R - g)$$

continued

where g is the long-run growth rate. So we have:

$$P_3 = \$10.985 \times 1.10/(.20 - .10) = \$120.835$$

To determine the value today, we need the present value of this amount plus the present value of the total dividends:

$$P_0 = \frac{D_1}{(1+R)^1} + \frac{D_2}{(1+R)^2} + \frac{D_3}{(1+R)^3} + \frac{P_3}{(1+R)^3}$$

$$= \frac{\$6.50}{1.20} + \frac{8.45}{1.20^2} + \frac{10.985}{1.20^3} + \frac{120.835}{1.20^3}$$

$$= \$5.42 + 5.87 + 6.36 + 69.93$$

$$= \$87.58$$

The total value of the stock today is thus \$87.58 million. If there were, for example, 20 million shares, then the stock would be worth \$87.58/20 = \$4.38 per share.

Components of the Required Return

Thus far, we have taken the required return, or discount rate, R, as given. We will have quite a bit to say on this subject in Chapters 12 and 13. For now, we want to examine the implications of the dividend growth model for this required return. Earlier, we calculated P_0 as:

$$P_0 = D_1/(R - g)$$

If we rearrange this to solve for R, we get:

$$R - g = D_1/P_0$$

$$R = D_1/P_0 + g \qquad [8.5]$$

This tells us that the total return, R, has two components. The first of these, D_1/P_0, is called the **dividend yield**. Because this is calculated as the expected cash dividend divided by the current price, it is conceptually similar to the current yield on a bond.

dividend yield
A stock's expected cash dividend divided by its current price.

The second part of the total return is the growth rate, g. We know that the dividend growth rate is also the rate at which the stock price grows (see Example 8.3). Thus, this growth rate can be interpreted as the **capital gains yield**, that is, the rate at which the value of the investment grows.[2]

capital gains yield
The dividend growth rate, or the rate at which the value of an investment grows.

To illustrate the components of the required return, suppose we observe a stock selling for \$20 per share. The next dividend will be \$1 per share. You think that the dividend will grow by 10 percent per year more or less indefinitely. What return does this stock offer you if this is correct?

The dividend growth model calculates total return as:

$$R = \text{Dividend yield} + \text{Capital gains yield}$$

$$R = D_1/P_0 + g$$

In this case, total return works out to be:

$$R = \$1/20 + 10\%$$

$$= 5\% + 10\%$$

$$= 15\%$$

This stock, therefore, has an expected return of 15 percent.

[2]Here and elsewhere, we use the term *capital gains* a little loosely. For the record, a capital gain (or loss) is, strictly speaking, something defined by the IRS. For our purposes, it would be more accurate (but less common) to use the term *price appreciation* instead of *capital gain*.

We can verify this answer by calculating the price in one year, P_1, using 15 percent as the required return. Based on the dividend growth model, this price is:

$$\begin{aligned} P_1 &= D_1 \times (1 + g)/(R - g) \\ &= \$1 \times 1.10/(.15 - .10) \\ &= \$1.10/.05 \\ &= \$22 \end{aligned}$$

Notice that this \$22 is \$20 × 1.1, so the stock price has grown by 10 percent as it should. If you pay \$20 for the stock today, you will get a \$1 dividend at the end of the year, and you will have a \$22 − 20 = \$2 gain. Your dividend yield is thus \$1/20 = 5%. Your capital gains yield is \$2/20 = 10%, so your total return would be 5% + 10% = 15%.

To get a feel for actual numbers in this context, consider that, according to the 2004 Value Line *Investment Survey,* Procter & Gamble's dividends were expected to grow by 9 percent over the next 5 or so years, compared to a historical growth rate of 11 percent over the preceding 5 years and 11.5 percent over the preceding 10 years. In 2004, the projected dividend for the coming year was given as \$2.12. The stock price at that time was about \$105 per share. What is the return investors require on P&G? Here, the dividend yield is 2 percent and the capital gains yield is 9 percent, giving a total required return of 11 percent on P&G stock.

Our discussion of stock valuation is summarized in Table 8.1.

TABLE 8.1 >>

Summary of Stock Valuation

I. The General Case

In general, the price today of a share of stock, P_0, is the present value of all of its future dividends, $D_1, D_2, D_3, \ldots$:

$$P_0 = \frac{D_1}{(1 + R)^1} + \frac{D_2}{(1 + R)^2} + \frac{D_3}{(1 + R)^3} + \cdots$$

where R is the required return.

II. Constant Growth Case

If the dividend grows at a steady rate, g, then the price can be written as:

$$P_0 = \frac{D_1}{R - g}$$

This result is called the *dividend growth model.*

III. Supernormal Growth

If the dividend grows steadily after t periods, then the price can be written as:

$$P_0 = \frac{D_1}{(1 + R)^1} + \frac{D_2}{(1 + R)^2} + \cdots + \frac{D_t}{(1 + R)^t} + \frac{P_t}{(1 + R)^t}$$

where

$$P_t = \frac{D_t \times (1 + g)}{(R - g)}$$

IV. The Required Return

The required return, R, can be written as the sum of two things:

$$R = D_1/P_0 + g$$

where D_1/P_0 is the *dividend yield* and g is the *capital gains yield* (which is the same thing as the growth rate in dividends for the steady growth case).

Concept Questions

8.1a What are the relevant cash flows for valuing a share of common stock?

8.1b Does the value of a share of stock depend on how long you expect to keep it?

8.1c What is the value of a share of stock when the dividend grows at a constant rate?

SOME FEATURES OF COMMON AND PREFERRED STOCKS 8.2

In discussing common stock features, we focus on shareholder rights and dividend payments. For preferred stock, we explain what the "preferred" means, and we also debate whether preferred stock is really debt or equity.

Common Stock Features

The term **common stock** means different things to different people, but it is usually applied to stock that has no special preference either in receiving dividends or in bankruptcy.

common stock
Equity without priority for dividends or in bankruptcy.

Shareholder Rights The conceptual structure of the corporation assumes that shareholders elect directors who, in turn, hire management to carry out their directives. Shareholders, therefore, control the corporation through the right to elect the directors. Generally, only shareholders have this right.

Directors are elected each year at an annual meeting. Although there are exceptions (discussed next), the general idea is "one share, one vote" (*not* one share*holder,* one vote). Corporate democracy is thus very different from our political democracy. With corporate democracy, the "golden rule" prevails absolutely.[3]

Directors are elected at an annual shareholders' meeting by a vote of the holders of a majority of shares who are present and entitled to vote. However, the exact mechanism for electing directors differs across companies. The most important difference is whether shares must be voted cumulatively or voted straight.

To illustrate the two different voting procedures, imagine that a corporation has two shareholders: Smith with 20 shares and Jones with 80 shares. Both want to be a director. Jones does not want Smith, however. We assume there are a total of four directors to be elected.

The effect of **cumulative voting** is to permit minority participation.[4] If cumulative voting is permitted, the total number of votes that each shareholder may cast is determined first. This is usually calculated as the number of shares (owned or controlled) multiplied by the number of directors to be elected.

cumulative voting
A procedure in which a shareholder may cast all votes for one member of the board of directors.

With cumulative voting, the directors are elected all at once. In our example, this means that the top four vote getters will be the new directors. A shareholder can distribute votes however he/she wishes.

Will Smith get a seat on the board? If we ignore the possibility of a five-way tie, then the answer is yes. Smith will cast $20 \times 4 = 80$ votes, and Jones will cast $80 \times 4 = 320$ votes. If Smith gives all his votes to himself, he is assured of a directorship. The reason is that

[3]The golden rule: Whosoever has the gold makes the rules.

[4]By minority participation, we mean participation by shareholders with relatively small amounts of stock.

Jones can't divide 320 votes among four candidates in such a way as to give all of them more than 80 votes, so Smith will finish fourth at worst.

In general, if there are N directors up for election, then $1/(N + 1)$ percent of the stock plus one share will guarantee you a seat. In our current example, this is $1/(4 + 1) = 20\%$. So the more seats that are up for election at one time, the easier (and cheaper) it is to win one.

straight voting
A procedure in which a shareholder may cast all votes for each member of the board of directors.

With **straight voting**, the directors are elected one at a time. Each time, Smith can cast 20 votes and Jones can cast 80. As a consequence, Jones will elect all of the candidates. The only way to guarantee a seat is to own 50 percent plus one share. This also guarantees that you will win every seat, so it's really all or nothing.

EXAMPLE 8.5 >> Buying the Election

Stock in JRJ Corporation sells for $20 per share and features cumulative voting. There are 10,000 shares outstanding. If three directors are up for election, how much does it cost to ensure yourself a seat on the board?

The question here is how many shares of stock it will take to get a seat. The answer is 2,501, so the cost is 2,501 × $20 = $50,020. Why 2,501? Because there is no way the remaining 7,499 votes can be divided among three people to give all of them more than 2,501 votes. For example, suppose two people receive 2,502 votes and the first two seats. A third person can receive at most 10,000 − 2,502 − 2,502 − 2,501 = 2,495, so the third seat is yours.

As we've illustrated, straight voting can "freeze out" minority shareholders; that is the reason many states have mandatory cumulative voting. In states where cumulative voting is mandatory, devices have been worked out to minimize its impact.

One such device is to stagger the voting for the board of directors. With staggered elections, only a fraction of the directorships are up for election at a particular time. Thus, if only two directors are up for election at any one time, it will take $1/(2 + 1) = 33.33\%$ of the stock plus one share to guarantee a seat.

Overall, staggering has two basic effects:

1. Staggering makes it more difficult for a minority to elect a director when there is cumulative voting because there are fewer directors to be elected at one time.
2. Staggering makes takeover attempts less likely to be successful because it makes it more difficult to vote in a majority of new directors.

We should note that staggering may serve a beneficial purpose. It provides "institutional memory," that is, continuity on the board of directors. This may be important for corporations with significant long-range plans and projects.

proxy
A grant of authority by a shareholder allowing another individual to vote his/her shares.

Proxy Voting A **proxy** is the grant of authority by a shareholder to someone else to vote his/her shares. For convenience, much of the voting in large public corporations is actually done by proxy.

As we have seen, with straight voting, each share of stock has one vote. The owner of 10,000 shares has 10,000 votes. Large companies have hundreds of thousands or even millions of shareholders. Shareholders can come to the annual meeting and vote in person, or they can transfer their right to vote to another party.

Obviously, management always tries to get as many proxies as possible transferred to it. However, if shareholders are not satisfied with management, an "outside" group of shareholders can try to obtain votes via proxy. They can vote by proxy in an attempt to replace management by electing enough directors. The resulting battle is called a *proxy fight.*

Classes of Stock Some firms have more than one class of common stock. Often, the classes are created with unequal voting rights. The Ford Motor Company, for example, has Class B common stock, which is not publicly traded (it is held by Ford family interests and trusts). This class has 40 percent of the voting power, even though it represents less than 10 percent of the total number of shares outstanding.

There are many other cases of corporations with different classes of stock. For example, at one time, General Motors had its "GM Classic" shares (the original) and two additional classes, Class E ("GME") and Class H ("GMH"). These classes were created to help pay for two large acquisitions, Electronic Data Systems and Hughes Aircraft. Another good example is Google, the Web search company, which only recently became publicly owned. Google has two classes of common stock, A and B. The Class A shares are held by the public, and each share has one vote. The Class B shares are held by company insiders, and each Class B share has 10 votes. As a result, Google's founders and management control the company.

Historically, the New York Stock Exchange did not allow companies to create classes of publicly traded common stock with unequal voting rights. Exceptions (e.g., Ford) appear to have been made. In addition, many non-NYSE companies have dual classes of common stock.

A primary reason for creating dual or multiple classes of stock has to do with control of the firm. If such stock exists, management of a firm can raise equity capital by issuing nonvoting or limited-voting stock while maintaining control.

The subject of unequal voting rights is controversial in the United States, and the idea of one share, one vote has a strong following and a long history. Interestingly, however, shares with unequal voting rights are quite common in the United Kingdom and elsewhere around the world.

Other Rights The value of a share of common stock in a corporation is directly related to the general rights of shareholders. In addition to the right to vote for directors, shareholders usually have the following rights:

1. The right to share proportionally in dividends paid.
2. The right to share proportionally in assets remaining after liabilities have been paid in a liquidation.
3. The right to vote on stockholder matters of great importance, such as a merger. Voting is usually done at the annual meeting or a special meeting.

In addition, stockholders sometimes have the right to share proportionally in any new stock sold. This is called the *preemptive right.*

Essentially, a preemptive right means that a company that wishes to sell stock must first offer it to the existing stockholders before offering it to the general public. The purpose is to give a stockholder the opportunity to protect his/her proportionate ownership in the corporation.

Dividends A distinctive feature of corporations is that they have shares of stock on which they are authorized by law to pay dividends to their shareholders. **Dividends** paid to shareholders represent a return on the capital directly or indirectly contributed to the corporation by the shareholders. The payment of dividends is at the discretion of the board of directors.

dividends
Payments by a corporation to shareholders, made in either cash or stock.

Some important characteristics of dividends include the following:

1. Unless a dividend is declared by the board of directors of a corporation, it is not a liability of the corporation. A corporation cannot default on an undeclared dividend. As a consequence, corporations cannot become bankrupt because of nonpayment of dividends. The amount of the dividend and even whether it is paid are decisions based on the business judgment of the board of directors.
2. The payment of dividends by the corporation is not a business expense. Dividends are not deductible for corporate tax purposes. In short, dividends are paid out of the corporation's aftertax profits.
3. Dividends received by individual shareholders are for the most part considered ordinary income by the IRS and are fully taxable. However, corporations that own stock in other corporations are permitted to exclude 70 percent of the dividend amounts they receive and are taxed only on the remaining 30 percent.[5]

Preferred Stock Features

preferred stock
Stock with dividend priority over common stock, normally with a fixed dividend rate, sometimes without voting rights.

Preferred stock differs from common stock because it has preference over common stock in the payment of dividends and in the distribution of corporation assets in the event of liquidation. *Preference* means only that the holders of the preferred shares must receive a dividend (in the case of an ongoing firm) before holders of common shares are entitled to anything.

Preferred stock is a form of equity from a legal and tax standpoint. It is important to note, however, that holders of preferred stock sometimes have no voting privileges.

Stated Value Preferred shares have a stated liquidating value, usually $100 per share. The cash dividend is described in terms of dollars per share. For example, General Motors "$5 preferred" easily translates into a dividend yield of 5 percent of stated value.

Cumulative and Noncumulative Dividends A preferred dividend is *not* like interest on a bond. The board of directors may decide not to pay the dividends on preferred shares, and their decision may have nothing to do with the current net income of the corporation.

Dividends payable on preferred stock are either *cumulative* or *noncumulative;* most are cumulative. If preferred dividends are cumulative and are not paid in a particular year, they will be carried forward as an *arrearage.* Usually, both the accumulated (past) preferred dividends and the current preferred dividends must be paid before the common shareholders can receive anything.

Unpaid preferred dividends are *not* debts of the firm. Directors elected by the common shareholders can defer preferred dividends indefinitely. However, in such cases, common shareholders must also forgo dividends. In addition, holders of preferred shares are often granted voting and other rights if preferred dividends have not been paid for some time. For example, as of summer 1996, USAir had failed to pay dividends on one of its preferred stock issues for six quarters. As a consequence, the holders of the shares were allowed to nominate two people to represent their interests on the airline's board. Because preferred

[5] For the record, the 70 percent exclusion applies when the recipient owns less than 20 percent of the outstanding stock in a corporation. If a corporation owns more than 20 percent but less than 80 percent, the exclusion is 80 percent. If more than 80 percent is owned, the corporation can file a single "consolidated" return and the exclusion is effectively 100 percent.

stockholders receive no interest on the accumulated dividends, some have argued that firms have an incentive to delay paying preferred dividends, but, as we have seen, this may mean sharing control with preferred stockholders.

Is Preferred Stock Really Debt? A good case can be made that preferred stock is really debt in disguise, a kind of equity bond. Preferred shareholders receive a stated dividend only, and, if the corporation is liquidated, preferred shareholders get a stated value. Often, preferred stocks carry credit ratings much like those of bonds. Furthermore, preferred stock is sometimes convertible into common stock, and preferred stocks are often callable.

In addition, many issues of preferred stock have obligatory sinking funds. The existence of such a sinking fund effectively creates a final maturity because it means that the entire issue will ultimately be retired. For these reasons, preferred stock seems to be a lot like debt. However, for tax purposes, preferred dividends are treated like common stock dividends.

In the 1990s, firms began to sell securities that looked a lot like preferred stocks but are treated as debt for tax purposes. The new securities were given interesting acronyms like TOPrS (trust-originated preferred securities, or toppers), MIPS (monthly income preferred securities), and QUIPS (quarterly income preferred securities), among others. Because of various specific features, these instruments can be counted as debt for tax purposes, making the interest payments tax deductible. Payments made to investors in these instruments are treated as interest for personal income taxes for individuals. Until 2003, interest payments and dividends were taxed at the same marginal tax rate. When the tax rate on dividend payments was reduced, these instruments were not included, so individuals must still pay their higher income tax rate on dividend payments received from these instruments.

Concept Questions

8.2a What rights do stockholders have?

8.2b What is a proxy?

8.2c Why is preferred stock called preferred?

THE STOCK MARKETS 8.3

Back in Chapter 1, we very briefly mentioned that shares of stock are bought and sold on various stock exchanges, the two most important of which are the New York Stock Exchange and the NASDAQ. From our earlier discussion, recall that the stock market consists of a **primary market** and a **secondary market**. In the primary, or new-issue, market, shares of stock are first brought to the market and sold to investors. In the secondary market, existing shares are traded among investors.

In the primary market, companies sell securities to raise money. We will discuss this process in detail in a later chapter. We therefore focus mainly on secondary-market activity in this section. We conclude with a discussion of how stock prices are quoted in the financial press.

primary market
The market in which new securities are originally sold to investors.

secondary market
The market in which previously issued securities are traded among investors.

Dealers and Brokers

Because most securities transactions involve dealers and brokers, it is important to understand exactly what is meant by the terms *dealer* and *broker.* A **dealer** maintains an

dealer
An agent who buys and sells securities from inventory.

broker
An agent who arranges security transactions among investors.

inventory and stands ready to buy and sell at any time. In contrast, a **broker** brings buyers and sellers together, but does not maintain an inventory. Thus, when we speak of used car dealers and real estate brokers, we recognize that the used car dealer maintains an inventory, whereas the real estate broker does not.

In the securities markets, a dealer stands ready to buy securities from investors wishing to sell them and sell securities to investors wishing to buy them. Recall from our previous chapter that the price the dealer is willing to pay is called the bid price. The price at which the dealer will sell is called the ask price (sometimes called the asked, offered, or offering price). The difference between the bid and ask prices is called the spread, and it is the basic source of dealer profits.

How big is the bid-ask spread on your favorite stock? Check out the latest quotes at www.bloomberg.com.

Dealers exist in all areas of the economy, not just the stock markets. For example, your local college bookstore is probably both a primary- and a secondary-market textbook dealer. If you buy a new book, this is a primary-market transaction. If you buy a used book, this is a secondary-market transaction, and you pay the store's ask price. If you sell the book back, you receive the store's bid price, often half of the ask price. The bookstore's spread is the difference between the two prices.

In contrast, a securities broker arranges transactions between investors, matching investors wishing to buy securities with investors wishing to sell securities. The distinctive characteristic of security brokers is that they do not buy or sell securities for their own accounts. Facilitating trades by others is their business.

Organization of the NYSE

The New York Stock Exchange, or NYSE, popularly known as the Big Board, celebrated its bicentennial a few years ago. It has occupied its current location on Wall Street since the turn of the twentieth century. Measured in terms of dollar volume of activity and the total value of shares listed, it is the largest stock market in the world.

member
The owner of a seat on the NYSE.

Members

The NYSE has about 1,400 exchange **members**, who are said to own "seats" on the exchange. Collectively, the members of the exchange are its owners. Exchange seat owners can buy and sell securities on the exchange floor without paying commissions. For this and other reasons, exchange seats are valuable assets and are regularly bought and sold. In 2004, seats were selling for about \$1.5 million. The record price is \$2.65 million in 1999. Interestingly, prior to 1986, the highest seat price paid was \$625,000, just before the 1929 market crash. Since then, the lowest seat price paid has been \$55,000, in 1977.

commission brokers
NYSE members who execute customer orders to buy and sell stock transmitted to the exchange floor.

The largest number of NYSE members are registered as **commission brokers**. The business of a commission broker is to execute customer orders to buy and sell stocks. A commission broker's primary responsibility to customers is to get the best possible prices for their orders. The exact number varies, but, usually, about 500 NYSE members are commission brokers. NYSE commission brokers typically are employees of brokerage companies such as Merrill Lynch.

specialist
A NYSE member acting as a dealer in a small number of securities on the exchange floor; often called a market maker.

Second in number of NYSE members are **specialists**, so named because each of them acts as an assigned dealer for a small set of securities. With a few exceptions, each security listed for trading on the NYSE is assigned to a single specialist. Specialists are also called "market makers" because they are obligated to maintain a fair, orderly market for the securities assigned to them.

Specialists post bid prices and ask prices for securities assigned to them. Specialists make a market by standing ready to buy at bid prices and sell at asked prices when there is a temporary disparity between the flow of buy orders and that of sell orders for a security. In this capacity, they act as dealers for their own accounts.

Third in number of exchange members are **floor brokers**. Floor brokers are used by commission brokers who are too busy to handle certain orders themselves. Such commission brokers will delegate some orders to floor brokers for execution. Floor brokers are sometimes called $2 brokers, a name earned at a time when the standard fee for their service was only $2.

floor brokers
NYSE members who execute orders for commission brokers on a fee basis; sometimes called $2 brokers.

In recent years, floor brokers have become less important on the exchange floor because of the efficient **SuperDOT system** (the *DOT* stands for Designated Order Turnaround), which allows orders to be transmitted electronically directly to the specialist. SuperDOT trading now accounts for a substantial percentage of all trading on the NYSE, particularly on smaller orders.

SuperDOT system
An electronic NYSE system allowing orders to be transmitted directly to the specialist.

Finally, a small number of NYSE members are **floor traders** who independently trade for their own accounts. Floor traders try to anticipate temporary price fluctuations and profit from them by buying low and selling high. In recent decades, the number of floor traders has declined substantially, suggesting that it has become increasingly difficult to profit from short-term trading on the exchange floor.

floor traders
NYSE members who trade for their own accounts, trying to anticipate temporary price fluctuations.

Operations

Now that we have a basic idea of how the NYSE is organized and who the major players are, we turn to the question of how trading actually takes place. Fundamentally, the business of the NYSE is to attract and process **order flow**. The term *order flow* means the flow of customer orders to buy and sell stocks. The customers of the NYSE are the millions of individual investors and tens of thousands of institutional investors who place their orders to buy and sell shares in NYSE-listed companies. The NYSE has been quite successful in attracting order flow. Currently, it is not unusual for well over a billion shares to change hands in a single day.

order flow
The flow of customer orders to buy and sell securities.

Floor Activity

It is quite likely that you have seen footage of the NYSE trading floor on television, or you may have visited the NYSE and viewed exchange floor activity from the visitors' gallery (it's worth the trip). Either way, you would have seen a big room, about the size of a basketball gym. This big room is called, technically, "the Big Room." There are a few other, smaller rooms that you normally don't see, one of which is called "the Garage" because that is what it was before it was taken over for trading.

Take a virtual field trip to the New York Stock Exchange at www.nyse.com.

On the floor of the exchange are a number of stations, each with a roughly figure-eight shape. These stations have multiple counters with numerous terminal screens above and on the sides. People operate behind and in front of the counters in relatively stationary positions.

Other people move around on the exchange floor, frequently returning to the many telephones positioned along the exchange walls. In all, you may be reminded of worker ants moving around an ant colony. It is natural to wonder: "What are all those people doing down there (and why are so many wearing funny-looking coats)?"

As an overview of exchange floor activity, here is a quick look at what goes on. Each of the counters at a figure-eight–shaped station is a **specialist's post**. Specialists normally operate in front of their posts to monitor and manage trading in the stocks assigned to them. Clerical employees working for the specialists operate behind the counter. Moving from the many telephones lining the walls of the exchange out to the exchange floor and back again are swarms of commission brokers, receiving telephoned customer orders, walking out to specialists' posts where the orders can be executed, and returning to confirm order executions and receive new customer orders.

specialist's post
A fixed place on the exchange floor where the specialist operates.

To better understand activity on the NYSE trading floor, imagine yourself as a commission broker. Your phone clerk has just handed you an order to sell 20,000 shares of Wal-Mart for a customer of the brokerage company that employs you. The customer wants to sell the stock at the best possible price as soon as possible. You immediately walk (running violates exchange rules) to the specialist's post where Wal-Mart stock is traded.

As you approach the specialist's post where Wal-Mart is traded, you check the terminal screen for information on the current market price. The screen reveals that the last executed trade was at 60.25 and that the specialist is bidding 60 per share. You could immediately sell to the specialist at 60, but that would be too easy.

Instead, as the customer's representative, you are obligated to get the best possible price. It is your job to "work" the order, and your job depends on providing satisfactory order execution service. So, you look around for another broker who represents a customer who wants to buy Wal-Mart stock. Luckily, you quickly find another broker at the specialist's post with an order to buy 20,000 shares. Noticing that the dealer is asking 60.10 per share, you both agree to execute your orders with each other at a price of 60.05. This price is exactly halfway between the specialist's bid and ask prices, and it saves each of your customers $.05 \times 20{,}000 = \$1{,}000$ as compared to dealing at the posted prices.

For a very actively traded stock, there may be many buyers and sellers around the specialist's post, and most of the trading will be done directly between brokers. This is called trading in the "crowd." In such cases, the specialist's responsibility is to maintain order and to make sure that all buyers and sellers receive a fair price. In other words, the specialist essentially functions as a referee.

More often, however, there will be no crowd at the specialist's post. Going back to our Wal-Mart example, suppose you are unable to quickly find another broker with an order to buy 20,000 shares. Because you have an order to sell immediately, you may have no choice but to sell to the specialist at the bid price of 60. In this case, the need to execute an order quickly takes priority, and the specialist provides the liquidity necessary to allow immediate order execution.

Finally, note that colored coats are worn by many of the people on the floor of the exchange. The color of the coat indicates the person's job or position. Clerks, runners, visitors, exchange officials, and so on wear particular colors to identify themselves. Also, things can get a little hectic on a busy day, with the result that good clothing doesn't last long; the cheap coats offer some protection.

NASDAQ Operations

In terms of total dollar volume of trading, the second largest stock market in the United States is NASDAQ (say "Naz-dak"). The somewhat odd name originally was an acronym for the National Association of Securities Dealers Automated Quotations system, but NASDAQ is now a name in its own right.

Introduced in 1971, the NASDAQ market is a computer network of securities dealers and others that disseminates timely security price quotes to computer screens worldwide. NASDAQ dealers act as market makers for securities listed on NASDAQ. As market makers, NASDAQ dealers post bid and ask prices at which they accept sell and buy orders, respectively. With each price quote, they also post the number of stock shares that they obligate themselves to trade at their quoted prices.

Like NYSE specialists, NASDAQ market makers trade on an inventory basis, that is, using their inventory as a buffer to absorb buy and sell order imbalances. Unlike the NYSE specialist system, NASDAQ features multiple market makers for actively traded stocks.

Thus, there are two key differences between the NYSE and NASDAQ:

1. NASDAQ is a computer network and has no physical location where trading takes place.
2. NASDAQ has a multiple market maker system rather than a specialist system.

Traditionally, a securities market largely characterized by dealers who buy and sell securities for their own inventories is called an **over-the-counter (OTC) market**. Consequently, NASDAQ is often referred to as an OTC market. However, in their efforts to promote a distinct image, NASDAQ officials prefer that the term OTC not be used when referring to the NASDAQ market. Nevertheless, old habits die hard, and many people still refer to NASDAQ as an OTC market.

over-the-counter (OTC) market
Securities market in which trading is almost exclusively done through dealers who buy and sell for their own inventories.

By 2004, the NASDAQ had grown to the point that it was, by some measures, bigger than the NYSE. For example, on April 30, 2004, 2.2 billion shares were traded on the NASDAQ versus 1.7 billion on the NYSE. In dollars, NASDAQ trading volume for the day was $41 billion compared to $52 billion for the NYSE.

NASDAQ (www.nasdaq.com) has a *great* Web site; check it out!

The NASDAQ is actually made up of two separate markets, the NASDAQ National Market (NNM) and the NASDAQ SmallCap Market. As the market for NASDAQ's larger and more actively traded securities, the NASDAQ National Market lists about 2,600 companies, including some of the best-known companies in the world. The NASDAQ SmallCap Market is for small companies and lists about 700 individual companies. As you might guess, an important difference in the two markets is that the National Market has more stringent listing requirements. Of course, as SmallCap companies become more established, they may move up to the National Market.

NASDAQ Participants As we mentioned previously, the NASDAQ has historically been a dealer market, characterized by competing market makers. Typically, there have been about a dozen or so per stock. The biggest market makers cover thousands of stocks.

In a very important development, in the late 1990s, the NASDAQ system was opened to so-called **electronic communications networks (ECNs)**. ECNs are basically Web sites that allow investors to trade directly with one another. Our nearby *Work the Web* box describes one of the biggest ECNs, INET (www.island.com), and contains important information about ECN "order books." Be sure to read it.

electronic communications network (ECN)
A Web site that allows investors to trade directly with each other.

Investor buy and sell orders placed on ECNs are transmitted to the NASDAQ and displayed along with market maker bid and ask prices. As a result, the ECNs open up the NASDAQ by essentially allowing individual investors to enter orders, not just market makers. Thus, the ECNs act to increase liquidity and competition.

If you check prices on the Web for both NASDAQ- and NYSE-listed stocks, you'll notice an interesting difference. For NASDAQ issues, you can actually see the bid and ask prices as well as recent transactions information. The bid and ask prices for the NASDAQ listings represent the **inside quotes**, that is, the highest bid and the lowest ask prices. For a relatively small fee (or possibly free from your broker), you can even have access to "Level II" quotes, which show all of the posted bid and ask prices and, frequently, the identity of the market maker. Of course, NYSE specialists post bid and ask prices as well, they are just not disclosed to the general public (they are available by subscription at a cost substantially higher than that for Level II NASDAQ quotes).

inside quotes
Highest bid quotes and lowest ask quotes offered by dealers for a security.

The success of the NASDAQ National Market as a competitor to the NYSE and other organized exchanges can be judged by its ability to attract stock listings by companies that traditionally might have chosen to be listed on the NYSE. Such well-known companies

WORK THE WEB

You can actually watch trading take place on the Web by visiting one of the biggest ECNs, INET (www.island.com), formerly called Island. INET is somewhat unique in that the "order book," meaning the list of buy and sell orders, is public in real time.

As shown, we have captured a sample order book for Johnson & Johnson. On the left are the buy orders (bids); sell orders (asks) are on the right. All orders are "limit" orders, which means that the customer has specified the most she will pay (for buy orders) or the least she will accept (for sell orders). The inside quotes (the highest bid, or buy, and the lowest ask, or sell) in this market are the ones at the top, so we sometimes hear the expression "top of the book" quotes.

If you visit this site, you can see trading take place as orders are entered and executed. Notice that on this particular day, by about 3:00 PM, INET had traded about 13,000 shares of Johnson & Johnson. At that time, the inside quotes for Johnson & Johnson were 500 shares bid at $51.61 and a total of 600 shares offered at $51.64.

refresh | INET home | disclaimer | help

inet **JNJ**

GET STOCK: JNJ go

Symbol Search

LAST MATCH		TODAY'S ACTIVITY	
Price	51.6300	Orders	4,015
Time	15:03:47.952	Volume	12,811

BUY ORDERS		SELL ORDERS	
SHARES	PRICE	SHARES	PRICE
500	51.6100	100	51.6400
100	51.5400	500	51.6400
100	51.4000	400	51.6500
500	51.3600	400	51.9600
500	51.1100	500	51.9600
1,000	50.7100	500	52.1600
10	49.8400	50	52.2000
50	49.2000	50	52.4700
7	49.0100	50	52.4800
5	48.7600	1,000	52.5300
8	48.5200	6	52.8700
50	48.5200	7	53.1500
50	48.2700	50	53.3700
30	47.5400	50	53.4700
6	42.5100	24	53.5900
(1 more)		(4 more)	

as Microsoft, Apple Computer, Intel, Dell, Yahoo!, and Starbucks list their securities on NASDAQ.

Stock Market Reporting

If you look through the pages of *The Wall Street Journal* (or other financial newspaper), you will find information on a large number of stocks in several different markets. Figure 8.2 reproduces a small section of the stock page for the New York Stock Exchange from May 17, 2004. Information on most NASDAQ issues is reported in the same way. In Figure 8.2, locate the line for motorcycle maker Harley-Davidson (HarleyDav). With the column headings, the line reads:

YTD % CHG	52 WEEK HI	52 WEEK LO	STOCK (SYM)	DIV	YLD %	PE	VOL 100s	CLOSE	NET CHG
+15.6	59.86	38.06	HarleyDav HDI	.40f	.7	21	16938	54.95	1.13

The first number, +15.6, tells us the Harley's stock price has risen by 15.6 percent on a year-to-date (YTD) basis. The next two numbers, 59.86 and 38.06, are the highest and lowest prices for the stock over the past 52 weeks. The .40 is the annual dividend in dollars. Because Harley, like most companies, pays dividends quarterly, this $.40 is actually the latest quarterly dividend multiplied by 4. So, the cash dividend paid was $.40/4 = $.10, or 10 cents per share. The small *f* following the .40 indicates a footnote, which, in this case tells us the dividend was just increased.

You can get real-time stock quotes on the Web. See finance.yahoo.com for details.

Jumping ahead just a bit, "CLOSE" is the closing price on the day (i.e., the last price at which a trade took place before the NYSE closed for the day). The "NET CHG" of 1.13

<< FIGURE 8.2

Sample Stock Quotation from *The Wall Street Journal*

NEW YORK STOCK EXCHANGE COMPOSITE TRANSACTIONS

YTD % CHG	52-WEEK HI	52-WEEK LO	STOCK (SYM)	DIV	YLD %	PE	VOL 100s	CLOSE	NET CHG
-0.4	28.41	17.45	Disney **DIS**	.21	.9	24	69695	23.24	-0.06
-33.9	22	10.51	Dist&Srv ADS **DYS**	.54e	4.0	...	763	13.65	-0.26
-13.2	29.30	6	djOrthopedics **DJO**		...	31	934	23.25	-0.45
-15.7	23.40	15.39	DlrGenl **DG**	.16f	.9	20	18734	17.70	-0.10
-2.7	28.50	17.11♣	DlrThrfty **DTG**		...	29	649	25.24	-0.15
-2.7	29.50	23.05	DomResBlkWar **DOM**	2.45e	8.8	...	81	27.73	0.43
-2.1	65.95	58.05♣	DominRes **D**	2.58	4.1	61	16332	62.46	0.33
-10.6	13	10.18	Domtar **DTC**	.24g	...	...	749	11.16	-0.15
-11.3	30.75	19.86♣	Donaldson **DCI** s	.22	.8	23	2594	26.23	0.12
-3.5	32.50	21.62	Donnelly **RRD**	1.04	3.6	26	7161	29.10	0.16
-2.2	35.68	24.87♣	DoralFnl **DRL** s	.60f	1.9	11	5226	31.57	-0.12
-6.9	44.13	28.79	DoverCp **DOV**	.60	1.6	24	6101	36.99	-0.09
18.2	11.99	7.97	DoverDwns **DDE**	.24f	2.1	17	99	11.18	-0.05
25.7	5.53	3.12	Dover Motor **DVD**	.04	.9	dd	293	4.40	-0.15
-9.5	44.22	29.81	DowChem **DOW**	1.34	3.6	17	29486	37.64	-0.01
-4.8	53.62	37.70♣	DowJones **DJ**	1.00	2.1	32	3289	47.48	-0.44
-1.9	55.49	39.74	DowneyFnl **DSL**	.40	.8	17	681	48.34	0.34
-41.7	33.05	17.58	DrRdyLab ADS **RDY**	.11e	.6	...	2468	18.45	-0.38
31.5	40.67	15.55♣	DrewInd **DW**		...	17	233	36.55	0.20
-1.8	20.80	14.41	DrilQuip **DRQ**		...	29	306	16	-0.04
-9.2	46.25	38.60	DuPont **DD**	1.40	3.4	39	38540	41.69	-0.42
-4.3	18.53	12.85	DuaneReade **DRD**		...	38	9056	16.19	-0.30
-14.0	17.60	14.35	DucatiMtr **DMH**		...	...	10	14.70	0.30
-14.3	25.65	12.60	Ducommun **DCO**		...	13	167	19.16	-0.11
-5.2	22.90	16.75	DukeEngy **DUK**	1.10	5.7	dd	36843	19.39	0.01
-10.4	16.28	11.93	DukeEngy un	2.06a	16.6	...	1130	12.40	-0.04
-10.1	16.30	12.50	DukeEngy 8%	2.00	15.5	...	263	12.87	0.03
-5.4	35.16	26.10	DukeRlty **DRE**	1.84	6.3	...	3285	29.32	0.24
3.1	57.01	36.40	DunBradst **DNB**		...	21	5481	52.28	-0.50
-1.0	20.50	13.68	DuquesneLight **DQE**	1.00	5.5	8	1612	18.15	0.25
-16.4	29.80	11.64	DycomInd **DY**		...	24	4372	22.41	0.74
-8.6	5.43	2.80	Dynegy A **DYN**		...	3	26543	3.91	...
11.5	7.78	4.79	DynexCap **DX**		...	dd	19	6.80	-0.04
-13.1	27.20	14.97♣	EDO **EDO**	.12	.6	25	618	21.43	-0.52
-19.0	**15.80**	**9**	**EMC Cp EMC**		**...**	**40**	**267643**	**10.46**	**-0.68**
-10.2	54.30	33	EmcorGp **EME**		...	26	1162	39.44	0.46
17.3	54.75	37.70♣	EOG Res **EOG**	.24	.4	16	11899	54.17	1.05
-0.5	69.90	48.28	E.ON **EON**	2.46e	3.8	...	340	65.10	0.79
-14.6	15.40	6.17	E Trade **ET**		...	15	37807	10.80	-0.28
14.2	66.09	33.75	EagleMat **EXP** s	1.20	1.9	17	880	61.99	0.69
8.3	64.30	52.40	EagleMat B **EXPB** n	.60e	1.0	...	376	60.65	0.65
-16.6	27.80	19.75	EstAm Spers **NGT**	1.82e	8.4	...	109	21.72	0.52
-9.3	36	25.45	EastGroup **EGP**	1.92f	6.5	41	1015	29.37	0.52
12.9	45.12	30.04	EmanChm **EMN**	1.76	3.9	dd	5726	44.63	-0.27
-2.1	32.46	20.39	EKodak **EK**	.50	2.0	26	17237	25.13	-0.10
7.0	62.13	38.23	Eaton **ETN** s	1.08	1.9	20	7815	57.78	0.18
-6.7	40.02	27.85	EatonVance **EV**	.48	1.4	22	2712	34.20	-0.48
5.9	30.17	23.78	Ecolab **ECL** s	.32	1.1	27	6843	28.99	0.13
2.4	24.85	15.21	EdisonInt **EIX**	.40e	1.8	9	10554	22.45	-0.05
0.4	41.80	29.50	EdwardsAG **AGE**	.64	1.8	18	3591	36.37	-0.40
16.4	35.99	25.77	EdwardsLife **EW**		...	cc	2699	35.02	0.17
-8.6	18.75	8.94	eFunds **EFD**		...	23	823	15.85	-0.25
-15.5	9.89	5.97	ElPaso **EP**	.16	2.3	dd	40739	6.92	0.16
4.6	14.89	10.90♣	ElPasoElec **EE**		...	28	878	13.96	...
222.9	**24.77**	**4.05**	**Elan ADS ELN**		**...**	**dd**	**77298**	**22.25**	**2.06**
2.8	31.15	19.65	ElecDePort **EDP**	2.14e	7.9	...	58	27.10	0.08

YTD % CHG	52-WEEK HI	52-WEEK LO	STOCK (SYM)	DIV	YLD %	PE	VOL 100s	CLOSE	NET CHG
-7.7	16.22	10.55	GrayTlvsn **GTN**	.12f	.9	...	2222	13.95	-0.04
-10.6	17.25	13.06	GreatAmFnl **GFR**	.10	.7	11	413	14.50	-0.55
-13.5	11.85	5.01	GtAtlPac **GAP**		...	dd	924	7.27	-0.04
-12.2	28	19.51	GtLakesChm **GLK**	.38	1.6	dd	3882	23.86	-0.07
-3.8	98.50	72	GtNorIron **GNI**	6.80e	7.6	13	12	89.25	-1.00
-6.7	35.69	26.36	GrtPlnsEngy **GXP**	1.66	5.6	13	3539	29.70	0.45
4.4	26.29	20	GreenMtPwr **GMP**	.88	3.6	13	10	24.64	-0.06
-12.2	20.75	9.60	Greenbrier **GBX**		...	17	167	14.70	-0.12
-6.8	20.90	18.51	Greenhill **GHL** n		...	...	630	19.10	0.50
9.2	47.30	28.85	GrnPtFnl **GPT** s	1.20	3.1	10	3761	38.57	0.43
-2.2	38.65	18.63	Greif A **GEF**	.56	1.6	...	167	34.72	0.11
8.6	23.43	13.95	Griffon **GFF**		...	15	3587	22	-0.57
-15.7	40.19	26.22	Gp1Auto **GPI**		...	10	3855	30.51	0.31
25.4	7.30	3.45	Gruma ADS **GMK**	.24e	3.7	...	17	6.67	0.02
12.2	22.50	12.58	GpoAsur ADS B **ASR**	.48e	2.4	...	123	19.74	0.11
-1.1	27.67	10.75	GpoElektr ADS **EKT**	.37e	1.8	...	202	20.89	0.33
-12.1	22.64	10.85	GpoImsa ADS **IMY**	.46e	2.6	...	29	17.55	0.15
-44.4	11.28	1.50	GpoIusacell ADS **CEL**		...	...	116	5.15	-0.03
-25.5	**7.50**	**3.05**	**GpoRadio ADS RC**	**.28e**	**5.5**	**...**	**224**	**5.20**	**-0.55**
4.4	49.30	28.36	GpoTelevsa ADS **TV**	4.72e	11.3	...	4498	41.61	0.75
-39.9	4.56	1.45	GpoTMM ADS **TMM**		...	...	379	2.55	0.01
3.3	64.95	33.30♣	Gtech **GTK**	.68	1.3	18	17414	51.14	1.79
-13.8	18.50	8.30	GungshnRail **GSH**	1.24e	9.9	...	230	12.51	-0.29
18.1	19.58	3.86	Guess **GES**		...	46	786	14.25	-0.17
1.4	73.70	36.97♣	GuidantCp **GDT**	.40f	.7	52	19805	61.03	-0.82
▲ 1.8	21	20.85	GulfPwr nts **GUQ** n		...	...	29	21.23	0.38
-12.5	43	35	GulfTrEnPt **GTM**	2.84	7.6	25	820	37.15	0.03
-11.0	21.50	12.50	GndlSltEnvr **GSE**		...	...	219	18.47	-0.01

H

YTD % CHG	52-WEEK HI	52-WEEK LO	STOCK (SYM)	DIV	YLD %	PE	VOL 100s	CLOSE	NET CHG
-7.1	46.60	31.10	HCA **HCA**	.52f	1.3	17	22825	39.90	-0.36
-1.3	34.75	27.14♣	HCC InsHldg **HCC**	.30	1.0	12	1624	31.40	0.02
-14.9	**34.90**	**16.25**	**HDFC Bnk HDB**	**.24e**	**.9**	**...**	**2395**	**25.98**	**-3.72**
-11.1	45.71	27.27	HNI **HNI**	.56	1.5	22	1179	38.53	0.01
-10.3	11.39	8.25	HRPT Prop **HRP**	.80	8.8	15	7648	9.05	0.04
-10.1	82.90	56.61	HSBC ADS **HBC**	3.65e	5.2	...	3755	70.83	-0.37
10.5	32.50	16.30	Haemonetic **HAE**		...	22	1808	26.40	-0.41
12.1	32.70	20.50	Hallibrtn **HAL**	.50	1.7	dd	23745	29.15	-0.19
-8.8	19.02	13	HnckFabrcs **HKF**	.48f	3.6	14	583	13.21	-0.18
6.5	26.47	15.09	Handleman **HDL**	.21e	1.0	13	1134	21.87	-0.48
3.7	19.25	9.59	HangerOrtho **HGR**		...	50	929	16.14	0.18
-4.7	13.49	8.82	HanovrCmprsr **HC**		...	dd	7445	10.63	-0.25
-0.6	42.75	26.55	Hanson ADS **HAN**	1.53e	4.2	...	107	36.29	-0.38
7.7	32.50	23	Harland **JH**	.40	1.4	15	1072	29.41	0.02
15.6	59.86	38.06	HarleyDav **HDI**	.40f	.7	21	16938	54.95	1.13
-1.3	87.25	33.95	HarmanInt **HAR** s	.05	.1	35	4029	73.02	-0.69
-34.8	17.80	10.03	HrmnyGld ADS **HMY**	.25e	2.4	...	9178	10.58	0.13
4.5	57.50	38.60	HarrahEntn **HET**	1.20	2.3	20	10943	52.03	0.35
14.0	51.19	28.55	Harris **HRS**	.40	.9	30	5493	43.25	-0.15
-5.9	48.78	33.16	Harsco **HSC**	1.10	2.7	18	991	41.25	-0.32
6.9	24.88	17.58	HarteHanks **HHS**	.16f	.7	23	616	23.24	-0.09
6.7	67.71	43.49	HrtfrdFnl **HIG**	1.12	1.8	dd	15068	63	-0.43
2.5	65.40	47.20	HrtfrdFnl un	3.00	5.0	...	122	60.58	-0.36
2.5	66.99	49.40	HrtfrdFnl 7.0un n	3.50	5.6	...	2389	62.17	-0.40

tells us that the closing price of \$54.95 is \$1.13 higher than it was the day before; so, we say that Harley was up 1.13 for the day.

The column marked "YLD %" gives the dividend yield based on the current dividend and the closing price. For Harley, this is \$.40/54.95 = .0073, or about .7 percent, the number shown. The next column, labeled "PE," is the price-earnings ratio we discussed in Chapter 3. It is calculated as the closing price divided by annual earnings per share (based on the most recent four quarters). In the jargon of Wall Street, we might say that Harley "sells for 21 times earnings."

Finally, the column marked "VOL 100s" tells us how many shares traded during the day (in hundreds). For example, the 16938 for Harley tells us that 1,693,800, or close to 2 million shares, changed hands on this day alone. If the average price during the day was \$55 or so, then the dollar volume of transactions was on the order of \$55 × 2 million = \$110 million worth for Harley alone. This was a fairly routine day of trading in Harley shares, so this amount is not unusual and serves to illustrate how active the market can be for well-known companies.

If you look over Figure 8.2, you will notice quite a few other footnote indicators (small letters) and special symbols. To learn more about these, pick up any *Wall Street Journal* and consult the stock pages.

Concept Questions

8.3a What is the difference between a securities broker and a securities dealer?

8.3b Which is bigger, the bid price or the ask price? Why?

8.3c What are the four types of members of the New York Stock Exchange, or NYSE?

8.3d How does NASDAQ differ from the NYSE?

8.4 SUMMARY AND CONCLUSIONS

This chapter has covered the basics of stocks and stock valuation. The key points include:

1. The cash flows from owning a share of stock come in the form of future dividends. We saw that in certain special cases it is possible to calculate the present value of all the future dividends and thus come up with a value for the stock.
2. As the owner of shares of common stock in a corporation, you have various rights, including the right to vote to elect corporate directors. Voting in corporate elections can be either cumulative or straight. Most voting is actually done by proxy, and a proxy battle breaks out when competing sides try to gain enough votes to have their candidates for the board elected.
3. In addition to common stock, some corporations have issued preferred stock. The name stems from the fact that preferred stockholders must be paid first, before common stockholders can receive anything. Preferred stock has a fixed dividend.
4. The two biggest stock markets in the United States are the NYSE and the NASDAQ. We discussed the organization and operation of these two markets, and we saw how stock price information is reported in the financial press.

This chapter completes Part 3 of our book. By now, you should have a good grasp of what we mean by present value. You should also be familiar with how to calculate present values, loan payments, and so on. In Part 4, we cover capital budgeting decisions. As you will see, the techniques you learned in Chapters 5–8 form the basis for our approach to evaluating business investment decisions.

Chapter Review and Self-Test Problems

8.1 **Dividend Growth and Stock Valuation** The Brigapenski Co. has just paid a cash dividend of $2 per share. Investors require a 16 percent return from investments such as this. If the dividend is expected to grow at a steady 8 percent per year, what is the current value of the stock? What will the stock be worth in five years?

8.2 **More Dividend Growth and Stock Valuation** In Self-Test Problem 8.1, what would the stock sell for today if the dividend was expected to grow at 20 percent per year for the next three years and then settle down to 8 percent per year, indefinitely?

Answers to Chapter Review and Self-Test Problems

8.1 The last dividend, D_0, was $2. The dividend is expected to grow steadily at 8 percent. The required return is 16 percent. Based on the dividend growth model, we can say that the current price is:

$$\begin{aligned} P_0 &= D_1/(R - g) = D_0 \times (1 + g)/(R - g) \\ &= \$2 \times 1.08/(.16 - .08) \\ &= \$2.16/.08 \\ &= \$27 \end{aligned}$$

We could calculate the price in five years by calculating the dividend in five years and then using the growth model again. Alternatively, we could recognize that the stock price will increase by 8 percent per year and calculate the future price directly. We'll do both. First, the dividend in five years will be:

$$\begin{aligned} D_5 &= D_0 \times (1 + g)^5 \\ &= \$2 \times 1.08^5 \\ &= \$2.9387 \end{aligned}$$

The price in five years would therefore be:

$$\begin{aligned} P_5 &= D_5 \times (1 + g)/(R - g) \\ &= \$2.9387 \times 1.08/.08 \\ &= \$3.1738/.08 \\ &= \$39.67 \end{aligned}$$

Once we understand the dividend model, however, it's easier to notice that:

$$\begin{aligned} P_5 &= P_0 \times (1 + g)^5 \\ &= \$27 \times 1.08^5 \\ &= \$27 \times 1.4693 \\ &= \$39.67 \end{aligned}$$

Notice that both approaches yield the same price in five years.

8.2 In this scenario, we have supernormal growth for the next three years. We'll need to calculate the dividends during the rapid-growth period and the stock price in three years. The dividends are:

$$\begin{aligned} D_1 &= \$2.00 \times 1.20 = \$2.400 \\ D_2 &= \$2.40 \times 1.20 = \$2.880 \\ D_3 &= \$2.88 \times 1.20 = \$3.456 \end{aligned}$$

After three years, the growth rate falls to 8 percent indefinitely. The price at that time, P_3, is thus:

$$\begin{aligned} P_3 &= D_3 \times (1 + g)/(R - g) \\ &= \$3.456 \times 1.08/(.16 - .08) \\ &= \$3.7325/.08 \\ &= \$46.656 \end{aligned}$$

To complete the calculation of the stock's present value, we have to determine the present value of the three dividends and the future price:

$$\begin{aligned} P_0 &= \frac{D_1}{(1+R)^1} + \frac{D_2}{(1+R)^2} + \frac{D_3}{(1+R)^3} + \frac{P_3}{(1+R)^3} \\ &= \frac{\$2.40}{1.16} + \frac{2.88}{1.16^2} + \frac{3.456}{1.16^3} + \frac{46.656}{1.16^3} \\ &= \$2.07 + 2.14 + 2.21 + 29.89 \\ &= \$36.31 \end{aligned}$$

Visit us at www.mhhe.com/rwj

Concepts Review and Critical Thinking Questions

1. **Stock Valuation** Why does the value of a share of stock depend on dividends?
2. **Stock Valuation** A substantial percentage of the companies listed on the NYSE and the NASDAQ don't pay dividends, but investors are nonetheless willing to buy shares in them. How is this possible given your answer to the previous question?
3. **Dividend Policy** Referring to the previous questions, under what circumstances might a company choose not to pay dividends?
4. **Dividend Growth Model** Under what two assumptions can we use the dividend growth model presented in the chapter to determine the value of a share of stock? Comment on the reasonableness of these assumptions.
5. **Common versus Preferred Stock** Suppose a company has a preferred stock issue and a common stock issue. Both have just paid a \$2 dividend. Which do you think will have a higher price, a share of the preferred or a share of the common?
6. **Dividend Growth Model** Based on the dividend growth model, what are the two components of the total return on a share of stock? Which do you think is typically larger?
7. **Growth Rate** In the context of the dividend growth model, is it true that the growth rate in dividends and the growth rate in the price of the stock are identical?
8. **Voting Rights** When it comes to voting in elections, what are the differences between U.S. political democracy and U.S. corporate democracy?
9. **Corporate Ethics** Is it unfair or unethical for corporations to create classes of stock with unequal voting rights?
10. **Voting Rights** Some companies, such as Reader's Digest, have created classes of stock with no voting rights at all. Why would investors buy such stock?
11. **Stock Valuation** Evaluate the following statement: Managers should not focus on the current stock value because doing so will lead to an overemphasis on short-term profits at the expense of long-term profits.

Questions and Problems

BASIC
(Questions 1–8)

1. **Stock Values** The Jackson–Timberlake Wardrobe Co., just paid a dividend of $1.40 per share on its stock. The dividends are expected to grow at a constant rate of 6 percent per year, indefinitely. If investors require a 12 percent return on The Jackson–Timberlake Wardrobe Co., stock, what is the current price? What will the price be in three years? In 15 years?
2. **Stock Values** The next dividend payment by MUG, Inc., will be $3.10 per share. The dividends are anticipated to maintain a 5 percent growth rate, forever. If MUG stock currently sells for $48.00 per share, what is the required return?
3. **Stock Values** For the company in the previous problem, what is the dividend yield? What is the expected capital gains yield?
4. **Stock Values** Warren Corporation will pay a $3.60 per share dividend next year. The company pledges to increase its dividend by 4.5 percent per year, indefinitely. If you require a 13 percent return on your investment, how much will you pay for the company's stock today?
5. **Stock Valuation** Joe Elvis Co. is expected to maintain a constant 6 percent growth rate in its dividends, indefinitely. If the company has a dividend yield of 3.9 percent, what is the required return on the company's stock?
6. **Stock Valuation** Suppose you know that a company's stock currently sells for $70 per share and the required return on the stock is 12 percent. You also know that the total return on the stock is evenly divided between a capital gains yield and a dividend yield. If it's the company's policy to always maintain a constant growth rate in its dividends, what is the current dividend per share?
7. **Stock Valuation** Rocket Man Corp. pays a constant $12 dividend on its stock. The company will maintain this dividend for the next eight years and will then cease paying dividends forever. If the required return on this stock is 10 percent, what is the current share price?
8. **Valuing Preferred Stock** Ayden, Inc., has an issue of preferred stock outstanding that pays an $8.25 dividend every year, in perpetuity. If this issue currently sells for $113 per share, what is the required return?

INTERMEDIATE
(Questions 9–18)

9. **Stock Valuation** Smashed Pumpkin Farms (SPF) just paid a dividend of $3.00 on its stock. The growth rate in dividends is expected to be a constant 5 percent per year, indefinitely. Investors require a 16 percent return on the stock for the first three years, a 14 percent return for the next three years, and then an 11 percent return, thereafter. What is the current share price for SPF stock?
10. **Nonconstant Growth** Metallica Bearings, Inc., is a young start-up company. No dividends will be paid on the stock over the next nine years, because the firm needs to plow back its earnings to fuel growth. The company will pay an $8 per share dividend in 10 years and will increase the dividend by 6 percent per year, thereafter. If the required return on this stock is 13 percent, what is the current share price?
11. **Nonconstant Dividends** Corn, Inc., has an odd dividend policy. The company has just paid a dividend of $9 per share and has announced that it will increase the dividend by $3 per share for each of the next four years, and then never pay another dividend. If you require an 11 percent return on the company's stock, how much will you pay for a share today?
12. **Nonconstant Dividends** South Side Corporation is expected to pay the following dividends over the next four years: $8, $6, $3, and $2. Afterwards, the company pledges to maintain a constant 5 percent growth rate in dividends, forever. If the required return on the stock is 13 percent, what is the current share price?

13. **Supernormal Growth** Rizzi Co. is growing quickly. Dividends are expected to grow at a 25 percent rate for the next three years, with the growth rate falling off to a constant 7 percent thereafter. If the required return is 13 percent and the company just paid a $2.80 dividend, what is the current share price?
14. **Supernormal Growth** Janicek Corp. is experiencing rapid growth. Dividends are expected to grow at 30 percent per year during the next three years, 18 percent over the following year, and then 8 percent per year, indefinitely. The required return on this stock is 14 percent, and the stock currently sells for $70.00 per share. What is the projected dividend for the coming year?
15. **Negative Growth** Antiques R Us is a mature manufacturing firm. The company just paid a $10 dividend, but management expects to reduce the payout by 8 percent per year, indefinitely. If you require an 11 percent return on this stock, what will you pay for a share today?
16. **Finding the Dividend** Hollin Corporation stock currently sells for $50 per share. The market requires a 14 percent return on the firm's stock. If the company maintains a constant 8 percent growth rate in dividends, what was the most recent dividend per share paid on the stock?
17. **Valuing Preferred Stock** Mark Bank just issued some new preferred stock. The issue will pay a $9 annual dividend in perpetuity, beginning six years from now. If the market requires a 7 percent return on this investment, how much does a share of preferred stock cost today?
18. **Using Stock Quotes** You have found the following stock quote for RJW Enterprises, Inc., in the financial pages of today's newspaper. What was the closing price for this stock that appeared in *yesterday's* paper? If the company currently has 25 million shares of stock outstanding, what was net income for the most recent four quarters?

YTD	52 WEEK				YLD			VOL		NET
% CHG	HI	LO	STOCK	SYM	DIV	%	PE	100s	CLOSE	CHG
22.4	70.80	39.93	RJW	RJW	.15	.2	14	35215	??	2.20

Visit us at www.mhhe.com/rwj

CHALLENGE
(Questions 19–22)

19. **Capital Gains versus Income** Consider four different stocks, all of which have a required return of 15 percent and a most recent dividend of $4.50 per share. Stocks W, X, and Y are expected to maintain constant growth rates in dividends for the foreseeable future of 10 percent, 0 percent, and −5 percent per year, respectively. Stock Z is a growth stock that will increase its dividend by 20 percent for the next two years and then maintain a constant 12 percent growth rate, thereafter. What is the dividend yield for each of these four stocks? What is the expected capital gains yield? Discuss the relationship among the various returns that you find for each of these stocks.
20. **Stock Valuation** Most corporations pay quarterly dividends on their common stock rather than annual dividends. Barring any unusual circumstances during the year, the board raises, lowers, or maintains the current dividend once a year and then pays this dividend out in equal quarterly installments to its shareholders.
    - **a.** Suppose a company currently pays a $3.00 annual dividend on its common stock in a single annual installment, and management plans on raising this dividend by 6 percent per year, indefinitely. If the required return on this stock is 14 percent, what is the current share price?
    - **b.** Now suppose that the company in (*a*) actually pays its annual dividend in equal quarterly installments; thus, this company has just paid a $.75 dividend per share, as it has for the previous three quarters. What is your value for the current share price now? (Hint: Find the equivalent annual end-of-year dividend for each year.) Comment on whether or not you think that this model of stock valuation is appropriate.

21. **Nonconstant Growth** Storico Co. just paid a dividend of $3.50 per share. The company will increase its dividend by 20 percent next year and will then reduce its dividend growth rate by 5 percentage points per year until it reaches the industry average of 5 percent dividend growth, after which the company will keep a constant growth rate, forever. If the required return on Storico stock is 13 percent, what will a share of stock sell for today?
22. **Nonconstant Growth** This one's a little harder. Suppose the current share price for the firm in the previous problem is $98.65 and all the dividend information remains the same. What required return must investors be demanding on Storico stock? (Hint: Set up the valuation formula with all the relevant cash flows, and use trial and error to find the unknown rate of return.)

www.mhhe.com/edumarketinsight — S&P Problems

STANDARD &POOR'S

1. **Calculating Required Return** A drawback of the dividend growth model is the need to estimate the growth rate of dividends. One way to estimate this growth rate is to use the sustainable growth rate. Look back at Chapter 4 and find the formula for the sustainable growth rate. Using the annual income statement and balance sheet, calculate the sustainable growth rate for the Kellogg Company (K). Find the most recent closing monthly stock price under the "Mthly. Adj. Prices" link. Using the growth rate you calculated, the most recent dividend per share, and the most recent stock price, calculate the required return for Kellogg's shareholders. Does this number make sense? Why or why not?
2. **Calculating Growth Rates** Coca-Cola (KO) is a dividend-paying company. Recently, dividends for Coca-Cola have increased at about 8 percent per year. Find the most recent closing monthly stock price under the "Mthly. Adj. Prices" link. Locate the most recent annual dividend for KO and calculate the dividend yield. Using your answer and the 8 percent dividend growth rate, what is the required return for shareholders? Suppose instead that you know that the required return is 13 percent. What price should Coca-Cola stock sell for now? What if the required return is 15 percent?

What's On the Web?

8.1 **Dividend Discount Model** According to the 2004 Value Line *Investment Survey,* the dividend growth for ConocoPhillips (P) is 3.5 percent. Find the current price quote and dividend information at finance.yahoo.com. If the growth rate given in the Value Line *Investment Survey* is correct, what is the required return for ConocoPhillips? Does this number make sense to you?

8.2 **Dividend Discount Model** Go to www.dividenddiscountmodel.com and enter BA (for Boeing) as the ticker symbol. You can enter a required return in the Discount Rate box and the site will calculate the stock price using the dividend discount model. If you want an 11 percent return, what price should you be willing to pay for the stock? At what required return does the current stock price make sense? You will need to enter different required returns until you arrive at the current stock price. Does this required return make sense? Using this market required return for Boeing, how does the price change if the required return increases by 1 percent? What does this tell you about the sensitivity of the dividend discount model to the inputs of the equation?

8.3 **Market Operations** How does a stock trade take place? Go to www.nyse.com, click on "The Trading Floor" and "Anatomy of a Trade." Describe the process of a trade on the NYSE.

>> **MINI-CASE**

Financing S&S Air's Expansion Plans with a Bond Issue

Mark Sexton and Todd Story, the owners of S&S Air, have decided to expand their operations. They instructed their newly hired financial analyst, Chris Guthrie, to enlist an underwriter to help sell $20 million in new 10-year bonds to finance construction. Chris has entered into discussions with Danielle Ralston, an underwriter from the firm of Raines and Warren, about which bond features S&S Air should consider and what coupon rate the issue will likely have.

Although Chris is aware of the bond features, he is uncertain as to the costs and benefits of some features, so he isn't clear on how each feature would affect the coupon rate of the bond issue. You are Danielle's assistant, and she has asked you to prepare a memo to Chris describing the effect of each of the following bond features on the coupon rate of the bond. She would also like you to list any advantages or disadvantages of each feature.

1. The security of the bond, that is, whether the bond has collateral.
2. The seniority of the bond.
3. The presence of a sinking fund.
4. A call provision with specified call dates and call prices.
5. A deferred call accompanying the above call provision.
6. A make-whole call provision.
7. Any positive covenants. Also, discuss several possible positive covenants S&S Air might consider.
8. Any negative covenants. Also, discuss several possible negative covenants S&S Air might consider.
9. A conversion feature (note that S&S Air is not a publicly traded company).
10. A floating rate coupon.

9 Net Present Value and Other Investment Criteria

The video game industry is no longer a game. In the first quarter of 2004 alone, sales of video games and consoles totaled $1.8 billion. Console hardware sales amounted to about $336 million of this total. With numbers like these, it is not too surprising that companies would spend large amounts to get in the game.

One of the big-name companies in the console market is Microsoft, which spent many millions of dollars to develop and sell its Xbox game console. Unfortunately for the company, sales lagged far behind those of the industry leader, Sony's PlayStation 2. In 2002, in an effort to boost the Xbox, Microsoft announced a new online game service, Xbox *Live*. The price tag for Xbox *Live?* Over $1 *billion!*

Microsoft's announcement of Xbox *Live* is an example of a capital budgeting decision. A product introduction such as this one, with a price tag of over $1 billion, is obviously a major undertaking, and the risks and rewards must be carefully weighed. In this chapter, we discuss the basic tools used in making such decisions.

This chapter introduces you to the practice of capital budgeting. Back in Chapter 1, we saw that increasing the value of the stock in a company is the goal of financial management. Thus, what we need to learn is how to tell whether a particular investment will achieve that or not. This chapter considers a variety of techniques that are actually used in practice. More importantly, it shows how many of these techniques can be misleading, and it explains why the net present value approach is the right one.

In Chapter 1, we identified the three key areas of concern to the financial manager. The first of these involved the question: What fixed assets should we buy? We called this the *capital budgeting decision.* In this chapter, we begin to deal with the issues that arise in answering this question.

The process of allocating or budgeting capital is usually more involved than just deciding on whether or not to buy a particular fixed asset. We will frequently face broader issues like whether or not we should launch a new product or enter a new market. Decisions such as these will determine the nature of a firm's operations and products for years to come, primarily because fixed asset investments are generally long-lived and not easily reversed once they are made.

The most fundamental decision a business must make concerns its product line. What services will we offer or what will we sell? In what markets will we compete? What new products will we introduce? The answer to any of these questions will require that the firm commit its scarce and valuable capital to certain types of assets. As a result, all of these strategic issues fall under the general heading of capital budgeting. The process of capital budgeting could thus be given a more descriptive (not to mention impressive) name: *strategic asset allocation.*

For the reasons we have discussed, the capital budgeting question is probably the most important issue in corporate finance. How a firm chooses to finance its operations (the capital structure question) and how a firm manages its short-term operating activities (the working capital question) are certainly issues of concern, but it is the fixed assets that define the business of the firm. Airlines, for example, are airlines because they operate airplanes, regardless of how they finance them.

Any firm possesses a huge number of possible investments. Each possible investment is an option available to the firm. Some options are valuable and some are not. The essence of successful financial management, of course, is learning to identify which are which. With this in mind, our goal in this chapter is to introduce you to the techniques used to analyze potential business ventures to decide which are worth undertaking.

We present and compare a number of different procedures used in practice. Our primary goal is to acquaint you with the advantages and disadvantages of the various approaches. As we shall see, the most important concept in this area is the idea of net present value. We consider this next.

9.1 NET PRESENT VALUE

In Chapter 1, we argued that the goal of financial management is to create value for the stockholders. The financial manager must thus examine a potential investment in light of its likely effect on the price of the firm's shares. In this section, we describe a widely used procedure for doing this, the net present value approach.

The Basic Idea

An investment is worth undertaking if it creates value for its owners. In the most general sense, we create value by identifying an investment worth more in the marketplace than it costs us to acquire. How can something be worth more than it costs? It's a case of the whole being worth more than the cost of the parts.

For example, suppose you buy a run-down house for \$25,000 and spend another \$25,000 on painters, plumbers, and so on to get it fixed up. Your total investment is \$50,000. When the work is completed, you place the house back on the market and find that it's worth \$60,000. The market value (\$60,000) exceeds the cost (\$50,000) by \$10,000. What you have done here is to act as a manager and bring together some fixed assets (a house), some labor (plumbers, carpenters, and others), and some materials (carpeting, paint, and so on). The net result is that you have created \$10,000 in value. Put another way, this \$10,000 is the *value added* by management.

With our house example, it turned out *after the fact* that \$10,000 in value had been created. Things thus worked out very nicely. The real challenge, of course, would have been to somehow identify *ahead of time* whether or not investing the necessary \$50,000 was a good idea in the first place. This is what capital budgeting is all about, namely, trying to determine whether a proposed investment or project will be worth more, once it is in place, than it costs.

For reasons that will be obvious in a moment, the difference between an investment's market value and its cost is called the **net present value** of the investment, abbreviated **NPV**. In other words, net present value is a measure of how much value is created or added today by undertaking an investment. Given our goal of creating value for the stockholders, the capital budgeting process can be viewed as a search for investments with positive net present values.

With our run-down house, you can probably imagine how we would go about making the capital budgeting decision. We would first look at what comparable, fixed-up properties were selling for in the market. We would then get estimates of the cost of buying a particular property and bringing it to market. At this point, we would have an estimated total cost and an estimated market value. If the difference was positive, then this investment would be worth undertaking because it would have a positive estimated net present value. There is risk, of course, because there is no guarantee that our estimates will turn out to be correct.

net present value (NPV)
The difference between an investment's market value and its cost.

As our example illustrates, investment decisions are greatly simplified when there is a market for assets similar to the investment we are considering. Capital budgeting becomes much more difficult when we cannot observe the market price for at least roughly comparable investments. The reason is that we are then faced with the problem of estimating the value of an investment using only indirect market information. Unfortunately, this is precisely the situation the financial manager usually encounters. We examine this issue next.

Estimating Net Present Value

Imagine we are thinking of starting a business to produce and sell a new product, say, organic fertilizer. We can estimate the start-up costs with reasonable accuracy because we know what we will need to buy to begin production. Would this be a good investment? Based on our discussion, you know that the answer depends on whether or not the value of the new business exceeds the cost of starting it. In other words, does this investment have a positive NPV?

This problem is much more difficult than our "fixer upper" house example because entire fertilizer companies are not routinely bought and sold in the marketplace, so it is essentially impossible to observe the market value of a similar investment. As a result, we must somehow estimate this value by other means.

Based on our work in Chapters 5 and 6, you may be able to guess how we will go about estimating the value of our fertilizer business. We will first try to estimate the future cash flows we expect the new business to produce. We will then apply our basic discounted cash flow procedure to estimate the present value of those cash flows. Once we have this estimate, we will then estimate NPV as the difference between the present value of the future cash flows and the cost of the investment. As we mentioned in Chapter 5, this procedure is often called **discounted cash flow (DCF) valuation**.

discounted cash flow (DCF) valuation
The process of valuing an investment by discounting its future cash flows.

To see how we might go about estimating NPV, suppose we believe the cash revenues from our fertilizer business will be \$20,000 per year, assuming everything goes as expected. Cash costs (including taxes) will be \$14,000 per year. We will wind down the business in eight years. The plant, property, and equipment will be worth \$2,000 as salvage at that time. The project costs \$30,000 to launch. We use a 15 percent discount rate on new projects such as this one. Is this a good investment? If there are 1,000 shares of stock outstanding, what will be the effect on the price per share of taking this investment?

Find out more about capital budgeting for small businesses at www.smallbusinesslearning.net.

From a purely mechanical perspective, we need to calculate the present value of the future cash flows at 15 percent. The net cash inflow will be \$20,000 cash income less \$14,000 in costs per year for eight years. These cash flows are illustrated in Figure 9.1. As Figure 9.1 suggests, we effectively have an eight-year annuity of \$20,000 − 14,000 = \$6,000 per year, along with a single lump-sum inflow of \$2,000 in eight years. Calculating the present value of the future cash flows thus comes down to the same type of problem we considered in Chapter 6. The total present value is:

$$\begin{aligned}\text{Present value} &= \$6{,}000 \times [1 - (1/1.15^8)]/.15 + (2{,}000/1.15^8) \\ &= (\$6{,}000 \times 4.4873) + (2{,}000/3.0590) \\ &= \$26{,}924 + 654 \\ &= \$27{,}578\end{aligned}$$

FIGURE 9.1 >>

Project Cash Flows ($000)

Time (years)	0	1	2	3	4	5	6	7	8
Initial cost	−$30								
Inflows		$ 20	$ 20	$ 20	$ 20	$ 20	$ 20	$ 20	$ 20
Outflows		−14	−14	−14	−14	−14	−14	−14	−14
Net inflow		$ 6	$ 6	$ 6	$ 6	$ 6	$ 6	$ 6	$ 6
Salvage									2
Net cash flow	−$30	$ 6	$ 6	$ 6	$ 6	$ 6	$ 6	$ 6	$ 8

When we compare this to the $30,000 estimated cost, we see that the NPV is:

$$\text{NPV} = -\$30{,}000 + 27{,}578 = -\$2{,}422$$

Therefore, this is *not* a good investment. Based on our estimates, taking it would *decrease* the total value of the stock by $2,422. With 1,000 shares outstanding, our best estimate of the impact of taking this project is a loss of value of $2,422/1,000 = $2.42 per share.

Our fertilizer example illustrates how NPV estimates can be used to determine whether or not an investment is desirable. From our example, notice that if the NPV is negative, the effect on share value will be unfavorable. If the NPV were positive, the effect would be favorable. As a consequence, all we need to know about a particular proposal for the purpose of making an accept-reject decision is whether the NPV is positive or negative.

Given that the goal of financial management is to increase share value, our discussion in this section leads us to the *net present value rule:*

An investment should be accepted if the net present value is positive and rejected if it is negative.

In the unlikely event that the net present value turned out to be exactly zero, we would be indifferent between taking the investment and not taking it.

Two comments about our example are in order. First and foremost, it is not the rather mechanical process of discounting the cash flows that is important. Once we have the cash flows and the appropriate discount rate, the required calculations are fairly straightforward. The task of coming up with the cash flows and the discount rate in the first place is much more challenging. We will have much more to say about this in the next several chapters. For the remainder of this chapter, we take it as a given that we have estimates of the cash revenues and costs and, where needed, an appropriate discount rate.

The second thing to keep in mind about our example is that the −$2,422 NPV is an estimate. Like any estimate, it can be high or low. The only way to find out the true NPV would be to place the investment up for sale and see what we could get for it. We generally won't be doing this, so it is important that our estimates be reliable. Once again, we will have more to say about this later. For the rest of this chapter, we will assume the estimates are accurate.

EXAMPLE 9.1 >> Using the NPV Rule

Suppose we are asked to decide whether or not a new consumer product should be launched. Based on projected sales and costs, we expect that the cash flows over the five-year life of the project will be $2,000 in the first two years, $4,000 in the next two, and $5,000 in the last year. It will cost about $10,000 to begin production. We use a 10 percent discount rate to evaluate new products. What should we do here?

continued

Given the cash flows and discount rate, we can calculate the total value of the product by discounting the cash flows back to the present:

$$\begin{aligned}\text{Present value} &= (\$2{,}000/1.1) + (2{,}000/1.1^2) + (4{,}000/1.1^3) \\ &\quad + (4{,}000/1.1^4) + (5{,}000/1.1^5) \\ &= \$1{,}818 + 1{,}653 + 3{,}005 + 2{,}732 + 3{,}105 \\ &= \$12{,}313\end{aligned}$$

The present value of the expected cash flows is $12,313, but the cost of getting those cash flows is only $10,000, so the NPV is $12,313 − 10,000 = $2,313. This is positive; so, based on the net present value rule, we should take on the project.

As we have seen in this section, estimating NPV is one way of assessing the profitability of a proposed investment. It is certainly not the only way profitability is assessed, and we now turn to some alternatives. As we will see, when compared to NPV, each of the alternative ways of assessing profitability that we will examine is flawed in some key way; so NPV is the preferred approach in principle, if not always in practice.

Calculating NPVs with a Spreadsheet

SPREADSHEET STRATEGIES

Spreadsheets are commonly used to calculate NPVs. Examining the use of spreadsheets in this context also allows us to issue an important warning. Let's rework Example 9.1:

	A	B	C	D	E	F	G	H
1								
2	**Using a spreadsheet to calculate net present values**							
3								
4	From Example 9.1, the project's cost is $10,000. The cash flows are $2,000 per year for the first							
5	two years, $4,000 per year for the next two, and $5,000 in the last year. The discount rate is							
6	10 percent; what's the NPV?							
7								
8		Year	Cash flow					
9		0	-$10,000	Discount rate =		10%		
10		1	2,000					
11		2	2,000		**NPV =**	**$2,102.72**	(*wrong* answer)	
12		3	4,000		**NPV =**	**$2,312.99**	(*right* answer)	
13		4	4,000					
14		5	5,000					
15								
16	The formula entered in cell F11 is =NPV(F9, C9:C14). This gives the wrong answer because the							
17	NPV function actually calculates present values, not *net* present values.							
18								
19	The formula entered in cell F12 is =NPV(F9, C10:C14) + C9. This gives the right answer because the							
20	NPV function is used to calculate the present value of the cash flows and then the initial cost is							
21	subtracted to calculate the answer. Notice that we added cell C9 because it is already negative.							

You can get a freeware NPV calculator at www.wheatworks.com.

In our spreadsheet example, notice that we have provided two answers. By comparing the answers to that found in Example 9.1, we see that the first answer is wrong even though we used the spreadsheet's NPV formula. What happened is that the "NPV" function in our spreadsheet is actually a PV function; unfortunately, one of the original spreadsheet programs many years ago got the definition wrong, and subsequent spreadsheets have copied it! Our second answer shows how to use the formula properly.

The example here illustrates the danger of blindly using calculators or computers without understanding what is going on; we shudder to think of how many capital budgeting decisions in the real world are based on incorrect use of this particular function. We will see another example of something that can go wrong with a spreadsheet later in the chapter.

Concept Questions

9.1a What is the net present value rule?

9.1b If we say an investment has an NPV of $1,000, what exactly do we mean?

9.2 THE PAYBACK RULE

It is very common in practice to talk of the payback on a proposed investment. Loosely, the *payback* is the length of time it takes to recover our initial investment or "get our bait back." Because this idea is widely understood and used, we will examine it in some detail.

Defining the Rule

We can illustrate how to calculate a payback with an example. Figure 9.2 shows the cash flows from a proposed investment. How many years do we have to wait until the accumulated cash flows from this investment equal or exceed the cost of the investment? As Figure 9.2 indicates, the initial investment is $50,000. After the first year, the firm has recovered $30,000, leaving $20,000. The cash flow in the second year is exactly $20,000, so this investment "pays for itself" in exactly two years. Put another way, the **payback period** is two years. If we require a payback of, say, three years or less, then this investment is acceptable. This illustrates the *payback period rule:*

payback period
The amount of time required for an investment to generate cash flows sufficient to recover its initial cost.

Based on the payback rule, an investment is acceptable if its calculated payback period is less than some prespecified number of years.

In our example, the payback works out to be exactly two years. This won't usually happen, of course. When the numbers don't work out exactly, it is customary to work with fractional years. For example, suppose the initial investment is $60,000, and the cash flows are $20,000 in the first year and $90,000 in the second. The cash flows over the first two years are $110,000, so the project obviously pays back sometime in the second year. After the first year, the project has paid back $20,000, leaving $40,000 to be recovered. To figure out the fractional year, note that this $40,000 is $40,000/90,000 = 4/9 of the second year's cash flow. Assuming that the $90,000 cash flow is received uniformly throughout the year, the payback would be $1\frac{4}{9}$ years.

EXAMPLE 9.2 >> Calculating Payback

The projected cash flows from a proposed investment are:

Year	Cash Flow
1	$100
2	200
3	500

This project costs $500. What is the payback period for this investment?

The initial cost is $500. After the first two years, the cash flows total $300. After the third year, the total cash flow is $800, so the project pays back sometime between the end of Year 2 and the end of Year 3. Because the accumulated cash flows for the first two years are $300, we need to recover $200 in the third year. The third-year cash flow is $500, so we will have to wait $200/500 = .4 year to do this. The payback period is thus 2.4 years, or about two years and five months.

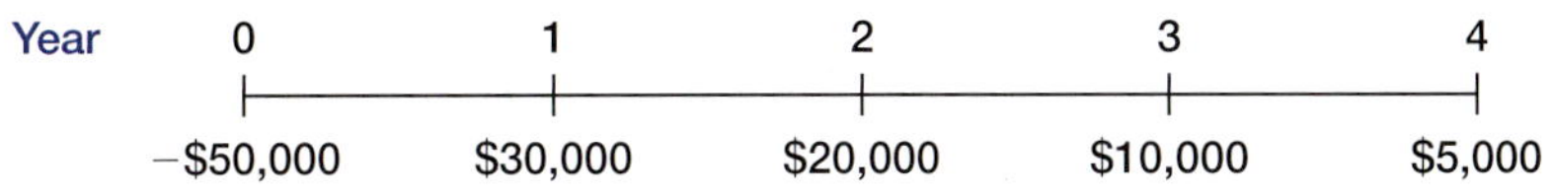

<< FIGURE 9.2

Net Project Cash Flows

<< TABLE 9.1

Expected Cash Flows for Projects A through E

Year	A	B	C	D	E
0	−$100	−$200	−$200	−$200	−$ 50
1	30	40	40	100	100
2	40	20	20	100	− 50,000,000
3	50	10	10	−200	
4	60		130	200	

Now that we know how to calculate the payback period on an investment, using the payback period rule for making decisions is straightforward. A particular cutoff time is selected, say, two years, and all investment projects that have payback periods of two years or less are accepted, and all of those that pay off in more than two years are rejected.

Table 9.1 illustrates cash flows for five different projects. The figures shown as the Year 0 cash flows are the costs of the investments. We examine these to indicate some peculiarities that can, in principle, arise with payback periods.

The payback for the first project, A, is easily calculated. The sum of the cash flows for the first two years is $70, leaving us with $100 − 70 = $30 to go. Because the cash flow in the third year is $50, the payback occurs sometime in that year. When we compare the $30 we need to the $50 that will be coming in, we get $30/50 = .6; so, payback will occur 60 percent of the way into the year. The payback period is thus 2.6 years.

Project B's payback is also easy to calculate: it *never* pays back because the cash flows never total up to the original investment. Project C has a payback of exactly four years because it supplies the $130 that B is missing in Year 4. Project D is a little strange. Because of the negative cash flow in Year 3, you can easily verify that it has two different payback periods, two years and four years. Which of these is correct? Both of them; the way the payback period is calculated doesn't guarantee a single answer. Finally, Project E is obviously unrealistic, but it does pay back in six months, thereby illustrating the point that a rapid payback does not guarantee a good investment.

Analyzing the Rule

When compared to the NPV rule, the payback period rule has some rather severe shortcomings. First of all, the payback period is calculated by simply adding up the future cash flows. There is no discounting involved, so the time value of money is completely ignored. The payback rule also fails to consider any risk differences. The payback would be calculated the same way for both very risky and very safe projects.

Perhaps the biggest problem with the payback period rule is coming up with the right cutoff period, because we don't really have an objective basis for choosing a particular number. Put another way, there is no economic rationale for looking at payback in the first place, so we have no guide as to how to pick the cutoff. As a result, we end up using a number that is arbitrarily chosen.

Suppose we have somehow decided on an appropriate payback period, say, two years or less. As we have seen, the payback period rule ignores the time value of money for the first two years. More seriously, cash flows after the second year are ignored entirely. To see this, consider the two investments, Long and Short, in Table 9.2. Both projects cost $250. Based

TABLE 9.2 >>

Investment Projected Cash Flows

Year	Long	Short
0	−$250	−$250
1	100	100
2	100	200
3	100	0
4	100	0

on our discussion, the payback on Long is 2 + (\$50/100) = 2.5 years, and the payback on Short is 1 + (\$150/200) = 1.75 years. With a cutoff of two years, Short is acceptable and Long is not.

Is the payback period rule guiding us to the right decisions? Maybe not. Suppose again that we require a 15 percent return on this type of investment. We can calculate the NPV for these two investments as:

$$\text{NPV(Short)} = -\$250 + (100/1.15) + (200/1.15^2) = -\$11.81$$
$$\text{NPV(Long)} = -\$250 + (100 \times \{[1 - (1/1.15^4)]/.15\}) = \$35.50$$

Now we have a problem. The NPV of the shorter-term investment is actually negative, meaning that taking it diminishes the value of the shareholders' equity. The opposite is true for the longer-term investment—it increases share value.

Our example illustrates two primary shortcomings of the payback period rule. First, by ignoring time value, we may be led to take investments (like Short) that actually are worth less than they cost. Second, by ignoring cash flows beyond the cutoff, we may be led to reject profitable long-term investments (like Long). More generally, using a payback period rule will tend to bias us towards shorter-term investments.

Redeeming Qualities of the Rule

Despite its shortcomings, the payback period rule is often used by large and sophisticated companies when they are making relatively minor decisions. There are several reasons for this. The primary reason is that many decisions simply do not warrant detailed analysis because the cost of the analysis would exceed the possible loss from a mistake. As a practical matter, it can be said that an investment that pays back rapidly and has benefits extending beyond the cutoff period probably has a positive NPV.

Small investment decisions are made by the hundreds every day in large organizations. Moreover, they are made at all levels. As a result, it would not be uncommon for a corporation to require, for example, a two-year payback on all investments of less than \$10,000. Investments larger than this would be subjected to greater scrutiny. The requirement of a two-year payback is not perfect for reasons we have seen, but it does exercise some control over expenditures and thus has the effect of limiting possible losses.

In addition to its simplicity, the payback rule has two other positive features. First, because it is biased towards short-term projects, it is biased towards liquidity. In other words, a payback rule tends to favor investments that free up cash for other uses more quickly. This could be very important for a small business; it would be less so for a large corporation. Second, the cash flows that are expected to occur later in a project's life are probably more uncertain. Arguably, a payback period rule adjusts for the extra riskiness of later cash flows, but it does so in a rather draconian fashion—by ignoring them altogether.

We should note here that some of the apparent simplicity of the payback rule is an illusion. The reason is that we still must come up with the cash flows first, and, as we discussed earlier, this is not at all easy to do. Thus, it would probably be more accurate to say that the *concept* of a payback period is both intuitive and easy to understand.

Summary of the Rule

To summarize, the payback period is a kind of "break-even" measure. Because time value is ignored, you can think of the payback period as the length of time it takes to break even in an accounting sense, but not in an economic sense. The biggest drawback to the payback period rule is that it doesn't ask the right question. The relevant issue is the impact an investment will have on the value of our stock, not how long it takes to recover the initial investment.

Nevertheless, because it is so simple, companies often use it as a screen for dealing with the myriad of minor investment decisions they have to make. There is certainly nothing wrong with this practice. As with any simple rule of thumb, there will be some errors in using it, but it wouldn't have survived all this time if it weren't useful. Now that you understand the rule, you can be on the alert for those circumstances under which it might lead to problems. To help you remember, the following table lists the pros and cons of the payback period rule.

Advantages and Disadvantages of the Payback Period Rule

Advantages	Disadvantages
1. Easy to understand.	1. Ignores the time value of money.
2. Adjusts for uncertainty of later cash flows.	2. Requires an arbitrary cutoff point.
	3. Ignores cash flows beyond the cutoff date.
3. Biased towards liquidity.	4. Biased against long-term projects, such as research and development, and new projects.

Concept Questions

9.2a In words, what is the payback period? The payback period rule?

9.2b Why do we say that the payback period is, in a sense, an accounting break-even measure?

THE DISCOUNTED PAYBACK 9.3

We saw that one of the shortcomings of the payback period rule was that it ignored time value. There is a variation of the payback period, the discounted payback period, that fixes this particular problem. The **discounted payback period** is the length of time until the sum of the discounted cash flows is equal to the initial investment. The *discounted payback rule* would be:

discounted payback period
The length of time required for an investment's discounted cash flows to equal its initial cost.

Based on the discounted payback rule, an investment is acceptable if its discounted payback is less than some prespecified number of years.

To see how we might calculate the discounted payback period, suppose that we require a 12.5 percent return on new investments. We have an investment that costs $300 and has

TABLE 9.3 >>

Ordinary and Discounted Payback

	Cash Flow		Accumulated Cash Flow	
Year	Undiscounted	Discounted	Undiscounted	Discounted
1	$100	$89	$100	$ 89
2	100	79	200	168
3	100	70	300	238
4	100	62	400	300
5	100	55	500	355

cash flows of $100 per year for five years. To get the discounted payback, we have to discount each cash flow at 12.5 percent and then start adding them. We do this in Table 9.3. In Table 9.3, we have both the discounted and the undiscounted cash flows. Looking at the accumulated cash flows, we see that the regular payback is exactly three years (look for the highlighted figure in Year 3). The discounted cash flows total $300 only after four years, however, so the discounted payback is four years, as shown.[1]

How do we interpret the discounted payback? Recall that the ordinary payback is the time it takes to break even in an accounting sense. Because it includes the time value of money, the discounted payback is the time it takes to break even in an economic or financial sense. Loosely speaking, in our example, we get our money back, along with the interest we could have earned elsewhere, in four years.

Figure 9.3 illustrates this idea by comparing the *future* value at 12.5 percent of the $300 investment to the *future* value of the $100 annual cash flows at 12.5 percent. Notice that the two lines cross at exactly four years. This tells us that the value of the project's cash flows catches up and then passes the original investment in four years.

Table 9.3 and Figure 9.3 illustrate another interesting feature of the discounted payback period. If a project ever pays back on a discounted basis, then it must have a positive NPV.[2] This is true because, by definition, the NPV is zero when the sum of the discounted cash flows equals the initial investment. For example, the present value of all the cash flows in Table 9.3 is $355. The cost of the project was $300, so the NPV is obviously $55. This $55 is the value of the cash flow that occurs *after* the discounted payback (see the last line in Table 9.3). In general, if we use a discounted payback rule, we won't accidentally take any projects with a negative estimated NPV.

Based on our example, the discounted payback would seem to have much to recommend it. You may be surprised to find out that it is rarely used in practice. Why? Probably because it really isn't any simpler to use than NPV. To calculate a discounted payback, you have to discount cash flows, add them up, and compare them to the cost, just as you do with NPV. So, unlike an ordinary payback, the discounted payback is not especially simple to calculate.

A discounted payback period rule has a couple of other significant drawbacks. The biggest one is that the cutoff still has to be arbitrarily set and cash flows beyond that point are ignored.[3] As a result, a project with a positive NPV may be found unacceptable because

[1] In this case, the discounted payback is an even number of years. This won't ordinarily happen, of course. However, calculating a fractional year for the discounted payback period is more involved than it is for the ordinary payback, and it is not commonly done.

[2] This argument assumes the cash flows, other than the first, are all positive. If they are not, then these statements are not necessarily correct. Also, there may be more than one discounted payback.

[3] If the cutoff were forever, then the discounted payback rule would be the same as the NPV rule. It would also be the same as the profitability index rule considered in a later section.

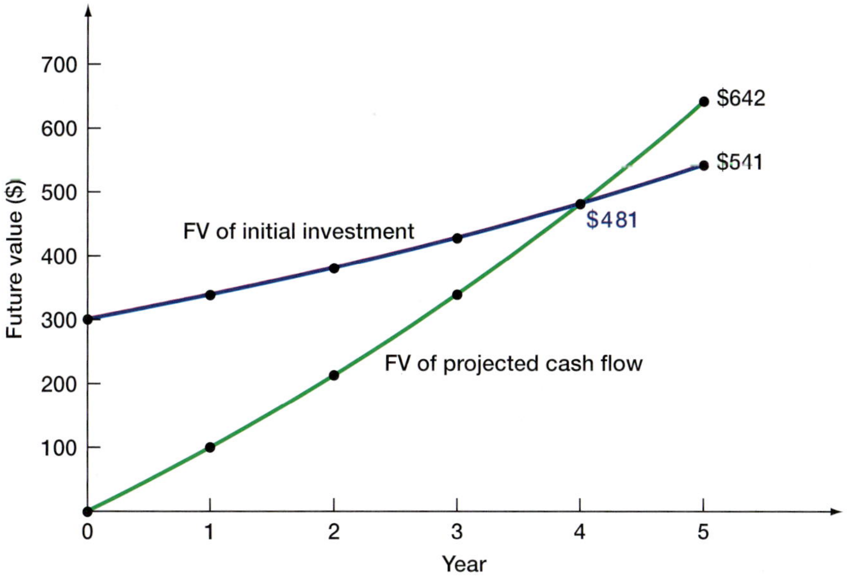

Future Value at 12.5%		
Year	$100 Annuity (projected cash flow)	$300 Lump Sum (projected investment)
0	$ 0	$300
1	100	338
2	213	380
3	339	427
4	**481**	**481**
5	642	541

<< FIGURE 9.3

Future Value of Project Cash Flows

the cutoff is too short. Also, just because one project has a shorter discounted payback than another does not mean it has a larger NPV.

All things considered, the discounted payback is a compromise between a regular payback and NPV that lacks the simplicity of the first and the conceptual rigor of the second. Nonetheless, if we need to assess the time it will take to recover the investment required by a project, then the discounted payback is better than the ordinary payback because it considers time value. In other words, the discounted payback recognizes that we could have invested the money elsewhere and earned a return on it. The ordinary payback does not take this into account. The advantages and disadvantages of the discounted payback rule are summarized in the following table.

Advantages and Disadvantages of the Discounted Payback Period Rule	
Advantages	**Disadvantages**
1. Includes time value of money. 2. Easy to understand. 3. Does not accept negative estimated NPV investments. 4. Biased towards liquidity.	1. May reject positive NPV investments. 2. Requires an arbitrary cutoff point. 3. Ignores cash flows beyond the cutoff date. 4. Biased against long-term projects, such as research and development, and new projects.

EXAMPLE 9.3 >> **Calculating Discounted Payback**

Consider an investment that costs $400 and pays $100 per year forever. We use a 20 percent discount rate on this type of investment. What is the ordinary payback? What is the discounted payback? What is the NPV?

The NPV and ordinary payback are easy to calculate in this case because the investment is a perpetuity. The present value of the cash flows is $100/.2 = $500, so the NPV is $500 − 400 = $100. The ordinary payback is obviously four years.

To get the discounted payback, we need to find the number of years such that a $100 annuity has a present value of $400 at 20 percent. In other words, the present value annuity factor is $400/100 = 4, and the interest rate is 20 percent per period; so what's the number of periods? If we solve for the number of periods, we find that the answer is a little less than nine years, so this is the discounted payback.

Concept Questions

9.3a In words, what is the discounted payback period? Why do we say it is, in a sense, a financial or economic break-even measure?

9.3b What advantage(s) does the discounted payback have over the ordinary payback?

9.4 THE AVERAGE ACCOUNTING RETURN

Another attractive, but flawed, approach to making capital budgeting decisions involves the **average accounting return (AAR)**. There are many different definitions of the AAR. However, in one form or another, the AAR is always defined as:

$$\frac{\text{Some measure of average accounting profit}}{\text{Some measure of average accounting value}}$$

The specific definition we will use is:

$$\frac{\text{Average net income}}{\text{Average book value}}$$

average accounting return (AAR)
An investment's average net income divided by its average book value.

To see how we might calculate this number, suppose we are deciding whether or not to open a store in a new shopping mall. The required investment in improvements is $500,000. The store would have a five-year life because everything reverts to the mall owners after that time. The required investment would be 100 percent depreciated (straight-line) over five years, so the depreciation would be $500,000/5 = $100,000 per year. The tax rate is 25 percent. Table 9.4 contains the projected revenues and expenses. Net income in each year, based on these figures, is also shown.

To calculate the average book value for this investment, we note that we started out with a book value of $500,000 (the initial cost) and ended up at $0. The average book value during the life of the investment is thus ($500,000 + 0)/2 = $250,000. As long as we use straight-line depreciation, the average investment will always be one-half of the initial investment.[4]

[4]We could, of course, calculate the average of the six book values directly. In thousands, we would have ($500 + 400 + 300 + 200 + 100 + 0)/6 = $250.

<< TABLE 9.4

Projected Yearly Revenue and Costs for Average Accounting Return

	Year 1	Year 2	Year 3	Year 4	Year 5
Revenue	$433,333	$450,000	$266,667	$200,000	$133,333
Expenses	$200,000	$150,000	$100,000	$100,000	$100,000
Earnings before depreciation	$233,333	$300,000	$166,667	$100,000	$ 33,333
Depreciation	$100,000	$100,000	$100,000	$100,000	$100,000
Earnings before taxes	$133,333	$200,000	$ 66,667	$ 0	−$ 66,667
Taxes (25%)	33,333	50,000	16,667	0	− 16,667
Net income	$100,000	$150,000	$ 50,000	$ 0	−$ 50,000

$$\text{Average net income} = \frac{\$100{,}000 + 150{,}000 + 50{,}000 + 0 - 50{,}000}{5} = \$50{,}000$$

$$\text{Average book value} = \frac{\$500{,}000 + 0}{2} = \$250{,}000$$

Looking at Table 9.4, we see that net income is $100,000 in the first year, $150,000 in the second year, $50,000 in the third year, $0 in Year 4, and −$50,000 in Year 5. The average net income, then, is:

$$[\$100{,}000 + 150{,}000 + 50{,}000 + 0 + (-50{,}000)]/5 = \$50{,}000$$

The average accounting return is:

$$\text{AAR} = \frac{\text{Average net income}}{\text{Average book value}} = \frac{\$50{,}000}{\$250{,}000} = 20\%$$

If the firm has a target AAR less than 20 percent, then this investment is acceptable; otherwise it is not. The *average accounting return rule* is thus:

Based on the average accounting return rule, a project is acceptable if its average accounting return exceeds a target average accounting return.

As we will now see, the use of this rule has a number of problems.

You should recognize the chief drawback to the AAR immediately. Above all else, the AAR is not a rate of return in any meaningful economic sense. Instead, it is the ratio of two accounting numbers, and it is not comparable to the returns offered, for example, in financial markets.[5]

One of the reasons the AAR is not a true rate of return is that it ignores time value. When we average figures that occur at different times, we are treating the near future and the more distant future in the same way. There was no discounting involved when we computed the average net income, for example.

The second problem with the AAR is similar to the problem we had with the payback period rule concerning the lack of an objective cutoff period. Because a calculated AAR is really not comparable to a market return, the target AAR must somehow be specified. There is no generally agreed-upon way to do this. One way of doing it is to calculate the AAR for the firm as a whole and use this as a benchmark, but there are lots of other ways as well.

[5]The AAR is closely related to the return on assets (ROA) discussed in Chapter 3. In practice, the AAR is sometimes computed by first calculating the ROA for each year, and then averaging the results. This produces a number that is similar, but not identical, to the one we computed.

The third, and perhaps worst, flaw in the AAR is that it doesn't even look at the right things. Instead of cash flow and market value, it uses net income and book value. These are both poor substitutes. As a result, an AAR doesn't tell us what the effect on share price will be of taking an investment, so it doesn't tell us what we really want to know.

Does the AAR have any redeeming features? About the only one is that it almost always can be computed. The reason is that accounting information will almost always be available, both for the project under consideration and for the firm as a whole. We hasten to add that once the accounting information is available, we can always convert it to cash flows, so even this is not a particularly important fact. The AAR is summarized in the following table.

Advantages and Disadvantages of the Average Accounting Return

Advantages	Disadvantages
1. Easy to calculate.	1. Not a true rate of return; time value of money is ignored.
2. Needed information will usually be available.	2. Uses an arbitrary benchmark cutoff rate.
	3. Based on accounting (book) values, not cash flows and market values.

Concept Questions

9.4a What is an average accounting rate of return (AAR)?

9.4b What are the weaknesses of the AAR rule?

9.5 THE INTERNAL RATE OF RETURN

internal rate of return (IRR)
The discount rate that makes the NPV of an investment zero.

We now come to the most important alternative to NPV, the **internal rate of return**, universally known as the **IRR**. As we will see, the IRR is closely related to NPV. With the IRR, we try to find a single rate of return that summarizes the merits of a project. Furthermore, we want this rate to be an "internal" rate in the sense that it depends only on the cash flows of a particular investment, not on rates offered elsewhere.

To illustrate the idea behind the IRR, consider a project that costs \$100 today and pays \$110 in one year. Suppose you were asked, "What is the return on this investment?" What would you say? It seems both natural and obvious to say that the return is 10 percent because, for every dollar we put in, we get \$1.10 back. In fact, as we will see in a moment, 10 percent is the internal rate of return, or IRR, on this investment.

Is this project with its 10 percent IRR a good investment? Once again, it would seem apparent that this is a good investment only if our required return is less than 10 percent. This intuition is also correct and illustrates the *IRR rule:*

Based on the IRR rule, an investment is acceptable if the IRR exceeds the required return. It should be rejected otherwise.

Imagine that we want to calculate the NPV for our simple investment. At a discount rate of R, the NPV is:

$$\text{NPV} = -\$100 + [110/(1 + R)]$$

Now, suppose we don't know the discount rate. This presents a problem, but we can still ask how high the discount rate would have to be before this project was deemed unacceptable. We know that we are indifferent between taking and not taking this investment when its NPV is just equal to zero. In other words, this investment is *economically* a break-even proposition when the NPV is zero because value is neither created nor destroyed. To find the break-even discount rate, we set NPV equal to zero and solve for R:

$$\begin{aligned} \text{NPV} &= 0 = -\$100 + [110/(1 + R)] \\ \$100 &= \$110/(1 + R) \\ 1 + R &= \$110/100 = 1.1 \\ R &= 10\% \end{aligned}$$

This 10 percent is what we already have called the return on this investment. What we have now illustrated is that the internal rate of return on an investment (or just "return" for short) is the discount rate that makes the NPV equal to zero. This is an important observation, so it bears repeating:

The IRR on an investment is the required return that results in a zero NPV when it is used as the discount rate.

The fact that the IRR is simply the discount rate that makes the NPV equal to zero is important because it tells us how to calculate the returns on more complicated investments. As we have seen, finding the IRR turns out to be relatively easy for a single-period investment. However, suppose you were now looking at an investment with the cash flows shown in Figure 9.4. As illustrated, this investment costs \$100 and has a cash flow of \$60 per year for two years, so it's only slightly more complicated than our single-period example. However, if you were asked for the return on this investment, what would you say? There doesn't seem to be any obvious answer (at least not to us). However, based on what we now know, we can set the NPV equal to zero and solve for the discount rate:

$$\text{NPV} = 0 = -\$100 + [60/(1 + \text{IRR})] + [60/(1 + \text{IRR})^2]$$

Unfortunately, the only way to find the IRR in general is by trial and error, either by hand or by calculator. This is precisely the same problem that came up in Chapter 5 when we found the unknown rate for an annuity and in Chapter 7 when we found the yield to maturity on a bond. In fact, we now see that, in both of those cases, we were finding an IRR.

In this particular case, the cash flows form a two-period, \$60 annuity. To find the unknown rate, we can try some different rates until we get the answer. If we were to start with a 0 percent rate, the NPV would obviously be \$120 − 100 = \$20. At a 10 percent discount rate, we would have:

$$\text{NPV} = -\$100 + (60/1.1) + (60/1.1^2) = \$4.13$$

Now, we're getting close. We can summarize these and some other possibilities as shown in Table 9.5. From our calculations, the NPV appears to be zero with a discount rate between 10 percent and 15 percent, so the IRR is somewhere in that range. With a little more

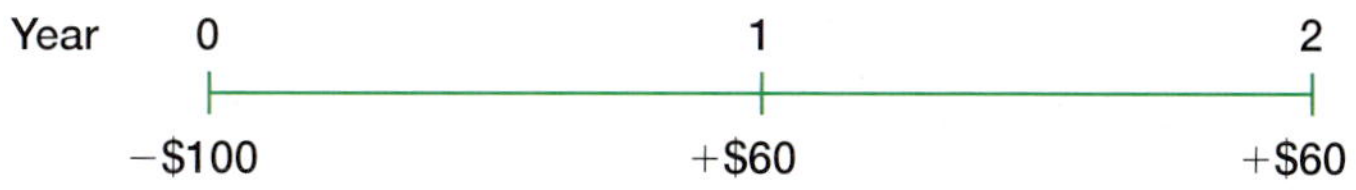

<< FIGURE 9.4

Project Cash Flows

TABLE 9.5 >>

NPV at Different Discount Rates

Discount Rate	NPV
0%	$20.00
5%	11.56
10%	4.13
15%	− 2.46
20%	− 8.33

FIGURE 9.5 >>

An NPV Profile

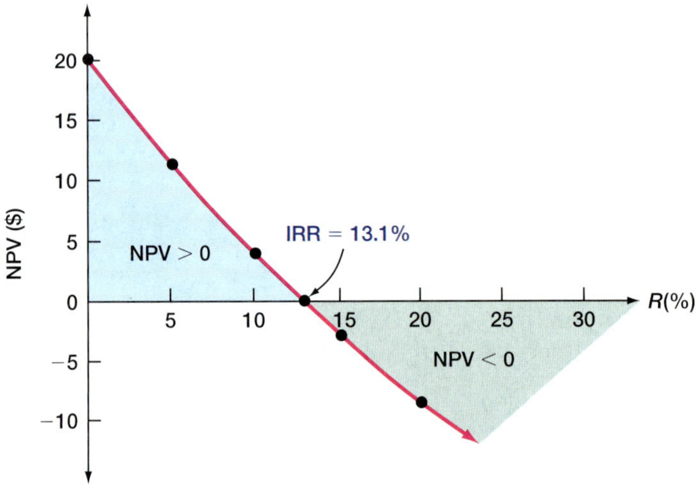

effort, we can find that the IRR is about 13.1 percent.[6] So, if our required return were less than 13.1 percent, we would take this investment. If our required return exceeded 13.1 percent, we would reject it.

By now, you have probably noticed that the IRR rule and the NPV rule appear to be quite similar. In fact, the IRR is sometimes simply called the *discounted cash flow,* or *DCF, return.* The easiest way to illustrate the relationship between NPV and IRR is to plot the numbers we calculated for Table 9.5. We put the different NPVs on the vertical axis, or y-axis, and the discount rates on the horizontal axis, or x-axis. If we had a very large number of points, the resulting picture would be a smooth curve called a **net present value profile**. Figure 9.5 illustrates the NPV profile for this project. Beginning with a 0 percent discount rate, we have $20 plotted directly on the y-axis. As the discount rate increases, the NPV declines smoothly. Where will the curve cut through the x-axis? This will occur where the NPV is just equal to zero, so it will happen right at the IRR of 13.1 percent.

net present value profile
A graphical representation of the relationship between an investment's NPVs and various discount rates.

In our example, the NPV rule and the IRR rule lead to identical accept-reject decisions. We will accept an investment using the IRR rule if the required return is less than 13.1 percent. As Figure 9.5 illustrates, however, the NPV is positive at any discount rate less than 13.1 percent, so we would accept the investment using the NPV rule as well. The two rules give equivalent results in this case.

[6] With a lot more effort (or a personal computer), we can find that the IRR is approximately (to 9 decimal places) 13.066238629 percent, not that anybody would ever want this many decimal places

Calculating the IRR

<< EXAMPLE 9.4

A project has a total up-front cost of $435.44. The cash flows are $100 in the first year, $200 in the second year, and $300 in the third year. What's the IRR? If we require an 18 percent return, should we take this investment?

We'll describe the NPV profile and find the IRR by calculating some NPVs at different discount rates. You should check our answers for practice. Beginning with 0 percent, we have:

Discount Rate	NPV
0%	$164.56
5%	100.36
10%	46.15
15%	0.00
20%	− 39.61

The NPV is zero at 15 percent, so 15 percent is the IRR. If we require an 18 percent return, then we should not take the investment. The reason is that the NPV is negative at 18 percent (verify that it is −$24.47). The IRR rule tells us the same thing in this case. We shouldn't take this investment because its 15 percent return is below our required 18 percent return.

At this point, you may be wondering if the IRR and NPV rules always lead to identical decisions. The answer is yes, as long as two very important conditions are met. First, the project's cash flows must be *conventional,* meaning that the first cash flow (the initial investment) is negative and all the rest are positive. Second, the project must be *independent,* meaning that the decision to accept or reject this project does not affect the decision to accept or reject any other. The first of these conditions is typically met, but the second often is not. In any case, when one or both of these conditions are not met, problems can arise. We discuss some of these next.

Calculating IRRs with a Spreadsheet

SPREADSHEET STRATEGIES

Because IRRs are so tedious to calculate by hand, financial calculators and, especially, spreadsheets are generally used. The procedures used by various financial calculators are too different for us to illustrate here, so we will focus on using a spreadsheet (financial calculators are covered in Appendix D). As the following example illustrates, using a spreadsheet is very easy.

	A	B	C	D	E	F	G	H
1								
2	Using a spreadsheet to calculate internal rates of return							
3								
4	Suppose we have a four-year project that costs $500. The cash flows over the four-year life will be							
5	$100, $200, $300, and $400. What is the IRR?							
6								
7		Year	Cash flow					
8		0	-$500					
9		1	100		IRR =	27.3%		
10		2	200					
11		3	300					
12		4	400					
13								
14								
15	The formula entered in cell F9 is =IRR(C8:C12). Notice that the Year 0 cash flow has a negative							
16	sign representing the initial cost of the project.							
17								

Problems with the IRR

The problems with the IRR come about when the cash flows are not conventional or when we are trying to compare two or more investments to see which is best. In the first case, surprisingly, the simple question: What's the return? can become very difficult to answer. In the second case, the IRR can be a misleading guide.

Nonconventional Cash Flows Suppose we have a strip-mining project that requires a $60 investment. Our cash flow in the first year will be $155. In the second year, the mine will be depleted, but we will have to spend $100 to restore the terrain. As Figure 9.6 illustrates, both the first and third cash flows are negative.

To find the IRR on this project, we can calculate the NPV at various rates:

Discount Rate	NPV
0%	−$5.00
10%	− 1.74
20%	− 0.28
30%	0.06
40%	− 0.31

The NPV appears to be behaving in a very peculiar fashion here. First, as the discount rate increases from 0 percent to 30 percent, the NPV starts out negative and becomes positive. This seems backwards because the NPV is rising as the discount rate rises. It then starts getting smaller and becomes negative again. What's the IRR? To find out, we draw the NPV profile as shown in Figure 9.7.

In Figure 9.7, notice that the NPV is zero when the discount rate is 25 percent, so this is the IRR. Or is it? The NPV is also zero at $33\frac{1}{3}$ percent. Which of these is correct? The answer is both or neither; more precisely, there is no unambiguously correct answer. This is the **multiple rates of return** problem. Many financial computer packages (including a best-seller for personal computers) aren't aware of this problem and just report the first IRR that is found. Others report only the smallest positive IRR, even though this answer is no better than any other.

multiple rates of return
The possibility that more than one discount rate will make the NPV of an investment zero.

In our current example, the IRR rule breaks down completely. Suppose our required return is 10 percent. Should we take this investment? Both IRRs are greater than 10 percent, so, by the IRR rule, maybe we should. However, as Figure 9.7 shows, the NPV is negative at any discount rate less than 25 percent, so this is not a good investment. When should we take it? Looking at Figure 9.7 one last time, we see that the NPV is positive only if our required return is between 25 percent and $33\frac{1}{3}$ percent.

Nonconventional cash flows can occur in a variety of ways. For example, Northeast Utilities, owner of the Connecticut-located Millstone nuclear power plant, had to shut down the plant's three reactors in November 1995. The reactors were expected to be back on-line in January 1997. By some estimates, the cost of the shutdown would run about $334 million. In fact, all nuclear plants eventually have to be shut down for good, and the costs associated with "decommissioning" a plant are enormous, creating large negative cash flows at the end of the project's life.

FIGURE 9.6 >>
Project Cash Flows

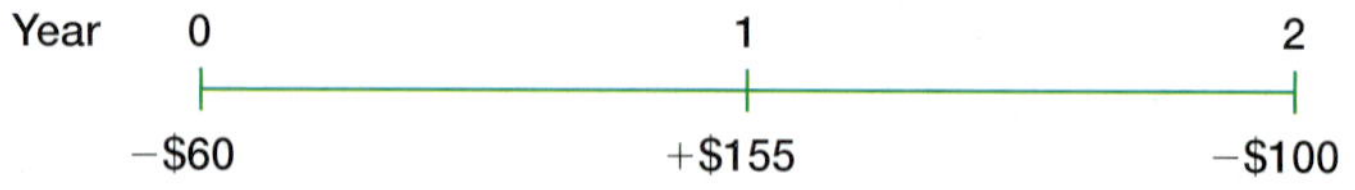

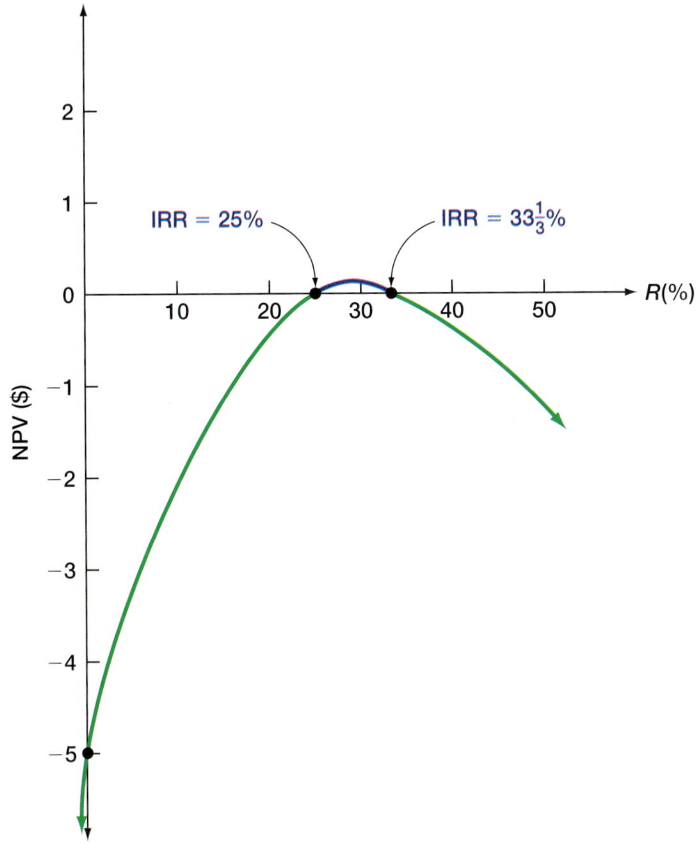

<< FIGURE 9.7

NPV Profile

The moral of the story is that when the cash flows aren't conventional, strange things can start to happen to the IRR. This is not anything to get upset about, however, because the NPV rule, as always, works just fine. This illustrates the fact that, oddly enough, the obvious question—What's the rate of return?—may not always have a good answer.

What's the IRR?

<< **EXAMPLE 9.5**

You are looking at an investment that requires you to invest $51 today. You'll get $100 in one year, but you must pay out $50 in two years. What is the IRR on this investment?

You're on the alert now for the nonconventional cash flow problem, so you probably wouldn't be surprised to see more than one IRR. However, if you start looking for an IRR by trial and error, it will take you a long time. The reason is that there is no IRR. The NPV is negative at every discount rate, so we shouldn't take this investment under any circumstances. What's the return on this investment? Your guess is as good as ours.

"I Think; Therefore, I Know How Many IRRs There Can Be."

<< **EXAMPLE 9.6**

We've seen that it's possible to get more than one IRR. If you wanted to make sure that you had found all of the possible IRRs, how could you do it? The answer comes from the great mathematician, philosopher, and financial analyst Descartes (of "I think; therefore I am" fame). Descartes' Rule of Sign says that the maximum number of IRRs that there

continued

can be is equal to the number of times that the cash flows change sign from positive to negative and/or negative to positive.[7]

In our example with the 25 percent and $33\frac{1}{3}$ percent IRRs, could there be yet another IRR? The cash flows flip from negative to positive, then back to negative, for a total of two sign changes. Therefore, according to Descartes' rule, the maximum number of IRRs is two and we don't need to look for any more. Note that the actual number of IRRs can be less than the maximum (see Example 9.5).

mutually exclusive investment decisions
A situation in which taking one investment prevents the taking of another.

Mutually Exclusive Investments

Even if there is a single IRR, another problem can arise concerning **mutually exclusive investment decisions**. If two investments, X and Y, are mutually exclusive, then taking one of them means that we cannot take the other. Two projects that are not mutually exclusive are said to be independent. For example, if we own one corner lot, then we can build a gas station or an apartment building, but not both. These are mutually exclusive alternatives.

Thus far, we have asked whether or not a given investment is worth undertaking. There is a related question, however, that comes up very often: Given two or more mutually exclusive investments, which one is the best? The answer is simple enough: the best one is the one with the largest NPV. Can we also say that the best one has the highest return? As we show, the answer is no.

To illustrate the problem with the IRR rule and mutually exclusive investments, consider the following cash flows from two mutually exclusive investments:

Year	Investment A	Investment B
0	−$100	−$100
1	50	20
2	40	40
3	40	50
4	30	60

The IRR for A is 24 percent, and the IRR for B is 21 percent. Because these investments are mutually exclusive, we can only take one of them. Simple intuition suggests that Investment A is better because of its higher return. Unfortunately, simple intuition is not always correct.

To see why Investment A is not necessarily the better of the two investments, we've calculated the NPV of these investments for different required returns:

Discount Rate	NPV(A)	NPV(B)
0%	$60.00	$70.00
5	43.13	47.88
10	29.06	29.79
15	17.18	14.82
20	7.06	2.31
25	− 1.63	− 8.22

[7]To be more precise, the number of IRRs that are bigger than −100 percent is equal to the number of sign changes, or it differs from the number of sign changes by an even number. Thus, for example, if there are five sign changes, there are either five IRRs, three IRRs, or one IRR. If there are two sign changes, there are either two IRRs or no IRRs.

The IRR for A (24 percent) is larger than the IRR for B (21 percent). However, if you compare the NPVs, you'll see that which investment has the higher NPV depends on our required return. B has greater total cash flow, but it pays back more slowly than A. As a result, it has a higher NPV at lower discount rates.

In our example, the NPV and IRR rankings conflict for some discount rates. If our required return is 10 percent, for instance, then B has the higher NPV and is thus the better of the two even though A has the higher return. If our required return is 15 percent, then there is no ranking conflict: A is better.

The conflict between the IRR and NPV for mutually exclusive investments can be illustrated by plotting the investments' NPV profiles as we have done in Figure 9.8. In Figure 9.8, notice that the NPV profiles cross at about 11 percent. Notice also that at any discount rate less than 11 percent, the NPV for B is higher. In this range, taking B benefits us more than taking A, even though A's IRR is higher. At any rate greater than 11 percent, Project A has the greater NPV.

This example illustrates that when we have mutually exclusive projects, we shouldn't rank them based on their returns. More generally, anytime we are comparing investments to determine which is best, looking at IRRs can be misleading. Instead, we need to look at the relative NPVs to avoid the possibility of choosing incorrectly. Remember, we're ultimately interested in creating value for the shareholders, so the option with the higher NPV is preferred, regardless of the relative returns.

If this seems counterintuitive, think of it this way. Suppose you have two investments. One has a 10 percent return and makes you $100 richer immediately. The other has a 20 percent return and makes you $50 richer immediately. Which one do you like better? We would rather have $100 than $50, regardless of the returns, so we like the first one better.

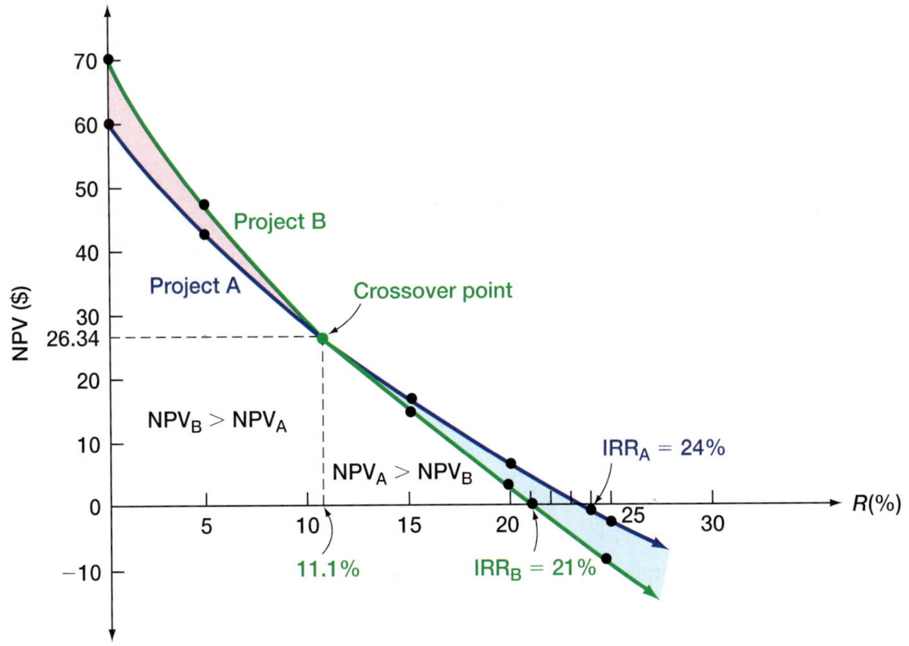

FIGURE 9.8

NPV Profiles for Mutually Exclusive Investments

EXAMPLE 9.7 >> Calculating the Crossover Rate

In Figure 9.8, the NPV profiles cross at about 11 percent. How can we determine just what this crossover point is? The *crossover rate,* by definition, is the discount rate that makes the NPVs of two projects equal. To illustrate, suppose we have the following two mutually exclusive investments:

Year	Investment A	Investment B
0	−$400	−$500
1	250	320
2	280	340

What's the crossover rate?

To find the crossover, first consider moving out of Investment A and into Investment B. If you make the move, you'll have to invest an extra $100 ($500 − 400). For this $100 investment, you'll get an extra $70 ($320 − 250) in the first year and an extra $60 ($340 − 280) in the second year. Is this a good move? In other words, is it worth investing the extra $100?

Based on our discussion, the NPV of the switch, NVP(B − A), is:

$$\text{NPV(B} - \text{A)} = -\$100 + [70/(1 + R)] + [60/(1 + R)^2]$$

We can calculate the return on this investment by setting the NPV equal to zero and solving for the IRR:

$$\text{NPV(B} - \text{A)} = 0 = -\$100 + [70/(1 + R)] + [60/(1 + R)^2]$$

If you go through this calculation, you will find the IRR is exactly 20 percent. What this tells us is that at a 20 percent discount rate, we are indifferent between the two investments because the NPV of the difference in their cash flows is zero. As a consequence, the two investments have the same value, so this 20 percent is the crossover rate. Check to see that the NPV at 20 percent is $2.78 for both investments.

In general, you can find the crossover rate by taking the difference in the cash flows and calculating the IRR using the difference. It doesn't make any difference which one you subtract from which. To see this, find the IRR for (A − B); you'll see it's the same number. Also, for practice, you might want to find the exact crossover in Figure 9.8 (hint: it's 11.0704 percent).

Redeeming Qualities of the IRR

Despite its flaws, the IRR is very popular in practice, more so than even the NPV. It probably survives because it fills a need that the NPV does not. In analyzing investments, people in general, and financial analysts in particular, seem to prefer talking about rates of return rather than dollar values.

In a similar vein, the IRR also appears to provide a simple way of communicating information about a proposal. One manager might say to another, "Remodeling the clerical wing has a 20 percent return." This may somehow seem simpler than saying, "At a 10 percent discount rate, the net present value is $4,000."

Finally, under certain circumstances, the IRR may have a practical advantage over the NPV. We can't estimate the NPV unless we know the appropriate discount rate, but we can still estimate the IRR. Suppose we didn't know the required return on an investment, but we found, for example, that it had a 40 percent return. We would probably be inclined to take it because it would be very unlikely that the required return would be that high. The advantages and disadvantages of the IRR are summarized as follows.

Advantages and Disadvantages of the Internal Rate of Return	
Advantages	**Disadvantages**
1. Closely related to NPV, often leading to identical decisions. 2. Easy to understand and communicate.	1. May result in multiple answers or not deal with nonconventional cash flows. 2. May lead to incorrect decisions in comparisons of mutually exclusive investments.

Concept Questions

9.5a Under what circumstances will the IRR and NPV rules lead to the same accept-reject decisions? When might they conflict?

9.5b Is it generally true that an advantage of the IRR rule over the NPV rule is that we don't need to know the required return to use the IRR rule?

THE PROFITABILITY INDEX 9.6

Another tool used to evaluate projects is called the **profitability index (PI)**, or benefit-cost ratio. This index is defined as the present value of the future cash flows divided by the initial investment. So, if a project costs $200 and the present value of its future cash flows is $220, the profitability index value would be $220/200 = 1.1. Notice that the NPV for this investment is $20, so it is a desirable investment.

profitability index (PI) The present value of an investment's future cash flows divided by its initial cost. Also, benefit-cost ratio

More generally, if a project has a positive NPV, then the present value of the future cash flows must be bigger than the initial investment. The profitability index would thus be bigger than 1 for a positive NPV investment and less than 1 for a negative NPV investment.

How do we interpret the profitability index? In our example, the PI was 1.1. This tells us that, per dollar invested, $1.10 in value or $.10 in NPV results. The profitability index thus measures "bang for the buck," that is, the value created per dollar invested. For this reason, it is often proposed as a measure of performance for government or other not-for-profit investments. Also, when capital is scarce, it may make sense to allocate it to those projects with the highest PIs. We will return to this issue in a later chapter.

The PI is obviously very similar to the NPV. However, consider an investment that costs $5 and has a $10 present value and an investment that costs $100 with a $150 present value. The first of these investments has an NPV of $5 and a PI of 2. The second has an NPV of $50 and a PI of 1.5. If these are mutually exclusive investments, then the second one is preferred even though it has a lower PI. This ranking problem is very similar to the IRR ranking problem we saw in the previous section. In all, there seems to be little reason to rely on the PI instead of the NPV. Our discussion of the PI is summarized as follows.

Advantages and Disadvantages of the Profitability Index	
Advantages	**Disadvantages**
1. Closely related to NPV, generally leading to identical decisions. 2. Easy to understand and communicate. 3. May be useful when available investment funds are limited.	1. May lead to incorrect decisions in comparisons of mutually exclusive investments.

Concept Questions

9.6a What does the profitability index measure?

9.6b How would you state the profitability index rule?

9.7 THE PRACTICE OF CAPITAL BUDGETING

Given that NPV seems to be telling us directly what we want to know, you might be wondering why there are so many other procedures and why alternative procedures are commonly used. Recall that we are trying to make an investment decision and that we are frequently operating under considerable uncertainty about the future. We can only *estimate* the NPV of an investment in this case. The resulting estimate can be very "soft," meaning that the true NPV might be quite different.

Because the true NPV is unknown, the astute financial manager seeks clues to help in assessing whether or not the estimated NPV is reliable. For this reason, firms would typically use multiple criteria for evaluating a proposal. For example, suppose we have an investment with a positive estimated NPV. Based on our experience with other projects, this one appears to have a short payback and a very high AAR. In this case, the different indicators seem to agree that it's "all systems go." Put another way, the payback and the AAR are consistent with the conclusion that the NPV is positive.

On the other hand, suppose we had a positive estimated NPV, a long payback, and a low AAR. This could still be a good investment, but it looks like we need to be much more careful in making the decision because we are getting conflicting signals. If the estimated NPV is based on projections in which we have little confidence, then further analysis is probably in order. We will consider how to evaluate NPV estimates in more detail in the next two chapters.

Capital expenditures by individual corporations can add up to enormous sums for the economy as a whole. For example, ExxonMobil spent about $13.9 billion on capital expenditures in 2002, and an additional $15.5 billion in 2003. The company also announced plans to spend another $15 billion in both 2004 and 2005. Home-improvement retailer Home Depot planned to spend $3.5 billion in 2004 and another $3.7 billion in 2005.

Capital spending boosts are often an industrywide occurrence. For example, in 2004, hospitals planned to boost capital spending by 14 percent per year over the next five years, considerably more than the 1 percent annual increase for 1997 to 2001. But not all industries were spending as much. Chip-maker Intel was expected to spend about $3.8 billion in 2004, only about 10 percent of revenues. Historically, Intel's capital spending was about 15 to 20 percent of revenue. Other chip-makers were expected to follow suit as industry sales slowed.

According to information released by the U.S. Census Bureau in 2003, capital investment for the economy as a whole was actually $1.01 trillion in 2002, $1.11 trillion in 2001, and $1.17 trillion in 2000. The totals for the three years therefore exceeded $3.29 trillion! Given the sums at stake, it is not too surprising that careful analysis of capital expenditures is something at which successful corporations seek to become adept.

There have been a number of surveys conducted asking firms what types of investment criteria they actually use. Table 9.6 summarizes the results of several of these. Panel A of

TABLE 9.6 >> Capital Budgeting Techniques in Practice

A. Historical Comparison of the Primary Use of Various Capital Budgeting Techniques

	1959	1964	1970	1975	1977	1979	1981
Payback period	34%	24%	12%	15%	9%	10%	5.0%
Average accounting return (AAR)	34	30	26	10	25	14	10.7
Internal rate of return (IRR)	19	38	57	37	54	60	65.3
Net present value (NPV)	—	—	—	26	10	14	16.5
IRR or NPV	19	38	57	63	64	74	81.8

B. Percentage of CFOs Who Always or Almost Always Use a Given Technique in 1999

Capital Budgeting Technique	Percentage Always or Almost Always Use	Average Score Scale is 4 (always) to 0 (never)		
		Overall	Large Firms	Small Firms
Internal rate of return	76%	3.09	3.41	2.87
Net present value	75	3.08	3.42	2.83
Payback period	57	2.53	2.25	2.72
Discounted payback period	29	1.56	1.55	1.58
Accounting rate of return	20	1.34	1.25	1.41
Profitability index	12	0.83	0.75	0.88

SOURCES: J. R. Graham and C. R. Harvey, "The Theory and Practice of Corporate Finance: Evidence from the Field," *Journal of Financial Economics,* May–June 2001, pp. 187–244; J. S. Moore and A. K. Reichert, "An Analysis of the Financial Management Techniques Currently Employed by Large U.S. Corporations," *Journal of Business Finance and Accounting,* Winter 1983, pp. 623–45; M. T. Stanley and S. R. Block, "A Survey of Multinational Capital Budgeting," *The Financial Review,* March 1984, pp. 36–51.

the table is a historical comparison looking at the primary capital budgeting techniques used by large firms through time. In 1959, only 19 percent of the firms surveyed used either IRR or NPV, and 68 percent used either payback periods or accounting returns. It is clear that, by the 1980s, IRR and NPV had become the dominant criteria.

Panel B of Table 9.6 summarizes the results of a 1999 survey of chief financial officers (CFOs) at both large and small firms in the United States. A total of 392 CFOs responded. What is shown is the percentage of CFOs who always or almost always use the various capital budgeting techniques we described in this chapter. Not surprisingly, IRR and NPV are the two most widely used techniques, particularly at larger firms. However, over half of the respondents always, or almost always, use the payback criterion as well. In fact, among smaller firms, payback is used just about as much as NPV and IRR. Less commonly used are discounted payback, accounting rates of return, and the profitability index. For future reference, the various criteria we have discussed are summarized in Table 9.7.

Concept Questions

9.7a What are the most commonly used capital budgeting procedures?

9.7b If NPV is conceptually the best procedure for capital budgeting, why do you think multiple measures are used in practice?

TABLE 9.7 >>

Summary of Investment Criteria

I. Discounted Cash Flow Criteria

A. *Net present value (NPV).* The NPV of an investment is the difference between its market value and its cost. The NPV rule is to take a project if its NPV is positive. NPV is frequently estimated by calculating the present value of the future cash flows (to estimate market value) and then subtracting the cost. NPV has no serious flaws; it is the preferred decision criterion.

B. *Internal rate of return (IRR).* The IRR is the discount rate that makes the estimated NPV of an investment equal to zero; it is sometimes called the *discounted cash flow (DCF) return.* The IRR rule is to take a project when its IRR exceeds the required return. IRR is closely related to NPV, and it leads to exactly the same decisions as NPV for conventional, independent projects. When project cash flows are not conventional, there may be no IRR or there may be more than one. More seriously, the IRR cannot be used to rank mutually exclusive projects; the project with the highest IRR is not necessarily the preferred investment.

C. *Profitability index (PI).* The PI, also called the *benefit-cost ratio,* is the ratio of present value to cost. The PI rule is to take an investment if the index exceeds 1. The PI measures the present value of an investment per dollar invested. It is quite similar to NPV, but, like IRR, it cannot be used to rank mutually exclusive projects. However, it is sometimes used to rank projects when a firm has more positive NPV investments than it can currently finance.

II. Payback Criteria

A. *Payback period.* The payback period is the length of time until the sum of an investment's cash flows equals its cost. The payback period rule is to take a project if its payback is *less* than some cutoff. The payback period is a flawed criterion, primarily because it ignores risk, the time value of money, and cash flows beyond the cutoff point.

B. *Discounted payback period.* The discounted payback period is the length of time until the sum of an investment's discounted cash flows equals its cost. The discounted payback period rule is to take an investment if the discounted payback is *less* than some cutoff. The discounted payback rule is flawed, primarily because it ignores cash flows after the cutoff.

III. Accounting Criterion

A. *Average accounting return (AAR).* The AAR is a measure of accounting profit relative to book value. It is *not* related to the IRR, but it is similar to the accounting return on assets (ROA) measure in Chapter 3. The AAR rule is to take an investment if its AAR exceeds a benchmark AAR. The AAR is seriously flawed for a variety of reasons, and it has little to recommend it.

9.8 SUMMARY AND CONCLUSIONS

This chapter has covered the different criteria used to evaluate proposed investments. The six criteria, in the order we discussed them, are:

1. Net present value (NPV)
2. Payback period
3. Discounted payback period
4. Average accounting return (AAR)
5. Internal rate of return (IRR)
6. Profitability index (PI)

We illustrated how to calculate each of these and discussed the interpretation of the results. We also described the advantages and disadvantages of each of them. Ultimately, a good capital budgeting criterion must tell us two things. First, is a particular project a good investment? Second, if we have more than one good project, but we can take only one of them, which one should we take? The main point of this chapter is that only the NPV criterion can always provide the correct answer to both questions.

For this reason, NPV is one of the two or three most important concepts in finance, and we will refer to it many times in the chapters ahead. When we do, keep two things in mind: (1) NPV is always just the difference between the market value of an asset or project and its cost, and (2) the financial manager acts in the shareholders' best interests by identifying and taking positive NPV projects.

Finally, we noted that NPVs can't normally be observed in the market; instead, they must be estimated. Because there is always the possibility of a poor estimate, financial managers use multiple criteria for examining projects. The other criteria provide additional information about whether or not a project truly has a positive NPV.

Chapter Review and Self-Test Problems

9.1 Investment Criteria This problem will give you some practice calculating NPVs and paybacks. A proposed overseas expansion has the following cash flows:

Year	Cash Flow
0	−$200
1	50
2	60
3	70
4	200

Calculate the payback, the discounted payback, and the NPV at a required return of 10 percent.

9.2 Mutually Exclusive Investments Consider the following two mutually exclusive investments. Calculate the IRR for each and the crossover rate. Under what circumstances will the IRR and NPV criteria rank the two projects differently?

Year	Investment A	Investment B
0	−$75	−$75
1	20	60
2	40	50
3	70	15

9.3 Average Accounting Return You are looking at a three-year project with a projected net income of $2,000 in Year 1, $4,000 in Year 2, and $6,000 in Year 3. The cost is $12,000, which will be depreciated straight-line to zero over the three-year life of the project. What is the average accounting return (AAR)?

Answers to Chapter Review and Self-Test Problems

9.1 In the following table, we have listed the cash flow, cumulative cash flow, discounted cash flow (at 10 percent), and cumulative discounted cash flow for the proposed project.

	Cash Flow		Accumulated Cash Flow	
Year	**Undiscounted**	**Discounted**	**Undiscounted**	**Discounted**
1	$ 50	$ 45.45	$ 50	$ 45.45
2	60	49.59	110	95.04
3	70	52.59	180	147.63
4	200	136.60	380	284.23

Recall that the initial investment was $200. When we compare this to accumulated undiscounted cash flows, we see that payback occurs between Years 3 and 4. The cash flows for the first three years are $180 total, so, going into the fourth year, we are short by $20. The total cash flow in Year 4 is $200, so the payback is 3 + ($20/200) = 3.10 years.

Looking at the accumulated discounted cash flows, we see that the discounted payback occurs between Years 3 and 4. The sum of the discounted cash flows is $284.23, so the NPV is $84.23. Notice that this is the present value of the cash flows that occur after the discounted payback.

9.2 To calculate the IRR, we might try some guesses, as in the following table:

Discount Rate	NPV(A)	NPV(B)
0%	$55.00	$50.00
10	28.83	32.14
20	9.95	18.40
30	− 4.09	7.57
40	− 14.80	− 1.17

Several things are immediately apparent from our guesses. First, the IRR on A must be between 20 percent and 30 percent (why?). With some more effort, we find that it's 26.79 percent. For B, the IRR must be a little less than 40 percent (again, why?); it works out to be 38.54 percent. Also, notice that at rates between 0 percent and 10 percent, the NPVs are very close, indicating that the crossover is in that vicinity.

To find the crossover exactly, we can compute the IRR on the difference in the cash flows. If we take the cash flows from A minus the cash flows from B, the resulting cash flows are:

Year	A − B
0	$ 0
1	− 40
2	− 10
3	55

These cash flows look a little odd, but the sign only changes once, so we can find an IRR. With some trial and error, you'll see that the NPV is zero at a discount rate of 5.42 percent, so this is the crossover rate.

The IRR for B is higher. However, as we've seen, A has the larger NPV for any discount rate less than 5.42 percent, so the NPV and IRR rankings will conflict in that range. Remember, if there's a conflict, we will go with the higher NPV.

Our decision rule is thus very simple: take A if the required return is less than 5.42 percent, take B if the required return is between 5.42 percent and 38.54 percent (the IRR on B), and take neither if the required return is more than 38.54 percent.

9.3 Here we need to calculate the ratio of average net income to average book value to get the AAR. Average net income is:

Average net income = ($2,000 + 4,000 + 6,000)/3 = $4,000

Average book value is:

Average book value = $12,000/2 = $6,000

So the average accounting return is:

AAR = $4,000/6,000 = 66.67%

This is an impressive return. Remember, however, that it isn't really a rate of return like an interest rate or an IRR, so the size doesn't tell us a lot. In particular, our money is probably not going to grow at a rate of 66.67 percent per year, sorry to say.

Concepts Review and Critical Thinking Questions

1. **Payback Period and Net Present Value** If a project with conventional cash flows has a payback period less than the project's life, can you definitively state the algebraic sign of the NPV? Why or why not? If you know that the discounted payback period is less than the project's life, what can you say about the NPV? Explain.
2. **Net Present Value** Suppose a project has conventional cash flows and a positive NPV. What do you know about its payback? Its discounted payback? Its profitability index? Its IRR? Explain.
3. **Payback Period** Concerning payback:
   - **a.** Describe how the payback period is calculated and describe the information this measure provides about a sequence of cash flows. What is the payback criterion decision rule?
   - **b.** What are the problems associated with using the payback period as a means of evaluating cash flows?
   - **c.** What are the advantages of using the payback period to evaluate cash flows? Are there any circumstances under which using payback might be appropriate? Explain.
4. **Discounted Payback** Concerning discounted payback:
   - **a.** Describe how the discounted payback period is calculated and describe the information this measure provides about a sequence of cash flows. What is the discounted payback criterion decision rule?
   - **b.** What are the problems associated with using the discounted payback period as a means of evaluating cash flows?
   - **c.** What conceptual advantage does the discounted payback method have over the regular payback method? Can the discounted payback ever be longer than the regular payback? Explain.
5. **Average Accounting Return** Concerning AAR:
   - **a.** Describe how the average accounting return is usually calculated and describe the information this measure provides about a sequence of cash flows. What is the AAR criterion decision rule?
   - **b.** What are the problems associated with using the AAR as a means of evaluating a project's cash flows? What underlying feature of AAR is most troubling to you from a financial perspective? Does the AAR have any redeeming qualities?

6. **Net Present Value** Concerning NPV:
   a. Describe how NPV is calculated and describe the information this measure provides about a sequence of cash flows. What is the NPV criterion decision rule?
   b. Why is NPV considered to be a superior method of evaluating the cash flows from a project? Suppose the NPV for a project's cash flows is computed to be $2,500. What does this number represent with respect to the firm's shareholders?
7. **Internal Rate of Return** Concerning IRR:
   a. Describe how the IRR is calculated and describe the information this measure provides about a sequence of cash flows. What is the IRR criterion decision rule?
   b. What is the relationship between IRR and NPV? Are there any situations in which you might prefer one method over the other? Explain.
   c. Despite its shortcomings in some situations, why do most financial managers use IRR along with NPV when evaluating projects? Can you think of a situation in which IRR might be a more appropriate measure to use than NPV? Explain.
8. **Profitability Index** Concerning the profitability index:
   a. Describe how the profitability index is calculated and describe the information this measure provides about a sequence of cash flows. What is the profitability index decision rule?
   b. What is the relationship between the profitability index and NPV? Are there any situations in which you might prefer one method over the other? Explain.
9. **Payback and Internal Rate of Return** A project has perpetual cash flows of C per period, a cost of I, and a required return of R. What is the relationship between the project's payback and its IRR? What implications does your answer have for long-lived projects with relatively constant cash flows?
10. **International Investment Projects** In 1996, Fuji Film, the Japanese manufacturer of photo film and related products, broke ground on a film plant in South Carolina. Fuji apparently thought that it would be better able to compete and create value with a U.S.-based facility. Other companies, such as BMW and Mercedes-Benz, have reached similar conclusions and taken similar actions. What are some of the reasons that foreign manufacturers of products as diverse as photo film and luxury automobiles might arrive at this same conclusion?
11. **Capital Budgeting Problems** What are some of the difficulties that might come up in actual applications of the various criteria we discussed in this chapter? Which one would be the easiest to implement in actual applications? The most difficult?
12. **Capital Budgeting in Not-for-Profit Entities** Are the capital budgeting criteria we discussed applicable to not-for-profit corporations? How should such entities make capital budgeting decisions? What about the U.S. government? Should it evaluate spending proposals using these techniques?

Questions and Problems

BASIC
(Questions 1–18)

1. **Calculating Payback** What is the payback period for the following set of cash flows?

Year	Cash Flow
0	−$4,800
1	1,200
2	2,500
3	3,400
4	1,700

2. **Calculating Payback** An investment project provides cash inflows of $840 per year for eight years. What is the project payback period if the initial cost is $3,000? What if the initial cost is $5,000? What if it is $7,000?

3. **Calculating Payback** Old Country, Inc., imposes a payback cutoff of three years for its international investment projects. If the company has the following two projects available, should they accept either of them?

Year	Cash Flow (A)	Cash Flow (B)
0	−$50,000	−$ 70,000
1	30,000	9,000
2	18,000	25,000
3	10,000	35,000
4	5,000	425,000

4. **Calculating Discounted Payback** An investment project has annual cash inflows of $7,000, $7,500, $8,000, and $8,500, and a discount rate of 14 percent. What is the discounted payback period for these cash flows if the initial cost is $8,000? What if the initial cost is $13,000? What if it is $18,000?

5. **Calculating Discounted Payback** An investment project costs $10,000 and has annual cash flows of $2,100 for six years. What is the discounted payback period if the discount rate is zero percent? What if the discount rate is 5 percent? If it is 15 percent?

6. **Calculating AAR** You're trying to determine whether or not to expand your business by building a new manufacturing plant. The plant has an installation cost of $15 million, which will be depreciated straight-line to zero over its four-year life. If the plant has projected net income of $1,416,000, $1,868,000, $1,562,000, and $985,000 over these four years, what is the project's average accounting return (AAR)?

7. **Calculating IRR** A firm evaluates all of its projects by applying the IRR rule. If the required return is 18 percent, should the firm accept the following project?

Year	Cash Flow
0	−$30,000
1	20,000
2	14,000
3	11,000

8. **Calculating NPV** For the cash flows in the previous problem, suppose the firm uses the NPV decision rule. At a required return of 11 percent, should the firm accept this project? What if the required return was 30 percent?

9. **Calculating NPV and IRR** A project that provides annual cash flows of $14,000 for nine years costs $70,000 today. Is this a good project if the required return is 8 percent? What if it's 16 percent? At what discount rate would you be indifferent between accepting the project and rejecting it?

10. **Calculating IRR** What is the IRR of the following set of cash flows?

Year	Cash Flow
0	−$8,000
1	3,200
2	4,000
3	6,100

11. **Calculating NPV** For the cash flows in the previous problem, what is the NPV at a discount rate of zero percent? What if the discount rate is 10 percent? If it is 20 percent? If it is 30 percent?

12. **NPV versus IRR** Bumble's Bees, Inc., has identified the following two mutually exclusive projects:

Year	Cash Flow (A)	Cash Flow (B)
0	−$34,000	−$34,000
1	16,500	5,000
2	14,000	10,000
3	10,000	18,000
4	6,000	19,000

  a. What is the IRR for each of these projects? If you apply the IRR decision rule, which project should the company accept? Is this decision necessarily correct?
  b. If the required return is 11 percent, what is the NPV for each of these projects? Which project will you choose if you apply the NPV decision rule?
  c. Over what range of discount rates would you choose Project A? Project B? At what discount rate would you be indifferent between these two projects? Explain.

13. **NPV versus IRR** Consider the following two mutually exclusive projects:

Year	Cash Flow (X)	Cash Flow (Y)
0	−$5,000	−$5,000
1	2,700	2,300
2	1,700	1,800
3	2,300	2,700

Sketch the NPV profiles for X and Y over a range of discount rates from zero to 25 percent. What is the crossover rate for these two projects?

14. **Problems with IRR** Cutler Petroleum, Inc., is trying to evaluate a generation project with the following cash flows:

Year	Cash Flow
0	−$28,000,000
1	53,000,000
2	− 8,000,000

  a. If the company requires a 10 percent return on its investments, should it accept this project? Why?
  b. Compute the IRR for this project. How many IRRs are there? If you apply the IRR decision rule, should you accept the project or not? What's going on here?

15. **Calculating Profitability Index** What is the profitability index for the following set of cash flows if the relevant discount rate is 10 percent? What if the discount rate is 15 percent? If it is 22 percent?

Year	Cash Flow
0	−$7,000
1	3,200
2	3,900
3	2,600

16. Problems with Profitability Index The Robb Computer Corporation is trying to choose between the following two mutually exclusive design projects:

Year	Cash Flow (I)	Cash Flow (II)
0	−$30,000	−$5,000
1	15,000	2,800
2	15,000	2,800
3	15,000	2,800

a. If the required return is 10 percent and Robb Computer applies the profitability index decision rule, which project should the firm accept?
b. If the company applies the NPV decision rule, which project should it take?
c. Explain why your answers in (*a*) and (*b*) are different.

17. Comparing Investment Criteria Consider the following two mutually exclusive projects:

Year	Cash Flow (A)	Cash Flow (B)
0	−$210,000	−$21,000
1	15,000	11,000
2	30,000	9,000
3	30,000	11,000
4	370,000	9,000

Whichever project you choose, if any, you require a 15 percent return on your investment.
a. If you apply the payback criterion, which investment will you choose? Why?
b. If you apply the discounted payback criterion, which investment will you choose? Why?
c. If you apply the NPV criterion, which investment will you choose? Why?
d. If you apply the IRR criterion, which investment will you choose? Why?
e. If you apply the profitability index criterion, which investment will you choose? Why?
f. Based on your answers in (*a*) through (*e*), which project will you finally choose? Why?

18. NPV and Discount Rates An investment has an installed cost of $568,240. The cash flows over the four-year life of the investment are projected to be $289,348, $196,374, $114,865, and $93,169. If the discount rate is zero, what is the NPV? If the discount rate is infinite, what is the NPV? At what discount rate is the NPV just equal to zero? Sketch the NPV profile for this investment based on these three points.

INTERMEDIATE
(Questions 19–20)

19. NPV and the Profitability Index If we define the NPV index as the ratio of NPV to cost, what is the relationship between this index and the profitability index?

20. Cash Flow Intuition A project has an initial cost of I, has a required return of R, and pays C annually for N years.
a. Find C in terms of I and N such that the project has a payback period just equal to its life.
b. Find C in terms of I, N, and R such that this is a profitable project according to the NPV decision rule.
c. Find C in terms of I, N, and R such that the project has a benefit-cost ratio of 2.

CHALLENGE
(Questions 21–23)

21. **Payback and NPV** An investment under consideration has a payback of seven years and a cost of $483,000. If the required return is 12 percent, what is the worst-case NPV? The best-case NPV? Explain. Assume the cash flows are conventional.

22. **Multiple IRRs** This problem is useful for testing the ability of financial calculators and computer software. Consider the following cash flows. How many different IRRs are there (hint: search between 20 percent and 70 percent)? When should we take this project?

Year	Cash Flow
0	−$ 504
1	2,862
2	− 6,070
3	5,700
4	− 2,000

23. **NPV Valuation** The Yurdone Corporation wants to set up a private cemetery business. According to the CFO, Barry M. Deep, business is "looking up." As a result, the cemetery project will provide a net cash inflow of $50,000 for the firm during the first year, and the cash flows are projected to grow at a rate of 6 percent per year forever. The project requires an initial investment of $780,000.
   a. If Yurdone requires a 13 percent return on such undertakings, should the cemetery business be started?
   b. The company is somewhat unsure about the assumption of a 6 percent growth rate in its cash flows. At what constant growth rate would the company just break even if it still required a 13 percent return on investment?

What's On the Web?

9.1 **Net Present Value** You have a project that has an initial cash outflow of −$20,000 and cash inflows of $6,000, $5,000, $4,000 and $3,000, respectively, for the next four years. Go to www.datadynamica.com, and follow the "Online IRR NPV Calculator" link. Enter the cash flows. If the required return is 12 percent, what is the IRR of the project? The NPV?

9.2 **Internal Rate of Return** Using the online calculator from the previous problem, find the IRR for a project with cash flows of −$500, $1,200, and −$400. What is going on here?

10 Making Capital Investment Decisions

Verizon Wireless is one of the leaders in the rapidly growing cell phone industry. In 2004, the company made headlines when it announced plans to spend $3 billion over the next two years to speed up its networks and build a new, next-generation wireless network. With 3G technology, this new network is designed to allow users to download music and video to cell phones, as well as to send videos from their cell phones. Capital expenditures such as this are not new to Verizon, which spent about $55 billion between 2000 and 2003 on its infrastructure.

As you no doubt recognize from your study of the previous chapter, Verizon's expenditures represent capital budgeting decisions. In this chapter, we further investigate capital budgeting decisions, how they are made, and how to look at them objectively.

This chapter follows up on our previous one by delving more deeply into capital budgeting. We have two main tasks. First, recall that in the last chapter, we saw that cash flow estimates are the critical input into a net present value analysis, but we didn't say very much about where these cash flows come from; so we will now examine this question in some detail. Our second goal is to learn how to critically examine NPV estimates, and, in particular, how to evaluate the sensitivity of NPV estimates to assumptions made about the uncertain future.

So far, we've covered various parts of the capital budgeting decision. Our task in this chapter is to start bringing these pieces together. In particular, we will show you how to "spread the numbers" for a proposed investment or project and, based on those numbers, make an initial assessment about whether or not the project should be undertaken.

In the discussion that follows, we focus on the process of setting up a discounted cash flow analysis. From the last chapter, we know that the projected future cash flows are the key element in such an evaluation. Accordingly, we emphasize working with financial and accounting information to come up with these figures.

In evaluating a proposed investment, we pay special attention to deciding what information is relevant to the decision at hand and what information is not. As we shall see, it is easy to overlook important pieces of the capital budgeting puzzle.

We will wait until the next chapter to describe in detail how to go about evaluating the results of our discounted cash flow analysis. Also, where needed, we will assume that we know the relevant required return, or discount rate. We continue to defer in-depth discussion of this subject to Part 5.

10.1 PROJECT CASH FLOWS: A FIRST LOOK

The effect of taking a project is to change the firm's overall cash flows today and in the future. To evaluate a proposed investment, we must consider these changes in the firm's cash flows and then decide whether or not they add value to the firm. The first (and most important) step, therefore, is to decide which cash flows are relevant and which are not.

Relevant Cash Flows

What is a relevant cash flow for a project? The general principle is simple enough: a relevant cash flow for a project is a change in the firm's overall future cash flow that comes about as a direct consequence of the decision to take that project. Because the relevant cash flows are defined in terms of changes in, or increments to, the firm's existing cash flow, they are called the **incremental cash flows** associated with the project.

The concept of incremental cash flow is central to our analysis, so we will state a general definition and refer back to it as needed:

incremental cash flows
The difference between a firm's future cash flows with a project and those without the project.

The incremental cash flows for project evaluation consist of *any and all* changes in the firm's future cash flows that are a direct consequence of taking the project.

This definition of incremental cash flows has an obvious and important corollary: Any cash flow that exists regardless of *whether or not* a project is undertaken is *not* relevant.

The Stand-Alone Principle

In practice, it would be very cumbersome to actually calculate the future total cash flows to the firm with and without a project, especially for a large firm. Fortunately, it is not really necessary to do so. Once we identify the effect of undertaking the proposed project on the firm's cash flows, we need only focus on the project's resulting incremental cash flows. This is called the **stand-alone principle**.

What the stand-alone principle says is that, once we have determined the incremental cash flows from undertaking a project, we can view that project as a kind of "minifirm" with its own future revenues and costs, its own assets, and, of course, its own cash flows. We will then be primarily interested in comparing the cash flows from this minifirm to the cost of acquiring it. An important consequence of this approach is that we will be evaluating the proposed project purely on its own merits, in isolation from any other activities or projects.

stand-alone principle
The assumption that evaluation of a project may be based on the project's incremental cash flows.

Concept Questions

10.1a What are the relevant incremental cash flows for project evaluation?

10.1b What is the stand-alone principle?

10.2 INCREMENTAL CASH FLOWS

We are concerned here only with those cash flows that are incremental and that result from a project. Looking back at our general definition, we might think it would be easy enough to decide whether or not a cash flow is incremental. Even so, there are a few situations in which it is easy to make mistakes. In this section, we describe some of the common pitfalls and how to avoid them.

Sunk Costs

A **sunk cost**, by definition, is a cost we have already paid or have already incurred the liability to pay. Such a cost cannot be changed by the decision today to accept or reject a project. Put another way, the firm will have to pay this cost no matter what. Based on our general definition of incremental cash flow, such a cost is clearly not relevant to the decision at hand. So, we will always be careful to exclude sunk costs from our analysis.

sunk cost
A cost that has already been incurred and cannot be removed and therefore should not be considered in an investment decision.

That a sunk cost is not relevant seems obvious given our discussion. Nonetheless, it's easy to fall prey to the fallacy that a sunk cost should be associated with a project. For example, suppose General Milk Company hires a financial consultant to help evaluate whether or not a line of chocolate milk should be launched. When the consultant turns in the report, General Milk objects to the analysis because the consultant did not include the hefty consulting fee as a cost of the chocolate milk project.

Who is correct? By now, we know that the consulting fee is a sunk cost, because the consulting fee must be paid whether or not the chocolate milk line is actually launched (this is an attractive feature of the consulting business).

Opportunity Costs

When we think of costs, we normally think of out-of-pocket costs, namely, those that require us to actually spend some amount of cash. An **opportunity cost** is slightly different; it requires us to give up a benefit. A common situation arises in which a firm already owns some of the assets a proposed project will be using. For example, we might be thinking of converting an old rustic cotton mill we bought years ago for $100,000 into upmarket condominiums.

opportunity cost
The most valuable alternative that is given up if a particular investment is undertaken.

If we undertake this project, there will be no direct cash outflow associated with buying the old mill because we already own it. For purposes of evaluating the condo project, should we then treat the mill as "free"? The answer is no. The mill is a valuable resource used by the project. If we didn't use it here, we could do something else with it. Like what? The obvious answer is that, at a minimum, we could sell it. Using the mill for the condo complex thus has an opportunity cost: we give up the valuable opportunity to do something else with the mill.[1]

There is another issue here. Once we agree that the use of the mill has an opportunity cost, how much should we charge the condo project for this use? Given that we paid $100,000, it might seem that we should charge this amount to the condo project. Is this correct? The answer is no, and the reason is based on our discussion concerning sunk costs.

The fact that we paid $100,000 some years ago is irrelevant. That cost is sunk. At a minimum, the opportunity cost that we charge the project is what the mill would sell for today (net of any selling costs) because this is the amount that we give up by using the mill instead of selling it.[2]

[1] Economists sometimes use the acronym TANSTAAFL, which is short for "There ain't no such thing as a free lunch," to describe the fact that only very rarely is something truly free.

[2] If the asset in question is unique, then the opportunity cost might be higher because there might be other valuable projects we could undertake that would use it. However, if the asset in question is of a type that is routinely bought and sold (a used car, perhaps), then the opportunity cost is always the going price in the market because that is the cost of buying another similar asset.

Side Effects

Remember that the incremental cash flows for a project include all the resulting changes in the *firm's* future cash flows. It would not be unusual for a project to have side, or spillover, effects, both good and bad. For example, in 2002, Japanese automaker Nissan introduced an all new version of its Altima sedan. The new model was larger all around and, in fact, looked a lot like a freshened-up version of its big brother, the Maxima. Many observers predicted that some portion of the Altima's sales would simply come at the expense of the Maxima. A negative impact on the cash flows of an existing product from the introduction of a new product is called **erosion**, and the same general problem anticipated by Nissan could occur for any multiline consumer product producer or seller.[3] In this case, the cash flows from the new line should be adjusted downwards to reflect lost profits on other lines.

erosion
The cash flows of a new project that come at the expense of a firm's existing projects.

In accounting for erosion, it is important to recognize that any sales lost as a result of launching a new product might be lost anyway because of future competition. Erosion is only relevant when the sales would not otherwise be lost.

Side effects show up in a lot of different ways. For example, one of Walt Disney Company's concerns when it built Euro Disney was that the new park would drain visitors from the Florida park, a popular vacation destination for Europeans. To give an example from the world of professional sports, when the L.A. Lakers signed Shaquille O'Neal, Coca-Cola Co. decided not to renew a marketing agreement with the Lakers worth an estimated $1 million a year because Shaq was a high-profile endorser of Pepsi.

There are beneficial spillover effects, of course. For example, you might think that Hewlett-Packard would have been concerned when the price of a printer that sold for $500 to $600 in 1994 declined to below $100 by 2005, but they weren't. What HP realized was that the big money is in the consumables that printer owners buy to keep their printers going, such as ink-jet cartridges, laser toner cartridges, and special paper. The profit margins for these products are substantial.

Net Working Capital

Normally, a project will require that the firm invest in net working capital in addition to long-term assets. For example, a project will generally need some amount of cash on hand to pay any expenses that arise. In addition, a project will need an initial investment in inventories and accounts receivable (to cover credit sales). Some of the financing for this will be in the form of amounts owed to suppliers (accounts payable), but the firm will have to supply the balance. This balance represents the investment in net working capital.

It's easy to overlook an important feature of net working capital in capital budgeting. As a project winds down, inventories are sold, receivables are collected, bills are paid, and cash balances can be drawn down. These activities free up the net working capital originally invested. So, the firm's investment in project net working capital closely resembles a loan. The firm supplies working capital at the beginning and recovers it towards the end.

Financing Costs

In analyzing a proposed investment, we will *not* include interest paid or any other financing costs such as dividends or principal repaid, because we are interested in the cash flow generated by the assets of the project. As we mentioned in Chapter 2, interest paid, for example, is a component of cash flow to creditors, not cash flow from assets.

[3]More colorfully, erosion is sometimes called *piracy* or *cannibalism.*

More generally, our goal in project evaluation is to compare the cash flow from a project to the cost of acquiring that project in order to estimate NPV. The particular mixture of debt and equity a firm actually chooses to use in financing a project is a managerial variable and primarily determines how project cash flow is divided between owners and creditors. This is not to say that financing arrangements are unimportant. They are just something to be analyzed separately. We will cover this in later chapters.

Other Issues

There are some other things to watch out for. First, we are only interested in measuring cash flow. Moreover, we are interested in measuring it when it actually occurs, not when it accrues in an accounting sense. Second, we are always interested in *after-tax* cash flow because taxes are definitely a cash outflow. In fact, whenever we write "incremental cash flows," we mean after-tax incremental cash flows. Remember, however, that after-tax cash flow and accounting profit, or net income, are entirely different things.

Concept Questions

10.2a What is a sunk cost? An opportunity cost?

10.2b Explain what erosion is and why it is relevant.

10.2c Explain why interest paid is not a relevant cash flow for project evaluation.

PRO FORMA FINANCIAL STATEMENTS AND PROJECT CASH FLOWS

10.3

The first thing we need when we begin evaluating a proposed investment is a set of pro forma, or projected, financial statements. Given these, we can develop the projected cash flows from the project. Once we have the cash flows, we can estimate the value of the project using the techniques we described in the previous chapter.

Getting Started: Pro Forma Financial Statements

Pro forma financial statements are a convenient and easily understood means of summarizing much of the relevant information for a project. To prepare these statements, we will need estimates of quantities such as unit sales, the selling price per unit, the variable cost per unit, and total fixed costs. We will also need to know the total investment required, including any investment in net working capital.

pro forma financial statements
Financial statements projecting future years' operations.

To illustrate, suppose we think we can sell 50,000 cans of shark attractant per year at a price of $4 per can. It costs us about $2.50 per can to make the attractant, and a new product such as this one typically has only a three-year life (perhaps because the customer base dwindles rapidly). We require a 20 percent return on new products.

Fixed costs for the project, including such things as rent on the production facility, will run $12,000 per year.[4] Further, we will need to invest a total of $90,000 in manufacturing equipment. For simplicity, we will assume that this $90,000 will be 100 percent depreciated over the three-year life of the project.[5] Furthermore, the cost of removing the

[4] By fixed cost, we literally mean a cash outflow that will occur regardless of the level of sales. This should not be confused with some sort of accounting period charge.

[5] We will also assume that a full year's depreciation can be taken in the first year.

TABLE 10.1 >>

Projected Income Statement, Shark Attractant Project

Sales (50,000 units at $4/unit)	$200,000
Variable costs ($2.50/unit)	125,000
	$ 75,000
Fixed costs	12,000
Depreciation ($90,000/3)	30,000
EBIT	$ 33,000
Taxes (34%)	11,220
Net income	$ 21,780

TABLE 10.2 >>

Projected Capital Requirements, Shark Attractant Project

	Year			
	0	1	2	3
Net working capital	$ 20,000	$20,000	$20,000	$20,000
Net fixed assets	90,000	60,000	30,000	0
Total investment	$110,000	$80,000	$50,000	$20,000

equipment will roughly equal its actual value in three years, so it will be essentially worthless on a market value basis as well. Finally, the project will require an initial $20,000 investment in net working capital, and the tax rate is 34 percent.

In Table 10.1, we organize these initial projections by first preparing the pro forma income statement. Once again, notice that we have *not* deducted any interest expense. This will always be so. As we described earlier, interest paid is a financing expense, not a component of operating cash flow.

We can also prepare a series of abbreviated balance sheets that show the capital requirements for the project as we've done in Table 10.2. Here we have net working capital of $20,000 in each year. Fixed assets are $90,000 at the start of the project's life (Year 0), and they decline by the $30,000 in depreciation each year, ending up at zero. Notice that the total investment given here for future years is the total book, or accounting, value, not market value.

At this point, we need to start converting this accounting information into cash flows. We consider how to do this next.

Project Cash Flows

To develop the cash flows from a project, we need to recall (from Chapter 2) that cash flow from assets has three components: operating cash flow, capital spending, and changes in net working capital. To evaluate a project, or minifirm, we need to arrive at estimates for each of these.

Once we have estimates of the components of cash flow, we will calculate cash flow for our minifirm just as we did in Chapter 2 for an entire firm:

$$\begin{aligned}\text{Project cash flow} &= \text{Project operating cash flow}\\ &\quad - \text{Project change in net working capital}\\ &\quad - \text{Project capital spending}\end{aligned}$$

We consider these components next.

<< TABLE 10.3

Projected Income Statement, Abbreviated, Shark Attractant Project

Sales	$200,000
Variable costs	125,000
Fixed costs	12,000
Depreciation	30,000
EBIT	$ 33,000
Taxes (34%)	11,220
Net income	$ 21,780

<< TABLE 10.4

Projected Operating Cash Flow, Shark Attractant Project

EBIT	$33,000
Depreciation	+ 30,000
Taxes	− 11,220
Operating cash flow	$51,780

Project Operating Cash Flow To determine the operating cash flow associated with a project, we first need to recall the definition of operating cash flow:

Operating cash flow = Earnings before interest and taxes
+ Depreciation
− Taxes

To illustrate the calculation of operating cash flow, we will use the projected information from the shark attractant project. For ease of reference, Table 10.3 repeats the income statement in more abbreviated form.

Given the income statement in Table 10.3, calculating the operating cash flow is very straightforward. As we see in Table 10.4, projected operating cash flow for the shark attractant project is $51,780.

Project Net Working Capital and Capital Spending We next need to take care of the fixed asset and net working capital requirements. Based on our balance sheets, we know that the firm must spend $90,000 up front for fixed assets and invest an additional $20,000 in net working capital. The immediate outflow is thus $110,000. At the end of the project's life, the fixed assets will be worthless, but the firm will recover the $20,000 that was tied up in working capital.[6] This will lead to a $20,000 *inflow* in the last year.

On a purely mechanical level, notice that whenever we have an investment in net working capital, that same investment has to be recovered; in other words, the same number needs to appear at some time in the future with the opposite sign.

Projected Total Cash Flow and Value

Given the information we've accumulated, we can finish the preliminary cash flow analysis as illustrated in Table 10.5.

Now that we have cash flow projections, we are ready to apply the various criteria we discussed in the last chapter. First, the NPV at the 20 percent required return is:

$$\begin{aligned} \text{NPV} &= -\$110{,}000 + 51{,}780/1.2 + 51{,}780/1.2^2 + 71{,}780/1.2^3 \\ &= \$10{,}648 \end{aligned}$$

[6]In reality, the firm would probably recover something less than 100 percent of this amount because of bad debts, inventory loss, and so on. If we wanted to, we could just assume that, for example, only 90 percent was recovered and proceed from there.

TABLE 10.5 >>

Projected Total Cash Flows, Shark Attractant Project

	Year			
	0	1	2	3
Operating cash flow		$51,780	$51,780	$51,780
Changes in NWC	−$ 20,000			+ 20,000
Capital spending	− 90,000			
Total project cash flow	−$110,000	$51,780	$51,780	$71,780

So, based on these projections, the project creates over $10,000 in value and should be accepted. Also, the return on this investment obviously exceeds 20 percent (because the NPV is positive at 20 percent). After some trial and error, we find that the IRR works out to be about 25.8 percent.

In addition, if required, we could go ahead and calculate the payback and the average accounting return, or AAR. Inspection of the cash flows shows that the payback on this project is just a little over two years (verify that it's about 2.1 years).[7]

From the last chapter, we know that the AAR is average net income divided by average book value. The net income each year is $21,780. The average (in thousands) of the four book values (from Table 10.2) for total investment is ($110 + 80 + 50 + 20)/4 = $65. So the AAR is $21,780/65,000 = 33.51 percent.[8] We've already seen that the return on this investment (the IRR) is about 26 percent. The fact that the AAR is larger illustrates again why the AAR cannot be meaningfully interpreted as the return on a project.

Concept Questions

10.3a What is the definition of project operating cash flow? How does this differ from net income?

10.3b For the shark attractant project, why did we add back the firm's net working capital investment in the final year?

10.4 MORE ON PROJECT CASH FLOW

In this section, we take a closer look at some aspects of project cash flow. In particular, we discuss project net working capital in more detail. We then examine current tax laws regarding depreciation. Finally, we work through a more involved example of the capital investment decision.

A Closer Look at Net Working Capital

In calculating operating cash flow, we did not explicitly consider the fact that some of our sales might be on credit. Also, we may not have actually paid some of the costs shown. In either case, the cash flow in question would not yet have occurred. We show here that these

[7]We're guilty of a minor inconsistency here. When we calculated the NPV and the IRR, we assumed that all the cash flows occurred at end of year. When we calculated the payback, we assumed that the cash flows occurred uniformly throughout the year.

[8]Notice that the average total book value is not the initial total of $110,000 divided by 2. The reason is that the $20,000 in working capital doesn't "depreciate."

possibilities are not a problem as long as we don't forget to include changes in net working capital in our analysis. This discussion thus emphasizes the importance and the effect of doing so.

Suppose that during a particular year of a project we have the following simplified income statement:

Sales	$500
Costs	310
Net income	$190

Depreciation and taxes are zero. No fixed assets are purchased during the year. Also, to illustrate a point, we assume that the only components of net working capital are accounts receivable and payable. The beginning and ending amounts for these accounts are as follows:

	Beginning of Year	End of Year	Change
Accounts receivable	$880	$910	+$30
Accounts payable	550	605	+ 55
Net working capital	$330	$305	−$25

Based on this information, what is total cash flow for the year? We can first just mechanically apply what we have been discussing to come up with the answer. Operating cash flow in this particular case is the same as EBIT because there are no taxes or depreciation and thus it equals $190. Also, notice that net working capital actually *declined* by $25. This just means that $25 was freed up during the year. There was no capital spending, so the total cash flow for the year is:

$$\begin{aligned}\text{Total cash flow} &= \text{Operating cash flow} - \text{Change in NWC} - \text{Capital spending}\\ &= \$190 - (-\ 25) - 0\\ &= \$215\end{aligned}$$

Now, we know that this $215 total cash flow has to be "dollars in" less "dollars out" for the year. We could therefore ask a different question: What were cash revenues for the year? Also, what were cash costs?

To determine cash revenues, we need to look more closely at net working capital. During the year, we had sales of $500. However, accounts receivable rose by $30 over the same time period. What does this mean? The $30 increase tells us that sales exceeded collections by $30. In other words, we haven't yet received the cash from $30 of the $500 in sales. As a result, our cash inflow is $500 − 30 = $470. In general, cash income is sales minus the increase in accounts receivable.

Cash outflows can be similarly determined. We show costs of $310 on the income statement, but accounts payable increased by $55 during the year. This means that we have not yet paid $55 of the $310, so cash costs for the period are just $310 − 55 = $255. In other words, in this case, cash costs equal costs less the increase in accounts payable.[9]

[9]If there were other accounts, we might have to make some further adjustments. For example, a net increase in inventory would be a cash outflow.

IN THEIR OWN WORDS . . .

Samuel Weaver on Capital Budgeting at Hershey Foods Corporation

>> **The capital program** at Hershey Foods Corporation and most Fortune 500 or Fortune 1,000 companies involves a three-phase approach: planning or budgeting, evaluation, and postcompletion reviews.

The first phase involves identification of likely projects at strategic planning time. These are selected to support the strategic objectives of the corporation. This identification is generally broad in scope with minimal financial evaluation attached. As the planning process focuses more closely on the short-term plans, major capital expenditures are scrutinized more rigorously. Project costs are more closely honed, and specific projects may be reconsidered.

Each project is then individually reviewed and authorized. Planning, developing, and refining cash flows underlie capital analysis at Hershey Foods. Once the cash flows have been determined, the application of capital evaluation techniques such as those using net present value, internal rate of return, and payback period is routine. Presentation of the results is enhanced using sensitivity analysis, which plays a major role for management in assessing the critical assumptions and resulting impact.

The final phase relates to postcompletion reviews in which the original forecasts of the project's performance are compared to actual results and/or revised expectations.

Capital expenditure analysis is only as good as the assumptions that underlie the project. The old cliché of GIGO (garbage in, garbage out) applies in this case. Incremental cash flows primarily result from incremental sales or margin improvements (cost savings). For the most part, a range of incremental cash flows can be identified from marketing research or engineering studies. However, for a number of projects, correctly discerning the implications and the relevant cash flows is analytically challenging. For example, when a new product is introduced and is expected to generate millions of dollars' worth of sales, the appropriate analysis focuses on the incremental sales after accounting for cannibalization of existing products.

One of the problems that we face at Hershey Foods deals with the application of net present value, NPV, versus internal rate of return, IRR. NPV offers us the correct investment indication when dealing with mutually exclusive alternatives. However, decision makers at all levels sometimes find it difficult to comprehend the result. Specifically, an NPV of, say, $535,000 needs to be interpreted. It is not enough to know that the NPV is positive or even that it is more positive than an alternative. Decision makers seek to determine a level of "comfort" regarding how profitable the investment is by relating it to other standards.

Although the IRR may provide a misleading indication of which project to select, the result is provided in a way that can be interpreted by all parties. The resulting IRR can be mentally compared to expected inflation, current borrowing rates, the cost of capital, an equity portfolio's return, and so on. An IRR of, say, 18 percent is readily interpretable by management. Perhaps this ease of understanding is why surveys indicate that most Fortune 500 or Fortune 1,000 companies use the IRR method as a primary evaluation technique.

In addition to the NPV versus IRR problem, there are a limited number of projects for which traditional capital expenditure analysis is difficult to apply because the cash flows can't be determined. When new computer equipment is purchased, an office building is renovated, or a parking lot is repaved, it is essentially impossible to identify the cash flows, so the use of traditional evaluation techniques is limited. These types of "capital expenditure" decisions are made using other techniques that hinge on management's judgment.

Samuel Weaver, Ph.D., is the former director, financial planning and analysis, for Hershey Chocolate North America. He is a certified management accountant. His position combined the theoretical with the pragmatic and involved the analysis of many different facets of finance in addition to capital expenditure analysis.

Putting this information together, we calculate that cash inflows less cash outflows is $470 − 255 = $215, just as we had before. Notice that:

$$\begin{aligned}\text{Cash flow} &= \text{Cash inflow} - \text{Cash outflow}\\ &= (\$500 - 30) - (310 - 55)\\ &= (\$500 - 310) - (30 - 55)\\ &= \text{Operating cash flow} - \text{Change in NWC}\\ &= \$190 - (-25)\\ &= \$215\end{aligned}$$

More generally, this example illustrates that including net working capital changes in our calculations has the effect of adjusting for the discrepancy between accounting sales and costs and actual cash receipts and payments.

Cash Collections and Costs

<< **EXAMPLE 10.1**

For the year just completed, the Combat Wombat Telestat Co. (CWT) reports sales of $998 and costs of $734. You have collected the following beginning and ending balance sheet information:

	Beginning	Ending
Accounts receivable	$100	$110
Inventory	100	80
Accounts payable	100	70
Net working capital	$100	$120

Based on these figures, what are cash inflows? Cash outflows? What happened to each account? What is net cash flow?

Sales were $998, but receivables rose by $10. So cash collections were $10 less than sales, or $988. Costs were $734, but inventories fell by $20. This means that we didn't replace $20 worth of inventory, so costs are actually overstated by this amount. Also, payables fell by $30. This means that, on a net basis, we actually paid our suppliers $30 more than we received from them, resulting in a $30 understatement of costs. Adjusting for these events, we calculate that cash costs are $734 − 20 + 30 = $744. Net cash flow is $988 − 744 = $244.

Finally, notice that net working capital increased by $20 overall. We can check our answer by noting that the original accounting sales less costs of $998 − 734 is $264. In addition, CWT spent $20 on net working capital, so the net result is a cash flow of $264 − 20 = $244, as we calculated.

Depreciation

As we note elsewhere, accounting depreciation is a noncash deduction. As a result, depreciation has cash flow consequences only because it influences the tax bill. The way that depreciation is computed for tax purposes is thus the relevant method for capital investment decisions. Not surprisingly, the procedures are governed by tax law. We now discuss some specifics of the depreciation system enacted by the Tax Reform Act of 1986. This system is a modification of the **accelerated cost recovery system (ACRS)** instituted in 1981.

accelerated cost recovery system (ACRS)
A depreciation method under U.S. tax law allowing for the accelerated write-off of property under various classifications.

Modified ACRS Depreciation (MACRS) Calculating depreciation is normally very mechanical. Although there are a number of *ifs, ands,* and *buts* involved, the basic idea under MACRS is that every asset is assigned to a particular class. An asset's class establishes its life for tax purposes. Once an asset's tax life is determined, the depreciation for each year is computed by multiplying the cost of the asset by a fixed percentage.[10] The expected salvage value (what we think the asset will be worth when we dispose of it) and the expected economic life (how long we expect the asset to be in service) are not explicitly considered in the calculation of depreciation.

[10]Under certain circumstances, the cost of the asset may be adjusted before computing depreciation. The result is called the *depreciable basis,* and depreciation is calculated using this number instead of the actual cost.

TABLE 10.6 >>

Modified ACRS Property Classes

Class	Examples
3-year	Equipment used in research
5-year	Autos, computers
7-year	Most industrial equipment

TABLE 10.7 >>

Modified ACRS Depreciation Allowances

	Property Class		
Year	3-Year	5-Year	7-Year
1	33.33%	20.00%	14.29%
2	44.44	32.00	24.49
3	14.82	19.20	17.49
4	7.41	11.52	12.49
5		11.52	8.93
6		5.76	8.93
7			8.93
8			4.45

Some typical depreciation classes are given in Table 10.6, and associated percentages (rounded to two decimal places) are shown in Table 10.7.[11]

A nonresidential real property, such as an office building, is depreciated over 31.5 years using straight-line depreciation. A residential real property, such as an apartment building, is depreciated straight-line over 27.5 years. Remember that land cannot be depreciated.[12]

To illustrate how depreciation is calculated, we consider an automobile costing $12,000. Autos are normally classified as five-year property. Looking at Table 10.7, we see that the relevant figure for the first year of a five-year asset is 20 percent.[13] The depreciation in the first year is thus $12,000 × .20 = $2,400. The relevant percentage in the second year is 32 percent, so the depreciation in the second year is $12,000 × .32 = $3,840, and so on. We can summarize these calculations as follows:

Year	MACRS Percentage	Depreciation
1	20.00%	.2000 × $12,000 = $ 2,400.00
2	32.00%	.3200 × 12,000 = 3,840.00
3	19.20%	.1920 × 12,000 = 2,304.00
4	11.52%	.1152 × 12,000 = 1,382.40
5	11.52%	.1152 × 12,000 = 1,382.40
6	5.76%	.0576 × 12,000 = 691.20
	100.00%	$12,000.00

[11]For the curious, these depreciation percentages are derived from a double-declining balance scheme with a switch to straight-line when the latter becomes advantageous. Further, there is a half-year convention, meaning that all assets are assumed to be placed in service midway through the tax year. This convention is maintained unless more than 40 percent of an asset's cost is incurred in the final quarter. In this case, a midquarter convention is used.

[12]There are, however, depletion allowances for firms in extraction-type lines of business (e.g., mining). These are somewhat similar to depreciation allowances.

[13]It may appear odd that five-year property is depreciated over six years. As described elsewhere, the tax accounting reason is that it is assumed we have the asset for only six months in the first year and, consequently, six months in the last year. As a result, there are five 12-month periods, but we have some depreciation in each of six different tax years.

<< TABLE 10.8

MACRS Book Values

Year	Beginning Book Value	Depreciation	Ending Book Value
1	$12,000.00	$2,400.00	$9,600.00
2	9,600.00	3,840.00	5,760.00
3	5,760.00	2,304.00	3,456.00
4	3,456.00	1,382.40	2,073.60
5	2,073.60	1,382.40	691.20
6	691.20	691.20	0.00

Notice that the MACRS percentages sum up to 100 percent. As a result, we write off 100 percent of the cost of the asset, or $12,000 in this case.

Book Value versus Market Value In calculating depreciation under current tax law, the economic life and future market value of the asset are not an issue. As a result, the book value of an asset can differ substantially from its actual market value. For example, with our $12,000 car, book value after the first year is $12,000 less the first year's depreciation of $2,400, or $9,600. The remaining book values are summarized in Table 10.8. After six years, the book value of the car is zero.

Suppose that we wanted to sell the car after five years. Based on historical averages, it would be worth, say, 25 percent of the purchase price, or .25 × $12,000 = $3,000. If we actually sold it for this, then we would have to pay taxes at the ordinary income tax rate on the difference between the sale price of $3,000 and the book value of $691.20. For a corporation in the 34 percent bracket, the tax liability would be .34 × $2,308.80 = $784.99.[14]

The reason that taxes must be paid in this case is that the difference between market value and book value is "excess" depreciation, and it must be "recaptured" when the asset is sold. What this means is that, as it turns out, we overdepreciated the asset by $3,000 − 691.20 = $2,308.80. Because we deducted $2,308.80 too much in depreciation, we paid $784.99 too little in taxes, and we simply have to make up the difference.

Notice that this is *not* a tax on a capital gain. As a general (albeit rough) rule, a capital gain occurs only if the market price exceeds the original cost. However, what is and what is not a capital gain is ultimately up to taxing authorities, and the specific rules can be very complex. We will ignore capital gain taxes for the most part.

Finally, if the book value exceeds the market value, then the difference is treated as a loss for tax purposes. For example, if we sell the car after two years for $4,000, then the book value exceeds the market value by $1,760. In this case, a tax saving of .34 × $1,760 = $598.40 occurs.

[14]The rules are different and more complicated with real property. Essentially, in this case, only the difference between the actual book value and the book value that would have existed if straight-line depreciation had been used is recaptured. Anything above the straight-line book value is considered a capital gain.

MACRS Depreciation << EXAMPLE 10.2

The Staple Supply Co. has just purchased a new computerized information system with an installed cost of $160,000. The computer is treated as five-year property. What are the yearly depreciation allowances? Based on historical experience, we think that the system will be worth only $10,000 when Staple gets rid of it in four years. What are the tax consequences of the sale? What is the total after-tax cash flow from the sale?

continued

The yearly depreciation allowances are calculated by just multiplying $160,000 by the five-year percentages found in Table 10.7:

Year	MACRS Percentage	Depreciation	Ending Book Value
1	20.00%	.2000 × $160,000 = $ 32,000	$128,000
2	32.00	.3200 × 160,000 = 51,200	76,800
3	19.20	.1920 × 160,000 = 30,720	46,080
4	11.52	.1152 × 160,000 = 18,432	27,648
5	11.52	.1152 × 160,000 = 18,432	9,216
6	5.76	.0576 × 160,000 = 9,216	0
	100.00%	$160,000	

Notice that we have also computed the book value of the system as of the end of each year. The book value at the end of Year 4 is $27,648. If Staple sells the system for $10,000 at that time, it will have a loss of $17,648 (the difference) for tax purposes. This loss, of course, is like depreciation because it isn't a cash expense.

What really happens? Two things. First, Staple gets $10,000 from the buyer. Second, it saves .34 × $17,648 = $6,000 in taxes. So the total after-tax cash flow from the sale is a $16,000 cash inflow.

An Example: The Majestic Mulch and Compost Company (MMCC)

At this point, we want to go through a somewhat more involved capital budgeting analysis. Keep in mind as you read that the basic approach here is exactly the same as that in the shark attractant example used earlier. We have only added on some more real-world detail (and a lot more numbers).

MMCC is investigating the feasibility of a new line of power mulching tools aimed at the growing number of home composters. Based on exploratory conversations with buyers for large garden shops, MMCC projects unit sales as follows:

Year	Unit Sales
1	3,000
2	5,000
3	6,000
4	6,500
5	6,000
6	5,000
7	4,000
8	3,000

The new power mulcher will be priced to sell at $120 per unit to start. When the competition catches up after three years, however, MMCC anticipates that the price will drop to $110.

The power mulcher project will require $20,000 in net working capital at the start. Subsequently, total net working capital at the end of each year will be about 15 percent of sales for that year. The variable cost per unit is $60, and total fixed costs are $25,000 per year.

TABLE 10.9
Projected Revenues, Power Mulcher Project

Year	Unit Price	Unit Sales	Revenues
1	$120	3,000	$360,000
2	120	5,000	600,000
3	120	6,000	720,000
4	110	6,500	715,000
5	110	6,000	660,000
6	110	5,000	550,000
7	110	4,000	440,000
8	110	3,000	330,000

TABLE 10.10
Annual Depreciation, Power Mulcher Project

Year	MACRS Percentage	Depreciation	Ending Book Value
1	14.29%	.1429 × $800,000 = $114,320	$685,680
2	24.49	.2449 × 800,000 = 195,920	489,760
3	17.49	.1749 × 800,000 = 139,920	349,840
4	12.49	.1249 × 800,000 = 99,920	249,920
5	8.93	.0893 × 800,000 = 71,440	178,480
6	8.93	.0893 × 800,000 = 71,440	107,040
7	8.93	.0893 × 800,000 = 71,440	35,600
8	4.45	.0445 × 800,000 = 35,600	0
	100.00%	$800,000	

It will cost about $800,000 to buy the equipment necessary to begin production. This investment is primarily in industrial equipment, which qualifies as seven-year MACRS property. The equipment will actually be worth about 20 percent of its cost in eight years, or .20 × $800,000 = $160,000. The relevant tax rate is 34 percent, and the required return is 15 percent. Based on this information, should MMCC proceed?

Operating Cash Flows There is a lot of information here that we need to organize. The first thing we can do is calculate projected sales. Sales in the first year are projected at 3,000 units at $120 apiece, or $360,000 total. The remaining figures are shown in Table 10.9.

Next, we compute the depreciation on the $800,000 investment in Table 10.10. With this information, we can prepare the pro forma income statements, as shown in Table 10.11. From here, computing the operating cash flows is straightforward. The results are illustrated in the first part of Table 10.13.

Change in NWC Now that we have the operating cash flows, we need to determine the changes in NWC. By assumption, net working capital requirements change as sales change. In each year, MMCC will generally either add to or recover some of its project net working capital. Recalling that NWC starts out at $20,000 and then rises to 15 percent of sales, we can calculate the amount of NWC for each year as illustrated in Table 10.12.

As illustrated, during the first year, net working capital grows from $20,000 to .15 × $360,000 = $54,000. The increase in net working capital for the year is thus $54,000 − 20,000 = $34,000. The remaining figures are calculated in the same way.

Remember that an increase in net working capital is a cash outflow, so we use a negative sign in this table to indicate an additional investment that the firm makes in net working capital. A positive sign represents net working capital returning to the firm. Thus, for

TABLE 10.11 >> Projected Income Statements, Power Mulcher Project

	Year							
	1	2	3	4	5	6	7	8
Unit price	$ 120	$ 120	$ 120	$ 110	$ 110	$ 110	$ 110	$ 110
Unit sales	3,000	5,000	6,000	6,500	6,000	5,000	4,000	3,000
Revenues	$360,000	$600,000	$720,000	$715,000	$660,000	$550,000	$440,000	$330,000
Variable costs	180,000	300,000	360,000	390,000	360,000	300,000	240,000	180,000
Fixed costs	25,000	25,000	25,000	25,000	25,000	25,000	25,000	25,000
Depreciation	114,320	195,920	139,920	99,920	71,440	71,440	71,440	35,600
EBIT	$ 40,680	$ 79,080	$195,080	$200,080	$203,560	$153,560	$103,560	$ 89,400
Taxes (34%)	13,831	26,887	66,327	68,027	69,210	52,210	35,210	30,396
Net income	$ 26,849	$ 52,193	$128,753	$132,053	$134,350	$101,350	$ 68,350	$ 59,004

TABLE 10.12 >> Changes in Net Working Capital, Power Mulcher Project

Year	Revenues	Net Working Capital	Cash Flow
0		$ 20,000	−$20,000
1	$360,000	54,000	− 34,000
2	600,000	90,000	− 36,000
3	720,000	108,000	− 18,000
4	715,000	107,250	750
5	660,000	99,000	8,250
6	550,000	82,500	16,500
7	440,000	66,000	16,500
8	330,000	49,500	16,500

example, $16,500 in NWC flows back to the firm in Year 6. Over the project's life, net working capital builds to a peak of $108,000 and declines from there as sales begin to drop off.

We show the result for changes in net working capital in the second part of Table 10.13. Notice that at the end of the project's life, there is $49,500 in net working capital still to be recovered. Therefore, in the last year, the project returns $16,500 of NWC during the year and then returns the remaining $49,500 at the end of the year for a total of $66,000.

Capital Spending Finally, we have to account for the long-term capital invested in the project. In this case, MMCC invests $800,000 at Year 0. By assumption, this equipment will be worth $160,000 at the end of the project. It will have a book value of zero at that time. As we discussed earlier, this $160,000 excess of market value over book value is taxable, so the after-tax proceeds will be $160,000 × (1 − .34) = $105,600. These figures are shown in the third part of Table 10.13.

Total Cash Flow and Value We now have all the cash flow pieces, and we put them together in Table 10.14. In addition to the total project cash flows, we have calculated the cumulative cash flows and the discounted cash flows. At this point, it's essentially plug-and-chug to calculate the net present value, internal rate of return, and payback.

If we sum the discounted flows and the initial investment, the net present value (at 15 percent) works out to be $65,488. This is positive, so, based on these preliminary

TABLE 10.13 >> Projected Cash Flows, Power Mulcher Project

	Year								
	0	1	2	3	4	5	6	7	8
I. Operating Cash Flow									
EBIT		$ 40,680	$ 79,080	$195,080	$200,080	$203,560	$153,560	$103,560	$ 89,400
Depreciation		114,320	195,920	139,920	99,920	71,440	71,440	71,440	35,600
Taxes		− 13,831	− 26,887	− 66,327	− 68,027	− 69,210	− 52,210	− 35,210	− 30,396
Operating cash flow		$141,169	$248,113	$268,673	$231,973	$205,790	$172,790	$139,790	$ 94,604
II. Net Working Capital									
Initial NWC	−$ 20,000								
Change in NWC		−$ 34,000	−$ 36,000	−$ 18,000	$ 750	$ 8,250	$ 16,500	$ 16,500	$ 16,500
NWC recovery									49,500
Total change in NWC	−$ 20,000	−$ 34,000	−$ 36,000	−$ 18,000	$ 750	$ 8,250	$ 16,500	$ 16,500	$ 66,000
III. Capital Spending									
Initial outlay	−$800,000								
After-tax salvage									$105,600
Capital spending	−$800,000								$105,600

TABLE 10.14 >> Projected Total Cash Flows, Power Mulcher Project

	Year								
	0	1	2	3	4	5	6	7	8
Operating cash flow		$141,169	$248,113	$268,673	$231,973	$205,790	$172,790	$139,790	$ 94,604
Change in NWC	−$ 20,000	− 34,000	− 36,000	− 18,000	750	8,250	16,500	16,500	66,000
Capital spending	− 800,000								105,600
Total project cash flow	−$820,000	$107,169	$212,113	$250,673	$232,723	$214,040	$189,290	$156,290	$266,204
Cumulative cash flow	−$820,000	−$712,831	−$500,718	−$250,045	−$ 17,322	$196,718	$386,008	$542,298	$808,502
Discounted cash flow @ 15%	− 820,000	93,190	160,388	164,821	133,060	106,416	81,835	58,755	87,023

Net present value (15%) = $65,488
Internal rate of return = 17.24%
Payback = 4.08 years

projections, the power mulcher project is acceptable. The internal, or DCF, rate of return is greater than 15 percent because the NPV is positive. It works out to be 17.24 percent, again indicating that the project is acceptable.

Looking at the cumulative cash flows, we can see that the project has almost paid back after four years because the table shows that the cumulative cash flow is almost zero at that time. As indicated, the fractional year works out to be $17,322/214,040 = .08, so the payback is 4.08 years. We can't say whether or not this is good because we don't have a benchmark for MMCC. This is the usual problem with payback periods.

Conclusion This completes our preliminary DCF analysis. Where do we go from here? If we have a great deal of confidence in our projections, then there is no further analysis to be done. MMCC should begin production and marketing immediately. It is unlikely that this will be the case. It is important to remember that the result of our analysis is an estimate of NPV, and we will usually have less than complete confidence in our projections. This means we have more work to do. In particular, we will almost surely want to spend some time evaluating the quality of our estimates. We will take up this subject in the next chapter. For now, we take a look at some alternative definitions of operating cash flow, and we illustrate some different cases that arise in capital budgeting.

Concept Questions

10.4a Why is it important to consider changes in net working capital in developing cash flows? What is the effect of doing so?

10.4b How is depreciation calculated for fixed assets under current tax law? What effects do expected salvage value and estimated economic life have on the calculated depreciation deduction?

10.5 ALTERNATIVE DEFINITIONS OF OPERATING CASH FLOW

The analysis we went through in the previous section is quite general and can be adapted to just about any capital investment problem. In the next section, we illustrate some particularly useful variations. Before we do so, we need to discuss the fact that there are different definitions of project operating cash flow that are commonly used, both in practice and in finance texts.

As we will see, the different approaches to operating cash flow that exist all measure the same thing. If they are used correctly, they all produce the same answer, and one is not necessarily any better or more useful than another. Unfortunately, the fact that alternative definitions are used does sometimes lead to confusion. For this reason, we examine several of these variations next to see how they are related.

In the discussion that follows, keep in mind that when we speak of cash flow, we literally mean dollars in less dollars out. This is all we are concerned with. Different definitions of operating cash flow simply amount to different ways of manipulating basic information about sales, costs, depreciation, and taxes to get at cash flow.

For a particular project and year under consideration, suppose we have the following estimates:

$$\text{Sales} = \$1{,}500$$
$$\text{Costs} = \$700$$
$$\text{Depreciation} = \$600$$

With these estimates, notice that EBIT is:

$$\begin{aligned}\text{EBIT} &= \text{Sales} - \text{Costs} - \text{Depreciation}\\ &= \$1{,}500 - 700 - 600\\ &= \$200\end{aligned}$$

Once again, we assume that no interest is paid, so the tax bill is:

$$\begin{aligned}\text{Taxes} &= \text{EBIT} \times \text{T} \\ &= \$200 \times .34 = \$68\end{aligned}$$

where T, the corporate tax rate, is 34 percent.

When we put all of this together, we see that project operating cash flow, OCF, is:

$$\begin{aligned}\text{OCF} &= \text{EBIT} + \text{Depreciation} - \text{Taxes} \\ &= \$200 + 600 - 68 = \$732\end{aligned}$$

It turns out there are some other ways to determine OCF that could be (and are) used. We consider these next.

The Bottom-Up Approach

Because we are ignoring any financing expenses, such as interest, in our calculations of project OCF, we can write project net income as:

$$\begin{aligned}\text{Project net income} &= \text{EBIT} - \text{Taxes} \\ &= \$200 - 68 \\ &= \$132\end{aligned}$$

If we simply add the depreciation to both sides, we arrive at a slightly different and very common expression for OCF:

$$\begin{aligned}\text{OCF} &= \text{Net Income} + \text{Depreciation} \\ &= \$132 + 600 \qquad \textbf{[10.1]} \\ &= \$732\end{aligned}$$

This is the *bottom-up* approach. Here, we start with the accountant's bottom line (net income) and add back any noncash deductions such as depreciation. It is crucial to remember that this definition of operating cash flow as net income plus depreciation is correct only if there is no interest expense subtracted in the calculation of net income.

For the shark attractant project, net income was \$21,780 and depreciation was \$30,000, so the bottom-up calculation is:

$$\text{OCF} = \$21{,}780 + 30{,}000 = \$51{,}780$$

This is exactly the same OCF we had previously.

The Top-Down Approach

Perhaps the most obvious way to calculate OCF is:

$$\begin{aligned}\text{OCF} &= \text{Sales} - \text{Costs} - \text{Taxes} \qquad \textbf{[10.2]} \\ &= \$1{,}500 - 700 - 68 = \$732\end{aligned}$$

This is the *top-down* approach, the second variation on the basic OCF definition. Here, we start at the top of the income statement with sales and work our way down to net cash flow by subtracting costs, taxes, and other expenses. Along the way, we simply leave out any strictly noncash items such as depreciation.

For the shark attractant project, the operating cash flow can be readily calculated using the top-down approach. With sales of \$200,000, total costs (fixed plus variable) of \$137,000, and a tax bill of \$11,220, the OCF is:

$$\text{OCF} = \$200{,}000 - 137{,}000 - 11{,}220 = \$51{,}780$$

This is just as we had before.

The Tax Shield Approach

The third variation on our basic definition of OCF is the *tax shield* approach. This approach will be very useful for some problems we consider in the next section. The tax shield definition of OCF is:

$$\text{OCF} = (\text{Sales} - \text{Costs}) \times (1 - T) + \text{Depreciation} \times T \quad [10.3]$$

where T is again the corporate tax rate. Assuming that $T = 34\%$, the OCF works out to be:

$$\begin{aligned}\text{OCF} &= (\$1{,}500 - 700) \times .66 + 600 \times .34\\ &= \$528 + 204\\ &= \$732\end{aligned}$$

This is just as we had before.

This approach views OCF as having two components. The first part is what the project's cash flow would be if there were no depreciation expense. In this case, this would-have-been cash flow is $528.

depreciation tax shield
The tax saving that results from the depreciation deduction, calculated as depreciation multiplied by the corporate tax rate.

The second part of OCF in this approach is the depreciation deduction multiplied by the tax rate. This is called the **depreciation tax shield**. We know that depreciation is a noncash expense. The only cash flow effect of deducting depreciation is to reduce our taxes, a benefit to us. At the current 34 percent corporate tax rate, every dollar in depreciation expense saves us 34 cents in taxes. So, in our example, the $600 depreciation deduction saves us $\$600 \times .34 = \$204$ in taxes.

For the shark attractant project we considered earlier in the chapter, the depreciation tax shield would be $\$30{,}000 \times .34 = \$10{,}200$. The after-tax value for sales less costs would be $(\$200{,}000 - 137{,}000) \times (1 - .34) = \$41{,}580$. Adding these together yields the value of OCF:

$$\text{OCF} = \$41{,}580 + 10{,}200 = \$51{,}780$$

This calculation verifies that the tax shield approach is completely equivalent to the approach we used before.

Conclusion

Now that we've seen that all of these approaches are the same, you're probably wondering why everybody doesn't just agree on one of them. One reason, as we will see in the next section, is that different approaches are useful in different circumstances. The best one to use is whichever happens to be the most convenient for the problem at hand.

Concept Questions

10.5a What are the top-down and bottom-up definitions of operating cash flow?

10.5b What is meant by the term *depreciation tax shield?*

10.6 SOME SPECIAL CASES OF DISCOUNTED CASH FLOW ANALYSIS

To finish our chapter, we look at three common cases involving discounted cash flow analysis. The first case involves investments that are primarily aimed at improving efficiency and thereby cutting costs. The second case we consider comes up when a firm is involved in submitting competitive bids. The third and final case arises in choosing between equipment options with different economic lives.

There are many other special cases we could consider, but these three are particularly important because problems similar to these are so common. Also, they illustrate some very diverse applications of cash flow analysis and DCF valuation.

Evaluating Cost-Cutting Proposals

One decision we frequently face is whether or not to upgrade existing facilities to make them more cost-effective. The issue is whether or not the cost savings are large enough to justify the necessary capital expenditure.

For example, suppose we are considering automating some part of an existing production process. The necessary equipment costs $80,000 to buy and install. The automation will save $22,000 per year (before taxes) by reducing labor and material costs. For simplicity, assume that the equipment has a five-year life and is depreciated to zero on a straight-line basis over that period. It will actually be worth $20,000 in five years. Should we automate? The tax rate is 34 percent, and the discount rate is 10 percent.

As always, the first step in making such a decision is to identify the relevant incremental cash flows. First, determining the relevant capital spending is easy enough. The initial cost is $80,000. The after-tax salvage value is $20,000 × (1 − .34) = $13,200 because the book value will be zero in five years. Second, there are no working capital consequences here, so we don't need to worry about changes in net working capital.

Operating cash flows are the third component to consider. Buying the new equipment affects our operating cash flows in two ways. First, we save $22,000 before taxes every year. In other words, the firm's operating income increases by $22,000, so this is the relevant incremental project operating income.

Second, and it's easy to overlook this, we have an additional depreciation deduction. In this case, the depreciation is $80,000/5 = $16,000 per year.

Because the project has an operating income of $22,000 (the annual pretax cost saving) and a depreciation deduction of $16,000, taking the project will increase the firm's EBIT by $22,000 − 16,000 = $6,000, so this is the project's EBIT.

Finally, because EBIT is rising for the firm, taxes will increase. This increase in taxes will be $6,000 × .34 = $2,040. With this information, we can compute operating cash flow in the usual way:

EBIT	$ 6,000
+ Depreciation	16,000
− Taxes	2,040
Operating cash flow	$19,960

So our after-tax operating cash flow is $19,960.

It might be somewhat more enlightening to calculate operating cash flow using a different approach. What is actually going on here is very simple. First, the cost savings increase our pretax income by $22,000. We have to pay taxes on this amount, so our tax bill increases by .34 × $22,000 = $7,480. In other words, the $22,000 pretax saving amounts to $22,000 × (1 − .34) = $14,520 after taxes.

Second, the extra $16,000 in depreciation isn't really a cash outflow, but it does reduce our taxes by $16,000 × .34 = $5,440. The sum of these two components is $14,520 + 5,440 = $19,960, just as we had before. Notice that the $5,440 is the depreciation tax shield we discussed earlier, and we have effectively used the tax shield approach here.

We can now finish off our analysis. Based on our discussion, the relevant cash flows are:

	Year					
	0	1	2	3	4	5
Operating cash flow		$19,960	$19,960	$19,960	$19,960	$19,960
Capital spending	−$80,000					13,200
Total cash flow	−$80,000	$19,960	$19,960	$19,960	$19,960	$33,160

At 10 percent, it's straightforward to verify that the NPV here is $3,860, so we should go ahead and automate.

EXAMPLE 10.3 >> To Buy or Not to Buy

We are considering the purchase of a $200,000 computer-based inventory management system. It will be depreciated straight-line to zero over its four-year life. It will be worth $30,000 at the end of that time. The system will save us $60,000 before taxes in inventory-related costs. The relevant tax rate is 39 percent. Because the new setup is more efficient than our existing one, we will be able to carry less total inventory and thus free up $45,000 in net working capital. What is the NPV at 16 percent? What is the DCF return (the IRR) on this investment?

We can first calculate the operating cash flow. The after-tax cost savings are $60,000 × (1 − .39) = $36,600. The depreciation is $200,000/4 = $50,000 per year, so the depreciation tax shield is $50,000 × .39 = $19,500. Operating cash flow is thus $36,600 + 19,500 = $56,100 per year.

The capital spending involves $200,000 up front to buy the system. The after-tax salvage is $30,000 × (1 − .39) = $18,300. Finally, and this is the somewhat tricky part, the initial investment in net working capital is a $45,000 *inflow* because the system frees up working capital. Furthermore, we will have to put this back in at the end of the project's life. What this really means is simple: While the system is in operation, we have $45,000 to use elsewhere.

To finish our analysis, we can compute the total cash flows:

	Year				
	0	1	2	3	4
Operating cash flow		$56,100	$56,100	$56,100	$56,100
Change in NWC	$ 45,000				− 45,000
Capital spending	− 200,000				18,300
Total cash flow	−$155,000	$56,100	$56,100	$56,100	$29,400

At 16 percent, the NPV is −$12,768, so the investment is not attractive. After some trial and error, we find that the NPV is zero when the discount rate is 11.48 percent, so the IRR on this investment is about 11.5 percent.

Setting the Bid Price

Early on, we used discounted cash flow analysis to evaluate a proposed new product. A somewhat different (and very common) scenario arises when we must submit a competitive bid to win a job. Under such circumstances, the winner is whoever submits the lowest bid.

There is an old joke concerning this process: The low bidder is whoever makes the biggest mistake. This is called the winner's curse. In other words, if you win, there is a good chance you underbid. In this section, we look at how to go about setting the bid price to avoid the winner's curse. The procedure we describe is useful anytime we have to set a price on a product or service.

As with any other capital budgeting project, you must be careful to account for all relevant cash flows. For example, in 2004, Goodrich Corporation lost a bidding contest with France's Snecma Group to supply landing gear for Boeing's newest jetliner, the 7E7, which is intended to replace the older 767. One industry analyst speculated the contract would call for a sales price that is below breakeven. Why would a manufacturer sell below breakeven? The answer is that they often sacrifice margin on the original equipment product to be the seller in the lucrative aftermarket, that is, the repair and replacement market.

To illustrate how to go about setting a bid price, imagine we are in the business of buying stripped-down truck platforms and then modifying them to customer specifications for resale. A local distributor has requested bids for 5 specially modified trucks each year for the next four years, for a total of 20 trucks in all.

We need to decide what price per truck to bid. The goal of our analysis is to determine the lowest price we can profitably charge. This maximizes our chances of being awarded the contract while guarding against the winner's curse.

Suppose we can buy the truck platforms for \$10,000 each. The facilities we need can be leased for \$24,000 per year. The labor and material cost to do the modification works out to be about \$4,000 per truck. Total cost per year will thus be \$24,000 + 5 × (10,000 + 4,000) = \$94,000.

We will need to invest \$60,000 in new equipment. This equipment will be depreciated straight-line to a zero salvage value over the four years. It will be worth about \$5,000 at the end of that time. We will also need to invest \$40,000 in raw materials inventory and other working capital items. The relevant tax rate is 39 percent. What price per truck should we bid if we require a 20 percent return on our investment?

We start out by looking at the capital spending and net working capital investment. We have to spend \$60,000 today for new equipment. The after-tax salvage value is \$5,000 × (1 − .39) = \$3,050. Furthermore, we have to invest \$40,000 today in working capital. We will get this back in four years.

We can't determine the operating cash flow just yet because we don't know the sales price. Thus, if we draw a time line, here is what we have so far:

	Year				
	0	1	2	3	4
Operating cash flow		+OCF	+OCF	+OCF	+OCF
Change in NWC	−\$ 40,000				\$40,000
Capital spending	− 60,000				3,050
Total cash flow	−\$100,000	+OCF	+OCF	+OCF	+OCF + \$43,050

With this in mind, note that the key observation is the following: The lowest possible price we can profitably charge will result in a zero NPV at 20 percent. The reason is that at that price, we earn exactly 20 percent on our investment.

Given this observation, we first need to determine what the operating cash flow must be for the NPV to be equal to zero. To do this, we calculate the present value of the \$43,050 nonoperating cash flow from the last year and subtract it from the \$100,000 initial investment:

$$\$100{,}000 - 43{,}050/1.20^4 = \$100{,}000 - 20{,}761 = \$79{,}239$$

Once we have done this, our time line is as follows:

	Year				
	0	1	2	3	4
Total cash flow	−\$79,239	+OCF	+OCF	+OCF	+OCF

As the time line suggests, the operating cash flow is now an unknown ordinary annuity amount. The four-year annuity factor for 20 percent is 2.58873, so we have:

$$\text{NPV} = 0 = -\$79{,}239 + \text{OCF} \times 2.58873$$

This implies that:

$$\text{OCF} = \$79{,}239/2.58873 = \$30{,}609$$

So the operating cash flow needs to be \$30,609 each year.

We're not quite finished. The final problem is to find out what sales price results in an operating cash flow of \$30,609. The easiest way to do this is to recall that operating cash flow can be written as net income plus depreciation, the bottom-up definition. The depreciation here is \$60,000/4 = \$15,000. Given this, we can determine what net income must be:

$$\begin{aligned}\text{Operating cash flow} &= \text{Net income} + \text{Depreciation}\\ \$30{,}609 &= \text{Net income} + \$15{,}000\\ \text{Net income} &= \$15{,}609\end{aligned}$$

From here, we work our way backwards up the income statement. If net income is \$15,609, then our income statement is as follows:

Sales	?
Costs	\$94,000
Depreciation	15,000
Taxes (39%)	?
Net income	\$15,609

So we can solve for sales by noting that:

$$\begin{aligned}\text{Net income} &= (\text{Sales} - \text{Costs} - \text{Depreciation}) \times (1 - T)\\ \$15{,}609 &= (\text{Sales} - \$94{,}000 - \$15{,}000) \times (1 - .39)\\ \text{Sales} &= \$15{,}609/.61 + 94{,}000 + 15{,}000\\ &= \$134{,}589\end{aligned}$$

Sales per year must be \$134,589. Because the contract calls for five trucks per year, the sales price has to be \$134,589/5 = \$26,918. If we round this up a bit, it looks as though we need to bid about \$27,000 per truck. At this price, were we to get the contract, our return would be just over 20 percent.

Evaluating Equipment Options with Different Lives

The final problem we consider involves choosing among different possible systems, equipment setups, or procedures. Our goal is to choose the most cost-effective. The approach we consider here is only necessary when two special circumstances exist. First, the possibilities under evaluation have different economic lives. Second, and just as important, we will need whatever we buy more or less indefinitely. As a result, when it wears out, we will buy another one.

We can illustrate this problem with a simple example. Imagine we are in the business of manufacturing stamped metal subassemblies. Whenever a stamping mechanism wears out, we have to replace it with a new one to stay in business. We are considering which of two stamping mechanisms to buy.

Machine A costs \$100 to buy and \$10 per year to operate. It wears out and must be replaced every two years. Machine B costs \$140 to buy and \$8 per year to operate. It lasts for three years and must then be replaced. Ignoring taxes, which one should we go with if we use a 10 percent discount rate?

In comparing the two machines, we notice that the first is cheaper to buy, but it costs more to operate and it wears out more quickly. How can we evaluate these trade-offs? We can start by computing the present value of the costs for each:

$$\begin{aligned}\text{Machine A: PV} &= -\$100 + -10/1.1 + -10/1.1^2 = -\$117.36\\ \text{Machine B: PV} &= -\$140 + -8/1.1 + -8/1.1^2 + -8/1.1^3\\ &= -\$159.89\end{aligned}$$

Notice that *all* the numbers here are costs, so they all have negative signs. If we stopped here, it might appear that A is the more attractive because the PV of the costs is less. However, all we have really discovered so far is that A effectively provides two years' worth of stamping service for \$117.36, whereas B effectively provides three years' worth for \$159.89. These costs are not directly comparable because of the difference in service periods.

We need to somehow work out a cost per year for these two alternatives. To do this, we ask the question, What amount, paid each year over the life of the machine, has the same PV of costs? This amount is called the **equivalent annual cost (EAC)**.

equivalent annual cost (EAC)
The present value of a project's costs calculated on an annual basis.

Calculating the EAC involves finding an unknown payment amount. For example, for Machine A, we need to find a two-year ordinary annuity with a PV of −\$117.36 at 10 percent. Going back to Chapter 6, we know that the two-year annuity factor is:

$$\text{Annuity factor} = (1 - 1/1.10^2)/.10 = 1.7355$$

For Machine A, then, we have:

$$\begin{aligned}\text{PV of costs} = -\$117.36 &= \text{EAC} \times 1.7355\\ \text{EAC} &= -\$117.36/1.7355\\ &= -\$67.62\end{aligned}$$

For Machine B, the life is three years, so we first need the three-year annuity factor:

$$\text{Annuity factor} = (1 - 1/1.10^3)/.10 = 2.4869$$

We calculate the EAC for B just as we did for A:

$$\begin{aligned}\text{PV of costs} = -\$159.89 &= \text{EAC} \times 2.4869\\ \text{EAC} &= -\$159.89/2.4869\\ &= -\$64.29\end{aligned}$$

Based on this analysis, we should purchase B because it effectively costs \$64.29 per year versus \$67.62 for A. In other words, all things considered, B is cheaper. In this case, the longer life and lower operating cost are more than enough to offset the higher initial purchase price.

EXAMPLE 10.4 >> Equivalent Annual Costs

This extended example illustrates what happens to the EAC when we consider taxes. You are evaluating two different pollution control options. A filtration system will cost \$1.1 million to install and \$60,000 annually, before taxes, to operate. It will have to be completely replaced every five years. A precipitation system will cost \$1.9 million to install, but only \$10,000 per year to operate. The precipitation equipment has an effective operating life of eight years. Straight-line depreciation is used throughout, and neither system has any salvage value. Which option should we select if we use a 12 percent discount rate? The tax rate is 34 percent.

We need to consider the EACs for the two systems because they have different service lives and they will be replaced as they wear out. The relevant information can be summarized as follows:

	Filtration System	Precipitation System
After-tax operating cost	−\$ 39,600	−\$ 6,600
Depreciation tax shield	74,800	80,750
Operating cash flow	\$ 35,200	\$ 74,150
Economic life	5 years	8 years
Annuity factor (12%)	3.6048	4.9676
Present value of operating cash flow	\$ 126,888	\$ 368,350
Capital spending	− 1,100,000	− 1,900,000
Total PV of costs	−\$ 973,112	−\$1,531,650

Notice that the operating cash flow is actually positive in both cases because of the large depreciation tax shields. This can occur whenever the operating cost is small relative to the purchase price.

To decide which system to purchase, we compute the EACs for both using the appropriate annuity factors:

$$\text{Filtration system: } -\$973{,}112 = \text{EAC} \times 3.6048$$
$$\text{EAC} = -\$269{,}951$$
$$\text{Precipitation system: } -\$1{,}531{,}650 = \text{EAC} \times 4.9676$$
$$\text{EAC} = -\$308{,}328$$

The filtration system is the cheaper of the two, so we select it. In this case, the longer life and smaller operating cost of the precipitation system are not sufficient to offset its higher initial cost.

Concept Questions

10.6a Under what circumstances do we have to worry about unequal economic lives? How do you interpret the EAC?

10.6b In setting a bid price, we used a zero NPV as our benchmark. Explain why this is appropriate.

SUMMARY AND CONCLUSIONS 10.7

This chapter has described how to go about putting together a discounted cash flow analysis. In it, we covered:

1. The identification of relevant project cash flows. We discussed project cash flows and described how to handle some issues that often come up, including sunk costs, opportunity costs, financing costs, net working capital, and erosion.
2. Preparing and using pro forma, or projected, financial statements. We showed how information from such financial statements is useful in coming up with projected cash flows, and we also looked at some alternative definitions of operating cash flow.
3. The role of net working capital and depreciation in determining project cash flows. We saw that including the change in net working capital was important in cash flow analysis because it adjusted for the discrepancy between accounting revenues and costs and cash revenues and costs. We also went over the calculation of depreciation expense under current tax law.
4. Some special cases encountered in using discounted cash flow analysis. Here we looked at three special issues: evaluating cost-cutting investments, how to go about setting a bid price, and the unequal lives problem.

The discounted cash flow analysis we've covered here is a standard tool in the business world. It is a very powerful tool, so care should be taken in its use. The most important thing is to get the cash flows identified in a way that makes economic sense. This chapter gives you a good start in learning to do this.

Chapter Review and Self-Test Problems

10.1 Capital Budgeting for Project X Based on the following information for Project X, should we undertake the venture? To answer, first prepare a pro forma income statement for each year. Next, calculate operating cash flow. Finish the problem by determining total cash flow and then calculating NPV assuming a 28 percent required return. Use a 34 percent tax rate throughout. For help, look back at our shark attractant and power mulcher examples.

Project X involves a new type of graphite composite in-line skate wheel. We think we can sell 6,000 units per year at a price of $1,000 each. Variable costs will run about $400 per unit, and the product should have a four-year life.

Fixed costs for the project will run $450,000 per year. Further, we will need to invest a total of $1,250,000 in manufacturing equipment. This equipment is seven-year MACRS property for tax purposes. In four years, the equipment will be worth about half of what we paid for it. We will have to invest $1,150,000 in net working capital at the start. After that, net working capital requirements will be 25 percent of sales.

10.2 Calculating Operating Cash Flow Mont Blanc Livestock Pens, Inc., has projected a sales volume of $1,650 for the second year of a proposed expansion project. Costs normally run 60 percent of sales, or about $990 in this case. The depreciation expense will be $100, and the tax rate is 35 percent. What is the operating cash flow? Calculate your answer using all of the approaches (including the top-down, bottom-up, and tax shield approaches) described in the chapter.

10.3 Spending Money to Save Money? For help on this one, refer back to the computerized inventory management system in Example 10.3. Here, we're contemplating a new automatic surveillance system to replace our current contract security system. It will cost $450,000 to get the new system. The cost will be depreciated straight-line to zero over the system's four-year expected life. The system is expected to be worth $250,000 at the end of four years after removal costs.

We think the new system will save us $125,000, before taxes, per year in contract security costs. The tax rate is 34 percent. What are the NPV and IRR on buying the new system? The required return is 17 percent.

Answers to Chapter Review and Self-Test Problems

10.1 To develop the pro forma income statements, we need to calculate the depreciation for each of the four years. The relevant MACRS percentages, depreciation allowances, and book values for the first four years are:

Year	MACRS Percentage	Depreciation	Ending Book Value
1	14.29%	.1429 × $1,250,000 = $178,625	$1,071,375
2	24.49	.2449 × 1,250,000 = 306,125	765,250
3	17.49	.1749 × 1,250,000 = 218,625	546,625
4	12.49	.1249 × 1,250,000 = 156,125	390,500

The projected income statements, therefore, are as follows:

	Year			
	1	2	3	4
Sales	$6,000,000	$6,000,000	$6,000,000	$6,000,000
Variable costs	2,400,000	2,400,000	2,400,000	2,400,000
Fixed costs	450,000	450,000	450,000	450,000
Depreciation	178,625	306,125	218,625	156,125
EBIT	$2,971,375	$2,843,875	$2,931,375	$2,993,875
Taxes (34%)	− 1,010,268	− 966,918	− 996,668	− 1,017,918
Net income	$1,961,108	$1,876,958	$1,934,708	$1,975,958

Based on this information, the operating cash flows are:

	Year			
	1	2	3	4
EBIT	$2,971,375	$2,843,875	$2,931,375	$2,993,875
Depreciation	178,625	306,125	218,625	156,125
Taxes	− 1,010,268	− 966,918	− 996,668	− 1,017,918
Operating cash flow	$2,139,732	$2,183,082	$2,153,332	$2,132,082

We now have to worry about the nonoperating cash flows. Net working capital starts out at $1,150,000 and then rises to 25 percent of sales, or $1,500,000. This is a $350,000 change in net working capital.

Finally, we have to invest \$1,250,000 to get started. In four years, the book value of this investment will be \$390,500, compared to an estimated market value of \$625,000 (half of the cost). The after-tax salvage is thus \$625,000 − .34 × (\$625,000 − 390,500) = \$545,270.

When we combine all this information, the projected cash flows for Project X are:

	Year				
	0	**1**	**2**	**3**	**4**
Operating cash flow		\$2,139,732	\$2,183,082	\$2,153,332	\$2,132,082
Change in NWC	−\$1,150,000	− 350,000			1,500,000
Capital spending	− 1,250,000				545,270
Total cash flow	−\$2,400,000	\$1,789,732	\$2,183,082	\$2,153,332	\$4,177,352

With these cash flows, the NPV at 28 percent is:

$$\begin{aligned} \text{NPV} &= -\$2{,}400{,}000 + 1{,}789{,}732/1.28 + 2{,}183{,}082/1.28^2 \\ &\quad + 2{,}153{,}332/1.28^3 + 4{,}177{,}352/1.28^4 \\ &= \$2{,}913{,}649 \end{aligned}$$

So this project appears quite profitable.

10.2 First, we can calculate the project's EBIT, its tax bill, and its net income.

$$\begin{aligned} \text{EBIT} &= \text{Sales} - \text{Costs} - \text{Depreciation} \\ &= \$1{,}650 - 990 - 100 = \$560 \\ \text{Taxes} &= \$560 \times .35 = \$196 \\ \text{Net income} &= \$560 - 196 = \$364 \end{aligned}$$

With these numbers, operating cash flow is:

$$\begin{aligned} \text{OCF} &= \text{EBIT} + \text{Depreciation} - \text{Taxes} \\ &= \$560 + 100 - 196 \\ &= \$464 \end{aligned}$$

Using the other OCF definitions, we have:

$$\begin{aligned} \text{Bottom-up OCF} &= \text{Net income} + \text{Depreciation} \\ &= \$364 + 100 \\ &= \$464 \\ \text{Top-down OCF} &= \text{Sales} - \text{Costs} - \text{Taxes} \\ &= \$1{,}650 - 990 - 196 \\ &= \$464 \\ \text{Tax shield OCF} &= (\text{Sales} - \text{Costs}) \times (1 - .35) \\ &\quad + \text{Depreciation} \times .35 \\ &= (\$1{,}650 - 990) \times .65 + 100 \times .35 \\ &= \$464 \end{aligned}$$

As expected, all of these definitions produce exactly the same answer.

10.3 The \$125,000 pretax saving amounts to (1 − .34) × \$125,000 = \$82,500 after taxes. The annual depreciation of \$450,000/4 = \$112,500 generates a tax shield of .34 × \$112,500 = \$38,250 each year. Putting these together, we calculate that the operating cash flow is \$82,500 + 38,250 = \$120,750. Because the book value is zero in four years, the after-tax salvage value is (1 − .34) × $250,000 = $165,000. There are no working capital consequences, so the cash flows are:

	Year				
	0	1	2	3	4
Operating cash flow		$120,750	$120,750	$120,750	$120,750
Capital spending	−$450,000				165,000
Total cash flow	−$450,000	$120,750	$120,750	$120,750	$285,750

You can verify that the NPV at 17 percent is −$30,702, and the return on the new surveillance system is only about 13.96 percent. The project does not appear to be profitable.

Concepts Review and Critical Thinking Questions

1. **Opportunity Cost** In the context of capital budgeting, what is an opportunity cost?
2. **Depreciation** Given the choice, would a firm prefer to use MACRS depreciation or straight-line depreciation? Why?
3. **Net Working Capital** In our capital budgeting examples, we assumed that a firm would recover all of the working capital it invested in a project. Is this a reasonable assumption? When might it not be valid?
4. **Stand-Alone Principle** Suppose a financial manager is quoted as saying, "Our firm uses the stand-alone principle. Because we treat projects like minifirms in our evaluation process, we include financing costs because they are relevant at the firm level." Critically evaluate this statement.
5. **Equivalent Annual Cost** When is EAC analysis appropriate for comparing two or more projects? Why is this method used? Are there any implicit assumptions required by this method that you find troubling? Explain.
6. **Cash Flow and Depreciation** "When evaluating projects, we're only concerned with the relevant incremental after-tax cash flows. Therefore, because depreciation is a noncash expense, we should ignore its effects when evaluating projects." Critically evaluate this statement.
7. **Capital Budgeting Considerations** A major college textbook publisher has an existing finance textbook. The publisher is debating whether or not to produce an "essentialized" version, meaning a shorter (and lower-priced) book. What are some of the considerations that should come into play?

To answer the next three questions, refer to the following example. In 2003, Porsche unveiled its new sports-utility vehicle (SUV), the Cayenne. With a price tag of over $40,000, the Cayenne goes from zero to 62 mph in 9.7 seconds. Porsche's decision to enter the SUV market was in response to the runaway success of other high-priced SUVs such as the Mercedes-Benz M-class. Vehicles in this class had generated years of very high profits. The Cayenne certainly spiced up the market, and Porsche subsequently introduced the Cayenne Turbo, which goes from zero to 62 mph in 5.6 seconds and has a top speed of 165 mph. The price tag for the Cayenne Turbo? Almost $100,000!

Some analysts questioned Porsche's entry into the luxury SUV market. The analysts were concerned not only that Porsche was a late entry into the market, but also that the introduction of the Cayenne would damage Porsche's reputation as a maker of high-performance automobiles.

8. **Erosion** In evaluating the Cayenne, would you consider the possible damage to Porsche's reputation erosion?
9. **Capital Budgeting** Porsche was one of the last manufacturers to enter the sports-utility vehicle market. Why would one company decide to proceed with a product when other companies, at least initially, decide not to enter the market?
10. **Capital Budgeting** In evaluating the Cayenne, what do you think Porsche needs to assume regarding the substantial profit margins that exist in this market? Is it likely they will be maintained as the market becomes more competitive, or will Porsche be able to maintain the profit margin because of its image and the performance of the Cayenne?

Questions and Problems

BASIC
(Questions 1–18)

1. **Relevant Cash Flows** Parker & Stone, Inc., is looking at setting up a new manufacturing plant in South Park to produce garden tools. The company bought some land six years ago for $5 million in anticipation of using it as a warehouse and distribution site, but the company has since decided to rent these facilities from a competitor instead. If the land were sold today, the company would net $5.4 million. The company wants to build its new manufacturing plant on this land; the plant will cost $10.4 million to build, and the site requires $650,000 worth of grading before it is suitable for construction. What is the proper cash flow amount to use as the initial investment in fixed assets when evaluating this project? Why?
2. **Relevant Cash Flows** Winnebagel Corp. currently sells 30,000 motor homes per year at $45,000 each, and 12,000 luxury motor coaches per year at $85,000 each. The company wants to introduce a new portable camper to fill out its product line; it hopes to sell 21,000 of these campers per year at $12,000 each. An independent consultant has determined that if Winnebagel introduces the new campers, it should boost the sales of its existing motor homes by 5,000 units per year, and reduce the sales of its motor coaches by 1,300 units per year. What is the amount to use as the annual sales figure when evaluating this project? Why?
3. **Calculating Projected Net Income** A proposed new investment has projected sales of $650,000. Variable costs are 60 percent of sales, and fixed costs are $158,000; depreciation is $75,000. Prepare a pro forma income statement assuming a tax rate of 35 percent. What is the projected net income?
4. **Calculating OCF** Consider the following income statement:

Sales	$912,400
Costs	593,600
Depreciation	135,000
EBIT	?
Taxes (34%)	?
Net income	?

Fill in the missing numbers and then calculate the OCF. What is the depreciation tax shield?

5. **OCF from Several Approaches** A proposed new project has projected sales of $85,000, costs of $43,000, and depreciation of $3,000. The tax rate is 35 percent.

Calculate operating cash flow using the four different approaches described in the chapter and verify that the answer is the same in each case.

6. **Calculating Depreciation** A piece of newly purchased industrial equipment costs $847,000 and is classified as seven-year property under MACRS. Calculate the annual depreciation allowances and end-of-the-year book values for this equipment.
7. **Calculating Salvage Value** Consider an asset that costs $440,000 and is depreciated straight-line to zero over its eight-year tax life. The asset is to be used in a five-year project; at the end of the project, the asset can be sold for $55,000. If the relevant tax rate is 35 percent, what is the after-tax cash flow from the sale of this asset?
8. **Calculating Salvage Value** An asset used in a four-year project falls in the five-year MACRS class for tax purposes. The asset has an acquisition cost of $9,300,000 and will be sold for $2,100,000 at the end of the project. If the tax rate is 35 percent, what is the after-tax salvage value of the asset?
9. **Calculating Project OCF** Down Under Boomerang, Inc., is considering a new three-year expansion project that requires an initial fixed asset investment of $2.7 million. The fixed asset will be depreciated straight-line to zero over its three-year tax life, after which time it will be worthless. The project is estimated to generate $2,400,000 in annual sales, with costs of $960,000. If the tax rate is 35 percent, what is the OCF for this project?
10. **Calculating Project NPV** In the previous problem, suppose the required return on the project is 15 percent. What is the project's NPV?
11. **Calculating Project Cash Flow from Assets** In the previous problem, suppose the project requires an initial investment in net working capital of $300,000 and the fixed asset will have a market value of $210,000 at the end of the project. What is the project's Year 0 net cash flow? Year 1? Year 2? Year 3? What is the new NPV?
12. **NPV and Modified ACRS** In the previous problem, suppose the fixed asset actually falls into the three-year MACRS class. All the other facts are the same. What is the project's Year 1 net cash flow now? Year 2? Year 3? What is the new NPV?
13. **Project Evaluation** Dog Up! Franks is looking at a new sausage system with an installed cost of $390,000. This cost will be depreciated straight-line to zero over the project's five-year life, at the end of which the sausage system can be scrapped for $60,000. The sausage system will save the firm $120,000 per year in pretax operating costs, and the system requires an initial investment in net working capital of $28,000. If the tax rate is 34 percent and the discount rate is 10 percent, what is the NPV of this project?
14. **Project Evaluation** Your firm is contemplating the purchase of a new $925,000 computer-based order entry system. The system will be depreciated straight-line to zero over its five-year life. It will be worth $90,000 at the end of that time. You will save $360,000 before taxes per year in order processing costs and you will be able to reduce working capital by $125,000 (this is a one-time reduction). If the tax rate is 35 percent, what is the IRR for this project?
15. **Project Evaluation** In the previous problem, suppose your required return on the project is 20 percent and your pretax cost savings are $400,000 per year. Will you accept the project? What if the pretax cost savings are $300,000 per year? At what level of pretax cost savings would you be indifferent between accepting the project and not accepting it?
16. **Calculating EAC** A five-year project has an initial fixed asset investment of $210,000, an initial NWC investment of $20,000, and an annual OCF of −$32,000.

The fixed asset is fully depreciated over the life of the project and has no salvage value. If the required return is 15 percent, what is this project's equivalent annual cost, or EAC?

17. **Calculating EAC** You are evaluating two different silicon wafer milling machines. The Techron I costs $210,000, has a three-year life, and has pretax operating costs of $34,000 per year. The Techron II costs $320,000, has a five-year life, and has pretax operating costs of $23,000 per year. For both milling machines, use straight-line depreciation to zero over the project's life and assume a salvage value of $20,000. If your tax rate is 35 percent and your discount rate is 14 percent, compute the EAC for both machines. Which do you prefer? Why?

18. **Calculating a Bid Price** Guthrie Enterprises needs someone to supply it with 150,000 cartons of machine screws per year to support its manufacturing needs over the next five years, and you've decided to bid on the contract. It will cost you $780,000 to install the equipment necessary to start production; you'll depreciate this cost straight-line to zero over the project's life. You estimate that in five years, this equipment can be salvaged for $50,000. Your fixed production costs will be $240,000 per year, and your variable production costs should be $8.50 per carton. You also need an initial investment in net working capital of $75,000. If your tax rate is 35 percent and you require a 16 percent return on your investment, what bid price should you submit?

INTERMEDIATE
(Questions 19–24)

19. **Cost-Cutting Proposals** Massey Machine Shop is considering a four-year project to improve its production efficiency. Buying a new machine press for $480,000 is estimated to result in $160,000 in annual pretax cost savings. The press falls in the MACRS five-year class, and it will have a salvage value at the end of the project of $70,000. The press also requires an initial investment in spare parts inventory of $20,000, along with an additional $3,000 in inventory for each succeeding year of the project. If the shop's tax rate is 35 percent and its discount rate is 14 percent, should Massey buy and install the machine press?

20. **Comparing Mutually Exclusive Projects** Hagar Industrial Systems Company (HISC) is trying to decide between two different conveyor belt systems. System A costs $430,000, has a four-year life, and requires $120,000 in pretax annual operating costs. System B costs $540,000, has a six-year life, and requires $80,000 in pretax annual operating costs. Both systems are to be depreciated straight-line to zero over their lives and will have zero salvage value. Whichever project is chosen, it will *not* be replaced when it wears out. If the tax rate is 34 percent and the discount rate is 20 percent, which project should the firm choose?

21. **Comparing Mutually Exclusive Projects** Suppose in the previous problem that HISC always needs a conveyor belt system; when one wears out, it must be replaced. Which project should the firm choose now?

22. **Calculating a Bid Price** Consider a project to supply 80 million postage stamps per year to the U.S. Postal Service for the next five years. You have an idle parcel of land available that cost $1,000,000 five years ago; if the land were sold today, it would net you $1,200,000, after-tax. You will need to install $3.1 million in new manufacturing plant and equipment to actually produce the stamps; this plant and equipment will be depreciated straight-line to zero over the project's five-year life. The equipment can be sold for $600,000 at the end of the project. You will also need $600,000 in initial net working capital for the project, and an additional investment of $50,000 in every year thereafter. Your production costs are 0.5 cents per stamp, and you have fixed costs of $800,000 per year. If your tax rate is 34 percent and your required return on this project is 15 percent, what bid price should you submit on the contract?

Visit us at www.mhhe.com/rwj

23. **Interpreting a Bid Price** In the previous problem, suppose you were going to use a three-year MACRS depreciation schedule for your manufacturing equipment, and that you felt you could keep working capital investments down to only $25,000 per year. How would this new information affect your calculated bid price?

24. **Comparing Mutually Exclusive Projects** Vandalay Industries is considering the purchase of a new machine for the production of latex. Machine A costs $2,100,000 and will last for six years. Variable costs are 35 percent of sales, and fixed costs are $150,000 per year. Machine B costs $4,500,000 and will last for nine years. Variable costs for this machine are 30 percent and fixed costs are $100,000 per year. The sales for each machine will be $9 million per year. The required return is 10 percent and the tax rate is 35 percent. Both machines will be depreciated on a straight-line basis. If the company plans to replace the machine when it wears out on a perpetual basis, which machine should you choose?

CHALLENGE
(Questions 25–29)

25. **Project Evaluation** Aguilera Acoustics (AAI), Inc., projects unit sales for a new 7-octave voice emulation implant as follows:

Year	Unit Sales
1	85,000
2	98,000
3	106,000
4	114,000
5	93,000

Production of the implants will require $1,500,000 in net working capital to start and additional net working capital investments each year equal to 15 percent of the projected sales increase for the following year. Total fixed costs are $900,000 per year, variable production costs are $240 per unit, and the units are priced at $325 each. The equipment needed to begin production has an installed cost of $21,000,000. Because the implants are intended for professional singers, this equipment is considered industrial machinery and thus qualifies as seven-year MACRS property. In five years, this equipment can be sold for about 20 percent of its acquisition cost. AAI is in the 35 percent marginal tax bracket and has a required return on all its projects of 18 percent. Based on these preliminary project estimates, what is the NPV of the project? What is the IRR?

26. **Calculating Required Savings** A proposed cost-saving device has an installed cost of $480,000. The device will be used in a five-year project, but is classified as three-year MACRS property for tax purposes. The required initial net working capital investment is $40,000, the marginal tax rate is 35 percent, and the project discount rate is 12 percent. The device has an estimated Year 5 salvage value of $45,000. What level of pretax cost savings do we require for this project to be profitable?

27. **Financial Break-Even Analysis** To solve the bid price problem presented in the text, we set the project NPV equal to zero and found the required price using the definition of OCF. Thus the bid price represents a financial break-even level for the project. This type of analysis can be extended to many other types of problems.
    a. In Problem 18, assume that the price per carton is $13 and find the project NPV. What does your answer tell you about your bid price? What do you know about the number of cartons you can sell and still break even? How about your level of costs?

b. Solve Problem 18 again with the price still at \$13 but find the quantity of cartons per year that you can supply and still break even. Hint: It's less than 150,000.

c. Repeat (*b*) with a price of \$13 and a quantity of 150,000 cartons per year, and find the highest level of fixed costs you could afford and still break even. Hint: It's more than \$240,000.

28. Calculating a Bid Price Your company has been approached to bid on a contract to sell 10,000 voice recognition (VR) computer keyboards a year for four years. Due to technological improvements, beyond that time they will be outdated and no sales will be possible. The equipment necessary for the production will cost \$2.4 million and will be depreciated on a straight-line basis to a zero salvage value. Production will require an investment in net working capital of \$75,000 to be returned at the end of the project and the equipment can be sold for \$200,000 at the end of production. Fixed costs are \$500,000 per year, and variable costs are \$165 per unit. In addition to the contract, you feel your company can sell 3,000, 6,000, 8,000, and 5,000 additional units to companies in other countries over the next four years, respectively, at a price of \$275. This price is fixed. The tax rate is 40 percent, and the required return is 13 percent. Additionally, the president of the company will only undertake the project if it has an NPV of \$100,000. What bid price should you set for the contract?

29. Replacement Decisions Suppose we are thinking about replacing an old computer with a new one. The old one cost us \$390,000; the new one will cost \$780,000. The new machine will be depreciated straight-line to zero over its five-year life. It will probably be worth about \$140,000 after five years.

The old computer is being depreciated at a rate of \$130,000 per year. It will be completely written off in three years. If we don't replace it now, we will have to replace it in two years. We can sell it now for \$230,000; in two years, it will probably be worth \$90,000. The new machine will save us \$125,000 per year in operating costs. The tax rate is 38 percent and the discount rate is 14 percent.

a. Suppose we recognize that if we don't replace the computer now, we will be replacing it in two years. Should we replace now or should we wait? Hint: What we effectively have here is a decision either to "invest" in the old computer (by not selling it) or to invest in the new one. Notice that the two investments have unequal lives.

b. Suppose we only consider whether or not we should replace the old computer now without worrying about what's going to happen in two years. What are the relevant cash flows? Should we replace it or not? Hint: Consider the net change in the firm's after-tax cash flows if we do the replacement.

Visit us at www.mhhe.com/rwj

11 Project Analysis and Evaluation

Computer chip makers are always striving to build better, faster CPUs. As Intel and Hewlett-Packard learned, however, just building a faster chip doesn't mean buyers will necessarily come. Intel and Hewlett-Packard joined forces in 1992 to build the new 64-bit Itanium chip. Originally expected to be brought to market by 1997, the chip wasn't ready until 2002. The project took 10 years and cost the companies $5 billion. When it finally reached the market, sales were far below expectations. How bad did things go for the new Itanium chip? In early 2004, Intel announced it was upgrading its more popular Xeon chip to 64-bit technology. And, a week later, Hewlett-Packard announced it would use a chip from Intel rival Advanced Micro Systems in some of its new servers.

Obviously, Intel and Hewlett-Packard didn't *plan* to spend $5 billion developing a chip that didn't sell. However, as the lack of sales for the Itanium chip shows, projects don't always go as companies think they will. This chapter explores how this can happen and what companies can do to analyze and possibly avoid these situations.

In our previous chapter, we discussed how to identify and organize the relevant cash flows for capital investment decisions. Our primary interest there was in coming up with a preliminary estimate of the net present value for a proposed project. In this chapter, we focus on assessing the reliability of such an estimate and on some additional considerations in project analysis.

We begin by discussing the need for an evaluation of cash flow and NPV estimates. We go on to develop some tools that are useful for such an evaluation. We also examine some additional complications and concerns that can arise in project evaluation.

EVALUATING NPV ESTIMATES 11.1

As we discussed in Chapter 9, an investment has a positive net present value if its market value exceeds its cost. Such an investment is desirable because it creates value for its owner. The primary problem in identifying such opportunities is that most of the time we can't actually observe the relevant market value. Instead, we estimate it. Having done so, it is only natural to wonder whether or not our estimates are at least close to the true values. We consider this question next.

The Basic Problem

Suppose we are working on a preliminary DCF analysis along the lines we described in the previous chapter. We carefully identify the relevant cash flows, avoiding such things as sunk costs, and we remember to consider working capital requirements. We add back any depreciation; we account for possible erosion; and we pay attention to opportunity costs. Finally, we double-check our calculations, and, when all is said and done, the bottom line is that the estimated NPV is positive.

Now what? Do we stop here and move on to the next proposal? Probably not. The fact that the estimated NPV is positive is definitely a good sign, but, more than anything, this tells us that we need to take a closer look.

If you think about it, there are two circumstances under which a discounted cash flow analysis could lead us to conclude that a project has a positive NPV. The first possibility is that the project really does have a positive NPV. That's the good news. The bad news is the second possibility: A project may appear to have a positive NPV because our estimate is inaccurate.

Notice that we could also err in the opposite way. If we conclude that a project has a negative NPV when the true NPV is positive, then we lose a valuable opportunity.

Projected versus Actual Cash Flows

There is a somewhat subtle point we need to make here. When we say something like "The projected cash flow in Year 4 is $700," what exactly do we mean? Does this mean that we think the cash flow will actually be $700? Not really. It could happen, of course, but we would be surprised to see it turn out exactly that way. The reason is that the $700 projection is based only on what we know today. Almost anything could happen between now and then to change that cash flow.

Loosely speaking, we really mean that, if we took all the possible cash flows that could occur in four years and averaged them, the result would be $700. So, we don't really expect a projected cash flow to be exactly right in any one case. What we do expect is that, if we evaluate a large number of projects, our projections will be right on average.

Forecasting Risk

The key inputs into a DCF analysis are projected future cash flows. If the projections are seriously in error, then we have a classic GIGO (garbage in, garbage out) system. In such a case, no matter how carefully we arrange the numbers and manipulate them, the resulting answer can still be grossly misleading. This is the danger in using a relatively sophisticated technique like DCF. It is sometimes easy to get caught up in number crunching and forget the underlying nuts-and-bolts economic reality.

The possibility that we will make a bad decision because of errors in the projected cash flows is called **forecasting risk** (or *estimation risk*). Because of forecasting risk, there is

forecasting risk
The possibility that errors in projected cash flows will lead to incorrect decisions. Also, estimation risk.

the danger that we will think a project has a positive NPV when it really does not. How is this possible? It happens if we are overly optimistic about the future, and, as a result, our projected cash flows don't realistically reflect the possible future cash flows.

Forecasting risk can take many forms. For example, Microsoft spent several billion dollars developing and bringing the Xbox game console to market. Technologically more sophisticated, the Xbox was the best way to play against competitors over the Internet. Unfortunately, Microsoft sold only 9 million Xboxes in the first 14 months of sales, at the low end of Microsoft's expected range. The Xbox was arguably the best available game console at the time, so why didn't it sell better? The reason given by analysts was that there were far fewer games made for the Xbox. For example, the Playstation enjoyed a 2-to-1 edge in the number of games made for it.

So far, we have not explicitly considered what to do about the possibility of errors in our forecasts, so one of our goals in this chapter is to develop some tools that are useful in identifying areas where potential errors exist and where they might be especially damaging. In one form or another, we will be trying to assess the economic "reasonableness" of our estimates. We will also be wondering how much damage will be done by errors in those estimates.

Sources of Value

The first line of defense against forecasting risk is simply to ask: "What is it about this investment that leads to a positive NPV?" We should be able to point to something specific as the source of value. For example, if the proposal under consideration involved a new product, then we might ask questions such as the following: Are we certain that our new product is significantly better than that of the competition? Can we truly manufacture at lower cost, or distribute more effectively, or identify undeveloped market niches, or gain control of a market?

These are just a few of the potential sources of value. There are many others. For example, in 2004, Google announced a new, free e-mail service, g-mail. Why? Free e-mail service is widely available from big hitters like Microsoft and Yahoo! and, obviously, it's free! The answer is that Google's mail service will be integrated with its acclaimed search engine, thereby giving it an edge. Also, offering e-mail will let Google expand its lucrative key-word based advertising delivery. So, Google's source of value is leveraging its proprietary web search and ad delivery technologies.

A key factor to keep in mind is the degree of competition in the market. It is a basic principle of economics that positive NPV investments will be rare in a highly competitive environment. Therefore, proposals that appear to show significant value in the face of stiff competition are particularly troublesome, and the likely reaction of the competition to any innovations must be closely examined.

To give an example, in 2004, demand for flat screen LCD televisions was high, prices were high, and profit margins were fat for retailers. But, also in 2004, manufacturers of the screens were projected to pour about $10 billion into new production facilities. Thus, anyone thinking of entering this highly profitable market would do well to reflect on what the supply (and profit margin) situation will look like in just a few years.

It is also necessary to think about *potential* competition. For example, suppose home improvement retailer Lowe's identifies an area that is underserved and is thinking about opening a store. If the store is successful, what will happen? The answer is that Home Depot (or another competitor) will very likely also build a store, thereby driving down volume and profits. So, we always need to keep in mind that success attracts imitators and competitors.

The point to remember is that positive NPV investments are probably not all that common, and the number of positive NPV projects is almost certainly limited for any given firm. If we can't articulate some sound economic basis for thinking ahead of time that we have found something special, then the conclusion that our project has a positive NPV should be viewed with some suspicion.

Concept Questions

11.1a What is forecasting risk? Why is it a concern for the financial manager?

11.1b What are some potential sources of value in a new project?

SCENARIO AND OTHER WHAT-IF ANALYSES

11.2

Our basic approach to evaluating cash flow and NPV estimates involves asking what-if questions. Accordingly, we discuss some organized ways of going about a what-if analysis. Our goal in performing such an analysis is to assess the degree of forecasting risk and to identify those components that are the most critical to the success or failure of an investment.

Getting Started

We are investigating a new project. Naturally, the first thing we do is estimate NPV based on our projected cash flows. We will call this initial set of projections the *base case*. Now, however, we recognize the possibility of error in these cash flow projections. After completing the base case, we thus wish to investigate the impact of different assumptions about the future on our estimates.

One way to organize this investigation is to put an upper and lower bound on the various components of the project. For example, suppose we forecast sales at 100 units per year. We know this estimate may be high or low, but we are relatively certain it is not off by more than 10 units in either direction. We thus pick a lower bound of 90 and an upper bound of 110. We go on to assign such bounds to any other cash flow components we are unsure about.

When we pick these upper and lower bounds, we are not ruling out the possibility that the actual values could be outside this range. What we are saying, again loosely speaking, is that it is unlikely that the true average (as opposed to our estimated average) of the possible values is outside this range.

An example is useful to illustrate the idea here. The project under consideration costs $200,000, has a five-year life, and has no salvage value. Depreciation is straight-line to zero. The required return is 12 percent, and the tax rate is 34 percent. In addition, we have compiled the following information:

	Base Case	Lower Bound	Upper Bound
Unit sales	6,000	5,500	6,500
Price per unit	$80	$75	$85
Variable costs per unit	$60	$58	$62
Fixed costs per year	$50,000	$45,000	$55,000

With this information, we can calculate the base-case NPV by first calculating net income:

Sales	$480,000
Variable costs	360,000
Fixed costs	50,000
Depreciation	40,000
EBIT	$ 30,000
Taxes (34%)	10,200
Net income	$ 19,800

Operating cash flow is thus $30,000 + 40,000 − 10,200 = $59,800 per year. At 12 percent, the five-year annuity factor is 3.6048, so the base-case NPV is:

$$\begin{aligned}\text{Base-case NPV} &= -\$200{,}000 + 59{,}800 \times 3.6048\\ &= \$15{,}567\end{aligned}$$

Thus, the project looks good so far.

Scenario Analysis

scenario analysis
The determination of what happens to NPV estimates when we ask what-if questions.

The basic form of what-if analysis is called **scenario analysis**. What we do is investigate the changes in our NPV estimates that result from asking questions like, What if unit sales realistically should be projected at 5,500 units instead of 6,000?

Once we start looking at alternative scenarios, we might find that most of the plausible ones result in positive NPVs. In this case, we have some confidence in proceeding with the project. If a substantial percentage of the scenarios look bad, then the degree of forecasting risk is high and further investigation is in order.

There are a number of possible scenarios we can consider. A good place to start is with the worst-case scenario. This will tell us the minimum NPV of the project. If this turns out to be positive, we will be in good shape. While we are at it, we will go ahead and determine the other extreme, the best case. This puts an upper bound on our NPV.

To get the worst case, we assign the least favorable value to each item. This means *low* values for items like units sold and price per unit and *high* values for costs. We do the reverse for the best case. For our project, these values would be:

	Worst Case	Best Case
Unit sales	5,500	6,500
Price per unit	$75	$85
Variable costs per unit	$62	$58
Fixed costs per year	$55,000	$45,000

With this information, we can calculate the net income and cash flows under each scenario (check these for yourself):

Scenario	Net Income	Cash Flow	Net Present Value	IRR
Base case	$19,800	$59,800	$ 15,567	15.1%
Worst case*	− 15,510	24,490	− 111,719	−14.4
Best case	59,730	99,730	159,504	40.9

*We assume a tax credit is created in our worst-case scenario.

What we learn is that under the worst scenario, the cash flow is still positive at $24,490. That's good news. The bad news is that the return is −14.4 percent in this case, and the NPV is −$111,719. Because the project costs $200,000, we stand to lose a little more than half of the original investment under the worst possible scenario. The best case offers an attractive 41 percent return.

The terms *best case* and *worst case* are very commonly used, and we will stick with them, but we should note they are somewhat misleading. The absolutely best thing that could happen would be something absurdly unlikely, such as launching a new diet soda and subsequently learning that our (patented) formulation also just happens to cure the common cold. Similarly, the true worst case would involve some incredibly remote possibility of total disaster. We're not claiming that these things don't happen; once in a while they do. Some products, such as personal computers, succeed beyond the wildest of expectations, and some, such as asbestos, turn out to be absolute catastrophes. Instead, our point is that in assessing the reasonableness of an NPV estimate, we need to stick to cases that are reasonably likely to occur.

Instead of *best* and *worst,* then, it is probably more accurate to use the words *optimistic* and *pessimistic*. In broad terms, if we were thinking about a reasonable range for, say, unit sales, then what we call the best case would correspond to something near the upper end of that range. The worst case would simply correspond to the lower end.

Depending on the project, the best and worst case estimates can vary greatly. For example, in February 2004, Ivanhoe Mines discussed its assessment report of a copper and gold mine in Mongolia. The company used base metal prices of $400 an ounce for gold and $0.90 an ounce for copper. Their report also used average life-of-mine recovery rates for both of the deposits. However, the company also reported that the base case numbers were only considered accurate to within plus or minus 35 percent, so this 35 percent range could be used as the basis for developing best case and worst case scenarios.

As we have mentioned, there is an unlimited number of different scenarios that we could examine. At a minimum, we might want to investigate two intermediate cases by going halfway between the base amounts and the extreme amounts. This would give us five scenarios in all, including the base case.

Beyond this point, it is hard to know when to stop. As we generate more and more possibilities, we run the risk of experiencing "paralysis of analysis." The difficulty is that no matter how many scenarios we run, all we can learn are possibilities, some good and some bad. Beyond that, we don't get any guidance as to what to do. Scenario analysis is thus useful in telling us what can happen and in helping us gauge the potential for disaster, but it does not tell us whether or not to take the project.

Unfortunately, in practice, even the worst case scenarios may not be low enough. Two recent examples show what we mean. The Eurotunnel, or Chunnel, may be one of the new Seven Wonders of the World. The tunnel under the English Channel connects England to France and covers 24 miles. It took 8,000 workers eight years to remove 9.8 million cubic yards of rock. When the tunnel was finally built, it cost $17.9 billion, or slightly more than twice the original estimate of $8.8 billion. And things only got worse. Forecasts called for 16.8 million passengers in the first year, but only 4 million actually used it. Revenue estimates for 2003 were $2.88 billion, but actual revenue was only about one-third of that. The major problems faced by the Eurotunnel were the increased competition from ferry services, which dropped their prices, and the rise of low-cost airlines.

Another example is the human transporter, or Segway. Trumpeted by inventor Dean Kamen as the replacement for automobiles in cities, the Segway came to market with great expectations. At the end of September 2003, the company recalled all of the transporters due to a mandatory software upgrade. Worse, the company had projected sales of 50,000 to 100,000 units by January of 2003, but by September of 2003, only 6,000 had been sold.

Sensitivity Analysis

sensitivity analysis
Investigation of what happens to NPV when only one variable is changed.

Sensitivity analysis is a variation on scenario analysis that is useful in pinpointing the areas where forecasting risk is especially severe. The basic idea with a sensitivity analysis is to freeze all of the variables except one and then see how sensitive our estimate of NPV is to changes in that one variable. If our NPV estimate turns out to be very sensitive to relatively small changes in the projected value of some component of project cash flow, then the forecasting risk associated with that variable is high.

To illustrate how sensitivity analysis works, we go back to our base case for every item except unit sales. We can then calculate cash flow and NPV using the largest and smallest unit sales figures.

Scenario	Unit Sales	Cash Flow	Net Present Value	IRR
Base case	6,000	$59,800	$15,567	15.1%
Worst case	5,500	53,200	−8,226	10.3
Best case	6,500	66,400	39,357	19.7

A cash flow sensitivity analysis spreadsheet is available at www.toolkit.cch.com/tools/cfsens_m.asp.

By way of comparison, we now freeze everything except fixed costs and repeat the analysis:

Scenario	Fixed Costs	Cash Flow	Net Present Value	IRR
Base case	$50,000	$59,800	$15,567	15.1%
Worst case	55,000	56,500	3,670	12.7
Best case	45,000	63,100	27,461	17.4

What we see here is that, given our ranges, the estimated NPV of this project is more sensitive to changes in projected unit sales than it is to changes in projected fixed costs. In fact, under the worst case for fixed costs, the NPV is still positive.

The results of our sensitivity analysis for unit sales can be illustrated graphically as in Figure 11.1. Here we place NPV on the vertical axis and unit sales on the horizontal axis. When we plot the combinations of unit sales versus NPV, we see that all possible combinations fall on a straight line. The steeper the resulting line is, the greater the sensitivity of the estimated NPV to changes in the projected value of the variable being investigated.

FIGURE 11.1 >>

Sensitivity Analysis for Unit Sales

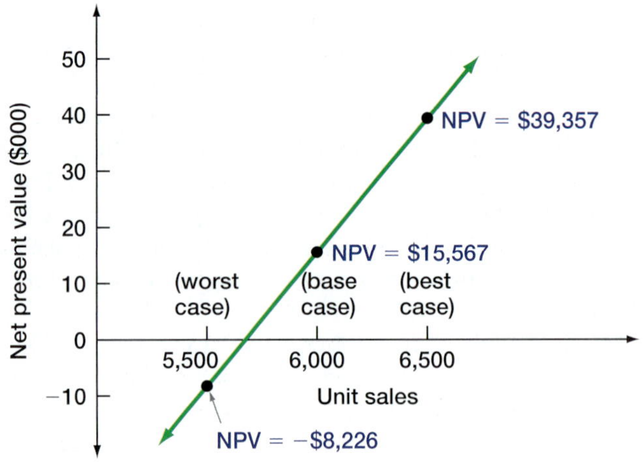

As we have illustrated, sensitivity analysis is useful in pinpointing those variables that deserve the most attention. If we find that our estimated NPV is especially sensitive to changes in a variable that is difficult to forecast (such as unit sales), then the degree of forecasting risk is high. We might decide that further market research would be a good idea in this case.

Because sensitivity analysis is a form of scenario analysis, it suffers from the same drawbacks. Sensitivity analysis is useful for pointing out where forecasting errors will do the most damage, but it does not tell us what to do about possible errors.

Simulation Analysis

Scenario analysis and sensitivity analysis are widely used. With scenario analysis, we let all the different variables change, but we let them take on only a small number of values. With sensitivity analysis, we let only one variable change, but we let it take on a large number of values. If we combine the two approaches, the result is a crude form of **simulation analysis**.

simulation analysis
A combination of scenario and sensitivity analysis.

If we want to let all the items vary at the same time, we have to consider a very large number of scenarios, and computer assistance is almost certainly needed. In the simplest case, we start with unit sales and assume that any value in our 5,500 to 6,500 range is equally likely. We start by randomly picking one value (or by instructing a computer to do so). We then randomly pick a price, a variable cost, and so on.

Once we have values for all the relevant components, we calculate an NPV. We repeat this sequence as much as we desire, probably several thousand times. The result is a large number of NPV estimates that we summarize by calculating the average value and some measure of how spread out the different possibilities are. For example, it would be of some interest to know what percentage of the possible scenarios result in negative estimated NPVs.

Because simulation analysis (or simulation) is an extended form of scenario analysis, it has the same problems. Once we have the results, there is no simple decision rule that tells us what to do. Also, we have described a relatively simple form of simulation. To really do it right, we would have to consider the interrelationships between the different cash flow components. Furthermore, we assumed that the possible values were equally likely to occur. It is probably more realistic to assume that values near the base case are more likely than extreme values, but coming up with the probabilities is difficult, to say the least.

For these reasons, the use of simulation is somewhat limited in practice. However, recent advances in computer software and hardware (and user sophistication) lead us to believe it may become more common in the future, particularly for large-scale projects.

Concept Questions

11.2a What are scenario, sensitivity, and simulation analysis?

11.2b What are the drawbacks to the various types of what-if analysis?

BREAK-EVEN ANALYSIS 11.3

It will frequently turn out that the crucial variable for a project is sales volume. If we are thinking of a new product or entering a new market, for example, the hardest thing to forecast accurately is how much we can sell. For this reason, sales volume is usually analyzed more closely than other variables.

Break-even analysis is a popular and commonly used tool for analyzing the relationship between sales volume and profitability. There are a variety of different break-even measures, and we have already seen several types. For example, we discussed (in Chapter 9) how the payback period can be interpreted as the length of time until a project breaks even, ignoring time value.

All break-even measures have a similar goal. Loosely speaking, we will always be asking: "How bad do sales have to get before we actually begin to lose money?" Implicitly, we will also be asking: "Is it likely that things will get that bad?" To get started on this subject, we first discuss fixed and variable costs.

Fixed and Variable Costs

In discussing break-even, the difference between fixed and variable costs becomes very important. As a result, we need to be a little more explicit about the difference than we have been so far.

variable costs
Costs that change when the quantity of output changes.

Variable Costs By definition, **variable costs** change as the quantity of output changes, and they are zero when production is zero. For example, direct labor costs and raw material costs are usually considered variable. This makes sense because if we shut down operations tomorrow, there will be no future costs for labor or raw materials.

We will assume that variable costs are a constant amount per unit of output. This simply means that total variable cost is equal to the cost per unit multiplied by the number of units. In other words, the relationship between total variable cost (VC), cost per unit of output (v), and total quantity of output (Q) can be written simply as:

$$\text{Total variable cost} = \text{Total quantity of output} \times \text{Cost per unit of output}$$
$$\text{VC} = Q \times v$$

For example, suppose variable costs (v) are \$2 per unit. If total output (Q) is 1,000 units, what will total variable costs (VC) be?

$$\begin{aligned} \text{VC} &= Q \times v \\ &= 1{,}000 \times \$2 \\ &= \$2{,}000 \end{aligned}$$

Similarly, if Q is 5,000 units, then VC will be 5,000 × \$2 = \$10,000. Figure 11.2 illustrates the relationship between output level and variable costs in this case. In Figure 11.2, notice that increasing output by one unit results in variable costs rising by \$2, so "the rise over the run" (the slope of the line) is given by \$2/1 = \$2.

EXAMPLE 11.1 >> Variable Costs

The Blume Corporation is a manufacturer of pencils. It has received an order for 5,000 pencils, and the company has to decide whether or not to accept the order. From recent experience, the company knows that each pencil requires 5 cents in raw materials and 50 cents in direct labor costs. These variable costs are expected to continue to apply in the future. What will Blume's total variable costs be if it accepts the order?

In this case, the cost per unit is 50 cents in labor plus 5 cents in material for a total of 55 cents per unit. At 5,000 units of output, we have:

$$\begin{aligned} \text{VC} &= Q \times v \\ &= 5{,}000 \times \$.55 \\ &= \$2{,}750 \end{aligned}$$

Therefore, total variable costs will be \$2,750.

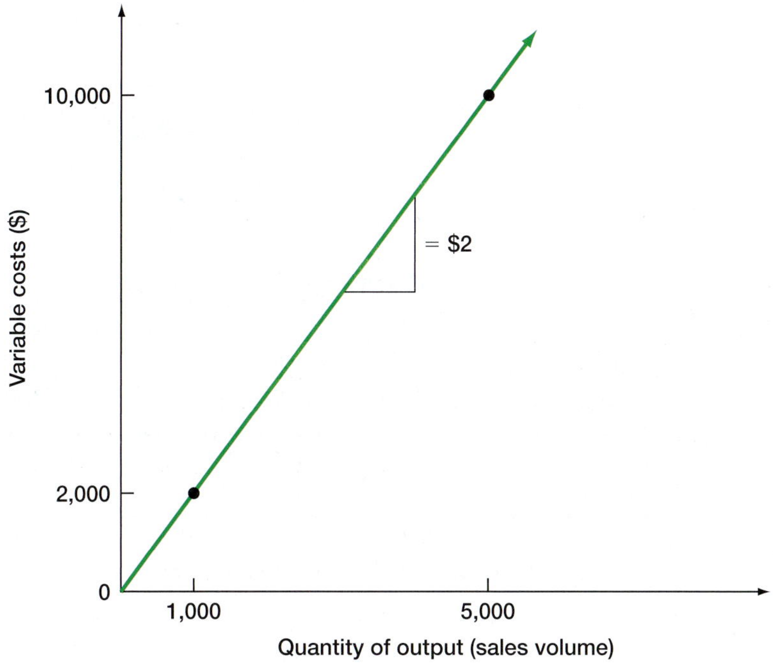

<< FIGURE 11.2

Output Level and Variable Costs

Fixed Costs **Fixed costs**, by definition, do not change during a specified time period. So, unlike variable costs, they do not depend on the amount of goods or services produced during a period (at least within some range of production). For example, the lease payment on a production facility and the company president's salary are fixed costs, at least over some period.

fixed costs
Costs that do not change when the quantity of output changes during a particular time period.

Naturally, fixed costs are not fixed forever. They are only fixed during some particular time, say, a quarter or a year. Beyond that time, leases can be terminated and executives "retired." More to the point, any fixed cost can be modified or eliminated given enough time; so, in the long run, all costs are variable.

Notice that during the time that a cost is fixed, that cost is effectively a sunk cost because we are going to have to pay it no matter what.

Total Costs Total costs (TC) for a given level of output are the sum of variable costs (VC) and fixed costs (FC):

$$\begin{aligned} \text{TC} &= \text{VC} + \text{FC} \\ &= v \times Q + \text{FC} \end{aligned}$$

So, for example, if we have variable costs of $3 per unit and fixed costs of $8,000 per year, our total cost is:

$$\text{TC} = \$3 \times Q + 8{,}000$$

If we produce 6,000 units, our total production cost will be $3 × 6,000 + 8,000 = $26,000. At other production levels, we have:

Quantity Produced	Total Variable Costs	Fixed Costs	Total Costs
0	$ 0	$8,000	$ 8,000
1,000	3,000	8,000	11,000
5,000	15,000	8,000	23,000
10,000	30,000	8,000	38,000

FIGURE 11.3 >>

Output Level and Total Costs

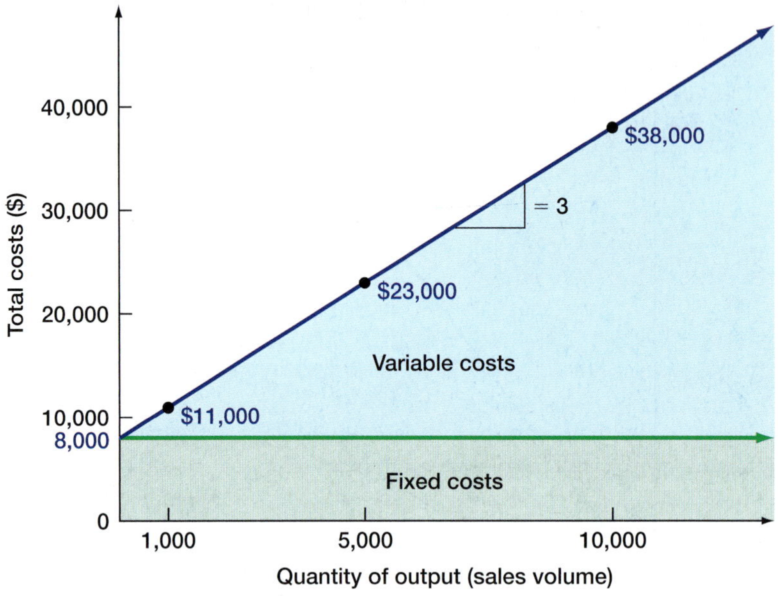

marginal, or incremental, cost The change in costs that occurs when there is a small change in output.

By plotting these points in Figure 11.3, we see that the relationship between quantity produced and total costs is given by a straight line. In Figure 11.3, notice that total costs are equal to fixed costs when sales are zero. Beyond that point, every one-unit increase in production leads to a $3 increase in total costs, so the slope of the line is 3. In other words, the **marginal**, or **incremental**, **cost** of producing one more unit is $3.

EXAMPLE 11.2 >> Average Cost versus Marginal Cost

Suppose the Blume Corporation has a variable cost per pencil of 55 cents. The lease payment on the production facility runs $5,000 per month. If Blume produces 100,000 pencils per year, what are the total costs of production? What is the average cost per pencil?

The fixed costs are $5,000 per month, or $60,000 per year. The variable cost is $.55 per pencil. So the total cost for the year, assuming that Blume produces 100,000 pencils, is:

$$\begin{aligned}\text{Total cost} &= v \times Q + \text{FC}\\ &= \$.55 \times 100{,}000 + 60{,}000\\ &= \$115{,}000\end{aligned}$$

The average cost per pencil is $115,000/100,000 = $1.15.

Now suppose that Blume has received a special, one-shot order for 5,000 pencils. Blume has sufficient capacity to manufacture the 5,000 pencils on top of the 100,000 already produced, so no additional fixed costs will be incurred. Also, there will be no effect on existing orders. If Blume can get 75 cents per pencil for this order, should the order be accepted?

What this boils down to is a very simple proposition. It costs 55 cents to make another pencil. Anything Blume can get for this pencil in excess of the 55-cent incremental cost contributes in a positive way towards covering fixed costs. The 75-cent

continued

marginal, or **incremental**, **revenue** exceeds the 55-cent marginal cost, so Blume should take the order.

The fixed cost of $60,000 is not relevant to this decision because it is effectively sunk, at least for the current period. In the same way, the fact that the average cost is $1.15 is irrelevant because this average reflects the fixed cost. As long as producing the extra 5,000 pencils truly does not cost anything beyond the 55 cents per pencil, then Blume should accept anything over that 55 cents.

marginal, or incremental, revenue
The change in revenue that occurs when there is a small change in output.

Accounting Break-Even

The most widely used measure of break-even is **accounting break-even**. The accounting break-even point is simply the sales level that results in a zero project net income.

accounting break-even
The sales level that results in zero project net income.

To determine a project's accounting break-even, we start off with some common sense. Suppose we retail one-terabyte computer diskettes for $5 apiece. We can buy diskettes from a wholesale supplier for $3 apiece. We have accounting expenses of $600 in fixed costs and $300 in depreciation. How many diskettes do we have to sell to break even, that is, for net income to be zero?

For every diskette we sell, we pick up $5 − 3 = $2 towards covering our other expenses (this $2 difference between the selling price and the variable cost is often called the *contribution margin per unit*). We have to cover a total of $600 + 300 = $900 in accounting expenses, so we obviously need to sell $900/2 = 450 diskettes. We can check this by noting that, at a sales level of 450 units, our revenues are $5 × 450 = $2,250 and our variable costs are $3 × 450 = $1,350. The income statement is thus:

Sales	$2,250
Variable costs	1,350
Fixed costs	600
Depreciation	300
EBIT	$ 0
Taxes (34%)	0
Net income	$ 0

Remember, because we are discussing a proposed new project, we do not consider any interest expense in calculating net income or cash flow from the project. Also, notice that we include depreciation in calculating expenses here, even though depreciation is not a cash outflow. That is why we call it an accounting break-even. Finally, notice that when net income is zero, so are pretax income and, of course, taxes. In accounting terms, our revenues are equal to our costs, so there is no profit to tax.

Figure 11.4 presents another way to see what is happening. This figure looks a lot like Figure 11.3 except that we add a line for revenues. As indicated, total revenues are zero when output is zero. Beyond that, each unit sold brings in another $5, so the slope of the revenue line is 5.

From our preceding discussion, we know that we break even when revenues are equal to total costs. The line for revenues and the line for total costs cross right where output is at 450 units. As illustrated, at any level of output below 450, our accounting profit is negative, and, at any level above 450, we have a positive net income.

FIGURE 11.4 >>

Accounting Break-Even

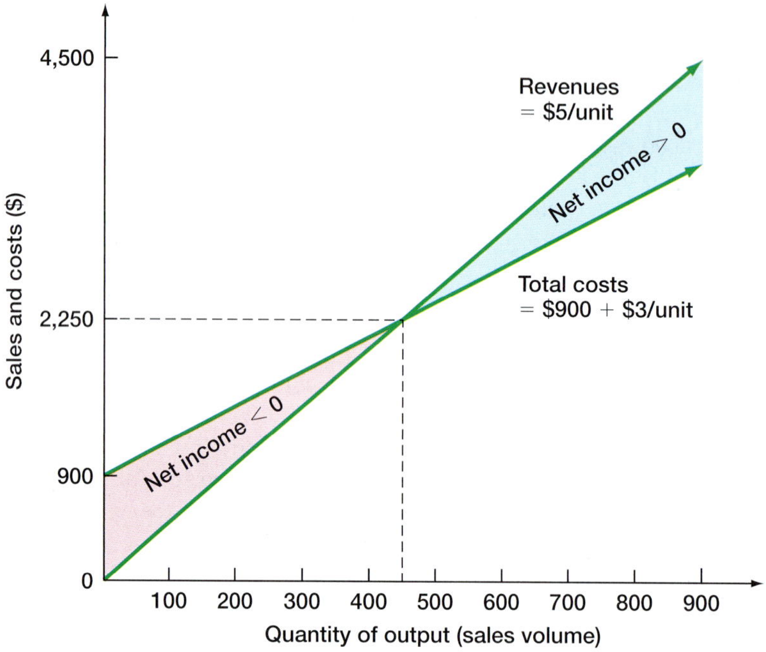

Accounting Break-Even: A Closer Look

In our numerical example, notice that the break-even level is equal to the sum of fixed costs and depreciation, divided by price per unit less variable costs per unit. This is always true. To see why, we recall all of the following variables:

P = Selling price per unit
v = Variable cost per unit
Q = Total units sold
S = Total sales = $P \times Q$
VC = Total variable costs = $v \times Q$
FC = Fixed costs
D = Depreciation
T = Tax rate

Project net income is given by:

$$\begin{aligned}\text{Net income} &= (\text{Sales} - \text{Variable costs} - \text{Fixed costs} - \text{Depreciation}) \times (1 - T)\\ &= (S - \text{VC} - \text{FC} - D) \times (1 - T)\end{aligned}$$

From here, it is not difficult to calculate the break-even point. If we set this net income equal to zero, we get:

$$\text{Net income} \overset{\text{SET}}{=} 0 = (S - \text{VC} - \text{FC} - D) \times (1 - T)$$

Divide both sides by $(1 - T)$ to get:

$$S - \text{VC} - \text{FC} - D = 0$$

As we have seen, this says that when net income is zero, so is pretax income. If we recall that $S = P \times Q$ and $\text{VC} = v \times Q$, then we can rearrange the equation to solve for the break-even level:

$$S - \text{VC} = \text{FC} + D$$
$$P \times Q - v \times Q = FC + D$$
$$(P - v) \times Q = FC + D$$
$$Q = (\text{FC} + D)/(P - v) \qquad [11.1]$$

This is the same result we described earlier.

Uses for the Accounting Break-Even

Why would anyone be interested in knowing the accounting break-even point? To illustrate how it can be useful, suppose we are a small specialty ice cream manufacturer with a strictly local distribution. We are thinking about expanding into new markets. Based on the estimated cash flows, we find that the expansion has a positive NPV.

Going back to our discussion of forecasting risk, we know that it is likely that what will make or break our expansion is sales volume. The reason is that, in this case at least, we probably have a fairly good idea of what we can charge for the ice cream. Further, we know relevant production and distribution costs with a fair degree of accuracy because we are already in the business. What we do not know with any real precision is how much ice cream we can sell.

Given the costs and selling price, however, we can immediately calculate the break-even point. Once we have done so, we might find that we need to get 30 percent of the market just to break even. If we think that this is unlikely to occur, because, for example, we have only 10 percent of our current market, then we know our forecast is questionable and there is a real possibility that the true NPV is negative. On the other hand, we might find that we already have firm commitments from buyers for about the break-even amount, so we are almost certain we can sell more. In this case, the forecasting risk is much lower, and we have greater confidence in our estimates.

There are several other reasons why knowing the accounting break-even can be useful. First, as we will discuss in more detail later, accounting break-even and payback period are very similar measures. Like payback period, accounting break-even is relatively easy to calculate and explain.

Second, managers are often concerned with the contribution a project will make to the firm's total accounting earnings. A project that does not break even in an accounting sense actually reduces total earnings.

Third, a project that just breaks even on an accounting basis loses money in a financial or opportunity cost sense. This is true because we could have earned more by investing elsewhere. Such a project does not lose money in an out-of-pocket sense. As described in the following pages, we get back exactly what we put in. For noneconomic reasons, opportunity losses may be easier to live with than out-of-pocket losses.

Concept Questions

11.3a How are fixed costs similar to sunk costs?

11.3b What is net income at the accounting break-even point? What about taxes?

11.3c Why might a financial manager be interested in the accounting break-even point?

11.4 OPERATING CASH FLOW, SALES VOLUME, AND BREAK-EVEN

Accounting break-even is one tool that is useful for project analysis. Ultimately, however, we are more interested in cash flow than accounting income. So, for example, if sales volume is the critical variable, then we need to know more about the relationship between sales volume and cash flow than just the accounting break-even.

Our goal in this section is to illustrate the relationship between operating cash flow and sales volume. We also discuss some other break-even measures. To simplify matters somewhat, we will ignore the effect of taxes. We start off by looking at the relationship between accounting break-even and cash flow.

Accounting Break-Even and Cash Flow

Now that we know how to find the accounting break-even, it is natural to wonder what happens with cash flow. To illustrate, suppose the Wettway Sailboat Corporation is considering whether or not to launch its new Margo-class sailboat. The selling price will be \$40,000 per boat. The variable costs will be about half that, or \$20,000 per boat, and fixed costs will be \$500,000 per year.

The Base Case The total investment needed to undertake the project is \$3,500,000. This amount will be depreciated straight-line to zero over the five-year life of the equipment. The salvage value is zero, and there are no working capital consequences. Wettway has a 20 percent required return on new projects.

Based on market surveys and historical experience, Wettway projects total sales for the five years at 425 boats, or about 85 boats per year. Ignoring taxes, should this project be launched?

To begin, ignoring taxes, the operating cash flow at 85 boats per year is:

$$\begin{aligned}\text{Operating cash flow} &= \text{EBIT} + \text{Depreciation} - \text{Taxes}\\ &= (S - \text{VC} - \text{FC} - D) + D - 0\\ &= 85 \times (\$40{,}000 - 20{,}000) - 500{,}000\\ &= \$1{,}200{,}000 \text{ per year}\end{aligned}$$

At 20 percent, the five-year annuity factor is 2.9906, so the NPV is:

$$\begin{aligned}\text{NPV} &= -\$3{,}500{,}000 + 1{,}200{,}000 \times 2.9906\\ &= -\$3{,}500{,}000 + 3{,}588{,}720\\ &= \$88{,}720\end{aligned}$$

In the absence of additional information, the project should be launched.

Calculating the Break-Even Level To begin looking a little closer at this project, you might ask a series of questions. For example, how many new boats does Wettway need to sell for the project to break even on an accounting basis? If Wettway does break even, what will be the annual cash flow from the project? What will be the return on the investment in this case?

Before fixed costs and depreciation are considered, Wettway generates \$40,000 − 20,000 = \$20,000 per boat (this is revenue less variable cost). Depreciation is \$3,500,000/5 = \$700,000 per year. Fixed costs and depreciation together total \$1.2 million, so Wettway needs to sell $(\text{FC} + D)/(P - v) = \$1.2 \text{ million}/20{,}000 = 60$ boats per year to break even on an accounting basis. This is 25 boats less than projected sales; so, assuming that Wettway is confident its projection is accurate to within, say, 15 boats, it appears unlikely that the new investment will fail to at least break even on an accounting basis.

To calculate Wettway's cash flow in this case, we note that if 60 boats are sold, net income will be exactly zero. Recalling from the previous chapter that operating cash flow for a project can be written as net income plus depreciation (the bottom-up definition), we can see that the operating cash flow is equal to the depreciation, or $700,000 in this case. The internal rate of return is exactly zero (why?).

Payback and Break-Even As our example illustrates, whenever a project breaks even on an accounting basis, the cash flow for that period will be equal to the depreciation. This result makes perfect accounting sense. For example, suppose we invest $100,000 in a five-year project. The depreciation is straight-line to a zero salvage, or $20,000 per year. If the project exactly breaks even every period, then the cash flow will be $20,000 per period.

The sum of the cash flows for the life of this project is 5 × $20,000 = $100,000, the original investment. What this shows is that a project's payback period is exactly equal to its life if the project breaks even every period. Similarly, a project that does better than break even has a payback that is shorter than the life of the project and has a positive rate of return.

The bad news is that a project that just breaks even on an accounting basis has a negative NPV and a zero return. For our sailboat project, the fact that Wettway will almost surely break even on an accounting basis is partially comforting because it means that the firm's "downside" risk (its potential loss) is limited, but we still don't know if the project is truly profitable. More work is needed.

Sales Volume and Operating Cash Flow

At this point, we can generalize our example and introduce some other break-even measures. From our discussion in the previous section, we know that, ignoring taxes, a project's operating cash flow, OCF, can be written simply as EBIT plus depreciation:

$$\begin{aligned} \text{OCF} &= [(P - v) \times Q - \text{FC} - D] + D \\ &= (P - v) \times Q - \text{FC} \end{aligned} \quad [11.2]$$

For the Wettway sailboat project, the general relationship (in thousands of dollars) between operating cash flow and sales volume is thus:

$$\begin{aligned} \text{OCF} &= (P - v) \times Q - \text{FC} \\ &= (\$40 - 20) \times Q - 500 \\ &= -\$500 + 20 \times Q \end{aligned}$$

What this tells us is that the relationship between operating cash flow and sales volume is given by a straight line with a slope of $20 and a *y*-intercept of −$500. If we calculate some different values, we get:

Quantity Sold	Operating Cash Flow
0	−$ 500
15	− 200
30	100
50	500
75	1,000

FIGURE 11.5 >>

Operating Cash Flow and Sales Volume

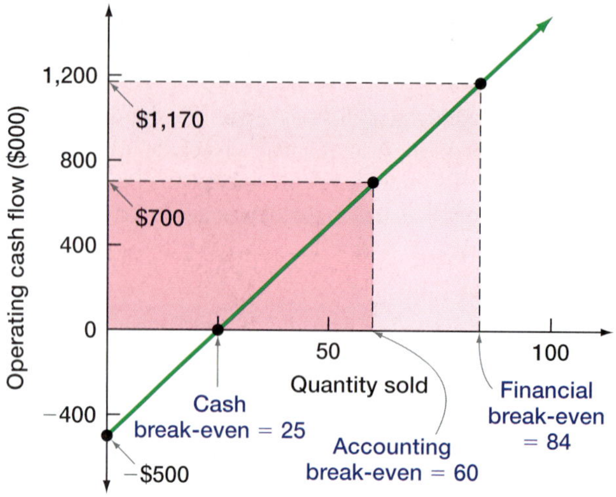

These points are plotted in Figure 11.5. In Figure 11.5, we have indicated three different break-even points. We discuss these next.

Cash Flow, Accounting, and Financial Break-Even Points

We know from the preceding discussion that the relationship between operating cash flow and sales volume (ignoring taxes) is:

$$\text{OCF} = (P - v) \times Q - \text{FC}$$

If we rearrange this and solve for Q, we get:

$$Q = (\text{FC} + \text{OCF})/(P - v) \quad \textbf{[11.3]}$$

This tells us what sales volume (Q) is necessary to achieve any given OCF, so this result is more general than the accounting break-even. We use it to find the various break-even points in Figure 11.5.

Accounting Break-Even Revisited Looking at Figure 11.5, suppose that operating cash flow is equal to depreciation (D). Recall that this situation corresponds to our break-even point on an accounting basis. To find the sales volume, we substitute the $700 depreciation amount for OCF in our general expression:

$$\begin{aligned} Q &= (\text{FC} + \text{OCF})/(P - v) \\ &= (\$500 + 700)/20 \\ &= 60 \end{aligned}$$

This is the same quantity we had before.

Cash Break-Even We have seen that a project that breaks even on an accounting basis has a net income of zero, but it still has a positive cash flow. At some sales level below the accounting break-even, the operating cash flow actually goes negative. This is a particularly unpleasant occurrence. If it happens, we actually have to supply additional cash to the project just to keep it afloat.

To calculate the **cash break-even** (the point where operating cash flow is equal to zero), we put in a zero for OCF:

cash break-even
The sales level that results in a zero operating cash flow.

$$
\begin{aligned}
Q &= (\text{FC} + 0)/(P - v) \\
&= \$500/20 \\
&= 25
\end{aligned}
$$

Wettway must therefore sell 25 boats to cover the $500 in fixed costs. As we show in Figure 11.5, this point occurs right where the operating cash flow line crosses the horizontal axis.

Notice that a project that just breaks even on a cash flow basis can cover its own fixed operating costs, but that is all. It never pays back anything, so the original investment is a complete loss (the IRR is −100 percent).

Financial Break-Even

The last case we consider is that of **financial break-even**, the sales level that results in a zero NPV. To the financial manager, this is the most interesting case. What we do is first determine what operating cash flow has to be for the NPV to be zero. We then use this amount to determine the sales volume.

financial break-even
The sales level that results in a zero NPV.

To illustrate, recall that Wettway requires a 20 percent return on its $3,500 (in thousands) investment. How many sailboats does Wettway have to sell to break even once we account for the 20 percent per year opportunity cost?

The sailboat project has a five-year life. The project has a zero NPV when the present value of the operating cash flows equals the $3,500 investment. Because the cash flow is the same each year, we can solve for the unknown amount by viewing it as an ordinary annuity. The five-year annuity factor at 20 percent is 2.9906, and the OCF can be determined as follows:

$$
\begin{aligned}
\$3{,}500 &= \text{OCF} \times 2.9906 \\
\text{OCF} &= \$3{,}500/2.9906 \\
&= \$1{,}170
\end{aligned}
$$

Wettway thus needs an operating cash flow of $1,170 each year to break even. We can now plug this OCF into the equation for sales volume:

$$
\begin{aligned}
Q &= (\$500 + 1{,}170)/20 \\
&= 83.5
\end{aligned}
$$

So, Wettway needs to sell about 84 boats per year. This is not good news.

As indicated in Figure 11.5, the financial break-even is substantially higher than the accounting break-even point. This will often be the case. Moreover, what we have discovered is that the sailboat project has a substantial degree of forecasting risk. We project sales of 85 boats per year, but it takes 84 just to earn the required return.

Conclusion

Overall, it seems unlikely that the Wettway sailboat project would fail to break even on an accounting basis. However, there appears to be a very good chance that the true NPV is negative. This illustrates the danger in looking at just the accounting break-even.

What should Wettway do? Is the new project all wet? The decision at this point is essentially a managerial issue—a judgment call. The crucial questions are:

1. How much confidence do we have in our projections?

TABLE 11.1 >>

Summary of Break-Even Measures

I. The General Break-Even Expression

Ignoring taxes, the relation between operating cash flow (OCF) and quantity of output or sales volume (Q) is:

$$Q = \frac{FC + OCF}{P - v}$$

where

FC = Total fixed costs
P = Price per unit
v = Variable cost per unit

As shown next, this relation can be used to determine the accounting, cash, and financial break-even points.

II. The Accounting Break-Even Point

Accounting break-even occurs when net income is zero. Operating cash flow is equal to depreciation when net income is zero, so the accounting break-even point is:

$$Q = \frac{FC + D}{P - v}$$

A project that always just breaks even on an accounting basis has a payback exactly equal to its life, a negative NPV, and an IRR of zero.

III. The Cash Break-Even Point

Cash break-even occurs when operating cash flow is zero. The cash break-even point is thus:

$$Q = \frac{FC}{P - v}$$

A project that always just breaks even on a cash basis never pays back, has an NPV that is negative and equal to the initial outlay, and has an IRR of −100 percent.

IV. The Financial Break-Even Point

Financial break-even occurs when the NPV of the project is zero. The financial break-even point is thus:

$$Q = \frac{FC + OCF^*}{P - v}$$

where OCF* is the level of OCF that results in a zero NPV. A project that breaks even on a financial basis has a discounted payback equal to its life, a zero NPV, and an IRR just equal to the required return.

2. How important is the project to the future of the company?
3. How badly will the company be hurt if sales do turn out to be low? What options are available to the company in this case?

We will consider questions such as these in a later section. For future reference, our discussion of the different break-even measures is summarized in Table 11.1.

Concept Questions

11.4a If a project breaks even on an accounting basis, what is its operating cash flow?

11.4b If a project breaks even on a cash basis, what is its operating cash flow?

11.4c If a project breaks even on a financial basis, what do you know about its *discounted* payback?

OPERATING LEVERAGE 11.5

We have discussed how to calculate and interpret various measures of break-even for a proposed project. What we have not explicitly discussed is what determines these points and how they might be changed. We now turn to this subject.

The Basic Idea

Operating leverage is the degree to which a project or firm is committed to fixed production costs. A firm with low operating leverage will have low fixed costs compared to a firm with high operating leverage. Generally speaking, projects with a relatively heavy investment in plant and equipment will have a relatively high degree of operating leverage. Such projects are said to be *capital intensive*.

operating leverage The degree to which a firm or project relies on fixed costs.

Anytime we are thinking about a new venture, there will normally be alternative ways of producing and delivering the product. For example, Wettway Corporation can purchase the necessary equipment and build all of the components for its sailboats in-house. Alternatively, some of the work could be farmed out to other firms. The first option involves a greater investment in plant and equipment, greater fixed costs and depreciation, and, as a result, a higher degree of operating leverage.

Implications of Operating Leverage

Regardless of how it is measured, operating leverage has important implications for project evaluation. Fixed costs act like a lever in the sense that a small percentage change in operating revenue can be magnified into a large percentage change in operating cash flow and NPV. This explains why we call it operating "leverage."

The higher the degree of operating leverage, the greater is the potential danger from forecasting risk. The reason is that relatively small errors in forecasting sales volume can get magnified, or "levered up," into large errors in cash flow projections.

From a managerial perspective, one way of coping with highly uncertain projects is to keep the degree of operating leverage as low as possible. This will generally have the effect of keeping the break-even point (however measured) at its minimum level. We will illustrate this point in a bit, but first we need to discuss how to measure operating leverage.

Measuring Operating Leverage

One way of measuring operating leverage is to ask, If quantity sold rises by 5 percent, what will be the percentage change in operating cash flow? In other words, the **degree of operating leverage (DOL)** is defined such that:

degree of operating leverage (DOL) The percentage change in operating cash flow relative to the percentage change in quantity sold.

$$\text{Percentage change in OCF} = \text{DOL} \times \text{Percentage change in } Q$$

Based on the relationship between OCF and Q, DOL can be written as:[1]

$$\text{DOL} = 1 + \text{FC}/\text{OCF} \qquad [11.4]$$

[1] To see this, note that if Q goes up by one unit, OCF will go up by $(P - v)$. In this case, the percentage change in Q is $1/Q$, and the percentage change in OCF is $(P - v)/\text{OCF}$. Given this, we have:

$$\begin{aligned}\text{Percentage change in OCF} &= \text{DOL} \times \text{Percentage change in } Q\\ (P - v)/\text{OCF} &= \text{DOL} \times 1/Q\\ \text{DOL} &= (P - v) \times Q/\text{OCF}\end{aligned}$$

Also, based on our definitions of OCF:

$$\text{OCF} + \text{FC} = (P - v) \times Q$$

Thus, DOL can be written as:

$$\begin{aligned}\text{DOL} &= (\text{OCF} + \text{FC})/\text{OCF}\\ &= 1 + \text{FC}/\text{OCF}\end{aligned}$$

The ratio FC/OCF simply measures fixed costs as a percentage of total operating cash flow. Notice that zero fixed costs would result in a DOL of 1, implying that percentage changes in quantity sold would show up one for one in operating cash flow. In other words, no magnification, or leverage, effect would exist.

To illustrate this measure of operating leverage, we go back to the Wettway sailboat project. Fixed costs were \$500 and $(P - v)$ was \$20, so OCF was:

$$\text{OCF} = -\$500 + 20 \times Q$$

Suppose Q is currently 50 boats. At this level of output, OCF is $-\$500 + 1{,}000 = \$500$.

If Q rises by 1 unit to 51, then the percentage change in Q is $(51 - 50)/50 = .02$, or 2%. OCF rises to \$520, a change of $P - v = \$20$. The percentage change in OCF is $(\$520 - 500)/500 = .04$, or 4%. So a 2 percent increase in the number of boats sold leads to a 4 percent increase in operating cash flow. The degree of operating leverage must be exactly 2.00. We can check this by noting that:

$$\begin{aligned}\text{DOL} &= 1 + \text{FC}/\text{OCF}\\ &= 1 + \$500/500\\ &= 2\end{aligned}$$

This verifies our previous calculations.

Our formulation of DOL depends on the current output level, Q. However, it can handle changes from the current level of any size, not just one unit. For example, suppose Q rises from 50 to 75, a 50 percent increase. With DOL equal to 2, operating cash flow should increase by 100 percent, or exactly double. Does it? The answer is yes, because, at a Q of 75, OCF is:

$$\text{OCF} = -\$500 + 20 \times 75 = \$1{,}000$$

Notice that operating leverage declines as output (Q) rises. For example, at an output level of 75, we have:

$$\begin{aligned}\text{DOL} &= 1 + \$500/1{,}000\\ &= 1.50\end{aligned}$$

The reason DOL declines is that fixed costs, considered as a percentage of operating cash flow, get smaller and smaller, so the leverage effect diminishes.

EXAMPLE 11.3 >> Operating Leverage

The Sasha Corp. currently sells gourmet dog food for \$1.20 per can. The variable cost is 80 cents per can, and the packaging and marketing operations have fixed costs of \$360,000 per year. Depreciation is \$60,000 per year. What is the accounting break-even? Ignoring taxes, what will be the increase in operating cash flow if the quantity sold rises to 10 percent above the break-even point?

The accounting break-even is \$420,000/.40 = 1,050,000 cans. As we know, the operating cash flow is equal to the \$60,000 depreciation at this level of production, so the degree of operating leverage is:

$$\begin{aligned}\text{DOL} &= 1 + \text{FC}/\text{OCF}\\ &= 1 + \$360{,}000/60{,}000\\ &= 7\end{aligned}$$

continued

Given this, a 10 percent increase in the number of cans of dog food sold will increase operating cash flow by a substantial 70 percent.

To check this answer, we note that if sales rise by 10 percent, then the quantity sold will rise to 1,050,000 × 1.1 = 1,155,000. Ignoring taxes, the operating cash flow will be 1,155,000 × $.40 − 360,000 = $102,000. Compared to the $60,000 cash flow we had, this is exactly 70 percent more: $102,000/60,000 = 1.70.

Operating Leverage and Break-Even

We illustrate why operating leverage is an important consideration by examining the Wettway sailboat project under an alternative scenario. At a Q of 85 boats, the degree of operating leverage for the sailboat project under the original scenario is:

$$\begin{aligned} \text{DOL} &= 1 + \text{FC}/\text{OCF} \\ &= 1 + \$500/1{,}200 \\ &= 1.42 \end{aligned}$$

Also, recall that the NPV at a sales level of 85 boats was $88,720, and that the accounting break-even was 60 boats.

An option available to Wettway is to subcontract production of the boat hull assemblies. If the company does this, the necessary investment falls to $3,200,000 and the fixed operating costs fall to $180,000. However, variable costs will rise to $25,000 per boat because subcontracting is more expensive than producing in-house. Ignoring taxes, evaluate this option.

For practice, see if you don't agree with the following:

$$\begin{aligned} \text{NPV at 20\% (85 units)} &= \$74{,}720 \\ \text{Accounting break-even} &= 55 \text{ boats} \\ \text{Degree of operating leverage} &= 1.16 \end{aligned}$$

What has happened? This option results in a slightly lower estimated net present value, and the accounting break-even point falls to 55 boats from 60 boats.

Given that this alternative has the lower NPV, is there any reason to consider it further? Maybe there is. The degree of operating leverage is substantially lower in the second case. If Wettway is worried about the possibility of an overly optimistic projection, then it might prefer to subcontract.

There is another reason why Wettway might consider the second arrangement. If sales turned out to be better than expected, the company would always have the option of starting to produce in-house at a later date. As a practical matter, it is much easier to increase operating leverage (by purchasing equipment) than to decrease it (by selling off equipment). As we discuss in a later chapter, one of the drawbacks to discounted cash flow analysis is that it is difficult to explicitly include options of this sort in the analysis, even though they may be quite important.

Concept Questions

11.5a What is operating leverage?

11.5b How is operating leverage measured?

11.5c What are the implications of operating leverage for the financial manager?

11.6 CAPITAL RATIONING

capital rationing The situation that exists if a firm has positive NPV projects but cannot find the necessary financing.

Capital rationing is said to exist when we have profitable (positive NPV) investments available but we can't get the funds needed to undertake them. For example, as division managers for a large corporation, we might identify $5 million in excellent projects, but find that, for whatever reason, we can spend only $2 million. Now what? Unfortunately, for reasons we will discuss, there may be no truly satisfactory answer.

Soft Rationing

soft rationing The situation that occurs when units in a business are allocated a certain amount of financing for capital budgeting.

The situation we have just described is called **soft rationing**. This occurs when, for example, different units in a business are allocated some fixed amount of money each year for capital spending. Such an allocation is primarily a means of controlling and keeping track of overall spending. The important thing to note about soft rationing is that the corporation as a whole isn't short of capital; more can be raised on ordinary terms if management so desires.

If we face soft rationing, the first thing to do is to try to get a larger allocation. Failing that, one common suggestion is to generate as large a net present value as possible within the existing budget. This amounts to choosing those projects with the largest benefit-cost ratio (profitability index).

Strictly speaking, this is the correct thing to do only if the soft rationing is a one-time event, that is, it won't exist next year. If the soft rationing is a chronic problem, then something is amiss. The reason goes all the way back to Chapter 1. Ongoing soft rationing means we are constantly bypassing positive NPV investments. This contradicts our goal of the firm. If we are not trying to maximize value, then the question of which projects to take becomes ambiguous because we no longer have an objective goal in the first place.

Hard Rationing

hard rationing The situation that occurs when a business cannot raise financing for a project under any circumstances.

With **hard rationing**, a business cannot raise capital for a project under any circumstances. For large, healthy corporations, this situation probably does not occur very often. This is fortunate because, with hard rationing, our DCF analysis breaks down, and the best course of action is ambiguous.

The reason DCF analysis breaks down has to do with the required return. Suppose we say our required return is 20 percent. Implicitly, we are saying we will take a project with a return that exceeds this. However, if we face hard rationing, then we are not going to take a new project no matter what the return on that project is, so the whole concept of a required return is ambiguous. About the only interpretation we can give this situation is that the required return is so large that no project has a positive NPV in the first place.

Hard rationing can occur when a company experiences financial distress, meaning that bankruptcy is a possibility. Also, a firm may not be able to raise capital without violating a preexisting contractual agreement. We discuss these situations in greater detail in a later chapter.

Concept Questions

11.6a What is capital rationing? What types are there?

11.6b What problems does capital rationing create for discounted cash flow analysis?

SUMMARY AND CONCLUSIONS 11.7

In this chapter, we looked at some ways of evaluating the results of a discounted cash flow analysis. We also touched on some of the problems that can come up in practice. We saw that:

1. Net present value estimates depend on projected future cash flows. If there are errors in those projections, then our estimated NPVs can be misleading. We called this possibility *forecasting risk.*
2. Scenario and sensitivity analysis are useful tools for identifying which variables are critical to the success of a project and where forecasting problems can do the most damage.
3. Break-even analysis in its various forms is a particularly common type of scenario analysis that is useful for identifying critical levels of sales.
4. Operating leverage is a key determinant of break-even levels. It reflects the degree to which a project or a firm is committed to fixed costs. The degree of operating leverage tells us the sensitivity of operating cash flow to changes in sales volume.
5. Projects usually have future managerial options associated with them. These options may be very important, but standard discounted cash flow analysis tends to ignore them.
6. Capital rationing occurs when apparently profitable projects cannot be funded. Standard discounted cash flow analysis is troublesome in this case because NPV is not necessarily the appropriate criterion anymore.

The most important thing to carry away from reading this chapter is that estimated NPVs or returns should not be taken at face value. They depend critically on projected cash flows. If there is room for significant disagreement about those projected cash flows, the results from the analysis have to be taken with a grain of salt.

Despite the problems we have discussed, discounted cash flow analysis is still *the* way of attacking problems, because it forces us to ask the right questions. What we have learned in this chapter is that knowing the questions to ask does not guarantee we will get all the answers.

Chapter Review and Self-Test Problems

Use the following base-case information to work the self-test problems.

A project under consideration costs $750,000, has a five-year life, and has no salvage value. Depreciation is straight-line to zero. The required return is 17 percent, and the tax rate is 34 percent. Sales are projected at 500 units per year. Price per unit is $2,500, variable cost per unit is $1,500, and fixed costs are $200,000 per year.

11.1 Scenario Analysis Suppose you think that the unit sales, price, variable cost, and fixed cost projections given here are accurate to within 5 percent. What are the upper and lower bounds for these projections? What is the base-case NPV? What are the best- and worst-case scenario NPVs?

11.2 Break-Even Analysis Given the base-case projections in the previous problem, what are the cash, accounting, and financial break-even sales levels for this project? Ignore taxes in answering.

Answers to Chapter Review and Self-Test Problems

11.1 We can summarize the relevant information as follows:

	Base Case	Lower Bound	Upper Bound
Unit sales	500	475	525
Price per unit	$ 2,500	$ 2,375	$ 2,625
Variable cost per unit	$ 1,500	$ 1,425	$ 1,575
Fixed cost per year	$200,000	$190,000	$210,000

Depreciation is $150,000 per year; knowing this, we can calculate the cash flows under each scenario. Remember that we assign high costs and low prices and volume for the worst-case and just the opposite for the best-case scenario.

Scenario	Unit Sales	Unit Price	Unit Variable Cost	Fixed Costs	Cash Flow
Base case	500	$2,500	$1,500	$200,000	$249,000
Best case	525	2,625	1,425	190,000	341,400
Worst case	475	2,375	1,575	210,000	163,200

At 17 percent, the five-year annuity factor is 3.19935, so the NPVs are:

$$\begin{aligned}\text{Base-case NPV} &= -\$750{,}000 + 3.19935 \times \$249{,}000 \\ &= \$46{,}638 \\ \text{Best-case NPV} &= -\$750{,}000 + 3.19935 \times \$341{,}400 \\ &= \$342{,}258 \\ \text{Worst-case NPV} &= -\$750{,}000 + 3.19935 \times \$163{,}200 \\ &= -\$227{,}866\end{aligned}$$

11.2 In this case, we have $200,000 in cash fixed costs to cover. Each unit contributes $2,500 − 1,500 = $1,000 towards covering fixed costs. The cash break-even is thus $200,000/$1,000 = 200 units. We have another $150,000 in depreciation, so the accounting break-even is ($200,000 + 150,000)/$1,000 = 350 units.

To get the financial break-even, we need to find the OCF such that the project has a zero NPV. As we have seen, the five-year annuity factor is 3.19935 and the project costs $750,000, so the OCF must be such that:

$$\$750{,}000 = \text{OCF} \times 3.19935$$

So, for the project to break even on a financial basis, the project's cash flow must be $750,000/3.19935, or $234,423 per year. If we add this to the $200,000 in cash fixed costs, we get a total of $434,423 that we have to cover. At $1,000 per unit, we need to sell $434,423/$1,000 = 435 units.

Concepts Review and Critical Thinking Questions

1. **Forecasting Risk** What is forecasting risk? In general, would the degree of forecasting risk be greater for a new product or a cost-cutting proposal? Why?
2. **Sensitivity Analysis and Scenario Analysis** What is the essential difference between sensitivity analysis and scenario analysis?

3. **Marginal Cash Flows** A co-worker claims that looking at all this marginal this and incremental that is just a bunch of nonsense, and states: "Listen, if our average revenue doesn't exceed our average cost, then we will have a negative cash flow, and we will go broke!" How do you respond?
4. **Operating Leverage** At one time at least, many Japanese companies had a "no layoff" policy (for that matter, so did IBM). What are the implications of such a policy for the degree of operating leverage a company faces?
5. **Operating Leverage** Airlines offer an example of an industry in which the degree of operating leverage is fairly high. Why?
6. **Break-Even** As a shareholder of a firm that is contemplating a new project, would you be more concerned with the accounting break-even point, the cash break-even point, or the financial break-even point? Why?
7. **Break-Even** Assume a firm is considering a new project that requires an initial investment and has equal sales and costs over its life. Will the project reach the accounting, cash, or financial break-even point first? Which will it reach next? Last? Will this ordering always apply?
8. **Capital Rationing** How are soft rationing and hard rationing different? What are the implications if a firm is experiencing soft rationing? Hard rationing?
9. **Capital Rationing** Going all the way back to Chapter 1, recall that we saw that partnerships and proprietorships can face difficulties when it comes to raising capital. In the context of this chapter, the implication is that small businesses will generally face what problem?

Questions and Problems

BASIC
(Questions 1–15)

1. **Calculating Costs and Break-Even** Bob's Bikes Inc. (BBI) manufactures biotech sunglasses. The variable materials cost is \$1.43 per unit and the variable labor cost is \$2.44 per unit.
   a. What is the variable cost per unit?
   b. Suppose BBI incurs fixed costs of \$650,000 during a year in which total production is 320,000 units. What are the total costs for the year?
   c. If the selling price is \$10.00 per unit, does BBI break even on a cash basis? If depreciation is \$190,000 per year, what is the accounting break-even point?
2. **Computing Average Cost** Everest Everwear Corporation can manufacture mountain climbing shoes for \$16.15 per pair in variable raw material costs and \$18.50 per pair in variable labor expense. The shoes sell for \$105 per pair. Last year, production was 150,000 pairs. Fixed costs were \$800,000. What were total production costs? What is the marginal cost per pair? What is the average cost? If the company is considering a one-time order for an extra 10,000 pairs, what is the minimum acceptable total revenue from the order? Explain.
3. **Scenario Analysis** Bellevue Transmissions, Inc., has the following estimates for its new gear assembly project: price = \$1,900 per unit; variable costs = \$170 per unit; fixed costs = \$6 million; quantity = 105,000 units. Suppose the company believes all of its estimates are accurate only to within ±15 percent. What values should the company use for the four variables given here when it performs its best-case scenario analysis? What about the worst-case scenario?
4. **Sensitivity Analysis** For the company in the previous problem, suppose management is most concerned about the impact of its price estimate on the project's

profitability. How could you address this concern for Bellevue Transmissions? Describe how you would calculate your answer. What values would you use for the other forecast variables?

5. **Sensitivity Analysis and Break-Even** We are evaluating a project that costs $896,000, has a eight-year life, and has no salvage value. Assume that depreciation is straight-line to zero over the life of the project. Sales are projected at 100,000 units per year. Price per unit is $38, variable cost per unit is $25, and fixed costs are $900,000 per year. The tax rate is 35 percent, and we require a 15 percent return on this project.
   a. Calculate the accounting break-even point. What is the degree of operating leverage at the accounting break-even point?
   b. Calculate the base-case cash flow and NPV. What is the sensitivity of NPV to changes in the sales figure? Explain what your answer tells you about a 500-unit decrease in projected sales.
   c. What is the sensitivity of OCF to changes in the variable cost figure? Explain what your answer tells you about a $1 decrease in estimated variable costs.
6. **Scenario Analysis** In the previous problem, suppose the projections given for price, quantity, variable costs, and fixed costs are all accurate to within ±10 percent. Calculate the best-case and worst-case NPV figures.
7. **Calculating Break-Even** In each of the following cases, calculate the accounting break-even and the cash break-even points. Ignore any tax effects in calculating the cash break-even.

Unit Price	Unit Variable Cost	Fixed Costs	Depreciation
$3,000	$2,275	$15,000,000	$6,500,000
39	27	73,000	140,000
8	3	1,200	840

8. **Calculating Break-Even** In each of the following cases, find the unknown variable.

Accounting Break-Even	Unit Price	Unit Variable Cost	Fixed Costs	Depreciation
130,200	$ 41	$30	$ 820,000	?
135,000	?	56	3,200,000	$1,150,000
5,478	105	?	160,000	105,000

9. **Calculating Break-Even** A project has the following estimated data: price = $70 per unit; variable costs = $37 per unit; fixed costs = $6,000; required return = 15 percent; initial investment = $12,000; life = four years. Ignoring the effect of taxes, what is the accounting break-even quantity? The cash break-even quantity? The financial break-even quantity? What is the degree of operating leverage at the financial break-even level of output?
10. **Using Break-Even Analysis** Consider a project with the following data: accounting break-even quantity = 19,000 units; cash break-even quantity = 13,000 units; life = five years; fixed costs = $120,000; variable costs = $23 per unit; required return = 16 percent. Ignoring the effect of taxes, find the financial break-even quantity.

11. **Calculating Operating Leverage** At an output level of 40,000 units, you calculate that the degree of operating leverage is 2.5. If output rises to 47,000 units, what will the percentage change in operating cash flow be? Will the new level of operating leverage be higher or lower? Explain.
12. **Leverage** In the previous problem, suppose fixed costs are $150,000. What is the operating cash flow at 35,000 units? The degree of operating leverage?
13. **Operating Cash Flow and Leverage** A proposed project has fixed costs of $45,000 per year. The operating cash flow at 8,000 units is $71,000. Ignoring the effect of taxes, what is the degree of operating leverage? If units sold rises from 8,000 to 8,500, what will be the increase in operating cash flow? What is the new degree of operating leverage?
14. **Cash Flow and Leverage** At an output level of 10,000 units, you have calculated that the degree of operating leverage is 2.75. The operating cash flow is $16,000 in this case. Ignoring the effect of taxes, what are fixed costs? What will the operating cash flow be if output rises to 11,000 units? If output falls to 9,000 units?
15. **Leverage** In the previous problem, what will be the new degree of operating leverage in each case?

INTERMEDIATE
(Questions 16–22)

16. **Break-Even Intuition** Consider a project with a required return of $R\%$ that costs $\$I$ and will last for N years. The project uses straight-line depreciation to zero over the N-year life; there is no salvage value or net working capital requirements.
    - **a.** At the accounting break-even level of output, what is the IRR of this project? The payback period? The NPV?
    - **b.** At the cash break-even level of output, what is the IRR of this project? The payback period? The NPV?
    - **c.** At the financial break-even level of output, what is the IRR of this project? The payback period? The NPV?
17. **Sensitivity Analysis** Consider a four-year project with the following information: initial fixed asset investment = $420,000; straight-line depreciation to zero over the four-year life; zero salvage value; price = $28; variable costs = $19; fixed costs = $190,000; quantity sold = 110,000 units; tax rate = 34 percent. How sensitive is OCF to changes in quantity sold?
18. **Operating Leverage** In the previous problem, what is the degree of operating leverage at the given level of output? What is the degree of operating leverage at the accounting break-even level of output?
19. **Project Analysis** You are considering a new product launch. The project will cost $720,000, have a four-year life, and have no salvage value; depreciation is straight-line to zero. Sales are projected at 190 units per year; price per unit will be $21,000, variable cost per unit will be $15,000, and fixed costs will be $225,000 per year. The required return on the project is 15 percent, and the relevant tax rate is 35 percent.
    - **a.** Based on your experience, you think the unit sales, variable cost, and fixed cost projections given here are probably accurate to within ± 10 percent. What are the upper and lower bounds for these projections? What is the base-case NPV? What are the best-case and worst-case scenarios?
    - **b.** Evaluate the sensitivity of your base-case NPV to changes in fixed costs.
    - **c.** What is the cash break-even level of output for this project (ignoring taxes)?
    - **d.** What is the accounting break-even level of output for this project? What is the degree of operating leverage at the accounting break-even point? How do you interpret this number?

20. **Project Analysis** McGilla Golf has decided to sell a new line of golf clubs. The clubs will sell for \$700 per set and have a variable cost of \$320 per set. The company has spent \$150,000 for a marketing study that determined the company will sell 55,000 sets per year for seven years. The marketing study also determined that the company will lose sales of 13,000 sets of its high-priced clubs. The high-priced clubs sell at \$1,100 and have variable costs of \$600. The company will also increase sales of its cheap clubs by 10,000 sets. The cheap clubs sell for \$400 and have variable costs of \$180 per set. The fixed costs each year will be \$7,500,000. The company has also spent \$1,000,000 on research and development for the new clubs. The plant and equipment required will cost \$18,200,000 and will be depreciated on a straight-line basis. The new clubs will also require an increase in net working capital of \$950,000 that will be returned at the end of the project. The tax rate is 40 percent, and the cost of capital is 14 percent. Calculate the payback period, the NPV, and the IRR.

21. **Scenario Analysis** In the previous problem, you feel that the values are accurate to within only $\pm$10 percent. What are the best-case and worst-case NPVs? (Hint: The price and variable costs for the two existing sets of clubs are known with certainty; only the sales gained or lost are uncertain.)

22. **Sensitivity Analysis** McGilla Golf would like to know the sensitivity of NPV to changes in the price of the new clubs and the quantity of new clubs sold. What is the sensitivity of the NPV to each of these variables?

CHALLENGE
(Questions 23–28)

23. **Break-Even and Taxes** This problem concerns the effect of taxes on the various break-even measures.
    a. Show that, when we consider taxes, the general relationship between operating cash flow, OCF, and sales volume, Q, can be written as:

$$Q = \frac{\text{FC} + \dfrac{\text{OCF} - T \times D}{1 - T}}{P - v}$$

    b. Use the expression in part (a) to find the cash, accounting, and financial break-even points for the Wettway sailboat example in the chapter. Assume a 38 percent tax rate.
    c. In part (b), the accounting break-even should be the same as before. Why? Verify this algebraically.

24. **Operating Leverage and Taxes** Show that if we consider the effect of taxes, the degree of operating leverage can be written as:

$$\text{DOL} = 1 + [\text{FC} \times (1 - T) - T \times D]/\text{OCF}$$

Notice that this reduces to our previous result if $T = 0$. Can you interpret this in words?

25. **Scenario Analysis** Consider a project to supply Detroit with 40,000 tons of machine screws annually for automobile production. You will need an initial \$1,700,000 investment in threading equipment to get the project started; the project will last for five years. The accounting department estimates that annual fixed costs will be \$450,000 and that variable costs should be \$210 per ton; accounting will depreciate the initial fixed asset investment straight-line to zero over the five-year project life. It also estimates a salvage value of \$500,000 after dismantling costs. The marketing department estimates that the automakers will let the contract at a selling price of \$230 per ton. The engineering department estimates you will need an initial net working

capital investment of \$450,000. You require a 13 percent return and face a marginal tax rate of 38 percent on this project.

a. What is the estimated OCF for this project? The NPV? Should you pursue this project?

b. Suppose you believe that the accounting department's initial cost and salvage value projections are accurate only to within ±15 percent; the marketing department's price estimate is accurate only to within ±10 percent; and the engineering department's net working capital estimate is accurate only to within ±5 percent. What is your worst-case scenario for this project? Your best-case scenario? Do you still want to pursue the project?

26. Sensitivity Analysis In Problem 25, suppose you're confident about your own projections, but you're a little unsure about Detroit's actual machine screw requirement. What is the sensitivity of the project OCF to changes in the quantity supplied? What about the sensitivity of NPV to changes in quantity supplied? Given the sensitivity number you calculated, is there some minimum level of output below which you wouldn't want to operate? Why?

27. Break-Even Analysis Use the results of Problem 23 to find the accounting, cash, and financial break-even quantities for the company in Problem 25.

28. Operating Leverage Use the results of Problem 24 to find the degree of operating leverage for the company in Problem 25 at the base-case output level of 40,000 units. How does this number compare to the sensitivity figure you found in Problem 26? Verify that either approach will give you the same OCF figure at any new quantity level.

>> MINI-CASE

Conch Republic Electronics

Conch Republic Electronics is a midsized electronics manufacturer located in Key West, Florida. The company president is Shelly Couts, who inherited the company. When it was founded over 70 years ago, the company originally repaired radios and other household appliances. Over the years, the company expanded into manufacturing and is now a reputable manufacturer of various electronic items. Jay McCanless, a recent MBA graduate, has been hired by the company's finance department.

One of the major revenue producing items manufactured by Conch Republic is a Personal Digital Assistant (PDA). Conch Republic currently has one PDA model on the market and sales have been excellent. The PDA is a unique item in that it comes in a variety of tropical colors and is preprogrammed to play Jimmy Buffett music. However, as with any electronic item, technology changes rapidly, and the current PDA has limited features in comparison with newer models. Conch Republic spent $750,000 to develop a prototype for a new PDA that has all the features of the existing PDA, but adds new features such as cell phone capability. The company has spent a further $200,000 for a marketing study to determine the expected sales figures for the new PDA.

Conch Republic can manufacture the new PDA for $86 each in variable costs. Fixed costs for the operation are estimated to run $3 million per year. The estimated sales volume is 70,000, 80,000, 100,000, 85,000, and 75,000 per each year for the next five years, respectively. The unit price of the new PDA will be $250. The necessary equipment can be purchased for $15 million and will be depreciated on a seven-year MACRS schedule. It is believed the value of the equipment in five years will be $3 million.

As previously stated, Conch Republic currently manufactures a PDA. Production of the existing model is expected to be terminated in two years. If Conch Republic does not introduce the new PDA, sales will be 80,000 units and 60,000 units for the next two years, respectively. The price of the existing PDA is $240 per unit, with variable costs of $68 each and fixed costs of $1,800,000 per year. If Conch Republic does introduce the new PDA, sales of the existing PDA will fall by 15,000 units per year, and the price of the existing units will have to be lowered to $220 each. Net working capital for the PDAs will be 20 percent of sales and will occur with the timing of the cash flows for the year; for example, there is no initial outlay for NWC, but changes in NWC will first occur in Year 1 with the first year's sales. Conch Republic has a 35 percent corporate tax rate and a 12 percent required return.

Shelly has asked Jay to prepare a report that answers the following questions:

1. What is the payback period of the project?
2. What is the profitability index of the project?
3. What is the IRR of the project?
4. What is the NPV of the project?
5. How sensitive is the NPV to changes in the price of the new PDA?
6. How sensitive is the NPV to changes in the quantity sold?
7. Should Conch Republic produce the new PDA?

Visit us at www.mhhe.com/rwj

PART FIVE

Risk and Return

12 Some Lessons from Capital Market History

With the NASDAQ stock market index up 50 percent in 2003, the stock market was a good place to be for investors. In fact, it was a great year for investors in Millcom International Cellular, which gained a whopping 1,209 percent! XM Satellite Radio investors also had to be pleased with the 880 percent gain of that stock. Of course, not all stocks increased in value during the year. Turnstone Systems stock fell almost 96 percent during the year, and HealtheTech stock dropped almost 89 percent. These examples show that there were tremendous potential profits to be made during 2003, but there was also the risk of losing money, and lots of it. So what should you, as a stock market investor, expect when you invest your own money? In this chapter, we study almost eight decades of market history to find out.

Thus far, we haven't had much to say about what determines the required return on an investment. In one sense, the answer is very simple: The required return depends on the risk of the investment. The greater the risk, the greater is the required return.

Having said this, we are left with a somewhat more difficult problem. How can we measure the amount of risk present in an investment? Put another way, what does it mean to say that one investment is riskier than another? Obviously, we need to define what we mean by risk if we are going to answer these questions. This is our task in the next two chapters.

From the last several chapters, we know that one of the responsibilities of the financial manager is to assess the value of proposed real asset investments. In doing this, it is important that we first look at what financial investments have to offer. At a minimum, the return we require from a proposed nonfinancial investment must be greater than what we can get by buying financial assets of similar risk.

The number of Web sites devoted to financial markets and instruments is astounding, and increasing daily. Be sure to check out the RWJ Web page for links to finance-related sites! (www.mhhe.com/rwj)

Our goal in this chapter is to provide a perspective on what capital market history can tell us about risk and return. The most important thing to get out of this chapter is a feel for the numbers. What is a high return? What is a low one? More generally, what returns should we expect from financial assets and what are the risks of such investments? This perspective is essential for understanding how to analyze and value risky investment projects.

We start our discussion of risk and return by describing the historical experience of investors in U.S. financial markets. In 1931, for example, the stock market lost 43 percent of its value. Just two years later, the stock market gained 54 percent. In more recent memory, the market lost about 25 percent of its value on October 19, 1987, alone. What lessons, if any, can financial managers learn from such shifts in the stock market? We will explore the last half century (and then some) of market history to find out.

Not everyone agrees on the value of studying history. On the one hand, there is philosopher George Santayana's famous comment, "Those who do not remember the past are condemned to repeat it." On the other hand, there is industrialist Henry Ford's equally famous comment, "History is more or less bunk." Nonetheless, perhaps everyone would agree with Mark Twain's observation, "October. This is one of the peculiarly dangerous months to speculate in stocks in. The others are July, January, September, April, November, May, March, June, December, August, and February."

There are two central lessons that emerge from our study of market history. First, there is a reward for bearing risk. Second, the greater the potential reward is, the greater is the risk. To illustrate these facts about market returns, we devote much of this chapter to reporting the statistics and numbers that make up the modern capital market history of the United States. In the next chapter, these facts provide the foundation for our study of how financial markets put a price on risk.

12.1 RETURNS

We wish to discuss historical returns on different types of financial assets. The first thing we need to do, then, is to briefly discuss how to calculate the return from investing.

Dollar Returns

If you buy an asset of any sort, your gain (or loss) from that investment is called the *return on your investment.* This return will usually have two components. First, you may receive some cash directly while you own the investment. This is called the *income component* of your return. Second, the value of the asset you purchase will often change. In this case, you have a capital gain or capital loss on your investment.[1]

How did the market do today? Find out at finance.yahoo.com.

To illustrate, suppose the Video Concept Company has several thousand shares of stock outstanding. You purchased some of these shares of stock in the company at the beginning of the year. It is now year-end, and you want to determine how well you have done on your investment.

First, over the year, a company may pay cash dividends to its shareholders. As a stockholder in Video Concept Company, you are a part owner of the company. If the company is profitable, it may choose to distribute some of its profits to shareholders (we discuss the details of dividend policy in Chapter 18). So, as the owner of some stock, you will receive some cash. This cash is the income component from owning the stock.

In addition to the dividend, the other part of your return is the capital gain or capital loss on the stock. This part arises from changes in the value of your investment. For example, consider the cash flows illustrated in Figure 12.1. At the beginning of the year, the stock was selling for \$37 per share. If you had bought 100 shares, you would have had a total outlay of \$3,700. Suppose, over the year, the stock paid a dividend of \$1.85 per share. By the end of the year, then, you would have received income of:

$$\text{Dividend} = \$1.85 \times 100 = \$185$$

Also, the value of the stock has risen to \$40.33 per share by the end of the year. Your 100 shares are now worth \$4,033, so you have a capital gain of:

$$\text{Capital gain} = (\$40.33 - 37) \times 100 = \$333$$

[1]As we mentioned in an earlier chapter, strictly speaking, what is and what is not a capital gain (or loss) is determined by the IRS. We thus use the terms loosely.

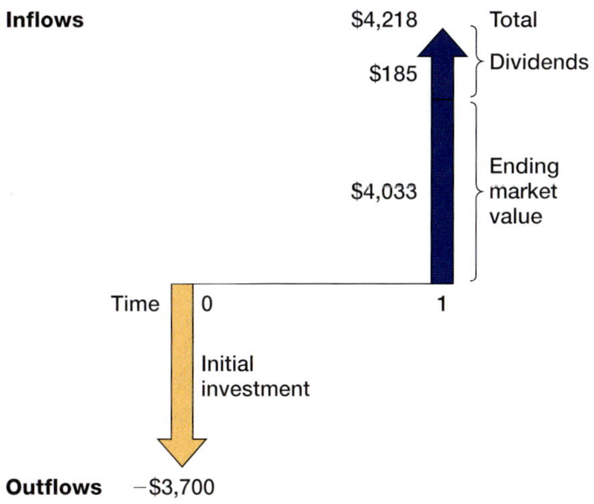

<< FIGURE 12.1

Dollar Returns

On the other hand, if the price had dropped to, say, $34.78, you would have a capital loss of:

$$\text{Capital loss} = (\$34.78 - 37) \times 100 = -\$222$$

Notice that a capital loss is the same thing as a negative capital gain.

The total dollar return on your investment is the sum of the dividend and the capital gain:

$$\text{Total dollar return} = \text{Dividend income} + \text{Capital gain (or loss)} \quad [12.1]$$

In our first example, the total dollar return is thus given by:

$$\text{Total dollar return} = \$185 + 333 = \$518$$

Notice that, if you sold the stock at the end of the year, the total amount of cash you would have would equal your initial investment plus the total return. In the preceding example, then:

$$\begin{aligned} \text{Total cash if stock is sold} &= \text{Initial investment} + \text{Total return} \quad [12.2] \\ &= \$3{,}700 + 518 \\ &= \$4{,}218 \end{aligned}$$

As a check, notice that this is the same as the proceeds from the sale of the stock plus the dividends:

$$\begin{aligned} \text{Proceeds from stock sale} + \text{Dividends} &= \$40.33 \times 100 + 185 \\ &= \$4{,}033 + 185 \\ &= \$4{,}218 \end{aligned}$$

Suppose you hold on to your Video Concept stock and don't sell it at the end of the year. Should you still consider the capital gain as part of your return? Isn't this only a "paper" gain and not really a cash flow if you don't sell the stock?

The answer to the first question is a strong yes, and the answer to the second is an equally strong no. The capital gain is every bit as much a part of your return as the dividend, and you should certainly count it as part of your return. That you actually decided to keep the stock and not sell (you don't "realize" the gain) is irrelevant because you could have converted it to cash if you had wanted to. Whether you choose to do so or not is up to you.

After all, if you insisted on converting your gain to cash, you could always sell the stock at year-end and immediately reinvest by buying the stock back. There is no net difference between doing this and just not selling (assuming, of course, that there are no tax consequences from selling the stock). Again, the point is that whether you actually cash out and buy sodas (or whatever) or reinvest by not selling doesn't affect the return you earn.

Percentage Returns

It is usually more convenient to summarize information about returns in percentage terms, rather than dollar terms, because that way your return doesn't depend on how much you actually invest. The question we want to answer is: How much do we get for each dollar we invest?

To answer this question, let P_t be the price of the stock at the beginning of the year and let D_{t+1} be the dividend paid on the stock during the year. Consider the cash flows in Figure 12.2. These are the same as those in Figure 12.1, except that we have now expressed everything on a per-share basis.

Go to www.smartmoney.com/marketmap for a cool Java applet that shows today's returns by market sector.

In our example, the price at the beginning of the year was \$37 per share and the dividend paid during the year on each share was \$1.85. As we discussed in Chapter 8, expressing the dividend as a percentage of the beginning stock price results in the dividend yield:

$$\begin{aligned}\text{Dividend yield} &= D_{t+1}/P_t \\ &= \$1.85/37 = .05 = 5\%\end{aligned}$$

This says that, for each dollar we invest, we get five cents in dividends.

FIGURE 12.2 >>

Percentage Returns

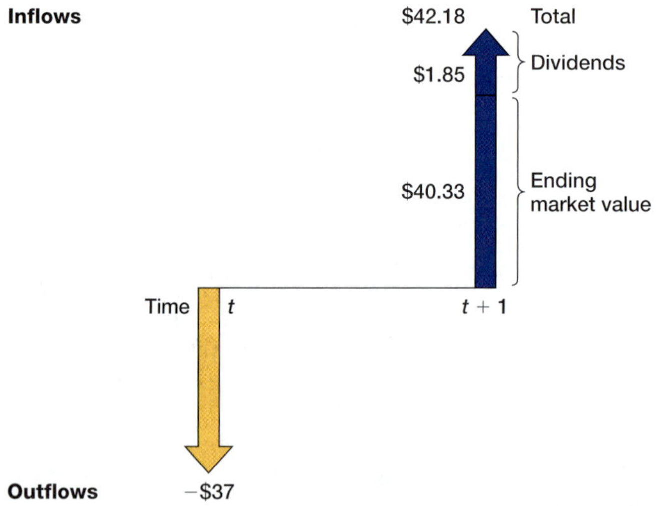

$$\text{Percentage return} = \frac{\text{Dividends paid at end of period} + \text{Change in market value over period}}{\text{Beginning market value}}$$

$$1 + \text{Percentage return} = \frac{\text{Dividends paid at end of period} + \text{Market value at end of period}}{\text{Beginning market value}}$$

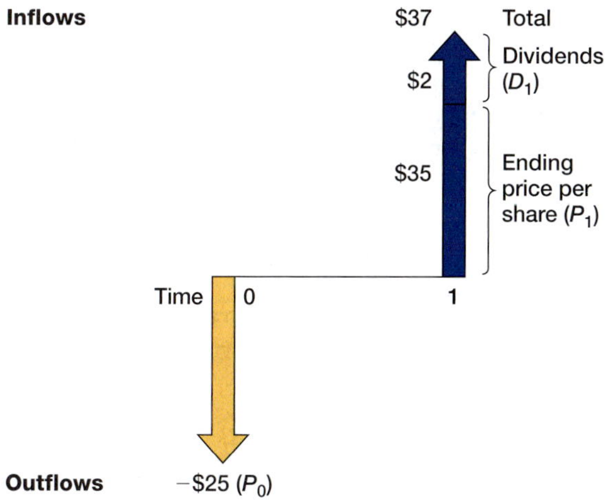

<< FIGURE 12.3

Cash Flow—An Investment Example

The second component of our percentage return is the capital gains yield. Recall (from Chapter 8) that this is calculated as the change in the price during the year (the capital gain) divided by the beginning price:

$$\begin{aligned}\text{Capital gains yield} &= (P_{t+1} - P_t)/P_t \\ &= (\$40.33 - 37)/37 \\ &= \$3.33/37 \\ &= 9\%\end{aligned}$$

So, per dollar invested, we get nine cents in capital gains.

Putting it together, per dollar invested, we get 5 cents in dividends and 9 cents in capital gains; so we get a total of 14 cents. Our percentage return is 14 cents on the dollar, or 14 percent.

To check this, notice that we invested \$3,700 and ended up with \$4,218. By what percentage did our \$3,700 increase? As we saw, we picked up \$4,218 − 3,700 = \$518. This is a \$518/3,700 = 14% increase.

Calculating Returns

<< EXAMPLE 12.1

Suppose you bought some stock at the beginning of the year for \$25 per share. At the end of the year, the price is \$35 per share. During the year, you got a \$2 dividend per share. This is the situation illustrated in Figure 12.3. What is the dividend yield? The capital gains yield? The percentage return? If your total investment was \$1,000, how much do you have at the end of the year?

Your \$2 dividend per share works out to a dividend yield of:

$$\begin{aligned}\text{Dividend yield} &= D_{t+1}/P_t \\ &= \$2/25 = .08 = 8\%\end{aligned}$$

The per-share capital gain is \$10, so the capital gains yield is:

$$\begin{aligned}\text{Capital gains yield} &= (P_{t+1} - P_t)/P_t \\ &= (\$35 - 25)/25 \\ &= \$10/25 \\ &= 40\%\end{aligned}$$

The total percentage return is thus 48 percent.

continued

If you had invested $1,000, you would have $1,480 at the end of the year, representing a 48 percent increase. To check this, note that your $1,000 would have bought you $1,000/25 = 40 shares. Your 40 shares would then have paid you a total of 40 × $2 = $80 in cash dividends. Your $10 per share gain would give you a total capital gain of $10 × 40 = $400. Add these together, and you get the $480 increase.

To give a more concrete example, stock in ExxonMobil (XOM) began 2002 at $34.94 a share. XOM paid dividends of $0.98 during 2002, and the stock price at the end of the year was $41.00. What was the return on XOM for the year? For practice, see if you agree that the answer is 20.15 percent. Of course, negative returns occur as well. For example, in 2003, AT&T's stock price at the beginning of the year was $26.11 per share, and 2003 dividends of $0.85 were paid. The stock ended the year at $20.30 per share. Verify the loss was 19.00 percent for the year.

Concept Questions

12.1a What are the two parts of total return?

12.1b Why are unrealized capital gains or losses included in the calculation of returns?

12.1c What is the difference between a dollar return and a percentage return? Why are percentage returns more convenient?

12.2 THE HISTORICAL RECORD

Roger Ibbotson and Rex Sinquefield conducted a famous set of studies dealing with rates of return in U.S. financial markets.[2] They presented year-to-year historical rates of return on five important types of financial investments. The returns can be interpreted as what you would have earned if you had held portfolios of the following:

For more on market history, visit www.globalfindata.com.

1. Large-company stocks. This common stock portfolio is based on the Standard & Poor's (S&P) 500 index, which contains 500 of the largest companies (in terms of total market value of outstanding stock) in the United States.
2. Small-company stocks. This is a portfolio composed of the stock corresponding to the smallest 20 percent of the companies listed on the New York Stock Exchange, again as measured by market value of outstanding stock.
3. Long-term corporate bonds. This is based on high-quality bonds with 20 years to maturity.
4. Long-term U.S. government bonds. This is based on U.S. government bonds with 20 years to maturity.
5. U.S. Treasury bills. This is based on Treasury bills (T-bills for short) with a three-month maturity.

These returns are not adjusted for inflation or taxes; thus, they are nominal, pretax returns.

In addition to the year-to-year returns on these financial instruments, the year-to-year percentage change in the consumer price index (CPI) is also computed. This is a commonly used measure of inflation, so we can calculate real returns using this as the inflation rate.

[2]R. G. Ibbotson and R. A. Sinquefield, *Stocks, Bonds, Bills, and Inflation* [SBBI] (Charlottesville, Va.: Financial Analysis Research Foundation, 1982).

A First Look

Before looking closely at the different portfolio returns, we take a look at the big picture. Figure 12.4 shows what happened to $1 invested in these different portfolios at the beginning of 1925. The growth in value for each of the different portfolios over the 78-year period ending in 2003 is given separately (the long-term corporate bonds are omitted). Notice that to get everything on a single graph, some modification in scaling is used. As is

FIGURE 12.4 >> **A $1 Investment in Different Types of Portfolios: 1926–2003 (Year-End 1925 = $1)**

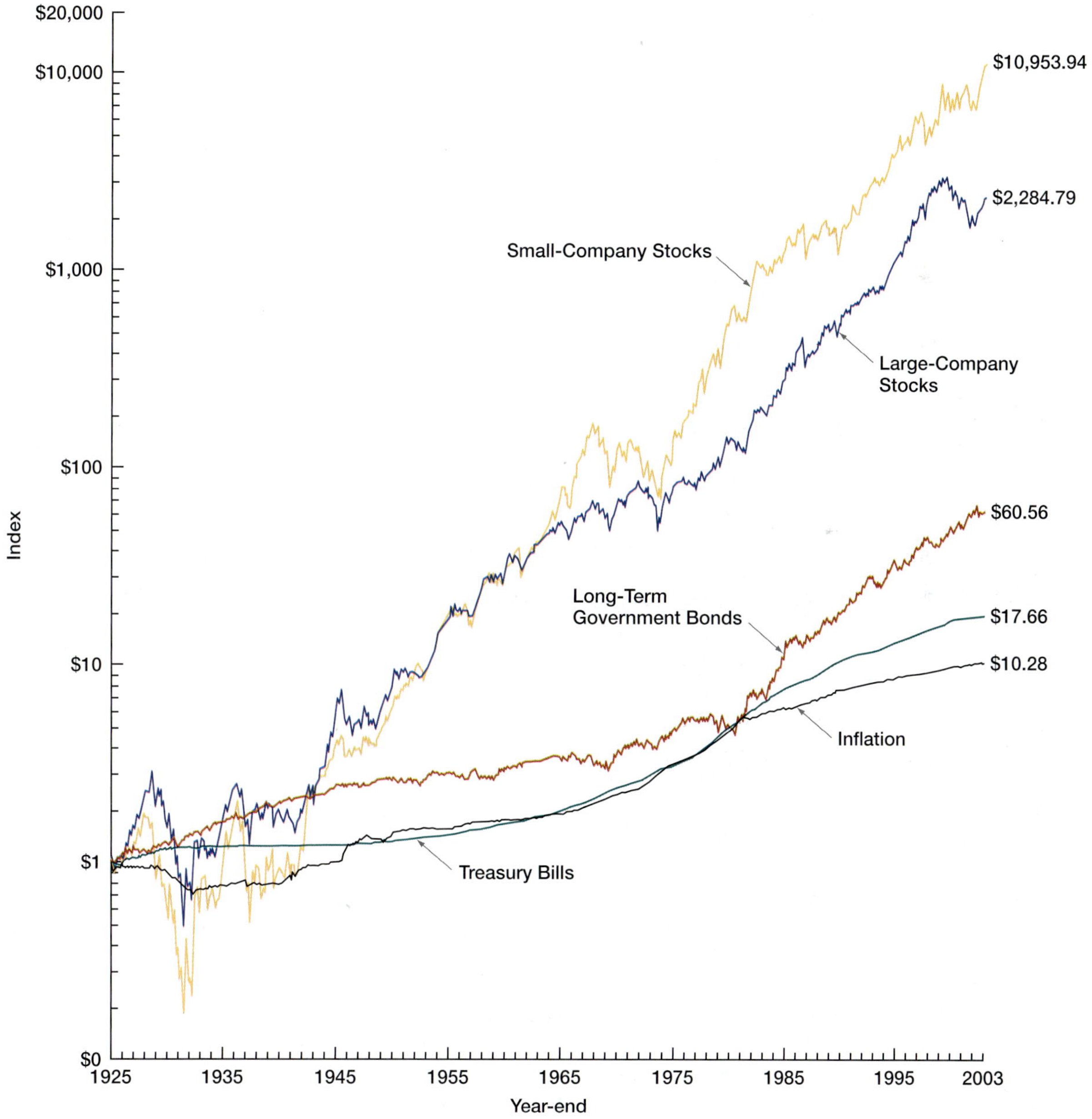

SOURCE: © *Stocks, Bonds, Bills, and Inflation 2004 Yearbook™*, Ibbotson Associates, Inc., Chicago (annually updates work by Roger G. Ibbotson and Rex A. Sinquefield). All rights reserved.

FIGURE 12.5 >>

Year-to-Year Total Returns on Large-Company Stocks: 1926–2003

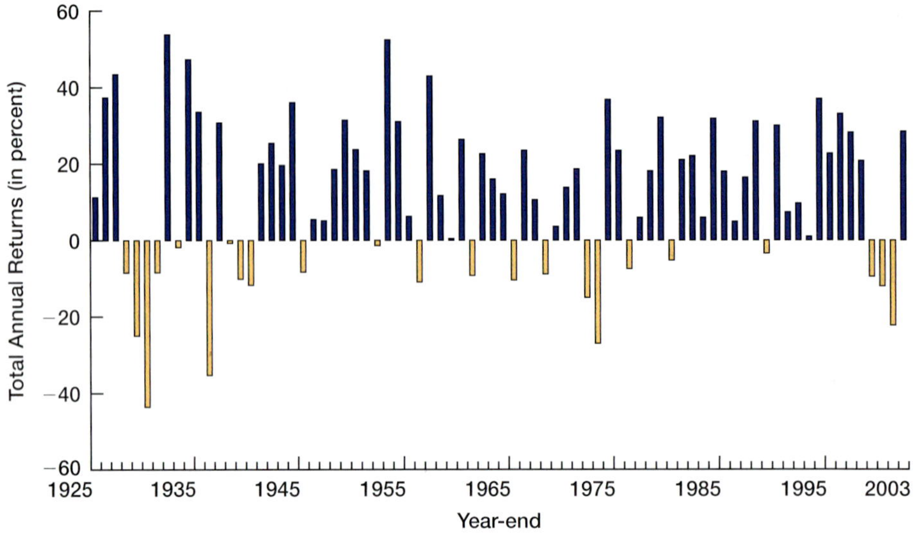

SOURCE: © *Stocks, Bonds, Bills, and Inflation 2004 Yearbook*™, Ibbotson Associates, Inc., Chicago (annually updates work by Roger G. Ibbotson and Rex A. Sinquefield). All rights reserved.

commonly done with financial series, the vertical axis is scaled such that equal distances measure equal percentage (as opposed to dollar) changes in values.[3]

Go to www.bigcharts.marketwatch.com to see both intraday and long-term charts.

Looking at Figure 12.4, we see that the "small-cap" (short for small-capitalization) investment did the best overall. Every dollar invested grew to a remarkable $10,953.94 over the 78 years. The large-company common stock portfolio did less well; a dollar invested in it grew to $2,284.79.

At the other end, the T-bill portfolio grew to only $17.66. This is even less impressive when we consider the inflation over the period in question. As illustrated, the increase in the price level was such that $10.28 was needed at the end of the period just to replace the original $1.

Given the historical record, why would anybody buy anything other than small-cap stocks? If you look closely at Figure 12.4, you will probably see the answer. The T-bill portfolio and the long-term government bond portfolio grew more slowly than did the stock portfolios, but they also grew much more steadily. The small stocks ended up on top, but as you can see, they grew quite erratically at times. For example, the small stocks were the worst performers for about the first 10 years and had a smaller return than long-term government bonds for almost 15 years.

A Closer Look

To illustrate the variability of the different investments, Figures 12.5 through 12.8 plot the year-to-year percentage returns in the form of vertical bars drawn from the horizontal axis. The height of the bar tells us the return for the particular year. For example, looking at the long-term government bonds (Figure 12.7), we see that the largest historical return (44.44 percent) occurred in 1982. This was a good year for bonds. In comparing these charts, notice the differences in the vertical axis scales. With these differences in mind, you can see how predictably the Treasury bills (Figure 12.7) behaved compared to the small stocks (Figure 12.6).

The returns shown in these bar graphs are sometimes very large. Looking at the graphs, for example, we see that the largest single-year return is a remarkable 142.87 percent for

[3]In other words, the scale is logarithmic.

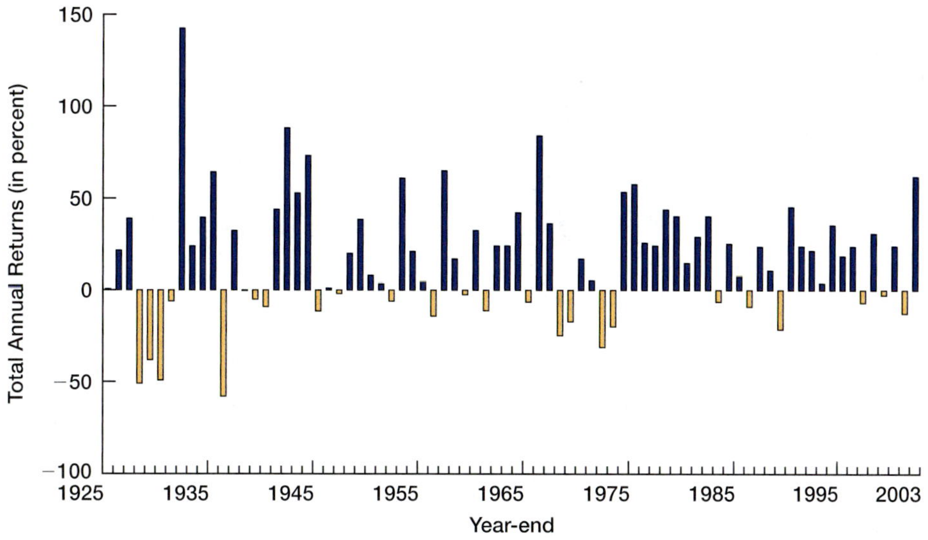

<< FIGURE 12.6

Year-to-Year Total Returns on Small-Company Stocks: 1926–2003

SOURCE: © *Stocks, Bonds, Bills, and Inflation 2004 Yearbook*™, Ibbotson Associates, Inc., Chicago (annually updates work by Roger G. Ibbotson and Rex A. Sinquefield).

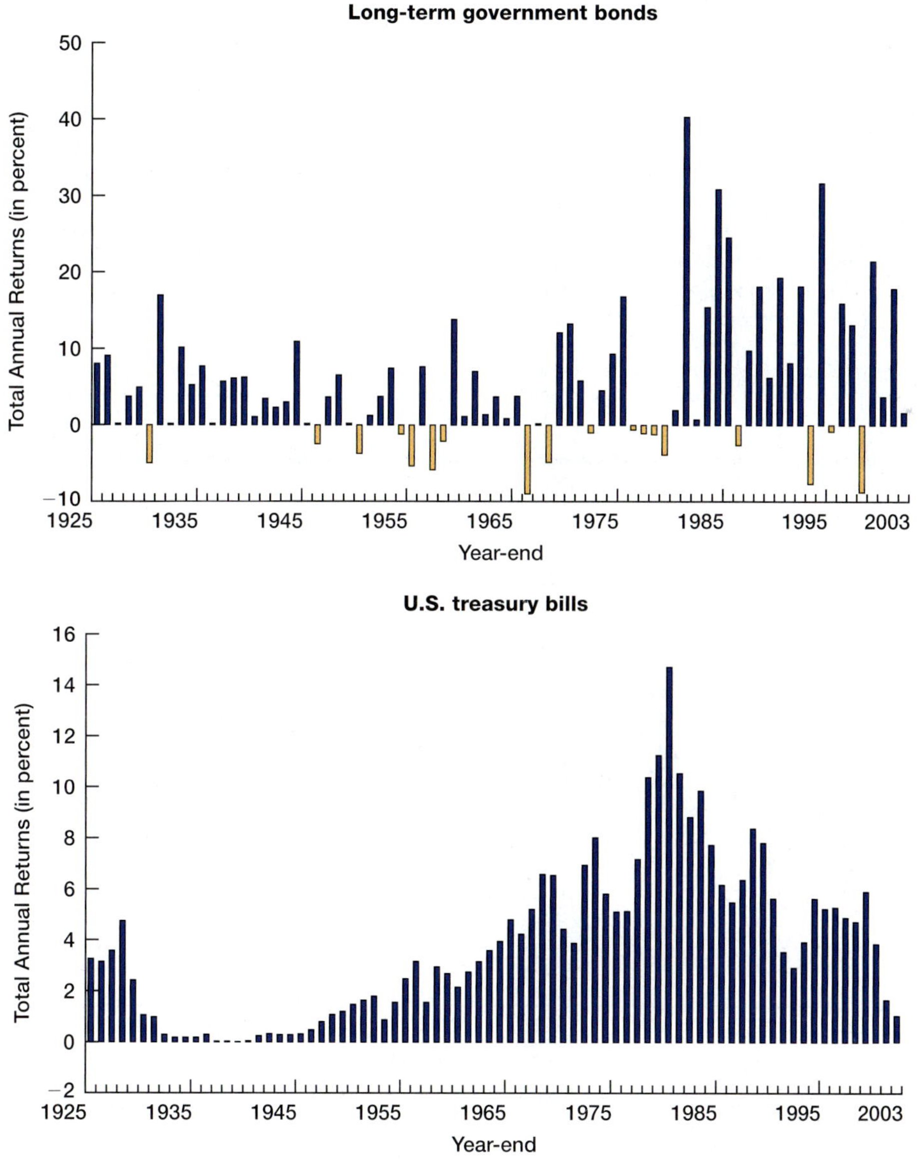

<< FIGURE 12.7

Year-to-Year Total Returns on Bonds and Bills: 1926–2003

SOURCE: © *Stocks, Bonds, Bills, and Inflation 2004 Yearbook*™, Ibbotson Associates, Inc., Chicago (annually updates work by Roger G. Ibbotson and Rex A. Sinquefield).

IN THEIR OWN WORDS . . .

Roger Ibbotson on Capital Market History

>> **The financial markets** are the most carefully documented human phenomena in history. Every day, approximately 2,000 NYSE stocks are traded, and at least 6,000 more stocks are traded on other exchanges and in over-the-counter markets. Bonds, commodities, futures, and options also provide a wealth of data. These data daily fill more than a dozen pages of *The Wall Street Journal* (and numerous other newspapers), and these pages are only summaries of the day's transactions. A record actually exists of every transaction, providing not only a real-time database, but a historical record extending back, in many cases, more than a century.

The global market adds another dimension to this wealth of data. The Japanese stock market trades a billion shares on active days, and the London exchange reports trades on over 10,000 domestic and foreign issues a day.

The data generated by these transactions are quantifiable, quickly analyzed and disseminated, and made easily accessible by computer. Because of this, finance has increasingly come to resemble one of the exact sciences. The use of financial market data ranges from the simple, such as using the S&P 500 to measure the performance of a portfolio, to the incredibly complex. For example, only a quarter of a century ago, the bond market was the most staid province on Wall Street. Today, it attracts swarms of traders seeking to exploit arbitrage opportunities—small temporary mispricings—using real-time data and computers to analyze them.

Financial market data are the foundation for the extensive empirical understanding we now have of the financial markets. The following is a list of some of the principal findings of such research:

- Risky securities, such as stocks, have higher average returns than riskless securities such as Treasury bills.
- Stocks of small companies have higher average returns than those of larger companies.
- Long-term bonds have higher average yields and returns than short-term bonds.
- The cost of capital for a company, project, or division can be predicted using data from the markets.

Because phenomena in the financial markets are so well measured, finance is the most readily quantifiable branch of economics. Researchers are able to do more extensive empirical research than in any other economic field, and the research can be quickly translated into action in the marketplace.

Roger Ibbotson is professor in the practice of management at the Yale School of Management. He is the founder and president of Ibbotson Associates, a major supplier of financial databases to the financial services industry. An outstanding scholar, he is best known for his original estimates of the historical rates of return realized by investors in different markets and for his research on new issues.

FIGURE 12.8 >>

Year-to-Year Inflation: 1926–2003

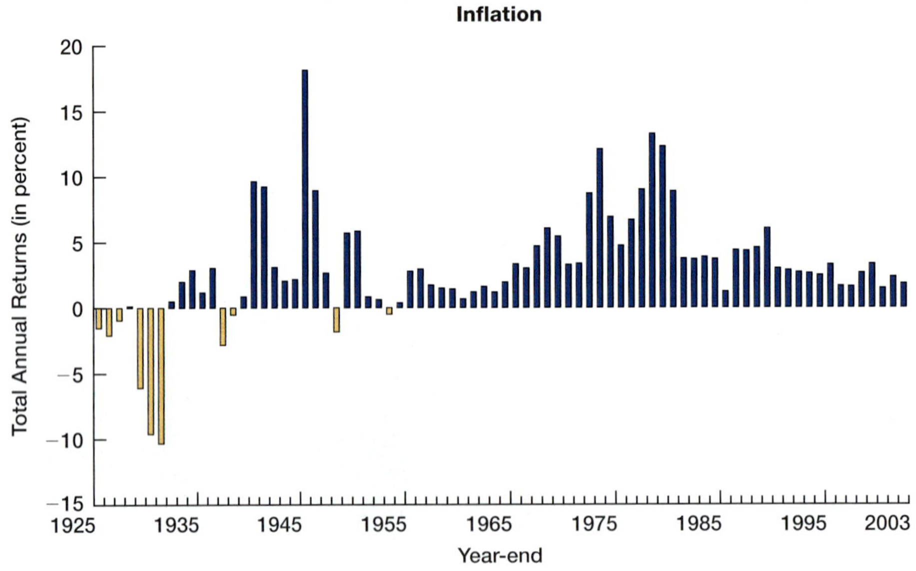

SOURCE: © *Stocks, Bonds, Bills, and Inflation 2004 Yearbook™*, Ibbotson Associates, Inc., Chicago (annually updates work by Roger G. Ibbotson and Rex A. Sinquefield). All rights reserved.

the small-cap stocks in 1933. In the same year, the large-company stocks "only" returned 52.94 percent. In contrast, the largest Treasury bill return was 15.21 percent, in 1981. For future reference, the actual year-to-year returns for the S&P 500, long-term government bonds, Treasury bills, and the CPI are shown in Table 12.1. As of 2004, the U.S. Treasury

TABLE 12.1 >> **Year-to-Year Total Returns: 1926–2003**

Year	Large-Company Stocks	Long-Term Government Bonds	U.S. Treasury Bills	Consumer Price Index	Year	Large-Company Stocks	Long-Term Government Bonds	U.S. Treasury Bills	Consumer Price Index
1926	13.75%	5.69%	3.30%	−1.12%	1965	12.38%	0.93%	4.06%	1.92%
1927	35.70	6.58	3.15	−2.26	1966	−10.06	5.12	4.94	3.46
1928	45.08	1.15	4.05	−1.16	1967	23.98	−2.86	4.39	3.04
1929	−8.80	4.39	4.47	0.58	1968	11.03	2.25	5.49	4.72
1930	−25.13	4.47	2.27	−6.40	1969	−8.43	−5.63	6.90	6.20
1931	−43.60	−2.15	1.15	−9.32	1970	3.94	18.92	6.50	5.57
1932	−8.75	8.51	0.88	−10.27	1971	14.30	11.24	4.36	3.27
1933	52.95	1.92	0.52	0.76	1972	18.99	2.39	4.23	3.41
1934	−2.31	7.59	0.27	1.52	1973	−14.69	3.30	7.29	8.71
1935	46.79	4.20	0.17	2.99	1974	−26.47	4.00	7.99	12.34
1936	32.49	5.13	0.17	1.45	1975	37.23	5.52	5.87	6.94
1937	−35.45	1.44	0.27	2.86	1976	23.93	15.56	5.07	4.86
1938	31.63	4.21	0.06	−2.78	1977	−7.16	0.38	5.45	6.70
1939	−1.43	3.84	0.04	0.00	1978	6.57	−1.26	7.64	9.02
1940	−10.36	5.70	0.04	0.71	1979	18.61	1.26	10.56	13.29
1941	−12.02	0.47	0.14	9.93	1980	32.50	−2.48	12.10	12.52
1942	20.75	1.80	0.34	9.03	1981	−4.92	4.04	14.60	8.92
1943	25.38	2.01	0.38	2.96	1982	21.55	44.28	10.94	3.83
1944	19.49	2.27	0.38	2.30	1983	22.56	1.29	8.99	3.79
1945	36.21	5.29	0.38	2.25	1984	6.27	15.29	9.90	3.95
1946	−8.42	0.54	0.38	18.13	1985	31.73	32.27	7.71	3.80
1947	5.05	−1.02	0.62	8.84	1986	18.67	22.39	6.09	1.10
1948	4.99	2.66	1.06	2.99	1987	5.25	−3.03	5.88	4.43
1949	17.81	4.58	1.12	−2.07	1988	16.61	6.84	6.94	4.42
1950	30.05	−0.98	1.22	5.93	1989	31.69	18.54	8.44	4.65
1951	23.79	−0.20	1.56	6.00	1990	−3.10	7.74	7.69	6.11
1952	18.39	2.43	1.75	0.75	1991	30.46	19.36	5.43	3.06
1953	−1.07	2.28	1.87	0.75	1992	7.62	7.34	3.48	2.90
1954	52.23	3.08	0.93	−0.74	1993	10.08	13.06	3.03	2.75
1955	31.62	−0.73	1.80	0.37	1994	1.32	−7.32	4.39	2.67
1956	6.91	−1.72	2.66	2.99	1995	37.58	25.94	5.61	2.54
1957	−10.50	6.82	3.28	2.90	1996	22.96	0.13	5.14	3.32
1958	43.57	−1.72	1.71	1.76	1997	33.36	12.02	5.19	1.70
1959	12.01	−2.02	3.48	1.73	1998	28.58	14.45	4.86	1.61
1960	0.47	11.21	2.81	1.36	1999	21.04	−7.51	4.80	2.68
1961	26.84	2.20	2.40	0.67	2000	−9.10	17.22	5.98	3.39
1962	−8.75	5.72	2.82	1.33	2001	−11.89	5.51	3.33	1.55
1963	22.70	1.79	3.23	1.64	2002	−22.10	15.15	1.61	2.72
1964	16.43	3.71	3.62	0.97	2003	28.69	0.54	1.03	1.88

SOURCES: Authors' calculation based on data obtained from *Global Financial Data* and other sources.

was no longer issuing bonds with maturities longer than 10 years, so the long-term government bond returns in the table reflect issues with 10 years to maturity.

Concept Questions

12.2a With 20/20 hindsight, what do you say was the best investment for the period from 1926 through 1935?

12.2b Why doesn't everyone just buy small stocks as investments?

12.2c What was the smallest return observed over the 78 years for each of these investments? Approximately when did it occur?

12.2d About how many times did large-company stocks return more than 30 percent? How many times did they return less than −20 percent?

12.2e What was the longest "winning streak" (years without a negative return) for large-company stocks? For long-term government bonds?

12.2f How often did the T-bill portfolio have a negative return?

12.3 AVERAGE RETURNS: THE FIRST LESSON

As you've probably begun to notice, the history of capital market returns is too complicated to be of much use in its undigested form. We need to begin summarizing all these numbers. Accordingly, we discuss how to go about condensing the detailed data. We start out by calculating average returns.

Calculating Average Returns

The obvious way to calculate the average returns on the different investments in Table 12.1 is simply to add up the yearly returns and divide by 78. The result is the historical average of the individual values.

For example, if you add up the returns for the large-company stocks in Figure 12.5 for the 78 years, you will get about 9.67. The average annual return is thus 9.67/78 = 12.4%. You interpret this 12.4 percent just like any other average. If you were to pick a year at random from the 78-year history and you had to guess what the return in that year was, the best guess would be 12.4 percent.

Average Returns: The Historical Record

Table 12.2 shows the average returns for the investments we have discussed. As shown, in a typical year, the small-company stocks increased in value by 17.5 percent. Notice also how much larger the stock returns are than the bond returns.

These averages are, of course, nominal because we haven't worried about inflation. Notice that the average inflation rate was 3.1 percent per year over this 78-year span. The nominal return on U.S. Treasury bills was 3.8 percent per year. The average real return on Treasury bills was thus approximately .7 percent per year; so the real return on T-bills has been quite low historically.

At the other extreme, small stocks had an average real return of about 17.5% − 3.1 = 14.4%, which is relatively large. If you remember the Rule of 72 (Chapter 5), then you know that a quick back-of-the-envelope calculation tells us that 14.4 percent real growth doubles your buying power about every five years. Notice also that the real value of the large-company stock portfolio increased by over 9 percent in a typical year.

<< TABLE 12.2

Average Annual Returns: 1926–2003

Investment	Average Return
Large-company stocks	12.4%
Small-company stocks	17.5
Long-term corporate bonds	6.2
Long-term government bonds	5.8
U.S. Treasury bills	3.8
Inflation	3.1

SOURCE: © *Stocks, Bonds, Bills, and Inflation 2004 Yearbook*™, Ibbotson Associates, Inc., Chicago (annually updates work by Roger G. Ibbotson and Rex A. Sinquefield). All rights reserved.

<< TABLE 12.3

Average Annual Returns and Risk Premiums: 1926–2003

Investment	Average Return	Risk Premium
Large-company stocks	12.4%	8.6%
Small-company stocks	17.5	13.7
Long-term corporate bonds	6.2	2.4
Long-term government bonds	5.8	2.0
U.S. Treasury bills	3.8	0.0

SOURCE: © *Stocks, Bonds, Bills, and Inflation 2004 Yearbook*™, Ibbotson Associates, Inc., Chicago (annually updates work by Roger G. Ibbotson and Rex A. Sinquefield). All rights reserved.

Risk Premiums

Now that we have computed some average returns, it seems logical to see how they compare with each other. One such comparison involves government-issued securities. These are free of much of the variability we see in, for example, the stock market.

The government borrows money by issuing bonds. These bonds come in different forms. The ones we will focus on are the Treasury bills. These have the shortest time to maturity of the different government bonds. Because the government can always raise taxes to pay its bills, the debt represented by T-bills is virtually free of any default risk over its short life. Thus, we will call the rate of return on such debt the *risk-free return,* and we will use it as a kind of benchmark.

A particularly interesting comparison involves the virtually risk-free return on T-bills and the very risky return on common stocks. The difference between these two returns can be interpreted as a measure of the *excess return* on the average risky asset (assuming that the stock of a large U.S. corporation has about average risk compared to all risky assets).

We call this the "excess" return because it is the additional return we earn by moving from a relatively risk-free investment to a risky one. Because it can be interpreted as a reward for bearing risk, we will call it a **risk premium**.

risk premium
The excess return required from an investment in a risky asset over that required from a risk-free investment.

Using Table 12.2, we can calculate the risk premiums for the different investments; these are shown in Table 12.3. We report only the nominal risk premiums because there is only a slight difference between the historical nominal and real risk premiums.

The risk premium on T-bills is shown as zero in the table because we have assumed that they are riskless.

The First Lesson

Looking at Table 12.3, we see that the average risk premium earned by a typical large-company stock is 12.4% − 3.8 = 8.6%. This is a significant reward. The fact that it exists historically is an important observation, and it is the basis for our first lesson: Risky assets, on average, earn a risk premium. Put another way, there is a reward for bearing risk.

Why is this so? Why, for example, is the risk premium for small stocks so much larger than the risk premium for large stocks? More generally, what determines the relative sizes of the risk premiums for the different assets? The answers to these questions are at the heart of modern finance, and the next chapter is devoted to them. For now, part of the answer can be found by looking at the historical variability of the returns on these different investments. So, to get started, we now turn our attention to measuring variability in returns.

Concept Questions

12.3a What do we mean by excess return and risk premium?

12.3b What was the real (as opposed to nominal) risk premium on the common stock portfolio?

12.3c What was the nominal risk premium on corporate bonds? The real risk premium?

12.3d What is the first lesson from capital market history?

12.4 THE VARIABILITY OF RETURNS: THE SECOND LESSON

We have already seen that the year-to-year returns on common stocks tend to be more volatile than the returns on, say, long-term government bonds. We now discuss measuring this variability of stock returns so we can begin examining the subject of risk.

Frequency Distributions and Variability

To get started, we can draw a *frequency distribution* for the common stock returns like the one in Figure 12.9. What we have done here is to count up the number of times the annual

FIGURE 12.9 >> **Frequency Distribution of Returns on Large-Company Stocks: 1926–2003**

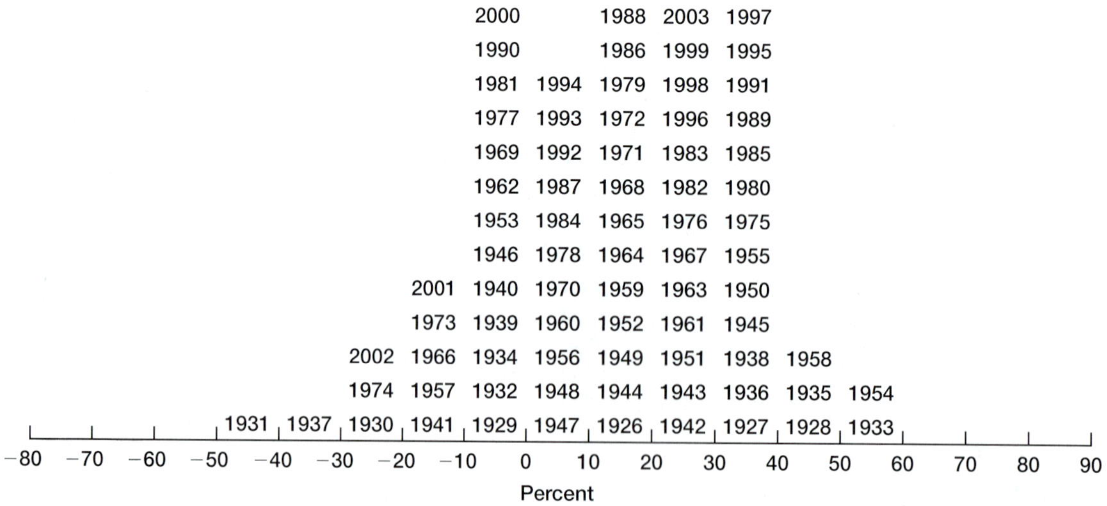

SOURCE: © *Stocks, Bonds, Bills, and Inflation 2004 Yearbook*™, Ibbotson Associates, Inc., Chicago (annually updates work by Roger G. Ibbotson and Rex A. Sinquefield).

return on the common stock portfolio falls within each 10 percent range. For example, in Figure 12.9, the height of 13 in the range of 10 to 20 percent means that 13 of the 78 annual returns were in that range.

What we need to do now is to actually measure the spread in returns. We know, for example, that the return on small stocks in a typical year was 17.5 percent. We now want to know how much the actual return deviates from this average in a typical year. In other words, we need a measure of how volatile the return is. The **variance** and its square root, the **standard deviation**, are the most commonly used measures of volatility. We describe how to calculate them next.

variance
The average squared difference between the actual return and the average return.

standard deviation
The positive square root of the variance.

The Historical Variance and Standard Deviation

The variance essentially measures the average squared difference between the actual returns and the average return. The bigger this number is, the more the actual returns tend to differ from the average return. Also, the larger the variance or standard deviation is, the more spread out the returns will be.

The way we will calculate the variance and standard deviation will depend on the specific situation. In this chapter, we are looking at historical returns; so the procedure we describe here is the correct one for calculating the *historical* variance and standard deviation. If we were examining projected future returns, then the procedure would be different. We describe this procedure in the next chapter.

To illustrate how we calculate the historical variance, suppose a particular investment had returns of 10 percent, 12 percent, 3 percent, and −9 percent over the last four years. The average return is $(.10 + .12 + .03 - .09)/4 = 4\%$. Notice that the return is never actually equal to 4 percent. Instead, the first return deviates from the average by $.10 - .04 = .06$, the second return deviates from the average by $.12 - .04 = .08$, and so on. To compute the variance, we square each of these deviations, add them up, and divide the result by the number of returns less 1, or 3 in this case. Most of this information is summarized in the table below.

For an easy-to-read review of basic stats, check out www.robertniles.com/stats.

	(1) Actual Return	(2) Average Return	(3) Deviation (1) − (2)	(4) Squared Deviation
	.10	.04	.06	.0036
	.12	.04	.08	.0064
	.03	.04	−.01	.0001
	−.09	.04	−.13	.0169
Totals	.16		.00	.0270

In the first column, we write down the four actual returns. In the third column, we calculate the difference between the actual returns and the average by subtracting out 4 percent. Finally, in the fourth column, we square the numbers in the third column to get the squared deviations from the average.

The variance can now be calculated by dividing .0270, the sum of the squared deviations, by the number of returns less 1. Let Var(R), or σ^2 (read this as "sigma squared"), stand for the variance of the return:

$$\text{Var}(R) = \sigma^2 = .027/(4 - 1) = .009$$

The standard deviation is the square root of the variance. So, if SD(R), or σ, stands for the standard deviation of return:

$$\text{SR}(R) = \sigma = \sqrt{.009} = .09487$$

The square root of the variance is used because the variance is measured in "squared" percentages and thus is hard to interpret. The standard deviation is an ordinary percentage, so the answer here could be written as 9.487 percent.

In the preceding table, notice that the sum of the deviations is equal to zero. This will always be the case, and it provides a good way to check your work. In general, if we have T historical returns, where T is some number, we can write the historical variance as:

$$\text{Var}(R) = \frac{1}{T-1}[(R_1 - \bar{R})^2 + \cdots + (R_T - \bar{R})^2] \qquad [12.3]$$

This formula tells us to do just what we did above: Take each of the T individual returns ($R_1, R_2, \ldots$) and subtract the average return, $\bar{R}$; square the results, and add them all up; and finally, divide this total by the number of returns less 1 ($T - 1$). The standard deviation is always the square root of Var(R). Standard deviations are a widely used measure of volatility. Our nearby *Work the Web* box gives a real-world example.

EXAMPLE 12.2 >> Calculating the Variance and Standard Deviation

Suppose the Supertech Company and the Hyperdrive Company have experienced the following returns in the last four years:

Year	Supertech Return	Hyperdrive Return
2001	−.20	.05
2002	.50	.09
2003	.30	−.12
2004	.10	.20

What are the average returns? The variances? The standard deviations? Which investment was more volatile?

To calculate the average returns, we add up the returns and divide by 4. The results are:

Supertech average return = $\bar{R}$ = .70/4 = .175

Hyperdrive average return = $\bar{R}$ = .22/4 = .055

To calculate the variance for Supertech, we can summarize the relevant calculations as follows:

Year	(1) Actual Return	(2) Average Return	(3) Deviation (1) − (2)	(4) Squared Deviation
2001	−.20	.175	−.375	.140625
2002	.50	.175	.325	.105625
2003	.30	.175	.125	.015625
2004	.10	.175	−.075	.005625
Totals	.70		.000	.267500

Because there are four years of returns, we calculate the variance by dividing .2675 by (4 − 1) = 3:

	Supertech	Hyperdrive
Variance (σ^2)	.2675/3 = .0892	.0529/3 = .0176
Standard deviation (σ)	$\sqrt{.0892}$ = .2987	$\sqrt{.0176}$ = .1327

continued

For practice, verify that you get the same answer as we do for Hyperdrive. Notice that the standard deviation for Supertech, 29.87 percent, is a little more than twice Hyperdrive's 13.27 percent; Supertech is thus the more volatile investment.

The Historical Record

Figure 12.10 summarizes much of our discussion of capital market history so far. It displays average returns, standard deviations, and frequency distributions of annual returns on a common scale. In Figure 12.10, for example, notice that the standard deviation for the small-stock portfolio (33.3 percent per year) is more than 10 times larger than the T-bill portfolio's standard deviation (3.1 percent per year). We will return to these figures momentarily.

Normal Distribution

For many different random events in nature, a particular frequency distribution, the **normal distribution** (or *bell curve*), is useful for describing the probability of ending up in a given range. For example, the idea behind "grading on a curve" comes from the fact that exam score distributions often resemble a bell curve.

normal distribution
A symmetric, bell-shaped frequency distribution that is completely defined by its mean and standard deviation.

WORK THE WEB

Standard deviations are widely reported for mutual funds. For example, the Fidelity Magellan fund was the second largest mutual fund in the United States at the time this was written. How volatile is it? To find out, we went to www.morningstar.com, entered the ticker symbol FMAGX, and the "Risk Measures" link. Here is what we found:

Fidelity Magellan FMAGX See Fund Family Data ▸▸

Volatility Measurements	Trailing 3-Yr through 04-30-04	*Trailing 5-Yr through 04-30-04	
Standard Deviation	15.90	Sharpe Ratio	-0.37
Mean	-2.84	Bear Market Decile Rank*	8

Modern Portfolio Theory Statistics		Trailing 3-Yr through 04-30-04
	Standard Index S&P 500	**Best Fit Index** Standard & Poor's 500
R-Squared	99	99
Beta	0.99	0.99
Alpha	-1.84	-1.84

The standard deviation for the Fidelity Magellan Fund is 15.90 percent. When you consider that the average stock has a standard deviation of about 50 percent, this seems like a low number. The reason for the low standard deviation has to do with the power of diversification, a topic we discuss in the next chapter. The mean is the average return, so over the last three years, investors in the Magellan Fund lost 2.84 percent per year. Also, under the Volatility Measurements section, you will see the Sharpe ratio. The Sharpe ratio is calculated as the risk premium of the asset divided by the standard deviation. As such, it is a measure of return relative to the level of risk taken (as measured by standard deviation). The "beta" for the Fidelity Magellan Fund is 0.99. We will have more to say about this number—lots more—in the next chapter.

FIGURE 12.10 >>

Historical Returns, Standard Deviations, and Frequency Distributions: 1926–2003

Series	Average Annual Return	Standard Deviation
Large-Company Stocks	12.4%	20.4%
Small-Company Stocks	17.5	33.3
Long-Term Corporate Bonds	6.2	8.6
Long-Term Government	5.8	9.4
Intermediate-Term Government	5.5	5.7
U.S. Treasury Bills	3.8	3.1
Inflation	3.1	4.3

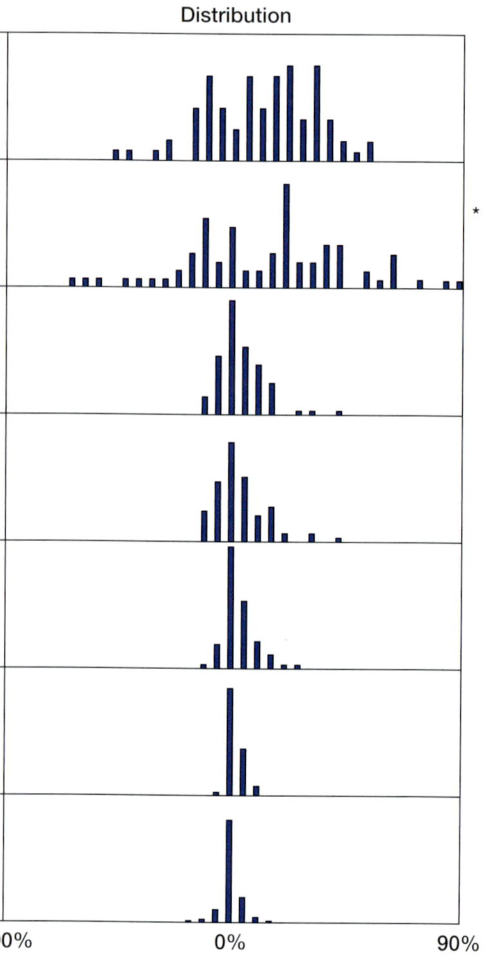

*The 1933 Small-Company Stocks Total Return was 142.9 percent.

SOURCE: © *Stocks, Bonds, Bills, and Inflation 2004 Yearbook*™, Ibbotson Associates, Inc., Chicago (annually updates work by Roger G. Ibbotson and Rex A. Sinquefield). All rights reserved.

Figure 12.11 illustrates a normal distribution and its distinctive bell shape. As you can see, this distribution has a much cleaner appearance than the actual return distributions illustrated in Figure 12.10. Even so, like the normal distribution, the actual distributions do appear to be at least roughly mound shaped and symmetric. When this is true, the normal distribution is often a very good approximation.

Also, keep in mind that the distributions in Figure 12.10 are based on only 78 yearly observations, whereas Figure 12.11 is, in principle, based on an infinite number. So, if we had been able to observe returns for, say, 1,000 years, we might have filled in a lot of the irregularities and ended up with a much smoother picture in Figure 12.10. For our purposes, it is enough to observe that the returns are at least roughly normally distributed.

The usefulness of the normal distribution stems from the fact that it is completely described by the average and the standard deviation. If you have these two numbers, then there is nothing else to know. For example, with a normal distribution, the probability that we will end up within one standard deviation of the average is about 2/3. The probability

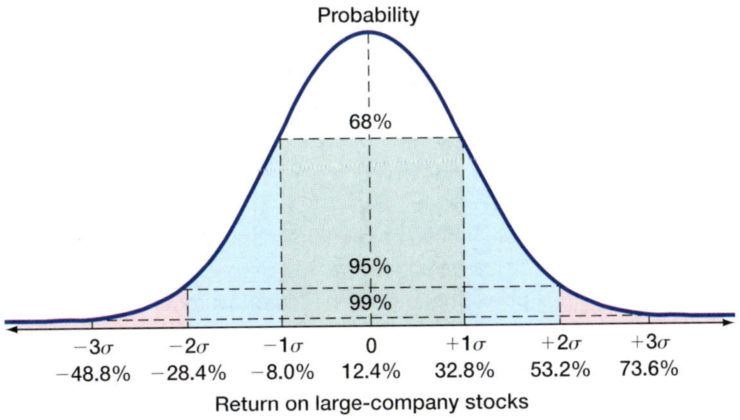

<< FIGURE 12.11

The Normal Distribution. Illustrated returns are based on the historical return and standard deviation for a portfolio of large-firm common stocks.

that we will end up within two standard deviations is about 95 percent. Finally, the probability of being more than three standard deviations away from the average is less than 1 percent. These ranges and the probabilities are illustrated in Figure 12.11.

To see why this is useful, recall from Figure 12.10 that the standard deviation of returns on the large-company stocks is 20.4 percent. The average return is 12.4 percent. So, assuming that the frequency distribution is at least approximately normal, the probability that the return in a given year is in the range of −8.0 to 32.8 percent (12.4 percent plus or minus one standard deviation, 20.4 percent) is about 2/3. This range is illustrated in Figure 12.11. In other words, there is about one chance in three that the return will be *outside* this range. This literally tells you that, if you buy stocks in large companies, you should expect to be outside this range in one year out of every three. This reinforces our earlier observations about stock market volatility. However, there is only a 5 percent chance (approximately) that we would end up outside the range of −28.4 to 53.2 percent (12.4 percent plus or minus $2 \times 20.4\%$). These points are also illustrated in Figure 12.11.

The Second Lesson

Our observations concerning the year-to-year variability in returns are the basis for our second lesson from capital market history. On average, bearing risk is handsomely rewarded, but in a given year, there is a significant chance of a dramatic change in value. Thus, our second lesson is this: the greater the potential reward, the greater is the risk.

Using Capital Market History

Based on the discussion in this section, you should begin to have an idea of the risks and rewards from investing. For example, in mid-2004, Treasury bills were paying about 1.4 percent. Suppose we had an investment that we thought had about the same risk as a portfolio of large-firm common stocks. At a minimum, what return would this investment have to offer for us to be interested?

From Table 12.3, we see that the risk premium on large-company stocks has been 8.6 percent historically, so a reasonable estimate of our required return would be this premium plus the T-bill rate, $1.4\% + 8.6\% = 10\%$. This may strike you as being high, but, if we were thinking of starting a new business, then the risks of doing so might resemble those of investing in small-company stocks. In this case, the historical risk premium is 13.7 percent, so we might require as much as 15.1 percent from such an investment at a minimum.

We will discuss the relationship between risk and required return in more detail in the next chapter. For now, you should notice that a projected internal rate of return, or IRR, on a risky investment in the 10 to 20 percent range isn't particularly outstanding. It depends on how much risk there is. This, too, is an important lesson from capital market history.

EXAMPLE 12.3 >> Investing in Growth Stocks

The term *growth stock* is frequently used as a euphemism for small-company stock. Are such investments suitable for "widows and orphans"? Before answering, you should consider the historical volatility. For example, from the historical record, what is the approximate probability that you will actually lose more than 16 percent of your money in a single year if you buy a portfolio of stocks of such companies?

Looking back at Figure 12.10, we see that the average return on small-company stocks is 17.5 percent and the standard deviation is 33.3 percent. Assuming the returns are approximately normal, there is about a 1/3 probability that you will experience a return outside the range of −15.8 to 50.8 percent (17.5% ± 33.3%).

Because the normal distribution is symmetric, the odds of being above or below this range are equal. There is thus a 1/6 chance (half of 1/3) that you will lose more than 15.8 percent. So you should expect this to happen once in every six years, on average. Such investments can thus be *very* volatile, and they are not well suited for those who cannot afford the risk.

Concept Questions

12.4a In words, how do we calculate a variance? A standard deviation?

12.4b With a normal distribution, what is the probability of ending up more than one standard deviation below the average?

12.4c Assuming that long-term corporate bonds have an approximately normal distribution, what is the approximate probability of earning 14.7 percent or more in a given year? With T-bills, roughly what is this probability?

12.4d What is the second lesson from capital market history?

12.5 MORE ON AVERAGE RETURNS

Thus far in this chapter, we have looked closely at simple average returns. But there is another way of computing an average return. The fact that average returns are calculated two different ways leads to some confusion, so our goal in this section is to explain the two approaches and also the circumstances under which each is appropriate.

Arithmetic versus Geometric Averages

Let's start with a simple example. Suppose you buy a particular stock for $100. Unfortunately, the first year you own it, it falls to $50. The second year you own it, it rises back to $100, leaving you where you started (no dividends were paid).

What was your average return on this investment? Common sense seems to say that your average return must be exactly zero since you started with $100 and ended with $100. But if we calculate the returns year-by-year, we see that you lost 50 percent the first year (you lost half of your money). The second year, you made 100 percent (you doubled your money). Your average return over the two years was thus (−50% + 100%)/2 = 25%!

So which is correct, 0 percent or 25 percent? The answer is that both are correct: They just answer different questions. The 0 percent is called the **geometric average return**. The 25 percent is called the **arithmetic average return**. The geometric average return answers the question *"What was your average compound return per year over a particular period?"* The arithmetic average return answers the question *"What was your return in an average year over a particular period?"*

geometric average return
The average compound return earned per year over a multiyear period.

arithmetic average return
The return earned in an average year over a multiyear period.

Notice that, in previous sections, the average returns we calculated were all arithmetic averages, so we already know how to calculate them. What we need to do now is (1) learn how to calculate geometric averages and (2) learn the circumstances under which one average is more meaningful than the other.

Calculating Geometric Average Returns

First, to illustrate how we calculate a geometric average return, suppose a particular investment had annual returns of 10 percent, 12 percent, 3 percent, and −9 percent over the last four years. The geometric average return over this four-year period is calculated as $(1.10 \times 1.12 \times 1.03 \times .91)^{1/4} - 1 = 3.66\%$. In contrast, the average arithmetic return we have been calculating is $(.10 + .12 + .03 - .09)/4 = 4.0\%$.

In general, if we have T years of returns, the geometric average return over these T years is calculated using this formula:

$$\text{Geometric average return} = [(1 + R_1) \times (1 + R_2) \times \cdots \times (1 + R_T)]^{1/T} - 1 \qquad [12.4]$$

This formula tells us that four steps are required:

1. Take each of the T annual returns $R_1, R_2, \ldots, R_T$ and add a one to each (after converting them to decimals!).
2. Multiply all the numbers from step 1 together.
3. Take the result from step 2 and raise it to the power of $1/T$.
4. Finally, subtract one from the result of step 3. The result is the geometric average return.

Calculating the Geometric Average Return

<< **EXAMPLE 12.4**

Calculate the geometric average return for S&P 500 large-cap stocks for the first five years in Table 12.1, 1926–1930.

First, convert percentages to decimal returns, add one, and then calculate their product:

S&P 500 Returns	Product
13.75	1.1375
35.70	×1.3570
45.08	×1.4508
−8.80	×0.9120
−25.13	×0.7487
	1.5291

Notice that the number 1.5291 is what our investment is worth after five years if we started with a one dollar investment. The geometric average return is then calculated as

$$\text{Geometric average return} = 1.5291^{1/5} - 1 = 0.0887, \text{ or } 8.87\%$$

Thus the geometric average return is about 8.87 percent in this example. Here is a tip: If you are using a financial calculator, you can put $1 in as the present value, $1.5291 as the future value, and 5 as the number of periods. Then, solve for the unknown rate. You should get the same answer we did.

TABLE 12.4 >>

Geometric versus Arithmetic Average Returns: 1926–2003

Series	Average Return: Geometric	Average Return: Arithmetic	Standard Deviation
Large-company stocks	10.4%	12.4%	20.4%
Small-company stocks	12.7	17.5	33.3
Long-term corporate bonds	5.9	6.2	8.6
Long-term government bonds	5.4	5.8	9.4
Intermediate-term government bonds	5.4	5.5	5.7
U.S. Treasury bills	3.7	3.8	3.1
Inflation	3.0	3.1	4.3

One thing you may have noticed in our examples thus far is that the geometric average returns seem to be smaller. It turns out that this will always be true (as long as the returns are not all identical, in which case the two "averages" would be the same). To illustrate, Table 12.4 shows the arithmetic averages and standard deviations from Figure 12.10, along with the geometric average returns.

As shown in Table 12.4, the geometric averages are all smaller, but the magnitude of the difference varies quite a bit. The reason is that the difference is greater for more volatile investments. In fact, there is useful approximation. Assuming all the numbers are expressed in decimals (as opposed to percentages), the geometric average return is approximately equal to the arithmetic average return minus half the variance. For example, looking at the large-company stocks, the arithmetic average is .124 and the standard deviation is .204, implying that the variance is .041616. The approximate geometric average is thus $.124 - .041616/2 = .1032$, which is quite close to the actual value.

EXAMPLE 12.5 >> More Geometric Averages

Take a look back at Figure 12.4. There, we showed the value of a $1 investment after 78 years. Use the value for the large-company stock investment to check the geometric average in Table 12.4.

In Figure 12.4, the large-company investment grew to $2,284.79 over 78 years. The geometric average return is thus

$$\text{Geometric average return} = 2{,}284.79^{1/78} - 1 = .1042, \text{ or } 10.4\%$$

This 10.4% is the value shown in Table 12.4. For practice, check some of the other numbers in Table 12.4 the same way.

Arithmetic Average Return or Geometric Average Return?

When we look at historical returns, the difference between the geometric and arithmetic average returns isn't too hard to understand. To put it slightly differently, the geometric average tells you what you actually earned per year on average, compounded annually. The arithmetic average tells you what you earned in a typical year. You should use whichever one answers the question you want answered.

A somewhat trickier question concerns which average return to use when forecasting future wealth levels, and there's a lot of confusion on this point among analysts and financial planners. First, let's get one thing straight: If you *know* the true arithmetic average return, then this is what you should use in your forecast. So, for example, if you know the arithmetic return is 10 percent, then your best guess of the value of a $1,000 investment in 10 years is the future value of $1,000 at 10 percent for 10 years, or $2,593.74.

The problem we face, however, is that we usually only have *estimates* of the arithmetic and geometric returns, and estimates have errors. In this case, the arithmetic average return is probably too high for longer periods and the geometric average is probably too low for shorter periods. So, you should regard long-run projected wealth levels calculated using arithmetic averages as optimistic. Short-run projected wealth levels calculated using geometric averages are probably pessimistic.

As a practical matter, if you are using averages calculated over a long period of time (such as the 78 years we use) to forecast up to a decade or so into the future, then you should use the arithmetic average. If you are forecasting a few decades into the future (such as you might do for retirement planning), then you should just split the difference between the arithmetic and geometric average returns. Finally, if for some reason you are doing very long forecasts covering many decades, use the geometric average.

This concludes our discussion of geometric versus arithmetic averages. One last note: In the future, when we say "average return," we mean arithmetic unless we explicitly say otherwise.

Concept Questions

12.5a If you wanted to forecast what the stock market is going to do over the next year, should you use an arithmetic or geometric average?

12.5b If you wanted to forecast what the stock market is going to do over the next century, should you use an arithmetic or geometric average?

CAPITAL MARKET EFFICIENCY 12.6

Capital market history suggests that the market values of stocks and bonds can fluctuate widely from year to year. Why does this occur? At least part of the answer is that prices change because new information arrives, and investors reassess asset values based on that information.

The behavior of market prices has been extensively studied. A question that has received particular attention is whether prices adjust quickly and correctly when new information arrives. A market is said to be "efficient" if this is the case. To be more precise, in an **efficient capital market**, current market prices fully reflect available information. By this we simply mean that, based on available information, there is no reason to believe that the current price is too low or too high.

efficient capital market
A market in which security prices reflect available information.

The concept of market efficiency is a rich one, and much has been written about it. A full discussion of the subject goes beyond the scope of our study of corporate finance. However, because the concept figures so prominently in studies of market history, we briefly describe the key points here.

Price Behavior in an Efficient Market

To illustrate how prices behave in an efficient market, suppose the F-Stop Camera Corporation (FCC) has, through years of secret research and development, developed a camera with an autofocusing system whose speed will double that of the autofocusing systems now available. FCC's capital budgeting analysis suggests that launching the new camera will be a highly profitable move; in other words, the NPV appears to be positive and substantial.

The key assumption thus far is that FCC has not released any information about the new system; so, the fact of its existence is "inside" information only.

Now consider a share of stock in FCC. In an efficient market, its price reflects what is known about FCC's current operations and profitability, and it reflects market opinion about FCC's potential for future growth and profits. The value of the new autofocusing system is not reflected, however, because the market is unaware of the system's existence.

If the market agrees with FCC's assessment of the value of the new project, FCC's stock price will rise when the decision to launch is made public. For example, assume the announcement is made in a press release on Wednesday morning. In an efficient market, the price of shares in FCC will adjust quickly to this new information. Investors should not be able to buy the stock on Wednesday afternoon and make a profit on Thursday. This would imply that it took the stock market a full day to realize the implication of the FCC press release. If the market is efficient, the price of shares of FCC stock on Wednesday afternoon will already reflect the information contained in the Wednesday morning press release.

Figure 12.12 presents three possible stock price adjustments for FCC. In Figure 12.12, Day 0 represents the announcement day. As illustrated, before the announcement, FCC's stock sells for $140 per share. The NPV per share of the new system is, say, $40, so the new price will be $180 once the value of the new project is fully reflected.

The solid line in Figure 12.12 represents the path taken by the stock price in an efficient market. In this case, the price adjusts immediately to the new information and no further changes in the price of the stock take place. The broken line in Figure 12.12 depicts a delayed reaction. Here it takes the market eight days or so to fully absorb the information. Finally, the dotted line illustrates an overreaction and subsequent adjustment to the correct price.

The broken line and the dotted line in Figure 12.12 illustrate paths that the stock price might take in an inefficient market. If, for example, stock prices don't adjust immediately to new information (the broken line), then buying stock immediately following the release

FIGURE 12.12 >>

Reaction of Stock Price to New Information in Efficient and Inefficient Markets

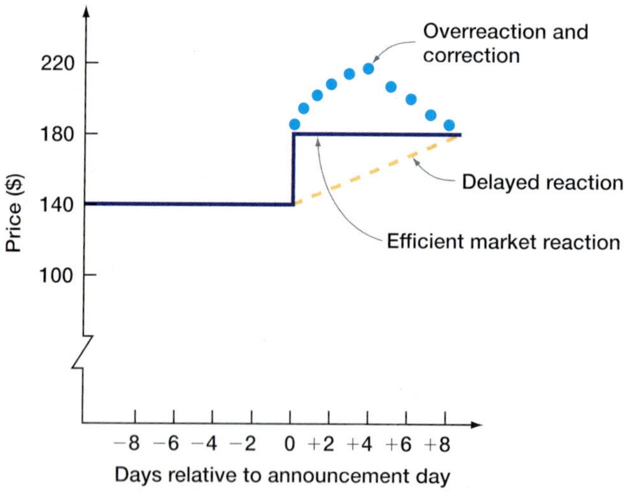

Efficient market reaction: The price instantaneously adjusts to and fully reflects new information; there is no tendency for subsequent increases and decreases to occur.
Delayed reaction: The price partially adjusts to the new information; 8 days elapse before the price completely reflects the new information.
Overreaction: The price overadjusts to the new information; it overshoots the new price and subsequently corrects.

of new information and then selling it several days later would be a positive NPV activity because the price is too low for several days after the announcement.

The Efficient Markets Hypothesis

efficient markets hypothesis (EMH)
The hypothesis that actual capital markets, such as the NYSE, are efficient.

The **efficient markets hypothesis (EMH)** asserts that well-organized capital markets, such as the NYSE, are efficient markets, at least as a practical matter. In other words, an advocate of the EMH might argue that although inefficiencies may exist, they are relatively small and not common.

If a market is efficient, then there is a very important implication for market participants: All investments in that market are *zero* NPV investments. The reason is not complicated. If prices are neither too low nor too high, then the difference between the market value of an investment and its cost is zero; hence, the NPV is zero. As a result, in an efficient market, investors get exactly what they pay for when they buy securities, and firms receive exactly what their stocks and bonds are worth when they sell them.

Look under the "contents" link at www.investorhome.com for more info on the EMH.

What makes a market efficient is competition among investors. Many individuals spend their entire lives trying to find mispriced stocks. For any given stock, they study what has happened in the past to the stock price and the stock's dividends. They learn, to the extent possible, what a company's earnings have been, how much the company owes to creditors, what taxes it pays, what businesses it is in, what new investments are planned, how sensitive it is to changes in the economy, and so on.

Not only is there a great deal to know about any particular company, but there is also a powerful incentive for knowing it, namely, the profit motive. If you know more about some company than other investors in the marketplace, you can profit from that knowledge by investing in the company's stock if you have good news and by selling it if you have bad news.

The logical consequence of all this information gathering and analysis is that mispriced stocks will become fewer and fewer. In other words, because of competition among investors, the market will become increasingly efficient. A kind of equilibrium comes into being with which there is just enough mispricing around for those who are best at identifying it to make a living at it. For most other investors, the activity of information gathering and analysis will not pay.[4]

Some Common Misconceptions about the EMH

No other idea in finance has attracted as much attention as that of efficient markets, and not all of the attention has been flattering. Rather than rehash the arguments here, we will be content to observe that some markets are more efficient than others. For example, financial markets on the whole are probably much more efficient than real asset markets.

Having said this, however, we can also say that much of the criticism of the EMH is misguided because it is based on a misunderstanding of what the hypothesis says and what it doesn't say. For example, when the notion of market efficiency was first publicized and debated in the popular financial press, it was often characterized by words to the effect that "throwing darts at the financial page will produce a portfolio that can be expected to do as well as any managed by professional security analysts."[5]

---

[4] The idea behind the EMH can be illustrated by the following short story: A student was walking down the hall with her finance professor when they both saw a $20 bill on the ground. As the student bent down to pick it up, the professor shook his head slowly and, with a look of disappointment on his face, said patiently to the student, "Don't bother. If it were really there, someone else would have picked it up already." The moral of the story reflects the logic of the efficient markets hypothesis: If you think you have found a pattern in stock prices or a simple device for picking winners, you probably have not.

[5] B. G. Malkiel, *A Random Walk Down Wall Street,* (revised and updated ed.) (New York: Norton, 2003).

IN THEIR OWN WORDS . . .

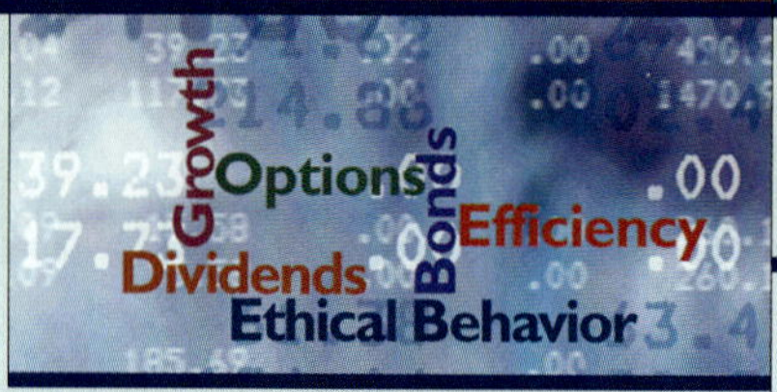

Richard Roll on Market Efficiency

>> **The concept of** an efficient market is a special application of the "no free lunch" principle. In an efficient financial market, costless trading policies will not generate "excess" returns. After adjusting for the riskiness of the policy, the trader's return will be no larger than the return of a randomly selected portfolio, at least on average.

This is often thought to imply something about the amount of "information" reflected in asset prices. However, it really doesn't mean that prices reflect all information nor even that they reflect publicly available information. Instead, it means that the connection between unreflected information and prices is too subtle and tenuous to be easily or costlessly detected.

Relevant information is difficult and expensive to uncover and evaluate. Thus, if costless trading policies are ineffective, there must exist some traders who make a living by "beating the market." They cover their costs (including the opportunity cost of their time) by trading. The existence of such traders is actually a necessary precondition for markets to become efficient. Without such professional traders, prices would fail to reflect everything that is cheap and easy to evaluate.

Efficient market prices should approximate a random walk, meaning that they will appear to fluctuate more or less randomly. Prices can fluctuate nonrandomly to the extent that their departure from randomness is expensive to discern. Also, observed price series can depart from apparent randomness due to changes in preferences and expectations, but this is really a technicality and does not imply a free lunch relative to current investor sentiments.

Richard Roll is Allstate Professor of Finance at UCLA. He is a preeminent financial researcher, and he has written extensively in almost every area of modern finance. He is particularly well known for his insightful analyses and great creativity in understanding empirical phenomena.

Confusion over statements of this sort has often led to a failure to understand the implications of market efficiency. For example, sometimes it is wrongly argued that market efficiency means that it doesn't matter how you invest your money because the efficiency of the market will protect you from making a mistake. However, a random dart thrower might wind up with all of the darts sticking into one or two high-risk stocks that deal in genetic engineering. Would you really want all of your money in two such stocks?

A contest run by *The Wall Street Journal* provides a good example of the controversy surrounding market efficiency. Each month, the *Journal* asked four professional money managers to pick one stock each. At the same time, it threw four darts at the stock page to select a comparison group. In the 147 five-and one-half month contests from July 1990 to September 2002, the pros won 90 times. When the returns on the portfolios are compared to the Dow Jones Industrial Average, the score is 80 to 67 in favor of the pros.

The fact that the pros are ahead of the darts by 90 to 57 suggests that markets are not efficient. Or does it? One problem is that the darts naturally tend to select stocks of average risk. The pros, however, are playing to win and naturally select riskier stocks, or so it is argued. If this is true, then, on average, we *expect* the pros to win. Furthermore, the pros' picks are announced to the public at the start. This publicity may boost the prices of the shares involved somewhat, leading to a partially self-fulfilling prophecy. Unfortunately, the *Journal* discontinued the contest in 2002, so this test of market efficiency is no longer ongoing.

More than anything else, what efficiency implies is that the price a firm will obtain when it sells a share of its stock is a "fair" price in the sense that it reflects the value of that stock given the information available about the firm. Shareholders do not have to worry that they are paying too much for a stock with a low dividend or some other sort of characteristic because the market has already incorporated that characteristic into the price. We sometimes say that the information has been "priced out."

The concept of efficient markets can be explained further by replying to a frequent objection. It is sometimes argued that the market cannot be efficient because stock prices fluctuate from day to day. If the prices are right, the argument goes, then why do they change so much and so often? From our discussion of the market, we can see that these price movements are in no way inconsistent with efficiency. Investors are bombarded with information every day. The fact that prices fluctuate is, at least in part, a reflection of that information flow. In fact, the absence of price movements in a world that changes as rapidly as ours would suggest inefficiency.

The Forms of Market Efficiency

It is common to distinguish between three forms of market efficiency. Depending on the degree of efficiency, we say that markets are either *weak form efficient, semistrong form efficient,* or *strong form efficient.* The difference between these forms relates to what information is reflected in prices.

We start with the extreme case. If the market is strong form efficient, then *all* information of *every* kind is reflected in stock prices. In such a market, there is no such thing as inside information. Therefore, in our FCC example, we apparently were assuming that the market was not strong form efficient.

Casual observation, particularly in recent years, suggests that inside information does exist and it can be valuable to possess. Whether it is lawful or ethical to use that information is another issue. In any event, we conclude that private information about a particular stock may exist that is not currently reflected in the price of the stock. For example, prior knowledge of a takeover attempt could be very valuable.

The second form of efficiency, semistrong form efficiency, is the most controversial. If a market is semistrong form efficient, then all *public* information is reflected in the stock price. The reason this form is controversial is that it implies that a security analyst who tries to identify mispriced stocks using, for example, financial statement information is wasting time because that information is already reflected in the current price.

The third form of efficiency, weak form efficiency, suggests that, at a minimum, the current price of a stock reflects the stock's own past prices. In other words, studying past prices in an attempt to identify mispriced securities is futile if the market is weak form efficient. Although this form of efficiency might seem rather mild, it implies that searching for patterns in historical prices that will be useful in identifying mispriced stocks will not work (this practice is quite common).

What does capital market history say about market efficiency? Here again, there is great controversy. At the risk of going out on a limb, we can say that the evidence does seem to tell us three things. First, prices do appear to respond very rapidly to new information, and the response is at least not grossly different from what we would expect in an efficient market. Second, the future of market prices, particularly in the short run, is very difficult to predict based on publicly available information. Third, if mispriced stocks do exist, then there is no obvious means of identifying them. Put another way, simpleminded schemes based on public information will probably not be successful.

Concept Questions

12.6a What is an efficient market?

12.6b What are the forms of market efficiency?

12.7 SUMMARY AND CONCLUSIONS

This chapter has explored the subject of capital market history. Such history is useful because it tells us what to expect in the way of returns from risky assets. We summed up our study of market history with two key lessons:

1. Risky assets, on average, earn a risk premium. There is a reward for bearing risk.
2. The greater the potential reward from a risky investment, the greater is the risk.

These lessons have significant implications for the financial manager. We will be considering these implications in the chapters ahead.

We also discussed the concept of market efficiency. In an efficient market, prices adjust quickly and correctly to new information. Consequently, asset prices in efficient markets are rarely too high or too low. How efficient capital markets (such as the NYSE) are is a matter of debate, but, at a minimum, they are probably much more efficient than most real asset markets.

Visit us at www.mhhe.com/rwj

Chapter Review and Self-Test Problems

12.1 Recent Return History Use Table 12.1 to calculate the average return over the years 1996 through 2000 for large-company stocks, long-term government bonds, and Treasury bills.

12.2 More Recent Return History Calculate the standard deviation for each security type using information from Problem 12.1. Which of the investments was the most volatile over this period?

Answers to Chapter Review and Self-Test Problems

12.1 We calculate the averages as follows:

Actual Returns			
Year	**Large-Company Stocks**	**Long-Term Government Bonds**	**Treasury Bills**
1996	0.2296	0.0013	0.0514
1997	0.3336	0.1202	0.0519
1998	0.2858	0.1445	0.0486
1999	0.2104	−0.0751	0.0480
2000	−0.0910	0.1722	0.0598
Average	0.1937	0.0726	0.0519

12.2 We first need to calculate the deviations from the average returns. Using the averages from Problem 12.1, we get:

Deviations from Average Returns			
Year	**Large-Company Stocks**	**Long-Term Government Bonds**	**Treasury Bills**
1996	0.0359	−0.0713	−0.0005
1997	0.1400	0.0476	0.0000
1998	0.0921	0.0719	−0.0033
1999	0.0167	−0.1477	−0.0039
2000	−0.2847	0.0996	0.0079
Total	0.0000	0.0000	0.0000

We square these deviations and calculate the variances and standard deviations:

Squared Deviations from Average Returns			
Year	**Large-Company Stocks**	**Long-Term Government Bonds**	**Treasury Bills**
1996	0.0012906	0.0050865	0.0000003
1997	0.0195872	0.0022639	0.0000000
1998	0.0084837	0.0051667	0.0000112
1999	0.0002801	0.0218212	0.0000155
2000	0.0810670	0.0099162	0.0000618
Variance	0.0276771	0.0110636	0.0000222
Std dev	0.1663645	0.1051838	0.0047104

To calculate the variances, we added up the squared deviations and divided by 4, the number of returns less 1. Notice that the stocks had much more volatility than the bonds with a much larger average return. For large company stocks, this was a particularly good period; the average return was 19.37 percent.

Concepts Review and Critical Thinking Questions

1. **Investment Selection** Given that Millcom International Cellular was up by over 1,200 percent for 2003, why didn't all investors hold Millcom International Cellular?
2. **Investment Selection** Given that Turnstone Systems was down by almost 96 percent for 2003, why did some investors hold the stock? Why didn't they sell out before the price declined so sharply?
3. **Risk and Return** We have seen that, over long periods of time, stock investments have tended to substantially outperform bond investments. However, it is not at all uncommon to observe investors with long horizons holding entirely bonds. Are such investors irrational?
4. **Market Efficiency Implications** Explain why a characteristic of an efficient market is that investments in that market have zero NPVs.
5. **Efficient Markets Hypothesis** A stock market analyst is able to identify mispriced stocks by comparing the average price for the last 10 days to the average price for the last 60 days. If this is true, what do you know about the market?

6. **Semistrong Efficiency** If a market is semistrong form efficient, is it also weak form efficient? Explain.
7. **Efficient Markets Hypothesis** What are the implications of the efficient markets hypothesis for investors who buy and sell stocks in an attempt to "beat the market"?
8. **Stocks versus Gambling** Critically evaluate the following statement: Playing the stock market is like gambling. Such speculative investing has no social value, other than the pleasure people get from this form of gambling.
9. **Efficient Markets Hypothesis** There are several celebrated investors and stock pickers frequently mentioned in the financial press who have recorded huge returns on their investments over the past two decades. Is the success of these particular investors an invalidation of the EMH? Explain.
10. **Efficient Markets Hypothesis** For each of the following scenarios, discuss whether profit opportunities exist from trading in the stock of the firm under the conditions that (1) the market is not weak form efficient, (2) the market is weak form but not semistrong form efficient, (3) the market is semistrong form but not strong form efficient, and (4) the market is strong form efficient.
    a. The stock price has risen steadily each day for the past 30 days.
    b. The financial statements for a company were released three days ago, and you believe you've uncovered some anomalies in the company's inventory and cost control reporting techniques that are causing the firm's true liquidity strength to be understated.
    c. You observe that the senior management of a company has been buying a lot of the company's stock on the open market over the past week.

Questions and Problems

BASIC
(Questions 1–12)

1. **Calculating Returns** Suppose a stock had an initial price of $64 per share, paid a dividend of $1.75 per share during the year, and had an ending share price of $72. Compute the percentage total return.
2. **Calculating Yields** In Problem 1, what was the dividend yield? The capital gains yield?
3. **Return Calculations** Rework Problems 1 and 2 assuming the ending share price is $55.
4. **Calculating Returns** Suppose you bought a 9 percent coupon bond one year ago for $1,050. The bond sells for $1,080 today.
    a. Assuming a $1,000 face value, what was your total dollar return on this investment over the past year?
    b. What was your total nominal rate of return on this investment over the past year?
    c. If the inflation rate last year was 4 percent, what was your total real rate of return on this investment?
5. **Nominal versus Real Returns** What was the average annual return on large-company stock from 1926 through 2003:
    a. In nominal terms?
    b. In real terms?
6. **Bond Returns** What is the historical real return on long-term government bonds? On long-term corporate bonds?

7. **Calculating Returns and Variability** Using the following returns, calculate the arithmetic average returns, the variances, and the standard deviations for X and Y.

	Returns	
Year	**X**	**Y**
1	14%	29%
2	20	− 7
3	− 9	−12
4	3	56
5	17	8

8. **Risk Premiums** Refer to Table 12.1 in the text and look at the period from 1970 through 1975.
   - **a.** Calculate the arithmetic average returns for large-company stocks and T-bills over this time period.
   - **b.** Calculate the standard deviation of the returns for large-company stocks and T-bills over this time period.
   - **c.** Calculate the observed risk premium in each year for the large-company stocks versus the T-bills. What was the average risk premium over this period? What was the standard deviation of the risk premium over this period?
   - **d.** Is it possible for the risk premium to be negative before an investment is undertaken? Can the risk premium be negative after the fact? Explain.
9. **Calculating Returns and Variability** You've observed the following returns on Crash-n-Burn Computer's stock over the past five years: 9 percent, −12 percent, 16 percent, 38 percent, and 11 percent.
   - **a.** What was the arithmetic average return on Crash-n-Burn's stock over this five-year period?
   - **b.** What was the variance of Crash-n-Burn's returns over this period? The standard deviation?
10. **Calculating Real Returns and Risk Premiums** For Problem 9, suppose the average inflation rate over this period was 3.5 percent and the average T-bill rate over the period was 4.2 percent.
    - **a.** What was the average real return on Crash-n-Burn's stock?
    - **b.** What was the average nominal risk premium on Crash-n-Burn's stock?
11. **Calculating Real Rates** Given the information in Problem 10, what was the average real risk-free rate over this time period? What was the average real risk premium?
12. **Effects of Inflation** Look at Table 12.1 and Figure 12.7 in the text. When were T-bill rates at their highest over the period from 1926 through 2003? Why do you think they were so high during this period? What relationship underlies your answer?

INTERMEDIATE
(Questions 13–19)

13. **Calculating Investment Returns** You bought one of Great White Shark Repellant Co.'s 8 percent coupon bonds one year ago for $980. These bonds make annual payments and mature six years from now. Suppose you decide to sell your bonds today, when the required return on the bonds is 9 percent. If the inflation rate was 4.2 percent over the past year, what was your total real return on investment?
14. **Calculating Returns and Variability** You find a certain stock that had returns of 8 percent, −13 percent, −7 percent, and 29 percent for four of the last five years.

If the average return of the stock over this period was 11 percent, what was the stock's return for the missing year? What is the standard deviation of the stock's return?

15. Arithmetic and Geometric Returns A stock has had returns of 29 percent, 14 percent, 23 percent, −8 percent, 9 percent, and −14 percent over the last six years. What are the arithmetic and geometric returns for the stock?

16. Arithmetic and Geometric Returns A stock has had the following year-end prices and dividends:

Year	Price	Dividend
1	$43.12	—
2	49.07	$0.55
3	51.19	0.60
4	47.24	0.63
5	56.09	0.72
6	67.21	0.81

What are the arithmetic and geometric returns for the stock?

17. Using Return Distributions Suppose the returns on long-term government bonds are normally distributed. Based on the historical record, what is the approximate probability that your return on these bonds will be less than −3.6 percent in a given year? What range of returns would you expect to see 95 percent of the time? What range would you expect to see 99 percent of the time?

18. Using Return Distributions Assuming that the returns from holding small-company stocks are normally distributed, what is the approximate probability that your money will double in value in a single year? What about triple in value?

19. Distributions In Problem 18, what is the probability that the return is less than −100 percent (think)? What are the implications for the distribution of returns?

CHALLENGE
(Questions 20–21)

20. Using Probability Distributions Suppose the returns on large-company stocks are normally distributed. Based on the historical record, use the cumulative normal probability table (rounded to the nearest table value) in the appendix of the text to determine the probability that in any given year you will lose money by investing in common stock.

21. Using Probability Distributions Suppose the returns on long-term corporate bonds and T-bills are normally distributed. Based on the historical record, use the cumulative normal probability table (rounded to the nearest table value) in the appendix of the text to answer the following questions:

a. What is the probability that in any given year, the return on long-term corporate bonds will be greater than 10 percent? Less than 0 percent?

b. What is the probability that in any given year, the return on T-bills will be greater than 10 percent? Less than 0 percent?

c. In 1979, the return on long-term corporate bonds was −4.18 percent. How likely is it that this low of a return will recur at some point in the future? T-bills had a return of 10.32 percent in this same year. How likely is it that this high of a return on T-bills will recur at some point in the future?

S&P Problems

1. **Calculating Yields** Download the historical stock prices for Duke Energy (DUK) under the "Mthly. Adj. Prices" link. Find the closing stock price for the beginning and end of the prior two years. Now use the annual financial statements to find the dividend for each of these years. What was the capital gains yield and dividend yield for Duke Energy stock for each of these years? Now calculate the capital gains yield and dividend for Tommy Hilfiger (TOM). How do the returns for these two companies compare?
2. **Calculating Average Returns** Download the Monthly Adjusted Prices for Microsoft (MSFT). What is the return on the stock over the past 12 months? Now use the 1 Month Total Return and calculate the average monthly return. Is this one-twelfth of the annual return you calculated? Why or why not? What is the monthly standard deviation of Microsoft's stock over the past year?

What's On the Web?

12.1 Market Risk Premium You want to find the current market risk premium. Go to money.cnn.com, follow the "Bonds & Rates" link, and the "Latest Rates" link. What is the shortest maturity interest rate shown? What is the interest rate for this maturity? Using the large-company stock return in Table 12.3, what is the current market risk premium? What assumption are you making when calculating the risk premium?

12.2 Historical Interest Rates Go to the St. Louis Federal Reserve Web site at www.stls.frb.org and follow the "FRED II®/Data" link and the "Interest Rates" link. You will find a list of links for different historical interest rates. Follow the "10-Year Treasury Constant Maturity Rate" link and you will find the monthly 10-year Treasury note interest rates. Calculate the average annual 10-year Treasury interest rate for 2002 and 2003 using the rates for each month. Compare this number to the long-term government bond returns and the U.S. Treasury bill returns found in Table 12.1. How does the 10-year Treasury interest rate compare to these numbers? Do you expect this relationship to always hold? Why or why not?

12.3. Market Efficiency What are the best performing stocks over the past year? Go to finance.yahoo.com and select the "Stock Screener" link. You will see a "Performance" category and a pull-down menu labeled "1 Yr Stock Perf." Select "Up more than 200%" and "Find Stocks." How many stocks have increased more than 200% over the past year? Now go back and select "Down more than 90%." How many stocks have dropped more than 90% in value over the past year? What does this say about market efficiency?

13

Return, Risk, and the Security Market Line

After the market closed on May 13, 2004, Dell Computer announced record sales of $731 million and an earnings increase of 22 percent for the second quarter. Unfortunately for Dell stockholders, the stock dropped 3.4 percent the next day. Just five days later, rival Hewlett-Packard announced its second quarter earnings. HP reported a 12 percent increase in revenue and a 34 percent increase in profits. HP's stock jumped by 7.6 percent the next day.

Both of these announcements would seem to be positive, but one stock fell on the news, and the other rose. So when is good news really good news? The answer is fundamental to understanding risk and return, and—the good news is—this chapter explores it in some detail.

In our last chapter, we learned some important lessons from capital market history. Most important, we learned that there is a reward, on average, for bearing risk. We called this reward a *risk premium.* The second lesson is that this risk premium is larger for riskier investments. This chapter explores the economic and managerial implications of this basic idea.

Thus far, we have concentrated mainly on the return behavior of a few large portfolios. We need to expand our consideration to include individual assets. Specifically, we have two tasks to accomplish. First, we have to define risk and discuss how to measure it. We then must quantify the relationship between an asset's risk and its required return.

When we examine the risks associated with individual assets, we find there are two types of risk: systematic and unsystematic. This distinction is crucial because, as we will see, systematic risk affects almost all assets in the economy, at least to some degree, whereas unsystematic risk affects at most a small number of assets. We then develop the principle of diversification, which shows that highly diversified portfolios will tend to have almost no unsystematic risk.

The principle of diversification has an important implication: To a diversified investor, only systematic risk matters. It follows that in deciding whether or not to buy a particular individual asset, a diversified investor will only be concerned with that asset's systematic risk. This is a key observation, and it allows us to say a great deal about the risks and returns on individual assets. In particular, it is the basis for a famous relationship between risk and return called the *security market line,* or SML. To develop the SML, we introduce the equally famous "beta" coefficient, one of the centerpieces of modern finance. Beta and the SML are key concepts because they supply us with at least part of the answer to the question of how to go about determining the required return on an investment.

EXPECTED RETURNS AND VARIANCES 13.1

In our previous chapter, we discussed how to calculate average returns and variances using historical data. We now begin to discuss how to analyze returns and variances when the information we have concerns future possible returns and their probabilities.

Expected Return

We start with a straightforward case. Consider a single period of time, say, a year. We have two stocks, L and U, which have the following characteristics: Stock L is expected to have a return of 25 percent in the coming year. Stock U is expected to have a return of 20 percent for the same period.

In a situation like this, if all investors agreed on the expected returns, why would anyone want to hold Stock U? After all, why invest in one stock when the expectation is that another will do better? Clearly, the answer must depend on the risk of the two investments. The return on Stock L, although it is *expected* to be 25 percent, could actually turn out to be higher or lower.

For example, suppose the economy booms. In this case, we think Stock L will have a 70 percent return. If the economy enters a recession, we think the return will be −20 percent. In this case, we say that there are two *states of the economy,* which means that these are the only two possible situations. This setup is oversimplified, of course, but it allows us to illustrate some key ideas without a lot of computation.

Suppose we think a boom and a recession are equally likely to happen, for a 50–50 chance of each. Table 13.1 illustrates the basic information we have described and some additional information about Stock U. Notice that Stock U earns 30 percent if there is a recession and 10 percent if there is a boom.

Obviously, if you buy one of these stocks, say Stock U, what you earn in any particular year depends on what the economy does during that year. However, suppose the probabilities stay the same through time. If you hold U for a number of years, you'll earn 30 percent about half the time and 10 percent the other half. In this case, we say that your **expected return** on Stock U, $E(R_U)$, is 20 percent:

expected return
The return on a risky asset expected in the future.

$$E(R_U) = .50 \times 30\% + .50 \times 10\% = 20\%$$

In other words, you should expect to earn 20 percent from this stock, on average.

For Stock L, the probabilities are the same, but the possible returns are different. Here, we lose 20 percent half the time, and we gain 70 percent the other half. The expected return on L, $E(R_L)$, is thus 25 percent:

$$E(R_L) = .50 \times -20\% + .50 \times 70\% = 25\%$$

Table 13.2 illustrates these calculations.

TABLE 13.1 States of the Economy and Stock Returns

State of Economy	Probability of State of Economy	Rate of Return if State Occurs	
		Stock L	Stock U
Recession	.50	−20%	30%
Boom	.50	70	10
	1.00		

TABLE 13.2 >>

Calculation of Expected Return

		Stock L		Stock U	
(1) State of Economy	(2) Probability of State of Economy	(3) Rate of Return if State Occurs	(4) Product (2) × (3)	(5) Rate of Return if State Occurs	(6) Product (2) × (5)
Recession	.50	−.20	−.10	.30	.15
Boom	.50	.70	.35	.10	.05
	1.00		$E(R_L) = .25 = 25\%$		$E(R_U) = .20 = 20\%$

In our previous chapter, we defined the risk premium as the difference between the return on a risky investment and that on a risk-free investment, and we calculated the historical risk premiums on some different investments. Using our projected returns, we can calculate the *projected,* or *expected, risk premium* as the difference between the expected return on a risky investment and the certain return on a risk-free investment.

For example, suppose risk-free investments are currently offering 8 percent. We will say that the risk-free rate, which we label as R_f, is 8 percent. Given this, what is the projected risk premium on Stock U? On Stock L? Because the expected return on Stock U, $E(R_U)$, is 20 percent, the projected risk premium is:

$$\begin{aligned}\text{Risk premium} &= \text{Expected return} - \text{Risk-free rate} \\ &= E(R_U) - R_f \\ &= 20\% - 8\% \\ &= 12\%\end{aligned} \qquad \textbf{[13.1]}$$

Similarly, the risk premium on Stock L is 25% − 8 = 17%.

In general, the expected return on a security or other asset is simply equal to the sum of the possible returns multiplied by their probabilities. So, if we had 100 possible returns, we would multiply each one by its probability and then add up the results. The result would be the expected return. The risk premium would then be the difference between this expected return and the risk-free rate.

EXAMPLE 13.1 >> Unequal Probabilities

Look again at Tables 13.1 and 13.2. Suppose you think a boom will only occur 20 percent of the time instead of 50 percent. What are the expected returns on Stocks U and L in this case? If the risk-free rate is 10 percent, what are the risk premiums?

The first thing to notice is that a recession must occur 80 percent of the time (1 − .20 = .80) because there are only two possibilities. With this in mind, we see that Stock U has a 30 percent return in 80 percent of the years and a 10 percent return in 20 percent of the years. To calculate the expected return, we again just multiply the possibilities by the probabilities and add up the results:

$$E(R_U) = .80 \times 30\% + .20 \times 10\% = 26\%$$

Table 13.3 summarizes the calculations for both stocks. Notice that the expected return on L is −2 percent.

The risk premium for Stock U is 26% − 10% = 16% in this case. The risk premium for Stock L is negative: −2% − 10% = −12%. This is a little odd, but, for reasons we discuss later, it is not impossible.

<< TABLE 13.3

Calculation of Expected Return

		Stock L		Stock U	
(1) State of Economy	**(2) Probability of State of Economy**	**(3) Rate of Return if State Occurs**	**(4) Product (2) × (3)**	**(5) Rate of Return if State Occurs**	**(6) Product (2) × (5)**
Recession	.80	−.20	−.16	.30	.24
Boom	.20	.70	.14	.10	.02
			$E(R_L) = -2\%$		$E(R_U) = 26\%$

Calculating the Variance

To calculate the variances of the returns on our two stocks, we first determine the squared deviations from the expected return. We then multiply each possible squared deviation by its probability. We add these up, and the result is the variance. The standard deviation, as always, is the square root of the variance.

To illustrate, let us return to the Stock U we originally discussed, which has an expected return of $E(R_U) = 20\%$. In a given year, it will actually return either 30 percent or 10 percent. The possible deviations are thus 30% − 20% = 10% and 10% − 20% = −10%. In this case, the variance is:

$$\text{Variance} = \sigma^2 = .50 \times (10\%)^2 + .50 \times (-10\%)^2 = .01$$

The standard deviation is the square root of this:

$$\text{Standard deviation} = \sigma = \sqrt{.01} = .10 = 10\%$$

Table 13.4 summarizes these calculations for both stocks. Notice that Stock L has a much larger variance.

When we put the expected return and variability information for our two stocks together, we have:

	Stock L	**Stock U**
Expected return, $E(R)$	25%	20%
Variance, σ^2	.2025	.0100
Standard deviation, σ	45%	10%

Stock L has a higher expected return, but U has less risk. You could get a 70 percent return on your investment in L, but you could also lose 20 percent. Notice that an investment in U will always pay at least 10 percent.

Which of these two stocks should you buy? We can't really say; it depends on your personal preferences. We can be reasonably sure that some investors would prefer L to U and some would prefer U to L.

You've probably noticed that the way we have calculated expected returns and variances here is somewhat different from the way we did it in the last chapter. The reason is that in Chapter 12, we were examining actual historical returns, so we estimated the average return and the variance based on some actual events. Here, we have projected *future* returns and their associated probabilities, so this is the information with which we must work.

TABLE 13.4 >>

Calculation of Variance

(1) State of Economy	(2) Probability of State of Economy	(3) Return Deviation from Expected Return	(4) Squared Return Deviation from Expected Return	(5) Product (2) × (4)
Stock L				
Recession	.50	$-.20 - .25 = -.45$	$-.45^2 = .2025$	.10125
Boom	.50	$.70 - .25 = .45$	$.45^2 = .2025$	.10125
				$\sigma_L^2 = .20250$
Stock U				
Recession	.50	$.30 - .20 = .10$	$.10^2 = .01$	.005
Boom	.50	$.10 - .20 = -.10$	$-.10^2 = .01$	.005
				$\sigma_U^2 = .010$

EXAMPLE 13.2 >> More Unequal Probabilities

Going back to Example 13.1, what are the variances on the two stocks once we have unequal probabilities? The standard deviations?

We can summarize the needed calculations as follows:

(1) State of Economy	(2) Probability of State of Economy	(3) Return Deviation from Expected Return	(4) Squared Return Deviation from Expected Return	(5) Product (2) × (4)
Stock L				
Recession	.80	$-.20 - (-.02) = -.18$	.0324	.02592
Boom	.20	$.70 - (-.02) = .72$	.5184	.10368
				$\sigma_L^2 = .12960$
Stock U				
Recession	.80	$.30 - .26 = .04$	.0016	.00128
Boom	.20	$.10 - .26 = -.16$	.0256	.00512
				$\sigma_U^2 = .00640$

Based on these calculations, the standard deviation for L is $\sigma_L = \sqrt{.1296} = .36 = 36\%$. The standard deviation for U is much smaller, $\sigma_U = \sqrt{.0064} = .08$ or 8%.

Concept Questions

13.1a How do we calculate the expected return on a security?

13.1b In words, how do we calculate the variance of the expected return?

13.2 PORTFOLIOS

Thus far in this chapter, we have concentrated on individual assets considered separately. However, most investors actually hold a **portfolio** of assets. All we mean by this is that investors tend to own more than just a single stock, bond, or other asset. Given that this is so, portfolio return and portfolio risk are of obvious relevance. Accordingly, we now discuss portfolio expected returns and variances.

Portfolio Weights

There are many equivalent ways of describing a portfolio. The most convenient approach is to list the percentage of the total portfolio's value that is invested in each portfolio asset. We call these percentages the **portfolio weights**.

For example, if we have \$50 in one asset and \$150 in another, then our total portfolio is worth \$200. The percentage of our portfolio in the first asset is \$50/\$200 = .25. The percentage of our portfolio in the second asset is \$150/\$200, or .75. Our portfolio weights are thus .25 and .75. Notice that the weights have to add up to 1.00 because all of our money is invested somewhere.[1]

portfolio
A group of assets such as stocks and bonds held by an investor.

Portfolio Expected Returns

Let's go back to Stocks L and U. You put half your money in each. The portfolio weights are obviously .50 and .50. What is the pattern of returns on this portfolio? The expected return?

portfolio weight
A percentage of a portfolio's total value that is in a particular asset.

To answer these questions, suppose the economy actually enters a recession. In this case, half your money (the half in L) loses 20 percent. The other half (the half in U) gains 30 percent. Your portfolio return, R_P, in a recession is thus:

$$R_P = .50 \times -20\% + .50 \times 30\% = 5\%$$

Table 13.5 summarizes the remaining calculations. Notice that when a boom occurs, your portfolio will return 40 percent:

$$R_P = .50 \times 70\% + .50 \times 10\% = 40\%$$

As indicated in Table 13.5, the expected return on your portfolio, $E(R_P)$, is 22.5 percent.

We can save ourselves some work by calculating the expected return more directly. Given these portfolio weights, we could have reasoned that we expect half of our money to earn 25 percent (the half in L) and half of our money to earn 20 percent (the half in U). Our portfolio expected return is thus:

Want more information on investing? Take a look at TheStreet.com's investing basics at www.thestreet.com/basics.

$$\begin{aligned} E(R_P) &= .50 \times E(R_L) + .50 \times E(R_U) \\ &= .50 \times 25\% + .50 \times 20\% \\ &= 22.5\% \end{aligned}$$

This is the same portfolio expected return we calculated previously.

This method of calculating the expected return on a portfolio works no matter how many assets there are in the portfolio. Suppose we had n assets in our portfolio, where n is any number. If we let x_i stand for the percentage of our money in Asset i, then the expected return would be:

$$E(R_P) = x_1 \times E(R_1) + x_2 \times E(R_2) + \ldots + x_n \times E(R_n) \quad [13.2]$$

This says that the expected return on a portfolio is a straightforward combination of the expected returns on the assets in that portfolio. This seems somewhat obvious, but, as we will examine next, the obvious approach is not always the right one.

[1] Some of it could be in cash, of course, but we would then just consider the cash to be one of the portfolio assets.

TABLE 13.5 >>

Expected Return on an Equally Weighted Portfolio of Stock L and Stock U

(1) State of Economy	(2) Probability of State of Economy	(3) Portfolio Return if State Occurs	(4) Product (2) × (3)
Recession	.50	$.50 \times -20\% + .50 \times 30\% = 5\%$	.025
Boom	.50	$.50 \times 70\% + .50 \times 10\% = 40\%$	.200
			$E(R_P) \times 22.5\%$

EXAMPLE 13.3 >> Portfolio Expected Return

Suppose we have the following projections on three stocks:

State of Economy	Probability of State of Economy	Returns if State Occurs		
		Stock A	Stock B	Stock C
Boom	.40	10%	15%	20%
Bust	.60	8	4	0

We want to calculate portfolio expected returns in two cases. First, what would be the expected return on a portfolio with equal amounts invested in each of the three stocks? Second, what would be the expected return if half of the portfolio were in A, with the remainder equally divided between B and C?

Based on what we've learned from our earlier discussions, we can determine that the expected returns on the individual stocks are (check these for practice):

$$E(R_A) = 8.8\%$$
$$E(R_B) = 8.4\%$$
$$E(R_C) = 8.0\%$$

If a portfolio has equal investments in each asset, the portfolio weights are all the same. Such a portfolio is said to be *equally weighted.* Because there are three stocks in this case, the weights are all equal to ⅓. The portfolio expected return is thus:

$$E(R_P) = (1/3) \times 8.8\% + (1/3) \times 8.4\% + (1/3) \times 8\% = 8.4\%$$

In the second case, verify that the portfolio expected return is 8.5 percent.

Portfolio Variance

From our earlier discussion, the expected return on a portfolio that contains equal investment in Stocks U and L is 22.5 percent. What is the standard deviation of return on this portfolio? Simple intuition might suggest that because half of the money has a standard deviation of 45 percent and the other half has a standard deviation of 10 percent, the portfolio's standard deviation might be calculated as:

$$\sigma_P = .50 \times 45\% + .50 \times 10\% = 27.5\%$$

Unfortunately, this approach is completely incorrect!

Let's see what the standard deviation really is. Table 13.6 summarizes the relevant calculations. As we see, the portfolio's variance is about .031, and its standard deviation is less than we thought—it's only 17.5 percent. What is illustrated here is that the variance on

(1) State of Economy	(2) Probability of State of Economy	(3) Portfolio Return if State Occurs	(4) Squared Deviation from Expected Return	(5) Product (2) × (4)
Recession	.50	5%	$(.05 - .225)^2 = .030625$	.0153125
Boom	.50	40	$(.40 - .225)^2 = .030625$	.0153125
				$\sigma_P^2 = .030625$
				$\sigma_P = \sqrt{.030625} = 17.5\%$

<< TABLE 13.6

Variance on an Equally Weighted Portfolio of Stock L and Stock U

a portfolio is not generally a simple combination of the variances of the assets in the portfolio.

We can illustrate this point a little more dramatically by considering a slightly different set of portfolio weights. Suppose we put 2/11 (about 18 percent) in L and the other 9/11 (about 82 percent) in U. If a recession occurs, this portfolio will have a return of:

$$R_P = (2/11) \times -20\% + (9/11) \times 30\% = 20.91\%$$

If a boom occurs, this portfolio will have a return of:

$$R_P = (2/11) \times 70\% + (9/11) \times 10\% = 20.91\%$$

Notice that the return is the same no matter what happens. No further calculations are needed: This portfolio has a zero variance. Apparently, combining assets into portfolios can substantially alter the risks faced by the investor. This is a crucial observation, and we will begin to explore its implications in the next section.

Portfolio Variance and Standard Deviation

<< EXAMPLE 13.4

In Example 13.3, what are the standard deviations on the two portfolios? To answer, we first have to calculate the portfolio returns in the two states. We will work with the second portfolio, which has 50 percent in Stock A and 25 percent in each of Stocks B and C. The relevant calculations can be summarized as follows:

State of Economy	Probability of State of Economy	Rate of Return if State Occurs			
		Stock A	Stock B	Stock C	Portfolio
Boom	.40	10%	15%	20%	13.75%
Bust	.60	8	4	0	5.00

The portfolio return when the economy booms is calculated as:

$$.50 \times 10\% + .25 \times 15\% + .25 \times 20\% = 13.75\%$$

The return when the economy goes bust is calculated the same way. The expected return on the portfolio is 8.5 percent. The variance is thus:

$$\sigma^2 = .40 \times (.1375 - .085)^2 + .60 \times (.05 - .085)^2$$
$$= .0018375$$

The standard deviation is thus about 4.3 percent. For our equally weighted portfolio, check to see that the standard deviation is about 5.4 percent.

Concept Questions

13.2a What is a portfolio weight?

13.2b How do we calculate the expected return on a portfolio?

13.2c Is there a simple relationship between the standard deviation on a portfolio and the standard deviations of the assets in the portfolio?

13.3 ANNOUNCEMENTS, SURPRISES, AND EXPECTED RETURNS

Now that we know how to construct portfolios and evaluate their returns, we begin to describe more carefully the risks and returns associated with individual securities. Thus far, we have measured volatility by looking at the difference between the actual return on an asset or portfolio, R, and the expected return, $E(R)$. We now look at why those deviations exist.

Expected and Unexpected Returns

To begin, for concreteness, we consider the return on the stock of a company called Flyers. What will determine this stock's return in, say, the coming year?

The return on any stock traded in a financial market is composed of two parts. First, the normal, or expected, return from the stock is the part of the return that shareholders in the market predict or expect. This return depends on the information shareholders have that bears on the stock, and it is based on the market's understanding today of the important factors that will influence the stock in the coming year.

The second part of the return on the stock is the uncertain, or risky, part. This is the portion that comes from unexpected information revealed within the year. A list of all possible sources of such information would be endless, but here are a few examples:

www.quicken.com is a great site for stock info.

News about Flyers research

Government figures released on gross domestic product (GDP)

The results from the latest arms control talks

The news that Flyers's sales figures are higher than expected

A sudden, unexpected drop in interest rates

Based on this discussion, one way to express the return on Flyers stock in the coming year would be:

$$\text{Total return} = \text{Expected return} + \text{Unexpected return}$$
$$R = E(R) + U \qquad [13.3]$$

where R stands for the actual total return in the year, $E(R)$ stands for the expected part of the return, and U stands for the unexpected part of the return. What this says is that the actual return, R, differs from the expected return, $E(R)$, because of surprises that occur during the year. In any given year, the unexpected return will be positive or negative, but, through time, the average value of U will be zero. This simply means that on average, the actual return equals the expected return.

Announcements and News

We need to be careful when we talk about the effect of news items on the return. For example, suppose Flyers's business is such that the company prospers when GDP grows at a relatively high rate and suffers when GDP is relatively stagnant. In this case, in deciding what return to expect this year from owning stock in Flyers, shareholders either implicitly or explicitly must think about what GDP is likely to be for the year.

When the government actually announces GDP figures for the year, what will happen to the value of Flyers's stock? Obviously, the answer depends on what figure is released. More to the point, however, the impact depends on how much of that figure is *new* information.

At the beginning of the year, market participants will have some idea or forecast of what the yearly GDP will be. To the extent that shareholders have predicted GDP, that prediction will already be factored into the expected part of the return on the stock, E(R). On the other hand, if the announced GDP is a surprise, then the effect will be part of U, the unanticipated portion of the return. As an example, suppose shareholders in the market had forecast that the GDP increase this year would be .5 percent. If the actual announcement this year is exactly .5 percent, the same as the forecast, then the shareholders don't really learn anything, and the announcement isn't news. There will be no impact on the stock price as a result. This is like receiving confirmation of something that you suspected all along; it doesn't reveal anything new.

To give a more concrete example, in July 2001, electronics manufacturer Motorola announced that sales had fallen by 19 percent, producing a loss of 35 cents per share. The next day, the company announced that it would cut 4,000 jobs. This seems like big-time bad news, but the stock price rose by more than 17 percent over the two-day period. Why? Because market participants had expected an even bigger loss.

A common way of saying that an announcement isn't news is to say that the market has already "discounted" the announcement. The use of the word *discount* here is different from the use of the term in computing present values, but the spirit is the same. When we discount a dollar in the future, we say it is worth less to us because of the time value of money. When we discount an announcement or a news item, we say that it has less of an impact on the market because the market already knew much of it.

Going back to Flyers, suppose the government announces that the actual GDP increase during the year has been 1.5 percent. Now shareholders have learned something, namely, that the increase is one percentage point higher than they had forecast. This difference between the actual result and the forecast, one percentage point in this example, is sometimes called the *innovation* or the *surprise.*

This distinction explains why what seems to be good news can actually be bad news (and vice versa). For example, in May 2004, Deere & Company, makers of the famous green tractors, announced record net income of $477.3 million for the second quarter. The company had earnings per share of $1.88, which handily surpassed the market estimate of $1.76 per share. Good news, right? Wrong. The stock slid 1.3 percent on the announcement. Investors were concerned that the company's performance was so strong that there was little room for improvement. In fact, Deere announced that it had operated at 110 percent of normal market conditions, and operations for the company typically topped out at 120 percent of normal market conditions, so there was little room left for future growth.

A key idea to keep in mind about news and price changes is that news about the future is what matters. Going back to the Dell example we used to open the chapter, analysts welcomed the good news about revenues and earnings, but also noted that those numbers were, in a very real sense, yesterday's news. Looking to the future, these same analysts noted that

Dell's average price on shipped products had declined by $50 per unit from the year before. At the same time, certain component prices had risen, so Dell's profit margins actually declined slightly, suggesting that future profit growth might not be so robust.

To summarize, an announcement can be broken into two parts, the anticipated, or expected, part and the surprise, or innovation:

$$\text{Announcement} = \text{Expected part} + \text{Surprise} \quad [13.4]$$

The expected part of any announcement is the part of the information that the market uses to form the expectation, E(R), of the return on the stock. The surprise is the news that influences the unanticipated return on the stock, U.

Our discussion of market efficiency in the previous chapter bears on this discussion. We are assuming that relevant information known today is already reflected in the expected return. This is identical to saying that the current price reflects relevant publicly available information. We are thus implicitly assuming that markets are at least reasonably efficient in the semistrong form sense.

Henceforth, when we speak of news, we will mean the surprise part of an announcement and not the portion that the market has expected and therefore already discounted.

Concept Questions

13.3a What are the two basic parts of a return?

13.3b Under what conditions will a company's announcement have no effect on common stock prices?

13.4 RISK: SYSTEMATIC AND UNSYSTEMATIC

The unanticipated part of the return, that portion resulting from surprises, is the true risk of any investment. After all, if we always receive exactly what we expect, then the investment is perfectly predictable and, by definition, risk-free. In other words, the risk of owning an asset comes from surprises—unanticipated events.

There are important differences, though, among various sources of risk. Look back at our previous list of news stories. Some of these stories are directed specifically at Flyers, and some are more general. Which of the news items are of specific importance to Flyers?

Announcements about interest rates or GDP are clearly important for nearly all companies, whereas the news about Flyers's president, its research, or its sales is of specific interest to Flyers. We will distinguish between these two types of events, because, as we shall see, they have very different implications.

Systematic and Unsystematic Risk

systematic risk
A risk that influences a large number of assets. Also, market risk.

The first type of surprise, the one that affects a large number of assets, we will label **systematic risk**. A systematic risk is one that influences a large number of assets, each to a greater or lesser extent. Because systematic risks have marketwide effects, they are sometimes called *market risks*.

The second type of surprise we will call **unsystematic risk**. An unsystematic risk is one that affects a single asset or a small group of assets. Because these risks are unique to individual companies or assets, they are sometimes called *unique* or *asset-specific risks.* We will use these terms interchangeably.

unsystematic risk
A risk that affects at most a small number of assets. Also, unique or asset-specific risk.

As we have seen, uncertainties about general economic conditions, such as GDP, interest rates, or inflation, are examples of systematic risks. These conditions affect nearly all companies to some degree. An unanticipated increase, or surprise, in inflation, for example, affects wages and the costs of the supplies that companies buy; it affects the value of the assets that companies own; and it affects the prices at which companies sell their products. Forces such as these, to which all companies are susceptible, are the essence of systematic risk.

In contrast, the announcement of an oil strike by a company will primarily affect that company and, perhaps, a few others (such as primary competitors and suppliers). It is unlikely to have much of an effect on the world oil market, however, or on the affairs of companies not in the oil business, so this is an unsystematic event.

Systematic and Unsystematic Components of Return

The distinction between a systematic risk and an unsystematic risk is never really as exact as we make it out to be. Even the most narrow and peculiar bit of news about a company ripples through the economy. This is true because every enterprise, no matter how tiny, is a part of the economy. It's like the tale of a kingdom that was lost because one horse lost a shoe. This is mostly hairsplitting, however. Some risks are clearly much more general than others. We'll see some evidence on this point in just a moment.

The distinction between the types of risk allows us to break down the surprise portion, U, of the return on the Flyers stock into two parts. Earlier, we had the actual return broken down into its expected and surprise components:

$$R = \mathrm{E}(R) + U$$

We now recognize that the total surprise component for Flyers, U, has a systematic and an unsystematic component, so:

$$R = \mathrm{E}(R) + \text{Systematic portion} + \text{Unsystematic portion} \qquad [13.5]$$

Because it is traditional, we will use the Greek letter epsilon, ϵ, to stand for the unsystematic portion. Because systematic risks are often called market risks, we will use the letter m to stand for the systematic part of the surprise. With these symbols, we can rewrite the formula for the total return:

$$\begin{aligned} R &= \mathrm{E}(R) + U \\ &= \mathrm{E}(R) + m + \epsilon \end{aligned}$$

The important thing about the way we have broken down the total surprise, U, is that the unsystematic portion, ϵ, is more or less unique to Flyers. For this reason, it is unrelated to the unsystematic portion of return on most other assets. To see why this is important, we need to return to the subject of portfolio risk.

Concept Questions

13.4a What are the two basic types of risk?

13.4b What is the distinction between the two types of risk?

13.5 DIVERSIFICATION AND PORTFOLIO RISK

We've seen earlier that portfolio risks can, in principle, be quite different from the risks of the assets that make up the portfolio. We now look more closely at the riskiness of an individual asset versus the risk of a portfolio of many different assets. We will once again examine some market history to get an idea of what happens with actual investments in U.S. capital markets.

For more on risk and diversification, visit www.investopedia.com/university.

The Effect of Diversification: Another Lesson from Market History

In our previous chapter, we saw that the standard deviation of the annual return on a portfolio of 500 large common stocks has historically been about 20 percent per year. Does this mean that the standard deviation of the annual return on a typical stock in that group of 500 is about 20 percent? As you might suspect by now, the answer is *no.* This is an extremely important observation.

To allow examination of the relationship between portfolio size and portfolio risk, Table 13.7 illustrates typical average annual standard deviations for equally weighted portfolios that contain different numbers of randomly selected NYSE securities.

In Column 2 of Table 13.7, we see that the standard deviation for a "portfolio" of one security is about 49 percent. What this means is that if you randomly selected a single NYSE stock and put all your money into it, your standard deviation of return would typically be a substantial 49 percent per year. If you were to randomly select two stocks and invest half your money in each, your standard deviation would be about 37 percent on average, and so on.

TABLE 13.7 >>

Standard Deviations of Annual Portfolio Returns

(1) Number of Stocks in Portfolio	(2) Average Standard Deviation of Annual Portfolio Returns	(3) Ratio of Portfolio Standard Deviation to Standard Deviation of a Single Stock
1	49.24%	1.00
2	37.36	.76
4	29.69	.60
6	26.64	.54
8	24.98	.51
10	23.93	.49
20	21.68	.44
30	20.87	.42
40	20.46	.42
50	20.20	.41
100	19.69	.40
200	19.42	.39
300	19.34	.39
400	19.29	.39
500	19.27	.39
1,000	19.21	.39

These figures are from Table 1 in M. Statman, "How Many Stocks Make a Diversified Portfolio?" *Journal of Financial and Quantitative Analysis* 22 (September 1987), pp. 353–64. They were derived from E. J. Elton and M. J. Gruber, "Risk Reduction and Portfolio Size: An Analytic Solution," *Journal of Business* 50 (October 1977), pp. 415–37.

The important thing to notice in Table 13.7 is that the standard deviation declines as the number of securities is increased. By the time we have 100 randomly chosen stocks, the portfolio's standard deviation has declined by about 60 percent, from 49 percent to about 20 percent. With 500 securities, the standard deviation is 19.27 percent, similar to the 20 percent we saw in our previous chapter for the large common stock portfolio. The small difference exists because the portfolio securities and time periods examined are not identical.

The Principle of Diversification

Figure 13.1 illustrates the point we've been discussing. What we have plotted is the standard deviation of return versus the number of stocks in the portfolio. Notice in Figure 13.1 that the benefit in terms of risk reduction from adding securities drops off as we add more and more. By the time we have 10 securities, most of the effect is already realized, and by the time we get to 30 or so, there is very little remaining benefit.

Figure 13.1 illustrates two key points. First, some of the riskiness associated with individual assets can be eliminated by forming portfolios. The process of spreading an investment across assets (and thereby forming a portfolio) is called *diversification.* The **principle of diversification** tells us that spreading an investment across many assets will eliminate some of the risk. The blue shaded area in Figure 13.1, labeled "diversifiable risk," is the part that can be eliminated by diversification.

principle of diversification Spreading an investment across a number of assets will eliminate some, but not all, of the risk.

The second point is equally important. There is a minimum level of risk that cannot be eliminated simply by diversifying. This minimum level is labeled "nondiversifiable risk" in Figure 13.1. Taken together, these two points are another important lesson from capital market history: diversification reduces risk, but only up to a point. Put another way, some risk is diversifiable and some is not.

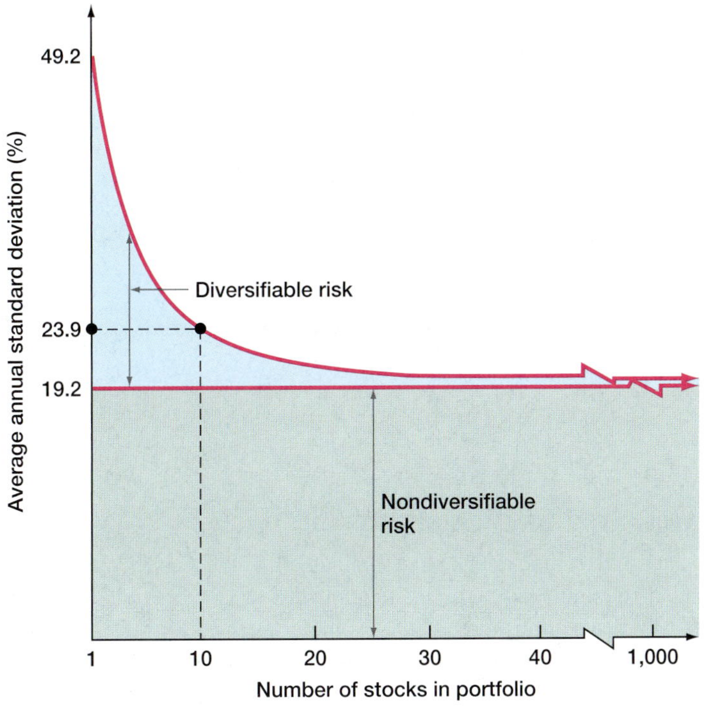

<< FIGURE 13.1

Portfolio Diversification

To give a recent example of the impact of diversification, the Dow Jones Industrial Average (DJIA), which is a widely followed stock market index of 30 large, well-known U.S. stocks, was up about 25 percent in 2003. As we saw in our previous chapter, this represents a pretty good year for a portfolio of large-cap stocks. The biggest individual gainers for the year were Intel (up 107 percent), Caterpillar (up 86 percent), and Alcoa (up 71 percent). But not all 30 stocks were up: The losers included Eastman Kodak (down 24 percent), AT&T (down 19 percent), and Merck (down 11 percent).

In contrast to 2003, consider 2002 when the DJIA was down about 17 percent, a fairly bad year. The big losers in this year were Home Depot (down 52 percent), and Intel (down 50 percent). Working to offset these losses was Eastman Kodak (up 20 percent). Again, the lesson is clear: Diversification reduces exposure to extreme outcomes, both good and bad.

Diversification and Unsystematic Risk

From our discussion of portfolio risk, we know that some of the risk associated with individual assets can be diversified away and some cannot. We are left with an obvious question: Why is this so? It turns out that the answer hinges on the distinction we made earlier between systematic and unsystematic risk.

By definition, an unsystematic risk is one that is particular to a single asset or, at most, a small group. For example, if the asset under consideration is stock in a single company, the discovery of positive NPV projects such as successful new products and innovative cost savings will tend to increase the value of the stock. Unanticipated lawsuits, industrial accidents, strikes, and similar events will tend to decrease future cash flows and thereby reduce share values.

Here is the important observation: If we only held a single stock, then the value of our investment would fluctuate because of company-specific events. If we hold a large portfolio, on the other hand, some of the stocks in the portfolio will go up in value because of positive company-specific events and some will go down in value because of negative events. The net effect on the overall value of the portfolio will be relatively small, however, because these effects will tend to cancel each other out.

Now we see why some of the variability associated with individual assets is eliminated by diversification. When we combine assets into portfolios, the unique, or unsystematic, events—both positive and negative—tend to "wash out" once we have more than just a few assets.

This is an important point that bears repeating:

Unsystematic risk is essentially eliminated by diversification, so a portfolio with many assets has almost no unsystematic risk.

In fact, the terms *diversifiable risk* and *unsystematic risk* are often used interchangeably.

Diversification and Systematic Risk

We've seen that unsystematic risk can be eliminated by diversifying. What about systematic risk? Can it also be eliminated by diversification? The answer is no because, by definition, a systematic risk affects almost all assets to some degree. As a result, no matter how many assets we put into a portfolio, the systematic risk doesn't go away. Thus, for obvious reasons, the terms *systematic risk* and *nondiversifiable risk* are used interchangeably.

Because we have introduced so many different terms, it is useful to summarize our discussion before moving on. What we have seen is that the total risk of an investment, as measured by the standard deviation of its return, can be written as:

$$\text{Total risk} = \text{Systematic risk} + \text{Unsystematic risk} \quad [13.6]$$

Systematic risk is also called *nondiversifiable risk* or *market risk.* Unsystematic risk is also called *diversifiable risk, unique risk,* or *asset-specific risk.* For a well-diversified portfolio, the unsystematic risk is negligible. For such a portfolio, essentially all of the risk is systematic.

Concept Questions

13.5a What happens to the standard deviation of return for a portfolio if we increase the number of securities in the portfolio?

13.5b What is the principle of diversification?

13.5c Why is some risk diversifiable? Why is some risk not diversifiable?

13.5d Why can't systematic risk be diversified away?

SYSTEMATIC RISK AND BETA 13.6

The question that we now begin to address is: What determines the size of the risk premium on a risky asset? Put another way, why do some assets have a larger risk premium than other assets? The answer to these questions, as we discuss next, is also based on the distinction between systematic and unsystematic risk.

The Systematic Risk Principle

Thus far, we've seen that the total risk associated with an asset can be decomposed into two components: systematic and unsystematic risk. We have also seen that unsystematic risk can be essentially eliminated by diversification. The systematic risk present in an asset, on the other hand, cannot be eliminated by diversification.

Based on our study of capital market history, we know that there is a reward, on average, for bearing risk. However, we now need to be more precise about what we mean by risk. The **systematic risk principle** states that the reward for bearing risk depends only on the systematic risk of an investment. The underlying rationale for this principle is straightforward: Because unsystematic risk can be eliminated at virtually no cost (by diversifying), there is no reward for bearing it. Put another way, the market does not reward risks that are borne unnecessarily.

systematic risk principle
The expected return on a risky asset depends only on that asset's systematic risk.

The systematic risk principle has a remarkable and very important implication:

The expected return on an asset depends only on that asset's systematic risk.

For more on beta, see www.wallstreetcity.com and moneycentral.msn.com.

There is an obvious corollary to this principle: no matter how much total risk an asset has, only the systematic portion is relevant in determining the expected return (and the risk premium) on that asset.

TABLE 13.8 >>

Beta Coefficients for Selected Companies

	Beta Coefficient (β_i)
Coca-Cola Bottling	0.45
General Mills	0.55
ExxonMobil	0.80
3M	0.90
American Electric Power	1.05
General Motors	1.25
eBay	1.55
Yahoo!	1.85

SOURCE: *Value Line Investment Survey*, 2004.

Measuring Systematic Risk

beta coefficient
The amount of systematic risk present in a particular risky asset relative to that in an average risky asset.

Because systematic risk is the crucial determinant of an asset's expected return, we need some way of measuring the level of systematic risk for different investments. The specific measure we will use is called the **beta coefficient**, for which we will use the Greek symbol β. A beta coefficient, or beta for short, tells us how much systematic risk a particular asset has relative to an average asset. By definition, an average asset has a beta of 1.0 relative to itself. An asset with a beta of .50, therefore, has half as much systematic risk as an average asset; an asset with a beta of 2.0 has twice as much.

Table 13.8 contains the estimated beta coefficients for the stocks of some well-known companies. (This particular source rounds numbers to the nearest .05.) The range of betas in Table 13.8 is typical for stocks of large U.S. corporations. Betas outside this range occur, but they are less common.

The important thing to remember is that the expected return, and thus the risk premium, on an asset depends only on its systematic risk. Because assets with larger betas have greater systematic risks, they will have greater expected returns. Thus, from Table 13.8, an investor who buys stock in ExxonMobil, with a beta of .80, should expect to earn less, on average, than an investor who buys stock in General Motors, with a beta of about 1.25.

One cautionary note is in order: not all betas are created equal. Different providers use somewhat different methods for estimating betas, and significant differences sometimes occur. As a result, it is a good idea to look at several sources. See our nearby *Work the Web* box for more on beta.

EXAMPLE 13.5 >> Total Risk versus Beta

Consider the following information on two securities. Which has greater total risk? Which has greater systematic risk? Greater unsystematic risk? Which asset will have a higher risk premium?

	Standard Deviation	Beta
Security A	40%	0.50
Security B	20	1.50

From our discussion in this section, Security A has greater total risk, but it has substantially less systematic risk. Because total risk is the sum of systematic and unsystematic risk, Security A must have greater unsystematic risk. Finally, from the systematic risk principle, Security B will have a higher risk premium and a greater expected return, despite the fact that it has less total risk.

WORK THE WEB

Suppose you want to find the beta for a company like Amazon.com. One way is to hit the Web. We went to finance.yahoo.com, entered the ticker symbol AMZN for Amazon and followed the "Key Statistics" link. Here is an abbreviated look at the results:

FINANCIAL HIGHLIGHTS	
Fiscal Year	
Fiscal Year Ends:	31-Dec
Most Recent Quarter (mrq):	31-Mar-04
Profitability	
Profit Margin (ttm):	2.75%
Operating Margin (ttm):	5.99%
Management Effectiveness	
Return on Assets (ttm):	8.77%
Return on Equity (ttm):	N/A
Income Statement	
Revenue (ttm):	5.71B
Revenue Per Share (ttm):	13.707
Revenue Growth (lfy)[3]:	33.80%
Gross Profit (ttm)[2]:	1.26B
EBITDA (ttm):	343.64M
Net Income Avl to Common (ttm):	156.54M
Diluted EPS (ttm):	0.361
Earnings Growth (lfy)[3]:	N/A

Stock Price History	
Beta:	2.18
52-Week Change:	24.18%
52-Week Change (relative to S&P500):	6.24%
52-Week High (21-Oct-03):	61.15
52-Week Low (27-May-03):	31.16
50-Day Moving Average:	44.08
200-Day Moving Average:	48.34
Share Statistics	
Average Volume (3 month):	7,079,227
Average Volume (10 day):	7,350,000
Shares Outstanding:	405.02M
Float:	281.50M
% Held by Insiders:	30.50%
% Held by Institutions:	58.95%
Shares Short (as of 7-Apr-04):	35.32M
Daily Volume (as of 7-Apr-04):	N/A
Short Ratio (as of 7-Apr-04):	5.266
Short % of Float (as of 7-Apr-04):	12.55%
Shares Short (prior month):	28.05M

The reported beta for Amazon.com is 2.18, which means that Amazon has over two times the systematic risk of a typical stock. You would expect that the company is very risky, and, looking at the other numbers, we agree. If you look at ROE, you will see that nothing is reported. Why? Amazon's losses over the years have reduced its book equity to a negative number! So, if you calculate ROE, you get a negative number. For a company with negative equity, the more the company makes, the *worse* the ROE becomes, which doesn't make sense. In all, Amazon appears to be a good candidate for a high beta.

Portfolio Betas

Earlier, we saw that the riskiness of a portfolio has no simple relationship to the risks of the assets in the portfolio. A portfolio beta, however, can be calculated, just like a portfolio expected return. For example, looking again at Table 13.8, suppose you put half of your money in ExxonMobil and half in Yahoo!. What would the beta of this combination be? Because ExxonMobil has a beta of .80 and Yahoo! has a beta of 1.85, the portfolio's beta, β_P, would be:

$$
\begin{aligned}
\beta_P &= .50 \times \beta_{ExxonMobil} + .50 \times \beta_{Yahoo!} \\
&= .50 \times .80 + .50 \times 1.85 \\
&= 1.325
\end{aligned}
$$

In general, if we had a large number of assets in a portfolio, we would multiply each asset's beta by its portfolio weight and then add the results up to get the portfolio's beta.

EXAMPLE 13.6 >> Portfolio Betas

Suppose we had the following investments:

Security	Amount Invested	Expected Return	Beta
Stock A	$1,000	8%	.80
Stock B	2,000	12	.95
Stock C	3,000	15	1.10
Stock D	4,000	18	1.40

What is the expected return on this portfolio? What is the beta of this portfolio? Does this portfolio have more or less systematic risk than an average asset?

To answer, we first have to calculate the portfolio weights. Notice that the total amount invested is $10,000. Of this, $1,000/10,000 = 10% is invested in Stock A. Similarly, 20 percent is invested in Stock B, 30 percent is invested in Stock C, and 40 percent is invested in Stock D. The expected return, $E(R_P)$, is thus:

$$\begin{aligned} E(R_P) &= .10 \times E(R_A) + .20 \times E(R_B) + .30 \times E(R_C) + .40 \times E(R_D) \\ &= .10 \times 8\% + .20 \times 12\% + .30 \times 15\% + .40 \times 18\% \\ &= 14.9\% \end{aligned}$$

Similarly, the portfolio beta, β_P, is:

$$\begin{aligned} \beta_P &= .10 \times \beta_A + .20 \times \beta_B + .30 \times \beta_C + .40 \times \beta_D \\ &= .10 \times .80 + .20 \times .95 + .30 \times 1.10 + .40 \times 1.40 \\ &= 1.16 \end{aligned}$$

This portfolio thus has an expected return of 14.9 percent and a beta of 1.16. Because the beta is larger than 1, this portfolio has greater systematic risk than an average asset.

Betas are easy to find on the Web. Try finance. yahoo.com and money.cnn.com.

Concept Questions

13.6a What is the systematic risk principle?

13.6b What does a beta coefficient measure?

13.6c How do you calculate a portfolio beta?

13.6d True or false: The expected return on a risky asset depends on that asset's total risk. Explain.

13.7 THE SECURITY MARKET LINE

We're now in a position to see how risk is rewarded in the marketplace. To begin, suppose that Asset A has an expected return of $E(R_A) = 20\%$ and a beta of $\beta_A = 1.6$. Furthermore, suppose that the risk-free rate is $R_f = 8\%$. Notice that a risk-free asset, by definition, has no systematic risk (or unsystematic risk), so a risk-free asset has a beta of zero.

Beta and the Risk Premium

Consider a portfolio made up of Asset A and a risk-free asset. We can calculate some different possible portfolio expected returns and betas by varying the percentages invested in these two assets. For example, if 25 percent of the portfolio is invested in Asset A, then the expected return is:

$$\begin{aligned} E(R_P) &= .25 \times E(R_A) + (1 - .25) \times R_f \\ &= .25 \times 20\% + .75 \times 8\% \\ &= 11\% \end{aligned}$$

Similarly, the beta on the portfolio, β_P, would be:

$$\begin{aligned} \beta_P &= .25 \times \beta_A + (1 - .25) \times 0 \\ &= .25 \times 1.6 \\ &= .40 \end{aligned}$$

Notice that, because the weights have to add up to 1, the percentage invested in the risk-free asset is equal to 1 minus the percentage invested in Asset A.

One thing that you might wonder about is whether or not it is possible for the percentage invested in Asset A to exceed 100 percent. The answer is yes. This can happen if the investor borrows at the risk-free rate. For example, suppose an investor has \$100 and borrows an additional \$50 at 8 percent, the risk-free rate. The total investment in Asset A would be \$150, or 150 percent of the investor's wealth. The expected return in this case would be:

$$\begin{aligned} E(R_P) &= 1.50 \times E(R_A) + (1 - 1.50) \times R_f \\ &= 1.50 \times 20\% - .50 \times 8\% \\ &= 26\% \end{aligned}$$

The beta on the portfolio would be:

$$\begin{aligned} \beta_P &= 1.50 \times \beta_A + (1 - 1.50) \times 0 \\ &= 1.50 \times 1.6 \\ &= 2.4 \end{aligned}$$

We can calculate some other possibilities, as follows:

Percentage of Portfolio in Asset A	Portfolio Expected Return	Portfolio Beta
0%	8%	.0
25	11	.4
50	14	.8
75	17	1.2
100	20	1.6
125	23	2.0
150	26	2.4

In Figure 13.2A, these portfolio expected returns are plotted against the portfolio betas. Notice that all the combinations fall on a straight line.

The Reward-to-Risk Ratio What is the slope of the straight line in Figure 13.2A? As always, the slope of a straight line is equal to "the rise over the run." In this case, as we move out of the risk-free asset into Asset A, the beta increases from zero to 1.6 (a "run" of 1.6). At the same time, the expected return goes from 8 percent to 20 percent, a "rise" of 12 percent. The slope of the line is thus $12\%/1.6 = 7.5\%$.

FIGURE 13.2A >>

Portfolio Expected Returns and Betas for Asset A

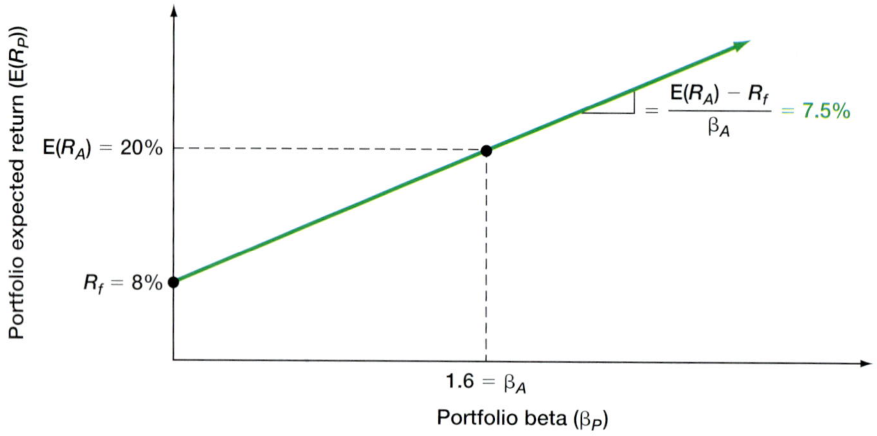

Notice that the slope of our line is just the risk premium on Asset A, $E(R_A) - R_f$, divided by Asset A's beta, β_A:

$$\text{Slope} = \frac{E(R_A) - R_f}{\beta_A}$$

$$= \frac{20\% - 8\%}{1.6} = 7.5\%$$

What this tells us is that Asset A offers a *reward-to-risk* ratio of 7.5 percent.[2] In other words, Asset A has a risk premium of 7.50 percent per "unit" of systematic risk.

The Basic Argument

Now suppose we consider a second asset, Asset B. This asset has a beta of 1.2 and an expected return of 16 percent. Which investment is better, Asset A or Asset B? You might think that, once again, we really cannot say—some investors might prefer A; some investors might prefer B. Actually, however, we can say: A is better because, as we will demonstrate, B offers inadequate compensation for its level of systematic risk, at least, relative to A.

To begin, we calculate different combinations of expected returns and betas for portfolios of Asset B and a risk-free asset, just as we did for Asset A. For example, if we put 25 percent in Asset B and the remaining 75 percent in the risk-free asset, the portfolio's expected return will be:

$$\begin{aligned} E(R_P) &= .25 \times E(R_B) + (1 - .25) \times R_f \\ &= .25 \times 16\% + .75 \times 8\% \\ &= 10\% \end{aligned}$$

Similarly, the beta on the portfolio, β_P, would be:

$$\begin{aligned} \beta_P &= .25 \times \beta_B + (1 - .25) \times 0 \\ &= .25 \times 1.2 \\ &= .30 \end{aligned}$$

[2]This ratio is sometimes called the *Treynor index,* after one of its originators.

Some other possibilities are as follows:

Percentage of Portfolio in Asset B	Portfolio Expected Return	Portfolio Beta
0%	8%	.0
25	10	.3
50	12	.6
75	14	.9
100	16	1.2
125	18	1.5
150	20	1.8

When we plot these combinations of portfolio expected returns and portfolio betas in Figure 13.2B, we get a straight line just as we did for Asset A.

The key thing to notice is that when we compare the results for Assets A and B, as in Figure 13.2C, the line describing the combinations of expected returns and betas for Asset A is higher than the one for Asset B. What this tells us is that for any given level of systematic risk (as measured by β), some combination of Asset A and the risk-free asset always offers a larger return. This is why we were able to state that Asset A is a better investment than Asset B.

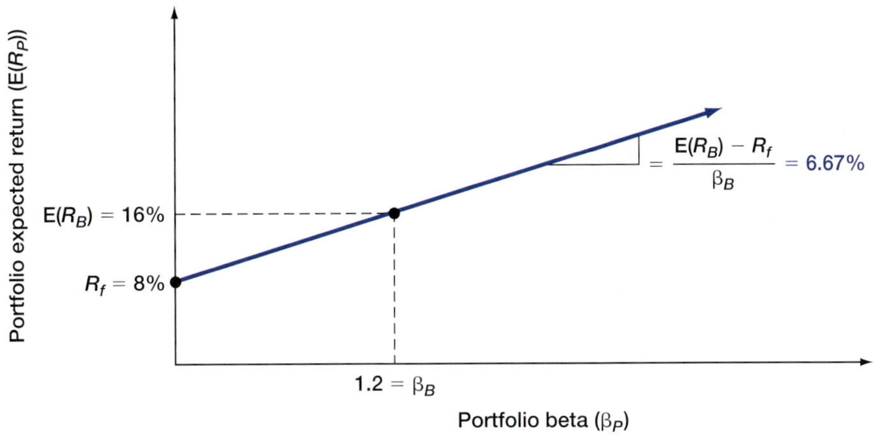

<< FIGURE 13.2B

Portfolio Expected Returns and Betas for Asset B

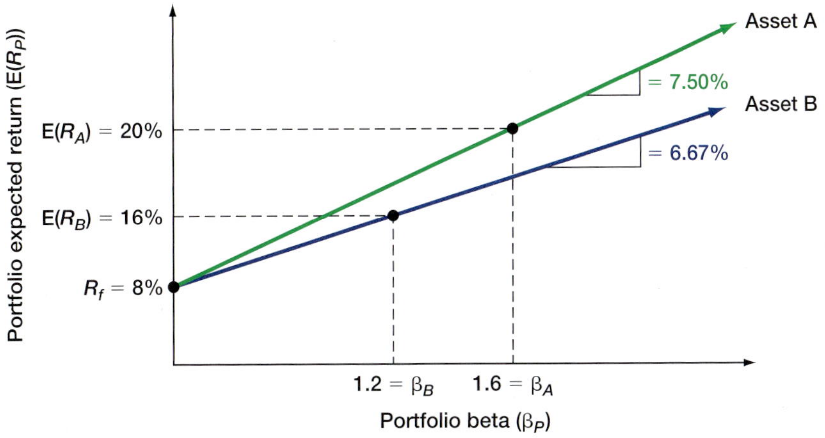

<< FIGURE 13.2C

Portfolio Expected Returns and Betas for Both Assets

Another way of seeing that A offers a superior return for its level of risk is to note that the slope of our line for Asset B is:

$$\text{Slope} = \frac{E(R_B) - R_f}{\beta_B}$$

$$= \frac{16\% - 8\%}{1.2} = 6.67\%$$

Thus, Asset B has a reward-to-risk ratio of 6.67 percent, which is less than the 7.5 percent offered by Asset A.

The Fundamental Result The situation we have described for Assets A and B could not persist in a well-organized, active market, because investors would be attracted to Asset A and away from Asset B. As a result, Asset A's price would rise and Asset B's price would fall. Because prices and returns move in opposite directions, A's expected return would decline and B's would rise.

This buying and selling would continue until the two assets plotted on exactly the same line, which means they would offer the same reward for bearing risk. In other words, in an active, competitive market, we must have the situation that:

$$\frac{E(R_A) - R_f}{\beta_A} = \frac{E(R_B) - R_f}{\beta_B}$$

This is the fundamental relationship between risk and return.

Our basic argument can be extended to more than just two assets. In fact, no matter how many assets we had, we would always reach the same conclusion:

The reward-to-risk ratio must be the same for all the assets in the market.

This result is really not so surprising. What it says is that, for example, if one asset has twice as much systematic risk as another asset, its risk premium will simply be twice as large.

Because all of the assets in the market must have the same reward-to-risk ratio, they all must plot on the same line. This argument is illustrated in Figure 13.3. As shown, Assets A

FIGURE 13.3 >>

Expected Returns and Systematic Risk

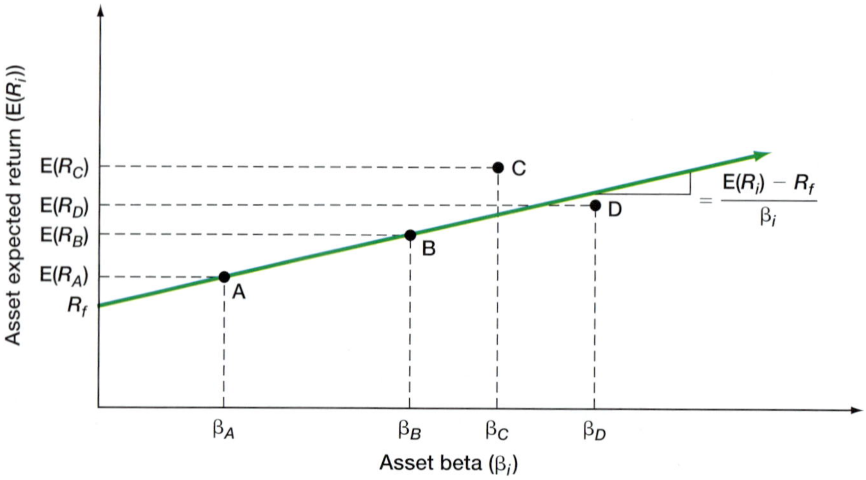

The fundamental relationship between beta and expected return is that all assets must have the same reward-to-risk ratio, $[E(R_i) - R_f]/\beta_i$. This means that they would all plot on the same straight line. Assets A and B are examples of this behavior. Asset C's expected return is too high; Asset D's is too low.

and B plot directly on the line and thus have the same reward-to-risk ratio. If an asset plotted above the line, such as C in Figure 13.3, its price would rise and its expected return would fall until it plotted exactly on the line. Similarly, if an asset plotted below the line, such as D in Figure 13.3, its expected return would rise until it too plotted directly on the line.

The arguments we have presented apply to active, competitive, well-functioning markets. The financial markets, such as the NYSE, best meet these criteria. Other markets, such as real asset markets, may or may not. For this reason, these concepts are most useful in examining financial markets. We will thus focus on such markets here. However, as we discuss in a later section, the information about risk and return gleaned from financial markets is crucial in evaluating the investments that a corporation makes in real assets.

Buy Low, Sell High

<< **EXAMPLE 13.7**

An asset is said to be *overvalued* if its price is too high given its expected return and risk. Suppose you observe the following situation:

Security	Beta	Expected Return
SWMS Co.	1.3	14%
Insec Co.	.8	10

The risk-free rate is currently 6 percent. Is one of the two securities overvalued relative to the other?

To answer, we compute the reward-to-risk ratio for both. For SWMS, this ratio is (14% − 6%)/1.3 = 6.15%. For Insec, this ratio is 5 percent. What we conclude is that Insec offers an insufficient expected return for its level of risk, at least, relative to SWMS. Because its expected return is too low, its price is too high. In other words, Insec is overvalued relative to SWMS, and we would expect to see its price fall relative to SWMS's. Notice that we could also say SWMS is undervalued relative to Insec.

The Security Market Line

The line that results when we plot expected returns and beta coefficients is obviously of some importance, so it's time we gave it a name. This line, which we use to describe the relationship between systematic risk and expected return in financial markets, is usually called the **security market line (SML)**. After NPV, the SML is arguably the most important concept in modern finance.

security market line (SML)
A positively sloped straight line displaying the relationship between expected return and beta.

Market Portfolios It will be very useful to know the equation of the SML. There are many different ways we could write it, but one way is particularly common. Suppose we consider a portfolio made up of all of the assets in the market. Such a portfolio is called a market portfolio, and we will express the expected return on this market portfolio as $\mathrm{E}(R_M)$.

Because all the assets in the market must plot on the SML, so must a market portfolio made up of those assets. To determine where it plots on the SML, we need to know the beta of the market portfolio, β_M. Because this portfolio is representative of all of the assets in the market, it must have average systematic risk. In other words, it has a beta of 1. We could therefore express the slope of the SML as:

$$\text{SML slope} = \frac{\mathrm{E}(R_M) - R_f}{\beta_M} = \frac{\mathrm{E}(R_M) - R_f}{1} = \mathrm{E}(R_M) - R_f$$

The term $\mathrm{E}(R_M) - R_f$ is often called the **market risk premium** because it is the risk premium on a market portfolio.

market risk premium
The slope of the SML, the difference between the expected return on a market portfolio and the risk-free rate.

The Capital Asset Pricing Model To finish up, if we let $E(R_i)$ and β_i stand for the expected return and beta, respectively, on any asset in the market, then we know that asset must plot on the SML. As a result, we know that its reward-to-risk ratio is the same as the overall market's:

$$\frac{E(R_i) - R_f}{\beta_i} = E(R_M) - R_f$$

If we rearrange this, then we can write the equation for the SML as:

$$E(R_i) = R_f + [E(R_M) - R_f] \times \beta_i \quad [13.7]$$

capital asset pricing model (CAPM)
The equation of the SML showing the relationship between expected return and beta.

This result is the famous **capital asset pricing model (CAPM)**.

What the CAPM shows is that the expected return for a particular asset depends on three things:

1. *The pure time value of money.* As measured by the risk-free rate, R_f, this is the reward for merely waiting for your money, without taking any risk.
2. *The reward for bearing systematic risk.* As measured by the market risk premium, $E(R_M) - R_f$, this component is the reward the market offers for bearing an average amount of systematic risk in addition to waiting.
3. *The amount of systematic risk.* As measured by β_i, this is the amount of systematic risk present in a particular asset or portfolio, relative to that in an average asset.

By the way, the CAPM works for portfolios of assets just as it does for individual assets. In an earlier section, we saw how to calculate a portfolio's β. To find the expected return on a portfolio, we simply use this β in the CAPM equation.

Figure 13.4 summarizes our discussion of the SML and the CAPM. As before, we plot expected return against beta. Now we recognize that, based on the CAPM, the slope of the SML is equal to the market risk premium, $E(R_M) - R_f$.

This concludes our presentation of concepts related to the risk-return trade-off. For future reference, Table 13.9 summarizes the various concepts in the order in which we discussed them.

FIGURE 13.4 >>

The Security Market Line (SML)

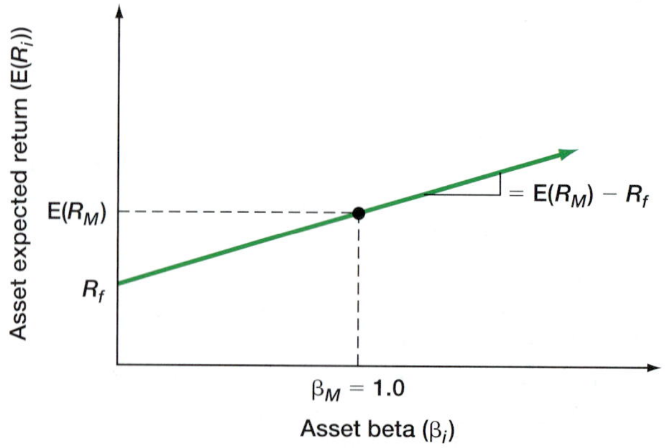

The slope of the security market line is equal to the market risk premium; i.e., the reward for bearing an average amount of systematic risk. The equation describing the SML can be written:

$$E(R_i) = R_f + \beta_i \times [E(R_M) - R_f]$$

which is the capital asset pricing model (CAPM).

<< TABLE 13.9

Summary of Risk and Return

I. Total Risk

The *total risk* of an investment is measured by the variance or, more commonly, the standard deviation of its return.

II. Total Return

The *total return* on an investment has two components: the expected return and the unexpected return. The unexpected return comes about because of unanticipated events. The risk from investing stems from the possibility of an unanticipated event.

III. Systematic and Unsystematic Risks

Systematic risks (also called *market risks*) are unanticipated events that affect almost all assets to some degree because the effects are economywide. *Unsystematic risks* are unanticipated events that affect single assets or small groups of assets. Unsystematic risks are also called *unique* or *asset-specific risks.*

IV. The Effect of Diversification

Some, but not all, of the risk associated with a risky investment can be eliminated by diversification. The reason is that unsystematic risks, which are unique to individual assets, tend to wash out in a large portfolio, but systematic risks, which affect all of the assets in a portfolio to some extent, do not.

V. The Systematic Risk Principle and Beta

Because unsystematic risk can be freely eliminated by diversification, the *systematic risk principle* states that the reward for bearing risk depends only on the level of systematic risk. The level of systematic risk in a particular asset, relative to the average, is given by the beta of that asset.

VI. The Reward-to-Risk Ratio and the Security Market Line

The *reward-to-risk ratio* for Asset i is the ratio of its risk premium, $E(R_i) - R_f$, to its beta, β_i:

$$\frac{E(R_i) - R_f}{\beta_i}$$

In a well-functioning market, this ratio is the same for every asset. As a result, when asset expected returns are plotted against asset betas, all assets plot on the same straight line, called the *security market line* (SML).

VII. The Capital Asset Pricing Model

From the SML, the expected return on Asset i can be written:

$$E(R_i) = R_f + [E(R_M) - R_f] \times \beta_i$$

This is the *capital asset pricing model* (CAPM). The expected return on a risky asset thus has three components. The first is the pure time value of money (R_f), the second is the market risk premium $[E(R_M) - R_f]$, and the third is the beta for that asset, (β_i).

Risk and Return

<< **EXAMPLE 13.8**

Suppose the risk-free rate is 4 percent, the market risk premium is 8.6 percent, and a particular stock has a beta of 1.3. Based on the CAPM, what is the expected return on this stock? What would the expected return be if the beta were to double?

With a beta of 1.3, the risk premium for the stock is 1.3 × 8.6%, or 11.18 percent. The risk-free rate is 4 percent, so the expected return is 15.18 percent. If the beta were to double to 2.6, the risk premium would double to 22.36 percent, so the expected return would be 26.36 percent.

Concept Questions

13.7a What is the fundamental relationship between risk and return in well-functioning markets?

13.7b What is the security market line? Why must all assets plot directly on it in a well-functioning market?

13.7c What is the capital asset pricing model (CAPM)? What does it tell us about the required return on a risky investment?

13.8 THE SML AND THE COST OF CAPITAL: A PREVIEW

Our goal in studying risk and return is twofold. First, risk is an extremely important consideration in almost all business decisions, so we want to discuss just what risk is and how it is rewarded in the market. Our second purpose is to learn what determines the appropriate discount rate for future cash flows. We briefly discuss this second subject now; we will discuss it in more detail in a subsequent chapter.

The Basic Idea

The security market line tells us the reward for bearing risk in financial markets. At an absolute minimum, any new investment our firm undertakes must offer an expected return that is no worse than what the financial markets offer for the same risk. The reason for this is simply that our shareholders can always invest for themselves in the financial markets.

The only way we benefit our shareholders is by finding investments with expected returns that are superior to what the financial markets offer for the same risk. Such an investment will have a positive NPV. So, if we ask, "What is the appropriate discount rate?" the answer is that we should use the expected return offered in financial markets on investments with the same systematic risk.

In other words, to determine whether or not an investment has a positive NPV, we essentially compare the expected return on that new investment to what the financial market offers on an investment with the same beta. This is why the SML is so important; it tells us the "going rate" for bearing risk in the economy.

The Cost of Capital

cost of capital
The minimum required return on a new investment.

The appropriate discount rate on a new project is the minimum expected rate of return an investment must offer to be attractive. This minimum required return is often called the **cost of capital** associated with the investment. It is called this because the required return is what the firm must earn on its capital investment in a project just to break even. It can thus be interpreted as the opportunity cost associated with the firm's capital investment.

Notice that when we say an investment is attractive if its expected return exceeds what is offered in financial markets for investments of the same risk, we are effectively using the internal rate of return (IRR) criterion that we developed and discussed in Chapter 9. The only difference is that now we have a much better idea of what determines the required return on an investment. This understanding will be critical when we discuss cost of capital and capital structure in Part 7 of our book.

Concept Questions

13.8a If an investment has a positive NPV, would it plot above or below the SML? Why?

13.8b What is meant by the term cost of capital?

SUMMARY AND CONCLUSIONS 13.9

This chapter has covered the essentials of risk. Along the way, we have introduced a number of definitions and concepts. The most important of these is the security market line, or SML. The SML is important because it tells us the reward offered in financial markets for bearing risk. Once we know this, we have a benchmark against which we compare the returns expected from real asset investments to determine if they are desirable.

Because we have covered quite a bit of ground, it's useful to summarize the basic economic logic underlying the SML as follows:

1. Based on capital market history, there is a reward for bearing risk. This reward is the risk premium on an asset.
2. The total risk associated with an asset has two parts: systematic risk and unsystematic risk. Unsystematic risk can be freely eliminated by diversification (this is the principle of diversification), so only systematic risk is rewarded. As a result, the risk premium on an asset is determined by its systematic risk. This is the systematic risk principle.
3. An asset's systematic risk, relative to the average, can be measured by its beta coefficient, β_i. The risk premium on an asset is then given by its beta coefficient multiplied by the market risk premium, $[E(R_M) - R_f] \times \beta_i$.
4. The expected return on an asset, $E(R_i)$, is equal to the risk-free rate, R_f, plus the risk premium:

   $$E(R_i) = R_f + [E(R_M) - R_f] \times \beta_i$$

   This is the equation of the SML, and it is often called the capital asset pricing model (CAPM).

This chapter completes our discussion of risk and return. Now that we have a better understanding of what determines a firm's cost of capital for an investment, the next several chapters will examine more closely how firms raise the long-term capital needed for investment.

Chapter Review and Self-Test Problems

13.1 Expected Return and Standard Deviation This problem will give you some practice calculating measures of prospective portfolio performance. There are two assets and three states of the economy:

State of Economy	Probability of State of Economy	Rate of Return if State Occurs	
		Stock A	Stock B
Recession	.20	−.15	.20
Normal	.50	.20	.30
Boom	.30	.60	.40

What are the expected returns and standard deviations for these two stocks?

13.2 Portfolio Risk and Return Using the information in the previous problem, suppose you have \$20,000 total. If you put \$15,000 in Stock A and the remainder in Stock B, what will be the expected return and standard deviation of your portfolio?

13.3 Risk and Return Suppose you observe the following situation:

Security	Beta	Expected Return
Cooley, Inc.	1.8	22.00%
Moyer Co.	1.6	20.24%

If the risk-free rate is 7 percent, are these securities correctly priced? What would the risk-free rate have to be if they are correctly priced?

13.4 CAPM Suppose the risk-free rate is 8 percent. The expected return on the market is 16 percent. If a particular stock has a beta of .7, what is its expected return based on the CAPM? If another stock has an expected return of 24 percent, what must its beta be?

Answers to Chapter Review and Self-Test Problems

13.1 The expected returns are just the possible returns multiplied by the associated probabilities:

$$\text{E}(R_A) = (.20 \times -.15) + (.50 \times .20) + (.30 \times .60) = 25\%$$
$$\text{E}(R_B) = (.20 \times .20) + (.50 \times .30) + (.30 \times .40) = 31\%$$

The variances are given by the sums of the squared deviations from the expected returns multiplied by their probabilities:

$$\begin{aligned}\sigma_A^2 &= .20 \times (-.15 - .25)^2 + .50 \times (.20 - .25)^2 + .30 \times (.60 - .25)^2\\ &= (.20 \times -.40^2) + (.50 \times -.05^2) + (.30 \times .25^2)\\ &= (.20 \times .16) + (.50 \times .0025) + (.30 \times .1225)\\ &= .0700\end{aligned}$$

$$\begin{aligned}\sigma_B^2 &= .20 \times (.20 - .31)^2 + .50 \times (.30 - .31)^2 + .30 \times (.40 - .31)^2\\ &= (.20 \times .11^2) + (.50 \times -.01^2) + (.30 \times .09^2)\\ &= (.20 \times .0121) + (.50 \times .0001) + (.30 \times .0081)\\ &= .0049\end{aligned}$$

The standard deviations are thus:

$$\sigma_A = \sqrt{.0700} = 26.46\%$$
$$\sigma_B = \sqrt{.0049} = 7\%$$

13.2 The portfolio weights are \$15,000/20,000 = .75 and \$5,000/20,000 = .25. The expected return is thus:

$$\begin{aligned}\text{E}(R_P) &= .75 \times \text{E}(R_A) + .25 \times \text{E}(R_B)\\ &= (.75 \times 25\%) + (.25 \times 31\%)\\ &= 26.5\%\end{aligned}$$

Alternatively, we could calculate the portfolio's return in each of the states:

State of Economy	Probability of State of Economy	Portfolio Return if State Occurs
Recession	.20	(.75 × −.15) + (.25 × .20) = −.0625
Normal	.50	(.75 × .20) + (.25 × .30) = .2250
Boom	.30	(.75 × .60) + (.25 × .40) = .5500

The portfolio's expected return is:

$$E(R_P) = (.20 \times -.0625) + (.50 \times .2250) + (.30 \times .5500) = 26.5\%$$

This is the same as we had before.

The portfolio's variance is:

$$\sigma_P^2 = .20 \times (-.0625 - .265)^2 + .50 \times (.225 - .265)^2 + .30 \times (.55 - .265)^2 = 0.0466$$

So the standard deviation is $\sqrt{.0466} = 21.59\%$.

13.3 If we compute the reward-to-risk ratios, we get $(22\% - 7\%)/1.8 = 8.33\%$ for Cooley versus 8.4% for Moyer. Relative to that of Cooley, Moyer's expected return is too high, so its price is too low.

If they are correctly priced, then they must offer the same reward-to-risk ratio. The risk-free rate would have to be such that:

$$(22\% - R_f)/1.8 = (20.44\% - R_f)/1.6$$

With a little algebra, we find that the risk-free rate must be 8 percent:

$$22\% - R_f = (20.44\% - R_f)(1.8/1.6)$$
$$22\% - 20.44\% \times 1.125 = R_f - R_f \times 1.125$$
$$R_f = 8\%$$

13.4 Because the expected return on the market is 16 percent, the market risk premium is $16\% - 8\% = 8\%$. The first stock has a beta of .7, so its expected return is $8\% + .7 \times 8\% = 13.6\%$.

For the second stock, notice that the risk premium is $24\% - 8\% = 16\%$. Because this is twice as large as the market risk premium, the beta must be exactly equal to 2. We can verify this using the CAPM:

$$E(R_i) = R_f + [E(R_M) - R_f] \times \beta_i$$
$$24\% = 8\% + (16\% - 8\%) \times \beta_i$$
$$\beta_i = 16\%/8\% = 2.0$$

Concepts Review and Critical Thinking Questions

1. **Diversifiable and Nondiversifiable Risks** In broad terms, why is some risk diversifiable? Why are some risks nondiversifiable? Does it follow that an investor can control the level of unsystematic risk in a portfolio, but not the level of systematic risk?
2. **Information and Market Returns** Suppose the government announces that, based on a just-completed survey, the growth rate in the economy is likely to be 2 percent

in the coming year, as compared to 5 percent for the year just completed. Will security prices increase, decrease, or stay the same following this announcement? Does it make any difference whether or not the 2 percent figure was anticipated by the market? Explain.

3. **Systematic versus Unsystematic Risk** Classify the following events as mostly systematic or mostly unsystematic. Is the distinction clear in every case?
   a. Short-term interest rates increase unexpectedly.
   b. The interest rate a company pays on its short-term debt borrowing is increased by its bank.
   c. Oil prices unexpectedly decline.
   d. An oil tanker ruptures, creating a large oil spill.
   e. A manufacturer loses a multimillion-dollar product liability suit.
   f. A Supreme Court decision substantially broadens producer liability for injuries suffered by product users.
4. **Systematic versus Unsystematic Risk** Indicate whether the following events might cause stocks in general to change price, and whether they might cause Big Widget Corp.'s stock to change price.
   a. The government announces that inflation unexpectedly jumped by 2 percent last month.
   b. Big Widget's quarterly earnings report, just issued, generally fell in line with analysts' expectations.
   c. The government reports that economic growth last year was at 3 percent, which generally agreed with most economists' forecasts.
   d. The directors of Big Widget die in a plane crash.
   e. Congress approves changes to the tax code that will increase the top marginal corporate tax rate. The legislation had been debated for the previous six months.
5. **Expected Portfolio Returns** If a portfolio has a positive investment in every asset, can the expected return on the portfolio be greater than that on every asset in the portfolio? Can it be less than that on every asset in the portfolio? If you answer yes to one or both of these questions, give an example to support your answer.
6. **Diversification** True or false: The most important characteristic in determining the expected return of a well-diversified portfolio is the variances of the individual assets in the portfolio. Explain.
7. **Portfolio Risk** If a portfolio has a positive investment in every asset, can the standard deviation on the portfolio be less than that on every asset in the portfolio? What about the portfolio beta?
8. **Beta and CAPM** Is it possible that a risky asset could have a beta of zero? Explain. Based on the CAPM, what is the expected return on such an asset? Is it possible that a risky asset could have a negative beta? What does the CAPM predict about the expected return on such an asset? Can you give an explanation for your answer?
9. **Corporate Downsizing** In recent years, it has been common for companies to experience significant stock price changes in reaction to announcements of massive layoffs. Critics charge that such events encourage companies to fire longtime employees and that Wall Street is cheering them on. Do you agree or disagree?
10. **Earnings and Stock Returns** As indicated by a number of examples in this chapter, earnings announcements by companies are closely followed by, and frequently result in, share price revisions. Two issues should come to mind. First, earnings

announcements concern past periods. If the market values stocks based on expectations of the future, why are numbers summarizing past performance relevant? Second, these announcements concern accounting earnings. Going back to Chapter 2, such earnings may have little to do with cash flow, so, again, why are they relevant?

Questions and Problems

BASIC
(Questions 1–20)

1. **Determining Portfolio Weights** What are the portfolio weights for a portfolio that has 70 shares of Stock A that sell for \$40 per share and 110 shares of Stock B that sell for \$22 per share?
2. **Portfolio Expected Return** You own a portfolio that has \$1,200 invested in Stock A and \$1,900 invested in Stock B. If the expected returns on these stocks are 11 percent and 16 percent, respectively, what is the expected return on the portfolio?
3. **Portfolio Expected Return** You own a portfolio that is 50 percent invested in Stock X, 30 percent in Stock Y, and 20 percent in Stock Z. The expected returns on these three stocks are 11 percent, 17 percent, and 14 percent, respectively. What is the expected return on the portfolio?
4. **Portfolio Expected Return** You have \$10,000 to invest in a stock portfolio. Your choices are Stock X with an expected return of 14 percent and Stock Y with an expected return of 9 percent. If your goal is to create a portfolio with an expected return of 12.2 percent, how much money will you invest in Stock X? In Stock Y?
5. **Calculating Expected Return** Based on the following information, calculate the expected return.

State of Economy	Probability of State of Economy	Rate of Return if State Occurs
Recession	.30	−.08
Boom	.70	.28

6. **Calculating Expected Return** Based on the following information, calculate the expected return.

State of Economy	Probability of State of Economy	Rate of Return if State Occurs
Recession	.20	−.05
Normal	.50	.12
Boom	.30	.25

7. **Calculating Returns and Standard Deviations** Based on the following information, calculate the expected return and standard deviation for the two stocks.

State of Economy	Probability of State of Economy	Rate of Return if State Occurs	
		Stock A	Stock B
Recession	.10	.06	−.20
Normal	.60	.07	.13
Boom	.30	.11	.33

8. **Calculating Expected Returns** A portfolio is invested 20 percent in Stock G, 70 percent in Stock J, and 10 percent in Stock K. The expected returns on these stocks are 8 percent, 15 percent, and 24 percent, respectively. What is the portfolio's expected return? How do you interpret your answer?

9. **Returns and Standard Deviations** Consider the following information:

State of Economy	Probability of State of Economy	Rate of Return if State Occurs		
		Stock A	Stock B	Stock C
Boom	.70	.07	.15	.33
Bust	.30	.13	.03	−.06

   a. What is the expected return on an equally weighted portfolio of these three stocks?

   b. What is the variance of a portfolio invested 20 percent each in A and B, and 60 percent in C?

10. **Returns and Standard Deviations** Consider the following information:

State of Economy	Probability of State of Economy	Rate of Return if State Occurs		
		Stock A	Stock B	Stock C
Boom	.30	.30	.45	.33
Good	.40	.12	.10	.15
Poor	.25	.01	−.15	−.05
Bust	.05	−.06	−.30	−.09

   a. Your portfolio is invested 30 percent each in A and C, and 40 percent in B. What is the expected return of the portfolio?

   b. What is the variance of this portfolio? The standard deviation?

11. **Calculating Portfolio Betas** You own a stock portfolio invested 25 percent in Stock Q, 20 percent in Stock R, 15 percent in Stock S, and 40 percent in Stock T. The betas for these four stocks are .6, 1.70, 1.15, and 1.34, respectively. What is the portfolio beta?

12. **Calculating Portfolio Betas** You own a portfolio equally invested in a risk-free asset and two stocks. If one of the stocks has a beta of 1.9 and the total portfolio is equally as risky as the market, what must the beta be for the other stock in your portfolio?

13. **Using CAPM** A stock has a beta of 1.3, the expected return on the market is 14 percent, and the risk-free rate is 5 percent. What must the expected return on this stock be?

14. **Using CAPM** A stock has an expected return of 14 percent, the risk-free rate is 4 percent, and the market risk premium is 6 percent. What must the beta of this stock be?

15. **Using CAPM** A stock has an expected return of 11 percent, its beta is .85, and the risk-free rate is 5.5 percent. What must the expected return on the market be?

16. **Using CAPM** A stock has an expected return of 17 percent, a beta of 1.9, and the expected return on the market is 11 percent. What must the risk-free rate be?

17. **Using CAPM** A stock has a beta of 1.2 and an expected return of 16 percent. A risk-free asset currently earns 5 percent.
    a. What is the expected return on a portfolio that is equally invested in the two assets?
    b. If a portfolio of the two assets has a beta of .75, what are the portfolio weights?
    c. If a portfolio of the two assets has an expected return of 8 percent, what is its beta?
    d. If a portfolio of the two assets has a beta of 2.40, what are the portfolio weights? How do you interpret the weights for the two assets in this case? Explain.
18. **Using the SML** Asset W has an expected return of 16 percent and a beta of 1.3. If the risk-free rate is 5 percent, complete the following table for portfolios of Asset W and a risk-free asset. Illustrate the relationship between portfolio expected return and portfolio beta by plotting the expected returns against the betas. What is the slope of the line that results?

Percentage of Portfolio in Asset W	Portfolio Expected Return	Portfolio Beta
0%		
25		
50		
75		
100		
125		
150		

19. **Reward-to-Risk Ratios** Stock Y has a beta of 1.50 and an expected return of 17 percent. Stock Z has a beta of .80 and an expected return of 10.5 percent. If the risk-free rate is 5.5 percent and the market risk premium is 7.5 percent, are these stocks correctly priced?
20. **Reward-to-Risk Ratios** In the previous problem, what would the risk-free rate have to be for the two stocks to be correctly priced?

INTERMEDIATE (Questions 21–27)

21. **Portfolio Returns** Using information from the previous chapter on capital market history, determine the return on a portfolio that is equally invested in large-company stocks and long-term government bonds. What is the return on a portfolio that is equally invested in small-company stocks and Treasury bills?
22. **CAPM** Using the CAPM, show that the ratio of the risk premiums on two assets is equal to the ratio of their betas.
23. **Portfolio Returns and Deviations** Consider the following information on three stocks:

State of Economy	Probability of State of Economy	Rate of Return if State Occurs		
		Stock A	Stock B	Stock C
Boom	.4	.20	.35	.60
Normal	.4	.15	.12	.05
Bust	.2	.01	−.25	−.50

a. If your portfolio is invested 40 percent each in A and B and 20 percent in C, what is the portfolio expected return? The variance? The standard deviation?

b. If the expected T-bill rate is 3.80 percent, what is the expected risk premium on the portfolio?

c. If the expected inflation rate is 3.50 percent, what are the approximate and exact expected real returns on the portfolio? What are the approximate and exact expected real risk premiums on the portfolio?

24. Analyzing a Portfolio You want to create a portfolio equally as risky as the market, and you have $1,000,000 to invest. Given this information, fill in the rest of the following table:

Asset	Investment	Beta
Stock A	$200,000	.80
Stock B	$250,000	1.30
Stock C		1.50
Risk-free asset		

25. Analyzing a Portfolio You have $100,000 to invest in a portfolio containing Stock X, Stock Y, and a risk-free asset. You must invest all of your money. Your goal is to create a portfolio that has an expected return of 13.5 percent and that has only 70 percent of the risk of the overall market. If X has an expected return of 31 percent and a beta of 1.8, Y has an expected return of 20 percent and a beta of 1.3, and the risk-free rate is 7 percent, how much money will you invest in Stock X? How do you interpret your answer?

26. Systematic versus Unsystematic Risk Consider the following information on Stocks I and II:

State of Economy	Probability of State of Economy	Rate of Return if State Occurs	
		Stock I	Stock II
Recession	.15	.09	−.30
Normal	.70	.42	.12
Irrational exuberance	.15	.26	.44

The market risk premium is 10 percent, and the risk-free rate is 4 percent. Which stock has the most systematic risk? Which one has the most unsystematic risk? Which stock is "riskier"? Explain.

27. SML Suppose you observe the following situation:

Security	Beta	Expected Return
Pete Corp.	1.3	.23
Repete Co.	.6	.13

Assume these securities are correctly priced. Based on the CAPM, what is the expected return on the market? What is the risk-free rate?

www.mhhe.com/edumarketinsight — S&P Problems

STANDARD & POOR'S

1. **Using CAPM** You can find estimates of beta for each company under the "Mthly. Val. Data" link. Locate the beta for Amazon.com (AMZN) and Dow Chemical (DOW). How has the beta for each of these companies changed over the period reported? Using the historical risk-free rate and market risk premium found in the chapter, calculate the expected return for each company based on the most recent beta. Is the expected return for each company what you would expect? Why or why not?

What's On the Web?

13.1 Expected Return You want to find the expected return for Honeywell using the CAPM. First you need the market risk premium. Go to www.cnnfn.com, follow the "Bonds & Rates" link, and the "Latest Rates" link. Find the current interest rate for three-month Treasury bills. Use the average large-company stock return in Table 12.3 to calculate the market risk premium. Next, go to finance.yahoo.com, enter the ticker symbol HON for Honeywell, and follow the "Profile" link. In the Statistics at a Glance section you will find the beta for Honeywell. What is the expected return for Honeywell using CAPM? What assumptions have you made to arrive at this number?

13.2 Portfolio Beta You have decided to invest in an equally weighted portfolio consisting of American Express, Procter & Gamble, Home Depot, and DuPont and need to find the beta of your portfolio. Go to finance.yahoo.com and follow the "Global Symbol Lookup" link to find the ticker symbols for each of these companies. Next, go back to finance.yahoo.com, enter one of the ticker symbols and get a stock quote. Follow the "Profile" link to find the beta for this company. You will then need to find the beta for each of the companies. What is the beta for your portfolio?

13.3 Beta Which companies currently have the highest and lowest betas? Go to www.amex.com and follow the "Screening" link. Enter 0 as the maximum beta and enter search. How many stocks currently have a beta less than 0? What is the lowest beta? Go back to the stock screener and enter 3 as the minimum. How many stocks have a beta above 3? What stock has the highest beta?

13.4 Security Market Line Go to finance.yahoo.com and enter the ticker symbol IP for International Paper. Follow the "Profile" link to get the beta for the company. Next, follow the "Research" link to find the estimated price in 12 months according to market analysts. Using the current share price and the mean target price, compute the expected return for this stock. Don't forget to include the expected dividend payments over the next year. Now go to money.cnn.com, follow the "Bonds & Rates" link, the "Latest Rates" link and find the current interest rate for three-month Treasury bills. Using this information, calculate the expected return on the market using the reward-to-risk ratio. Does this number make sense? Why or why not?

PART FIVE

Risk and Return

14 Options and Corporate Finance

For many workers, from senior management on down, employee stock options have become a very important part of their overall compensation. For example, in 2003, online auctioneer eBay gave its overseas employees an average of approximately $34,000 in stock options. U.S. employees did even better. They received an average of approximately $69,000 in stock options! In the same year, search provider Google granted employee stock options worth about $219 million to its employees.

Employee stock options are just one kind of option. This chapter introduces you to options and explains their features and what determines their value. The chapter also shows you that options show up in many places in corporate finance. In fact, once you know what to look for, they show up just about everywhere, so understanding how they work is essential.

option
A contract that gives its owner the right to buy or sell some asset at a fixed price on or before a given date.

Options are a part of everyday life. "Keep your options open" is sound business advice, and "We're out of options" is a sure sign of trouble. In finance, an **option** is an arrangement that gives its owner the right to buy or sell an asset at a fixed price anytime on or before a given date. The most familiar options are stock options. These are options to buy and sell shares of common stock, and we will discuss them in some detail in the following pages.

Of course, stock options are not the only options. In fact, at the root of it, many different kinds of financial decisions amount to the evaluation of options. For example, we will show how understanding options adds several important details to the NPV analysis we have discussed in earlier chapters.

Also, virtually all corporate securities have implicit or explicit option features, and the use of such features is growing. As a result, understanding securities that possess option features requires a general knowledge of the factors that determine an option's value.

This chapter starts with a description of different types of options. We identify and discuss the general factors that determine option values and show how ordinary debt and equity have optionlike characteristics. We then examine employee stock options and the important role of options in capital budgeting. We conclude by illustrating how option features are incorporated into corporate securities by discussing warrants, convertible bonds, and other optionlike securities.

OPTIONS: THE BASICS 14.1

An option is a contract that gives its owner the right to buy or sell some asset at a fixed price on or before a given date. For example, an option on a building might give the holder of the option the right to buy the building for $1 million anytime on or before the Saturday prior to the third Wednesday of January 2010.

Options are a unique type of financial contract because they give the buyer the right, but not the obligation, to do something. The buyer uses the option only if it is profitable to do so; otherwise, the option can be thrown away.

There is a special vocabulary associated with options. Here are some important definitions:

1. **Exercising the option**. The act of buying or selling the underlying asset via the option contract is called *exercising the option.*
2. **Strike price**, or exercise price. The fixed price specified in the option contract at which the holder can buy or sell the underlying asset is called the *strike price* or *exercise price.* The strike price is often called the *striking price.*
3. **Expiration date**. An option usually has a limited life. The option is said to expire at the end of its life. The last day on which the option may be exercised is called the *expiration date.*
4. **American** and **European options**. An American option may be exercised anytime up to and including the expiration date. A European option may be exercised only on the expiration date.

exercising the option
The act of buying or selling the underlying asset via the option contract.

strike price
The fixed price in the option contract at which the holder can buy or sell the underlying asset. Also, the exercise price or striking price.

expiration date
The last day on which an option may be exercised.

American option
An option that may be exercised at any time until its expiration date.

European option
An option that may only be exercised on the expiration date.

Puts and Calls

Options come in two basic types: puts and calls. A **call option** gives the owner the right to *buy* an asset at a fixed price during a particular time period. It may help you to remember that a call option gives you the right to "call in" an asset.

A **put option** is essentially the opposite of a call option. Instead of giving the holder the right to buy some asset, it gives the holder the right to *sell* that asset for a fixed exercise price. If you buy a put option, you can force the seller of the option to buy the asset from you for a fixed price and thereby "put it to them."

What about an investor who *sells* a call option? The seller receives money up front and has the *obligation* to sell the asset at the exercise price if the option holder wants it. Similarly, an investor who *sells* a put option receives cash up front and is then obligated to buy the asset at the exercise price if the option holder demands it.[1]

The asset involved in an option can be anything. The options that are most widely bought and sold, however, are stock options. These are options to buy and sell shares of stock. Because these are the best-known types of options, we will study them first. As we discuss stock options, keep in mind that the general principles apply to options involving any asset, not just shares of stock.

call option
The right to buy an asset at a fixed price during a particular period of time.

put option
The right to sell an asset at a fixed price during a particular period of time. The opposite of a call option.

Stock Option Quotations

On April 26, 1973, the Chicago Board Options Exchange (CBOE) opened and began organized trading in stock options. Put and call options involving stock in some of the best-known corporations in the United States are traded there. The CBOE is still the largest

[1] An investor who sells an option is often said to have "written" the option.

organized options market, but options are traded in a number of other places today, including the New York, American, and Philadelphia stock exchanges. Almost all such options are American (as opposed to European).

A simplified *Wall Street Journal* quotation (from the online edition) for a CBOE option might look something like this:

Prices at close June 15, 2005							
RWJ (*RWJ*)					**Underlying stock price: 100.00**		
		Call			**Put**		
Expiration	**Strike**	**Last**	**Volume**	**Open Interest**	**Last**	**Volume**	**Open Interest**
Jun	95	6	120	400	2	80	1000
July	95	6.50	40	200	2.80	100	4600
Aug	95	8	70	600	4	20	800

The first thing to notice here is the company identifier, RWJ. This tells us that these options involve the right to buy or sell shares of stock in the RWJ Corporation. To the right of company identifier is the closing price on the stock. As of the close of business on the day before this quotation, RWJ was selling for $100 per share.

The first column in the table shows the expiration months (June, July, and August). All CBOE options expire following the third Friday of the expiration month. The next column shows the strike price. The RWJ options listed here have an exercise price of $95.

Check out these options exchanges:
www.cboe.com
www.pacificex.com
www.phlx.com
www.kcbt.com
www.liffe.com
www.euronext.com

The next three columns give us information on call options. The first thing given is the most recent price (Last). Next we have volume, which tells us the number of option *contracts* that were traded that day. One option contract involves the right to buy (for a call option) or sell (for a put option) 100 shares of stock, and all trading actually takes place in contracts. Option prices, however, are quoted on a per-share basis.

The last piece of information given for the call options is the open interest. This is the number of contracts of each type currently outstanding. The three columns of information for call options (price, volume, and open interest) are followed by the same three columns for put options.

For example, the first option listed would be described as the "RWJ June 95 call." The price for this option is $6. If you pay the $6, then you have the right anytime between now and the third Friday of June to buy one share of RWJ stock for $95. Because trading takes place in round lots (multiples of 100 shares), one option contract costs you $6 × 100 = $600.

The other quotations are similar. For example, the July 95 put option costs $2.80. If you pay $2.80 × 100 = $280, then you have the right to sell 100 shares of RWJ stock anytime between now and the third Friday in July at a price of $95 per share.

Table 14.1 contains a more detailed CBOE quote reproduced from *The Wall Street Journal* (online). From our discussion in the preceding paragraphs, we know that these are Apple Computer (AAPL) options and that AAPL closed at 30.69 per share. Notice that there are multiple strike prices instead of just one. As shown, puts and calls with strike prices ranging from 22.50 up to 35 are available. The symbol "..." in a quote means that that particular contract didn't trade that day or that the contract is not currently available.

To check your understanding of option quotes, suppose you want the right to sell 100 shares of AAPL for $30 anytime up until the third Friday in July. What should you tell your broker and how much will it cost you?

Because you want the right to sell the stock for $30, you need to buy a *put* option with a $30 exercise price. So you call up your broker and place an order for one AAPL July 30

AppleC (*AAPL*)						**Underlying stock price*: 30.69**	
		Call			**Put**		
Expiration	**Strike**	**Last**	**Volume**	**Open Interest**	**Last**	**Volume**	**Open Interest**
Oct	22.50	. . .	. . .	286	0.30	39	2790
Jan	22.50	. . .	. . .	3497	0.65	2	2031
Jun	25.00	5.90	30	1300	. . .	. . .	5101
Jul	25.00	5.90	208	9465	0.10	465	9484
Oct	25.00	6.60	27	1195	0.65	12	3218
Jan	25.00	7.10	103	18045	1.15	66	11359
Jun	27.50	3.21	68	10283	. . .	. . .	3618
Jul	27.50	3.80	167	17887	0.30	2787	9468
Oct	27.50	4.70	39	5104	1.25	10	3908
Jan	27.50	5.70	197	7478	1.80	10	3162
Jun	30.00	0.85	1549	7662	0.15	1406	2417
Jul	30.00	1.85	860	34929	1.05	2613	8318
Oct	30.00	3.30	367	8898	2.20	391	2023
Jan	30.00	4.00	391	31627	2.75	187	2032
Jun	32.50	0.05	2	2641	1.55	5	339
Jul	32.50	0.80	141	34663	2.35	335	1413
Oct	32.50	2.00	60	4502	3.40	10	344
Jan	32.50	2.90	5	4069	4.00	3	73
Jul	35.00	0.30	227	182	. . .	. . .	. . .
Oct	35.00	1.05	34	10717	5.00	20	451
Jan	35.00	1.85	100	10693	. . .	. . .	292

<< TABLE 14.1

A Sample *Wall Street Journal* Option Quotation

**Underlying stock price* represents listed exchange price only. It may not match the composite closing price.

SOURCE: Reprinted with permission from *The Wall Street Journal,* June 16, 2004

put contract. Because the July 30 put is quoted at $1.05, you will have to pay $1.05 per share, or $105 in all (plus commission).

Of course, you can look up option prices on the Web. To do so, however, you have to know the relevant ticker symbol. It turns out the option ticker symbols are a bit more complicated than stock tickers, so our nearby *Work the Web* box shows you how to get them along with the associated option price quotes.

Option Payoffs

Looking at Table 14.1, suppose you buy 50 January 30 call contracts. The option is quoted at $4, so the contracts cost $400 each. You spend a total of 50 × $400 = $20,000. You wait awhile, and the expiration date rolls around.

Now what? You have the right to buy AAPL stock for $30 per share. If AAPL is selling for less than $30 a share, then this option isn't worth anything, and you throw it away. In this case, we say that the option has finished "out of the money" because the stock price is less than the exercise price. Your $20,000 is, alas, a complete loss.

If AAPL is selling for more than $30 per share, then you need to exercise your option. In this case, the option is "in the money" because the stock price exceeds the exercise price. Suppose AAPL has risen to, say, $50 per share. Because you have the right to buy AAPL at $30, you make a $20 profit on each share upon exercise. Each contract involves 100 shares, so you make $20 per share × 100 shares per contract = $2,000 per contract. Finally, you

WORK THE WEB

How do you find option prices for options that are currently traded? To find out, we went to finance.yahoo.com, got a stock quote for J.C. Penney (JCP), and followed the Options link. As you can see below, there were seven call option contracts and five put option contracts trading for J.C. Penney with a June 2004 expiration date.

View By Expiration: **Jun 04** | Jul 04 | Aug 04 | Nov 04 | Jan 05 | Jan 06

CALL OPTIONS — Expire at close Fri, Jun 18, 2004

Strike	Symbol	Last	Chg	Bid	Ask	Vol	Open Int
27.50	JCPFY.X	7.80	0.00	8.10	8.30	0	233
30.00	JCPFF.X	5.30	0.00	5.70	5.80	0	313
32.50	JCPFZ.X	3.00	0.00	3.30	3.40	0	2,964
35.00	JCPFG.X	1.25	↑0.10	1.15	1.25	109	3,039
37.50	JCPFU.X	0.15	↓0.05	0.15	0.20	190	1,156
40.00	JCPFH.X	0.10	0.00	N/A	0.05	10	157
42.50	JCPFV.X	0.00	0.00	N/A	0.05	0	150

PUT OPTIONS — Expire at close Fri, Jun 18, 2004

Strike	Symbol	Last	Chg	Bid	Ask	Vol	Open Int
27.50	JCPRY.X	0.05	0.00	N/A	0.05	0	210
30.00	JCPRF.X	0.05	0.00	N/A	0.05	10	809
32.50	JCPRZ.X	0.10	↓0.05	0.10	0.15	229	4,453
35.00	JCPRG.X	0.50	↓0.10	0.50	0.55	21	1,750
37.50	JCPRU.X	2.15	0.00	1.90	2.05	0	486

The Chicago Board Options Exchange (CBOE) sets the strike prices for traded options. The strike prices are centered around the current stock price, and the number of strike prices depends in part on the trading volume in the stock. If you examine the prices for the call options, you see the quotes behave as you might expect. As the strike price of the call option increases, the option contract becomes less valuable. Examining the put option prices, we see that two of the contracts with different strike prices traded at the same price. How is this possible? There are two reasons: First, as you have already noticed, the option contracts for J.C. Penney are not very actively traded, at least during this period. The prices for the $27.50 and $30 strike price put options never existed at the same point in time. In fact, no put option contracts with a $27.50 strike price traded on this day. Second, options traded on the exchange have a 5-cent "tick." This means that any change in price is a minimum of 5 cents. So, while you can price an option to the penny, you just can't trade on the "Penney."

own 50 contracts, so the value of your options is a handsome $100,000. Notice that, because you invested $20,000, your net profit is $80,000.

As our example indicates, the gains and losses from buying call options can be quite large. To illustrate further, suppose you simply purchase the stock with the $20,000 instead of buying call options. In this case, you will have about $20,000/30.69 = 651.68 shares. We can now compare what you have when the option expires for different stock prices:

Ending Stock Price	Option Value (50 contracts)	Net Profit or Loss (50 contracts)	Stock Value (651.68 shares)	Net Profit or Loss (651.68 shares)
$10	$ 0	−$ 20,000	$ 6,517	−$13,483
20	0	− 20,000	13,034	− 6,966
30	0	− 20,000	19,550	− 450
40	50,000	30,000	26,067	6,067
50	100,000	80,000	32,584	12,584
60	150,000	130,000	39,101	19,101

The option position clearly magnifies the gains and losses on the stock by a substantial amount. The reason is that the payoff on your 50 option contracts is based on 50 × 100 = 5,000 shares of stock instead of just 651.68.

In our example, notice that, if the stock price ends up below the exercise price, then you lose all $20,000 with the option. With the stock, you still have about what you started with. Also notice that the option can never be worth less than zero because you can always just throw it away. As a result, you can never lose more than your original investment (the $20,000 in our example).

It is important to recognize that stock options are a zero-sum game. By this we mean that whatever the buyer of a stock option makes, the seller loses, and vice versa. To illustrate, suppose, in our example just preceding, you *sell* 50 option contracts. You receive $20,000 up front, and you will be obligated to sell the stock for $30 if the buyer of the option wishes to exercise it. In this situation, if the stock price ends up below $30, you will be $20,000 ahead. If the stock price ends up above $30, you will have to sell something for less than it is worth, so you will lose the difference. For example, if the stock price is $50, you will have to sell 50 × 100 = 5,000 shares at $30 per share, so you will be out $50 − 30 = $20 per share, or $100,000 total. Because you received $20,000 up front, your net loss is $80,000. We can summarize some other possibilities as follows:

Ending Stock Price	Net Profit to Option Seller
$10	+$20,000
20	+ 20,000
30	+ 20,000
40	− 30,000
50	− 80,000
60	−130,000

Notice that the net profits to the option buyer (calculated previously) are just the opposites of these amounts.

Put Payoffs

<< **EXAMPLE 14.1**

Looking at Table 14.1, suppose you buy 10 AAPL January 32.50 put contracts. How much does this cost (ignoring commissions)? Just before the option expires, AAPL is selling for $22.50 per share. Is this good news or bad news? What is your net profit?

The option is quoted at 4, so one contract costs 100 × 4 = $400. Your 10 contracts total $4,000. You now have the right to sell 1,000 shares of AAPL for $32.50 per share. If the stock is currently selling for $22.50 per share, then this is most definitely good news. You can buy 1,000 shares at $22.50 and sell them for $32.50. Your puts are thus worth $32.50 − 22.50 = $10 per share, or $10 × 1,000 = $10,000 in all. Because you paid $4,000, your net profit is $10,000 − 4,000 = $6,000.

Concept Questions

14.1a What is a call option? A put option?

14.1b If you thought that a stock was going to drop sharply in value, how might you use stock options to profit from the decline?

14.2 FUNDAMENTALS OF OPTION VALUATION

Now that we understand the basics of puts and calls, we can discuss what determines their values. We will focus on call options in the discussion that follows, but the same type of analysis can be applied to put options.

Value of a Call Option at Expiration

We have already described the payoffs from call options for different stock prices. In continuing this discussion, the following notation will be useful:

To learn more about options, visit www.financial-guide.ch/ica/derivatives.

S_1 = Stock price at expiration (in one period)
S_0 = Stock price today
C_1 = Value of the call option on the expiration date (in one period)
C_0 = Value of the call option today
E = Exercise price on the option

From our previous discussion, remember that, if the stock price (S_1) ends up below the exercise price (E) on the expiration date, then the call option (C_1) is worth zero. In other words:

$$C_1 = 0 \quad \text{if } S_1 \leq E$$

Or, equivalently:

$$C_1 = 0 \quad \text{if } S_1 - E \leq 0 \qquad \textbf{[14.1]}$$

This is the case in which the option is out of the money when it expires.

If the option finishes in the money, then $S_1 > E$, and the value of the option at expiration is equal to the difference:

$$C_1 = S_1 - E \quad \text{if } S_1 > E$$

Or, equivalently:

$$C_1 = S_1 - E \quad \text{if } S_1 - E > 0 \qquad \textbf{[14.2]}$$

For example, suppose we have a call option with an exercise price of \$10. The option is about to expire. If the stock is selling for \$8, then we have the right to pay \$10 for something worth only \$8. Our option is thus worth exactly zero because the stock price is less than the exercise price on the option ($S_1 \leq E$). If the stock is selling for \$12, then the option has value. Because we can buy the stock for \$10, the option is worth $S_1 - E = \$12 - 10 = \$2$.

Figure 14.1 plots the value of a call option at expiration against the stock price. The result looks something like a hockey stick. Notice that for every stock price less than E, the value of the option is zero. For every stock price greater than E, the value of the call option

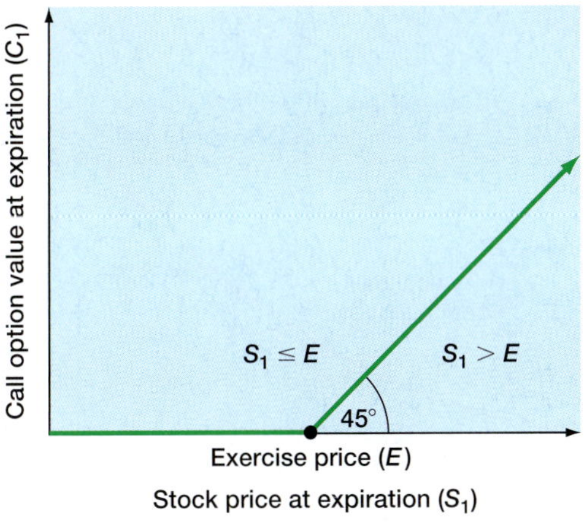

<< FIGURE 14.1

Value of a Call Option at Expiration for Different Stock Prices

As shown, the value of a call option at expiration is equal to zero if the stock price is less than or equal to the exercise price. The value of the call is equal to the stock price minus the exercise price ($S_1 - E$) if the stock price exceeds the exercise price. The resulting "hockey stick" shape is highlighted.

is $S_1 - E$. Also, once the stock price exceeds the exercise price, the option's value goes up dollar for dollar with the stock price.

The Upper and Lower Bounds on a Call Option's Value

Now that we know how to determine C_1, the value of the call at expiration, we turn to a somewhat more challenging question: How can we determine C_0, the value sometime *before* expiration? We will be discussing this in the next several sections. For now, we will establish the upper and lower bounds for the value of a call option.

The Upper Bound What is the most that a call option can sell for? If you think about it, the answer is obvious. A call option gives you the right to buy a share of stock, so it can never be worth more than the stock itself. This tells us the upper bound on a call's value: A call option will always sell for no more than the underlying asset. So, in our notation, the upper bound is:

$$C_0 \leq S_0 \qquad [14.3]$$

The Lower Bound What is the least a call option can sell for? The answer here is a little less obvious. First of all, the call can't sell for less than zero, so $C_0 \geq 0$. Furthermore, if the stock price is greater than the exercise price, the call option is worth at least $S_0 - E$.

To see why, suppose we have a call option selling for \$4. The stock price is \$10, and the exercise price is \$5. Is there a profit opportunity here? The answer is yes because you could buy the call for \$4 and immediately exercise it by spending an additional \$5. Your total cost of acquiring the stock would be \$4 + 5 = \$9. If you were to turn around and immediately sell the stock for \$10, you would pocket a \$1 certain profit.

Opportunities for riskless profits such as this one are called *arbitrages* (say "are-bi-trazh," with the accent on the first syllable) or *arbitrage opportunities*. One who arbitrages is called an *arbitrageur,* or just "arb" for short. The root for the term *arbitrage* is the same as the root for the word *arbitrate,* and an arbitrageur essentially arbitrates prices. In a well-organized market, significant arbitrages will, of course, be rare.

FIGURE 14.2 >>

Value of a Call Option Before Expiration for Different Stock Prices

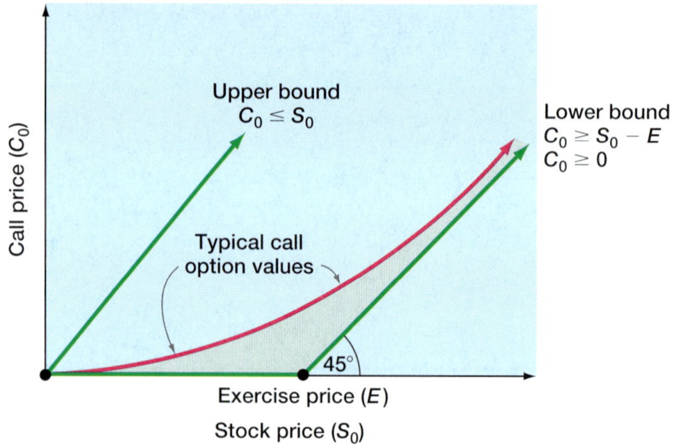

As shown, the upper bound on a call's value is given by the value of the stock ($C_0 \leq S_0$). The lower bound is either $S_0 - E$ or zero, whichever is larger. The highlighted curve illustrates the value of a call option prior to maturity for different stock prices.

In the case of a call option, to prevent arbitrage, the value of the call today must be greater than the stock price less the exercise price:

$$C_0 \geq S_0 - E$$

If we put our two conditions together, we have:

$$\begin{aligned} C_0 &\geq 0 && \text{if } S_0 - E < 0 \\ C_0 &\geq S_0 - E && \text{if } S_0 - E \geq 0 \end{aligned} \qquad [14.4]$$

These conditions simply say that the lower bound on the call's value is either zero or $S_0 - E$, whichever is bigger.

intrinsic value
The lower bound of an option's value, or what the option would be worth if it were about to expire.

Our lower bound is called the **intrinsic value** of the option, and it is simply what the option would be worth if it were about to expire. With this definition, our discussion thus far can be restated as follows: at expiration, an option is worth its intrinsic value; it will generally be worth more than that anytime before expiration.

Figure 14.2 displays the upper and lower bounds on the value of a call option. Also plotted is a curve representing typical call option values for different stock prices prior to maturity. The exact shape and location of this curve depends on a number of factors. We begin our discussion of these factors in the next section.

A Simple Model: Part I

Option pricing can be a complex subject, and we defer a detailed discussion to a later chapter. Fortunately, as is often the case, many of the key insights can be illustrated with a simple example. Suppose we are looking at a call option with one year to expiration and an exercise price of $105. The stock currently sells for $100, and the risk-free rate, R_f, is 20 percent.

The value of the stock in one year is uncertain, of course. To keep things simple, suppose we know that the stock price will be either $110 or $130. It is important to note that we *don't* know the odds associated with these two prices. In other words, we know the possible values for the stock, but not the probabilities associated with those values.

Because the exercise price on the option is $105, we know that the option will be worth either $110 − 105 = $5 or $130 − 105 = $25, but, once again, we don't know which. We do know one thing, however: Our call option is certain to finish in the money.

The Basic Approach Here is the crucial observation: It is possible to exactly duplicate the payoffs on the stock using a combination of the option and the risk-free asset. How? Do the following: Buy one call option and invest \$87.50 in a risk-free asset (such as a T-bill).

What will you have in a year? Your risk-free asset will earn 20 percent, so it will be worth \$87.50 × 1.20 = \$105. Your option will be worth \$5 or \$25, so the total value will be either \$110 or \$130, just like the value of the stock:

Stock Value	vs.	Risk-Free Asset Value	+	Call Value	=	Total Value
\$110		\$105		\$ 5		\$110
130		105		25		130

As illustrated, these two strategies—buying a share of stock or buying a call and investing in the risk-free asset—have exactly the same payoffs in the future.

Because these two strategies have the same future payoffs, they must have the same value today or else there would be an arbitrage opportunity. The stock sells for \$100 today, so the value of the call option today, C_0, is:

$$\begin{aligned} \$100 &= \$87.50 + C_0 \\ C_0 &= \$12.50 \end{aligned}$$

Where did we get the \$87.50? This is just the present value of the exercise price on the option, calculated at the risk-free rate:

$$E/(1 + R_f) = \$105/1.20 = \$87.50$$

Given this, our example shows that the value of a call option in this simple case is given by:

$$\begin{aligned} S_0 &= C_0 + E/(1 + R_f) \\ C_0 &= S_0 - E/(1 + R_f) \end{aligned} \qquad [14.5]$$

In words, the value of the call option is equal to the stock price minus the present value of the exercise price.

A More Complicated Case Obviously, our assumption that the stock price in one year will be either \$110 or \$130 is a vast oversimplification. We can now develop a more realistic model by assuming that the stock price in one year can be *anything* greater than or equal to the exercise price. Once again, we don't know how likely the different possibilities are, but we are certain that the option will finish somewhere in the money.

We again let S_1 stand for the stock price in one year. Now consider our strategy of investing \$87.50 in a riskless asset and buying one call option. The riskless asset will again be worth \$105 in one year, and the option will be worth S_1 − \$105, the value of which will depend on what the stock price is.

When we investigate the combined value of the option and the riskless asset, we observe something very interesting:

$$\begin{aligned} \text{Combined value} &= \text{Riskless asset value} + \text{Option value} \\ &= \$105 + (S_1 - 105) \\ &= S_1 \end{aligned}$$

Just as we had before, buying a share of stock has exactly the same payoff as buying a call option and investing the present value of the exercise price in the riskless asset.

Once again, to prevent arbitrage, these two strategies must have the same cost, so the value of the call option is equal to the stock price less the present value of the exercise price:[2]

$$C_0 = S_0 - E/(1 + R_f)$$

Our conclusion from this discussion is that determining the value of a call option is not difficult as long as we are certain that the option will finish somewhere in the money.

Four Factors Determining Option Values

For information on options and the underlying companies, see www.optionsnewsletter.com.

If we continue to suppose that our option is certain to finish in the money, then we can readily identify four factors that determine an option's value. There is a fifth factor that comes into play if the option can finish out of the money. We will discuss this last factor in the next section.

For now, if we assume that the option expires in t periods, then the present value of the exercise price is $E/(1 + R_f)^t$, and the value of the call is:

$$\text{Call option value} = \text{Stock value} - \text{Present value of the exercise price}$$
$$C_0 = S_0 - E/(1 + R_f)^t \quad \textbf{[14.6]}$$

If we take a look at this expression, we see that the value of the call obviously depends on four things:

1. *The stock price.* The higher the stock price (S_0) is, the more the call is worth. This comes as no surprise because the option gives us the right to buy the stock at a fixed price.
2. *The exercise price.* The higher the exercise price (E) is, the less the call is worth. This is also not a surprise because the exercise price is what we have to pay to get the stock.
3. *The time to expiration.* The longer the time to expiration is (the bigger t is), the more the option is worth. Once again, this is obvious. Because the option gives us the right to buy for a fixed length of time, its value goes up as that length of time increases.
4. *The risk-free rate.* The higher the risk-free rate (R_f) is, the more the call is worth. This result is a little less obvious. Normally, we think of asset values as going down as rates rise. In this case, the exercise price is a cash *outflow,* a liability. The current value of that liability goes down as the discount rate goes up.

Concept Questions

14.2a What is the value of a call option at expiration?

14.2b What are the upper and lower bounds on the value of a call option anytime before expiration?

14.2c Assuming that the stock price is certain to be greater than the exercise price on a call option, what is the value of the call? Why?

[2] You're probably wondering what would happen if the stock price were less than the present value of the exercise price, which would result in a negative value for the call option. This can't happen because we are certain that the stock price will be at least E in one year because we know the option will finish in the money. If the current price of the stock is less than $E/(1 + R_f)$, then the return on the stock is certain to be greater than the risk-free rate, which creates an arbitrage opportunity. For example, if the stock is currently selling for \$80, then the minimum return will be (\$105 − 80)/80 = 31.25%. Because we can borrow at 20 percent, we can earn a certain minimum return of 11.25 percent per dollar borrowed. This, of course, is an arbitrage opportunity.

VALUING A CALL OPTION

14.3

We now investigate the value of a call option when there is the possibility that the option will finish out of the money. We will again examine the simple case of two possible future stock prices. This case will let us identify the remaining factor that determines an option's value.

A Simple Model: Part II

From our previous example, we have a stock that currently sells for \$100. It will be worth either \$110 or \$130 in a year, and we don't know which. The risk-free rate is 20 percent. We are now looking at a different call option, however. This one has an exercise price of \$120 instead of \$105. What is the value of this call option?

The Philadelphia Stock Exchange has a good discussion of options: www.phlx.com/products.

This case is a little harder. If the stock ends up at \$110, the option is out of the money and worth nothing. If the stock ends up at \$130, the option is worth \$130 − 120 = \$10.

Our basic approach to determining the value of the call option will be the same. We will show once again that it is possible to combine the call option and a risk-free investment in a way that exactly duplicates the payoff from holding the stock. The only complication is that it's a little harder to determine how to do it.

For example, suppose we bought one call and invested the present value of the exercise price in a riskless asset as we did before. In one year, we would have \$120 from the riskless investment plus an option worth either zero or \$10. The total value would be either \$120 or \$130. This is not the same as the value of the stock (\$110 or \$130), so the two strategies are not comparable.

Instead, consider investing the present value of \$110 (the lower stock price) in a riskless asset. This guarantees us a \$110 payoff. If the stock price is \$110, then any call options we own are worthless, and we have exactly \$110 as desired.

When the stock is worth \$130, the call option is worth \$10. Our risk-free investment is worth \$110, so we are \$130 − 110 = \$20 short. Because each call option is worth \$10, we need to buy two of them to replicate the value of the stock.

Thus, in this case, investing the present value of the lower stock price in a riskless asset and buying two call options exactly duplicates owning the stock. When the stock is worth \$110, we have \$110 from our risk-free investment. When the stock is worth \$130, we have \$110 from the risk-free investment plus two call options worth \$10 each.

Because these two strategies have exactly the same value in the future, they must have the same value today, or else arbitrage would be possible:

$$S_0 = \$100 = 2 \times C_0 + \$110/(1 + R_f)$$
$$2 \times C_0 = \$100 - 110/1.20$$
$$C_0 = \$4.17$$

Each call option is thus worth \$4.17.

EXAMPLE 14.2

Don't Call Us, We'll Call You

We are looking at two call options on the same stock, one with an exercise price of \$20 and one with an exercise price of \$30. The stock currently sells for \$35. Its future price will be either \$25 or \$50. If the risk-free rate is 10 percent, what are the values of these call options?

continued

The first case (with the \$20 exercise price) is not difficult because the option is sure to finish in the money. We know that the value is equal to the stock price less the present value of the exercise price:

$$\begin{aligned} C_0 &= S_0 - E/(1 + R_f) \\ &= \$35 - 20/1.1 \\ &= \$16.82 \end{aligned}$$

In the second case, the exercise price is \$30, so the option can finish out of the money. At expiration, the option is worth \$0 if the stock is worth \$25. The option is worth \$50 − 30 = \$20 if it finishes in the money.

As before, we start by investing the present value of the lowest stock price in the risk-free asset. This costs \$25/1.1 = \$22.73. At expiration, we have \$25 from this investment.

If the stock price is \$50, then we need an additional \$25 to duplicate the stock payoff. Because each option is worth \$20 in this case, we need \$25/20 = 1.25 options. So, to prevent arbitrage, investing the present value of \$25 in a risk-free asset and buying 1.25 call options must have the same value as the stock:

$$\begin{aligned} S_0 &= 1.25 \times C_0 + \$25/(1 + R_f) \\ \$35 &= 1.25 \times C_0 + \$25/(1 + .10) \\ C_0 &= \$9.82 \end{aligned}$$

Notice that this second option had to be worth less because it has the higher exercise price.

The Fifth Factor

We now illustrate the fifth (and last) factor that determines an option's value. Suppose everything in our example is the same as before except that the stock price can be \$105 or \$135 instead of \$110 or \$130. Notice that the effect of this change is to make the stock's future price more volatile than before.

We investigate the same strategy that we used previously: Invest the present value of the lowest stock price (\$105 in this case) in the risk-free asset and buy two call options. If the stock price is \$105, then, as before, the call options have no value and we have \$105 in all.

If the stock price is \$135, then each option is worth $S_1 - E = \$135 - 120 = \$15$. We have two calls, so our portfolio is worth $\$105 + 2 \times 15 = \$135$. Once again, we have exactly replicated the value of the stock.

What has happened to the option's value? More to the point, the variance of the return on the stock has increased. Does the option's value go up or down? To find out, we need to solve for the value of the call just as we did before:

$$\begin{aligned} S_0 = \$100 &= 2 \times C_0 + \$105/(1 + R_f) \\ 2 \times C_0 &= \$100 - 105/1.20 \\ C_0 &= \$6.25 \end{aligned}$$

The value of the call option has gone up from \$4.17 to \$6.25.

Based on our example, the fifth and final factor that determines an option's value is the variance of the return on the underlying asset. Furthermore, the *greater* that variance is, the *more* the option is worth. This result appears a little odd at first, and it may be somewhat surprising to learn that increasing the risk (as measured by return variance) on the underlying asset increases the value of the option.

The reason that increasing the variance on the underlying asset increases the value of the option isn't hard to see in our example. Changing the lower stock price to \$105 from \$110 doesn't hurt a bit because the option is worth zero in either case. However, moving the upper possible price to \$135 from \$130 makes the option worth more when it is in the money.

More generally, increasing the variance of the possible future prices on the underlying asset doesn't affect the option's value when the option finishes out of the money. The value is always zero in this case. On the other hand, increasing that variance increases the possible payoffs when the option is in the money, so the net effect is to increase the option's value. Put another way, because the downside risk is always limited, the only effect is to increase the upside potential.

In later discussion, we will use the usual symbol, σ^2, to stand for the variance of the return on the underlying asset.

A Closer Look

Before moving on, it will be useful to consider one last example. Suppose the stock price is \$100, and it will move either up or down by 20 percent. The risk-free rate is 5 percent. What is the value of a call option with a \$90 exercise price?

The stock price will be either \$80 or \$120. The option is worth zero when the stock is worth \$80, and it's worth \$120 − 90 = \$30 when the stock is worth \$120. We will therefore invest the present value of \$80 in the risk-free asset and buy some call options.

When the stock finishes at \$120, our risk-free asset pays \$80, leaving us \$40 short. Each option is worth \$30 in this case, so we need \$40/30 = 4/3 options to match the payoff on the stock. The option's value must thus be given by:

$$\begin{aligned} S_0 &= \$100 = 4/3 \times C_0 + \$80/1.05 \\ C_0 &= (3/4) \times (\$100 - 76.19) \\ &= \$17.86 \end{aligned}$$

To make our result a little bit more general, notice that the number of options that you need to buy to replicate the value of the stock is always equal to $\Delta S/\Delta C$, where ΔS is the difference in the possible stock prices and ΔC is the difference in the possible option values. In our current case, for example, ΔS would be \$120 − 80 = \$40 and ΔC would be \$30 − 0 = \$30, so $\Delta S/\Delta C$ would be \$40/30 = 4/3, as we calculated.

Notice also that when the stock is certain to finish in the money, $\Delta S/\Delta C$ is always exactly equal to one, so one call option is always needed. Otherwise, $\Delta S/\Delta C$ is greater than one, so more than one call option is needed.

This concludes our discussion of option valuation. The most important thing to remember is that the value of an option depends on five factors. Table 14.2 summarizes these factors and the direction of their influence for both puts and calls. In Table 14.2, the sign in parentheses indicates the direction of the influence.[3] In other words, the sign tells us whether the value of the option goes up or down when the value of a factor increases. For example, notice that increasing the exercise price reduces the value of a call option. Increasing any of the other four factors increases the value of the call. Notice also that the time to expiration and the variance of return act the same for puts and calls. The other three factors have opposite signs in the two cases.

[3] The signs in Table 14.2 are for American options. For a European put option, the effect of increasing the time to expiration is ambiguous, and the direction of the influence can be positive or negative.

TABLE 14.2 >>

Five Factors That Determine Option Values

Factor	Direction of Influence: Calls	Direction of Influence: Puts
Current value of the underlying asset	(+)	(−)
Exercise price on the option	(−)	(+)
Time to expiration on the option	(+)	(+)
Risk-free rate	(+)	(−)
Variance of return on the underlying asset	(+)	(+)

We have not considered how to value a call option when the option can finish out of the money and the stock price can take on more than two values. A very famous result, the Black-Scholes option pricing model, is needed in this case. We cover this subject in a later chapter.

Concept Questions

14.3a What are the five factors that determine an option's value?

14.3b What is the effect of an increase in each of the five factors on the value of a call option? Give an intuitive explanation for your answer.

14.3c What is the effect of an increase in each of the five factors on the value of a put option? Give an intuitive explanation for your answer.

14.4 EMPLOYEE STOCK OPTIONS

Options are important in corporate finance in a lot of different ways. In this section, we begin to examine some of these by taking a look at **employee stock options**, or ESOs. An ESO is, in essence, a call option that a firm gives to employees giving them the right to buy shares of stock in the company. The practice of granting options to employees has become widespread. It is almost universal for upper management, but some companies, like The Gap and Starbucks, grant options to almost every employee. Thus, an understanding of ESOs is important. Why? Because you may very soon be an ESO holder!

employee stock option (ESO)
An option granted to an employee by a company giving the employee the right to buy shares of stock in the company at a fixed price for a fixed time.

ESO Features

Since ESOs are basically call options, we have already covered most of the important aspects. However, ESOs have a few features that make them different from regular stock options. The details differ from company to company, but a typical ESO has a 10-year life, which is much longer than most ordinary options. Unlike traded options, ESOs cannot be sold. They also have what is known as a "vesting" period. Often, for up to three years or so, an ESO cannot be exercised and also must be forfeited if an employee leaves the company. After this period, the options "vest," which means they can be exercised. Sometimes, employees who resign with vested options are given a limited time to exercise their options.

See www.esopassociation.org for a site devoted to employee stock options.

Why are ESOs granted? There are basically two reasons. First, going back to Chapter 1, the owners of a corporation (the shareholders) face the basic problem of aligning shareholder and management interests and also of providing incentives for employees to focus on corporate goals. ESOs are a powerful motivator because, as we have seen, the payoffs on options can be very large. High-level executives in particular stand to gain enormous wealth if they are successful in creating value for stockholders.

The second reason some companies rely heavily on ESOs is that an ESO has no immediate, upfront, out-of-pocket cost to the corporation. In smaller, possibly cash-strapped, companies, ESOs are simply a substitute for ordinary wages. Employees are willing to accept them instead of cash, hoping for big payoffs in the future. In fact, ESOs are a major recruiting tool, allowing businesses to attract talent that they otherwise could not afford.

ESO Repricing

ESOs are almost always "at the money" when they are issued, meaning that the stock price is equal to the strike price. Notice that, in this case, the intrinsic value is zero, so there is no value from immediate exercise. Of course, even though the intrinsic value is zero, an ESO is still quite valuable because of, among other things, its very long life.

If the stock falls significantly after an ESO is granted, then the option is said to be "underwater." On occasion, a company will decide to lower the strike price on underwater options. Such options are said to be "restruck" or "repriced."

For an employee stock option calculator, visit www.stock-options.com.

The practice of repricing ESOs is very controversial. Companies that do it argue that once an ESO becomes deeply out of the money, it loses its incentive value because employees recognize there is only a small chance that the option will finish in the money. In fact, employees may leave and join other companies where they receive a fresh options grant.

For example, Cosi, the sandwich shop chain, repriced more than 800,000 options for top executives in early 2004. The biggest winner in the repricing appeared to be cofounder and VP Jay Wainwright. The exercise price on the 360,521 options he held dropped to $2.26 a share. The original strike prices ranged from $5.30 to $12.25. In defense of the repricing, Cosi stated that its goal was to motivate employees as part of a turnaround effort.

Critics of repricing point out that a lowered strike price is, in essence, a reward for failing. They also point out that if employees know that options will be repriced, then much of the incentive effect is lost. Because of this controversy, many companies do not reprice options or have voted against repricing. For example, pharmaceutical giant Bristol-Myers Squibb's explicit policy prohibiting option repricing states that: "It is the Board of Directors' policy that the company will not, without stockholder approval, amend any employee or non-employee director stock option to reduce the exercise price (except for appropriate adjustment in the case of a stock split or similar change in capitalization)." However, other equally well-known companies have no such policy, and some have been labeled "serial repricers." The accusation is that such companies routinely drop strike prices following stock price declines.

For more information on ESOs, try the National Center for Employee Ownership at www.nceo.org.

Today, many companies award options on a regular basis, perhaps annually or even quarterly. That way, an employee will always have at least some options that are near the money even if others are underwater. Also, regular grants ensure that employees always have unvested options, which gives them an added incentive to stay with their current employer rather than forfeit the potentially valuable options.

Concept Questions

14.4a What are the key differences between a traded stock option and an ESO?

14.4b What is ESO repricing? Why is it controversial?

EQUITY AS A CALL OPTION ON THE FIRM'S ASSETS 14.5

Now that we understand the basic determinants of an option's value, we turn to examining some of the many ways that options appear in corporate finance. One of the most important insights we gain from studying options is that the common stock in a leveraged firm (one that has issued debt) is effectively a call option on the assets of the firm. This is a remarkable observation, and we explore it next.

Looking at an example is the easiest way to get started. Suppose a firm has a single debt issue outstanding. The face value is \$1,000, and the debt is coming due in a year. There are no coupon payments between now and then, so the debt is effectively a pure discount bond. In addition, the current market value of the firm's assets is \$950, and the risk-free rate is 12.5 percent.

In a year, the stockholders will have a choice. They can pay off the debt for \$1,000 and thereby acquire the assets of the firm free and clear, or they can default on the debt. If they default, the bondholders will own the assets of the firm.

In this situation, the stockholders essentially have a call option on the assets of the firm with an exercise price of \$1,000. They can exercise the option by paying the \$1,000, or they can choose not to exercise the option by defaulting. Whether or not they will choose to exercise obviously depends on the value of the firm's assets when the debt becomes due.

If the value of the firm's assets exceeds \$1,000, then the option is in the money, and the stockholders will exercise by paying off the debt. If the value of the firm's assets is less than \$1,000, then the option is out of the money, and the stockholders will optimally choose to default. What we now illustrate is that we can determine the values of the debt and equity using our option pricing results.

Case I: The Debt Is Risk-Free

Suppose that in one year the firm's assets will be worth either \$1,100 or \$1,200. What is the value today of the equity in the firm? The value of the debt? What is the interest rate on the debt?

To answer these questions, we first recognize that the option (the equity in the firm) is certain to finish in the money because the value of the firm's assets (\$1,100 or \$1,200) will always exceed the face value of the debt. In this case, from our discussion in previous sections, we know that the option value is simply the difference between the value of the underlying asset and the present value of the exercise price (calculated at the risk-free rate). The present value of \$1,000 in one year at 12.5 percent is \$888.89. The current value of the firm is \$950, so the option (the firm's equity) is worth \$950 − 888.89 = \$61.11.

What we see is that the equity, which is effectively an option to purchase the firm's assets, must be worth \$61.11. The debt must therefore actually be worth \$888.89. In fact, we really didn't need to know about options to handle this example, because the debt is risk-free. The reason is that the bondholders are certain to receive \$1,000. Because the debt is risk-free, the appropriate discount rate (and the interest rate on the debt) is the risk-free rate, and we therefore know immediately that the current value of the debt is \$1,000/1.125 = \$888.89. The equity is thus worth \$950 − 888.89 = \$61.11, as we calculated.

Case II: The Debt Is Risky

Suppose now that the value of the firm's assets in one year will be either \$800 or \$1,200. This case is a little more difficult because the debt is no longer risk-free. If the value of the assets turns out to be \$800, then the stockholders will not exercise their option and will thereby default. The stock is worth nothing in this case. If the assets are worth \$1,200, then the stockholders will exercise their option to pay off the debt and will enjoy a profit of \$1,200 − 1,000 = \$200.

What we see is that the option (the equity in the firm) will be worth either zero or \$200. The assets will be worth either \$1,200 or \$800. Based on our discussion in previous sections,

IN THEIR OWN WORDS . . .

Robert C. Merton on Applications of Options Analysis

>> **Organized markets for** trading options on stocks, fixed-income securities, currencies, financial futures, and a variety of commodities are among the most successful financial innovations of the past generation. Commercial success is not, however, the reason that option pricing analysis has become one of the cornerstones of finance theory. Instead, its central role derives from the fact that optionlike structures permeate virtually every part of the field.

From the first observation 30 years ago that leveraged equity has the same payoff structure as a call option, option pricing theory has provided an integrated approach to the pricing of corporate liabilities, including all types of debt, preferred stocks, warrants, and rights. The same methodology has been applied to the pricing of pension fund insurance, deposit insurance, and other government loan guarantees. It has also been used to evaluate various labor contract provisions such as wage floors and guaranteed employment including tenure.

A significant and recent extension of options analysis has been to the evaluation of operating or "real" options in capital budgeting decisions. For example, a facility that can use various inputs to produce various outputs provides the firm with operating options not available from a specialized facility that uses a fixed set of inputs to produce a single type of output. Similarly, choosing among technologies with different proportions of fixed and variable costs can be viewed as evaluating alternative options to change production levels, including abandonment of the project. Research and development projects are essentially options to either establish new markets, expand market share, or reduce production costs. As these examples suggest, options analysis is especially well suited to the task of evaluating the "flexibility" components of projects. These are precisely the components whose values are particularly difficult to estimate by using traditional capital budgeting techniques.

Robert C. Merton is the John and Natty McArthur University Professor at Harvard University. He was previously the J.C. Penney Professor of Management at MIT. He received the 1997 Nobel Prize in Economics for his work on pricing options and other contingent claims and for his work on risk and uncertainty.

a portfolio that has the present value of \$800 invested in a risk-free asset and (\$1,200 − 800)/(200 − 0) = 2 call options exactly replicates the value of the assets of the firm.

The present value of \$800 at the risk-free rate of 12.5 percent is \$800/1.125 = \$711.11. This amount, plus the value of the two call options, is equal to \$950, the current value of the firm:

$$\$950 = 2 \times C_0 + \$711.11$$
$$C_0 = \$119.44$$

Because the call option in this case is actually the firm's equity, the value of the equity is \$119.44. The value of the debt is thus \$950 − 119.44 = \$830.56.

Finally, because the debt has a \$1,000 face value and a current value of \$830.56, the interest rate is (\$1,000/830.56) − 1 = 20.4%. This exceeds the risk-free rate, of course, because the debt is now risky.

Equity as a Call Option

<< **EXAMPLE 14.3**

Swenson Software has a pure discount debt issue with a face value of \$100. The issue is due in a year. At that time, the assets of the firm will be worth either \$55 or \$160, depending on the sales success of Swenson's latest product. The assets of the firm are currently worth \$110. If the risk-free rate is 10 percent, what is the value of the equity in Swenson? The value of the debt? The interest rate on the debt?

To replicate the value of the assets of the firm, we first need to invest the present value of \$55 in the risk-free asset. This costs \$55/1.10 = \$50. If the assets turn out to be worth \$160, then the option is worth \$160 − 100 = \$60. Our risk-free asset will be worth \$55,

continued

so we need ($160 − 55)/60 = 1.75 call options. Because the firm is currently worth $110, we have:

$$\$110 = 1.75 \times C_0 + \$50$$
$$C_0 = \$34.29$$

The equity is thus worth $34.29; the debt is worth $110 − 34.29 = $75.71. The interest rate on the debt is about ($100/75.71) − 1 = 32.1%.

Concept Questions

14.5a Why do we say that the equity in a leveraged firm is effectively a call option on the firm's assets?

14.5b All other things being the same, would the stockholders of a firm prefer to increase or decrease the volatility of the firm's return on assets? Why? What about the bondholders? Give an intuitive explanation.

14.6 OPTIONS AND CAPITAL BUDGETING

real option
An option that involves real assets as opposed to financial assets such as shares of stock.

Most of the options we have discussed so far are financial options because they involve the right to buy or sell financial assets such as shares of stock. In contrast, **real options** involve real assets. As we will discuss in this section, our understanding of capital budgeting can be greatly enhanced by recognizing that many corporate investment decisions really amount to the evaluation of real options.

To give a simple example of a real option, imagine that you are shopping for a used car. You find one that you like for $4,000, but you are not completely sure. So, you give the owner of the car $150 to hold the car for you for one week, meaning that you have one week to buy the car or else you forfeit your $150. As you probably recognize, what you have done here is to purchase a call option, giving you the right to buy the car at a fixed price for a fixed time. It's a real option because the underlying asset (the car) is a real asset.

The use of options such as the one in our car example is very common in the business world. For example, real estate developers frequently need to purchase several smaller tracts of land from different owners to assemble a single larger tract. The development can't go forward unless all of the smaller properties are obtained. In this case, the developer will often buy options on the individual properties, but only exercise those options if all of the necessary pieces can be obtained.

These examples involve explicit options. As it turns out, almost all capital budgeting decisions contain numerous *implicit* options. We discuss the most important types of these next.

The Investment Timing Decision

Consider a business that is examining a new project of some sort. What this normally means is management must decide whether to make an investment outlay to acquire the new assets needed for the project. If you think about it, what management has is the right, but not the obligation, to pay some fixed amount (the initial investment) and thereby acquire a real asset (the project). In other words, essentially all proposed projects are real options!

Based on our discussion in previous chapters, you already know how to analyze proposed business investments. You would identify and analyze the relevant cash flows and assess the net present value (NPV) of the proposal. If the NPV is positive, you would recommend taking the project, where taking the project amounts to exercising the option.

There is a very important qualification to this discussion that involves mutually exclusive investments. Remember that two (or more) investments are said to be mutually exclusive if we can take only one of them. A standard example is a situation in which we own a piece of land that we wish to build on. We are considering building either a gasoline station or an apartment building. We further think that both projects have positive NPVs, but, of course, we can take only one. Which one do we take? The obvious answer is that we take the one with the larger NPV.

Here is the key point. Just because an investment has a positive NPV doesn't mean we should take it today. That sounds like a complete contradiction of what we have said all along, but it isn't. The reason is that if we take a project today, we can't take it later. Put differently, almost all projects compete with themselves in time. We can take a project now, a month from now, a year from now, and so on. We therefore have to compare the NPV of taking the project now versus the NPV of taking it later. Deciding when to take a project is called the **investment timing decision**.

investment timing decision
The evaluation of the optimal time to begin a project.

A simple example is useful to illustrate the investment timing decision. A project costs \$100 and has a single future cash flow. If we take it today, the cash flow will be \$120 in one year. If we wait one year, the project will still cost \$100, but the cash flow the following year (i.e., two years from now) will be \$130 because the potential market is bigger. If these are the only two options, and the relevant discount rate is 10 percent, what should we do?

To answer this question, we need to compute the two NPVs. If we take it today, the NPV is:

$$\text{NPV} = -\$100 + 120/1.1 = \$9.09$$

If we wait one year, the NPV at that time would be:

$$\text{NPV} = -\$100 + 130/1.1 = \$18.18$$

This \$18.18 is the NPV one year from now. We need the value today, so we discount back one period:

$$\text{NPV} = \$18.18/1.1 = \$16.53$$

So, the choice is clear. If we wait, the NPV is \$16.53 today compared to \$9.09 if we start immediately, so the optimal time to begin the project is one year from now.

The fact that we do not have to take a project immediately is often called the "option to wait." In our simple example, the value of the option to wait is the difference in NPVs, \$16.53 − 9.09 = \$7.44. This \$7.44 is the extra value created by deferring the start of the project as opposed to taking it today.

As our example illustrates, the option to wait can be very valuable. Just how valuable depends on the type of project. If we were thinking about a consumer product intended to capitalize on a current fashion or trend, then the option to wait is probably not very valuable because the window of opportunity is probably short. In contrast, suppose the project in question is a proposal to replace an existing production facility with a new, higher-efficiency one. This type of investment can be made now or later. In this case, the option to wait may be very valuable.

EXAMPLE 14.4 >> The Investment Timing Decision

A project costs $200 and has a future cash flow of $42 per year forever. If we wait one year, the project will cost $240 because of inflation, but the cash flows will be $48 per year forever. If these are the only two options, and the relevant discount rate is 12 percent, what should we do? What is the value of the option to wait?

In this case, the project is a simple perpetuity. If we take it today, the NPV is:

$$\text{NPV} = -\$200 + 42/.12 = \$150$$

If we wait one year, the NPV at that time would be:

$$\text{NPV} = -\$240 + 48/.12 = \$160$$

So, $160 is the NPV one year from now, but we need to know the value today. Discounting back one period, we get:

$$\text{NPV} = \$160/1.12 = \$142.86.$$

If we wait, the NPV is $142.86 today compared to $150 if we start immediately, so the optimal time to begin the project is now.

What's the value of the option to wait? It is tempting to say that it is $142.86 − $150 = −$7.14, but that's wrong. Why? Because, as we discussed earlier, an option can never have a negative value. In this case, the option to wait has a zero value.

There is another important aspect regarding the option to wait. Just because a project has a negative NPV today doesn't mean that we should permanently reject it. For example, suppose an investment costs $120 and has a perpetual cash flow of $10 per year. If the discount rate is 10 percent, then the NPV is $10/.10 − 120 = −$20, so the project should not be taken now.

We should not just forget about this project forever, though. Suppose that next year, for some reason, the relevant discount rate fell to 5 percent. Then the NPV would be $10/.05 − $120 = $80, and we would take the project (assuming that further waiting isn't even more valuable). More generally, as long as there is some possible future scenario under which a project has a positive NPV, then the option to wait is valuable, and we should just shelve the project proposal for now.

Managerial Options

Once we decide the optimal time to launch a project, other real options come into play. In our capital budgeting analysis thus far, we have more or less ignored the impact of managerial actions that might take place *after* a project is launched. In effect, we assumed that, once a project is launched, its basic features cannot be changed.

managerial options Opportunities that managers can exploit if certain things happen in the future.

In reality, depending on what actually happens in the future, there will always be opportunities to modify a project. These opportunities, which are an important type of real options, are often called **managerial options**. There are a great number of these options. The ways in which a product is priced, manufactured, advertised, and produced can all be changed, and these are just a few of the possibilities.

For example, look at Krispy Kreme. When the company first went public in 2000, consumers craved the company's doughnuts, and investors had the same craving for the company's stock. In fact, for the next four years, the company's stock was one of the best performers on Wall Street. By 2004, however, the company's business had grown stale, highlighted by the announcement of a $24.4 million loss in the first quarter of the year. Company management placed much of the blame on the unexpected popularity of the low-carb Atkins diet, which, needless to say, reduced demand for Krispy Kreme's carb-heavy doughnuts.

Faced with falling sales, management announced several new initiatives for the company. Hoping to attract Atkins dieters back into its stores, the company expanded its product lines. Among the list of new items were sugar-free doughnuts, small packages of doughnuts at convenience stores, bags of coffee, frozen coffee at all of its stores, mini-rings, doughnut holes, and gift cards.

In addition to introducing new products, the company said it would only open 100 stores in 2004, down from the original forecast of 120 stores. This lowered capital spending for the year to $75 million, down from the original estimate of $110 million. And the company also planned to use at least two other design formats. The first design was an outside kiosk intended to make purchases more convenient for customers. The second design plan called for a smaller store that would sit on one-half to three-quarters of an acre, less than the typical one acre used by existing stores.

As the case of Krispy Kreme suggests, the possibility of future action is important. Unexpected events occur, and it is the job of management to respond to them. We discuss some of the most common types of managerial actions in the next few sections.

Contingency Planning The various what-if procedures, particularly the break-even measures we discussed in an earlier chapter, have a use beyond that of simply evaluating cash flow and NPV estimates. We can also view these procedures and measures as primitive ways of exploring the dynamics of a project and investigating managerial options. What we think about in this case are some of the possible futures that could come about and what actions we might take if they do.

For example, we might find that a project fails to break even when sales drop below 10,000 units. This is a fact that is interesting to know, but the more important thing is to then go on and ask: What actions are we going to take if this actually occurs? This is called **contingency planning**, and it amounts to an investigation of some of the managerial options implicit in a project.

contingency planning Taking into account the managerial options implicit in a project.

There is no limit to the number of possible futures or contingencies that we could investigate. However, there are some broad classes, and we consider these next.

The Option to Expand One particularly important option we have not explicitly addressed is the option to expand. If we truly find a positive NPV project, then there is an obvious consideration. Can we expand the project or repeat it to get an even larger NPV? Our static analysis implicitly assumes that the scale of the project is fixed.

For example, if the sales demand for a particular product were to greatly exceed expectations, we might investigate increasing production. If this is not feasible for some reason, then we could always increase cash flow by raising the price. Either way, the potential cash flow is higher than we have indicated because we have implicitly assumed that no expansion or price increase is possible. Overall, because we ignore the option to expand in our analysis, we *underestimate* NPV (all other things being equal).

The Option to Abandon At the other extreme, the option to scale back or even abandon a project is also quite valuable. For example, if a project does not break even on a cash flow basis, then it can't even cover its own expenses. We would be better off if we just abandoned it. Our DCF analysis implicitly assumes that we would keep operating even in this case.

Sometimes, the best thing to do is punt. For example, consider the fate of Oldsmobile, the 106-year-old carmaker. The company was formed in 1897, and it joined General Motors (GM) in 1908. Oldsmobile was among the first to mass produce gasoline powered cars, to use chrome to dress up its cars, and to offer automatic transmissions. Over time, however, sales began to flag for a variety of reasons, despite repeated attempts by GM to revive them. Unable to turn things around, GM finally pulled the plug, closing Olds for good in April 2004.

More generally, if sales demand were significantly below expectations, we might be able to sell off some capacity or put it to another use. Maybe the product or service could be redesigned or otherwise improved. Regardless of the specifics, we once again *underestimate* NPV if we assume that the project must last for some fixed number of years, no matter what happens in the future.

The Option to Suspend or Contract Operations An option that is closely related to the option to abandon is the option to suspend operations. Very frequently, we see companies choosing to temporarily shut down an activity of some sort. For example, automobile manufacturers sometimes find themselves with too many vehicles of a particular type. In this case, production is often halted until the excess supply is worked off. At some point in the future, production resumes.

The option to suspend operations is particularly valuable in natural resource extraction, which includes such things as mining and pumping oil. Suppose you own a gold mine. If gold prices fall dramatically, then your analysis might show that it costs more to extract an ounce of gold than you can sell the gold for, so you quit mining. The gold just stays in the ground, however, and you can always resume operations if the price rises sufficiently. In fact, operations might be suspended and restarted many times over the life of the mine.

Companies also sometimes choose to permanently scale back an activity. If a new product does not sell as well as planned, production might be cut back and the excess capacity put to some other use. This case is really just the opposite of the option to expand, so we will label it the option to contract.

For example, supermarket operator Winn-Dixie exercised its option to contract in April 2004 when it announced the closing of 156 stores. Battered by events such as Wal-Mart's expansion into the grocery business, the company closed 45 unprofitable stores along with all of its 111 stores in the Midwest. It closed three distribution centers and, at the same time, announced it would try to sell various manufacturing operations. Winn-Dixie's planned contraction would leave it with 922 stores, 10,000 fewer employees, and, the company hopes, leaner, more profitable operations.

Options in Capital Budgeting: An Example Suppose we are examining a new project. To keep things relatively simple, let's say that we expect to sell 100 units per year at $1 net cash flow apiece into perpetuity. We thus expect that the cash flow will be $100 per year.

In one year, we will know more about the project. In particular, we will have a better idea of whether or not it is successful. If it looks like a long-run success, the expected sales will be revised upwards to 150 units per year. If it does not, the expected sales will be revised downwards to 50 units per year. Success and failure are equally likely. Notice that, because there is an even chance of selling 50 or 150 units, the expected sales are still 100 units, as we originally projected. The cost is $550, and the discount rate is 20 percent. The project can be dismantled and sold in one year for $400, if we decide to abandon it. Should we take it?

A standard DCF analysis is not difficult. The expected cash flow is $100 per year forever, and the discount rate is 20 percent. The PV of the cash flows is $\$100/.20 = \$500$, so the NPV is $\$500 - 550 = -\$50$. We shouldn't take the project.

This analysis ignores valuable options, however. In one year, we can sell out for \$400. How can we account for this? What we have to do is to decide what we are going to do one year from now. In this simple case, there are only two contingencies we need to evaluate, an upward revision and a downward revision, so the extra work is not great.

In one year, if the expected cash flows are revised to \$50, then the PV of the cash flows is revised downwards to \$50/.20 = \$250. We get \$400 by abandoning the project, so that is what we will do (the NPV of keeping the project in one year is \$250 − 400 = −\$150).

If the demand is revised upwards, then the PV of the future cash flows at Year 1 is \$150/.20 = \$750. This exceeds the \$400 abandonment value, so we will keep the project.

We now have a project that costs \$550 today. In one year, we expect a cash flow of \$100 from the project. In addition, this project will be worth either \$400 (if we abandon it because it is a failure) or \$750 (if we keep it because it succeeds). These outcomes are equally likely, so we expect the project to be worth (\$400 + 750)/2, or \$575.

Summing up, in one year, we expect to have \$100 in cash plus a project worth \$575, or \$675 total. At a 20 percent discount rate, this \$675 is worth \$562.50 today, so the NPV is \$562.50 − 550 = \$12.50. We should take the project.

The NPV of our project has increased by \$62.50. Where did this come from? Our original analysis implicitly assumed we would keep the project even if it was a failure. At Year 1, however, we saw that we were \$150 better off (\$400 versus \$250) if we abandoned. There was a 50 percent chance of this happening, so the expected gain from abandoning is \$75. The PV of this amount is the value of the option to abandon, \$75/1.20 = \$62.50.

Strategic Options Companies sometimes undertake new projects just to explore possibilities and evaluate potential future business strategies. This is a little like testing the water by sticking a toe in before diving. Such projects are difficult to analyze using conventional DCF methods because most of the benefits come in the form of **strategic options**, that is, options for future, related business moves. Projects that create such options may be very valuable, but that value is difficult to measure. Research and development, for example, is an important and valuable activity for many firms, precisely because it creates options for new products and procedures.

strategic options
Options for future, related business products or strategies.

To give another example, a large manufacturer might decide to open a retail outlet as a pilot study. The primary goal is to gain some market insight. Because of the high start-up costs, this one operation won't break even. However, using the sales experience gained from the pilot, the firm can then evaluate whether or not to open more outlets, to change the product mix, to enter new markets, and so on. The information gained and the resulting options for actions are all valuable, but coming up with a reliable dollar figure is probably not feasible.

Conclusion We have seen that incorporating options into capital budgeting analysis is not easy. What can we do about them in practice? The answer is that we need to keep them in mind as we work with the projected cash flows. We will tend to underestimate NPV by ignoring options. The damage might be small for a highly structured, very specific proposal, but it might be great for an exploratory one.

Concept Questions

14.6a Why do we say that almost every capital budgeting proposal involves mutually exclusive alternatives?

14.6b What are the options to expand, abandon, and suspend operations?

14.6c What are strategic options?

14.7 OPTIONS AND CORPORATE SECURITIES

In this section, we return to financial assets by considering some of the most common ways options appear in corporate securities and other financial assets. We begin by examining warrants and convertible bonds.

Warrants

warrant
A security that gives the holder the right to purchase shares of stock at a fixed price over a given period of time.

A **warrant** is a corporate security that looks a lot like a call option. It gives the holder the right, but not the obligation, to buy shares of common stock directly from a company at a fixed price for a given time period. Each warrant specifies the number of shares of stock that the holder can buy, the exercise price, and the expiration date.

The differences in contractual features between the call options that trade on the Chicago Board Options Exchange and warrants are relatively minor. Warrants usually have much longer maturity periods, however. In fact, some warrants are actually perpetual and have no fixed expiration date.

Warrants are often called *sweeteners* or *equity kickers* because they are often issued in combination with privately placed loans or bonds. Throwing in some warrants is a way of making the deal a little more attractive to the lender, and it is a very common practice. Also, warrants have been listed and traded on the NYSE since April 13, 1970. In 2004, however, there were fewer than 20 issues of warrants listed.

In many cases, warrants are attached to the bonds when issued. The loan agreement will state whether the warrants are detachable from the bond. Usually, the warrant can be detached immediately and sold by the holder as a separate security.

The Difference between Warrants and Call Options As we have explained, from the holder's point of view, warrants are very similar to call options on common stock. A warrant, like a call option, gives its holder the right to buy common stock at a specified price. From the firm's point of view, however, a warrant is very different from a call option sold on the company's common stock.

The most important difference between call options and warrants is that call options are issued by individuals and warrants are issued by firms. When a call option is exercised, one investor buys stock from another investor. The company is not involved. When a warrant is exercised, the firm must issue new shares of stock. Each time a warrant is exercised, then, the firm receives some cash and the number of shares outstanding increases. Notice that the employee stock options we discussed earlier in the chapter are issued by corporations, so, strictly speaking, they are warrants rather than options.

To illustrate, suppose the Endrun Company issues a warrant giving holders the right to buy one share of common stock at $25. Further suppose the warrant is exercised. Endrun must print one new stock certificate. In exchange for the stock certificate, it receives $25 from the holder.

In contrast, when a call option is exercised, there is no change in the number of shares outstanding. Suppose Ms. Enger purchases a call option on the common stock of the Endrun Company from Mr. Swift. The call option gives Ms. Enger the right to buy (from Mr. Swift) one share of common stock of the Endrun Company for $25.

If Ms. Enger chooses to exercise the call option, Mr. Swift is obligated to give her one share of Endrun's common stock in exchange for $25. If Mr. Swift does not already own a share, he must go into the stock market and buy one.

The call option amounts to a side bet between Ms. Enger and Mr. Swift on the value of the Endrun Company's common stock. When a call option is exercised, one investor gains and the other loses. The total number of shares outstanding of the Endrun Company remains constant, and no new funds are made available to the company.

Earnings Dilution Warrants and (as we shall see) convertible bonds frequently cause the number of shares to increase. This happens (1) when the warrants are exercised and (2) when the bonds are converted, causing the firm's net income to be spread over a larger number of shares. Earnings per share therefore decrease.

Firms with significant numbers of warrants and convertible issues outstanding will generally calculate and report earnings per share on a *diluted basis.* This means that the calculation is based on the number of shares that would be outstanding if all the warrants were exercised and all the convertibles were converted. Because this increases the number of shares, diluted EPS will be lower than "basic" EPS, which are calculated only on the basis of shares actually outstanding.

Convertible Bonds

A **convertible bond** is similar to a bond with warrants. The most important difference is that a bond with warrants can be separated into distinct securities (a bond and some warrants), but a convertible bond cannot. A convertible bond gives the holder the right to exchange the bond for a fixed number of shares of stock anytime up to and including the maturity date of the bond.

convertible bond
A bond that can be exchanged for a fixed number of shares of stock for a specified amount of time.

Preferred stock can frequently be converted into common stock. A convertible preferred stock is the same as a convertible bond except that it has an infinite maturity date.[4]

Features of a Convertible Bond The basic features of a convertible bond can be illustrated by examining a particular issue. In May 2004, Internet services company Digital River issued $175 million in convertible bonds. The bonds have a 1.25 percent coupon rate, mature in 2024, and can be converted into Digital River common stock at a **conversion price** of $44.063. Because each bond has a face value of $1,000, the owner can receive $\$1{,}000/44.063 = 22.6948$ shares of Digital River's stock. The number of shares per bond, 22.6948 in this case, is called the **conversion ratio**.

conversion price
The dollar amount of a bond's par value that is exchangeable for one share of stock.

conversion ratio
The number of shares per bond received for conversion into stock.

When Digital River issued its convertible bonds, its common stock was trading at $33.13 per share. The conversion price was thus $(\$44.063 - 33.13)/33.13 = 33$ percent higher than its actual stock price. This 33 percent is called the **conversion premium**. It reflects the fact that the conversion option in Digital River's bonds was well out of the money at the time of issuance; this is usually the case.

conversion premium
The difference between the conversion price and the current stock price, divided by the current stock price.

Value of a Convertible Bond Even though the conversion feature of the convertible bond cannot be detached like a warrant, the value of the bond can still be decomposed into the bond value and the value of the conversion feature. We discuss how this is done next.

The easiest way to illustrate convertible bond valuation is with an example. Suppose a company called Micron Origami (MO) has an outstanding convertible bond issue. The coupon rate is 7 percent and the conversion ratio is 15. There are 12 remaining coupons, and the stock is trading for $68.

Straight Bond Value The **straight bond value** is what the convertible bond would sell for if it could not be converted into common stock. This value will depend on the general level of interest rates on debentures and on the default risk of the issuer.

straight bond value
The value a convertible bond would have if it could not be converted into common stock.

[4]The dividends paid are, of course, not tax deductible for the corporation. Interest paid on a convertible bond is tax deductible.

Suppose straight debentures issued by MO are rated B, and B-rated bonds are priced to yield 8 percent. We can determine the straight bond value of MO convertible bonds by discounting the \$35 semiannual coupon payment and maturity value at 8 percent, just as we did in Chapter 6:

$$\begin{aligned}\text{Straight bond value} &= \$35 \times (1 - 1/1.04^{12})/.04 + 1{,}000/1.04^{12} \\ &= \$328.48 + 624.60 \\ &= \$953.08\end{aligned}$$

The straight bond value of a convertible bond is a minimum value in the sense that the bond is always worth at least this amount. As we discuss, it will usually be worth more.

conversion value
The value a convertible bond would have if it were to be immediately converted into common stock.

Conversion Value

The **conversion value** of a convertible bond is what the bond would be worth if it were immediately converted into common stock. This value is computed by multiplying the current price of the stock by the number of shares that will be received when the bond is converted.

For example, each MO convertible bond can be converted into 15 shares of MO common stock. MO common was selling for \$68. Thus, the conversion value was 15 × \$68 = \$1,020.

A convertible cannot sell for less than its conversion value, or an arbitrage opportunity exists. If MO's convertible had sold for less than \$1,020, investors would have bought the bonds and converted them into common stock and sold the stock. The arbitrage profit would have been the difference between the value of the stock and the bond's conversion value.

For more on convertible bonds, see www.convertbond.com.

Floor Value

As we have seen, convertible bonds have two *floor values:* the straight bond value and the conversion value. The minimum value of a convertible bond is given by the greater of these two values. For the MO issue, the conversion value is \$1,020 and the straight bond value is \$953.08. At a minimum, this bond is thus worth \$1,020.

Figure 14.3 plots the minimum value of a convertible bond against the value of the stock. The conversion value is determined by the value of the firm's underlying common stock. As the value of the common stock rises and falls, the conversion value rises and falls with it. For example, if the value of MO's common stock increases by \$1, the conversion value of its convertible bonds will increase by \$15.

FIGURE 14.3 >>

Minimum Value of a Convertible Bond versus the Value of the Stock for a Given Interest Rate

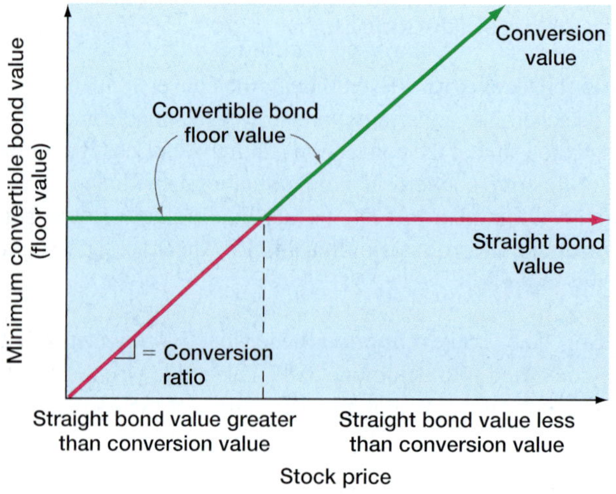

As shown, the minimum, or floor, value of a convertible bond is either its straight bond value or its conversion value, whichever is greater.

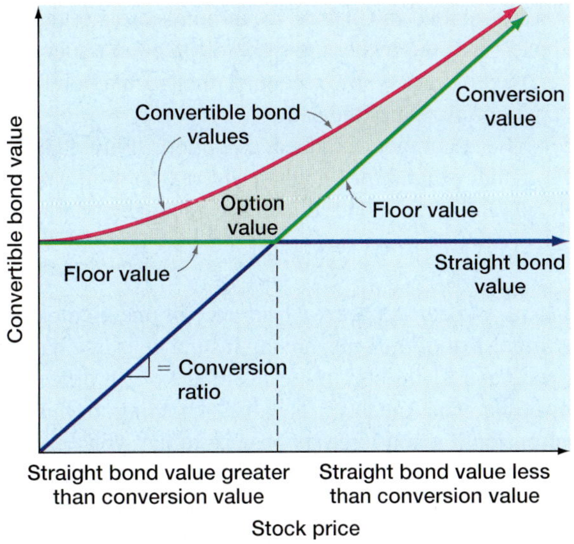

As shown, the value of a convertible bond is the sum of its floor value and its option value (highlighted region).

<< FIGURE 14.4

Value of a Convertible Bond versus the Value of the Stock for a Given Interest Rate

In Figure 14.3, we have implicitly assumed that the convertible bond is default-free. In this case, the straight bond value does not depend on the stock price, so it is plotted as a horizontal line. Given the straight bond value, the minimum value of the convertible depends on the value of the stock. When the stock price is low, the minimum value of a convertible is most significantly influenced by the underlying value as straight debt. However, when the value of the firm is very high, the value of a convertible bond is mostly determined by the underlying conversion value. This is also illustrated in Figure 14.3.

Option Value The value of a convertible bond will always exceed the straight bond value and the conversion value unless the firm is in default or the bondholders are forced to convert. The reason is that holders of convertibles do not have to convert immediately. Instead, by waiting, they can take advantage of whichever is greater in the future, the straight bond value or the conversion value.

This option to wait has value, and it raises the value of the convertible bond over its floor value. The total value of the convertible is thus equal to the sum of the floor value and the option value. This is illustrated in Figure 14.4. Notice the similarity between this picture and the representation of the value of a call option in Figure 14.2, referenced in our earlier discussion.

Other Options

We've discussed two of the more common optionlike securities, warrants and convertibles. Options appear in many other places. We briefly describe a few in this section.

The Call Provision on a Bond As we discussed in Chapter 7, most corporate bonds are callable. A call provision allows a corporation to buy the bonds at a fixed price for a fixed period of time. In other words, the corporation has a call option on the bonds. The cost of the call feature to the corporation is the cost of the option.

Convertible bonds are almost always callable. This means that a convertible bond is really a package of three securities: a straight bond, a call option held by the bondholder (the conversion feature), and a call option held by the corporation (the call provision).

Put Bonds As we discussed in Chapter 7, put bonds are a relatively new innovation. Recall that such a bond gives the owner the right to force the issuer to buy the bond back at a fixed price for a fixed time. We now recognize that such a bond is a combination of a straight bond and a put option, hence the name.

A given bond can have a number of embedded options. For example, one popular type of bond is a LYON, which stands for "liquid yield option note." A LYON is a callable, putable, convertible, pure discount bond. It is thus a package of a pure discount bond, two call options, and a put option.

Insurance and Loan Guarantees Insurance of one kind or another is a financial feature of everyday life. Most of the time, having insurance is like having a put option. For example, suppose you have $1 million in fire insurance on an office building. One night, your building burns down, which reduces its value to nothing. In this case, you will effectively exercise your put option and force the insurer to pay you $1 million for something worth very little.

Loan guarantees are a form of insurance. If you loan money to someone and they default, then, with a guaranteed loan, you can collect from someone else, often the government. For example, when you loan money to a commercial bank (by making a deposit), your loan is guaranteed (up to $100,000) by the government.

In two particularly well-known cases of loan guarantees, Lockheed (now Lockheed Martin) Corporation (in 1971) and Chrysler (now DaimlerChrysler) Corporation (in 1980) were saved from impending financial doom when the U.S. government came to the rescue by agreeing to guarantee new loans. Under the guarantees, if Lockheed or Chrysler had defaulted, the lenders could have obtained the full value of their claims from the U.S. government. From the lenders' point of view, the loans were as risk-free as Treasury bonds. These guarantees enabled Lockheed and Chrysler to borrow large amounts of cash and to get through difficult times.

Loan guarantees are not cost-free. The U.S. government, with a loan guarantee, has provided a put option to the holders of risky bonds. The value of the put option is the cost of the loan guarantee. This point has been made abundantly clear by the collapse of the U.S. savings and loan industry in the early 1980s. The final cost to U.S. taxpayers of making good on the guaranteed deposits in these institutions was a staggering $150 billion.

In more recent times, following the September 11, 2001, terrorist attacks, Congress established the Air Transportation Stabilization Board (ATSB). The ATSB was authorized to issue up to $10 billion in loan guarantees to U.S. air carriers that suffered losses as a result of the attacks. By mid-2004, $1.56 billion in guarantees had been issued to six borrowers. Interestingly, recipients of loan guarantees are required to compensate the government for the risk being borne by the taxpayers. This compensation came in the form of cash fees and warrants to buy stock. These warrants represent between 10 and 33 percent of each company's equity. Because of recoveries (and, thus, stock price increases) at some borrowers, the ATSB's warrant portfolio became quite valuable, worth about $100 million in mid-2004.

Concept Questions

14.7a How are warrants and call options different?

14.7b What is the minimum value of a convertible bond?

14.7c Explain how car insurance acts like a put option.

14.7d Explain why U.S. government loan guarantees are not free.

SUMMARY AND CONCLUSIONS 14.8

This chapter has described the basics of option valuation and discussed optionlike corporate securities. In it, we saw that:

1. Options are contracts giving the right, but not the obligation, to buy and sell underlying assets at a fixed price during a specified time period. The most familiar options are puts and calls involving shares of stock. These options give the holder the right, but not the obligation, to sell (the put option) or buy (the call option) shares of common stock at a given price.

   As we discussed, the value of any option depends only on five factors:

   a. The price of the underlying asset

   b. The exercise price

   c. The expiration date

   d. The interest rate on risk-free bonds

   e. The volatility of the underlying asset's value
2. Companies have begun to use employee stock options (ESO) in rapidly growing numbers. Such options are similar to call options and serve to motivate employees to boost stock prices. ESOs are also an important form of compensation for many workers, particularly at more senior management levels.
3. Almost all capital budgeting proposals can be viewed as real options. Also, projects and operations contain implicit options, such as the option to expand, the option to abandon, and the option to suspend or contract operations.
4. A warrant gives the holder the right to buy shares of common stock directly from the company at a fixed exercise price for a given period of time. Typically, warrants are issued in a package with bonds. Afterwards, they often can be detached and traded separately.
5. A convertible bond is a combination of a straight bond and a call option. The holder can give up the bond in exchange for a fixed number of shares of stock. The minimum value of a convertible bond is given by its straight bond value or its conversion value, whichever is greater.
6. Many other corporate securities have option features. Bonds with call provisions, bonds with put provisions, and bonds backed by a loan guarantee are just a few examples.

Chapter Review and Self-Test Problems

14.1 Value of a Call Option Stock in the Nantucket Corporation is currently selling for \$25 per share. In one year, the price will be either \$20 or \$30. T-bills with one year to maturity are paying 10 percent. What is the value of a call option with a \$20 exercise price? A \$26 exercise price?

14.2 Convertible Bonds Old Cycle Corporation (OCC), publisher of *Ancient Iron* magazine, has a convertible bond issue that is currently selling in the market for \$950. Each bond can be exchanged for 100 shares of stock at the holder's option.

The bond has a 7 percent coupon, payable annually, and it will mature in 10 years. OCC's debt is BBB-rated. Debt with this rating is priced to yield 12 percent. Stock in OCC is trading at \$7 per share.

What is the conversion ratio on this bond? The conversion price? The conversion premium? What is the floor value of the bond? What is its option value?

Answers to Chapter Review and Self-Test Problems

14.1 With a \$20 exercise price, the option can't finish out of the money (it can finish "at the money" if the stock price is \$20). We can replicate the value of the stock by investing the present value of \$20 in T-bills and buying one call option. Buying the T-bill will cost \$20/1.1 = \$18.18.

If the stock ends up at \$20, the call option will be worth zero and the T-bill will pay \$20. If the stock ends up at \$30, the T-bill will again pay \$20, and the option will be worth \$30 − 20 = \$10, so the package will be worth \$30. Because the T-bill–call option combination exactly duplicates the payoff on the stock, it has to be worth \$20 or arbitrage is possible. Using the notation from the chapter, we can calculate the value of the call option:

$$S_0 = C_0 + E/(1 + R_f)$$
$$\$25 = C_0 + \$18.18$$
$$C_0 = \$6.82$$

With the \$26 exercise price, we start by investing the present value of the lower stock price in T-bills. This guarantees us \$20 when the stock price is \$20. If the stock price is \$30, then the option is worth \$30 − 26 = \$4. We have \$20 from our T-bill, so we need \$10 from the options in order to match the stock. Because each option is worth \$4 in this case, we need to buy \$10/4 = 2.5 call options. Notice that the difference in the possible stock prices (ΔS) is \$10 and the difference in the possible option prices (ΔC) is \$4, so $\Delta S/\Delta C = 2.5$.

To complete the calculation, we note that the present value of the \$20 plus 2.5 call options has to be \$25 to prevent arbitrage, so:

$$\$25 = 2.5 \times C_0 + \$20/1.1$$
$$C_0 = \$6.82/2.5$$
$$= \$2.73$$

14.2 Because each bond can be exchanged for 100 shares, the conversion ratio is 100. The conversion price is the face value of the bond (\$1,000) divided by the conversion ratio, or \$1,000/100 = \$10. The conversion premium is the percentage difference between the current price and the conversion price, or (\$10 − 7)/7 = 43%.

The floor value of the bond is the greater of its straight bond value or its conversion value. Its conversion value is what the bond is worth if it is immediately converted: 100 × \$7 = \$700. The straight bond value is what the bond would be worth if it were not convertible. The annual coupon is \$70, and the bond matures in 10 years. At a 12 percent required return, the straight bond value is:

$$\text{Straight bond value} = \$70 \times (1 - 1/1.12^{10})/.12 + 1{,}000/1.12^{10}$$
$$= \$395.52 + 321.97$$
$$= \$717.49$$

This exceeds the conversion value, so the floor value of the bond is \$717.49. Finally, the option value is the value of the convertible in excess of its floor value. Because the bond is selling for \$950, the option value is:

$$\text{Option value} = \$950 - 717.49$$
$$= \$232.51$$

Concepts Review and Critical Thinking Questions

1. **Options** What is a call option? A put option? Under what circumstances might you want to buy each? Which one has greater *potential* profit? Why?
2. **Options** Complete the following sentence for each of these investors:
   a. A buyer of call options
   b. A buyer of put options
   c. A seller (writer) of call options
   d. A seller (writer) of put options

   "The (buyer/seller) of a (put/call) option (pays/receives) money for the (right/obligation) to (buy/sell) a specified asset at a fixed price for a fixed length of time."
3. **Intrinsic Value** What is the intrinsic value of a call option? How do we interpret this value?
4. **Put Options** What is the value of a put option at maturity? Based on your answer, what is the intrinsic value of a put option?
5. **Option Pricing** You notice that shares of stock in the Patel Corporation are going for $50 per share. Call options with an exercise price of $35 per share are selling for $10. What's wrong here? Describe how you can take advantage of this mispricing if the option expires today.
6. **Options and Stock Risk** If the risk of a stock increases, what is likely to happen to the price of call options on the stock? To the price of put options? Why?
7. **Option Rise** True or false: The unsystematic risk of a share of stock is irrelevant in valuing the stock because it can be diversified away; therefore, it is also irrelevant for valuing a call option on the stock. Explain.
8. **Option Pricing** Suppose a certain stock currently sells for $30 per share. If a put option and a call option are available with $30 exercise prices, which do you think will sell for more, the put or the call? Explain.
9. **Option Price and Interest Rates** Suppose the interest rate on T-bills suddenly and unexpectedly rises. All other things being the same, what is the impact on call option values? On put option values?
10. **Contingent Liabilities** When you take out an ordinary student loan, it is usually the case that whoever holds that loan is given a guarantee by the U.S. government, meaning that the government will make up any payments you skip. This is just one example of the many loan guarantees made by the U.S. government. Such guarantees don't show up in calculations of government spending or in official deficit figures. Why not? Should they show up?
11. **Option to Abandon** What is the option to abandon? Explain why we underestimate NPV if we ignore this option.
12. **Option to Expand** What is the option to expand? Explain why we underestimate NPV if we ignore this option.
13. **Capital Budgeting Options** In Chapter 10, we discussed Porsche's launch of its new Cayenne. Suppose sales of the Cayenne go extremely well and Porsche is forced to expand output to meet demand. Porsche's action in this case would be an example of exploiting what kind of option?
14. **Option to Suspend** Natural resource extraction facilities (e.g., oil wells or gold mines) provide a good example of the value of the option to suspend operations. Why?

15. **Employee Stock Options** You own stock in the Hendrix Guitar Company. The company has implemented a plan to award employee stock options. As a shareholder, does the plan benefit you? If so, what are the benefits?

Questions and Problems

BASIC
(Questions 1–13)

1. **Calculating Option Values** T-bills currently yield 5.5 percent. Stock in Nina Manufacturing is currently selling for $55 per share. There is no possibility that the stock will be worth less than $50 per share in one year.
   a. What is the value of a call option with a $45 exercise price? What is the intrinsic value?
   b. What is the value of a call option with a $35 exercise price? What is the intrinsic value?
   c. What is the value of a put option with a $45 exercise price? What is the intrinsic value?
2. **Understanding Option Quotes** Use the option quote information shown here to answer the questions that follow. The stock is currently selling for $83.

Option and NY Close	Expiration	Strike Price	Calls		Puts	
			Vol.	Last	Vol.	Last
RWJ						
	Mar	80	230	2.80	160	0.80
	Apr	80	170	6	127	1.40
	Jul	80	139	8.05	43	3.90
	Oct	80	60	10.20	11	3.65

   a. Are the call options in the money? What is the intrinsic value of an RWJ Corp. call option?
   b. Are the put options in the money? What is the intrinsic value of an RWJ Corp. put option?
   c. Two of the options are clearly mispriced. Which ones? At a minimum, what should the mispriced options sell for? Explain how you could profit from the mispricing in each case.
3. **Calculating Payoffs** Use the option quote information shown here to answer the questions that follow. The stock is currently selling for $114.

Option and NY Close	Expiration	Strike Price	Calls		Puts	
			Vol.	Last	Vol.	Last
Macrosoft						
	Feb	110	85	7.60	40	.60
	Mar	110	61	8.80	22	1.55
	May	110	22	10.25	11	2.85
	Aug	110	3	13.05	3	4.70

   a. Suppose you buy 10 contracts of the February 110 call option. How much will you pay, ignoring commissions?

b. In part (*a*), suppose that Macrosoft stock is selling for $140 per share on the expiration date. How much is your options investment worth? What if the terminal stock price is $125? Explain.

c. Suppose you buy 10 contracts of the August 110 put option. What is your maximum gain? On the expiration date, Macrosoft is selling for $104 per share. How much is your options investment worth? What is your net gain?

d. In part (*c*), suppose you *sell* 10 of the August 110 put contracts. What is your net gain or loss if Macrosoft is selling for $103 at expiration? For $132? What is the break-even price, that is, the terminal stock price that results in a zero profit?

4. **Calculating Option Values** The price of Ervin Corp. stock will be either $75 or $95 at the end of the year. Call options are available with one year to expiration. T-bills currently yield 6 percent.

a. Suppose the current price of Ervin stock is $80. What is the value of the call option if the exercise price is $70 per share?

b. Suppose the exercise price is $90 in part (*a*). What is the value of the call option now?

5. **Calculating Option Values** The price of Tara, Inc., stock will be either $60 or $80 at the end of the year. Call options are available with one year to expiration. T-bills currently yield 5 percent.

a. Suppose the current price of Tara stock is $70. What is the value of the call option if the exercise price is $45 per share?

b. Suppose the exercise price is $70 in part (*a*). What is the value of the call option now?

6. **Using the Pricing Equation** A one-year call option *contract* on Cheesy Poofs Co. stock sells for $1,200. In one year, the stock will be worth $45 or $65 per share. The exercise price on the call option is $60. What is the current value of the stock if the risk-free rate is 5 percent?

7. **Equity as an Option** Rackin Pinion Corporation's assets are currently worth $1,050. In one year, they will be worth either $1,000 or $1,400. The risk-free interest rate is 5 percent. Suppose Rackin Pinion has an outstanding debt issue with a face value of $1,000.

a. What is the value of the equity?

b. What is the value of the debt? The interest rate on the debt?

c. Would the value of the equity go up or down if the risk-free rate were 20 percent? Why? What does your answer illustrate?

8. **Equity as an Option** Buckeye Industries has a bond issue with a face value of $1,000 that is coming due in one year. The value of Buckeye's assets is currently $1,200. Jim Tressell, the CEO, believes that the assets in the firm will be worth either $800 or $1,400 in a year. The going rate on one-year T-bills is 4 percent.

a. What is the value of Buckeye's equity? The value of the debt?

b. Suppose Buckeye can reconfigure its existing assets in such a way that the value in a year will be $500 or $1,700. If the current value of the assets is unchanged, will the stockholders favor such a move? Why or why not?

9. **Calculating Conversion Value** A $1,000 par convertible debenture has a conversion price for common stock of $80 per share. With the common stock selling at $90, what is the conversion value of the bond?

10. Convertible Bonds The following facts apply to a convertible bond making semiannual payments:

Conversion price	$40/share
Coupon rate	7.5%
Par value	$1,000
Yield on nonconvertible debentures of same quality	9%
Maturity	20 years
Market price of stock	$38/share

a. What is the minimum price at which the convertible should sell?

b. What accounts for the premium of the market price of a convertible bond over the total market value of the common stock into which it can be converted?

11. Calculating Values for Convertibles You have been hired to value a new 30-year callable, convertible bond. The bond has a 7 percent coupon, payable annually, and its face value is $1,000. The conversion price is $65 and the stock currently sells for $50.

a. What is the minimum value of the bond? Comparable nonconvertible bonds are priced to yield 9 percent.

b. What is the conversion premium for this bond?

12. Calculating Warrant Values A bond with 25 detachable warrants has just been offered for sale at $1,000. The bond matures in 15 years and has an annual coupon of $105. Each warrant gives the owner the right to purchase two shares of stock in the company at $15 per share. Ordinary bonds (with no warrants) of similar quality are priced to yield 12 percent. What is the value of one warrant?

13. Option to Wait Your company is deciding whether to invest in a new machine. The new machine will increase cash flow by $280,000 per year. You believe the technology used in the machine has a 10-year life; in other words, no matter when you purchase the machine, it will be obsolete 10 years from today. The machine is currently priced at $1,500,000. The cost of the machine will decline by $125,000 per year until it reaches $1,000,000, where it will remain. If your required return is 12 percent, should you purchase the machine? If so, when should you purchase it?

INTERMEDIATE
(Questions 14–19)

14. Abandonment Value We are examining a new project. We expect to sell 7,000 units per year at $60 net cash flow apiece for the next 10 years. In other words, the annual operating cash flow is projected to be $\$60 \times 7{,}000 = \$420{,}000$. The relevant discount rate is 16 percent, and the initial investment required is $1,800,000.

a. What is the base-case NPV?

b. After the first year, the project can be dismantled and sold for $1,400,000. If expected sales are revised based on the first year's performance, when would it make sense to abandon the investment? In other words, at what level of expected sales would it make sense to abandon the project?

c. Explain how the $1,400,000 abandonment value can be viewed as the opportunity cost of keeping the project in one year.

15. Abandonment In the previous problem, suppose you think it is likely that expected sales will be revised upwards to 9,000 units if the first year is a success and revised downwards to 4,000 units if the first year is not a success.

a. If success and failure are equally likely, what is the NPV of the project? Consider the possibility of abandonment in answering.

b. What is the value of the option to abandon?

16. Abandonment and Expansion In the previous problem, suppose the scale of the project can be doubled in one year in the sense that twice as many units can be produced and sold. Naturally, expansion would only be desirable if the project is a success. This implies that if the project is a success, projected sales after expansion will be 18,000. Again assuming that success and failure are equally likely, what is the NPV of the project? Note that abandonment is still an option if the project is a failure. What is the value of the option to expand?

17. Intuition and Option Value Suppose a share of stock sells for $65. The risk-free rate is 5 percent, and the stock price in one year will be either $75 or $85.

a. What is the value of a call option with a $75 exercise price?

b. What's wrong here? What would you do?

18. Intuition and Convertibles Which of the following two sets of relationships, at time of issuance of convertible bonds, is more typical? Why?

	A	B
Offering price of bond	$ 800	$1,000
Bond value (straight debt)	800	950
Conversion value	1,000	900

19. Convertible Calculations Alicia, Inc., has a $1,000 face value convertible bond issue that is currently selling in the market for $950. Each bond is exchangeable at any time for 20 shares of the company's stock. The convertible bond has an 8 percent coupon, payable semiannually. Similar nonconvertible bonds are priced to yield 10 percent. The bond matures in 10 years. Stock in Alicia sells for $46 per share.

a. What are the conversion ratio, conversion price, and conversion premium?

b. What is the straight bond value? The conversion value?

c. In part (*b*), what would the stock price have to be for the conversion value and the straight bond value to be equal?

d. What is the option value of the bond?

CHALLENGE
(Questions 20–21)

20. Pricing Convertibles You have been hired to value a new 25-year callable, convertible bond. The bond has a 6.80 percent coupon, payable annually. The conversion price is $150, and the stock currently sells for $44.75. The stock price is expected to grow at 12 percent per year. The bond is callable at $1,200, but, based on prior experience, it won't be called unless the conversion value is $1,300. The required return on this bond is 10 percent. What value would you assign?

21. Abandonment Decisions For some projects, it may be advantageous to terminate the project early. For example, if a project is losing money, you might be able to reduce your losses by scrapping out the assets and terminating the project, rather than continuing to lose money all the way through to the project's completion. Consider the following project of Hand Clapper, Inc. The company is considering a four-year project to manufacture clap-command garage door openers. This project requires an initial investment of $8 million that will be depreciated straight-line to zero over the project's life. An initial investment in net working capital of $2 million is required to support spare parts inventory; this cost is fully recoverable whenever the project ends. The company believes it can generate $7 million in pretax revenues with $3 million in total pretax operating costs. The tax rate is 38 percent and the discount rate is 16 percent. The market value of the equipment over the life of the project is as follows:

Year	Market Value (millions)
1	$6.50
2	6.00
3	3.00
4	0.00

a. Assuming Hand Clapper operates this project for four years, what is the NPV?

b. Now compute the project NPV assuming the project is abandoned after only one year, after two years, and after three years. What economic life for this project maximizes its value to the firm? What does this problem tell you about not considering abandonment possibilities when evaluating projects?

What's On the Web?

14.1 Option Prices You want to find the option prices for ConAgra Foods (CAG). Go to finance.yahoo.com, get a stock quote, and follow the "Options" link. What is the option premium and strike price for the highest and lowest strike price options that are nearest to expiring? What are the option premium and strike price for the highest and lowest strike price options expiring next month?

14.2 Option Symbol Construction What is the option symbol for a call option on Cisco Systems (CSCO) with a strike price of $40 that expires in October. Go to www.cboe.com, follow the "Trading Tools" link, then the "Symbol Directory" link. Find the basic ticker symbol for Cisco Systems options. Next, follow the "Strike Price Code" link. Find the codes for the expiration month and strike price and construct the ticker symbol. Now construct the ticker symbol for a put option with the same strike price and expiration.

14.3 Option Expiration Go to www.cboe.com, highlight the "Trading Tools" tab, then follow the "Expiration Calendar" link. On what day do equity options expire in the current month? On what day do they expire next month?

14.4 LEAPS. Go to www.cboe.com, highlight the "Products" tab, then follow the "LEAPS®" link. What are LEAPS? What are the two types of LEAPS? What are the benefits of equity LEAPS? What are the benefits of index LEAPS?

14.5 FLEX Options Go to www.cboe.com, highlight the "Institutional" tab, then follow the "FLEX Options" link. What is a FLEX option? When do FLEX options expire? What is the minimum size of a FLEX option?

>> MINI-CASE

S&S Air's Convertible Bond

S&S Air is preparing its first public securities offering. In consultation with Danielle Ralston of underwriter Raines and Warren, Chris Guthrie decided that a convertible bond with a 20-year maturity was the way to go. He met the owners, Mark and Todd, and presented his analysis of the convertible bond issue. Since the company is not publicly traded, Chris looked at comparable publicly traded companies and determined the average PE ratio for the industry is 12.5. Earnings per share for the company are $1.60. With this in mind, Chris has suggested a conversion price of $25 per share.

Several days later, Todd, Mark, and Chris met again to discuss the potential bond issue. Both Todd and Mark researched convertible bonds and have questions for Chris. Todd begins by asking Chris if the convertible bond issue will have a lower coupon rate than a comparable bond without a conversion feature. Chris informs him that a par value convertible bond issue would require a 6 percent coupon rate with a conversion value of $800, while a plain vanilla bond would have a 10 percent coupon rate. Todd nods in agreement and explains that the convertible bonds are a win-win form of financing. He states that if the value of the company stock does not rise above the conversion price, the company has issued debt at a cost below the market rate (6 percent instead of 10 percent). If the company's stock does rise to the conversion value, the company has effectively issued stock at a price above the current value.

Mark immediately disagrees, saying that convertible bonds are a no-win form of financing. He argues that if the value of the company stock rises to more than $25, the company is forced to sell stock at the conversion price. This means the new shareholders, in other words those who bought the convertible bonds, benefit from a bargain price. Put another way, if the company prospers, it would have been better to have issued straight debt so that the gains would not be shared.

Chris has gone back to Danielle for help. As Danielle's assistant, you've been asked to prepare another memo answering the following questions:

1. Why do you think Chris is suggesting a conversion price of $25? Given that the company is not publicly traded, does it even make sense to talk about a conversion price?
2. Is there anything wrong with Todd's argument that it is cheaper to issue a bond with a convertible feature because the required coupon is lower?
3. Is there anything wrong with Mark's argument that a convertible bond is a bad idea because it allows new shareholders to participate in gains made by the company?
4. How can you reconcile the arguments made by Todd and Mark?
5. In the course of the debate, a question comes up concerning whether or not the bonds should have an ordinary (not make-whole) call feature. Chris confuses everybody by stating: "The call feature lets S&S Air force conversion, thereby minimizing the problem that Mark has identified." What is he talking about? Is he making sense?

Visit us at www.mhhe.com/rwj

PART SIX

Cost of Capital and Long-Term Financial Policy

15 Cost of Capital

Eastman Chemical is a leading international chemical company and maker of plastic such as that used in soft drink containers. It was created on December 31, 1993, when its former parent company, Eastman Kodak, split off the division as a separate company. Soon thereafter, Eastman Chemical adopted a new motivational program for its employees. Everyone who works for the company, from hourly workers up to the CEO, gets a bonus that depends on the amount by which Eastman's return on capital for the year exceeds its cost of capital. With this approach, Eastman joined the many firms that tie compensation packages to how good a job the firm does in providing an adequate return for its investors. In this chapter, we learn how to compute a firm's cost of capital and find out what it means to the firm and its investors.

Suppose you have just become the president of a large company and the first decision you face is whether to go ahead with a plan to renovate the company's warehouse distribution system. The plan will cost the company $50 million, and it is expected to save $12 million per year after taxes over the next six years.

This is a familiar problem in capital budgeting. To address it, you would determine the relevant cash flows, discount them, and, if the net present value is positive, take on the project; if the NPV is negative, you would scrap it. So far, so good; but what should you use as the discount rate?

From our discussion of risk and return, you know that the correct discount rate depends on the riskiness of the project to renovate the warehouse distribution system. In particular, the new project will have a positive NPV only if its return exceeds what the financial markets offer on investments of similar risk. We called this minimum required return the *cost of capital* associated with the project.[1]

Thus, to make the right decision as president, you must examine what the capital markets have to offer and use this information to arrive at an estimate of the project's cost of capital. Our primary purpose in this chapter is to describe how to go about doing this. There are a variety of approaches to this task, and a number of conceptual and practical issues arise.

One of the most important concepts we develop is that of the *weighted average cost of capital* (WACC). This is the cost of capital for the firm as a whole, and it can be interpreted as the required return on the overall firm. In discussing the WACC, we will recognize the fact that a firm will normally raise capital in a variety of forms and that these different forms of capital may have different costs associated with them.

[1]The term *cost of money* is also used.

We also recognize in this chapter that taxes are an important consideration in determining the required return on an investment, because we are always interested in valuing the aftertax cash flows from a project. We will therefore discuss how to incorporate taxes explicitly into our estimates of the cost of capital.

THE COST OF CAPITAL: SOME PRELIMINARIES 15.1

In Chapter 13, we developed the security market line, or SML, and used it to explore the relationship between the expected return on a security and its systematic risk. We concentrated on how the risky returns from buying securities looked from the viewpoint of, for example, a shareholder in the firm. This helped us understand more about the alternatives available to an investor in the capital markets.

In this chapter, we turn things around a bit and look more closely at the other side of the problem, which is how these returns and securities look from the viewpoint of the companies that issue them. The important fact to note is that the return an investor in a security receives is the cost of that security to the company that issued it.

Required Return versus Cost of Capital

When we say that the required return on an investment is, say, 10 percent, we usually mean that the investment will have a positive NPV only if its return exceeds 10 percent. Another way of interpreting the required return is to observe that the firm must earn 10 percent on the investment just to compensate its investors for the use of the capital needed to finance the project. This is why we could also say that 10 percent is the cost of capital associated with the investment.

To illustrate the point further, imagine that we are evaluating a risk-free project. In this case, how to determine the required return is obvious: We look at the capital markets and observe the current rate offered by risk-free investments, and we use this rate to discount the project's cash flows. Thus, the cost of capital for a risk-free investment is the risk-free rate.

If a project is risky, then, assuming that all the other information is unchanged, the required return is obviously higher. In other words, the cost of capital for this project, if it is risky, is greater than the risk-free rate, and the appropriate discount rate would exceed the risk-free rate.

We will henceforth use the terms *required return, appropriate discount rate,* and *cost of capital* more or less interchangeably because, as the discussion in this section suggests, they all mean essentially the same thing. The key fact to grasp is that the cost of capital associated with an investment depends on the risk of that investment. This is one of the most important lessons in corporate finance, so it bears repeating:

The cost of capital depends primarily on the use of the funds, not the source.

It is a common error to forget this crucial point and fall into the trap of thinking that the cost of capital for an investment depends primarily on how and where the capital is raised.

Financial Policy and Cost of Capital

We know that the particular mixture of debt and equity a firm chooses to employ—its capital structure—is a managerial variable. In this chapter, we will take the firm's financial policy as given. In particular, we will assume that the firm has a fixed debt-equity ratio that it maintains. This ratio reflects the firm's *target* capital structure. How a firm might choose that ratio is the subject of our next chapter.

From the preceding discussion, we know that a firm's overall cost of capital will reflect the required return on the firm's assets as a whole. Given that a firm uses both debt and equity capital, this overall cost of capital will be a mixture of the returns needed to compensate its creditors and those needed to compensate its stockholders. In other words, a firm's cost of capital will reflect both its cost of debt capital and its cost of equity capital. We discuss these costs separately in the sections that follow.

Concept Questions

15.1a What is the primary determinant of the cost of capital for an investment?

15.1b What is the relationship between the required return on an investment and the cost of capital associated with that investment?

15.2 THE COST OF EQUITY

cost of equity
The return that equity investors require on their investment in the firm.

We begin with the most difficult question on the subject of cost of capital: What is the firm's overall **cost of equity**? The reason this is a difficult question is that there is no way of directly observing the return that the firm's equity investors require on their investment. Instead, we must somehow estimate it. This section discusses two approaches to determining the cost of equity: the dividend growth model approach and the security market line, SML, approach.

The Dividend Growth Model Approach

The easiest way to estimate the cost of equity capital is to use the dividend growth model we developed in Chapter 8. Recall that, under the assumption that the firm's dividend will grow at a constant rate g, the price per share of the stock, P_0, can be written as:

$$P_0 = \frac{D_0 \times (1 + g)}{R_E - g} = \frac{D_1}{R_E - g}$$

where D_0 is the dividend just paid and D_1 is the next period's projected dividend. Notice that we have used the symbol R_E (the E stands for equity) for the required return on the stock.

As we discussed in Chapter 8, we can rearrange this to solve for R_E as follows:

$$R_E = D_1/P_0 + g \qquad [15.1]$$

Because R_E is the return that the shareholders require on the stock, it can be interpreted as the firm's cost of equity capital.

Implementing the Approach To estimate R_E using the dividend growth model approach, we obviously need three pieces of information: P_0, D_0, and g.[2] Of these, for a publicly traded, dividend-paying company, the first two can be observed directly, so they are easily obtained. Only the third component, the expected growth rate for dividends, must be estimated.

[2]Notice that if we have D_0 and g, we can simply calculate D_1 by multiplying D_0 by $(1 + g)$.

To illustrate how we estimate R_E, suppose Greater States Public Service, a large public utility, paid a dividend of \$4 per share last year. The stock currently sells for \$60 per share. You estimate that the dividend will grow steadily at a rate of 6 percent per year into the indefinite future. What is the cost of equity capital for Greater States?

Using the dividend growth model, we can calculate that the expected dividend for the coming year, D_1, is:

$$\begin{aligned} D_1 &= D_0 \times (1 + g) \\ &= \$4 \times 1.06 \\ &= \$4.24 \end{aligned}$$

Given this, the cost of equity, R_E, is:

$$\begin{aligned} R_E &= D_1/P_0 + g \\ &= \$4.24/60 + .06 \\ &= 13.07\% \end{aligned}$$

The cost of equity is thus 13.07 percent.

Estimating *g* To use the dividend growth model, we must come up with an estimate for g, the growth rate. There are essentially two ways of doing this: (1) use historical growth rates, or (2) use analysts' forecasts of future growth rates. Analysts' forecasts are available from a variety of sources. Naturally, different sources will have different estimates, so one approach might be to obtain multiple estimates and then average them.

Alternatively, we might observe dividends for the previous, say, five years, calculate the year-to-year growth rates, and average them. For example, suppose we observe the following for some company:

Year	Dividend
2001	\$1.10
2002	1.20
2003	1.35
2004	1.40
2005	1.55

Growth estimates can be found at www.zacks.com.

We can calculate the percentage change in the dividend for each year as follows:

Year	Dividend	Dollar Change	Percentage Change
2001	\$1.10	—	—
2002	1.20	\$.10	9.09%
2003	1.35	.15	12.50
2004	1.40	.05	3.70
2005	1.55	.15	10.71

Notice that we calculated the change in the dividend on a year-to-year basis and then expressed the change as a percentage. Thus, in 2002 for example, the dividend rose from \$1.10 to \$1.20, an increase of \$.10. This represents a $\$.10/1.10 = 9.09\%$ increase.

If we average the four growth rates, the result is $(9.09 + 12.50 + 3.70 + 10.71)/4 = 9\%$, so we could use this as an estimate for the expected growth rate, g. Notice that this

9 percent growth rate we have calculated is a simple, or arithmetic average. Going back to Chapter 12, we also could calculate a geometric growth rate. Here, the dividend grows from \$1.10 to \$1.55 over a four-year period. What's the compound, or geometric growth rate? See if you don't agree that it's 8.95 percent; you can view this as a simple time value of money problem where \$1.10 is the present value and \$1.55 is the future value.

As usual, the geometric average (8.95 percent) is lower than the arithmetic average (9.09 percent), but the difference here is not likely to be of any practical significance. In general, if the dividend has grown at a relatively steady rate, as we assume when we use this approach, then it can't make much difference which way we calculate the average dividend growth rate.

Advantages and Disadvantages of the Approach The primary advantage of the dividend growth model approach is its simplicity. It is both easy to understand and easy to use. There are a number of associated practical problems and disadvantages.

First and foremost, the dividend growth model is obviously only applicable to companies that pay dividends. This means that the approach is useless in many cases. Furthermore, even for companies that do pay dividends, the key underlying assumption is that the dividend grows at a constant rate. As our previous example illustrates, this will never be *exactly* the case. More generally, the model is really only applicable to cases in which reasonably steady growth is likely to occur.

A second problem is that the estimated cost of equity is very sensitive to the estimated growth rate. For a given stock price, an upward revision of g by just one percentage point, for example, increases the estimated cost of equity by at least a full percentage point. Because D_1 will probably be revised upwards as well, the increase will actually be somewhat larger than that.

Finally, this approach really does not explicitly consider risk. Unlike the SML approach (which we consider next), there is no direct adjustment for the riskiness of the investment. For example, there is no allowance for the degree of certainty or uncertainty surrounding the estimated growth rate for dividends. As a result, it is difficult to say whether or not the estimated return is commensurate with the level of risk.[3]

The SML Approach

In Chapter 13, we discussed the security market line, or SML. Our primary conclusion was that the required or expected return on a risky investment depends on three things:

1. The risk-free rate, R_f
2. The market risk premium, $E(R_M) - R_f$
3. The systematic risk of the asset relative to average, which we called its beta coefficient, β

Using the SML, we can write the expected return on the company's equity, $E(R_E)$, as:

$$E(R_E) = R_f + \beta_E \times [E(R_M) - R_f]$$

where β_E is the estimated beta. To make the SML approach consistent with the dividend growth model, we will drop the Es denoting expectations and henceforth write the required return from the SML, R_E, as:

$$R_E = R_f + \beta_E \times (R_M - R_f) \quad [15.2]$$

[3]There is an implicit adjustment for risk because the current stock price is used. All other things being equal, the higher the risk, the lower is the stock price. Further, the lower the stock price, the greater is the cost of equity, again assuming all the other information is the same.

Implementing the Approach To use the SML approach, we need a risk-free rate, R_f, an estimate of the market risk premium, $R_M - R_f$, and an estimate of the relevant beta, β_E. In Chapter 12 (Table 12.3), we saw that one estimate of the market risk premium (based on large common stocks) is 8.6 percent. U.S. Treasury bills are paying about 1.5 percent as this chapter is being written, so we will use this as our risk-free rate. Beta coefficients for publicly traded companies are widely available.[4]

Betas and T-bill rates can both be found at www.bloomberg.com.

To illustrate, in Chapter 13, we saw that GM had an estimated beta of 1.25 (Table 13.8). We could thus estimate GM's cost of equity as:

$$\begin{aligned} R_{GM} &= R_f + \beta_{GM} \times (R_M - R_f) \\ &= 1.5\% + 1.25 \times 8.6\% \\ &= 12.25\% \end{aligned}$$

Thus, using the SML approach, we calculate that GM's cost of equity is about 12.25 percent.

Advantages and Disadvantages of the Approach The SML approach has two primary advantages. First, it explicitly adjusts for risk. Second, it is applicable to companies other than just those with steady dividend growth. Thus, it may be useful in a wider variety of circumstances.

There are drawbacks, of course. The SML approach requires that two things be estimated, the market risk premium and the beta coefficient. To the extent that our estimates are poor, the resulting cost of equity will be inaccurate. For example, our estimate of the market risk premium, 8.6 percent, is based on about 80 years of returns on a particular portfolio of stocks. Using different time periods or different stocks could result in very different estimates.

Finally, as with the dividend growth model, we essentially rely on the past to predict the future when we use the SML approach. Economic conditions can change very quickly, so, as always, the past may not be a good guide to the future. In the best of all worlds, both approaches (the dividend growth model and the SML) are applicable and the two result in similar answers. If this happens, we might have some confidence in our estimates. We might also wish to compare the results to those for other, similar, companies as a reality check.

The Cost of Equity

<< **EXAMPLE 15.1**

Suppose stock in Alpha Air Freight has a beta of 1.2. The market risk premium is 8 percent, and the risk-free rate is 6 percent. Alpha's last dividend was \$2 per share, and the dividend is expected to grow at 8 percent indefinitely. The stock currently sells for \$30. What is Alpha's cost of equity capital?

We can start off by using the SML. Doing this, we find that the expected return on the common stock of Alpha Air Freight is:

$$\begin{aligned} R_E &= R_f + \beta_E \times (R_M - R_f) \\ &= 6\% + 1.2 \times 8\% \\ &= 15.6\% \end{aligned}$$

continued

[4]Beta coefficients can also be estimated directly by using historical data. For a discussion of how to do this, see Chapters 9, 10, and 12 in S. A. Ross, R. W. Westerfield, and J. J. Jaffe, *Corporate Finance,* 7th ed. (New York: McGraw-Hill, 2005).

This suggests that 15.6 percent is Alpha's cost of equity. We next use the dividend growth model. The projected dividend is $D_0 \times (1 + g) = \$2 \times 1.08 = \$2.16$, so the expected return using this approach is:

$$R_E = D_1/P_0 + g$$
$$= \$2.16/30 + .08$$
$$= 15.2\%$$

Our two estimates are reasonably close, so we might just average them to find that Alpha's cost of equity is approximately 15.4 percent.

Concept Questions

15.2a What do we mean when we say that a corporation's cost of equity capital is 16 percent?

15.2b What are two approaches to estimating the cost of equity capital?

15.3 THE COSTS OF DEBT AND PREFERRED STOCK

In addition to ordinary equity, firms use debt and, to a lesser extent, preferred stock to finance their investments. As we discuss next, determining the costs of capital associated with these sources of financing is much easier than determining the cost of equity.

The Cost of Debt

cost of debt
The return that lenders require on the firm's debt.

The **cost of debt** is the return that the firm's creditors demand on new borrowing. In principle, we could determine the beta for the firm's debt and then use the SML to estimate the required return on debt just as we estimated the required return on equity. This isn't really necessary, however.

Unlike a firm's cost of equity, its cost of debt can normally be observed either directly or indirectly, because the cost of debt is simply the interest rate the firm must pay on new borrowing, and we can observe interest rates in the financial markets. For example, if the firm already has bonds outstanding, then the yield to maturity on those bonds is the market-required rate on the firm's debt.

Alternatively, if we know that the firm's bonds are rated, say, AA, then we can simply find out what the interest rate on newly issued AA-rated bonds is. Either way, there is no need to estimate a beta for the debt because we can directly observe the rate we want to know.

There is one thing to be careful about, though. The coupon rate on the firm's outstanding debt is irrelevant here. That rate just tells us roughly what the firm's cost of debt was back when the bonds were issued, not what the cost of debt is today.[5] This is why we have to look at the yield on the debt in today's marketplace. For the sake of consistency with our other notation, we will use the symbol R_D for the cost of debt.

[5]The firm's cost of debt based on its historic borrowing is sometimes called the *embedded debt cost.*

The Cost of Debt

EXAMPLE 15.2

Suppose the General Tool Company issued a 30-year, 7 percent bond 8 years ago. The bond is currently selling for 96 percent of its face value, or $960. What is General Tool's cost of debt?

Going back to Chapter 7, we need to calculate the yield to maturity on this bond. Because the bond is selling at a discount, the yield is apparently greater than 7 percent, but not much greater because the discount is fairly small. You can check to see that the yield to maturity is about 7.37 percent, assuming annual coupons. General Tool's cost of debt, R_D, is thus 7.37 percent.

The Cost of Preferred Stock

Determining the *cost of preferred stock* is quite straightforward. As we discussed in Chapters 6 and 8, preferred stock has a fixed dividend paid every period forever, so a share of preferred stock is essentially a perpetuity. The cost of preferred stock, R_P, is thus:

$$R_P = D/P_0 \quad [15.3]$$

where D is the fixed dividend and P_0 is the current price per share of the preferred stock. Notice that the cost of preferred stock is simply equal to the dividend yield on the preferred stock. Alternatively, because preferred stocks are rated in much the same way as bonds, the cost of preferred stock can be estimated by observing the required returns on other, similarly rated shares of preferred stock.

Alabama Power Co.'s Cost of Preferred Stock

EXAMPLE 15.3

On June 16, 2004, Alabama Power Co. had two issues of ordinary preferred stock that traded on the NYSE. One issue paid $1.30 annually per share and sold for $23.78 per share. The other paid $1.46 per share annually and sold for $24.30 per share. What is Alabama Power's cost of preferred stock?

Using the first issue, we calculate that the cost of preferred stock is:

$$\begin{aligned} R_P &= D/P_0 \\ &= \$1.30/23.78 \\ &= 5.5\% \end{aligned}$$

Using the second issue, we calculate that the cost is:

$$\begin{aligned} R_P &= D/P_0 \\ &= \$1.46/24.30 \\ &= 6\% \end{aligned}$$

So, Alabama Power's cost of preferred stock appears to be in the 5.5 to 6 percent range.

Concept Questions

15.3a How can the cost of debt be calculated?

15.3b How can the cost of preferred stock be calculated?

15.3c Why is the coupon rate a bad estimate of a firm's cost of debt?

15.4 THE WEIGHTED AVERAGE COST OF CAPITAL

Now that we have the costs associated with the main sources of capital the firm employs, we need to worry about the specific mix. As we mentioned earlier, we will take this mix, which is the firm's capital structure, as given for now. Also, we will focus mostly on debt and ordinary equity in this discussion.

In Chapter 3, we mentioned that financial analysts frequently focus on a firm's total capitalization, which is the sum of its long-term debt and equity. This is particularly true in determining cost of capital; short-term liabilities are often ignored in the process. We will not explicitly distinguish between total value and total capitalization in the following discussion; the general approach is applicable with either.

The Capital Structure Weights

We will use the symbol E (for equity) to stand for the *market* value of the firm's equity. We calculate this by taking the number of shares outstanding and multiplying it by the price per share. Similarly, we will use the symbol D (for debt) to stand for the *market* value of the firm's debt. For long-term debt, we calculate this by multiplying the market price of a single bond by the number of bonds outstanding.

If there are multiple bond issues (as there normally would be), we repeat this calculation of D for each and then add up the results. If there is debt that is not publicly traded (because it is held by a life insurance company, for example), we must observe the yield on similar, publicly traded debt and then estimate the market value of the privately held debt using this yield as the discount rate. For short-term debt, the book (accounting) values and market values should be somewhat similar, so we might use the book values as estimates of the market values.

Finally, we will use the symbol V (for value) to stand for the combined market value of the debt and equity:

$$V = E + D \qquad [15.4]$$

If we divide both sides by V, we can calculate the percentages of the total capital represented by the debt and equity:

$$100\% = E/V + D/V \qquad [15.5]$$

These percentages can be interpreted just like portfolio weights, and they are often called the *capital structure weights.*

For example, if the total market value of a company's stock were calculated as $200 million and the total market value of the company's debt were calculated as $50 million, then the combined value would be $250 million. Of this total, E/V = $200 million/250 million = 80%, so 80 percent of the firm's financing would be equity and the remaining 20 percent would be debt.

We emphasize here that the correct way to proceed is to use the *market* values of the debt and equity. Under certain circumstances, such as when calculating figures for a privately owned company, it may not be possible to get reliable estimates of these quantities. In this case, we might go ahead and use the accounting values for debt and equity. Although this would probably be better than nothing, we would have to take the answer with a grain of salt.

Taxes and the Weighted Average Cost of Capital

There is one final issue we need to discuss. Recall that we are always concerned with aftertax cash flows. If we are determining the discount rate appropriate to those cash flows, then the discount rate also needs to be expressed on an aftertax basis.

As we discussed previously in various places in this book (and as we will discuss later), the interest paid by a corporation is deductible for tax purposes. Payments to stockholders, such as dividends, are not. What this means, effectively, is that the government pays some of the interest. Thus, in determining an aftertax discount rate, we need to distinguish between the pretax and the aftertax cost of debt.

To illustrate, suppose a firm borrows \$1 million at 9 percent interest. The corporate tax rate is 34 percent. What is the aftertax interest rate on this loan? The total interest bill will be \$90,000 per year. This amount is tax deductible, however, so the \$90,000 interest reduces the firm's tax bill by $.34 \times \$90{,}000 = \$30{,}600$. The aftertax interest bill is thus $\$90{,}000 - 30{,}600 = \$59{,}400$. The aftertax interest rate is thus $\$59{,}400/1$ million $=$ 5.94%.

Notice that, in general, the aftertax interest rate is simply equal to the pretax rate multiplied by 1 minus the tax rate. [If we use the symbol T_C to stand for the corporate tax rate, then the aftertax rate that we use can be written as $R_D \times (1 - T_C)$.] For example, using the numbers from the preceding paragraph, we find that the aftertax interest rate is $9\% \times (1 - .34) = 5.94\%$.

To get a feel for actual, industry-level WACCs, visit www.ibbotson.com.

Bringing together the various topics we have discussed in this chapter, we now have the capital structure weights along with the cost of equity and the aftertax cost of debt. To calculate the firm's overall cost of capital, we multiply the capital structure weights by the associated costs and add them up. The total is the **weighted average cost of capital (WACC)**.

weighted average cost of capital (WACC)
The weighted average of the cost of equity and the aftertax cost of debt.

$$\text{WACC} = (E/V) \times R_E + (D/V) \times R_D \times (1 - T_C) \qquad [15.6]$$

This WACC has a very straightforward interpretation. It is the overall return the firm must earn on its existing assets to maintain the value of its stock. It is also the required return on any investments by the firm that have essentially the same risks as existing operations. So, if we were evaluating the cash flows from a proposed expansion of our existing operations, this is the discount rate we would use.

If a firm uses preferred stock in its capital structure, then our expression for the WACC needs a simple extension. If we define P/V as the percentage of the firm's financing that comes from preferred stock, then the WACC is simply:

$$\text{WACC} = (E/V) \times R_E + (P/V) \times R_P + (D/V) \times R_D \times (1 - T_C) \qquad [15.7]$$

where R_P is the cost of preferred stock.

Calculating the WACC

<< EXAMPLE 15.4

The B. B. Lean Co. has 1.4 million shares of stock outstanding. The stock currently sells for \$20 per share. The firm's debt is publicly traded and was recently quoted at 93 percent of face value. It has a total face value of \$5 million, and it is currently priced to yield 11 percent. The risk-free rate is 8 percent, and the market risk premium is 7 percent. You've estimated that Lean has a beta of .74. If the corporate tax rate is 34 percent, what is the WACC of Lean Co.?

We can first determine the cost of equity and the cost of debt. Using the SML, we find that the cost of equity is $8\% + .74 \times 7\% = 13.18\%$. The total value of the equity is

continued

1.4 million × \$20 = \$28 million. The pretax cost of debt is the current yield to maturity on the outstanding debt, 11 percent. The debt sells for 93 percent of its face value, so its current market value is .93 × \$5 million = \$4.65 million. The total market value of the equity and debt together is \$28 million + 4.65 million = \$32.65 million.

From here, we can calculate the WACC easily enough. The percentage of equity used by Lean to finance its operations is \$28 million/\$32.65 million = 85.76%. Because the weights have to add up to 1, the percentage of debt is 1 − .8576 = 14.24%. The WACC is thus:

$$\begin{aligned} \text{WACC} &= (E/V) \times R_E + (D/V) \times R_D \times (1 - T_C) \\ &= .8576 \times 13.18\% + .1424 \times 11\% \times (1 - .34) \\ &= 12.34\% \end{aligned}$$

B. B. Lean thus has an overall weighted average cost of capital of 12.34 percent.

Calculating the WACC for Eastman Chemical

In this section, we illustrate how to calculate the WACC for Eastman Chemical, the company we discussed at the beginning of the chapter. Our goal is to take you through, on a step-by-step basis, the process of finding and using the information needed using online sources. As you will see, there is a fair amount of detail involved, but the necessary information is, for the most part, readily available.

Eastman's Cost of Equity Our first stop is the key statistics screen for Eastman available at finance.yahoo.com (ticker: EMN). As of mid-2004, the relevant pieces of what we found are shown in the next two boxes:

EASTMAN CHEM (NYSE:EMN) Quote data by Reuters			
Last Trade:	**46.23**	Day's Range:	45.98 - 46.65
Trade Time:	4:01PM ET	52wk Range:	30.39 - 46.67
Change:	↓0.11 (0.24%)	Volume:	731,600
Prev Close:	46.34	Avg Vol (3m):	701,772
Open:	46.34	Market Cap:	3.57B
Bid:	N/A	P/E (ttm):	N/A
Ask:	N/A	EPS (ttm):	-3.848
1y Target Est:	44.50	Div & Yield:	1.76 (3.80%)

According to the screen on the next page, Eastman has 77 million shares of stock outstanding. The book value per share is \$12.861, but the stock sells for \$46.23. Total equity is therefore about \$990 million on a book value basis, but it is closer to \$3.570 billion on a market value basis.

To estimate Eastman's cost of equity, we assume a market risk premium of 8.6 percent, similar to what we calculated in Chapter 12. Eastman's beta on Yahoo! is 0.908, which is only slightly lower than the beta of the average stock. To check this number, we went to www.hoovers.com and www.moneycentral.msn.com. The beta estimates we found there were both 0.90, so we will use the estimate from Yahoo!. According to the bond section of finance.yahoo.com, T-bills were paying about 1.4 percent. Using the CAPM to estimate the

VALUATION MEASURES	
Market Cap (intraday):	3.57B
Enterprise Value (1-Jun-04)³:	5.75B
Trailing P/E (ttm, intraday):	N/A
Forward P/E (fye 31-Dec-05)¹:	15.16
PEG Ratio (5 yr expected)¹:	3.86
Price/Sales (ttm):	0.60
Price/Book (mrq):	3.60
Enterprise Value/Revenue (ttm)³:	0.97
Enterprise Value/EBITDA (ttm)³:	130.76

FINANCIAL HIGHLIGHTS

Balance Sheet	
Total Cash (mrq):	42.00M
Total Cash Per Share (mrq):	0.54
Total Debt (mrq)²:	2.21B
Total Debt/Equity (mrq):	2.227
Current Ratio (mrq):	1.741
Book Value Per Share (mrq):	12.861

TRADING INFORMATION

Stock Price History	
Beta:	0.908
52-Week Change:	41.76%
52-Week Change (relative to S&P500):	21.88%
52-Week High (27-May-04):	46.67
52-Week Low (3-Jul-03):	30.39
50-Day Moving Average:	43.32
200-Day Moving Average:	38.61

Share Statistics	
Average Volume (3 month):	701,772
Average Volume (10 day):	732,000
Shares Outstanding:	77.29M
Float:	71.90M
% Held by Insiders:	6.97%
% Held by Institutions:	85.41%
Shares Short (as of 10-May-04):	4.32M
Daily Volume (as of 10-May-04):	N/A
Short Ratio (as of 10-May-04):	6.695
Short % of Float (as of 10-May-04):	6.01%
Shares Short (prior month):	3.39M

Dividends & Splits	
Annual Dividend:	1.76
Dividend Yield:	3.80%
Dividend Date:	1-Jul-04
Ex-Dividend Date:	11-Jun-04
Last Split Factor (new per old)²:	N/A
Last Split Date:	N/A

cost of equity, we find:

$$R_E = 0.014 + 0.908(0.086) = 0.0921 \text{ or } 9.21\%$$

Eastman has only paid dividends for a few years, so calculating the growth rate for the dividend discount model is problematic. However, under the analysts' estimates link at finance.yahoo.com, we found the following:

Growth Est	EMN	Industry	Sector	S&P 500
Current Qtr.	26.2%	36.0%	94.2%	19.7%
Next Qtr.	130.8%	32.9%	78.4%	11.3%
This Year	139.8%	47.3%	90.4%	17.9%
Next Year	29.8%	26.7%	29.3%	10.8%
Past 5 Years (per annum)	-21.4%	N/A	N/A	N/A
Next 5 Years (per annum)	5.1%	9.38%	10.01%	10.76%
Price/Earnings (avg. for comparison categories)	19.7	18.34	18.02	17.11
PEG Ratio (avg. for comparison categories)	3.86	1.95	1.80	1.59

Analysts estimate the growth in earnings per share for the company will be 5.1 percent for the next five years. For now, we will use this growth rate in the dividend discount model to estimate the cost of equity; the link between earnings growth and dividends is discussed in a later chapter. The estimated cost of equity using the dividend discount model is:

$$R_E = \left(\frac{\$1.76\ (1 + .051)}{\$46.23}\right) + .051 = .0910 \text{ or } 9.10\%$$

Notice that the estimates for the cost of equity are very close; however, this is not always the case. Remember that each method of estimating the cost of equity relies on different assumptions, so different estimates of the cost of equity should not surprise us. If the estimates are different, there are two simple solutions: First, we could ignore one of the estimates. We would look at each estimate to see if one of them seemed too high or too low to be reasonable. Second, we could average the two estimates. Averaging the two estimates of Eastman's cost of equity gives us a cost of equity of 9.15 percent. Since this seems like a reasonable number, we will use it in calculating the cost of capital in this example.

Eastman's Cost of Debt Eastman has six relatively long-term bond issues that account for essentially all of its long-term debt. To calculate the cost of debt, we will have to combine these six issues. What we will do is compute a weighted average. We went to www.nasdbondinfo.com to find quotes on the bonds. We should note here that finding the yield to maturity for all of a company's outstanding bond issues on a single day is unusual. If you remember our previous discussion on bonds, the bond market is not as liquid as the stock market, and, on many days, individual bond issues may not trade. To find the book value of the bonds, we went to www.sec.gov and found the 10Q report (i.e., the most recent quarterly financial report) dated March 31, 2004, and filed with the SEC on May 6, 2004. The basic information is as follows:[6]

Coupon Rate	Maturity	Book Value (Face value, in millions)	Price (% of par)	Yield to Maturity
3.25%	2008	$250	94.81	4.68%
7.00	2012	257	108.19	5.69
6.30	2018	405	98.54	6.46
7.60	2024	496	109.12	6.80
7.625	2024	200	112.76	6.48
7.60	2027	297	104.81	6.80

To calculate the weighted average cost of debt, we take the percentage of the total debt represented by each issue and multiply by the yield on the issue. We then add to get the overall weighted average debt cost. We use both book values and market values here for

[6]You might be wondering why the yield on the 7.625 percent issue maturing in 2024 is lower than that on the other two long-term issues with similar maturities. The reason is that this issue has a put feature (discussed in Chapter 7) that the other two issues do not. Such features are desirable from the buyer's standpoint, so this issue has a higher price and, thus, a lower yield.

comparison. The results of the calculations are as follows:

Coupon Rate	Book Value (Face value, in millions)	Percentage of Total	Market Value (in millions)	Percentage of Total	Yield to Maturity	Book Values	Market Values
3.25%	$250	.13	$237.0	.12	4.68%	0.56%	0.56
7.00	257	.13	278.1	.14	5.69	0.76	0.79
6.30	405	.21	399.1	.20	6.46	1.29	1.29
7.60	496	.26	541.2	.27	6.80	1.85	1.85
7.625	200	.10	225.5	.11	6.48	0.73	0.73
7.60	297	.16	311.3	.16	6.80	1.06	1.06
Total	$1,905	1.00	$1,992.2	1.00		6.29%	6.29%

As these calculations show, Eastman's cost of debt is 6.29 percent on a book value basis and also 6.29 percent on a market value basis. Thus, for Eastman, whether market values or book values are used makes no difference. The reason is simply that the market values and book values are similar to the total values. This will often be the case and explains why companies frequently use book values for debt in WACC calculations. Also, Eastman has no preferred stock, so we don't need to consider a cost of preferred.

Eastman's WACC We now have the various pieces necessary to calculate Eastman's WACC. First, we need to calculate the capital structure weights. On a book value basis, Eastman's equity and debt are worth \$0.99 billion and \$1.905 billion, respectively. The total value is \$2.895 billion, so the equity and debt percentages are \$0.99 billion/2.895 billion = .34 and \$1.905 billion/2.895 billion = .66. Assuming a tax rate of 35 percent, Eastman's WACC is:

$$\begin{aligned}\text{WACC} &= .34 \times 9.15\% + .66 \times 6.29\% \times (1 - .35)\\ &= 5.81\%\end{aligned}$$

Thus, using book value capital structure weights, we get about 5.8 percent for Eastman's WACC.

If we use market value weights, however, the WACC will be higher. To see why, notice that, on a market value basis, Eastman's equity and debt are worth \$3.570 billion and \$1.992 billion, respectively. The capital structure weights are therefore \$3.570 billion/5.562 billion = .64 and \$1.992 billion/5.562 billion = .36, so the equity percentage is much higher. With these weights, Eastman's WACC is:

$$\begin{aligned}\text{WACC} &= .64 \times 9.15\% + .36 \times 6.29\% \times (1 - .35)\\ &= 7.33\%\end{aligned}$$

Thus, using market value weights, we get 7.3 percent for Eastman's WACC, which is a full percent and one-half higher than the 5.8 percent WACC we got using book value weights.

As this example illustrates, using book values can lead to trouble, particularly if equity book values are used. Going back to Chapter 3, recall that we discussed the market-to-book ratio (the ratio of market value per share to book value per share). This ratio is usually substantially bigger than 1. For Eastman, for example, verify that it's about 3.6; so book values significantly overstate the percentage of Eastman's financing that comes from debt. In addition, if we were computing a WACC for a company that did not have publicly traded stock, we would try to come up with a suitable market-to-book ratio by looking at publicly traded companies, and we would then use this ratio to adjust the book value of the company under consideration. As we have seen, failure to do so can lead to significant underestimation of the WACC.

Our nearby *Work the Web* box explains more about the WACC and related topics.

WORK THE WEB

So how does our estimate of the WACC for Eastman Chemical compare to others? One place to find estimates for WACC is www.valuepro.net. We went there and found the following information for Eastman.

Online Valuation for EMN - 6 / 2 / 2004

Intrinsic Stock Value 130.49 | Recalculate | Value Another Stock

Excess Return Period (yrs)	10	Depreciation Rate (% of Rev)	6.33
Revenues ($mil)	5956.0	Investment Rate (% of Rev)	3.97
Growth Rate (%)	28.5	Working Capital (% of Rev)	5.84
Net Oper. Profit Margin (%)	1.64	Short-Term Assets ($mil)	1584.0
Tax Rate (%)	21.053	Short-Term Liab. ($mil)	773
Stock Price ($)	45.9800	Equity Risk Premium (%)	3
Shares Outstanding (mil)	77.3	Company Beta	0.9975
10-Yr Treasury Yield (%)	5	Value Debt Out. ($mil)	2213
Bond Spread Treasury (%)	1.5	Value Pref. Stock Out. ($mil)	0
Preferred Stock Yield (%)	7.5	Company WACC (%)	6.89

As you can see, ValuePro estimates the WACC (Cost of Capital) for Eastman as 6.89 percent, which is lower than our estimate of 7.33 percent. You can see why the estimates for WACC are different: Different inputs were used in the computations. For example, ValuePro uses a 5 percent risk-free rate, and an equity risk premium of only 3 percent. Calculating WACC requires the estimation of various inputs, and you must use your best (good) judgment in these estimates.

Solving the Warehouse Problem and Similar Capital Budgeting Problems

Now we can use the WACC to solve the warehouse problem we posed at the beginning of the chapter. However, before we rush to discount the cash flows at the WACC to estimate NPV, we need to make sure we are doing the right thing.

Going back to first principles, we need to find an alternative in the financial markets that is comparable to the warehouse renovation. To be comparable, an alternative must be of the same level of risk as the warehouse project. Projects that have the same risk are said to be in the same risk class.

The WACC for a firm reflects the risk and the target capital structure of the firm's existing assets as a whole. As a result, strictly speaking, the firm's WACC is the appropriate discount rate only if the proposed investment is a replica of the firm's existing operating activities.

In broader terms, whether or not we can use the firm's WACC to value the warehouse project depends on whether the warehouse project is in the same risk class as the firm. We will assume that this project is an integral part of the overall business of the firm. In such cases, it is natural to think that the cost savings will be as risky as the general cash flows of the firm, and the project will thus be in the same risk class as the overall firm. More generally, projects like the warehouse renovation that are intimately related to the firm's existing operations are often viewed as being in the same risk class as the overall firm.

We can now see what the president should do. Suppose the firm has a target debt-equity ratio of 1/3. From Chapter 3, we know that a debt-equity ratio of $D/E = 1/3$ implies that E/V is .75 and D/V is .25. The cost of debt is 10 percent, and the cost of equity is 20 percent. Assuming a 34 percent tax rate, the WACC will be:

$$\begin{aligned}\text{WACC} &= (E/V) \times R_E + (D/V) \times R_D \times (1 - T_C) \\ &= .75 \times 20\% + .25 \times 10\% \times (1 - .34) \\ &= 16.65\%\end{aligned}$$

Recall that the warehouse project had a cost of \$50 million and expected aftertax cash flows (the cost savings) of \$12 million per year for six years. The NPV (in millions) is thus:

$$\text{NPV} = -\$50 + \frac{12}{(1 + \text{WACC})^1} + \cdots + \frac{12}{(1 + \text{WACC})^6}$$

Because the cash flows are in the form of an ordinary annuity, we can calculate this NPV using 16.65 percent (the WACC) as the discount rate as follows:

$$\begin{aligned}\text{NPV} &= -\$50 + 12 \times \frac{1 - [1/(1 + .1665)^6]}{.1665} \\ &= -\$50 + 12 \times 3.6222 \\ &= -\$6.53\end{aligned}$$

Should the firm take on the warehouse renovation? The project has a negative NPV using the firm's WACC. This means that the financial markets offer superior projects in the same risk class (namely, the firm itself). The answer is clear: The project should be rejected. For future reference, our discussion of the WACC is summarized in Table 15.1.

TABLE 15.1 >>

Summary of Capital Cost Calculations

I. The Cost of Equity, R_E

A. Dividend growth model approach (from Chapter 8):

$$R_E = D_1/P_0 + g$$

where D_1 is the expected dividend in one period, g is the dividend growth rate, and P_0 is the current stock price.

B. SML approach (from Chapter 13):

$$R_E = R_f + \beta_E \times (R_M - R_f)$$

where R_f is the risk-free rate, R_M is the expected return on the overall market, and β_E is the systematic risk of the equity.

II. The Cost of Debt, R_D

A. For a firm with publicly held debt, the cost of debt can be measured as the yield to maturity on the outstanding debt. The coupon rate is irrelevant. Yield to maturity is covered in Chapter 7.

B. If the firm has no publicly traded debt, then the cost of debt can be measured as the yield to maturity on similarly rated bonds (bond ratings are discussed in Chapter 7).

III. The Weighted Average Cost of Capital, WACC

A. The firm's WACC is the overall required return on the firm as a whole. It is the appropriate discount rate to use for cash flows similar in risk to those of the overall firm.

B. The WACC is calculated as:

$$\text{WACC} = (E/V) \times R_E + (D/V) \times R_D \times (1 - T_C)$$

where T_C is the corporate tax rate, E is the *market* value of the firm's equity, D is the *market* value of the firm's debt, and $V = E + D$. Note that E/V is the percentage of the firm's financing (in market value terms) that is equity, and D/V is the percentage that is debt.

EXAMPLE 15.5 >> Using the WACC

A firm is considering a project that will result in initial aftertax cash savings of $5 million at the end of the first year. These savings will grow at the rate of 5 percent per year. The firm has a debt-equity ratio of .5, a cost of equity of 29.2 percent, and a cost of debt of 10 percent. The cost-saving proposal is closely related to the firm's core business, so it is viewed as having the same risk as the overall firm. Should the firm take on the project?

Assuming a 34 percent tax rate, the firm should take on this project if it costs less than $30 million. To see this, first note that the PV is:

$$\text{PV} = \frac{\$5 \text{ million}}{\text{WACC} - .05}$$

This is an example of a growing perpetuity as discussed in Chapter 6. The WACC is:

$$\begin{aligned}\text{WACC} &= (E/V) \times R_E + (D/V) \times R_D \times (1 - T_C)\\ &= 2/3 \times 29.2\% + 1/3 \times 10\% \times (1 - .34)\\ &= 21.67\%\end{aligned}$$

The PV is thus:

$$\text{PV} = \frac{\$5 \text{ million}}{.2167 - .05} = \$30 \text{ million}$$

The NPV will be positive only if the cost is less than $30 million.

Performance Evaluation: Another Use of the WACC

Looking back at the Eastman Chemical example we used to open the chapter, we see another use of the WACC: its use for performance evaluation. Probably the best-known approach in this area is the economic value added (EVA) method developed by Stern Stewart and Co. Companies such as AT&T, Coca-Cola, Quaker Oats, and Briggs and Stratton are among the firms that have been using EVA as a means of evaluating corporate performance. Similar approaches include market value added (MVA) and shareholder value added (SVA).

Visit www.sternstewart.com for more on EVA.

Although the details differ, the basic idea behind EVA and similar strategies is straightforward. Suppose we have \$100 million in capital (debt and equity) tied up in our firm, and our overall WACC is 12 percent. If we multiply these together, we get \$12 million. Referring back to Chapter 2, if our cash flow from assets is less than this, we are, on an overall basis, destroying value; if cash flow from assets exceeds \$12 million, we are creating value.

In practice, evaluation strategies such as these suffer to a certain extent from problems with implementation. For example, it appears that Eastman Chemical and others make extensive use of book values for debt and equity in computing cost of capital. Even so, by focusing on value creation, WACC-based evaluation procedures force employees and management to pay attention to the real bottom line: increasing share prices.

Concept Questions

15.4a How is the WACC calculated?

15.4b Why do we multiply the cost of debt by $(1 - T_C)$ when we compute the WACC?

15.4c Under what conditions is it correct to use the WACC to determine NPV?

DIVISIONAL AND PROJECT COSTS OF CAPITAL 15.5

As we have seen, using the WACC as the discount rate for future cash flows is only appropriate when the proposed investment is similar to the firm's existing activities. This is not as restrictive as it sounds. If we are in the pizza business, for example, and we are thinking of opening a new location, then the WACC is the discount rate to use. The same is true of a retailer thinking of a new store, a manufacturer thinking of expanding production, or a consumer products company thinking of expanding its markets.

Nonetheless, despite the usefulness of the WACC as a benchmark, there will clearly be situations in which the cash flows under consideration have risks distinctly different from those of the overall firm. We consider how to cope with this problem next.

The SML and the WACC

When we are evaluating investments with risks that are substantially different from those of the overall firm, the use of the WACC will potentially lead to poor decisions. Figure 15.1 illustrates why.

In Figure 15.1, we have plotted an SML corresponding to a risk-free rate of 7 percent and a market risk premium of 8 percent. To keep things simple, we consider an all-equity company with a beta of 1. As we have indicated, the WACC and the cost of equity are exactly equal to 15 percent for this company because there is no debt.

FIGURE 15.1 >>

The Security Market Line (SML) and the Weighted Average Cost of Capital (WACC)

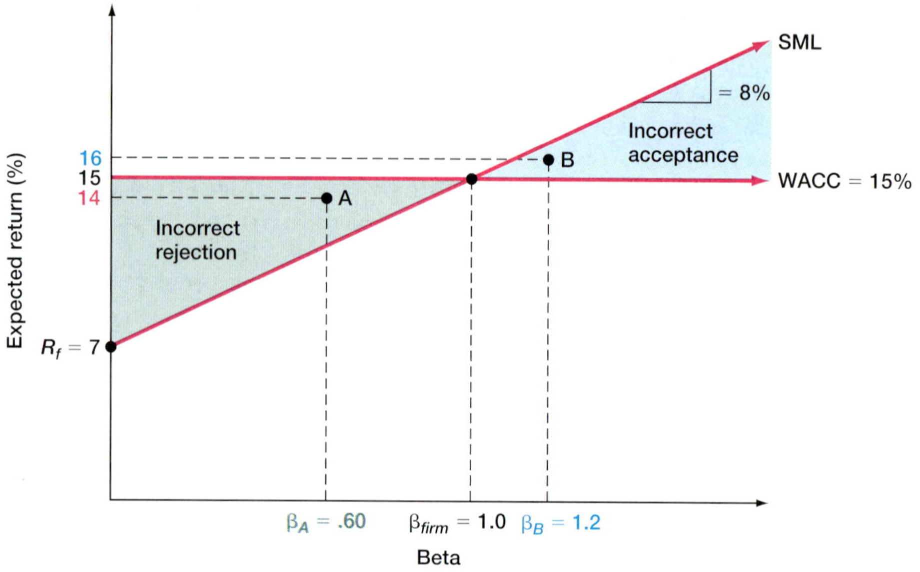

If a firm uses its WACC to make accept-reject decisions for all types of projects, it will have a tendency towards incorrectly accepting risky projects and incorrectly rejecting less risky projects.

Suppose our firm uses its WACC to evaluate all investments. This means that any investment with a return of greater than 15 percent will be accepted and any investment with a return of less than 15 percent will be rejected. We know from our study of risk and return, however, that a desirable investment is one that plots above the SML. As Figure 15.1 illustrates, using the WACC for all types of projects can result in the firm's incorrectly accepting relatively risky projects and incorrectly rejecting relatively safe ones.

For example, consider Point A. This project has a beta of $\beta_A = .60$, as compared to the firm's beta of 1.0. It has an expected return of 14 percent. Is this a desirable investment? The answer is yes, because its required return is only:

$$\begin{aligned}\text{Required return} &= R_f + \beta_A \times (R_M - R_f)\\ &= 7\% + .60 \times 8\%\\ &= 11.8\%\end{aligned}$$

However, if we use the WACC as a cutoff, then this project will be rejected because its return is less than 15 percent. This example illustrates that a firm that uses its WACC as a cutoff will tend to reject profitable projects with risks less than those of the overall firm.

At the other extreme, consider Point B. This project has a beta of $\beta_B = 1.2$. It offers a 16 percent return, which exceeds the firm's cost of capital. This is not a good investment, however, because, given its level of systematic risk, its return is inadequate. Nonetheless, if we use the WACC to evaluate it, it will appear to be attractive. So the second error that will arise if we use the WACC as a cutoff is that we will tend to make unprofitable investments with risks greater than those of the overall firm. As a consequence, through time, a firm that uses its WACC to evaluate all projects will have a tendency to both accept unprofitable investments and become increasingly risky.

Divisional Cost of Capital

The same type of problem with the WACC can arise in a corporation with more than one line of business. Imagine, for example, a corporation that has two divisions, a regulated telephone company and an electronics manufacturing operation. The first of these (the phone operation) has relatively low risk; the second has relatively high risk.

In this case, the firm's overall cost of capital is really a mixture of two different costs of capital, one for each division. If the two divisions were competing for resources, and the firm used a single WACC as a cutoff, which division would tend to be awarded greater funds for investment?

The answer is that the riskier division would tend to have greater returns (ignoring the greater risk), so it would tend to be the "winner." The less glamorous operation might have great profit potential that would end up being ignored. Large corporations in the United States are aware of this problem, and many work to develop separate divisional costs of capital.

The Pure Play Approach

We've seen that using the firm's WACC inappropriately can lead to problems. How can we come up with the appropriate discount rates in such circumstances? Because we cannot observe the returns on these investments, there generally is no direct way of coming up with a beta, for example. Instead, what we must do is examine other investments outside the firm that are in the same risk class as the one we are considering and use the market-required returns on these investments as the discount rate. In other words, we will try to determine what the cost of capital is for such investments by trying to locate some similar investments in the marketplace.

For example, going back to our telephone division, suppose we wanted to come up with a discount rate to use for that division. What we could do is identify several other phone companies that have publicly traded securities. We might find that a typical phone company has a beta of .80, AA-rated debt, and a capital structure that is about 50 percent debt and 50 percent equity. Using this information, we could develop a WACC for a typical phone company and use this as our discount rate.

Alternatively, if we were thinking of entering a new line of business, we would try to develop the appropriate cost of capital by looking at the market-required returns on companies already in that business. In the language of Wall Street, a company that focuses on a single line of business is called a *pure play*. For example, if you wanted to bet on the price of crude oil by purchasing common stocks, you would try to identify companies that dealt exclusively with this product because they would be the most affected by changes in the price of crude oil. Such companies would be called pure plays on the price of crude oil.

What we try to do here is to find companies that focus as exclusively as possible on the type of project in which we are interested. Our approach, therefore, is called the **pure play approach** to estimating the required return on an investment. To illustrate, suppose McDonald's decides to enter the personal computer and network server business with a line of machines called McPuters. The risks involved are quite different from those in the fast-food business. As a result, McDonald's would need to look at companies already in the personal computer business to compute a cost of capital for the new division. Two obvious "pure play" candidates would be Dell and Gateway, which are predominately in this line of business. IBM, on the other hand, would not be as good a choice because its primary focus is elsewhere, and it has many different product lines.

pure play approach
The use of a WACC that is unique to a particular project, based on companies in similar lines of business.

In Chapter 3, we discussed the subject of identifying similar companies for comparison purposes. The same problems we described there come up here. The most obvious one is that we may not be able to find any suitable companies. In this case, how to objectively determine a discount rate becomes a very difficult question. Even so, the important thing is to be aware of the issue so that we at least reduce the possibility of the kinds of mistakes that can arise when the WACC is used as a cutoff on all investments.

The Subjective Approach

Because of the difficulties that exist in objectively establishing discount rates for individual projects, firms often adopt an approach that involves making subjective adjustments to the overall WACC. To illustrate, suppose a firm has an overall WACC of 14 percent. It places all proposed projects into four categories as follows:

Category	Examples	Adjustment Factor	Discount Rate
High risk	New products	+6%	20%
Moderate risk	Cost savings, expansion of existing lines	+0	14
Low risk	Replacement of existing equipment	−4	10
Mandatory	Pollution control equipment	n/a	n/a

n/a = Not applicable.

The effect of this crude partitioning is to assume that all projects either fall into one of three risk classes or else are mandatory. In the last case, the cost of capital is irrelevant because the project must be taken. With the subjective approach, the firm's WACC may change through time as economic conditions change. As this happens, the discount rates for the different types of projects will also change.

Within each risk class, some projects will presumably have more risk than others, and the danger of making incorrect decisions still exists. Figure 15.2 illustrates this point. Comparing Figures 15.1 and 15.2, we see that similar problems exist, but the magnitude of the potential error is less with the subjective approach. For example, the project labeled A would be accepted if the WACC were used, but it is rejected once it is classified as a high-risk investment. What this illustrates is that some risk adjustment, even if it is subjective, is probably better than no risk adjustment.

FIGURE 15.2 >>

The Security Market Line (SML) and the Subjective Approach

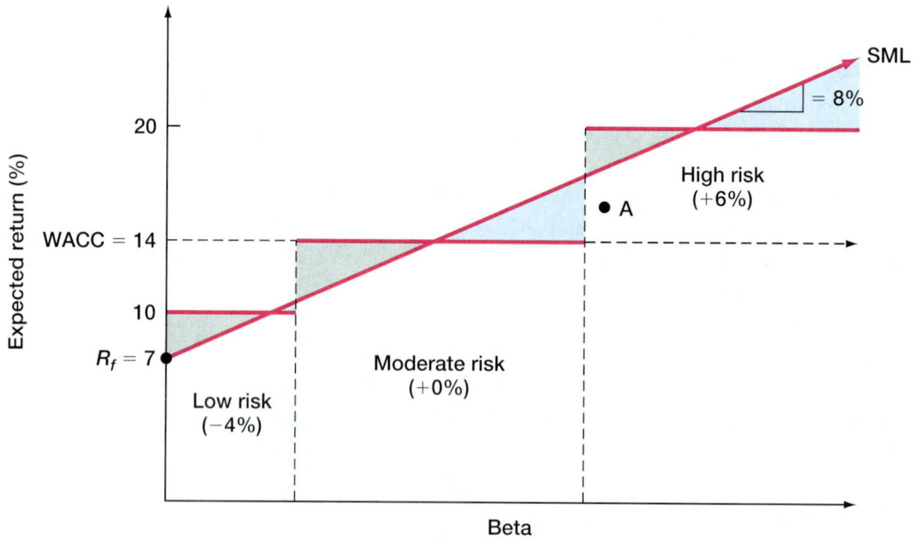

With the subjective approach, the firm places projects into one of several risk classes. The discount rate used to value the project is then determined by adding (for high risk) or subtracting (for low risk) an adjustment factor to or from the firm's WACC. This results in fewer incorrect decisions than if the firm simply used the WACC to make the decisions.

It would be better, in principle, to objectively determine the required return for each project separately. However, as a practical matter, it may not be possible to go much beyond subjective adjustments because either the necessary information is unavailable or else the cost and effort required are simply not worthwhile.

Concept Questions

15.5a What are the likely consequences if a firm uses its WACC to evaluate all proposed investments?

15.5b What is the pure play approach to determining the appropriate discount rate? When might it be used?

FLOTATION COSTS AND THE WEIGHTED AVERAGE COST OF CAPITAL 15.6

So far, we have not included issue, or flotation, costs in our discussion of the weighted average cost of capital. If a company accepts a new project, it may be required to issue, or float, new bonds and stocks. This means that the firm will incur some costs, which we call *flotation costs*. The nature and magnitude of flotation costs are discussed in some detail in Chapter 16.

Sometimes it is suggested that the firm's WACC should be adjusted upwards to reflect flotation costs. This is really not the best approach, because, once again, the required return on an investment depends on the risk of the investment, not the source of the funds. This is not to say that flotation costs should be ignored. Because these costs arise as a consequence of the decision to undertake a project, they are relevant cash flows. We therefore briefly discuss how to include them in a project analysis.

The Basic Approach

We start with a simple case. The Spatt Company, an all-equity firm, has a cost of equity of 20 percent. Because this firm is 100 percent equity, its WACC and its cost of equity are the same. Spatt is contemplating a large-scale $100 million expansion of its existing operations. The expansion would be funded by selling new stock.

Based on conversations with its investment banker, Spatt believes its flotation costs will run 10 percent of the amount issued. This means that Spatt's proceeds from the equity sale will be only 90 percent of the amount sold. When flotation costs are considered, what is the cost of the expansion?

As we discuss in more detail in Chapter 16, Spatt needs to sell enough equity to raise $100 million *after* covering the flotation costs. In other words:

$$\$100 \text{ million} = (1 - .10) \times \text{Amount raised}$$
$$\text{Amount raised} = \$100 \text{ million}/.90 = \$111.11 \text{ million}$$

Spatt's flotation costs are thus $11.11 million, and the true cost of the expansion is $111.11 million once we include flotation costs.

Things are only slightly more complicated if the firm uses both debt and equity. For example, suppose Spatt's target capital structure is 60 percent equity, 40 percent debt. The flotation costs associated with equity are still 10 percent, but the flotation costs for debt are less, say, 5 percent.

Earlier, when we had different capital costs for debt and equity, we calculated a weighted average cost of capital using the target capital structure weights. Here, we will do much the same thing. We can calculate a weighted average flotation cost, f_A, by multiplying the equity flotation cost, f_E, by the percentage of equity (E/V) and the debt flotation cost, f_D, by the percentage of debt (D/V) and then adding the two together:

$$
\begin{aligned}
f_A &= (E/V) \times f_E + (D/V) \times f_D \qquad [15.8]\\
&= 60\% \times .10 + 40\% \times .05\\
&= 8\%
\end{aligned}
$$

The weighted average flotation cost is thus 8 percent. What this tells us is that for every dollar in outside financing needed for new projects, the firm must actually raise $\$1/(1 - .08) = \$1.087$. In our example, the project cost is \$100 million when we ignore flotation costs. If we include them, then the true cost is \$100 million$/(1 - f_A) =$ \$100 million/.92 = \$108.7 million.

In taking issue costs into account, the firm must be careful not to use the wrong weights. The firm should use the target weights, even if it can finance the entire cost of the project with either debt or equity. The fact that a firm can finance a specific project with debt or equity is not directly relevant. If a firm has a target debt-equity ratio of 1, for example, but chooses to finance a particular project with all debt, it will have to raise additional equity later on to maintain its target debt-equity ratio. To take this into account, the firm should always use the target weights in calculating the flotation cost.

EXAMPLE 15.6 >> Calculating the Weighted Average Flotation Cost

The Weinstein Corporation has a target capital structure that is 80 percent equity, 20 percent debt. The flotation costs for equity issues are 20 percent of the amount raised; the flotation costs for debt issues are 6 percent. If Weinstein needs \$65 million for a new manufacturing facility, what is the true cost once flotation costs are considered?

We first calculate the weighted average flotation cost, f_A:

$$
\begin{aligned}
f_A &= (E/V) \times f_E + (D/V) \times f_D\\
&= 80\% \times .20 + 20\% \times .06\\
&= 17.2\%
\end{aligned}
$$

The weighted average flotation cost is thus 17.2 percent. The project cost is \$65 million when we ignore flotation costs. If we include them, then the true cost is \$65 million$/(1 - f_A)$ = \$65 million/.828 = \$78.5 million, again illustrating that flotation costs can be a considerable expense.

Flotation Costs and NPV

To illustrate how flotation costs can be included in an NPV analysis, suppose the Tripleday Printing Company is currently at its target debt-equity ratio of 100 percent. It is considering building a new \$500,000 printing plant in Kansas. This new plant is expected to generate aftertax cash flows of \$73,150 per year forever. The tax rate is 34 percent. There are two financing options:

1. A \$500,000 new issue of common stock. The issuance costs of the new common stock would be about 10 percent of the amount raised. The required return on the company's new equity is 20 percent.
2. A \$500,000 issue of 30-year bonds. The issuance costs of the new debt would be 2 percent of the proceeds. The company can raise new debt at 10 percent.

IN THEIR OWN WORDS . . .

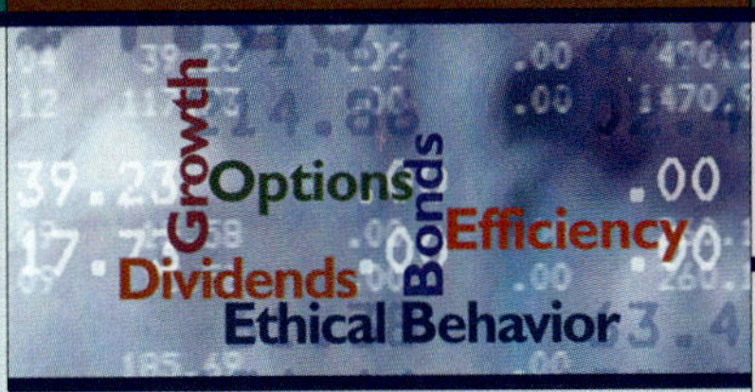

Samuel Weaver on Cost of Capital and Hurdle Rates at Hershey Foods Corporation

>> **At Hershey, we** reevaluate our cost of capital annually or as market conditions warrant. The calculation of the cost of capital essentially involves three different issues, each with a few alternatives:

- *Capital structure weighting*
  Historical book value
  Target capital structure
  Market-based weights
- *Cost of debt*
  Historical (coupon) interest rates
  Market-based interest rates
- *Cost of equity*
  Dividend growth model
  Capital asset pricing model, or CAPM

At Hershey, we calculate our cost of capital officially based upon the projected "target" capital structure at the end of our three-year intermediate planning horizon. This allows management to see the immediate impact of strategic decisions related to the planned composition of Hershey's capital pool. The cost of debt is calculated as the anticipated weighted average aftertax cost of debt in that final plan year based upon the coupon rates attached to that debt. The cost of equity is computed via the dividend growth model.

We recently conducted a survey of the 11 food processing companies that we consider our industry group competitors. The results of this survey indicated that the cost of capital for most of these companies was in the 10 to 12 percent range. Furthermore, without exception, all 11 of these companies employed the CAPM when calculating their cost of equity. Our experience has been that the dividend growth model works better for Hershey. We do pay dividends, and we do experience steady, stable growth in our dividends. This growth is also projected within our strategic plan. Consequently, the dividend growth model is technically applicable and appealing to management since it reflects their best estimate of the future long-term growth rate.

In addition to the calculation already described, the other possible combinations and permutations are calculated as barometers. Unofficially, the cost of capital is calculated using market weights, current marginal interest rates, and the CAPM cost of equity. For the most part, and due to rounding the cost of capital to the nearest whole percentage point, these alternative calculations yield approximately the same results.

From the cost of capital, individual project hurdle rates are developed using a subjectively determined risk premium based on the characteristics of the project. Projects are grouped into separate project categories, such as cost savings, capacity expansion, product line extension, and new products. For example, in general, a new product is more risky than a cost savings project. Consequently, each project category's hurdle rate reflects the level of risk and commensurate required return as perceived by senior management. As a result, capital project hurdle rates range from a slight premium over the cost of capital to the highest hurdle rate of approximately double the cost of capital.

Samuel Weaver, Ph.D., was formerly director, financial planning and analysis, for Hershey Chocolate North America. He is a certified management accountant. His position combined the theoretical with the pragmatic and involved the analysis of many different facets of finance in addition to capital expenditure analysis.

What is the NPV of the new printing plant?

To begin, because printing is the company's main line of business, we will use the company's weighted average cost of capital to value the new printing plant:

$$\begin{aligned}\text{WACC} &= (E/V) \times R_E + (D/V) \times R_D \times (1 - T_C) \\ &= .50 \times 20\% + .50 \times 10\% \times (1 - .34) \\ &= 13.3\%\end{aligned}$$

Because the cash flows are \$73,150 per year forever, the PV of the cash flows at 13.3 percent per year is:

$$\text{PV} = \frac{\$73{,}150}{.133} = \$550{,}000$$

If we ignore flotation costs, the NPV is:

$$\text{NPV} = \$550{,}000 - 500{,}000 = \$50{,}000$$

With no flotation costs, the project generates an NPV that is greater than zero, so it should be accepted.

What about financing arrangements and issue costs? Because new financing must be raised, the flotation costs are relevant. From the information given, we know that the flotation costs are 2 percent for debt and 10 percent for equity. Because Tripleday uses equal amounts of debt and equity, the weighted average flotation cost, f_A, is:

$$\begin{aligned} f_A &= (E/V) \times f_E + (D/V) \times f_D \\ &= .50 \times 10\% + .50 \times 2\% \\ &= 6\% \end{aligned}$$

Remember, the fact that Tripleday can finance the project with all debt or all equity is irrelevant. Because Tripleday needs \$500,000 to fund the new plant, the true cost, once we include flotation costs, is $\$500{,}000/(1 - f_A) = \$500{,}000/.94 = \$531{,}915$. Because the PV of the cash flows is \$550,000, the plant has an NPV of $\$550{,}000 - 531{,}915 = \$18{,}085$, so it is still a good investment. However, its value is less than we initially might have thought.

Concept Questions

15.6a What are flotation costs?

15.6b How are flotation costs included in an NPV analysis?

15.7 SUMMARY AND CONCLUSIONS

This chapter has discussed cost of capital. The most important concept is the weighted average cost of capital, or WACC, which we interpreted as the required rate of return on the overall firm. It is also the discount rate appropriate for cash flows that are similar in risk to those of the overall firm. We described how the WACC can be calculated, and we illustrated how it can be used in certain types of analyses.

We also pointed out situations in which it is inappropriate to use the WACC as the discount rate. To handle such cases, we described some alternative approaches to developing discount rates, such as the pure play approach. We also discussed how the flotation costs associated with raising new capital can be included in an NPV analysis.

Chapter Review and Self-Test Problems

15.1 Calculating the Cost of Equity Suppose stock in Watta Corporation has a beta of .80. The market risk premium is 6 percent, and the risk-free rate is 6 percent. Watta's last dividend was \$1.20 per share, and the dividend is expected to grow at 8 percent indefinitely. The stock currently sells for \$45 per share. What is Watta's cost of equity capital?

15.2 Calculating the WACC In addition to the information given in the previous problem, suppose Watta has a target debt-equity ratio of 50 percent. Its cost of debt is 9 percent, before taxes. If the tax rate is 35 percent, what is the WACC?

15.3 Flotation Costs Suppose in the previous problem Watta is seeking \$30 million for a new project. The necessary funds will have to be raised externally. Watta's flotation costs for selling debt and equity are 2 percent and 16 percent, respectively. If flotation costs are considered, what is the true cost of the new project?

Visit us at www.mhhe.com/rwj

Answers to Chapter Review and Self-Test Problems

15.1 We start off with the SML approach. Based on the information given, the expected return on Watta's common stock is:

$$\begin{aligned} R_E &= R_f + \beta_E \times (R_M - R_f) \\ &= 6\% + .80 \times 6\% \\ &= 10.80\% \end{aligned}$$

We now use the dividend growth model. The projected dividend is $D_0 \times (1 + g) = \$1.20 \times 1.08 = \$1.296$, so the expected return using this approach is:

$$\begin{aligned} R_E &= D_1/P_0 + g \\ &= \$1.296/45 + .08 \\ &= 10.88\% \end{aligned}$$

Because these two estimates, 10.80 percent and 10.88 percent, are fairly close, we will average them. Watta's cost of equity is approximately 10.84 percent.

15.2 Because the target debt-equity ratio is .50, Watta uses \$.50 in debt for every \$1 in equity. In other words, Watta's target capital structure is 1/3 debt and 2/3 equity. The WACC is thus:

$$\begin{aligned} \text{WACC} &= (E/V) \times R_E + (D/V) \times R_D \times (1 - T_C) \\ &= 2/3 \times 10.84\% + 1/3 \times 9\% \times (1 - .35) \\ &= 9.177\% \end{aligned}$$

15.3 Because Watta uses both debt and equity to finance its operations, we first need the weighted average flotation cost. As in the previous problem, the percentage of equity financing is 2/3, so the weighted average cost is:

$$\begin{aligned} f_A &= (E/V) \times f_E + (D/V) \times f_D \\ &= 2/3 \times 16\% + 1/3 \times 2\% \\ &= 11.33\% \end{aligned}$$

If Watta needs \$30 million after flotation costs, then the true cost of the project is \$30 million/$(1 - f_A)$ = \$30 million/.8867 = \$33.83 million.

Concepts Review and Critical Thinking Questions

1. **WACC** On the most basic level, if a firm's WACC is 12 percent, what does this mean?
2. **Book Values versus Market Values** In calculating the WACC, if you had to use book values for either debt or equity, which would you choose? Why?
3. **Project Risk** If you can borrow all the money you need for a project at 6 percent, doesn't it follow that 6 percent is your cost of capital for the project?
4. **WACC and Taxes** Why do we use an aftertax figure for cost of debt but not for cost of equity?
5. **DCF Cost of Equity Estimation** What are the advantages of using the DCF model for determining the cost of equity capital? What are the disadvantages? What specific piece of information do you need to find the cost of equity using this model? What are some of the ways in which you could get this estimate?
6. **SML Cost of Equity Estimation** What are the advantages of using the SML approach to finding the cost of equity capital? What are the disadvantages? What are the specific pieces of information needed to use this method? Are all of these variables observable, or do they need to be estimated? What are some of the ways in which you could get these estimates?

7. **Cost of Debt Estimation** How do you determine the appropriate cost of debt for a company? Does it make a difference if the company's debt is privately placed as opposed to being publicly traded? How would you estimate the cost of debt for a firm whose only debt issues are privately held by institutional investors?
8. **Cost of Capital** Suppose Tom O'Bedlam, president of Bedlam Products, Inc., has hired you to determine the firm's cost of debt and cost of equity capital.
   a. The stock currently sells for $50 per share, and the dividend per share will probably be about $5. Tom argues, "It will cost us $5 per share to use the stockholders' money this year, so the cost of equity is equal to 10 percent ($5/50)." What's wrong with this conclusion?
   b. Based on the most recent financial statements, Bedlam Products' total liabilities are $8 million. Total interest expense for the coming year will be about $1 million. Tom therefore reasons, "We owe $8 million, and we will pay $1 million interest. Therefore, our cost of debt is obviously $1 million/8 million = 12.5%." What's wrong with this conclusion?
   c. Based on his own analysis, Tom is recommending that the company increase its use of equity financing, because "debt costs 12.5 percent, but equity only costs 10 percent; thus equity is cheaper." Ignoring all the other issues, what do you think about the conclusion that the cost of equity is less than the cost of debt?
9. **Company Risk versus Project Risk** Both Dow Chemical Company, a large natural gas user, and Superior Oil, a major natural gas producer, are thinking of investing in natural gas wells near Houston. Both are all-equity–financed companies. Dow and Superior are looking at identical projects. They've analyzed their respective investments, which would involve a negative cash flow now and positive expected cash flows in the future. These cash flows would be the same for both firms. No debt would be used to finance the projects. Both companies estimate that their project would have a net present value of $1 million at an 18 percent discount rate and a −$1.1 million NPV at a 22 percent discount rate. Dow has a beta of 1.25, whereas Superior has a beta of .75. The expected risk premium on the market is 8 percent, and risk-free bonds are yielding 12 percent. Should either company proceed? Should both? Explain.
10. **Divisional Cost of Capital** Under what circumstances would it be appropriate for a firm to use different costs of capital for its different operating divisions? If the overall firm WACC were used as the hurdle rate for all divisions, would the riskier divisions or the more conservative divisions tend to get most of the investment projects? Why? If you were to try to estimate the appropriate cost of capital for different divisions, what problems might you encounter? What are two techniques you could use to develop a rough estimate for each division's cost of capital?

Questions and Problems

BASIC
(Questions 1–19)

1. **Calculating Cost of Equity** The Say Hey! Co. just issued a dividend of $2.45 per share on its common stock. The company is expected to maintain a constant 6 percent growth rate in its dividends indefinitely. If the stock sells for $45 a share, what is the company's cost of equity?
2. **Calculating Cost of Equity** The Tubby Ball Corporation's common stock has a beta of 1.3. If the risk-free rate is 4.5 percent and the expected return on the market is 12 percent, what is Tubby Ball's cost of equity capital?
3. **Calculating Cost of Equity** Stock in Parrothead Industries has a beta of 1.15. The market risk premium is 8 percent, and T-bills are currently yielding 4 percent.

Parrothead's most recent dividend was $1.80 per share, and dividends are expected to grow at a 5 percent annual rate indefinitely. If the stock sells for $34 per share, what is your best estimate of Parrothead's cost of equity?

4. **Estimating the DCF Growth Rate** Suppose Massey Ltd. just issued a dividend of $1.22 per share on its common stock. The company paid dividends of $.78, $.91, $.93, and $1.00 per share in the last four years. If the stock currently sells for $45, what is your best estimate of the company's cost of equity capital using the arithmetic average growth rate in dividends? What if you use the geometric average growth rate?
5. **Calculating Cost of Preferred Stock** Holdup Bank has an issue of preferred stock with a $6 stated dividend that just sold for $92 per share. What is the bank's cost of preferred stock?
6. **Calculating Cost of Debt** Advance, Inc., is trying to determine its cost of debt. The firm has a debt issue outstanding with 12 years to maturity that is quoted at 105 percent of face value. The issue makes semiannual payments and has an embedded cost of 8 percent annually. What is Advance's pretax cost of debt? If the tax rate is 35 percent, what is the aftertax cost of debt?
7. **Calculating Cost of Debt** Jiminy's Cricket Farm issued a 30-year, 10 percent semiannual bond 7 years ago. The bond currently sells for 108 percent of its face value. The company's tax rate is 35 percent.
   a. What is the pretax cost of debt?
   b. What is the aftertax cost of debt?
   c. Which is more relevant, the pretax or the aftertax cost of debt? Why?
8. **Calculating Cost of Debt** For the firm in Problem 7, suppose the book value of the debt issue is $20 million. In addition, the company has a second debt issue on the market, a zero coupon bond with seven years left to maturity; the book value of this issue is $80 million and the bonds sell for 58 percent of par. What is the company's total book value of debt? The total market value? What is your best estimate of the aftertax cost of debt now?
9. **Calculating WACC** Mullineaux Corporation has a target capital structure of 50 percent common stock, 5 percent preferred stock, and 45 percent debt. Its cost of equity is 16 percent, the cost of preferred stock is 7.5 percent, and the cost of debt is 9 percent. The relevant tax rate is 35 percent.
   a. What is Mullineaux's WACC?
   b. The company president has approached you about Mullineaux's capital structure. He wants to know why the company doesn't use more preferred stock financing, since it costs less than debt. What would you tell the president?
10. **Taxes and WACC** Miller Manufacturing has a target debt-equity ratio of .60. Its cost of equity is 18 percent and its cost of debt is 10 percent. If the tax rate is 35 percent, what is Miller's WACC?
11. **Finding the Target Capital Structure** Captain's Llamas has a weighted average cost of capital of 11.5 percent. The company's cost of equity is 16 percent and its cost of debt is 8.5 percent. The tax rate is 35 percent. What is Captain's target debt-equity ratio?
12. **Book Value versus Market Value** Filer Manufacturing has 9.5 million shares of common stock outstanding. The current share price is $53, and the book value per share is $5. Filer Manufacturing also has two bond issues outstanding. The first bond issue has a face value of $75 million, an 8 percent coupon, and sells for 93 percent of par. The second issue has a face value of $60 million, a 7.5 percent coupon, and

sells for 96.5 percent of par. The first issue matures in 10 years, the second in 6 years.

a. What are Filer's capital structure weights on a book value basis?

b. What are Filer's capital structure weights on a market value basis?

c. Which are more relevant, the book or market value weights? Why?

13. Calculating the WACC In Problem 12, suppose the most recent dividend was $4.10 and the dividend growth rate is 6 percent. Assume that the overall cost of debt is the weighted average of that implied by the two outstanding debt issues. Both bonds make semiannual payments. The tax rate is 35 percent. What is the company's WACC?

14. WACC Jungle, Inc., has a target debt-equity ratio of .80. Its WACC is 10.5 percent, and the tax rate is 35 percent.

a. If Jungle's cost of equity is 15 percent, what is its pretax cost of debt?

b. If instead you know that the aftertax cost of debt is 6.4 percent, what is the cost of equity?

15. Finding the WACC Given the following information for Huntington Power Co., find the WACC. Assume the company's tax rate is 35 percent.

Debt: 4,000 7 percent coupon bonds outstanding, $1,000 par value, 20 years to maturity, selling for 103 percent of par; the bonds make semiannual payments.

Common stock: 90,000 shares outstanding, selling for $57 per share; the beta is 1.10.

Preferred stock: 13,000 shares of 6 percent preferred stock outstanding, currently selling for $104 per share.

Market: 8 percent market risk premium and 6 percent risk-free rate.

16. Finding the WACC Titan Mining Corporation has 9 million shares of common stock outstanding, .5 million shares of 7 percent preferred stock outstanding, and 120,000 8.5 percent semiannual bonds outstanding, par value $1,000 each. The common stock currently sells for $34 per share and has a beta of 1.20, the preferred stock currently sells for $83 per share, and the bonds have 15 years to maturity and sell for 93 percent of par. The market risk premium is 10 percent, T-bills are yielding 5 percent, and Titan Mining's tax rate is 35 percent.

a. What is the firm's market value capital structure?

b. If Titan Mining is evaluating a new investment project that has the same risk as the firm's typical project, what rate should the firm use to discount the project's cash flows?

17. SML and WACC An all-equity firm is considering the following projects:

Project	Beta	Expected Return
W	.60	11%
X	.90	13
Y	1.20	14
Z	1.70	16

The T-bill rate is 5 percent, and the expected return on the market is 12 percent.

a. Which projects have a higher expected return than the firm's 12 percent cost of capital?

b. Which projects should be accepted?

c. Which projects would be incorrectly accepted or rejected if the firm's overall cost of capital were used as a hurdle rate?

18. Calculating Flotation Costs Suppose your company needs \$15 million to build a new assembly line. Your target debt-equity ratio is .90. The flotation cost for new equity is 10 percent, but the flotation cost for debt is only 4 percent. Your boss has decided to fund the project by borrowing money, because the flotation costs are lower and the needed funds are relatively small.

a. What do you think about the rationale behind borrowing the entire amount?

b. What is your company's weighted average flotation cost?

c. What is the true cost of building the new assembly line after taking flotation costs into account? Does it matter in this case that the entire amount is being raised from debt?

19. Calculating Flotation Costs Southern Alliance Company needs to raise \$25 million to start a new project and will raise the money by selling new bonds. The company has a target capital structure of 60 percent common stock, 10 percent preferred stock, and 30 percent debt. Flotation costs for issuing new common stock are 11 percent, for new preferred stock, 7 percent, and for new debt, 4 percent. What is the true initial cost figure Southern should use when evaluating its project?

INTERMEDIATE
(Questions 20–21)

20. WACC and NPV Och, Inc., is considering a project that will result in initial aftertax cash savings of \$3.5 million at the end of the first year, and these savings will grow at a rate of 5 percent per year indefinitely. The firm has a target debt-equity ratio of .65, a cost of equity of 15 percent, and an aftertax cost of debt of 5.5 percent. The cost-saving proposal is somewhat riskier than the usual project the firm undertakes; management uses the subjective approach and applies an adjustment factor of +2 percent to the cost of capital for such risky projects. Under what circumstances should Och take on the project?

21. Flotation Costs Knight, Inc., recently issued new securities to finance a new TV show. The project cost \$2.1 million and the company paid \$128,000 in flotation costs. In addition, the equity issued had a flotation cost of 8 percent of the amount raised, whereas the debt issued had a flotation cost of 3 percent of the amount raised. If Knight issued new securities in the same proportion as its target capital structure, what is the company's target debt-equity ratio?

CHALLENGE
(Questions 22–23)

22. Flotation Costs and NPV Photochronograph Corporation (PC) manufactures time series photographic equipment. It is currently at its target debt-equity ratio of 1.3. It's considering building a new \$45 million manufacturing facility. This new plant is expected to generate aftertax cash flows of \$5.7 million in perpetuity. There are three financing options:

1. A new issue of common stock. The flotation costs of the new common stock would be 8 percent of the amount raised. The required return on the company's new equity is 17 percent.
2. A new issue of 20-year bonds. The flotation costs of the new bonds would be 4 percent of the proceeds. If the company issues these new bonds at an annual coupon rate of 9 percent, they will sell at par.
3. Increased use of accounts payable financing. Because this financing is part of the company's ongoing daily business, it has no flotation costs and the company assigns it a cost that is the same as the overall firm WACC. Management has a target ratio of accounts payable to long-term debt of .20. (Assume there is no difference between the pretax and aftertax accounts payable cost.)

What is the NPV of the new plant? Assume that PC has a 35 percent tax rate.

23. Project Evaluation This is a comprehensive project evaluation problem bringing together much of what you have learned in this and previous chapters. Suppose you have been hired as a financial consultant to Defense Electronics, Inc. (DEI), a large, publicly traded firm that is the market share leader in radar detection systems (RDSs). The company is looking at setting up a manufacturing plant overseas to produce a new line of RDSs. This will be a five-year project. The company bought some land three years ago for $7 million in anticipation of using it as a toxic dump site for waste chemicals, but it built a piping system to safely discard the chemicals instead. The land was appraised last week for $9.6 million. The company wants to build its new manufacturing plant on this land; the plant will cost $15 million to build. The following market data on DEI's securities are current:

Debt:	15,000 7 percent coupon bonds outstanding, 15 years to maturity, selling for 92 percent of par; the bonds have a $1,000 par value each and make semiannual payments.
Common stock:	300,000 shares outstanding, selling for $75 per share; the beta is 1.3.
Preferred stock:	20,000 shares of 5 percent preferred stock outstanding, selling for $72 per share.
Market:	8 percent expected market risk premium; 5 percent risk-free rate.

DEI uses G. M. Wharton as its lead underwriter. Wharton charges DEI spreads of 9 percent on new common stock issues, 7 percent on new preferred stock issues, and 4 percent on new debt issues. Wharton has included all direct and indirect issuance costs (along with its profit) in setting these spreads. Wharton has recommended to DEI that it raise the funds needed to build the plant by issuing new shares of common stock. DEI's tax rate is 35 percent. The project requires $900,000 in initial net working capital investment to get operational.

a. Calculate the project's initial Time 0 cash flow, taking into account all side effects.

b. The new RDS project is somewhat riskier than a typical project for DEI, primarily because the plant is being located overseas. Management has told you to use an adjustment factor of +2 percent to account for this increased riskiness. Calculate the appropriate discount rate to use when evaluating DEI's project.

c. The manufacturing plant has an eight-year tax life, and DEI uses straight-line depreciation. At the end of the project (i.e., the end of Year 5), the plant can be scrapped for $5 million. What is the aftertax salvage value of this manufacturing plant?

d. The company will incur $400,000 in annual fixed costs. The plan is to manufacture 12,000 RDSs per year and sell them at $10,000 per machine; the variable production costs are $9,000 per RDS. What is the annual operating cash flow, OCF, from this project?

e. DEI's comptroller is primarily interested in the impact of DEI's investments on the bottom line of reported accounting statements. What will you tell her is the accounting break-even quantity of RDSs sold for this project?

f. Finally, DEI's president wants you to throw all your calculations, assumptions, and everything else into the report for the chief financial officer; all he wants to know is what the RDS project's internal rate of return, IRR, and net present value, NPV, are. What will you report?

16 Raising Capital

On August 19, 2004, in an eagerly awaited initial public offering (IPO), the Internet search engine company Google went public. Initially, the company expected to sell about 26 million shares of stock at a price of $108 to $135 per share through an unusual (for an IPO) "Dutch auction" process. Just before the company went public, it reduced the price to $85 per share and also reduced the number of shares to 19.6 million. Even with these reductions, the company's value when it first sold shares to investors was $23 billion. By the end of the first day of trading, the stock price had jumped 18 percent to just over $100, which meant that the company missed out on almost $300 million by pricing the stock too low. Even though Google's IPO was ultimately deemed to have been somewhat successful, the company experienced a lot of problems in the IPO process. These missteps included confusion over the Dutch auction process, the bidding rules, unregistered stock given to employees, and comments made in interviews given by the company's founders. In this chapter, we will examine the process by which companies such as Google sell stock to the public, the costs of doing so, and the role of investment banks in the process.

All firms must, at varying times, obtain capital. To do so, a firm must either borrow the money (debt financing), sell a portion of the firm (equity financing), or both. How a firm raises capital depends a great deal on the size of the firm, its life cycle stage, and its growth prospects.

In this chapter, we examine some of the ways in which firms actually raise capital. We begin by looking at companies in the early stages of their lives and the importance of venture capital for such firms. We then look at the process of going public and the role of investment banks. Along the way, we discuss many of the issues associated with selling securities to the public and their implications for all types of firms. We close the chapter with a discussion of sources of debt capital.[1]

[1]We are indebted to Jay R. Ritter of the University of Florida for helpful comments and suggestions on this chapter.

16.1 THE FINANCING LIFE CYCLE OF A FIRM: EARLY-STAGE FINANCING AND VENTURE CAPITAL

One day, you and a friend have a great idea for a new computer software product that helps users communicate using the next-generation meganet. Filled with entrepreneurial zeal, you christen the product Megacomm and set about bringing it to market.

Working nights and weekends, you are able to create a prototype of your product. It doesn't actually work, but at least you can show it around to illustrate your idea. To actually develop the product, you need to hire programmers, buy computers, rent office space, and so on. Unfortunately, because you are both college students, your combined assets are not sufficient to fund a pizza party, much less a start-up company. You need what is often referred to as OPM—other people's money.

Your first thought might be to approach a bank for a loan. You would probably discover, however, that banks are generally not interested in making loans to start-up companies with no assets (other than an idea) run by fledgling entrepreneurs with no track record. Instead, your search for capital would very likely lead you to the **venture capital (VC)** market.

venture capital (VC) Financing for new, often high-risk ventures.

Venture Capital

The term *venture capital* does not have a precise meaning, but it generally refers to financing for new, often high-risk ventures. For example, before it went public, Netscape Communications was VC financed. Individual venture capitalists invest their own money; so-called "angels" are usually individual VC investors, but they tend to specialize in smaller deals. Venture capital firms specialize in pooling funds from various sources and investing them. The underlying sources of funds for such firms include individuals, pension funds, insurance companies, large corporations, and even university endowment funds. The broad term *private equity* is often used to label the rapidly growing area of equity financing for nonpublic companies.[2]

Venture capitalists and venture capital firms recognize that many or even most new ventures will not fly, but the occasional one will. The potential profits are enormous in such cases. To limit their risk, venture capitalists generally provide financing in stages. At each stage, enough money is invested to reach the next milestone or planning stage. For example, the *first-stage financing* might be enough to get a prototype built and a manufacturing plan completed. Based on the results, the *second-stage financing* might be a major investment needed to actually begin manufacturing, marketing, and distribution. There might be many such stages, each of which represents a key step in the process of growing the company.

Venture capital firms often specialize in different stages. Some specialize in very early "seed money," or ground floor, financing. In contrast, financing in the later stages might come from venture capitalists specializing in so-called mezzanine level financing, where *mezzanine level* refers to the level just above the ground floor.

For a list of well-known VC firms, see www.vfinance.com.

The fact that financing is available in stages and is contingent on specified goals being met is a powerful motivating force for the firm's founders. Often, the founders receive relatively little in the way of salary and have substantial portions of their personal assets tied

[2]So-called vulture capitalists specialize in high-risk investments in established, but financially distressed, firms. Vulgar capitalists invest in firms that have bad taste (O.K., we made up this last bit).

up in the business. At each stage of financing, the value of the founder's stake grows and the probability of success rises.

In addition to providing financing, venture capitalists often actively participate in running the firm, providing the benefit of experience with previous start-ups as well as general business expertise. This is especially true when the firm's founders have little or no hands-on experience in running a company.

Some Venture Capital Realities

Although there is a large venture capital market, the truth is that access to venture capital is really very limited. Venture capital companies receive huge numbers of unsolicited proposals, the vast majority of which end up in the circular file unread. Venture capitalists rely heavily on informal networks of lawyers, accountants, bankers, and other venture capitalists to help identify potential investments. As a result, personal contacts are important in gaining access to the venture capital market; it is very much an "introduction" market.

Another simple fact about venture capital is that it is incredibly expensive. In a typical deal, the venture capitalist will demand (and get) 40 percent or more of the equity in the company. Venture capitalists frequently hold voting preferred stock, giving them various priorities in the event that the company is sold or liquidated. The venture capitalist will typically demand (and get) several seats on the company's board of directors and may even appoint one or more members of senior management.

Choosing a Venture Capitalist

The Internet is a tremendous source of venture capital information, both for suppliers and demanders of capital. For example, the site at www.dealflow.com prompts you to search the firm's database as either an entrepreneur (i.e., capital seeker) or a venture capitalist (i.e., capital supplier).

Some start-up companies, particularly those headed by experienced, previously successful entrepreneurs, will be in such demand that they will have the luxury of looking beyond the money in choosing a venture capitalist. There are some key considerations in such a case, some of which can be summarized as follows:

1. **Financial strength is important.** The venture capitalist needs to have the resources and financial reserves for additional financing stages should they become necessary. This doesn't mean that bigger is necessarily better, however, because of our next consideration.
2. **Style is important.** Some venture capitalists will wish to be very much involved in day-to-day operations and decision making, whereas others will be content with monthly reports. Which are better depends on the firm and also on the venture capitalists' business skills. In addition, a large venture capital firm may be less flexible and more bureaucratic than a smaller "boutique" firm.
3. **References are important.** Has the venture capitalist been successful with similar firms? Of equal importance, how has the venture capitalist dealt with situations that didn't work out?
4. **Contacts are important.** A venture capitalist may be able to help the business in ways other than helping with financing and management by providing introductions to potentially important customers, suppliers, and other industry contacts. Venture capitalist firms frequently specialize in a few particular industries, and such specialization could prove quite valuable.
5. **Exit strategy is important.** Venture capitalists are generally not long-term investors. How and under what circumstances the venture capitalist will "cash out" of the business should be carefully evaluated.

Conclusion

For more VC info and links, see www.globaltechnoscan.com.

If a start-up succeeds, the big payoff frequently comes when the company is sold to another company or goes public. Either way, investment bankers are often involved in the process. We discuss the process of selling securities to the public in the next several sections, paying particular attention to the process of going public.

Concept Questions

16.1a What is venture capital?

16.1b Why is venture capital often provided in stages?

16.2 SELLING SECURITIES TO THE PUBLIC: THE BASIC PROCEDURE

There are many rules and regulations surrounding the process of selling securities. The Securities Act of 1933 is the origin of federal regulations for all new interstate securities issues. The Securities Exchange Act of 1934 is the basis for regulating securities already outstanding. The Securities and Exchange Commission, or SEC, administers both acts.

There is a series of steps involved in issuing securities to the public. In general terms, the basic procedure is as follows:

registration statement
A statement filed with the SEC that discloses all material information concerning the corporation making a public offering.

1. Management's first step in issuing any securities to the public is to obtain approval from the board of directors. In some cases, the number of authorized shares of common stock must be increased. This requires a vote of the shareholders.
2. The firm must prepare a **registration statement** and file it with the SEC. The registration statement is required for all public, interstate issues of securities, with two exceptions:

   a. Loans that mature within nine months

   b. Issues that involve less than $5 million

   The second exception is known as the *small-issues exemption.* In such a case, simplified procedures are used. Under the basic small-issues exemption, issues of less than $5 million are governed by **Regulation A**, for which only a brief offering statement is needed. Normally, however, a registration statement contains many pages (50 or more) of financial information, including a financial history, details of the existing business, proposed financing, and plans for the future.

Regulation A
An SEC regulation that exempts public issues of less than $5 million from most registration requirements.

3. The SEC examines the registration statement during a waiting period. During this time, the firm may distribute copies of a preliminary **prospectus**. The prospectus contains much of the information put into the registration statement, and it is given to potential investors by the firm. The preliminary prospectus is sometimes called a **red herring**, in part because bold red letters are printed on the cover.

prospectus
A legal document describing details of the issuing corporation and the proposed offering to potential investors.

A registration statement becomes effective on the 20th day after its filing unless the SEC sends a *letter of comment* suggesting changes. In that case, after the changes are made, the 20-day waiting period starts again. It is important to note that the SEC does not consider the economic merits of the proposed sale; it merely makes sure that various rules and regulations are followed. Also, the SEC generally does not check the accuracy or truthfulness of information in the prospectus.

The registration statement does not initially contain the price of the new issue. Usually, a price amendment is filed at or near the end of the waiting period, and the registration becomes effective.

4. The company cannot sell these securities during the waiting period. However, oral offers can be made.
5. On the effective date of the registration statement, a price is determined and a full-fledged selling effort gets under way. A final prospectus must accompany the delivery of securities or confirmation of sale, whichever comes first.

red herring
A preliminary prospectus distributed to prospective investors in a new issue of securities.

Tombstone advertisements (or, simply, tombstones) are used by underwriters during and after the waiting period. An example is reproduced in Figure 16.1. The tombstone contains the name of the issuer (the World Wrestling Federation, or WWF, in this case). It provides some information about the issue, and it lists the investment banks (the underwriters) that are involved with selling the issue. The role of the investment banks in selling securities is discussed more fully in the following pages.

tombstone
An advertisement announcing a public offering.

The investment banks on the tombstone are divided into groups called *brackets* based on their participation in the issue, and the names of the banks are listed alphabetically within each bracket. The brackets are often viewed as a kind of pecking order. In general, the higher the bracket, the greater is the underwriter's prestige.

Concept Questions

16.2a What are the basic procedures in selling a new issue?

16.2b What is a registration statement?

Find out what firms are going public this week at cbs.marketwatch.com.

ALTERNATIVE ISSUE METHODS 16.3

When a company decides to issue a new security, it can sell it as a public issue or a private issue. In the case of a public issue, the firm is required to register the issue with the SEC. However, if the issue is to be sold to fewer than 35 investors, the sale can be carried out privately. In this case, a registration statement is not required.[3]

general cash offer
An issue of securities offered for sale to the general public on a cash basis.

For equity sales, there are two kinds of public issues: a **general cash offer** and a **rights offer** (or *rights offering*). With a cash offer, securities are offered to the general public. With a rights offer, securities are initially offered only to existing owners. Rights offers are fairly common in other countries, but they are relatively rare in the United States, particularly in recent years. We therefore focus primarily on cash offers in this chapter.

rights offer
A public issue of securities in which securities are first offered to existing shareholders. Also called a rights offering.

The first public equity issue that is made by a company is referred to as an **initial public offering**, IPO, or an *unseasoned new issue.* This issue occurs when a company decides to go public. Obviously, all initial public offerings are cash offers. If the firm's existing shareholders wanted to buy the shares, the firm wouldn't have to sell them publicly in the first place.

initial public offering
A company's first equity issue made available to the public. Also called an unseasoned new issue or an IPO.

[3]A variety of different arrangements can be made for private equity issues. Selling unregistered securities avoids the costs of complying with the Securities Exchange Act of 1934. Regulation significantly restricts the resale of unregistered equity securities. For example, the purchaser may be required to hold the securities for at least one year. Many of the restrictions were significantly eased in 1990 for very large institutional investors, however. The private placement of bonds is discussed in a later section.

FIGURE 16.1 >>

An Example of a Tombstone Advertisement

This announcement is neither an offer to sell nor a solicitation of an offer to buy any of these securities.
The offering is made only by the Prospectus.

New Issue

11,500,000 Shares

World Wrestling Federation Entertainment, Inc.

Class A Common Stock

Price $17.00 Per Share

Copies of the Prospectus may be obtained in any State in which this announcement is circulated from only such of the Underwriters, including the undersigned, as may lawfully offer these securities in such State.

U.S. Offering

9,200,000 Shares

This portion of the underwriting is being offered in the United States and Canada.

Bear, Stearns & Co. Inc.

Credit Suisse First Boston

Merrill Lynch & Co.

Wit Capital Corporation

Allen & Company Incorporated — Banc of America Securities LLC — Deutsche Banc Alex. Brown
Donaldson, Lufkin & Jenrette — A.G. Edwards & Sons, Inc. — Hambrecht & Quist — ING Barings
Prudential Securities — SG Cowen — Wassertein Perella Securities, Inc. — Advest, Inc.
Axiom Capital Management, Inc. — Blackford Securities Corp. — J.C. Bradford & Co.
Joseph Charles & Assoc., Inc. — Chatsworth Securities LLC — Gabelli & Company, Inc.
Gaines, Berland Inc. — Jefferies & Company, Inc. — Josephthal & Co. Inc. — Neuberger Berman, LLC
Raymond James & Associates, Inc. — Sanders Morris Mundy
Tucker Anthony Cleary Gull — Wachovia Securities, Inc.

International Offering

2,300,000 Shares

This portion of the underwriting is being offered outside of the United States and Canada.

Bear, Stearns International Limited

Credit Suisse First Boston

Merrill Lynch International

Method	Type	Definition
Public Traditional negotiated cash offer	Firm commitment cash offer	Company negotiates an agreement with an investment banker to underwrite and distribute the new shares. A specified number of shares are bought by underwriters and sold at a higher price.
	Best efforts cash offer	Company has investment bankers sell as many of the new shares as possible at the agreed-upon price. There is no guarantee concerning how much cash will be raised.
	Dutch auction cash offer	Company has investment bankers auction shares to determine the highest offer price obtainable for a given number of shares to be sold.
Privileged subscription	Direct rights offer	Company offers the new stock directly to its existing shareholders.
	Standby rights offer	Like the direct rights offer, this contains a privileged subscription arrangement with existing shareholders. The net proceeds are guaranteed by the underwriters.
Nontraditional cash offer	Shelf cash offer	Qualifying companies can authorize all shares they expect to sell over a two-year period and sell them when needed.
	Competitive firm cash offer	Company can elect to award the underwriting contract through a public auction instead of negotiation.
Private	Direct placement	Securities are sold directly to the purchaser, who, at least until recently, generally could not resell securities for at least two years.

<< TABLE 16.1

The Methods of Issuing New Securities

IPO information is widely available. Try www.ipohome.com and IPO Central at www.hoovers.com.

A **seasoned equity offering (SEO)** is a new issue for a company with securities that have been previously issued.[4] A seasoned equity offering of common stock can be made by using a cash offer or a rights offer.

These methods of issuing new securities are shown in Table 16.1. They are discussed in Sections 16.4 through 16.8.

seasoned equity offering (SEO)
A new equity issue of securities by a company that has previously issued securities to the public.

Concept Questions

16.3a Why is an initial public offering necessarily a cash offer?

16.3b What is the difference between a rights offer and a cash offer?

UNDERWRITERS **16.4**

If the public issue of securities is a cash offer, **underwriters** are usually involved. Underwriting is an important line of business for large investment firms such as Merrill Lynch. Underwriters perform services such as the following for corporate issuers:

1. Formulating the method used to issue the securities
2. Pricing the new securities
3. Selling the new securities

underwriters
Investment firms that act as intermediaries between a company selling securities and the investing public.

[4]The terms *follow-on offering* and *secondary offering* are also commonly used.

Typically, the underwriter buys the securities for less than the offering price and accepts the risk of not being able to sell them. Because underwriting involves risk, underwriters usually combine to form an underwriting group called a **syndicate** to share the risk and to help sell the issue.

syndicate
A group of underwriters formed to share the risk and to help sell an issue.

In a syndicate, one or more managers arrange, or co-manage, the offering. The lead manager typically has the responsibility of dealing with the issuer and pricing the securities. The other underwriters in the syndicate serve primarily to distribute the issue and produce research reports later on.

gross spread
Compensation to the underwriter, determined by the difference between the underwriter's buying price and offering price.

The difference between the underwriter's buying price and the offering price is called the **gross spread**, or underwriting discount. It is the basic compensation received by the underwriter. Sometimes, on smaller deals, the underwriter will get noncash compensation in the form of warrants and stock in addition to the spread.[5]

Choosing an Underwriter

A firm can offer its securities to the highest bidding underwriter on a *competitive offer* basis, or it can negotiate directly with an underwriter. Except for a few large firms, companies usually do new issues of debt and equity on a *negotiated offer* basis. The exception is public utility holding companies, which are essentially required to use competitive underwriting.

There is evidence that competitive underwriting is cheaper to use than negotiated underwriting. The underlying reasons for the dominance of negotiated underwriting in the United States are the subject of ongoing debate.

Types of Underwriting

Three basic types of underwriting are involved in a cash offer: firm commitment, best efforts, and dutch auction.

firm commitment underwriting
The type of underwriting in which the underwriter buys the entire issue, assuming full financial responsibility for any unsold shares.

Firm Commitment Underwriting

In **firm commitment underwriting**, the issuer sells the entire issue to the underwriters, who then attempt to resell it. This is the most prevalent type of underwriting in the United States. This is really just a purchase-resale arrangement, and the underwriter's fee is the spread. For a new issue of seasoned equity, the underwriters can look at the market price to determine what the issue should sell for, and more than 95 percent of all such new issues are firm commitments.

Learn more about investment banks at Merrill Lynch (www.ml.com).

If the underwriter cannot sell all of the issue at the agreed-upon offering price, it may have to lower the price on the unsold shares. Nonetheless, with firm commitment underwriting, the issuer receives the agreed-upon amount, and all the risk associated with selling the issue is transferred to the underwriter.

Because the offering price usually isn't set until the underwriters have investigated how receptive the market is to the issue, this risk is usually minimal. Also, because the offering price usually is not set until just before selling commences, the issuer doesn't know precisely what its net proceeds will be until that time.

best efforts underwriting
The type of underwriting in which the underwriter sells as much of the issue as possible, but can return any unsold shares to the issuer without financial responsibility.

Best Efforts Underwriting

In **best efforts underwriting**, the underwriter is legally bound to use "best efforts" to sell the securities at the agreed-upon offering price. Beyond this, the underwriter does not guarantee any particular amount of money to the issuer. This form of underwriting has become uncommon in recent years.

[5]Warrants are options to buy stock at a fixed price for some fixed period of time.

Dutch Auction Underwriting With **Dutch auction underwriting**, the underwriter does not set a fixed price for the shares to be sold. Instead, the underwriter conducts an auction in which investors bid for shares. The offer price is determined based on the submitted bids. A Dutch auction is also known by the more descriptive name *uniform price auction*. This approach to selling securities to the public is relatively new in the IPO market and has not been widely used there, but it is very common in the bond markets. For example, it is the sole procedure used by the U.S. Treasury to sell enormous quantities of notes, bonds, and bills to the public.

Dutch auction underwriting
The type of underwriting in which the offer price is set based on competitive bidding by investors. Also known as a *uniform price auction*.

Dutch auction underwriting was much in the news in 2004 because, as we mentioned to open the chapter, Web search company Google elected to use this approach. The best way to understand a Dutch or uniform price auction is to consider a simple example. Suppose the Rial Company wants to sell 400 shares to the public. The company receives five bids as follows:

Bidder	Quantity	Price
A	100 shares	$16
B	100 shares	14
C	200 shares	12
D	200 shares	12
E	200 shares	10

Thus, bidder A is willing buy 100 shares at $16 each, bidder B is willing to buy 100 shares at $14, and so on. The Rial Company examines the bids to determine the highest price that will result in all 400 shares being sold. So, for example, at $14, A and B would buy only 200 shares, so that price is too high. Working our way down, all 400 shares won't be sold until we hit a price of $12, so $12 will be the offer price in the IPO. Bidders A through D will receive shares; bidder E will not.

Learn all about Dutch auction IPOs at **www.wrhambrecht.com.**

There are two additional important points to observe in our example: First, all the winning bidders will pay $12, even bidders A and B, who actually bid a higher price. The fact that all successful bidders pay the same price is the reason for the name "uniform price auction." The idea in such an auction is to encourage bidders to bid aggressively by providing some protection against bidding a price that is too high.

Second, notice that at the $12 offer price, there are actually bids for 500 shares, which exceeds the 400 shares Rial wants to sell. Thus, there has to be some sort of allocation. How this is done varies a bit, but, in the IPO market, the approach has been to simply compute the ratio of shares offered to shares bid at the offer price or better, which, in our example, is $400/500 = .8$, and allocate bidders that percentage of their bids. In other words, bidders A through D would each receive 80 percent of the shares they bid at a price of $12 per share.

The Aftermarket

The period after a new issue is initially sold to the public is referred to as the *aftermarket*. During this time, the members of the underwriting syndicate generally do not sell securities for less than the offering price.

The principal underwriter is permitted to buy shares if the market price falls below the offering price. The purpose of this would be to support the market and stabilize the price against temporary downward pressure. If the issue remains unsold after a time (for example, 30 days), members can leave the group and sell their shares at whatever price the market will allow.[6]

The Green Shoe Provision

Green Shoe provision
A contract provision giving the underwriter the option to purchase additional shares from the issuer at the offering price. Also called the overallotment option.

Many underwriting contracts contain a **Green Shoe provision** (sometimes called the *overallotment option*), which gives the members of the underwriting group the option to purchase additional shares from the issuer at the offering price.[7] Essentially all IPOs and SEOs include this provision, but ordinary debt offerings generally do not. The stated reason for the Green Shoe option is to cover excess demand and oversubscriptions. Green Shoe options usually last for 30 days and involve 15 percent of the newly issued shares.

In practice, usually underwriters initially go ahead and sell 115 percent of the shares offered. If the demand for the issue is strong after the offering, the underwriters exercise the Green Shoe option to get the extra 15 percent from the company. If demand for the issue is weak, the underwriters buy the needed shares in the open market, thereby helping to support the price of the issue in the aftermarket.

Lockup Agreements

lockup agreement
The part of the underwriting contract that specifies how long insiders must wait after an IPO before they can sell stock.

Although they are not required by law, almost all underwriting contracts contain so-called **lockup agreements**. Such agreements specify how long insiders must wait after an IPO before they can sell some or all of their stock. Lockup periods have become fairly standardized in recent years at 180 days. Thus, following an IPO, insiders can't cash out until six months have gone by, which ensures that they maintain a significant economic interest in the company going public.

Lockup periods are also important because it is not unusual for the number of locked-up shares to exceed the number of shares held by the public, sometimes by a substantial multiple. On the day the lockup period expires, there is the possibility that a large number of shares will hit the market on the same day and thereby depress values. The evidence suggests that, on average, venture capital–backed companies are particularly likely to experience a loss in value on the lockup expiration day.

The Quiet Period

For 40 calendar days following an IPO, the SEC requires that a firm and its managing underwriters observe a "quiet period." This means that all communications with the public must be limited to ordinary announcements and other purely factual matters. The SEC's logic is that all relevant information should be contained in the prospectus. An important result of this requirement is that the underwriter's analysts are prohibited from making recommendations to investors. As soon as the quiet period ends, however, the managing underwriters typically publish research reports, usually accompanied by a favorable "buy" recommendation.

In 2004, two firms experienced notable quiet period-related problems. Just before Google's IPO, an interview with Google cofounders Sergy Brin and Larry Page appeared in *Playboy*. The interview almost caused a postponement of the IPO, but Google was able

---

[6]Occasionally, the price of a security falls dramatically when the underwriter ceases to stabilize the price. In such cases, Wall Street humorists (the ones who didn't buy any of the stock) have referred to the period following the aftermarket as the aftermath.

[7]The term *Green Shoe provision* sounds quite exotic, but the origin is relatively mundane. The term comes from the name of the Green Shoe Manufacturing Company, which, in 1963, was the first issuer that granted such an option.

to amend its prospectus in time. In May 2004, Salesforce.com's IPO was delayed because an interview with CEO Mark Benioff appeared in *The New York Times.* Salesforce.com finally went public two months later.

Concept Questions

16.4a What do underwriters do?

16.4b What is the Green Shoe provision?

IPOS AND UNDERPRICING 16.5

Determining the correct offering price is the most difficult thing an underwriter must do for an initial public offering. The issuing firm faces a potential cost if the offering price is set too high or too low. If the issue is priced too high, it may be unsuccessful and have to be withdrawn. If the issue is priced below the true market value, the issuer's existing shareholders will experience an opportunity loss when they sell their shares for less than they are worth.

Underpricing is fairly common. It obviously helps new shareholders earn a higher return on the shares they buy. However, the existing shareholders of the issuing firm are not helped by underpricing. To them, it is an indirect cost of issuing new securities. For example, on February 24, 2004, Kinetic Concepts, a medical technology company, went public, selling 18 million shares at a price of $30, thereby raising $540 million. At the end of the first day of trading, the stock sold for $40.40, up about 35 percent for the day. Based on these numbers, Kinetic Concepts' shares were apparently underpriced by about $10.40 each, which means that the company missed out on an additional $187 million. That's a lot of money, but it pales in comparison to the money "left on the table" by companies such as eToys, whose 8.2 million share 1999 IPO was underpriced by $57 per share, or almost a half a billion dollars in all! eToys could have used the money; it was bankrupt within two years.

IPO Underpricing: The 1999–2000 Experience

Table 16.2, along with Figures 16.2 and 16.3, shows that 1999 and 2000 were extraordinary years in the IPO market. Almost 900 companies went public, and the average first-day return across the two years was about 65 percent. During this time, 194 IPOs doubled, or more than doubled, in value on the first day. In contrast, only 39 percent did so in the preceding 24 years combined. One company, VA Linux, shot up 698 percent!

The dollar amount raised in 2000, $66 billion, was a record, followed closely by 1999 at $65 billion. The underpricing was so severe in 1999 that companies left another $36 billion "on the table," which was substantially more than 1990–1998 combined, and, in 2000, the amount was at least $27 billion. In other words, over the two-year period, companies missed out on $63 billion because of underpricing.

October 19, 1999, was one of the more memorable days during this time. The World Wrestling Federation (WWF) (now known as World Wrestling Entertainment, or WWE) and Martha Stewart Omnimedia both went public, so it was Martha Stewart versus "Stone Cold" Steve Austin in a Wall Street version of MTV's *Celebrity Deathmatch.* When the closing bell rang, it was a clear smack-down as Martha Stewart gained 98 percent on the first day compared to 48 percent for the WWF. If you're interested in finding out how IPOs have done recently, check out our nearby *Work the Web* box.

FIGURE 16.2 >> **Average Initial Returns by Month for SEC-Registered Initial Public Offerings: 1960–2003**

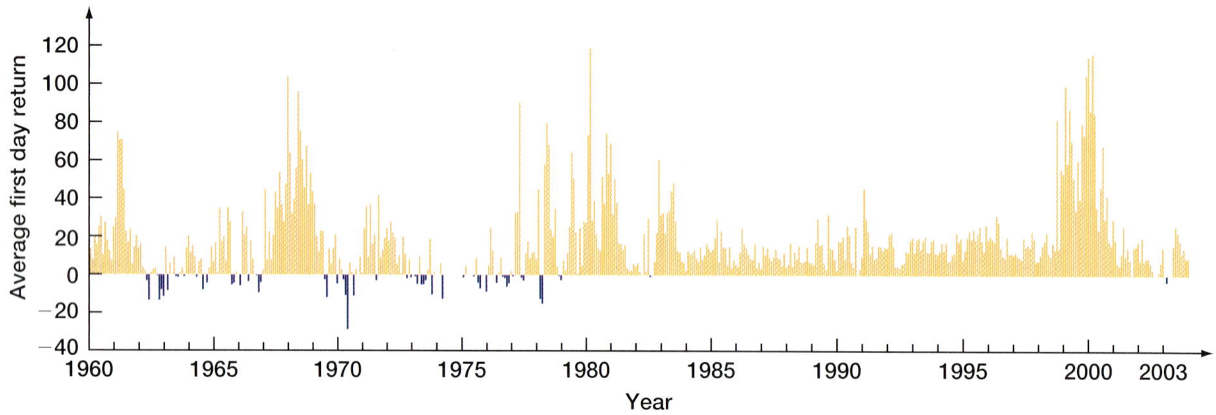

SOURCE: Roger G. Ibbotson, Jody L. Sindelar, and Jay R. Ritter, "The Market's Problems with the Pricing of Initial Public Offerings," *Journal of Applied Corporate Finance* 7 (Spring 1994), as updated by the authors.

FIGURE 16.3 >> **Number of Offerings by Month for SEC-Registered Initial Public Offerings: 1960–2003**

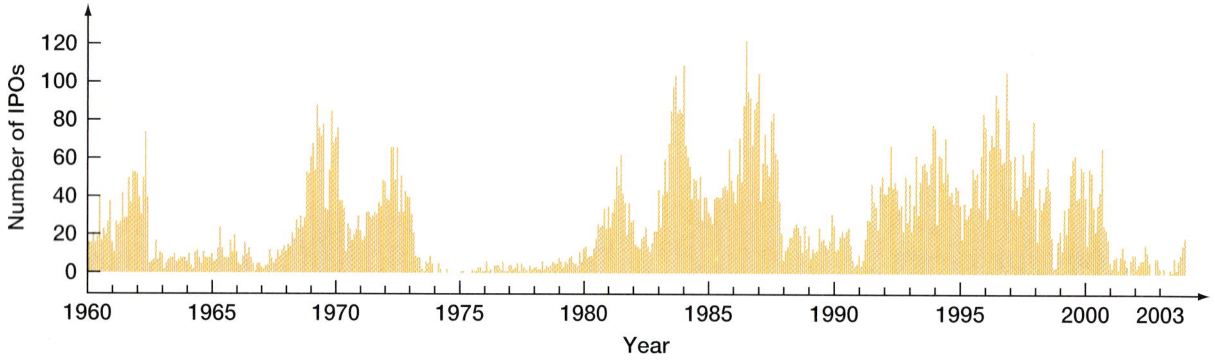

SOURCE: Roger G. Ibbotson, Jody L. Sindelar, and Jay R. Ritter, "The Market's Problems with the Pricing of Initial Public Offerings," *Journal of Applied Corporate Finance* 7 (Spring 1994), as updated by the authors.

Evidence on Underpricing

Figure 16.2 provides a more general illustration of the underpricing phenomenon. What is shown is the month-by-month history of underpricing for SEC-registered IPOs.[8] The period covered is 1960 through 2003. Figure 16.3 presents the number of offerings in each month for the same period.

Figure 16.2 shows that underpricing can be quite dramatic, exceeding 100 percent in some months. In such months, the average IPO more than doubled in value, sometimes in a matter of hours. Also, the degree of underpricing varies through time, and periods of

[8]The discussion in this section draws on Roger G. Ibbotson, Jody L. Sindelar, and Jay R. Ritter, "The Market's Problems with the Pricing of Initial Public Offerings," *Journal of Applied Corporate Finance* 7 (Spring 1994).

<< TABLE 16.2

Number of Offerings, Average First-Day Return, and Gross Proceeds of Initial Public Offerings: 1975–2003

Year	Number of Offerings*	Average First-Day Return, %†	Gross Proceeds, $ Millions‡
1975	12	−1.5	262
1976	26	1.9	214
1977	15	3.6	127
1978	20	11.2	209
1979	39	8.5	312
1980	75	13.9	934
1981	197	6.2	2,366
1982	82	10.6	1,064
1983	522	9.0	11,323
1984	222	2.6	2,841
1985	216	6.2	5,492
1986	485	5.9	16,349
1987	344	5.6	13,069
1988	129	5.4	4,181
1989	120	7.9	5,402
1990	113	10.4	4,480
1991	288	11.7	15,771
1992	397	10.0	22,204
1993	507	12.7	29,257
1994	416	9.7	18,300
1995	465	21.0	28,872
1996	666	16.5	42,479
1997	484	13.9	33,218
1998	319	20.0	35,112
1999	490	69.1	65,460
2000	385	55.4	65,677
2001	81	13.7	34,368
2002	71	8.5	22,220
2003	67	12.3	10,114
1975–79	112	5.7	1,124
1980–89	2,392	6.8	63,021
1990–99	4,145	20.9	295,153
2000–03	604	39.5	132,379
1975–2003	**7,253**	**17.6**	**491,677**

*The number of offerings excludes IPOs with an offer price of less than $5.00, ADRs; best efforts, units, and Regulation A offers (small issues, raising less than $1.5 million during the 1980s), real estate investment trusts (REITs), partnerships, and closed-end funds. Banks and S&Ls and non-CRSP-listed IPOs are included.

†First-day returns are computed as the percentage return from the offering price to the first closing market price.

‡Gross proceeds data are from Securities Data Co., and exclude overallotment options but include the international tranche, if any. No adjustments for inflation have been made.

SOURCE: Professor Jay R. Ritter, University of Florida.

severe underpricing ("hot issue" markets) are followed by periods of little underpricing ("cold issue" markets). For example, in the 1960s, the average IPO was underpriced by 21.2 percent. In the 1970s, the average underpricing was much smaller (9.0 percent), and the amount of underpricing was actually very small or even negative for much of that time. Underpricing in the 1980s ran about 6.8 percent. For 1990–99, IPOs were underpriced by 20.9 percent on average, and they were underpriced by 39.5 percent in 2000–03.

WORK THE WEB

So how much money have companies left on the table recently? We went to www.hoovers.com to see. Here is what we found for the first half of 2004:

Money Left On The Table

Company	Lead Underwriter	Offer Price	Pricing Valuation (mil.)	First Trade Price	First Trade Valuation (mil.)	Money on the Table (mil.)
Assurant, Inc.	Morgan Stanley & Co. Incorporated	$22.00	$1,760.0	$23.75	$1,900.0	$140.0
Eyetech Pharmaceuticals, Inc.	Merrill Lynch, Pierce, Fenner & Smith Incorporated	$21.00	$136.5	$30.00	$195.0	$58.5
Government Properties Trust, Inc.	Friedman, Billings, Ramsey & Co., Inc.	$10.00	$140.0	$13.90	$194.6	$54.6
Kinetic Concepts, Inc.	Merrill Lynch, Pierce, Fenner & Smith Incorporated	$30.00	$540.0	$33.00	$594.0	$54.0
Capital Lease Funding, Inc.	Friedman, Billings, Ramsey & Co., Inc.	$10.50	$210.0	$12.95	$259.0	$49.0

As you can see, Assurant led the list, leaving $140 million on the table because of underpricing. However, Eyetech Pharmaceutical may have been worse off: The company left $58.5 million on the table, which was over 40 percent of the initial amount raised by the company!

From Figure 16.3, it is apparent that the number of IPOs is also highly variable through time. Further, there are pronounced cycles in both the degree of underpricing and the number of IPOs. Comparing Figures 16.2 and 16.3, we see that increases in the number of new offerings tend to follow periods of significant underpricing by roughly 6 months. This probably occurs because companies decide to go public when they perceive that the market is highly receptive to new issues.

Table 16.2 contains a year-by-year summary of underpricing for the years 1975–2003. As indicated, a grand total of 7,253 companies were included in this analysis. The degree of underpricing averaged 17.6 percent overall for the 29 years examined. Securities were overpriced on average in only 1 of the 29 years; in 1975, the average decrease in value was −1.5 percent. At the other extreme, in 1999, the 490 issues were underpriced, on average, by a remarkable 69.1 percent.

Why Does Underpricing Exist?

Based on the evidence we've examined, an obvious question is, Why does underpricing continue to exist? As we discuss, there are various explanations, but, to date, there is a lack of complete agreement among researchers as to which is correct.

We present some pieces of the underpricing puzzle by stressing two important caveats to our preceding discussion. First, the average figures we have examined tend to obscure the fact that much of the apparent underpricing is attributable to the smaller, more highly speculative issues. This point is illustrated in Table 16.3, which shows the extent of underpricing for 6,086 firms over the period from 1980 through 2003. Here, the firms are grouped based on their total sales in the 12 months prior to the IPO.

As illustrated in Table 16.3, the underpricing tends to be higher for firms with little to no sales in the previous year. These firms tend to be young firms, and such young firms can be

IN THEIR OWN WORDS . . .

Jay Ritter on IPO Underpricing around the World

>> **The United States** is not the only country in which initial public offerings (IPOs) of common stock are underpriced. The phenomenon exists in every country with a stock market, although the extent of underpricing varies from country to country.

In general, countries with developed capital markets have more moderate underpricing than in emerging markets. During the Internet bubble of 1999–2000, however, underpricing in the developed capital markets increased dramatically. In the United States, for example, the average first-day return during 1999–2000 was 65 percent. At the same time that underpricing in the developed capital markets increased, the underpricing of IPOs sold to residents of China moderated. The Chinese average has come down to a mere 257 percent, which is lower than it had been in the early and mid 1990s. After the bursting of the Internet bubble in mid-2000, the level of underpricing in the United States, Germany, and other developed capital markets has returned to more traditional levels.

The table below gives a summary of the average first-day returns on IPOs in a number of countries around the world, with the figures collected from a number of studies by various authors.

Country	Sample Size	Time Period	Avg. Initial Return	Country	Sample Size	Time Period	Avg. Initial Return
Australia	381	1976–1995	12.1%	Mexico	37	1987–1990	33.0%
Austria	83	1984–2002	6.3	Netherlands	143	1982–1999	10.2
Belgium	86	1984–1999	14.6	New Zealand	201	1979–1999	23.0
Brazil	62	1979–1990	78.5	Nigeria	63	1989–1993	19.1
Canada	500	1971–1999	6.3	Norway	68	1984–1996	12.5
Chile	55	1982–1997	8.8	Philippines	104	1987–1997	22.7
China	432	1990–2000	256.9	Poland	140	1991–1998	27.4
Denmark	117	1984–1998	5.4	Portugal	21	1992–1998	10.6
Finland	99	1984–1997	10.1	Singapore	441	1973–2001	29.6
France	571	1983–2000	11.6	South Africa	118	1980–1991	32.7
Germany	407	1978–1999	27.7	Spain	99	1986–1998	10.7
Greece	338	1987–2002	49.0	Sweden	332	1980–1998	30.5
Hong Kong	857	1980–2001	17.3	Switzerland	120	1983–2000	34.9
India	98	1992–1993	35.3	Taiwan	293	1986–1998	31.1
Indonesia	237	1989–2001	19.7	Thailand	292	1987–1997	46.7
Israel	285	1990–1994	12.1	Turkey	163	1990–1996	13.1
Italy	181	1985–2001	21.7	United Kingdom	3,122	1959–2001	17.4
Japan	1,689	1970–2001	28.4	United States	14,978	1960–2003	18.3
Korea	477	1980–1996	74.3				
Malaysia	401	1980–1998	104.1				

Jay R. Ritter is Cordell Professor of Finance at the University of Florida. An outstanding scholar, he is well known for his insightful analyses of new issues and going public.

very risky investments. Arguably, they must be significantly underpriced, on average, just to attract investors, and this is one explanation for the underpricing phenomenon.

The second caveat is that relatively few IPO buyers will actually get the initial high average returns observed in IPOs, and many will actually lose money. Although it is true that, on average, IPOs have positive initial returns, a significant fraction of them have price drops. Furthermore, when the price is too low, the issue is often "oversubscribed." This means investors will not be able to buy all of the shares they want, and the underwriters will allocate the shares among investors.

TABLE 16.3 >> **Average First-Day Returns, Categorized by Sales, for IPOs: 1980–2003***

Annual Sales of Issuing Firms	1980–89 Number of Firms	1980–89 First-Day Average Return	1990–98 Number of Firms	1990–98 First-Day Average Return	1999–2000 Number of Firms	1999–2000 First-Day Average Return	2001–2003 Number of Firms	2001–2003 First-Day Average Return
$0 ≤ Sales < $10m	389	10.2%	642	16.9%	17	69.5%	28	7.2%
$10m ≤ Sales < $20m	247	8.8	358	18.2	128	81.0	11	14.3
$20m ≤ Sales < $50m	484	7.9	753	8.8	140	77.9	22	14.5
$50m ≤ Sales < $100m	334	6.5	562	13.1	83	62.5	26	14.4
$100m ≤ Sales < $200m	229	4.8	432	11.9	50	30.9	26	12.6
$200m ≤ Sales	264	3.6	603	8.9	82	25.0	96	11.2
All	1,947	7.3	3,350	14.8	800	65.1	209	11.7

*Sales, measured in millions, are for the last twelve months prior to going public. All sales have been converted into dollars of 2003 purchasing power, using the Consumer Price Index. There are 6,306 IPOs, after excluding IPOs with an offer price of less than $5.00 per share, units, REITs, ADRs, closed-end funds, banks and S&Ls, firms not listed on CRSP within six months of the offer date, and 85 firms with missing sales. The average first-day return is 18.7 percent.

SOURCE: Professor Jay R. Ritter, University of Florida.

The average investor will find it difficult to get shares in a "successful" offering (one in which the price increases) because there will not be enough shares to go around. On the other hand, an investor blindly submitting orders for IPOs tends to get more shares in issues that go down in price.

To illustrate, consider this tale of two investors. Smith knows very accurately what the Bonanza Corporation is worth when its shares are offered. She is confident that the shares are underpriced. Jones knows only that prices usually rise one month after an IPO. Armed with this information, Jones decides to buy 1,000 shares of every IPO. Does he actually earn an abnormally high return on the initial offering?

The answer is no, and at least one reason is Smith. Knowing about the Bonanza Corporation, Smith invests all her money in its IPO. When the issue is oversubscribed, the underwriters have to somehow allocate the shares between Smith and Jones. The net result is that when an issue is underpriced, Jones doesn't get to buy as much of it as he wanted.

Smith also knows that the Blue Sky Corporation IPO is overpriced. In this case, she avoids its IPO altogether, and Jones ends up with a full 1,000 shares. To summarize this tale, Jones gets fewer shares when more knowledgeable investors swarm to buy an underpriced issue and gets all he wants when the smart money avoids the issue.

This is an example of a "winner's curse," and it is thought to be another reason why IPOs have such a large average return. When the average investor "wins" and gets the entire allocation, it may be because those who knew better avoided the issue. The only way underwriters can counteract the winner's curse and attract the average investor is to underprice new issues (on average) so that the average investor still makes a profit.

Another reason for underpricing is that the underpricing is a kind of insurance for the investment banks. Conceivably, an investment bank could be sued successfully by angry customers if it consistently overpriced securities. Underpricing guarantees that, at least on average, customers will come out ahead.

A final reason for underpricing is that before the offer price is established, investment banks talk to big institutional investors to gauge the level of interest in the stock and to gather opinions about a suitable price. Underpricing is a way that the bank can reward these investors for truthfully revealing what they think the stock is worth and the number of shares they would like to buy.

Concept Questions

16.5a Why is underpricing a cost to the issuing firm?

16.5b Suppose a stockbroker calls you up out of the blue and offers to sell you "all the shares you want" of a new issue. Do you think the issue will be more or less underpriced than average?

NEW EQUITY SALES AND THE VALUE OF THE FIRM

16.6

We now turn to a consideration of seasoned offerings, which, as we discussed earlier, are offerings by firms that already have outstanding securities. It seems reasonable to believe that new long-term financing is arranged by firms after positive net present value projects are put together. As a consequence, when the announcement of external financing is made, the firm's market value should go up. Interestingly, this is not what happens. Stock prices tend to decline following the announcement of a new equity issue, although they tend to not change much following a debt announcement. A number of researchers have studied this issue. Plausible reasons for this strange result include the following:

1. **Managerial information.** If management has superior information about the market value of the firm, it may know when the firm is overvalued. If it does, it will attempt to issue new shares of stock when the market value exceeds the correct value. This will benefit existing shareholders. However, the potential new shareholders are not stupid, and they will anticipate this superior information and discount it in lower market prices at the new-issue date.
2. **Debt usage.** A company's issuing new equity may reveal that the company has too much debt or too little liquidity. One version of this argument says that the equity issue is a bad signal to the market. After all, if the new projects are favorable ones, why should the firm let new shareholders in on them? It could just issue debt and let the existing shareholders have all the gain.
3. **Issue costs.** As we discuss next, there are substantial costs associated with selling securities.

The drop in value of the existing stock following the announcement of a new issue is an example of an indirect cost of selling securities. This drop might typically be on the order of 3 percent for an industrial corporation (and somewhat smaller for a public utility), so, for a large company, it can represent a substantial amount of money. We label this drop the *abnormal return* in our discussion of the costs of new issues that follows.

To give a couple of recent examples, in June 2004, SS&C Technologies Inc. announced a seasoned issue of $87 million. Its stock fell about 3.76 percent on the day. Similarly, in March 2004, General Electric (GE) announced a secondary offering of 118 million shares to raise $3.8 billion. Its stock dropped about 2.9 percent on the news. In both of these cases, the stock price drop was about what we would expect.

Concept Questions

16.6a What are some possible reasons why the price of stock drops on the announcement of a new equity issue?

16.6b Explain why we might expect a firm with a positive NPV investment to finance it with debt instead of equity.

16.7 THE COSTS OF ISSUING SECURITIES

Issuing securities to the public isn't free, and the costs of different methods are important determinants of which is used. These costs associated with *floating* a new issue are generically called *flotation costs*. In this section, we take a closer look at the flotation costs associated with equity sales to the public.

The Costs of Selling Stock to the Public

The costs of selling stock are classified in the following table and fall into six categories: (1) the gross spread, (2) other direct expenses, (3) indirect expenses, (4) abnormal returns (discussed previously), (5) underpricing, and (6) the Green Shoe option.

The Costs of Issuing Securities

1. Gross spread	The gross spread consists of direct fees paid by the issuer to the underwriting syndicate—the difference between the price the issuer receives and the offer price.
2. Other direct expenses	These are direct costs, incurred by the issuer, that are not part of the compensation to underwriters. These costs include filing fees, legal fees, and taxes—all reported on the prospectus.
3. Indirect expenses	These costs are not reported on the prospectus and include the costs of management time spent working on the new issue.
4. Abnormal returns	In a seasoned issue of stock, the price of the existing stock drops on average by 3 percent upon the announcement of the issue. This drop is called the abnormal return.
5. Underpricing	For initial public offerings, losses arise from selling the stock below the true value.
6. Green Shoe option	The Green Shoe option gives the underwriters the right to buy additional shares at the offer price to cover overallotments.

Table 16.4 reports direct costs as a percentage of the gross amount raised for IPOs, SEOs, straight (ordinary) bonds, and convertible bonds sold by U.S. companies over the five-year period from 1990 through 2003. These are direct costs only. Not included are indirect expenses, the cost of the Green Shoe provision, underpricing (for IPOs), and abnormal returns (for SEOs).

As Table 16.4 shows, the direct costs alone can be very large, particularly for smaller issues (less than $10 million). On a smaller IPO, for example, the total direct costs amount to 15.36 percent of the amount raised. This means that if a company sells $10 million in stock, it will only net about $8.5 million; the other $1.5 million goes to cover the underwriter spread and other direct expenses. Typical underwriter spreads on an IPO range from about 5 percent up to 10 percent or so, but, for well over half of the IPOs in Table 16.4, the spread is exactly 7 percent, so this is, by far, the most common spread.

Overall, four clear patterns emerge from Table 16.4. First of all, with the possible exception of straight debt offerings (about which we will have more to say later), there are substantial economies of scale. The underwriter spreads are smaller on larger issues, and

TABLE 16.4 >> Direct Costs as a Percentage of Gross Proceeds for Equity (IPOs and SEOs) and Straight and Convertible Bonds Offered by Domestic Operating Companies: 1990–2003

	Equity								Bonds							
	IPOs				SEOs				Convertible Bonds				Straight Bonds			
Proceeds ($ in millions)	Number of Issues	Gross Spread	Other Direct Expense	Total Direct Cost	Number of Issues	Gross Spread	Other Direct Expense	Total Direct Cost	Number of Issues	Gross Spread	Other Direct Expense	Total Direct Cost	Number of Issues	Gross Spread	Other Direct Expense	Total Direct Cost
2–9.99	624	9.15%	6.21%	15.36%	267	7.56%	5.32%	12.88%	8	5.73%	2.78%	8.51%	70	1.39%	2.35%	3.74%
10–19.99	704	7.33	4.30	11.63	519	6.32	2.49	8.81	20	5.26	2.90	8.16	104	1.33	1.59	2.92
20–39.99	1336	6.99	2.82	9.81	904	5.73	1.51	7.24	27	4.74	1.72	6.46	159	1.22	0.90	2.12
40–59.99	771	6.96	2.25	9.21	677	5.28	0.92	6.20	33	3.29	1.01	4.30	152	0.72	0.63	1.35
60–79.99	403	6.88	1.77	8.65	489	5.07	0.74	5.81	61	2.70	0.61	3.31	113	1.52	0.76	2.28
80–99.99	245	6.79	1.55	8.34	292	4.95	0.61	5.56	17	2.16	0.56	2.72	159	1.39	0.56	1.95
100–199.99	438	6.48	1.19	7.67	657	4.57	0.43	5.00	100	2.56	0.39	2.95	677	1.60	0.52	2.12
200–499.99	197	5.91	0.81	6.72	275	3.99	0.27	4.26	53	2.34	0.22	2.56	333	1.43	0.37	1.80
500 and up	72	4.66	0.49	5.15	83	3.48	0.16	3.64	17	2.05	0.11	2.16	118	0.62	0.20	0.82
Total	4,790	7.17	3.22	10.39	4,163	5.37	1.35	6.72	336	2.99	0.81	3.80	1,885	1.36	0.61	1.97

SOURCE: Inmoo Lee, Scott Lochhead, Jay Ritter, and Quanshui Zhao, "The Costs of Raising Capital," *Journal of Financial Research* 19 (Spring 1996), updated by the authors.

the other direct costs fall sharply as a percentage of the amount raised, a reflection of the mostly fixed nature of such costs. Second, the costs associated with selling debt are substantially less than the costs of selling equity. Third, IPOs have higher expenses than SEOs, but the difference is not as great as might originally be guessed. Finally, straight bonds are cheaper to float than convertible bonds.

As we have discussed, the underpricing of IPOs is an additional cost to the issuer. To give a better idea of the total cost of going public, Table 16.5 combines the information in Table 16.4 for IPOs with data on the underpricing experienced by these firms. Comparing the total direct costs (in the fifth column) to the underpricing (in the sixth column), we see that they are roughly the same size, so the direct costs are only about half of the total. Overall, across all size groups, the total direct costs amount to 10 percent of the amount raised, and the underpricing amounts to 24 percent.

Finally, with regard to debt offerings, there is a general pattern in issue costs that is somewhat obscured in Table 16.4. Recall from Chapter 7 that bonds carry different credit ratings. Higher-rated bonds are said to be investment grade, whereas lower-rated bonds are noninvestment grade. Table 16.6 contains a breakdown of direct costs for bond issues after the investment and noninvestment grades have been separated.

Table 16.6 clarifies three things regarding debt issues. First, there are substantial economies of scale here as well. Second, investment-grade issues have much lower direct costs, particularly for straight bonds. Finally, there are relatively few noninvestment-grade issues in the smaller size categories, reflecting the fact that such issues are more commonly handled as private placements, which we discuss in a later section.

The Costs of Going Public: The Case of Symbion

On February 6, 2004, Symbion, Inc., the Nashville-based owner and operator of outpatient surgery centers, went public via an IPO. Symbion issued 7.2 million shares of stock at a price of $15.00 each, 2,584,000 of which were underwritten by Symbion's lead investment bank, Credit Suisse First Boston LLC, with the remaining 4,616,000 underwritten by a syndicate made up of seven other investment banks.

Even though the IPO raised a gross sum of $108 million, Symbion only got to keep about $96 million after expenses. The biggest expense was the 7 percent underwriter spread, which is very standard for an offering of this size. Symbion sold each of the 7.2 million shares to the underwriters for $13.95, and the underwriters in turn sold the shares to the public for $15.00 each. Thus, of the $108 million investors paid for the shares, Symbion received $100,440,000.

But wait, there's more. Symbion spent $10,048 in SEC registration fees, $12,000 in other filing fees, and $100,000 to be listed on the NASDAQ. The company also spent $1.29 million on accounting to obtain the necessary audits, $5,250 for a transfer agent to physically transfer the shares and maintain a list of shareholders, $565,000 for printing and engraving expenses, $1.16 million for legal fees and expenses, and, finally, $67,702 in miscellaneous expenses.

As Symbion's outlays show, an IPO can be a costly undertaking! In the end, Symbion's expenses totaled $11,904,000, of which $8,694,000 went to the underwriters and $3,210,000 went to other parties. The total cost to Symbion was 11 percent of the issue proceeds, which is a little higher than might be expected. At least part of the reason is that the company had filed to go public in 2003. Midway through the process, the company and its underwriters determined that the market conditions were not favorable for an IPO, so the company withdrew its registration. The costs for this previous registration were included in the 2004 IPO.

TABLE 16.5 >> Direct and Indirect Costs, in Percentages, of Equity IPOs: 1990–2003

Proceeds ($ in millions)	Number of Issues	Gross Spread	Other Direct Expense	Total Direct Cost	Underpricing
2–9.99	624	9.15%	6.21%	15.36%	18.18%
10–19.99	704	7.33	4.30	11.63	10.02
20–39.99	1336	6.99	2.82	9.81	17.91
40–59.99	771	6.96	2.25	9.21	29.57
60–79.99	403	6.88	1.77	8.65	39.20
80–99.99	245	6.79	1.55	8.34	45.36
100–199.99	438	6.48	1.19	7.67	37.10
200–499.99	197	5.91	0.81	6.72	17.12
500 and up	72	4.66	0.49	5.15	12.19
Total	4,790	7.17	3.22	10.39	23.55

SOURCE: Inmoo Lee, Scott Lochhead, Jay Ritter, and Quanshui Zhao, "The Costs of Raising Capital," *Journal of Financial Research* 19 (Spring 1996), updated by the authors.

TABLE 16.6 >> Average Gross Spreads and Total Direct Costs for Domestic Debt Issues: 1990–2003

	Convertible Bonds						Straight Bonds					
	Investment Grade			Noninvestment Grade			Investment Grade			Noninvestment Grade		
Proceeds ($ in millions)	Number of Issues	Gross Spread	Total Direct Cost	Number of Issues	Gross Spread	Total Direct Cost	Number of Issues	Gross Spread	Total Direct Cost	Number of Issues	Gross Spread	Total Direct Cost
2–9.99	0	—	—	0	—	—	40	0.62%	1.90%	0	—	—
10–19.99	0	—	—	1	4.00%	5.67%	68	0.50	1.35	2	2.74%	4.80%
20–39.99	0	—	—	11	3.47	5.02	119	0.58	1.21	13	3.06	4.36
40–59.99	3	1.92%	2.43%	21	3.33	4.48	132	0.39	0.86	12	3.01	3.93
60–79.99	4	1.65	2.09	47	2.78	3.40	68	0.57	0.97	43	2.99	4.07
80–99.99	3	0.89	1.16	9	2.54	3.19	100	0.66	0.94	56	2.74	3.66
100–199.99	28	2.22	2.55	50	2.57	3.00	341	0.55	0.80	321	2.71	3.39
200–499.99	26	1.99	2.18	17	2.62	2.85	173	0.50	0.81	156	2.49	2.90
500 and up	12	1.96	2.09	1	2.50	2.57	97	0.28	0.38	20	2.45	2.71
Total	76	1.99	2.26	157	2.81	3.47	1,138	0.51	0.85	623	2.68	3.35

SOURCE: Inmoo Lee, Scott Lochhead, Jay Ritter, and Quanshui Zhao, "The Costs of Raising Capital," *Journal of Financial Research* 19 (Spring 1996), updated by the authors.

Concept Questions

16.7a What are the different costs associated with security offerings?

16.7b What lessons do we learn from studying issue costs?

16.8 RIGHTS

When new shares of common stock are sold to the general public, the proportional ownership of existing shareholders is likely to be reduced. However, if a preemptive right is contained in the firm's articles of incorporation, then the firm must first offer any new issue of common stock to existing shareholders. If the articles of incorporation do not include a preemptive right, the firm has a choice of offering the issue of common stock directly to existing shareholders or to the public.

An issue of common stock offered to existing stockholders is called a *rights offering* (or *offer,* for short) or a *privileged subscription.* In a rights offering, each shareholder is issued rights to buy a specified number of new shares from the firm at a specified price within a specified time, after which time the rights are said to expire. The terms of the rights offering are evidenced by certificates known as share warrants or rights. Such rights are often traded on securities exchanges or over the counter.

Rights offerings have some interesting advantages relative to cash offers. For example, they appear to be cheaper for the issuing firm than cash offers. In fact, a firm can do a rights offering without using an underwriter; whereas, as a practical matter, an underwriter is almost a necessity in a cash offer. Despite this, rights offerings are fairly rare in the United States; however, in many other countries, they are more common than cash offers. Why this is true is a bit of a mystery and the source of much debate, but, to our knowledge, no definitive answer exists.

The Mechanics of a Rights Offering

To illustrate the various considerations a financial manager faces in a rights offering, we will examine the situation faced by the National Power Company, whose abbreviated initial financial statements are given in Table 16.7.

As indicated in Table 16.7, National Power earns \$2 million after taxes and has one million shares outstanding. Earnings per share are thus \$2, and the stock sells for \$20, or 10 times earnings (that is, the price-earnings ratio is 10). To fund a planned expansion, the company intends to raise \$5 million worth of new equity funds through a rights offering.

To execute a rights offering, the financial management of National Power will have to answer the following questions:

1. What should the price per share be for the new stock?
2. How many shares will have to be sold?
3. How many shares will each shareholder be allowed to buy?

Also, management will probably want to ask:

4. What is likely to be the effect of the rights offering on the per-share value of the existing stock?

It turns out that the answers to these questions are highly interrelated. We will get to them in just a moment.

The early stages of a rights offering are the same as those for the general cash offer. The difference between a rights offering and a general cash offer lies in how the shares are sold.

<< TABLE 16.7

National Power Company Financial Statements before Rights Offering

NATIONAL POWER COMPANY
Balance Sheet

Assets		Shareholders' Equity	
Assets	$15,000,000	Common stock	$ 5,000,000
		Retained earnings	10,000,000
Total	$15,000,000	Total	$15,000,000

Income Statement

Earnings before taxes	$ 3,030,303
Taxes (34%)	1,030,303
Net income	$ 2,000,000
Shares outstanding	1,000,000
Earnings per share	$ 2
Market price per share	$ 20
Total market value	$20,000,000

In a rights offer, National Power's existing shareholders are informed that they own one right for each share of stock they own. National Power will then specify how many rights a shareholder needs to buy one additional share at a specified price.

To take advantage of the rights offering, shareholders have to exercise the rights by filling out a subscription form and sending it, along with payment, to the firm's subscription agent (the subscription agent is usually a bank). Shareholders of National Power will actually have several choices: (1) exercise their rights and subscribe for some or all of the entitled shares, (2) order some or all of the rights sold, or (3) do nothing and let the rights expire. As we will discuss, this third course of action is inadvisable.

Number of Rights Needed to Purchase a Share

National Power wants to raise $5 million in new equity. Suppose the subscription price is set at $10 per share. How National Power arrives at that price is something we will discuss later, but notice that the subscription price is substantially less than the current $20 per share market price.

At $10 per share, National Power will have to issue 500,000 new shares. This can be determined by dividing the total amount of funds to be raised by the subscription price:

$$\text{Number of new shares} = \frac{\text{Funds to be raised}}{\text{Subscription price}} \qquad [16.1]$$

$$= \frac{\$5{,}000{,}000}{10} = 500{,}000 \text{ shares}$$

Because stockholders always get one right for each share of stock they own, one million rights will be issued by National Power. To determine how many rights will be needed to buy one new share of stock, we can divide the number of existing outstanding shares of stock by the number of new shares:

$$\begin{array}{c}\text{Number of rights needed}\\ \text{to buy a share of stock}\end{array} = \frac{\text{Old shares}}{\text{New Shares}} \qquad [16.2]$$

$$= \frac{1{,}000{,}000}{500{,}000} = 2 \text{ rights}$$

Thus, a shareholder will need to give up two rights plus $10 to receive a share of new stock. If all the stockholders do this, National Power will raise the required $5 million.

It should be clear that the subscription price, the number of new shares, and the number of rights needed to buy a new share of stock are interrelated. For example, National Power can lower the subscription price. If it does, more new shares will have to be issued to raise $5 million in new equity. Several alternatives are worked out here:

Subscription Price	Number of New Shares	Number of Rights Needed to Buy a Share of Stock
$20	250,000	4
10	500,000	2
5	1,000,000	1

The Value of a Right

Rights clearly have value. In the case of National Power, the right to buy a share of stock worth $20 for $10 is definitely worth something. In fact, if you think about it, a right is essentially a call option, and our discussion of such options in Chapter 14 applies here. The most important difference between a right and an ordinary call option is that rights are issued by the firm, so they more closely resemble warrants. In general, the valuation of options, rights, and warrants can be fairly complex, so we defer discussion of this subject to a later chapter. However, we can discuss the value of a right just prior to expiration to illustrate some important points.

Suppose a shareholder of National Power owns two shares of stock just before the rights offering is about to expire. This situation is depicted in Table 16.8. Initially, the price of National Power is $20 per share, so the shareholder's total holding is worth $2 \times \$20 = \$40$. The National Power rights offer gives shareholders with two rights the opportunity to purchase one additional share for $10. The additional share does not carry a right.

The stockholder who has two shares will receive two rights. The holding of the shareholder who exercises these rights and buys the new share will increase to three shares. The

TABLE 16.8 >>

The Value of Rights: The Individual Shareholder

Initial Position	
Number of shares	2
Share price	$20
Value of holding	$40
Terms of Offer	
Subscription price	$10
Number of rights issued	2
Number of rights for a new share	2
After Offer	
Number of shares	3
Value of holding	$50
Share price	$16.67
Value of one right: Old price − New price	$20 − 16.67 = $3.33

<< TABLE 16.9

National Power Company Rights Offering

Initial Position	
Number of shares	1 million
Share price	\$20
Value of firm	\$20 million
Terms of Offer	
Subscription price	\$10
Number of rights issued	1 million
Number of rights for a new share	2
After Offer	
Number of shares	1.5 million
Share price	\$16.67
Value of firm	\$25 million
Value of one right	\$20 − 16.67 = \$3.33

total investment will be \$40 + 10 = \$50 (the \$40 initial value plus the \$10 paid to the company).

The stockholder now holds three shares, all of which are identical because the new share does not have a right and the rights attached to the old shares have been exercised. Because the total cost of buying these three shares is \$40 + 10 = \$50, the price per share must end up at \$50/3 = \$16.67 (rounded to two decimal places).

Table 16.9 summarizes what happens to National Power's stock price. If all shareholders exercise their rights, the number of shares will increase to 1 million + .5 million = 1.5 million. The value of the firm will increase to \$20 million + 5 million = \$25 million. The value of each share will thus drop to \$25 million/1.5 million = \$16.67 after the rights offering.

The difference between the old share price of \$20 and the new share price of \$16.67 reflects the fact that the old shares carried rights to subscribe to the new issue. The difference must be equal to the value of one right, that is, \$20 − 16.67 = \$3.33.

An investor holding no shares of outstanding National Power stock who wants to subscribe to the new issue can do so by buying some rights. Suppose an outside investor buys two rights. This will cost \$3.33 × 2 = \$6.67 (to account for previous rounding). If the investor exercises the rights at a subscription price of \$10, the total cost will be \$10 + 6.67 = \$16.67. In return for this expenditure, the investor will receive a share of the new stock, which, as we have seen, is worth \$16.67.

Exercising Your Rights: Part I

<< **EXAMPLE 16.1**

In the National Power example, suppose the subscription price is set at \$8. How many shares will have to be sold? How many rights will you need to buy a new share? What is the value of a right? What will the price per share be after the rights offer?

To raise \$5 million, \$5 million/8 = 625,000 shares will need to be sold. There are one million shares outstanding, so it will take 1 million/625,000 = 8/5 = 1.6 rights to buy a new share of stock (you can buy five new shares for every eight you own). After the rights offer, there will be 1.625 million shares, worth \$25 million altogether, so the per-share value will be \$25/1.625 = \$15.38. The value of a right in this case is the \$20 original price less the \$15.38 ending price, or \$4.62.

Ex Rights

ex-rights date
The beginning of the period when stock is sold without a recently declared right, normally two trading days before the holder-of-record date.

holder-of-record date
The date on which existing shareholders on company records are designated as the recipients of stock rights. Also, the date of record.

National Power's rights have a substantial value. In addition, the rights offering will have a large impact on the market price of National Power's stock. That price will drop by $3.33 on the **ex-rights date**.

The standard procedure for issuing rights involves the firm's setting a **holder-of-record date**. Following stock exchange rules, the stock typically goes ex rights two trading days before the holder-of-record date. If the stock is sold before the ex-rights date—"rights on," "with rights," or "cum rights"—the new owner will receive the rights. After the ex-rights date, an investor who purchases the shares will not receive the rights. This is depicted for National Power in Figure 16.4.

As illustrated, on September 30, National Power announces the terms of the rights offering, stating that the rights will be mailed on, say, November 1 to stockholders of record as of October 15. Because October 13 is the ex-rights date, only those shareholders who own the stock on or before October 12 will receive the rights.

EXAMPLE 16.2 >> Exercising Your Rights: Part II

The Lagrange Point Co. has proposed a rights offering. The stock currently sells for $40 per share. Under the terms of the offer, stockholders will be allowed to buy one new share for every five that they own at a price of $25 per share. What is the value of a right? What is the ex-rights price?

You can buy five rights on shares for 5 × $40 = $200 and then exercise the rights for another $25. Your total investment is $225, and you end up with six ex-rights shares. The ex-rights price per share is $225/6 = $37.50. The rights are thus worth $40 − 37.50 = $2.50 apiece.

EXAMPLE 16.3 >> Right On

In Example 16.2, suppose the rights sell for only $2 instead of the $2.50 we calculated. What can you do?

You can get rich quick, because you have found a money machine. Here's the recipe: Buy five rights for $10. Exercise them and pay $25 to get a new share. Your total investment to get one ex-rights share is 5 × $2 + 25 = $35. Sell the share for $37.50 and pocket the $2.50 difference. Repeat as desired.

The Underwriting Arrangements

standby underwriting
The type of underwriting in which the underwriter agrees to purchase the unsubscribed portion of the issue.

standby fee
An amount paid to an underwriter participating in a standby underwriting agreement.

Rights offerings are typically arranged using **standby underwriting**. In standby underwriting, the issuer makes a rights offering, and the underwriter makes a firm commitment to "take up" (that is, purchase) the unsubscribed portion of the issue. The underwriter usually gets a **standby fee** and additional amounts based on the securities taken up.

Standby underwriting protects the firm against undersubscription, which can occur if investors throw away rights or if bad news causes the market price of the stock to fall below the subscription price.

In practice, only a small percentage (less than 10 percent) of shareholders fail to exercise valuable rights. This failure can probably be attributed to ignorance or vacations. Furthermore, shareholders are usually given an **oversubscription privilege**, which enables

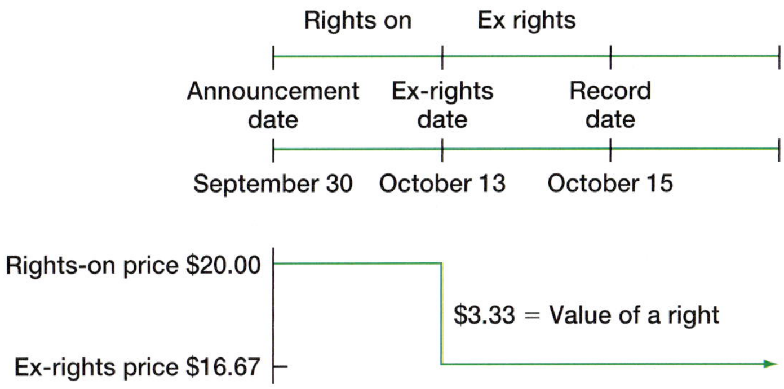

In a rights offering, there is a date of record, which is the last day that a shareholder can establish legal ownership. However, stocks are sold ex rights two business days before the record date. Before the ex-rights date, the stock sells rights on, which means that the purchaser receives the rights.

<< FIGURE 16.4

Ex-Rights Stock Prices

them to purchase unsubscribed shares at the subscription price. The oversubscription privilege makes it unlikely that the corporate issuer would have to turn to its underwriter for help.

oversubscription privilege
A privilege that allows shareholders to purchase unsubscribed shares in a rights offering at the subscription price.

Effects on Shareholders

Shareholders can exercise their rights or sell them. In either case, the stockholder will neither win nor lose because of the rights offering. The hypothetical holder of two shares of National Power has a portfolio worth $40. If the shareholder exercises the rights, they end up with three shares worth a total of $50. In other words, with an expenditure of $10, the investor's holding increases in value by $10, which means that the shareholder is neither better nor worse off.

On the other hand, if the shareholder sells the two rights for $3.33 each, he or she would obtain $3.33 × 2 = $6.67 and end up with two shares worth $16.67 and the cash from selling the right:

$$\begin{aligned} \text{Shares held} &= 2 \times \$16.67 = \$33.33 \\ \text{Rights sold} &= 2 \times \$3.33 = \underline{6.67} \\ \text{Total} &= \underline{\underline{\$40.00}} \end{aligned}$$

The new $33.33 market value plus $6.67 in cash is exactly the same as the original holding of $40. Thus, stockholders cannot lose or gain by exercising or selling rights.

It is obvious that after the rights offering, the new market price of the firm's stock will be lower than the price before the rights offering. As we have seen, however, stockholders have suffered no loss because of the rights offering. Thus, the stock price decline is very much like that in a stock split, a device that is described in Chapter 18. The lower the subscription price, the greater is the price decline resulting from a rights offering. It is important to emphasize that because shareholders receive rights equal in value to the price drop, the rights offering does *not* hurt stockholders.

There is one last issue. How do we set the subscription price in a rights offering? If you think about it, you will see that the subscription price really does not matter. It has to be below the market price of the stock in order for the rights to have value, but, beyond this, the price is arbitrary. In principle, it could be as low as we cared to make it as long as it was not zero. In other words, it is impossible to underprice a rights offer.

Concept Questions

16.8a How does a rights offering work?

16.8b What are the questions that financial management must answer in a rights offering?

16.8c How is the value of a right determined?

16.8d When does a rights offering affect the value of a company's shares?

16.8e Does a rights offering cause share prices to decrease? How are existing shareholders affected by a rights offering?

16.9 DILUTION

dilution
Loss in existing shareholders' value, in terms of either ownership, market value, book value, or EPS.

A subject that comes up quite a bit in discussions involving the selling of securities is **dilution**. Dilution refers to a loss in existing shareholders' value. There are several kinds:

1. Dilution of percentage ownership
2. Dilution of market value
3. Dilution of book value and earnings per share

The differences between these three types can be a little confusing, and there are some common misconceptions about dilution, so we discuss it in this section.

Dilution of Proportionate Ownership

The first type of dilution can arise whenever a firm sells shares to the general public. For example, Joe Smith owns 5,000 shares of Merit Shoe Company. Merit Shoe currently has 50,000 shares of stock outstanding; each share gets one vote. Joe thus controls 10 percent (5,000/50,000) of the votes and gets 10 percent of the dividends.

If Merit Shoe issues 50,000 new shares of common stock to the public via a general cash offer, Joe's ownership in Merit Shoe may be diluted. If Joe does not participate in the new issue, his ownership will drop to 5 percent (5,000/100,000). Notice that the value of Joe's shares is unaffected; he just owns a smaller percentage of the firm.

Because a rights offering would ensure Joe Smith an opportunity to maintain his proportionate 10 percent share, dilution of the ownership of existing shareholders can be avoided by using a rights offering.

Dilution of Value: Book versus Market Values

We now examine dilution of value by looking at some accounting numbers. We do this to illustrate a fallacy concerning dilution; we do not mean to suggest that accounting value dilution is more important than market value dilution. As we illustrate, quite the reverse is true.

Suppose Upper States Manufacturing (USM) wants to build a new electricity-generating plant to meet future anticipated demands. As shown in Table 16.10, USM currently has one million shares outstanding and no debt. Each share is selling for \$5, and the company has a \$5 million market value. USM's book value is \$10 million total, or \$10 per share.

USM has experienced a variety of difficulties in the past, including cost overruns, regulatory delays in building a nuclear-powered electricity-generating plant, and below-normal profits. These difficulties are reflected in the fact that USM's market-to-book ratio is \$5/10 = .50 (successful firms rarely have market prices below book values).

<< TABLE 16.10

New Issues and Dilution: The Case of Upper States Manufacturing

		After Taking on New Project	
	Initial	**With Dilution**	**With No Dilution**
Number of shares	1,000,000	1,400,000	1,400,000
Book value	\$10,000,000	\$12,000,000	\$12,000,000
Book value per share (*B*)	\$10	\$8.57	\$8.57
Market value	\$5,000,000	\$6,000,000	\$8,000,000
Market price (*P*)	\$5	\$4.29	\$5.71
Net income	\$1,000,000	\$1,200,000	\$1,600,000
Return on equity (ROE)	.10	.10	.13
Earnings per share (EPS)	\$1	\$.86	\$1.14
EPS/*P*	.20	.20	.20
P/EPS	5	5	5
P/*B*	.5	.5	.67
Project cost \$2,000,000		NPV = −\$1,000,000	NPV = \$1,000,000

Net income for USM is currently \$1 million. With one million shares, earnings per share are \$1, and the return on equity is \$1/10 = 10%.[9] USM thus sells for five times earnings (the price-earnings ratio is 5). USM has 200 shareholders, each of whom holds 5,000 shares. The new plant will cost \$2 million, so USM will have to issue 400,000 new shares (\$5 × 400,000 = \$2 million). There will thus be 1.4 million shares outstanding after the issue.

The ROE on the new plant is expected to be the same as for the company as a whole. In other words, net income is expected to go up by .10 × \$2 million = \$200,000. Total net income will thus be \$1.2 million. The following will result if the plant is built:

1. With 1.4 million shares outstanding, EPS will be \$1.2/1.4 = \$.857, down from \$1.
2. The proportionate ownership of each old shareholder will drop to 5,000/1.4 million = .36 percent from .50 percent.
3. If the stock continues to sell for five times earnings, then the value will drop to 5 × \$.857 = \$4.29, representing a loss of \$.71 per share.
4. The total book value will be the old \$10 million plus the new \$2 million, for a total of \$12 million. Book value per share will fall to \$12 million/1.4 million = \$8.57.

If we take this example at face value, then dilution of proportionate ownership, accounting dilution, and market value dilution all occur. USM's stockholders appear to suffer significant losses.

A Misconception Our example appears to show that selling stock when the market-to-book ratio is less than 1 is detrimental to the stockholders. Some managers claim that the resulting dilution occurs because EPS will go down whenever shares are issued when the market value is less than the book value.

When the market-to-book ratio is less than 1, increasing the number of shares does cause EPS to go down. Such a decline in EPS is accounting dilution, and accounting dilution will always occur under these circumstances.

Is it furthermore true that market value dilution will necessarily occur? The answer is *no*. There is nothing incorrect about our example, but why the market value has decreased is not obvious. We discuss this next.

[9]Return on equity, or ROE, is equal to earnings per share divided by book value per share, or, equivalently, net income divided by common equity. We discuss this and other financial ratios in some detail in Chapter 3.

The Correct Arguments In this example, the market price falls from $5 per share to $4.29. This is true dilution, but why does it occur? The answer has to do with the new project. USM is going to spend $2 million on the new plant. However, as shown in Table 16.10, the total market value of the company is going to rise from $5 million to $6 million, an increase of only $1 million. This simply means that the NPV of the new project is −$1 million. With 1.4 million shares, the loss per share is $1/1.4 = $.71, as we calculated before.

So, true dilution takes place for the shareholders of USM because the NPV of the project is negative, not because the market-to-book ratio is less than 1. This negative NPV causes the market price to drop, and the accounting dilution has nothing to do with it.

Suppose the new project has a positive NPV of $1 million. The total market value rises by $2 million + 1 million = $3 million. As shown in Table 16.10 (third column), the price per share rises to $5.71. Notice that accounting dilution still takes place because the book value per share still falls, but there is no economic consequence of that fact. The market value of the stock rises.

The $.71 increase in share value comes about because of the $1 million NPV, which amounts to an increase in value of about $.71 per share. Also, as shown, if the ratio of price to EPS remains at 5, then EPS must rise to $5.71/5 = $1.14. Total earnings (net income) rises to $1.14 per share × 1.4 million shares = $1.6 million. Finally, ROE will rise to $1.6 million/12 million = 13.33%.

Concept Questions

16.9a What are the different kinds of dilution?

16.9b Is dilution important?

16.10 ISSUING LONG-TERM DEBT

term loans
Direct business loans of, typically, one to five years.

private placements
Loans, usually long-term in nature, provided directly by a limited number of investors.

The general procedures followed in a public issue of bonds are the same as those for stocks. The issue must be registered with the SEC, there must be a prospectus, and so on. The registration statement for a public issue of bonds, however, is different from the one for common stock. For bonds, the registration statement must indicate an indenture.

Another important difference is that more than 50 percent of all debt is issued privately. There are two basic forms of direct private long-term financing: term loans and private placement.

Term loans are direct business loans. These loans have maturities of between one year and five years. Most term loans are repayable during the life of the loan. The lenders include commercial banks, insurance companies, and other lenders that specialize in corporate finance. **Private placements** are very similar to term loans except that the maturity is longer.

The important differences between direct private long-term financing and public issues of debt are:

1. A direct long-term loan avoids the cost of Securities and Exchange Commission registration.
2. Direct placement is likely to have more restrictive covenants.
3. It is easier to renegotiate a term loan or a private placement in the event of a default. It is harder to renegotiate a public issue because hundreds of holders are usually involved.

4. Life insurance companies and pension funds dominate the private-placement segment of the bond market. Commercial banks are significant participants in the term-loan market.
5. The costs of distributing bonds are lower in the private market.

The interest rates on term loans and private placements are usually higher than those on an equivalent public issue. This difference reflects the trade-off between a higher interest rate and more flexible arrangements in the event of financial distress, as well as the lower costs associated with private placements.

An additional, and very important, consideration is that the flotation costs associated with selling debt are much less than the comparable costs associated with selling equity.

Concept Questions

16.10a What is the difference between private and public bond issues?

16.10b A private placement is likely to have a higher interest rate than a public issue. Why?

SHELF REGISTRATION 16.11

To simplify the procedures for issuing securities, in March 1982 the SEC adopted Rule 415 on a temporary basis, and it was made permanent in November 1983. Rule 415 allows shelf registration. Both debt and equity securities can be shelf registered.

Shelf registration permits a corporation to register an offering that it reasonably expects to sell within the next two years and then sell the issue whenever it wants during that two-year period. For example, in April 2004, banking giant Wells Fargo & Co., filed with the SEC to offer $20.2 billion in debt securities, preferred stock, and other securities. This was quite a large amount for a company to put "on the shelf." Not all companies can use Rule 415. The primary qualifications are:

shelf registration
Registration permitted by SEC Rule 415, which allows a company to register all issues it expects to sell within two years at one time, with subsequent sales at any time within those two years.

1. The company must be rated investment grade.
2. The firm cannot have defaulted on its debt in the past three years.
3. The aggregate market value of the firm's outstanding stock must be more than $150 million.
4. The firm must not have had a violation of the Securities Act of 1934 in the past three years.

Shelf registration allows firms to use a *dribble* method of new equity issuance. In dribbling, a company registers the issue and hires an underwriter as its selling agent. The company sells shares in "dribs and drabs" from time to time directly via a stock exchange (for example, the NYSE). Companies that have used dribble programs include Niagara Mohawk, Pacific Gas and Electric, and The Southern Company.

The rule has been controversial. Arguments have been constructed against shelf registration:

1. The costs of new issues might go up because underwriters might not be able to provide as much current information to potential investors as they would otherwise, so investors would pay less. The expense of selling the issue piece by piece might therefore be higher than that of selling it all at once.
2. Some investment bankers have argued that shelf registration will cause a "market overhang" that will depress market prices. In other words, the possibility that the company may increase the supply of stock at any time will have a negative impact on the current stock price.

Shelf registration is much more common with bonds than stocks, but some equity shelf sales do occur. For example, in May 2004, the Internet travel service company Priceline.com filed a shelf registration to sell $100 million in common stock.

Concept Questions

16.11a What is shelf registration?

16.11b What are the arguments against shelf registration?

16.12 SUMMARY AND CONCLUSIONS

This chapter has looked at how corporate securities are issued. The following are the main points:

1. The costs of issuing securities can be quite large. They are much lower (as a percentage) for larger issues.
2. The direct and indirect costs of going public can be substantial. However, once a firm is public, it can raise additional capital with much greater ease.
3. Rights offerings are cheaper than general cash offers. Even so, most new equity issues in the United States are underwritten general cash offers.

Visit us at www.mhhe.com/rwj

Chapter Review and Self-Test Problems

16.1 Flotation Costs The L5 Corporation is considering an equity issue to finance a new space station. A total of $15 million in new equity is needed. If the direct costs are estimated at 7 percent of the amount raised, how large does the issue need to be? What is the dollar amount of the flotation cost?

16.2 Rights Offerings The Hadron Corporation currently has 3 million shares outstanding. The stock sells for $40 per share. To raise $20 million for a new particle accelerator, the firm is considering a rights offering at $25 per share. What is the value of a right in this case? The ex-rights price?

Answers to Chapter Review and Self-Test Problems

16.1 The firm needs to net $15 million after paying the 7 percent flotation costs. So the amount raised is given by:

Amount raised × (1 − .07) = $15 million

Amount raised = $15 million/.93 = $16.129 million

The total flotation cost is thus $1.129 million.

16.2 To raise $20 million at $25 per share, $20 million/25 = 800,000 shares will have to be sold. Before the offering, the firm is worth 3 million × $40 = $120 million. The issue will raise $20 million and there will be 3.8 million shares outstanding. The value of an ex-rights share will therefore be $140 million/3.8 million = $36.84. The value of a right is thus $40 − 36.84 = $3.16.

Concepts Review and Critical Thinking Questions

1. **Debt versus Equity Offering Size** In the aggregate, debt offerings are much more common than equity offerings and typically much larger as well. Why?

2. **Debt versus Equity Flotation Costs** Why are the costs of selling equity so much larger than the costs of selling debt?
3. **Bond Ratings and Flotation Costs** Why do noninvestment-grade bonds have much higher direct costs than investment-grade issues?
4. **Underpricing in Debt Offerings** Why is underpricing not a great concern with bond offerings?

   Use the following information to answer the next three questions. Eyetech Pharmaceuticals, Inc., a company that develops treatments for eye problems, went public in January 2004. Assisted by the investment bank Merrill Lynch, Eyetech sold 6.5 million shares at $21 each, thereby raising a total of $136.5 million. At the end of the first day of trading, the stock sold for $32.40 per share, down slightly from a high of $33.00. Based on the end-of-day numbers, Eyetech shares were apparently underpriced by about $11 each, meaning that the company missed out on an additional $67 million.
5. **IPO Pricing** The Eyetech IPO was underpriced by about 54 percent. Should Eyetech be upset at Merrill Lynch over the underpricing?
6. **IPO Pricing** In the previous question, would it affect your thinking to know that the company was incorporated less than four years earlier, had only $30 million in revenues for the first nine months of 2003, and had never earned a profit. Additionally, the company had only one product, Macugen, which had won fast-track status from the FDA, but still did not have approval to be sold.
7. **IPO Pricing** In the previous two questions, how would it affect your thinking to know that in addition to the 6.5 million shares offered in the IPO, Eyetech had an additional 32 million shares outstanding? Of those 32 million shares, 10 million shares were owned by pharmaceutical giant Pfizer, and 12 million shares were owned by the 13 directors and executive officers.
8. **Cash Offer versus Rights Offer** Ren-Stimpy International is planning to raise fresh equity capital by selling a large new issue of common stock. Ren-Stimpy is currently a publicly traded corporation, and it is trying to choose between an underwritten cash offer and a rights offering (not underwritten) to current shareholders. Ren-Stimpy management is interested in minimizing the selling costs and has asked you for advice on the choice of issue methods. What is your recommendation and why?
9. **IPO Underpricing** In 1980, a certain assistant professor of finance bought 12 initial public offerings of common stock. He held each of these for approximately one month and then sold. The investment rule he followed was to submit a purchase order for every firm commitment initial public offering of oil and gas exploration companies. There were 22 of these offerings, and he submitted a purchase order for approximately $1,000 in stock for each of the companies. With 10 of these, no shares were allocated to this assistant professor. With 5 of the 12 offerings that were purchased, fewer than the requested number of shares were allocated.

   The year 1980 was very good for oil and gas exploration company owners: On average, for the 22 companies that went public, the stocks were selling for 80 percent above the offering price a month after the initial offering date. The assistant professor looked at his performance record and found that the $8,400 invested in the 12 companies had grown to $10,000, representing a return of only about 20 percent (commissions were negligible). Did he have bad luck, or should he have expected to do worse than the average initial public offering investor? Explain.
10. **IPO Pricing** The following material represents the cover page and summary of the prospectus for the initial public offering of the Pest Investigation Control

Corporation (PICC), which is going public tomorrow with a firm commitment initial public offering managed by the investment banking firm of Erlanger and Ritter. Answer the following questions:

a. Assume that you know nothing about PICC other than the information contained in the prospectus. Based on your knowledge of finance, what is your prediction for the price of PICC tomorrow? Provide a short explanation of why you think this will occur.

b. Assume that you have several thousand dollars to invest. When you get home from class tonight, you find that your stockbroker, whom you have not talked to for weeks, has called. She has left a message that PICC is going public tomorrow and that she can get you several hundred shares at the offering price if you call her back first thing in the morning. Discuss the merits of this opportunity.

PROSPECTUS PICC

200,000 shares

PEST INVESTIGATION CONTROL CORPORATION

Of the shares being offered hereby, all 200,000 are being sold by the Pest Investigation Control Corporation, Inc. ("the Company"). Before the offering there has been no public market for the shares of PICC, and no guarantee can be given that any such market will develop.

These securities have not been approved or disapproved by the SEC nor has the commission passed upon the accuracy or adequacy of this prospectus. Any representation to the contrary is a criminal offense.

	Price to Public	Underwriting Discount	Proceeds to Company*
Per share	$11.00	$1.10	$9.90
Total	$2,200,000	$220,000	$1,980,000

*Before deducting expenses estimated at $27,000 and payable by the Company.

This is an initial public offering. The common shares are being offered, subject to prior sale, when, as, and if delivered to and accepted by the Underwriters and subject to approval of certain legal matters by their Counsel and by Counsel for the Company. The Underwriters reserve the right to withdraw, cancel, or modify such offer and to reject offers in whole or in part.

Erlanger and Ritter, Investment Bankers

July 12, 2005

Prospectus Summary

The Company	The Pest Investigation Control Corporation (PICC) breeds and markets toads and tree frogs as ecologically safe insect-control mechanisms.
The Offering	200,000 shares of common stock, no par value.
Listing	The Company will seek listing on NASDAQ and will trade over the counter.
Shares Outstanding	As of June 30, 2005, 400,000 shares of common stock were outstanding. After the offering, 600,000 shares of common stock will be outstanding.
Use of Proceeds	To finance expansion of inventory and receivables and general working capital, and to pay for country club memberships for certain finance professors.

Selected Financial Information
(amounts in thousands except per-share data)

	Fiscal Year Ended June 30				As of June 30, 2005	
	2003	2004	2005		Actual	As Adjusted for This Offering
Revenues	$60.00	$120.00	$240.00	Working capital	$ 8	$1,961
Net earnings	3.80	15.90	36.10	Total assets	511	2,464
Earnings per share	0.01	0.04	0.09	Stockholders' equity	423	2,376

Questions and Problems

BASIC
(Questions 1–8)

1. **Rights Offerings** Again, Inc., is proposing a rights offering. Presently there are 350,000 shares outstanding at $85 each. There will be 70,000 new shares offered at $70 each.
   a. What is the new market value of the company?
   b. How many rights are associated with one of the new shares?
   c. What is the ex-rights price?
   d. What is the value of a right?
   e. Why might a company have a rights offering rather than a general cash offer?
2. **Rights Offerings** The Clifford Corporation has announced a rights offer to raise $50 million for a new journal, the *Journal of Financial Excess.* This journal will review potential articles after the author pays a nonrefundable reviewing fee of $5,000 per page. The stock currently sells for $40 per share, and there are 5.2 million shares outstanding.
   a. What is the maximum possible subscription price? What is the minimum?
   b. If the subscription price is set at $35 per share, how many shares must be sold? How many rights will it take to buy one share?
   c. What is the ex-rights price? What is the value of a right?
   d. Show how a shareholder with 1,000 shares before the offering and no desire (or money) to buy additional shares is not harmed by the rights offer.
3. **Rights** Stone Shoe Co. has concluded that additional equity financing will be needed to expand operations and that the needed funds will be best obtained through a rights offering. It has correctly determined that as a result of the rights offering, the share price will fall from $80 to $74.50 ($80 is the rights-on price; $74.50 is the ex-rights price, also known as the *when-issued* price). The company is seeking $15 million in additional funds with a per-share subscription price equal to $40. How many shares are there currently, before the offering? (Assume that the increment to the market value of the equity equals the gross proceeds from the offering.)
4. **IPO Underpricing** The Woods Co. and the Garcia Co. have both announced IPOs at $40 per share. One of these is undervalued by $11, and the other is overvalued by $6, but you have no way of knowing which is which. You plan on buying 1,000 shares of each issue. If an issue is underpriced, it will be rationed, and only half your order will be filled. If you *could* get 1,000 shares in Woods and 1,000 shares in Garcia, what would your profit be? What profit do you actually expect? What principle have you illustrated?
5. **Calculating Flotation Costs** The St. Anger Corporation needs to raise $25 million to finance its expansion into new markets. The company will sell new shares of equity via a general cash offering to raise the needed funds. If the offer price is $35 per share and the company's underwriters charge an 8 percent spread, how many shares need to be sold?
6. **Calculating Flotation Costs** In the previous problem, if the SEC filing fee and associated administrative expenses of the offering are $900,000, how many shares need to be sold?
7. **Calculating Flotation Costs** The Green Hills Co. has just gone public. Under a firm commitment agreement, Green Hills received $19.75 for each of the 5 million shares sold. The initial offering price was $21 per share, and the stock rose to $26 per share

in the first few minutes of trading. Green Hills paid $800,000 in direct legal and other costs, and $250,000 in indirect costs. What was the flotation cost as a percentage of funds raised?

8. **Price Dilution** Raggio, Inc., has 100,000 shares of stock outstanding. Each share is worth $90, so the company's market value of equity is $9,000,000. Suppose the firm issues 20,000 new shares at the following prices: $90, $85, and $70. What will the effect be of each of these alternative offering prices on the existing price per share?

INTERMEDIATE
(Questions 9–15)

9. **Dilution** Teardrop Inc., wishes to expand its facilities. The company currently has 10 million shares outstanding and no debt. The stock sells for $50 per share, but the book value per share is $40. Net income for Teardrop is currently $15 million. The new facility will cost $35 million, and it will increase net income by $500,000.
   a. Assuming a constant price-earnings ratio, what will the effect be of issuing new equity to finance the investment? To answer, calculate the new book value per share, the new total earnings, the new EPS, the new stock price, and the new market-to-book ratio. What is going on here?
   b. What would the new net income for Teardrop have to be for the stock price to remain unchanged?

10. **Dilution** The Metallica Heavy Metal Mining (MHMM) Corporation wants to diversify its operations. Some recent financial information for the company is shown here:

Stock price	$ 98
Number of shares	14,000
Total assets	$6,000,000
Total liabilities	$2,400,000
Net income	$ 630,000

MHMM is considering an investment that has the same PE ratio as the firm. The cost of the investment is $1,100,000, and it will be financed with a new equity issue. The return on the investment will equal MHMM's current ROE. What will happen to the book value per share, the market value per share, and the EPS? What is the NPV of this investment? Does dilution take place?

11. **Dilution** In the previous problem, what would the ROE on the investment have to be if we wanted the price after the offering to be $98 per share (assume the PE ratio still remains constant)? What is the NPV of this investment? Does any dilution take place?

12. **Rights** Hoobastink Mfg. is considering a rights offer. The company has determined that the ex-rights price would be $52. The current price is $55 per share, and there are 5 million shares outstanding. The rights offer would raise a total of $60 million. What is the subscription price?

13. **Value of a Right** Show that the value of a right can be written as:

$$\text{Value of a right} = P_{RO} - P_X = (P_{RO} - P_S)/(N + 1)$$

where P_{RO}, P_S, and P_X stand for the rights-on price, the subscription price, and the ex-rights price, respectively, and N is the number of rights needed to buy one new share at the subscription price.

14. **Selling Rights** Wuttke Corp. wants to raise $3.65 million via a rights offering. The company currently has 490,000 shares of common stock outstanding that sell for $30 per share. Its underwriter has set a subscription price of $22 per share and will charge

Wuttke a 6 percent spread. If you currently own 6,000 shares of stock in the company and decide not to participate in the rights offering, how much money can you get by selling your rights?

15. Valuing a Right Mitsi Inventory Systems, Inc., has announced a rights offer. The company has announced that it will take four rights to buy a new share in the offering at a subscription price of $40. At the close of business the day before the ex-rights day, the company's stock sells for $80 per share. The next morning, you notice that the stock sells for $72 per share and the rights sell for $6 each. Are the stock and/or the rights correctly priced on the ex-rights day? Describe a transaction in which you could use these prices to create an immediate profit.

What's On the Web?

16.1 Initial Public Offerings What IPO had the biggest price jump (and which had the biggest price drop) in the most recent quarter? Go to www.hoovers.com, follow the "IPO Central" link, and find out.

16.2 IPO Filings You want to look at the most recent initial public offering filing with the SEC. Go to www.hoovers.com, follow the "IPO Central" link, and follow the "IPO Filings" link to find the most recent SEC filings. What is the name of the company with the most recent filing? Find the "SEC Filing" link. What is the name of the document filed with the SEC for the IPO? Now view the document. What does this company do? What does the company propose for the funds raised by the IPO?

16.3 Initial Public Offerings What was the largest IPO? Go to www.ipohome.com and follow the "IPO Marketwatch" link. What was the largest IPO ever? In what country was the company located? What is the largest IPO in the United States?

17 Financial Leverage and Capital Structure Policy

What do AmeriDebt, Parmalat USA, and the National School Fitness Foundation have in common? All three filed for bankruptcy in 2004. AmeriDebt's filing was one of the more ironic bankruptcy filings in recent history. The company is a credit counseling service in the business of educating customers about the proper management of debt! Parmalat USA is a subsidiary of Parmalat Finanziaria, the Italian dairy products company under scrutiny for financial fraud. Things turned sour when creditors found out that, among other things, a $4.9 billion bank account allegedly held by the company didn't exist, creating what the company called "a bit of a liquidity problem." In the case of the National School Fitness Foundation, the nonprofit company arranged to sell $77.5 million in exercise equipment to more than 600 schools. The company promised to reimburse the schools for the purchase from government grants or private donations, but couldn't do it and ran out of cash. As these three cases illustrate, companies that can't meet their financial obligations will fail. For this reason, firms must carefully consider how much debt to use in financing their operations. In this chapter, we discuss the basic ideas underlying optimal debt policies and how firms establish them.

Thus far, we have taken the firm's capital structure as given. Debt-equity ratios don't just drop on firms from the sky, of course, so now it's time to wonder where they do come from. Going back to Chapter 1, recall that we refer to decisions about a firm's debt-equity ratio as *capital structure decisions.*[1]

For the most part, a firm can choose any capital structure that it wants. If management so desired, a firm could issue some bonds and use the proceeds to buy back some stock, thereby increasing the debt-equity ratio. Alternatively, it could issue stock and use the money to pay off some debt, thereby reducing the debt-equity ratio. Activities such as these, that alter the firm's existing capital structure are called capital *restructurings.* In general, such restructurings take place whenever the firm substitutes one capital structure for another while leaving the firm's assets unchanged.

Because the assets of a firm are not directly affected by a capital restructuring, we can examine the firm's capital structure decision separately from its other activities. This means that a firm can consider capital restructuring decisions in isolation from its investment decisions. In this chapter, then, we will ignore investment decisions and focus on the long-term financing, or capital structure, question.

What we will see in this chapter is that capital structure decisions can have important implications for the value of the firm and its cost of capital. We will also find that important

[1]It is conventional to refer to decisions regarding debt and equity as *capital structure decisions.* However, the term *financial structure decisions* would be more accurate, and we use the terms interchangeably.

elements of the capital structure decision are easy to identify, but precise measures of these elements are generally not obtainable. As a result, we are only able to give an incomplete answer to the question of what the best capital structure might be for a particular firm at a particular time.

THE CAPITAL STRUCTURE QUESTION 17.1

How should a firm go about choosing its debt-equity ratio? Here, as always, we assume that the guiding principle is to choose the course of action that maximizes the value of a share of stock. As we discuss next, however, when it comes to capital structure decisions, this is essentially the same thing as maximizing the value of the whole firm, and, for convenience, we will tend to frame our discussion in terms of firm value.

Firm Value and Stock Value: An Example

The following example illustrates that the capital structure that maximizes the value of the firm is the one that financial managers should choose for the shareholders, so there is no conflict in our goals. To begin, suppose the market value of the J. J. Sprint Company is $1,000. The company currently has no debt, and J. J. Sprint's 100 shares sell for $10 each. Further suppose that J. J. Sprint restructures itself by borrowing $500 and then paying out the proceeds to shareholders as an extra dividend of $500/100 = $5 per share.

This restructuring will change the capital structure of the firm with no direct effect on the firm's assets. The immediate effect will be to increase debt and decrease equity. However, what will be the final impact of the restructuring? Table 17.1 illustrates three possible outcomes in addition to the original no-debt case. Notice that in Scenario II, the value of the firm is unchanged at $1,000. In Scenario I, firm value rises to $1,250; it falls by $250, to $750, in Scenario III. We haven't yet said what might lead to these changes. For now, we just take them as possible outcomes to illustrate a point.

Because our goal is to benefit the shareholders, we next examine, in Table 17.2, the net payoffs to the shareholders in these scenarios. We see that, if the value of the firm stays the same, then shareholders will experience a capital loss that will exactly offset the extra dividend. This is Scenario II. In Scenario I, the value of the firm increases to $1,250 and the shareholders come out ahead by $250. In other words, the restructuring has an NPV of $250 in this scenario. The NPV in Scenario III is −$250.

<< TABLE 17.1

Possible Firm Values: No Debt versus Debt plus Dividend

		Debt plus Dividend		
	No Debt	I	II	III
Debt	$ 0	$ 500	$ 500	$500
Equity	1,000	750	500	250
Firm value	$1,000	$1,250	$1,000	$750

<< TABLE 17.2

Possible Payoffs to Shareholders: Debt plus Dividend

	Debt plus Dividend		
	I	II	III
Equity value reduction	−$250	−$500	−$750
Dividends	500	500	500
Net effect	+$250	$ 0	−$250

The key observation to make here is that the change in the value of the firm is the same as the net effect on the stockholders. Financial managers can therefore try to find the capital structure that maximizes the value of the firm. Put another way, the NPV rule applies to capital structure decisions, and the change in the value of the overall firm is the NPV of a restructuring. Thus, J. J. Sprint should borrow $500 if it expects Scenario I. The crucial question in determining a firm's capital structure is, of course, which scenario is likely to occur.

Capital Structure and the Cost of Capital

In Chapter 15, we discussed the concept of the firm's weighted average cost of capital, or WACC. You may recall that the WACC tells us that the firm's overall cost of capital is a weighted average of the costs of the various components of the firm's capital structure. When we described the WACC, we took the firm's capital structure as given. Thus, one important issue that we will want to explore in this chapter is what happens to the cost of capital when we vary the amount of debt financing, or the debt-equity ratio.

A primary reason for studying the WACC is that the value of the firm is maximized when the WACC is minimized. To see this, recall that the WACC is the discount rate that is appropriate for the firm's overall cash flows. Because values and discount rates move in opposite directions, minimizing the WACC will maximize the value of the firm's cash flows.

Thus, we will want to choose the firm's capital structure so that the WACC is minimized. For this reason, we will say that one capital structure is better than another if it results in a lower weighted average cost of capital. Further, we say that a particular debt-equity ratio represents the *optimal capital structure* if it results in the lowest possible WACC. This optimal capital structure is sometimes called the firm's *target* capital structure as well.

Concept Questions

17.1a Why should financial managers choose the capital structure that maximizes the value of the firm?

17.1b What is the relationship between the WACC and the value of the firm?

17.1c What is an optimal capital structure?

17.2 THE EFFECT OF FINANCIAL LEVERAGE

The previous section described why the capital structure that produces the highest firm value (or the lowest cost of capital) is the one most beneficial to stockholders. In this section, we examine the impact of financial leverage on the payoffs to stockholders. As you may recall, *financial leverage* refers to the extent to which a firm relies on debt. The more debt financing a firm uses in its capital structure, the more financial leverage it employs.

As we describe, financial leverage can dramatically alter the payoffs to shareholders in the firm. Remarkably, however, financial leverage may not affect the overall cost of capital. If this is true, then a firm's capital structure is irrelevant because changes in capital structure won't affect the value of the firm. We will return to this issue a little later.

The Basics of Financial Leverage

We start by illustrating how financial leverage works. For now, we ignore the impact of taxes. Also, for ease of presentation, we describe the impact of leverage in terms of its effects on earnings per share, EPS, and return on equity, ROE. These are, of course, accounting numbers and, as such, are not our primary concern. Using cash flows instead of these accounting numbers would lead to precisely the same conclusions, but a little more work would be needed. We discuss the impact on market values in a subsequent section.

Financial Leverage, EPS, and ROE: An Example The Trans Am Corporation currently has no debt in its capital structure. The CFO, Ms. Morris, is considering a restructuring that would involve issuing debt and using the proceeds to buy back some of the outstanding equity. Table 17.3 presents both the current and proposed capital structures. As shown, the firm's assets have a market value of $8 million, and there are 400,000 shares outstanding. Because Trans Am is an all-equity firm, the price per share is $20.

The proposed debt issue would raise $4 million; the interest rate would be 10 percent. Because the stock sells for $20 per share, the $4 million in new debt would be used to purchase $4 million/20 = 200,000 shares, leaving 200,000. After the restructuring, Trans Am would have a capital structure that was 50 percent debt, so the debt-equity ratio would be 1. Notice that, for now, we assume that the stock price will remain at $20.

To investigate the impact of the proposed restructuring, Ms. Morris has prepared Table 17.4, which compares the firm's current capital structure to the proposed capital structure under three scenarios. The scenarios reflect different assumptions about the firm's

<< TABLE 17.3

Current and Proposed Capital Structures for the Trans Am Corporation

	Current	Proposed
Assets	$8,000,000	$8,000,000
Debt	$ 0	$4,000,000
Equity	$8,000,000	$4,000,000
Debt-equity ratio	0	1
Share price	$ 20	$ 20
Shares outstanding	400,000	200,000
Interest rate	10%	10%

<< TABLE 17.4

Capital Structure Scenarios for the Trans Am Corporation

Current Capital Structure: No Debt			
	Recession	Expected	Expansion
EBIT	$500,000	$1,000,000	$1,500,000
Interest	0	0	0
Net income	$500,000	$1,000,000	$1,500,000
ROE	6.25%	12.50%	18.75%
EPS	$ 1.25	$ 2.50	$ 3.75
Proposed Capital Structure: Debt = $4 million			
EBIT	$500,000	$1,000,000	$1,500,000
Interest	400,000	400,000	400,000
Net income	$100,000	$ 600,000	$1,100,000
ROE	2.50%	15.00%	27.50%
EPS	$ .50	$ 3.00	$ 5.50

FIGURE 17.1 >>

Financial Leverage: EPS and EBIT for the Trans Am Corporation

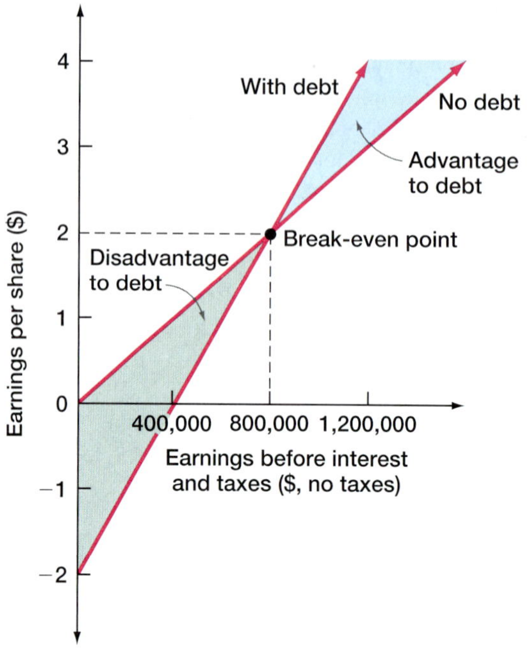

EBIT. Under the expected scenario, the EBIT is $1 million. In the recession scenario, EBIT falls to $500,000. In the expansion scenario, it rises to $1.5 million.

To illustrate some of the calculations behind the figures in Table 17.4, consider the expansion case. EBIT is $1.5 million. With no debt (the current capital structure) and no taxes, net income is also $1.5 million. In this case, there are 400,000 shares worth $8 million total. EPS is therefore $1.5 million/400,000 = $3.75. Also, because accounting return on equity, ROE, is net income divided by total equity, ROE is $1.5 million/8 million = 18.75%.[2]

With $4 million in debt (the proposed capital structure), things are somewhat different. Because the interest rate is 10 percent, the interest bill is $400,000. With EBIT of $1.5 million, interest of $400,000, and no taxes, net income is $1.1 million. Now there are only 200,000 shares worth $4 million total. EPS is therefore $1.1 million/200,000 = $5.50, versus the $3.75 that we calculated in the previous scenario. Furthermore, ROE is $1.1 million/4 million = 27.5%. This is well above the 18.75 percent we calculated for the current capital structure.

EPS versus EBIT The impact of leverage is evident when the effect of the restructuring on EPS and ROE is examined. In particular, the variability in both EPS and ROE is much larger under the proposed capital structure. This illustrates how financial leverage acts to magnify gains and losses to shareholders.

In Figure 17.1, we take a closer look at the effect of the proposed restructuring. This figure plots earnings per share, EPS, against earnings before interest and taxes, EBIT, for the current and proposed capital structures. The first line, labeled "No debt," represents the case of no leverage. This line begins at the origin, indicating that EPS would be zero if EBIT were zero. From there, every $400,000 increase in EBIT increases EPS by $1 (because there are 400,000 shares outstanding).

[2]ROE is discussed in some detail in Chapter 3.

The second line represents the proposed capital structure. Here, EPS is negative if EBIT is zero. This follows because \$400,000 of interest must be paid regardless of the firm's profits. Because there are 200,000 shares in this case, the EPS is −\$2 as shown. Similarly, if EBIT were \$400,000, EPS would be exactly zero.

The important thing to notice in Figure 17.1 is that the slope of the line in this second case is steeper. In fact, for every \$400,000 increase in EBIT, EPS rises by \$2, so the line is twice as steep. This tells us that EPS is twice as sensitive to changes in EBIT because of the financial leverage employed.

Another observation to make in Figure 17.1 is that the lines intersect. At that point, EPS is exactly the same for both capital structures. To find this point, note that EPS is equal to EBIT/400,000 in the no-debt case. In the with-debt case, EPS is (EBIT − \$400,000)/200,000. If we set these equal to each other, EBIT is:

$$\begin{aligned} \text{EBIT}/400{,}000 &= (\text{EBIT} - \$400{,}000)/200{,}000 \\ \text{EBIT} &= 2 \times (\text{EBIT} - \$400{,}000) \\ &= \$800{,}000 \end{aligned}$$

When EBIT is \$800,000, EPS is \$2 under either capital structure. This is labeled as the break-even point in Figure 17.1; we could also call it the indifference point. If EBIT is above this level, leverage is beneficial; if it is below this point, it is not.

There is another, more intuitive, way of seeing why the break-even point is \$800,000. Notice that, if the firm has no debt and its EBIT is \$800,000, its net income is also \$800,000. In this case, the ROE is 10 percent. This is precisely the same as the interest rate on the debt, so the firm earns a return that is just sufficient to pay the interest.

Break-Even EBIT

<< EXAMPLE 17.1

The MPD Corporation has decided in favor of a capital restructuring. Currently, MPD uses no debt financing. Following the restructuring, however, debt will be \$1 million. The interest rate on the debt will be 9 percent. MPD currently has 200,000 shares outstanding, and the price per share is \$20. If the restructuring is expected to increase EPS, what is the minimum level for EBIT that MPD's management must be expecting? Ignore taxes in answering.

To answer, we calculate the break-even EBIT. At any EBIT above this, the increased financial leverage will increase EPS, so this will tell us the minimum level for EBIT. Under the old capital structure, EPS is simply EBIT/200,000. Under the new capital structure, the interest expense will be \$1 million × .09 = \$90,000. Furthermore, with the \$1 million proceeds, MPD will repurchase \$1 million/20 = 50,000 shares of stock, leaving 150,000 outstanding. EPS will thus be (EBIT − \$90,000)/150,000.

Now that we know how to calculate EPS under both scenarios, we set them equal to each other and solve for the break-even EBIT:

$$\begin{aligned} \text{EBIT}/200{,}000 &= (\text{EBIT} - \$90{,}000)/150{,}000 \\ \text{EBIT} &= 4/3 \times (\text{EBIT} - \$90{,}000) \\ &= \$360{,}000 \end{aligned}$$

Verify that, in either case, EPS is \$1.80 when EBIT is \$360,000. Management at MPD is apparently of the opinion that EPS will exceed \$1.80.

Corporate Borrowing and Homemade Leverage

Based on Tables 17.3 and 17.4 and Figure 17.1, Ms. Morris draws the following conclusions:

1. The effect of financial leverage depends on the company's EBIT. When EBIT is relatively high, leverage is beneficial.
2. Under the expected scenario, leverage increases the returns to shareholders, as measured by both ROE and EPS.
3. Shareholders are exposed to more risk under the proposed capital structure because the EPS and ROE are much more sensitive to changes in EBIT in this case.
4. Because of the impact that financial leverage has on both the expected return to stockholders and the riskiness of the stock, capital structure is an important consideration.

The first three of these conclusions are clearly correct. Does the last conclusion necessarily follow? Surprisingly, the answer is no. As we discuss next, the reason is that shareholders can adjust the amount of financial leverage by borrowing and lending on their own. This use of personal borrowing to alter the degree of financial leverage is called **homemade leverage**.

homemade leverage The use of personal borrowing to change the overall amount of financial leverage to which the individual is exposed.

We will now illustrate that it actually makes no difference whether or not Trans Am adopts the proposed capital structure, because any stockholder who prefers the proposed capital structure can simply create it using homemade leverage. To begin, the first part of Table 17.5 shows what will happen to an investor who buys $2,000 worth of Trans Am stock if the proposed capital structure is adopted. This investor purchases 100 shares of stock. From Table 17.4, we know that EPS will be either $.50, $3, or $5.50, so the total earnings for 100 shares will be either $50, $300, or $550 under the proposed capital structure.

Now, suppose that Trans Am does not adopt the proposed capital structure. In this case, EPS will be $1.25, $2.50, or $3.75. The second part of Table 17.5 demonstrates how a stockholder who prefers the payoffs under the proposed structure can create them using personal borrowing. To do this, the stockholder borrows $2,000 at 10 percent on their own. Our investor uses this amount, along with the original $2,000, to buy 200 shares of stock. As shown, the net payoffs are exactly the same as those for the proposed capital structure.

How did we know to borrow $2,000 to create the right payoffs? We are trying to replicate Trans Am's proposed capital structure at the personal level. The proposed capital structure results in a debt-equity ratio of 1. To replicate this structure at the personal level, the stockholder must borrow enough to create this same debt-equity ratio. Because the

TABLE 17.5 >>

Proposed Capital Structure versus Original Capital Structure with Homemade Leverage

Proposed Capital Structure			
	Recession	Expected	Expansion
EPS	$ .50	$ 3.00	$ 5.50
Earnings for 100 shares	50.00	300.00	550.00
Net cost = 100 shares × $20 = $2,000			
Original Capital Structure and Homemade Leverage			
EPS	$ 1.25	$ 2.50	$ 3.75
Earnings for 200 shares	250.00	500.00	750.00
Less: Interest on $2,000 at 10%	200.00	200.00	200.00
Net earnings	$ 50.00	$300.00	$550.00
Net cost = 200 shares × $20 − Amount borrowed = $4,000 − 2,000 = $2,000			

stockholder has $2,000 in equity invested, the borrowing of another $2,000 will create a personal debt-equity ratio of 1.

This example demonstrates that investors can always increase financial leverage themselves to create a different pattern of payoffs. It thus makes no difference whether or not Trans Am chooses the proposed capital structure.

Unlevering the Stock

<< EXAMPLE 17.2

In our Trans Am example, suppose management adopts the proposed capital structure. Further suppose that an investor who owned 100 shares preferred the original capital structure. Show how this investor could "unlever" the stock to recreate the original payoffs.

To create leverage, investors borrow on their own. To undo leverage, investors must loan out money. In the case of Trans Am, the corporation borrowed an amount equal to half its value. The investor can unlever the stock by simply loaning out money in the same proportion. In this case, the investor sells 50 shares for $1,000 total and then loans out the $1,000 at 10 percent. The payoffs are calculated in the following table.

	Recession	Expected	Expansion
EPS (proposed structure)	$ .50	$ 3.00	$ 5.50
Earnings for 50 shares	25.00	150.00	275.00
Plus: Interest on $1,000	100.00	100.00	100.00
Total payoff	$125.00	$250.00	$375.00

These are precisely the payoffs the investor would have experienced under the original capital structure.

Concept Questions

17.2a What is the impact of financial leverage on stockholders?

17.2b What is homemade leverage?

17.2c Why is Trans Am's capital structure irrelevant?

CAPITAL STRUCTURE AND THE COST OF EQUITY CAPITAL

17.3

We have seen that there is nothing special about corporate borrowing because investors can borrow or lend on their own. As a result, whichever capital structure Trans Am chooses, the stock price will be the same. Trans Am's capital structure is thus irrelevant, at least in the simple world we have examined.

Our Trans Am example is based on a famous argument advanced by two Nobel laureates, Franco Modigliani and Merton Miller, whom we will henceforth call M&M. What we illustrated for the Trans Am Corporation is a special case of **M&M Proposition I**. M&M Proposition I states that it is completely irrelevant how a firm chooses to arrange its finances.

FIGURE 17.2 >>

Two Pie Models of Capital Structure

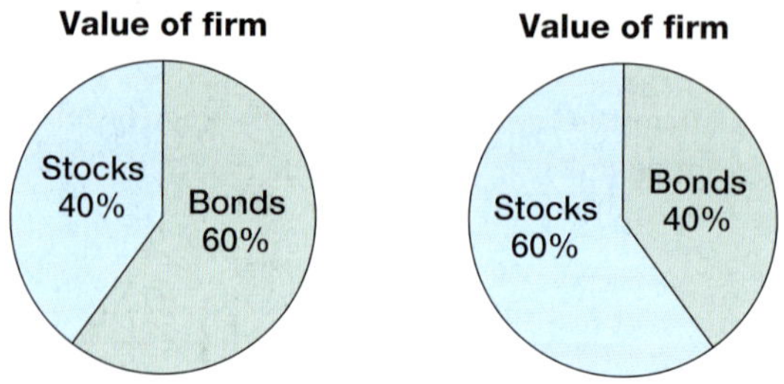

M&M Proposition I The proposition that the value of the firm is independent of the firm's capital structure.

M&M Proposition I: The Pie Model

One way to illustrate M&M Proposition I is to imagine two firms that are identical on the left-hand side of the balance sheet. Their assets and operations are exactly the same. The right-hand sides are different because the two firms finance their operations differently. In this case, we can view the capital structure question in terms of a "pie" model. Why we choose this name is apparent from Figure 17.2. Figure 17.2 gives two possible ways of cutting up the pie between the equity slice, E, and the debt slice, D: 40%–60% and 60%–40%. However, the size of the pie in Figure 17.2 is the same for both firms because the value of the assets is the same. This is precisely what M&M Proposition I states: The size of the pie doesn't depend on how it is sliced.

The Cost of Equity and Financial Leverage: M&M Proposition II

Although changing the capital structure of the firm does not change the firm's *total* value, it does cause important changes in the firm's debt and equity. We now examine what happens to a firm financed with debt and equity when the debt-equity ratio is changed. To simplify our analysis, we will continue to ignore taxes.

Based on our discussion in Chapter 15, if we ignore taxes, the weighted average cost of capital, WACC, is:

$$\text{WACC} = (E/V) \times R_E + (D/V) \times R_D$$

where $V = E + D$. We also saw that one way of interpreting the WACC is as the required return on the firm's overall assets. To remind us of this, we will use the symbol R_A to stand for the WACC and write:

$$R_A = (E/V) \times R_E + (D/V) \times R_D$$

If we rearrange this to solve for the cost of equity capital, we see that:

$$R_E = R_A + (R_A - R_D) \times (D/E) \quad [17.1]$$

M&M Proposition II The proposition that a firm's cost of equity capital is a positive linear function of the firm's capital structure.

This is the famous **M&M Proposition II**, which tells us that the cost of equity depends on three things: the required rate of return on the firm's assets, R_A, the firm's cost of debt, R_D, and the firm's debt-equity ratio, D/E.

Figure 17.3 summarizes our discussion thus far by plotting the cost of equity capital, R_E, against the debt-equity ratio. As shown, M&M Proposition II indicates that the cost of equity, R_E, is given by a straight line with a slope of $(R_A - R_D)$. The y-intercept corresponds to a firm with a debt-equity ratio of zero, so $R_A = R_E$ in that case. Figure 17.3 shows that, as the firm raises its debt-equity ratio, the increase in leverage raises the risk of the equity and therefore the required return or cost of equity (R_E).

Notice in Figure 17.3 that the WACC doesn't depend on the debt-equity ratio; it's the same no matter what the debt-equity ratio is. This is another way of stating M&M Proposition I: The firm's overall cost of capital is unaffected by its capital structure. As illustrated,

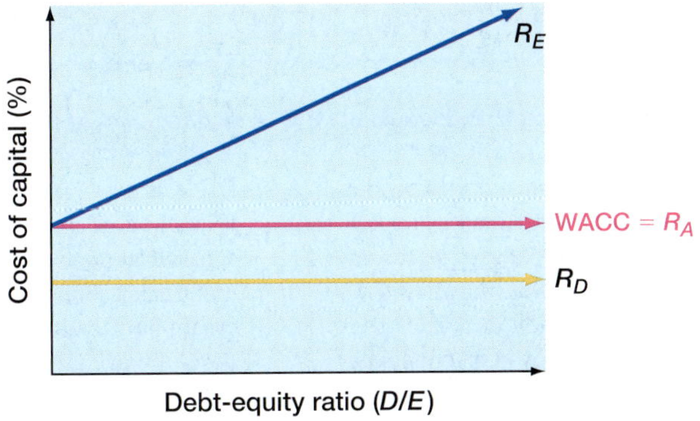

$R_E = R_A + (R_A - R_D) \times (D/E)$ by M&M Proposition II

$$R_A = \text{WACC} = \left(\frac{E}{V}\right) \times R_E + \left(\frac{D}{V}\right) \times R_D$$

where $V = D + E$

<< FIGURE 17.3

The Cost of Equity and the WACC: M&M Propositions I and II with No Taxes

the fact that the cost of debt is lower than the cost of equity is exactly offset by the increase in the cost of equity from borrowing. In other words, the change in the capital structure weights (E/V and D/V) is exactly offset by the change in the cost of equity (R_E), so the WACC stays the same.

<< EXAMPLE 17.3

The Cost of Equity Capital

The Ricardo Corporation has a weighted average cost of capital (ignoring taxes) of 12 percent. It can borrow at 8 percent. Assuming that Ricardo has a target capital structure of 80 percent equity and 20 percent debt, what is its cost of equity? What is the cost of equity if the target capital structure is 50 percent equity? Calculate the WACC using your answers to verify that it is the same.

According to M&M Proposition II, the cost of equity, R_E, is:

$$R_E = R_A + (R_A - R_D) \times (D/E)$$

In the first case, the debt-equity ratio is .2/.8 = .25, so the cost of the equity is:

$$\begin{aligned} R_E &= 12\% + (12\% - 8\%) \times .25 \\ &= 13\% \end{aligned}$$

In the second case, verify that the debt-equity ratio is 1.0, so the cost of equity is 16 percent.

We can now calculate the WACC assuming that the percentage of equity financing is 80 percent, the cost of equity is 13 percent, and the tax rate is zero:

$$\begin{aligned} \text{WACC} &= (E/V) \times R_E + (D/V) \times R_D \\ &= .80 \times 13\% + .20 \times 8\% \\ &= 12\% \end{aligned}$$

In the second case, the percentage of equity financing is 50 percent and the cost of equity is 16 percent. The WACC is:

$$\begin{aligned} \text{WACC} &= (E/V) \times R_E + (D/V) \times R_D \\ &= .50 \times 16\% + .50 \times 8\% \\ &= 12\% \end{aligned}$$

As we have calculated, the WACC is 12 percent in both cases.

IN THEIR OWN WORDS . . .

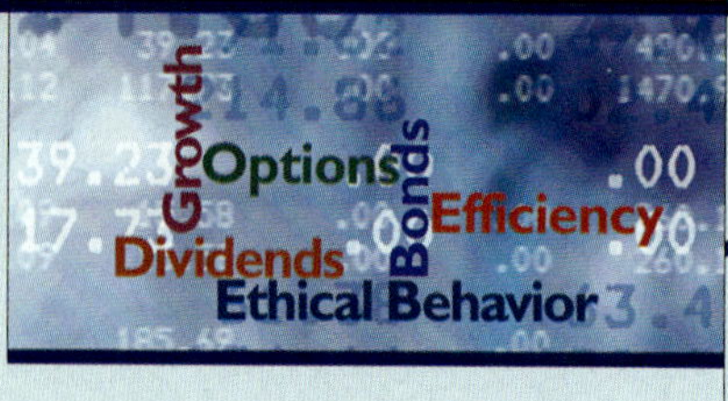

Merton H. Miller on Capital Structure: M&M 30 Years Later

>> **How difficult it** is to summarize briefly the contribution of these papers was brought home to me very clearly after Franco Modigliani was awarded the Nobel Prize in Economics, in part—but, of course, only in part—for the work in finance. The television camera crews from our local stations in Chicago immediately descended upon me. "We understand," they said, "that you worked with Modigliani some years back in developing these M&M theorems, and we wonder if you could explain them briefly to our television viewers." "How briefly?" I asked. "Oh, take 10 seconds," was the reply.

Ten seconds to explain the work of a lifetime! Ten seconds to describe two carefully reasoned articles, each running to more than 30 printed pages and each with 60 or so long footnotes! When they saw the look of dismay on my face, they said, "You don't have to go into details. Just give us the main points in simple, commonsense terms."

The main point of the cost-of-capital article was, in principle at least, simple enough to make. It said that in an economist's ideal world, the total market value of all the securities issued by a firm would be governed by the earning power and risk of its underlying real assets and would be independent of how the mix of securities issued to finance it was divided between debt instruments and equity capital. Some corporate treasurers might well think that they could enhance total value by increasing the proportion of debt instruments because yields on debt instruments, given their lower risk, are, by and large, substantially below those on equity capital. But, under the ideal conditions assumed, the added risk to the shareholders from issuing more debt will raise required yields on the equity by just enough to offset the seeming gain from use of low-cost debt.

Such a summary would not only have been too long, but it relied on shorthand terms and concepts that are rich in connotations to economists, but hardly so to the general public. I thought, instead, of an analogy that we ourselves had invoked in the original paper. "Think of the firm," I said, "as a gigantic tub of whole milk. The farmer can sell the whole milk as is. Or he can separate out the cream and sell it at a considerably higher price than the whole milk would bring. (Selling cream is the analog of a firm selling low-yield and hence high-priced debt securities.) But, of course, what the farmer would have left would be skim milk, with low butterfat content, and that would sell for much less than whole milk. Skim milk corresponds to the levered equity. The M&M proposition says that if there were no costs of separation (and, of course, no government dairy support programs), the cream plus the skim milk would bring the same price as the whole milk."

The television people conferred among themselves for a while. They informed me that it was still too long, too complicated, and too academic. "Have you anything simpler?" they asked. I thought of another way in which the M&M proposition is presented that stresses the role of securities as devices for "partitioning" a firm's payoffs among the group of its capital suppliers. "Think of the firm," I said, "as a gigantic pizza, divided into quarters. If, now, you cut each quarter in half into eighths, the M&M proposition says that you will have more pieces, but not more pizza."

Once again whispered conversation. This time, they shut the lights off. They folded up their equipment. They thanked me for my cooperation. They said they would get back to me. But I knew that I had somehow lost my chance to start a new career as a packager of economic wisdom for TV viewers in convenient 10-second sound bites. Some have the talent for it; and some just don't.

The late Merton H. Miller was famous for his pathbreaking work with Franco Modigliani on corporate capital structure, cost of capital, and dividend policy. He received the Nobel Prize in Economics for his contributions shortly after this essay was prepared.

Business and Financial Risk

M&M Proposition II shows that the firm's cost of equity can be broken down into two components. The first component, R_A, is the required return on the firm's assets overall, and it depends on the nature of the firm's operating activities. The risk inherent in a firm's operations is called the **business risk** of the firm's equity. Referring back to Chapter 13, note that this business risk depends on the systematic risk of the firm's assets. The greater a firm's business risk, the greater R_A will be, and, all other things being the same, the greater will be the firm's cost of equity.

business risk
The equity risk that comes from the nature of the firm's operating activities.

The second component in the cost of equity, $(R_A - R_D) \times (D/E)$, is determined by the firm's financial structure. For an all-equity firm, this component is zero. As the firm begins to rely on debt financing, the required return on equity rises. This occurs because the debt financing increases the risks borne by the stockholders. This extra risk that arises from the use of debt financing is called the **financial risk** of the firm's equity.

financial risk
The equity risk that comes from the financial policy (i.e., capital structure) of the firm.

The total systematic risk of the firm's equity thus has two parts: business risk and financial risk. The first part (the business risk) depends on the firm's assets and operations and is not affected by capital structure. Given the firm's business risk (and its cost of debt), the second part (the financial risk) is completely determined by financial policy. As we have illustrated, the firm's cost of equity rises when the firm increases its use of financial leverage because the financial risk of the equity increases while the business risk remains the same.

Concept Questions

17.3a What does M&M Proposition I state?

17.3b What are the three determinants of a firm's cost of equity?

17.3c The total systematic risk of a firm's equity has two parts. What are they?

M&M PROPOSITIONS I AND II WITH CORPORATE TAXES

17.4

Debt has two distinguishing features that we have not taken into proper account. First, as we have mentioned in a number of places, interest paid on debt is tax deductible. This is good for the firm, and it may be an added benefit of debt financing. Second, failure to meet debt obligations can result in bankruptcy. This is not good for the firm, and it may be an added cost of debt financing. Since we haven't explicitly considered either of these two features of debt, we realize that we may get a different answer about capital structure once we do. Accordingly, we consider taxes in this section and bankruptcy in the next one.

We can start by considering what happens to M&M Propositions I and II when we consider the effect of corporate taxes. To do this, we will examine two firms, Firm U (unlevered) and Firm L (levered). These two firms are identical on the left-hand side of the balance sheet, so their assets and operations are the same.

We assume that EBIT is expected to be $1,000 every year forever for both firms. The difference between the firms is that Firm L has issued $1,000 worth of perpetual bonds on which it pays 8 percent interest each year. The interest bill is thus .08 × $1,000 = $80 every year forever. Also, we assume that the corporate tax rate is 30 percent.

For our two firms, U and L, we can now calculate the following:

	Firm U	Firm L
EBIT	$1,000	$1,000
Interest	0	80
Taxable income	$1,000	$ 920
Taxes (30%)	300	276
Net income	$ 700	$ 644

The Interest Tax Shield

To simplify things, we will assume that depreciation is zero. We will also assume that capital spending is zero and that there are no changes in NWC. In this case, cash flow from assets is simply equal to EBIT − Taxes. For Firms U and L, we thus have:

Cash Flow from Assets	Firm U	Firm L
EBIT	$1,000	$1,000
− Taxes	300	276
Total	$ 700	$ 724

We immediately see that capital structure is now having some effect because the cash flows from U and L are not the same even though the two firms have identical assets.

To see what's going on, we can compute the cash flow to stockholders and bondholders.

Cash Flow	Firm U	Firm L
To stockholders	$700	$644
To bondholders	0	80
Total	$700	$724

What we are seeing is that the total cash flow to L is $24 more. This occurs because L's tax bill (which is a cash outflow) is $24 less. The fact that interest is deductible for tax purposes has generated a tax saving equal to the interest payment ($80) multiplied by the corporate tax rate (30 percent): $80 × .30 = $24. We call this tax saving the **interest tax shield**.

interest tax shield
The tax saving attained by a firm from interest expense.

Taxes and M&M Proposition I

Because the debt is perpetual, the same $24 shield will be generated every year forever. The aftertax cash flow to L will thus be the same $700 that U earns plus the $24 tax shield. Because L's cash flow is always $24 greater, Firm L is worth more than Firm U, the difference being the value of this $24 perpetuity.

Because the tax shield is generated by paying interest, it has the same risk as the debt, and 8 percent (the cost of debt) is therefore the appropriate discount rate. The value of the tax shield is thus:

$$\text{PV} = \frac{\$24}{.08} = \frac{.30 \times \$1{,}000 \times .08}{.08} = .30(\$1{,}000) = \$300$$

As our example illustrates, the present value of the interest tax shield can be written as:

$$\begin{aligned}\text{Present value of the interest tax shield} &= (T_C \times D \times R_D)/R_D \\ &= T_C \times D\end{aligned} \qquad [17.2]$$

We have now come up with another famous result, M&M Proposition I with corporate taxes. We have seen that the value of Firm L, V_L, exceeds the value of Firm U, V_U, by the present value of the interest tax shield, $T_C \times D$. M&M Proposition I with taxes therefore states that:

$$V_L = V_U + T_C \times D \qquad [17.3]$$

The effect of borrowing in this case is illustrated in Figure 17.4. We have plotted the value of the levered firm, V_L, against the amount of debt, D. M&M Proposition I with corporate taxes implies that the relationship is given by a straight line with a slope of T_C and a y-intercept of V_U.

In Figure 17.4, we have also drawn a horizontal line representing V_U. As indicated, the distance between the two lines is $T_C \times D$, the present value of the tax shield.

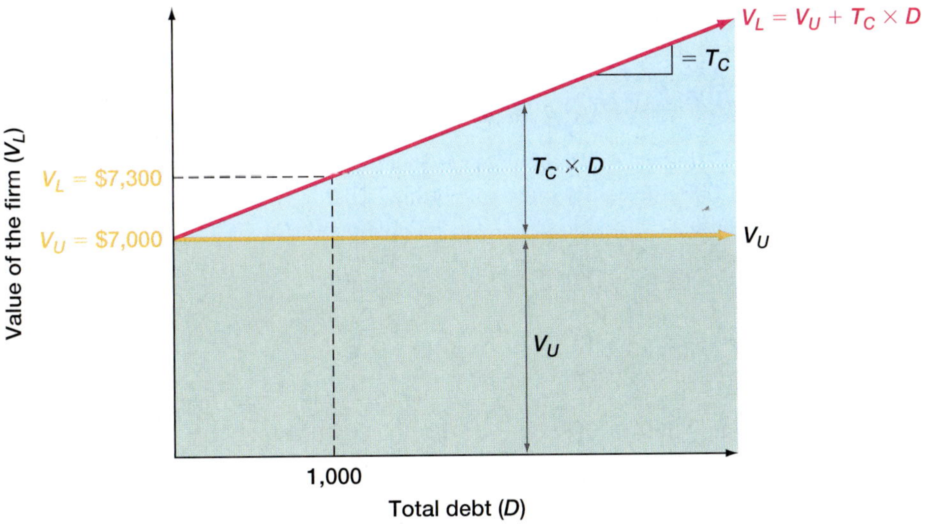

<< FIGURE 17.4

M&M Proposition I With Taxes

The value of the firm increases as total debt increases because of the interest tax shield. This is the basis of M&M Proposition I with taxes.

Suppose that the cost of capital for Firm U is 10 percent. We will call this the **unlevered cost of capital**, and we will use the symbol R_U to represent it. We can think of R_U as the cost of capital a firm would have if it had no debt. Firm U's cash flow is \$700 every year forever, and, because U has no debt, the appropriate discount rate is $R_U = 10\%$. The value of the unlevered firm, V_U, is simply:

unlevered cost of capital
The cost of capital of a firm that has no debt.

$$V_U = \frac{\text{EBIT} \times (1 - T_C)}{R_U}$$
$$= \frac{\$700}{.10}$$
$$= \$7{,}000$$

The value of the levered firm, V_L, is:

$$V_L = V_U + T_C \times D$$
$$= \$7{,}000 + .30 \times 1{,}000$$
$$= \$7{,}300$$

As Figure 17.4 indicates, the value of the firm goes up by \$.30 for every \$1 in debt. In other words, the NPV *per dollar* of debt is \$.30. It is difficult to imagine why any corporation would not borrow to the absolute maximum under these circumstances.

The result of our analysis in this section is the realization that, once we include taxes, capital structure definitely matters. However, we immediately reach the illogical conclusion that the optimal capital structure is 100 percent debt.

Taxes, the WACC, and Proposition II

The conclusion that the best capital structure is 100 percent debt also can be reached by examining the weighted average cost of capital. From our previous chapter, we know that, once we consider the effect of taxes, the WACC is:

$$\text{WACC} = (E/V) \times R_E + (D/V) \times R_D \times (1 - T_C)$$

To calculate this WACC, we need to know the cost of equity. M&M Proposition II with corporate taxes states that the cost of equity is:

$$R_E = R_U + (R_U - R_D) \times (D/E) \times (1 - T_C) \quad [17.4]$$

To illustrate, recall that we saw a moment ago that Firm L is worth $7,300 total. Because the debt is worth $1,000, the equity must be worth $7,300 − 1,000 = $6,300. For Firm L, the cost of equity is thus:

$$R_E = .10 + (.10 - .08) \times (\$1{,}000/6{,}300) \times (1 - .30)$$
$$= 10.22\%$$

The weighted average cost of capital is:

$$\text{WACC} = (\$6{,}300/7{,}300) \times 10.22\% + (1{,}000/7{,}300) \times 8\% \times (1 - .30)$$
$$= 9.6\%$$

Without debt, the WACC is over 10 percent, and, with debt, it is 9.6 percent. Therefore, the firm is better off with debt.

Conclusion

Figure 17.5 summarizes our discussion concerning the relationship between the cost of equity, the aftertax cost of debt, and the weighted average cost of capital. For reference, we have included R_U, the unlevered cost of capital. In Figure 17.5, we have the debt-equity ratio

FIGURE 17.5 >>

The Cost of Equity and the WACC: M&M Proposition II with Taxes

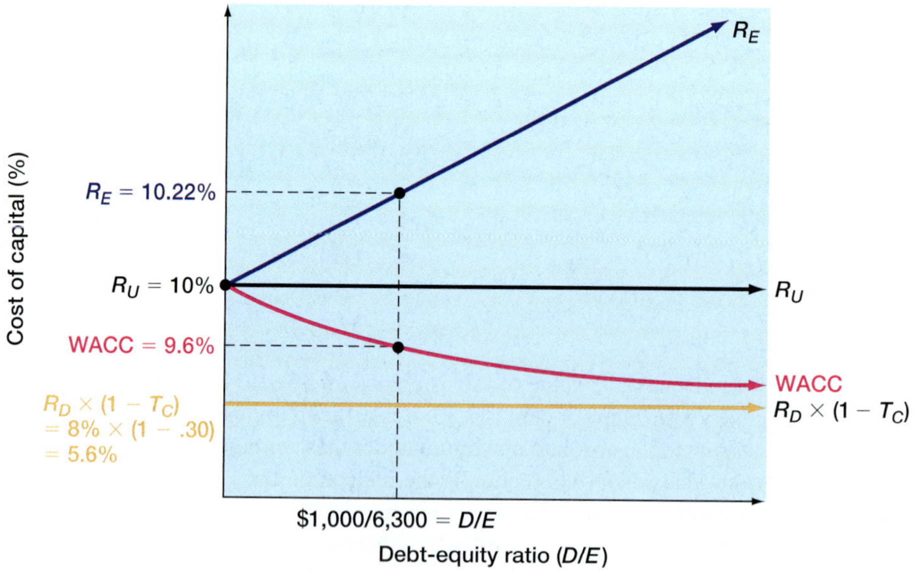

M&M Proposition I with taxes implies that a firm's WACC decreases as the firm relies more heavily on debt financing:

$$\text{WACC} = \left(\frac{E}{V}\right) \times R_E + \left(\frac{D}{V}\right) \times R_D \times (1 - T_C)$$

M&M Proposition II with taxes implies that a firm's cost of equity R_E, rises as the firm relies more heavily on debt financing:

$$R_E = R_U + (R_U - R_D) \times (D/E) \times (1 - T_C)$$

on the horizontal axis. Notice how the WACC declines as the debt-equity ratio grows. This illustrates again that the more debt the firm uses, the lower is its WACC. Table 17.6 summarizes the key results of our analysis of the M&M propositions for future reference.

The Cost of Equity and the Value of the Firm

<< EXAMPLE 17.4

This is a comprehensive example that illustrates most of the points we have discussed thus far. You are given the following information for the Format Co.:

$$\text{EBIT} = \$151.52$$
$$T_C = .34$$
$$D = \$500$$
$$R_U = .20$$

The cost of debt capital is 10 percent. What is the value of Format's equity? What is the cost of equity capital for Format? What is the WACC?

This one's easier than it looks. Remember that all the cash flows are perpetuities. The value of the firm if it has no debt, V_U, is:

$$V_U = \frac{\text{EBIT} - \text{Taxes}}{R_U} = \frac{\text{EBIT} \times (1 - T_C)}{R_U}$$
$$= \frac{\$100}{.20}$$
$$= \$500$$

From M&M Proposition I with taxes, we know that the value of the firm with debt is:

$$V_L = V_U + T_C \times D$$
$$= \$500 + .34 \times 500$$
$$= \$670$$

Because the firm is worth $670 total and the debt is worth $500, the equity is worth $170:

$$E = V_L - D$$
$$= \$670 - 500$$
$$= \$170$$

Based on M&M Proposition II with taxes, the cost of equity is:

$$R_E = R_U + (R_U - R_D) \times (D/E) \times (1 - T_C)$$
$$= .20 + (.20 - .10) \times (\$500/170) \times (1 - .34)$$
$$= 39.4\%$$

Finally, the WACC is:

$$\text{WACC} = (\$170/670) \times 39.4\% + (500/670) \times 10\% \times (1 - .34)$$
$$= 14.92\%$$

Notice that this is substantially lower than the cost of capital for the firm with no debt (R_U = 20%), so debt financing is highly advantageous.

TABLE 17.6 >>

Modigliani and Miller Summary

I. The No-Tax Case

A. Proposition I: The value of the firm levered (V_L) is equal to the value of the firm unlevered (V_U):

$$V_L = V_U$$

Implications of Proposition I:

1. A firm's capital structure is irrelevant.
2. A firm's weighted average cost of capital (WACC) is the same no matter what mixture of debt and equity is used to finance the firm.

B. Proposition II: The cost of equity, R_E, is:

$$R_E = R_A + (R_A - R_D) \times (D/E)$$

where R_A is the WACC, R_D is the cost of debt, and D/E is the debt-equity ratio.

Implications of Proposition II:

1. The cost of equity rises as the firm increases its use of debt financing.
2. The risk of the equity depends on two things: the riskiness of the firm's operations *(business risk)* and the degree of financial leverage *(financial risk).* Business risk determines R_A; financial risk is determined by D/E.

II. The Tax Case

A. Proposition I with taxes: The value of the firm levered (V_L) is equal to the value of the firm unlevered (V_U) plus the present value of the interest tax shield:

$$V_L = V_U + T_C \times D$$

where T_C is the corporate tax rate and D is the amount of debt.

Implications of Proposition I:

1. Debt financing is highly advantageous, and, in the extreme, a firm's optimal capital structure is 100 percent debt.
2. A firm's weighted average cost of capital (WACC) decreases as the firm relies more heavily on debt financing.

B. Proposition II with taxes: The cost of equity, R_E, is:

$$R_E = R_U + (R_U - R_D) \times (D/E) \times (1 - T_C)$$

where R_U is the *unlevered cost of capital,* that is, the cost of capital for the firm if it has no debt. Unlike the case with Proposition I, the general implications of Proposition II are the same whether there are taxes or not.

Concept Questions

17.4a What is the relationship between the value of an unlevered firm and the value of a levered firm once we consider the effect of corporate taxes?

17.4b If we only consider the effect of taxes, what is the optimal capital structure?

17.5 BANKRUPTCY COSTS

One limiting factor affecting the amount of debt a firm might use comes in the form of *bankruptcy costs.* As the debt-equity ratio rises, so too does the probability that the firm will be unable to pay its bondholders what was promised to them. When this happens, ownership of the firm's assets is ultimately transferred from the stockholders to the bondholders.

In principle, a firm becomes bankrupt when the value of its assets equals the value of its debt. When this occurs, the value of equity is zero, and the stockholders turn over control of the firm to the bondholders. When this takes place, the bondholders hold assets whose value is exactly equal to what is owed on the debt. In a perfect world, there are no costs associated with this transfer of ownership, and the bondholders don't lose anything.

This idealized view of bankruptcy is not, of course, what happens in the real world. Ironically, it is expensive to go bankrupt. As we discuss, the costs associated with bankruptcy may eventually offset the tax-related gains from leverage.

Direct Bankruptcy Costs

When the value of a firm's assets equals the value of its debt, then the firm is economically bankrupt in the sense that the equity has no value. However, the formal turning over of the assets to the bondholders is a *legal* process, not an economic one. There are legal and administrative costs to bankruptcy, and it has been remarked that bankruptcies are to lawyers what blood is to sharks.

For example, in December of 2001, energy products giant Enron filed for bankruptcy in the largest U.S. bankruptcy to date. Over two years later, in July of 2004, the company was still trying to emerge from bankruptcy. Its latest reorganization plan called for creditors of the company to receive 70 percent of what they were owed in stock and 30 percent in cash. Creditors of companies owned entirely by Enron would receive from about 23 percent to 17 percent of what was owed them. Just to give you an idea of the direct costs that can be associated with bankruptcy proceedings, in the first 30 months of bankruptcy, Enron spent about $665 million on lawyers, accountants, consultants, and examiners, and the final tally will probably be much larger.

Because of the expenses associated with bankruptcy, bondholders won't get all that they are owed. Some fraction of the firm's assets will "disappear" in the legal process of going bankrupt. These are the legal and administrative expenses associated with the bankruptcy proceeding. We call these costs **direct bankruptcy costs**.

These direct bankruptcy costs are a disincentive to debt financing. If a firm goes bankrupt, then, suddenly, a piece of the firm disappears. This amounts to a bankruptcy "tax." So a firm faces a trade-off: borrowing saves a firm money on its corporate taxes, but the more a firm borrows, the more likely it is that the firm will become bankrupt and have to pay the bankruptcy tax.

direct bankruptcy costs
The costs that are directly associated with bankruptcy, such as legal and administrative expenses.

Indirect Bankruptcy Costs

Because it is expensive to go bankrupt, a firm will spend resources to avoid doing so. When a firm is having significant problems in meeting its debt obligations, we say that it is experiencing financial distress. Some financially distressed firms ultimately file for bankruptcy, but most do not because they are able to recover or otherwise survive.

For example, in 2004, most of the older, larger airlines in the United States were in financial distress. United Airlines was already in bankruptcy. In May 2004, US Airways announced that it might seek bankruptcy protection. The company stated that its employee costs were not competitive with newer discount carriers such as America West and JetBlue Airways. Management said that if employees did not agree to wage concessions, the company would be forced back to bankruptcy court, even though it had emerged from bankruptcy only 13 months earlier. Similar problems existed at Delta Air Lines. Analysts estimated the company would be able to operate for only another six months unless wage concessions were reached with employees, particularly pilots. The company and its creditors had already met to attempt to find a way in which the company could avoid bankruptcy. Whether Delta and US Airways ultimately go bankrupt remains to be seen as this is written, but it is clear that the companies are expending significant time and resources to avoid that outcome.

The costs of avoiding a bankruptcy filing incurred by a financially distressed firm are called **indirect bankruptcy costs**. We use the term **financial distress costs** to refer

indirect bankruptcy costs
The costs of avoiding a bankruptcy filing incurred by a financially distressed firm.

financial distress costs
The direct and indirect costs associated with going bankrupt or experiencing financial distress.

generically to the direct and indirect costs associated with going bankrupt and/or avoiding a bankruptcy filing.

The problems that come up in financial distress are particularly severe, and the financial distress costs are thus larger, when the stockholders and the bondholders are different groups. Until the firm is legally bankrupt, the stockholders control it. They, of course, will take actions in their own economic interests. Because the stockholders can be wiped out in a legal bankruptcy, they have a very strong incentive to avoid a bankruptcy filing.

The bondholders, on the other hand, are primarily concerned with protecting the value of the firm's assets and will try to take control away from stockholders. They have a strong incentive to seek bankruptcy to protect their interests and keep stockholders from further dissipating the assets of the firm. The net effect of all this fighting is that a long, drawn-out, and potentially quite expensive legal battle gets started.

Meanwhile, as the wheels of justice turn in their ponderous way, the assets of the firm lose value because management is busy trying to avoid bankruptcy instead of running the business. Normal operations are disrupted, and sales are lost. Valuable employees leave, potentially fruitful programs are dropped to preserve cash, and otherwise profitable investments are not taken.

These are all indirect bankruptcy costs, or costs of financial distress. Whether or not the firm ultimately goes bankrupt, the net effect is a loss of value because the firm chose to use debt in its capital structure. It is this possibility of loss that limits the amount of debt that a firm will choose to use.

Concept Questions

17.5a What are direct bankruptcy costs?

17.5b What are indirect bankruptcy costs?

17.6 OPTIMAL CAPITAL STRUCTURE

Our previous two sections have established the basis for determining an optimal capital structure. A firm will borrow because the interest tax shield is valuable. At relatively low debt levels, the probability of bankruptcy and financial distress is low, and the benefit from debt outweighs the cost. At very high debt levels, the possibility of financial distress is a chronic, ongoing problem for the firm, so the benefit from debt financing may be more than offset by the financial distress costs. Based on our discussion, it would appear that an optimal capital structure exists somewhere in between these extremes.

The Static Theory of Capital Structure

static theory of capital structure The theory that a firm borrows up to the point where the tax benefit from an extra dollar in debt is exactly equal to the cost that comes from the increased probability of financial distress.

The theory of capital structure that we have outlined is called the **static theory of capital structure**. It says that firms borrow up to the point where the tax benefit from an extra dollar in debt is exactly equal to the cost that comes from the increased probability of financial distress. We call this the static theory because it assumes that the firm is fixed in terms of its assets and operations and it only considers possible changes in the debt-equity ratio.

The static theory is illustrated in Figure 17.6, which plots the value of the firm, V_L, against the amount of debt, D. In Figure 17.6, we have drawn lines corresponding to three different stories. The first represents M&M Proposition I with no taxes. This is the horizontal line extending from V_U, and it indicates that the value of the firm is unaffected by its

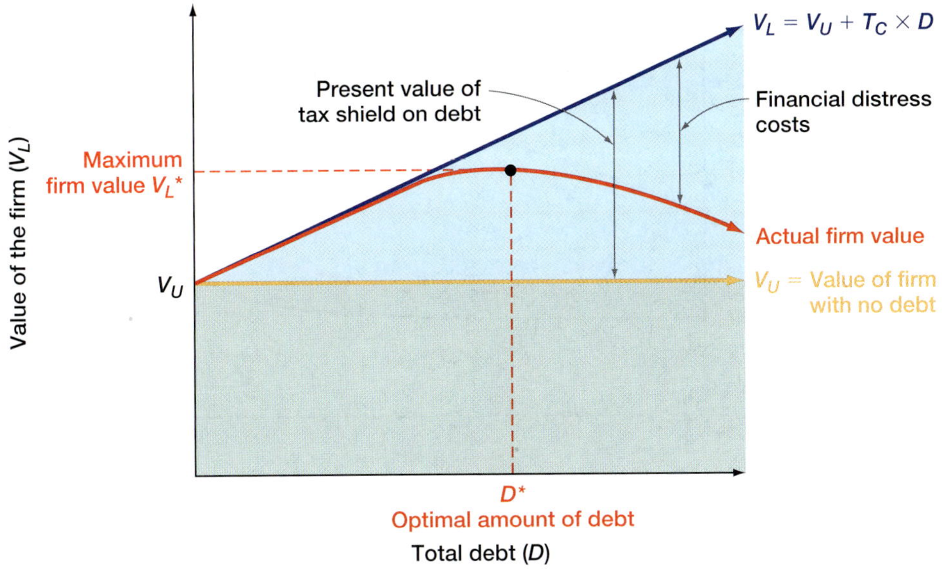

<< FIGURE 17.6

The Static Theory of Capital Structure: The Optimal Capital Structure and the Value of the Firm

According to the static theory, the gain from the tax shield on debt is offset by financial distress costs. An optimal capital structure exists that just balances the additional gain from leverage against the added financial distress cost.

capital structure. The second case, M&M Proposition I with corporate taxes, is represented by the upward-sloping straight line. These two cases are exactly the same as the ones we previously illustrated in Figure 17.4.

The third case in Figure 17.6 illustrates our current discussion: The value of the firm rises to a maximum and then declines beyond that point. This is the picture that we get from our static theory. The maximum value of the firm, V_L*, is reached at D*, so this point represents the optimal amount of borrowing. Put another way, the firm's optimal capital structure is composed of D^*/V_L^* in debt and $(1 - D^*/V_L^*)$ in equity.

The final thing to notice in Figure 17.6 is that the difference between the value of the firm in our static theory and the M&M value of the firm with taxes is the loss in value from the possibility of financial distress. Also, the difference between the static theory value of the firm and the M&M value with no taxes is the gain from leverage, net of distress costs.

Optimal Capital Structure and the Cost of Capital

As we discussed earlier, the capital structure that maximizes the value of the firm is also the one that minimizes the cost of capital. Figure 17.7 illustrates the static theory of capital structure in terms of the weighted average cost of capital and the costs of debt and equity. Notice in Figure 17.7 that we have plotted the various capital costs against the debt-equity ratio, D/E.

Figure 17.7 is much the same as Figure 17.5 except that we have added a new line for the WACC. This line, which corresponds to the static theory, declines at first. This occurs because the aftertax cost of debt is cheaper than equity, so, at least initially, the overall cost of capital declines.

At some point, the cost of debt begins to rise, and the fact that debt is cheaper than equity is more than offset by the financial distress costs. From this point, further increases in debt actually increase the WACC. As illustrated, the minimum WACC* occurs at the point D^*/E^*, just as we described before.

FIGURE 17.7 >>

The Static Theory of Capital Structure: The Optimal Capital Structure and the Cost of Capital

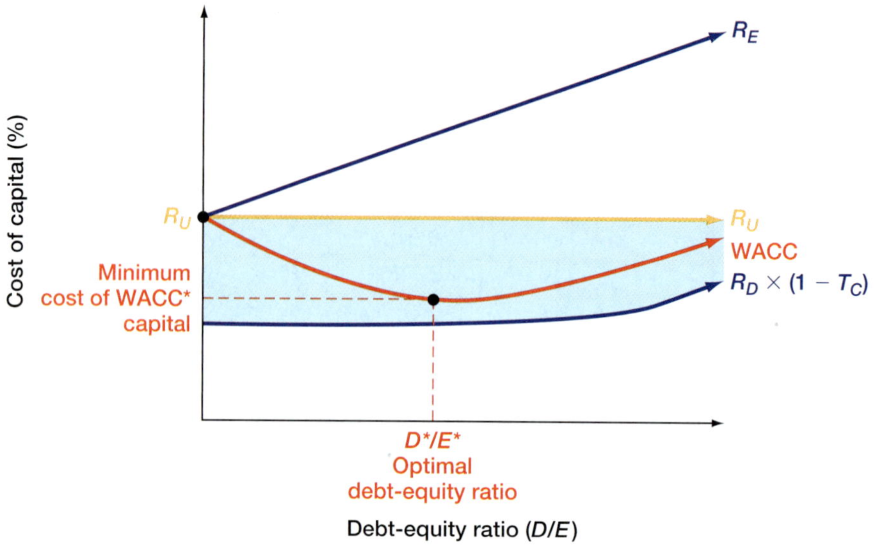

According to the static theory, the WACC falls initially because of the tax advantage of debt. Beyond the point D^*/E^*, it begins to rise because of financial distress costs.

Optimal Capital Structure: A Recap

With the help of Figure 17.8, we can recap (no pun intended) our discussion of capital structure and cost of capital. As we have noted, there are essentially three cases. We will use the simplest of the three cases as a starting point and then build up to the static theory of capital structure. Along the way, we will pay particular attention to the connection between capital structure, firm value, and cost of capital.

Figure 17.8 presents the original Modigliani and Miller no-tax, no-bankruptcy argument as Case I. This is the most basic case. In the top part of the figure, we have plotted the value of the firm, V_L, against total debt, D. When there are no taxes, bankruptcy costs, or other real-world imperfections, we know that the total value of the firm is not affected by its debt policy, so V_L is simply constant. The bottom part of Figure 17.8 tells the same story in terms of the cost of capital. Here, the weighted average cost of capital, WACC, is plotted against the debt-to-equity ratio, D/E. As with total firm value, the overall cost of capital is not affected by debt policy in this basic case, so the WACC is constant.

Next, we consider what happens to the original M&M argument once taxes are introduced. As Case II illustrates, we now see that the firm's value critically depends on its debt policy. The more the firm borrows, the more it is worth. From our earlier discussion, we know this happens because interest payments are tax deductible, and the gain in firm value is just equal to the present value of the interest tax shield.

In the bottom part of Figure 17.8, notice how the WACC declines as the firm uses more and more debt financing. As the firm increases its financial leverage, the cost of equity does increase, but this increase is more than offset by the tax break associated with debt financing. As a result, the firm's overall cost of capital declines.

To finish our story, we include the impact of bankruptcy or financial distress costs to get Case III. As shown in the top part of Figure 17.8, the value of the firm will not be as large as we previously indicated. The reason is that the firm's value is reduced by the present value of the potential future bankruptcy costs. These costs grow as the firm borrows more and more, and they eventually overwhelm the tax advantage of debt financing. The optimal

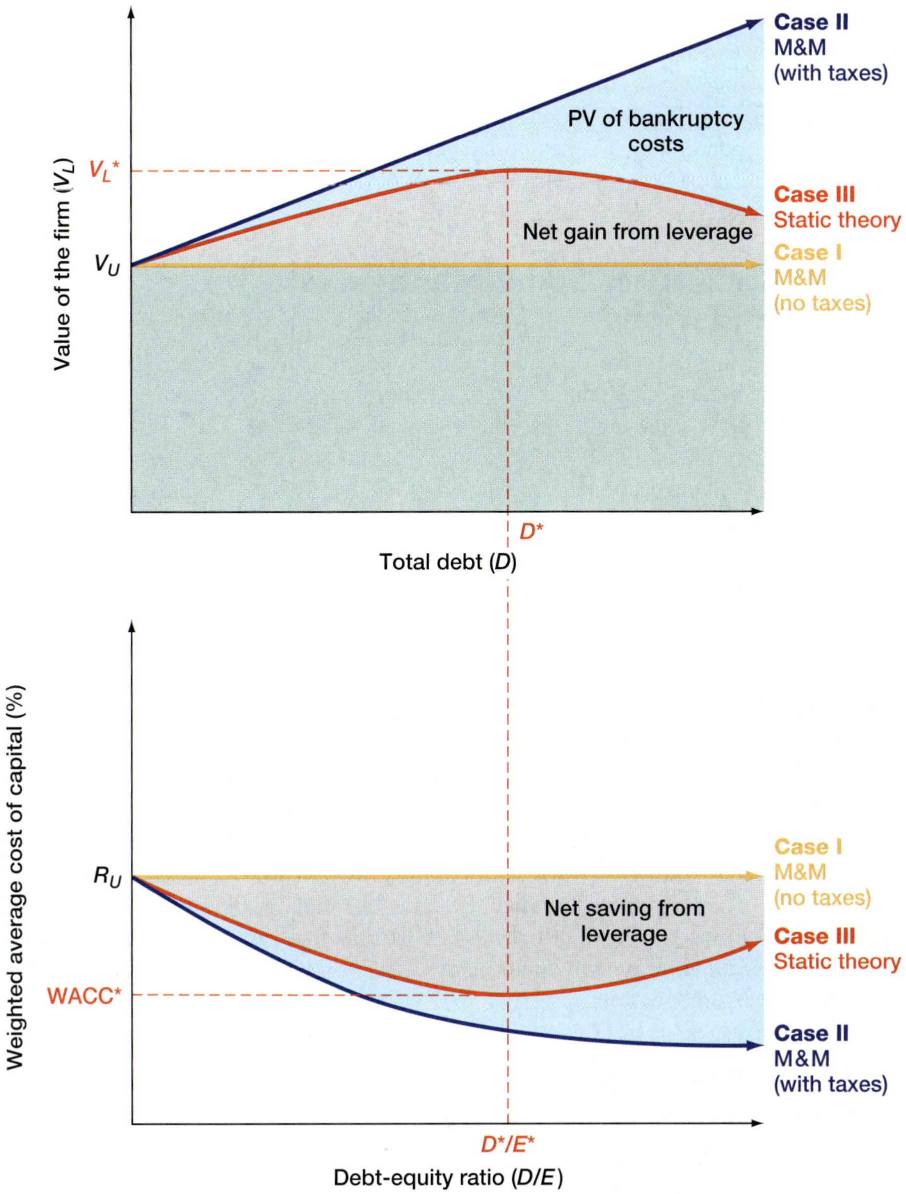

<< FIGURE 17.8

The Capital Structure Question

Case I
With no taxes or bankruptcy costs, the value of the firm and its weighted average cost of capital are not affected by capital structures.

Case II
With corporate taxes and no bankruptcy costs, the value of the firm increases and the weighted average cost of capital decreases as the amount of debt goes up.

Case III
With corporate taxes and bankruptcy costs, the value of the firm, V_L, reaches a maximum at D^*, the point representing the optimal amount of borrowing. At the same time, the weighted average cost of capital, WACC, is minimized at D^*/E^*.

capital structure occurs at D^*, the point at which the tax saving from an additional dollar in debt financing is exactly balanced by the increased bankruptcy costs associated with the additional borrowing. This is the essence of the static theory of capital structure.

The bottom part of Figure 17.8 presents the optimal capital structure in terms of the cost of capital. Corresponding to D^*, the optimal debt level, is the optimal debt-to-equity ratio, D^*/E^*. At this level of debt financing, the lowest possible weighted average cost of capital, WACC*, occurs.

Capital Structure: Some Managerial Recommendations

The static model that we have described is not capable of identifying a precise optimal capital structure, but it does point out two of the more relevant factors: taxes and financial distress. We can draw some limited conclusions concerning these.

Taxes First of all, the tax benefit from leverage is obviously only important to firms that are in a tax-paying position. Firms with substantial accumulated losses will get little value from the interest tax shield. Furthermore, firms that have substantial tax shields from other sources, such as depreciation, will get less benefit from leverage.

Also, not all firms have the same tax rate. The higher the tax rate, the greater the incentive to borrow.

Financial Distress Firms with a greater risk of experiencing financial distress will borrow less than firms with a lower risk of financial distress. For example, all other things being equal, the greater the volatility in EBIT, the less a firm should borrow.

In addition, financial distress is more costly for some firms than others. The costs of financial distress depend primarily on the firm's assets. In particular, financial distress costs will be determined by how easily ownership of those assets can be transferred.

For example, a firm with mostly tangible assets that can be sold without great loss in value will have an incentive to borrow more. For firms that rely heavily on intangibles, such as employee talent or growth opportunities, debt will be less attractive because these assets effectively cannot be sold.

Concept Questions

17.6a Can you describe the trade-off that defines the static theory of capital structure?

17.6b What are the important factors in making capital structure decisions?

17.7 THE PIE AGAIN

Although it is comforting to know that the firm might have an optimal capital structure when we take account of such real-world matters as taxes and financial distress costs, it is disquieting to see the elegant original M&M intuition (that is, the no-tax version) fall apart in the face of these matters.

Critics of the M&M theory often say that it fails to hold as soon as we add in real-world issues and that the M&M theory is really just that, a theory that doesn't have much to say about the real world that we live in. In fact, they would argue that it is the M&M theory that is irrelevant, not capital structure. As we discuss next, however, taking that view blinds critics to the real value of the M&M theory.

The Extended Pie Model

To illustrate the value of the original M&M intuition, we briefly consider an expanded version of the pie model that we introduced earlier. In the extended pie model, taxes just represent another claim on the cash flows of the firm. Because taxes are reduced as leverage is increased, the value of the government's claim (G) on the firm's cash flows decreases with leverage.

Bankruptcy costs are also a claim on the cash flows. They come into play as the firm comes close to bankruptcy and has to alter its behavior to attempt to stave off the event itself, and they become large when bankruptcy actually takes place. Thus, the value of this claim (B) on the cash flows rises with the debt-equity ratio.

The extended pie theory simply holds that all of these claims can be paid from only one source, the cash flows (CF) of the firm. Algebraically, we must have:

CF = Payments to stockholders + Payments to creditors
 + Payments to the government
 + Payments to bankruptcy courts and lawyers
 + Payments to any and all other claimants to the cash flows of the firm

The extended pie model is illustrated in Figure 17.9. Notice that we have added a few slices for the additional groups. Notice also the change in the relative sizes of the slices as the firm's use of debt financing is increased.

With the list we have developed, we have not even begun to exhaust the potential claims to the firm's cash flows. To give an unusual example, we might say that everyone reading this book has an economic claim on the cash flows of General Motors. After all, if you are injured in an accident, you might sue GM, and, win or lose, GM will expend some of its cash flow in dealing with the matter. For GM, or any other company, there should thus be a slice of the pie representing potential lawsuits. This is the essence of the M&M intuition and theory: The value of the firm depends on the total cash flow of the firm. The firm's capital structure just cuts that cash flow up into slices without altering the total. What we recognize now is that the stockholders and the bondholders may not be the only ones who can claim a slice.

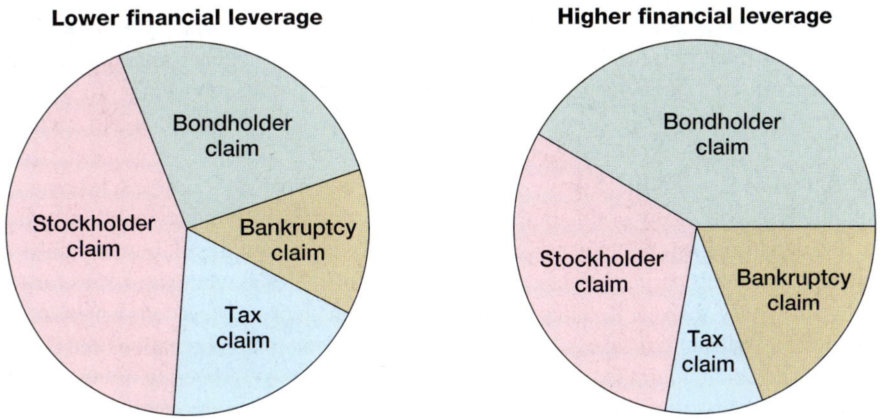

<< FIGURE 17.9

The Extended Pie Model

In the extended pie model, the value of all the claims against the firm's cash flows is not affected by capital structure, but the *relative* values of claims change as the amount of debt financing is increased.

Marketed Claims versus Nonmarketed Claims

With our extended pie model, there is an important distinction between claims such as those of stockholders and bondholders, on the one hand, and those of the government and potential litigants in lawsuits on the other. The first set of claims are *marketed claims,* and the second set are *nonmarketed claims.* A key difference is that the marketed claims can be bought and sold in financial markets and the nonmarketed claims cannot.

When we speak of the value of the firm, we are generally referring to just the value of the marketed claims, V_M, and not the value of the nonmarketed claims, V_N. If we write V_T for the total value of *all* the claims against a corporation's cash flows, then:

$$\begin{aligned} V_T &= E + D + G + B + \cdots \\ &= V_M + V_N \end{aligned}$$

The essence of our extended pie model is that this total value, V_T, of all the claims to the firm's cash flows is unaltered by capital structure. However, the value of the marketed claims, V_M, may be affected by changes in the capital structure.

Based on the pie theory, any increase in V_M must imply an identical decrease in V_N. The optimal capital structure is thus the one that maximizes the value of the marketed claims, or, equivalently, minimizes the value of nonmarketed claims such as taxes and bankruptcy costs.

Concept Questions

17.7a What are some of the claims to a firm's cash flows?

17.7b What is the difference between a marketed claim and a nonmarketed claim?

17.7c What does the extended pie model say about the value of all the claims to a firm's cash flows?

17.8 OBSERVED CAPITAL STRUCTURES

No two firms have identical capital structures. Nonetheless, there are some regular elements that we see when we start looking at actual capital structures. We discuss a few of these next.

The most striking thing we observe about capital structures, particularly in the United States, is that most corporations seem to have relatively low debt-equity ratios. In fact, most corporations use much less debt financing than equity financing. To illustrate, Table 17.7 presents median debt ratios and debt-equity ratios for various U.S. industries classified by SIC code (we discussed such codes in Chapter 3).

In Table 17.7, what is most striking is the wide variation across industries, ranging from essentially no debt for drug and computer companies to relatively heavy debt usage in the steel and department store industries. Notice that these last two industries are the only ones for which more debt is used than equity, and most of the other industries rely far more heavily on equity than debt. This is true even though many of the companies in these industries pay substantial taxes. Table 17.7 makes it clear that corporations have not, in general, issued debt up to the point that tax shelters have been completely used up, and we conclude that there must be limits to the amount of debt corporations can use. Take a look at our nearby *Work the Web* box for more on actual capital structures.

Because different industries have different operating characteristics in terms of, for example, EBIT volatility and asset types, there does appear to be some connection between these characteristics and capital structure. Our story involving tax savings and financial

Industry	Ratio of Debt to Total Capital*	Ratio of Debt to Equity	Number of Companies	SIC Code	Representative Companies
Dairy products	13.18%	15.47%	8	202	Ben and Jerry's, Dreyer's
Fabric apparel	23.04	29.93	38	23	VF Corp., Jones Apparel
Paper	37.09	58.99	30	26	Kimberly-Clark, Fort James
Drugs	2.75	2.83	161	283	Pfizer, Warner-Lambert
Petroleum refining	30.32	43.55	12	29	ExxonMobil, USX-Marathon
Rubber footwear	28.51	41.22	6	302	Nike, Reebok
Steel	55.84	126.46	28	331	Nucor, USX-US Steel
Computers	6.91	7.42	90	357	Cisco, Dell
Motor vehicles	41.59	71.21	39	371	Ford, General Motors
Aircraft	16.97	20.44	5	372	Boeing
Airlines	47.50	90.49	17	4512	Delta, Southwest
Cable television	39.77	68.66	8	484	Cablevision Sys, Cox Communications
Electric utilities	49.86	99.43	54	491	Southern Co.
Department stores	50.53	110.43	8	531	Sears, Kohl's
Eating places	28.31	39.49	62	5812	McDonald's, Wendy's

<< **TABLE 17.7**

Capital Structures for U.S. Industries

*Debt is the book value of preferred stock and long-term debt, including amounts due in one year. Equity is the market value of outstanding shares. Total capital is the sum of debt and equity. Median values are shown.

SOURCE: *Cost of Capital,* 2000 Yearbook (Chicago: Ibbotson Associates, Inc., 2000)

WORK THE WEB

When it comes to capital structure, all companies (and industries) are not created equal. To illustrate, we looked up some capital structure information on Allied Waste Industries (AW) and Johnson & Johnson (JNJ) using the Ratio Comparison area of yahoo.investor.reuters.com. Allied Waste's capital structure looks like this:

Financial Strength	Company	Industry	Sector	S&P 500
Quick Ratio (MRQ)	0.55	0.74	0.93	1.27
Current Ratio (MRQ)	0.69	0.94	1.48	1.78
LT Debt to Equity (MRQ)	3.08	1.47	0.69	0.66
Total Debt to Equity (MRQ)	3.13	1.57	0.79	0.83
Interest Coverage (TTM)	1.19	3.97	7.97	12.07

For every dollar of equity, Allied has long-term debt of \$3.08 and total debt of \$3.13. Compare this result to Johnson & Johnson:

Financial Strength	Company	Industry	Sector	S&P 500
Quick Ratio (MRQ)	1.38	1.10	1.96	1.27
Current Ratio (MRQ)	1.96	1.61	2.61	1.78
LT Debt to Equity (MRQ)	0.10	0.28	0.32	0.66
Total Debt to Equity (MRQ)	0.13	0.38	0.40	0.83
Interest Coverage (TTM)	51.86	20.24	15.25	12.07

For every dollar of equity, Johnson & Johnson has only \$0.10 of long-term debt and total debt of \$0.13. When we examine the industry and sector averages, the differences are again apparent. Although the choice of capital structure is a management decision, it is clearly influenced by industry characteristics.

distress costs undoubtedly supplies part of the reason, but, to date, there is no fully satisfactory theory that explains these regularities in capital structures.

Concept Questions

17.8a Do U.S. corporations rely heavily on debt financing?

17.8b What regularities do we observe in capital structures?

17.9 A QUICK LOOK AT THE BANKRUPTCY PROCESS

As we have discussed, one of the consequences of using debt is the possibility of financial distress, which can be defined in several ways:

1. *Business failure.* This term is usually used to refer to a situation in which a business has terminated with a loss to creditors, but even an all-equity firm can fail.
2. *Legal bankruptcy.* Firms or creditors bring petitions to a federal court for bankruptcy. **Bankruptcy** is a legal proceeding for liquidating or reorganizing a business.
3. *Technical insolvency.* Technical insolvency occurs when a firm is unable to meet its financial obligations.
4. *Accounting insolvency.* Firms with negative net worth are insolvent on the books. This happens when the total book liabilities exceed the book value of the total assets.

bankruptcy
A legal proceeding for liquidating or reorganizing a business.

The SEC has a good overview of the bankruptcy process in its "online publications" section: www.sec.gov.

We now very briefly discuss some of the terms and more relevant issues associated with bankruptcy and financial distress.

Liquidation and Reorganization

Firms that cannot or choose not to make contractually required payments to creditors have two basic options: liquidation or reorganization. **Liquidation** means termination of the firm as a going concern, and it involves selling off the assets of the firm. The proceeds, net of selling costs, are distributed to creditors in order of established priority. **Reorganization** is the option of keeping the firm a going concern; it often involves issuing new securities to replace old securities. Liquidation or reorganization is the result of a bankruptcy proceeding. Which occurs depends on whether the firm is worth more "dead or alive."

liquidation
Termination of the firm as a going concern.

reorganization
Financial restructuring of a failing firm to attempt to continue operations as a going concern.

Bankruptcy Liquidation Chapter 7 of the Federal Bankruptcy Reform Act of 1978 deals with "straight" liquidation. The following sequence of events is typical:

1. A petition is filed in a federal court. Corporations may file a voluntary petition, or involuntary petitions may be filed against the corporation by several of its creditors.
2. A trustee-in-bankruptcy is elected by the creditors to take over the assets of the debtor corporation. The trustee will attempt to liquidate the assets.
3. When the assets are liquidated, after payment of the bankruptcy administration costs, the proceeds are distributed among the creditors.
4. If any proceeds remain, after expenses and payments to creditors, they are distributed to the shareholders.

The distribution of the proceeds of the liquidation occurs according to the following priority list:

1. Administrative expenses associated with the bankruptcy
2. Other expenses arising after the filing of an involuntary bankruptcy petition but before the appointment of a trustee
3. Wages, salaries, and commissions
4. Contributions to employee benefit plans
5. Consumer claims
6. Government tax claims
7. Payment to unsecured creditors
8. Payment to preferred stockholders
9. Payment to common stockholders

This priority list for liquidation is a reflection of the **absolute priority rule (APR)**. The higher a claim is on this list, the more likely it is to be paid. In many of these categories, there are various limitations and qualifications that we omit for the sake of brevity.

absolute priority rule (APR)
The rule establishing priority of claims in liquidation.

Two qualifications to this list are in order. The first concerns secured creditors. Such creditors are entitled to the proceeds from the sale of the security and are outside this ordering. However, if the secured property is liquidated and provides cash insufficient to cover the amount owed, the secured creditors join with unsecured creditors in dividing the remaining liquidated value. In contrast, if the secured property is liquidated for proceeds greater than the secured claim, the net proceeds are used to pay unsecured creditors and others. The second qualification to the APR is that, in reality, what happens, and who gets what, in the event of bankruptcy is subject to much negotiation, and, as a result, the APR is frequently not followed.

Bankruptcy Reorganization Corporate reorganization takes place under Chapter 11 of the Federal Bankruptcy Reform Act of 1978. The general objective of a proceeding under Chapter 11 is to plan to restructure the corporation with some provision for repayment of creditors. A typical sequence of events follows:

Get the latest on bankruptcy at www.bankruptcydata.com.

1. A voluntary petition can be filed by the corporation, or an involuntary petition can be filed by creditors.
2. A federal judge either approves or denies the petition. If the petition is approved, a time for filing proofs of claims is set.
3. In most cases, the corporation (the "debtor in possession") continues to run the business.
4. The corporation (and, in certain cases, the creditors) submits a reorganization plan.
5. Creditors and shareholders are divided into classes. A class of creditors accepts the plan if a majority of the class agrees to the plan.
6. After its acceptance by creditors, the plan is confirmed by the court.
7. Payments in cash, property, and securities are made to creditors and shareholders. The plan may provide for the issuance of new securities.
8. For some fixed length of time, the firm operates according to the provisions of the reorganization plan.

The corporation may wish to allow the old stockholders to retain some participation in the firm. Needless to say, this may involve some protest by the holders of unsecured debt.

So-called prepackaged bankruptcies are a relatively common phenomenon. What happens is that the corporation secures the necessary approval of a bankruptcy plan from a majority of its creditors first, and then it files for bankruptcy. As a result, the company enters bankruptcy and reemerges almost immediately.

For example, MTS Inc., better known as Tower Records, filed for Chapter 11 bankruptcy in February 2004. The company claimed it would not be able to meet debt payments without affecting daily operations. The problems experienced by Tower were increased competition from retailers such as Wal-Mart, Virgin Megastores, and Best Buy, as well as both legal and illegal digital downloading (particularly by college students). Tower and its bondholders therefore began negotiating a prepackaged bankruptcy, or prepack, which amounts to agreeing to terms prior to the bankruptcy filing. Tower's bondholders agreed to eliminate $80 million of the company's debt in exchange for equity interest in the company. As a result of the prepack, MTS was able to exit the Chapter 11 bankruptcy process in about two months.

In some cases, the bankruptcy procedure is needed to invoke the "cram-down" power of the bankruptcy court. Under certain circumstances, a class of creditors can be forced to accept a bankruptcy plan even if they vote not to approve it, hence the remarkably apt description "cram down."

Financial Management and the Bankruptcy Process

It may seem a little odd, but the right to go bankrupt is very valuable. There are several reasons why this is true. First of all, from an operational standpoint, when a firm files for bankruptcy, there is an immediate "stay" on creditors, usually meaning that payments to creditors will cease, and creditors will have to await the outcome of the bankruptcy process to find out if and how much they will be paid. This stay gives the firm time to evaluate its options, and it prevents what is usually termed a "race to the courthouse steps" by creditors and others.

Beyond this, some bankruptcy filings are actually strategic actions intended to improve a firm's competitive position, and firms have filed for bankruptcy even though they were not insolvent at the time. Probably the most famous example is Continental Airlines. In 1983, following deregulation of the airline industry, Continental found itself competing with newly established airlines that had much lower labor costs. Continental filed for reorganization under Chapter 11 even though it was not insolvent.

Continental argued that, based on pro forma data, it would become insolvent in the future, and a reorganization was therefore necessary. By filing for bankruptcy, Continental was able to terminate its existing labor agreements, lay off large numbers of workers, and slash wages for the remaining employees. In other words, at least in the eyes of critics, Continental essentially used the bankruptcy process as a vehicle for reducing labor costs. Congress subsequently modified bankruptcy laws to make it more difficult, though not impossible, for companies to abrogate a labor contract through the bankruptcy process.

Other famous examples of strategic bankruptcies exist. For example, Manville (then known as Johns-Manville) and Dow Corning filed for bankruptcy because of expected future losses resulting from litigation associated with asbestos and silicone breast implants, respectively. In fact, by 2004, at least 70 companies had filed for Chapter 11 bankruptcy because of asbestos litigation. In 2000, for example, Owens Corning, known for its pink fiberglass insulation, threw in the towel after settling about 240,000 cases with no end in sight. As of June 2004, the company was still in bankruptcy. In that month, the company reached a tentative agreement to repay senior trade creditors, bondholders, and holders of bank debt an estimated 35.8 percent of the debt owed. Other well-known companies that filed for bankruptcy due to the asbestos nightmare include Congoleum, Federal Mogul, and two subsidiaries of Halliburton.

Agreements to Avoid Bankruptcy

When a firm defaults on an obligation, it can avoid a bankruptcy filing. Because the legal process of bankruptcy can be lengthy and expensive, it is often in everyone's best interest to devise a "workout" that avoids a bankruptcy filing. Much of the time, creditors can work with the management of a company that has defaulted on a loan contract. Voluntary arrangements to restructure or "reschedule" the company's debt can be and often are made. This may involve *extension,* which postpones the date of payment, or *composition,* which involves a reduced payment.

Concept Questions

17.9a What is the APR?

17.9b What is the difference between liquidation and reorganization?

SUMMARY AND CONCLUSIONS 17.10

The ideal mixture of debt and equity for a firm—its optimal capital structure—is the one that maximizes the value of the firm and minimizes the overall cost of capital. If we ignore taxes, financial distress costs, and any other imperfections, we find that there is no ideal mixture. Under these circumstances, the firm's capital structure is simply irrelevant.

If we consider the effect of corporate taxes, we find that capital structure matters a great deal. This conclusion is based on the fact that interest is tax deductible and thus generates a valuable tax shield. Unfortunately, we also find that the optimal capital structure is 100 percent debt, which is not something we observe in healthy firms.

We next introduce costs associated with bankruptcy, or, more generally, financial distress. These costs reduce the attractiveness of debt financing. We conclude that an optimal capital structure exists when the net tax saving from an additional dollar in interest just equals the increase in expected financial distress costs. This is the essence of the static theory of capital structure.

When we examine actual capital structures, we find two regularities. First, firms in the United States typically do not use great amounts of debt, but they pay substantial taxes. This suggests that there is a limit to the use of debt financing to generate tax shields. Second, firms in similar industries tend to have similar capital structures, suggesting that the nature of their assets and operations is an important determinant of capital structure.

Chapter Review and Self-Test Problems

17.1 EBIT and EPS Suppose the BDJ Corporation has decided in favor of a capital restructuring that involves increasing its existing $80 million in debt to $125 million. The interest rate on the debt is 9 percent and is not expected to change.

The firm currently has 10 million shares outstanding, and the price per share is \$45. If the restructuring is expected to increase the ROE, what is the minimum level for EBIT that BDJ's management must be expecting? Ignore taxes in your answer.

17.2 M&M Proposition II (no taxes) The Habitat Corporation has a WACC of 16 percent. Its cost of debt is 13 percent. If Habitat's debt-equity ratio is 2, what is its cost of equity capital? Ignore taxes in your answer.

17.3 M&M Proposition I (with corporate taxes) Gypco expects an EBIT of \$10,000 every year forever. Gypco can borrow at 7 percent. Suppose Gypco currently has no debt and its cost of equity is 17 percent. If the corporate tax rate is 35 percent, what is the value of the firm? What will the value be if Gypco borrows \$15,000 and uses the proceeds to repurchase stock?

Answers to Chapter Review and Self-Test Problems

17.1 To answer, we can calculate the break-even EBIT. At any EBIT above this, the increased financial leverage will increase EPS. Under the old capital structure, the interest bill is \$80 million × .09 = \$7,200,000. There are 10 million shares of stock, so, ignoring taxes, EPS is (EBIT − \$7.2 million)/10 million.

Under the new capital structure, the interest expense will be \$125 million × .09 = \$11.25 million. Furthermore, the debt rises by \$45 million. This amount is sufficient to repurchase \$45 million/\$45 = 1 million shares of stock, leaving 9 million outstanding. EPS is thus (EBIT − \$11.25 million)/9 million.

Now that we know how to calculate EPS under both scenarios, we set the two calculations equal to each other and solve for the break-even EBIT:

$$\begin{aligned}(\text{EBIT} - \$7.2 \text{ million})/10 \text{ million} &= (\text{EBIT} - \$11.25 \text{ million})/9 \text{ million}\\ \text{EBIT} - \$7.2 \text{ million} &= 1.11 \times (\text{EBIT} - \$11.25 \text{ million})\\ \text{EBIT} &= \$47{,}700{,}000\end{aligned}$$

Verify that, in either case, EPS is \$4.05 when EBIT is \$47.7 million.

17.2 According to M&M Proposition II (no taxes), the cost of equity is:

$$\begin{aligned}R_E &= R_A + (R_A - R_D) \times (D/E)\\ &= 16\% + (16\% - 13\%) \times 2\\ &= 22\%\end{aligned}$$

17.3 With no debt, Gypco's WACC is 17 percent. This is also the unlevered cost of capital. The aftertax cash flow is \$10,000 × (1 − .35) = \$6,500, so the value is just V_U = \$6,500/.17 = \$38,235.

After the debt issue, Gypco will be worth the original \$38,235 plus the present value of the tax shield. According to M&M Proposition I with taxes, the present value of the tax shield is $T_C \times D$, or .35 × \$15,000 = \$5,250, so the firm is worth \$38,235 + 5,250 = \$43,485.

Concepts Review and Critical Thinking Questions

1. **Business Risk versus Financial Risk** Explain what is meant by business and financial risk. Suppose Firm A has greater business risk than Firm B. Is it true that Firm A also has a higher cost of equity capital? Explain.

2. **M&M Propositions** How would you answer in the following debate?

   Q: Isn't it true that the riskiness of a firm's equity will rise if the firm increases its use of debt financing?

   A: Yes, that's the essence of M&M Proposition II.

   Q: And isn't it true that, as a firm increases its use of borrowing, the likelihood of default increases, thereby increasing the risk of the firm's debt?

   A: Yes.

   Q: In other words, increased borrowing increases the risk of the equity *and* the debt?

   A: That's right.

   Q: Well, given that the firm uses only debt and equity financing, and given that the risks of both are increased by increased borrowing, does it not follow that increasing debt increases the overall risk of the firm and therefore decreases the value of the firm?

   A: ??

3. **Optimal Capital Structure** Is there an easily identifiable debt-equity ratio that will maximize the value of a firm? Why or why not?
4. **Observed Capital Structures** Refer to the observed capital structures given in Table 17.7 of the text. What do you notice about the types of industries with respect to their average debt-equity ratios? Are certain types of industries more likely to be highly leveraged than others? What are some possible reasons for this observed segmentation? Do the operating results and tax history of the firms play a role? How about their future earnings prospects? Explain.
5. **Financial Leverage** Why is the use of debt financing referred to as financial "leverage"?
6. **Homemade Leverage** What is homemade leverage?
7. **Bankruptcy and Corporate Ethics** As mentioned in the text, some firms have filed for bankruptcy because of actual or likely litigation-related losses. Is this a proper use of the bankruptcy process?
8. **Bankruptcy and Corporate Ethics** Firms sometimes use the threat of a bankruptcy filing to force creditors to renegotiate terms. Critics argue that in such cases, the firm is using bankruptcy laws "as a sword rather than a shield." Is this an ethical tactic?
9. **Bankruptcy and Corporate Ethics** As mentioned in the text, Continental Airlines filed for bankruptcy, at least in part, as a means of reducing labor costs. Whether this move was ethical, or proper, was hotly debated. Give both sides of the argument.
10. **Capital Structure Goal** What is the basic goal of financial management with regard to capital structure?

Questions and Problems

BASIC (Questions 1–15)

1. **EBIT and Leverage** Money, Inc., has no debt outstanding and a total market value of $150,000. Earnings before interest and taxes, EBIT, are projected to be $14,000 if economic conditions are normal. If there is strong expansion in the economy, then EBIT will be 30 percent higher. If there is a recession, then EBIT will be 60 percent lower. Money is considering a $60,000 debt issue with a 5 percent interest rate. The

proceeds will be used to repurchase shares of stock. There are currently 2,500 shares outstanding. Ignore taxes for this problem.

a. Calculate earnings per share, EPS, under each of the three economic scenarios before any debt is issued. Also, calculate the percentage changes in EPS when the economy expands or enters a recession.

b. Repeat part (*a*) assuming that Money goes through with recapitalization. What do you observe?

2. **EBIT, Taxes, and Leverage** Repeat parts (*a*) and (*b*) in Problem 1 assuming Money has a tax rate of 35 percent.

3. **ROE and Leverage** Suppose the company in Problem 1 has a market-to-book ratio of 1.0.

   a. Calculate return on equity, ROE, under each of the three economic scenarios before any debt is issued. Also, calculate the percentage changes in ROE for economic expansion and recession, assuming no taxes.

   b. Repeat part (*a*) assuming the firm goes through with the proposed recapitalization.

   c. Repeat parts (*a*) and (*b*) of this problem assuming the firm has a tax rate of 35 percent.

4. **Break-Even EBIT** ZZ Pop Corporation is comparing two different capital structures, an all-equity plan (Plan I) and a levered plan (Plan II). Under Plan I, ZZ Pop would have 150,000 shares of stock outstanding. Under Plan II, there would be 60,000 shares of stock outstanding and $1.5 million in debt outstanding. The interest rate on the debt is 10 percent and there are no taxes.

   a. If EBIT is $200,000, which plan will result in the higher EPS?

   b. If EBIT is $700,000, which plan will result in the higher EPS?

   c. What is the break-even EBIT?

5. **M&M and Stock Value** In Problem 4, use M&M Proposition I to find the price per share of equity under each of the two proposed plans. What is the value of the firm?

6. **Break-Even EBIT and Leverage** Kolby Corp. is comparing two different capital structures. Plan I would result in 1,100 shares of stock and $16,500 in debt. Plan II would result in 900 shares of stock and $27,500 in debt. The interest rate on the debt is 10 percent.

   a. Ignoring taxes, compare both of these plans to an all-equity plan assuming that EBIT will be $10,000. The all-equity plan would result in 1,400 shares of stock outstanding. Which of the three plans has the highest EPS? The lowest?

   b. In part (*a*), what are the break-even levels of EBIT for each plan as compared to that for an all-equity plan? Is one higher than the other? Why?

   c. Ignoring taxes, when will EPS be identical for Plans I and II?

   d. Repeat parts (*a*), (*b*), and (*c*) assuming that the corporate tax rate is 40 percent. Are the break-even levels of EBIT different from before? Why or why not?

7. **Leverage and Stock Value** Ignoring taxes in Problem 6, what is the price per share of equity under Plan I? Plan II? What principle is illustrated by your answers?

8. **Homemade Leverage** Star, Inc., a prominent consumer products firm, is debating whether or not to convert its all-equity capital structure to one that is 40 percent debt.

Currently, there are 2,000 shares outstanding and the price per share is $70. EBIT is expected to remain at $16,000 per year forever. The interest rate on new debt is 8 percent, and there are no taxes.

a. Ms. Knowles, a shareholder of the firm, owns 100 shares of stock. What is her cash flow under the current capital structure, assuming the firm has a dividend payout rate of 100 percent?

b. What will Ms. Knowles' cash flow be under the proposed capital structure of the firm? Assume that she keeps all 100 of her shares.

c. Suppose Star does convert, but Ms. Knowles prefers the current all-equity capital structure. Show how she could unlever her shares of stock to recreate the original capital structure.

d. Using your answer to part (*c*), explain why Star's choice of capital structure is irrelevant.

9. Homemade Leverage and WACC ABC Co. and XYZ Co. are identical firms in all respects except for their capital structure. ABC is all-equity financed with $600,000 in stock. XYZ uses both stock and perpetual debt; its stock is worth $300,000 and the interest rate on its debt is 10 percent. Both firms expect EBIT to be $73,000. Ignore taxes.

a. Rico owns $30,000 worth of XYZ's stock. What rate of return is she expecting?

b. Show how Rico could generate exactly the same cash flows and rate of return by investing in ABC and using homemade leverage.

c. What is the cost of equity for ABC? What is it for XYZ?

d. What is the WACC for ABC? For XYZ? What principle have you illustrated?

10. M&M Nina Corp. uses no debt. The weighted average cost of capital is 13 percent. If the current market value of the equity is $35 million and there are no taxes, what is EBIT?

11. M&M and Taxes In the previous question, suppose the corporate tax rate is 35 percent. What is EBIT in this case? What is the WACC? Explain.

12. Calculating WACC Moon Beam Industries has a debt-equity ratio of 1.5. Its WACC is 12 percent, and its cost of debt is 12 percent. The corporate tax rate is 35 percent.

a. What is Moon Beam's cost of equity capital?

b. What is Moon Beam's unlevered cost of equity capital?

c. What would the cost of equity be if the debt-equity ratio were 2? What if it were 1.0? What if it were zero?

13. Calculating WACC Shadow Corp. has no debt but can borrow at 8 percent. The firm's WACC is currently 12 percent, and the tax rate is 35 percent.

a. What is Shadow's cost of equity?

b. If the firm converts to 25 percent debt, what will its cost of equity be?

c. If the firm converts to 50 percent debt, what will its cost of equity be?

d. What is Shadow's WACC in part (*b*)? In part (*c*)?

14. M&M and Taxes Bruce & Co. expects its EBIT to be $95,000 every year forever. The firm can borrow at 11 percent. Bruce currently has no debt, and its cost of equity is 22 percent. If the tax rate is 35 percent, what is the value of the firm? What will the value be if Bruce borrows $60,000 and uses the proceeds to repurchase shares?

15. **M&M and Taxes** In Problem 14, what is the cost of equity after recapitalization? What is the WACC? What are the implications for the firm's capital structure decision?

INTERMEDIATE
(Questions 16–17)

16. **M&M** Tool Manufacturing has an expected EBIT of $35,000 in perpetuity and a tax rate of 35 percent. The firm has $70,000 in outstanding debt at an interest rate of 9 percent, and its unlevered cost of capital is 14 percent. What is the value of the firm according to M&M Proposition I with taxes? Should Tool change its debt-equity ratio if the goal is to maximize the value of the firm? Explain.

17. **Firm Value** Old School Corporation expects an EBIT of $9,000 every year forever. Old School currently has no debt, and its cost of equity is 17 percent. The firm can borrow at 10 percent. If the corporate tax rate is 35 percent, what is the value of the firm? What will the value be if Old School converts to 50 percent debt? To 100 percent debt?

CHALLENGE
(Questions 18–21)

18. **Weighted Average Cost of Capital** In a world of corporate taxes only, show that the WACC can be written as WACC = $R_U \times [1 - T_C(D/V)]$.

19. **Cost of Equity and Leverage** Assuming a world of corporate taxes only, show that the cost of equity, R_E, is as given in the chapter by M&M Proposition II with corporate taxes.

20. **Business and Financial Risk** Assume a firm's debt is risk-free, so that the cost of debt equals the risk-free rate, R_f. Define β_A as the firm's *asset* beta, that is, the systematic risk of the firm's assets. Define β_E to be the beta of the firm's equity. Use the capital asset pricing model, CAPM, along with M&M Proposition II to show that $\beta_E = \beta_A \times (1 + D/E)$, where D/E is the debt-equity ratio. Assume the tax rate is zero.

21. **Stockholder Risk** Suppose a firm's business operations are such that they mirror movements in the economy as a whole very closely, that is, the firm's asset beta is 1.0. Use the result of Problem 20 to find the equity beta for this firm for debt-equity ratios of 0, 1, 5, and 20. What does this tell you about the relationship between capital structure and shareholder risk? How is the shareholders' required return on equity affected? Explain.

S&P Problems

STANDARD &POOR'S

1. **Capital Structure** Find the annual balance sheets for Pfizer (PFE), Ford (F), and McDonald's (MCD). For each company, calculate the long-term debt-to-equity ratio for the two most recent years. Why would these three companies use such different capital structures?

What's On the Web?

17.1 **Capital Structure** Go to yahoo.investors.reuters.com and enter the ticker symbol AMGM for Amgen, a biotechnology company. Follow the "Ratio Comparison" link and find long-term debt-to-equity and total debt-to-equity ratios. How does Amgen compare to the industry, sector, and S&P 500 in these areas? Now answer the same question for Edison International (EIX), the parent company of Southern California Edison, a utility company. How do the capital structures of Amgen and Edison International compare? Can you think of possible explanations for the difference between these two companies?

17.2 Capital Structure Go to finance.yahoo.com and follow the "Screener" link. Using the Total Debt/Equity screen on the Java Screener, how many companies have debt-to-equity ratios greater than 2? Greater than 5? Greater than 10? What company has the highest debt-to-equity ratio? What is the ratio? Now find how many companies have a negative debt-to-equity ratio. What is the lowest debt-to-equity ratio? What does it mean if a company has a negative debt-to-equity ratio? Repeat these screens for the Long-term debt/Equity screen.

PART SIX

Cost of Capital and Long-Term Financial Policy

18 Dividends and Dividend Policy

In May 2004, Northrop Grumman Corporation, the giant aerospace and defense contractor, announced a broad plan to reward stockholders for the recent success of the firm's business. Under the plan, Northrop would (1) boost its quarterly dividend by 15 percent from 40 cents to 46 cents per share, (2) undertake a two-for-one stock split, meaning each existing common share would be replaced with two new ones, and (3) continue its $700 million buyback of its common stock. Investors cheered, bidding up the stock price by 1.6 percent on the day of the announcement. Why were investors so pleased? To find out, this chapter explores all three of these actions and their implications for shareholders.

Dividend policy is an important subject in corporate finance, and dividends are a major cash outlay for many corporations. For example, among companies in the S&P 500, Citigroup and General Electric have the biggest outlays for dividends. How much? Both companies pay out in excess of $8 billion annually. In contrast, about 25 percent of the companies in the S&P 500 pay no dividends at all.

At first glance, it may seem obvious that a firm would always want to give as much as possible back to its shareholders by paying dividends. It might seem equally obvious, however, that a firm could always invest the money for its shareholders instead of paying it out. The heart of the dividend policy question is just this: Should the firm pay out money to its shareholders, or should the firm take that money and invest it for its shareholders?

It may seem surprising, but much research and economic logic suggest that dividend policy doesn't matter. In fact, it turns out that the dividend policy issue is much like the capital structure question. The important elements are not difficult to identify, but the interactions between those elements are complex and no easy answer exists.

Dividend policy is controversial. Many implausible reasons are given for why dividend policy might be important, and many of the claims made about dividend policy are economically illogical. Even so, in the real world of corporate finance, determining the most appropriate dividend policy is considered an important issue. It could be that financial managers who worry about dividend policy are wasting time, but it could also be true that we are missing something important in our discussions.

In part, all discussions of dividends are plagued by the "two-handed lawyer" problem. President Truman, while discussing the legal implications of a possible presidential decision, asked his staff to set up a meeting with a lawyer. Supposedly Mr. Truman said, "But I don't want one of those two-handed lawyers." When asked what a two-handed lawyer was, he replied, "You know, a lawyer who says, 'On the one hand I recommend you do so and so because of the following reasons, but on the other hand I recommend that you don't do it because of these other reasons.' "

Unfortunately, any sensible treatment of dividend policy will appear to have been written by a two-handed lawyer (or, in fairness, several two-handed financial economists). On the one hand, there are many good reasons for corporations to pay high dividends, but, on the other hand, there are also many good reasons to pay low dividends.

In this chapter, we will cover three broad topics that relate to dividends and dividend policy. First, we describe the various kinds of dividends and how dividends are paid. Second, we consider an idealized case in which dividend policy doesn't matter. We then discuss the limitations of this case and present some real-world arguments for both high- and low-dividend payouts. Finally, we conclude the chapter by looking at some strategies that corporations might employ to implement a dividend policy, and we discuss share repurchases as an alternative to dividends.

CASH DIVIDENDS AND DIVIDEND PAYMENT 18.1

The term **dividend** usually refers to cash paid out of earnings. If a payment is made from sources other than current or accumulated retained earnings, the term **distribution**, rather than *dividend,* is used. However, it is acceptable to refer to a distribution from earnings as a dividend and a distribution from capital as a liquidating dividend. More generally, any direct payment by the corporation to the shareholders may be considered a dividend or a part of dividend policy.

dividend
A payment made out of a firm's earnings to its owners, in the form of either cash or stock.

distribution
A payment made by a firm to its owners from sources other than current or accumulated retained earnings.

Dividends come in several different forms. The basic types of cash dividends are:

1. Regular cash dividends
2. Extra dividends
3. Special dividends
4. Liquidating dividends

Later in the chapter, we discuss dividends paid in stock instead of cash, and we also consider another alternative to cash dividends, stock repurchase.

Cash Dividends

The most common type of dividend is a cash dividend. Commonly, public companies pay **regular cash dividends** four times a year. As the name suggests, these are cash payments made directly to shareholders, and they are made in the regular course of business. In other words, management sees nothing unusual about the dividend and no reason why it won't be continued.

regular cash dividend
A cash payment made by a firm to its owners in the normal course of business, usually made four times a year.

Sometimes firms will pay a regular cash dividend and an *extra cash dividend.* By calling part of the payment "extra," management is indicating that the "extra" part may or may not be repeated in the future. A *special dividend* is similar, but the name usually indicates that this dividend is viewed as a truly unusual or one-time event and won't be repeated. For example, in December of 2004, Microsoft paid a special dividend of $3 per share. The total payout of $32 billion was the largest one-time corporate dividend in history. Founder Bill Gates received about $3 *billion,* which he pledged to donate to charity. Finally, the payment of a *liquidating dividend* usually means that some or all of the business has been liquidated, that is, sold off.

However it is labeled, a cash dividend payment reduces corporate cash and retained earnings, except in the case of a liquidating dividend (which may reduce paid-in capital).

FIGURE 18.1 >>

Example of Procedure for Dividend Payment

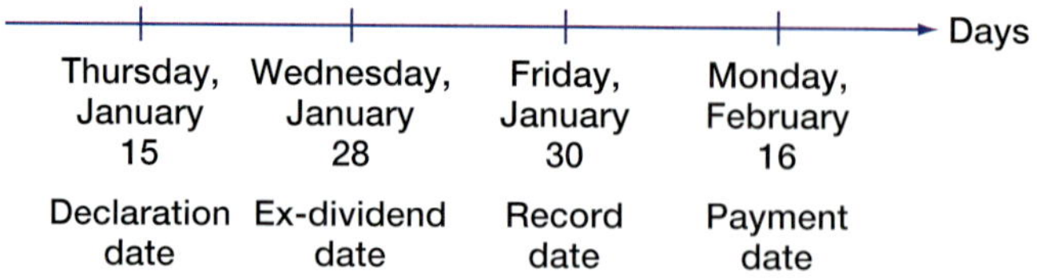

1. *Declaration date*: The board of directors declares a payment of dividends.
2. *Ex-dividend date*: A share of stock goes ex dividend on the date the seller is entitled to keep the dividend; under NYSE rules, shares are traded ex dividend on and after the second business day before the record date.
3. *Record date*: The declared dividends are distributable to those people who are shareholders of record as of this specific date.
4. *Payment date*: The dividend checks are mailed to shareholders of record.

Standard Method of Cash Dividend Payment

The decision to pay a dividend rests in the hands of the board of directors of the corporation. When a dividend has been declared, it becomes a debt of the firm and cannot be rescinded easily. Sometime after it has been declared, a dividend is distributed to all shareholders as of some specific date.

Commonly, the amount of the cash dividend is expressed in terms of dollars per share (*dividends per share*). As we have seen in other chapters, it is also expressed as a percentage of the market price (the *dividend yield*) or as a percentage of net income or earnings per share (the *dividend payout*).

Dividend Payment: A Chronology

declaration date
The date on which the board of directors passes a resolution to pay a dividend.

ex-dividend date
The date two business days before the date of record, establishing those individuals entitled to a dividend.

date of record
The date by which a holder must be on record in order to be designated to receive a dividend.

The mechanics of a cash dividend payment can be illustrated by the example in Figure 18.1 and the following description:

1. **Declaration date**. On January 15, the board of directors passes a resolution to pay a dividend of $1 per share on February 16 to all holders of record as of January 30.
2. **Ex-dividend date**. To make sure that dividend checks go to the right people, brokerage firms and stock exchanges establish an ex-dividend date. This date is two business days before the date of record (discussed next). If you buy the stock before this date, then you are entitled to the dividend. If you buy on this date or after, then the previous owner will get the dividend.

   In Figure 18.1, Wednesday, January 28, is the ex-dividend date. Before this date, the stock is said to trade "with dividend" or "cum dividend." Afterwards, the stock trades "ex dividend."

   The ex-dividend date convention removes any ambiguity about who is entitled to the dividend. Because the dividend is valuable, the stock price will be affected when the stock goes "ex." We examine this effect in a moment.
3. **Date of record**. Based on its records, the corporation prepares a list on January 30 of all individuals believed to be stockholders. These are the *holders of record,* and January 30 is the date of record (or record date). The word *believed* is important here. If you buy the stock just before this date, the corporation's records may not reflect that fact because of mailing or other delays. Without some modification, some of the dividend checks will get mailed to the wrong people. This is the reason for the ex-dividend day convention.

date of payment
The date that the dividend checks are mailed.

4. **Date of payment**. The dividend checks are mailed on February 16.

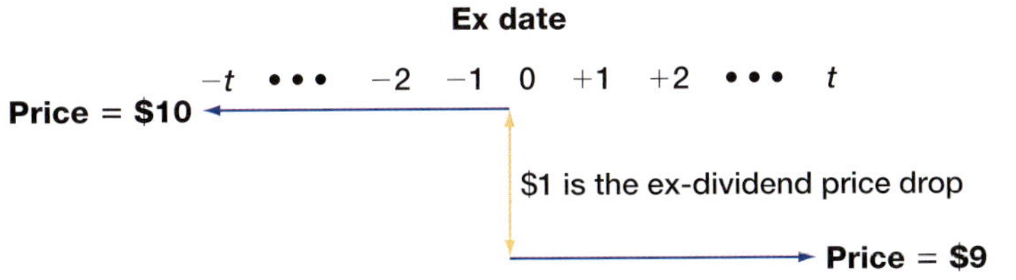

The stock price will fall by the amount of the dividend on the ex date (Time 0). If the dividend is $1 per share, the price will be $10 − 1 = $9 on the ex date:

Before ex date (Time −1), dividend = $0 Price = $10
On ex date (Time 0), dividend = $1 Price = $9

<< FIGURE 18.2

Price Behavior Around the Ex-Dividend Date for a $1 Cash Dividend

More on the Ex-Dividend Date

The ex-dividend date is important and is a common source of confusion. We examine what happens to the stock when it goes ex, meaning that the ex-dividend date arrives. To illustrate, suppose we have a stock that sells for $10 per share. The board of directors declares a dividend of $1 per share, and the record date is set to be Tuesday, June 12. Based on our previous discussion, we know that the ex date will be two business (not calendar) days earlier, on Friday, June 8.

If you buy the stock on Thursday, June 7, just as the market closes, you'll get the $1 dividend because the stock is trading cum dividend. If you wait and buy it just as the market opens on Friday, you won't get the $1 dividend. What happens to the value of the stock overnight?

If you think about it, you will see that the stock is worth about $1 less on Friday morning, so its price will drop by this amount between close of business on Thursday and the Friday opening. In general, we expect that the value of a share of stock will go down by about the dividend amount when the stock goes ex dividend. The key word here is *about.* Because dividends are taxed, the actual price drop might be closer to some measure of the aftertax value of the dividend. Determining this value is complicated because of the different tax rates and tax rules that apply for different buyers.

The series of events described here is illustrated in Figure 18.2.

<< EXAMPLE 18.1

"Ex" Marks the Day

The board of directors of Divided Airlines has declared a dividend of $2.50 per share payable on Tuesday, May 30, to shareholders of record as of Tuesday, May 9. Cal Icon buys 100 shares of Divided on Tuesday, May 2, for $150 per share. What is the ex date? Describe the events that will occur with regard to the cash dividend and the stock price.

The ex date is two business days before the date of record, Tuesday, May 9, so the stock will go ex on Friday, May 5. Cal buys the stock on Tuesday, May 2, so Cal purchases the stock cum dividend. In other words, Cal will get $2.50 × 100 = $250 in dividends. The check will be mailed on Tuesday, May 30. Just before the stock does go ex on Friday, its value will drop overnight by about $2.50 per share.

As a more concrete example, in the first quarter of 2004, McGraw-Hill, which we feel compelled to note is a very fine company,[1] boosted its dividend by 11.11 percent. In fact, dividends have been paid by the company since 1937 and have increased without fail since

[1]The reason we feel compelled to note this is that McGraw-Hill is the publisher of this textbook!

1974, growing at a compound rate of 10.4 percent over the following 31-year period. The dividend record date was February 25, with payment to be made on March 10. The new quarterly dividend was $.30 a share.

The record date was February 25, a Wednesday, so the ex date was Monday, the 23rd. When the market opened, McGraw-Hill's stock price dropped by $0.22, or only about 75 percent of the dividend. However, the market was active that day, so the dividend wasn't the only influence on the price.

Concept Questions

18.1a What are the different types of cash dividends?

18.1b What are the mechanics of the cash dividend payment?

18.1c How should the price of a stock change when it goes ex dividend?

18.2 DOES DIVIDEND POLICY MATTER?

To decide whether or not dividend policy matters, we first have to define what we mean by dividend *policy*. All other things being the same, of course dividends matter. Dividends are paid in cash, and cash is something that everybody likes. The question we will be discussing here is whether the firm should pay out cash now or invest the cash and pay it out later. Dividend policy, therefore, is the time pattern of dividend payout. In particular, should the firm pay out a large percentage of its earnings now or a small (or even zero) percentage? This is the dividend policy question.

An Illustration of the Irrelevance of Dividend Policy

A powerful argument can be made that dividend policy does not matter. We illustrate this by considering the simple case of Wharton Corporation. Wharton is an all-equity firm that has existed for 10 years. The current financial managers plan to dissolve the firm in two years. The total cash flows the firm will generate, including the proceeds from liquidation, will be $10,000 in each of the next two years.

Current Policy: Dividends Set Equal to Cash Flow At the present time, dividends at each date are set equal to the cash flow of $10,000. There are 100 shares outstanding, so the dividend per share is $100. In Chapter 6, we showed that the value of the stock is equal to the present value of the future dividends. Assuming a 10 percent required return, the value of a share of stock today, P_0, is:

$$P_0 = \frac{D_1}{(1+R)^1} + \frac{D_2}{(1+R)^2}$$

$$= \frac{\$100}{1.10} + \frac{100}{1.10^2} = \$173.55$$

The firm as a whole is thus worth 100 × $173.55 = $17,355.

Several members of the board of Wharton have expressed dissatisfaction with the current dividend policy and have asked you to analyze an alternative policy.

Alternative Policy: Initial Dividend Greater than Cash Flow Another possible policy is for the firm to pay a dividend of \$110 per share on the first date (Date 1), which is, of course, a total dividend of \$11,000. Because the cash flow is only \$10,000, an extra \$1,000 must somehow be raised. One way to do this is to issue \$1,000 worth of bonds or stock at Date 1. Assume that stock is issued. The new stockholders will desire enough cash flow at Date 2 so that they earn the required 10 percent return on their Date 1 investment.[2]

What is the value of the firm with this new dividend policy? The new stockholders invest \$1,000. They require a 10 percent return, so they will demand $\$1,000 \times 1.10 = \$1,100$ of the Date 2 cash flow, leaving only \$8,900 to the old stockholders. The dividends to the old stockholders will be as follows:

	Date 1	Date 2
Aggregate dividends to old stockholders	\$11,000	\$8,900
Dividends per share	110	89

The present value of the dividends per share is therefore:

$$P_0 = \frac{\$110}{1.10} + \frac{89}{1.10^2} = \$173.55$$

This is the same value we had before.

The value of the stock is not affected by this switch in dividend policy even though we have to sell some new stock just to finance the new dividend. In fact, no matter what pattern of dividend payout the firm chooses, the value of the stock will always be the same in this example. In other words, for the Wharton Corporation, dividend policy makes no difference. The reason is simple: Any increase in a dividend at some point in time is exactly offset by a decrease somewhere else, so the net effect, once we account for time value, is zero.

Homemade Dividends

There is an alternative and perhaps more intuitively appealing explanation of why dividend policy doesn't matter in our example. Suppose individual investor X prefers dividends per share of \$100 at both Dates 1 and 2. Would she be disappointed if informed that the firm's management was adopting the alternative dividend policy (dividends of \$110 and \$89 on the two dates, respectively)? Not necessarily, because she could easily reinvest the \$10 of unneeded funds received on Date 1 by buying some more Wharton stock. At 10 percent, this investment would grow to \$11 by Date 2. Thus, X would receive her desired net cash flow of $\$110 - 10 = \$100$ at Date 1 and $\$89 + 11 = \$100$ at Date 2.

Conversely, imagine that an investor Z, preferring \$110 of cash flow at Date 1 and \$89 of cash flow at Date 2, finds that management will pay dividends of \$100 at both Dates 1 and 2. This investor can simply sell \$10 worth of stock to boost his total cash at Date 1 to \$110. Because this investment returns 10 percent, Investor Z gives up \$11 at Date 2 ($\$10 \times 1.1$), leaving him with $\$100 - 11 = \$89$.

Our two investors are able to transform the corporation's dividend policy into a different policy by buying or selling on their own. The result is that investors are able to create a **homemade dividend policy**. This means that dissatisfied stockholders can alter the firm's

homemade dividend policy
The tailored dividend policy created by individual investors who undo corporate dividend policy by reinvesting dividends or selling shares of stock.

[2]The same results would occur after an issue of bonds, though the arguments would be less easily presented.

dividend policy to suit themselves. As a result, there is no particular advantage to any one dividend policy the firm might choose.

Many corporations actually assist their stockholders in creating homemade dividend policies by offering *automatic dividend reinvestment plans* (ADRs or DRIPs). McDonald's, Wal-Mart, Sears, and Procter & Gamble, plus over 1,000 more companies, have set up such plans, so they are relatively common. As the name suggests, with such a plan, stockholders have the option of automatically reinvesting some or all of their cash dividend in shares of stock. In some cases, they actually receive a discount on the stock, which makes such a plan very attractive.

A Test

Our discussion to this point can be summarized by considering the following true-false test questions:

1. True or false: Dividends are irrelevant.
2. True or false: Dividend policy is irrelevant.

The first statement is surely false, and the reason follows from common sense. Clearly, investors prefer higher dividends to lower dividends at any single date if the dividend level is held constant at every other date. To be more precise regarding the first question, if the dividend per share at a given date is raised while the dividend per share at every other date is held constant, the stock price will rise. The reason is that the present value of the future dividends must go up if this occurs. This action can be accomplished by management decisions that improve productivity, increase tax savings, strengthen product marketing, or otherwise improve cash flow.

The second statement is true, at least in the simple case we have been examining. Dividend policy by itself cannot raise the dividend at one date while keeping it the same at all other dates. Rather, dividend policy merely establishes the trade-off between dividends at one date and dividends at another date. Once we allow for time value, the present value of the dividend stream is unchanged. Thus, in this simple world, dividend policy does not matter, because managers choosing either to raise or to lower the current dividend do not affect the current value of their firm. However, we have ignored several real-world factors that might lead us to change our minds; we pursue some of these in subsequent sections.

Concept Questions

18.2a How can an investor create a homemade dividend?

18.2b Are dividends irrelevant?

18.3 REAL-WORLD FACTORS FAVORING A LOW PAYOUT

The example we used to illustrate the irrelevance of dividend policy ignored taxes and flotation costs. In this section, we will see that these factors might lead us to prefer a low-dividend payout.

Taxes

U.S. tax laws are complex, and they affect dividend policy in a number of ways. The key tax feature has to do with the taxation of dividend income and capital gains. For individual shareholders, *effective* tax rates on dividend income are higher than the tax rates on capital gains. Historically, dividends received have been taxed as ordinary income. Capital gains have been taxed at somewhat lower rates, and the tax on a capital gain is deferred until the stock is sold. This second aspect of capital gains taxation makes the effective tax rate much lower because the present value of the tax is less.[3]

A firm that adopts a low-dividend payout will reinvest the money instead of paying it out. This reinvestment increases the value of the firm and of the equity. All other things being equal, the net effect is that the expected capital gains portion of the return will be higher in the future. So, the fact that capital gains are taxed favorably may lead us to prefer this approach.

This tax disadvantage of dividends doesn't necessarily lead to a policy of paying no dividends. Suppose a firm has some excess cash after selecting all positive NPV projects (this type of excess cash is frequently referred to as *free cash flow*). The firm is considering two mutually exclusive uses of the excess cash: (1) pay dividends or (2) retain the excess cash for investment in securities. The correct dividend policy will depend upon the individual tax rate and the corporate tax rate.

To see why, suppose the Regional Electric Company has \$1,000 in extra cash. It can retain the cash and invest it in Treasury bills yielding 10 percent, or it can pay the cash to shareholders as a dividend. Shareholders can also invest in Treasury bills with the same yield. The corporate tax rate is 34 percent, and the individual tax rate is 28 percent. What is the amount of cash that investors will have after five years under each policy?

If dividends are paid now, shareholders will receive \$1,000 before taxes, or $\$1{,}000 \times (1 - .28) = \$720$ after taxes. This is the amount they will invest. If the rate on T-bills is 10 percent, before taxes, then the aftertax return is $10\% \times (1 - .28) = 7.2\%$ per year. Thus, in five years, the shareholders will have:

$$\$720 \times (1 + .072)^5 = \$1{,}019.31$$

If Regional Electric Company retains the cash, invests in Treasury bills, and pays out the proceeds five years from now, then \$1,000 will be invested today. However, because the corporate tax rate is 34 percent, the aftertax return from the T-bills will be $10\% \times (1 - .34) = 6.6\%$ per year. In five years, the investment will be worth:

$$\$1{,}000 \times (1 + .066)^5 = \$1{,}376.53$$

If this amount is then paid out as a dividend, the stockholders will receive (after tax):

$$\$1{,}376.53 \times (1 - .28) = \$991.10$$

In this case, dividends will be greater after taxes if the firm pays them now. The reason is that the firm simply cannot invest as profitably as the shareholders can on their own (on an aftertax basis).

This example shows that for a firm with extra cash, the dividend payout decision will depend on personal and corporate tax rates. All other things being the same, when personal tax rates are higher than corporate tax rates, a firm will have an incentive to reduce dividend payouts. However, if personal tax rates are lower than corporate tax rates, a firm will have an incentive to pay out any excess cash in dividends.

Recent tax law changes have led to a renewed interest in the effect of taxes on corporate dividend policies. As we previously noted, historically dividends have been taxed as ordinary income (at ordinary income tax rates). In 2003, this changed dramatically. Tax rates

[3]In fact, capital gains taxes can sometimes be avoided altogether. Although we do not recommend this particular tax-avoidance strategy, the capital gains tax may be avoided by dying. Your heirs are not considered to have a capital gain, so the tax liability dies when you do. In this instance, you can take it with you.

on dividends and long-term capital gains were lowered from a maximum in the 35–39 percent range to 15 percent. The new tax rate on dividends is therefore substantially less than the corporate tax rate, giving corporations a much larger tax incentive to pay dividends. However, note that capital gains are still taxed preferentially because of the deferment.

Expected Return, Dividends, and Personal Taxes

We illustrate the effect of personal taxes by considering an extreme situation in which dividends are taxed as ordinary income and capital gains are not taxed at all. We show that a firm that provides more return in the form of dividends will have a lower value (or a higher pretax required return) than one whose return is in the form of untaxed capital gains.

Suppose every investor is in a 25 percent tax bracket and is considering the stocks of Firm G and Firm D. Firm G pays no dividend, and Firm D pays a dividend. The current price of the stock of Firm G is $100, and next year's price is expected to be $120. The shareholder in Firm G thus expects a $20 capital gain. With no dividend, the return is $\$20/100 = 20\%$. If capital gains are not taxed, the pretax and aftertax returns must be the same.

Suppose the stock of Firm D is expected to pay a $20 dividend next year, and the ex-dividend price will then be $100. If the stocks of Firm G and Firm D are equally risky, the market prices must be set so that the aftertax expected returns of these stocks are equal. The aftertax return on Firm D will therefore have to be 20 percent.

What will be the price of stock in Firm D? The aftertax dividend is $\$20 \times (1 - .25) = \$15$, so our investor will have a total of $115 after taxes. At a 20 percent required rate of return (after taxes), the present value of this aftertax amount is:

$$\text{Present value} = \$115/1.20 = \$95.83$$

The market price of the stock in Firm D thus must be $95.83.

What we see is that Firm D is worth less because of its dividend policy. Another way to see the same thing is to look at the pretax required return for Firm D:

$$\text{Pretax return} = (\$120 - 95.83)/95.83 = 25.2\%$$

Firm D effectively has a higher cost of equity (25.2 percent versus 20 percent) because of its dividend policy. Shareholders demand the higher return as compensation for the extra tax liability.

Flotation Costs

In our example illustrating that dividend policy doesn't matter, we saw that the firm could sell some new stock if necessary to pay a dividend. As we mentioned in Chapter 16, selling new stock can be very expensive. If we include flotation costs in our argument, then we will find that the value of the stock decreases if we sell new stock.

More generally, imagine two firms identical in every way except that one pays out a greater percentage of its cash flow in the form of dividends. Because the other firm plows back more, its equity grows faster. If these two firms are to remain identical, then the one with the higher payout will have to periodically sell some stock to catch up. Because this is expensive, a firm might be inclined to have a low payout.

Dividend Restrictions

In some cases, a corporation may face restrictions on its ability to pay dividends. For example, as we discussed in Chapter 7, a common feature of a bond indenture is a covenant prohibiting dividend payments above some level. Also, a corporation may be prohibited by state law from paying dividends if the dividend amount exceeds the firm's retained earnings.

> ### Concept Questions
> **18.3a** What are the tax benefits of low dividends?
>
> **18.3b** Why do flotation costs favor a low payout?

REAL-WORLD FACTORS FAVORING A HIGH PAYOUT

18.4

In this section, we consider reasons why a firm might pay its shareholders higher dividends even if it means the firm must issue more shares of stock to finance the dividend payments.

In a classic textbook, Benjamin Graham, David Dodd, and Sidney Cottle have argued that firms should generally have high-dividend payouts because:

1. "The discounted value of near dividends is higher than the present worth of distant dividends."
2. Between "two companies with the same general earning power and same general position in an industry, the one paying the larger dividend will almost always sell at a higher price."[4]

Two additional factors favoring a high-dividend payout have also been mentioned frequently by proponents of this view: the desire for current income and the resolution of uncertainty.

Desire for Current Income

It has been argued that many individuals desire current income. The classic example is the group of retired people and others living on a fixed income, the proverbial widows and orphans. It is argued that this group is willing to pay a premium to get a higher dividend yield. If this is true, then it lends support to the second claim made by Graham, Dodd, and Cottle.

It is easy to see, however, that this argument is not relevant in our simple case. An individual preferring high current cash flow but holding low-dividend securities can easily sell off shares to provide the necessary funds. Similarly, an individual desiring a low current cash flow but holding high-dividend securities can just reinvest the dividend. This is just our homemade dividend argument again. Thus, in a world of no transaction costs, a policy of high current dividends would be of no value to the stockholder.

The current-income argument may have relevance in the real world. Here the sale of low-dividend stocks would involve brokerage fees and other transaction costs. These direct cash expenses could be avoided by an investment in high-dividend securities. In addition, the expenditure of the stockholder's own time in selling securities and the natural (though not necessarily rational) fear of consuming out of principal might further lead many investors to buy high-dividend securities.

Even so, to put this argument in perspective, it should be remembered that financial intermediaries such as mutual funds can (and do) perform these "repackaging" transactions

[4]B. Graham, D. Dodd, and S. Cottle, *Security Analysis* (New York: McGraw-Hill, 1962).

for individuals at very low cost. Such intermediaries could buy low-dividend stocks, and, through a controlled policy of realizing gains, they could pay their investors at a higher rate.

Uncertainty Resolution

We have just pointed out that investors with substantial current consumption needs will prefer high current dividends. In another classic treatment, Myron Gordon has argued that a high-dividend policy also benefits stockholders because it resolves uncertainty.[5]

According to Gordon, investors price a security by forecasting and discounting future dividends. Gordon then argues that forecasts of dividends to be received in the distant future have greater uncertainty than do forecasts of near-term dividends. Because investors dislike uncertainty, the stock price should be low for those companies that pay small dividends now in order to remit higher, less certain dividends at later dates.

Gordon's argument is essentially a bird-in-hand story. A $1 dividend in a shareholder's pocket is somehow worth more than that same $1 in a bank account held by the corporation. By now, you should see the problem with this argument. A shareholder can create a bird in hand very easily just by selling some of the stock.

Tax and Legal Benefits from High Dividends

Earlier, we saw that dividends were taxed unfavorably for individual investors (at least until very recently). This fact is a powerful argument for a low payout. However, there are a number of other investors who do not receive unfavorable tax treatment from holding high-dividend yield, rather than low-dividend yield, securities.

Corporate Investors A significant tax break on dividends occurs when a corporation owns stock in another corporation. A corporate stockholder receiving either common or preferred dividends is granted a 70 percent (or more) dividend exclusion. Since the 70 percent exclusion does not apply to capital gains, this group is taxed unfavorably on capital gains.

As a result of the dividend exclusion, high-dividend, low-capital gains stocks may be more appropriate for corporations to hold. As we discuss elsewhere, this is why corporations hold a substantial percentage of the outstanding preferred stock in the economy. This tax advantage of dividends also leads some corporations to hold high-yielding stocks instead of long-term bonds because there is no similar tax exclusion of interest payments to corporate bondholders.

Tax-Exempt Investors We have pointed out both the tax advantages and the tax disadvantages of a low-dividend payout. Of course, this discussion is irrelevant to those in zero tax brackets. This group includes some of the largest investors in the economy, such as pension funds, endowment funds, and trust funds.

There are some legal reasons for large institutions to favor high-dividend yields. First, institutions such as pension funds and trust funds are often set up to manage money for the benefit of others. The managers of such institutions have a *fiduciary responsibility* to invest the money prudently. It has been considered imprudent in courts of law to buy stock in companies with no established dividend record.

Second, institutions such as university endowment funds and trust funds are frequently prohibited from spending any of the principal. Such institutions might therefore prefer to

[5]M. Gordon, *The Investment, Financing and Valuation of the Corporation* (Burr Ridge, Ill.: Richard D. Irwin, 1961).

hold high-dividend yield stocks so they have some ability to spend. Like widows and orphans, this group thus prefers current income. However, unlike widows and orphans, this group is very large in terms of the amount of stock owned.

Conclusion

Overall, individual investors (for whatever reason) may have a desire for current income and may thus be willing to pay the dividend tax. In addition, some very large investors such as corporations and tax-free institutions may have a very strong preference for high-dividend payouts.

Concept Questions

18.4a Why might some individual investors favor a high-dividend payout?

18.4b Why might some nonindividual investors prefer a high-dividend payout?

A RESOLUTION OF REAL-WORLD FACTORS? 18.5

In the previous sections, we presented some factors that favor a low-dividend policy and others that favor a high-dividend policy. In this section, we discuss two important concepts related to dividends and dividend policy: the information content of dividends and the clientele effect. The first topic illustrates both the importance of dividends in general and the importance of distinguishing between dividends and dividend policy. The second topic suggests that, despite the many real-world considerations we have discussed, the dividend payout ratio may not be as important as we originally imagined.

Information Content of Dividends

To begin, we quickly review some of our earlier discussion. Previously, we examined three different positions on dividends:

1. Based on the homemade dividend argument, dividend policy is irrelevant.
2. Because of tax effects for individual investors and new issues costs, a low-dividend policy is best.
3. Because of the desire for current income and related factors, a high-dividend policy is best.

If you wanted to decide which of these positions is the right one, an obvious way to get started would be to look at what happens to stock prices when companies announce dividend changes. You would find with some consistency that stock prices rise when the current dividend is unexpectedly increased, and they generally fall when the dividend is unexpectedly decreased. What does this imply about any of the three positions just stated?

At first glance, the behavior we describe seems consistent with the third position and inconsistent with the other two. In fact, many writers have argued this. If stock prices rise in response to dividend increases and fall in response to dividend decreases, then isn't the market saying that it approves of higher dividends?

Other authors have pointed out that this observation doesn't really tell us much about dividend policy. Everyone agrees that dividends are important, all other things being equal. Companies cut dividends only with great reluctance. Thus, a dividend cut is often a signal that the firm is in trouble.

More to the point, a dividend cut is usually not a voluntary, planned change in dividend policy. Instead, it usually signals that management does not think that the current dividend policy can be maintained. As a result, expectations of future dividends should generally be revised downwards. The present value of expected future dividends falls, and so does the stock price.

In this case, the stock price declines following a dividend cut because future dividends are generally expected to be lower, not because the firm has changed the percentage of its earnings it will pay out in the form of dividends.

For a dramatic example, consider what happened to NUI Corporation when it announced that it would not pay a dividend. NUI is a diversified energy company that is engaged in the sale and distribution of natural gas, retail energy sales, and other activities. In May 2004, the company announced a loss of $2.82 per share, which was larger than expected. The company had a bond covenant that made it impossible to pay a dividend in any quarter in which its total capitalization was more than 60 percent debt. The big loss put the company over this limit, so the company announced that no dividend would be paid.

The next day was not pleasant for NUI shareholders. On a typical day, less than 100,000 shares of NUI stock trade on the NYSE. On that day, however, over 1.8 million shares traded hands. The stock had closed at $15.65 the previous day. When the market opened, the stock fell to $14.90 per share, but quickly dropped to $12.38 per share. At the end of the day, the stock closed at $12.80, a loss of about 18 percent. In other words, NUI lost almost 1/5 of its market value overnight. As this case illustrates, shareholders can react very negatively to unanticipated cuts in dividends.

In a similar vein, an unexpected increase in the dividend signals good news. Management will raise the dividend only when future earnings, cash flow, and general prospects are expected to rise to such an extent that the dividend will not have to be cut later. A dividend increase is management's signal to the market that the firm is expected to do well. The stock price reacts favorably because expectations of future dividends are revised upwards, not because the firm has increased its payout.

In both of these cases, the stock price reacts to the dividend change. The reaction can be attributed to changes in the expected amount of future dividends, not necessarily a change in dividend payout policy. This reaction is called the **information content effect** of the dividend. The fact that dividend changes convey information about the firm to the market makes it difficult to interpret the effect of the dividend policy of the firm.

information content effect
The market's reaction to a change in corporate dividend payout.

The Clientele Effect

In our earlier discussion, we saw that some groups (wealthy individuals, for example) have an incentive to pursue low-payout (or zero payout) stocks. Other groups (corporations, for example) have an incentive to pursue high-payout stocks. Companies with high payouts will thus attract one group, and low-payout companies will attract another.

These different groups are called *clienteles,* and what we have described is a **clientele effect**. The clientele effect argument states that different groups of investors desire different levels of dividends. When a firm chooses a particular dividend policy, the only effect is to attract a particular clientele. If a firm changes its dividend policy, then it just attracts a different clientele.

clientele effect
The observable fact that stocks attract particular groups based on dividend yield and the resulting tax effects.

What we are left with is a simple supply and demand argument. Suppose 40 percent of all investors prefer high dividends, but only 20 percent of the firms pay high dividends. Here the high-dividend firms will be in short supply; thus, their stock prices will rise. Consequently, low-dividend firms will find it advantageous to switch policies until 40 percent of all firms have high payouts. At this point, the *dividend market* is in equilibrium. Further changes in dividend policy are pointless because all of the clienteles are satisfied. The dividend policy for any individual firm is now irrelevant.

To see if you understand the clientele effect, consider the following statement: In spite of the theoretical argument that dividend policy is irrelevant or that firms should not pay dividends, many investors like high dividends; because of this fact, a firm can boost its share price by having a higher dividend payout ratio. True or false?

The answer is "false" if clienteles exist. As long as enough high-dividend firms satisfy the dividend-loving investors, a firm won't be able to boost its share price by paying high dividends. An unsatisfied clientele must exist for this to happen, and there is no evidence that this is the case.

Concept Questions

18.5a How does the market react to unexpected dividend changes? What does this tell us about dividends? About dividend policy?

18.5b What is a dividend clientele? All things considered, would you expect a risky firm with significant but highly uncertain growth prospects to have a low- or high-dividend payout?

ESTABLISHING A DIVIDEND POLICY 18.6

How do firms actually determine the level of dividends they will pay at a particular time? As we have seen, there are good reasons for firms to pay high dividends, and there are good reasons to pay low dividends.

We know some things about how dividends are paid in practice. Firms don't like to cut dividends. Consider the case of The Stanley Works, maker of Stanley tools and other building products. As of 2004, Stanley had paid dividends for 127 years, longer than any other industrial company listed on the NYSE. Furthermore, Stanley had boosted its dividend every year since 1968, a 36-year run of increases.

In the next section, we discuss a particular dividend policy strategy. In doing so, we emphasize the real-world features of dividend policy. We also analyze an increasingly important alternative to cash dividends, a stock repurchase.

Residual Dividend Approach

Earlier, we noted that firms with higher dividend payouts will have to sell stock more often. As we have seen, such sales are not very common, and they can be very expensive. Consistent with this, we will assume that the firm wishes to minimize the need to sell new equity. We will also assume that the firm wishes to maintain its current capital structure.

If a firm wishes to avoid new equity sales, then it will have to rely on internally generated equity to finance new positive NPV projects.[6] Dividends can only be paid out of what is left over. This leftover is called the *residual,* and such a dividend policy is called a **residual dividend approach**.

residual dividend approach
A policy under which a firm pays dividends only after meeting its investment needs while maintaining a desired debt-equity ratio.

With a residual dividend policy, the firm's objective is to meet its investment needs and maintain its desired debt-equity ratio before paying dividends. To illustrate, imagine that a

[6]Our discussion of sustainable growth in Chapter 4 is relevant here. We assumed there that a firm has a fixed capital structure, profit margin, and capital intensity. If the firm raises no new external equity and wishes to grow at some target rate, then there is only one payout ratio consistent with these assumptions.

firm has \$1,000 in earnings and a debt-equity ratio of .50. Notice that, because the debt-equity ratio is .50, the firm has 50 cents in debt for every \$1.50 in total value. The firm's capital structure is thus ⅓ debt and ⅔ equity.

The first step in implementing a residual dividend policy is to determine the amount of funds that can be generated without selling new equity. If the firm reinvests the entire \$1,000 and pays no dividend, then equity will increase by \$1,000. To keep the debt-equity ratio at .50, the firm must borrow an additional \$500. The total amount of funds that can be generated without selling new equity is thus \$1,000 + 500 = \$1,500.

The second step is to decide whether or not a dividend will be paid. To do this, we compare the total amount that can be generated without selling new equity (\$1,500 in this case) to planned capital spending. If funds needed exceed funds available, then no dividend will be paid. In addition, the firm will have to sell new equity to raise the needed financing or else (what is more likely) postpone some planned capital spending.

If funds needed are less than funds generated, then a dividend will be paid. The amount of the dividend will be the residual, that is, that portion of the earnings that is not needed to finance new projects. For example, suppose we have \$900 in planned capital spending. To maintain the firm's capital structure, this \$900 must be financed by ⅔ equity and ⅓ debt. So, the firm will actually borrow ⅓ × \$900 = \$300. The firm will spend ⅔ × \$900 = \$600 of the \$1,000 in equity available. There is a \$1,000 − 600 = \$400 residual, so the dividend will be \$400.

In sum, the firm has aftertax earnings of \$1,000. Dividends paid are \$400. Retained earnings are \$600, and new borrowing totals \$300. The firm's debt-equity ratio is unchanged at .50.

The relationship between physical investment and dividend payout is presented for six different levels of investment in Table 18.1 and illustrated in Figure 18.3. The first three rows of the table can be discussed together, because in each of these cases no dividends are paid.

In Row 1, for example, note that new investment is \$3,000. Additional debt of \$1,000 and equity of \$2,000 must be raised to keep the debt-equity ratio constant. Because this latter figure is greater than the \$1,000 in earnings, all earnings are retained. Additional stock to be issued is also \$1,000. In this example, because new stock is issued, dividends are not simultaneously paid out.

In Rows 2 and 3, investment drops. Additional debt needed goes down as well, because it is equal to ⅓ of investment. Because the amount of new equity needed is still greater than or equal to \$1,000, all earnings are retained and no dividend is paid.

We finally find a situation in Row 4 in which a dividend is paid. Here, total investment is \$1,000. To keep the debt-equity ratio constant, ⅓ of this investment, or \$333, is financed by debt. The remaining ⅔, or \$667, comes from internal funds, implying that the residual is \$1,000 − 667 = \$333. The dividend is equal to this \$333 residual.

In this case, note that no additional stock is issued. Because the needed investment is even lower in Rows 5 and 6, new debt is reduced further, retained earnings drop, and dividends increase. Again, no additional stock is issued.

TABLE 18.1 >>

Example of Dividend Policy Under the Residual Approach

Row	Aftertax Earnings	New Investment	Additional Debt	Retained Earnings	Additional Stock	Dividends
1	\$1,000	\$3,000	\$1,000	\$1,000	\$1,000	\$ 0
2	1,000	2,000	667	1,000	333	0
3	1,000	1,500	500	1,000	0	0
4	1,000	1,000	333	667	0	333
5	1,000	500	167	333	0	667
6	1,000	0	0	0	0	1,000

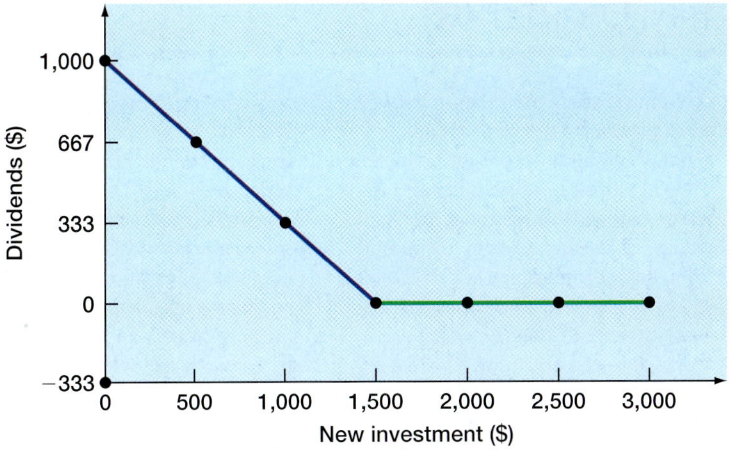

This figure illustrates that a firm with many investment opportunities will pay small amounts of dividends and a firm with few investment opportunities will pay relatively large amounts of dividends.

<< FIGURE 18.3

Relationship between Dividends and Investment in the Example of Residual Dividend Policy

Given our discussion, we expect those firms with many investment opportunities to pay a small percentage of their earnings as dividends and other firms with fewer opportunities to pay a high percentage of their earnings as dividends. This result appears to occur in the real world. Young, fast-growing firms commonly employ a low payout ratio, whereas older, slower-growing firms in more mature industries use a higher ratio.

Dividend Stability

The key point of the residual dividend approach is that dividends are paid only after all profitable investment opportunities are exhausted. Of course, a strict residual approach might lead to a very unstable dividend policy. If investment opportunities in one period are quite high, dividends will be low or zero. Conversely, dividends might be high in the next period if investment opportunities are considered less promising.

Consider the case of Big Department Stores, Inc., a retailer whose annual earnings are forecasted to be equal from year to year, but whose quarterly earnings change throughout the year. The earnings are low in each year's first quarter because of the post-Christmas business slump. Although earnings increase only slightly in the second and third quarters, they advance greatly in the fourth quarter as a result of the Christmas season. A graph of this firm's earnings is presented in Figure 18.4.

The firm can choose between at least two types of dividend policies. First, each quarter's dividend can be a fixed fraction of that quarter's earnings. Here, dividends will vary throughout the year. This is a cyclical dividend policy. Second, each quarter's dividend can be a fixed fraction of yearly earnings, implying that all dividend payments would be equal. This is a stable dividend policy. These two types of dividend policies are displayed in Figure 18.5. Corporate officials generally agree that a stable policy is in the interest of the firm and its stockholders, so the stable policy would be more common.

A Compromise Dividend Policy

In practice, many firms appear to follow what amounts to a compromise dividend policy. Such a policy is based on five main goals:

1. Avoid cutting back on positive NPV projects to pay a dividend.
2. Avoid dividend cuts.

IN THEIR OWN WORDS . . .

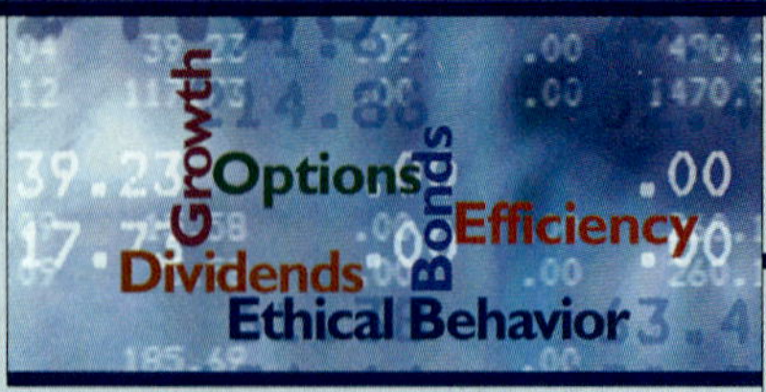

Fischer Black on Why Firms Pay Dividends

>> I think investors simply like dividends. They believe that dividends enhance stock value (given the firm's prospects), and they feel uncomfortable spending out of their capital.

We see evidence for this everywhere: investment advisors and institutions treat a high-yield stock as both attractive and safe, financial analysts value a stock by predicting and discounting its dividends, financial economists study the relation between stock prices and actual dividends, and investors complain about dividend cuts.

What if investors were neutral towards dividends? Investment advisors would tell clients to spend indifferently from income and capital and, if taxable, to avoid income; financial analysts would ignore dividends in valuing stocks; financial economists would treat stock price and the discounted value of dividends as equal, even when stocks are mispriced; and a firm would apologize to its taxable investors when forced by an accumulated earnings tax to pay dividends. This is not what we observe.

Furthermore, changing dividends seems a poor way to tell the financial markets about a firm's prospects. Public statements can better detail the firm's prospects and have more impact on both the speaker's and the firm's reputations.

I predict that under current tax rules, dividends will gradually disappear.

The late Fischer Black was a partner at Goldman Sachs and Co., an investment banking firm. Before that, he was a professor of finance at MIT. He is one of the fathers of option pricing theory, and he is widely regarded as one of the preeminent financial scholars. He is well known for his creative ideas, many of which were dismissed at first only to become part of accepted lore when others finally came to understand them. He is sadly missed by his colleagues.

3. Avoid the need to sell equity.
4. Maintain a target debt-equity ratio.
5. Maintain a target dividend payout ratio.

These goals are ranked more or less in order of their importance. In our strict residual approach, we assume that the firm maintains a fixed debt-equity ratio. Under the compromise approach, the debt-equity ratio is viewed as a long-range goal. It is allowed to vary in the short run if necessary to avoid a dividend cut or the need to sell new equity.

target payout ratio
A firm's long-term desired dividend-to-earnings ratio.

In addition to having a strong reluctance to cut dividends, financial managers tend to think of dividend payments in terms of a proportion of income, and they also tend to think investors are entitled to a "fair" share of corporate income. This share is the long-run **target payout ratio**, and it is the fraction of the earnings the firm expects to pay as dividends under ordinary circumstances. Again, this ratio is viewed as a long-range goal, so it

FIGURE 18.4 >>

Earnings for Big Department Stores, Inc.

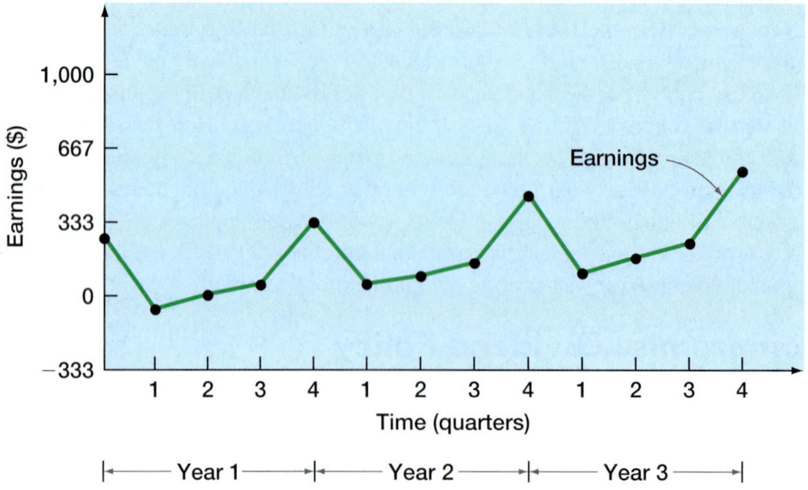

<< FIGURE 18.5

Alternative Dividend Policies for Big Department Stores, Inc.

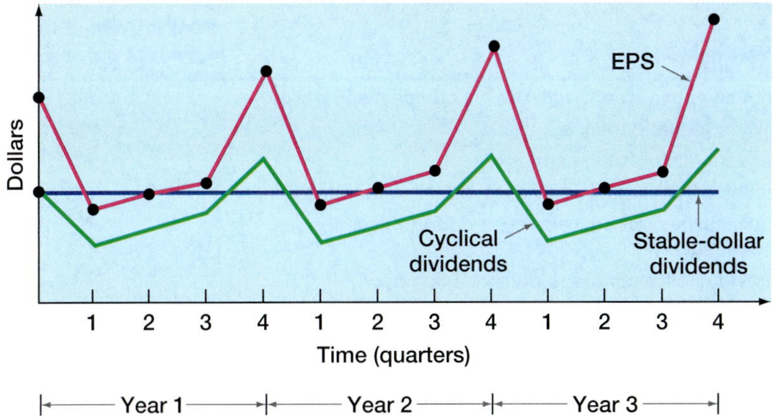

Cyclical dividend policy: Dividends are a constant proportion of earnings at each pay date.
Stable dividend policy: Dividends are a constant proportion of earnings over an earnings cycle.

might vary in the short run if this is necessary. As a result, in the long run, earnings growth is followed by dividend increases, but only with a lag.

One can minimize the problems of dividend instability by creating two types of dividends: regular and extra. For companies using this approach, the regular dividend would most likely be a relatively small fraction of permanent earnings, so that it could be sustained easily. Extra dividends would be granted when an increase in earnings was expected to be temporary.

Because investors look on an extra dividend as a bonus, there is relatively little disappointment when an extra dividend is not repeated. Although the extra-dividend approach appears quite sensible, few companies use it in practice. One reason is that a share repurchase, which we discuss a little later, does much the same thing with some extra advantages.

Some Survey Evidence on Dividends

A recent study surveyed a large number of financial executives regarding dividend policy. One of the questions asked was "Do these statements describe factors that affect your company's dividend decisions?" Table 18.2 shows some of the results.

<< TABLE 18.2

Survey Responses on Dividend Decisions*

Policy Statements	Percent Who Agree or Strongly Agree
1. We try to avoid reducing dividends per share.	93.8%
2. We try to maintain a smooth dividend from year to year.	89.6
3. We consider the level of dividends per share that we have paid in recent quarters.	88.2
4. We are reluctant to make dividend changes that might have to be reversed in the future.	77.9
5. We consider the change or growth in dividends per share.	66.7
6. We consider the cost of raising external capital to be smaller than the cost of cutting dividends.	42.8
7. We pay dividends to attract investors subject to "prudent man" investment restrictions.	41.7

*Survey respondents were asked the question, "Do these statements describe factors that affect your company's dividend decisions?"

SOURCE: Adapted from Table 4 of A. Brav, J.R. Graham, C.R. Harvey, and R. Michaely, "Payout Policy in the 21st Century," *Journal of Financial Economics,* forthcoming, 2005.

TABLE 18.3 >>

Survey Responses on Dividend Decisions*

Policy Statements	Percent Who Think This Is Important or Very Important
1. Maintaining consistency with our historic dividend policy.	84.1%
2. Stability of future earnings.	71.9
3. A sustainable change in earnings.	67.1
4. Attracting institutional investors to purchase our stock.	52.5
5. The availability of good investment opportunities for our firm to pursue.	47.6
6. Attracting retail investors to purchase our stock.	44.5
7. Personal taxes our stockholders pay when receiving dividends.	21.1
8. Flotation costs to issuing new equity.	9.3

*Survey respondents were asked the question, "How important are the following factors to your company's dividend decision?"

SOURCE: Adapted from Table 5 of A. Brav, J.R. Graham, C.R. Harvey, and R. Michaely, "Payout Policy in the 21st Century," *Journal of Financial Economics,* forthcoming, 2005.

As shown in Table 18.2, financial managers are very disinclined to cut dividends. Moreover, they are very conscious of their previous dividends and desire to maintain a relatively steady dividend. In contrast, the cost of external capital and the desire to attract "prudent man" investors (those with fiduciary duties) are less important.

Table 18.3 is drawn from the same survey, but here the responses are to the question, "How important are the following factors to your company's dividend decision?" Not surprisingly given the responses in Table 18.2 and our earlier discussion, the highest priority is maintaining a consistent dividend policy. The next several items are also consistent with our previous analysis. Financial managers are very concerned about earnings stability and future earnings levels in making dividend decisions, and they consider the availability of good investment opportunities. Survey respondents also believed that attracting both institutional and individual (retail) investors was relatively important.

In contrast to our discussion in the earlier part of this chapter on taxes and flotation costs, the financial managers in this survey did not think that personal taxes paid on dividends by shareholders are very important. And even fewer think that equity flotation costs are relevant.

Concept Questions

18.6a What is a residual dividend policy?

18.6b What is the chief drawback to a strict residual policy? What do many firms do in practice?

18.7 STOCK REPURCHASE: AN ALTERNATIVE TO CASH DIVIDENDS

When a firm wants to pay cash to its shareholders, it normally pays a cash dividend. Another way is to **repurchase** its own stock. In 2000, for example, 2,072 firms announced buyback programs totaling almost $300 billion.

In fact, net equity sales in the United States have actually been negative in some recent years. This has occurred because corporations have actually repurchased more stock than they have sold. Stock repurchasing has thus been a major financial activity, and it appears that it will continue to be one.

repurchase
Another method used to pay out a firm's earnings to its owners, which provides more preferable tax treatment than dividends.

Cash Dividends versus Repurchase

Imagine an all-equity company with excess cash of $300,000. The firm pays no dividends, and its net income for the year just ended is $49,000. The market value balance sheet at the end of the year is represented here.

Market Value Balance Sheet (before paying out excess cash)			
Excess cash	$ 300,000	Debt	$ 0
Other assets	700,000	Equity	1,000,000
Total	$1,000,000	Total	$1,000,000

There are 100,000 shares outstanding. The total market value of the equity is $1 million, so the stock sells for $10 per share. Earnings per share, EPS, are $49,000/100,000 = $.49, and the price-earnings ratio, PE, is $10/.49 = 20.4.

One option the company is considering is a $300,000/100,000 = $3 per share extra cash dividend. Alternatively, the company is thinking of using the money to repurchase $300,000/10 = 30,000 shares of stock.

If commissions, taxes, and other imperfections are ignored in our example, the stockholders shouldn't care which option is chosen. Does this seem surprising? It shouldn't, really. What is happening here is that the firm is paying out $300,000 in cash. The new balance sheet is represented here.

Market Value Balance Sheet (after paying out excess cash)			
Excess cash	$ 0	Debt	$ 0
Other assets	700,000	Equity	700,000
Total	$700,000	Total	$700,000

If the cash is paid out as a dividend, there are still 100,000 shares outstanding, so each is worth $7.

The fact that the per-share value fell from $10 to $7 isn't a cause for concern. Consider a stockholder who owns 100 shares. At $10 per share before the dividend, the total value is $1,000.

After the $3 dividend, this same stockholder has 100 shares worth $7 each, for a total of $700, plus 100 × $3 = $300 in cash, for a combined total of $1,000. This just illustrates what we saw early on: A cash dividend doesn't affect a stockholder's wealth if there are no imperfections. In this case, the stock price simply fell by $3 when the stock went ex dividend.

Also, because total earnings and the number of shares outstanding haven't changed, EPS is still 49 cents. The price-earnings ratio, however, falls to $7/.49 = 14.3. Why we are looking at accounting earnings and PE ratios will be apparent in just a moment.

Alternatively, if the company repurchases 30,000 shares, there are 70,000 left outstanding. The balance sheet looks the same.

Market Value Balance Sheet (after share repurchase)			
Excess cash	$ 0	Debt	$ 0
Other assets	700,000	Equity	700,000
Total	$700,000	Total	$700,000

The company is worth \$700,000 again, so each remaining share is worth \$700,000/70,000 = \$10. Our stockholder with 100 shares is obviously unaffected. For example, if they were so inclined, they could sell 30 shares and end up with \$300 in cash and \$700 in stock, just as they have if the firm pays the cash dividend. This is another example of a homemade dividend.

In this second case, EPS goes up because total earnings remain the same while the number of shares goes down. The new EPS is \$49,000/70,000 = \$.70. However, the important thing to notice is that the PE ratio is \$10/.70 = 14.3, just as it was following the dividend.

This example illustrates the important point that, if there are no imperfections, a cash dividend and a share repurchase are essentially the same thing. This is just another illustration of dividend policy irrelevance when there are no taxes or other imperfections.

Real-World Considerations in a Repurchase

The example we have just described shows that a repurchase and a cash dividend are the same thing in a world without taxes and transaction costs. In the real world, there are some accounting differences between a share repurchase and a cash dividend, but the most important difference is in the tax treatment.

Under current tax law, a repurchase has a significant tax advantage over a cash dividend. A dividend is fully taxed as ordinary income, and a shareholder has no choice about whether or not to receive the dividend. In a repurchase, a shareholder pays taxes only if (1) the shareholder actually chooses to sell and (2) the shareholder has a capital gain on the sale.

For example, suppose a dividend of \$1 per share is taxed at ordinary rates. Investors in the 28 percent tax bracket who own 100 shares of the security pay as much as \$100 × .28 = \$28 in taxes. Selling shareholders would pay far lower taxes if \$100 worth of stock were repurchased. This is because taxes are paid only on the profit from a sale. Thus, the gain on a sale would be only \$40 if shares sold at \$100 were originally purchased at \$60. The capital gains tax would be .28 × \$40 = \$11.20. Note that the recent reductions in dividend and capital gains tax rates do not change the fact that a repurchase has a potentially large tax edge.

If this example strikes you as being too good to be true, you are quite likely right. The IRS does not allow a repurchase solely for the purpose of avoiding taxes. There must be some other business-related reason for repurchasing. Probably the most common reason is that "the stock is a good investment." The second most common is that "investing in the stock is a good use for the money" or that "the stock is undervalued," and so on.

However it is justified, some corporations have engaged in massive repurchases in recent years. For example, in the first three months of 2004, Coca-Cola Company repurchased 9.9 million shares, spending \$486 million, and some analysts predicted the company would repurchase about \$1.5 billion worth of its stock each year for the next several years. Not to be outdone, PepsiCo Inc. repurchased nearly \$5 billion of its shares between 2002 and 2004, and expected to repurchase another \$2.5 billion worth of shares in 2004 alone. IBM is also well-known for its aggressive repurchasing policies. During 2002 and 2003, the company spent $8.6 billion to repurchase about 98 million shares of its stock. Then, in the first three months of 2004, the company repurchased $1.8 billion more of its stock. If that's not enough, the board of directors set aside another $4 billion for additional stock repurchases.

One thing to note is that not all announced stock repurchase plans are completed. It is difficult to get accurate information on how much is actually repurchased, but it has been estimated that only about one-third of all share repurchases are ever completed.

Share Repurchase and EPS

You may read in the popular financial press that a share repurchase is beneficial because it causes earnings per share to increase. As we have seen, this will happen. The reason is simply that a share repurchase reduces the number of outstanding shares, but it has no effect on total earnings. As a result, EPS rises.

However, the financial press may place undue emphasis on EPS figures in a repurchase agreement. In our preceding example, we saw that the value of the stock wasn't affected by the EPS change. In fact, the price-earnings ratio was exactly the same when we compared a cash dividend to a repurchase.

Because the increase in earnings per share is exactly tracked by the increase in the price per share, there is no net effect. Put another way, the increase in EPS is just an accounting adjustment that reflects (correctly) the change in the number of shares outstanding.

In the real world, to the extent that repurchases benefit the firm, we would argue that they do so primarily because of the tax considerations we discussed before.

Concept Questions

18.7a Why might a stock repurchase make more sense than an extra cash dividend?

18.7b Why don't all firms use stock repurchases instead of cash dividends?

STOCK DIVIDENDS AND STOCK SPLITS 18.8

Another type of dividend is paid out in shares of stock. This type of dividend is called a **stock dividend**. A stock dividend is not a true dividend because it is not paid in cash. The effect of a stock dividend is to increase the number of shares that each owner holds. Because there are more shares outstanding, each is simply worth less.

stock dividend
A payment made by a firm to its owners in the form of stock, diluting the value of each share outstanding.

A stock dividend is commonly expressed as a percentage; for example, a 20 percent stock dividend means that a shareholder receives one new share for every five currently owned (a 20 percent increase). Because every shareholder receives 20 percent more stock, the total number of shares outstanding rises by 20 percent. As we will see in a moment, the result is that each share of stock is worth about 20 percent less.

A **stock split** is essentially the same thing as a stock dividend, except that a split is expressed as a ratio instead of a percentage. When a split is declared, each share is split up to create additional shares. For example, in a three-for-one stock split, each old share is split into three new shares.

stock split
An increase in a firm's shares outstanding without any change in owners' equity.

Some Details on Stock Splits and Stock Dividends

Stock splits and stock dividends have essentially the same impacts on the corporation and the shareholder: They increase the number of shares outstanding and reduce the value per share. The accounting treatment is not the same, however, and it depends on two things:

(1) whether the distribution is a stock split or a stock dividend and (2) the size of the stock dividend if it is called a dividend.

By convention, stock dividends of less than 20 to 25 percent are called *small stock dividends.* The accounting procedure for such a dividend is discussed next. A stock dividend greater than this value of 20 to 25 percent is called a *large stock dividend.* Large stock dividends are not uncommon. For example, in April 2004, National Semiconductor, Cognizant Technology Solutions, and Eon Labs all announced 100 percent stock dividends, to name a few. Except for some relatively minor accounting differences, this has the same effect as a two-for-one stock split.

Example of a Small Stock Dividend The Peterson Co., a consulting firm specializing in difficult accounting problems, has 10,000 shares of stock outstanding, each selling at \$66. The total market value of the equity is \$66 × 10,000 = \$660,000. With a 10 percent stock dividend, each stockholder receives one additional share for each 10 owned, and the total number of shares outstanding after the dividend is 11,000.

Before the stock dividend, the equity portion of Peterson's balance sheet might look like this:

Common stock (\$1 par, 10,000 shares outstanding)	\$ 10,000
Capital in excess of par value	200,000
Retained earnings	290,000
Total owners' equity	\$500,000

A seemingly arbitrary accounting procedure is used to adjust the balance sheet after a small stock dividend. Because 1,000 new shares are issued, the common stock account is increased by \$1,000 (1,000 shares at \$1 par value each), for a total of \$11,000. The market price of \$66 is \$65 greater than the par value, so the "excess" of \$65 × 1,000 shares = \$65,000 is added to the capital surplus account (capital in excess of par value), producing a total of \$265,000.

Total owners' equity is unaffected by the stock dividend because no cash has come in or out, so retained earnings is reduced by the entire \$66,000, leaving \$224,000. The net effect of these machinations is that Peterson's equity accounts now look like this:

Common stock (\$1 par, 11,000 shares outstanding)	\$ 11,000
Capital in excess of par value	265,000
Retained earnings	224,000
Total owners' equity	\$500,000

Example of a Stock Split A stock split is conceptually similar to a stock dividend, but it is commonly expressed as a ratio. For example, in a three-for-two split, each shareholder receives one additional share of stock for each two held originally, so a three-for-two split amounts to a 50 percent stock dividend. Again, no cash is paid out, and the percentage of the entire firm that each shareholder owns is unaffected.

The accounting treatment of a stock split is a little different from (and simpler than) that of a stock dividend. Suppose Peterson decides to declare a two-for-one stock split. The number of shares outstanding will double to 20,000, and the par value will be halved to \$.50 per share. The owners' equity after the split is represented as:

Common stock ($.50 par, 20,000 shares outstanding)	$ 10,000
Capital in excess of par value	200,000
Retained earnings	290,000
Total owners' equity	$500,000

For a list of recent stock splits, try www.stocksplits.net.

Note that, for all three of the categories, the figures on the right are completely unaffected by the split. The only changes are in the par value per share and the number of shares outstanding. Because the number of shares has doubled, the par value of each is cut in half.

Example of a Large Stock Dividend In our example, if a 100 percent stock dividend were declared, 10,000 new shares would be distributed, so 20,000 shares would be outstanding. At a $1 par value per share, the common stock account would rise by $10,000, for a total of $20,000. The retained earnings account would be reduced by $10,000, leaving $280,000. The result would be the following:

Common stock ($1 par, 20,000 shares outstanding)	$ 20,000
Capital in excess of par value	200,000
Retained earnings	280,000
Total owners' equity	$500,000

Value of Stock Splits and Stock Dividends

The laws of logic tell us that stock splits and stock dividends can (1) leave the value of the firm unaffected, (2) increase its value, or (3) decrease its value. Unfortunately, the issues are complex enough that one cannot easily determine which of the three relationships holds.

The Benchmark Case A strong case can be made that stock dividends and splits do not change either the wealth of any shareholder or the wealth of the firm as a whole. In our preceding example, the equity had a total market value of $660,000. With the small stock dividend, the number of shares increased to 11,000, so it seems that each would be worth $660,000/11,000 = $60.

For example, a shareholder who had 100 shares worth $66 each before the dividend would have 110 shares worth $60 each afterwards. The total value of the stock is $6,600 either way; so the stock dividend doesn't really have any economic effect.

After the stock split, there are 20,000 shares outstanding, so each should be worth $660,000/20,000 = $33. In other words, the number of shares doubles and the price halves. From these calculations, it appears that stock dividends and splits are just paper transactions.

Although these results are relatively obvious, there are reasons that are often given to suggest that there may be some benefits to these actions. The typical financial manager is aware of many real-world complexities, and, for that reason, the stock split or stock dividend decision is not treated lightly in practice.

Popular Trading Range Proponents of stock dividends and stock splits frequently argue that a security has a proper **trading range**. When the security is priced above this level, many investors do not have the funds to buy the common trading unit of 100 shares, called a *round lot.* Although securities can be purchased in *odd-lot* form (fewer than

trading range
The price range between the highest and lowest prices at which a stock is traded.

100 shares), the commissions are greater. Thus, firms will split the stock to keep the price in this trading range.

For example, in early 2003, Microsoft announced a two-for-one stock split. This was the ninth split for Microsoft since the company went public in 1986. The stock had split three-for-two on two occasions and two-for-one a total of seven times. So, for every share of Microsoft you owned in 1986 when the company first went public, you would own 288 shares as of the most recent stock split. Similarly, since Wal-Mart went public in 1970, it has split its stock two-for-one eleven times, and Dell Computer has split three-for-two once and two-for-one six times since going public in 1988.

Although this argument is a popular one, its validity is questionable for a number of reasons. Mutual funds, pension funds, and other institutions have steadily increased their trading activity since World War II and now handle a sizable percentage of total trading volume (on the order of 80 percent of NYSE trading volume, for example). Because these institutions buy and sell in huge amounts, the individual share price is of little concern.

Furthermore, we sometimes observe share prices that are quite large that do not appear to cause problems. To take a well-known case, Berkshire-Hathaway, a widely respected company headed by legendary investor Warren Buffett, sold for as much as $95,650 per share in 2004.

Finally, there is evidence that stock splits may actually decrease the liquidity of the company's shares. Following a two-for-one split, the number of shares traded should more than double if liquidity is increased by the split. This doesn't appear to happen, and the reverse is sometimes observed.

Reverse Splits

reverse split
A stock split in which a firm's number of shares outstanding is reduced.

A less frequently encountered financial maneuver is the **reverse split**. For example, in June 2003, Priceline.com underwent a one-for-six reverse stock split, and Stamps.com undertook a one-for-two reverse stock split in April 2004. In a one-for-three reverse split, each investor exchanges three old shares for one new share. The par value is tripled in the process. As with stock splits and stock dividends, a case can be made that a reverse split has no real effect.

Given real-world imperfections, three related reasons are cited for reverse splits. First, transaction costs to shareholders may be less after the reverse split. Second, the liquidity and marketability of a company's stock might be improved when its price is raised to the popular trading range. Third, stocks selling at prices below a certain level are not considered respectable, meaning that investors underestimate these firms' earnings, cash flow, growth, and stability. Some financial analysts argue that a reverse split can achieve instant respectability. As was the case with stock splits, none of these reasons is particularly compelling, especially not the third one.

There are two other reasons for reverse splits. First, stock exchanges have minimum price per share requirements. A reverse split may bring the stock price up to such a minimum. In 2001–2002, in the wake of a bear market, this motive became an increasingly important one. In 2001, 106 companies asked their shareholders to approve reverse splits. There were 111 reverse splits in 2002 and 75 in 2003, but only 14 by mid-year 2004. The most common reason for these reverse splits is that NASDAQ delists companies whose stock price drops below $1 per share for 30 days. A large number of companies, particularly Internet-related technology companies, found themselves in danger of being delisted and used reverse splits to boost their stock prices. Second, companies sometimes perform reverse splits and, at the same time, buy out any stockholders who end up with less than a certain number of shares.

For example, in November 2003, Arlington Hospitality, Inc., completed a one-for-100 reverse stock split, followed by a cash purchase of all holdings less than one share. The goal was to buy out all shareholders who held less than one hundred shares (pre-split) to save in mailing and other costs. The company planned to repurchase about 35,000 shares from some 900 stockholders. What made the proposal especially imaginative was that immediately after the reverse stock split, the company underwent a 100-for-one split to restore the stock to its original cost!

Concept Questions

18.8a What is the effect of a stock split on stockholder wealth?

18.8b How does the accounting treatment of a stock split differ from that used with a small stock dividend?

SUMMARY AND CONCLUSIONS 18.9

In this chapter, we first discussed the types of dividends and how they are paid. We then defined dividend policy and examined whether or not dividend policy matters. Next, we illustrated how a firm might establish a dividend policy and described an important alternative to cash dividends, a share repurchase.

In covering these subjects, we saw that:

1. Dividend policy is irrelevant when there are no taxes or other imperfections because shareholders can effectively undo the firm's dividend strategy. Shareholders who receive dividends greater than desired can reinvest the excess. Conversely, shareholders who receive dividends smaller than desired can sell off extra shares of stock.
2. Individual shareholder income taxes and new issue flotation costs are real-world considerations that favor a low-dividend payout. With taxes and new issue costs, the firm should pay out dividends only after all positive NPV projects have been fully financed.
3. There are groups in the economy that may favor a high payout. These include many large institutions such as pension plans. Recognizing that some groups prefer a high payout and some prefer a low payout, the clientele effect argument supports the idea that dividend policy responds to the needs of stockholders. For example, if 40 percent of the stockholders prefer low dividends and 60 percent of the stockholders prefer high dividends, approximately 40 percent of companies will have a low-dividend payout, and 60 percent will have a high payout. This sharply reduces the impact of any individual firm's dividend policy on its market price.
4. A firm wishing to pursue a strict residual dividend payout will have an unstable dividend. Dividend stability is usually viewed as highly desirable. We therefore discussed a compromise strategy that provides for a stable dividend and appears to be quite similar to the dividend policies many firms follow in practice.
5. A stock repurchase acts much like a cash dividend, but has a significant tax advantage. Stock repurchases are therefore a very useful part of overall dividend policy.

To close out our discussion of dividends, we emphasize one last time the difference between dividends and dividend policy. Dividends are important, because the value of a share of stock is ultimately determined by the dividends that will be paid. What is less clear is whether or not the time pattern of dividends (more now versus more later) matters. This is the dividend policy question, and it is not easy to give a definitive answer to it.

Chapter Review and Self-Test Problems

18.1 Residual Dividend Policy The Readata Corporation practices a strict residual dividend policy and maintains a capital structure of 60 percent debt, 40 percent equity. Earnings for the year are \$5,000. What is the maximum amount of capital spending possible without selling new equity? Suppose that planned investment outlays for the coming year are \$12,000. Will Readata be paying a dividend? If so, how much?

18.2 Repurchase versus Cash Dividend Gothic Corporation is deciding whether to pay out \$500 in excess cash in the form of an extra dividend or a share repurchase. Current earnings are \$2.50 per share, and the stock sells for \$25. The market value balance sheet before paying out the \$500 is as follows:

Market Value Balance Sheet (before paying out excess cash)

Excess cash	\$ 500	Debt	\$ 500
Other assets	2,500	Equity	2,500
Total	\$3,000	Total	\$3,000

Evaluate the two alternatives in terms of the effect on the price per share of the stock, the EPS, and the PE ratio.

Answers to Chapter Review and Self-Test Problems

18.1 Readata has a debt-equity ratio of .60/.40 = 1.50. If the entire \$5,000 in earnings were reinvested, then \$5,000 × 1.50 = \$7,500 in new borrowing would be needed to keep the debt-equity ratio unchanged. Total new financing possible without external equity is thus \$5,000 + 7,500 = \$12,500.

If planned outlays are \$12,000, then this amount will be financed with 40 percent equity. The needed equity is thus \$12,000 × .40 = \$4,800. This is less than the \$5,000 in earnings, so a dividend of \$5,000 − 4,800 = \$200 will be paid.

18.2 The market value of the equity is \$2,500. The price per share is \$25, so there are 100 shares outstanding. The cash dividend would amount to \$500/100 = \$5 per share. When the stock goes ex dividend, the price will drop by \$5 per share to \$20. Put another way, the total assets decrease by \$500, so the equity value goes down by this amount to \$2,000. With 100 shares, the new stock price is \$20 per share. After the dividend, EPS will be the same, \$2.50, but the PE ratio will be \$20/2.50 = 8 times.

With a repurchase, \$500/25 = 20 shares will be bought up, leaving 80. The equity will again be worth \$2,000 total. With 80 shares, this is \$2,000/80 = \$25 per share, so the price doesn't change. Total earnings for Gothic must be \$2.50 × 100 = \$250. After the repurchase, EPS will be higher at \$250/80 = \$3.125. The PE ratio, however, will be \$25/3.125 = 8 times.

Concepts Review and Critical Thinking Questions

1. **Dividend Policy Irrelevance** How is it possible that dividends are so important, but, at the same time, dividend policy is irrelevant?
2. **Stock Repurchases** What is the impact of a stock repurchase on a company's debt ratio? Does this suggest another use for excess cash?
3. **Dividend Policy** What is the chief drawback to a strict residual dividend policy? Why is this a problem? How does a compromise policy work? How does it differ from a strict residual policy?

4. **Dividend Chronology** On Tuesday, December 8, Hometown Power Co.'s board of directors declares a dividend of 75 cents per share payable on Wednesday, January 17, to shareholders of record as of Wednesday, January 3. When is the ex-dividend date? If a shareholder buys stock before that date, who gets the dividends on those shares, the buyer or the seller?

5. **Alternative Dividends** Some corporations, like one British company that offers its large shareholders free crematorium use, pay dividends in kind (that is, offer their services to shareholders at below-market cost). Should mutual funds invest in stocks that pay these dividends in kind? (The fundholders do not receive these services.)

6. **Dividends and Stock Price** If increases in dividends tend to be followed by (immediate) increases in share prices, how can it be said that dividend policy is irrelevant?

7. **Dividends and Stock Price** Last month, Central Virginia Power Company, which had been having trouble with cost overruns on a nuclear power plant that it had been building, announced that it was "temporarily suspending payments due to the cash flow crunch associated with its investment program." The company's stock price dropped from $28.50 to $25 when this announcement was made. How would you interpret this change in the stock price (that is, what would you say caused it)?

8. **Dividend Reinvestment Plans** The DRK Corporation has recently developed a dividend reinvestment plan, or DRIP. The plan allows investors to reinvest cash dividends automatically in DRK in exchange for new shares of stock. Over time, investors in DRK will be able to build their holdings by reinvesting dividends to purchase additional shares of the company.

   Over 1,000 companies offer dividend reinvestment plans. Most companies with DRIPs charge no brokerage or service fees. In fact, the shares of DRK will be purchased at a 10 percent discount from the market price.

   A consultant for DRK estimates that about 75 percent of DRK's shareholders will take part in this plan. This is somewhat higher than the average.

   Evaluate DRK's dividend reinvestment plan. Will it increase shareholder wealth? Discuss the advantages and disadvantages involved here.

9. **Dividend Policy** For initial public offerings of common stock, 2000 was a very big year, with over $80.6 billion raised by the process. Relatively few of the 452 firms involved paid cash dividends. Why do you think that most chose not to pay cash dividends?

10. **Investment and Dividends** The Phew Charitable Trust pays no taxes on its capital gains or on its dividend income or interest income. Would it be irrational for it to have low-dividend, high-growth stocks in its portfolio? Would it be irrational for it to have municipal bonds in its portfolio? Explain.

    Use the following information to answer the next two questions:

    Historically, the U.S. tax code treated dividend payments made to shareholders as ordinary income. Thus, dividends were taxed at the investor's marginal tax rate, which was as high as 38.6 percent in 2002. Capital gains were taxed at a capital gains tax rate, which was the same for most investors, and fluctuated through the years. In 2002, the capital gains tax rate stood at 20 percent. In an effort to stimulate the economy, President George W. Bush presided over a tax plan overhaul that included changes in dividend and capital gains tax rates. The new tax plan, which was implemented in 2003, called for a 15 percent tax rate on both dividends and capital gains for investors in higher tax brackets. For lower-tax bracket investors, the tax rate on dividends and capital gains was set at 5 percent through 2007, dropping to zero in 2008.

11. Ex-Dividend Stock Prices How do you think this tax law change affects ex-dividend stock prices?

12. Stock Repurchases How do you think this tax law change affected the relative attractiveness of stock repurchases compared to dividend payments?

Questions and Problems

BASIC
(Questions 1–13)

1. Dividends and Taxes Lee Ann, Inc., has declared a $6.00 per share dividend. Suppose capital gains are not taxed, but dividends are taxed at 15 percent. New IRS regulations require that taxes be withheld at the time the dividend is paid. Lee Ann sells for $80 per share, and the stock is about to go ex dividend. What do you think the ex-dividend price will be?

2. Stock Dividends The owners' equity accounts for Hexagon International are shown here:

Common stock ($1 par value)	$ 10,000
Capital surplus	180,000
Retained earnings	586,500
Total owners' equity	$776,500

a. If Hexagon stock currently sells for $25 per share and a 10 percent stock dividend is declared, how many new shares will be distributed? Show how the equity accounts would change.

b. If Hexagon declared a 25 percent stock dividend, how would the accounts change?

3. Stock Splits For the company in Problem 2, show how the equity accounts will change if:

a. Hexagon declares a four-for-one stock split. How many shares are outstanding now? What is the new par value per share?

b. Hexagon declares a one-for-five reverse stock split. How many shares are outstanding now? What is the new par value per share?

4. Stock Splits and Stock Dividends Rooster Rocks Corporation (RRC) currently has 150,000 shares of stock outstanding that sell for $65 per share. Assuming no market imperfections or tax effects exist, what will the share price be after:

a. RRC has a five-for-three stock split?

b. RRC has a 15 percent stock dividend?

c. RRC has a 42.5 percent stock dividend?

d. RRC has a four-for-seven reverse stock split?

e. Determine the new number of shares outstanding in parts (*a*) through (*d*).

5. Regular Dividends The balance sheet for Cherry Pie Corp. is shown here in market value terms. There are 5,000 shares of stock outstanding.

Market Value Balance Sheet			
Cash	$ 20,000	Equity	$175,000
Fixed assets	155,000		
Total	$175,000	Total	$175,000

The company has declared a dividend of $1.50 per share. The stock goes ex dividend tomorrow. Ignoring any tax effects, what is the stock selling for today?

What will it sell for tomorrow? What will the balance sheet look like after the dividends are paid?

6. **Share Repurchase** In the previous problem, suppose Cherry Pie has announced it is going to repurchase $4,025 worth of stock. What effect will this transaction have on the equity of the firm? How many shares will be outstanding? What will the price per share be after the repurchase? Ignoring tax effects, show how the share repurchase is effectively the same as a cash dividend.

7. **Stock Dividends** The market value balance sheet for Outbox Manufacturing is shown here. Outbox has declared a 25 percent stock dividend. The stock goes ex dividend tomorrow (the chronology for a stock dividend is similar to that for a cash dividend). There are 15,000 shares of stock outstanding. What will the ex dividend price be?

Market Value Balance Sheet

Cash	$190,000	Debt	$160,000
Fixed assets	330,000	Equity	360,000
Total	$520,000	Total	$520,000

8. **Stock Dividends** The company with the common equity accounts shown here has declared a 12 percent stock dividend at a time when the market value of its stock is $20 per share. What effects on the equity accounts will the distribution of the stock dividend have?

Common stock ($1 par value)	$ 350,000
Capital surplus	1,650,000
Retained earnings	3,000,000
Total owners' equity	$5,000,000

9. **Stock Splits** In the previous problem, suppose the company instead decides on a five-for-one stock split. The firm's 70-cent per share cash dividend on the new (post-split) shares represents an increase of 10 percent over last year's dividend on the pre-split stock. What effect does this have on the equity accounts? What was last year's dividend per share?

10. **Residual Dividend Policy** Soprano, Inc., a litter recycling company, uses a residual dividend policy. A debt-equity ratio of .80 is considered optimal. Earnings for the period just ended were $1,200, and a dividend of $480 was declared. How much in new debt was borrowed? What were total capital outlays?

11. **Residual Dividend Policy** Worthington Corporation has declared an annual dividend of $0.80 per share. For the year just ended, earnings were $7 per share.
    a. What is Worthington's payout ratio?
    b. Suppose Worthington has seven million shares outstanding. Borrowing for the coming year is planned at $18 million. What are planned investment outlays assuming a residual dividend policy? What target capital structure is implicit in these calculations?

12. **Residual Dividend Policy** Red Zeppelin Corporation follows a strict residual dividend policy. Its debt-equity ratio is 3.
    a. If earnings for the year are $180,000, what is the maximum amount of capital spending possible with no new equity?

b. If planned investment outlays for the coming year are $760,000, will Red Zeppelin pay a dividend? If so, how much?

c. Does Red Zeppelin maintain a constant dividend payout? Why or why not?

13. Residual Dividend Policy Preti Rock (PR), Inc., predicts that earnings in the coming year will be $56 million. There are 12 million shares, and PR maintains a debt-equity ratio of 2.

a. Calculate the maximum investment funds available without issuing new equity and the increase in borrowing that goes along with it.

b. Suppose the firm uses a residual dividend policy. Planned capital expenditures total $72 million. Based on this information, what will the dividend per share be?

c. In part (*b*), how much borrowing will take place? What is the addition to retained earnings?

d. Suppose PR plans no capital outlays for the coming year. What will the dividend be under a residual policy? What will new borrowing be?

INTERMEDIATE
(Questions 14–16)

14. Homemade Dividends You own 1,000 shares of stock in Avondale Corporation. You will receive a 70-cent per share dividend in one year. In two years, Avondale will pay a liquidating dividend of $40 per share. The required return on Avondale stock is 15 percent. What is the current share price of your stock (ignoring taxes)? If you would rather have equal dividends in each of the next two years, show how you can accomplish this by creating homemade dividends. Hint: Dividends will be in the form of an annuity.

15. Homemade Dividends In the previous problem, suppose you want only $200 total in dividends the first year. What will your homemade dividend be in two years?

16. Stock Repurchase Flychucker Corporation is evaluating an extra dividend versus a share repurchase. In either case, $5,000 would be spent. Current earnings are $0.95 per share, and the stock currently sells for $40 per share. There are 200 shares outstanding. Ignore taxes and other imperfections in answering the first two questions.

a. Evaluate the two alternatives in terms of the effect on the price per share of the stock and shareholder wealth.

b. What will be the effect on Flychucker's EPS and PE ratio under the two different scenarios?

c. In the real world, which of these actions would you recommend? Why?

CHALLENGE
(Questions 17–18)

17. Expected Return, Dividends, and Taxes The Gecko Company and the Gordon Company are two firms whose business risk is the same but that have different dividend policies. Gecko pays no dividend, whereas Gordon has an expected dividend yield of 6 percent. Suppose the capital gains tax rate is zero, whereas the income tax rate is 35 percent. Gecko has an expected earnings growth rate of 15 percent annually, and its stock price is expected to grow at this same rate. If the aftertax expected returns on the two stocks are equal (because they are in the same risk class), what is the pretax required return on Gordon's stock?

18. Dividends and Taxes As discussed in the text, in the absence of market imperfections and tax effects, we would expect the share price to decline by the amount of the dividend payment when the stock goes ex dividend. Once we consider the role of taxes, however, this is not necessarily true. One model has been proposed that incorporates tax effects into determining the ex-dividend price:[7]

$$(P_0 - P_X)/D = (1 - T_P)/(1 - T_G)$$

[7]N. Elton and M. Gruber, "Marginal Stockholder Tax Rates and the Clientele Effect," *Review of Economics and Statistics* 52 (February 1970).

where P_0 is the price just before the stock goes ex, P_X is the ex-dividend share price, D is the amount of the dividend per share, T_P is the relevant marginal personal tax rate on dividends, and T_G is the effective marginal tax rate on capital gains.

a. If $T_P = T_G = 0$, how much will the share price fall when the stock goes ex?

b. If $T_P = 15$ percent and $T_G = 0$, how much will the share price fall?

c. If $T_P = 15$ percent and $T_G = 20$ percent, how much will the share price fall?

d. Suppose the only owners of stock are corporations. Recall that corporations get at least a 70 percent exemption from taxation on the dividend income they receive, but they do not get such an exemption on capital gains. If the corporation's income and capital gains tax rates are both 35 percent, what does this model predict the ex-dividend share price will be?

e. What does this problem tell you about real-world tax considerations and the dividend policy of the firm?

S&P Problem

1. Dividend Payouts Use the annual financial statements for General Mills (GIS), Boston Beer (SAM), and US Steel (X) to find the dividend payout ratio for each company for the last three years. Why would these companies pay out a different percentage of income as dividends? Is there anything unusual about the dividends paid by US Steel? How is this possible?

What's On the Web?

18.1 Dividend Reinvestment Plans As we mentioned in the chapter, dividend reinvestment plans (DRIPs) permit shareholders to automatically reinvest cash dividends in the company. To find out more about DRIPs go to www.fool.com, follow the "Fool's School" link and then the "DRIP Investing" link. What are the advantages Motley Fool lists for DRIPs? What are the different types of DRIPs? What is a Direct Purchase Plan? How does a Direct Purchase Plan differ from a DRIP?

18.2 Dividends Go to www.companyboardroom.com and scroll down until you see the section titled Today's Highlighted Dividends and follow the "Full List" link. How many companies went "ex" on this day? What is the largest declared dividend? For the stocks going "ex" today, what is the longest time until the payable date?

18.3 Stock Splits Go to www.companyboardroom.com and scroll down until you see the section titled Today's Highlighted Splits and follow the "Full List" link. How many stock splits are listed? How many are reverse splits? What is the largest split and the largest reverse split in terms of shares? Pick a company and follow the link. What type of information do you find?

18.4 Dividend Yields Which stock has the highest dividend yield? To answer this (and more), go to finance.yahoo.com and follow the "Screener" link. Use the minimum value box for the dividend yield on the Java version of the screener to find out how many stocks have a dividend yield above 3 percent. Above 5 percent? Now use the dividend amount to find out how many stocks have an annual dividend above $2. Above $4?

18.5 Stock Splits How many times has Procter & Gamble stock split? Go to the web page at www.pg.com, and you will find a pull-down menu listed under "Investing." Follow the "Stock Information" link, then the "Splits & Dividends." When did Procter & Gamble stock first split? What was the split? When was the most recent stock split?

Visit us at www.mhhe.com/rwj

>> MINI-CASE

Cost of Capital for Hubbard Computer, Inc.

You have recently been hired by Hubbard Computer, Inc., (HCI) in its relatively new treasury management department. HCI was founded eight years ago by Bob Hubbard and currently operates 74 stores in the Southeast. The company is privately owned by Bob and his family, and it had sales of $97 million last year.

HCI primarily sells to customers who shop in the stores. Customers come to the store and talk with a sales representative. The sales representative assists the customer in determining the type of computer and peripherals that are necessary for the individual customer's computing needs. After the order is taken, the customer pays for the order immediately, and the computer is made to fill the order. Delivery of the computer averages 15 days, and it is guaranteed in 30 days.

HCI's growth to date has come from its profits. When the company had sufficient capital, it would open a new store. Other than scouting locations, relatively little formal analysis has been used in its capital budgeting process. Bob has just read about capital budgeting techniques and has come to you for help. For starters, the company has never attempted to determine its cost of capital, and Bob would like you to perform the analysis. Since the company is privately owned, it is difficult to determine the cost of equity for the company. Bob wants you to use the pure play approach to estimating the cost of capital for HCI, and he has chosen Dell as a representative company. The following steps will allow you to calculate this estimate.

1. Most publicly traded corporations are required to submit quarterly (10Q) and annual reports (10K) to the SEC detailing the financial operations of the company over the past quarter or year, respectively. These corporate filings are available on the SEC Web site at www.sec.gov. Go to the SEC Web site, follow the "Search for Company Filings" link, the "Companies & Other Files" link, enter "Dell Computer," and search for SEC filings made by Dell. Find the most recent 10Q or 10K and download the form. Look on the balance sheet to find the book value of debt and the book value of equity. If you look further down the report, you should find a section titled "Long-term Debt and Interest Rate Risk Management" that will provide a breakdown of Dell's long-term debt.
2. To estimate the cost of equity for Dell, go to finance.yahoo.com and enter the ticker symbol DELL. Follow the links to answer the following questions: What is the most recent stock price listed for Dell? What is the market value of equity, or market capitalization? How many shares of stock does Dell have outstanding? What is the most recent annual dividend? Can you use the dividend discount model in this case? What is the beta for Dell? Now go back to finance.yahoo.com and follow the "Bonds" link. What is the yield on 3-month Treasury bills? Using the historical market risk premium, what is the cost of equity for Dell using CAPM?
3. You now need to calculate the cost of debt for Dell. Go to www.nasdbondinfo.com, enter Dell as the company and find the yield to maturity for each of Dell's bonds. What is the weighted average cost of debt for Dell using the book value weights and using the market value weights? Does it make a difference in this case if you use book value weights or market value weights?
4. You now have all the necessary information to calculate the weighted average cost of capital for Dell. Calculate the weighted average cost of capital for Dell using book value weights and market value weights assuming Dell has a 35 percent marginal tax rate. Which number is more relevant?
5. You used Dell as a pure play company to estimate the cost of capital for HCI. Are there any potential problems with this approach in this situation?

19 Short-Term Finance and Planning

The spring of 2004 brought record gasoline prices in the United States, which created problems for automobile manufacturers. Especially hard hit were sales of high-priced, high-margin sport utility vehicles (SUVs). For example, sales of the BMW X5 dropped 6 percent from the previous year. Lower sales meant that SUV inventories grew to a 100-day supply, substantially greater than the 60 to 65 days the industry prefers. To reduce inventory and increase sales, manufacturers were forced to offer cash rebates, ranging from $500 to $5,000, which reduced profits. As this chapter explores, the length of time goods are carried in inventory until they are sold is an important element of short-term financial management, and industries such as the automobile industry pay close attention to it.

To this point, we have described many of the decisions of long-term finance, such as those of capital budgeting, dividend policy, and financial structure. In this chapter, we begin to discuss short-term finance. Short-term finance is primarily concerned with the analysis of decisions that affect current assets and current liabilities.

Frequently, the term *net working capital* is associated with short-term financial decision making. As we describe in Chapter 2 and elsewhere, net working capital is the difference between current assets and current liabilities. Often, short-term financial management is called *working capital management.* These terms mean the same thing.

Interested in a career in short-term finance? Visit the Treasury Management Association Web site at www.treasurymanagement.com.

There is no universally accepted definition of short-term finance. The most important difference between short-term and long-term finance is in the timing of cash flows. Short-term financial decisions typically involve cash inflows and outflows that occur within a year or less. For example, short-term financial decisions are involved when a firm orders raw materials, pays in cash, and anticipates selling finished goods in one year for cash. In contrast, long-term financial decisions are involved when a firm purchases a special machine that will reduce operating costs over, say, the next five years.

What types of questions fall under the general heading of short-term finance? To name just a very few:

1. What is a reasonable level of cash to keep on hand (in a bank) to pay bills?
2. How much should the firm borrow in the short term?
3. How much credit should be extended to customers?

This chapter introduces the basic elements of short-term financial decisions. First, we discuss the short-term operating activities of the firm. We then identify some alternative short-term financial policies. Finally, we outline the basic elements in a short-term financial plan and describe short-term financing instruments.

19.1 TRACING CASH AND NET WORKING CAPITAL

In this section, we examine the components of cash and net working capital as they change from one year to the next. We have already discussed various aspects of this subject in Chapters 2, 3, and 4. We briefly review some of that discussion as it relates to short-term financing decisions. Our goal is to describe the short-term operating activities of the firm and their impact on cash and working capital.

To begin, recall that *current assets* are cash and other assets that are expected to convert to cash within the year. Current assets are presented on the balance sheet in order of their accounting liquidity—the ease with which they can be converted to cash and the time it takes to convert them. Four of the most important items found in the current asset section of a balance sheet are cash and cash equivalents, marketable securities, accounts receivable, and inventories.

Analogous to their investment in current assets, firms use several kinds of short-term debt, called *current liabilities*. Current liabilities are obligations that are expected to require cash payment within one year (or within the operating period if it is longer than one year). Three major items found as current liabilities are accounts payable, expenses payable (including accrued wages and taxes), and notes payable.

Because we want to focus on changes in cash, we start off by defining cash in terms of the other elements of the balance sheet. This lets us isolate the cash account and explore the impact on cash from the firm's operating and financing decisions. The basic balance sheet identity can be written as:

$$\text{Net working capital} + \text{Fixed assets} = \text{Long-term debt} + \text{Equity} \qquad [19.1]$$

Net working capital is cash plus other current assets, less current liabilities, that is:

$$\text{Net working capital} = (\text{Cash} + \text{Other current assets}) - \text{Current liabilities} \qquad [19.2]$$

If we substitute this for net working capital in the basic balance sheet identity and rearrange things a bit, we see that cash is:

$$\begin{aligned}\text{Cash} = {} & \text{Long-term debt} + \text{Equity} + \text{Current liabilities} \\ & - \text{Current assets other than cash} - \text{Fixed assets}\end{aligned} \qquad [19.3]$$

This tells us in general terms that some activities naturally increase cash and some activities decrease it. We can list these various activities, along with an example of each, as follows:

Activities that increase cash

Increasing long-term debt (borrowing over the long term)
Increasing equity (selling some stock)
Increasing current liabilities (getting a 90-day loan)
Decreasing current assets other than cash (selling some inventory for cash)
Decreasing fixed assets (selling some property)

Activities that decrease cash

Decreasing long-term debt (paying off a long-term debt)
Decreasing equity (repurchasing some stock)
Decreasing current liabilities (paying off a 90-day loan)
Increasing current assets other than cash (buying some inventory for cash)
Increasing fixed assets (buying some property)

Notice that our two lists are exact opposites. For example, floating a long-term bond issue increases cash (at least until the money is spent). Paying off a long-term bond issue decreases cash.

As we discussed in Chapter 3, those activities that increase cash are called *sources of cash.* Those activities that decrease cash are called *uses of cash.* Looking back at our list, we see that sources of cash always involve increasing a liability (or equity) account or decreasing an asset account. This makes sense because increasing a liability means that we have raised money by borrowing it or by selling an ownership interest in the firm. A decrease in an asset means that we have sold or otherwise liquidated an asset. In either case, there is a cash inflow.

Uses of cash are just the reverse. A use of cash involves decreasing a liability by paying it off, perhaps, or increasing assets by purchasing something. Both of these activities require that the firm spend some cash.

EXAMPLE 19.1

Sources and Uses

Here is a quick check of your understanding of sources and uses: If accounts payable go up by $100, does this indicate a source or a use? What if accounts receivable go up by $100?

Accounts payable are what we owe our suppliers. This is a short-term debt. If it rises by $100, we have effectively borrowed the money, which is a *source* of cash. Receivables are what our customers owe to us, so an increase of $100 in accounts receivable means that we have loaned the money; this is a *use* of cash.

Concept Questions

19.1a What is the difference between net working capital and cash?

19.1b Will net working capital always increase when cash increases?

19.1c List five potential uses of cash.

19.1d List five potential sources of cash.

THE OPERATING CYCLE AND THE CASH CYCLE 19.2

The primary concern in short-term finance is the firm's short-run operating and financing activities. For a typical manufacturing firm, these short-run activities might consist of the following sequence of events and decisions:

Event	Decision
1. Buying raw materials	1. How much inventory to order
2. Paying cash	2. Whether to borrow or draw down cash balances
3. Manufacturing the product	3. What choice of production technology to use
4. Selling the product	4. Whether credit should be extended to a particular customer
5. Collecting cash	5. How to collect

These activities create patterns of cash inflows and cash outflows. These cash flows are both unsynchronized and uncertain. They are unsynchronized because, for example, the payment of cash for raw materials does not happen at the same time as the receipt of cash from selling the product. They are uncertain because future sales and costs cannot be precisely predicted.

Defining the Operating and Cash Cycles

We can start with a simple case. One day, call it Day 0, we purchase \$1,000 worth of inventory on credit. We pay the bill 30 days later, and, after 30 more days, someone buys the \$1,000 in inventory for \$1,400. Our buyer does not actually pay for another 45 days. We can summarize these events chronologically as follows:

Day	Activity	Cash Effect
0	Acquire inventory	None
30	Pay for inventory	−\$1,000
60	Sell inventory on credit	None
105	Collect on sale	+\$1,400

operating cycle
The time period between the acquisition of inventory and the collection of cash from receivables.

inventory period
The time it takes to acquire and sell inventory.

accounts receivable period
The time between sale of inventory and collection of the receivable.

The Operating Cycle

There are several things to notice in our example. First, the entire cycle, from the time we acquire some inventory to the time we collect the cash, takes 105 days. This is called the **operating cycle**.

As we illustrate, the operating cycle is the length of time it takes to acquire inventory, sell it, and collect for it. This cycle has two distinct components. The first part is the time it takes to acquire and sell the inventory. This period, a 60-day span in our example, is called the **inventory period**. The second part is the time it takes to collect on the sale, 45 days in our example. This is called the **accounts receivable period**.

Based on our definitions, the operating cycle is obviously just the sum of the inventory and accounts receivable periods:

$$\text{Operating cycle} = \text{Inventory period} + \text{Accounts receivable period} \quad [19.4]$$

$$105 \text{ days} = 60 \text{ days} + 45 \text{ days}$$

What the operating cycle describes is how a product moves through the current asset accounts. The product begins life as inventory, it is converted to a receivable when it is sold, and it is finally converted to cash when we collect from the sale. Notice that, at each step, the asset is moving closer to cash.

accounts payable period
The time between receipt of inventory and payment for it.

cash cycle
The time between cash disbursement and cash collection.

The Cash Cycle

The second thing to notice is that the cash flows and other events that occur are not synchronized. For example, we don't actually pay for the inventory until 30 days after we acquire it. The intervening 30-day period is called the **accounts payable period**. Next, we spend cash on Day 30, but we don't collect until Day 105. Somehow, we have to arrange to finance the \$1,000 for 105 − 30 = 75 days. This period is called the **cash cycle**.

The cash cycle, therefore, is the number of days that pass before we collect the cash from a sale, measured from when we actually pay for the inventory. Notice that, based on our definitions, the cash cycle is the difference between the operating cycle and the

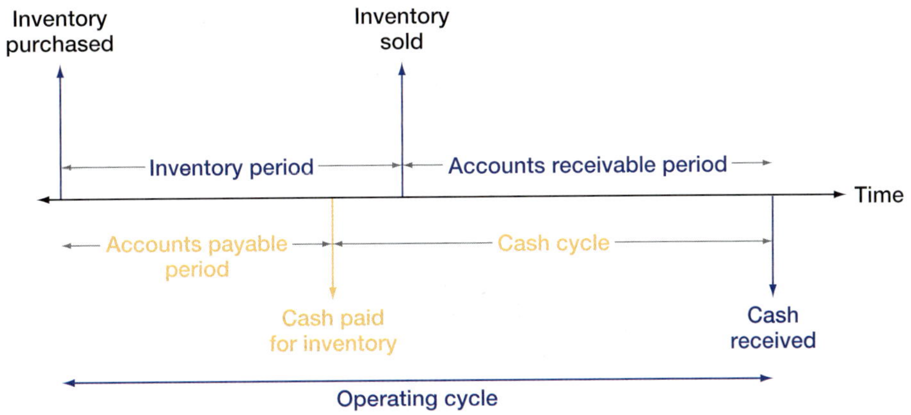

<< FIGURE 19.1

Cash Flow Time Line and the Short-Term Operating Activities of a Typical Manufacturing Firm

The operating cycle is the time period from inventory purchase until the receipt of cash. (The operating cycle may not include the time from placement of the order until arrival of the stock.) The cash cycle is the time period from when cash is paid out to when cash is received.

accounts payable period:

$$\text{Cash cycle} = \text{Operating cycle} - \text{Accounts payable period} \quad [19.5]$$
$$75 \text{ days} = 105 \text{ days} - 30 \text{ days}$$

Figure 19.1 depicts the short-term operating activities and cash flows for a typical manufacturing firm by way of a cash flow time line. As shown, the **cash flow time line** presents the operating cycle and the cash cycle in graphical form. In Figure 19.1, the need for short-term financial management is suggested by the gap between the cash inflows and the cash outflows. This is related to the lengths of the operating cycle and the accounts payable period.

cash flow time line
A graphical representation of the operating cycle and the cash cycle.

The gap between short-term inflows and outflows can be filled either by borrowing or by holding a liquidity reserve in the form of cash or marketable securities. Alternatively, the gap can be shortened by changing the inventory, receivable, and payable periods. These are all managerial options that we discuss in the following sections and in subsequent chapters.

Learn more about outsourcing accounts management at www.businessdebts.com and www.opiglobal.com.

Internet-based bookseller and retailer Amazon.com provides an interesting example of the importance of managing the cash cycle. By mid-2004, the market value of Amazon.com was higher than (in fact almost ten times as much as) that of Barnes & Noble, king of the brick-and-mortar bookstores, even though Barnes & Noble's sales were greater than Amazon's.

How could Amazon.com be worth so much more? There are multiple reasons, but short-term management is one factor. During 2003, Amazon turned over its inventory about 19 times per year, 5 times faster than Barnes & Noble, so its inventory period is dramatically shorter. Even more striking, Amazon charges a customer's credit card when it ships a book, and it usually gets paid by the credit card firm within a day. This means Amazon has a *negative* cash cycle! In fact, during 2003, Amazon's cash cycle was a negative 24 days. Every sale therefore generates a cash inflow that can be put to work immediately.

Amazon is not the only company with a negative cash cycle. Consider aircraft manufacturer Boeing Company. During 2003, Boeing had an inventory period of 178 days and a receivables period of 136 days, so its operating cycle was a lengthy 314 days. Boeing's cash cycle must be fairly long, right? Wrong. Boeing had a payables period of 460 days, so its cash cycle was a negative 146 days!

The Operating Cycle and the Firm's Organizational Chart

Before we examine the operating and cash cycles in greater detail, it is useful for us to take a look at the people involved in managing a firm's current assets and liabilities. As Table 19.1 illustrates, short-term financial management in a large corporation involves a number of different financial and nonfinancial managers. Examining Table 19.1, we see that selling on credit involves at least three different entities: the credit manager, the marketing manager, and the controller. Of these three, only two are responsible to the vice president of finance (the marketing function is usually associated with the vice president of marketing). Thus, there is the potential for conflict, particularly if different managers concentrate on only part of the picture. For example, if marketing is trying to land a new account, it may seek more liberal credit terms as an inducement. However, this may increase the firm's investment in receivables or its exposure to bad-debt risk, and conflict can result.

Calculating the Operating and Cash Cycles

In our example, the lengths of time that made up the different periods were obvious. If all we have is financial statement information, we will have to do a little more work. We illustrate these calculations next.

To begin, we need to determine various things such as how long it takes, on average, to sell inventory and how long it takes, on average, to collect. We start by gathering some balance sheet information such as the following (in thousands):

Item	Beginning	Ending	Average
Inventory	$2,000	$3,000	$2,500
Accounts receivable	1,600	2,000	1,800
Accounts payable	750	1,000	875

Also, from the most recent income statement, we might have the following figures (in thousands):

Net sales	$11,500
Cost of goods sold	8,200

TABLE 19.1 >>

Managers Who Deal with Short-Term Financial Problems

Title of Manager	Duties Related to Short-Term Financial Management	Assets/Liabilities Influenced
Cash manager	Collection, concentration, disbursement; short-term investments; short-term borrowing; banking relations	Cash, marketable securities, short-term loans
Credit manager	Monitoring and control of accounts receivable; credit policy decisions	Accounts receivable
Marketing manager	Credit policy decisions	Accounts receivable
Purchasing manager	Decisions on purchases, suppliers; may negotiate payment terms	Inventory, accounts payable
Production manager	Setting of production schedules and materials requirements	Inventory, accounts payable
Payables manager	Decisions on payment policies and on whether to take discounts	Accounts payable
Controller	Accounting information on cash flows; reconciliation of accounts payable; application of payments to accounts receivable	Accounts receivable, accounts payable

We now need to calculate some financial ratios. We discussed these in some detail in Chapter 3; here, we just define them and use them as needed.

The Operating Cycle First of all, we need the inventory period. We spent \$8.2 million on inventory (our cost of goods sold). Our average inventory was \$2.5 million. We thus turned our inventory over \$8.2/2.5 times during the year:[1]

$$\text{Inventory turnover} = \frac{\text{Cost of goods sold}}{\text{Average inventory}} = \frac{\$8.2 \text{ million}}{2.5 \text{ million}} = 3.28 \text{ times}$$

Loosely speaking, this tells us that we bought and sold off our inventory 3.28 times during the year. This means that, on average, we held our inventory for:

$$\text{Inventory period} = \frac{365 \text{ days}}{\text{Inventory turnover}} = \frac{365}{3.28} = 111.3 \text{ days}$$

So, the inventory period is about 111 days. On average, in other words, inventory sat for about 111 days before it was sold.[2]

Similarly, receivables averaged \$1.8 million, and sales were \$11.5 million. Assuming that all sales were credit sales, the receivables turnover is:[3]

$$\text{Receivables turnover} = \frac{\text{Credit sales}}{\text{Average accounts receivable}} = \frac{\$11.5 \text{ million}}{1.8 \text{ million}} = 6.4 \text{ times}$$

If we turn over our receivables 6.4 times, then the receivables period is:

$$\text{Receivables period} = \frac{365 \text{ days}}{\text{Receivables turnover}} = \frac{365}{6.4} = 57 \text{ days}$$

The receivables period is also called the *days' sales in receivables* or the *average collection period.* Whatever it is called, it tells us that our customers took an average of 57 days to pay.

The operating cycle is the sum of the inventory and receivables periods:

$$\text{Operating cycle} = \text{Inventory period} + \text{Accounts receivable period} = 111 \text{ days} + 57 \text{ days} = 168 \text{ days}$$

This tells us that, on average, 168 days elapse between the time we acquire inventory and, having sold it, collect for the sale.

---

[1]Notice that in calculating inventory turnover here, we use the *average* inventory instead of using the ending inventory as we did in Chapter 3. Both approaches are used in the real world. To gain some practice using average figures, we will stick with this approach in calculating various ratios throughout this chapter.

[2]This measure is conceptually identical to the days' sales in inventory figure we discussed in Chapter 3.

[3]If fewer than 100 percent of our sales were credit sales, then we would just need a little more information, namely, credit sales for the year. See Chapter 3 for more discussion of this measure.

The Cash Cycle We now need the payables period. From the information given earlier, we know that average payables were \$875,000 and cost of goods sold was \$8.2 million. Our payables turnover is:

$$\text{Payables turnover} = \frac{\text{Cost of goods sold}}{\text{Average payables}}$$

$$= \frac{\$8.2 \text{ million}}{\$.875 \text{ million}} = 9.4 \text{ times}$$

The payables period is:

$$\text{Payables period} = \frac{365 \text{ days}}{\text{Payables turnover}}$$

$$= \frac{365}{9.4} = 39 \text{ days}$$

Thus, we took an average of 39 days to pay our bills.

Finally, the cash cycle is the difference between the operating cycle and the payables period:

$$\text{Cash cycle} = \text{Operating cycle} - \text{Accounts payable period}$$
$$= 168 \text{ days} - 39 \text{ days} = 129 \text{ days}$$

So, on average, there is a 129-day delay between the time we pay for merchandise and the time we collect on the sale.

EXAMPLE 19.2 >> The Operating and Cash Cycles

You have collected the following information for the Slowpay Company.

Item	Beginning	Ending
Inventory	\$5,000	\$7,000
Accounts receivable	1,600	2,400
Accounts payable	2,700	4,800

Credit sales for the year just ended were \$50,000, and cost of goods sold was \$30,000. How long does it take Slowpay to collect on its receivables? How long does merchandise stay around before it is sold? How long does Slowpay take to pay its bills?

We can first calculate the three turnover ratios:

$$\text{Inventory turnover} = \$30{,}000/6{,}000 = 5 \text{ times}$$
$$\text{Receivables turnover} = \$50{,}000/2{,}000 = 25 \text{ times}$$
$$\text{Payables turnover} = \$30{,}000/3{,}750 = 8 \text{ times}$$

We use these to get the various periods:

$$\text{Inventory period} = 365/5 = 73 \text{ days}$$
$$\text{Receivables period} = 365/25 = 14.6 \text{ days}$$
$$\text{Payables period} = 365/8 = 45.6 \text{ days}$$

All told, Slowpay collects on a sale in 14.6 days, inventory sits around for 73 days, and bills get paid after about 46 days. The operating cycle here is the sum of the inventory and receivables periods: 73 + 14.6 = 87.6 days. The cash cycle is the difference between the operating cycle and the payables period: 87.6 − 45.6 = 42 days.

Interpreting the Cash Cycle

Our examples show that the cash cycle depends on the inventory, receivables, and payables periods. The cash cycle increases as the inventory and receivables periods get longer. It decreases if the company is able to defer payment of payables and thereby lengthen the payables period.

Unlike Amazon.com, most firms have a positive cash cycle, and they thus require financing for inventories and receivables. The longer the cash cycle, the more financing is required. Also, changes in the firm's cash cycle are often monitored as an early-warning measure. A lengthening cycle can indicate that the firm is having trouble moving inventory or collecting on its receivables. Such problems can be masked, at least partially, by an increased payables cycle, so both cycles should be monitored.

The link between the firm's cash cycle and its profitability can be easily seen by recalling that one of the basic determinants of profitability and growth for a firm is its total asset turnover, which is defined as Sales/Total assets. In Chapter 3, we saw that the higher this ratio is, the greater is the firm's accounting return on assets, ROA, and return on equity, ROE. Thus, all other things being the same, the shorter the cash cycle is, the lower is the firm's investment in inventories and receivables. As a result, the firm's total assets are lower, and total turnover is higher.

Concept Questions

19.2a What does it mean to say that a firm has an inventory turnover ratio of 4?

19.2b Describe the operating cycle and the cash cycle. What are the differences?

19.2c Explain the connection between a firm's accounting-based profitability and its cash cycle.

SOME ASPECTS OF SHORT-TERM FINANCIAL POLICY 19.3

The short-term financial policy that a firm adopts will be reflected in at least two ways:

1. *The size of the firm's investment in current assets.* This is usually measured relative to the firm's level of total operating revenues. A *flexible,* or accommodative, short-term financial policy would maintain a relatively high ratio of current assets to sales. A *restrictive* short-term financial policy would entail a low ratio of current assets to sales.[4]
2. *The financing of current assets.* This is measured as the proportion of short-term debt (that is, current liabilities) and long-term debt used to finance current assets. A restrictive short-term financial policy means a high proportion of short-term debt relative to long-term financing, and a flexible policy means less short-term debt and more long-term debt.

If we take these two areas together, we see that a firm with a flexible policy would have a relatively large investment in current assets, and it would finance this investment with relatively less in short-term debt. The net effect of a flexible policy is thus a relatively high level of net working capital. Put another way, with a flexible policy, the firm maintains a higher overall level of liquidity.

[4]Some people use the term *conservative* in place of *flexible* and the term *aggressive* in place of *restrictive.*

The Size of the Firm's Investment in Current Assets

Short-term financial policies that are flexible with regard to current assets include such actions as:

1. Keeping large balances of cash and marketable securities
2. Making large investments in inventory
3. Granting liberal credit terms, which results in a high level of accounts receivable

Restrictive short-term financial policies would be just the opposite:

1. Keeping low cash balances and making little investment in marketable securities
2. Making small investments in inventory
3. Allowing few or no credit sales, thereby minimizing accounts receivable

Determining the optimal level of investment in short-term assets requires an identification of the different costs of alternative short-term financing policies. The objective is to trade off the cost of a restrictive policy against the cost of a flexible one to arrive at the best compromise.

Current asset holdings are highest with a flexible short-term financial policy and lowest with a restrictive policy. So, flexible short-term financial policies are costly in that they require a greater investment in cash and marketable securities, inventory, and accounts receivable. However, we expect that future cash inflows will be higher with a flexible policy. For example, sales are stimulated by the use of a credit policy that provides liberal financing to customers. A large amount of finished inventory on hand ("on the shelf") enables quick delivery service to customers and may increase sales. Similarly, a large inventory of raw materials may result in fewer production stoppages because of inventory shortages.

A more restrictive short-term financial policy probably reduces future sales to levels below those that would be achieved under flexible policies. It is also possible that higher prices can be charged to customers under flexible working capital policies. Customers may be willing to pay higher prices for the quick delivery service and more liberal credit terms implicit in flexible policies.

Managing current assets can be thought of as involving a trade-off between costs that rise and costs that fall with the level of investment. Costs that rise with increases in the level of investment in current assets are called **carrying costs**. The larger the investment a firm makes in its current assets, the higher its carrying costs will be. Costs that fall with increases in the level of investment in current assets are called **shortage costs**.

carrying costs
Costs that rise with increases in the level of investment in current assets.

shortage costs
Costs that fall with increases in the level of investment in current assets.

In a general sense, carrying costs are the opportunity costs associated with current assets. The rate of return on current assets is very low when compared to that on other assets. For example, the rate of return on U.S. Treasury bills is usually a good deal less than 10 percent. This is very low compared to the rate of return firms would like to achieve overall. (U.S. Treasury bills are an important component of cash and marketable securities.)

Shortage costs are incurred when the investment in current assets is low. If a firm runs out of cash, it will be forced to sell marketable securities. Of course, if a firm runs out of cash and cannot readily sell marketable securities, it may have to borrow or default on an obligation. This situation is called a *cash-out.* A firm may lose customers if it runs out of inventory (a *stock-out*) or if it cannot extend credit to customers.

More generally, there are two kinds of shortage costs:

1. *Trading, or order, costs.* Order costs are the costs of placing an order for more cash (brokerage costs, for example) or more inventory (production setup costs, for example).

2. *Costs related to lack of safety reserves.* These are costs of lost sales, lost customer goodwill, and disruption of production schedules.

The top part of Figure 19.2 illustrates the basic trade-off between carrying costs and shortage costs. On the vertical axis, we have costs measured in dollars, and, on the horizontal axis, we have the amount of current assets. Carrying costs start out at zero when current assets are zero and then climb steadily as current assets grow. Shortage costs start out very high and then decline as we add current assets. The total cost of holding current assets is the sum of the two. Notice how the combined costs reach a minimum at CA*. This is the optimal level of current assets.

Optimal current asset holdings are highest under a flexible policy. This policy is one in which the carrying costs are perceived to be low relative to shortage costs. This is Case A in Figure 19.2. In comparison, under restrictive current asset policies, carrying costs are perceived to be high relative to shortage costs, resulting in lower current asset holdings. This is Case B in Figure 19.2.

Alternative Financing Policies for Current Assets

In previous sections, we looked at the basic determinants of the level of investment in current assets, and we thus focused on the asset side of the balance sheet. Now we turn to the financing side of the question. Here we are concerned with the relative amounts of short-term and long-term debt, assuming that the investment in current assets is constant.

An Ideal Case We start off with the simplest possible case: an "ideal" economy. In such an economy, short-term assets can always be financed with short-term debt, and long-term assets can be financed with long-term debt and equity. In this economy, net working capital is always zero.

Consider a simplified case for a grain elevator operator. Grain elevator operators buy crops after harvest, store them, and sell them during the year. They have high inventories of grain after the harvest and end up with low inventories just before the next harvest.

Bank loans with maturities of less than one year are used to finance the purchase of grain and the storage costs. These loans are paid off from the proceeds of the sale of grain.

The situation is shown in Figure 19.3. Long-term assets are assumed to grow over time, whereas current assets increase at the end of the harvest and then decline during the year. Short-term assets end up at zero just before the next harvest. Current (short-term) assets are financed by short-term debt, and long-term assets are financed with long-term debt and equity. Net working capital—current assets minus current liabilities—is always zero. Figure 19.3 displays a "sawtooth" pattern that we will see again when we get to our discussion on cash management in the next chapter. For now, we need to discuss some alternative policies for financing current assets under less idealized conditions.

Different Policies for Financing Current Assets In the real world, it is not likely that current assets will ever drop to zero. For example, a long-term rising level of sales will result in some permanent investment in current assets. Moreover, the firm's investments in long-term assets may show a great deal of variation.

A growing firm can be thought of as having a total asset requirement consisting of the current assets and long-term assets needed to run the business efficiently. The total asset requirement may exhibit change over time for many reasons, including (1) a general growth trend, (2) seasonal variation around the trend, and (3) unpredictable day-to-day and

FIGURE 19.2 >>

Carrying Costs and Shortage Costs

Short-term financial policy: the optimal investment in current assets

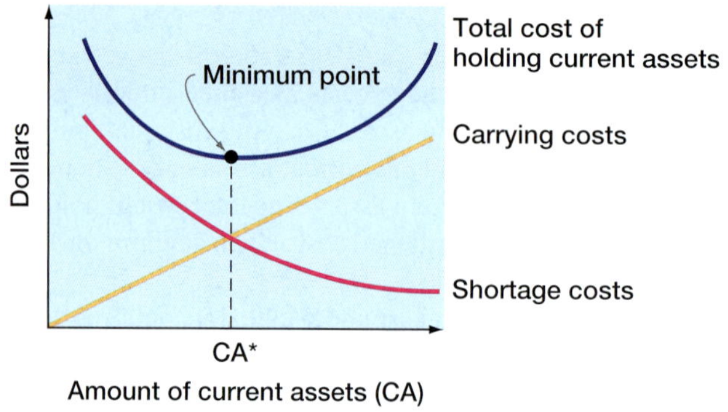

CA* represents the optimal amount of current assets. Holding this amount minimizes total costs.

Carrying costs increase with the level of investment in current assets. They include the costs of maintaining economic value and opportunity costs. Shortage costs decrease with increases in the level of investment in current assets. They include trading costs and the costs related to being short of the current asset (for example, being short of cash). The firm's policy can be characterized as flexible or restrictive.

A. Flexible policy

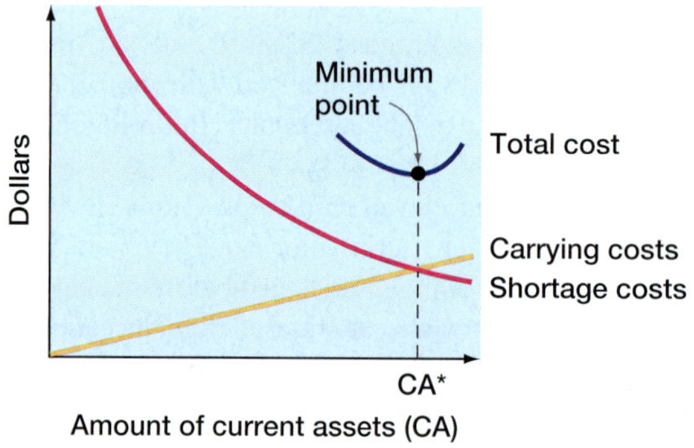

A flexible policy is most appropriate when carrying costs are low relative to shortage costs.

B. Restrictive policy

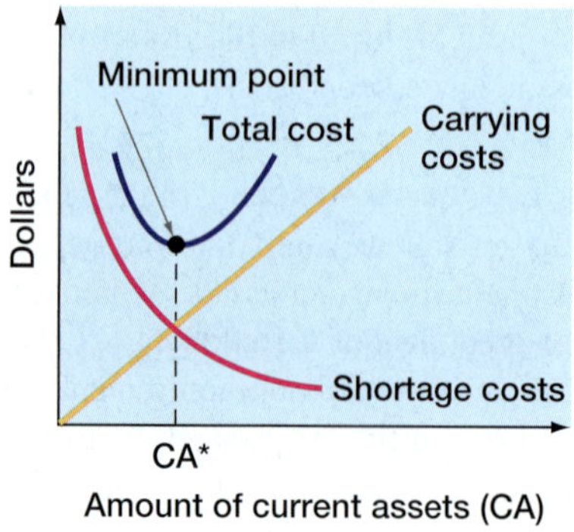

A restrictive policy is most appropriate when carrying costs are high relative to shortage costs.

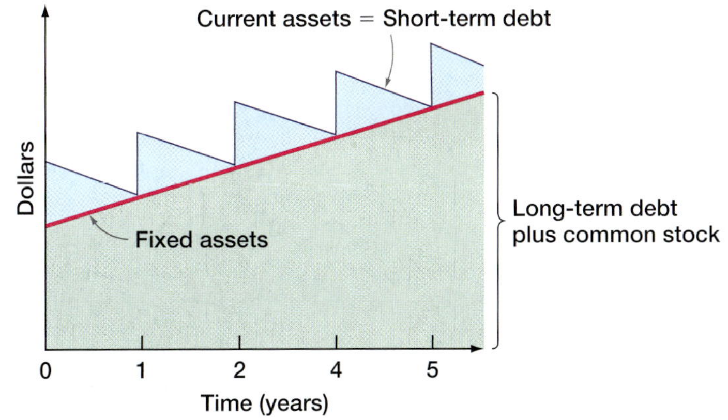

In an ideal world, net working capital is always zero because short-term assets are financed by short-term debt.

<< FIGURE 19.3

Financing Policy for an Ideal Economy

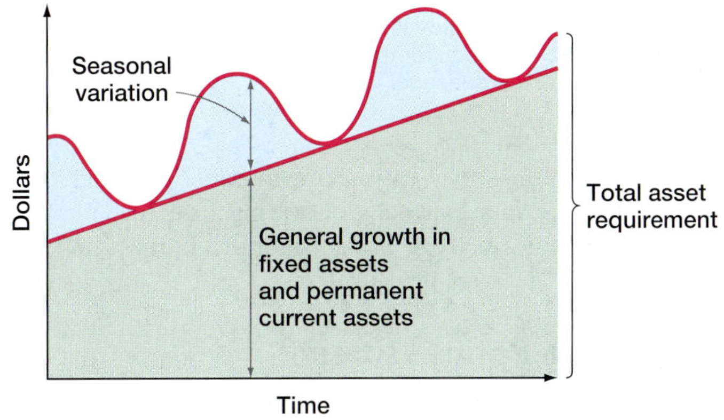

<< FIGURE 19.4

The Total Asset Requirement over Time

month-to-month fluctuations. This fluctuation is depicted in Figure 19.4. (We have not tried to show the unpredictable day-to-day and month-to-month variations in the total asset requirement.)

The peaks and valleys in Figure 19.4 represent the firm's total asset needs through time. For example, for a lawn and garden supply firm, the peaks might represent inventory buildups prior to the spring selling season. The valleys would come about because of lower off-season inventories. There are two strategies such a firm might consider to meet its cyclical needs. First, the firm could keep a relatively large pool of marketable securities. As the need for inventory and other current assets began to rise, the firm would sell off marketable securities and use the cash to purchase whatever was needed. Once the inventory was sold and inventory holdings began to decline, the firm would reinvest in marketable securities. This approach is the flexible policy illustrated in Figure 19.5 as Policy F. Notice that the firm essentially uses a pool of marketable securities as a buffer against changing current asset needs.

At the other extreme, the firm could keep relatively little in marketable securities. As the need for inventory and other assets began to rise, the firm would simply borrow the needed cash on a short-term basis. The firm would repay the loans as the need for assets cycled back down. This approach is the restrictive policy illustrated in Figure 19.5 as Policy R.

In comparing the two strategies illustrated in Figure 19.5, notice that the chief difference is the way in which the seasonal variation in asset needs is financed. In the flexible case, the

FIGURE 19.5 >> **Alternative Asset Financing Policies**

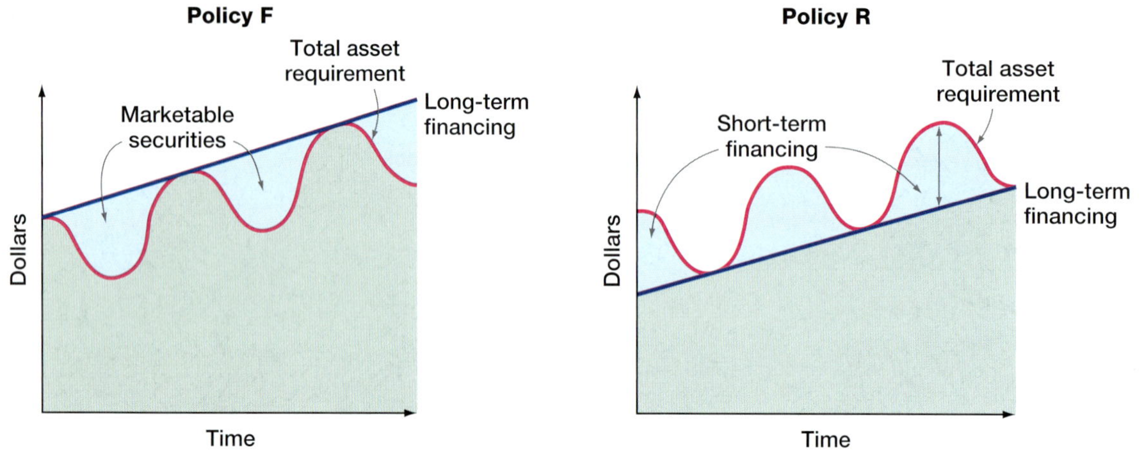

Policy F always implies a short-term cash surplus and a large investment in cash and marketable securities.

Policy R uses long-term financing for permanent asset requirements only and short-term borrowing for seasonal variations.

firm finances internally, using its own cash and marketable securities. In the restrictive case, the firm finances the variation externally, borrowing the needed funds on a short-term basis. As we discussed previously, all else being the same, a firm with a flexible policy will have a greater investment in net working capital.

Which Financing Policy Is Best?

What is the most appropriate amount of short-term borrowing? There is no definitive answer. Several considerations must be included in a proper analysis:

1. *Cash reserves.* The flexible financing policy implies surplus cash and little short-term borrowing. This policy reduces the probability that a firm will experience financial distress. Firms may not have to worry as much about meeting recurring, short-run obligations. However, investments in cash and marketable securities are zero net present value investments at best.
2. *Maturity hedging.* Most firms attempt to match the maturities of assets and liabilities. They finance inventories with short-term bank loans and fixed assets with long-term financing. Firms tend to avoid financing long-lived assets with short-term borrowing. This type of maturity mismatching would necessitate frequent refinancing and is inherently risky because short-term interest rates are more volatile than longer-term rates.
3. *Relative interest rates.* Short-term interest rates are usually lower than long-term rates. This implies that it is, on the average, more costly to rely on long-term borrowing as compared to short-term borrowing.

The two policies, F and R, we depict in Figure 19.5 are, of course, extreme cases. With F, the firm never does any short-term borrowing, and with R, the firm never has a cash reserve (an investment in marketable securities). Figure 19.6 illustrates these two policies along with a compromise, Policy C.

With this compromise approach, the firm borrows in the short term to cover peak financing needs, but it maintains a cash reserve in the form of marketable securities during

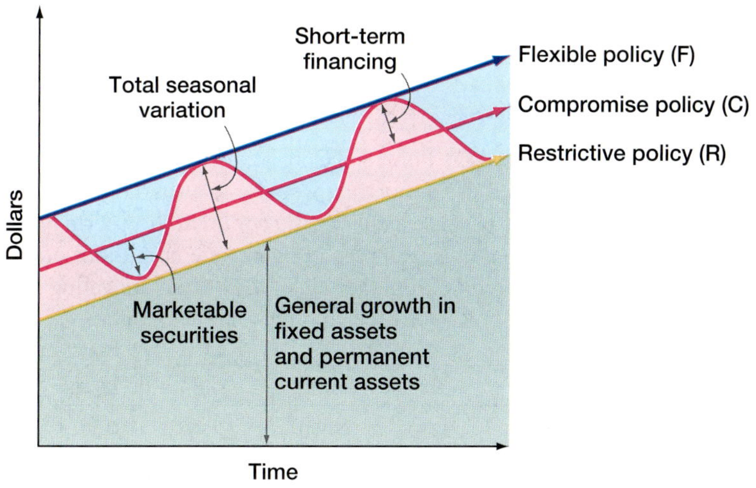

<< FIGURE 19.6

A Compromise Financing Policy

With a compromise policy, the firm keeps a reserve of liquidity that it uses to initially finance seasonal variations in current asset needs. Short-term borrowing is used when the reserve is exhausted.

slow periods. As current assets build up, the firm draws down this reserve before doing any short-term borrowing. This allows for some run-up in current assets before the firm has to resort to short-term borrowing.

Current Assets and Liabilities in Practice

Short-term assets represent a significant portion of a typical firm's overall assets. For U.S. manufacturing, mining, and trade corporations, current assets were about 50 percent of total assets in the 1960s. Today, this figure is closer to 40 percent. Most of the decline is due to more efficient cash and inventory management. Over this same period, current liabilities rose from about 20 percent of total liabilities and equity to almost 30 percent. The result is that liquidity (as measured by the ratio of net working capital to total assets) has declined, signaling a move to more restrictive short-term policies.

Concept Questions

19.3a What keeps the real world from being an ideal one in which net working capital could always be zero?

19.3b What considerations determine the optimal size of the firm's investment in current assets?

19.3c What considerations determine the optimal compromise between flexible and restrictive net working capital policies?

THE CASH BUDGET 19.4

The **cash budget** is a primary tool in short-run financial planning. It allows the financial manager to identify short-term financial needs and opportunities. An important function of the cash budget is to help the manager explore the need for short-term borrowing. The idea

cash budget
A forecast of cash receipts and disbursements for the next planning period.

of the cash budget is simple: it records estimates of cash receipts (cash in) and disbursements (cash out). The result is an estimate of the cash surplus or deficit.

Sales and Cash Collections

We start with an example involving the Fun Toys Corporation. We will prepare a quarterly cash budget. We could just as well use a monthly, weekly, or even daily basis. We choose quarters for convenience and also because a quarter is a common short-term business planning period. (Note that, throughout this example, all figures are in millions of dollars.)

All of Fun Toys's cash inflows come from the sale of toys. Cash budgeting for Fun Toys must therefore start with a sales forecast for the coming year, by quarter:

	Q1	Q2	Q3	Q4
Sales (in millions)	\$200	\$300	\$250	\$400

Note that these are predicted sales, so there is forecasting risk here, and actual sales could be more or less. Fun Toys started the year with accounts receivable equal to \$120.

Fun Toys has a 45-day receivables, or average collection, period. This means that half of the sales in a given quarter will be collected the following quarter. This happens because sales made during the first 45 days of a quarter will be collected in that quarter, whereas sales made in the second 45 days will be collected in the next quarter. Note that we are assuming that each quarter has 90 days, so the 45-day collection period is the same as a half-quarter collection period.

Based on the sales forecasts, we now need to estimate Fun Toys's projected cash collections. First, any receivables that we have at the beginning of a quarter will be collected within 45 days, so all of them will be collected sometime during the quarter. Second, as we discussed, any sales made in the first half of the quarter will be collected, so total cash collections are:

$$\text{Cash collections} = \text{Beginning accounts receivable} + 1/2 \times \text{Sales} \quad [19.6]$$

For example, in the first quarter, cash collections would be the beginning receivables of \$120 plus half of sales, $1/2 \times \$200 = \$100$, for a total of \$220.

Because beginning receivables are all collected along with half of sales, ending receivables for a particular quarter will be the other half of sales. First-quarter sales are projected at \$200, so ending receivables will be \$100. This will be the beginning receivables in the second quarter. Cash collections in the second quarter will thus be \$100 plus half of the projected \$300 in sales, or \$250 total.

Continuing this process, we can summarize Fun Toys's projected cash collections as shown in Table 19.2.

See the Finance Tools section of www.toolkit.cch.com/tools/tools.asp for several useful templates including a cash flow budget.

TABLE 19.2 >>

Cash Collection for Fun Toys (in Millions)

	Q1	Q2	Q3	Q4
Beginning receivables	\$120	\$100	\$150	\$125
Sales	200	300	250	400
Cash collections	220	250	275	325
Ending receivables	100	150	125	200

Collections = Beginning receivables + 1/2 × Sales

Ending receivables = Beginning receivables + Sales − Collections

= 1/2 × Sales

In Table 19.2, collections are shown as the only source of cash. Of course, this need not be the case. Other sources of cash could include asset sales, investment income, and receipts from planned long-term financing.

Cash Outflows

Next, we consider the cash disbursements, or payments. These come in four basic categories:

1. *Payments of accounts payable.* These are payments for goods or services rendered by suppliers, such as raw materials. Generally, these payments will be made sometime after purchases.
2. *Wages, taxes, and other expenses.* This category includes all other regular costs of doing business that require actual expenditures. Depreciation, for example, is often thought of as a regular cost of business, but it requires no cash outflow and is not included.
3. *Capital expenditures.* These are payments of cash for long-lived assets.
4. *Long-term financing expenses.* This category includes, for example, interest payments on long-term debt outstanding and dividend payments to shareholders.

Fun Toys's purchases from suppliers (in dollars) in a quarter are equal to 60 percent of the next quarter's predicted sales. Fun Toys's payments to suppliers are equal to the previous quarter's purchases, so the accounts payable period is 90 days. For example, in the quarter just ended, Fun Toys ordered $.60 \times \$200 = \$120$ in supplies. This will actually be paid in the first quarter (Q1) of the coming year.

Wages, taxes, and other expenses are routinely 20 percent of sales; interest and dividends are currently $20 per quarter. In addition, Fun Toys plans a major plant expansion (a capital expenditure) costing $100 in the second quarter. If we put all this information together, the cash outflows are as shown in Table 19.3.

The Cash Balance

The predicted *net cash inflow* is the difference between cash collections and cash disbursements. The net cash inflow for Fun Toys is shown in Table 19.4. What we see immediately is that there is a cash surplus in the first and third quarters and a cash deficit in the second and fourth.

<< TABLE 19.3

Cash Disbursements for Fun Toys (in Millions)

	Q1	Q2	Q3	Q4
Payment of accounts (60% of sales)	$120	$180	$150	$240
Wages, taxes, other expenses	40	60	50	80
Capital expenditures	0	100	0	0
Long-term financing expenses (interest and dividends)	20	20	20	20
Total cash disbursements	$180	$360	$220	$340

<< TABLE 19.4

Net Cash Inflow for Fun Toys (in Millions)

	Q1	Q2	Q3	Q4
Total cash collections	$220	$250	$275	$325
Total cash disbursements	180	360	220	340
Net cash inflow	$ 40	−$110	$ 55	−$ 15

TABLE 19.5 >>

Cash Balance for Fun Toys (in Millions)

	Q1	Q2	Q3	Q4
Beginning cash balance	$20	$ 60	−$50	$ 5
Net cash inflow	40	− 110	55	− 15
Ending cash balance	$60	−$ 50	$ 5	−$10
Minimum cash balance	− 10	− 10	− 10	− 10
Cumulative surplus (deficit)	$50	−$ 60	−$ 5	−$20

We will assume that Fun Toys starts the year with a \$20 cash balance. Furthermore, Fun Toys maintains a \$10 minimum cash balance to guard against unforeseen contingencies and forecasting errors. So, the company starts the first quarter with \$20 in cash. This amount rises by \$40 during the quarter, and the ending balance is \$60. Of this, \$10 is reserved as a minimum, so we subtract it out and find that the first quarter surplus is \$60 − 10 = \$50.

Fun Toys starts the second quarter with \$60 in cash (the ending balance from the previous quarter). There is a net cash inflow of −\$110, so the ending balance is \$60 − 110 = −\$50. We need another \$10 as a buffer, so the total deficit is −\$60. These calculations and those for the last two quarters are summarized in Table 19.5.

At the beginning of the second quarter, Fun Toys has a cash shortfall of \$60. This occurs because of the seasonal pattern of sales (higher towards the end of the second quarter), the delay in collections, and the planned capital expenditure.

The cash situation at Fun Toys is projected to improve to a \$5 deficit in the third quarter, but, by year's end, Fun Toys still has a \$20 deficit. Without some sort of financing, this deficit will carry over into the next year. We explore this subject in the next section.

For now, we can make the following general comments on Fun Toys's cash needs:

1. Fun Toys's large outflow in the second quarter is not necessarily a sign of trouble. It results from delayed collections on sales and a planned capital expenditure (presumably a worthwhile one).
2. The figures in our example are based on a forecast. Sales could be much worse (or better) than the forecasted figures.

Concept Questions

19.4a How would you do a sensitivity analysis (discussed in Chapter 11) for Fun Toys's net cash balance?

19.4b What could you learn from such an analysis?

19.5 SHORT-TERM BORROWING

Fun Toys has a short-term financing problem. It cannot meet the forecasted cash outflows in the second quarter using internal sources. How it will finance that shortfall depends on its financial policy. With a very flexible policy, Fun Toys might seek up to \$60 million in long-term debt financing.

In addition, note that much of the cash deficit comes from the large capital expenditure. Arguably, this is a candidate for long-term financing. Nonetheless, because we have discussed long-term financing elsewhere, we will concentrate here on two short-term borrowing options: (1) unsecured borrowing and (2) secured borrowing.

Unsecured Loans

The most common way to finance a temporary cash deficit is to arrange a short-term unsecured bank loan. Firms that use short-term bank loans often arrange for a line of credit. A **line of credit** is an agreement under which a firm is authorized to borrow up to a specified amount. To ensure that the line is used for short-term purposes, the lender will sometimes require the borrower to pay the line down to zero and keep it there for some period during the year, typically 60 days (called a *cleanup period*).

line of credit
A formal (committed) or informal (noncommitted) prearranged, short-term bank loan.

Short-term lines of credit are classified as either *committed* or *noncommitted.* The latter type is an informal arrangement that allows firms to borrow up to a previously specified limit without going through the normal paperwork (much as they would with a credit card). A *revolving credit arrangement* (or just *revolver*) is similar to a line of credit, but it is usually open for two or more years, whereas a line of credit would usually be evaluated on an annual basis.

Committed lines of credit are more formal legal arrangements and usually involve a commitment fee paid by the firm to the bank (usually the fee is on the order of .25 percent of the total committed funds per year). The interest rate on the line of credit is usually set equal to the bank's prime lending rate plus an additional percentage, and the rate will usually float. A firm that pays a commitment fee for a committed line of credit is essentially buying insurance to guarantee that the bank can't back out of the agreement (absent some material change in the borrower's status).

Compensating Balances

As a part of a credit line or other lending arrangement, banks will sometimes require that the firm keep some amount of money on deposit. This is called a compensating balance. A **compensating balance** is some of the firm's money kept by the bank in low-interest or non-interest-bearing accounts. By leaving these funds with the bank and receiving little or no interest, the firm further increases the effective interest rate earned by the bank on the line of credit, thereby "compensating" the bank. A compensating balance might be on the order of 2 to 5 percent of the amount borrowed.

compensating balance
Money kept by the firm with a bank in low-interest or non-interest-bearing accounts as part of a loan agreement.

Firms also use compensating balances to pay for noncredit bank services such as cash management services. A traditionally contentious issue is whether the firm should pay for bank credit and noncredit services with fees or with compensating balances. Most major firms have now negotiated for banks to use the corporation's collected funds for compensation and use fees to cover any shortfall. Arrangements such as this one and some similar approaches discussed in the next chapter make the subject of minimum balances less of an issue than it once was.

Cost of a Compensating Balance

A compensating balance requirement has an obvious opportunity cost because the money often must be deposited in an account with a zero or low interest rate. For example, suppose that we have a $100,000 line of credit with a 10 percent compensating balance requirement. This means that 10 percent of the amount actually used must be left on deposit in a non-interest-bearing account.

The quoted interest rate on the credit line is 16 percent. Suppose we need $54,000 to purchase some inventory. How much do we have to borrow? What interest rate are we effectively paying?

If we need $54,000, we have to borrow enough so that $54,000 is left over after we take out the 10 percent compensating balance:

$$\$54{,}000 = (1 - .10) \times \text{Amount borrowed}$$
$$\$60{,}000 = \$54{,}000/.90 = \text{Amount borrowed}$$

The interest on the \$60,000 for one year at 16 percent is $\$60{,}000 \times .16 = \$9{,}600$. We're actually only getting \$54,000 to use, so the effective interest rate is:

$$\begin{aligned}\text{Effective interest rate} &= \text{Interest paid/Amount available}\\ &= \$9{,}600/54{,}000\\ &= 17.78\%\end{aligned}$$

Notice that what effectively happens here is that we pay 16 cents in interest on every 90 cents we borrow because we don't get to use the 10 cents tied up in the compensating balance. The interest rate is thus $.16/.90 = 17.78\%$, as we calculated.

Several points bear mentioning. First, compensating balances are usually computed as a monthly *average* of the daily balances. This means that the effective interest rate may be lower than our example illustrates. Second, it has become common for compensating balances to be based on the *unused* amount of the credit line. The requirement of such a balance amounts to an implicit commitment fee. Third, and most important, the details of any short-term business lending arrangements are highly negotiable. Banks will generally work with firms to design a package of fees and interest.

Letters of Credit A *letter of credit* is a common arrangement in international finance. With a letter of credit, the bank issuing the letter promises to make a loan if certain conditions are met. Typically, the letter guarantees payment on a shipment of goods provided that the goods arrive as promised. A letter of credit can be revocable (subject to cancellation) or irrevocable (not subject to cancellation if the specified conditions are met).

Secured Loans

Banks and other finance companies often require security for a short-term loan just as they do for a long-term loan. Security for short-term loans usually consists of accounts receivable, inventories, or both.

accounts receivable financing
A secured short-term loan that involves either the assignment or the factoring of receivables.

Accounts Receivable Financing **Accounts receivable financing** involves either *assigning* receivables or *factoring* receivables. Under assignment, the lender has the receivables as security, but the borrower is still responsible if a receivable can't be collected. With *conventional factoring,* the receivable is discounted and sold to the lender (the factor). Once it is sold, collection is the factor's problem, and the factor assumes the full risk of default on bad accounts. With *maturity factoring,* the factor forwards the money on an agreed-upon future date.

For more on factoring, see www.factors.com.

Factors play a particularly important role in the retail industry. Retailers in the clothing business, for example, must buy large amounts of new clothes at the beginning of the season. Because this is typically a long time before they have sold anything, they wait to pay their suppliers, sometimes 30 to 60 days. If an apparel maker can't wait that long, it turns to factors, who buy the receivables and take over collection. In fact, the garment industry accounts for about 80 percent of all factoring in the United States.

Factoring can also be important elsewhere. For instance, in May 2004, Moody's upgraded the credit rating of graphite and carbon products specialist Graftech International. One of the reasons given for the upgrade was the increased liquidity Graftech had because of its accounts receivable factoring.

Cost of Factoring

<< EXAMPLE 19.3

For the year just ended, LuLu's Pies had an average of $50,000 in accounts receivable. Credit sales were $500,000. LuLu's factors its receivables by discounting them 3 percent, in other words, by selling them for 97 cents on the dollar. What is the effective interest rate on this source of short-term financing?

To determine the interest rate, we first have to know the accounts receivable, or average collection, period. During the year, LuLu's turned over its receivables $500,000/50,000 = 10 times. The average collection period is therefore 365/10 = 36.5 days.

The interest paid here is a form of discount interest (discussed in Chapter 6). In this case, LuLu's is paying 3 cents in interest on every 97 cents of financing. The interest rate per 36.5 days is thus .03/.97 = 3.09%. The APR is 10 × 3.09% = 30.9%, but the effective annual rate is:

$$\text{EAR} = 1.0309^{10} - 1 = 35.6\%$$

Factoring is a relatively expensive source of money in this case.

We should note that, if the factor takes on the risk of default by a buyer, then the factor is providing insurance as well as immediate cash. More generally, the factor essentially takes over the firm's credit operations. This can result in a significant saving. The interest rate we calculated is therefore overstated, particularly if default is a significant possibility.

inventory loan
A secured short-term loan to purchase inventory.

Inventory Loans **Inventory loans**, short-term loans to purchase inventory, come in three basic forms: blanket inventory liens, trust receipts, and field warehouse financing:

1. *Blanket inventory lien.* A blanket lien gives the lender a lien against all the borrower's inventories (the blanket "covers" everything).
2. *Trust receipt.* A trust receipt is a device by which the borrower holds specific inventory in "trust" for the lender. Automobile dealer financing, for example, is done by use of trust receipts. This type of secured financing is also called *floor planning,* in reference to inventory on the showroom floor. However, it is somewhat cumbersome to use trust receipts for, say, wheat grain.
3. *Field warehouse financing.* In field warehouse financing, a public warehouse company (an independent company that specializes in inventory management) acts as a control agent to supervise the inventory for the lender.

Other Sources

There are a variety of other sources of short-term funds employed by corporations. Two of the most important are *commercial paper* and *trade credit.*

Commercial paper consists of short-term notes issued by large and highly rated firms. Typically, these notes are of short maturity, ranging up to 270 days (beyond that limit, the firm must file a registration statement with the SEC). Because the firm issues these directly and because it usually backs the issue with a special bank line of credit, the interest rate the firm obtains is often significantly below the rate a bank would charge for a direct loan.

Another option available to a firm is to increase the accounts payable period; in other words, the firm may take longer to pay its bills. This amounts to borrowing from suppliers in the form of trade credit. This is an extremely important form of financing for smaller businesses in particular. As we discuss in Chapter 21, a firm using trade credit may end up paying a much higher price for what it purchases, so this can be a very expensive source of financing.

Concept Questions

19.5a What are the two basic forms of short-term financing?

19.5b Describe two types of secured loans.

19.6 A SHORT-TERM FINANCIAL PLAN

To illustrate a completed short-term financial plan, we will assume that Fun Toys arranges to borrow any needed funds on a short-term basis. The interest rate is a 20 percent APR, and it is calculated on a quarterly basis. From Chapter 5, we know that the rate is 20%/4 = 5% per quarter. We will assume that Fun Toys starts the year with no short-term debt.

From Table 19.5, we know that Fun Toys has a second-quarter deficit of $60 million. The firm will have to borrow this amount. Net cash inflow in the following quarter is $55 million. The firm will now have to pay $60 million × .05 = $3 million in interest out of that, leaving $52 million to reduce the borrowing.

Fun Toys still owes $60 million − 52 million = $8 million at the end of the third quarter. Interest in the last quarter will thus be $8 million × .05 = $.4 million. In addition, net inflows in the last quarter are −$15 million, so the company will have to borrow a total of $15.4 million, bringing total borrowing up to $15.4 million + 8 million = $23.4 million. Table 19.6 extends Table 19.5 to include these calculations.

Notice that the ending short-term debt is just equal to the cumulative deficit for the entire year, $20 million, plus the interest paid during the year, $3 million + .4 million = $3.4 million, for a total of $23.4 million.

Our plan is very simple. For example, we ignored the fact that the interest paid on the short-term debt is tax deductible. We also ignored the fact that the cash surplus in the first quarter would earn some interest (which would be taxable). We could add on a number of refinements. Even so, our plan highlights the fact that in about 90 days, Fun Toys will need to borrow $60 million or so on a short-term basis. It's time to start lining up the source of the funds.

TABLE 19.6 >>

Short-Term Financial Plan for Fun Toys (in Millions)

	Q1	Q2	Q3	Q4
Beginning cash balance	$20	$ 60	$10	$10.0
Net cash inflow	40	− 110	55	− 15.0
New short-term borrowing	—	60	—	15.4
Interest on short-term borrowing	—	—	− 3	− .4
Short-term borrowing repaid	—	—	− 52	—
Ending cash balance	$60	$ 10	$10	$10.0
Minimum cash balance	− 10	− 10	− 10	− 10.0
Cumulative surplus (deficit)	$50	$ 0	$ 0	$ 0.0
Beginning short-term borrowing	0	0	60	8.0
Change in short-term debt	0	60	− 52	15.4
Ending short-term debt	$ 0	$ 60	$ 8	$23.4

Our plan also illustrates that financing the firm's short-term needs will cost about $3.4 million in interest (before taxes) for the year. This is a starting point for Fun Toys to begin evaluating alternatives to reduce this expense. For example, can the $100 million planned expenditure be postponed or spread out? At 5 percent per quarter, short-term credit is expensive.

Also, if Fun Toys's sales are expected to keep growing, then the deficit of $20 million plus will probably also keep growing, and the need for additional financing will be permanent. Fun Toys may wish to think about raising money on a long-term basis to cover this need.

Concept Questions

19.6a In Table 19.6, does Fun Toys have a projected deficit or surplus?

19.6b In Table 19.6, what would happen to Fun Toys's deficit or surplus if the minimum cash balance was reduced to $5?

SUMMARY AND CONCLUSIONS 19.7

1. This chapter has introduced the management of short-term finance. Short-term finance involves short-lived assets and liabilities. We trace and examine the short-term sources and uses of cash as they appear on the firm's financial statements. We see how current assets and current liabilities arise in the short-term operating activities and the cash cycle of the firm.
2. Managing short-term cash flows involves the minimizing of costs. The two major costs are carrying costs, the return forgone by keeping too much invested in short-term assets such as cash, and shortage costs, the cost of running out of short-term assets. The objective of managing short-term finance and doing short-term financial planning is to find the optimal trade-off between these two costs.
3. In an ideal economy, the firm could perfectly predict its short-term uses and sources of cash, and net working capital could be kept at zero. In the real world we live in, cash and net working capital provide a buffer that lets the firm meet its ongoing obligations. The financial manager seeks the optimal level of each of the current assets.
4. The financial manager can use the cash budget to identify short-term financial needs. The cash budget tells the manager what borrowing is required or what lending will be possible in the short run. The firm has available to it a number of possible ways of acquiring funds to meet short-term shortfalls, including unsecured and secured loans.

Chapter Review and Self-Test Problems

19.1 The Operating and Cash Cycles Consider the following financial statement information for the Route 66 Company:

Item	Beginning		Ending
Inventory	$1,273		$1,401
Accounts receivable	3,782		3,368
Accounts payable	1,795		2,025
Net sales		$14,750	
Cost of goods sold		11,375	

Calculate the operating and cash cycles.

19.2 Cash Balance for Greenwell Corporation The Greenwell Corporation has a 60-day average collection period and wishes to maintain a $160 million minimum cash balance. Based on this and the information given in the following cash budget, complete the cash budget. What conclusions do you draw?

GREENWELL CORPORATION **Cash Budget** **(in millions)**				
	Q1	**Q2**	**Q3**	**Q4**
Beginning receivables	$240			
Sales	150	$165	$180	$135
Cash collections				
Ending receivables				
Total cash collections				
Total cash disbursements	170	160	185	190
Net cash inflow				
Beginning cash balance	$ 45			
Net cash inflow				
Ending cash balance				
Minimum cash balance				
Cumulative surplus (deficit)				

Answers to Chapter Review and Self-Test Problems

19.1 We first need the turnover ratios. Note that we use the average values for all balance sheet items and that we base the inventory and payables turnover measures on cost of goods sold.

$$\text{Inventory turnover} = \$11{,}375/[(1{,}273 + 1{,}401)/2] = 8.51 \text{ times}$$
$$\text{Receivables turnover} = \$14{,}750/[(3{,}782 + 3{,}368)/2] = 4.13 \text{ times}$$
$$\text{Payables turnover} = \$11{,}375/[(1{,}795 + 2{,}025)/2] = 5.96 \text{ times}$$

We can now calculate the various periods:

$$\text{Inventory period} = 365 \text{ days}/8.51 \text{ times} = 42.89 \text{ days}$$
$$\text{Receivables period} = 365 \text{ days}/4.13 \text{ times} = 88.38 \text{ days}$$
$$\text{Payables period} = 365 \text{ days}/5.96 \text{ times} = 61.24 \text{ days}$$

So the time it takes to acquire inventory and sell it is about 43 days. Collection takes another 88 days, and the operating cycle is thus 43 + 88 = 131 days. The cash cycle is thus 131 days less the payables period, 131 − 61 = 70 days.

19.2 Because Greenwell has a 60-day collection period, only those sales made in the first 30 days of the quarter will be collected in the same quarter. Total cash collections in the first quarter will thus equal 30/90 = ⅓ of sales plus beginning receivables, or ⅓ × $150 + 240 = $290. Ending receivables for the first quarter (and the second-quarter beginning receivables) are the other ⅔ of sales, or ⅔ × $150 = $100. The remaining calculations are straightforward, and the completed budget follows.

GREENWELL CORPORATION Cash Budget (in millions)				
	Q1	**Q2**	**Q3**	**Q4**
Beginning receivables	$240	$100	$110	$120
Sales	150	165	180	135
Cash collections	290	155	170	165
Ending receivables	$100	$110	$120	$ 90
Total cash collections	$290	$155	$170	$165
Total cash disbursements	170	160	185	190
Net cash inflow	$120	−$ 5	−$ 15	−$ 25
Beginning cash balance	$ 45	$165	$160	$145
Net cash inflow	120	− 5	− 15	− 25
Ending cash balance	$165	$160	$145	$120
Minimum cash balance	− 160	− 160	− 160	− 160
Cumulative surplus (deficit)	$ 5	$ 0	−$ 15	−$ 40

The primary conclusion from this schedule is that, beginning in the third quarter, Greenwell's cash surplus becomes a cash deficit. By the end of the year, Greenwell will need to arrange for $40 million in cash beyond what will be available.

Concepts Review and Critical Thinking Questions

1. **Operating Cycle** What are some of the characteristics of a firm with a long operating cycle?
2. **Cash Cycle** What are some of the characteristics of a firm with a long cash cycle?
3. **Sources and Uses** For the year just ended, you have gathered the following information on the Holly Corporation:
   a. A $200 dividend was paid.
   b. Accounts payable increased by $500.
   c. Fixed asset purchases were $900.
   d. Inventories increased by $625.
   e. Long-term debt decreased by $1,200.
   Label each as a source or use of cash and describe its effect on the firm's cash balance.
4. **Cost of Current Assets** Loftis Manufacturing, Inc., has recently installed a just-in-time (JIT) inventory system. Describe the effect this is likely to have on the company's carrying costs, shortage costs, and operating cycle.
5. **Operating and Cash Cycles** Is it possible for a firm's cash cycle to be longer than its operating cycle? Explain why or why not.

   Use the following information to answer Questions 6–10: Last month, BlueSky Airline announced that it would stretch out its bill payments to 45 days from 30 days. The reason given was that the company wanted to "control costs and optimize cash flow." The increased payables period will be in effect for all of the company's 4,000 suppliers.

6. **Operating and Cash Cycles** What impact did this change in payables policy have on BlueSky's operating cycle? Its cash cycle?
7. **Operating and Cash Cycles** What impact did the announcement have on BlueSky's suppliers?
8. **Corporate Ethics** Is it ethical for large firms to unilaterally lengthen their payables periods, particularly when dealing with smaller suppliers?
9. **Payables Period** Why don't all firms simply increase their payables periods to shorten their cash cycles?
10. **Payables Period** BlueSky lengthened its payables period to "control costs and optimize cash flow." Exactly what is the cash benefit to BlueSky from this change?

Questions and Problems

BASIC
(Questions 1–11)

1. **Changes in the Cash Account** Indicate the impact of the following corporate actions on cash, using the letter *I* for an increase, *D* for a decrease, or *N* when no change occurs.
   - **a.** A dividend is paid with funds received from a sale of debt.
   - **b.** Real estate is purchased and paid for with short-term debt.
   - **c.** Inventory is bought on credit.
   - **d.** A short-term bank loan is repaid.
   - **e.** Next year's taxes are prepaid.
   - **f.** Preferred stock is redeemed.
   - **g.** Sales are made on credit.
   - **h.** Interest on long-term debt is paid.
   - **i.** Payments for previous sales are collected.
   - **j.** The accounts payable balance is reduced.
   - **k.** A dividend is paid.
   - **l.** Production supplies are purchased and paid for with a short-term note.
   - **m.** Utility bills are paid.
   - **n.** Cash is paid for raw materials purchased for inventory.
   - **o.** Marketable securities are sold.
2. **Cash Equation** Kaleb's Korndog Corp. has a book net worth of $9,300. Long-term debt is $1,900. Net working capital, other than cash, is $2,450. Fixed assets are $2,300. How much cash does the company have? If current liabilities are $1,250, what are current assets?
3. **Changes in the Operating Cycle** Indicate the effect that the following will have on the operating cycle. Use the letter *I* to indicate an increase, the letter *D* for a decrease, and the letter *N* for no change.
   - **a.** Average receivables goes up.
   - **b.** Credit repayment times for customers are increased.
   - **c.** Inventory turnover goes from 3 times to 6 times.
   - **d.** Payables turnover goes from 6 times to 11 times.
   - **e.** Receivables turnover goes from 7 times to 9 times.
   - **f.** Payments to suppliers are accelerated.

4. **Changes in Cycles** Indicate the impact of the following on the cash and operating cycles, respectively. Use the letter *I* to indicate an increase, the letter *D* for a decrease, and the letter *N* for no change.
   a. The terms of cash discounts offered to customers are made less favorable.
   b. The cash discounts offered by suppliers are decreased; thus, payments are made earlier.
   c. An increased number of customers begin to pay in cash instead of with credit.
   d. Fewer raw materials than usual are purchased.
   e. A greater percentage of raw material purchases are paid for with credit.
   f. More finished goods are produced for inventory instead of for order.
5. **Calculating Cash Collections** The Kolby Coffee Company has projected the following quarterly sales amounts for the coming year:

	Q1	Q2	Q3	Q4
Sales	$800	$760	$940	$870

   a. Accounts receivable at the beginning of the year are $300. Kolby has a 45-day collection period. Calculate cash collections in each of the four quarters by completing the following:

	Q1	Q2	Q3	Q4
Beginning receivables				
Sales				
Cash collections				
Ending receivables				

   b. Rework (*a*) assuming a collection period of 60 days.
   c. Rework (*a*) assuming a collection period of 30 days.
6. **Calculating Cycles** Consider the following financial statement information for the Bulldog Icers Corporation:

Item	Beginning		Ending
Inventory	$8,413		$10,158
Accounts receivable	5,108		5,439
Accounts payable	6,927		7,625
Net sales		$67,312	
Cost of goods sold		52,827	

   Calculate the operating and cash cycles. How do you interpret your answer?
7. **Factoring Receivables** Your firm has an average collection period of 34 days. Current practice is to factor all receivables immediately at a 2 percent discount. What is the effective cost of borrowing in this case? Assume that default is extremely unlikely.

8. Calculating Payments Iron Man Products has projected the following sales for the coming year:

	Q1	Q2	Q3	Q4
Sales	$540	$630	$710	$785

Sales in the year following this one are projected to be 15 percent greater in each quarter.

a. Calculate payments to suppliers assuming that Iron Man places orders during each quarter equal to 30 percent of projected sales for the next quarter. Assume that Iron Man pays immediately. What is the payables period in this case?

	Q1	Q2	Q3	Q4
Payment of accounts	$	$	$	$

b. Rework (*a*) assuming a 90-day payables period.

	Q1	Q2	Q3	Q4
Payment of accounts	$	$	$	$

c. Rework (*a*) assuming a 60-day payables period.

	Q1	Q2	Q3	Q4
Payment of accounts	$	$	$	$

9. Calculating Payments The Thunder Dan Corporation's purchases from suppliers in a quarter are equal to 75 percent of the next quarter's forecasted sales. The payables period is 60 days. Wages, taxes, and other expenses are 20 percent of sales, and interest and dividends are $60 per quarter. No capital expenditures are planned.

Projected quarterly sales are:

	Q1	Q2	Q3	Q4
Sales	$750	$920	$890	$790

Sales for the first quarter of the following year are projected at $970. Calculate Thunder's cash outlays by completing the following:

	Q1	Q2	Q3	Q4
Payment of accounts				
Wages, taxes, other expenses				
Long-term financing expenses (interest and dividends)				
Total				

10. Calculating Cash Collections The following is the sales budget for Duck-n-Run, Inc., for the first quarter of 2004:

	January	February	March
Sales budget	$150,000	$173,000	$194,000

Credit sales are collected as follows:

65 percent in the month of the sale
20 percent in the month after the sale
15 percent in the second month after the sale

The accounts receivable balance at the end of the previous quarter was $57,000 ($41,000 of which was uncollected December sales).

a. Compute the sales for November.

b. Compute the sales for December.

c. Compute the cash collections from sales for each month from January through March.

11. Calculating the Cash Budget Here are some important figures from the budget of Nashville Nougats, Inc., for the second quarter of 2004:

	April	May	June
Credit sales	$380,000	$396,000	$438,000
Credit purchases	147,000	175,500	200,500
Cash disbursements			
Wages, taxes, and expenses	39,750	48,210	50,300
Interest	11,400	11,400	11,400
Equipment purchases	83,000	91,000	0

The company predicts that 5 percent of its credit sales will never be collected, 35 percent of its sales will be collected in the month of the sale, and the remaining 60 percent will be collected in the following month. Credit purchases will be paid in the month following the purchase.

In March 2004, credit sales were $210,000, and credit purchases were $156,000. Using this information, complete the following cash budget:

	April	May	June
Beginning cash balance	$280,000		
Cash receipts			
Cash collections from credit sales			
Total cash available			
Cash disbursements			
Purchases			
Wages, taxes, and expenses			
Interest			
Equipment purchases			
Total cash disbursements			
Ending cash balance			

INTERMEDIATE
(Questions 12–15)

12. **Costs of Borrowing** You've worked out a line of credit arrangement that allows you to borrow up to $60 million at any time. The interest rate is .61 percent per month. In addition, 4 percent of the amount that you borrow must be deposited in a non-interest-bearing account. Assume that your bank uses compound interest on its line of credit loans.
    a. What is the effective annual interest rate on this lending arrangement?
    b. Suppose you need $15 million today and you repay it in six months. How much interest will you pay?

13. **Costs of Borrowing** A bank offers your firm a revolving credit arrangement for up to $100 million at an interest rate of 2.20 percent per quarter. The bank also requires you to maintain a compensating balance of 5 percent against the *unused* portion of the credit line, to be deposited in a non-interest-bearing account. Assume you have a short-term investment account at the bank that pays 1.40 percent per quarter, and assume that the bank uses compound interest on its revolving credit loans.
    a. What is your effective annual interest rate (an opportunity cost) on the revolving credit arrangement if your firm does not use it during the year?
    b. What is your effective annual interest rate on the lending arrangement if you borrow $60 million immediately and repay it in one year?
    c. What is your effective annual interest rate if you borrow $100 million immediately and repay it in one year?

14. **Calculating the Cash Budget** Wildcat, Inc., has estimated sales (in millions) for the next four quarters as:

	Q1	Q2	Q3	Q4
Sales	$230	$195	$270	$290

Sales for the first quarter of the year after this one are projected at $250 million. Accounts receivable at the beginning of the year were $79 million. Wildcat has a 45-day collection period.

Wildcat's purchases from suppliers in a quarter are equal to 45 percent of the next quarter's forecasted sales, and suppliers are normally paid in 36 days. Wages, taxes, and other expenses run about 30 percent of sales. Interest and dividends are $15 million per quarter.

Wildcat plans a major capital outlay in the second quarter of $90 million. Finally, the company started the year with a $73 million cash balance and wishes to maintain a $30 million minimum balance.

a. Complete a cash budget for Wildcat by filling in the following:

WILDCAT, INC.
Cash Budget
(in millions)

	Q1	Q2	Q3	Q4
Beginning cash balance	$73			
Net cash inflow				
Ending cash balance				
Minimum cash balance	30			
Cumulative surplus (deficit)				

b. Assume that Wildcat can borrow any needed funds on a short-term basis at a rate of 3 percent per quarter, and can invest any excess funds in short-term marketable securities at a rate of 2 percent per quarter. Prepare a short-term financial plan by filling in the following schedule. What is the net cash cost (total interest paid minus total investment income earned) for the year?

WILDCAT, INC.
Short-Term Financial Plan
(in millions)

	Q1	Q2	Q3	Q4
Beginning cash balance	$73			
Net cash inflow				
New short-term investments				
Income from short-term investments				
Short-term investments sold				
New short-term borrowing				
Interest on short-term borrowing				
Short-term borrowing repaid				
Ending cash balance				
Minimum cash balance	30			
Cumulative surplus (deficit)				
Beginning short-term investments				
Ending short-term investments				
Beginning short-term debt				
Ending short-term debt				

15. Cash Management Policy Rework Problem 14 assuming:

a. Wildcat maintains a minimum cash balance of $45 million.

b. Wildcat maintains a minimum cash balance of $15 million.

Based on your answers in (*a*) and (*b*), do you think the firm can boost its profit by changing its cash management policy? Are there other factors that must be considered as well? Explain.

CHALLENGE
(Questions 16–17)

16. Costs of Borrowing In exchange for a $500 million fixed commitment line of credit, your firm has agreed to do the following:

1. Pay 1.3 percent per quarter on any funds actually borrowed
2. Maintain a 4 percent compensating balance on any funds actually borrowed
3. Pay an up-front commitment fee of .105 percent of the amount of the line

Based on this information, answer the following:

a. Ignoring the commitment fee, what is the effective annual interest rate on this line of credit?

b. Suppose your firm immediately uses $210 million of the line and pays it off in one year. What is the effective annual interest rate on this $210 million loan?

17. Costs of Borrowing Stream Bank offers your firm an 8 percent *discount* interest loan for up to $8 million, and in addition requires you to maintain a 6 percent compensating balance against the amount borrowed. What is the effective annual interest rate on this lending arrangement?

S&P Problems

1. **Cash and Operating Cycles** Find the most recent financial statements for Dell Computer (DELL) and Boeing (BA). Calculate the cash and operating cycle for each company for the most recent year. Are the numbers similar for these companies? Why or why not?
2. **Cash and Operating Cycles** Download the most recent quarterly financial statements for Wal-Mart (WMT). Calculate the operating and cash cycle for Wal-Mart over each of the last four quarters. Comment on any changes in the operating or cash cycle over this period.

What's On the Web?

19.1 Cash Cycle Go to www.investor.reuters.com. You will need to find the most recent annual income statement and two most recent balance sheets for BJ Services Company (BJS) and Avon Products (AVP). Both companies are on the S&P 500 Index. BJS is provider of pressure pumping and other oilfield services, while AVP is a manufacturer and marketer of beauty and related products. Calculate the cash cycle for each company and comment on any similarities or differences.

19.2 Operating Cycle Using the information you gathered in the previous problem, calculate the operating cycle for each company. What are the similarities or differences? Is this what you would expect from companies in each of these industries?

20

Cash and Liquidity Management

PART SEVEN

Short-Term Financial Planning and Management

Most often, when news breaks about a firm's cash supply, it's because the company is running low. But that wasn't the case for many companies in the middle of 2004. By July 2004, cash on hand for all nonfinancial companies in the S&P 500 was expected to top half a *trillion* dollars for the first time. Microsoft was the cash leader with about $51 billion in cash, with General Motors a distant second at $37.5 billion. Intel held $15.7 billion in cash, which was about 9 percent of its total market value. These companies certainly had ample cash reserves; in fact, the word *enormous* might be more appropriate. Why would these firms hold such large quantities of cash? We examine cash management in this chapter to find out.

This chapter is about how firms manage cash. The basic objective in cash management is to keep the investment in cash as low as possible while still keeping the firm operating efficiently and effectively. This goal usually reduces to the dictum "Collect early and pay late." Accordingly, we discuss ways of accelerating collections and managing disbursements.

In addition, firms must invest temporarily idle cash in short-term marketable securities. As we discuss in various places, these securities can be bought and sold in the financial markets. As a group, they have very little default risk, and most are highly marketable. There are different types of these so-called money market securities, and we discuss a few of the most important ones.

20.1 REASONS FOR HOLDING CASH

John Maynard Keynes, in his classic work *The General Theory of Employment, Interest, and Money*, identified three motives for liquidity: the speculative motive, the precautionary motive, and the transaction motive. We discuss these next.

The Speculative and Precautionary Motives

speculative motive
The need to hold cash to take advantage of additional investment opportunities, such as bargain purchases.

The **speculative motive** is the need to hold cash in order to be able to take advantage of, for example, bargain purchases that might arise, attractive interest rates, and (in the case of international firms) favorable exchange rate fluctuations.

For most firms, reserve borrowing ability and marketable securities can be used to satisfy speculative motives. Thus, there might be a speculative motive for maintaining liquidity, but not necessarily for holding cash per se. Think of it this way: If you have a credit card with a very large credit limit, then you can probably take advantage of any unusual bargains that come along without carrying any cash.

This is also true, to a lesser extent, for precautionary motives. The **precautionary motive** is the need for a safety supply to act as a financial reserve. Once again, there probably is a precautionary motive for maintaining liquidity. However, given that the value of money market instruments is relatively certain and that instruments such as T-bills are extremely liquid, there is no real need to hold substantial amounts of cash for precautionary purposes.

precautionary motive
The need to hold cash as a safety margin to act as a financial reserve.

The Transaction Motive

Cash is needed to satisfy the **transaction motive**, the need to have cash on hand to pay bills. Transaction-related needs come from the normal disbursement and collection activities of the firm. The disbursement of cash includes the payment of wages and salaries, trade debts, taxes, and dividends.

Cash is collected from product sales, the selling of assets, and new financing. The cash inflows (collections) and outflows (disbursements) are not perfectly synchronized, and some level of cash holdings is necessary to serve as a buffer.

As electronic funds transfers and other high-speed, "paperless" payment mechanisms continue to develop, even the transaction demand for cash may all but disappear. Even if it does, however, there will still be a demand for liquidity and a need to manage it efficiently.

transaction motive
The need to hold cash to satisfy normal disbursement and collection activities associated with a firm's ongoing operations.

Compensating Balances

Compensating balances are another reason to hold cash. As we discussed in the previous chapter, cash balances are kept at commercial banks to compensate for banking services the firm receives. A minimum compensating balance requirement may impose a lower limit on the level of cash a firm holds.

Costs of Holding Cash

When a firm holds cash in excess of some necessary minimum, it incurs an opportunity cost. The opportunity cost of excess cash (held in currency or bank deposits) is the interest income that could be earned in the next best use, such as investment in marketable securities.

Given the opportunity cost of holding cash, why would a firm hold cash in excess of its compensating balance requirements? The answer is that a cash balance must be maintained to provide the liquidity necessary for transaction needs—paying bills. If the firm maintains too small a cash balance, it may run out of cash. If this happens, the firm may have to raise cash on a short-term basis. This could involve, for example, selling marketable securities or borrowing.

Activities such as selling marketable securities and borrowing involve various costs. As we've discussed, holding cash has an opportunity cost. To determine the appropriate cash balance, the firm must weigh the benefits of holding cash against these costs. We discuss this subject in more detail in the sections that follow.

Cash Management versus Liquidity Management

Before we move on, we should note that it is important to distinguish between true cash management and a more general subject, liquidity management. The distinction is a source of confusion because the word *cash* is used in practice in two different ways. First of all, it has its literal meaning, actual cash on hand. However, financial managers frequently use the word to describe a firm's holdings of cash along with its marketable securities, and marketable securities are sometimes called cash equivalents or near-cash. In our discussion of Microsoft's and GM's cash positions at the beginning of the chapter, for example, what was actually being described was their total cash and cash equivalents.

The distinction between liquidity management and cash management is straightforward. Liquidity management concerns the optimal quantity of liquid assets a firm should have on hand, and it is one particular aspect of the current asset management policies we discussed in our previous chapter. Cash management is much more closely related to optimizing mechanisms for collecting and disbursing cash, and it is this subject that we primarily focus on in this chapter.

Concept Questions

20.1a What is the transaction motive, and how does it lead firms to hold cash?

20.1b What is the cost to the firm of holding excess cash?

UNDERSTANDING FLOAT 20.2

As you no doubt know, the amount of money you have according to your checkbook can be very different from the amount of money that your bank thinks you have. The reason is that some of the checks you have written haven't yet been presented to the bank for payment. The same thing is true for a business. The cash balance that a firm shows on its books is called the firm's *book, or ledger, balance.* The balance shown in its bank account as available to spend is called its *available, or collected, balance*. The difference between the available balance and the ledger balance is called the **float**, and it represents the net effect of checks in the process of *clearing* (moving through the banking system).

float
The difference between book cash and bank cash, representing the net effect of checks in the process of clearing.

Disbursement Float

Checks written by a firm generate *disbursement float,* causing a decrease in the firm's book balance but no change in its available balance. For example, suppose General Mechanics, Inc. (GMI), currently has $100,000 on deposit with its bank. On June 8, it buys some raw materials and pays with a check for $100,000. The company's book balance is immediately reduced by $100,000 as a result.

GMI's bank, however, will not find out about this check until it is presented to GMI's bank for payment on, say, June 14. Until the check is presented, the firm's available balance is greater than its book balance by $100,000. In other words, before June 8, GMI has a zero float:

$$\begin{aligned}\text{Float} &= \text{Firm's available balance} - \text{Firm's book balance}\\ &= \$100{,}000 - 100{,}000\\ &= \$0\end{aligned}$$

GMI's position from June 8 to June 14 is:

$$\begin{aligned}\text{Disbursement float} &= \text{Firm's available balance} - \text{Firm's book balance}\\ &= \$100{,}000 - 0\\ &= \$100{,}000\end{aligned}$$

During this period of time that the check is clearing, GMI has a balance with the bank of $100,000. It can obtain the benefit of this cash while the check is clearing. For example, the available balance could be temporarily invested in marketable securities and thus earn some interest. We will return to this subject a little later.

Collection Float and Net Float

Checks received by the firm create *collection float.* Collection float increases book balances but does not immediately change available balances. For example, suppose GMI receives a check from a customer for $100,000 on October 8. Assume, as before, that the company has $100,000 deposited at its bank and a zero float. It deposits the check and increases its book balance by $100,000 to $200,000. However, the additional cash is not available to GMI until its bank has presented the check to the customer's bank and received $100,000. This will occur on, say, October 14. In the meantime, the cash position at GMI will reflect a collection float of $100,000. We can summarize these events. Before October 8, GMI's position is:

$$\begin{aligned}\text{Float} &= \text{Firm's available balance} - \text{Firm's book balance}\\ &= \$100{,}000 - 100{,}000\\ &= \$0\end{aligned}$$

GMI's position from October 8 to October 14 is:

$$\begin{aligned}\text{Collection float} &= \text{Firm's available balance} - \text{Firm's book balance}\\ &= \$100{,}000 - 200{,}000\\ &= -\$100{,}000\end{aligned}$$

In general, a firm's payment (disbursement) activities generate disbursement float, and its collection activities generate collection float. The net effect, that is, the sum of the total collection and disbursement floats, is the net float. The net float at a point in time is simply the overall difference between the firm's available balance and its book balance. If the net float is positive, then the firm's disbursement float exceeds its collection float, and its available balance exceeds its book balance. If the available balance is less than the book balance, then the firm has a net collection float.

A firm should be concerned with its net float and available balance more than with its book balance. If a financial manager knows that a check written by the company will not clear for several days, that manager will be able to keep a lower cash balance at the bank than might be possible otherwise. This can generate a great deal of money.

For example, take the case of ExxonMobil. The average daily sales of ExxonMobil are about $690 million. If ExxonMobil's collections could be speeded up by a single day, then

ExxonMobil could free up $690 million for investing. At a relatively modest .01 percent daily rate, the interest earned would be on the order of $69,000 *per day*.

EXAMPLE 20.1

Staying Afloat

Suppose you have $5,000 on deposit. One day, you write a check for $1,000 to pay for books, and you deposit $2,000. What are your disbursement, collection, and net floats?

After you write the $1,000 check, you show a balance of $4,000 on your books, but the bank shows $5,000 while the check is clearing. The difference is a disbursement float of $1,000.

After you deposit the $2,000 check, you show a balance of $6,000. Your available balance doesn't rise until the check clears. This results in a collection float of −$2,000. Your net float is the sum of the collection and disbursement floats, or −$1,000.

Overall, you show $6,000 on your books. The bank shows a $7,000 balance, but only $5,000 is available because your deposit has not been cleared. The discrepancy between your available balance and your book balance is the net float (−$1,000), and it is bad for you. If you write another check for $5,500, there may not be sufficient available funds to cover it, and it might bounce. This is the reason that financial managers have to be more concerned with available balances than book balances.

Float Management

For a real-world example of float management services, visit www.epaymentsystems.com.

Float management involves controlling the collection and disbursement of cash. The objective in cash collection is to speed up collections and reduce the lag between the time customers pay their bills and the time the cash becomes available. The objective in cash disbursement is to control payments and minimize the firm's costs associated with making payments.

Total collection or disbursement times can be broken down into three parts: mailing time, processing delay, and availability delay:

1. *Mailing time* is the part of the collection and disbursement process during which checks are trapped in the postal system.
2. *Processing delay* is the time it takes the receiver of a check to process the payment and deposit it in a bank for collection.
3. *Availability delay* refers to the time required to clear a check through the banking system.

Speeding up collections involves reducing one or more of these components. Slowing up disbursements involves increasing one of them. We will describe some procedures for managing collection and disbursement times later. First, we need to discuss how float is measured.

Measuring Float The size of the float depends on both the dollars and the time delay involved. For example, suppose you mail a check for $500 to another state each month. It takes five days in the mail for the check to reach its destination (the mailing time) and one day for the recipient to get over to the bank (the processing delay). The recipient's bank holds out-of-state checks for three days (availability delay). The total delay is $5 + 1 + 3 = 9$ days.

In this case, what is your average daily disbursement float? There are two equivalent ways of calculating the answer. First, you have a $500 float for nine days, so we say that the total float is $9 \times \$500 = \$4{,}500$. Assuming 30 days in the month, the average daily float is $\$4{,}500/30 = \$150$.

Alternatively, your disbursement float is $500 for 9 days out of the month and zero the other 21 days (again assuming 30 days in a month). Your average daily float is thus:

$$\begin{aligned}\text{Average daily float} &= (9 \times \$500 + 21 \times 0)/30 \\ &= 9/30 \times \$500 + 21/30 \times 0 \\ &= \$4{,}500/30 \\ &= \$150\end{aligned}$$

This means that, on an average day, your book balance is $150 less than your available balance, representing a $150 average disbursement float.

Things are only a little more complicated when there are multiple disbursements or receipts. To illustrate, suppose Concepts, Inc., receives two items each month as follows:

Amount	Processing and availability delay	Total float
Item 1: $5,000,000	× 9	= $45,000,000
Item 2: $3,000,000	× 5	= $15,000,000
Total $8,000,000		$60,000,000

The average daily float is equal to:

$$\begin{aligned}\text{Average daily float} &= \frac{\text{Total float}}{\text{Total days}} \\ &= \frac{\$60 \text{ million}}{30} = \$2 \text{ million}\end{aligned} \qquad [20.1]$$

So, on an average day, there is $2 million that is uncollected and not available.

Another way to see this is to calculate the average daily receipts and multiply by the weighted average delay. Average daily receipts are:

$$\text{Average daily receipts} = \frac{\text{Total receipts}}{\text{Total days}} = \frac{\$8 \text{ million}}{30} = \$266{,}666.67$$

Of the $8 million total receipts, $5 million, or ⅝ of the total, is delayed for nine days. The other ⅜ is delayed for five days. The weighted average delay is thus:

$$\begin{aligned}\text{Weighted average delay} &= (5/8) \times 9 \text{ days} + (3/8) \times 5 \text{ days} \\ &= 5.625 + 1.875 = 7.50 \text{ days}\end{aligned}$$

The average daily float is thus:

$$\begin{aligned}\text{Average daily float} &= \text{Average daily receipts} \times \text{Weighted average delay} \\ &= \$266{,}666.67 \times 7.50 \text{ days} = \$2 \text{ million}\end{aligned} \qquad [20.2]$$

Some Details In measuring float, there is an important difference to note between collection and disbursement float. We defined float as the difference between the firm's available cash balance and its book balance. With a disbursement, the firm's book balance goes down when the check is *mailed,* so the mailing time is an important component in disbursement float. However, with a collection, the firm's book balance isn't increased until the check is *received,* so mailing time is not a component of collection float.

<< FIGURE 20.1

Buildup of the Float

	Day 1	Day 2	Day 3	Day 4	Day 5	. . .
Beginning float	$ 0	$1,000	$2,000	$3,000	$3,000	. . .
Checks received	1,000	1,000	1,000	1,000	1,000	. . .
Checks cleared (cash available)	− 0	− 0	− 0	− 1,000	− 1,000	. . .
Ending float	$1,000	$2,000	$3,000	$3,000	$3,000	. . .

This doesn't mean that mailing time is not important. The point is that when collection *float* is calculated, mailing time should not be considered. As we will discuss, when total collection *time* is considered, the mailing time is a crucial component.

Also, when we talk about availability delay, how long it actually takes a check to clear isn't really crucial. What matters is how long we must wait before the bank grants availability, that is, use of the funds. Banks actually have availability schedules that are used to determine how long a check is held based on time of deposit and other factors. Beyond this, availability delay can be a matter of negotiation between the bank and a customer. In a similar vein, for outgoing checks, what matters is the date our account is debited, not when the recipient is granted availability.

Cost of the Float The basic cost of collection float to the firm is simply the opportunity cost of not being able to use the cash. At a minimum, the firm could earn interest on the cash if it were available for investing.

Suppose the Lambo Corporation has average daily receipts of $1,000 and a weighted average delay of three days. The average daily float is thus 3 × $1,000 = $3,000. This means that, on a typical day, there is $3,000 that is not earning interest. Suppose Lambo could eliminate the float entirely. What would be the benefit? If it costs $2,000 to eliminate the float, what is the NPV of doing so?

Try www.cfoasia.com for an international view on cash management.

Figure 20.1 illustrates the situation for Lambo. Suppose Lambo starts with a zero float. On a given day, Day 1, Lambo receives and deposits a check for $1,000. The cash will become available three days later on Day 4. At the end of the day on Day 1, the book balance is $1,000 more than the available balance, so the float is $1,000. On Day 2, the firm receives and deposits another check. It will collect three days later on Day 5. Now, at the end of Day 2, there are two uncollected checks, and the books show a $2,000 balance. The bank, however, still shows a zero available balance; so the float is $2,000. The same sequence occurs on Day 3, and the float rises to a total of $3,000.

On Day 4, Lambo again receives and deposits a check for $1,000. However, it also collects $1,000 from the Day 1 check. The change in book balance and the change in available balance are identical, +$1,000; so the float stays at $3,000. The same thing happens every day after Day 4; the float therefore stays at $3,000 forever.[1]

Figure 20.2 illustrates what happens if the float is eliminated entirely on some day *t* in the future. After the float is eliminated, daily receipts are still $1,000. The firm collects the same day because the float is eliminated, so daily collections are also still $1,000. As Figure 20.2 illustrates, the only change occurs the first day. On that day, as usual, Lambo collects $1,000 from the sale made three days before. Because the float is gone, it also collects on the sales made two days before, one day before, and that same day, for an additional $3,000. Total collections on Day *t* are thus $4,000 instead of $1,000.

[1]This permanent float that exists forever is sometimes called the *steady-state float*.

FIGURE 20.2 >>

Effect of Eliminating the Float

	Day			
	t	$t + 1$	$t + 2$	. . .
Beginning float	$3,000	$ 0	$ 0	. . .
Checks received	1,000	1,000	1,000	. . .
Checks cleared (cash available)	− 4,000	− 1,000	− 1,000	. . .
Ending float	$ 0	$ 0	$ 0	. . .

What we see is that Lambo generates an extra $3,000 on Day *t* by eliminating the float. On every subsequent day, Lambo receives $1,000 in cash just as it did before the float was eliminated. Thus, the only change in the firm's cash flows from eliminating the float is this extra $3,000 that comes in immediately. No other cash flows are affected, so Lambo is $3,000 richer.

In other words, the PV of eliminating the float is simply equal to the total float. Lambo could pay this amount out as a dividend, invest it in interest-bearing assets, or do anything else with it. If it costs $2,000 to eliminate the float, then the NPV is $3,000 − 2,000 = $1,000; so Lambo should do it.

EXAMPLE 20.2 >> Reducing the Float: Part I

Instead of eliminating the float, suppose Lambo can reduce it to one day. What is the maximum Lambo should be willing to pay for this?

If Lambo can reduce the float from three days to one day, then the amount of the float will fall from $3,000 to $1,000. From our discussion immediately preceding, we see right away that the PV of doing this is just equal to the $2,000 float reduction. Lambo should thus be willing to pay up to $2,000.

EXAMPLE 20.3 >> Reducing the Float: Part II

Look back at Example 20.2. A large bank is willing to provide the float reduction service for $175 per year, payable at the end of each year. The relevant discount rate is 8 percent. Should Lambo hire the bank? What is the NPV of the investment? How do you interpret this discount rate? What is the most per year that Lambo should be willing to pay?

The PV to Lambo is still $2,000. The $175 would have to be paid out every year forever to maintain the float reduction; so the cost is perpetual, and its PV is $175/.08 = $2,187.50. The NPV is $2,000 − 2,187.50 = −$187.50; therefore, the service is not a good deal.

Ignoring the possibility of bounced checks, the discount rate here corresponds most closely to the cost of short-term borrowing. The reason is that Lambo could borrow $1,000 from the bank every time a check was deposited and pay it back three days later. The cost would be the interest that Lambo would have to pay.

The most Lambo would be willing to pay is whatever charge results in an NPV of zero. This zero NPV occurs when the $2,000 benefit exactly equals the PV of the costs, that is, when $2,000 = *C*/.08, where *C* is the annual cost. Solving for *C*, we find that *C* = .08 × $2,000 = $160 per year.

Ethical and Legal Questions The cash manager must work with collected bank cash balances and not the firm's book balance (which reflects checks that have been deposited but not collected). If this is not done, a cash manager could be drawing on uncollected cash as a source of funds for short-term investing. Most banks charge a penalty rate for the use of uncollected funds. However, banks may not have good enough accounting and control procedures to be fully aware of the use of uncollected funds. This raises some ethical and legal questions for the firm.

For example, in May 1985, Robert Fomon, chairman of E. F. Hutton (a large investment bank), pleaded guilty to 2,000 charges of mail and wire fraud in connection with a scheme the firm had operated from 1980 to 1982. E. F. Hutton employees had written checks totaling hundreds of millions of dollars against uncollected cash. The proceeds had then been invested in short-term money market assets. This type of systematic overdrafting of accounts (or check *kiting,* as it is sometimes called) is neither legal nor ethical and is apparently not a widespread practice among corporations. Also, the particular inefficiencies in the banking system that Hutton was exploiting have been largely eliminated.

For its part, E. F. Hutton paid a $2 million fine, reimbursed the government (the U.S. Department of Justice) $750,000, and reserved an additional $8 million for restitution to defrauded banks. We should note that the key issue in the case against Hutton was not its float management per se, but, rather, its practice of writing checks for no economic reason other than to exploit float.

Despite the stiff penalties for check kiting, the practice apparently continues to go on. For example, in November 2003, a car dealership owner in Arizona was sentenced to seven years in prison for engaging in a three-year check kiting scheme worth $3.8 million.

Electronic Data Interchange: The End of Float?

Electronic data interchange (EDI) is a general term that refers to the growing practice of direct, electronic information exchange between all types of businesses. One important use of EDI, often called financial EDI, or FEDI, is to electronically transfer financial information and funds between parties, thereby eliminating paper invoices, paper checks, mailing, and handling. For example, it is now possible to arrange to have your checking account directly debited each month to pay many types of bills, and corporations now routinely directly deposit paychecks into employee accounts. More generally, EDI allows a seller to send a bill electronically to a buyer, thereby avoiding the mail. The seller can then authorize payment, which also occurs electronically. Its bank then transfers the funds to the seller's account at a different bank. The net effect is that the length of time required to initiate and complete a business transaction is shortened considerably, and much of what we normally think of as float is sharply reduced or eliminated. As the use of FEDI increases (which it will), float management will evolve to focus much more on issues surrounding computerized information exchange and funds transfers.

One of the drawbacks of EDI (and FEDI) is that it is expensive and complex to set up. However, with the growth of the Internet, a new form of EDI has emerged, Internet e-commerce. For example, networking giant Cisco Systems books about $13 million in orders each day on its Web site from resellers around the world. Cisco estimates that it saved $2.1 billion in technical support, marketing, distribution, and working capital management costs in 2003 by exploiting the Web. Firms are also linking to critical suppliers and customers via "extranets," which are business networks that extend a company's internal network. Because of security concerns and lack of standardization, don't look for e-commerce and extranets to eliminate the need for EDI anytime soon. In fact, these are complementary systems that will most likely be used in tandem as the future unfolds.

Concept Questions

20.2a Which would a firm be most interested in reducing, collection or disbursement float? Why?

20.2b How is daily average float calculated?

20.2c What is the benefit from reducing or eliminating float?

20.3 CASH COLLECTION AND CONCENTRATION

From our previous discussion, we know that collection delays work against the firm. All other things being the same, then, a firm will adopt procedures to speed up collections and thereby decrease collection times. In addition, even after cash is collected, firms need procedures to funnel, or concentrate, that cash where it can be best used. We discuss some common collection and concentration procedures next.

Components of Collection Time

Based on our previous discussion, we can depict the basic parts of the cash collection process as follows: The total time in this process is made up of mailing time, check-processing delay, and the bank's availability delay.

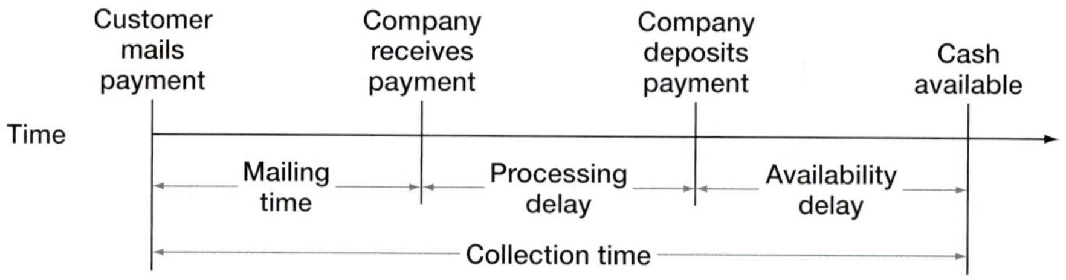

The amount of time that cash spends in each part of the cash collection process depends on where the firm's customers and banks are located and how efficient the firm is in collecting cash.

Cash Collection

How a firm collects from its customers depends in large part on the nature of the business. The simplest case would be a business such as a restaurant chain. Most of its customers will pay with cash, check, or credit card at the point of sale (this is called *over-the-counter collection*), so there is no problem with mailing delay. Normally, the funds will be deposited in a local bank, and the firm will have some means (discussed later) of gaining access to the funds.

When some or all of the payments a company receives are checks that arrive through the mail, all three components of collection time become relevant. The firm may choose to have all the checks mailed to one location, or, more commonly, the firm might have a number of different mail collection points to reduce mailing times. Also, the firm may run its collection operation itself or might hire an outside firm that specializes in cash collection. We discuss these issues in more detail in the following pages.

Other approaches to cash collection exist. One that is becoming more common is the preauthorized payment arrangement. With this arrangement, the payment amounts and payment dates are fixed in advance. When the agreed-upon date arrives, the amount is automatically transferred from the customer's bank account to the firm's bank account, which sharply reduces or even eliminates collection delays. The same approach is used by firms that have online terminals, meaning that when a sale is rung up, the money is immediately transferred to the firm's accounts.

Lockboxes

When a firm receives its payments by mail, it must decide where the checks will be mailed and how the checks will be picked up and deposited. Careful selection of the number and locations of collection points can greatly reduce collection times. Many firms use special post office boxes called **lockboxes** to intercept payments and speed cash collection.

lockboxes
Special post office boxes set up to intercept and speed up accounts receivable payments.

Figure 20.3 illustrates a lockbox system. The collection process is started by customers' mailing their checks to a post office box instead of sending them to the firm. The lockbox is maintained by a local bank. A large corporation may actually maintain more than 20 lockboxes around the country.

<< FIGURE 20.3

Overview of Lockbox Processing

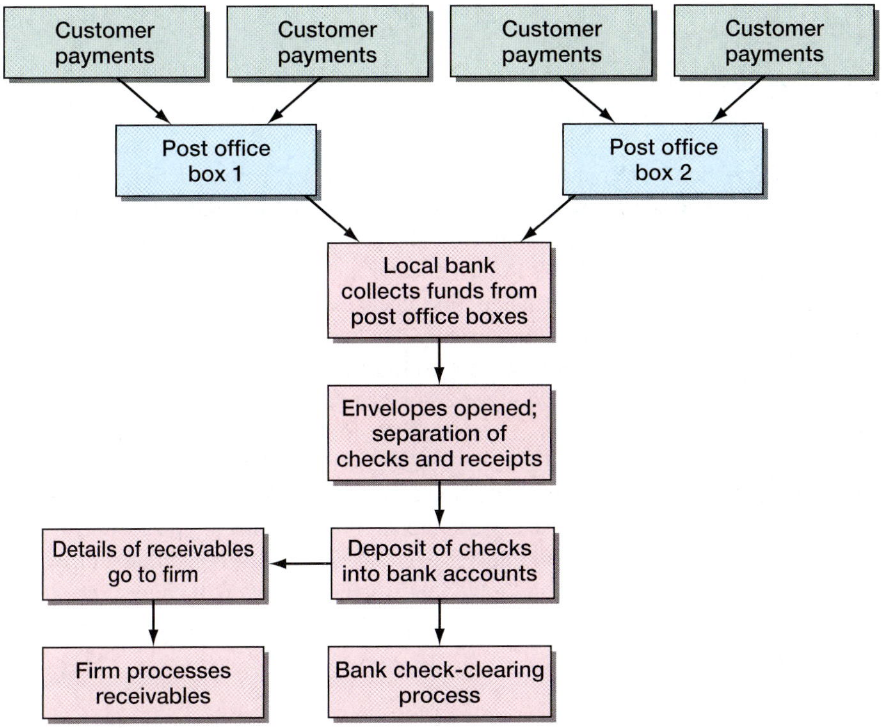

The flow starts when a corporate customer mails remittances to a post office box instead of to the corporation. Several times a day the bank collects the lockbox receipts from the post office. The checks are then put into the company bank accounts.

In the typical lockbox system, the local bank collects the lockbox checks several times a day. The bank deposits the checks directly to the firm's account. Details of the operation are recorded (in some computer-usable form) and sent to the firm.

A lockbox system reduces mailing time because checks are received at a nearby post office instead of at corporate headquarters. Lockboxes also reduce the processing time because the corporation doesn't have to open the envelopes and deposit checks for collection. In all, a bank lockbox system should enable a firm to get its receipts processed, deposited, and cleared faster than if it were to receive checks at its headquarters and deliver them itself to the bank for deposit and clearing.

Recently, some firms, such as Tulsa National Bank, are turning to what are called "electronic lockboxes" as an alternative to traditional lockboxes. In one version of an electronic lockbox, customers use the telephone or the Internet to access their account, say, their credit card account at a bank, review their bill, and authorize payment without paper ever having changed hands on either end of the transaction. Clearly, an electronic lockbox system is far superior to traditional bill payment methods, at least from the biller's perspective. Look for systems like this to continue to grow in popularity.

Cash Concentration

cash concentration
The practice of and procedures for moving cash from multiple banks into the firm's main accounts.

As we discussed earlier, a firm will typically have a number of cash collection points, and, as a result, cash collections may end up in many different banks and bank accounts. From here, the firm needs procedures to move the cash into its main accounts. This is called **cash concentration**. By routinely pooling its cash, the firm greatly simplifies its cash management by reducing the number of accounts that must be tracked. Also, by having a larger pool of funds available, a firm may be able to negotiate or otherwise obtain a better rate on any short-term investments.

In setting up a concentration system, firms will typically use one or more *concentration banks*. A concentration bank pools the funds obtained from local banks contained within some geographic region. Concentration systems are often used in conjunction with lockbox systems. Figure 20.4 illustrates how an integrated cash collection and cash concentration system might look. As Figure 20.4 illustrates, a key part of the cash collection and concentration process is the transfer of funds to the concentration bank. There are several options available for accomplishing this transfer. The cheapest is a *depository transfer check (DTC),* which is a preprinted check that usually needs no signature and is valid only for transferring funds between specific accounts within the *same* firm. The money becomes available one to two days later. *Automated clearinghouse* (*ACH*) transfers are basically electronic versions of paper checks. These may be more expensive, depending on the circumstances, but the funds are available the next day. The most expensive means of transfer are *wire transfers,* which provide same-day availability. Which approach a firm will choose depends on the number and size of payments. For example, a typical ACH transfer might be $200, whereas a typical wire transfer would be several million dollars. Firms with a large number of collection points and relatively small payments will choose the cheaper route, whereas firms that receive smaller numbers of relatively large payments may choose more expensive procedures.

Global Treasury News has current info on cash management, especially on international issues. (www.gtnews.com)

Accelerating Collections: An Example

The decision of whether or not to use a bank cash management service incorporating lockboxes and concentration banks depends on where a firm's customers are located and the

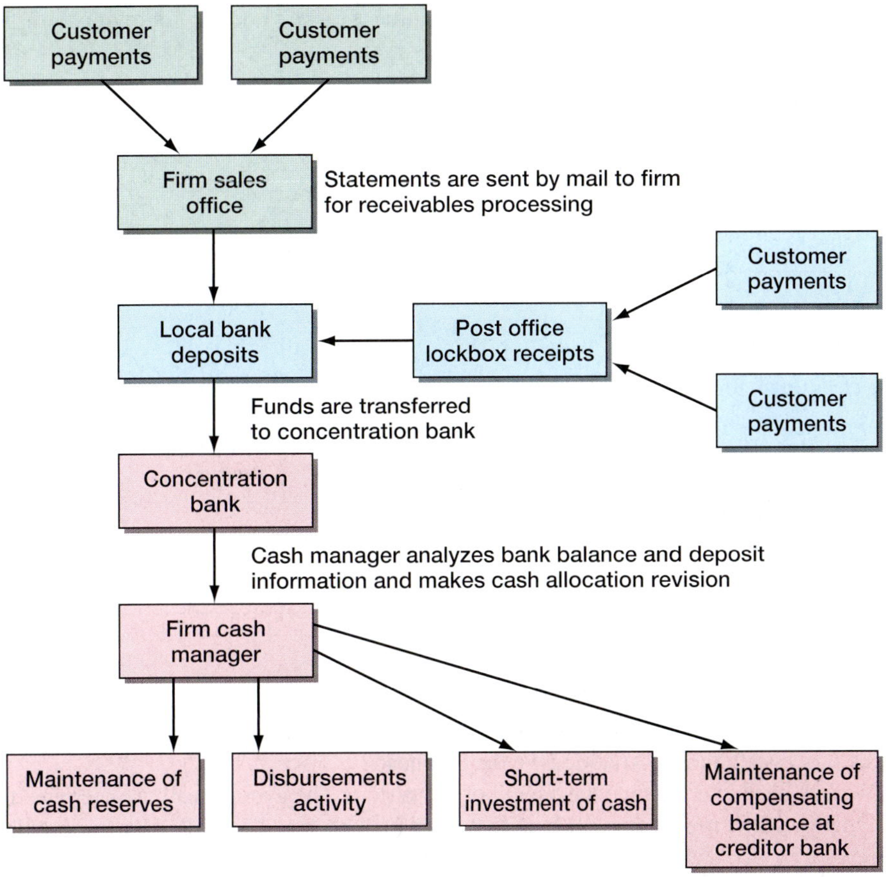

<< FIGURE 20.4

Lockboxes and Concentration Banks in a Cash Management System

speed of the U.S. postal system. Suppose Atlantic Corporation, located in Philadelphia, is considering a lockbox system. Its collection delay is currently eight days.

Atlantic does business in the southwestern part of the country (New Mexico, Arizona, and California). The proposed lockbox system would be located in Los Angeles and operated by Pacific Bank. Pacific Bank has analyzed Atlantic's cash-gathering system and has concluded that it can decrease collection time by two days. Specifically, the bank has come up with the following information on the proposed lockbox system:

Reduction in mailing time	= 1.0 day
Reduction in clearing time	= .5 day
Reduction in firm processing time	= .5 day
Total	= 2.0 days

The following is also known:

Daily interest on Treasury bills	= .025%
Average number of daily payments to lockboxes	= 2,000
Average size of payment	= $600

The cash flows for the current collection operation are shown in the following cash flow time chart:

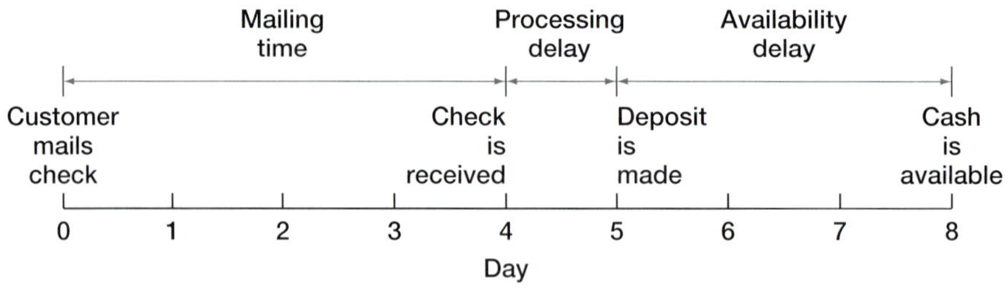

The cash flows for the lockbox collection operation will be as follows:

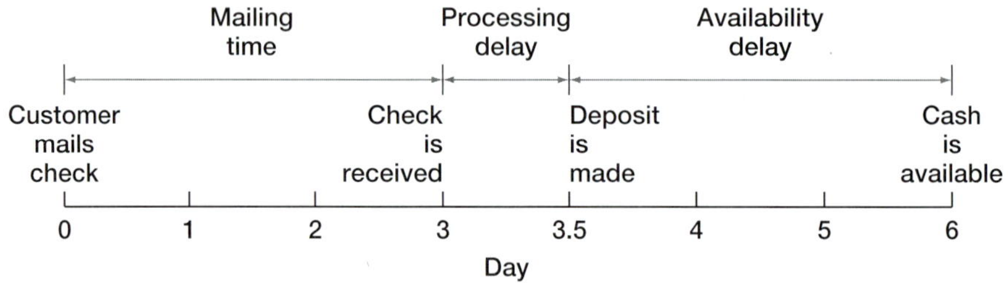

The Pacific Bank has agreed to operate this lockbox system for a fee of 25 cents per check processed. Should Atlantic give the go-ahead?

We first need to determine the benefit of the system. The average daily collections from the southwestern region are $1.2 million (2,000 × $600). The collection time will be decreased by two days, so the lockbox system will increase the collected bank balance by $1.2 million × 2 = $2.4 million. In other words, the lockbox system releases $2.4 million to the firm by reducing processing, mailing, and clearing time by two days. From our earlier discussion, we know that this $2.4 million is the PV of the proposal.

To calculate the NPV, we need to determine the PV of the costs. There are several different ways to proceed. First, at 2,000 checks per day and $.25 per check, the daily cost is $500. This cost will be incurred every day forever. At an interest rate of .025 percent per day, the PV is therefore $500/.00025 = $2 million. The NPV is thus $2.4 million − 2 million = $400,000, and the system appears to be desirable.

Alternatively, Atlantic could invest the $2.4 million at .025 percent per day. The interest earned would be $2.4 million × .00025 = $600 per day. The cost of the system is $500 per day; so, running it obviously generates a profit in the amount of $100 per day. The PV of $100 per day forever is $100/.00025 = $400,000, just as we had before.

Finally, and most simply, each check is for $600 and is available two days sooner if the system is used. The interest on $600 for two days is 2 × $600 × .00025 = $.30. The cost is 25 cents per check, so Atlantic makes a nickel ($.30 − .25) on every check. With 2,000 checks per day, the profit is $.05 × 2,000 checks = $100 per day, as we calculated.

EXAMPLE 20.4 >> Accelerating Collections

In our example concerning the Atlantic Corporation's proposed lockbox system, suppose the Pacific Bank wants a $20,000 fixed fee (paid annually) in addition to the 25 cents per check. Is the system still a good idea?

continued

To answer, we need to calculate the PV of the fixed fee. The daily interest rate is .025 percent. The annual rate is therefore $1.00025^{365} - 1 = 9.553\%$. The PV of the fixed fee (which is paid each year forever) is $20,000/.09553 = $209,358. Because the NPV without the fee is $400,000, the NPV with the fee is $400,000 − 209,358 = $190,642. It's still a good idea.

Concept Questions

20.3a What is a lockbox? What purpose does it serve?

20.3b What is a concentration bank? What purpose does it serve?

MANAGING CASH DISBURSEMENTS 20.4

From the firm's point of view, disbursement float is desirable, so the goal in managing disbursement float is to slow down disbursements. To do this, the firm may develop strategies to *increase* mail float, processing float, and availability float on the checks it writes. Beyond this, firms have developed procedures for minimizing cash held for payment purposes. We discuss the most common of these in this section.

Increasing Disbursement Float

As we have seen, slowing down payments comes from the time involved in mail delivery, check processing, and collection of funds. Disbursement float can be increased by writing a check on a geographically distant bank. For example, a New York supplier might be paid with checks drawn on a Los Angeles bank. This will increase the time required for the checks to clear through the banking system. Mailing checks from remote post offices is another way firms slow down disbursement.

For a free cash budgeting spreadsheet, go to www.toolkit.cch.com/tools/tools.asp.

Tactics for maximizing disbursement float are debatable on both ethical and economic grounds. First, as we discuss in some detail in the next chapter, payment terms very frequently offer a substantial discount for early payment. The discount is usually much larger than any possible savings from "playing the float game." In such cases, increasing mailing time will be of no benefit if the recipient dates payments based on the date received (as is common) as opposed to the postmark date.

Beyond this, suppliers are not likely to be fooled by attempts to slow down disbursements. The negative consequences of poor relations with suppliers can be costly. In broader terms, intentionally delaying payments by taking advantage of mailing times or unsophisticated suppliers may amount to avoiding paying bills when they are due, an unethical business procedure.

Controlling Disbursements

We have seen that maximizing disbursement float is probably poor business practice. However, a firm will still wish to tie up as little cash as possible in disbursements. Firms have therefore developed systems for efficiently managing the disbursement process. The general idea in such systems is to have no more than the minimum amount necessary to pay bills on deposit in the bank. We discuss some approaches to accomplishing this goal next.

Zero-Balance Accounts With a **zero-balance account** system, the firm, in cooperation with its bank, maintains a master account and a set of subaccounts. When a check

FIGURE 20.5 >> Zero-Balance Accounts

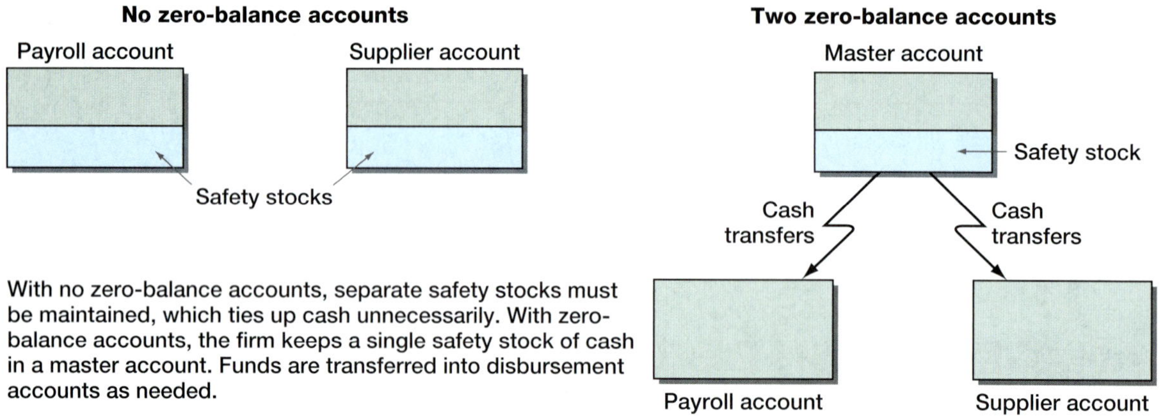

With no zero-balance accounts, separate safety stocks must be maintained, which ties up cash unnecessarily. With zero-balance accounts, the firm keeps a single safety stock of cash in a master account. Funds are transferred into disbursement accounts as needed.

zero-balance account
A disbursement account in which the firm maintains a zero balance, transferring funds in from a master account only as needed to cover checks presented for payment.

written on one of the subaccounts must be paid, the necessary funds are transferred in from the master account. Figure 20.5 illustrates how such a system might work. In this case, the firm maintains two disbursement accounts, one for suppliers and one for payroll. As shown, if the firm does not use zero-balance accounts, then each of these accounts must have a safety stock of cash to meet unanticipated demands. If the firm does use zero-balance accounts, then it can keep one safety stock in a master account and transfer the funds to the two subsidiary accounts as needed. The key is that the total amount of cash held as a buffer is smaller under the zero-balance arrangement, which frees up cash to be used elsewhere.

controlled disbursement account
A disbursement account to which the firm transfers an amount that is sufficient to cover demands for payment.

Controlled Disbursement Accounts With a **controlled disbursement account** system, almost all payments that must be made in a given day are known in the morning. The bank informs the firm of the total, and the firm transfers (usually by wire) the amount needed.

Concept Questions

20.4a Is maximizing disbursement float a sound business practice?

20.4b What is a zero-balance account? What is the advantage of such an account?

20.5 INVESTING IDLE CASH

If a firm has a temporary cash surplus, it can invest in short-term securities. As we have mentioned at various times, the market for short-term financial assets is called the *money market.* The maturity of short-term financial assets that trade in the money market is one year or less.

Most large firms manage their own short-term financial assets, carrying out transactions through banks and dealers. Some large firms and many small firms use money market mutual funds. These are funds that invest in short-term financial assets for a management fee. The management fee is compensation for the professional expertise and diversification provided by the fund manager.

Among the many money market mutual funds, some specialize in corporate customers. In addition, banks offer arrangements in which the bank takes all excess available funds at the close of each business day and invests them for the firm.

Temporary Cash Surpluses

Firms have temporary cash surpluses for various reasons. Two of the most important are the financing of seasonal or cyclical activities of the firm and the financing of planned or possible expenditures.

Seasonal or Cyclical Activities Some firms have a predictable cash flow pattern. They have surplus cash flows during part of the year and deficit cash flows the rest of the year. For example, Toys "Я" Us, a retail toy firm, has a seasonal cash flow pattern influenced by Christmas.

A firm such as Toys "Я" Us may buy marketable securities when surplus cash flows occur and sell marketable securities when deficits occur. Of course, bank loans are another short-term financing device. The use of bank loans and marketable securities to meet temporary financing needs is illustrated in Figure 20.6. In this case, the firm is following a compromise working capital policy in the sense we discussed in the previous chapter.

Planned or Possible Expenditures Firms frequently accumulate temporary investments in marketable securities to provide the cash for a plant construction program, dividend payment, or other large expenditure. Thus, firms may issue bonds and stocks before the cash is needed, investing the proceeds in short-term marketable securities and then selling the securities to finance the expenditures. Also, firms may face the possibility of having to make a large cash outlay. An obvious example would involve the possibility of losing a large lawsuit. Firms may build up cash surpluses against such a contingency.

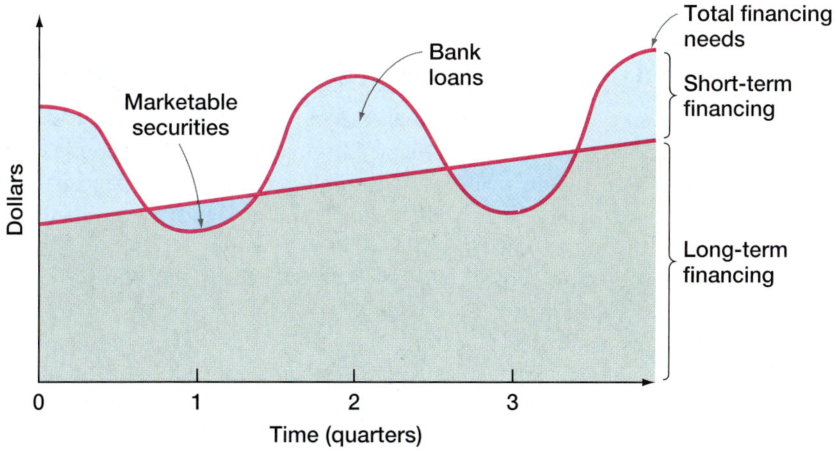

Time 1: A surplus cash flow exists. Seasonal demand for assets is low. The surplus cash flow is invested in short-term marketable securities.

Time 2: A deficit cash flow exists. Seasonal demand for assets is high. The financial deficit is financed by the selling of marketable securities and by bank borrowing.

<< FIGURE 20.6

Seasonal Cash Demands

Characteristics of Short-Term Securities

Given that a firm has some temporarily idle cash, there are a variety of short-term securities available for investing. The most important characteristics of these short-term marketable securities are their maturity, default risk, marketability, and taxability.

Maturity From Chapter 7, we know that for a given change in the level of interest rates, the prices of longer-maturity securities will change more than those of shorter-maturity securities. As a consequence, firms that invest in long-term securities are accepting greater risk than firms that invest in securities with short-term maturities.

We called this type of risk *interest rate risk*. Firms often limit their investments in marketable securities to those maturing in less than 90 days to avoid the risk of losses in value from changing interest rates. Of course, the expected return on securities with short-term maturities is usually less than the expected return on securities with longer maturities.

Default Risk *Default risk* refers to the probability that interest and principal will not be paid in the promised amounts on the due dates (or will not be paid at all). In Chapter 7, we observed that various financial reporting agencies, such as Moody's Investors Service and Standard and Poor's, compile and publish ratings of various corporate and other publicly held securities. These ratings are connected to default risk. Of course, some securities have negligible default risk, such as U.S. Treasury bills. Given the purposes of investing idle corporate cash, firms typically avoid investing in marketable securities with significant default risk.

Marketability *Marketability* refers to how easy it is to convert an asset to cash; so marketability and liquidity mean much the same thing. Some money market instruments are much more marketable than others. At the top of the list are U.S. Treasury bills, which can be bought and sold very cheaply and very quickly.

Taxes Interest earned on money market securities that are not some kind of government obligation (either federal or state) is taxable at the local, state, and federal levels. U.S. Treasury obligations such as T-bills are exempt from state taxation, but other government-backed debt is not. Municipal securities are exempt from federal taxes, but they may be taxed at the state level.

Some Different Types of Money Market Securities

Money market securities are generally highly marketable and short-term. They usually have low risk of default. They are issued by the U.S. government (for example, U.S. Treasury bills), domestic and foreign banks (for example, certificates of deposit), and business corporations (for example, commercial paper). There are many types in all, and we illustrate only a few of the most common here.

U.S. Treasury bills are obligations of the U.S. government that mature in 30, 90, or 180 days. Bills are sold by auction every week.

Short-term tax-exempts are short-term securities issued by states, municipalities, local housing agencies, and urban renewal agencies. Because these are all considered municipal securities, they are exempt from federal taxes. RANs, BANs, and TANs, for example, are revenue, bond, and tax anticipation notes, respectively. In other words, they represent short-term borrowing by municipalities in anticipation of cash receipts.

Short-term tax-exempts have more default risk than U.S. Treasury issues and are less marketable. Because the interest is exempt from federal income tax, the pretax yield on tax-exempts is lower than that on comparable securities such as Treasury bills. Also, corporations face restrictions on holding tax-exempts as investments.

Commercial paper is short-term securities issued by finance companies, banks, and corporations. Typically, commercial paper is unsecured. Maturities range from a few weeks to 270 days.

There is no especially active secondary market in commercial paper. As a consequence, the marketability can be low; however, firms that issue commercial paper will often repurchase it directly before maturity. The default risk of commercial paper depends on the financial strength of the issuer. Moody's and S&P publish quality ratings for commercial paper. These ratings are similar to the bond ratings we discussed in Chapter 7.

Check out short-term rates online at www.bloomberg.com.

Certificates of deposit (CDs) are short-term loans to commercial banks. The most common are jumbo CDs—those in excess of $100,000. There are active markets in CDs of 3-month, 6-month, 9-month, and 12-month maturities.

Repurchase agreements (repos) are sales of government securities (for example, U.S. Treasury bills) by a bank or securities dealer with an agreement to repurchase. Typically, an investor buys some Treasury securities from a bond dealer and simultaneously agrees to sell them back at a later date at a specified higher price. Repurchase agreements usually involve a very short term—overnight to a few days.

Because 70 to 80 percent of the dividends received by one corporation from another is exempt from taxation, the relatively high dividend yields on preferred stock provide a strong incentive for investment. The only problem is that the dividend is fixed with ordinary preferred stock, so the price can fluctuate more than is desirable in a short-term investment. However, money market preferred stock is a fairly recent innovation featuring a floating dividend. The dividend is reset fairly often (usually every 49 days), so this type of preferred has much less price volatility than ordinary preferred, and it has become a popular short-term investment.

Concept Questions

20.5a What are some reasons why firms find themselves with idle cash?

20.5b What are some types of money market securities?

20.5c Why are money market preferred stocks an attractive short-term investment?

SUMMARY AND CONCLUSIONS **20.6**

In this chapter, we have examined cash and liquidity management. We saw that:

1. A firm holds cash to conduct transactions and to compensate banks for the various services they render.
2. The difference between a firm's available balance and its book balance is the firm's net float. The float reflects the fact that some checks have not cleared and are thus uncollected. The financial manager must always work with collected cash balances and not with the company's book balance. To do otherwise is to use the bank's cash without the bank's knowing it, which raises ethical and legal questions.
3. The firm can make use of a variety of procedures to manage the collection and disbursement of cash in such a way as to speed up the collection of cash and slow down the payments. Some methods to speed up the collection are the use of lockboxes, concentration banking, and wire transfers.
4. Because of seasonal and cyclical activities, to help finance planned expenditures, or as a contingency reserve, firms temporarily hold a cash surplus. The money market offers a variety of possible vehicles for "parking" this idle cash.

Chapter Review and Self-Test Problem

20.1 Float Measurement On a typical day, a firm writes checks totaling $3,000. These checks clear in seven days. Simultaneously, the firm receives $1,700. The cash is available in two days on average. Calculate the disbursement, the collection, and the net floats. How do you interpret the answer?

Answer to Chapter Review and Self-Test Problem

20.1 The disbursement float is 7 days × $3,000 = $21,000. The collection float is 2 days × (−$1,700) = −$3,400. The net float is $21,000 + (−3,400) = $17,600. In other words, at any given time, the firm typically has uncashed checks outstanding of $21,000. At the same time, it has uncollected receipts of $3,400. Thus, the firm's book balance is typically $17,600 less than its available balance, for a positive $17,600 net float.

Concepts Review and Critical Thinking Questions

1. **Cash Management** Is it possible for a firm to have too much cash? Why would shareholders care if a firm accumulates large amounts of cash?
2. **Cash Management** What options are available to a firm if it believes it has too much cash? How about too little?
3. **Agency Issues** Are stockholders and creditors likely to agree on how much cash a firm should keep on hand?
4. **Motivations for Holding Cash** In the chapter opening, we discussed the enormous cash positions of several companies. Why would firms such as these hold such large quantities of cash?
5. **Cash Management versus Liquidity Management** What is the difference between cash management and liquidity management?
6. **Short-Term Investments** Why is a preferred stock with a dividend tied to short-term interest rates an attractive short-term investment for corporations with excess cash?
7. **Collection and Disbursement Floats** Which would a firm prefer: a net collection float or a net disbursement float? Why?
8. **Float** Suppose a firm has a book balance of $2 million. At the automatic teller machine (ATM), the cash manager finds out that the bank balance is $2.5 million. What is the situation here? If this is an ongoing situation, what ethical dilemma arises?
9. **Short-Term Investments** For each of the short-term marketable securities given here, provide an example of the potential disadvantages the investment has for meeting a corporation's cash management goals.
   a. U.S. Treasury bills
   b. Ordinary preferred stock
   c. Negotiable certificates of deposit (NCDs)
   d. Commercial paper
   e. Revenue anticipation notes
   f. Repurchase agreements
10. **Agency Issues** It is sometimes argued that excess cash held by a firm can aggravate agency problems (discussed in Chapter 1) and, more generally, reduce incentives for shareholder wealth maximization. How would you frame the issue here?

11. **Use of Excess Cash** One option a firm usually has with any excess cash is to pay its suppliers more quickly. What are the advantages and disadvantages of this use of excess cash?
12. **Use of Excess Cash** Another option usually available is to reduce the firm's outstanding debt. What are the advantages and disadvantages of this use of excess cash?
13. **Float** An unfortunately common practice goes like this (warning: don't try this at home): Suppose you are out of money in your checking account; however, your local grocery store will, as a convenience to you as a customer, cash a check for you. So, you cash a check for $200. Of course, this check will bounce unless you do something. To prevent this, you go to the grocery the next day and cash another check for $200. You take this $200 and deposit it. You repeat this process every day, and, in doing so, you make sure that no checks bounce. Eventually, manna from heaven arrives (perhaps in the form of money from home), and you are able to cover your outstanding checks.

    To make it interesting, suppose you are absolutely certain that no checks will bounce along the way. Assuming this is true, and ignoring any question of legality (what we have described is probably illegal check kiting), is there anything unethical about this? If you say yes, then why? In particular, who is harmed?

Questions and Problems

BASIC
(Questions 1–10)

1. **Calculating Float** In a typical month, the Timmons Corporation receives 90 checks totaling $85,000. These are delayed six days on average. What is the average daily float?
2. **Calculating Net Float** Each business day, on average, a company writes checks totaling $25,000 to pay its suppliers. The usual clearing time for the checks is four days. Meanwhile, the company is receiving payments from its customers each day, in the form of checks, totaling $40,000. The cash from the payments is available to the firm after two days.
    a. Calculate the company's disbursement float, collection float, and net float.
    b. How would your answer to part (*a*) change if the collected funds were available in one day instead of two?
3. **Costs of Float** Purple Feet Wine, Inc., receives an average of $9,000 in checks per day. The delay in clearing is typically four days. The current interest rate is .025 percent per day.
    a. What is the company's float?
    b. What is the most Purple Feet should be willing to pay today to eliminate its float entirely?
    c. What is the highest daily fee the company should be willing to pay to eliminate its float entirely?
4. **Float and Weighted Average Delay** Your neighbor goes to the post office once a month and picks up two checks, one for $16,000 and one for $3,000. The larger check takes four days to clear after it is deposited; the smaller one takes five days.
    a. What is the total float for the month?
    b. What is the average daily float?
    c. What are the average daily receipts and weighted average delay?
5. **NPV and Collection Time** Your firm has an average receipt size of $80. A bank has approached you concerning a lockbox service that will decrease your total collection time by two days. You typically receive 12,000 checks per day. The daily interest rate

is .016 percent. If the bank charges a fee of $190 per day, should the lockbox project be accepted? What would the net annual savings be if the service were adopted?

6. **Using Weighted Average Delay** A mail-order firm processes 5,000 checks per month. Of these, 65 percent are for $50 and 35 percent are for $70. The $50 checks are delayed two days on average; the $70 checks are delayed three days on average.
   a. What is the average daily collection float? How do you interpret your answer?
   b. What is the weighted average delay? Use the result to calculate the average daily float.
   c. How much should the firm be willing to pay to eliminate the float?
   d. If the interest rate is 7 percent per year, calculate the daily cost of the float.
   e. How much should the firm be willing to pay to reduce the weighted average float by 1.5 days?

7. **Value of Lockboxes** Paper Submarine Manufacturing is investigating a lockbox system to reduce its collection time. It has determined the following:

Average number of payments per day	400
Average value of payment	$1,400
Variable lockbox fee (per transaction)	$.75
Daily interest rate on money market securities	.02%

   The total collection time will be reduced by three days if the lockbox system is adopted.
   a. What is the PV of adopting the system?
   b. What is the NPV of adopting the system?
   c. What is the net cash flow per day from adopting? Per check?

8. **Lockboxes and Collections** It takes Cookie Cutter Modular Homes, Inc., about six days to receive and deposit checks from customers. Cookie Cutter's management is considering a lockbox system to reduce the firm's collection times. It is expected that the lockbox system will reduce receipt and deposit times to three days total. Average daily collections are $140,000, and the required rate of return is 9 percent per year.
   a. What is the reduction in outstanding cash balances as a result of implementing the lockbox system?
   b. What is the dollar return that could be earned on these savings?
   c. What is the maximum monthly charge Cookie Cutter should pay for this lockbox system?

9. **Value of Delay** No More Pencils, Inc., disburses checks every two weeks that average $70,000 and take seven days to clear. How much interest can the company earn annually if it delays transfer of funds from an interest-bearing account that pays .02 percent per day for these seven days? Ignore the effects of compounding interest.

10. **NPV and Reducing Float** No More Books Corporation has an agreement with Lollipop Bank whereby the bank handles $8 million in collections a day and requires a $500,000 compensating balance. No More Books is contemplating canceling the agreement and dividing its eastern region so that two other banks will handle its business. Banks A and B will each handle $4 million of collections a day, and each requires a compensating balance of $300,000. No More Books's financial management expects that collections will be accelerated by one day if the eastern region is divided. Should the company proceed with the new system? What will be the annual net savings? Assume that the T-bill rate is 5 percent annually.

INTERMEDIATE
(Questions 11–12)

11. **Lockboxes and Collection Time** Bird's Eye Treehouses, Inc., a Kentucky company, has determined that a majority of its customers are located in the Pennsylvania area. It therefore is considering using a lockbox system offered by a bank located in Pittsburgh. The bank has estimated that use of the system will reduce collection time by two days. Based on the following information, should the lockbox system be adopted?

Average number of payments per day	600
Average value of payment	\$1,100
Variable lockbox fee (per transaction)	\$.35
Annual interest rate on money market securities	6.0%

How would your answer change if there were a fixed charge of \$1,000 per year in addition to the variable charge?

12. **Calculating Transactions Required** Cow Chips, Inc., a large fertilizer distributor based in California, is planning to use a lockbox system to speed up collections from its customers located on the East Coast. A Philadelphia-area bank will provide this service for an annual fee of \$25,000 plus 10 cents per transaction. The estimated reduction in collection and processing time is one day. If the average customer payment in this region is \$5,500, how many customers each day, on average, are needed to make the system profitable for Cow Chips? Treasury bills are currently yielding 5 percent per year.

CHALLENGE
(Question 13)

13. **Concentration Banking** Mojo Corporation currently employs a lockbox system with collection centers in San Francisco, St. Louis, Atlanta, and Boston. Each lockbox center, on average, handles \$130,000 in payments every day. Mojo's current policy is to invest these payments in short-term marketable securities daily at the collection center banks. Every two weeks, the investment accounts are swept and the proceeds are wire-transferred to Mojo's headquarters in Dallas to meet the company's payroll. The investment accounts pay .015 percent per day, and wire transfers cost .15 percent of the amount transferred.
   a. What is Mojo's total net cash flow available from its lockbox system to meet the payroll?
   b. Suppose Late Nite Bank, located just outside Dallas, offers to set up a concentration bank system for Mojo. Late Nite will accept each of the lockbox center's daily payments via automated clearinghouse, ACH, transfers (in lieu of wire transfers) and deposit the funds in the same marketable securities investments yielding .015 percent per day. ACH-transferred funds are not available for use for one day. If the ACH transfers cost \$700 each, should Mojo proceed with the concentration bank plan?
   c. In part (*b*), at what cost of ACH transfers would Mojo be indifferent between the two systems?

What's On the Web?

20.1 Commercial Paper Rates What are the highest and lowest historical interest rates for commercial paper? Go to www.stlouisfed.org and follow the "FRED II®" link. Look under the "Interest Rate" link to find the 1-, 2-, and 3-month AA nonfinancial commercial paper rates. Looking at the monthly series, what were the highest and lowest interest rates for 1-, 2-, and 3-month nonfinancial commercial paper over the time reported? When did they occur?

20.2 ACH Services One provider of float reduction services is ePayment Systems. You can find their Web site at www.epaymentsystems.com. Follow the "Services" link and then the "Electronic Check Conversion" link. What does an electronic check conversion accomplish? How does the system work? How long does it take for the funds to be deposited in the merchant's account?

20A DETERMINING THE TARGET CASH BALANCE

target cash balance
A firm's desired cash level as determined by the trade-off between carrying costs and shortage costs.

adjustment costs
The costs associated with holding too little cash. Also, shortage costs.

Based on our general discussion of current assets in the previous chapter, the **target cash balance** involves a trade-off between the opportunity costs of holding too much cash (the carrying costs) and the costs of holding too little (the shortage costs, also called **adjustment costs**). The nature of these costs depends on the firm's working capital policy.

If the firm has a flexible working capital policy, then it will probably maintain a marketable securities portfolio. In this case, the adjustment, or shortage, costs will be the trading costs associated with buying and selling securities. If the firm has a restrictive working capital policy, it will probably borrow in the short term to meet cash shortages. The costs in this case will be the interest and other expenses associated with arranging a loan.

In our discussion that follows, we will assume that the firm has a flexible policy. Its cash management, then, consists of moving money in and out of marketable securities. This is a very traditional approach to the subject, and it is a nice way of illustrating the costs and benefits of holding cash. Keep in mind, however, that the distinction between cash and money market investments is becoming increasingly blurred.

For example, how do we classify a money market fund with check-writing privileges? Such near-cash arrangements are becoming more and more common. It may be that the prime reason they are not universal is regulation limiting their usage. We will return to this subject of such arrangements at various points in the following discussion.

The Basic Idea

Figure 20A.1 presents the cash management problem for our flexible firm. If a firm tries to keep its cash holdings too low, it will find itself running out of cash more often than is desirable, and thus selling marketable securities (and perhaps later buying marketable securities to replace those sold) more frequently than would be the case if the cash balance were higher. Thus, trading costs will be high when the cash balance is small. These costs will fall as the cash balance becomes larger.

In contrast, the opportunity costs of holding cash are very low if the firm holds very little cash. These costs increase as the cash holdings rise because the firm is giving up more and more in interest that could have been earned.

In Figure 20A.1, the sum of the costs is given by the total cost curve. As shown, the minimum total cost occurs where the two individual cost curves cross at Point C^*. At this point, the opportunity costs and the trading costs are equal. This point represents the target cash balance, and it is the point the firm should try to find.

Figure 20A.1 is essentially the same as Figure 19.2 in the previous chapter. As we discuss next, however, we can now say more about the optimum investment in cash and the factors that influence it.

The BAT Model

The Baumol-Allais-Tobin (BAT) model is a classic means of analyzing our cash management problem. We will show how this model can be used to actually establish the target

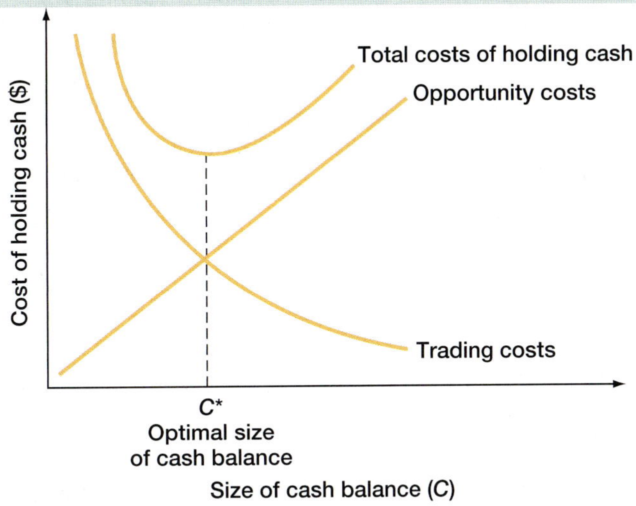

Trading costs are increased when the firm must sell securities to establish a cash balance. Opportunity costs are increased when there is a cash balance because there is no return on cash.

<< FIGURE 20A.1

Cost of Holding Cash

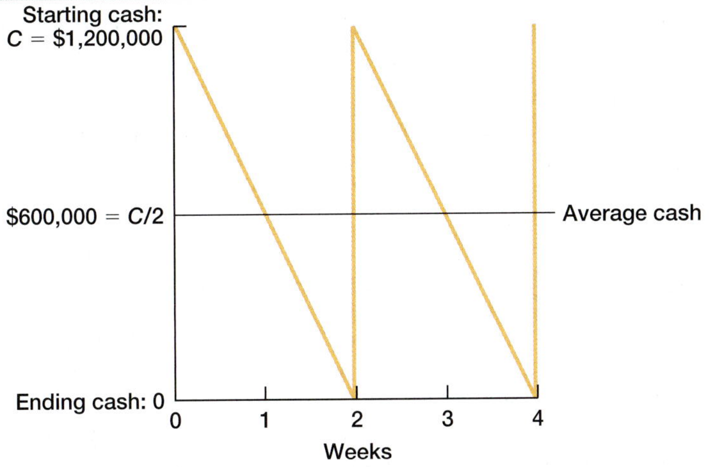

The Golden Socks Corporation starts at Week 0 with cash of $1,200,000. The balance drops to zero by the second week. The average cash balance is $C/2 = \$1{,}200{,}000/2 = \$600{,}000$ over the period.

<< FIGURE 20A.2

Cash Balances for the Golden Socks Corporation

cash balance. It is a straightforward model and very useful for illustrating the factors in cash management and, more generally, current asset management.

To develop the BAT model, suppose the Golden Socks Corporation starts off at Week 0 with a cash balance of $C = \$1.2$ million. Each week, outflows exceed inflows by $600,000. As a result, the cash balance will drop to zero at the end of Week 2. The average cash balance will be the beginning balance ($1.2 million) plus the ending balance ($0) divided by 2, or ($\$1.2$ million $+ 0)/2 = \$600{,}000$, over the two-week period. At the end of Week 2, Golden Socks replenishes its cash by depositing another $1.2 million.

As we have described, the cash management strategy for Golden Socks is very simple and boils down to depositing $1.2 million every two weeks. This policy is shown in Figure 20A.2. Notice how the cash balance declines by $600,000 per week. Because the company brings the account up to $1.2 million, the balance hits zero every two weeks. This results in the sawtooth pattern displayed in Figure 20A.2.

Implicitly, we assume that the net cash outflow is the same every day and that it is known with certainty. These two assumptions make the model easy to handle. We will indicate in the next section what happens when they do not hold.

If C were set higher, say, at $2.4 million, cash would last four weeks before the firm would have to sell marketable securities, but the firm's average cash balance would increase to $1.2 million (from $600,000). If C were set at $600,000, cash would run out in one week, and the firm would have to replenish cash more frequently, but the average cash balance would fall from $600,000 to $300,000.

Because transactions costs (for example, the brokerage costs of selling marketable securities) must be incurred whenever cash is replenished, establishing large initial balances will lower the trading costs connected with cash management. However, the larger the average cash balance, the greater is the opportunity cost (the return that could have been earned on marketable securities).

To determine the optimal strategy, Golden Socks needs to know the following three things:

F = The fixed cost of making a securities trade to replenish cash.

T = The total amount of new cash needed for transactions purposes over the relevant planning period, say, one year.

R = The opportunity cost of holding cash. This is the interest rate on marketable securities.

With this information, Golden Socks can determine the total costs of any particular cash balance policy. It can then determine the optimal cash balance policy.

The Opportunity Costs To determine the opportunity costs of holding cash, we have to find out how much interest is forgone. Golden Socks has, on average, $C/2$ in cash. This amount could be earning interest at rate R. So the total dollar opportunity costs of cash balances are equal to the average cash balance multiplied by the interest rate:

$$\text{Opportunity costs} = (C/2) \times R \qquad \textbf{[20A.1]}$$

For example, the opportunity costs of various alternatives are given here assuming that the interest rate is 10 percent:

Initial Cash Balance	Average Cash Balance	Opportunity Cost (R = .10)
C	$C/2$	$(C/2) \times R$
$4,800,000	$2,400,000	$240,000
2,400,000	1,200,000	120,000
1,200,000	600,000	60,000
600,000	300,000	30,000
300,000	150,000	15,000

In our original case, in which the initial cash balance is $1.2 million, the average balance is $600,000. The interest Golden Socks could have earned on this (at 10 percent) is $60,000, so this is what the firm gives up with this strategy. Notice that the opportunity costs increase as the initial (and average) cash balance rises.

The Trading Costs To determine the total trading costs for the year, we need to know how many times Golden Socks will have to sell marketable securities during the year. First of all, the total amount of cash disbursed during the year is \$600,000 per week, so T = \$600,000 × 52 weeks = \$31.2 million. If the initial cash balance is set at C = \$1.2 million, then Golden Socks will sell \$1.2 million in marketable securities T/C = \$31.2 million/1.2 million = 26 times per year. It costs F dollars each time, so trading costs are given by:

$$\frac{\$31.2 \text{ million}}{\$1.2 \text{ million}} \times F = 26 \times F$$

In general, the total trading costs will be given by:

$$\text{Trading costs} = (T/C) \times F \qquad [20A.2]$$

In this example, if F were \$1,000 (an unrealistically large amount), then the trading costs would be \$26,000.

We can calculate the trading costs associated with some different strategies as follows:

Total Amount of Disbursements during Relevant Period	Initial Cash Balance	Trading Costs (F = \$1,000)
T	C	$(T/C) \times F$
\$31,200,000	\$4,800,000	\$ 6,500
31,200,000	2,400,000	13,000
31,200,000	1,200,000	26,000
31,200,000	600,000	52,000
31,200,000	300,000	104,000

The Total Cost Now that we have the opportunity costs and the trading costs, we can calculate the total cost by adding them together:

$$\begin{aligned}\text{Total cost} &= \text{Opportunity costs} + \text{Trading costs}\\ &= (C/2) \times R + (T/C) \times F\end{aligned} \qquad [20A.3]$$

Using the numbers generated earlier, we have:

Cash Balance	Opportunity Costs	+	Trading Costs	=	Total Cost
\$4,800,000	\$240,000		\$ 6,500		\$246,500
2,400,000	120,000		13,000		133,000
1,200,000	60,000		26,000		86,000
600,000	30,000		52,000		82,000
300,000	15,000		104,000		119,000

Notice how the total cost starts out at almost \$250,000 and declines to about \$82,000 before starting to rise again.

The Solution We can see from the preceding schedule that a \$600,000 cash balance results in the lowest total cost of the possibilities presented: \$82,000. But what about \$700,000 or \$500,000 or other possibilities? It appears that the optimum balance is somewhere between \$300,000 and \$1.2 million. With this in mind, we could easily proceed by trial and error to find the optimum balance. It is not difficult to find it directly, however, so we do this next.

Take a look back at Figure 20A.1. As the figure is drawn, the optimal size of the cash balance, C^*, occurs right where the two lines cross. At this point, the opportunity costs and the trading costs are exactly equal. So, at C^*, we must have that:

$$\text{Opportunity costs} = \text{Trading costs}$$
$$(C^*/2) \times R = (T/C^*) \times F$$

With a little algebra, we can write:

$$C^{*2} = (2T \times F)/R$$

To solve for C^*, we take the square root of both sides to get:

$$C^* = \sqrt{(2T \times F)/R} \qquad [20A.4]$$

This is the optimum initial cash balance.

For Golden Socks, we have T = \$31.2 million, F = \$1,000, and R = 10%. We can now find the optimum cash balance:

$$\begin{aligned} C^* &= \sqrt{(2 \times \$31{,}200{,}000 \times 1{,}000)/.10} \\ &= \sqrt{\$624 \text{ billion}} \\ &= \$789{,}937 \end{aligned}$$

We can verify this answer by calculating the various costs at this balance, as well as a little above and a little below:

Cash Balance	Opportunity Costs	+	Trading Costs	=	Total Cost
$850,000	$42,500		$36,706		$79,206
800,000	40,000		39,000		79,000
789,937	39,497		39,497		78,994
750,000	37,500		41,600		79,100
700,000	35,000		44,571		79,571

The total cost at the optimum cash level is $78,994, and it does appear to increase as we move in either direction.

EXAMPLE 20A.1 >> The BAT Model

The Vulcan Corporation has cash outflows of $100 per day, seven days a week. The interest rate is 5 percent, and the fixed cost of replenishing cash balances is $10 per transaction. What is the optimal initial cash balance? What is the total cost?

The total cash needed for the year is 365 days × \$100 = \$36,500. From the BAT model, we have that the optimal initial balance is:

$$\begin{aligned} C^* &= \sqrt{(2T \times F)/R} \\ &= \sqrt{(2 \times \$36{,}500 \times 10)/.05} \\ &= \sqrt{\$14.6 \text{ million}} \\ &= \$3{,}821 \end{aligned}$$

The average cash balance is \$3,821/2 = \$1,911, so the opportunity cost is \$1,911 × .05 = \$96. Because Vulcan needs \$100 per day, the \$3,821 balance will last \$3,821/100 = 38.21 days. The firm needs to resupply the account 365/38.21 = 9.6 times per year, so the trading (order) cost is \$96. The total cost is \$192.

Conclusion The BAT model is possibly the simplest and most stripped-down sensible model for determining the optimal cash position. Its chief weakness is that it assumes steady, certain cash outflows. We next discuss a more involved model designed to deal with this limitation.

The Miller-Orr Model: A More General Approach

We now describe a cash management system designed to deal with cash inflows and outflows that fluctuate randomly from day to day. With this model, we again concentrate on the cash balance, but, in contrast to the situation with the BAT model, we assume that this balance fluctuates up and down randomly and that the average change is zero.

The Basic Idea Figure 20A.3 shows how the system works. It operates in terms of an upper limit to the amount of cash (U^*) and a lower limit (L), and a target cash balance (C^*). The firm allows its cash balance to wander around between the lower and upper limits. As long as the cash balance is somewhere between U^* and L, nothing happens.

When the cash balance reaches the upper limit (U^*), such as it does at Point X, the firm moves $U^* - C^*$ dollars out of the account and into marketable securities. This action moves the cash balance down to C^*. In the same way, if the cash balance falls to the lower limit (L), as it does at Point Y, the firm will sell $C^* - L$ worth of securities and deposit the cash in the account. This action takes the cash balance up to C^*.

Using the Model To get started, management sets the lower limit (L). This limit essentially defines a safety stock; so, where it is set depends on how much risk of a cash shortfall the firm is willing to tolerate. Alternatively, the minimum might just equal a required compensating balance.

As with the BAT model, the optimal cash balance depends on trading costs and opportunity costs. Once again, the cost per transaction of buying and selling marketable securities, F, is assumed to be fixed. Also, the opportunity cost of holding cash is R, the interest rate per period on marketable securities.

<< FIGURE 20A.3

The Miller-Orr Model

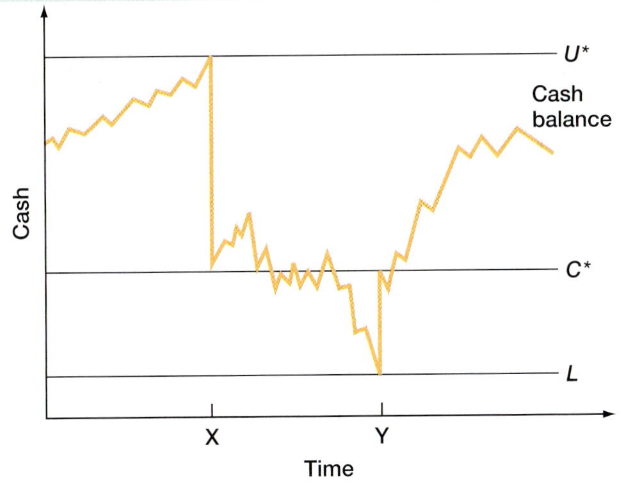

U^* is the upper control limit. L is the lower control limit. The target cash balance is C^*. As long as cash is between L and U^*, no transaction is made.

The only extra piece of information needed is σ^2, the variance of the net cash flow per period. For our purposes, the period can be anything, a day or a week, for example, as long as the interest rate and the variance are based on the same length of time.

Given L, which is set by the firm, Miller and Orr show that the cash balance target, C^*, and the upper limit, U^*, that minimize the total costs of holding cash are:[2]

$$C^* = L + (3/4 \times F \times \sigma^2/R)^{(1/3)} \qquad \textbf{[20A.5]}$$

$$U^* = 3 \times C^* - 2 \times L \qquad \textbf{[20A.6]}$$

Also, the average cash balance in the Miller-Orr model is:

$$\text{Average cash balance} = (4 \times C^* - L)/3 \qquad \textbf{[20A.7]}$$

The derivation of these expressions is relatively complex, so we will not present it here. Fortunately, as we illustrate next, the results are not difficult to use.

For example, suppose $F = \$10$, the interest rate is 1 percent per month, and the standard deviation of the monthly net cash flows is \$200. The variance of the monthly net cash flows is:

$$\sigma^2 = \$200^2 = \$40{,}000$$

We assume a minimum cash balance of $L = \$100$. We can calculate the cash balance target, C^*, as:

$$\begin{aligned} C^* &= L + (3/4 \times F \times \sigma^2/R)^{(1/3)} \\ &= \$100 + (3/4 \times 10 \times 40{,}000/.01)^{(1/3)} \\ &= \$100 + 30{,}000{,}000^{(1/3)} \\ &= \$100 + 311 = \$411 \end{aligned}$$

The upper limit, U^*, is thus:

$$\begin{aligned} U^* &= 3 \times C^* - 2 \times L \\ &= 3 \times \$411 - 2 \times 100 \\ &= \$1{,}033 \end{aligned}$$

Finally, the average cash balance will be:

$$\begin{aligned} \text{Average cash balance} &= (4 \times C^* - L)/3 \\ &= (4 \times \$411 - 100)/3 \\ &= \$515 \end{aligned}$$

Implications of the BAT and Miller-Orr Models

Our two cash management models differ in complexity, but they have some similar implications. In both cases, all other things being equal, we see that:

1. The greater the interest rate, the lower is the target cash balance.
2. The greater the order cost, the higher is the target balance.

These implications are both fairly obvious. The advantage of the Miller-Orr model is that it improves our understanding of the problem of cash management by considering the effect of uncertainty as measured by the variation in net cash inflows.

[2]M. H. Miller and D. Orr, "A Model of the Demand for Money by Firms," *Quarterly Journal of Economics,* August 1966.

The Miller-Orr model shows that the greater the uncertainty is (the higher σ^2 is), the greater is the difference between the target balance and the minimum balance. Similarly, the greater the uncertainty is, the higher is the upper limit and the higher is the average cash balance. These statements all make intuitive sense. For example, the greater the variability is, the greater is the chance that the balance will drop below the minimum. We thus keep a higher balance to guard against this happening.

Other Factors Influencing the Target Cash Balance

Before moving on, we briefly discuss two additional considerations that affect the target cash balance.

First, in our discussion of cash management, we assume that cash is invested in marketable securities such as Treasury bills. The firm obtains cash by selling these securities. Another alternative is to borrow cash. Borrowing introduces additional considerations to cash management:

1. Borrowing is likely to be more expensive than selling marketable securities because the interest rate is likely to be higher.
2. The need to borrow will depend on management's desire to hold low cash balances. A firm is more likely to have to borrow to cover an unexpected cash outflow the greater its cash flow variability and the lower its investment in marketable securities.

Second, for large firms, the trading costs of buying and selling securities are very small when compared to the opportunity costs of holding cash. For example, suppose a firm has $1 million in cash that won't be needed for 24 hours. Should the firm invest the money or leave it sitting?

Suppose the firm can invest the money at an annualized rate of 7.57 percent per year. The daily rate in this case is about two basis points (.02 percent or .0002).[3] The daily return earned on $1 million is thus .0002 × $1 million = $200. In many cases, the order cost will be much less than this; so a large firm will buy and sell securities very often before it will leave substantial amounts of cash idle.

Concept Questions

20A.1a What is a target cash balance?

20A.1b What is the basic trade-off in the BAT model?

20A.1c Describe how the Miller-Orr model works.

Appendix Review and Self-Test Problem

20A.1 The BAT Model Given the following information, calculate the target cash balance using the BAT model:

Annual interest rate	12%
Fixed order cost	$100
Total cash needed	$240,000

[3]A basis point is 1 percent of 1 percent. Also, the annual interest rate is calculated as $(1 + R)^{365} = 1.0757$, implying a daily rate of .02 percent.

What are the opportunity cost of holding cash, the trading cost, and the total cost? What would these be if $15,000 were held instead? If $25,000 were held?

Answer to Appendix Review and Self-Test Problem

20A.1 From the BAT model, we know that the target cash balance is:

$$\begin{aligned} C^* &= \sqrt{(2T \times F)/R} \\ &= \sqrt{(2 \times \$240{,}000 \times 100)/.12} \\ &= \sqrt{\$400{,}000{,}000} \\ &= \$20{,}000 \end{aligned}$$

The average cash balance will be $C^*/2 = \$20{,}000/2 = \$10{,}000$. The opportunity cost of holding $10,000 when the going rate is 12 percent is $\$10{,}000 \times .12 = \$1{,}200$. There will be $\$240{,}000/20{,}000 = 12$ orders during the year, so the order cost, or trading cost, is also $12 \times \$100 = \$1{,}200$. The total cost is thus $2,400.

If $15,000 is held, then the average balance is $7,500. Verify that the opportunity, trading, and total costs in this case are $900, $1,600, and $2,500, respectively. If $25,000 is held, these numbers are $1,500, $960, and $2,460, respectively.

Questions and Problems

Visit us at www.mhhe.com/rwj

BASIC
(Questions 1–10)

1. **Changes in Target Cash Balances** Indicate the likely impact of each of the following on a company's target cash balance. Use the letter *I* to denote an increase and *D* to denote a decrease. Briefly explain your reasoning in each case.
   a. Commissions charged by brokers decrease.
   b. Interest rates paid on money market securities rise.
   c. The compensating balance requirement of a bank is raised.
   d. The firm's credit rating improves.
   e. The cost of borrowing increases.
   f. Direct fees for banking services are established.
2. **Using the BAT Model** Given the following information, calculate the target cash balance using the BAT model:

Annual interest rate	7%
Fixed order cost	$10
Total cash needed	$5,000

   How do you interpret your answer?
3. **Opportunity versus Trading Costs** White Whale Corporation has an average daily cash balance of $400. Total cash needed for the year is $25,000. The interest rate is 5 percent, and replenishing the cash costs $6 each time. What are the opportunity cost of holding cash, the trading cost, and the total cost? What do you think of White Whale's strategy?
4. **Costs and the BAT Model** Debit and Credit Bookkeepers needs a total of $4,000 in cash during the year for transactions and other purposes. Whenever cash runs low, it sells off $300 in securities and transfers the cash in. The interest rate is 6 percent per year, and selling off securities costs $25 per sale.

a. What is the opportunity cost under the current policy? The trading cost? With no additional calculations, would you say that Debit and Credit keeps too much or too little cash? Explain.

b. What is the target cash balance derived using the BAT model?

5. **Determining Optimal Cash Balances** The Joe Elvis Company is currently holding $700,000 in cash. It projects that over the next year its cash outflows will exceed cash inflows by $360,000 per month. How much of the current cash holding should be retained and how much should be used to increase the company's holdings of marketable securities? Each time these securities are bought or sold through a broker, the company pays a fee of $500. The annual interest rate on money market securities is 6.5 percent. After the initial investment of excess cash, how many times during the next 12 months will securities be sold?

6. **Interpreting Miller-Orr** Econoline Crush, Inc., uses a Miller-Orr cash management approach with a lower limit of $40,000, an upper limit of $125,000, and a target balance of $60,000. Explain what each of these points represents and then explain how the system will work.

7. **Using Miller-Orr** Slap Shot Corporation has a fixed cost associated with buying and selling marketable securities of $100. The interest rate is currently .021 percent per day, and the firm has estimated that the standard deviation of its daily net cash flows is $75. Management has set a lower limit of $1,100 on cash holdings. Calculate the target cash balance and upper limit using the Miller-Orr model. Describe how the system will work.

8. **Interpreting Miller-Orr** Based on the Miller-Orr model, describe what will happen to the lower limit, the upper limit, and the spread (the distance between the two) if the variation in net cash flow grows. Give an intuitive explanation for why this happens. What happens if the variance drops to zero?

9. **Using Miller-Orr** The variance of the daily cash flows for the Pele Bicycle Shop is $960,000. The opportunity cost to the firm of holding cash is 7 percent per year. What should be the target cash level and the upper limit if the tolerable lower limit has been established as $150,000? The fixed cost of buying and selling securities is $500 per transaction.

10. **Using BAT** All Night Corporation has determined that its target cash balance if it uses the BAT model is $2,200. The total cash needed for the year is $21,000, and the order cost is $10. What interest rate must All Night be using?

21 Credit and Inventory Management

In April 2004, retailing giant Wal-Mart Stores began using radio-frequency identification (RFID) tags on cases and pallets in a small group of stores in the Dallas area. These high-tech tags are replacing bar codes because they can be read from a distance. RFID tag sales are expected to grow from about $1 billion in 2003 to about $4.6 billion in 2007. So why the rapid growth in a high-tech bar code? Look no further than Wal-Mart for the answer. The company is expected to save billions each year when RFIDs are fully implemented across the company. Specifically, it will save $6.7 billion in labor costs by eliminating the need to scan each pallet individually, $600 million by reducing out-of-stock items, $575 million by reducing theft, $300 million with better tracking, and $180 million by reducing inventory. The total cost savings for Wal-Mart is estimated at $8.35 *billion* per year! As this example suggests, proper management of inventory can have a significant impact on the profitability of a company and the value investors place on it.

CREDIT AND RECEIVABLES 21.1

When a firm sells goods and services, it can demand cash on or before the delivery date or it can extend credit to customers and allow some delay in payment. The next few sections provide an idea of what is involved in the firm's decision to grant credit to its customers. Granting credit is making an investment in a customer, an investment tied to the sale of a product or service.

Why do firms grant credit? Not all do, but the practice is extremely common. The obvious reason is that offering credit is a way of stimulating sales. The costs associated with granting credit are not trivial. First, there is the chance that the customer will not pay. Second, the firm has to bear the costs of carrying the receivables. The credit policy decision thus involves a trade-off between the benefits of increased sales and the costs of granting credit.

From an accounting perspective, when credit is granted, an account receivable is created. Such receivables include credit to other firms, called *trade credit,* and credit granted consumers, called *consumer credit.* About one-sixth of all the assets of U.S. industrial firms are in the form of accounts receivable, so receivables obviously represent a major investment of financial resources by U.S. businesses.

Components of Credit Policy

If a firm decides to grant credit to its customers, then it must establish procedures for extending credit and collecting. In particular, the firm will have to deal with the following components of credit policy:

1. **Terms of sale**. The terms of sale establish how the firm proposes to sell its goods and services. A basic decision is whether the firm will require cash or will extend credit. If the firm does grant credit to a customer, the terms of sale will specify (perhaps implicitly) the credit period, the cash discount and discount period, and the type of credit instrument.
2. **Credit analysis**. In granting credit, a firm determines how much effort to expend trying to distinguish between customers who will pay and customers who will not pay. Firms use a number of devices and procedures to determine the probability that customers will not pay, and, put together, these are called credit analysis.
3. **Collection policy**. After credit has been granted, the firm has the potential problem of collecting the cash, for which it must establish a collection policy.

terms of sale
The conditions under which a firm sells its goods and services for cash or credit.

credit analysis
The process of determining the probability that customers will not pay.

collection policy
The procedures followed by a firm in collecting accounts receivable.

In the next several sections, we will discuss these components of credit policy that collectively make up the decision to grant credit.

The Cash Flows from Granting Credit

In a previous chapter, we described the accounts receivable period as the time it takes to collect on a sale. There are several events that occur during this period. These events are the cash flows associated with granting credit, and they can be illustrated with a cash flow diagram:

The Cash Flows of Granting Credit

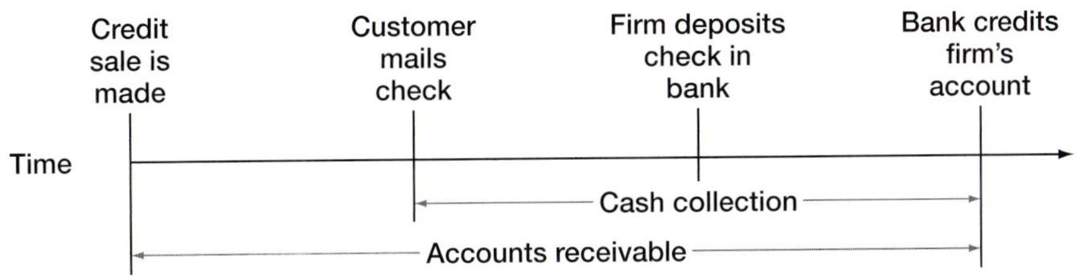

These companies assist businesses with working capital management: www.treasury.pncbank.com and www.treasurystrat.com/corp.

As our time line indicates, the typical sequence of events when a firm grants credit is as follows: (1) the credit sale is made, (2) the customer sends a check to the firm, (3) the firm deposits the check, and (4) the firm's account is credited for the amount of the check.

Based on our discussion in the previous chapter, it is apparent that one of the factors influencing the receivables period is float. Thus, one way to reduce the receivables period is to speed up the check mailing, processing, and clearing. Because we cover this subject elsewhere, we will ignore float in the subsequent discussion and focus on what is likely to be the major determinant of the receivables period, credit policy.

The Investment in Receivables

The investment in accounts receivable for any firm depends on the amount of credit sales and the average collection period. For example, if a firm's average collection period, ACP, is 30 days, then at any given time, there will be 30 days' worth of sales outstanding. If credit sales run \$1,000 per day, the firm's accounts receivable will then be equal to 30 days $\times$ \$1,000 per day = \$30,000, on average.

As our example illustrates, a firm's receivables generally will be equal to its average daily sales multiplied by its average collection period, or ACP:

$$\text{Accounts receivable} = \text{Average daily sales} \times \text{ACP} \qquad [21.1]$$

Thus, a firm's investment in accounts receivable depends on factors that influence credit sales and collections.

We have seen the average collection period in various places, including Chapter 3 and Chapter 19. Recall that we use the terms *days' sales in receivables, receivables period,* and *average collection period* interchangeably to refer to the length of time it takes for the firm to collect on a sale.

Concept Questions

21.1a What are the basic components of credit policy?

21.1b What are the basic components of the terms of sale if a firm chooses to sell on credit?

21.2 TERMS OF THE SALE

As we described previously, the terms of a sale are made up of three distinct elements:

1. The period for which credit is granted (the credit period)
2. The cash discount and the discount period
3. The type of credit instrument

Within a given industry, the terms of sale are usually fairly standard, but these terms vary quite a bit across industries. In many cases, the terms of sale are remarkably archaic and literally date to previous centuries. Organized systems of trade credit that resemble current practice can be easily traced to the great fairs of medieval Europe, and they almost surely existed long before then.

The Basic Form

The easiest way to understand the terms of sale is to consider an example. Terms such as 2/10, net 60 are common. This means that customers have 60 days from the invoice date (discussed a bit later) to pay the full amount; however, if payment is made within 10 days, a 2 percent cash discount can be taken.

Consider a buyer who places an order for $1,000, and assume that the terms of the sale are 2/10, net 60. The buyer has the option of paying $\$1{,}000 \times (1 - .02) = \$980$ in 10 days, or paying the full $1,000 in 60 days. If the terms are stated as just net 30, then the customer has 30 days from the invoice date to pay the entire $1,000, and no discount is offered for early payment.

In general, credit terms are interpreted in the following way:

<take this discount off the invoice price> / <if you pay in this many days>,

<else pay the full invoice amount in this many days>

Thus, 5/10, net 45 means take a 5 percent discount from the full price if you pay within 10 days, or else pay the full amount in 45 days.

For more on the credit process for small businesses, see www.newyorkfed.org/education/addpub/credit.html.

The Credit Period

The **credit period** is the basic length of time for which credit is granted. The credit period varies widely from industry to industry, but it is almost always between 30 and 120 days. If a cash discount is offered, then the credit period has two components: the net credit period and the cash discount period.

credit period
The length of time for which credit is granted.

The net credit period is the length of time the customer has to pay. The cash discount period is the time during which the discount is available. With 2/10, net 30, for example, the net credit period is 30 days and the cash discount period is 10 days.

The Invoice Date

The invoice date is the beginning of the credit period. An **invoice** is a written account of merchandise shipped to the buyer. For individual items, by convention, the invoice date is usually the shipping date or the billing date, *not* the date that the buyer receives the goods or the bill.

invoice
A bill for goods or services provided by the seller to the purchaser.

Many other arrangements exist. For example, the terms of sale might be ROG, for *receipt of goods*. In this case, the credit period starts when the customer receives the order. This might be used when the customer is in a remote location.

With EOM dating, all sales made during a particular month are assumed to be made at the end of that month. This is useful when a buyer makes purchases throughout the month, but the seller only bills once a month.

For example, terms of 2/10th, EOM tell the buyer to take a 2 percent discount if payment is made by the 10th of the month; otherwise the full amount is due. Confusingly, the end of the month is sometimes taken to be the 25th day of the month. MOM, for middle of month, is another variation.

Seasonal dating is sometimes used to encourage sales of seasonal products during the off-season. A product sold primarily in the summer (suntan oil?) can be shipped in January with credit terms of 2/10, net 30. However, the invoice might be dated May 1, so that the credit period actually begins at that time. This practice encourages buyers to order early.

Length of the Credit Period

Several factors influence the length of the credit period. Two important ones are the *buyer's* inventory period and operating cycle. All else equal, the shorter these are, the shorter the credit period will be.

From Chapter 19, the operating cycle has two components: the inventory period and the receivables period. The buyer's inventory period is the time it takes the buyer to acquire inventory (from us), process it, and sell it. The buyer's receivables period is the time it then takes the buyer to collect on the sale. Note that the credit period we offer is effectively the buyer's payables period.

By extending credit, we finance a portion of our buyer's operating cycle and thereby shorten that buyer's cash cycle (see Figure 19.1). If our credit period exceeds the buyer's inventory period, then we are not only financing the buyer's inventory purchases, but part of the buyer's receivables as well.

Furthermore, if our credit period exceeds our buyer's operating cycle, then we are effectively providing financing for aspects of our customer's business beyond the immediate purchase and sale of our merchandise. The reason is that the buyer effectively has a loan from us even after the merchandise is resold, and the buyer can use that credit for other purposes. For this reason, the length of the buyer's operating cycle is often cited as an appropriate upper limit to the credit period.

There are a number of other factors that influence the credit period. Many of these also influence our customer's operating cycles; so, once again, these are related subjects. Among the most important are:

1. *Perishability and collateral value.* Perishable items have relatively rapid turnover and relatively low collateral value. Credit periods are thus shorter for such goods. For example, a food wholesaler selling fresh fruit and produce might use net seven days. Alternatively, jewelry might be sold for 5/30, net four months.
2. *Consumer demand.* Products that are well established generally have more rapid turnover. Newer or slow-moving products will often have longer credit periods associated with them to entice buyers. Also, as we have seen, sellers may choose to extend much longer credit periods for off-season sales (when customer demand is low).
3. *Cost, profitability, and standardization.* Relatively inexpensive goods tend to have shorter credit periods. The same is true for relatively standardized goods and raw materials. These all tend to have lower markups and higher turnover rates, both of which lead to shorter credit periods. There are exceptions. Auto dealers, for example, generally pay for cars as they are received.
4. *Credit risk.* The greater the credit risk of the buyer, the shorter the credit period is likely to be (assuming that credit is granted at all).
5. *Size of the account.* If an account is small, the credit period may be shorter because small accounts cost more to manage, and the customers are less important.
6. *Competition.* When the seller is in a highly competitive market, longer credit periods may be offered as a way of attracting customers.
7. *Customer type.* A single seller might offer different credit terms to different buyers. A food wholesaler, for example, might supply groceries, bakeries, and restaurants. Each group would probably have different credit terms. More generally, sellers often have both wholesale and retail customers, and they frequently quote different terms to the two types.

Cash Discounts

cash discount
A discount given to induce prompt payment. Also, sales discount.

As we have seen, **cash discounts** are often part of the terms of sale. The practice of granting discounts for cash purchases in the United States dates to the Civil War and is widespread today. One reason discounts are offered is to speed up the collection of receivables. This will have the effect of reducing the amount of credit being offered, and the firm must trade this off against the cost of the discount.

Notice that when a cash discount is offered, the credit is essentially free during the discount period. The buyer only pays for the credit after the discount expires. With 2/10, net 30, a rational buyer either pays in 10 days to make the greatest possible use of the free credit or pays in 30 days to get the longest possible use of the money in exchange for giving up the discount. By giving up the discount, the buyer effectively gets $30 - 10 = 20$ days' credit.

Another reason for cash discounts is that they are a way of charging higher prices to customers that have had credit extended to them. In this sense, cash discounts are a convenient way of charging for the credit granted to customers.

Cost of the Credit In our examples, it might seem that the discounts are rather small. With 2/10, net 30, for example, early payment only gets the buyer a 2 percent discount. Does this provide a significant incentive for early payment? The answer is yes because the implicit interest rate is extremely high.

Visit the National Association of Credit Management at www.nacm.org.

To see why the discount is important, we will calculate the cost to the buyer of not paying early. To do this, we will find the interest rate that the buyer is effectively paying for the trade credit. Suppose the order is for $1,000. The buyer can pay $980 in 10 days or wait another 20 days and pay $1,000. It's obvious that the buyer is effectively borrowing $980 for 20 days and that the buyer pays $20 in interest on the "loan." What's the interest rate?

This interest is ordinary discount interest, which we discussed in Chapter 5. With $20 in interest on $980 borrowed, the rate is $\$20/980 = 2.0408\%$. This is relatively low, but remember that this is the rate per 20-day period. There are $365/20 = 18.25$ such periods in a year, so, by not taking the discount, the buyer is paying an effective annual rate, EAR, of:

$$\text{EAR} = 1.020408^{18.25} - 1 = 44.6\%$$

From the buyer's point of view, this is an expensive source of financing!

Given that the interest rate is so high here, it is unlikely that the seller benefits from early payment. Ignoring the possibility of default by the buyer, the decision of a customer to forgo the discount almost surely works to the seller's advantage.

Trade Discounts In some circumstances, the discount is not really an incentive for early payment but is instead a *trade discount,* a discount routinely given to some type of buyer. For example, with our 2/10th, EOM terms, the buyer takes a 2 percent discount if the invoice is paid by the 10th, but the bill is considered due on the 10th, and overdue after that. Thus, the credit period and the discount period are effectively the same, and there is no reward for paying before the due date.

The Cash Discount and the ACP To the extent that a cash discount encourages customers to pay early, it will shorten the receivables period and, all other things being equal, reduce the firm's investment in receivables.

For example, suppose a firm currently has terms of net 30 and an average collection period, ACP, of 30 days. If it offers terms of 2/10, net 30, then perhaps 50 percent of its customers (in terms of volume of purchases) will pay in 10 days. The remaining customers will still take an average of 30 days to pay. What will the new ACP be? If the firm's annual sales are $15 million (before discounts), what will happen to the investment in receivables?

If half of the customers take 10 days to pay and half take 30, then the new average collection period will be:

$$\text{New ACP} = .50 \times 10 \text{ days} + .50 \times 30 \text{ days} = 20 \text{ days}$$

The ACP thus falls from 30 days to 20 days. Average daily sales are $\$15 \text{ million}/365 = \$41{,}096$ per day. Receivables will thus fall by $\$41{,}096 \times 10 = \$410{,}960$.

Credit Instruments

credit instrument The evidence of indebtedness.

The **credit instrument** is the basic evidence of indebtedness. Most trade credit is offered on *open account.* This means that the only formal instrument of credit is the invoice, which is sent with the shipment of goods and which the customer signs as evidence that the goods have been received. Afterwards, the firm and its customers record the exchange on their books of account.

At times, the firm may require that the customer sign a *promissory note.* This is a basic IOU and might be used when the order is large, when there is no cash discount involved, or when the firm anticipates a problem in collections. Promissory notes are not common, but they can eliminate possible controversies later about the existence of debt.

One problem with promissory notes is that they are signed after delivery of the goods. One way to obtain a credit commitment from a customer before the goods are delivered is to arrange a *commercial draft.* Typically, the firm draws up a commercial draft calling for the customer to pay a specific amount by a specified date. The draft is then sent to the customer's bank with the shipping invoices.

If immediate payment is required on the draft, it is called a *sight draft.* If immediate payment is not required, then the draft is a *time draft.* When the draft is presented and the buyer "accepts" it, meaning that the buyer promises to pay it in the future, then it is called a *trade acceptance* and is sent back to the selling firm. The seller can then keep the acceptance or sell it to someone else. If a bank accepts the draft, meaning that the bank is guaranteeing payment, then the draft becomes a *banker's acceptance.* This arrangement is common in international trade, and banker's acceptances are actively traded in the money market.

A firm can also use a conditional sales contract as a credit instrument. With such an arrangement, the firm retains legal ownership of the goods until the customer has completed payment. Conditional sales contracts usually are paid in instalments and have an interest cost built into them.

Concept Questions

21.2a What considerations enter into the determination of the terms of sale?

21.2b Explain what terms of "3/45, net 90" mean. What is the effective interest rate?

21.3 ANALYZING CREDIT POLICY

In this section, we take a closer look at the factors that influence the decision to grant credit. Granting credit makes sense only if the NPV from doing so is positive. We thus need to look at the NPV of the decision to grant credit.

Credit Policy Effects

In evaluating credit policy, there are five basic factors to consider:

1. *Revenue effects.* If the firm grants credit, then there will be a delay in revenue collections as some customers take advantage of the credit offered and pay later. However, the firm may be able to charge a higher price if it grants credit and it may be able to increase the quantity sold. Total revenues may thus increase.
2. *Cost effects.* Although the firm may experience delayed revenues if it grants credit, it will still incur the costs of sales immediately. Whether the firm sells for cash or credit, it will still have to acquire or produce the merchandise (and pay for it).

3. *The cost of debt.* When the firm grants credit, it must arrange to finance the resulting receivables. As a result, the firm's cost of short-term borrowing is a factor in the decision to grant credit.[1]
4. *The probability of nonpayment.* If the firm grants credit, some percentage of the credit buyers will not pay. This can't happen, of course, if the firm sells for cash.
5. *The cash discount.* When the firm offers a cash discount as part of its credit terms, some customers will choose to pay early to take advantage of the discount.

Evaluating a Proposed Credit Policy

To illustrate how credit policy can be analyzed, we will start with a relatively simple case. Locust Software has been in existence for two years, and it is one of several successful firms that develop computer programs. Currently, Locust sells for cash only.

Locust is evaluating a request from some major customers to change its current policy to net one month (30 days). To analyze this proposal, we define the following:

P = Price per unit

v = Variable cost per unit

Q = Current quantity sold per month

Q' = Quantity sold under new policy

R = Monthly required return

For now, we ignore discounts and the possibility of default. Also, we ignore taxes because they don't affect our conclusions.

NPV of Switching Policies To illustrate the NPV of switching credit policies, suppose we have the following for Locust:

$P = \$49$

$v = \$20$

$Q = 100$

$Q' = 110$

If the required return, R, is 2 percent per month, should Locust make the switch?

Currently, Locust has monthly sales of $P \times Q = \$4{,}900$. Variable costs each month are $v \times Q = \$2{,}000$, so the monthly cash flow from this activity is:

$$\begin{aligned}\text{Cash flow with old policy} &= (P - v)Q \\ &= (\$49 - 20) \times 100 \\ &= \$2{,}900\end{aligned} \tag{21.2}$$

This is not the total cash flow for Locust, of course, but it is all that we need to look at because fixed costs and other components of cash flow are the same whether or not the switch is made.

[1]The cost of short-term debt is not necessarily the required return on receivables, although it is commonly assumed to be. As always, the required return on an investment depends on the risk of the investment, not the source of the financing. The *buyer's* cost of short-term debt is closer in spirit to the correct rate. We will maintain the implicit assumption that the seller and the buyer have the same short-term debt cost. In any case, the time periods in credit decisions are relatively short, so a relatively small error in the discount rate will not have a large effect on our estimated NPV.

If Locust does switch to net 30 days on sales, then the quantity sold will rise to $Q' = 110$. Monthly revenues will increase to $P \times Q'$, and costs will be $v \times Q'$. The monthly cash flow under the new policy will thus be:

$$\begin{aligned}\text{Cash flow with new policy} &= (P - v)\,Q' \\ &= (\$49 - 20) \times 110 \\ &= \$3{,}190\end{aligned} \qquad \textbf{[21.3]}$$

Going back to Chapter 8, we know that the relevant incremental cash flow is the difference between the new and old cash flows:

$$\begin{aligned}\text{Incremental cash inflow} &= (P - v)(Q' - Q) \\ &= (\$49 - 20) \times (110 - 100) \\ &= \$290\end{aligned}$$

This says that the benefit each month of changing policies is equal to the gross profit per unit sold, $P - v = \$29$, multiplied by the increase in sales, $Q' - Q = 10$. The present value of the future incremental cash flows is thus:

$$\text{PV} = [(P - v)(Q' - Q)]/R \qquad \textbf{[21.4]}$$

For Locust, this present value works out to be:

$$\text{PV} = (\$29 \times 10)/.02 = \$14{,}500$$

Notice that we have treated the monthly cash flow as a perpetuity because the same benefit will be realized each month forever.

Now that we know the benefit of switching, what's the cost? There are two components to consider. First, because the quantity sold will rise from Q to Q', Locust will have to produce $Q' - Q$ more units at a cost of $v(Q' - Q) = \$20 \times (110 - 100) = \$200$. Second, the sales that would have been collected this month under the current policy ($P \times Q = \$4{,}900$) will not be collected. Under the new policy, the sales made this month won't be collected until 30 days later. The cost of the switch is the sum of these two components:

$$\text{Cost of switching} = PQ + v(Q' - Q) \qquad \textbf{[21.5]}$$

For Locust, this cost would be $4,900 + 200 = $5,100.

Putting it all together, we see that the NPV of the switch is:

$$\text{NPV of switching} = -[PQ + v(Q' - Q)] + [(P - v)(Q' - Q)]/R \qquad \textbf{[21.6]}$$

For Locust, the cost of switching is $5,100. As we saw earlier, the benefit is $290 per month, forever. At 2 percent per month, the NPV is:

$$\begin{aligned}\text{NPV} &= -\$5{,}100 + 290/.02 \\ &= -\$5{,}100 + 14{,}500 \\ &= \$9{,}400\end{aligned}$$

Therefore, the switch is very profitable.

EXAMPLE 21.1 >> We'd Rather Fight than Switch

Suppose a company is considering a switch from all cash to net 30, but the quantity sold is not expected to change. What is the NPV of the switch? Explain.

In this case, $Q' - Q$ is zero, so the NPV is just $-PQ$. What this says is that the effect of the switch is simply to postpone one month's collections forever, with no benefit from doing so.

A Break-Even Application Based on our discussion thus far, the key variable for Locust is $Q' - Q$, the increase in unit sales. The projected increase of 10 units is only an estimate, so there is some forecasting risk. Under the circumstances, it's natural to wonder what increase in unit sales is necessary to break even.

Earlier, the NPV of the switch was defined as:

$$\text{NPV} = -[PQ + v(Q' - Q)] + [(P - v)(Q' - Q)]/R$$

We can calculate the break-even point explicitly by setting the NPV equal to zero and solving for $(Q' - Q)$:

$$\begin{aligned} \text{NPV} = 0 &= -[PQ + v(Q' - Q)] + [(P - v)(Q' - Q)]/R \\ Q' - Q &= PQ/[(P - v)/R - v] \end{aligned} \qquad [21.7]$$

For Locust, the break-even sales increase is thus:

$$\begin{aligned} Q' - Q &= \$4{,}900/(29/.02 - 20) \\ &= 3.43 \text{ units} \end{aligned}$$

This tells us that the switch is a good idea as long as Locust is confident that it can sell at least 3.43 more units per month.

Concept Questions

21.3a What are the important effects to consider in a decision to offer credit?

21.3b Explain how to estimate the NPV of a credit policy switch.

OPTIMAL CREDIT POLICY 21.4

So far, we've discussed how to compute net present values for a switch in credit policy. We have not discussed the optimal amount of credit or the optimal credit policy. In principle, the optimal amount of credit is determined by the point at which the incremental cash flows from increased sales are exactly equal to the incremental costs of carrying the increase in investment in accounts receivable.

For business reports on credit visit www.creditworthy.com.

The Total Credit Cost Curve

The trade-off between granting credit and not granting credit isn't hard to identify, but it is difficult to quantify precisely. As a result, we can only describe an optimal credit policy.

To begin, the carrying costs associated with granting credit come in three forms:

1. The required return on receivables
2. The losses from bad debts
3. The costs of managing credit and credit collections

We have already discussed the first and second of these. The third cost, the cost of managing credit, consists of the expenses associated with running the credit department. Firms that don't grant credit have no such department and no such expense. These three costs will all increase as credit policy is relaxed.

If a firm has a very restrictive credit policy, then all of the associated costs will be low. In this case, the firm will have a "shortage" of credit, so there will be an opportunity cost. This opportunity cost is the extra potential profit from credit sales that is lost because credit is refused. This forgone benefit comes from two sources, the increase in quantity sold, Q'

FIGURE 21.1 >>

The Costs of Granting Credit

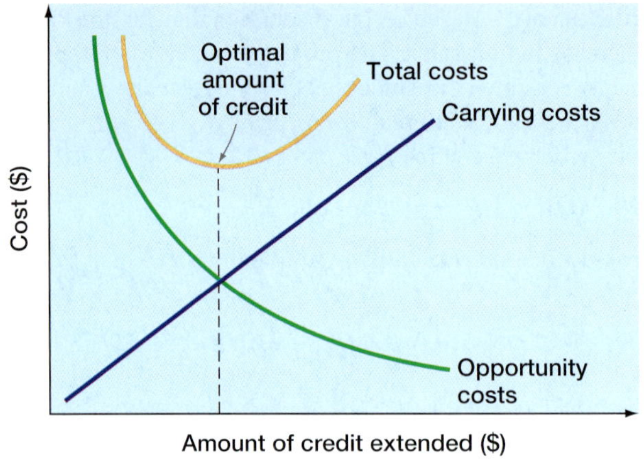

Carrying costs are the cash flows that must be incurred when credit is granted. They are positively related to the amount of credit extended.

Opportunity costs are the lost sales resulting from refusing credit. These costs go down when credit is granted.

minus Q, and, potentially, a higher price. The opportunity costs go down as credit policy is relaxed.

The sum of the carrying costs and the opportunity costs of a particular credit policy is called the total **credit cost curve**. We have drawn such a curve in Figure 21.1. As Figure 21.1 illustrates, there is a point where the total credit cost is minimized. This point corresponds to the optimal amount of credit or, equivalently, the optimal investment in receivables.

credit cost curve
A graphical representation of the sum of the carrying costs and the opportunity costs of a credit policy.

If the firm extends more credit than this minimum, the additional net cash flow from new customers will not cover the carrying costs of the investment in receivables. If the level of receivables is below this amount, then the firm is forgoing valuable profit opportunities.

In general, the costs and benefits from extending credit will depend on characteristics of particular firms and industries. All other things being equal, for example, it is likely that firms with (1) excess capacity, (2) low variable operating costs, and (3) repeat customers will extend credit more liberally than other firms. See if you can explain why each of these characteristics contributes to a more liberal credit policy.

Organizing the Credit Function

Firms that grant credit have the expense of running a credit department. In practice, firms often choose to contract out all or part of the credit function to a factor, an insurance company, or a captive finance company. Chapter 19 discusses factoring, an arrangement in which the firm sells its receivables. Depending on the specific arrangement, the factor may have full responsibility for credit checking, authorization, and collection. Smaller firms may find such an arrangement cheaper than running a credit department.

Firms that manage internal credit operations are self-insured against default. An alternative is to buy credit insurance through an insurance company. The insurance company offers coverage up to a preset dollar limit for accounts. As you would expect, accounts with a higher credit rating merit higher insurance limits. This type of insurance is particularly important for exporters, and government insurance is available for certain types of exports.

captive finance company
A wholly owned subsidiary that handles the credit function for the parent company.

Large firms often extend credit through a **captive finance company**, which is simply a wholly owned subsidiary that handles the credit function for the parent company. General

Motors Acceptance Corporation, GMAC, is a well-known example. General Motors sells to car dealers who in turn sell to customers. GMAC finances the dealer's inventory of cars and also finances customers who buy the cars.

Why would a firm choose to set up a separate company to handle the credit function? There are a number of reasons, but a primary one is to separate the production and financing of the firm's products for purposes of management, financing, and reporting. For example, the finance subsidiary is able to borrow in its own name, using its receivables as collateral, and the subsidiary often carries a better credit rating than the parent. This may allow the firm to achieve a lower overall cost of debt than could be obtained if production and financing were commingled.

Concept Questions

21.4a What are the carrying costs of granting credit?

21.4b What are the opportunity costs of not granting credit?

21.4c What is a captive finance subsidiary?

CREDIT ANALYSIS 21.5

Thus far, we have focused on establishing credit terms. Once a firm decides to grant credit to its customers, it must then establish guidelines for determining who will and who will not be allowed to buy on credit. Credit analysis refers to the process of deciding whether or not to extend credit to a particular customer. It usually involves two steps: gathering relevant information and determining creditworthiness.

Credit analysis is important simply because potential losses on receivables can be substantial. Companies report the amount of receivables they expect not to collect on their balance sheets. In 2003, IBM reported that $865 million of accounts receivable were doubtful, and GE reported a staggering $6.256 billion as an allowance for losses.

When Should Credit Be Granted?

Imagine that a firm is trying to decide whether or not to grant credit to a customer. This decision can get complicated. For example, note that the answer depends on what will happen if credit is refused. Will the customer simply pay cash or will the customer not make the purchase at all? To avoid being bogged down by this and other difficulties, we will use some special cases to illustrate the key points.

A One-Time Sale We start by considering the simplest case. A new customer wishes to buy one unit on credit at a price of P per unit. If credit is refused, then the customer will not make the purchase.

Furthermore, we assume that, if credit is granted, then, in one month, the customer will either pay up or default. The probability of the second of these events is π. In this case, the probability (π) can be interpreted as the percentage of *new* customers who will not pay. Our business does not have repeat customers, so this is strictly a one-time sale. Finally, the required return on receivables is R per month, and the variable cost is v per unit.

The analysis here is straightforward. If the firm refuses credit, then the incremental cash flow is zero. If it grants credit, then it spends v (the variable cost) this month and expects to collect $(1 - \pi)P$ next month. The NPV of granting credit is:

$$\text{NPV} = -v + (1 - \pi)P/(1 + R) \qquad [21.8]$$

For example, for Locust Software, this NPV is:

$$\text{NPV} = -\$20 + (1 - \pi) \times 49/1.02$$

With, say, a 20 percent rate of default, this works out to be:

$$\text{NPV} = -\$20 + .80 \times 49/1.02 = \$18.43$$

Therefore, credit should be granted. Notice that we have divided by $(1 + R)$ here instead of by R because we now assume that this is a one-time transaction.

Our example illustrates an important point. In granting credit to a new customer, a firm risks its variable cost (v). It stands to gain the full price (P). For a new customer, then, credit may be granted even if the default probability is high. For example, the break-even probability in this case can be determined by setting the NPV equal to zero and solving for π:

$$\begin{aligned} \text{NPV} = 0 &= -\$20 + (1 - \pi) \times 49/1.02 \\ 1 - \pi &= \$20/49 \times 1.02 \\ \pi &= 58.4\% \end{aligned}$$

Locust should extend credit as long as there is a $1 - .584 = 41.6\%$ chance or better of collecting. This explains why firms with higher markups will tend to have looser credit terms.

This percentage (58.4%) is the maximum acceptable default probability for a *new* customer. If an old, cash-paying customer wanted to switch to a credit basis, the analysis would be different, and the maximum acceptable default probability would be much lower.

The important difference is that, if we extend credit to an old customer, then we risk the total sales price (P), because this is what we collect if we don't extend credit. If we extend credit to a new customer, we only risk our variable cost.

Repeat Business A second, very important factor to keep in mind is the possibility of repeat business. We can illustrate this by extending our one-time sale example. We make one important assumption: A new customer who does not default the first time around will remain a customer forever and never default.

If the firm grants credit, it spends v this month. Next month, it gets nothing if the customer defaults, or it gets P if the customer pays. If the customer pays, then the customer will buy another unit on credit and the firm will spend v again. The net cash inflow for the month is thus $P - v$. In every subsequent month, this same $P - v$ will occur as the customer pays for the previous month's order and places a new one.

It follows from our discussion that, in one month, the firm will receive \$0 with probability π. With probability $(1 - \pi)$, however, the firm will have a permanent new customer. The value of a new customer is equal to the present value of $(P - v)$ every month forever:

$$\text{PV} = (P - v)/R$$

The NPV of extending credit is therefore:

$$\text{NPV} = -v + (1 - \pi)(P - v)/R \qquad [21.9]$$

For Locust, this is:

$$\begin{aligned} \text{NPV} &= -\$20 + (1 - \pi) \times (49 - 20)/.02 \\ &= -\$20 + (1 - \pi) \times 1{,}450 \end{aligned}$$

Even if the probability of default is 90 percent, the NPV is:

$$\text{NPV} = -\$20 + .10 \times 1{,}450 = \$125$$

Locust should extend credit unless default is a virtual certainty. The reason is that it only costs \$20 to find out who is a good customer and who is not. A good customer is worth \$1,450, however, so Locust can afford quite a few defaults.

Our repeat business example probably exaggerates the acceptable default probability, but it does illustrate that it will often turn out that the best way to do credit analysis is simply to extend credit to almost anyone. It also points out that the possibility of repeat business is a crucial consideration. In such cases, the important thing is to control the amount of credit initially offered to any one customer so that the possible loss is limited. The amount can be increased with time. Most often, the best predictor of whether or not someone will pay in the future is whether or not they have paid in the past.

Credit Information

If a firm does want credit information on customers, there are a number of sources. Information sources commonly used to assess creditworthiness include the following:

Web-surfing students should peruse the Dun & Bradstreet home page—this major supplier of credit information can be found at www.dnb.com.

1. *Financial statements.* A firm can ask a customer to supply financial statements such as balance sheets and income statements. Minimum standards and rules of thumb based on financial ratios like the ones we discussed in Chapter 3 can then be used as a basis for extending or refusing credit.
2. *Credit reports on the customer's payment history with other firms.* Quite a few organizations sell information on the credit strength and credit history of business firms. The best-known and largest firm of this type is Dun & Bradstreet, which provides subscribers with credit reports on individual firms. Experian is another well-known credit-reporting firm. Ratings and information are available for a huge number of firms, including very small ones. Equifax, Transunion, and Experian are the major suppliers of consumer credit information.
3. *Banks.* Banks will generally provide some assistance to their business customers in acquiring information on the creditworthiness of other firms.
4. *The customer's payment history with the firm.* The most obvious way to obtain information about the likelihood of customers not paying is to examine whether they have settled past obligations (and how quickly).

Credit Evaluation and Scoring

five *Cs* of credit
The five basic credit factors to be evaluated: character, capacity, capital, collateral, and conditions.

There are no magical formulas for assessing the probability that a customer will not pay. In very general terms, the classic **five *Cs* of credit** are the basic factors to be evaluated:

1. *Character.* The customer's willingness to meet credit obligations.
2. *Capacity.* The customer's ability to meet credit obligations out of operating cash flows.
3. *Capital.* The customer's financial reserves.
4. *Collateral.* An asset pledged in the case of default.
5. *Conditions.* General economic conditions in the customer's line of business.

credit scoring
The process of quantifying the probability of default when granting consumer credit.

Credit scoring is the process of calculating a numerical rating for a customer based on information collected; credit is then granted or refused based on the result. For example, a firm might rate a customer on a scale of 1 (very poor) to 10 (very good) on each of the five *Cs* of credit using all the information available about the customer. A credit score could then be calculated by totaling these ratings. Based on experience, a firm might choose to grant credit only to customers with a score above, say, 30.

Firms such as credit card issuers have developed statistical models for credit scoring. Usually, all of the legally relevant and observable characteristics of a large pool of customers are studied to find their historic relation to defaults. Based on the results, it is possible to determine the variables that best predict whether a customer will pay and then calculate a credit score based on those variables.

Because credit-scoring models and procedures determine who is and who is not creditworthy, it is not surprising that they have been the subject of government regulation. In particular, the kinds of background and demographic information that can be used in the credit decision are limited.

Concept Questions

21.5a What is credit analysis?

21.5b What are the five Cs of credit?

21.6 COLLECTION POLICY

Collection policy is the final element in credit policy. Collection policy involves monitoring receivables to spot trouble and obtaining payment on past-due accounts.

Monitoring Receivables

To keep track of payments by customers, most firms will monitor outstanding accounts. First of all, a firm will normally keep track of its average collection period, ACP, through time. If a firm is in a seasonal business, the ACP will fluctuate during the year, but unexpected increases in the ACP are a cause for concern. Either customers in general are taking longer to pay, or some percentage of accounts receivable is seriously overdue.

To see just how important timely collection of receivables is to investors, consider the case of Art Technology Group (ATG), a company that provides Internet customer relationship management and e-commerce software. In late 2000, ATG announced an unusual sale of accounts receivable to a bank. The sale helped lower ATG's reported September days' sales outstanding, an important indicator of receivables management. However, after this information became public, investors became concerned about the quality of the firm's sales, and ATG's stock sank 18 percent.

aging schedule
A compilation of accounts receivable by the age of each account.

The **aging schedule** is a second basic tool for monitoring receivables. To prepare one, the credit department classifies accounts by age.[2] Suppose a firm has $100,000 in receivables. Some of these accounts are only a few days old, but others have been outstanding for quite some time. The following is an example of an aging schedule.

Aging Schedule

Age of Account	Amount	Percentage of Total Value of Accounts Receivable
0–10 days	$ 50,000	50%
11–60 days	25,000	25
61–80 days	20,000	20
Over 80 days	5,000	5
	$100,000	100%

[2]Aging schedules are used elsewhere in business such as inventory tracking.

If this firm has a credit period of 60 days, then 25 percent of its accounts are late. Whether or not this is serious depends on the nature of the firm's collections and customers. It is often the case that accounts beyond a certain age are almost never collected. Monitoring the age of accounts is very important in such cases.

Firms with seasonal sales will find the percentages on the aging schedule changing during the year. For example, if sales in the current month are very high, then total receivables will also increase sharply. This means that the older accounts, as a percentage of total receivables, become smaller and might appear less important. Some firms have refined the aging schedule so that they have an idea of how it should change with peaks and valleys in their sales.

Collection Effort

A firm usually goes through the following sequence of procedures for customers whose payments are overdue:

1. It sends out a delinquency letter informing the customer of the past-due status of the account.
2. It makes a telephone call to the customer.
3. It employs a collection agency.
4. It takes legal action against the customer.

At times, a firm may refuse to grant additional credit to customers until arrearages are cleared up. This may antagonize a normally good customer, which points to a potential conflict between the collections department and the sales department.

In probably the worst case, the customer files for bankruptcy. When this happens, the credit-granting firm is just another unsecured creditor. The firm can simply wait, or it can sell its receivable. For example, when FoxMeyer Health filed for bankruptcy in August 1996, it owed $20 million to Bristol-Myers Squibb for drug purchases. Once FoxMeyer filed for bankruptcy, Bristol-Myers tried to sell its receivable at a discount. The purchaser would then have been the creditor in the bankruptcy proceedings and would have gotten paid when the bankruptcy was settled. Similar trade claims against FoxMeyer initially traded as high as 49 cents on the dollar, but settled to about 20 cents less than a month later. Thus, if Bristol-Myers had cashed out at that price, it would have sold its $20 million claim for about $4 million, a hefty discount. Of course, Bristol-Myers would have gotten its money immediately rather than waiting for an uncertain future amount.

Concept Questions

21.6a What tools can a manager use to monitor receivables?

21.6b What is an aging schedule?

INVENTORY MANAGEMENT 21.7

Like receivables, inventories represent a significant investment for many firms. For a typical manufacturing operation, inventories will often exceed 15 percent of assets. For a retailer, inventories could represent more than 25 percent of assets. From our discussion in Chapter 19, we know that a firm's operating cycle is made up of its inventory period and its receivables period. This is one reason for considering credit and inventory policy in the same chapter. Beyond this, both credit policy and inventory policy are used to drive sales, and the two must be coordinated to ensure that the process of acquiring inventory, selling it, and collecting on the sale proceeds smoothly. For example, changes in credit policy designed to stimulate sales must be accompanied by planning for adequate inventory.

The Financial Manager and Inventory Policy

Despite the size of a typical firm's investment in inventories, the financial manager of a firm will not normally have primary control over inventory management. Instead, other functional areas such as purchasing, production, and marketing will usually share decision-making authority regarding inventory. Inventory management has become an increasingly important specialty in its own right, and financial management will often only have input into the decision. For this reason, we will only survey some basics of inventory and inventory policy.

Visit the Society for Inventory Management Benchmarking Analysis at www.simba.org.

Inventory Types

For a manufacturer, inventory is normally classified into one of three categories. The first category is *raw material.* This is whatever the firm uses as a starting point in its production process. Raw materials might be something as basic as iron ore for a steel manufacturer or something as sophisticated as disk drives for a computer manufacturer.

The second type of inventory is *work-in-progress,* which is just what the name suggests—unfinished product. How big this portion of inventory is depends in large part on the length of the production process. For an airframe manufacturer, for example, work-in-progress can be substantial. The third and final type of inventory is *finished goods,* that is, products ready to ship or sell.

There are three things to keep in mind concerning inventory types. First, the names for the different types can be a little misleading because one company's raw materials can be another's finished goods. For example, going back to our steel manufacturer, iron ore would be a raw material, and steel would be the final product. An auto body panel stamping operation will have steel as its raw material and auto body panels as its finished goods, and an automobile assembler will have body panels as raw materials and automobiles as finished products.

The second thing to keep in mind is that the various types of inventory can be quite different in terms of their liquidity. Raw materials that are commodity-like or relatively standardized can be easy to convert to cash. Work-in-progress, on the other hand, can be quite illiquid and have little more than scrap value. As always, the liquidity of finished goods depends on the nature of the product.

Finally, a very important distinction between finished goods and other types of inventories is that the demand for an inventory item that becomes a part of another item is usually termed *derived* or *dependent demand* because the firm's need for these inventory types depends on its need for finished items. In contrast, the firm's demand for finished goods is not derived from demand for other inventory items, so it is sometimes said to be *independent.*

Inventory Costs

As we discussed in Chapter 19, there are two basic types of costs associated with current assets in general and with inventory in particular. The first of these is *carrying costs.* Here, carrying costs represent all of the direct and opportunity costs of keeping inventory on hand. These include:

1. Storage and tracking costs
2. Insurance and taxes

3. Losses due to obsolescence, deterioration, or theft
4. The opportunity cost of capital on the invested amount

The sum of these costs can be substantial, ranging roughly from 20 to 40 percent of inventory value per year.

The other type of costs associated with inventory is *shortage costs.* Shortage costs are costs associated with having inadequate inventory on hand. The two components of shortage costs are restocking costs and costs related to safety reserves. Depending on the firm's business, restocking or order costs are either the costs of placing an order with suppliers or the costs of setting up a production run. The costs related to safety reserves are opportunity losses such as lost sales and loss of customer goodwill that result from having inadequate inventory.

A basic trade-off exists in inventory management because carrying costs increase with inventory levels, whereas shortage or restocking costs decline with inventory levels. The basic goal of inventory management is thus to minimize the sum of these two costs. We consider ways to reach this goal in the next section.

Just to give you an idea of how important it is to balance carrying costs with shortage costs, consider the case of restaurant chain Applebee's. In 2003, the company ran out of its signature riblets for its all-you-can-eat promotion. So, in 2004, the company found additional suppliers and increased its inventory. In regrettable planning, the company began promoting its honey barbecue ribs, which were a big hit. At the same time, it removed riblets from its appetizer sampler and dropped pictures of the riblets from the menu. The result was far more riblets in stock than could be sold, so in July 2004, the company wrote off $2.3 million in riblet inventory (and probably took a lot of ribbing from the competition).

Concept Questions

21.7a What are the different types of inventory?

21.7b What are three things to remember when examining inventory types?

21.7c What is the basic goal of inventory management?

INVENTORY MANAGEMENT TECHNIQUES **21.8**

As we described earlier, the goal of inventory management is usually framed as cost minimization. Three techniques are discussed in this section, ranging from the relatively simple to the very complex.

The ABC Approach

The ABC approach is a simple approach to inventory management in which the basic idea is to divide inventory into three (or more) groups. The underlying rationale is that a small portion of inventory in terms of quantity might represent a large portion in terms of inventory value. For example, this situation would exist for a manufacturer that uses some relatively expensive, high-tech components and some relatively inexpensive basic materials in producing its products.

Figure 21.2 illustrates an ABC comparison of items in terms of the percentage of inventory value represented by each group versus the percentage of items represented. As

FIGURE 21.2 >>

ABC Inventory Analysis

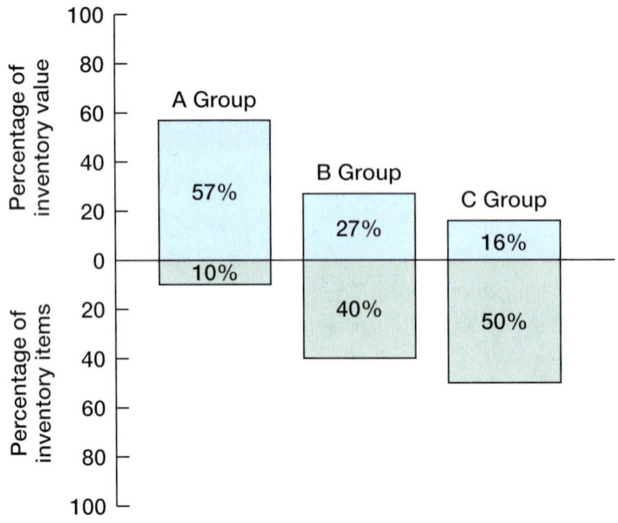

Figure 21.2 shows, the A Group constitutes only 10 percent of inventory by item count, but it represents over half of the value of inventory. The A Group items are thus monitored closely, and inventory levels are kept relatively low. At the other end, basic inventory items, such as nuts and bolts, also exist, but, because these are crucial and inexpensive, large quantities are ordered and kept on hand. These would be C Group items. The B Group is made up of in-between items.

The Economic Order Quantity Model

The economic order quantity (EOQ) model is the best-known approach for explicitly establishing an optimal inventory level. The basic idea is illustrated in Figure 21.3, which plots the various costs associated with holding inventory (on the vertical axis) against inventory levels (on the horizontal axis). As shown, inventory carrying costs rise and restocking costs decrease as inventory levels increase. From our general discussion in Chapter 19 and our discussion of the total credit cost curve in this chapter, the general shape of the total inventory cost curve is familiar. With the EOQ model, we will attempt to specifically locate the minimum total cost point, Q^*.

In our discussion that follows, an important point to keep in mind is that the actual cost of the inventory itself is not included. The reason is that the *total* amount of inventory the firm needs in a given year is dictated by sales. What we are analyzing here is how much the firm should have on hand at any particular time. More precisely, we are trying to determine what order size the firm should use when it restocks its inventory.

Inventory Depletion To develop the EOQ, we will assume that the firm's inventory is sold off at a steady rate until it hits zero. At that point, the firm restocks its inventory back to some optimal level. For example, suppose the Eyssell Corporation starts out today with 3,600 units of a particular item in inventory. Annual sales of this item are 46,800 units, which is about 900 per week. If Eyssell sells off 900 units of inventory each week, then, after four weeks, all the available inventory will be sold, and Eyssell will restock by ordering (or manufacturing) another 3,600 and start over. This selling and restocking process produces a sawtooth pattern for inventory holdings; this pattern is illustrated in

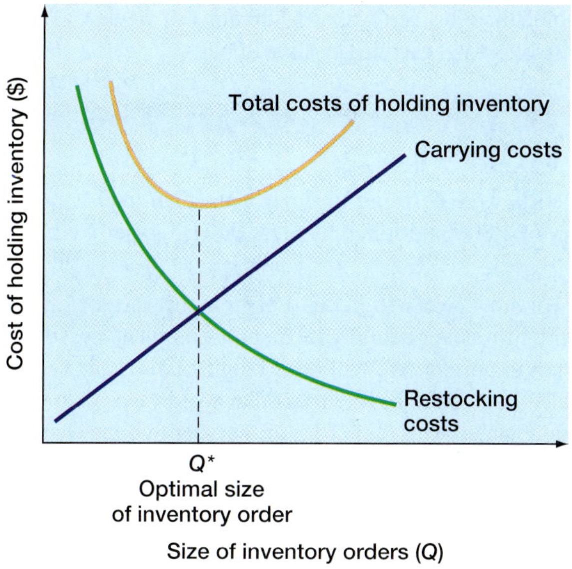

<< FIGURE 21.3

Costs of Holding Inventory

Restocking costs are greatest when the firm holds a small quantity of inventory. Carrying costs are greatest when there is a large quantity of inventory on hand. Total costs are the sum of the carrying and restocking costs.

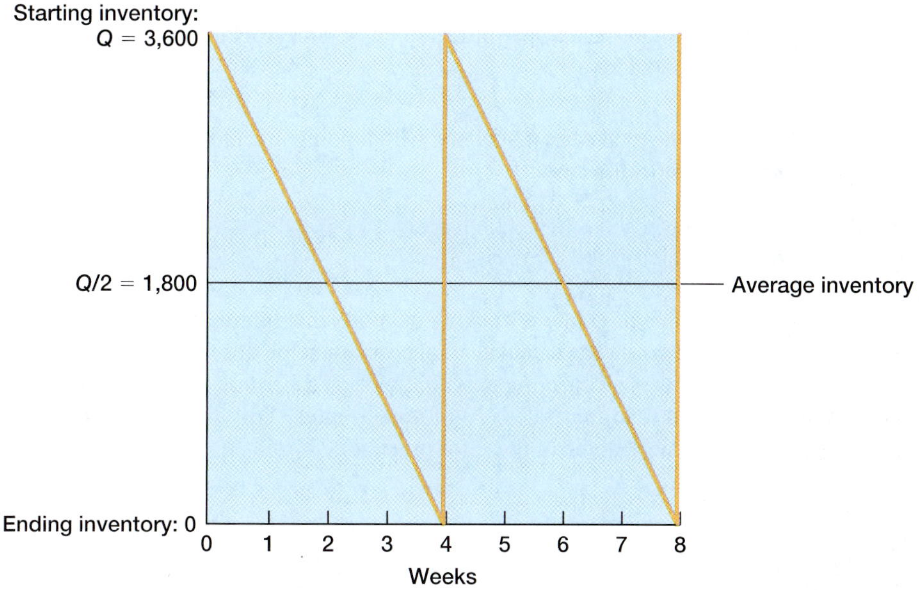

<< FIGURE 21.4

Inventory Holdings for the Eyssell Corporation

The Eyssell Corporation starts with inventory of 3,600 units. The quantity drops to zero by the end of the fourth week. The average inventory is $Q/2 = 3{,}600/2 = 1{,}800$ over the period.

Figure 21.4. As the figure shows, Eyssell always starts with 3,600 units in inventory and ends up at zero. On average, then, inventory is half of 3,600, or 1,800 units.

The Carrying Costs As Figure 21.3 illustrates, carrying costs are normally assumed to be directly proportional to inventory levels. Suppose we let Q be the quantity of inventory that Eyssell orders each time (3,600 units); we will call this the restocking quantity. Average inventory would then just be $Q/2$, or 1,800 units. If we let CC be the carrying cost per unit per year, Eyssell's total carrying costs will be:

$$\begin{aligned}\text{Total carrying costs} &= \text{Average inventory} \times \text{Carrying costs per unit} \\ &= (Q/2) \times \text{CC}\end{aligned} \quad [21.10]$$

In Eyssell's case, if carrying costs were \$.75 per unit per year, then total carrying costs would be the average inventory of 1,800 multiplied by \$.75, or \$1,350 per year.

The Shortage Costs For now, we will focus only on the restocking costs. In essence, we will assume that the firm never actually runs short on inventory, so that costs relating to safety reserves are not important. We will return to this issue later.

Restocking costs are normally assumed to be fixed. In other words, every time we place an order, there are fixed costs associated with that order (remember that the cost of the inventory itself is not considered here). Suppose we let T be the firm's total unit sales per year. If the firm orders Q units each time, then it will need to place a total of T/Q orders. For Eyssell, annual sales are 46,800, and the order size is 3,600. Eyssell thus places a total of 46,800/3,600 = 13 orders per year. If the fixed cost per order is F, the total restocking cost for the year would be:

$$\begin{aligned}\text{Total restocking cost} &= \text{Fixed cost per order} \times \text{Number of orders} \\ &= F \times (T/Q)\end{aligned} \quad [21.11]$$

For Eyssell, order costs might be \$50 per order, so the total restocking cost for 13 orders would be \$50 × 13 = \$650 per year.

The Total Costs The total costs associated with holding inventory are the sum of the carrying costs and the restocking costs:

$$\begin{aligned}\text{Total costs} &= \text{Carrying costs} + \text{Restocking costs} \\ &= (Q/2) \times \text{CC} + F \times (T/Q)\end{aligned} \quad [21.12]$$

Our goal is to find the value of Q, the restocking quantity, that minimizes this cost. To see how we might go about this, we can calculate total costs for some different values of Q. For the Eyssell Corporation, we had carrying costs (CC) of \$.75 per unit per year, fixed costs (F) of \$50 per order, and total unit sales (T) of 46,800 units. With these numbers, some possible total costs are (check some of these for practice):

Restocking Quantity (Q)	Carrying Costs (Q/2 × CC)	+	Restocking Costs (F × T/Q)	=	Total Costs
500	\$ 187.5		\$4,680.0		\$4,867.5
1,000	375.0		2,340.0		2,715.0
1,500	562.5		1,560.0		2,122.5
2,000	750.0		1,170.0		1,920.0
2,500	**937.5**		**936.0**		**1,873.5**
3,000	1,125.0		780.0		1,905.0
3,500	1,312.5		668.6		1,981.1

Inspecting the numbers, we see that total costs start out at almost \$5,000 and decline to just under \$1,900. The cost-minimizing quantity is about 2,500.

To find the cost-minimizing quantity, we can look back at Figure 21.3. What we notice is that the minimum point occurs right where the two lines cross. At this point, carrying costs and restocking costs are the same. For the particular types of costs we have assumed here, this will always be true, so we can find the minimum point just by setting these costs equal to each other and solving for Q^*:

$$\begin{aligned}\text{Carrying costs} &= \text{Restocking costs}\\ (Q^*/2) \times \text{CC} &= F \times (T/Q^*)\end{aligned} \quad [21.13]$$

With a little algebra, we get:

$$Q^{*2} = \frac{2T \times F}{\text{CC}} \quad [21.14]$$

To solve for Q^*, we take the square root of both sides to find:

$$Q^* = \sqrt{\frac{2T \times F}{\text{CC}}} \quad [21.15]$$

This reorder quantity, which minimizes the total inventory cost, is called the **economic order quantity (EOQ)**. For the Eyssell Corporation, the EOQ is:

economic order quantity (EOQ) The restocking quantity that minimizes the total inventory costs.

$$\begin{aligned}Q^* &= \sqrt{\frac{2T \times F}{\text{CC}}} \quad [21.16]\\ &= \sqrt{\frac{(2 \times 46{,}800) \times \$50}{.75}}\\ &= \sqrt{6{,}240{,}000}\\ &= 2{,}498 \text{ units}\end{aligned}$$

Thus, for Eyssell, the economic order quantity is 2,498 units. At this level, verify that the restocking costs and carrying costs are both \$936.75.

Carrying Costs

<< **EXAMPLE 21.2**

Thiewes Shoes begins each period with 100 pairs of hiking boots in stock. This stock is depleted each period and reordered. If the carrying cost per pair of boots per year is \$3, what are the total carrying costs for the hiking boots?

Inventories always start at 100 items and end up at zero, so average inventory is 50 items. At an annual cost of \$3 per item, total carrying costs are \$150.

Restocking Costs

<< **EXAMPLE 21.3**

In our previous example (Example 21.2), suppose Thiewes sells a total of 600 pairs of boots in a year. How many times per year does Thiewes restock? Suppose the restocking cost is \$20 per order. What are total restocking costs?

Thiewes orders 100 items each time. Total sales are 600 items per year, so Thiewes restocks six times per year, or about every two months. The restocking costs would be 6 orders × \$20 per order = \$120.

EXAMPLE 21.4 >> The EOQ

Based on our previous two examples, what size orders should Thiewes place to minimize costs? How often will Thiewes restock? What are the total carrying and restocking costs? The total costs?

We have that the total number of pairs of boots ordered for the year (T) is 600. The restocking cost (F) is \$20 per order, and the carrying cost (CC) is \$3. We can calculate the EOQ for Thiewes as follows:

$$\begin{aligned} \text{EOQ} &= \sqrt{\frac{2T \times F}{\text{CC}}} \\ &= \sqrt{\frac{(2 \times 600) \times \$20}{3}} \\ &= \sqrt{8{,}000} \\ &= 89.44 \text{ units} \end{aligned}$$

Because Thiewes sells 600 pairs per year, it will restock 600/89.44 = 6.71 times. The total restocking costs will be \$20 × 6.71 = \$134.16. Average inventory will be 89.44/2 = 44.72. The carrying costs will be \$3 × 44.72 = \$134.16, the same as the restocking costs. The total costs are thus \$268.33.

Extensions to the EOQ Model

Thus far, we have assumed that a company will let its inventory run down to zero and then reorder. In reality, a company will wish to reorder before its inventory goes to zero, for two reasons. First, by always having at least some inventory on hand, the firm minimizes the risk of a stock-out and the resulting losses of sales and customers. Second, when a firm does reorder, there will be some time lag before the inventory arrives. Thus, to finish our discussion of the EOQ, we consider two extensions, safety stocks and reordering points.

Safety Stocks A *safety stock* is the minimum level of inventory that a firm keeps on hand. Inventories are reordered whenever the level of inventory falls to the safety stock level. The top of Figure 21.5 illustrates how a safety stock can be incorporated into an EOQ model. Notice that adding a safety stock simply means that the firm does not run its inventory all the way down to zero. Other than this, the situation here is identical to that described in our earlier discussion of the EOQ.

Reorder Points To allow for delivery time, a firm will place orders before inventories reach a critical level. The *reorder points* are the times at which the firm will actually place its inventory orders. These points are illustrated in the middle of Figure 21.5. As shown, the reorder points simply occur some fixed number of days (or weeks or months) before inventories are projected to reach zero.

One of the reasons that a firm will keep a safety stock is to allow for uncertain delivery times. We can therefore combine our reorder point and safety stock discussions in the bottom part of Figure 21.5. The result is a generalized EOQ model in which the firm orders in advance of anticipated needs and also keeps a safety stock of inventory.

<< FIGURE 21.5

Safety Stocks and Reorder Points

A. Safety stocks

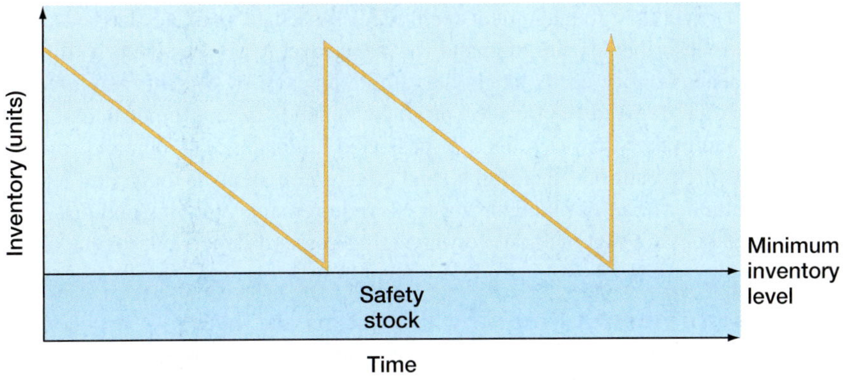

With a safety stock, the firm reorders when inventory reaches a minimum level.

B. Reorder points

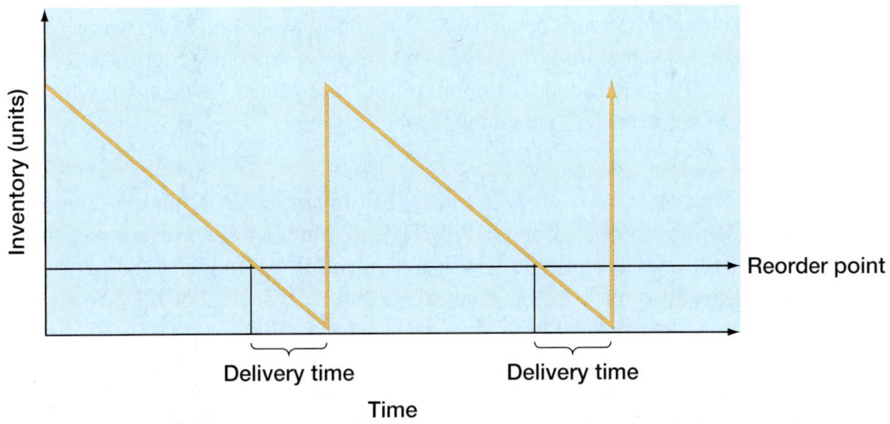

When there are lags in delivery or production times, the firm reorders when inventory reaches the reorder point.

C. Combined reorder points and safety stocks

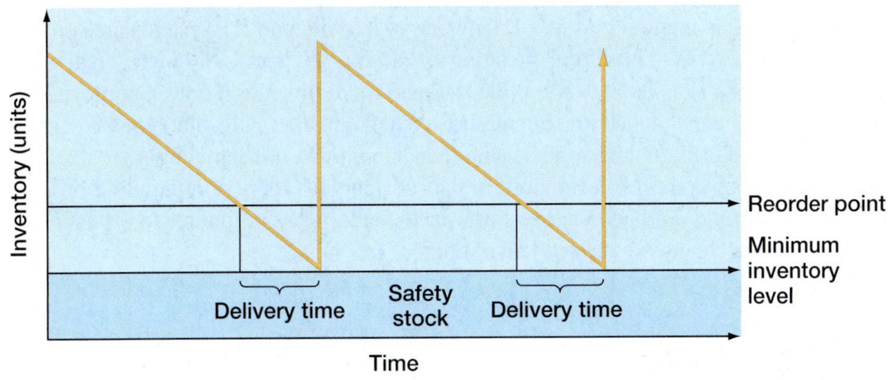

By combining safety stocks and reorder points, the firm maintains a buffer against unforeseen events.

Managing Derived-Demand Inventories

The third type of inventory management technique is used to manage derived-demand inventories. As we described earlier, demand for some inventory types is derived from or dependent on other inventory needs. A good example is given by the auto manufacturing industry, in which the demand for finished products depends on consumer demand, marketing programs, and other factors related to projected unit sales. The demand for inventory items such as tires, batteries, headlights, and other components is then completely determined by the number of autos planned. Materials requirements planning and just-in-time inventory management are two methods for managing demand-dependent inventories.

materials requirements planning (MRP)
A set of procedures used to determine inventory levels for demand-dependent inventory types such as work-in-progress and raw materials.

Materials Requirements Planning Production and inventory specialists have developed computer-based systems for ordering and/or scheduling production of demand-dependent types of inventories. These systems fall under the general heading of **materials requirements planning (MRP)**. The basic idea behind MRP is that, once finished goods inventory levels are set, it is possible to determine what levels of work-in-progress inventories must exist to meet the need for finished goods. From there, it is possible to calculate the quantity of raw materials that must be on hand. This ability to schedule backwards from finished goods inventories stems from the dependent nature of work-in-progress and raw materials inventories. MRP is particularly important for complicated products for which a variety of components are needed to create the finished product.

just-in-time (JIT) inventory
A system for managing demand-dependent inventories that minimizes inventory holdings.

Just-in-Time Inventory **Just-in-time (JIT) inventory** is a modern approach to managing dependent inventories. The goal of JIT is to minimize such inventories, thereby maximizing turnover. The approach began in Japan, and it is a fundamental part of Japanese manufacturing philosophy. As the name suggests, the basic goal of JIT is to have only enough inventory on hand to meet immediate production needs.

The result of the JIT system is that inventories are reordered and restocked frequently. Making such a system work and avoiding shortages requires a high degree of cooperation among suppliers. Japanese manufacturers often have a relatively small, tightly integrated group of suppliers with whom they work closely to achieve the needed coordination. These suppliers are a part of a large manufacturer's (such as Toyota's) industrial group, or *keiretsu*. Each large manufacturer tends to have its own *keiretsu*. It also helps to have suppliers located nearby, a situation that is common in Japan.

The *kanban* is an integral part of a JIT inventory system, and JIT systems are sometimes called *kanban systems*. The literal meaning of *kanban* is "card" or "sign," but, broadly speaking, a kanban is a signal to a supplier to send more inventory. For example, a kanban can literally be a card attached to a bin of parts. When a worker pulls that bin, the card is detached and routed back to the supplier, who then supplies a replacement bin.

A JIT inventory system is an important part of a larger production planning process. A full discussion of it would necessarily shift our focus away from finance to production and operations management, so we will leave it here.

Concept Questions

21.8a What does the EOQ model determine for the firm?

21.8b Which cost component of the EOQ model does JIT inventory minimize?

SUMMARY AND CONCLUSIONS 21.9

This chapter has covered the basics of credit and inventory policy. The major topics we discussed include:

1. The components of credit policy. We discussed the terms of sale, credit analysis, and collection policy. Under the general subject of terms of sale, the credit period, the cash discount and discount period, and the credit instrument were described.
2. Credit policy analysis. We developed the cash flows from the decision to grant credit and showed how the credit decision can be analyzed in an NPV setting. The NPV of granting credit depends on five factors: revenue effects, cost effects, the cost of debt, the probability of nonpayment, and the cash discount.
3. Optimal credit policy. The optimal amount of credit the firm should offer depends on the competitive conditions under which the firm operates. These conditions will determine the carrying costs associated with granting credit and the opportunity costs of the lost sales resulting from refusing to offer credit. The optimal credit policy minimizes the sum of these two costs.
4. Credit analysis. We looked at the decision to grant credit to a particular customer. We saw that two considerations are very important: the cost relative to the selling price and the possibility of repeat business.
5. Collection policy. Collection policy determines the method of monitoring the age of accounts receivable and dealing with past-due accounts. We described how an aging schedule can be prepared and the procedures a firm might use to collect on past-due accounts.
6. Inventory types. We described the different inventory types and how they differ in terms of liquidity and demand.
7. Inventory costs. The two basic inventory costs are carrying and restocking costs; we discussed how inventory management involves a trade-off between these two costs.
8. Inventory management techniques. We described the ABC approach and the EOQ model approach to inventory management. We also briefly touched on materials requirements planning, MRP, and just-in-time, or JIT, inventory management.

Chapter Review and Self-Test Problems

21.1 Credit Policy The Cold Fusion Corp. (manufacturer of the Mr. Fusion home power plant) is considering a new credit policy. The current policy is cash only. The new policy would involve extending credit for one period. Based on the following information, determine if a switch is advisable. The interest rate is 2.0 percent per period.

	Current Policy	New Policy
Price per unit	$ 175	$ 175
Cost per unit	$ 130	$ 130
Sales per period in units	1,000	1,100

21.2 Credit Where Credit Is Due You are trying to decide whether or not to extend credit to a particular customer. Your variable cost is \$15 per unit; the selling price is \$22. This customer wants to buy 1,000 units today and pay in 30 days. You think there is a 15 percent chance of default. The required return is 3 percent per 30 days. Should you extend credit? Assume that this is a one-time sale and that the customer will not buy if credit is not extended.

21.3 The EOQ Annondale Manufacturing starts each period with 10,000 "Long John" golf clubs in stock. This stock is depleted each month and reordered. If the carrying cost per golf club is \$1, and the fixed order cost is \$5, is Annondale following an economically advisable strategy?

Answers to Chapter Review and Self-Test Problems

21.1 If the switch is made, an extra 100 units per period will be sold at a gross profit of \$175 − 130 = \$45 each. The total benefit is thus \$45 × 100 = \$4,500 per period. At 2.0 percent per period forever, the PV is \$4,500/.02 = \$225,000.

The cost of the switch is equal to this period's revenue of \$175 × 1,000 units = \$175,000 plus the cost of producing the extra 100 units, 100 × \$130 = \$13,000. The total cost is thus \$188,000, and the NPV is \$225,000 − 188,000 = \$37,000. The switch should be made.

21.2 If the customer pays in 30 days, then you will collect \$22 × 1,000 = \$22,000. There's only an 85 percent chance of collecting this; so you expect to get \$22,000 × .85 = \$18,700 in 30 days. The present value of this is \$18,700/1.03 = \$18,155.34. Your cost is \$15 × 1,000 = \$15,000; so the NPV is \$18,155.34 − 15,000 = \$3,155.34. Credit should be extended.

21.3 We can answer by first calculating Annondale's carrying and restocking costs. The average inventory is 5,000 clubs, and, because the carrying costs are \$1 per club, total carrying costs are \$5,000. Annondale restocks every month at a fixed order cost of \$5, so the total restocking costs are \$60. What we see is that carrying costs are large relative to reorder costs, so Annondale is carrying too much inventory.

To determine the optimal inventory policy, we can use the EOQ model. Because Annondale orders 10,000 golf clubs 12 times per year, total needs (T) are 120,000 golf clubs. The fixed order cost is \$5, and the carrying cost per unit (CC) is \$1. The EOQ is therefore:

$$\begin{aligned} EOQ &= \sqrt{\frac{2T \times F}{\text{CC}}} \\ &= \sqrt{\frac{(2 \times 120{,}000) \times \$5}{1}} \\ &= \sqrt{1{,}200{,}000} \\ &= 1{,}095.45 \text{ units} \end{aligned}$$

We can check this by noting that the average inventory is about 550 clubs, so the carrying cost is \$550. Annondale will have to reorder 120,000/1,095.45 = 109.54 ≈ 110 times. The fixed order cost is \$5, so the total restocking cost is also \$550.

Concepts Review and Critical Thinking Questions

1. **Credit Instruments** Describe each of the following:
   a. Sight draft
   b. Time draft
   c. Banker's acceptance
   d. Promissory note
   e. Trade acceptance
2. **Trade Credit Forms** In what form is trade credit most commonly offered? What is the credit instrument in this case?
3. **Receivables Costs** What are the costs associated with carrying receivables? What are the costs associated with not granting credit? What do we call the sum of the costs for different levels of receivables?
4. **Five *C*s of Credit** What are the five *C*s of credit? Explain why each is important.
5. **Credit Period Length** What are some of the factors that determine the length of the credit period? Why is the length of the buyer's operating cycle often considered an upper bound on the length of the credit period?
6. **Credit Period Length** In each of the following pairings, indicate which firm would probably have a longer credit period and explain your reasoning.
   a. Firm A sells a miracle cure for baldness; Firm B sells toupees.
   b. Firm A specializes in products for landlords; Firm B specializes in products for renters.
   c. Firm A sells to customers with an inventory turnover of 10 times; Firm B sells to customers with an inventory turnover of 20 times.
   d. Firm A sells fresh fruit; Firm B sells canned fruit.
   e. Firm A sells and installs carpeting; Firm B sells rugs.
7. **Inventory Types** What are the different inventory types? How do the types differ? Why are some types said to have dependent demand whereas other types are said to have independent demand?
8. **Just-in-Time Inventory** If a company moves to a JIT inventory management system, what will happen to inventory turnover? What will happen to total asset turnover? What will happen to return on equity, ROE? (Hint: remember the Du Pont equation from Chapter 3.)
9. **Inventory Costs** If a company's inventory carrying costs are $5 million per year and its fixed order costs are $8 million per year, do you think the firm keeps too much inventory on hand or too little? Why?
10. **Inventory Period** At least part of Dell's corporate profits can be traced to its inventory management. Using just-in-time inventory, Dell typically maintains an inventory of three to four days' sales. Competitors such as Hewlett-Packard and IBM have attempted to match Dell's inventory policies, but lag far behind. In an industry where the price of PC components continues to decline, Dell clearly has a competitive advantage. Why would you say that it is to Dell's advantage to have such a short inventory period? If doing this is valuable, why don't all other PC manufacturers switch to Dell's approach?

Questions and Problems

BASIC
(Questions 1–12)

1. **Cash Discounts** You place an order for 200 units of inventory at a unit price of $95. The supplier offers terms of 2/10, net 30.
   a. How long do you have to pay before the account is overdue? If you take the full period, how much should you remit?
   b. What is the discount being offered? How quickly must you pay to get the discount? If you do take the discount, how much should you remit?
   c. If you don't take the discount, how much interest are you paying implicitly? How many days' credit are you receiving?
2. **Size of Accounts Receivable** The Graham Corporation has annual sales of $65 million. The average collection period is 48 days. What is Graham's average investment in accounts receivable as shown on the balance sheet?
3. **ACP and Accounts Receivable** Kyoto Joe, Inc., sells earnings forecasts for Japanese securities. Its credit terms are 2/10, net 30. Based on experience, 65 percent of all customers will take the discount.
   a. What is the average collection period for Kyoto Joe?
   b. If Kyoto Joe sells 1,200 forecasts every month at a price of $2,200 each, what is its average balance sheet amount in accounts receivable?
4. **Size of Accounts Receivable** Vitale, Baby!, Inc., has weekly credit sales of $18,000, and the average collection period is 29 days. The cost of production is 80 percent of the selling price. What is Vitale's average accounts receivable figure?
5. **Terms of Sale** A firm offers terms of 2/9, net 40. What effective annual interest rate does the firm earn when a customer does not take the discount? Without doing any calculations, explain what will happen to this effective rate if:
   a. The discount is changed to 3 percent.
   b. The credit period is increased to 60 days.
   c. The discount period is increased to 15 days.
6. **ACP and Receivables Turnover** Music City, Inc., has an average collection period of 52 days. Its average daily investment in receivables is $46,000. What are annual credit sales? What is the receivables turnover?
7. **Size of Accounts Receivable** Essence of Skunk Fragrances, Ltd., sells 4,000 units of its perfume collection each year at a price per unit of $400. All sales are on credit with terms of 2/15, net 40. The discount is taken by 60 percent of the customers. What is the amount of the company's accounts receivable? In reaction to sales by its main competitor, Sewage Spray, Essence of Skunk is considering a change in its credit policy to terms of 4/10, net 30 to preserve its market share. How will this change in policy affect accounts receivable?
8. **Size of Accounts Receivable** The Orbison Corporation sells on credit terms of net 25. Its accounts are, on average, 9 days past due. If annual credit sales are $8 million, what is the company's balance sheet amount in accounts receivable?
9. **Evaluating Credit Policy** Air Spares is a wholesaler that stocks engine components and test equipment for the commercial aircraft industry. A new customer has placed an order for 8 high-bypass turbine engines, which increase fuel economy. The variable cost is $1.5 million per unit, and the credit price is $1.8 million each. Credit is extended for one period, and based on historical experience, payment for about 1 out of every 200 such orders is never collected. The required return is 2.5 percent per period.

a. Assuming that this is a one-time order, should it be filled? The customer will not buy if credit is not extended.

b. What is the break-even probability of default in part (*a*)?

c. Suppose that customers who don't default become repeat customers and place the same order every period forever. Further assume that repeat customers never default. Should the order be filled? What is the break-even probability of default?

d. Describe in general terms why credit terms will be more liberal when repeat orders are a possibility.

10. Credit Policy Evaluation Champions, Inc., is considering a change in its cash-only sales policy. The new terms of sale would be net one month. Based on the following information, determine if Champions should proceed or not. Describe the buildup of receivables in this case. The required return is 1.5 percent per month.

	Current Policy	New Policy
Price per unit	$ 800	$ 800
Cost per unit	$ 475	$ 475
Unit sales per month	1,130	1,195

11. EOQ Redan Manufacturing uses 2,000 switch assemblies per week and then reorders another 2,000. If the relevant carrying cost per switch assembly is $20, and the fixed order cost is $2,600, is Redan's inventory policy optimal? Why or why not?

12. EOQ The Trektronics store begins each week with 180 phasers in stock. This stock is depleted each week and reordered. If the carrying cost per phaser is $51 per year and the fixed order cost is $150, what is the total carrying cost? What is the restocking cost? Should Trektronics increase or decrease its order size? Describe an optimal inventory policy for Trektronics in terms of order size and order frequency.

INTERMEDIATE
(Questions 13–15)

13. EOQ Derivation Prove that when carrying costs and restocking costs are as described in the chapter, the EOQ must occur at the point where the carrying costs and restocking costs are equal.

14. Credit Policy Evaluation The Jungle Corporation is considering a change in its cash-only policy. The new terms would be net one period. Based on the following information, determine if Jungle should proceed or not. The required return is 3 percent per period.

	Current Policy	New Policy
Price per unit	$ 75	$ 80
Cost per unit	$ 43	$ 43
Unit sales per month	3,200	3,500

15. Credit Policy Evaluation Happiness Systems currently has an all-cash credit policy. It is considering making a change in the credit policy by going to terms of net 30 days. Based on the following information, what do you recommend? The required return is 2 percent per month.

	Current Policy	New Policy
Price per unit	$ 340	$ 345
Cost per unit	$ 260	$ 265
Unit sales per month	1,800	1,850

CHALLENGE
(Questions 16–19)

16. **Break-Even Quantity** In Problem 14, what is the break-even quantity for the new credit policy?
17. **Credit Markup** In Problem 14, what is the break-even price per unit that should be charged under the new credit policy? Assume that the sales figure under the new policy is 3,300 units and all other values remain the same.
18. **Credit Markup** In Problem 15, what is the break-even price per unit under the new credit policy? Assume all other values remain the same.
19. **Safety Stocks and Order Points** Saché, Inc., expects to sell 700 of its designer suits every week. The store is open seven days a week and expects to sell the same number of suits every day. The company has an EOQ of 500 suits and a safety stock of 100 suits. Once an order is placed, it takes three days for Saché to get the suits in. How many orders does the company place per year? Assume that it is Monday morning before the store opens, and a shipment of suits has just arrived. When will Saché place its next order?

What's On the Web?

21.1 **Banker's Acceptance Rates** What are the highest and lowest historical interest rates for banker's acceptances? Go to www.economagic.com and follow the "Interest Rates" link. Find the highest and lowest interest rates for one-, two- and three-month banker's acceptances over the time reported. When did they occur?

21A MORE ON CREDIT POLICY ANALYSIS

This appendix takes a closer look at credit policy analysis by investigating some alternative approaches and by examining the effect of cash discounts and the possibility of nonpayment.

Two Alternative Approaches

From our chapter discussion, we know how to analyze the NPV of a proposed credit policy switch. We now discuss two alternative approaches: the one-shot approach and the accounts receivable approach. These are very common means of analysis; our goal is to show that these two and our NPV approach are all the same. Afterwards, we will use whichever of the three is most convenient.

The One-Shot Approach Looking back at our example for Locust Software (in Section 21.3), we see that if the switch is not made, Locust will have a net cash flow this month of $(P - v)Q = \$29 \times 100 = \$2{,}900$. If the switch is made, Locust will invest $vQ' = \$20 \times 110 = \$2{,}200$ this month and will receive $PQ' = \$49 \times 110 = \$5{,}390$ next month. Suppose we ignore all other months and cash flows and view this as a one-shot investment. Is Locust better off with $2,900 in cash this month, or should Locust invest the $2,200 to get $5,390 next month?

The present value of the $5,390 to be received next month is $\$5{,}390/1.02 = \$5{,}284.31$; the cost is $2,200, so the net benefit is $\$5{,}284.31 - 2{,}200 = \$3{,}084.31$. If we compare this to the net cash flow of $2,900 under the current policy, then we see that Locust should switch. The NPV is $\$3{,}084.31 - 2{,}900 = \$184.31$.

In effect, Locust can repeat this one-shot investment every month and thereby generate an NPV of \$184.31 every month (including the current one). The PV of this series of NPVs is:

$$\text{Present value} = \$184.31 + 184.31/.02 = \$9{,}400$$

This PV is the same as our answer in Section 21.3.

The Accounts Receivable Approach Our second approach is the one that is most commonly discussed and is very useful. By extending credit, the firm increases its cash flow through increased gross profits. However, the firm must increase its investment in receivables and bear the carrying cost of doing so. The accounts receivable approach focuses on the expense of the incremental investment in receivables as compared to the increased gross profit.

As we have seen, the monthly benefit from extending credit is given by the gross profit per unit $(P - v)$ multiplied by the increase in quantity sold $(Q' - Q)$. For Locust, this benefit is $(\$49 - 20) \times (110 - 100) = \$290$ per month.

If Locust makes the switch, then receivables will rise from zero (because there are currently no credit sales) to PQ', so Locust must invest in receivables. The necessary investment has two components. The first part is what Locust would have collected under the old policy (PQ). Locust must carry this amount in receivables each month because collections are delayed by 30 days.

The second part is related to the increase in receivables that results from the increase in sales. Because unit sales increase from Q to Q', Locust must produce the latter quantity today even though it won't collect for 30 days. The actual cost to Locust of producing the extra quantity is equal to v per unit, so the investment necessary to provide the extra quantity sold is $v(Q' - Q)$.

In sum, if Locust switches, its investment in receivables will be equal to the $P \times Q$ in revenues plus an additional $v(Q' - Q)$ in production costs:

$$\text{Incremental investment in receivables} = PQ + v(Q' - Q)$$

The required return on this investment (the carrying cost of the receivables) is R per month; so, for Locust, the accounts receivable carrying cost is:

$$\begin{aligned}\text{Carrying cost} &= [PQ + v(Q' - Q)] \times R \\ &= (\$4{,}900 + 200) \times .02 \\ &= \$102 \text{ per month}\end{aligned}$$

Because the monthly benefit is \$290 and the cost per month is only \$102, the net benefit is \$290 − 102 = \$188 per month. Locust earns this \$188 every month, so the PV of the switch is:

$$\begin{aligned}\text{Present value} &= \$188/.02 \\ &= \$9{,}400\end{aligned}$$

Again, this is the same figure we previously calculated.

One of the advantages of looking at the accounts receivable approach is that it helps us interpret our earlier NPV calculation. As we have seen, the investment in receivables necessary to make the switch is $PQ + v(Q' - Q)$. If you take a look back at our original NPV calculation, you'll see that this is precisely what we had as the cost to Locust of making the switch. Our earlier NPV calculation thus amounts to a comparison of the incremental investment in receivables to the PV of the increased future cash flows.

There is one final thing to notice. The increase in accounts receivable is PQ', and this amount corresponds to the amount of receivables shown on the balance sheet. However, the incremental investment in receivables is $PQ + v(Q' - Q)$. It is straightforward to verify that this second quantity is smaller by $(P - v)(Q' - Q)$. This difference is the gross profit on the new sales, which Locust does not actually have to put up in order to switch credit policies.

Put another way, whenever we extend credit to a new customer who would not otherwise buy, all we risk is our cost, not the full sales price. This is the same issue that we discussed in Section 21.5.

EXAMPLE 21A.1 >> Extra Credit

Looking back at Locust Software, determine the NPV of the switch if the quantity sold is projected to increase by only 5 units instead of 10. What will be the investment in receivables? What is the carrying cost? What is the monthly net benefit from switching?

If the switch is made, Locust gives up $P \times Q$ = \$4,900 today. An extra five units have to be produced at a cost of \$20 each, so the cost of switching is \$4,900 + 5 × 20 = \$5,000. The benefit each month of selling the extra five units is 5 × (\$49 − 20) = \$145. The NPV of the switch is −\$5,000 + 145/.02 = \$2,250, so the switch is still profitable.

The \$5,000 cost of switching can be interpreted as the investment in receivables. At 2 percent per month, the carrying cost is .02 × \$5,000 = \$100. Because the benefit each month is \$145, the net benefit from switching is \$45 per month (\$145 − 100). Notice that the PV of \$45 per month forever at 2 percent is \$45/.02 = \$2,250, as we calculated.

Discounts and Default Risk

We now take a look at cash discounts, default risk, and the relationship between the two. To get started, we define the following:

π = Percentage of credit sales that go uncollected

d = Percentage discount allowed for cash customers

P' = Credit price (the no-discount price)

Notice that the cash price, P, is equal to the credit price, P', multiplied by $(1 - d)$: $P = P'(1 - d)$, or, equivalently, $P' = P/(1 - d)$.

The situation at Locust is now a little more complicated. If a switch is made from the current policy of no credit, then the benefit from the switch will come from both the higher price (P') and, potentially, the increased quantity sold (Q').

Furthermore, in our previous case, it was reasonable to assume that all customers took the credit, because it was free. Now, not all customers will take the credit because a discount is offered. In addition, of the customers who do take the credit offered, a certain percentage (π) will not pay.

To simplify the discussion that follows, we will assume that the quantity sold (Q) is not affected by the switch. This assumption isn't crucial, but it does cut down on the work (see Problem 5 at the end of the appendix). We will also assume that all customers take the credit terms. This assumption isn't crucial either. It actually doesn't matter what percentage of the customers take the offered credit.[3]

[3]The reason is that all customers are offered the same terms. If the NPV of offering credit is \$100, assuming that all customers switch, then it will be \$50 if only 50 percent of our customers switch. The hidden assumption is that the default rate is a constant percentage of credit sales.

NPV of the Credit Decision Currently, Locust sells Q units at a price of $P = \$49$. Locust is considering a new policy that involves 30 days' credit and an increase in price to $P' = \$50$ on credit sales. The cash price will remain at \$49, so Locust is effectively allowing a discount of $(\$50 - 49)/50 = 2\%$ for cash.

What is the NPV to Locust of extending credit? To answer, note that Locust is already receiving $(P - v)Q$ every month. With the new, higher price, this will rise to $(P' - v)Q$, assuming that everybody pays. However, because π percent of sales will not be collected, Locust will only collect on $(1 - \pi) \times P'Q$; so net receipts will be $[(1 - \pi)P' - v] \times Q$.

The net effect of the switch for Locust is thus the difference between the cash flows under the new policy and those under the old policy:

$$\text{Net incremental cash flow} = [(1 - \pi)P' - v] \times Q - (P - v) \times Q$$

Because $P = P' \times (1 - d)$, this simplifies to:[4]

$$\text{Net incremental cash flow} = P'Q \times (d - \pi) \qquad [21A.1]$$

If Locust does make the switch, then the cost in terms of the investment in receivables is just $P \times Q$ since $Q = Q'$. The NPV of the switch is thus:

$$\text{NPV} = -PQ + P'Q \times (d - \pi)/R \qquad [21A.2]$$

For example, suppose that, based on industry experience, the percentage of "deadbeats" (π) is expected to be 1 percent. What is the NPV of changing credit terms for Locust? We can plug in the relevant numbers as follows:

$$\begin{aligned} \text{NPV} &= -PQ + P'Q \times (d - \pi)/R \\ &= -\$49 \times 100 + 50 \times 100 \times (.02 - .01)/.02 \\ &= -\$2{,}400 \end{aligned}$$

Because the NPV of the change is negative, Locust shouldn't switch.

In our expression for NPV, the key elements are the cash discount percentage (d) and the default rate (π). One thing we see immediately is that, if the percentage of sales that goes uncollected exceeds the discount percentage, then $d - \pi$ is negative. Obviously, the NPV of the switch would then be negative as well. More generally, our result tells us that the decision to grant credit here is a trade-off between getting a higher price, thereby increasing sales revenues, and not collecting on some fraction of those sales.

With this in mind, note that $P'Q \times (d - \pi)$ is the increase in sales less the portion of that increase that won't be collected. This is the incremental cash inflow from the switch in credit policy. If d is 5 percent and π is 2 percent, for example, then, loosely speaking, revenues are increasing by 5 percent because of the higher price, but collections only rise by 3 percent because the default rate is 2 percent. Unless $d > \pi$, we will actually have a decrease in cash inflows from the switch.

A Break-Even Application Because the discount percentage (d) is controlled by the firm, the key unknown in this case is the default rate (π). What is the break-even default rate for Locust Software?

[4] To see this, note that the net incremental cash flow is:

$$\begin{aligned} \text{Net incremental cash flow} &= [(1 - \pi)P' - v] \times Q - (P - v) \times Q \\ &= [(1 - \pi)P' - P] \times Q \end{aligned}$$

Because $P = P' \times (1 - d)$, this can be written as:

$$\begin{aligned} \text{Net incremental cash flow} &= [(1 - \pi)P' - (1 - d)P'] \times Q \\ &= P'Q \times (d - \pi) \end{aligned}$$

We can answer by finding the default rate that makes the NPV equal to zero:

$$\text{NPV} = 0 = -PQ + P'Q \times (d - \pi)/R$$

Rearranging things a bit, we have:

$$PR = P'(d - \pi)$$
$$\pi = d - R \times (1 - d)$$

For Locust, the break-even default rate works out to be:

$$\pi = .02 - .02 \times (.98)$$
$$= .0004$$
$$= .04\%$$

This is quite small because the implicit interest rate Locust will be charging its credit customers (2 percent discount interest per month, or about .02/.98 = 2.0408%) is only slightly greater than the required return of 2 percent per month. As a result, there's not much room for defaults if the switch is going to make sense.

Concept Questions

21A.1a What is the incremental investment that a firm must make in receivables if credit is extended?

21A.1b Describe the trade-off between the default rate and the cash discount.

Appendix Review and Self-Test Problems

21A.1 Credit Policy Rework Chapter Review and Self-Test Problem 21.1 using the one-shot and accounts receivable approaches. As before, the required return is 2.0 percent per period, and there will be no defaults. The basic information is:

	Current Policy	New Policy
Price per unit	$ 175	$ 175
Cost per unit	$ 130	$ 130
Sales per period in units	1,000	1,100

21A.2 Discounts and Default Risk The De Long Corporation is considering a change in credit policy. The current policy is cash only, and sales per period are 2,000 units at a price of $110. If credit is offered, the new price will be $120 per unit and the credit will be extended for one period. Unit sales are not expected to change, and all customers are expected to take the credit. De Long anticipates that 4 percent of its customers will default. If the required return is 2 percent per period, is the change a good idea? What if only half the customers take the offered credit?

Answers to Appendix Review and Self-Test Problems

21A.1 As we saw earlier, if the switch is made, an extra 100 units per period will be sold at a gross profit of $175 − 130 = $45 each. The total benefit is thus $45 × 100 = $4,500 per period. At 2.0 percent per period forever, the PV is $4,500/.02 = $225,000.

Visit us at www.mhhe.com/rwj

The cost of the switch is equal to this period's revenue of $175 × 1,000 units = $175,000 plus the cost of producing the extra 100 units, 100 × $130 = $13,000. The total cost is thus $188,000, and the NPV is $225,000 − 188,000 = $37,000. The switch should be made.

For the accounts receivable approach, we interpret the $188,000 cost as the investment in receivables. At 2.0 percent per period, the carrying cost is $188,000 × .02 = $3,760 per period. The benefit per period we calculated as $4,500; so the net gain per period is $4,500 − 3,760 = $740. At 2.0 percent per period, the PV of this is $740/.02 = $37,000.

Finally, for the one-shot approach, if credit is not granted, the firm will generate ($175 − 130) × 1,000 = $45,000 this period. If credit is extended, the firm will invest $130 × 1,100 = $143,000 today and receive $175 × 1,100 = $192,500 in one period. The NPV of this second option is $192,500/1.02 − 143,000 = $45,725.49. The firm is $45,725.49 − 45,000 = $725.49 better off today and in each future period because of granting credit. The PV of this stream is $725.49 + 725.49/.02 = $37,000 (allowing for a rounding error).

21A.2 The costs per period are the same whether or not credit is offered; so we can ignore the production costs. The firm currently has sales of, and collects, $110 × 2,000 = $220,000 per period. If credit is offered, sales will rise to $120 × 2,000 = $240,000.

Defaults will be 4 percent of sales, so the cash inflow under the new policy will be .96 × $240,000 = $230,400. This amounts to an extra $10,400 every period. At 2 percent per period, the PV is $10,400/.02 = $520,000. If the switch is made, De Long will give up this month's revenues of $220,000; so the NPV of the switch is $300,000. If only half of the customers take the credit, then the NPV is half as large: $150,000. So, regardless of what percentage of customers take the credit, the NPV is positive. Thus, the change is a good idea.

Questions and Problems

BASIC
(Questions 1–5)

1. **Evaluating Credit Policy** Bismark Co. is in the process of considering a change in its terms of sale. The current policy is cash only; the new policy will involve one period's credit. Sales are 70,000 units per period at a price of $530 per unit. If credit is offered, the new price will be $552. Unit sales are not expected to change, and all customers are expected to take the credit. Bismark estimates that 2 percent of credit sales will be uncollectible. If the required return is 2 percent per period, is the change a good idea?
2. **Credit Policy Evaluation** The Johnson Company sells 3,000 pairs of running shoes per month at a cash price of $90 per pair. The firm is considering a new policy that involves 30 days' credit and an increase in price to $91.84 per pair on credit sales. The cash price will remain at $90, and the new policy is not expected to affect the quantity sold. The discount period will be 10 days. The required return is 1 percent per month.
   - **a.** How would the new credit terms be quoted?
   - **b.** What is the investment in receivables required under the new policy?
   - **c.** Explain why the variable cost of manufacturing the shoes is not relevant here.
   - **d.** If the default rate is anticipated to be 10 percent, should the switch be made? What is the break-even credit price? The break-even cash discount?

3. **Credit Analysis** Silicon Wafers, Inc. (SWI), is debating whether or not to extend credit to a particular customer. SWI's products, primarily used in the manufacture of semiconductors, currently sell for $1,850 per unit. The variable cost is $1,200 per unit. The order under consideration is for 12 units today; payment is promised in 30 days.
   a. If there is a 20 percent chance of default, should SWI fill the order? The required return is 2 percent per month. This is a one-time sale, and the customer will not buy if credit is not extended.
   b. What is the break-even probability in part (*a*)?
   c. This part is a little harder. In general terms, how do you think your answer to part (*a*) will be affected if the customer will purchase the merchandise for cash if the credit is refused? The cash price is $1,700 per unit.
4. **Credit Analysis** Consider the following information on two alternative credit strategies:

	Refuse Credit	Grant Credit
Price per unit	$ 51	$ 55
Cost per unit	$ 29	$ 31
Quantity sold per quarter	3,300	3,500
Probability of payment	1.0	.90

   The higher cost per unit reflects the expense associated with credit orders, and the higher price per unit reflects the existence of a cash discount. The credit period will be 90 days, and the cost of debt is .75 percent per month.
   a. Based on this information, should credit be granted?
   b. In part (*a*), what does the credit price per unit have to be to break even?
   c. In part (*a*), suppose we can obtain a credit report for $2 per customer. Assuming that each customer buys one unit and that the credit report correctly identifies all customers who will not pay, should credit be extended?
5. **NPV of Credit Policy Switch** Suppose a corporation currently sells Q units per month for a cash-only price of P. Under a new credit policy that allows one month's credit, the quantity sold will be Q' and the price per unit will be P'. Defaults will be π percent of credit sales. The variable cost is v per unit and is not expected to change. The percentage of customers who will take the credit is α, and the required return is R per month. What is the NPV of the decision to switch? Interpret the various parts of your answer.

>> MINI-CASE

Piepkorn Manufacturing Working Capital Management

You have recently been hired by Piepkorn Manufacturing to work in the newly established treasury department. Piepkorn Manufacturing is a small company that produces cardboard boxes in a variety of sizes for different purchasers. Gary Piepkorn, the owner of the company, works primarily in the sales and production areas of the company. Currently, the company puts all receivables in one shoe box and all payables in another. Because of the disorganized system, the finance area needs work, and that's what you've been brought in to do.

The company currently has a cash balance of $164,000, and plans to purchase new box folding machinery in the fourth quarter at a cost of $240,000. The purchase of the machinery will be made with cash because of a discount offered. The company's policy is to maintain a minimum cash balance of $100,000. All sales and all purchases are made on credit.

Gary Piepkorn has projected the following gross sales for each of the next four quarters:

	Q1	Q2	Q3	Q4
Gross sales	$695,000	$708,000	$741,000	$757,000

Also, gross sales for the first quarter of next year are projected at $784,000. Piepkorn currently has an accounts receivable period of 57 days, and an accounts receivable balance of $426,000. Ten percent of the accounts receivable balance is from a company that has just entered bankruptcy, and it is likely this portion of the accounts receivable will never be collected.

Piepkorn typically orders 50 percent of next quarter's projected gross sales in the current quarter, and suppliers are typically paid in 53 days. Wages, taxes, and other costs run about 25 percent of gross sales. The company has a quarterly interest payment of $85,000 on its long-term debt.

The company uses a local bank for its short-term financial needs. It pays 1.5 percent per quarter in all short-term borrowing and maintains a money market account that pays 1 percent per quarter on all short-term deposits.

Gary has asked you to prepare a cash budget and short-term financial plan for the company under the current policies. He has also asked you to prepare additional plans based on changes in several inputs.

1. Use the numbers given to complete the cash budget and short-term financial plan.
2. Rework the cash budget and short-term financial plan assuming Piepkorn changes to a minimum balance of $80,000.
3. You have looked at the credit policy offered by your competitors and have determined that the industry standard credit policy is 1/10, net 45. The discount will begin to be offered on the first day of the first quarter. You want to examine how this credit policy would affect the cash budget and short-term financial plan. If this credit policy is implemented, you believe that 25 percent of all sales will take advantage of it, and the accounts receivable period will decline to 38 days. Rework the cash budget and short-term financial plan under the new credit policy and a minimum cash balance of $80,000. What interest rate are you effectively offering customers?
4. You have talked to the company's suppliers about the credit terms Piepkorn receives. Currently, the company receives terms of net 45. The suppliers have stated that they would offer new credit terms of 2/15, net 40. The discount would begin to be offered in the first day of the first quarter. What interest rate are the suppliers offering the company? Rework the cash budget and short-term financial plan assuming you take the credit terms on all orders and the minimum cash balance is $80,000.

PIEPKORN MANUFACTURING
Cash Budget

	Q1	Q2	Q3	Q4
Beginning cash balance				
Net cash inflow				
Ending cash balance				
Minimum cash balance				
Cumulative surplus (deficit)				

Visit us at www.mhhe.com/rwj

PIEPKORN MANUFACTURING Short-Term Financial Plan				
	Q1	Q2	Q3	Q4
Beginning cash balance				
Net cash inflow				
New short-term investments				
Income from short-term investments				
Short-term investments sold				
New short-term borrowing				
Interest on short-term borrowing				
Short-term borrowing repaid				
Ending cash balance				
Minimum cash balance				
Cumulative surplus (deficit)				
Beginning short-term investments				
Ending short-term investments				
Beginning short-term debt				
Ending short-term debt				

22

International Corporate Finance

PART EIGHT

Topics in Corporate Finance

In early 2002, major currencies such as the German mark, Italian lira, and French franc became footnotes in history, replaced by the euro (€). In an extraordinary turn of events, the 11 countries that originally made up the European Economic and Monetary Union (EMU) turned their sovereign currencies and much of the control of their monetary policies over to the new European Central Bank. Some of the major proponents of the new system were businesses in these 11 countries; many business leaders believed the union was necessary to enhance competitiveness with countries such as the United States. And the euro will continue to grow. In May 2004, 10 more countries began the process that leads to adoption of the euro, and several more were moving in that direction. As the euro spreads, it will become more widely used than the U.S. dollar and will play an increasingly important role in the global economy. In this chapter, we explore the role played by currencies and exchange rates, along with a number of other key topics in international finance.

Corporations with significant foreign operations are often called *international corporations* or *multinationals.* Such corporations must consider many financial factors that do not directly affect purely domestic firms. These include foreign exchange rates, differing interest rates from country to country, complex accounting methods for foreign operations, foreign tax rates, and foreign government intervention.

The basic principles of corporate finance still apply to international corporations; like domestic companies, these firms seek to invest in projects that create more value for the shareholders than they cost and to arrange financing that raises cash at the lowest possible cost. In other words, the net present value principle holds for both foreign and domestic operations, although it is usually more complicated to apply the NPV rule to foreign investments.

One of the most significant complications of international finance is foreign exchange. The foreign exchange markets provide important information and opportunities for an international corporation when it undertakes capital budgeting and financing decisions. As we will discuss, international exchange rates, interest rates, and inflation rates are closely related. We will spend much of this chapter exploring the connection between these financial variables.

We won't have much to say here about the role of cultural and social differences in international business. Neither will we be discussing the implications of differing political and economic systems. These factors are of great importance to international businesses, but it would take another book to do them justice. Consequently, we will focus only on some purely financial considerations in international finance and some key aspects of foreign exchange markets.

See www.adr.com for more.

22.1 TERMINOLOGY

American Depositary Receipt (ADR)
A security issued in the United States representing shares of a foreign stock and allowing that stock to be traded in the United States.

cross-rate
The implicit exchange rate between two currencies (usually non-U.S.) quoted in some third currency (usually the U.S. dollar).

Eurobonds
International bonds issued in multiple countries but denominated in a single currency (usually the issuer's currency).

Eurocurrency
Money deposited in a financial center outside of the country whose currency is involved.

foreign bonds
International bonds issued in a single country, usually denominated in that country's currency.

gilts
British and Irish government securities.

London Interbank Offer Rate (LIBOR)
The rate most international banks charge one another for overnight Eurodollar loans.

A common buzzword for the student of business finance is *globalization.* The first step in learning about the globalization of financial markets is to conquer the new vocabulary. As with any specialty, international finance is rich in jargon. Accordingly, we get started on the subject with a highly eclectic vocabulary exercise.

The terms that follow are presented alphabetically, and they are not all of equal importance. We choose these particular ones because they appear frequently in the financial press or because they illustrate the colorful nature of the language of international finance.

1. An **American Depositary Receipt (ADR)** is a security issued in the United States that represents shares of a foreign stock, allowing that stock to be traded in the United States. Foreign companies use ADRs, which are issued in U.S. dollars, to expand the pool of potential U.S. investors. ADRs are available in two forms for a large and growing number of foreign companies: company sponsored, which are listed on an exchange, and unsponsored, which usually are held by the investment bank that makes a market in the ADR. Both forms are available to individual investors, but only company-sponsored issues are quoted daily in newspapers.
2. The **cross-rate** is the implicit exchange rate between two currencies (usually non-U.S.) when both are quoted in some third currency, usually the U.S. dollar.
3. A **Eurobond** is a bond issued in multiple countries, but denominated in a single currency, usually the issuer's home currency. Such bonds have become an important way to raise capital for many international companies and governments. Eurobonds are issued outside the restrictions that apply to domestic offerings and are syndicated and traded mostly from London. Trading can and does take place anywhere there is a buyer and a seller.
4. **Eurocurrency** is money deposited in a financial center outside of the country whose currency is involved. For instance, Eurodollars—the most widely used Eurocurrency—are U.S. dollars deposited in banks outside the U.S. banking system.
5. **Foreign bonds**, unlike Eurobonds, are issued in a single country and are usually denominated in that country's currency. Often, the country in which these bonds are issued will draw distinctions between them and bonds issued by domestic issuers, including different tax laws, restrictions on the amount issued, and tougher disclosure rules.

   Foreign bonds often are nicknamed for the country where they are issued: Yankee bonds (United States), Samurai bonds (Japan), Rembrandt bonds (the Netherlands), Bulldog bonds (Britain). Partly because of tougher regulations and disclosure requirements, the foreign-bond market hasn't grown in past years with the vigor of the Eurobond market.
6. **Gilts**, technically, are British and Irish government securities, although the term also includes issues of local British authorities and some overseas public-sector offerings.
7. The **London Interbank Offer Rate (LIBOR)** is the rate that most international banks charge one another for loans of Eurodollars overnight in the London market. LIBOR is a cornerstone in the pricing of money market issues and other short-term debt issues by both government and corporate borrowers. Interest rates are frequently quoted as some spread over LIBOR, and they then float with the LIBOR rate.
8. There are two basic kinds of **swaps**: interest rate and currency. An interest rate swap occurs when two parties exchange a floating-rate payment for a fixed-rate payment or vice versa. Currency swaps are agreements to deliver one currency in exchange for another. Often, both types of swaps are used in the same transaction when debt

denominated in different currencies is swapped. Chapter 23 contains a more detailed discussion of swaps.

swaps
Agreements to exchange two securities or currencies.

Concept Questions

22.1a What are the differences between a Eurobond and a foreign bond?

22.1b What are Eurodollars?

For current LIBOR rates, see www.bloomberg.com.

FOREIGN EXCHANGE MARKETS AND EXCHANGE RATES

22.2

The **foreign exchange market** is undoubtedly the world's largest financial market. It is the market where one country's currency is traded for another's. Most of the trading takes place in a few currencies: the U.S. dollar ($), the British pound sterling (£), the Japanese yen (¥), and the euro (€). Table 22.1 lists some of the more common currencies and their symbols.

foreign exchange market
The market in which one country's currency is traded for another's.

The foreign exchange market is an over-the-counter market, so there is no single location where traders get together. Instead, market participants are located in the major commercial and investment banks around the world. They communicate using computer terminals, telephones, and other telecommunications devices. For example, one communications network for foreign transactions is maintained by the Society for Worldwide Interbank Financial Telecommunications (SWIFT), a Belgian not-for-profit cooperative. Using data transmission lines, a bank in New York can send messages to a bank in London via SWIFT regional processing centers.

The many different types of participants in the foreign exchange market include the following:

1. Importers who pay for goods using foreign currencies
2. Exporters who receive foreign currency and may want to convert to the domestic currency
3. Portfolio managers who buy or sell foreign stocks and bonds

Visit SWIFT at www.swift.com.

TABLE 22.1 International Currency Symbols

Country	Currency	Symbol
Australia	Dollar	A$
Canada	Dollar	Can$
Denmark	Krone	DKr
EMU	Euro	€
India	Rupee	Rs
Iran	Rial	Rl
Japan	Yen	¥
Kuwait	Dinar	KD
Mexico	Peso	Ps
Norway	Krone	NKr
Saudi Arabia	Riyal	SR
Singapore	Dollar	S$
South Africa	Rand	R
Sweden	Krona	SKr
Switzerland	Franc	SF
United Kingdom	Pound	£
United States	Dollar	$

4. Foreign exchange brokers who match buy and sell orders
5. Traders who "make a market" in foreign currencies
6. Speculators who try to profit from changes in exchange rates

Exchange Rates

exchange rate
The price of one country's currency expressed in terms of another country's currency.

An **exchange rate** is simply the price of one country's currency expressed in terms of another country's currency. In practice, almost all trading of currencies takes place in terms of the U.S. dollar. For example, both the Swiss franc and the Japanese yen are traded with their prices quoted in U.S. dollars. Exchange rates are constantly changing. Our nearby *Work the Web* box shows you how to get up-to-the-minute rates.

Exchange Rate Quotations Figure 22.1 reproduces exchange rate quotations as they appeared in *The Wall Street Journal* in 2004. The first two columns (labeled "U.S. $ equivalent") give the number of dollars it takes to buy one unit of foreign currency. Because this is the price in dollars of a foreign currency, it is called a *direct* or *American quote* (remember that "Americans are direct"). For example, the Australian dollar is quoted at .7002, which means that you can buy one Australian dollar with U.S. $.7002.

Get up-to-the-minute exchange rates at www.xe.com and www.exchangerate.com.

The third and fourth columns show the *indirect,* or *European, exchange rate* (even though the currency may not be European). This is the amount of foreign currency per U.S. dollar. The Australian dollar is quoted here at 1.4282, so you can get 1.4282 Australian dollars for one U.S. dollar. Naturally, this second exchange rate is just the reciprocal of the first one (possibly with a little rounding error), $1/.7002 = 1.4282$.

EXAMPLE 22.1 >> A Yen for Euros

Suppose you have $1,000. Based on the rates in Figure 22.1, how many Japanese yen can you get? Alternatively, if a Porsche costs € 100,000 (recall that € is the symbol for the euro), how many dollars will you need to buy it?

The exchange rate in terms of yen per dollar (third column) is 107.90. Your $1,000 will thus get you:

$1,000 × 107.90 yen per $1 = 107,900 yen

Because the exchange rate in terms of dollars per euro (first column) is 1.2186, you will need:

€100,000 × $1.2186 per € = $121,860

WORK THE WEB

You just returned from your dream vacation to Jamaica and feel rich because you have 10,000 Jamaican dollars left over. You now need to convert this to U.S. dollars. How much will you have? You can look up the current exchange rate and do the conversion yourself, or simply work the Web. We went to www.xe.com and used the currency converter on the site to find out. This is what we found:

xe.com Universal Currency Converter® Results

Live mid-market rates as of 2004.07.01 00:15:32 GMT.

10,000.00 JMD = 163.826 USD
Jamaica Dollars — United States Dollars

1 JMD = 0.0163826 USD — 1 USD = 61.0402 JMD

Another Conversion? | Bookmark Us

Looks like you left Jamaica just before you ran out of money.

<< FIGURE 22.1

Exchange Rate Quotations

Key Currency Cross Rates

Late New York Trading Monday, June 28, 2004

	Dollar	Euro	Pound	SFranc	Peso	Yen	CdnDlr
Canada	1.3468	1.6412	2.4648	1.0785	.11727	.01248	...
Japan	107.90	131.48	197.46	86.405	9.395	...	80.114
Mexico	11.4850	13.9956	21.019	9.1972	...	.10644	8.5276
Switzerland	1.2488	1.5217	2.2853	...	.10873	.01157	.9272
U.K.	.54640	.6659	...	.4376	.04758	.00506	.40572
Euro	.82060	...	1.5018	.65715	.07145	.00761	.60931
U.S.	...	1.2186	1.8301	.80080	.08707	.00927	.74250

Source: Reuters

Exchange Rates

June 28, 2004

The foreign exchange mid-range rates below apply to trading among banks in amounts of $1 million and more, as quoted at 4 p.m. Eastern time by Reuters and other sources. Retail transactions provide fewer units of foreign currency per dollar.

	U.S. $ EQUIVALENT		CURRENCY PER U.S. $	
Country	**Mon**	**Fri**	**Mon**	**Fri**
Argentina (Peso)-y	.3375	.3384	2.9630	2.9551
Australia (Dollar)	.7002	.7001	1.4282	1.4284
Bahrain (Dinar)	2.6525	2.6526	.3770	.3770
Brazil (Real)	.3198	.3215	3.1270	3.1104
Canada (Dollar)	.7425	.7405	1.3468	1.3504
1-month forward	.7420	.7401	1.3477	1.3512
3-months forward	.7415	.7394	1.3486	1.3524
6-months forward	.7409	.7389	1.3497	1.3534
Chile (Peso)	.001577	.001579	634.12	633.31
China (Renminbi)	.1208	.1208	8.2781	8.2781
Colombia (Peso)	.0003707	.0003713	2697.60	2693.24
Czech. Rep. (Koruna)				
Commercial rate	.03818	.03833	26.192	26.089
Denmark (Krone)	.1640	.1636	6.0976	6.1125
Ecuador (US Dollar)	1.0000	1.0000	1.0000	1.0000
Egypt (Pound)-y	.1613	.1614	6.2000	6.1950
Hong Kong (Dollar)	.1282	.1283	7.8003	7.7942
Hungary (Forint)	.004813	.004790	207.77	208.77
India (Rupee)	.02181	.02184	45.851	45.788
Indonesia (Rupiah)	.0001061	.0001061	9425	9425
Israel (Shekel)	.2224	.2222	4.4964	4.5005
Japan (Yen)	.009268	.009289	107.90	107.65
1-month forward	.009279	.009300	107.77	107.53
3-months forward	.009306	.009327	107.46	107.22
6-months forward	.009358	.009377	106.86	106.64
Jordan (Dinar)	1.4104	1.4104	.7090	.7090
Kuwait (Dinar)	3.3920	3.3936	.2948	.2947
Lebanon (Pound)	.0006603	.0006603	1514.46	1514.46
Malaysia (Ringgit)-b	.2632	.2632	3.7994	3.7994
Malta (Lira)	2.8624	2.8563	.3494	.3501
Mexico (Peso)				
Floating rate	.0871	.0882	11.4850	11.3366

	U.S. $ EQUIVALENT		CURRENCY PER U.S. $	
Country	**Mon**	**Fri**	**Mon**	**Fri**
New Zealand (Dollar)	.6414	.6362	1.5591	1.5718
Norway (Krone)	.1462	.1464	6.8399	6.8306
Pakistan (Rupee)	.01743	.01726	57.372	57.937
Peru (new Sol)	.2881	.2882	3.4710	3.4698
Philippines (Peso)	.01781	.01783	56.148	56.085
Poland (Zloty)	.2686	.2667	3.7230	3.7495
Russia (Ruble)-a	.03445	.03446	29.028	29.019
Saudi Arabia (Riyal)	.2666	.2667	3.7509	3.7495
Singapore (Dollar)	.5842	.5854	1.7117	1.7082
Slovak Rep. (Koruna)	.03054	.03048	32.744	32.808
South Africa (Rand)	.1622	.1586	6.1652	6.3052
South Korea (Won)	.0008677	.0008705	1152.47	1148.77
Sweden (Krona)	.1334	.1326	7.4963	7.5415
Switzerland (Franc)	.8008	.8004	1.2488	1.2494
1-month forward	.8014	.8010	1.2478	1.2484
3-months forward	.8031	.8026	1.2452	1.2460
6-months forward	.8056	.8051	1.2413	1.2421
Taiwan (Dollar)	.02976	.02980	33.602	33.557
Thailand (Baht)	.02446	.02449	40.883	40.833
Turkey (Lira)	.00000067	.00000067	1492537	1492537
U.K. (Pound)	1.8301	1.8255	.5464	.5478
1-month forward	1.8252	1.8205	.5479	.5493
3-months forward	1.8153	1.8106	.5509	.5523
6-months forward	1.8022	1.7975	.5549	.5563
United Arab (Dirham)	.2723	.2722	3.6724	3.6738
Uruguay (Peso)				
Financial	.03360	.03370	29.762	29.674
Venezuela (Bolivar)	.000521	.000521	1919.39	1919.39
SDR	1.4695	1.4676	.6805	.6814
Euro	1.2186	1.2159	.8206	.8224

Special Drawing Rights (SDR) are based on exchange rates for the U.S., British, and Japanese currencies. Source: International Monetary Fund.

a-Russian Central Bank rate. b-Government rate. y-Floating rate.

Cross-Rates and Triangle Arbitrage Using the U.S. dollar as the common denominator in quoting exchange rates greatly reduces the number of possible cross-currency quotes. For example, with five major currencies, there would potentially be 10 exchange rates instead of just 4.[1] Also, the fact that the dollar is used throughout cuts down on inconsistencies in the exchange rate quotations.

Earlier, we defined the cross-rate as the exchange rate for a non-U.S. currency expressed in terms of another non-U.S. currency. For example, suppose we observe the following for

[1]There are four exchange rates instead of five because one exchange rate would involve the exchange of a currency for itself. More generally, it might seem that there should be 25 exchange rates with five currencies. There are 25 different combinations, but, of these, 5 involve the exchange of a currency for itself. Of the remaining 20, half are redundant because they are just the reciprocals of another exchange rate. Of the remaining 10, 6 can be eliminated by using a common denominator.

the euro (€) and the Swiss franc (SF):

€ per \$1 = 1.00
SF per \$1 = 2.00

Suppose the cross-rate is quoted as:

€ per SF = .40

What do you think?

The cross-rate here is inconsistent with the exchange rates. To see this, suppose you have \$100. If you convert this to Swiss francs, you will receive:

$\$100 \times \text{SF } 2 \text{ per } \$1 = \text{SF } 200$

If you convert this to euros at the cross-rate, you will have:

$\text{SF } 200 \times € .4 \text{ per SF } 1 = €80$

However, if you just convert your dollars to euros without going through Swiss francs, you will have:

$\$100 \times €1 \text{ per } \$1 = €100$

What we see is that the euro has two prices, €1 per \$1 and €.80 per \$1, with the price we pay depending on how we get the euros.

To make money, we want to buy low and sell high. The important thing to note is that euros are cheaper if you buy them with dollars because you get 1 euro instead of just .8. You should proceed as follows:

1. Buy 100 euros for \$100.
2. Use the 100 euros to buy Swiss francs at the cross-rate. Because it takes .4 euros to buy a Swiss franc, you will receive €100/.4 = SF 250.
3. Use the SF 250 to buy dollars. Because the exchange rate is SF 2 per dollar, you receive SF 250/2 = \$125, for a round-trip profit of \$25.
4. Repeat steps 1 through 3.

This particular activity is called *triangle arbitrage* because the arbitrage involves moving through three different exchange rates:

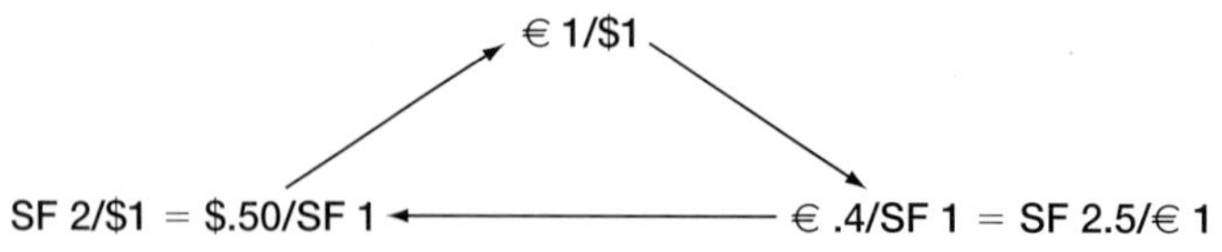

To prevent such opportunities, it is not difficult to see that because a dollar will buy you either 1 euro or 2 Swiss francs, the cross-rate must be:

$(€1/\$1)/(\text{SF } 2/\$1) = €1/\text{SF } 2$

That is, the cross-rate must be one euro per two Swiss francs. If it were anything else, there would be a triangle arbitrage opportunity.

Shedding Some Pounds

EXAMPLE 22.2

Suppose the exchange rates for the British pound and Swiss franc are:

Pounds per $1 = .60
SF per $1 = 2.00

The cross-rate is three francs per pound. Is this consistent? Explain how to go about making some money.

The cross-rate should be SF 2.00/£.60 = SF 3.33 per pound. You can buy a pound for SF 3 in one market, and you can sell a pound for SF 3.33 in another. So we want to first get some francs, then use the francs to buy some pounds, and then sell the pounds. Assuming you have $100, you could:

1. Exchange dollars for francs: $100 × 2 = SF 200.
2. Exchange francs for pounds: SF 200/3 = £66.67.
3. Exchange pounds for dollars: £66.67/.60 = $111.12.

This would result in an $11.12 round-trip profit.

For international news and events, visit www.ft.com.

Types of Transactions There are two basic types of trades in the foreign exchange market: spot trades and forward trades. A **spot trade** is an agreement to exchange currency "on the spot," which actually means that the transaction will be completed or settled within two business days. The exchange rate on a spot trade is called the **spot exchange rate**. Implicitly, all of the exchange rates and transactions we have discussed so far have referred to the spot market.

spot trade
An agreement to trade currencies based on the exchange rate today for settlement within two business days.

spot exchange rate
The exchange rate on a spot trade.

A **forward trade** is an agreement to exchange currency at some time in the future. The exchange rate that will be used is agreed upon today and is called the **forward exchange rate**. A forward trade will normally be settled sometime in the next 12 months.

If you look back at Figure 22.1, you will see forward exchange rates quoted for some of the major currencies. For example, the spot exchange rate for the Swiss franc is SF 1 = $.8008. The 180-day (6-month) forward exchange rate is SF 1 = $.8056. This means that you can buy a Swiss franc today for $.8008 or you can agree to take delivery of a Swiss franc in 180 days and pay $.8056 at that time.

forward trade
An agreement to exchange currency at some time in the future.

forward exchange rate
The agreed-upon exchange rate to be used in a forward trade.

Notice that the Swiss franc is more expensive in the forward market ($.8056 versus $.8008). Because the Swiss franc is more expensive in the future than it is today, it is said to be selling at a *premium* relative to the dollar. For the same reason, the dollar is said to be selling at a *discount* relative to the Swiss franc.

Why does the forward market exist? One answer is that it allows businesses and individuals to lock in a future exchange rate today, thereby eliminating any risk from unfavorable shifts in the exchange rate.

Looking Forward

EXAMPLE 22.3

Suppose you are expecting to receive a million British pounds in six months, and you agree to a forward trade to exchange your pounds for dollars. Based on Figure 22.1, how many dollars will you get in six months? Is the pound selling at a discount or a premium relative to the dollar?

In Figure 22.1, the spot exchange rate and the 180-day forward rate in terms of dollars per pound are $1.8301 = £1 and $1.8022 = £1, respectively. If you expect £1 million in

continued

180 days, then you will get £1 million × \$1.8022 per pound = \$1.8022 million. Because it is cheaper to buy a pound in the forward market than in the spot market (\$1.8022 versus \$1.8301), the pound is said to be selling at a discount relative to the dollar.

As we mentioned earlier, it is standard practice around the world (with a few exceptions) to quote exchange rates in terms of the U.S. dollar. This means that rates are quoted as the amount of currency per U.S. dollar. For the remainder of this chapter, we will stick with this form. Things can get extremely confusing if you forget this. Thus, when we say things like "the exchange rate is expected to rise," it is important to remember that we are talking about the exchange rate quoted as units of foreign currency per dollar.

Concept Questions

22.2a What is triangle arbitrage?

22.2b What do we mean by the 90-day forward exchange rate?

22.2c If we say that the exchange rate is SF 1.90, what do we mean?

22.3 PURCHASING POWER PARITY

Now that we have discussed what exchange rate quotations mean, we can address an obvious question: What determines the level of the spot exchange rate? In addition, because we know that exchange rates change through time, we can ask the related question, What determines the rate of change in exchange rates? At least part of the answer in both cases goes by the name of **purchasing power parity (PPP)**, the idea that the exchange rate adjusts to keep purchasing power constant among currencies. As we discuss next, there are two forms of PPP, *absolute* and *relative*.

purchasing power parity (PPP)
The idea that the exchange rate adjusts to keep purchasing power constant among currencies.

Absolute Purchasing Power Parity

The basic idea behind *absolute purchasing power parity* is that a commodity costs the same regardless of what currency is used to purchase it or where it is selling. This is a very straightforward concept. If a beer costs £2 in London, and the exchange rate is £.60 per dollar, then a beer costs £2/.60 = \$3.33 in New York. In other words, absolute PPP says that \$1 will buy you the same number of, say, cheeseburgers anywhere in the world.

More formally, let S_0 be the spot exchange rate between the British pound and the U.S. dollar today (Time 0), and remember that we are quoting exchange rates as the amount of foreign currency per dollar. Let P_{US} and P_{UK} be the current U.S. and British prices, respectively, on a particular commodity, say, apples. Absolute PPP simply says that:

$$P_{UK} = S_0 \times P_{US}$$

This tells us that the British price for something is equal to the U.S. price for that same something multiplied by the exchange rate.

The rationale behind PPP is similar to that behind triangle arbitrage. If PPP did not hold, arbitrage would be possible (in principle) if apples were moved from one country to another. For example, suppose apples are selling in New York for \$4 per bushel, whereas in London the price is £2.40 per bushel. Absolute PPP implies that:

$$\begin{aligned} P_{UK} &= S_0 \times P_{US} \\ £2.40 &= S_0 \times \$4 \\ S_0 &= £2.40/\$4 = £.60 \end{aligned}$$

That is, the implied spot exchange rate is £.60 per dollar. Equivalently, a pound is worth $1/£.60 = $1.67.

Suppose that, instead, the actual exchange rate is £.50. Starting with $4, a trader could buy a bushel of apples in New York, ship it to London, and sell it there for £2.40. Our trader could then convert the £2.40 into dollars at the prevailing exchange rate, S_0 = £.50, yielding a total of £2.40/.50 = $4.80. The round-trip gain would bc 80 cents.

Because of this profit potential, forces are set in motion to change the exchange rate and/or the price of apples. In our example, apples would begin moving from New York to London. The reduced supply of apples in New York would raise the price of apples there, and the increased supply in Britain would lower the price of apples in London.

In addition to moving apples around, apple traders would be busily converting pounds back into dollars to buy more apples. This activity would increase the supply of pounds and simultaneously increase the demand for dollars. We would expect the value of a pound to fall. This means that the dollar would be getting more valuable, so it would take more pounds to buy one dollar. Because the exchange rate is quoted as pounds per dollar, we would expect the exchange rate to rise from £.50.

For absolute PPP to hold absolutely, several things must be true:

1. The transactions costs of trading apples—shipping, insurance, spoilage, and so on—must be zero.
2. There must be no barriers to trading apples—no tariffs, taxes, or other political barriers.
3. Finally, an apple in New York must be identical to an apple in London. It won't do for you to send red apples to London if the English eat only green apples.

Given the fact that the transactions costs are not zero and that the other conditions are rarely exactly met, it is not surprising that absolute PPP is really applicable only to traded goods, and then only to very uniform ones.

For this reason, absolute PPP does not imply that a Mercedes costs the same as a Ford or that a nuclear power plant in France costs the same as one in New York. In the case of the cars, they are not identical. In the case of the power plants, even if they were identical, they are expensive and would be very difficult to ship. On the other hand, we would be very surprised to see a significant violation of absolute PPP for gold.

As an example of a violation of absolute PPP, in late 2003 the euro was going for about $1.30. Porsche's new, and very desirable, Carrera GT sold for about $440,000 in the United States. This converted to a euro price of €338,462 before tax and €392,615 after tax. The price of the car in Germany was €452,690, which means that if German residents could ship the car for less than €60,000 they would be better off buying it in the United States.

Violations of PPP are actually sought out by corporations. For example, in the middle of 2004, Alcoa announced that it would build a $1 billion aluminum smelter plant on the Caribbean island of Trinidad. At the same time, the company was breaking ground on another $1 billion plant in Iceland and looking into other locations including China, Brunei, Bahrain, Brazil, and Canada. In all cases, low energy costs were the attraction (aluminum smelting is very energy-intensive). Meanwhile, the company had several plants in the Pacific Northwest that were closed because higher electricity prices in this region made the plants unprofitable.

Relative Purchasing Power Parity

As a practical matter, a relative version of purchasing power parity has evolved. *Relative purchasing power parity* does not tell us what determines the absolute level of the exchange rate. Instead, it tells what determines the *change* in the exchange rate over time.

The Basic Idea Suppose the British pound–U.S. dollar exchange rate is currently $S_0 = £.50$. Further suppose that the inflation rate in Britain is predicted to be 10 percent over the coming year, and (for the moment) the inflation rate in the United States is predicted to be zero. What do you think the exchange rate will be in a year?

If you think about it, you see that a dollar currently costs .50 pounds in Britain. With 10 percent inflation, we expect prices in Britain to generally rise by 10 percent. So we expect that the price of a dollar will go up by 10 percent, and the exchange rate should rise to £.50 × 1.1 = £.55.

If the inflation rate in the United States is not zero, then we need to worry about the *relative* inflation rates in the two countries. For example, suppose the U.S. inflation rate is predicted to be 4 percent. Relative to prices in the United States, prices in Britain are rising at a rate of 10% − 4% = 6% per year. So we expect the price of the dollar to rise by 6 percent, and the predicted exchange rate is £.50 × 1.06 = £.53.

The Result In general, relative PPP says that the change in the exchange rate is determined by the difference in the inflation rates of the two countries. To be more specific, we will use the following notation:

S_0 = Current (Time 0) spot exchange rate (foreign currency per dollar)
$E(S_t)$ = Expected exchange rate in t periods
h_{US} = Inflation rate in the United States
h_{FC} = Foreign country inflation rate

Based on our discussion just preceding, relative PPP says that the expected percentage change in the exchange rate over the next year, $[E(S_1) - S_0]/S_0$, is:

$$[E(S_1) - S_0]/S_0 = h_{FC} - h_{US} \tag{22.1}$$

In words, relative PPP simply says that the expected percentage change in the exchange rate is equal to the difference in inflation rates. If we rearrange this slightly, we get:

$$E(S_1) = S_0 \times [1 + (h_{FC} - h_{US})] \tag{22.2}$$

This result makes a certain amount of sense, but care must be used in quoting the exchange rate.

In our example involving Britain and the United States, relative PPP tells us that the exchange rate will rise by $h_{FC} - h_{US} = 10\% - 4\% = 6\%$ per year. Assuming the difference in inflation rates doesn't change, the expected exchange rate in two years, $E(S_2)$, will therefore be:

$$\begin{aligned} E(S_2) &= E(S_1) \times (1 + .06) \\ &= .53 \times 1.06 \\ &= .562 \end{aligned}$$

Notice that we could have written this as:

$$\begin{aligned} E(S_2) &= .53 \times 1.06 \\ &= .50 \times (1.06 \times 1.06) \\ &= .50 \times 1.06^2 \end{aligned}$$

In general, relative PPP says that the expected exchange rate at some time in the future, $E(S_t)$, is:

$$E(S_t) = S_0 \times [1 + (h_{FC} - h_{US})]^t \tag{22.3}$$

As we will see, this is a very useful relationship.

Because we don't really expect absolute PPP to hold for most goods, we will focus on relative PPP in our following discussion. Henceforth, when we refer to PPP without further qualification, we mean relative PPP.

It's All Relative

EXAMPLE 22.4

Suppose the Japanese exchange rate is currently 105 yen per dollar. The inflation rate in Japan over the next three years will run, say, 2 percent per year, whereas the U.S. inflation rate will be 6 percent. Based on relative PPP, what will the exchange rate be in three years?

Because the U.S. inflation rate is higher, we expect that a dollar will become less valuable. The exchange rate change will be 2% − 6% = −4% per year. Over three years, the exchange rate will fall to:

$$\begin{aligned} E(S_3) &= S_0 \times [1 + (h_{FC} - h_{US})]^3 \\ &= 105 \times [1 + (-.04)]^3 \\ &= 92.90 \end{aligned}$$

Currency Appreciation and Depreciation We frequently hear things like "the dollar strengthened (or weakened) in financial markets today" or "the dollar is expected to appreciate (or depreciate) relative to the pound." When we say that the dollar strengthens or appreciates, we mean that the value of a dollar rises, so it takes more foreign currency to buy a dollar.

What happens to the exchange rates as currencies fluctuate in value depends on how exchange rates are quoted. Because we are quoting them as units of foreign currency per dollar, the exchange rate moves in the same direction as the value of the dollar: it rises as the dollar strengthens, and it falls as the dollar weakens.

Relative PPP tells us that the exchange rate will rise if the U.S. inflation rate is lower than the foreign country's. This happens because the foreign currency depreciates in value and therefore weakens relative to the dollar.

Concept Questions

22.3a What does absolute PPP say? Why might it not hold for many types of goods?

22.3b According to relative PPP, what determines the change in exchange rates?

22.4 INTEREST RATE PARITY, UNBIASED FORWARD RATES, AND THE INTERNATIONAL FISHER EFFECT

The next issue we need to address is the relationship between spot exchange rates, forward exchange rates, and interest rates. To get started, we need some additional notation:

F_t = Forward exchange rate for settlement at time t

R_{US} = U.S. nominal risk-free interest rate

R_{FC} = Foreign country nominal risk-free interest rate

As before, we will use S_0 to stand for the spot exchange rate. You can take the U.S. nominal risk-free rate, R_{US}, to be the T-bill rate.

Covered Interest Arbitrage

Suppose we observe the following information about U.S. and Swiss currency in the market:

$$S_0 = \text{SF } 2.00$$
$$F_1 = \text{SF } 1.90$$
$$R_{US} = 10\%$$
$$R_S = 5\%$$

where R_S is the nominal risk-free rate in Switzerland. The period is one year, so F_1 is the 360-day forward rate.

For exchange rates and even pictures of non-U.S. currencies, see www.travlang.com/money.

Do you see an arbitrage opportunity here? There is one. Suppose you have \$1 to invest, and you want a riskless investment. One option you have is to invest the \$1 in a riskless U.S. investment such as a 360-day T-bill. If you do this, then, in one period, your \$1 will be worth:

$$\begin{aligned}\$ \text{ value in 1 period} &= \$1 \times (1 + R_{US})\\ &= \$1.10\end{aligned}$$

Alternatively, you can invest in the Swiss risk-free investment. To do this, you need to convert your \$1 to Swiss francs and simultaneously execute a forward trade to convert francs back to dollars in one year. The necessary steps would be as follows:

1. Convert your \$1 to $\$1 \times S_0 = \text{SF } 2.00$.
2. At the same time, enter into a forward agreement to convert Swiss francs back to dollars in one year. Because the forward rate is SF 1.90, you will get \$1 for every SF 1.90 that you have in one year.
3. Invest your SF 2.00 in Switzerland at R_S. In one year, you will have:

$$\begin{aligned}\text{SF value in 1 year} &= \text{SF } 2.00 \times (1 + R_S)\\ &= \text{SF } 2.00 \times 1.05\\ &= \text{SF } 2.10\end{aligned}$$

4. Convert your SF 2.10 back to dollars at the agreed-upon rate of SF 1.90 = \$1. You end up with:

$$\begin{aligned}\$ \text{ value in 1 year} &= \text{SF } 2.10/1.90\\ &= \$1.1053\end{aligned}$$

Notice that the value in one year resulting from this strategy can be written as:

$$\begin{aligned}\$ \text{ value in 1 year} &= \$1 \times S_0 \times (1 + R_S)/F_1\\ &= \$1 \times 2 \times 1.05/1.90\\ &= \$1.1053\end{aligned}$$

The return on this investment is apparently 10.53 percent. This is higher than the 10 percent we get from investing in the United States. Because both investments are risk-free, there is an arbitrage opportunity.

To exploit the difference in interest rates, you need to borrow, say, \$5 million at the lower U.S. rate and invest it at the higher Swiss rate. What is the round-trip profit from doing this? To find out, we can work through the steps outlined previously:

1. Convert the \$5 million at SF 2 = \$1 to get SF 10 million.
2. Agree to exchange Swiss francs for dollars in one year at SF 1.90 to the dollar.

3. Invest the SF 10 million for one year at $R_S = 5\%$. You end up with SF 10.5 million.
4. Convert the SF 10.5 million back to dollars to fulfill the forward contract. You receive SF 10.5 million/1.90 = \$5,526,316.
5. Repay the loan with interest. You owe \$5 million plus 10 percent interest, for a total of \$5.5 million. You have \$5,526,316, so your round-trip profit is a risk-free \$26,316.

The activity that we have illustrated here goes by the name of *covered interest arbitrage*. The term *covered* refers to the fact that we are covered in the event of a change in the exchange rate because we lock in the forward exchange rate today.

Interest Rate Parity

If we assume that significant covered interest arbitrage opportunities do not exist, then there must be some relationship between spot exchange rates, forward exchange rates, and relative interest rates. To see what this relationship is, note that, in general, Strategy 1, from the preceding discussion, investing in a riskless U.S. investment, gives us $1 + R_{US}$ for every dollar we invest. Strategy 2, investing in a foreign risk-free investment, gives us $S_0 \times (1 + R_{FC})/F_1$ for every dollar we invest. Because these have to be equal to prevent arbitrage, it must be the case that:

$$1 + R_{US} = S_0 \times (1 + R_{FC})/F_1$$

Rearranging this a bit gets us the famous **interest rate parity (IRP)** condition:

$$F_1/S_0 = (1 + R_{FC})/(1 + R_{US}) \quad [22.4]$$

interest rate parity (IRP)
The condition stating that the interest rate differential between two countries is equal to the percentage difference between the forward exchange rate and the spot exchange rate.

There is a very useful approximation for IRP that illustrates very clearly what is going on and is not difficult to remember. If we define the percentage forward premium or discount as $(F_1 - S_0)/S_0$, then IRP says that this percentage premium or discount is *approximately* equal to the difference in interest rates:

$$(F_1 - S_0)/S_0 = R_{FC} - R_{US} \quad [22.5]$$

Very loosely, what IRP says is that any difference in interest rates between two countries for some period is just offset by the change in the relative value of the currencies, thereby eliminating any arbitrage possibilities. Notice that we could also write:

$$F_1 = S_0 \times [1 + (R_{FC} - R_{US})] \quad [22.6]$$

In general, if we have t periods instead of just one, the IRP approximation is written as:

$$F_t = S_0 \times [1 + (R_{FC} - R_{US})]^t \quad [22.7]$$

Parity Check

<< **EXAMPLE 22.5**

Suppose the exchange rate for Japanese yen, S_0, is currently ¥120 = \$1. If the interest rate in the United States is R_{US} = 10% and the interest rate in Japan is R_J = 5%, then what must the forward rate be to prevent covered interest arbitrage?

From IRP, we have:

$$\begin{aligned} F_1 &= S_0 \times [1 + (R_J - R_{US})] \\ &= ¥120 \times [1 + (.05 - .10)] \\ &= ¥120 \times .95 \\ &= ¥114 \end{aligned}$$

Notice that the yen will sell at a premium relative to the dollar (why?).

Forward Rates and Future Spot Rates

In addition to PPP and IRP, there is one more basic relationship we need to discuss. What is the connection between the forward rate and the expected future spot rate? The **unbiased forward rates (UFR)** condition says that the forward rate, F_1, is equal to the *expected* future spot rate, $E(S_1)$:

unbiased forward rates (UFR)
The condition stating that the current forward rate is an unbiased predictor of the future spot exchange rate.

$$F_1 = E(S_1)$$

With *t* periods, UFR would be written as:

$$F_t = E(S_t)$$

Loosely, the UFR condition says that, on average, the forward exchange rate is equal to the future spot exchange rate.

How are the international markets doing? Find out at cbs.marketwatch.com.

If we ignore risk, then the UFR condition should hold. Suppose the forward rate for the Japanese yen is consistently lower than the future spot rate by, say, 10 yen. This means that anyone who wanted to convert dollars to yen in the future would consistently get more yen by not agreeing to a forward exchange. The forward rate would have to rise to get anyone interested in a forward exchange.

Similarly, if the forward rate were consistently higher than the future spot rate, then anyone who wanted to convert yen to dollars would get more dollars per yen by not agreeing to a forward trade. The forward exchange rate would have to fall to attract such traders.

For these reasons, the forward and actual future spot rates should be equal to each other on average. What the future spot rate will actually be is uncertain, of course. The UFR condition may not hold if traders are willing to pay a premium to avoid this uncertainty. If the condition does hold, then the 180-day forward rate that we see today should be an unbiased predictor of what the exchange rate will actually be in 180 days.

Putting It All Together

We have developed three relationships, PPP, IRP, and UFR, that describe the interaction between key financial variables such as interest rates, exchange rates, and inflation rates. We now explore the implications of these relationships as a group.

Uncovered Interest Parity To start, it is useful to collect our international financial market relationships in one place:

$$\text{PPP:}\quad E(S_1) = S_0 \times [1 + (h_{FC} - h_{US})]$$
$$\text{IRP:}\quad F_1 = S_0 \times [1 + (R_{FC} - R_{US})]$$
$$\text{UFR:}\quad F_1 = E(S_1)$$

We begin by combining UFR and IRP. Because we know that $F_1 = E(S_1)$ from the UFR condition, we can substitute $E(S_1)$ for F_1 in IRP. The result is:

$$\text{UIP: } E(S_1) = S_0 \times [1 + (R_{FC} - R_{US})] \qquad [22.8]$$

This important relationship is called **uncovered interest parity (UIP)**, and it will play a key role in our international capital budgeting discussion that follows. With *t* periods, UIP becomes:

uncovered interest parity (UIP)
The condition stating that the expected percentage change in the exchange rate is equal to the difference in interest rates.

$$E(S_t) = S_0 \times [1 + (R_{FC} - R_{US})]^t \qquad [22.9]$$

The International Fisher Effect Next, we compare PPP and UIP. Both of them have $E(S_1)$ on the left-hand side, so their right-hand sides must be equal. We thus have that:

$$S_0 \times [1 + (h_{FC} - h_{US})] = S_0 \times [1 + (R_{FC} - R_{US})]$$
$$h_{FC} - h_{US} = R_{FC} - R_{US}$$

This tells us that the difference in returns between the United States and a foreign country is just equal to the difference in inflation rates. Rearranging this slightly gives us the **international Fisher effect (IFE)**:

$$\text{IFE: } R_{US} - h_{US} = R_{FC} - h_{FC} \qquad [22.10]$$

international Fisher effect (IFE)
The theory that real interest rates are equal across countries.

The IFE says that *real* rates are equal across countries.[2]

The conclusion that real returns are equal across countries is really basic economics. If real returns were higher in, say, Brazil than in the United States, money would flow out of U.S. financial markets and into Brazilian markets. Asset prices in Brazil would rise and their returns would fall. At the same time, asset prices in the United States would fall and their returns would rise. This process acts to equalize real returns.

Having said all this, we need to note a couple of things. First of all, we really haven't explicitly dealt with risk in our discussion. We might reach a different conclusion about real returns once we do, particularly if people in different countries have different tastes and attitudes towards risk. Second, there are many barriers to the movement of money and capital around the world. Real returns might be different in two different countries for long periods of time if money can't move freely between them.

Despite these problems, we expect that capital markets will become increasingly internationalized. As this occurs, any differences in real rates that do exist will probably diminish. The laws of economics have very little respect for national boundaries.

Concept Questions

22.4a What is covered interest arbitrage?

22.4b What is the international Fisher effect?

INTERNATIONAL CAPITAL BUDGETING 22.5

Kihlstrom Equipment, a U.S.-based international company, is evaluating an overseas investment. Kihlstrom's exports of drill bits have increased to such a degree that it is considering building a distribution center in France. The project will cost €2 million to launch. The cash flows are expected to be €.9 million a year for the next three years.

The current spot exchange rate for euros is €.5. Recall that this is euros per dollar, so a euro is worth $1/.5 = $2. The risk-free rate in the United States is 5 percent, and the risk-free rate in "euroland" is 7 percent. Note that the exchange rate and the two interest rates are observed in financial markets, not estimated.[3] Kihlstrom's required return on dollar investments of this sort is 10 percent.

Should Kihlstrom take this investment? As always, the answer depends on the NPV, but how do we calculate the net present value of this project in U.S. dollars? There are two basic ways to go about doing this:

1. *The home currency approach.* Convert all the euro cash flows into dollars, and then discount at 10 percent to find the NPV in dollars. Notice that for this approach, we have to come up with the future exchange rates to convert the future projected euro cash flows into dollars.

[2]Notice that our result here is in terms of the approximate real rate, $R - h$ (see Chapter 7), because we used approximations for PPP and IRP. For the exact result, see Problem 15 at the end of the chapter.

[3]For example, the interest rates might be the short-term Eurodollar and euro deposit rates offered by large money center banks.

2. *The foreign currency approach.* Determine the required return on euro investments, and then discount the euro cash flows to find the NPV in euros. Then convert this euro NPV to a dollar NPV. This approach requires us to somehow convert the 10 percent dollar required return to the equivalent euro required return.

The difference between these two approaches is primarily a matter of when we convert from euros to dollars. In the first case, we convert before estimating the NPV. In the second case, we convert after estimating NPV.

It might appear that the second approach is superior because, for it, we only have to come up with one number, the euro discount rate. Furthermore, because the first approach requires us to forecast future exchange rates, it probably seems that there is greater room for error with this approach. As we illustrate next, however, based on our previous results, the two approaches are really the same.

Method 1: The Home Currency Approach

To convert the project future cash flows into dollars, we will invoke the uncovered interest parity, or UIP, relation to come up with the projected exchange rates. Based on our earlier discussion, the expected exchange rate at time t, $E(S_t)$, is:

$$E(S_t) = S_0 \times [1 + (R_€ - R_{US})]^t$$

where $R_€$ stands for the nominal risk-free rate in euroland. Because $R_€$ is 7 percent, R_{US} is 5 percent, and the current exchange rate (S_0) is €.5:

$$\begin{aligned} E(S_t) &= .5 \times [1 + (.07 - .05)]^t \\ &= .5 \times 1.02^t \end{aligned}$$

The projected exchange rates for the drill bit project are thus:

Year	Expected Exchange Rate
1	€.5 × 1.02^1 = €.5100
2	€.5 × 1.02^2 = €.5202
3	€.5 × 1.02^3 = €.5306

Using these exchange rates, along with the current exchange rate, we can convert all of the euro cash flows to dollars (note that all of the cash flows in this example are in millions):

Year	(1) Cash Flow in € mil	(2) Expected Exchange Rate	(3) Cash Flow in $mil (1)/(2)
0	−€2.0	€.5000	−$4.00
1	.9	.5100	1.76
2	.9	.5202	1.73
3	.9	.5306	1.70

To finish off, we calculate the NPV in the ordinary way:

$$\begin{aligned} NPV_\$ &= -\$4 + \$1.76/1.10 + \$1.73/1.10^2 + \$1.70/1.10^3 \\ &= \$.3 \text{ million} \end{aligned}$$

So the project appears to be profitable.

Method 2: The Foreign Currency Approach

Kihlstrom requires a nominal return of 10 percent on the dollar-denominated cash flows. We need to convert this to a rate suitable for euro-denominated cash flows. Based on the international Fisher effect, we know that the difference in the nominal rates is:

$$\begin{aligned} R_{€} - R_{US} &= h_{€} - h_{US} \\ &= 7\% - 5\% = 2\% \end{aligned}$$

The appropriate discount rate for estimating the euro cash flows from the drill bit project is approximately equal to 10 percent plus an extra 2 percent to compensate for the greater euro inflation rate.

If we calculate the NPV of the euro cash flows at this rate, we get:

$$\begin{aligned} \text{NPV}_{€} &= -€2 + €.9/1.12 + €.9/1.12^2 + €.9/1.12^3 \\ &= €.16 \text{ million} \end{aligned}$$

The NPV of this project is €.16 million. Taking this project makes us €.16 million richer today. What is this in dollars? Because the exchange rate today is €.5, the dollar NPV of the project is:

$$\text{NPV}_{\$} = \text{NPV}_{€}/S_0 = €.16/.5 = \$.3 \text{ million}$$

This is the same dollar NPV that we previously calculated.

The important thing to recognize from our example is that the two capital budgeting procedures are actually the same and will always give the same answer.[4] In this second approach, the fact that we are implicitly forecasting exchange rates is simply hidden. Even so, the foreign currency approach is computationally a little easier.

Unremitted Cash Flows

The previous example assumed that all aftertax cash flows from the foreign investment could be remitted to (paid out to) the parent firm. Actually, substantial differences can exist between the cash flows generated by a foreign project and the amount that can actually be remitted, or "repatriated," to the parent firm.

A foreign subsidiary can remit funds to a parent in many forms, including the following:

1. Dividends
2. Management fees for central services
3. Royalties on the use of trade names and patents

However cash flows are repatriated, international firms must pay special attention to remittances, because there may be current and future controls on remittances. Many governments are sensitive to the charge of being exploited by foreign national firms. In such cases, governments are tempted to limit the ability of international firms to remit cash flows. Funds that cannot currently be remitted are sometimes said to be *blocked.*

Concept Questions

22.5a What financial complications arise in international capital budgeting? Describe two procedures for estimating NPV in the case of an international project.

22.5b What are blocked funds?

[4]Actually, there will be a slight difference because we are using the approximate relationships. If we calculate the required return as $1.10 \times (1 + .02) - 1 = 12.2\%$, then we get exactly the same NPV. See Problem 15 for more detail.

22.6 EXCHANGE RATE RISK

exchange rate risk The risk related to having international operations in a world where relative currency values vary.

Exchange rate risk is the natural consequence of international operations in a world where relative currency values move up and down. Managing exchange rate risk is an important part of international finance. As we discuss next, there are three different types of exchange rate risk, or exposure: short-run exposure, long-run exposure, and translation exposure. Chapter 23 contains a more detailed discussion of the issues raised in this section.

Short-Run Exposure

The day-to-day fluctuations in exchange rates create short-run risks for international firms. Most such firms have contractual agreements to buy and sell goods in the near future at set prices. When different currencies are involved, such transactions have an extra element of risk.

For example, imagine that you are importing imitation pasta from Italy and reselling it in the United States under the Impasta brand name. Your largest customer has ordered 10,000 cases of Impasta. You place the order with your supplier today, but you won't pay until the goods arrive in 60 days. Your selling price is \$6 per case. Your cost is 8.4 euros per case, and the exchange rate is currently €1.50, so it takes 1.50 euros to buy \$1.

At the current exchange rate, your cost in dollars of filling the order is €8.4/1.5 = \$5.60 per case, so your pretax profit on the order is 10,000 × (\$6 − 5.60) = \$4,000. However, the exchange rate in 60 days will probably be different, so your profit will depend on what the future exchange rate turns out to be.

For example, if the rate goes to €1.6, your cost is €8.4/1.6 = \$5.25 per case. Your profit goes to \$7,500. If the exchange rate goes to, say, €1.4, then your cost is €8.4/1.4 = \$6, and your profit is zero.

The short-run exposure in our example can be reduced or eliminated in several ways. The most obvious way is by entering into a forward exchange agreement to lock in an exchange rate. For example, suppose the 60-day forward rate is €1.58. What will be your profit if you hedge? What profit should you expect if you don't?

If you hedge, you lock in an exchange rate of €1.58. Your cost in dollars will thus be €8.4/1.58 = \$5.32 per case, so your profit will be 10,000 × (\$6 − 5.32) = \$6,800. If you don't hedge, then, assuming that the forward rate is an unbiased predictor (in other words, assuming the UFR condition holds), you should expect that the exchange rate will actually be €1.58 in 60 days. You should expect to make \$6,800.

Alternatively, if this strategy is not feasible, you could simply borrow the dollars today, convert them into euros, and invest the euros for 60 days to earn some interest. Based on IRP, this amounts to entering into a forward contract.

Long-Run Exposure

In the long run, the value of a foreign operation can fluctuate because of unanticipated changes in relative economic conditions. For example, imagine that we own a labor-intensive assembly operation located in another country to take advantage of lower wages. Through time, unexpected changes in economic conditions can raise the foreign wage levels to the point where the cost advantage is eliminated or even becomes negative.

The impact of changes in exchange rate levels can be substantial. For example, during 2003 and the early part of 2004, the U.S. dollar continued to weaken against other currencies. This meant foreign manufacturers took home less for each dollar's worth of sales they made, which can lead to big profit swings. Volkswagen estimated that it lost €1.2 billion

($1.5 billion) due to currency swings in 2003. And Peugeot Citroën of France estimated it might lose as much as €600 million ($744 million) in 2004.

Hedging long-run exposure is more difficult than hedging short-term risks. For one thing, organized forward markets don't exist for such long-term needs. Instead, the primary option that firms have is to try to match up foreign currency inflows and outflows. The same thing goes for matching foreign currency–denominated assets and liabilities. For example, a firm that sells in a foreign country might try to concentrate its raw material purchases and labor expense in that country. That way, the dollar values of its revenues and costs will move up and down together. Probably the best examples of this type of hedging are the so-called transplant auto manufacturers such as BMW, Honda, Mercedes, and Toyota, which now build a substantial portion of the cars they sell in the United States, thereby obtaining some degree of immunization against exchange rate movements.

For example, BMW produces 160,000 cars in South Carolina and exports about 100,000 of them. The costs of manufacturing the cars are paid mostly in dollars, and, when BMW exports the cars to Europe, it receives euros. When the dollar weakens, these vehicles become more profitable for BMW. At the same time, BMW exports about 217,000 cars to the United States each year. The costs of manufacturing these imported cars are mostly in euros, so they become less profitable when the dollar weakens. Taken together, these gains and losses tend to offset each other and provide BMW with a natural hedge.

Similarly, a firm can reduce its long-run exchange rate risk by borrowing in the foreign country. Fluctuations in the value of the foreign subsidiary's assets will then be at least partially offset by changes in the value of the liabilities.

Translation Exposure

When a U.S. company calculates its accounting net income and EPS for some period, it must "translate" everything into dollars. This can create some problems for the accountants when there are significant foreign operations. In particular, two issues arise:

1. What is the appropriate exchange rate to use for translating each balance sheet account?
2. How should balance sheet accounting gains and losses from foreign currency translation be handled?

To illustrate the accounting problem, suppose we started a small foreign subsidiary in Lilliputia a year ago. The local currency is the gulliver, abbreviated GL. At the beginning of the year, the exchange rate was GL 2 = $1, and the balance sheet in gullivers looked like this:

Assets	GL 1,000	Liabilities	GL 500
		Equity	500

At 2 gullivers to the dollar, the beginning balance sheet in dollars was as follows:

Assets	$500	Liabilities	$250
		Equity	250

Lilliputia is a quiet place, and nothing at all actually happened during the year. As a result, net income was zero (before consideration of exchange rate changes). However, the exchange rate did change to 4 gullivers = $1 purely because the Lilliputian inflation rate is much higher than the U.S. inflation rate.

Because nothing happened, the accounting ending balance sheet in gullivers is the same as the beginning one. However, if we convert it to dollars at the new exchange rate, we get:

Assets	$250	Liabilities	$125
		Equity	125

Notice that the value of the equity has gone down by $125, even though net income was exactly zero. Despite the fact that absolutely nothing really happened, there is a $125 accounting loss. How to handle this $125 loss has been a controversial accounting question.

One obvious and consistent way to handle this loss is simply to report the loss on the parent's income statement. During periods of volatile exchange rates, this kind of treatment can dramatically impact an international company's reported EPS. This is a purely accounting phenomenon, but, even so, such fluctuations are disliked by some financial managers.

The current approach to handling translation gains and losses is based on rules set out in the Financial Accounting Standards Board (FASB) Statement of Financial Accounting Standards No. 52 (FASB 52), issued in December 1981. For the most part, FASB 52 requires that all assets and liabilities be translated from the subsidiary's currency into the parent's currency using the exchange rate that currently prevails.

Any translation gains and losses that occur are accumulated in a special account within the shareholders' equity section of the balance sheet. This account might be labeled something like "unrealized foreign exchange gains (losses)." The amounts involved can be substantial, at least from an accounting standpoint. For example, IBM's December 31, 2003, fiscal year-end balance sheet shows a deduction from equity in the amount of $539 million for translation adjustments related to assets and liabilities of non-U.S. subsidiaries. These gains and losses are not reported on the income statement. As a result, the impact of translation gains and losses will not be recognized explicitly in net income until the underlying assets and liabilities are sold or otherwise liquidated.

Managing Exchange Rate Risk

For a large multinational firm, the management of exchange rate risk is complicated by the fact that there can be many different currencies involved in many different subsidiaries. It is very likely that a change in some exchange rate will benefit some subsidiaries and hurt others. The net effect on the overall firm depends on its net exposure.

For example, suppose a firm has two divisions. Division A buys goods in the United States for dollars and sells them in Britain for pounds. Division B buys goods in Britain for pounds and sells them in the United States for dollars. If these two divisions are of roughly equal size in terms of their inflows and outflows, then the overall firm obviously has little exchange rate risk.

In our example, the firm's net position in pounds (the amount coming in less the amount going out) is small, so the exchange rate risk is small. However, if one division, acting on its own, were to start hedging its exchange rate risk, then the overall firm's exchange rate risk would go up. The moral of the story is that multinational firms have to be conscious of the overall position that the firm has in a foreign currency. For this reason, management of exchange rate risk is probably best handled on a centralized basis.

Concept Questions

22.6a What are the different types of exchange rate risk?

22.6b How can a firm hedge short-run exchange rate risk? Long-run exchange rate risk?

POLITICAL RISK

22.7

One final element of risk in international investing is **political risk**. Political risk refers to changes in value that arise as a consequence of political actions. This is not a problem faced exclusively by international firms. For example, changes in U.S. tax laws and regulations may benefit some U.S. firms and hurt others, so political risk exists nationally as well as internationally.

political risk
Risk related to changes in value that arise because of political actions.

Some countries do have more political risk than others, however. When firms have operations in these riskier countries, the extra political risk may lead the firms to require higher returns on overseas investments to compensate for the possibility that funds may be blocked, critical operations interrupted, and contracts abrogated. In the most extreme case, the possibility of outright confiscation may be a concern in countries with relatively unstable political environments.

Political risk also depends on the nature of the business; some businesses are less likely to be confiscated because they are not particularly valuable in the hands of a different owner. An assembly operation supplying subcomponents that only the parent company uses would not be an attractive "takeover" target, for example. Similarly, a manufacturing operation that requires the use of specialized components from the parent is of little value without the parent company's cooperation.

A great site for evaluating the political risk of a country is www.cia.gov/cia/publications/factbook.

Natural resource developments, such as copper mining or oil drilling, are just the opposite. Once the operation is in place, much of the value is in the commodity. The political risk for such investments is much higher for this reason. Also, the issue of exploitation is more pronounced with such investments, again increasing the political risk.

Political risk can be hedged in several ways, particularly when confiscation or nationalization is a concern. The use of local financing, perhaps from the government of the foreign country in question, reduces the possible loss because the company can refuse to pay on the debt in the event of unfavorable political activities. Based on our discussion in this section, structuring the operation in such a way that it requires significant parent company involvement to function is another way to reduce political risk.

Concept Questions

22.7a What is political risk?

22.7b What are some ways of hedging political risk?

SUMMARY AND CONCLUSIONS

22.8

The international firm has a more complicated life than the purely domestic firm. Management must understand the connection between interest rates, foreign currency exchange rates, and inflation, and it must become aware of a large number of different financial market regulations and tax systems. This chapter is intended to be a concise introduction to some of the financial issues that come up in international investing.

Our coverage has been necessarily brief. The main topics we discussed are the following:

1. Some basic vocabulary. We briefly defined some exotic terms such as *LIBOR* and *Eurocurrency*.
2. The basic mechanics of exchange rate quotations. We discussed the spot and forward markets and how exchange rates are interpreted.

3. The fundamental relationships between international financial variables:
   a. Absolute and relative purchasing power parity, PPP
   b. Interest rate parity, IRP
   c. Unbiased forward rates, UFR

   Absolute purchasing power parity states that \$1 should have the same purchasing power in each country. This means that an orange costs the same whether you buy it in New York or in Tokyo.

   Relative purchasing power parity means that the expected percentage change in exchange rates between the currencies of two countries is equal to the difference in their inflation rates.

   Interest rate parity implies that the percentage difference between the forward exchange rate and the spot exchange rate is equal to the interest rate differential. We showed how covered interest arbitrage forces this relationship to hold.

   The unbiased forward rates condition indicates that the current forward rate is a good predictor of the future spot exchange rate.
4. International capital budgeting. We showed that the basic foreign exchange relationships imply two other conditions:
   a. Uncovered interest parity
   b. The international Fisher effect

   By invoking these two conditions, we learned how to estimate NPVs in foreign currencies and how to convert foreign currencies into dollars to estimate NPV in the usual way.
5. Exchange rate and political risk. We described the various types of exchange rate risk and discussed some commonly used approaches to managing the effect of fluctuating exchange rates on the cash flows and value of the international firm. We also discussed political risk and some ways of managing exposure to it.

Chapter Review and Self-Test Problems

22.1 Relative Purchasing Power Parity The inflation rate in the United States is projected at 3 percent per year for the next several years. The New Zealand inflation rate is projected to be 5 percent during that time. The exchange rate is currently NZ\$ 1.66. Based on relative PPP, what is the expected exchange rate in two years?

22.2 Covered Interest Arbitrage The spot and 360-day forward rates on the Swiss franc are SF 2.1 and SF 1.9, respectively. The risk-free interest rate in the United States is 6 percent, and the risk-free rate in Switzerland is 4 percent. Is there an arbitrage opportunity here? How would you exploit it?

Answers to Chapter Review and Self-Test Problems

22.1 Based on relative PPP, the expected exchange rate in two years, $E(S_2)$, is:

$$E(S_2) = S_0 \times [1 + (h_{NZ} - h_{US})]^2$$

where h_{NZ} is the New Zealand inflation rate. The current exchange rate is NZ\$ 1.66, so the expected exchange rate is:

$$\begin{aligned} E(S_2) &= \text{NZ\$ } 1.66 \times [1 + (.05 - .03)]^2 \\ &= \text{NZ\$ } 1.66 \times 1.02^2 \\ &= \text{NZ\$ } 1.73 \end{aligned}$$

22.2 Based on interest rate parity, the forward rate should be (approximately):

$$F_1 = S_0 \times [1 + (R_{FC} - R_{US})]$$
$$= 2.1 \times [1 + (.04 - .06)]$$
$$= 2.06$$

Because the forward rate is actually SF 1.9, there is an arbitrage opportunity.

To exploit the arbitrage opportunity, you first note that dollars are selling for SF 1.9 each in the forward market. Based on IRP, this is too cheap because they should be selling for SF 2.06. So you want to arrange to buy dollars with Swiss francs in the forward market. To do this, you can:

1. Today: Borrow, say, $1 million for 360 days. Convert it to SF 2.1 million in the spot market, and buy a forward contract at SF 1.9 to convert it back to dollars in 360 days. Invest the SF 2.1 million at 4 percent.
2. In one year: Your investment has grown to SF 2.1 million × 1.04 = SF 2.184 million. Convert this to dollars at the rate of SF 1.9 = $1. You will have SF 2.184 million/1.9 = $1,149,474. Pay off your loan with 6 percent interest at a cost of $1 million × 1.06 = $1,060,000 and pocket the difference of $89,474.

Concepts Review and Critical Thinking Questions

1. **Spot and Forward Rates** Suppose the exchange rate for the Swiss franc is quoted as SF 1.50 in the spot market and SF 1.53 in the 90-day forward market.
   a. Is the dollar selling at a premium or a discount relative to the franc?
   b. Does the financial market expect the franc to strengthen relative to the dollar? Explain.
   c. What do you suspect is true about relative economic conditions in the United States and Switzerland?
2. **Purchasing Power Parity** Suppose the rate of inflation in Mexico will run about 3 percent higher than the U.S. inflation rate over the next several years. All other things being the same, what will happen to the Mexican peso versus dollar exchange rate? What relationship are you relying on in answering?
3. **Exchange Rates** The exchange rate for the Australian dollar is currently A$1.40. This exchange rate is expected to rise by 10 percent over the next year.
   a. Is the Australian dollar expected to get stronger or weaker?
   b. What do you think about the relative inflation rates in the United States and Australia?
   c. What do you think about the relative nominal interest rates in the United States and Australia? Relative real rates?
4. **Yankee Bonds** Which of the following most accurately describes a Yankee bond?
   a. A bond issued by General Motors in Japan with the interest payable in U.S. dollars
   b. A bond issued by General Motors in Japan with the interest payable in yen
   c. A bond issued by Toyota in the United States with the interest payable in yen
   d. A bond issued by Toyota in the United States with the interest payable in dollars
   e. A bond issued by Toyota worldwide with the interest payable in dollars
5. **Exchange Rates** Are exchange rate changes necessarily good or bad for a particular company?
6. **International Risks** At one point, Duracell International confirmed that it was planning to open battery-manufacturing plants in China and India. Manufacturing in

these countries allows Duracell to avoid import duties of between 30 and 35 percent that have made alkaline batteries prohibitively expensive for some consumers. What additional advantages might Duracell see in this proposal? What are some of the risks to Duracell?

7. **Multinational Corporations** Given that many multinationals based in many countries have much greater sales outside their domestic markets than within them, what is the particular relevance of their domestic currency?
8. **Exchange Rate Movements** Are the following statements true or false? Explain why.
   - **a.** If the general price index in Great Britain rises faster than that in the United States, we would expect the pound to appreciate relative to the dollar.
   - **b.** Suppose you are a German machine tool exporter, and you invoice all of your sales in foreign currency. Further suppose that the euroland monetary authorities begin to undertake an expansionary monetary policy. If it is certain that the easy money policy will result in higher inflation rates in euroland relative to those in other countries, then you should use the forward markets to protect yourself against future losses resulting from the deterioration in the value of the euro.
   - **c.** If you could accurately estimate differences in the relative inflation rates of two countries over a long period of time, while other market participants were unable to do so, you could successfully speculate in spot currency markets.
9. **Exchange Rate Movements** Some countries encourage movements in their exchange rate relative to those of some other country as a short-term means of addressing foreign trade imbalances. For each of the following scenarios, evaluate the impact the announcement would have on an American importer and an American exporter doing business with the foreign country.
   - **a.** Officials in the administration of the United States government announce that they are comfortable with a rising euro relative to the dollar.
   - **b.** British monetary authorities announce that they feel the pound has been driven too low by currency speculators relative to the dollar.
   - **c.** The Brazilian government announces that it will print billions of new cruzeiros and inject them into the economy in an effort to reduce the country's unemployment rate.
10. **International Capital Market Relationships** We discussed five international capital market relationships: relative PPP, IRP, UFR, UIP, and the international Fisher effect. Which of these would you expect to hold most closely? Which do you think would be most likely to be violated?

Questions and Problems

BASIC
(Questions 1–13)

1. **Using Exchange Rates** Take a look back at Figure 22.1 to answer the following questions:
   - **a.** If you have $100, how many euros can you get?
   - **b.** How much is one euro worth?
   - **c.** If you have five million euros, how many dollars do you have?
   - **d.** Which is worth more, a New Zealand dollar or a Singapore dollar?
   - **e.** Which is worth more, a Mexican peso or a Chilean peso?
   - **f.** How many Mexican pesos can you get for a euro? What do you call this rate?
   - **g.** Per unit, what is the most valuable currency of those listed? The least valuable?

2. **Using the Cross-Rate** Use the information in Figure 22.1 to answer the following questions:
   a. Which would you rather have, \$100 or £100? Why?
   b. Which would you rather have, 100 Swiss francs (SF) or £100? Why?
   c. What is the cross-rate for Swiss francs in terms of British pounds? For British pounds in terms of Swiss francs?
3. **Forward Exchange Rates** Use the information in Figure 22.1 to answer the following questions:
   a. What is the six-month forward rate for the Japanese yen in yen per U.S. dollar? Is the yen selling at a premium or a discount? Explain.
   b. What is the three-month forward rate for Canadian dollars in U.S. dollars per Canadian dollar? Is the dollar selling at a premium or a discount? Explain.
   c. What do you think will happen to the value of the dollar relative to the yen and the Canadian dollar, based on the information in the figure? Explain.
4. **Using Spot and Forward Exchange Rates** Suppose the spot exchange rate for the Canadian dollar is Can\$1.26 and the six-month forward rate is Can\$1.22.
   a. Which is worth more, a U.S. dollar or a Canadian dollar?
   b. Assuming absolute PPP holds, what is the cost in the United States of an Elkhead beer if the price in Canada is Can\$2.19? Why might the beer actually sell at a different price in the United States?
   c. Is the U.S. dollar selling at a premium or a discount relative to the Canadian dollar?
   d. Which currency is expected to appreciate in value?
   e. Which country do you think has higher interest rates—the United States or Canada? Explain.
5. **Cross-Rates and Arbitrage** Suppose the Japanese yen exchange rate is ¥115 = \$1, and the British pound exchange rate is £1 = \$1.70.
   a. What is the cross-rate in terms of yen per pound?
   b. Suppose the cross-rate is ¥185 = £1. Is there an arbitrage opportunity here? If there is, explain how to take advantage of the mispricing.
6. **Interest Rate Parity** Use Figure 22.1 to answer the following questions. Suppose interest rate parity holds, and the current six-month risk-free rate in the United States is 2.5 percent. What must the six-month risk-free rate be in Great Britain? In Japan? In Switzerland?
7. **Interest Rates and Arbitrage** The treasurer of a major U.S. firm has \$30 million to invest for three months. The annual interest rate in the United States is .45 percent per month. The interest rate in Great Britain is .6 percent per month. The spot exchange rate is £.56, and the three-month forward rate is £.59. Ignoring transactions costs, in which country would the treasurer want to invest the company's funds? Why?
8. **Inflation and Exchange Rates** Suppose the current exchange rate for the Polish zloty is Z 3.84. The expected exchange rate in three years is Z 3.92. What is the difference in the annual inflation rates for the United States and Poland over this period? Assume that the anticipated rate is constant for both countries. What relationship are you relying on in answering?
9. **Exchange Rate Risk** Suppose your company imports computer motherboards from Singapore. The exchange rate is given in Figure 22.1. You have just placed an order

for 30,000 motherboards at a cost to you of 168.5 Singapore dollars each. You will pay for the shipment when it arrives in 90 days. You can sell the motherboards for $145 each. Calculate your profit if the exchange rate goes up or down by 10 percent over the next 90 days. What is the break-even exchange rate? What percentage rise or fall does this represent in terms of the Singapore dollar versus the U.S. dollar?

10. Exchange Rates and Arbitrage Suppose the spot and six-month forward rates on the Norwegian krone are Kr 6.43 and Kr 6.56, respectively. The annual risk-free rate in the United States is 5 percent, and the annual risk-free rate in Norway is 8 percent.

a. Is there an arbitrage opportunity here? If so, how would you exploit it?

b. What must the six-month forward rate be to prevent arbitrage?

11. The International Fisher Effect You observe that the inflation rate in the United States is 3.5 percent per year and that T-bills currently yield 3.9 percent annually. What do you estimate the inflation rate to be in:

a. Australia, if short-term Australian government securities yield 5 percent per year?

b. Canada, if short-term Canadian government securities yield 7 percent per year?

c. Taiwan, if short-term Taiwanese government securities yield 10 percent per year?

12. Spot versus Forward Rates Suppose the spot and three-month forward rates for the yen are ¥131.30 and ¥129.76, respectively.

a. Is the yen expected to get stronger or weaker?

b. What would you estimate is the difference between the inflation rates of the United States and Japan?

13. Expected Spot Rates Suppose the spot exchange rate for the Hungarian forint is HUF 215. Interest rates in the United States are 3.5 percent per year. They are 8.6 percent in Hungary. What do you predict the exchange rate will be in one year? In two years? In five years? What relationship are you using?

INTERMEDIATE
(Question 14)

14. Capital Budgeting You are evaluating a proposed expansion of an existing subsidiary located in Switzerland. The cost of the expansion would be SF 27.0 million. The cash flows from the project would be SF 7.5 million per year for the next five years. The dollar required return is 13 percent per year, and the current exchange rate is SF 1.72. The going rate on Eurodollars is 8 percent per year. It is 7 percent per year on Euroswiss.

a. What do you project will happen to exchange rates over the next four years?

b. Based on your answer in (*a*), convert the projected franc flows into dollar flows and calculate the NPV.

c. What is the required return on franc flows? Based on your answer, calculate the NPV in francs and then convert to dollars.

CHALLENGE
(Question 15)

15. Using the Exact International Fisher Effect From our discussion of the Fisher effect in Chapter 7, we know that the actual relationship between a nominal rate, R, a real rate, r, and an inflation rate, h, can be written as:

$$1 + r = (1 + R)/(1 + h)$$

This is the *domestic* Fisher effect.

a. What is the nonapproximate form of the international Fisher effect?

b. Based on your answer in (*a*), what is the exact form for UIP? (Hint: Recall the exact form of IRP and use UFR.)

c. What is the exact form for relative PPP? (Hint: Combine your previous two answers.)

d. Recalculate the NPV for the Kihlstrom drill bit project (discussed in Section 22.5) using the exact forms for UIP and the international Fisher effect. Verify that you get precisely the same answer either way.

S&P Problems

STANDARD &POOR'S

1. American Depositary Receipts Nestlé S. A. has American Depositary Receipts listed on the over-the-counter market. Many ADRs listed on U.S. exchanges are for fractional shares. In the case of Nestlé, 4 ADRs are equal to one registered share of stock. Find the information for Nestlé using the ticker symbol "3NSRGY."

a. Click on the "Mthly. Adj. Prices" link and find Nestlé's closing price for May 2004. Assume the exchange rate on that day was \$/SFr 1.231 and Nestlé shares traded for SFr 21.50. Is there an arbitrage opportunity available? If so, how would you take advantage of it?

b. What exchange rate is necessary to eliminate the arbitrage opportunity available in *a*?

c. Dividend payments made to ADR shareholders are in U.S. dollars. Suppose you own 90 Nestlé ADRs. Assume the current exchange rate is the rate you calculated in *b*. Nestlé declares a dividend of SFr 1.15. What U.S. dollar dividend payment will you receive?

What's On the Web?

22.1 Purchasing Power Parity One of the more famous examples of a violation of absolute purchasing power parity is the Big Mac index calculated by *The Economist*. This index calculates the dollar price of a McDonald's Big Mac in different countries. You can find the Big Mac index by going to www.economist.com, following the "Markets & Data" link and then the "Big Mac index" link. Using the most recent index, which country has the most expensive Big Macs? Which country has the cheapest Big Macs? Why is the price of a Big Mac not the same in every country?

22.2 Inflation and Exchange Rates Go to www.marketvector.com and follow the "Exchange Rates" link. Select the "Australian Dollar" link. Is the U.S. dollar expected to appreciate or depreciate compared to the Australian dollar over the next six months? What is the difference in the annual inflation rates for the United States and Australia over this period? Assume that the anticipated rate is constant for both countries. What relationship are you relying on in answering?

22.3 Interest Rate Parity Go to the *Financial Times* site at www.ft.com, click on the "Markets" link and then the "Currencies" link. Find the current exchange rate between the U.S. dollar and the euro. Next, follow the "Currencies home" link and the "Money rates" link to find the U.S. dollar LIBOR and the Euro LIBOR interest rates. What must the one-year forward rate be to prevent arbitrage? What principle are you relying on in your answer?

PART EIGHT

Topics in Corporate Finance

23 Risk Management: An Introduction to Financial Engineering

For airlines, jet fuel can make up as much as 15 percent of operating expenses and is their second biggest cost after labor. Airlines combat the effects of increasing fuel costs through various hedging techniques. In 2004, for example, Southwest Airlines was more than 80 percent hedged for the year according to industry reports. As a result, Southwest locked in a cost that corresponded to a price of $24 per barrel of oil. As prices hit $40 per barrel in the summer, Southwest's savings were enormous. Airlines use a variety of sophisticated financial tools to deal with risks associated with volatile fuel costs, including heating oil futures contracts, jet fuel swaps, and call options. As we will see in this chapter, these techniques are among the tools commonly used by firms to manage risk.

Since the early 1970s, prices for all types of goods and services have become increasingly volatile. This is a cause for concern because sudden and unexpected shifts in prices can create expensive disruptions in operating activities for even very well run firms. As a result, firms are increasingly taking steps to shield themselves from price volatility through the use of new and innovative financial arrangements.

The purpose of this chapter is to introduce you to some of the basics of financial risk management. The activities we discuss here are on the frontier of modern, real-world financial management. By describing one of the rapidly developing areas in corporate finance, we hope to leave you with a sense of how the art and practice of financial management evolve in response to changes in the financial environment.

Check out the "Internet Resource for Derivatives" for information on derivative instruments and markets at www.numa.com.

HEDGING AND PRICE VOLATILITY 23.1

In broad terms, reducing a firm's exposure to price or rate fluctuations is called **hedging**. The term *immunization* is sometimes used as well. As we will discuss, there are many different types of hedging and many different techniques. Frequently, when a firm desires to hedge a particular risk, there will be no direct way of doing so. The financial manager's job in such cases is to create a way by using available financial instruments to create new ones. This process has come to be called *financial engineering*.

hedging
Reducing a firm's exposure to price or rate fluctuations. Also, immunization.

Corporate risk management often involves the buying and selling of **derivative securities**. A derivative security is a financial asset that represents a claim to another financial asset. For example, a stock option gives the owner the right to buy or sell stock, a financial asset, so stock options are derivative securities.

The International Financial Risk Institute (riskinstitute.ch) promotes education on risk management.

Financial engineering frequently involves creating new derivative securities, or else combining existing derivatives to accomplish specific hedging goals. In a world where prices were very stable and changed only slowly, there would be very little demand for financial engineering. As this is being written, however, financial engineering is very much a growth industry. As we discuss next, the reason is that the financial world has become more risky.

derivative security
A financial asset that represents a claim to another financial asset.

Price Volatility: A Historical Perspective

In trying to understand why we claim that the financial world has become more risky, you will find it useful to look back at the history of prices. Figure 23.1 provides a very long-term view of price levels for the United States. The price-level series shown begins in 1820 and runs through 2003. The remarkable fact revealed by this series is that for the first 100 years, prices changed very little (except in wartime). In contrast, in the last 40 or 50 years, prices have increased dramatically.

As we saw in Chapter 12, the rate of change in prices has slowed in recent years. The important lesson, however, is that even though the inflation rate is now relatively low in the

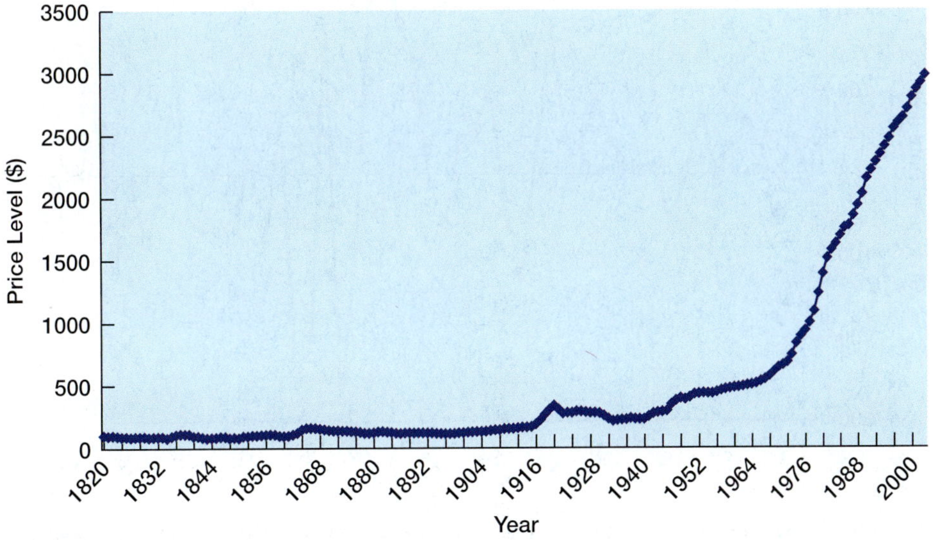

<< FIGURE 23.1

Price Levels in the United States (1820 = 100)

SOURCE: Author calculations using the U.S. BLS Consumer Price Index from Global Financial Data, Inc.

United States, the uncertainty about the future rate of inflation remains. Beyond the unexpected changes in overall price levels, there are three specific areas of particular importance to businesses in which volatility has also increased dramatically: interest rates, exchange rates, and commodity prices.

Interest Rate Volatility

We know that debt is a vital source of financing for corporations, and interest rates are a key component of a firm's cost of capital. Up until 1979, interest rates in the United States were relatively stable because the Federal Reserve actively managed rates to keep them that way. This goal has since been abandoned, and interest rate volatility has increased sharply. Figure 23.2 illustrates this increase by plotting the changes in ten-year Treasury bond rates. The increase in volatility following 1979 is readily apparent.

Before 1979, U.S. firms were able to plan for and predict their future borrowing costs with some confidence. In today's financial world, because of the increased uncertainty surrounding interest rates, this is no longer the case.

Exchange Rate Volatility

As we discuss in an earlier chapter, international operations have become increasingly important to U.S. businesses. Consequently, exchange rates and exchange rate volatility have also become increasingly important. Figure 23.3 plots percentage changes in the U.K. pound–U.S. dollar exchange rate and illustrates that exchange rate volatility has increased enormously since the early 1970s.

The reason for the increase in exchange rate volatility was the breakdown of the so-called Bretton Woods accord. Under the Bretton Woods system, exchange rates were fixed for the most part and significant changes occurred only rarely. As a result, importers and exporters could predict with relative certainty what exchange rates were likely to be in the

FIGURE 23.2 >>

Annual Changes in Ten-Year Treasury Rates: 1950–2003

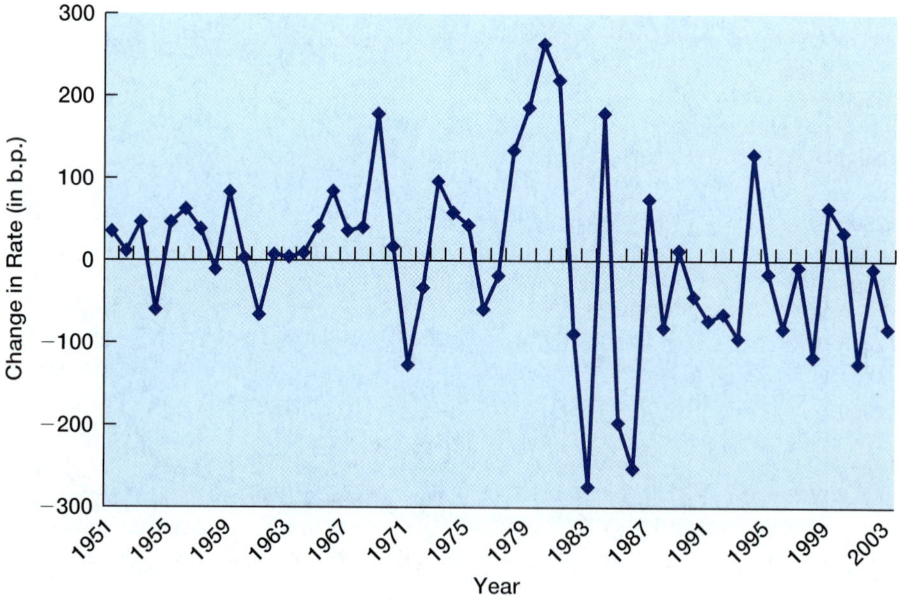

The rate changes in this figure are changes in year-end and are measured in basis points, where one basis point is 1 percent of 1 percent, that is .0001.

SOURCE: Author calculations using data from Global Financial Data, Inc.

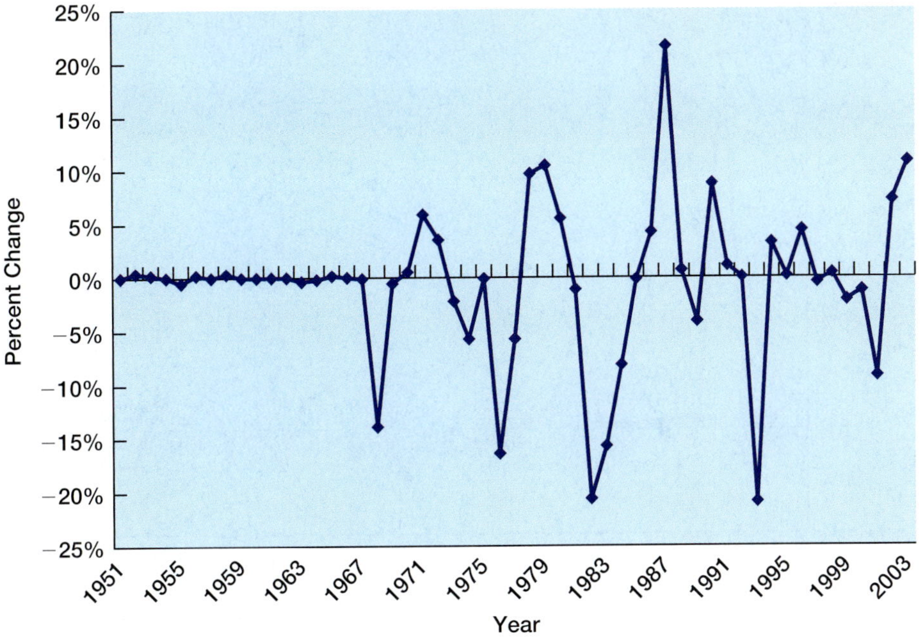

The percentage changes in this figure are based on year-end rates.

SOURCE: Author calculations using data from Global Financial Data, Inc.

<< FIGURE 23.3

Annual Percentage Changes in the U.S. Dollar–British Pound Exchange Rate: 1950–2003

future. In today's post–Bretton Woods era, exchange rates are set by market forces, and future exchange rates are very difficult to predict with precision.

Commodity Price Volatility

Commodity prices (the prices for basic goods and materials) are the third major area in which volatility has risen. Oil is one of the most important commodities, and, as Figure 23.4 shows (and recent experience confirms), oil prices can change dramatically from one year to the next (what caused the big spike in the early '70s?).

The behavior of oil prices is not unique; many other key commodities have experienced increased volatility over the past two decades.

Applied Derivatives Trading **is a Web magazine covering derivatives and risk management (www.adtrading.com).**

The Impact of Financial Risk: The U.S. Savings and Loan Industry

The best-known example of the effect of financial risk is the collapse of the once-thriving U.S. savings and loan, or S&L, industry. At one time, the S&L industry was relatively simple. S&Ls accepted short-term deposits, and they made long-term, fixed-rate home mortgage loans. Before the increases in interest rate volatility came about, short-term interest rates were almost always lower than long-term rates, so the S&Ls simply profited from the spread.

When short-term interest rates became highly volatile, they exceeded long-term rates on various occasions, sometimes by substantial amounts. Suddenly, the S&L business got very complicated. Depositors removed their funds because higher rates were available elsewhere, but home owners held on to their low-interest-rate mortgages. S&Ls were forced into borrowing over the short term at very high rates. They began taking greater risks in lending in an attempt to earn higher returns, but this frequently resulted in much higher default rates, another problem with which the S&Ls were unfamiliar.

FIGURE 23.4 >>

Annual Percentage Changes in Oil Prices: 1970–2003

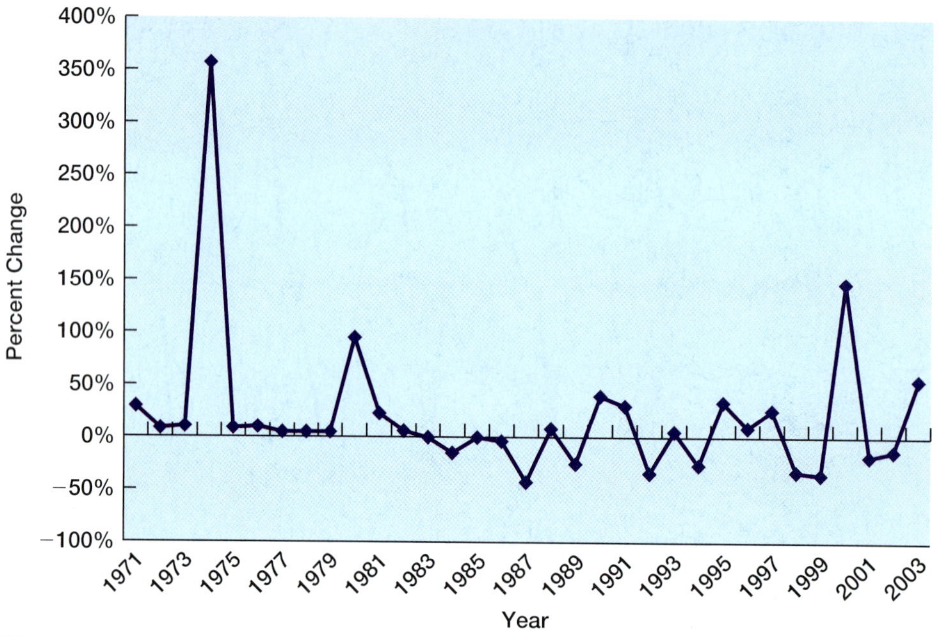

The percentage changes in this figure are based on annual prices.

SOURCE: Author calculations using data from the United States Department of Energy.

There were other economic and political factors that contributed to the astounding size of the S&L disaster, but the root cause was the increase in interest rate volatility. Today, financial institutions take specific steps to insulate themselves from interest rate volatility.

Concept Questions

23.1a What is hedging?

23.1b Why do firms place greater emphasis on hedging now than they did in the past?

23.2 MANAGING FINANCIAL RISK

We've seen that price and rate volatility have increased in recent decades. Whether or not this is a cause for concern for a particular firm depends on the nature of the firm's operations and its financing. For example, an all-equity firm would not be as concerned about interest rate fluctuations as a highly leveraged one. Similarly, a firm with little or no international activity would not be overly concerned about exchange rate fluctuations.

To effectively manage financial risk, financial managers need to identify the types of price fluctuations that have the greatest impact on the value of the firm. Sometimes these will be obvious, but sometimes they will not be. For example, consider a forest products company. If interest rates increase, then its borrowing costs will clearly rise. Beyond this, however, the demand for housing typically declines as interest rates rise. As housing demand falls, so does demand for lumber. An increase in interest rates thus leads to increased financing costs and, at the same time, decreased revenues.

IN THEIR OWN WORDS . . .

Charles W. Smithson on Who Uses What

>> **For the second** consecutive year, the Wharton School has surveyed the use of derivatives by nonfinancial U.S. corporations. In October 1995, questionnaires were sent to 1,999 randomly selected corporations and an additional 159 Fortune 500 firms. Responses were received from 350 firms (a response rate of 16 percent).

The percentage of respondents reporting derivatives use increased to 41 percent, from 35 percent in 1994. Of firms that responded to both surveys, the proportion using derivatives rose only slightly, from 37 percent to 38 percent in 1995. Derivatives use continued to be related to firm size. Only 13 percent of the 1995 respondents with a market value of less than $50 million said they used derivatives, compared with 48 percent of firms valued at $50–250 million and 59 percent of companies worth more than $250 million. The figure for the largest firms was slightly lower than in 1994 but medium-size firms have become far more likely to use derivatives. In 1994, only 30 percent of respondents in the $50–250 million bracket said they used them.

Firms that do not use derivatives were asked to rank their most important reasons for this from a list of seven. The most frequently cited was "lack of significant exposure" (65 percent put this as either their first, second, or third most important reason). The next most frequently cited reasons were "expected costs exceeded the benefits" and "concerns about the perceptions of derivatives among investors, regulators, or the public."

Of derivatives users, the vast majority employed the instruments to manage their foreign exchange and interest rate exposures (76 percent and 73 percent, respectively). Many also used derivatives to manage commodity exposures (37 percent) but only a small percentage for equity exposures (12 percent). Forward contracts were the dominant tool for foreign exchange risk management, swaps for interest rate risk management, futures for commodity price risk management, and OTC options for equity exposures.

Derivatives users were asked to rank their risk management objectives. Most put managing volatility as "most important"—in cash flows by 49 percent or in earnings (42 percent). Hedging to manage market value directly was ranked "most important" by only 8 percent and balance sheet hedging (also referred to as translation hedging) by only 1 percent.

Firms were most likely to use foreign exchange derivatives to hedge firm commitments and transactions that were anticipated to occur within a year. Anticipated transactions beyond one year were "frequently" hedged by only 11 percent of derivatives users although "sometimes" hedged by 43 percent. This suggests that many firms have a long horizon for their foreign currency risk management. Reported hedging of economic exposure decreased in 1995, with only 8 percent of derivatives users indicating they "frequently" hedged for that reason, down from 16 percent in 1994. Hedging the balance sheet (translation exposure) "frequently" was also down in 1995, falling from 22 percent in 1994 to 14 percent in 1995. The main reason firms used interest rate derivatives was to alter the interest rate sensitivity of existing debt.

To assess the influence of a firm's market view on its derivatives activity, the 1995 survey asked derivatives users to indicate how often their market view led them to take an active position or to alter the timing or size of hedges. With respect to foreign exchange risk management, only 6 percent indicated that they actively took positions on a frequent basis. For firms that "frequently" altered the size or timing of hedges based on a market view, the figures were only 12 percent and 11 percent, respectively. But, higher proportions "sometimes" altered their hedging policy, 33 percent, 48 percent, and 61 percent, respectively. The frequency with which firms altered their interest rate risk management strategy based on a market view was essentially identical.

The "train wrecks" in 1994 and 1995 brought derivatives a great deal of publicity—much of it negative. To gauge the impact of this on end-users, the survey asked respondents to indicate their degree of concern about various issues mentioned frequently in the press. The greatest source of concern was credit risk, specified by 33 percent. Users also expressed concern about evaluating the risks of derivatives transactions and uncertainty over accounting treatment. Given the concern about evaluating the risks of derivatives transactions, it is not surprising that end-users have enhanced their capacity to do this. The survey found that tools for evaluating derivatives risk, such as scenario analysis, were in widespread use.

Charles W. Smithson is the former managing director for research in the global risk management sector of Chase Manhattan Bank. He has been actively involved in the developing discipline of financial risk management. In addition to his articles in academic and professional journals, he is author of *Managing Financial Risk* and coeditor of *The Handbook of Financial Engineering* (with C. W. Smith). He is also coauthor of *Managerial Economics* (with S. C. Maurice and C. R. Thomas) and an economic perspective on commodity "crises," *The Doomsday Myth* (with S.C. Maurice). He is currently the managing partner of Rutter Associates.

The Risk Profile

The basic tool for identifying and measuring a firm's exposure to financial risk is the **risk profile**. The risk profile is a plot showing the relationship between changes in the price of some good, service, or rate and changes in the value of the firm. Constructing a risk profile is conceptually very similar to performing a sensitivity analysis (described in Chapter 11).

To illustrate, consider an agricultural products company that has a large-scale wheat-farming operation. Because wheat prices can be very volatile, we might wish to investigate the firm's exposure to wheat price fluctuations, that is, its risk profile with regard to wheat prices. To do this, we plot changes in the value of the firm (ΔV) versus unexpected changes in wheat prices (ΔP_{wheat}). Figure 23.5 shows the result.

risk profile
A plot showing how the value of the firm is affected by changes in prices or rates.

The risk profile in Figure 23.5 tells us two things. First, because the line slopes up, increases in wheat prices will increase the value of the firm. Because wheat is an output, this comes as no surprise. Second, because the line has a fairly steep slope, this firm has a significant exposure to wheat price fluctuations, and it may wish to take steps to reduce that exposure.

Reducing Risk Exposure

Erisk is an online publication dealing with risk management (www.erisk.com).

Fluctuations in the price of any particular good or service can have very different effects on different types of firms. Going back to wheat prices, we now consider the case of a food processing operation. The food processor buys large quantities of wheat and has a risk profile like that illustrated in Figure 23.6. As with the agricultural products firm, the value of this firm is sensitive to wheat prices, but, because wheat is an input, increases in wheat prices lead to decreases in firm value.

Both the agricultural products firm and the food processor are exposed to wheat price fluctuations, but any fluctuations have opposite effects for the two firms. If these two firms get together, then much of the risk can be eliminated. The grower and the processor can simply

FIGURE 23.5 >>

Risk Profile for a Wheat Grower

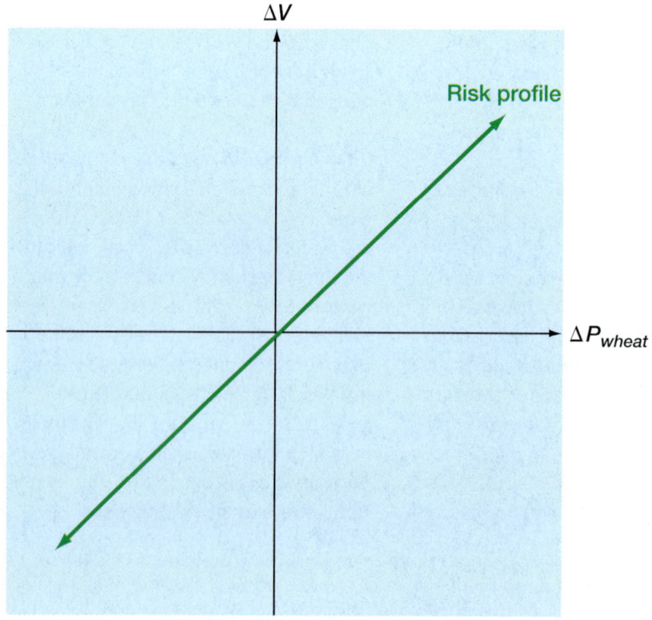

For a grower, unexpected increases in wheat prices increase the value of the firm.

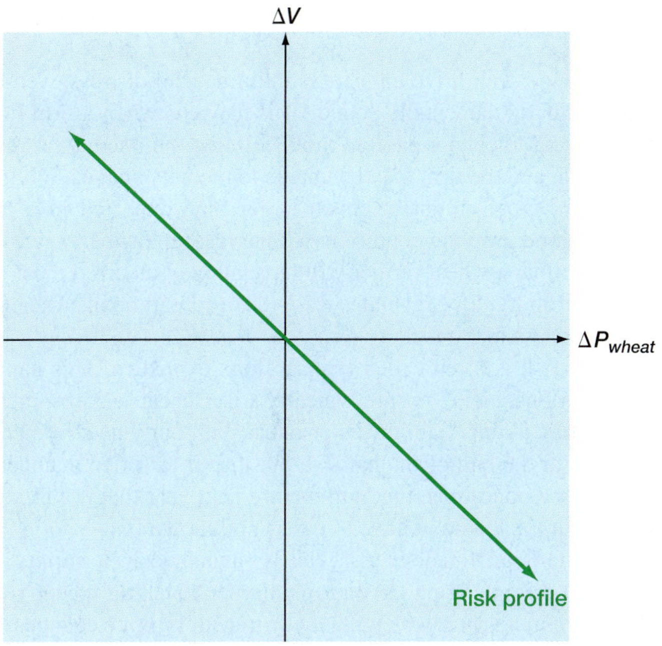

<< FIGURE 23.6

Risk Profile for a Wheat Buyer

For a buyer, unexpected increases in wheat prices decrease the value of the firm.

agree that, at set dates in the future, the grower will deliver a certain quantity of wheat, and the processor will pay a set price. Once the agreement is signed, both firms will have locked in the price of wheat for as long as the contract is in effect, and both of their risk profiles with regard to wheat prices will be completely flat during that time.

We should note that, in reality, a firm that hedges financial risk usually won't be able to create a completely flat risk profile. For example, our wheat grower doesn't actually know what the size of the crop will be ahead of time. If the crop is larger than expected, then some portion of the crop will be unhedged. If the crop is small, then the grower will have to buy more to fulfill the contract and will thereby be exposed to the risk of price changes. Either way, there is some exposure to wheat price fluctuations, but, by hedging, that exposure is sharply reduced.

There are a number of other reasons why perfect hedging is usually impossible, but this is not really a problem. With most financial risk management, the goal is to reduce the risk to more bearable levels and thereby flatten out the risk profile, not necessarily to eliminate the risk altogether.

In thinking about financial risk, there is an important distinction to be made. Price fluctuations have two components. Short-run, essentially temporary, changes are the first component. The second component has to do with more long-run, essentially permanent, changes. As we discuss next, these two types of changes have very different implications for the firm.

Hedging Short-Run Exposure

Short-run, temporary changes in prices result from unforeseen events or shocks. Some examples are sudden increases in orange juice prices because of a late Florida freeze, increases in oil prices because of political turmoil, and increases in lumber prices because available supplies are low following a hurricane. Price fluctuations of this sort are often called *transitory* changes.

Short-run price changes can drive a business into financial distress even though, in the long run, the business is fundamentally sound. This happens when a firm finds itself with sudden cost increases that it cannot pass on to its customers immediately. A negative cash flow position is created, and the firm may be unable to meet its financial obligations.

For example, wheat crops might be much larger than expected in a particular year because of unusually good growing conditions. At harvest time, wheat prices will be unexpectedly low. By that time, a wheat farmer will have already incurred most of the costs of production. If prices drop too low, revenues from the crop will be insufficient to cover the costs, and financial distress may result.

transactions exposure
Short-run financial risk arising from the need to buy or sell at uncertain prices or rates in the near future.

Short-run financial risk is often called **transactions exposure**. This name stems from the fact that short-term financial exposure typically arises because a firm must make transactions in the near future at uncertain prices or rates. With our wheat farmer, for example, the crop must be sold at the end of the harvest, but the wheat price is uncertain. Alternatively, a firm may have a bond issue that will mature next year that it will need to replace, but the interest rate that the firm will have to pay is not known.

As we will see, short-run financial risk can be managed in a variety of ways. The opportunities for short-term hedging have grown tremendously in recent years, and firms in the United States are increasingly hedging away transitory price changes.

Cash Flow Hedging: A Cautionary Note

One thing to notice is that, in our discussion thus far, we have talked conceptually about hedging the value of the firm. In our example concerning wheat prices, however, what is really hedged is the firm's near-term cash flow. In fact, at the risk of ignoring some subtleties, we will say that hedging short-term financial exposure, hedging transactions exposure, and hedging near-term cash flows amount to much the same thing.

It will usually be the case that directly hedging the value of the firm is not really feasible, and, instead, the firm will try to reduce the uncertainty of its near-term cash flows. If the firm is thereby able to avoid expensive disruptions, then cash flow hedging will act to hedge the value of the firm, but the linkage is indirect. In such cases, care must be taken to ensure that the cash flow hedging does have the desired effect.

For example, imagine a vertically integrated firm with an oil-producing division and a gasoline-retailing division. Both divisions are affected by fluctuations in oil prices. However, it may well be that the firm as a whole has very little transactions exposure because any transitory shifts in oil prices simply benefit one division and cost the other. The overall firm's risk profile with regard to oil prices is essentially flat. Put another way, the firm's net exposure is small. If one division, acting on its own, were to begin hedging its cash flows, then the firm as a whole would suddenly be exposed to financial risk. The point is that cash flow hedging should not be done in isolation. Instead, a firm needs to worry about its net exposure. As a result, any hedging activities should probably be done on a centralized, or at least cooperative, basis.

Hedging Long-Term Exposure

Price fluctuations can also be longer-run, more permanent changes. These result from fundamental shifts in the underlying economics of a business. If improvements in agricultural technology come about, for example, then wheat prices will permanently decline (in the absence of agricultural price subsidies!). If a firm is unable to adapt to the new technology, then it will not be economically viable over the long run.

A firm's exposure to long-run financial risks is often called its **economic exposure**. Because long-term exposure is rooted in fundamental economic forces, it is much more difficult, if not impossible, to hedge on a permanent basis. For example, is it possible that a wheat farmer and a food processor could permanently eliminate exposure to wheat price fluctuations by agreeing on a fixed price forever?

economic exposure
Long-term financial risk arising from permanent changes in prices or other economic fundamentals.

The answer is no, and, in fact, the effect of such an agreement might even be the opposite of the one desired. The reason is that if, over the long run, wheat prices were to change on a permanent basis, one party to this agreement would ultimately be unable to honor it. Either the buyer would be paying too much, or the seller would be receiving too little. In either case, the loser would become uncompetitive and fail. Something of the sort happened in the 1970s when public utilities and other energy consumers entered into long-run contracts with natural gas producers. Natural gas prices plummeted in later years, and a great deal of turmoil followed.

Conclusion

In the long run, either a business is economically viable or it will fail. No amount of hedging can change this simple fact. Nonetheless, by hedging over the near term, a firm gives itself time to adjust its operations and thereby adapt to new conditions without expensive disruptions. So, drawing our discussion in this section together, we can say that, by managing financial risks, the firm can accomplish two important things. The first is that the firm insulates itself from otherwise troublesome transitory price fluctuations. The second is that the firm gives itself a little breathing room to adapt to fundamental changes in market conditions.

Concept Questions

23.2a What is a risk profile? Describe the risk profiles with regard to oil prices for an oil producer and a gasoline retailer.

23.2b What can a firm accomplish by hedging financial risk?

HEDGING WITH FORWARD CONTRACTS 23.3

Forward contracts are among the oldest and most basic tools for managing financial risk. Our goal in this section is to describe forward contracts and discuss how they are used to hedge financial risk.

Forward Contracts: The Basics

A **forward contract** is a legally binding agreement between two parties calling for the sale of an asset or product in the future at a price agreed upon today. The terms of the contract call for one party to deliver the goods to the other on a certain date in the future, called the *settlement date*. The other party pays the previously agreed-upon *forward price* and takes the goods. Looking back, note that the agreement we discussed between the wheat grower and the food processor was, in fact, a forward contract.

forward contract
A legally binding agreement between two parties calling for the sale of an asset or product in the future at a price agreed upon today.

Forward contracts can be bought and sold. The *buyer* of a forward contract has the obligation to take delivery and pay for the goods; the *seller* has the obligation to make delivery and accept payment. The buyer of a forward contract benefits if prices increase because the buyer will have locked in a lower price. Similarly, the seller wins if prices fall

FIGURE 23.7 >> Payoff Profiles for a Forward Contract

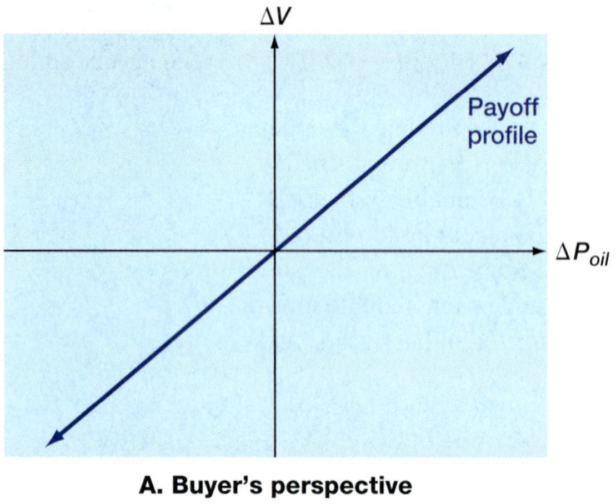

because a higher selling price has been locked in. Note that one party to a forward contract can win only at the expense of the other, so a forward contract is a zero-sum game.

The Payoff Profile

payoff profile
A plot showing the gains and losses that will occur on a contract as the result of unexpected price changes.

The **payoff profile** is the key to understanding how forward contracts and other contracts that we discuss later are used to hedge financial risks. In general, a payoff profile is a plot showing the gains and losses on a contract that result from unexpected price changes. For example, suppose we were examining a forward contract on oil. Based on our discussion, the buyer of the forward contract is obligated to accept delivery of a specified quantity of oil at a future date and pay a set price. Part A of Figure 23.7 shows the resulting payoff profile on the forward contract from the buyer's perspective.

What Figure 23.7 shows is that, as oil prices increase, the buyer of the forward contract benefits by having locked in a lower-than-market price. If oil prices decrease, then the buyer loses because that buyer ends up paying a higher-than-market price. For the seller of the forward contract, things are simply reversed. The payoff profile of the seller is illustrated in Part B of Figure 23.7.

Hedging with Forwards

To illustrate how forward contracts can be used to hedge, we consider the case of a public utility that uses oil to generate power. The prices that our utility can charge are regulated and cannot be changed rapidly. As a result, sudden increases in oil prices are a source of financial risk.[1] The utility's risk profile is illustrated in Figure 23.8.

If we compare the risk profile in Figure 23.8 to the buyer's payoff profile on a forward contract shown in Figure 23.7, we see what the utility needs to do. The payoff profile for the buyer of a forward contract on oil is exactly the opposite of the utility's risk profile with respect to oil. If the utility buys a forward contract, its exposure to unexpected changes in oil prices will be eliminated. This result is shown in Figure 23.9.

Our public utility example illustrates the fundamental approach to managing financial risk. We first identify the firm's exposure to financial risk using a risk profile. We then try

[1]Actually, many utilities are allowed to automatically pass on oil price increases

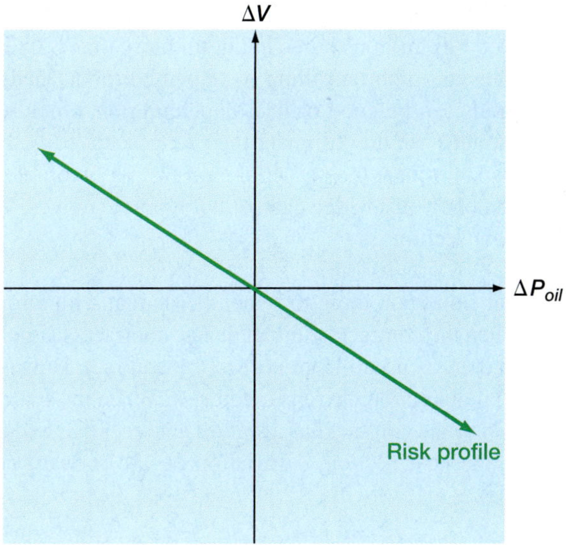

<< FIGURE 23.8

Risk Profile for an Oil Buyer

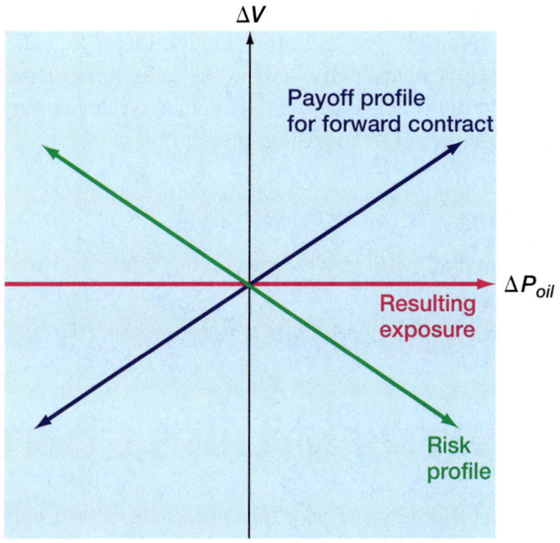

<< FIGURE 23.9

Hedging with Forward Contracts

to find a financial arrangement, such as a forward contract, that has an offsetting payoff profile.

A Caveat Figure 23.9 shows that the utility's net exposure to oil price fluctuations is zero. If oil prices rise, then the gains on the forward contract will offset the damage from increased costs. However, if oil prices decline, the benefit from lower costs will be offset by losses on the forward contract.

For example, in January of 2000, America Online (AOL) announced that it would buy Time Warner, forming the company then known as AOL Time Warner. Following the announcement, stock in Time Warner soared to more than $90 per share. Time Warner Vice Chairman (and well-known media mogul) Ted Turner had previously entered into a hedging arrangement under which he locked in a maximum possible price of $30 per share on

4 million shares of stock he owned. As a result, he missed out on $240 million in gains—good thing he owned over 100 million shares in all, up more than $2.8 billion on the day!

This example illustrates an important thing to remember about hedging with forward contracts. Price fluctuations can be good or bad, depending on which way they go. If we hedge with forward contracts, we do eliminate the risk associated with an adverse price change. However, we also eliminate the potential gain from a favorable move. You might wonder if we couldn't somehow just hedge against unfavorable moves. We can, and we describe how in a subsequent section.

Credit Risk Another important thing to remember is that with a forward contract, no money changes hands when the contract is initiated. The contract is simply an agreement to transact in the future, so there is no up-front cost to the contract. However, because a forward contract is a financial obligation, there is credit risk. When the settlement date arrives, the party on the losing end of the contract has a significant incentive to default on the agreement. As we discuss in the next section, a variation on the forward contract exists that greatly diminishes this risk.

Forward Contracts in Practice Where are forward contracts commonly used to hedge? Because exchange rate fluctuations can have disastrous consequences for firms that have significant import or export operations, forward contracts are routinely used by such firms to hedge exchange rate risk. For example, Jaguar, the U.K. auto manufacturer (and subsidiary of Ford Motor Co.), historically hedged the U.S. dollar–British pound exchange rate for six months into the future. (The subject of exchange rate hedging with forward contracts is discussed in greater detail in an earlier chapter.)

Concept Questions

23.3a What is a forward contract? Describe the payoff profiles for the buyer and the seller of a forward contract.

23.3b Explain how a firm can alter its risk profile using forward contracts.

23.4 HEDGING WITH FUTURES CONTRACTS

futures contract
A forward contract with the feature that gains and losses are realized each day rather than only on the settlement date.

A **futures contract** is exactly the same as a forward contract with one exception. With a forward contract, the buyer and seller realize gains or losses only on the settlement date. With a futures contract, gains and losses are realized on a daily basis. If we buy a futures contract on oil, then, if oil prices rise today, we have a profit and the seller of the contract has a loss. The seller pays up, and we start again tomorrow with neither party owing the other.

The daily resettlement feature found in futures contracts is called *marking-to-market.* As we mentioned earlier, there is a significant risk of default with forward contracts. With daily marking-to-market, this risk is greatly reduced. This is probably why organized trading is much more common in futures contracts than in forward contracts (outside of international trade).

Trading in Futures

In the United States and elsewhere around the world, futures contracts for a remarkable variety of items are routinely bought and sold. The types of contracts available are traditionally divided into two groups, commodity futures and financial futures. With a financial future, the underlying goods are financial assets such as stocks, bonds, or currencies. With a commodity future, the underlying goods can be just about anything other than a financial asset.

There are commodity futures contracts on a wide variety of agricultural products such as corn, orange juice, and, yes, pork bellies. There is even a contract on fertilizer. There are commodity contracts on precious metals such as gold and silver, and there are contracts on basic goods such as copper and lumber. There are contracts on various petroleum products such as crude oil, heating oil, and gasoline. Wherever there is price volatility, there may be a demand for a futures contract, and new futures contracts are introduced on a fairly regular basis.

Futures Exchanges

There are a number of futures exchanges in the United States and elsewhere, and more are being established. The Chicago Board of Trade (CBT) is among the largest. Other notable exchanges include the Chicago Mercantile Exchange (CME), the London International Financial Futures and Options Exchange (LIFFE), and the New York Mercantile Exchange (NYM).

Surf over to these home pages at www.cbot.com, www.cme.com, and www.liffe.com. All of these Web sites provide a great deal of information about the services and financial products found on the respective exchanges.

Table 23.1 gives a partial *Wall Street Journal* listing for selected futures contracts. Taking a look at the corn contracts in the left portion of the table, note that the contracts trade on the CBT, one contract calls for the delivery of 5,000 bushels of corn, and prices are quoted in cents per bushel. The months in which the contracts mature are given in the first column.

For the corn contract with a July maturity, the first number in the row is the opening price (250.25 cents per bushel), the next number is the high price for the day (252), and the following number is the low price for the day (248.50). The *settlement price* is the fourth number (249.50), and it is essentially the closing price for the day. For purposes of marking-to-market, this is the figure used. The change listed next, is the movement in the settlement price since the previous trading session (. . . means no change). The highest price (342) and lowest price (227.75) over the life of the contract are shown next. Finally, the *open interest* (7,552), the number of contracts outstanding at the end of the day, is shown. At the end of a section, the volume of trading in all maturities is shown for that day (78,872) and the previous day (112,232), along with the total open interest for all maturities (547,475) and the change in the total open interest (−8,967).

To get some real-world experience at very low cost, visit the fascinating futures exchange at the University of Iowa: www.biz.uiowa.edu/iem.

To see how large futures trading can be, we take a look at the CBT Treasury bond contracts (under the interest rate heading). One contract is for long-term Treasury bonds with a face, or par, value of $100,000. The total open interest for all months is about 500,000 contracts. The total face value outstanding is therefore $500 billion for this one type of contract!

Hedging with Futures

Hedging with futures contracts is conceptually identical to hedging with forward contracts, and the payoff profile on a futures contract is drawn just like the profile for a forward contract. The only difference in hedging with futures is that the firm will have to maintain an account with a broker so that gains and losses can be credited or debited each day as a part of the marking-to-market process.

Even though there is a large variety of futures contracts, it is unlikely that a particular firm will be able to find the precise hedging instrument it needs. For example, we might produce a particular grade or variety of oil, and find that no contract exists for exactly that grade. However, all oil prices tend to move together, so we could hedge our output using futures contracts on other grades of oil. For example, as we mentioned to open the chapter,

TABLE 23.1 >>

Sample *Wall Street Journal* Futures Price Quotations

FUTURES

Exchange Abbreviations

For commodity futures and futures options

CBT-Chicago Board of Trade
CME-Chicago Mercantile Exchange
CMX-COMEX (Div. of New York Mercantile Exchange)
EUREX-European Exchange
FINEX-Financial Exchange (Div. of New York Board of Trade)
IPE-International Petroleum Exchange
KC-Kansas City Board of Trade
LIFFE-London International Financial Futures Exchange
MATIF-Marche a Terme International de France
ME-Montreal Exchange
MPLS-Minneapolis Grain Exchange
NQLX-NQLX (unit of Euronext.liffe)
NYBOT-New York Board of Trade
NYFE-New York Futures Exchange (Sub. of New York Board of Trade)
NYM-New York Mercantile Exchange
ONE-OneChicago
SFE-Sydney Futures Exchange
SGX-Singapore Exchange Ltd.

Futures prices reflect day and overnight trading
Open interest reflects previous day's trading

Wednesday, July 7, 2004

Grain and Oilseed Futures

Corn (CBT)-5,000 bu.; cents per bu.

	OPEN	HIGH	LOW	SETTLE	CHG	LIFETIME HIGH	LIFETIME LOW	OPEN INT
July	250.25	252.00	248.50	249.50	...	342.00	227.75	7,552
Sept	254.00	256.50	252.50	253.75	-.25	341.00	229.75	167,492
Dec	258.75	261.75	257.50	258.50	...	341.50	232.50	296,072
Mr05	265.50	269.00	264.75	266.00	...	342.00	239.00	40,371
May	271.50	274.25	270.50	271.50	...	344.00	243.50	12,853
Dec	266.00	266.00	262.00	264.50	1.25	288.50	235.00	9,803

Est vol 78,872; vol Tue 112,232; open int 547,475, -8,967.

Oats (CBT)-5,000 bu.; cents per bu.

	OPEN	HIGH	LOW	SETTLE	CHG	LIFETIME HIGH	LIFETIME LOW	OPEN INT
Sept	139.00	140.50	137.25	137.25	-1.25	190.00	134.00	3,373
Dec	146.00	148.00	143.50	144.00	-1.50	193.00	141.00	6,758

Est vol 988; vol Tue 1,158; open int 10,498, -153.

Soybeans (CBT)-5,000 bu.; cents per bu.

	OPEN	HIGH	LOW	SETTLE	CHG	LIFETIME HIGH	LIFETIME LOW	OPEN INT
July	980.00	1035.00	955.00	961.50	-18.00	1064.00	520.00	8,880
Aug	820.25	869.50	818.00	821.50	2.00	1026.00	521.00	44,898
Sept	683.50	725.00	678.25	685.50	1.50	904.50	528.00	11,761
Nov	651.00	685.00	646.00	660.50	8.50	802.00	483.00	88,090
Ja05	654.50	687.00	651.00	663.00	9.50	800.00	573.00	4,749
Mar	657.00	685.00	657.00	664.50	7.50	787.00	570.00	3,879
May	653.00	681.00	653.00	660.00	9.00	775.00	642.00	3,928

Est vol 95,795; vol Tue 75,179; open int 168,379, -4,918.

Food and Fiber Futures

Lumber (CME)-110,000 bd. ft., $ per 1,000 bd. ft.

	OPEN	HIGH	LOW	SETTLE	CHG	LIFETIME HIGH	LIFETIME LOW	OPEN INT
July	385.00	385.00	381.80	384.20	.40	429.50	282.00	1,320
Sept	370.00	370.00	365.00	368.00	1.70	398.00	309.90	2,486
Nov	339.30	341.70	338.40	341.20	2.90	364.50	318.80	594

Est vol 827; vol Tue 1,001; open int 4,522, -81.

Milk (CME)-200,000 lbs., cents per lb.

	OPEN	HIGH	LOW	SETTLE	CHG	LIFETIME HIGH	LIFETIME LOW	OPEN INT
July	14.75	14.85	14.73	14.82	...	17.75	11.60	5,983
Aug	13.65	13.80	13.65	13.75	.07	17.50	11.65	5,218
Sept	13.90	14.30	13.90	14.25	.30	16.90	12.10	5,031
Oct	13.55	13.70	13.55	13.61	.11	15.50	11.89	3,114
Nov	12.90	13.05	12.90	13.05	.15	14.05	11.39	2,037
Ja05	12.34	12.35	12.34	12.35	.01	12.44	11.50	558
Feb	12.26	12.31	12.21	12.31	.03	12.35	11.50	510
Mar	12.28	12.32	12.25	12.32	.02	12.35	11.50	349

Est vol 698; vol Tue 546; open int 25,703, -5,394.

Cocoa (NYBOT)-10 metric tons; $ per ton.

	OPEN	HIGH	LOW	SETTLE	CHG	LIFETIME HIGH	LIFETIME LOW	OPEN INT
July	...	...	...	1,414	76	2,307	1,299	229
Sept	1,345	1,425	1,345	1,419	81	2,402	1,298	47,334
Dec	1,365	1,435	1,365	1,433	80	2,065	1,315	17,175
Mr05	1,388	1,455	1,388	1,451	77	1,810	1,340	10,262
Sept	1,430	1,430	1,430	1,494	76	1,580	1,385	4,802

Est vol 22,622; vol Tue 9,057; open int 106,874, +1,530.

Silver (CMX)-5,000 troy oz.; cnts per troy oz.

	OPEN	HIGH	LOW	SETTLE	CHG	LIFETIME HIGH	LIFETIME LOW	OPEN INT
July	598.0	614.0	598.0	611.0	14.6	849.0	436.0	1,448
Sept	598.5	616.0	598.5	612.5	14.5	830.0	477.0	49,307
Dec	602.0	620.0	602.0	615.6	14.5	848.0	440.0	19,346
Mr05	613.0	620.0	613.0	618.7	14.5	828.0	485.0	4,904
Dc06	653.0	653.0	653.0	640.5	14.5	840.0	469.0	1,204

Est vol 10,000; vol Tue 11,090; open int 82,761, -269.

Petroleum Futures

Crude Oil, Light Sweet (NYM)-1,000 bbls.; $ per bbl.

	OPEN	HIGH	LOW	SETTLE	CHG	LIFETIME HIGH	LIFETIME LOW	OPEN INT
Aug	39.58	39.84	38.75	39.08	-0.57	42.30	20.84	174,308
Sept	39.64	39.90	38.85	39.20	-0.52	41.85	20.82	116,659
Oct	39.38	39.56	38.55	38.89	-0.57	41.24	23.75	48,460
Nov	39.05	39.25	38.45	38.59	-0.59	40.62	24.75	29,682
Dec	38.69	38.91	38.00	38.27	-0.59	40.07	16.35	60,114
Ja05	38.05	38.05	37.77	37.85	-0.56	39.45	23.25	23,914
Feb	37.55	37.55	37.30	37.45	-0.54	38.87	23.85	13,581
Mar	37.59	37.59	37.00	37.11	-0.52	38.21	23.05	12,305
Apr	36.80	36.90	36.80	36.77	-0.50	37.60	23.25	10,684
June	36.22	36.60	36.00	36.15	-0.48	36.85	22.40	20,991
Nov	34.95	34.95	34.95	35.09	-0.40	35.40	26.00	3,185
Dec	34.90	35.15	34.75	34.90	-0.39	35.30	17.00	46,118
Dc06	33.50	33.50	33.10	33.11	-0.30	33.50	19.10	32,600
Dc07	31.65	31.90	31.65	31.66	-0.25	31.90	19.50	13,302
Dc08	30.90	31.00	30.90	30.66	-0.25	31.00	19.75	11,955
Dc09	30.20	30.20	30.20	29.91	-0.25	30.20	22.50	10,982
Dc10	29.80	29.85	29.80	29.55	-0.25	29.85	27.15	15,887

Est vol 186,476; vol Tue 175,477; open int 699,223, +5,574.

Heating Oil No. 2 (NYM)-42,000 gal.; $ per gal.

	OPEN	HIGH	LOW	SETTLE	CHG	LIFETIME HIGH	LIFETIME LOW	OPEN INT
Aug	1.0905	1.0970	1.0620	1.0791	-.0140	1.1060	.6455	64,701
Sept	1.0981	1.1031	1.0710	1.0867	-.0150	1.1130	.6585	23,079
Oct	1.1041	1.1082	1.0870	1.0937	-.0135	1.1150	.6655	14,910
Nov	1.1096	1.1145	1.0875	1.0997	-.0125	1.1180	.6820	11,026
Dec	1.1116	1.1140	1.0900	1.1042	-.0115	1.1230	.6937	23,009
Ja05	1.1125	1.1125	1.0960	1.1062	-.0105	1.1260	.7160	10,302
Feb	1.0950	1.0950	1.0870	1.0902	-.0090	1.1100	.7140	10,071
Mar	1.0600	1.0670	1.0580	1.0612	-.0060	1.0800	.7033	9,260
Apr	1.0225	1.0225	1.0150	1.0202	-.0045	1.0400	.7025	1,901
May	.9845	.9845	.9750	.9817	-.0030	.9880	.7015	1,794
June	.9505	.9585	.9500	.9567	-.0020	.9610	.7050	3,869

Est vol 41,751; vol Tue 30,287; open int 187,760, -436.

Gasoline-NY Unleaded (NYM)-42,000 gal.; $ per gal.

	OPEN	HIGH	LOW	SETTLE	CHG	LIFETIME HIGH	LIFETIME LOW	OPEN INT
Aug	1.2680	1.2780	1.2530	1.2735	.0014	1.3200	.8400	61,649
Sept	1.2371	1.2480	1.2265	1.2456	.0030	1.2550	.8530	25,379
Oct	1.1671	1.1750	1.1575	1.1746	.0015	1.1765	.8300	9,767
Nov	1.1221	1.1290	1.1210	1.1306	-.0005	1.1350	.8300	5,875
Dec	1.0940	1.1000	1.0910	1.1006	-.0015	1.1050	.7990	11,905
Ja05	1.0820	1.0840	1.0740	1.0916	-.0005	1.0967	.8070	2,670
Feb	1.0905	1.0905	1.0905	1.0911	.0005	1.0905	.8450	3,491
May	1.1510	1.1510	1.1510	1.1541	.0005	1.1510	1.0800	6,318

Est vol 44,201; vol Tue 37,066; open int 137,738, +3,216.

Interest Rate Futures

Treasury Bonds (CBT)-$100,000; pts 32nds of 100%

	OPEN	HIGH	LOW	SETTLE	CHG	LIFETIME HIGH	LIFETIME LOW	OPEN INT
Sept	107-27	108-01	107-20	107-27	1	114-30	101-24	482,663
Dec	106-23	106-25	106-15	106-21	1	113-07	100-24	16,958

Est vol 126,645; vol Tue 171,830; open int 499,822, -22,592.

Currency Futures

Japanese Yen (CME)-¥12,500,000; $ per ¥

	OPEN	HIGH	LOW	SETTLE	CHG	LIFETIME HIGH	LIFETIME LOW	OPEN INT
Sept	.9160	.9270	.9156	.9246	.0082	.9705	.8575	87,216
Dec	.9244	.9303	.9208	.9293	.0082	.9740	.8800	12,290

Est vol 20,286; vol Tue 19,935; open int 99,512, -1,919.

Canadian Dollar (CME)-CAD 100,000; $ per CAD

	OPEN	HIGH	LOW	SETTLE	CHG	LIFETIME HIGH	LIFETIME LOW	OPEN INT
Sept	.7527	.7580	.7523	.7555	.0018	.7815	.6505	56,562
Dec	.7554	.7572	.7528	.7551	.0018	.7800	.6940	4,528
Mr05	.7550	.7560	.7539	.7547	.0018	.7775	.7150	669
June	.7570	.7570	.7530	.7543	.0018	.7760	.7150	201

Est vol 13,256; vol Tue 15,642; open int 62,007, +1,659.

airlines hedge jet fuel costs using heating oil contracts. Using a contract on a related, but not identical, asset as a means of hedging is called **cross-hedging**.

cross-hedging
Hedging an asset with contracts written on a closely related, but not identical, asset.

When a firm does cross-hedge, it does not actually want to buy or sell the underlying asset. This presents no problem because the firm can reverse its futures position at some point before maturity. This simply means that if the firm sells a futures contract to hedge something, it will buy the same contract at a later date, thereby eliminating its futures position. In fact, futures contracts are very rarely held to maturity by anyone (despite horror stories of individuals waking up to find mountains of soybeans in their front yards), and, as a result, actual physical delivery very rarely takes place.

A related issue has to do with contract maturity. A firm might wish to hedge over a relatively long period of time, but the available contracts might have shorter maturities. A firm could therefore decide to roll over short-term contracts, but this entails some risks. For example, Metallgesellschaft AG, a German firm, nearly went bankrupt in 1993 after losing more than $1 billion in the oil markets, mainly through derivatives. The trouble began in 1992 when MG Corp., a U.S. subsidiary, began marketing gasoline, heating oil, and diesel fuel. It entered into contracts to supply products for fixed prices for up to 10 years. Thus, if the price of oil rose, the firm stood to lose money. MG protected itself by, among other things, buying short-term oil futures that fluctuated with near-term energy prices. Under these contracts, if the price of oil rose, the derivatives gained in value. Unfortunately for MG, oil prices dropped, and the firm incurred huge losses on its short-term derivatives positions without an immediate, offsetting benefit on its long-term contracts. Thus, its primary problem was that it was hedging a long-term contract with short-term contracts, a less-than-ideal approach.

For information on the regulation of futures contracts, go to the Commodity Futures Trading Commission at www.cftc.gov.

Concept Questions

23.4a What is a futures contract? How does it differ from a forward contract?

23.4b What is cross-hedging? Why is it important?

HEDGING WITH SWAP CONTRACTS **23.5**

As the name suggests, a **swap contract** is an agreement by two parties to exchange, or swap, specified cash flows at specified intervals. Swaps are a recent innovation; they were first introduced to the public in 1981 when IBM and the World Bank entered into a swap agreement. The market for swaps has grown tremendously since that time.

swap contract
An agreement by two parties to exchange, or swap, specified cash flows at specified intervals in the future.

A swap contract is really just a portfolio, or series, of forward contracts. Recall that with a forward contract, one party promises to exchange an asset (e.g., bushels of wheat) for another asset (cash) on a specific future date. With a swap, the only difference is that there are multiple exchanges instead of just one. In principle, a swap contract could be tailored to exchange just about anything. In practice, most swap contracts fall into one of three basic categories: currency swaps, interest rate swaps, and commodity swaps. Other types will surely develop, but we will concentrate on just these three.

Currency Swaps

With a *currency swap,* two companies agree to exchange a specific amount of one currency for a specific amount of another at specific dates in the future. For example, suppose a U.S. firm has a German subsidiary and wishes to obtain debt financing for an expansion of the subsidiary's operations. Because most of the subsidiary's cash flows are in euros, the company would like the subsidiary to borrow and make payments in euros, thereby hedging against changes in the euro-dollar exchange rate. Unfortunately, the company has good access to U.S. debt markets, but not to German debt markets.

A great place to get information about swaps is the International Swaps and Derivatives Association Web site at www.isda.org.

At the same time, a German firm would like to obtain U.S. dollar financing. It can borrow cheaply in euros, but not in dollars. Both firms face a similar problem. They can borrow at favorable rates, but not in the desired currency. A currency swap is a solution. These two firms simply agree to exchange dollars for euros at a fixed rate at specific future dates (the payment dates on the loans). Each firm thus obtains the best possible rate and then arranges to eliminate exposure to exchange rate changes by agreeing to exchange currencies, a neat solution.

Interest Rate Swaps

Imagine a firm that wishes to obtain a fixed-rate loan, but can only get a good deal on a floating-rate loan, that is, a loan for which the payments are adjusted periodically to reflect changes in interest rates. Another firm can obtain a fixed-rate loan, but wishes to obtain the lowest possible interest rate and is therefore willing to take a floating-rate loan. (Rates on floating-rate loans are generally lower than rates on fixed-rate loans; why?) Both firms could accomplish their objectives by agreeing to exchange loan payments; in other words, the two firms would make each other's loan payments. This is an example of an *interest rate swap;* what is really being exchanged is a floating interest rate for a fixed one.

Interest rate swaps and currency swaps are often combined. One firm obtains floating-rate financing in a particular currency and swaps it for fixed-rate financing in another currency. Also, note that payments on floating-rate loans are always based on some index, such as the one-year Treasury rate. An interest rate swap might involve exchanging one floating-rate loan for another as a way of changing the underlying index.

Commodity Swaps

As the name suggests, a *commodity swap* is an agreement to exchange a fixed quantity of a commodity at fixed times in the future. For example, as we mentioned to open the chapter, airlines hedge fuel costs using jet fuel swaps. Commodity swaps are the newest type of swap, and the market for them is small relative to that for other types. The potential for growth is enormous, however.

Swap contracts for oil have been engineered. For example, say that an oil user has a need for 20,000 barrels every quarter. The oil user could enter into a swap contract with an oil producer to supply the needed oil. What price would they agree on? As we mentioned previously, they can't fix a price forever. Instead, they could agree that the price would be equal to the *average* daily oil price from the previous 90 days. As a result of their using an average price, the impact of the relatively large daily price fluctuations in the oil market would be reduced, and both firms would benefit from a reduction in transactions exposure.

The Swap Dealer

Unlike futures contracts, swap contracts are not traded on organized exchanges. The main reason is that they are not sufficiently standardized. Instead, the *swap dealer* plays a key role in the swaps market. In the absence of a swap dealer, a firm that wished to enter into a swap would have to track down another firm that wanted the opposite end of the deal. This search would probably be expensive and time-consuming.

Instead, a firm wishing to enter into a swap agreement contacts a swap dealer, and the swap dealer takes the other side of the agreement. The swap dealer will then try to find an offsetting transaction with some other party or parties (perhaps another firm or another dealer). Failing this, a swap dealer will hedge its exposure using futures contracts.

Commercial banks are the dominant swap dealers in the United States. As a large swap dealer, a bank would be involved in a variety of contracts. It would be swapping fixed-rate loans for floating-rate loans with some parties and doing just the opposite with other participants. The total collection of contracts in which a dealer is involved is called the swap *book*. The dealer will try to keep a balanced book to limit its net exposure. A balanced book is often called a *matched* book.

Interest Rate Swaps: An Example

To get a better understanding of swap contracts and the role of the swap dealer, we consider a floating-for-fixed interest rate swap. Suppose Company A can borrow at a floating rate equal to prime plus 1 percent or at a fixed rate of 10 percent. Company B can borrow at a floating rate of prime plus 2 percent or at a fixed rate of 9.5 percent. Company A desires a fixed-rate loan, whereas Company B desires a floating-rate loan. Clearly, a swap is in order.

Company A contacts a swap dealer, and a deal is struck. Company A borrows the money at a rate of prime plus 1 percent. The swap dealer agrees to cover the loan payments, and, in exchange, the company agrees to make fixed-rate payments to the swap dealer at a rate of, say, 9.75 percent. Notice that the swap dealer is making floating-rate payments and receiving fixed-rate payments. The company is making fixed-rate payments, so it has swapped a floating payment for a fixed one.

Company B also contacts a swap dealer. The deal here calls for Company B to borrow the money at a fixed rate of 9.5 percent. The swap dealer agrees to cover the fixed loan payments, and the company agrees to make floating-rate payments to the swap dealer at a rate of prime plus, say, 1.5 percent. In this second arrangement, the swap dealer is making fixed-rate payments and receiving floating-rate payments.

What's the net effect of these machinations? First, Company A gets a fixed-rate loan at a rate of 9.75 percent, which is cheaper than the 10 percent rate it can obtain on its own. Second, Company B gets a floating-rate loan at prime plus 1.5 instead of prime plus 2. The swap benefits both companies.

The swap dealer also wins. When all the dust settles, the swap dealer receives (from Company A) fixed-rate payments at a rate of 9.75 percent and makes fixed-rate payments (for Company B) at a rate of 9.5 percent. At the same time, it makes floating-rate payments (for Company A) at a rate of prime plus 1 percent and receives floating-rate payments at a rate of prime plus 1.5 percent (from Company B). Notice that the swap dealer's book is perfectly balanced, in terms of risk, and it has no exposure to interest rate volatility.

Figure 23.10 illustrates the transactions in our interest rate swap. Notice that the essence of the swap transactions is that one company swaps a fixed payment for a floating payment, while the other exchanges a floating payment for a fixed one. The swap dealer acts as an intermediary and profits from the spread between the rates it charges and the rates it receives.

Concept Questions

23.5a What is a swap contract? Describe three types.

23.5b Describe the role of the swap dealer.

23.5c Explain the cash flows in Figure 23.10.

FIGURE 23.10 >>

Illustration of an Interest Rate Swap

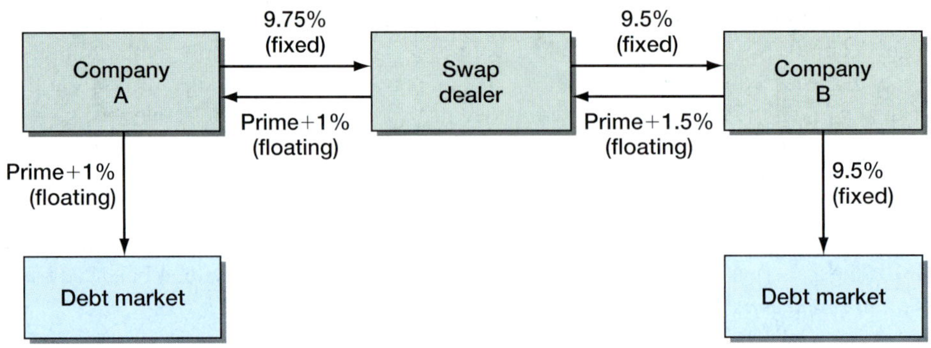

Company A borrows at prime plus 1% and swaps for a 9.75% fixed rate. Company B borrows at 9.5% fixed and swaps for a prime plus 1.5% floating rate.

23.6 HEDGING WITH OPTION CONTRACTS

The contracts we have discussed thus far—forwards, futures, and swaps—are conceptually similar. In each case, two parties agree to transact on a future date or dates. The key is that both parties are obligated to complete the transaction.

In contrast, an **option contract** is an agreement that gives the owner the right, but not the obligation, to buy or sell (depending on the option type) some asset at a specified price for a specified time. Options are covered in detail elsewhere in our book. Here we will only quickly discuss some option basics and then focus on using options to hedge volatility in commodity prices, interest rates, and exchange rates. In doing so, we will sidestep a wealth of detail concerning option terminology, option trading strategies, and option valuation.

option contract
An agreement that gives the owner the right, but not the obligation, to buy or sell a specific asset at a specific price for a set period of time.

Option Terminology

Recall that options come in two flavors, puts and calls. The owner of a **call option** has the right, but not the obligation, to *buy* an underlying asset at a fixed price, called the *strike price* or *exercise price,* for a specified time. The owner of a **put option** has the right, but not the obligation, to sell an underlying asset at a fixed price for a specified time.

call option
An option that gives the owner the right, but not the obligation, to buy an asset.

put option
An option that gives the owner the right, but not the obligation, to sell an asset.

The act of buying or selling the underlying asset using the option contract is called *exercising* the option. Some options ("American" options) can be exercised anytime up to and including the *expiration date* (the last day); other options ("European" options) can be exercised only on the expiration date. Most options are American.

Because the buyer of a call option has the right to buy the underlying asset by paying the strike price, the seller of a call option is obligated to deliver the asset and accept the strike price if the option is exercised. Similarly, the buyer of the put option has the right to sell the underlying asset and receive the strike price. In this case, the seller of the put option must accept the asset and pay the strike price.

Options versus Forwards

The Chicago Board Options Exchange (CBOE) is the world's largest options exchange. Make a virtual visit at www.cboe.com.

There are two key differences between an option contract and a forward contract. The first is obvious. With a forward contract, both parties are obligated to transact; one party delivers the asset, and the other party pays for it. With an option, the transaction occurs only if the owner of the option chooses to exercise it.

The second difference between an option and a forward contract is that, whereas no money changes hands when a forward contract is created, the buyer of an option contract gains a valuable right and must pay the seller for that right. The price of the option is frequently called the *option premium.*

Option Payoff Profiles

Figure 23.11 shows the general payoff profile for a call option from the owner's viewpoint. The horizontal axis shows the difference between the asset's value and the strike price on the option. As illustrated, if the price of the underlying asset rises above the strike price, then the owner of the option will exercise the option and enjoy a profit. If the value of the asset falls below the strike price, the owner of the option will not exercise it. Notice that this payoff profile does not consider the premium that the buyer paid for the option.

A good introduction to the options markets is available at www.optionscentral.com.

The payoff profile that results from buying a call is repeated in Part A of Figure 23.12. Part B shows the payoff profile on a call option from the seller's side. A call option is a zero-sum game, so the seller's payoff profile is exactly the opposite of the buyer's.

Part C of Figure 23.12 shows the payoff profile for the buyer of a put option. In this case, if the asset's value falls below the strike price, then the buyer profits because the seller of the put must pay the strike price. Part D shows that the seller of the put option loses out when the price falls below the strike price.

Option Hedging

Suppose a firm has a risk profile that looks like the one in Part A of Figure 23.13. If the firm wishes to hedge against adverse price movements using options, what should it do? Examining the different payoff profiles in Figure 23.12, we see that the one that has the desirable shape is C, buying a put. If the firm buys a put, then its net exposure is as illustrated in Part B of Figure 23.13.

In this case, by buying a put option, the firm has eliminated the downside risk, that is, the risk of an adverse price movement. However, the firm has retained the upside potential. In other words, the put option acts as a kind of insurance policy. Remember that this desirable insurance is not free; the firm pays for it when it buys the put option.

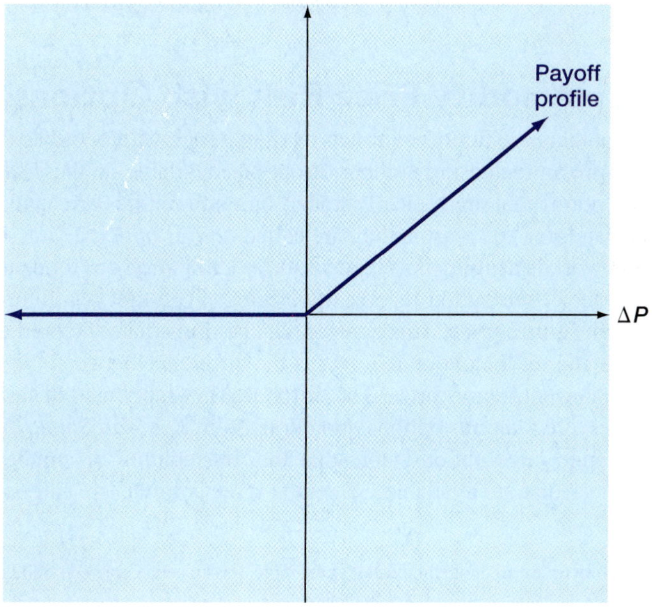

<< FIGURE 23.11

Call Option Payoff Profile for an Option Buyer

FIGURE 23.12 >> Option Payoff Profiles

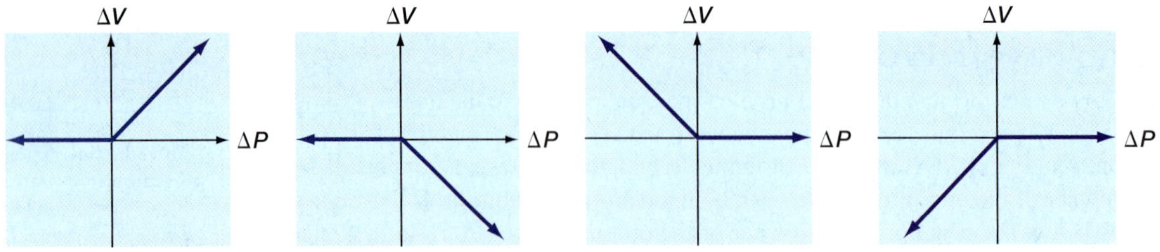

A. Buying a call **B. Selling a call** **C. Buying a put** **D. Selling a put**

FIGURE 23.13 >> Hedging with Options

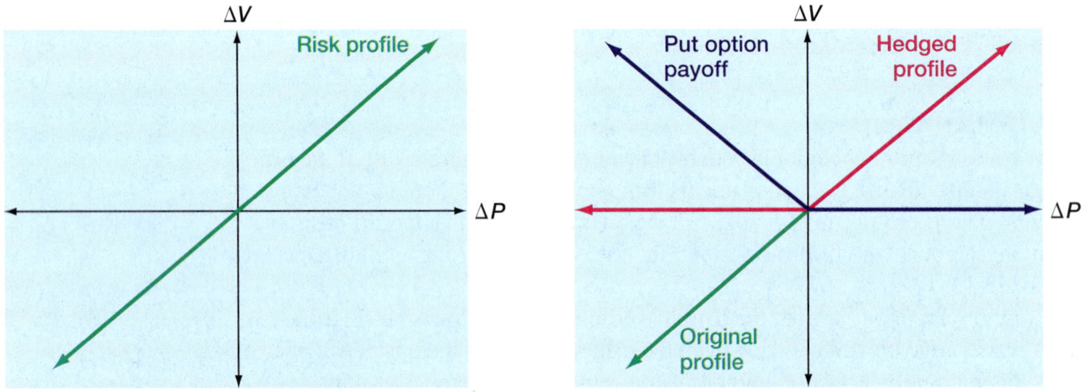

A. The unhedged risk profile

B. The hedged risk profile

The hedged profile is created by purchasing a put option, thereby eliminating the downside risk.

Hedging Commodity Price Risk with Options

We saw earlier that there are futures contracts available for a variety of basic commodities. In addition, there are an increasing number of options available on these same commodities. In fact, the options that are typically traded on commodities are actually options on futures contracts, and, for this reason, they are called *futures options.*

The Derivatives 'Zine at www.margrabe.com covers risk management.

The way these work is as follows: When a futures call option on, for example, wheat is exercised, the owner of the option receives two things. The first is a futures contract on wheat at the current futures price. This contract can be immediately closed at no cost. The second thing the owner of the option receives is the difference between the strike price on the option and the current futures price. The difference is simply paid in cash.

Information on commodity futures and options can be found at www.futuresbasics.com.

Table 23.2 gives a few futures options quotations from *The Wall Street Journal.* Briefly, looking at the orange juice options, note that the first column of numbers tells us the different strike prices that are available.[2] The next three columns are call option prices (or

[2] Notice that the strike prices are all quoted in cents; for example, the first entry for oil is 3800, meaning $38 per barrel.

<< TABLE 23.2

Sample *Wall Street Journal* Futures Option Price Quotations

FUTURES OPTIONS PRICES

Wednesday, July 7, 2004

Final or settlement prices of selected contracts. Volume and open interest are totals in all contract months.

STRIKE CALLS-SETTLE PUTS-SETTLE

Food and Fiber

Cotton (NYBOT)

50,000 lbs.; cents per lb.

Price	Oct	Dec	Mar	Oct	Dec	Mar
47	3.83	5.13	6.92	1.98	2.62	2.54
48	3.28	4.59	6.33	2.44	3.07	2.94
49	2.79	4.10	5.78	2.94	3.57	3.38
50	2.36	3.64	5.27	3.51	4.10	3.85
51	1.98	3.22	4.78	4.12	4.68	4.36
52	1.65	2.85	4.33	4.79	5.30	4.90

Est vol 4,285 Tu 3,314 calls 2,186 puts
Op int Tues 90,016 calls 44,886 puts

Orange Juice (NYBOT)

15,000 lbs.; cents per lb.

Price	Aug	Sep	Nov	Aug	Sep	Nov
60	7.85	8.40	10.00	.05	.60	1.20
65	3.25	4.55	6.50	.40	1.85	2.35
70	.65	2.30	4.15	2.80	4.40	5.15
75	.05	1.30	3.00	7.20	8.40	8.70
80	.05	.80	1.90	12.15	12.90	12.75
85	.05	.55	1.45	17.15	17.55	17.15

Est vol 1,658 Tu 1,845 calls 452 puts
Op int Tues 30,654 calls 9,661 puts

Petroleum

Crude Oil (NYM)

1,000 bbls.; $ per bbl.

Price	Aug	Sep	Oct	Aug	Sep	Oct
3800	1.49	2.47	2.79	0.41	1.27	1.90
3850	1.17	2.19	2.53	0.59	1.49	2.14
3900	0.89	1.93	2.29	0.81	1.73	2.40
3950	0.67	1.70	2.07	1.09	2.00	2.68
4000	0.49	1.50	1.88	1.41	2.30	2.99
4050	0.35	1.32	1.71	1.77	2.62	3.31

Est vol 50,143 Tu 19,192 calls 20,733 puts
Op int Tues 439,295 calls 566,699 puts

STRIKE CALLS-SETTLE PUTS-SETTLE

Metals

Copper (CMX)

25,000 lbs.; cents per lb.

Price	Aug	Sep	Oct	Aug	Sep	Oct
118	8.75	10.30	11.10	1.20	2.80	4.55
120	7.25	9.00	9.90	1.65	3.50	5.35
122	...	7.80	...	...	4.30	...
124	4.65	6.70	7.80	3.05	5.20	7.25
126	...	5.75	...	...	6.25	...
128	2.80	4.85	...	5.20	7.35	...

Est vol 500 Tu 262 calls 67 puts
Op int Tues 15,286 calls 10,561 puts

Gold (CMX)

100 troy ounces; $ per troy ounce

Price	Aug	Sep	Oct	Aug	Sep	Oct
380	23.60	26.50	28.60	0.90	2.60	4.70
385	18.10	22.60	25.00	1.30	3.70	6.00
390	14.90	19.00	21.60	2.20	5.10	7.70
395	11.50	15.80	18.60	3.80	6.80	9.60
400	8.40	12.90	15.80	5.70	8.90	11.80
405	5.90	10.40	13.30	8.20	11.40	14.30

Est vol 42,000 Tu 5,343 calls 5,820 puts
Op int Tues 414,313 calls 224,732 puts

Currency

Japanese Yen (CME)

12,500,000 yen; cents per 100 yen

Price	Jly	Aug	Sep	Jly	Aug	Sep
9150	1.05	1.63	1.97	0.09	0.67	1.01
9200	0.63	1.34	1.68	0.17	0.88	1.22
9250	0.33	1.08	1.44	0.37	1.12	1.48
9300	0.18	0.86	1.22	0.72	1.40	1.76
9350	0.10	0.69	1.03	1.14	1.73	2.07
9400	0.05	0.55	0.87	1.59	...	2.41

Est vol 1,597 Tu 665 calls 327 puts
Op int Tues 28,479 calls 20,314 puts

Canadian Dollar (CME)

100,000 Can.$, cents per Can.$

Price	Jly	Aug	Sep	Jly	Aug	Sep
7450	1.09	...	1.58	0.04	0.31	0.53
7500	0.64	1.02	1.27	0.09	0.47	0.72

premiums) for three different months of expiration. The final three columns are put option prices for the same three months.

Suppose you buy the November 80 orange juice futures call option. You will pay $1.90 per pound for the option (they're actually sold in multiples of 15,000, but we'll ignore this). If you exercise your option, you will receive a futures contract on orange juice and the difference between the current futures price and the strike price of $80 in cash.

Hedging Exchange Rate Risk with Options

Table 23.2 shows that there are futures options available on foreign currencies as well as on commodities. These work in exactly the same way as commodities futures options. In addition, there are other traded options with which the underlying asset is just currency rather than a futures contract on a currency. Firms with significant exposure to exchange rate risk will frequently purchase put options to protect against adverse exchange rate changes.

Hedging Interest Rate Risk with Options

The use of options to hedge against interest rate risk is a very common practice, and there are a variety of options available to serve this purpose. Some are futures options like the ones we have been discussing, and these trade on organized exchanges. For example, we mentioned the Treasury bond contract in our discussion of futures. There are options available on this contract and a number of other financial futures as well. Beyond this, there is a thriving over-the-counter market in interest rate options. We will describe some of these options in this section.

The Association of Corporate Treasurers (www.treasurers.org) has lots of information on a variety of subjects, including risk management.

A Preliminary Note

Some interest rate options are actually options on interest-bearing assets such as bonds (or on futures contracts for bonds). Most of the options that are traded on exchanges fall into this category. As we will discuss in a moment, some others are actually options on interest rates. The distinction is important if we are thinking about using one type or the other to hedge. To illustrate, suppose we want to protect ourselves against an increase in interest rates using options; what should we do?

We need to buy an option that increases in value as interest rates go up. One thing we can do is buy a *put* option on a bond. Why a put? Remember that when interest rates go up, bond values go down, so one way to hedge against interest rate increases is to buy put options on bonds. The other way to hedge is to buy a *call* option on interest rates. We discuss this alternative in more detail in the next section.

We actually saw interest rate options in Chapter 7 when we discussed the call feature on a bond. Remember that the call provision gives the issuer the right to buy back the bond at a set price, known as the *call price.* What happens is that if interest rates fall, the bond's price will rise. If it rises above the call price, the buyer will exercise its option and acquire the bond at a bargain price. The call provision can thus be viewed as either a call option on a bond or a put option on interest rates.

Interest Rate Caps

An *interest rate cap* is a call option on an interest rate. Suppose a firm has a floating-rate loan. It is concerned that interest rates will rise sharply and the firm will experience financial distress because of the increased loan payment. To guard against this, the firm can purchase an interest rate cap from a bank (there are banks that specialize in such products). What will happen is that if the loan payment ever rises above an agreed-upon limit (the "ceiling"), the bank will pay the difference between the actual payment and the ceiling to the firm in cash.

A *floor* is a put option on an interest rate. If a firm buys a cap and sells a floor, the result is a *collar.* By selling the put and buying the call, the firm protects itself against increases in interest rates beyond the ceiling by the cap. However, if interest rates drop below the floor, the put will be exercised against the firm. The result is that the rate the firm pays will not drop below the floor rate. In other words, the rate the firm pays will always be between the floor and the ceiling.

Other Interest Rate Options

We will close out our chapter by briefly mentioning two relatively new types of interest rate options. Suppose a firm has a floating-rate loan. The firm is comfortable with its floating-rate loan, but it would like to have the right to convert it to a fixed-rate loan in the future.

What can the firm do? What it wants is the right, but not the obligation, to swap its floating-rate loan for a fixed-rate loan. In other words, the firm needs to buy an option on a swap. Swap options exist, and they have the charming name *swaptions.*

We've seen that there are options on futures contracts and options on swap contracts, but what about options on options? Such options are called *compound* options. As we have just discussed, a cap is a call option on interest rates. Suppose a firm thinks that, depending on interest rates, it might like to buy a cap in the future. As you can probably guess, in this case, what the firm might want to do today is buy an option on a cap. Inevitably, it seems, an option on a cap is called a *caption,* and there is a large market for these instruments.

Concept Questions

23.6a Suppose that the unhedged risk profile in Figure 23.13 sloped down instead of up. What option-based hedging strategy would be suitable in this case?

23.6b What is a futures option?

23.6c What is a caption? Who might want to buy one?

SUMMARY AND CONCLUSIONS 23.7

This chapter has introduced some of the basic principles of financial risk management and financial engineering. The motivation for risk management and financial engineering stems from the fact that a firm will frequently have an undesirable exposure to some type of risk. This is particularly true today because of the increased volatility in key financial variables such as interest rates, exchange rates, and commodity prices.

We describe a firm's exposure to a particular risk with a risk profile. The goal of financial risk management is to alter the firm's risk profile through the buying and selling of derivative assets such as futures contracts, swap contracts, and options contracts. By finding instruments with appropriate payoff profiles, a firm can reduce or even eliminate its exposure to many types of risk.

Hedging cannot change the fundamental economic reality of a business. What it can do is allow a firm to avoid expensive and troublesome disruptions that might otherwise result from short-run, temporary price fluctuations. Hedging also gives a firm time to react and adapt to changing market conditions. Because of the price volatility and rapid economic change that characterize modern business, intelligently dealing with volatility has become an increasingly important task for financial managers.

There are many other option types available in addition to those we have discussed, and more are created every day. One very important aspect of financial risk management that we have not discussed is that options, forwards, futures, and swaps can be combined in a wide variety of ways to create new instruments. These basic contract types are really just the building blocks used by financial engineers to create new and innovative products for corporate risk management.

Visit us at www.mhhe.com/rwj

Chapter Review and Self-Test Problems

23.1 Futures Contracts Suppose Golden Grain Farms (GGF) expects to harvest 50,000 bushels of wheat in September. GGF is concerned about the possibility of price fluctuations between now and September. The futures price for September wheat is $2 per bushel, and the relevant contract calls for 5,000 bushels. What action should GGF take to lock in the $2 price? Suppose the price of wheat actually turns out to be $3. Evaluate GGF's gains and losses. Do the same for a price of $1. Ignore marking-to-market.

23.2 Options Contracts In the previous question, suppose that September futures put options with a strike price of $2 per bushel cost $.15 per bushel. Assuming that GGF hedges using put options, evaluate its gains and losses for wheat prices of $1, $2, and $3.

Answers to Chapter Review and Self-Test Problems

23.1 GGF wants to deliver wheat and receive a fixed price, so it needs to *sell* futures contracts. Each contract calls for delivery of 5,000 bushels, so GGF needs to sell 10 contracts. No money changes hands today.

If wheat prices actually turn out to be \$3, then GGF will receive \$150,000 for its crop, but it will have a loss of \$50,000 on its futures position when it closes that position because the contracts require it to sell 50,000 bushels of wheat at \$2, when the going price is \$3. It thus nets \$100,000 overall.

If wheat prices turn out to be \$1 per bushel, then the crop will be worth only \$50,000. However, GGF will have a profit of \$50,000 on its futures position, so GGF again nets \$100,000.

23.2 If GGF wants to insure against a price decline only, it can buy 10 put contracts. Each contract is for 5,000 bushels, so the cost per contract is $5{,}000 \times \$.15 = \$750$. For 10 contracts, the cost will be \$7,500.

If wheat prices turn out to be \$3, then GGF will not exercise the put options (why not?). Its crop is worth \$150,000, but it is out the \$7,500 cost of the options, so it nets \$142,500.

If wheat prices fall to \$1, the crop is worth \$50,000. GGF will exercise its puts (why?) and thereby force the seller of the puts to pay \$2 per bushel. GGF receives a total of \$100,000. If we subtract the cost of the puts, we see that GGF's net is \$92,500. In fact, verify that its net at any price of \$2 or lower is \$92,500.

Concepts Review and Critical Thinking Questions

1. **Hedging Strategies** If a firm is selling futures contracts on lumber as a hedging strategy, what must be true about the firm's exposure to lumber prices?
2. **Hedging Strategies** If a firm is buying call options on pork belly futures as a hedging strategy, what must be true about the firm's exposure to pork belly prices?
3. **Forwards and Futures** What is the difference between a forward contract and a futures contract? Why do you think that futures contracts are much more common? Are there any circumstances under which you might prefer to use forwards instead of futures? Explain.
4. **Hedging Commodities** Bubbling Crude Corporation, a large Texas oil producer, would like to hedge against adverse movements in the price of oil, since this is the firm's primary source of revenue. What should the firm do? Provide at least two reasons why it probably will not be possible to achieve a completely flat risk profile with respect to oil prices.
5. **Sources of Risk** A company produces an energy intensive product and uses natural gas as the energy source. The competition primarily uses oil. Explain why this company is exposed to fluctuations in both oil and natural gas prices.
6. **Hedging Commodities** If a textile manufacturer wanted to hedge against adverse movements in cotton prices, it could buy cotton futures contracts or buy call options on cotton futures contracts. What would be the pros and cons of the two approaches?
7. **Options** Explain why a put option on a bond is conceptually the same as a call option on interest rates.

Visit us at www.mhhe.com/rwj

8. **Hedging Interest Rates** A company has a large bond issue maturing in one year. When it matures, the company will float a new issue. Current interest rates are attractive, and the company is concerned that rates next year will be higher. What are some hedging strategies that the company might use in this case?
9. **Swaps** Explain why a swap is effectively a series of forward contracts. Suppose a firm enters into a swap agreement with a swap dealer. Describe the nature of the default risk faced by both parties.
10. **Swaps** Suppose a firm enters into a fixed-for-floating interest rate swap with a swap dealer. Describe the cash flows that will occur as a result of the swap.
11. **Transaction versus Economic Exposure** What is the difference between transactions and economic exposure? Which can be hedged more easily? Why?
12. **Hedging Exchange Rate Risk** Refer to Table 23.1 in the text to answer this question. If a U.S. company exports its goods to Japan, how would it use a futures contract on Japanese yen to hedge its exchange rate risk? Would it buy or sell yen futures? In answering, pay attention to how the exchange rate is quoted in the futures contract.
13. **Hedging Strategies** For the following scenarios, describe a hedging strategy using futures contracts that might be considered. If you think that a cross-hedge would be appropriate, discuss the reasons for your choice of contract.
    a. A public utility is concerned about rising costs.
    b. A candy manufacturer is concerned about rising costs.
    c. A corn farmer fears that this year's harvest will be at record high levels across the country.
    d. A manufacturer of photographic film is concerned about rising costs.
    e. A natural gas producer believes there will be excess supply in the market this year.
    f. A bank derives all its income from long-term, fixed-rate residential mortgages.
    g. A stock mutual fund invests in large, blue-chip stocks and is concerned about a decline in the stock market.
    h. A U.S. importer of Swiss army knives will pay for its order in six months in Swiss francs.
    i. A U.S. exporter of construction equipment has agreed to sell some cranes to a German construction firm. The U.S. firm will be paid in euros in three months.
14. **Swaps** In May 2004, Sysco Corporation, the distributor of food and food-related products (not to be confused with Cisco Systems), announced it had signed an interest rate swap. The interest rate swap effectively converted the company's $100 million, 4.6 percent interest rate bonds for a variable rate payment, which would be the six-month LIBOR minus 0.52 percent. Why would Sysco use a swap agreement? In other words, why didn't Sysco just go ahead and issue floating rate bonds since the net effect of issuing fixed-rate bonds and then doing a swap is to create a variable-rate bond?

Questions and Problems

BASIC (Questions 1–4)

1. **Futures Quotes** Refer to Table 23.1 in the text to answer this question. Suppose you purchase a March 2005 cocoa futures contract on July 7, 2004, at the last price of the day. What will your profit or loss be if cocoa prices turn out to be $1,402 per metric ton at expiration?

2. **Futures Quotes** Refer to Table 23.1 in the text to answer this question. Suppose you sell five March 2005 silver futures contracts on July 7, 2004, at the last price of the day. What will your profit or loss be if silver prices turn out to be $6.45 per ounce at expiration? What if silver prices are $5.86 per ounce at expiration?
3. **Futures Options Quotes** Refer to Table 23.2 in the text to answer this question. Suppose you purchase the October 2004 call option on crude oil futures with a strike price of $39.50. How much does your option cost per barrel of oil? What is the total cost? Suppose the price of oil futures is $35.45 per barrel at expiration of the option contract. What is your net profit or loss from this position? What if oil futures prices are $43.24 per barrel at expiration?
4. **Put and Call Payoffs** Suppose a financial manager buys call options on 50,000 barrels of oil with an exercise price of $35 per barrel. She simultaneously sells a put option on 50,000 barrels of oil with the same exercise price of $35 per barrel. Consider her gains and losses if oil prices are $30, $32, $35, $38, and $40. What do you notice about the payoff profile?

INTERMEDIATE
(Questions 5–6)

5. **Hedging with Futures** Refer to Table 23.1 in the text to answer this question. Suppose today is July 7, 2004, and your firm produces breakfast cereal and needs 75,000 bushels of corn in December 2004 for an upcoming promotion. You would like to lock in your costs today because you are concerned that corn prices might go up between now and December.
   - **a.** How could you use corn futures contracts to hedge your risk exposure? What price would you effectively be locking in based on the closing price of the day?
   - **b.** Suppose corn prices are $2.64 per pound in December. What is the profit or loss on your futures position? Explain how your futures position has eliminated your exposure to price risk in the corn market.
6. **Interest Rate Swaps** ABC Company and XYZ Company need to raise funds to pay for capital improvements at their manufacturing plants. ABC Company is a well-established firm with an excellent credit rating in the debt market; it can borrow funds either at 11 percent fixed rate or at LIBOR + 1 percent floating rate. XYZ Company is a fledgling start-up firm without a strong credit history. It can borrow funds either at 10 percent fixed rate or at LIBOR + 3 percent floating rate.
   - **a.** Is there an opportunity here for ABC and XYZ to benefit by means of an interest rate swap?
   - **b.** Suppose you've just been hired at a bank that acts as a dealer in the swaps market, and your boss has shown you the borrowing rate information for your clients ABC and XYZ. Describe how you could bring these two companies together in an interest rate swap that would make both firms better off, while netting your bank a 2.0 percent profit.

CHALLENGE
(Question 7)

7. **Financial Engineering** Suppose there were call options and forward contracts available on coal, but no put options. Show how a financial engineer could synthesize a put option using the available contracts. What does your answer tell you about the general relationship between puts, calls, and forwards?

What's On the Web?

23.1 **Contract Specifications** You want to find the contract specifications for futures contracts. Go to the Chicago Board of Trade at www.cbot.com and find the contract specifications for corn, cattle, and lean hogs. What are the contract sizes? What contract months are available for each?

23.2 Futures Quotes You want to find the price of a future on light sweet crude oils. Go to the New York Mercantile Exchange at www.nymex.com and find the contract size for the light sweet crude oil futures. Next, find the price quotes for these futures. What is the most recent settlement price for the shortest-term contract? For the longest-term contract? Based on these prices, what is the total dollar value of each contract?

23.3 New York Board of Trade Go to the New York Board of Trade Web site at www.nybot.com to answer the following questions: What contracts are traded on the New York Board of Trade? What does FCOJ stand for? What are the trading months for FCOJ futures contracts? What are the position limits for FCOJ futures contracts? What is the last trading day of the expiration month for FCOJ futures? What are the trading months and last trading day for FCOJ options contracts? What is the FCOJ differential contract?

23.4 Hedging with Futures You are working for a company that processes beef and will take delivery of 200,000 pounds of cattle in August. You would like to lock on your costs today because you are concerned about an increase in cattle prices. Go to the Chicago Mercantile Exchange (CME) at www.cme.com and find the contract specifications for cattle futures. How many futures contracts will you need to hedge your exposure? Will you buy or sell futures? Now find the current price quote for cattle futures on the Web site. What price are you effectively locking in if you traded at the last price? Suppose cattle prices increase 5 percent before the expiration. What is your profit or loss on the futures position? What if prices decrease by 5 percent? Explain how your futures position has eliminated your exposure to price risk in the live cattle market.

PART EIGHT

Topics in Corporate Finance

24 Option Valuation

On July 2, 2004, the closing stock prices for Estée Lauder, American Express, and Amazon.com were $48.34, $51.24, and $52.59, respectively. Each company had a call option trading on the Chicago Board Options Exchange with a $50 strike price and an expiration date of October 16, 74 days away. You would expect that the prices on these call options would be similar, but they weren't. The Estée Lauder options sold for $1.45, American Express options traded at $2.90, and Amazon.com options traded at $6.30. Why would options on these three similarly priced stocks be priced so differently when the strike prices and the time to expiration are exactly the same? If you go back to our earlier chapter on options, the volatility of the underlying stock is an important determinant of an option's underlying value; in fact, these three stocks have very different volatilities. In this chapter, we explore this issue—and many others—in much greater depth using the Nobel prize-winning Black-Scholes Option Pricing Model.

In an earlier chapter, we explored the basics of options, but we didn't discuss how to value them in much detail. Our goal in this chapter is to take this next step and examine how to actually estimate what an option is worth. To do this, we will explore two very famous results, the put-call parity condition and the Black-Scholes Option Pricing Model.

An understanding of option valuation lets us illustrate and explore some very important ideas in corporate finance. For example, we will show why certain types of mergers are a bad idea. We will also examine some conflicts between bondholder and stockholder interests. We will even provide some examples under which companies have an incentive to take negative NPV projects. In each case, option-related effects underlie the issue.

The Options Industry Council has a Web page featuring a lot of educational materials: www.888options.com.

PUT-CALL PARITY

24.1

From our earlier discussions, recall that the purchaser of a call option pays for the right, but not the obligation, to buy an asset for a fixed time at a fixed price. The purchaser of a put option pays for the right to sell an asset for a fixed time at a fixed price. The fixed price is called the *exercise* or *strike* price.

Protective Puts

Consider the following investment strategy. Today, you buy one share of Microsoft for $110. At the same time, you also buy one put option with a $105 strike price. The put option has a life of one year, and the premium is $5. Your total investment is $115, and your plan is to hold this investment for one year and then sell out.[1]

What have you accomplished here? To answer, we created Table 24.1, which shows your gains and losses one year from now for different stock prices. In the table, notice that the worst thing that ever happens to you is that the value of your investment falls to $105. The reason is that if Microsoft's stock price is below $105 per share one year from now, you will exercise your put option and sell your stock for the strike price of $105, so that is the least you can possibly receive.

Thus, by purchasing the put option, you have limited your "downside" risk to a maximum potential loss of $10 (i.e., $115 − $105). This particular strategy of buying a stock and also buying a put on the stock is called a **protective put** strategy because it protects you against losses beyond a certain point. Notice that the put option acts as a kind of insurance policy that pays off in the event that an asset you own (the stock) declines in value.

protective put
The purchase of stock and a put option on the stock to limit the downside risk associated with the stock.

In our example, we picked a strike price of $105. You could have picked a higher strike price and limited your downside risk to even less. Of course, a higher strike price would mean that you would have to pay more for the put option, so there is a trade-off between the amount of protection and the cost of that protection.

An Alternative Strategy

Now consider a different strategy. You take your $115 and purchase a one-year *call* option on Microsoft with a strike price of $105. The premium is $15. That leaves you with $100, which you decide to invest in a riskless asset such as a T-bill. The risk-free rate is 5 percent.

What does this strategy accomplish? Once again, we will create a table to illustrate your gains and losses. Notice that in Table 24.2 your $100 grows to $105 based on a 5 percent interest rate. If you compare Table 24.2 to our previous Table 24.1, you will make an interesting discovery. No matter what the stock price is one year from now, the two strategies *always* have the same value in one year!

The fact that the two strategies always have exactly the same value in one year explains why they have the same cost today. If one of these strategies were cheaper than the other today, there would be an arbitrage opportunity involving buying the one that's cheaper and simultaneously selling the one that's more expensive.

The Result

Our example illustrates a very important pricing relationship. What it shows is that a protective put strategy can be exactly duplicated by a combination of a call option (with the

[1]Of course, in reality, you can't buy an option on just one share, so you would need to buy 100 shares of Microsoft and one put contract at a minimum to actually implement this strategy. We're really just explaining the calculations on a per-share basis.

TABLE 24.1 >>

Gains and Losses in One Year.
Original investment: purchase 1 share at $110 plus a one-year put option with a strike price of $105 for $5. Total cost is $115.

Stock Price in One Year	Value of Put Option (Strike Price = $105)	Combined Value	Total Gain or Loss (Combined Value Less $115)
$125	$ 0	$125	$10
120	0	120	5
115	0	115	0
110	0	110	−5
105	0	105	−10
100	5	105	−10
95	10	105	−10
80	25	105	−10

TABLE 24.2 >>

Gains and Losses in One Year.
Original investment: purchase a one-year call option with a strike price of $105 for $15. Invest $100 in risk-free asset paying 5 percent. Total cost is $115.

Stock Price in One Year	Value of Call Option (Strike Price = $105)	Value of Risk-Free Asset	Combined Value	Total Gain or Loss (Combined Value Less $115)
$125	$20	$105	$125	$10
120	15	105	120	5
115	10	105	115	0
110	5	105	110	−5
105	0	105	105	−10
100	0	105	105	−10
95	0	105	105	−10
90	0	105	105	−10

same strike price as the put option) and a riskless investment. In our example, notice that the investment in the riskless asset, $100, is exactly equal to the present value of the strike price on the option calculated at the risk-free rate, $105/1.05 = $100.

put-call parity (PCP) The relationship between the prices of the underlying stock, a call option, a put option, and a riskless asset.

Putting it all together, what we have discovered is the **put-call parity (PCP)** condition. It says that:

$$\text{Share of stock} + \text{a put option} = \text{Present value of strike price} + \text{a call option} \quad [24.1]$$

In symbols, we can write:

$$S + P = \text{PV}(E) + C \quad [24.2]$$

where S and P are stock and put values, and $\text{PV}(E)$ and C are the present value of the exercise price and the value of the call option.

Because the present value of the exercise price is calculated using the risk-free rate, you can think of it as the price of a risk-free, pure discount instrument (i.e., a T-bill) with a face value equal to the strike price. In our experience, the easiest way to remember the PCP condition is to remember that "stock plus put equals T-bill plus call."

The PCP condition is an algebraic expression, meaning that it can be rearranged. For example, suppose we know that the risk-free rate is .5 percent per month. A call with a strike price of $40 sells for $4, and a put with the same strike price sells for $3. Both have a three-month maturity. What's the stock price?

To answer, we just use the PCP condition to solve for the stock price:

$$\begin{aligned} S &= \text{PV}(E) + C - P \quad [24.3] \\ &= \$40/1.005^3 + 4 - 3 \\ &= \$40.41 \end{aligned}$$

The PCP condition really says that between a riskless asset (like a T-bill), a call option, a put option, and a share of stock, we can always figure out the price of any one of the four given the prices of the other three.

<< EXAMPLE 24.1

Put-Call Parity

Suppose a share of stock sells for \$60. A six-month call option with a \$70 strike price sells for \$2. The risk-free rate is .4 percent per month. What's the price of a six-month put option with a \$70 strike?

If we just use the PCP condition to solve for the put price, we get:

$$\begin{aligned} P &= \text{PV}(E) + C - S \\ &= \$70/1.004^6 + 2 - \$60 \\ &= \$10.34 \end{aligned}$$

Notice that, in this example, the put option is worth a lot more than the call. Why?

<< EXAMPLE 24.2

More Parity

Suppose a share of stock sells for \$110. A one-year, at-the-money call option sells for \$15. An at-the-money put with the same maturity sells for \$5. Can you create a risk-free investment by combining these three instruments? How? What's the risk-free rate?

Here, we can use the PCP condition to solve for the present value of the strike price:

$$\begin{aligned} \text{PV}(E) &= S + P - C \\ &= \$110 + 5 - 15 \\ &= \$100 \end{aligned}$$

The present value of the strike price is thus \$100. Notice that because the options are at the money, the strike is the same as the stock price, \$110. So, if you put \$100 in a riskless investment today and receive \$110 in one year, the implied risk-free rate is obviously 10 percent.

Continuous Compounding: A Refresher Course

Back in Chapter 6, we saw that the effective annual interest rate (EAR) on an investment depends on compounding frequency. We also saw that, in the extreme, compounding can occur every instant, or continuously. So, as a quick refresher, suppose you invest \$100 at a rate of 6 percent per year compounded continuously. How much will you have in one year? How about in two years?

In Chapter 6, we saw that the EAR with continuous compounding is:

$$\text{EAR} = e^q - 1$$

where q is the quoted rate (6 percent, or .06, in this case) and e is the number 2.71828 . . . , the base of the natural logarithms. Plugging in the numbers, we get:

$$\begin{aligned} \text{EAR} &= e^q - 1 \\ &= 2.71828^{.06} - 1 \\ &= .06184 \end{aligned}$$

or about 6.2 percent. Notice that most calculators have a key labeled "e^x," so doing this calculation is simply a matter of entering .06 and then pressing this key. With an EAR of

6.184 percent, your \$100 investment will grow to \$106.18 in one year. In two years, it will grow to:

$$\begin{aligned}\text{Future value} &= \$100 \times 1.06184^2 \\ &= \$100 \times 1.1275 \\ &= \$112.75\end{aligned}$$

When we move into option valuation, continuous compounding shows up quite a bit, and it helps to have some shortcuts. In our examples here, we first converted the continuously compounded rate to an EAR and then did our calculations. It turns out that we don't need to do the conversion at all. Instead, we can calculate present and future values directly. In particular, the future value of \$1 for t periods at a continuously compounded rate of R per period is simply:

$$\text{Future value} = \$1 \times e^{Rt}$$

For example, looking back at the problem we just solved, the future value of \$100 in two years at a continuously compounded rate of 6 percent is

$$\begin{aligned}\text{Future value} &= \$100\, e^{.06(2)} \\ &= \$100 \times 2.71828^{.12} \\ &= \$100 \times 1.1275 \\ &= \$112.75\end{aligned}$$

which is exactly what we had before.

Similarly, we can calculate the present value of \$1 to be received in t periods at a continuously compounded rate of R per period as follows:

$$\text{Present value} = \$1 \times e^{-Rt}$$

So, if we want the present value of \$15,000 to be received in five years at 8 percent compounded continuously, we would calculate:

$$\begin{aligned}\text{Present value} &= \$15{,}000 \times e^{-.08(5)} \\ &= \$15{,}000 \times 2.71828^{-.4} \\ &= \$15{,}000 \times .67032 \\ &= \$10{,}054.80\end{aligned}$$

EXAMPLE 24.3 >> Continuous Compounding

What is the present value of \$500 to be received in six months if the discount rate is 9 percent per year, compounded continuously?

In this case, notice that the number of periods is equal to one-half because six months is half of a year. Thus, the present value is:

$$\begin{aligned}\text{Present value} &= \$500 \times e^{-.09(1/2)} \\ &= \$500 \times 2.71828^{-.045} \\ &= \$500 \times .956 \\ &= \$478\end{aligned}$$

Looking back at our PCP condition, we wrote:

$$S + P = \text{PV}(E) + C$$

If we assume that R is the continuously compounded risk-free rate per year, then we could write this as:

$$S + P = E \times e^{-Rt} + C \qquad [24.4]$$

where t is the time to maturity (in years) on the options.

Finally, suppose we are given an EAR and we need to convert it to a continuously compounded rate. For example, if the risk-free rate is 8 percent per year compounded annually, what's the continuously compounded risk-free rate?

Going back to our first formula, we had that:

$$\text{EAR} = e^q - 1$$

Now, we need to solve for q, the continuously compounded rate. Plugging in the numbers, we have:

$$.08 = e^q - 1$$
$$e^q = 1.08$$

We need to take the natural logarithm (ln) of both sides to solve for q:

$$\ln(e^q) = \ln(1.08)$$
$$q = .07696$$

or about 7.7 percent. Notice that most calculators have a button labeled "ln," so doing this calculation involves entering 1.08 and then pressing this key.

EXAMPLE 24.4

Even More Parity

Suppose a share of stock sells for $30. A three-month call option with a $25 strike sells for $7. A three-month put with the same maturity sells for $1. What's the continuously compounded risk-free rate?

We need to plug the relevant numbers into the PCP condition:

$$S + P = E \times e^{-Rt} + C$$
$$\$30 + 1 = \$25 \times e^{-R(1/4)} + 7$$

Notice that we used one-fourth for the number of years because three months is a quarter of a year. We now need to solve for R:

$$\$24 = \$25 \times e^{-R(1/4)}$$
$$.96 = e^{-R(1/4)}$$
$$\ln(.96) = \ln(e^{-R(1/4)})$$
$$-.0408 = -R(1/4)$$
$$R = .1632$$

or about 16.32 percent, which would be a very high risk-free rate!

Concept Questions

24.1a What is a protective put strategy?

24.1b What strategy exactly duplicates a protective put?

24.2 THE BLACK-SCHOLES OPTION PRICING MODEL

We're now in a position to discuss one of the most celebrated results in modern finance, the Black-Scholes Option Pricing Model (OPM). The OPM is a sufficiently important discovery that it was the basis for the Nobel Prize in Economics in 1997. The underlying development of the Black-Scholes OPM is fairly complex, so we will focus only on the main result and how to use it.

The Call Option Pricing Formula

Black and Scholes showed that the value of a European-style call option on a non-dividend paying stock, C, can be written as follows:

$$C = S \times \mathrm{N}(d_1) - E \times e^{-Rt} \times \mathrm{N}(d_2) \qquad [24.5]$$

where S, E, and e^{-Rt} are as we previously defined them and $\mathrm{N}(d_1)$ and $\mathrm{N}(d_2)$ are probabilities that must be calculated. More specifically, $\mathrm{N}(d_1)$ is the probability that a standardized, normally distributed random variable (widely known as a "z" variable) is less than or equal to d_1, and $\mathrm{N}(d_2)$ is the probability of a value less than or equal to d_2. Determining these probabilities requires a table such as Table 24.3.

To illustrate, suppose we are given the following information:

There's a Black-Scholes calculator (and a lot more) at www.numa.com.

$$\begin{aligned} S &= \$100 \\ E &= \$90 \\ R_f &= 4\% \text{ per year, continuously compounded} \\ d_1 &= .60 \\ d_2 &= .30 \\ t &= 9 \text{ months} \end{aligned}$$

Based on this information, what is the value of the call option, C?

To answer, we need to determine $\mathrm{N}(d_1)$ and $\mathrm{N}(d_2)$. In Table 24.3, we first find the row corresponding to a d of .60. The corresponding probability $\mathrm{N}(d)$ is .7258, so this is $\mathrm{N}(d_1)$. For d_2, the associated probability $\mathrm{N}(d_2)$ is .6179. Using the Black-Scholes OPM, we calculate that the value of the call option is:

$$\begin{aligned} C &= S \times \mathrm{N}(d_1) - E \times e^{-Rt} \times \mathrm{N}(d_2) \\ &= \$100 \times .7258 - \$90 \times e^{-.04(3/4)} \times .6179 \\ &= \$18.61 \end{aligned}$$

Notice that t, the time to expiration, is 9 months, which is $9/12 = 3/4$ of one year.

As this example illustrates, if we are given values for d_1 and d_2 (and the table), then using the Black-Scholes model is not difficult. Generally, however, we would not be given the values of d_1 and d_2, and we must calculate them. This requires a little extra effort. The values for d_1 and d_2 for the Black-Scholes OPM are given by:

$$\begin{aligned} d_1 &= [\ln(S/E) + (R + \sigma^2/2) \times t]/(\sigma \times \sqrt{t}) \\ d_2 &= d_1 - \sigma \times \sqrt{t} \end{aligned} \qquad [24.6]$$

In these expressions, σ is the standard deviation of the rate of return on the underlying asset. Also, $\ln(S/E)$ is the natural logarithm of the current stock price divided by the exercise price.

TABLE 24.3 >> Cumulative Normal Distribution

d	N(*d*)	*d*	N(*d*)	*d*	N(*d*)	*d*	N(*d*)	*d*	N(*d*)	*d*	N(*d*)
−3.00	.0013	−1.58	.0571	−0.76	.2236	0.06	.5239	0.86	.8051	1.66	.9515
−2.95	.0016	−1.56	.0594	−0.74	.2297	0.08	.5319	0.88	.8106	1.68	.9535
−2.90	.0019	−1.54	.0618	−0.72	.2358	0.10	.5398	0.90	.8159	1.70	.9554
−2.85	.0022	−1.52	.0643	−0.70	.2420	0.12	.5478	0.92	.8212	1.72	.9573
−2.80	.0026	−1.50	.0668	−0.68	.2483	0.14	.5557	0.94	.8264	1.74	.9591
−2.75	.0030	−1.48	.0694	−0.66	.2546	0.16	.5636	0.96	.8315	1.76	.9608
−2.70	.0035	−1.46	.0721	−0.64	.2611	0.18	.5714	0.98	.8365	1.78	.9625
−2.65	.0040	−1.44	.0749	−0.62	.2676	0.20	.5793	1.00	.8414	1.80	.9641
−2.60	.0047	−1.42	.0778	−0.60	.2743	0.22	.5871	1.02	.8461	1.82	.9656
−2.55	.0054	−1.40	.0808	−0.58	.2810	0.24	.5948	1.04	.8508	1.84	.9671
−2.50	.0062	−1.38	.0838	−0.56	.2877	0.26	.6026	1.06	.8554	1.86	.9686
−2.45	.0071	−1.36	.0869	−0.54	.2946	0.28	.6103	1.08	.8599	1.88	.9699
−2.40	.0082	−1.34	.0901	−0.52	.3015	0.30	.6179	1.10	.8643	1.90	.9713
−2.35	.0094	−1.32	.0934	−0.50	.3085	0.32	.6255	1.12	.8686	1.92	.9726
−2.30	.0107	−1.30	.0968	−0.48	.3156	0.34	.6331	1.14	.8729	1.94	.9738
−2.25	.0122	−1.28	.1003	−0.46	.3228	0.36	.6406	1.16	.8770	1.96	.9750
−2.20	.0139	−1.26	.1038	−0.44	.3300	0.38	.6480	1.18	.8810	1.98	.9761
−2.15	.0158	−1.24	.1075	−0.42	.3373	0.40	.6554	1.20	.8849	2.00	.9772
−2.10	.0179	−1.22	.1112	−0.40	.3446	0.42	.6628	1.22	.8888	2.05	.9798
−2.05	.0202	−1.20	.1151	−0.38	.3520	0.44	.6700	1.24	.8925	2.10	.9821
−2.00	.0228	−1.18	.1190	−0.36	.3594	0.46	.6773	1.26	.8962	2.15	.9842
−1.98	.0239	−1.16	.1230	−0.34	.3669	0.48	.6844	1.28	.8997	2.20	.9861
−1.96	.0250	−1.14	.1271	−0.32	.3745	0.50	.6915	1.30	.9032	2.25	.9878
−1.94	.0262	−1.12	.1314	−0.30	.3821	0.52	.6985	1.32	.9066	2.30	.9893
−1.92	.0274	−1.10	.1357	−0.28	.3897	0.54	.7054	1.34	.9099	2.35	.9906
−1.90	.0287	−1.08	.1401	−0.26	.3974	0.56	.7123	1.36	.9131	2.40	.9918
−1.88	.0301	−1.06	.1446	**−0.24**	**.4052**	0.58	.7191	1.38	.9162	2.45	.9929
−1.86	.0314	−1.04	.1492	−0.22	.4129	0.60	.7258	1.40	.9192	2.50	.9938
−1.84	.0329	−1.02	.1539	−0.20	.4207	0.62	.7324	1.42	.9222	2.55	.9946
−1.82	.0344	−1.00	.1587	−0.18	.4286	0.64	.7389	1.44	.9251	2.60	.9953
−1.80	.0359	−0.98	.1635	−0.16	.4365	0.66	.7454	1.46	.9279	2.65	.9960
−1.78	.0375	−0.96	.1685	−0.14	.4443	0.68	.7518	1.48	.9306	2.70	.9965
−1.76	.0392	−0.94	.1736	−0.12	.4523	0.70	.7580	1.50	.9332	2.75	.9970
−1.74	.0409	−0.92	.1788	−0.10	.4602	0.72	.7642	1.52	.9357	2.80	.9974
−1.72	.0427	−0.90	.1841	−0.08	.4681	0.74	.7704	1.54	.9382	2.85	.9978
−1.70	.0446	−0.88	.1894	−0.06	.4761	0.76	.7764	1.56	.9406	2.90	.9981
−1.68	.0465	−0.86	.1949	−0.04	.4841	0.78	.7823	1.58	.9429	2.95	.9984
−1.66	.0485	−0.84	.2005	−0.02	.4920	0.80	.7882	1.60	.9452	3.00	.9986
−1.64	.0505	−0.82	.2061	0.00	.5000	0.82	.7939	1.62	.9474	3.05	.9989
−1.62	.0526	−0.80	.2119	0.02	.5080	0.84	.7996	1.64	.9495		
−1.60	.0548	−0.78	.2177	0.04	.5160						

This table shows the probability [N(*d*)] of observing a value less than or equal to *d*. For example, as illustrated, if *d* is −.24, then N(*d*) is .4052.

The formula for d_1 looks a little intimidating, but it is mostly a matter of plug-and-chug with a calculator. To illustrate, suppose we have the following:

$S = \$70$
$E = \$80$
$R = 4\%$ per year, continuously compounded
$\sigma = 60\%$ per year
$t = 3$ months

With these numbers, d_1 is:

$$\begin{aligned} d_1 &= [\ln(S/E) + (R + \sigma^2/2) \times t]/(\sigma \times \sqrt{t}) \\ &= [\ln(70/80) + (.04 + .6^2/2) \times \tfrac{1}{4}]/(.6 \times \sqrt{\tfrac{1}{4}}) \\ &= -.26 \\ d_2 &= d_1 - \sigma \times \sqrt{t} \\ &= -.26 - .6 \times \sqrt{\tfrac{1}{4}} \\ &= -.56 \end{aligned}$$

Referring to Table 24.3, the values of $N(d_1)$ and $N(d_2)$ are .3974 and .2877, respectively. Plugging all the numbers in:

$$\begin{aligned} C &= S \times N(d_1) - E \times e^{-Rt} \times N(d_2) \\ &= \$70 \times .3974 - \$80 \times e^{-.04(1/4)} \times .2877 \\ &= \$5.03 \end{aligned}$$

If you take a look at the Black-Scholes formula and our examples, you will see that the price of a call option depends on five, and only five, factors. These are the same factors that we identified earlier: namely, the stock price, the strike price, the time to maturity, the risk-free rate, and the standard deviation of the return on the stock.

EXAMPLE 24.5 >> Call Option Pricing

Suppose you are given the following:

$S = \$40$
$E = \$36$
$R = 4\%$ per year, continuously compounded
$\sigma = 70\%$ per year
$t = 3$ months

What's the value of a call option on the stock?

We need to use the Black-Scholes OPM. So, we first need to calculate d_1 and d_2:

$$\begin{aligned} d_1 &= [\ln(S/E) + (R + \sigma^2/2) \times t]/(\sigma \times \sqrt{t}) \\ &= [\ln(40/36) + (.04 + .7^2/2) \times \tfrac{1}{4}]/(.7 \times \sqrt{\tfrac{1}{4}}) \\ &= .50 \\ d_2 &= d_1 - \sigma \times \sqrt{t} \\ &= .50 - .7 \times \sqrt{\tfrac{1}{4}} \\ &= .15 \end{aligned}$$

continued

Referring to Table 24.3, the values of N(d_1) and N(d_2) are .6915 and .5597, respectively. To get the second of these, we averaged the two numbers on each side, (.5557 + .5636)/2 = .5597. Plugging all the numbers in:

$$\begin{aligned} C &= S \times \mathrm{N}(d_1) - E \times e^{-Rt} \times \mathrm{N}(d_2) \\ &= \$40 \times .6915 - \$36 \times e^{-.04(1/4)} \times .5597 \\ &= \$7.71 \end{aligned}$$

A question that sometimes comes up concerns the probabilities N(d_1) and N(d_2). Just what are they the probabilities of? In other words, how do we interpret them? The answer is that they don't really correspond to anything in the real world. We mention this because there is a common misconception about N(d_2) in particular. It is frequently thought to be the probability that the stock price will exceed the strike price on the expiration day, which is also the probability that a call option will finish in the money. Unfortunately, that's not correct, at least not unless the expected return on the stock is equal to the risk-free rate.

Tables such as Table 24.3 are the traditional means of looking up "z" values, but they have been mostly replaced by computers. They are not as accurate because of rounding, and they also have only a limited number of values. Our nearby *Spreadsheet Strategies* box shows how to calculate Black-Scholes call option prices using a spreadsheet. Because this is so much easier and more accurate, we will do all the calculations in the rest of this chapter using computers instead of tables.

SPREADSHEET STRATEGIES

	A	B	C	D	E	F	G	H	I	J	K
1											
2	**Using a spreadsheet to calculate Black-Scholes option prices**										
3											
4	XYZ stock has a price of $65 and an annual return standard deviation of 50%. The riskless										
5	interest rate is 5%. Calculate call and put option prices with a strike of $60 and a 3-month										
6	time to expiration.										
7											
8	Stock =	65		d1 =	0.4952		N(d1) =	0.6898			
9	Strike =	60									
10	Sigma =	0.5		d2 =	0.2452		N(d2) =	0.5968			
11	Time =	0.25									
12	Rate =	0.05									
13											
14		Call = Stock x N(d1) – Strike x exp(– Rate x Time) x N(d2) =									$9.47
15											
16		Put = Strike x exp(– Rate x Time) + Call – Stock						=			$3.72
17											
18	Formula entered in E8 is =(LN(B8/B9)+(B12+0.5*B10^2)*B11)/(B10*SQRT(B11))										
19	Formula entered in E10 is =E8–B10*SQRT(B11)										
20	Formula entered in H8 is =NORMSDIST(E8)										
21	Formula entered in K10 is =NORMSDIST(E10)										
22	Formula entered in K14 is =B8*H8–B9*EXP(–B12*B11)*H10										
23	Formula entered in K16 is =B9*EXP(–B12*B11)+K14–B8										

Put Option Valuation

Our examples thus far have focused only on call options. Only a little extra work is needed to value put options. Basically, we just pretend that a put option is a call option and use the Black-Scholes formula to value it. We then use the put-call parity (PCP) condition to solve for the put value. To see how this works, suppose we have the following:

$S = \$40$
$E = \$40$
$R = 4\%$ per year, continuously compounded
$\sigma = 80\%$ per year
$t = 4$ months

What's the value of a *put* option on the stock?

For practice, calculate the Black-Scholes call option price and see if you agree that a call option would be worth about \$7.52. Now, recall the PCP condition:

$$S + P = E \times e^{-Rt} + C$$

which we can rearrange to solve for the put price:

$$P = E \times e^{-Rt} + C - S$$

Plugging in the relevant numbers, we get:

$$\begin{aligned} P &= \$40 \times e^{-.04(1/3)} + 7.52 - 40 \\ &= \$6.99 \end{aligned}$$

Thus, the value of a put option is \$6.99. So, once we know how to value call options, we also know how to value put options.

A Cautionary Note

For practice, let's consider another put option value. Suppose we have the following:

$S = \$70$
$E = \$90$
$R = 8\%$ per year, continuously compounded
$\sigma = 20\%$ per year
$t = 12$ months

What's the value of a put option on the stock?

For practice, calculate the call option's value and see if you get \$1.61. Once again, we use PCP to solve for the put price:

$$P = E \times e^{-Rt} + C - S$$

The put value we get is:

$$\begin{aligned} P &= \$90 \times e^{-.08(1)} + 1.61 - 70 \\ &= \$14.69 \end{aligned}$$

Is there something about our put option value that seems odd? The answer is yes. Since the stock price is \$70 and the strike price is \$90, you could get \$20 by exercising the put immediately, so it looks like we have an arbitrage possibility. Unfortunately, we don't. This example illustrates that we have to be careful with assumptions. The Black-Scholes formula is for *European*-style options (remember that European-style options can be exercised only on the final day, whereas American-style options can be exercised anytime). In fact, our PCP condition is only for European-style options.

What our example shows is that an American-style put option is worth more than a European-style put. The reason is not hard to understand. Suppose you buy a put with a strike price of $80. The very best thing that can happen is for the stock price to fall to zero. If the stock price did fall to zero, no further gain on your option is possible, so you would want to exercise it immediately rather than wait. If the option is American style, you can, but not if it is European style. More generally, it often pays to exercise a put option once it is well into the money because any additional potential gains are limited, so American-style exercise is valuable.

What about call options? Here the answer is a little more encouraging. As long as we stick to non-dividend-paying stocks, it will never be optimal to exercise a call option early. Again, the reason is not complicated. A call option is worth more alive than dead, meaning you would always be better off selling the option than exercising it. In other words, for a call option, the exercise style is irrelevant.

Here is a challenge for the more mathematically inclined among you. We have a formula for a European-style put option. What about for an American-style put? Despite a great deal of effort, this problem has never been solved, so no formula is known. Just to be clear, we have numerical procedures for valuing put options, but no explicit formula. Call us if you figure one out.

Concept Questions

24.2a What are the five factors that determine an option's value?

24.2b Which is worth more, an American-style put or a European-style put? Why?

MORE ON BLACK-SCHOLES 24.3

In this section, we take a closer look at the inputs into the option pricing formula and their effects on option values. Table 24.4 summarizes the inputs and their impacts (positive or negative) on option values. In the table, a plus sign means that increasing the input increases the option's value and vice versa.

Table 24.4 also indicates that four of the five effects have common names. For fairly obvious reasons given their names, these effects are collectively called the "greeks." We will discuss them in the next several sections. In some cases, the calculations can be fairly involved, but the good news is that options calculators are widely available on the Web. See our nearby *Work the Web* box for one example.

<< TABLE 24.4

Five Inputs Determining the Value of an American Option on a Non-Dividend-Paying Stock

	Impact on Option Price from an Increase in Input		
Input	**Call Options**	**Put Options**	**Common Name**
Stock price (S)	+	–	Delta
Strike price (E)	–	+	
Time to expiration (t)	+	+	Theta
Standard deviation of return on stock (σ)	+	+	Vega
Risk-free rate (R)	+	–	Rho

NOTE: The effect of increasing the time to maturity is positive for an American put option, but the impact is ambiguous for a European put.

WORK THE WEB

The Black-Scholes OPM is a wonderful tool, but as we have seen, the calculations can get somewhat tedious. One way to find the price of an option without the effort is to work the Web. We went to the options calculator at www.ivolatility.com and entered "MSFT," the ticker symbol for Microsoft. As shown, the current stock price is \$27.74, the standard deviation of the stock's return is 16.17 percent per year, and the risk-free rate is 1.94 percent. Here is what we get:

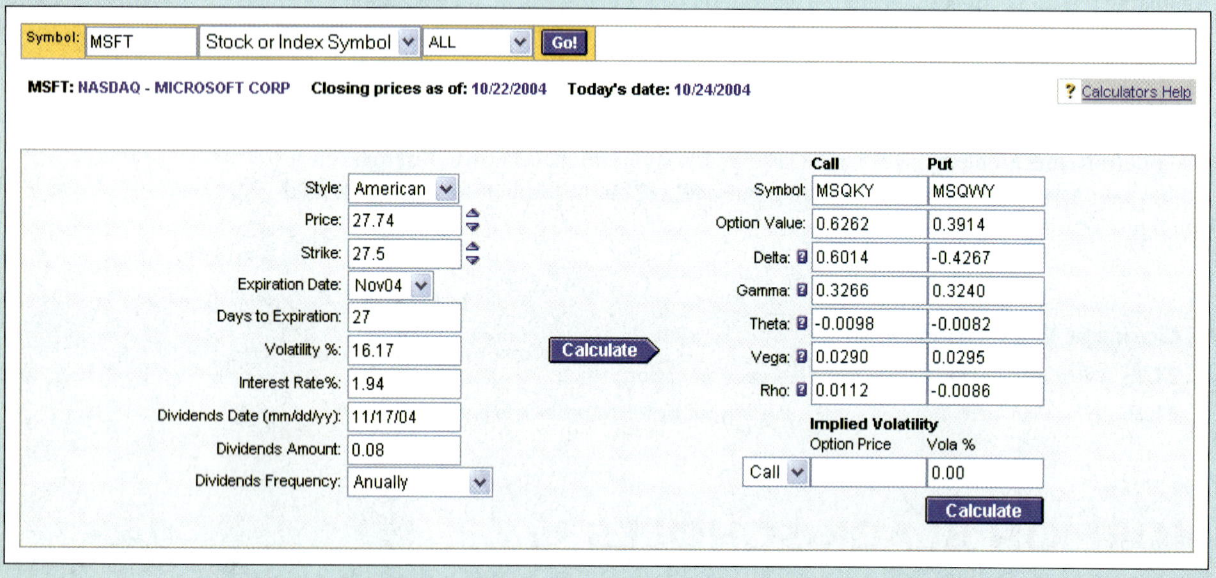

As you can see, a call option on MSFT should sell for \$.6262 and a put option should sell for \$.3914. Now that's easy! Notice that the "greeks" are also calculated. What does "gamma" tell you? Visit the site to learn more.

Varying the Stock Price

The effect that the stock price has on put and call values is pretty obvious. Increasing the stock price increases call values and decreases put values. However, the strength of the effect varies depending on the "moneyness" of the option (i.e., how far in or out of the money it is).

Another good options calculator can be found at www.margrabe.com/optionpricing.html

For a given set of input values, we illustrate the relationship between call and put option prices and the underlying stock price in Figure 24.1. In the figure, stock prices are measured on the horizontal axis and option prices are measured on the vertical axis. Notice that the lines for put and call values are bowed. The reason is that the value of an option that is far out of the money is not as sensitive to a change in the underlying stock price as an in-the-money option.

delta
Measures the effect on an option's value of a small change in the value of the underlying stock.

The sensitivity of an option's value to small changes in the price of the underlying stock is called the option's **delta**. For European options, we can directly measure the deltas as follows:

$$\text{Call option delta} = \text{N}(d_1)$$
$$\text{Put option delta} = \text{N}(d_1) - 1$$

FIGURE 24.1 >> Put and Call Option Prices

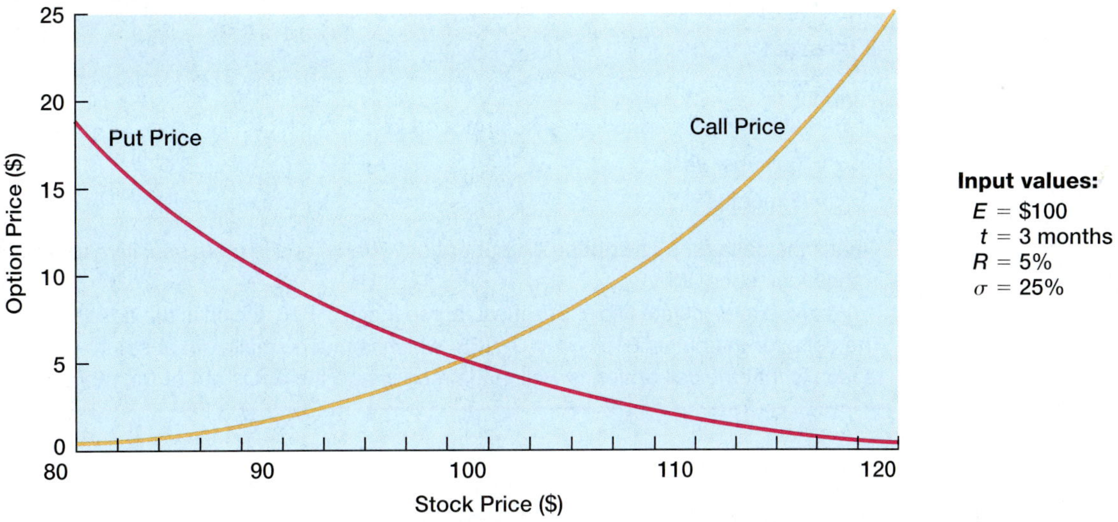

The "N(d_1)" that we need to calculate these deltas is the same one we used to calculate option values, so we already know how to do it. Remember that N(d_1) is a probability, so its value ranges somewhere between zero and one.

For a small change in the stock price, the change in an option's price is approximately equal to its delta multiplied by the change in the stock price:

Change in option value ≈ Delta × Change in stock value

To illustrate this, suppose we are given the following:

$S = \$120$

$E = \$100$

$R = 8\%$ per year, continuously compounded

$\sigma = 80\%$ per year

$t = 6$ months

Using the Black-Scholes formula, the value of a call option is $37.72. The delta (N($d_1$)) is .75, which tells us that if the stock price changes by, say, $1, the option's value will change in the same direction by $.75.

We can check this directly by changing the stock price to $121 and recalculating the option value. If we do this, the new value of the call is $38.47, an increase of $.75, so the approximation is pretty accurate (it is off in the third decimal point).

If we price a put option using these same inputs, the value is $13.94. The delta is $.75 - 1$, or $-.25$. If we increase the stock price to $121, the new put value is 13.70, a change of $-.24$, so, again, the approximation is fairly accurate as long as we stick to relatively small changes.

Looking back at our graph in Figure 24.1, we now see why the lines get progressively steeper as the stock price rises for calls and falls for puts. The delta for a deeply in-the-money option is close to one, whereas the delta for a deeply out-of-the-money option is close to zero.

EXAMPLE 24.6 >> Delta

Suppose you are given the following:

$S = \$40$
$E = \$30$
$R = 6\%$ per year, continuously compounded
$\sigma = 90\%$ per year
$t = 3$ months

What's the delta for a call option? A put option? Which one is more sensitive to a change in the stock price. Why?

We need to calculate $N(d_1)$. See if you agree that it's .815, which is the delta for the call. The delta for the put is $.815 - 1 = -.185$, which is much smaller (in absolute value). The reason is that the call option is well in the money and the put is out of the money.

Varying the Time to Expiration

The impact of changing the time to maturity on American-style options is also fairly obvious. Since an American-style option can be exercised any time, increasing the option's time to expiration can't possibly hurt and, especially for out-of-the-money options, might help. Thus, for both puts and calls, increasing the time to expiration has a positive effect.

For a European-style call option, increasing the time to expiration also never hurts because, as we discussed earlier, the option is always worth more alive than dead and any extra time to expiration only adds to its "alive" value. With a European-style put, however, increasing the time to expiration may or may not increase the value of the option. As we have discussed, for a deep in-the-money put, immediate exercise is often desirable, so increasing the time to expiration only reduces the value of the option. If a put is out-of-the-money, then increasing the time to expiration will probably increase its value.

Figure 24.2 shows the effect of increasing the time to expiration on a put and a call. As in Figure 24.1, the options are exactly at the money. In the figure, notice that once time to maturity reaches about six months, further increases have little impact on the put's value. The call's value, in contrast, just keeps on rising.

theta
Measures the sensitivity of an option's value to a change in the time to expiration.

The sensitivity of an option's value to the passage of time is called its **theta**. There is a formula for theta, but it is fairly complicated, so we will not present it. The important thing to realize is that option values are sensitive to the passage of time (especially call option values). To see why this is important, imagine you buy an option today and you hold it for a month. During the month, the stock price never changes. What happens to the value of your option?

The answer is that the value of your option declines because time to expiration has gotten shorter even though the underlying asset has not changed in value. We sometimes say that an option is a "wasting" asset, meaning that its value declines as time goes by, all else held constant. The tendency of an option's value to decline as time passes is also called "time decay." An option's theta is thus a measure of the rate of time decay.

Recall from our earlier chapter on options that the intrinsic value of an option is:

$$\text{Call intrinsic value} = \text{Max}[S - E, 0]$$
$$\text{Put intrinsic value} = \text{Max}[E - S, 0]$$

FIGURE 24.2 >> **Option Prices and Time to Expiration**

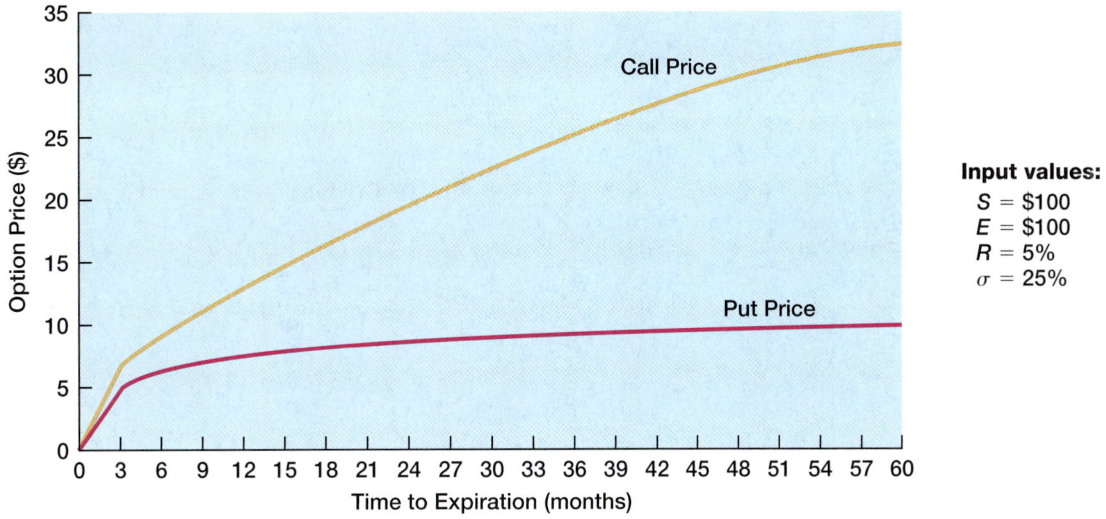

where "Max[$S - E$, 0]" just means $S - E$ or 0, whichever is bigger. American-style options can never sell for less than their intrinsic value because, if one did, there would be an arbitrage opportunity. For example, suppose a stock sells for $60. A three-month call option with a $50 strike price sells for $8. What do you think?

You think you are going to be rich because you can buy the option for $8, exercise it for $50, then sell the stock for $60 for a $2 riskless profit. To prevent this type of simple arbitrage, the option has to sell for at least its intrinsic value of $60 − 50 = $10. In reality, the option might sell for $11. The extra $1 in value over the intrinsic value is called the "time premium." In other words, an option's value can be written as:

Option value = Intrinsic value + Time premium

It is the time premium that wastes away or decays as time goes by. The reason is that the day an option expires, it is worth exactly its intrinsic value because, on that day, it must be exercised or torn up. The existence of the time premium also explains our earlier observation that a call option is always worth more alive than dead. If you exercise an option, you receive the intrinsic value. If you sell it, you get the intrinsic value plus any remaining time premium.

Time Premiums

<< **EXAMPLE 24.7**

At the end of Fall 2004, shares in Microsoft were going for about $27.74. A call option expiring in April of 2005 with a $30 strike was quoted at $.50. A put with the same strike was quoted at $2.70. For both options, what are the intrinsic value and time premium?

Beginning with the call option, we see that it is out of the money because the $30 strike price is higher than the $27.74 stock price. The intrinsic value is zero, and the entire $.50 is therefore time premium. The put is in the money, and its intrinsic value is $30 − 27.74 = $2.26. The put's value is $2.70, so the time premium is $2.70 − 2.26 = $.44.

FIGURE 24.3 >> Option Prices and Sigma

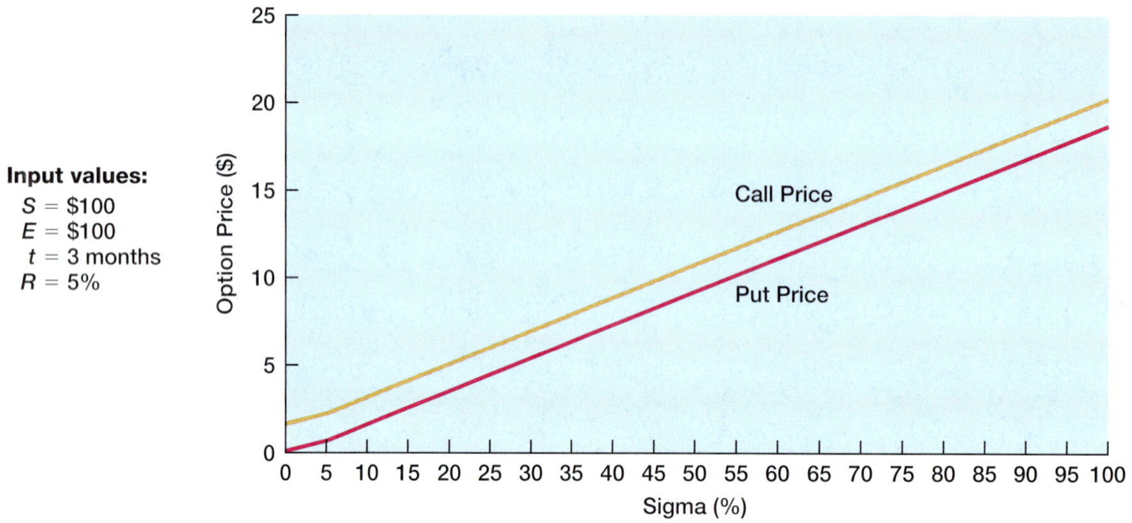

Varying the Standard Deviation

Figure 24.3 illustrates the impact on option values of varying the standard deviation of the return on the underlying asset. As shown, the effect is positive and pronounced for both puts and calls. In fact, increasing the standard deviation has an almost identical effect on them.

The sensitivity of an option's value to the volatility of the underlying asset is called its **vega**.[2] Once again, the formula is somewhat complicated, so we will omit it. The main thing to understand from Figure 24.3 is that option values are very sensitive to standard deviations, and changes in the volatility of the underlying asset's return can have a strong impact on option values.

vega
Measures the sensitivity of an option's value to a change in the standard deviation of the return on the underlying asset.

Varying the Risk-Free Rate

We illustrate the effect of changing the risk-free rate on option values in Figure 24.4. As shown, increasing the risk-free rate has a positive impact on call values and a negative impact on put values. Notice, however, that for realistic changes in interest rates, option values don't change a lot. In other words, option values are not as sensitive to changes in interest rates as they are to, say, changes in volatilities. An option's sensitivity to interest rate changes is called its **rho**.

rho
Measures the sensitivity of an option's value to a change in the risk-free rate.

There are a few other greeks in addition to the ones we have discussed, but we will end our Greek lesson here. What we now discuss is a very important use of Black-Scholes: the calculation of implied volatilities.

[2]The Greek scholars among you will recognize that "vega" is not a Greek letter. (It is a star in the constellation Lyra and also a particularly forgettable automobile manufactured by Chevrolet in the 1960s and 1970s.)

FIGURE 24.4 >> Options Prices and Interest Rates

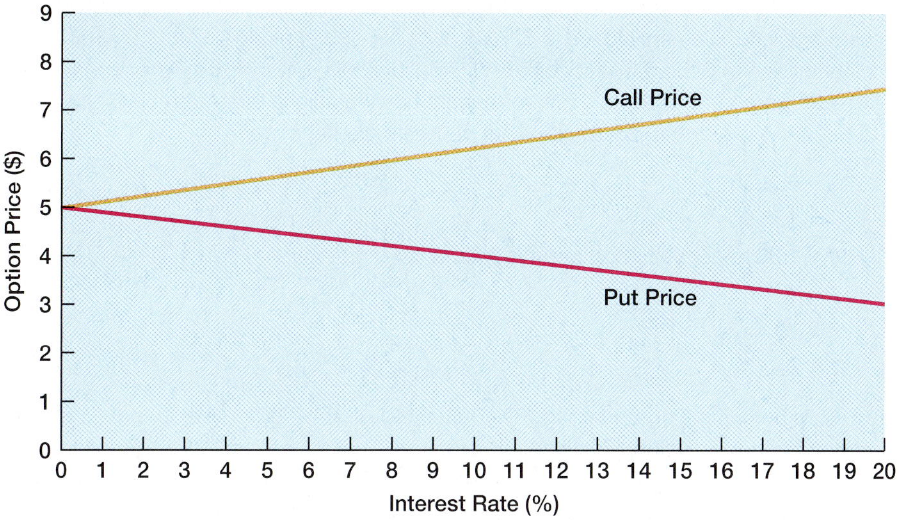

Input values:
S = \$100
E = \$100
t = 3 months
σ = 25%

Implied Standard Deviations

Thus far, we have focused on using the Black-Scholes OPM to calculate option values, but there is another, very important, use. Of the five factors that determine an option's value, four can be directly observed: the stock price, the strike price, the risk-free rate, and the life of the option. Only the standard deviation must be estimated.

For an option-oriented Web site focusing on volatilities, visit www.ivolatility.com.

The standard deviation we use in the OPM is actually a prediction of what the standard deviation of the underlying asset's return is going to be over the life of the option. Often, we already know the value of an option because we observe its price in the financial markets. In such cases, we can use the value of the option, along with the four observable inputs, to back out a value for the standard deviation. When we solve for the standard deviation this way, the result is called the **implied standard deviation** (ISD, which some people pronounce as "iz-dee"), also known as the implied volatility.

To illustrate this calculation, suppose we are given the following:

S = \$12
E = \$8
R = 5% per year, continuously compounded
t = 6 months

implied standard deviation
An estimate of the future standard deviation of the return on an asset obtained from the Black-Scholes OPM.

We also know that the call option sells for \$4.59. Based on this information, how volatile is the stock expected to be over the next three months?

If we plug all this information into the Black-Scholes formula, we would be left with one unknown, the standard deviation (σ). However, it's not possible to directly solve for σ, so trial and error must be used. In other words, we just start plugging in values for σ until we find one that produces the call price of \$4.59.

For a stock option, .50 is a good place to start. If you plug this in, you will see that the calculated call value is \$4.38, which is too low. Recall that option values increase as we increase σ, so we might try .60. Now the option value is \$4.52, so we're getting close, but we're still low. At .65, the calculated value is \$4.61, which is just a little too high. After a little more work, we discover that the implied volatility is .64, or 64 percent.

EXAMPLE 24.8 >> ISD

Here is an actual example. On July 2, 2004, common stock in network hardware manufacturer Cisco Systems closed at \$22.95. A call option expiring on October 16, 2004, with a strike price of \$22.50 traded for \$1.70. Treasury bills maturing on October 14 were paying 1.28 percent. Based on this information, how volatile is the return on Cisco predicted to be? Just to summarize, the relevant numbers we have are:

S = \$22.95

E = \$22.50

R = 1.28% per year, compounded annually

σ = ?

t = 74 days

C = \$1.70

From here, it's plug and chug. As you have probably figured out by now, it's easier to use an options calculator to solve this problem. That's what we did; the implied standard deviation is about 35 percent. Our nearby *Work the Web* box shows you how to do this.

In principle, to solve this problem, we need to convert the interest rate of 1.28 percent to a continuously compounded rate. If we do this, we get 1.272 percent. However, we've seen that option values are not very sensitive to small changes in interest rates, and in this case, it actually makes almost no difference. For this reason, in practice, the continuous compounding issue is often ignored, especially when rates are low.

WORK THE WEB

From our discussion of implied standard deviation, you can see that solving for ISD when you know the option price is simply trial and error. Fortunately, most option calculators will do the work for you. To illustrate, we found the ISD for the Cisco call option we discussed in Example 24.8. Just to refresh your memory, Cisco stock closed at \$22.95. A call option with a strike price of \$25 and a maturity of 74 days was selling for \$1.70. Treasury bills with the same maturity had a yield of 1.28 percent. What is the ISD of Cisco stock? We went to www.numa.com and used the options calculator at the site. After entering all the information, this is what we found:

implied volatility for european call option

INPUT DATA	Share Price:	22.950	Strike Price:	22.500	Maturity(yrs):	0.203
	Dividend Yld:	0	Interest Rate:	1.28	Option Price:	1.700

Implied Volatility = 35.16			
Intrinsic Value:	0.450	Time Value:	1.250

Notice the calculator changes the days to maturity to 0.203, which is 74/365 of a year. So, Cisco stock has an ISD of 35.16 percent per year.

Concept Questions

24.3a What are an option's delta, rho, theta, and vega?

24.3b What is an ISD?

VALUATION OF EQUITY AND DEBT IN A LEVERAGED FIRM

24.4

In our earlier chapter on options, we pointed out that the equity in a leveraged corporation (i.e., a corporation that has borrowed money) can be viewed as a call option on the assets of the business. The reason is that, when a debt comes due, the stockholders have the option to pay off the debt, and thereby acquire the assets free and clear, or else default. The act of paying off the debt amounts to exercising an in-the-money call option to acquire the assets. Defaulting amounts to letting an out-of-the-money call option expire. In this section, we expand on the idea of equity as a call option in several ways.

Valuing the Equity in a Leveraged Firm

Consider a firm that has a single zero-coupon bond issue outstanding with a face value of $10 million. It matures in six years. The firms' assets have a current *market* value of $12 million. The volatility (standard deviation) of the return on the firm's assets is 40 percent per year. The continuously compounded risk-free rate is 6 percent. What is the current market value of the firm's equity? Its debt? What is its continuously compounded cost of debt?

What this case amounts to is that the stockholders have the right, but not the obligation, to pay $10 million in six years. If they do, they get the assets of the firm. If they don't, they default and get nothing. So, the equity in the firm is a call option with a strike price of $10 million.

Using the Black-Scholes formula in this case can be a little confusing because now we are solving for the stock price. So, the symbol "C" is the value of the stock and the symbol "S" is the value of the firm's assets. With this in mind, we can value the equity of the firm by plugging the numbers into the Black-Scholes OPM with S = $12 million and E = $10 million. When we do so, we get $6.516 million as the value of the equity, with a delta of .849.

Now that we know the value of the equity, we can calculate the value of the debt using the standard balance sheet identity. The firm's assets are worth $12 million and the equity is worth $6.516 million, so the debt is worth $12 million − $6.516 million = $5.484 million.

To calculate the firm's continuously compounded cost of debt, we observe that the present value is $5.484 million and the future value in six years is the $10 million face value. We need to solve for a continuously compounded rate, R_D, as follows:

$$
\begin{aligned}
\$5.484 &= \$10 \times e^{-R_D(6)} \\
.5484 &= e^{-R_D(6)} \\
R_D &= -1/6 \times \ln(.5484) \\
&= .10
\end{aligned}
$$

So, the firm's cost of debt is 10 percent, compared to a risk-free rate of 6 percent. The extra 4 percent is the default risk premium, i.e., the extra compensation the bondholders demand because of the risk that the firm will default and bondholders will receive assets worth less than $10 million.

We also have that the delta of the option here is .849. How do we interpret this? In the context of valuing equity as a call option, the delta tells us what happens to the value of the equity when the value of the firm's assets changes. This is an important consideration. For example, suppose the firm undertakes a project with an NPV of $100 thousand, meaning that the value of the firm's assets will rise by $100 thousand. We now see that the value of the stock will rise (approximately) by only .849 × $100 thousand = $84.9 thousand.[3] Why?

The reason is that the firm has made its assets more valuable, which means that default is less likely to occur in the future. As a result, the bonds gain value, too. How much do they gain? The answer is $100 − 84.9 = $15.1, in other words, whatever value the stockholders don't get.

EXAMPLE 24.9 >> Equity as a Call Option

Consider a firm that has a single zero-coupon bond issue outstanding with a face value of $40 million. It matures in five years. The risk-free rate is 4 percent. The firm's assets have a current market value of $35 million, and the firm's equity is worth $15 million. If the firm takes a project with a $200 thousand NPV, approximately how much will the stockholders gain?

To answer this question, we need to know the delta, so we need to calculate $N(d_1)$. To do this, we need to know the relevant standard deviation, which we don't have. We do have the value of the option ($15 million), though, so we can calculate the ISD. If we use C = $15 million, S = $35 million, and E = $40 million along with the risk-free rate of 4 percent and time to expiration of five years, we get that the ISD is 48.2 percent. With this value, the delta is .725, so, if $200,000 in value is created, the stockholders will get 72.5 percent of it, or $145,000.

Options and the Valuation of Risky Bonds

Let's continue with the case we just examined of a firm with $12 million in assets and a six-year, zero-coupon bond with a face value of $10 million. Given the other numbers, we showed that the bonds were worth $5.484 million. Suppose that the holders of these bonds wish to eliminate the risk of default. In other words, the holders want to turn their risky bonds into risk-free bonds. How can they do this?

The answer is that the bondholders can do a protective put along the lines we described earlier in the chapter. In this case, the bondholders want to make sure that their bonds will never be worth less than their face value of $10 million, so the bondholders need to purchase a put option with a six-year life and a $10 million face value. The put option is an option to sell the assets of the firm for $10 million.

Remember that if the assets of the firm are worth more than $10 million in six years, the shareholders will pay the $10 million. If the assets are worth less than $10 million, the stockholders will default, and the bondholders will receive the assets of the firm. At that point, however, the bondholders will exercise their put and sell the assets for $10 million. Either way, the bondholders get their $10 million.

So, what we have discovered is that a risk-free bond is the same thing as a combination of a risky bond and a put option on the assets of the firm with a matching maturity and a

[3]Delta is used to evaluate the effect of a small change in the underlying asset's value, so it might look like we shouldn't use it to evaluate a shift of $100 thousand. "Small" is relative, however, and $100 thousand is small relative to the $12 million total asset value.

strike price equal to the face value of the bond:

$$\text{Value of risky bond} + \text{put option} = \text{Value of risk-free bond} \qquad [24.7]$$

In our example, the face value of the debt is \$10 million, and the risk-free rate is 6 percent, so the value of the bonds if they were risk free is:

$$\begin{aligned}\text{Value of risk-free bonds} &= \$10 \text{ million} \times e^{-.06(6)} \\ &= \$6.977 \text{ million}\end{aligned}$$

If we compare this to the value of the risky bonds, \$5.484 million, we see that the put option is worth \$6.977 − 5.484 = \$1.493 million. Notice that the value of the risk-free bonds is also the present value of the strike price at the risk-free rate.

We can check that this put value is correct. We know the value of the underlying assets is \$12 million, value of the call option (the stock) is \$6.516 million, and the present value of the strike price is \$6.977 million. Using the PCP condition:

$$\begin{aligned}P &= \$6.977 + 6.516 - \$12 \\ &= \$1.493 \text{ million}\end{aligned}$$

which is exactly what we calculated.

We can restate our result here as follows:

$$\begin{aligned}\text{Value of risky bond} &= \text{Value of risk-free bond} - \text{put option} \\ &= E \times e^{-Rt} - P\end{aligned} \qquad [24.8]$$

This shows us that anything that increases the value of the put option *decreases* the value of the firm's bonds. With this in mind, we can use the PCP condition to bring together and unite a lot of our discussion in this chapter (and this book!).

Using the PCP condition, we can write:

$$S = C + E \times e^{-Rt} - P$$

Remember that, in this case, the stock is the underlying asset. Now, if we are thinking of the stock in a firm as being a call option on the assets of the firm, here is how we would interpret this:

$$\text{Value of assets } (S) = \text{Value of stock } (C) + (E \times e^{-Rt} - P) \qquad [24.9]$$

where E, the strike price, is the face value of the firm's debt. Notice that, as we have just seen, the term in parentheses is the value of the firm's risky bonds, so this expression is really just the balance sheet identity:

$$\text{Value of assets } (S) = \text{Value of stock } (C) + \text{Value of bonds } (E \times e^{-Rt} - P) \qquad [24.10]$$

Thus, the PCP condition and the balance sheet identity say the same thing, but recognizing the nature of the optionlike features of the equity and debt in a leveraged firm leads to a far richer understanding of corporate finance. We illustrate some important examples in the next section.

Concept Questions

24.4a Why do we say that the equity in a leveraged firm is a call option? What does the delta of the call option tell us in this context?

24.4b What is the connection between the standard balance sheet identity and the put-call parity (PCP condition)?

24.5 OPTIONS AND CORPORATE DECISIONS: SOME APPLICATIONS

In this section, we explore the implications of options analysis in two key areas, capital budgeting and mergers. We start with mergers and show a very surprising result. We then go on to show that the net present value rule has some important wrinkles in a leveraged firm.

Mergers and Diversification

Elsewhere in our book, we discuss mergers and acquisitions. There we mention that diversification is frequently cited as a reason for two firms to merge. Is diversification a good reason to merge? It might seem so. After all, in an earlier chapter, we spent a lot of time explaining why diversification is very valuable for investors in their own portfolios because of the elimination of unsystematic risk.

To investigate this issue, let's consider two companies, Sunshine Swimwear (SS) and Polar Winterwear (PW). For obvious reasons, both companies have very seasonal cash flows, and, in their respective off-seasons, both companies worry about cash flow. If the two companies were to merge, the combined company would have a much more stable cash flow. In other words, a merger would diversify away some of the seasonal variation and, in fact, would make bankruptcy much less likely.

Notice that the operations of the two firms are very different, so the proposed merger is a purely "financial" merger, which means that there are no "synergies" or other value-creating possibilities except, possibly, gains from risk reduction. Here is some premerger information:

	Sunshine Swimwear	Polar Winterwear
Market value of assets	\$30 million	\$10 million
Face value of pure discount debt	\$12 million	\$4 million
Debt maturity	3 years	3 years
Asset return standard deviation	50 percent	60 percent

The risk-free rate, continuously compounded, is 5 percent. Given this, we can calculate the following (check these for practice):

	Sunshine Swimwear	Polar Winterwear
Market value of equity	\$20.394 million	\$6.992 million
Market value of debt	\$ 9.606 million	\$3.008 million

If you do check these, you may get slightly different answers if you use Table 24.3 (we used an options calculator).

After the merger, the combined firm's assets will simply be the sum of the premerger values, \$30 + \$10 = \$40, because no value was created or destroyed. Similarly, the total face value of the debt is now \$16 million. However, we will assume that the combined firm's asset return standard deviation is 40 percent. This is lower than for either of the two individual firms because of the diversification effect.

So, what is the impact of this merger? To find out, we compute the postmerger value of the equity. Based on our discussion, here is the relevant information:

	Combined Firm
Market value of assets	$40 million
Face value of pure discount debt	$16 million
Debt maturity	3 years
Asset return standard deviation	40 percent

Once again, we can calculate equity and debt values:

	Combined Firm
Market value of equity	$26.602 million
Market value of debt	$13.398 million

What we notice is that this merger is a terrible idea, at least for the stockholders! Before the merger, the stock in the two separate firms was worth a total of $20.394 + 6.992 = $27.386 million compared to only $26.602 million postmerger, so the merger vaporized $27.386 − 26.602 = $.784 million, or almost $1 million, in equity.

Where did $1 million in equity go? It went to the bondholders. Their bonds were worth $9.606 + 3.008 = $12.614 million before the merger and $13.398 million after, a gain of exactly $.784 million. Thus, this merger neither created nor destroyed value, but it shifted it from the stockholders to the bondholders.

Our example shows that pure financial mergers are a bad idea, and it also shows why. The diversification works in the sense that it reduces the volatility of the firm's return on assets. This risk reduction benefits the bondholders by making default less likely. This is sometimes called the "co-insurance" effect. Essentially, by merging, the firms insure each other's bonds. The bonds are thus less risky, and they rise in value. If the bonds increase in value, and there is no net increase in asset values, then the equity must decrease in value. Thus, pure financial mergers are good for creditors, but not stockholders.

Another way to see this is that since the equity is a call option, a reduction in return variance on the underlying asset has to reduce its value. The reduction in value in the case of a purely financial merger has an interesting interpretation. The merger makes default (and, thus, bankruptcy) *less* likely to happen. That is obviously a good thing from a bondholder's perspective, but why is it a bad thing from a stockholder's perspective? The answer is simple: The right to go bankrupt is a valuable stockholder option. A purely financial merger reduces the value of that option.

Options and Capital Budgeting

In our earlier chapter on options, we discussed the many options embedded in capital budgeting decisions, including the option to wait, the option to abandon, and others. To add to these option-related issues, we now consider two additional issues. What we will show is that, for a leveraged firm, the shareholders might prefer a lower NPV project to a higher one. We then show that they might even prefer a *negative* NPV project to a positive NPV project.

As usual, we will illustrate these points first with an example. Here is the basic background information on the firm:

Market value of assets	$20 million
Face value of pure discount debt	$40 million
Debt maturity	5 years
Asset return standard deviation	50 percent

The risk-free rate is 4 percent. As we have now done many times, we can calculate equity and debt values:

Market value of equity	$5.724 million
Market value of debt	$14.276 million

This firm has a fairly high degree of leverage; the debt/equity ratio based on market values is $14.276/5.724 = 2.5, or 250 percent. This is high, but not unheard-of. Notice also that the option here is out of the money; as a result, the delta is .546.

The firm has two mutually exclusive investments under consideration. They both must be taken now or never, so there is no timing issue. The projects affect both the market value of the firm's assets and the firm's asset return standard deviation as follows:

	Project A	**Project B**
NPV	$4	$2
Market value of firm's assets ($20 + NPV)	$24	$22
Firm's asset return standard deviation	40 percent	60 percent

Which project is better? It is obvious that Project A has the higher NPV, but by now you are wary of the change in the firm's asset return standard deviation. One project reduces it, the other increases it. To see which project the stockholders like better, we have to go through our by now very familiar calculations:

	Project A	**Project B**
Market value of equity	$ 5.938	$ 8.730
Market value of debt	$18.062	$13.27

There is a dramatic difference between the two projects. Project A benefits both the stockholders and the bondholders, but most of the gain goes to the bondholders. Project B has a huge impact on the value of the equity plus it reduces the value of the debt. Clearly, the stockholders prefer B.

What are the implications of our analysis? Basically, what we have discovered is two things. First, when the equity has a delta significantly smaller than 1.0, any value created will go partially to bondholders. Second, stockholders have a strong incentive to increase the variance of the return on the firm's assets. More specifically, stockholders will have a strong preference for variance-increasing projects as opposed to variance-decreasing ones, even if that means a lower NPV.

Let's do one final example. Here is a different set of numbers:

Market value of assets	$20 million
Face value of pure discount debt	$100 million
Debt maturity	5 years
Asset return standard deviation	50 percent

The risk-free rate is 4 percent, so the equity and debt values are:

Market value of equity	$2 million
Market value of debt	$18 million

Notice that the change from our previous example is that the face value of the debt is now $100 million, so the option is far out of the money. The delta is only .24, so most of any value created will go to the bondholders.

The firm has an investment under consideration, which must be taken now or never. The project affects both the market value of the firm's assets and the firm's asset return standard deviation as follows:

Project NPV	−$1 million
Market value of firm's assets ($20 million + NPV)	$19 million
Firm's asset return standard deviation	70 percent

Thus, the project has a negative NPV, but it increases the standard deviation of the firm's return on assets. If the firm takes the project, here is the result:

Market value of equity	$4.821 million
Market value of debt	$14.179 million

This project more than doubles the value of the equity! Once again, what we are seeing is that stockholders have a strong incentive to increase volatility, particularly when the option is far out of the money. What is happening is that the shareholders have relatively little to lose because bankruptcy is the likely outcome. As a result, there is a strong incentive to go for a long shot, even if that long shot has a negative NPV. It's a bit like using your very last dollar on a lottery ticket. It's a bad investment, but there aren't a lot of other options!

Concept Questions

24.5a What is a pure financial merger?

24.5b Why might stockholders in a leveraged firm prefer a low NPV project over a higher NPV project?

SUMMARY AND CONCLUSIONS 24.6

This chapter introduces the wide world of option valuation and some of its more important implications for corporate finance. In it, we saw that:

1. The put-call parity (PCP) condition tells us that among a call option, a put option, a risk-free investment like a T-bill, and an underlying asset such as shares of stock, we can replicate any one using the other three.
2. The Black-Scholes Option Pricing Model (OPM) lets us explicitly value call options given values for the five relevant inputs, which are the price of the underlying asset, the strike price, the time to expiration, the risk-free rate, and the standard deviation of the return on the underlying asset.
3. The effect of changing the inputs into the Black-Scholes OPM varies. Some have positive effects, some negative. The magnitude also varies; relatively small changes in the risk-free rate don't have much of an effect, but changes in the standard deviation can have a very large effect. These various effects are known as the "greeks" because of the Greek (and quasi-Greek) letters used to identify them.

4. The equity in a leveraged corporation can be viewed as a call option on the assets of the firm. This gives the stockholders a strong incentive to increase the volatility of the return on the firm's assets, even if that means accepting projects with lower NPVs.

Chapter Review and Self-Test Problems

24.1 Put-Call Parity A share of stock sells for $40. The continuously compounded risk-free rate is 8 percent per year. A call option with one month to expiration and a strike price of $45 sells for $1. What's the value of a put option with the same expiration and strike?

24.2 Black-Scholes A share of stock sells for $40. The continuously compounded risk-free rate is 4 percent. The standard deviation of the return on the stock is 80 percent. What is the value of a put option with a strike of $45 and a three-month expiration?

Answers to Chapter Review and Self-Test Problems

24.1 The PCP condition says that:

$$S + P = E \times e^{-Rt} + C$$

Filling in the relevant numbers and rearranging to solve for P, the put price, we get:

$$\begin{aligned} P &= \$45 \times e^{-.08(1/12)} + 1 - 40 \\ &= \$5.70 \end{aligned}$$

24.2 We will do this one the long way and then check our answer using an options calculator. We will calculate the value of a call option and then convert it to a put using PCP. We first need d_1 and d_2:

$$\begin{aligned} d_1 &= [\ln(S/E) + (R + \sigma^2/2) \times t]/(\sigma \times \sqrt{t}) \\ &= [\ln(40/45) + (.04 + .8^2/2) \times \tfrac{1}{4}]/(.8 \times \sqrt{\tfrac{1}{4}}) \\ &= -.07 \\ d_2 &= d_1 - \sigma \times \sqrt{t} \\ &= -.47 \end{aligned}$$

Referring to Table 24.3, the values of $N(d_1)$ and $N(d_2)$ are .4721 and .3192, respectively. Notice that in both cases we average two values. Plugging all the numbers in:

$$\begin{aligned} C &= S \times N(d_1) - E \times e^{-Rt} \times N(d_2) \\ &= \$40 \times .4721 - \$45 \times e^{-.04(1/4)} \times .3192 \\ &= \$4.66 \end{aligned}$$

Converting to a put as in our previous question:

$$\begin{aligned} P &= \$45 \times e^{-.04(1/4)} + 4.66 - 40 \\ &= \$9.21 \end{aligned}$$

Using the options calculator at www.numa.com, we get $9.21, so our "by hand" approach was pretty accurate in this case.

Concepts Review and Critical Thinking Questions

1. **Options and Expiration Dates** What is the impact of lengthening the time to expiration on an option's value? Explain.
2. **Options and Stock Price Volatility** What is the impact of an increase in the volatility of the underlying stock's return on an option's value? Explain.

3. **Options and Interest Rates** How do interest rates affect option prices? Explain.
4. **Protective Puts** The protective put strategy we discussed in the chapter is sometimes referred to as "stock price insurance." Why?
5. **Intrinsic Value** What is the intrinsic value of a call option? Of a put option? How do we interpret this value?
6. **Time Value** What is the time value of a call option? Of a put option? What happens to the time value of a call option as the maturity increases? What about a put option?
7. **Option Valuation and NPV** You are CEO of Titan Industries and have just been awarded a large number of employee stock options. The company has two mutually exclusive projects available. The first project has a large NPV and will reduce the total risk of the company. The second project has a small NPV and will increase the total risk of the company. You have decided to accept the first project when you remember your employee stock options. How might this affect your decision?
8. **Put-Call Parity** You find a put and a call with the same exercise price and maturity. What do you know about the relative prices of the put and call? Prove your answer and provide an intuitive explanation.
9. **Put-Call Parity** A put and a call have the same maturity and strike price. If they have the same price, which one is in the money? Prove your answer and provide an intuitive explanation.
10. **Put-Call Parity** One thing put-call parity tells us is that given any three of a stock, a call, a put, and a T-bill, the fourth can be synthesized or replicated using the other three. For example, how can we replicate a share of stock using a call, a put, and a T-bill?

Questions and Problems

BASIC
(Questions 1–14)

1. **Continuous Compounding** If you have \$1,000 today, how much will it be worth in six years at 8 percent per year compounded continuously?
2. **Continuous Compounding** If you need \$10,000 in three years, how much will you need to deposit today if you can earn 9 percent per year compounded continuously?
3. **Put-Call Parity** A stock is currently selling for \$61 per share. A call option with an exercise price of \$65 sells for \$4.12 and expires in three months. If the risk-free rate of interest is 2.6 percent per year, compounded continuously, what is the price of a put option with the same exercise price?
4. **Put-Call Parity** A put option that expires in six months with an exercise price of \$50 sells for \$4.89. The stock is currently priced at \$53, and the risk-free rate is 3.6 percent per year, compounded continuously. What is the price of a call option with the same exercise price?
5. **Put-Call Parity** A put option and a call option with an exercise price of \$70 and three months to expiration sell for \$2.87 and \$4.68, respectively. If the risk-free rate is 4.8 percent per year, compounded continuously, what is the current stock price?
6. **Put-Call Parity** A put option and call option with an exercise price of \$65 expire in two months and sell for \$2.86 and \$4.08, respectively. If the stock is currently priced at \$65.80, what is the annual continuously compounded rate of interest?
7. **Put-Call Parity** A put option with a maturity of five months sells for \$4.80. A call with the same expiration sells for \$9.30. If the exercise price is \$80 and the stock is currently priced at \$83.12, what is the annual continuously compounded interest rate?

8. **Black-Scholes** What are the prices of a call option and a put option with the following characteristics?

Stock price	= $38
Exercise price	= $35
Risk-free rate	= 6% per year, compounded continuously
Maturity	= 3 months
Standard deviation	= 54% per year

9. **Black-Scholes** What are the prices of a call option and a put option with the following characteristics?

Stock price	= $86
Exercise price	= $90
Risk-free rate	= 4% per year, compounded continuously
Maturity	= 8 months
Standard deviation	= 62% per year

10. **Delta** What are the deltas of a call option and a put option with the following characteristics? What does the delta of the option tell you?

Stock price	= $87
Exercise price	= $85
Risk-free rate	= 5% per year, compounded continuously
Maturity	= 9 months
Standard deviation	= 56% per year

11. **Black-Scholes and Asset Value** You own a lot in Key West, Florida, that is currently unused. Similar lots have recently sold for $1.6 million. Over the past five years, the price of land in the area has increased 12 percent per year, with an annual standard deviation of 20 percent. A buyer has recently approached you and wants an option to buy the land in the next 12 months for $1.75 million. The risk-free rate of interest is 5 percent per year, compounded continuously. How much should you charge for the option?
12. **Black-Scholes and Asset Value** In the previous problem, suppose you wanted the option to sell the land to the buyer in one year. Assuming all the facts are the same, describe the transaction that would occur today. What is the price of the transaction today?
13. **Time Value of Options** You are given the following information concerning options on a particular stock:

Stock price	= $86
Exercise price	= $90
Risk-free rate	= 6% per year, compounded continuously
Maturity	= 6 months
Standard deviation	= 53% per year

a. What is the intrinsic value of the call option? Of the put option?

b. What is the time value of the call option? Of the put option?

c. Does the call or the put have the larger time value component? Would you expect this to be true in general?

14. Put-Call Parity A call option with an exercise price of $20 and four months to expiration has a price of $3.81. The stock is currently priced at $20.26, and the risk-free rate is 5 percent per year, compounded continuously. What is the price of a put option with the same exercise price?

INTERMEDIATE
(Questions 15–22)

15. Black-Scholes A call option matures in six months. The underlying stock price is $85, and the stock's return has a standard deviation of 20 percent per year. The risk-free rate is 4 percent per year, compounded continuously. If the exercise price is $0, what is the price of the call option?

16. Black-Scholes A call option has an exercise price of $80 and matures in six months. The current stock price is $84, and the risk-free rate is 5 percent per year, compounded continuously. What is the price of the call if the standard deviation of the stock is 0 percent per year?

17. Black-Scholes A stock is currently priced at $35. A call option with an expiration of one year has an exercise price of $50. The risk-free rate is 12 percent per year, compounded continuously, and the standard deviation of the stock's return is infinitely large. What is the price of the call option?

18. Equity as an Option Sunburn Sunscreen has a zero coupon bond issue outstanding with a $10,000 face value that matures in one year. The current market value of the firm's assets is $10,500. The standard deviation of the return on the firm's assets is 38 percent per year, and the annual risk-free rate is 5 percent per year, compounded continuously. Based on the Black-Scholes model, what is the market value of the firm's equity and debt?

19. Equity as an Option and NPV Suppose the firm in the previous problem is considering two mutually exclusive investments. Project A has an NPV of $700, and Project B has an NPV of $1,000. As the result of taking Project A, the standard deviation of the return on the firm's assets will increase to 55 percent per year. If Project B is taken, the standard deviation will fall to 34 percent per year.

a. What is the value of the firm's equity and debt if Project A is undertaken? If Project B is undertaken?

b. Which project would the stockholders prefer? Can you reconcile your answer with the NPV rule?

c. Suppose the stockholders and bondholders are in fact the same group of investors. Would this affect your answer to *b*?

d. What does this problem suggest to you about stockholder incentives?

20. Equity as an Option Frostbite Thermalwear has a zero coupon bond issue outstanding with a face value of $20,000 that matures in one year. The current market value of the firm's assets is $22,000. The standard deviation of the return on the firm's assets is 53 percent per year, and the annual risk-free rate is 5 percent per year, compounded continuously. Based on the Black-Scholes model, what is the market value of the firm's equity and debt? What is the firm's continuously compounded cost of debt?

21. Mergers and Equity as an Option Suppose Sunburn Sunscreen and Frostbite Thermalwear in the previous problems have decided to merge. Since the two companies have seasonal sales, the combined firm's return on assets will have a standard deviation of 31 percent per year.

a. What is the combined value of equity in the two existing companies? Value of debt?

b. What is the value of the new firm's equity? Value of debt?

c. What was the gain or loss for shareholders? For bondholders?

d. What happened to shareholder value here?

22. Equity as an Option and NPV A company has a single zero coupon bond outstanding which matures in 10 years with a face value of $30 million. The current value of the company's assets is $22 million, and the standard deviation of the return on the firm's assets is 39 percent per year. The risk-free rate is 6 percent per year, compounded continuously.

a. What is the current market value of the company's equity?

b. What is the current market value of the company's debt?

c. What is the company's continuously compounded cost of debt?

d. The company has a new project available. The project has an NPV of $750,000. If the company undertakes the project, what will be the new market value of equity? Assume volatility is unchanged.

e. Assuming the company undertakes the new project and does not borrow any additional funds, what is the new continuously compounded cost of debt? What is happening here?

CHALLENGE
(Questions 23–30)

23. Debt Valuation and Time to Maturity Christina Industries has a zero coupon bond issue that matures in two years with a face value of $30,000. The current value of the company's assets is $13,000, and the standard deviation of the return on assets is 60 percent per year.

a. Assume the risk-free rate is 5 percent per year, compounded continuously. What is the value of a risk-free bond with the same face value and maturity as the company's bond?

b. What price would the bondholders have to pay for a put option on the firm's assets with a strike price equal to the face value of the debt?

c. Using the answers from *a* and *b*, what is the value of the firm's debt? What is the continuously compounded yield on the company's debt?

d. From an examination of the value of the assets of Christina Industries, and the fact that the debt must be repaid in two years, it seems likely that the company will default on its debt. Management has approached bondholders and proposed a plan whereby the company would repay the same face value of debt, but the repayment would not occur for five years. What is the value of the debt under the proposed plan? What is the new continuously compounded yield on the debt? Explain why this occurs.

24. Debt Valuation and Asset Variance Ozzy Corp. has a zero coupon bond that matures in five years with a face value of $60,000. The current value of the company's assets is $57,000, and the standard deviation of its return on assets is 50 percent per year. The risk-free rate is 6 percent per year, compounded continuously.

a. What is the value of a risk-free bond with the same face value and maturity as the current bond?

b. What is the value of a put option on the firm's assets with a strike price equal to the face value of the debt?

c. Using the answers from *a* and *b*, what is the value of the firm's debt? What is the continuously compounded yield on the company's debt?

d. Assume the company can restructure its assets so that the standard deviation of its return on assets increases to 60 percent per year. What happens to the value of the debt? What is the new continuously compounded yield on the debt? Reconcile your answers in *c* and *d*.

e. What happens to bondholders if the company restructures its assets? What happens to shareholders? How does this create an agency problem?

25. Black-Scholes and Dividends In addition to the five factors discussed in the chapter, dividends also affect the price of an option. The Black-Scholes Option Pricing Model with dividends is:

$$C = S \times e^{-dt} \times \mathrm{N}(d_1) - E \times e^{-Rt} \times \mathrm{N}(d_2)$$
$$d_1 = [\ln(S/E) + (R - d + \sigma^2/2) \times t]/(\sigma \times \sqrt{t})$$
$$d_2 = d_1 - \sigma \times \sqrt{t}$$

All of the variables are the same as the Black-Scholes model without dividends except for the variable *d*, which is the continuously compounded dividend yield on the stock.

a. What effect do you think the dividend yield will have on the price of a call option? Explain.

b. A stock is currently priced at $84 per share, the standard deviation of its return is 50 percent per year, and the risk-free rate is 5 percent per year, compounded continuously. What is the price of a call option with a strike price of $80 and a maturity of 6 months if the stock has a dividend yield of 2 percent per year?

26. Put-Call Parity and Dividends The put-call parity condition is altered when dividends are paid. The dividend-adjusted put-call parity formula is:

$$S \times e^{-dt} + P = E \times e^{-Rt} + C$$

where *d* is again the continuously compounded dividend yield.

a. What effect do you think the dividend yield will have on the price of a put option? Explain.

b. From the previous question, what is the price of a put option with the same strike and time to expiration as the call option?

27. Put Delta In the chapter, we noted that the delta for a put option is $\mathrm{N}(d_1) - 1$. Is this the same thing as $-\mathrm{N}(-d_1)$? (Hint: Yes, but why?)

28. Black-Scholes Put Pricing Model Use the Black-Scholes model for pricing a call, put-call parity, and the previous question to show that the Black-Scholes model for directly pricing a put can be written as:

$$P = E \times e^{-Rt} \times \mathrm{N}(-d_2) - S \times \mathrm{N}(-d_1)$$

29. Black-Scholes A stock is currently priced at $50. The stock will never pay a dividend. The risk-free rate is 12 percent per year, compounded continuously, and the standard deviation of the stock's return is 60 percent. A European call option on the stock has a strike price of $100 and no expiration date, meaning that it has an infinite life. Based on Black-Scholes, what is the value of the call option? Do you see a paradox here? Do you see a way out of the paradox?

30. Delta You purchase one call and sell one put with the same strike price and expiration date. What is the delta of your portfolio? Why?

What's On the Web?

24.1 Black-Scholes Go to www.cfo.com. Find the stock options calculator under the "Tools" link. The call option and put option on a stock expire in 30 days. The strike price is $50 and the current stock price is $51.20. The standard deviation of the stock is 60 percent per year, and the risk-free rate is 4.8 percent per year, compounded continuously. What is the price of the call and the put? What are the deltas?

24.2 Black-Scholes Go to www.cboe.com, click on the "Trading Tools" tab, then the "Volatility Optimizer" link to find the options calculator. A stock is currently priced at $93 per share, and its return has a standard deviation of 48 percent per year. Options are available with an exercise price of $90, and the risk-free rate is 5.2 percent per year, compounded continuously. What is the price of the call and the put that expire next month? What are the deltas? How do your answers change for an exercise price of $95?

24.3 Implied Standard Deviation Go to www.numa.com and look under the section titled "Options" and follow the calculator link. You purchased a call option for $10.50 that matures in 51 days. The strike price is $100, and the underlying stock has a price of $102. If the risk-free rate is 4.8 percent, compounded continuously, what is the implied return standard deviation of the stock? Using this implied standard deviation, what is the price of a put option with the same characteristics?

24.4 Black-Scholes with Dividends Recalculate the first two problems assuming a dividend yield of 2 percent per year. How does this change your answers? Can you explain why dividends have the effect they do?

25 Mergers and Acquisitions

In 2004, Vodaphone (part owner of Verizon Wireless) and Cingular Wireless became involved in a heated battle to buy cell phone service provider AT&T Wireless, better known to investors by its ticker symbol, AWE. After a fast-paced series of higher and higher bids, Cingular ultimately emerged as the winner, with an all-cash offer of $41 billion, the largest such transaction ever. AWE-some! The deal made Cingular the biggest wireless company in the United States, but at a very high price. How do companies such as Cingular determine whether an acquisition like AWE is worthwhile? This chapter explores reasons mergers take place, and, just as important, reasons why they should not.

There is no more dramatic or controversial activity in corporate finance than the acquisition of one firm by another or the merger of two firms. It is the stuff of headlines in the financial press, and it is occasionally an embarrassing source of scandal.

The acquisition of one firm by another is, of course, an investment made under uncertainty, and the basic principles of valuation apply. One firm should acquire another only if doing so generates a positive net present value for the shareholders of the acquiring firm. However, because the NPV of an acquisition candidate can be difficult to determine, mergers and acquisitions, or M&A activities, are interesting topics in their own right.

An excellent source of merger data online is found at www.mergers.com.

Some of the special problems that come up in this area of finance include the following:

1. The benefits from acquisitions can depend on such things as strategic fits. Strategic fits are difficult to define precisely, and it is not easy to estimate the value of strategic fits using discounted cash flow techniques.
2. There can be complex accounting, tax, and legal effects that must be taken into account when one firm is acquired by another.
3. Acquisitions are an important control device for shareholders. Some acquisitions are a consequence of an underlying conflict between the interests of existing managers and those of shareholders. Agreeing to be acquired by another firm is one way that shareholders can remove existing managers.
4. Mergers and acquisitions sometimes involve "unfriendly" transactions. In such cases, when one firm attempts to acquire another, the activity does not always confine itself to quiet, genteel negotiations. The sought-after firm often resists takeover and may resort to defensive tactics with exotic names such as poison pills, greenmail, and white knights.

For up-to-date information on happenings in the world of M&A, go to cbs.marketwatch.com, then type "merger" into its search option.

We discuss these and other issues associated with mergers in the sections that follow. We begin by introducing the basic legal, accounting, and tax aspects of acquisitions.

IN THEIR OWN WORDS . . .

Michael C. Jensen on Mergers and Acquisitions

>> Economic analysis and evidence indicate that takeovers, LBOs, and corporate restructurings are playing an important role in helping the economy adjust to major competitive changes in the last two decades. The competition among alternative management teams and organizational structures for control of corporate assets has enabled vast economic resources to move more quickly to their highest-valued use. In the process, substantial benefits for the economy as a whole as well as for shareholders have been created. Overall gains to selling-firm shareholders from mergers, acquisitions, leveraged buyouts, and other corporate restructurings in the 12-year period from 1977 through 1988 total over $500 billion in 1988 dollars. I estimate gains to buying-firm shareholders to be at least $50 billion for the same period. These gains equal 53 percent of the total cash dividends (valued in 1988 dollars) paid to investors by the entire corporate sector in the same period.

Mergers and acquisitions are a response to new technologies or market conditions that require a strategic change in a company's direction or use of resources. Compared to current management, a new owner is often better able to accomplish major change in the existing organizational structure. Alternatively, leveraged buyouts bring about organizational change by creating entrepreneurial incentives for management and by eliminating the centralized bureaucratic obstacles to maneuverability that are inherent in large public corporations.

When managers have a substantial ownership interest in the organization, the conflicts of interest between shareholders and managers over the payout of the company's free cash flow are reduced. Management's incentives are focused on maximizing the value of the enterprise, rather than building empires—often through poorly conceived diversification acquisitions—without regard to shareholder value. Finally, the required repayment of debt replaces management's discretion in paying dividends and the tendency to overretain cash. Substantial increases in efficiency are thereby created.

Michael C. Jensen is Edsel Bryant Ford Professor of Business Administration at Harvard University. An outstanding scholar and researcher, he is famous for his pathbreaking analysis of the modern corporation and its relations with its stockholders.

25.1 THE LEGAL FORMS OF ACQUISITIONS

There are three basic legal procedures that one firm can use to acquire another firm:

1. Merger or consolidation
2. Acquisition of stock
3. Acquisition of assets

Although these forms are different from a legal standpoint, the financial press frequently does not distinguish between them. The term *merger* is often used regardless of the actual form of the acquisition.

In our discussion, we will frequently refer to the acquiring firm as the *bidder.* This is the company that will make an offer to distribute cash or securities to obtain the stock or assets of another company. The firm that is sought (and perhaps acquired) is often called the *target firm.* The cash or securities offered to the target firm are the *consideration* in the acquisition.

merger
The complete absorption of one company by another, wherein the acquiring firm retains its identity and the acquired firm ceases to exist as a separate entity.

Merger or Consolidation

A **merger** is the complete absorption of one firm by another. The acquiring firm retains its name and its identity, and it acquires all of the assets and liabilities of the acquired firm. After a merger, the acquired firm ceases to exist as a separate business entity.

A **consolidation** is the same as a merger except that an entirely new firm is created. In a consolidation, both the acquiring firm and the acquired firm terminate their previous legal existence and become part of a new firm. For this reason, the distinction between the acquiring and the acquired firm is not as important in a consolidation as it is in a merger.

consolidation
A merger in which an entirely new firm is created and both the acquired and acquiring firms cease to exist.

The rules for mergers and consolidations are basically the same. Acquisition by merger or consolidation results in a combination of the assets and liabilities of acquired and acquiring firms; the only difference lies in whether or not a new firm is created. We will henceforth use the term *merger* to refer generically to both mergers and consolidations.

There are some advantages and some disadvantages to using a merger to acquire a firm:

1. A primary advantage is that a merger is legally simple and does not cost as much as other forms of acquisition. The reason is that the firms simply agree to combine their entire operations. Thus, for example, there is no need to transfer title to individual assets of the acquired firm to the acquiring firm.
2. A primary disadvantage is that a merger must be approved by a vote of the stockholders of each firm.[1] Typically, two-thirds (or even more) of the share votes are required for approval. Obtaining the necessary votes can be time-consuming and difficult. Furthermore, as we discuss in greater detail a bit later, the cooperation of the target firm's existing management is almost a necessity for a merger. This cooperation may not be easily or cheaply obtained.

Acquisition of Stock

A second way to acquire another firm is to simply purchase the firm's voting stock with an exchange of cash, shares of stock, or other securities. This process will often start as a private offer from the management of one firm to that of another.

Regardless of how it starts, at some point the offer is taken directly to the target firm's stockholders. This can be accomplished by a tender offer. A **tender offer** is a public offer to buy shares. It is made by one firm directly to the shareholders of another firm.

tender offer
A public offer by one firm to directly buy the shares of another firm.

Those shareholders who choose to accept the offer tender their shares by exchanging them for cash or securities (or both), depending on the offer. A tender offer is frequently contingent on the bidder's obtaining some percentage of the total voting shares. If not enough shares are tendered, then the offer might be withdrawn or reformulated.

The tender offer is communicated to the target firm's shareholders by public announcements such as those made in newspaper advertisements. Sometimes, a general mailing is used in a tender offer. This is not common, however, because a general mailing requires the names and addresses of the stockholders of record. Obtaining such a list without the target firm's cooperation is not easy.

The following are some factors involved in choosing between an acquisition by stock and a merger:

1. In an acquisition by stock, no shareholder meetings have to be held and no vote is required. If the shareholders of the target firm don't like the offer, they are not required to accept it and need not tender their shares.
2. In an acquisition by stock, the bidding firm can deal directly with the shareholders of the target firm by using a tender offer. The target firm's management and board of directors can be bypassed.

What's new in mergers and acquisitions? Visit www.advisor-alliance.com to find out.

[1]Mergers between corporations require compliance with state laws. In virtually all states, the shareholders of each corporation must give their assent.

3. Acquisition is occasionally unfriendly. In such cases, a stock acquisition is used in an effort to circumvent the target firm's management, which is usually actively resisting acquisition. Resistance by the target firm's management often makes the cost of acquisition by stock higher than the cost of a merger.
4. Frequently, a significant minority of shareholders will hold out in a tender offer. The target firm cannot be completely absorbed when this happens, and this may delay realization of the merger benefits or may be costly in some other way. For example, if the bidder ends up with less than 80 percent of the target firm's shares, it must pay tax on 20 to 30 percent of any dividends paid by the target firm to the bidder.
5. Complete absorption of one firm by another requires a merger. Many acquisitions by stock are followed up with a formal merger later.

Acquisition of Assets

A firm can effectively acquire another firm by buying most or all of its assets. This accomplishes the same thing as buying the company. In this case, however, the target firm will not necessarily cease to exist; it will have just sold off its assets. The "shell" will still exist unless its stockholders choose to dissolve it.

This type of acquisition requires a formal vote of the shareholders of the selling firm. One advantage to this approach is that there is no problem with minority shareholders holding out. However, acquisition of assets may involve transferring titles to individual assets. The legal process of transferring assets can be costly.

Acquisition Classifications

Financial analysts typically classify acquisitions into three types:

1. *Horizontal acquisition.* This is acquisition of a firm in the same industry as the bidder. The firms compete with each other in their product markets. The Cingular/AT&T Wireless acquisition we discussed to open the chapter is a good example. Additional examples are easy to find, including the combination of regional telephone companies Bell Atlantic and GTE that produced telecommunications giant Verizon. Such mergers have been common in the banking industry. A recent example would be the 2004 combination of Wachovia and SouthTrust.

Got the urge to merge? See www.firstlist.com and www.mergernetwork.com for ideas.

2. *Vertical acquisition.* A vertical acquisition involves firms at different steps of the production process. The acquisition by an airline company of a travel agency would be a vertical acquisition. For example, America Online's (AOL's) purchase of Netscape for $4.21 billion in 1998 was essentially a vertical merger. AOL is a huge on-line service provider, while Netscape provides Internet and electronic commerce software.
3. *Conglomerate acquisition.* When the bidder and the target firm are not related to each other, the merger is called a conglomerate acquisition. The acquisition of a food products firm by a computer firm would be considered a conglomerate acquisition.

A Note on Takeovers

Takeover is a general and imprecise term referring to the transfer of control of a firm from one group of shareholders to another. A takeover thus occurs whenever one group takes control from another.[2] This can occur through any one of three means: acquisitions, proxy contests, and going-private transactions. Thus, takeovers encompass a broader set of activities

[2] Having *control* may be defined as having a majority vote on the board of directors.

than just acquisitions. These activities can be depicted as follows:

- Takeovers
  - Acquisition
    - Merger or consolidation
    - Acquisition of stock
    - Acquisition of assets
  - Proxy contest
  - Going private

proxy contest
An attempt to gain control of a firm by soliciting a sufficient number of stockholder votes to replace existing management.

As we have mentioned before, a takeover achieved by acquisition will occur by merger, tender offer, or purchase of assets. In mergers and tender offers, the bidder buys the voting common stock of the target firm.

Takeovers can also occur with proxy contests. **Proxy contests** occur when a group attempts to gain controlling seats on the board of directors by voting in new directors. A proxy is the right to cast someone else's votes. In a proxy contest, proxies are solicited by an unhappy group of shareholders from the rest of the shareholders.

In **going-private transactions**, all of the equity shares of a public firm are purchased by a small group of investors. Usually, the group includes members of incumbent management and some outside investors. Such transactions have come to be known generically as **leveraged buyouts (LBOs)** because a large percentage of the money needed to buy up the stock is usually borrowed. Such transactions are also termed *management buyouts (MBOs)* when existing management is heavily involved. The shares of the firm are delisted from stock exchanges and can no longer be purchased in the open market.

going-private transactions
Transactions in which all publicly owned stock in a firm is replaced with complete equity ownership by a private group.

leveraged buyouts (LBOs)
Going-private transactions in which a large percentage of the money used to buy the stock is borrowed. Oftentimes, incumbent management is involved.

LBOs have become increasingly common, and some recent ones have been quite large. For example, one of the largest cash acquisitions in history (and possibly the single largest private transaction ever of any kind) was the 1989 LBO of RJR Nabisco, the tobacco and food products giant. The acquisition price in that buyout was an astonishing $30.6 billion. In that LBO, as with most of the large ones, much of the financing came from junk bond sales (see Chapter 7 for a discussion of junk bonds).

Alternatives to Merger

Firms don't have to merge to combine their efforts. At a minimum, two (or more) firms can simply agree to work together. They can sell each other's products, perhaps under different brand names, or jointly develop a new product or technology. Firms will frequently establish a **strategic alliance**, which is usually a formal agreement to cooperate in pursuit of a joint goal. An even more formal arrangement is a **joint venture**, which commonly involves two firms putting up the money to establish a new firm. For example, Verizon Wireless is a joint venture between Verizon Communications and Vodaphone, and Cingular is a joint venture between SBC and BellSouth.

strategic alliance
Agreement between firms to cooperate in pursuit of a joint goal.

joint venture
Typically an agreement between firms to create a separate, co-owned entity established to pursue a joint goal.

Concept Questions

25.1a What is a merger? How does a merger differ from other acquisition forms?

25.1b What is a takeover?

TAXES AND ACQUISITIONS 25.2

If one firm buys another firm, the transaction may be taxable or tax-free. In a *taxable acquisition,* the shareholders of the target firm are considered to have sold their shares, and they will have capital gains or losses that will be taxed. In a *tax-free acquisition,* the acquisition is considered an exchange instead of a sale, so no capital gain or loss occurs at the time of the transaction.

Determinants of Tax Status

The general requirements for tax-free status are that the acquisition be for a business purpose, and not to avoid taxes, and that there be a continuity of equity interest. In other words, the stockholders in the target firm must retain an equity interest in the bidder.

The specific requirements for a tax-free acquisition depend on the legal form of the acquisition, but, in general, if the buying firm offers the selling firm cash for its equity, it will be a taxable acquisition. If shares of stock are offered, the transaction will generally be a tax-free acquisition.

In a tax-free acquisition, the selling shareholders are considered to have exchanged their old shares for new ones of equal value, so that no capital gains or losses are experienced.

Taxable versus Tax-Free Acquisitions

There are two factors to consider when comparing a tax-free acquisition and a taxable acquisition: the capital gains effect and the write-up effect. The *capital gains effect* refers to the fact that the target firm's shareholders may have to pay capital gains taxes in a taxable acquisition. They may demand a higher price as compensation, thereby increasing the cost of the merger. This is a cost of a taxable acquisition.

The tax status of an acquisition also affects the appraised value of the assets of the selling firm. In a taxable acquisition, the assets of the selling firm are revalued or "written up" from their historic book value to their estimated current market value. This is the *write-up effect,* and it is important because it means that the depreciation expense on the acquired firm's assets can be increased in taxable acquisitions. Remember that an increase in depreciation is a noncash expense, but it has the desirable effect of reducing taxes.

The benefit from the write-up effect was sharply curtailed by the Tax Reform Act of 1986. The reason is that the increase in value from writing up the assets is now considered a taxable gain. Before this change, taxable mergers were much more attractive, because the write-up was not taxed.

Concept Questions

25.2a What factors influence the choice between a taxable and a tax-free acquisition?

25.2b Under current tax law, why are taxable acquisitions less attractive than they once were?

25.3 ACCOUNTING FOR ACQUISITIONS

Prior to 2001, when one firm acquired another, the bidder had to decide whether the acquisition would be treated as a *purchase* or a *pooling of interests* for accounting purposes. Through the years, a great deal was written on the two approaches, discussing their pros and cons. This issue was made moot in 2001 because the Federal Accounting Standards Board (FASB) eliminated the pooling of interests option. We discuss both approaches next to illustrate some issues, but, because pooling is no longer allowed, our treatment of it is brief. In all of this, keep in mind that we are examining purely accounting-related issues. How a merger is treated for financial reporting purposes has no cash flow consequences.

The Purchase Method

The *purchase accounting method* of reporting acquisitions requires that the assets of the target firm be reported at their fair market value on the books of the bidder. With this method, an asset called *goodwill* is created for accounting purposes. Goodwill is the difference between the purchase price and the estimated fair market value of the net assets (assets less liabilities) acquired.

To illustrate, suppose Firm A acquires Firm B, thereby creating a new firm, AB. The balance sheets for the two firms on the date of the acquisition are shown in Table 25.1. Suppose Firm A pays $18 million in cash for Firm B. The money is raised by borrowing the full amount. The net fixed assets of Firm B, which are carried on the books at $8 million, are appraised at $14 million fair market value. Because the working capital is $2 million, the balance sheet assets are worth $16 million. Firm A thus pays **$2 million** in excess of the estimated market value of these net assets. This amount is the goodwill.[3]

The last balance sheet in Table 25.1 shows what the new firm looks like under purchase accounting. Notice that:

1. The total assets of Firm AB increase to **$38 million**. The fixed assets increase to **$30 million**. This is the sum of the fixed assets of Firm A and the revalued fixed assets of Firm B ($16 million + 14 million = **$30 million**).
2. The **$2 million** excess of the purchase price over the fair market value is reported as goodwill on the balance sheet.[4]

Pooling of Interests

Under a pooling of interests, the assets of the acquiring and acquired firms are pooled, meaning that the balance sheets are just added together. Using our previous example, assume that Firm A buys Firm B by giving B's shareholders $18 million worth of common stock. The result is shown in Table 25.2.

The new firm is owned jointly by all the stockholders of the previously separate firms. The accounting is much simpler here; we just add the two old balance sheets together. The total assets are unchanged by the acquisition, and no goodwill account is created.

More on Goodwill

As we just discussed, the purchase method generally leads to the creation of an intangible asset called goodwill. Pre-2001 guidelines required firms to amortize this goodwill, meaning that a portion of it was deducted as an expense every year over some period of time. In essence, the goodwill, like any asset, had to be depreciated until it was completely written off.

The amortization of goodwill was something that firms generally disliked because it reduced reported earnings. However, notice that the amortization deduction was strictly non-cash. Unlike true depreciation, it was not even a tax-deductible expense, so financial analysts just routinely ignored it.

Despite the cash flow irrelevance of goodwill amortization, FASB's decision to require purchase accounting caused a great deal of protest, much of it due to the treatment of

[3]Remember, there are assets such as employee talents, good customers, growth opportunities, and other intangibles that don't show up on the balance sheet. The $2 million excess pays for these.

[4]You might wonder what would happen if the purchase price were less than the estimated fair market value. Amusingly, to be consistent, it seems that the accountants would need to create a liability called *ill will!* Instead, the fair market value is revised downwards to equal the purchase price.

TABLE 25.1 >>

Accounting for Acquisitions: Purchase (in Millions)

Firm A				Firm B			
Working capital	$ 4	Equity	$20	Working capital	$ 2	Equity	$10
Fixed assets	16			Fixed assets	8		
Total	$20	Total	$20	Total	$10	Total	$10

Firm AB			
Working capital	$ 6	Debt	$18
Fixed assets	30	Equity	20
Goodwill	2		
Total	$38	Total	$38

The market value of the fixed assets of Firm B is $14 million. Firm A pays $18 million for Firm B by issuing debt.

TABLE 25.2 >>

Accounting for Acquisitions: Pooling of Interests (in Millions)

Firm A				Firm B			
Working capital	$ 4	Equity	$20	Working capital	$ 2	Equity	$10
Fixed assets	16			Fixed assets	8		
Total	$20	Total	$20	Total	$10	Total	$10

Firm AB			
Working capital	$ 6	Equity	$30
Fixed assets	24		
Total	$30	Total	$30

goodwill and its impact on reported earnings. As a compromise, in 2001 FASB eliminated the requirement that goodwill be amortized and put in place a new rule. In essence, the new rule says that each year firms must assess the value of the goodwill on their balance sheets. If the value has gone down (or become "impaired" in accounting-speak), the firm must deduct the decrease; otherwise, no amortization is required.

Concept Questions

25.3a What is the difference between a purchase and a pooling of interests?

25.3b What is "goodwill"?

25.4 GAINS FROM ACQUISITION

To determine the gains from an acquisition, we need to first identify the relevant incremental cash flows, or, more generally, the source of value. In the broadest sense, acquiring another firm makes sense only if there is some concrete reason to believe that the target firm will somehow be worth more in our hands than it is worth now. As we will see, there are a number of reasons why this might be so.

Try the "M&A" link at www.thedeal.com for current news.

Synergy

Suppose Firm A is contemplating acquiring Firm B. The acquisition will be beneficial if the combined firm will have value that is greater than the sum of the values of the separate firms. If we let V_{AB} stand for the value of the merged firm, then the merger makes sense only if:

$$V_{AB} > V_A + V_B$$

where V_A and V_B are the separate values. A successful merger thus requires that the value of the whole exceed the sum of the parts.

The difference between the value of the combined firm and the sum of the values of the firms as separate entities is the incremental net gain from the acquisition, ΔV:

$$\Delta V = V_{AB} - (V_A + V_B)$$

When ΔV is positive, the acquisition is said to generate **synergy**. For example, with the AT&T Wireless acquisition we discussed to open the chapter, Cingular estimated that operating synergies and savings on capital expenditures would total about \$1 billion in 2005 and over \$2 billion per year in subsequent years.

synergy
The positive incremental net gain associated with the combination of two firms through a merger or acquisition.

If Firm A buys Firm B, it gets a company worth V_B plus the incremental gain, ΔV. The value of Firm B to Firm A (V_B^*) is thus:

$$\text{Value of Firm B to Firm A} = V_B^* = \Delta V + V_B$$

We place an * on V_B^* to emphasize that we are referring to the value of Firm B to Firm A, not the value of Firm B as a separate entity.

V_B^* can be determined in two steps: (1) estimating V_B and (2) estimating ΔV. If B is a public company, then its market value as an independent firm under existing management (V_B) can be observed directly. If Firm B is not publicly owned, then its value will have to be estimated based on similar companies that are. Either way, the problem of determining a value for V_B^* requires determining a value for ΔV.

To determine the incremental value of an acquisition, we need to know the incremental cash flows. These are the cash flows for the combined firm less what A and B could generate separately. In other words, the incremental cash flow for evaluating a merger is the difference between the cash flow of the combined company and the sum of the cash flows for the two companies considered separately. We will label this incremental cash flow as ΔCF.

Synergy

<< **EXAMPLE 25.1**

Firms A and B are competitors with very similar assets and business risks. Both are all-equity firms with aftertax cash flows of \$10 per year forever, and both have an overall cost of capital of 10 percent. Firm A is thinking of buying Firm B. The aftertax cash flow from the merged firm would be \$21 per year. Does the merger generate synergy? What is V_B^*? What is ΔV?

The merger does generate synergy because the cash flow from the merged firm is ΔCF = \$1 greater than the sum of the individual cash flows (\$21 versus \$20). Assuming that the risks stay the same, the value of the merged firm is \$21/.10 = \$210. Firms A and B are each worth \$10/.10 = \$100, for a total of \$200. The incremental gain from the merger, ΔV, is thus \$210 − 200 = \$10. The total value of Firm B to Firm A, V_B^*, is \$100 (the value of B as a separate company) plus \$10 (the incremental gain), or \$110.

From our discussions in earlier chapters, we know that the incremental cash flow, ΔCF, can be broken down into four parts:

$$\begin{aligned}\Delta\text{CF} &= \Delta\text{EBIT} + \Delta\text{Depreciation} - \Delta\text{Tax} - \Delta\text{Capital requirements}\\ &= \Delta\text{Revenue} - \Delta\text{Cost} - \Delta\text{Tax} - \Delta\text{Capital requirements}\end{aligned}$$

where ΔRevenue is the difference in revenues, ΔCost is the difference in costs, ΔTax is the difference in taxes, and ΔCapital requirements is the change in new fixed assets and net working capital.

Based on this breakdown, the merger will make sense only if one or more of these cash flow components are beneficially affected by the merger. The possible cash flow benefits of mergers and acquisitions thus fall into four basic categories: revenue enhancement, cost reductions, lower taxes, and reductions in capital needs.

Revenue Enhancement

One important reason for an acquisition is that the combined firm may generate greater revenues than two separate firms. Increases in revenue may come from marketing gains, strategic benefits, and increases in market power.

Marketing Gains It is frequently claimed that mergers and acquisitions can produce greater operating revenues from improved marketing. For example, improvements might be made in the following areas:

1. Previously ineffective media programming and advertising efforts
2. A weak existing distribution network
3. An unbalanced product mix

In the AT&T Wireless acquisition, analysts noted enormous savings in marketing expenses. Cell phone providers advertise heavily, and essentially all of the money that AT&T Wireless was spending would no longer be necessary.

Strategic Benefits Some acquisitions promise a strategic advantage. This is an opportunity to take advantage of the competitive environment if certain things occur or, more generally, to enhance management flexibility with regard to the company's future operations. In this latter regard, a strategic benefit is more like an option than a standard investment opportunity.

For example, suppose a sewing machine manufacturer can use its technology to enter other businesses. The small-motor technology from the original business can provide opportunities to begin manufacturing small appliances and electric typewriters. Similarly, electronics expertise gained in producing typewriters can be used to manufacture electronic printers.

The word *beachhead* has been used in describing the process of entering a new industry to exploit perceived opportunities. The beachhead is used to spawn new opportunities based on "intangible" relationships. One example is Procter & Gamble's initial acquisition of the Charmin Paper Company as a beachhead that allowed Procter & Gamble to develop a highly interrelated cluster of paper products—disposable diapers, paper towels, feminine hygiene products, and bathroom tissue.[5]

Market Power One firm may acquire another to increase its market share and market power. In such mergers, profits can be enhanced through higher prices and reduced competition for customers. Of course, mergers that substantially reduce competition in the market may be challenged by the U.S. Department of Justice or the Federal Trade Commission on antitrust grounds.

---

[5]This example comes from Michael Porter, *Competitive Advantage* (New York: Free Press, 1985).

Cost Reductions

One of the most basic reasons to merge is that a combined firm may operate more efficiently than two separate firms. A firm can achieve greater operating efficiency in several different ways through a merger or an acquisition.

Economies of Scale Economies of scale relate to the average cost per unit of producing goods and services. If the per-unit cost of production falls as the level of production increases, then an economy of scale exists:

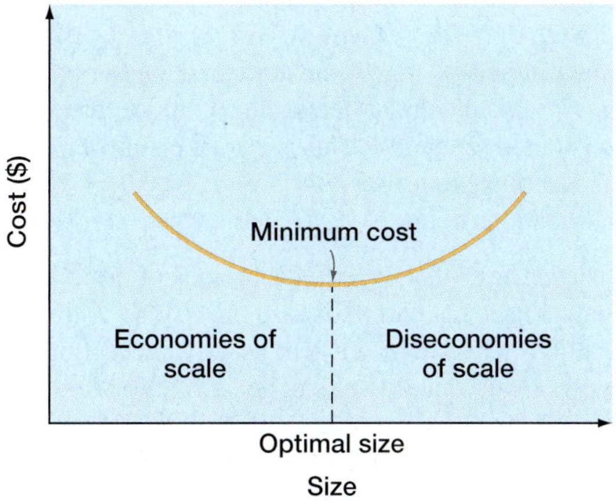

Frequently, the phrase *spreading overhead* is used in connection with economies of scale. This expression refers to the sharing of central facilities such as corporate headquarters, top management, and computer services. In the AT&T Wireless acquisition, Cingular specifically noted the enormous savings available from the elimination of redundant personnel and operations. In essence, even though the combined company would be much larger as a result of the acquisition, the operating and capital costs per customer would be much lower.

Economies of Vertical Integration Operating economies can be gained from vertical combinations as well as from horizontal combinations. The main purpose of vertical acquisitions is to make it easier to coordinate closely related operating activities. Benefits from vertical integration are probably the reason that most forest product firms that cut timber also own sawmills and hauling equipment. Economies of vertical integration may explain why some airline companies have purchased hotels and car rental companies.

Technology transfers are another reason for vertical integration. Very frequently, a company will decide that the cheapest—and fastest—way to acquire another firm's technological skills is to simply buy the firm. For obvious reasons, this rationale is particularly common in high-tech industries.

Complementary Resources Some firms acquire others to make better use of existing resources or to provide the missing ingredient for success. Think of a ski equipment store that could merge with a tennis equipment store to produce more even sales over both the winter and summer seasons, and thereby better use store capacity.

Lower Taxes

Tax gains are a powerful incentive for some acquisitions. The possible tax gains from an acquisition include the following:

1. The use of tax losses
2. The use of unused debt capacity
3. The use of surplus funds
4. The ability to write up the value of depreciable assets

Net Operating Losses Firms that lose money on a pretax basis will not pay taxes. Such firms can end up with tax losses they cannot use. These tax losses are referred to as *net operating losses (NOL).*

A firm with net operating losses may be an attractive merger partner for a firm with significant tax liabilities. Absent any other effects, the combined firm will have a lower tax bill than the two firms considered separately. This is a good example of how a firm can be more valuable merged than standing alone.

There are two qualifications to our NOL discussion:

1. Federal tax laws permit firms that experience periods of profit and loss to even things out through loss carry-back and carry-forward provisions. A firm that has been profitable in the past but has a loss in the current year can get refunds of income taxes paid in the past three years. After that, losses can be carried forward for up to 15 years. Thus, a merger to exploit unused tax shields must offer tax savings over and above what can be accomplished by firms via carry-overs.[6]
2. The IRS may disallow an acquisition if the principal purpose of the acquisition is to avoid federal tax by acquiring a deduction or credit that would not otherwise be available.

Unused Debt Capacity Some firms do not use as much debt as they are able. This makes them potential acquisition candidates. Adding debt can provide important tax savings, and many acquisitions are financed with debt. The acquiring company can deduct interest payments on the newly created debt and reduce taxes.

Surplus Funds Another quirk in the tax laws involves surplus funds. Consider a firm that has free cash flow—cash flow available after all taxes have been paid and after all positive net present value projects have been financed. In such a situation, aside from purchasing fixed-income securities, the firm has several ways to spend the free cash flow, including:

1. Paying dividends
2. Buying back its own shares
3. Acquiring shares in another firm

We discussed the first two options in Chapter 18. We saw that an extra dividend will increase the income tax paid by some investors. A share repurchase will reduce the taxes paid by shareholders as compared to paying dividends, but this is not a legal option if the sole purpose is to avoid taxes that would have otherwise been paid by shareholders.

---

[6]Under the 1986 Tax Reform Act, a corporation's ability to carry forward net operating losses (and other tax credits) is limited when more than 50 percent of the stock changes hands over a three-year period.

To avoid these problems, the firm can buy another firm. By doing this, the firm avoids the tax problem associated with paying a dividend. Also, the dividends received from the purchased firm are not taxed in a merger.

Asset Write-Ups We have previously observed that, in a taxable acquisition, the assets of the acquired firm can be revalued. If the value of the assets is increased, tax deductions for depreciation will be a benefit, but this benefit will usually be more than offset by taxes due on the write-up.

Reductions in Capital Needs

All firms must make investments in working capital and fixed assets to sustain an efficient level of operating activity. A merger may reduce the combined investments needed by the two firms. For example, it may be that Firm A needs to expand its manufacturing facilities whereas Firm B has significant excess capacity. It may be much cheaper for Firm A to buy Firm B than to build from scratch.

In addition, acquiring firms may see ways of more effectively managing existing assets. This can occur with a reduction in working capital resulting from more efficient handling of cash, accounts receivable, and inventory. Finally, the acquiring firm may also sell off certain assets that are not needed in the combined firm.

Firms will often cite a large number of reasons for merging. Typically, when firms agree to merge, they sign an *agreement of merger,* which contains, among other things, a list of the economic benefits that shareholders can expect from the merger. For example, the U.S. Steel and Marathon Oil agreement stated (emphasis added):

> U.S. Steel believes that the acquisition of Marathon provides U.S. Steel with an attractive opportunity to *diversify* into the energy business. Reasons for the merger include, but are not limited to, the facts that consummation of the merger will allow U.S. Steel to consolidate Marathon in U.S. Steel's federal *income tax return,* will also contribute to *greater efficiency,* and will enhance the *ability to manage capital* by permitting movements of cash between U.S. Steel and Marathon. Additionally, the merger will *eliminate the possibility of conflicts of interest* between the interests of minority and majority shareholders and will *enhance management flexibility.* The acquisition will provide Marathon shareholders with a substantial premium over historic market prices for their shares. However, [Marathon] shareholders will no longer continue to share in the future prospects of the company.

Avoiding Mistakes

Evaluating the benefit of a potential acquisition is more difficult than a standard capital budgeting analysis because so much of the value can come from intangible, or otherwise difficult to quantify, benefits. Consequently, there is a great deal of room for error. Here are some general rules that should be remembered:

1. *Do not ignore market values.* There is no point to and little gain from estimating the value of a publicly traded firm when that value can be directly observed. The current market value represents a consensus opinion of investors concerning the firm's value (under existing management). Use this value as a starting point. If the firm is not publicly held, then the place to start is with similar firms that are publicly held.
2. *Estimate only incremental cash flows.* It is important to estimate the incremental cash flows that will result from the acquisition. Only incremental cash flows from an acquisition will add value to the acquiring firm. Acquisition analysis should thus focus only on the newly created, incremental cash flows from the proposed acquisition.

3. *Use the correct discount rate.* The discount rate should be the required rate of return for the incremental cash flows associated with the acquisition. It should reflect the risk associated with the use of funds, not the source. In particular, if Firm A is acquiring Firm B, then Firm A's cost of capital is not particularly relevant. Firm B's cost of capital is a much more appropriate discount rate because it reflects the risk of Firm B's cash flows.
4. *Be aware of transactions costs.* An acquisition may involve substantial (and sometimes astounding) transactions costs. These will include fees to investment bankers, legal fees, and disclosure requirements.

A Note on Inefficient Management

There are firms whose value could be increased with a change in management. These are firms that are poorly run or otherwise do not efficiently use their assets to create shareholder value. Mergers are a means of replacing management in such cases.

The fact that a firm might benefit from a change in management does not necessarily mean that existing management is dishonest, incompetent, or negligent. Instead, just as some athletes are better than others, so might some management teams be better at running a business. This can be particularly true during times of technological change or other periods when innovations in business practice are occurring. In any case, to the extent that corporate "raiders" can identify poorly run firms or firms that, for other reasons, will benefit from a change in management, these raiders provide a valuable service to target-firm shareholders and society in general.

Concept Questions

25.4a What are the relevant incremental cash flows for evaluating a merger candidate?

25.4b What are some different sources of gain from acquisition?

25.5 SOME FINANCIAL SIDE EFFECTS OF ACQUISITIONS

In addition to the various possibilities we have discussed thus far, mergers can have some purely financial side effects, that is, things that occur regardless of whether the merger makes economic sense or not. Two such effects are particularly worth mentioning: EPS growth and diversification.

EPS Growth

An acquisition can create the appearance of growth in earnings per share, or EPS. This may fool investors into thinking that the firm is doing better than it really is. What happens is easiest to see with an example.

Suppose Global Resources, Ltd., acquires Regional Enterprises. The financial positions of Global and Regional before the acquisition are shown in Table 25.3. We assume that the merger creates no additional value, so the combined firm (Global Resources after acquiring Regional) has a value that is equal to the sum of the values of the two firms before the merger.

Before the merger, both Global and Regional have 100 shares outstanding. However, Global sells for $25 per share, versus a price of $10 per share for Regional. Global

<< TABLE 25.3

Financial Positions of Global Resources and Regional Enterprises

	Global Resources before Merger	Regional Enterprises before Merger	Global Resources after Merger: The Market Is Smart	Global Resources after Merger: The Market Is Fooled
Earnings per share	$1	$1	$1.43	$1.43
Price per share	$25	$10	$25	$35.71
Price-earnings ratio	25	10	17.5	25
Number of shares	100	100	140	140
Total earnings	$100	$100	$200	$200
Total value	$2,500	$1,000	$3,500	$5,000

Exchange ratio: 1 share in Global for 2.5 shares in Regional.

therefore acquires Regional by exchanging 1 of its shares for every 2.5 Regional shares. Because there are 100 shares in Regional, this will take $100/2.5 = 40$ shares in all.

After the merger, Global will have 140 shares outstanding, and several things will happen (see the third column of Table 25.3):

1. The market value of the combined firm is **$3,500**. This is equal to the sum of the values of the separate firms before the merger. If the market is "smart," it will realize that the combined firm is worth the sum of the values of the separate firms.
2. The earnings per share of the merged firm are **$1.43**. The acquisition enables Global to increase its earnings per share from $1 to $1.43, an increase of 43 percent.
3. Because the stock price of Global after the merger is the same as that before the merger, the price-earnings ratio must fall. This is true as long as the market is smart and recognizes that the total market value has not been altered by the merger.

If the market is "fooled," it might mistake the 43 percent increase in earnings per share for true growth. In this case, the price-earnings ratio of Global may not fall after the merger. Suppose the price-earnings ratio of Global remains equal to 25. Because the combined firm has earnings of **$200**, the total value of the combined firm will increase to **$5,000 (25 × $200)**. The per-share value for Global will increase to **$35.71 ($5,000/140)**.

This is earnings growth magic. Like all good magic, it is just illusion. For it to work, the shareholders of Global and Regional must receive something for nothing. This, of course, is unlikely with so simple a trick.

Diversification

Diversification is commonly mentioned as a benefit of a merger. We previously noted that U.S. Steel included diversification as a benefit in describing its acquisition of Marathon Oil. The problem is that diversification per se probably does not create value.

Going back to Chapter 13, recall that diversification reduces unsystematic risk. We also saw that the value of an asset depends on its systematic risk, and systematic risk is not directly affected by diversification. Because the unsystematic risk is not especially important, there is no particular benefit from reducing it.

An easy way to see why diversification isn't an important benefit of a merger is to consider someone who owned stock in U.S. Steel and Marathon Oil. Such a stockholder was already diversified between these two investments. The merger didn't do anything the stockholders couldn't do for themselves.

More generally, stockholders can get all the diversification they want by buying stock in different companies. As a result, they won't pay a premium for a merged company just for the benefit of diversification.

By the way, we are not saying that U.S. Steel (now USX) made a mistake. At the time of the merger, U.S. Steel was a cash-rich company (over 20 percent of its assets were in the form of cash and marketable securities). It is not uncommon to see firms with surplus cash articulating a "need" for diversification.

Concept Questions

25.5a Why can a merger create the appearance of earnings growth?

25.5b Why is diversification by itself not a good reason for a merger?

25.6 THE COST OF AN ACQUISITION

We've discussed some of the benefits of acquisition. We now need to discuss the cost of a merger.[7] We learned earlier that the net incremental gain from a merger is:

$$\Delta V = V_{AB} - (V_A + V_B)$$

Also, the total value of Firm B to Firm A, V_B^*, is:

$$V_B^* = V_B + \Delta V$$

The NPV of the merger is therefore:

$$\text{NPV} = V_B^* - \text{Cost to Firm A of the acquisition} \qquad [25.1]$$

To illustrate, suppose we have the following premerger information for Firm A and Firm B:

	Firm A	Firm B
Price per share	$ 20	$ 10
Number of shares	25	10
Total market value	$500	$100

Both of these firms are 100 percent equity. You estimate that the incremental value of the acquisition, ΔV, is $100.

The board of Firm B has indicated that it will agree to a sale if the price is $150, payable in cash or stock. This price for Firm B has two parts. Firm B is worth $100 as a standalone, so this is the minimum value that we could assign to Firm B. The second part, $50, is called the merger premium, and it represents the amount paid above the stand-alone value.

Should Firm A acquire Firm B? Should it pay in cash or stock? To answer, we need to determine the NPV of the acquisition under both alternatives. We can start by noting that the value of Firm B to Firm A is:

$$\begin{aligned} V_B^* &= \Delta V + V_B \\ &= \$100 + 100 = \$200 \end{aligned}$$

[7]For a more complete discussion of the costs of a merger and the NPV approach, see S. C. Myers, "A Framework for Evaluating Mergers," in *Modern Developments in Financial Management,* ed. S. C. Myers (New York: Praeger Publishers, 1976).

The total value received by A as a result of buying Firm B is thus \$200. The question then is, How much does Firm A have to give up? The answer depends on whether cash or stock is used as the means of payment.

Case I: Cash Acquisition

The cost of an acquisition when cash is used is just the cash itself. So, if Firm A pays \$150 in cash to purchase all of the shares of Firm B, the cost of acquiring Firm B is \$150. The NPV of a cash acquisition is:

$$\begin{aligned} \text{NPV} &= V_B^* - \text{Cost} \\ &= \$200 - 150 = \$50 \end{aligned}$$

The acquisition is therefore profitable.

After the merger, Firm AB will still have 25 shares outstanding. The value of Firm A after the merger is:

$$\begin{aligned} V_{AB} &= V_A + (V_B^* - \text{Cost}) \\ &= \$500 + 200 - 150 \\ &= \$550 \end{aligned}$$

This is just the premerger value of \$500 plus the \$50 NPV. The price per share after the merger is \$550/25 = \$22, representing a gain of \$2 per share.

Case II: Stock Acquisition

Things are somewhat more complicated when stock is the means of payment. In a cash merger, the shareholders in B receive cash for their stock, and, as in the U.S. Steel–Marathon Oil example, they no longer participate in the company. Thus, as we have seen, the cost of the acquisition in this case is the amount of cash needed to pay off B's stockholders.

In a stock merger, no cash actually changes hands. Instead, the shareholders of Firm B come in as new shareholders in the merged firm. The value of the merged firm in this case will be equal to the premerger values of Firms A and B plus the incremental gain from the merger, ΔV:

$$\begin{aligned} V_{AB} &= V_A + V_B + \Delta V \\ &= \$500 + 100 + 100 \\ &= \$700 \end{aligned}$$

To give \$150 worth of stock for Firm B, Firm A will have to give up \$150/20 = 7.5 shares. After the merger, there will be 25 + 7.5 = 32.5 shares outstanding, and the per-share value will be \$700/32.5 = \$21.54.

Notice that the per-share price after the merger is lower under the stock purchase option. The reason has to do with the fact that B's shareholders own stock in the new firm.

It appears that Firm A paid \$150 for Firm B. However, it actually paid more than that. When all is said and done, B's stockholders own 7.5 shares of stock in the merged firm. After the merger, each of these shares is worth \$21.54. The total value of the consideration received by B's stockholders is thus 7.5 × \$21.54 = \$161.55.

This \$161.55 is the true cost of the acquisition because it is what the sellers actually end up receiving. The NPV of the merger to Firm A is:

$$\begin{aligned} \text{NPV} &= V_B^* - \text{Cost} \\ &= \$200 - 161.55 = \$38.45 \end{aligned}$$

We can check this by noting that A started with 25 shares worth \$20 each. The gain to A of \$38.45 works out to be \$38.45/25 = \$1.54 per share. The value of the stock has increased to \$21.54, as we calculated.

When we compare the cash acquisition to the stock acquisition, we see that the cash acquisition is better in this case, because Firm A gets to keep all of the NPV if it pays in cash. If it pays in stock, Firm B's stockholders share in the NPV by becoming new stockholders in A.

Cash versus Common Stock

The distinction between cash and common stock financing in a merger is an important one. If cash is used, the cost of an acquisition is not dependent on the acquisition gains. All other things being the same, if common stock is used, the cost is higher because Firm A's shareholders must share the acquisition gains with the shareholders of Firm B. However, if the NPV of the acquisition is negative, then the loss will be shared between the two firms.

Whether a firm should finance an acquisition with cash or with shares of stock depends on several factors, including the following:

1. *Sharing gains.* If cash is used to finance an acquisition, the selling firm's shareholders will not participate in the potential gains from the merger. Of course, if the acquisition is not a success, the losses will not be shared, and shareholders of the acquiring firm will be worse off than if stock had been used.
2. *Taxes.* Acquisition by paying cash usually results in a taxable transaction. Acquisition by exchanging stock is generally tax-free.
3. *Control.* Acquisition by paying cash does not affect the control of the acquiring firm. Acquisition with voting shares may have implications for control of the merged firm.

In a typical year, in terms of the total number of deals, cash financing is much more common than stock financing. The same is usually true based on the total dollar values, though the difference is smaller. The reason is that stock financing becomes more common if we look at very large deals.

Concept Questions

25.6a Why does the true cost of a stock acquisition depend on the gain from the merger?

25.6b What are some important factors in deciding whether to use stock or cash in an acquisition?

25.7 DEFENSIVE TACTICS

Target-firm managers frequently resist takeover attempts. Resistance usually starts with press releases and mailings to shareholders that present management's viewpoint. It can eventually lead to legal action and solicitation of competing bids. Managerial action to defeat a takeover attempt may make target-firm shareholders better off if it elicits a higher offer premium from the bidding firm or another firm.

Of course, management resistance may simply reflect pursuit of self-interest at the expense of shareholders. This is a controversial subject. At times, management resistance has greatly increased the amount ultimately received by their shareholders. At other times, management resistance appears to have defeated all takeover attempts to the detriment of their shareholders.

In this section, we describe various defensive tactics that have been used by target firms' management to resist unfriendly attempts. The law surrounding these defenses is not settled, and some of these maneuvers may ultimately be deemed illegal or otherwise unsuitable.

The Corporate Charter

The *corporate charter* consists of the articles of incorporation and corporate bylaws that establish the governance rules of the firm. The corporate charter establishes the conditions that allow for a takeover. Firms frequently amend corporate charters to make acquisitions more difficult. For example, usually, two-thirds (67 percent) of the shareholders of record must approve a merger. Firms can make it more difficult to be acquired by changing this required percentage to 80 percent or so. Such a change is called a *supermajority amendment.*

Another device is to stagger the election of the board members. This makes it more difficult to elect a new board of directors quickly. Such a board is sometimes called a classified board. We discussed staggered elections in Chapter 8.

Repurchase and Standstill Agreements

Managers of target firms may attempt to negotiate *standstill agreements.* Standstill agreements are contracts wherein the bidding firm agrees to limit its holdings in the target firm. These agreements usually lead to the end of a takeover attempt.

Standstill agreements often occur at the same time that a *targeted repurchase* is arranged. In a targeted repurchase, a firm buys a certain amount of its own stock from an individual investor, usually at a substantial premium. These premiums can be thought of as payments to potential bidders to eliminate unfriendly takeover attempts. Critics of such payments view them as bribes and label them **greenmail**.

greenmail
In a targeted stock repurchase, payments made to potential bidders to eliminate unfriendly takeover attempts.

Poison Pills and Share Rights Plans

A **poison pill** is a tactic designed to repel would-be suitors. The term comes from the world of espionage. Agents are supposed to bite a pill of cyanide rather than permit capture. Presumably, this prevents enemy interrogators from learning important secrets.

poison pill
A financial device designed to make unfriendly takeover attempts unappealing, if not impossible.

In the equally colorful world of corporate finance, a poison pill is a financial device designed to make it impossible for a firm to be acquired without management's consent—unless the buyer is willing to commit financial suicide.

A majority of the largest firms in the United States have adopted poison pill provisions of one form or another, often calling them **share rights plans** (SRPs) or something similar. SRPs differ quite a bit in detail from company to company; we will describe a kind of generic approach here. In general, when a company adopts an SRP, it distributes share rights to its existing stockholders.[8] These rights allow shareholders to buy shares of stock (or preferred stock) at some fixed price.

share rights plans
Provisions allowing existing stockholders to purchase stock at some fixed price should an outside takeover bid come up, discouraging hostile takeover attempts.

The rights issued with an SRP have a number of unusual features. First, the exercise, or subscription, price on the right is usually set high enough so that the rights are well out of the money, meaning that the purchase price is much higher than the current stock price. The rights will often be good for 10 years, and the purchase, or exercise, price is usually a reasonable estimate of what the stock will be worth at the end of that time.

In addition, unlike ordinary stock rights, these rights can't be exercised immediately, and they can't be bought and sold separately from the stock. Also, they can essentially be canceled by management at any time; often, they can be redeemed (bought back) for a penny apiece, or some similarly trivial amount.

[8]We discussed ordinary share rights in Chapter 16.

Things get interesting when, under certain circumstances, the rights are "triggered." This means that the rights become exercisable, they can be bought and sold separately from the stock, and they are not easily canceled or redeemed. Typically, the rights will be triggered when someone acquires 20 percent of the common stock or announces a tender offer.

When the rights are triggered, they can be exercised. Because they are out of the money, this fact is not especially important. Certain other features come into play, however. The most important is the *flip-in provision.*

The flip-in provision is the "poison" in the pill. In the event of an unfriendly takeover attempt, the holder of a right can pay the exercise price and receive common stock in the target firm worth twice the exercise price. In other words, holders of the rights can buy stock in the target firm at half price. Simultaneously, the rights owned by the raider (the acquirer) are voided. The goal of the flip-in provision is to massively dilute the raider's ownership position.[9]

The rights issued in connection with an SRP are poison pills because anyone trying to force a merger will trigger the rights. When this happens, all the target firm's stockholders can effectively buy stock in the merged firm at half price. This greatly increases the cost of the merger to the bidder because the target firm's shareholders end up with a much larger percentage of the merged firm.

Notice that the flip-in provision doesn't prevent someone from acquiring control of a firm by purchasing a majority interest. It just acts to vastly increase the cost of doing so.

The intention of a poison pill is to force a bidder to negotiate with management. Frequently, merger offers are made with the contingency that the rights will be canceled by the target firm.

Some new varieties of poison pills have appeared on the scene in recent years. For example, a "chewable" pill, common in Canada but not in the United States, is a pill that is installed by shareholder vote and can be redeemed by shareholder vote. Then there's the "deadhand pill," which explicitly gives the directors who installed the pill, or their handpicked successors, the authority to remove the pill. This type of pill is controversial because it makes it virtually impossible for new directors elected by stockholders to remove an existing poison pill.

Going Private and Leveraged Buyouts

As we have previously discussed, going private is what happens when the publicly owned stock in a firm is replaced with complete equity ownership by a private group, which may include elements of existing management. As a consequence, the firm's stock is taken off the market (if it is an exchange-traded stock, it is delisted) and is no longer traded.

One result of going private is that takeovers via tender offer can no longer occur since there are no publicly held shares. In this sense, an LBO (or, more specifically, an MBO) can be a takeover defense. However, it's only a defense for management. From the stockholders' point of view, an LBO is a takeover because they are bought out.

Other Devices and Jargon of Corporate Takeovers

As corporate takeovers have become more common, a new vocabulary has developed. The terms are colorful, and, in no particular order, some of them are listed here:

1. *Golden parachute.* Some target firms provide compensation to top-level management if a takeover occurs. For example, shareholders in communications provider Sprint cheered when the firm agreed to be acquired by then high-flying WorldCom in 1999.

---

[9]Some plans also contain "flip-over" provisions. These allow the holders to buy stock in the merged company at half price.

As is very common, the chairman of Sprint, William Esrey had a golden parachute agreement. What came as a bit of a surprise was the size. Depending on who did the calculations, the value of Esrey's parachute was about $500 to $700 million! The opposite of a golden parachute is a "golden handcuff," which is an incentive package designed to get executives to stay on board once the acquisition is completed.

Depending on your perspective and the amounts involved, golden parachutes can be viewed as a payment to management to make it less concerned for its own welfare and more interested in stockholders when considering a takeover bid.

2. *Poison put.* A poison put is a variation on the poison pill we described earlier. A poison put forces the firm to buy securities back at some set price.
3. *Crown jewel.* Firms often sell or threaten to sell major assets—crown jewels—when faced with a takeover threat. This is sometimes referred to as the "scorched earth" strategy. This tactic often involves a lockup, which we discuss shortly.
4. *White knight.* A firm facing an unfriendly merger offer might arrange to be acquired by a different, friendly firm. The firm is thereby rescued by a white knight. Alternatively, the firm may arrange for a friendly entity to acquire a large block of stock. So-called white squires or big brothers are individuals, firms, or even mutual funds involved in friendly transactions of these types. Sometimes white knights or others are granted exceptional terms or otherwise compensated. Inevitably it seems, this has been called *whitemail.*
5. *Lockup.* A lockup is an option granted to a friendly suitor (a white knight, perhaps) giving them the right to purchase stock or some of the assets (the crown jewels, possibly) of a target firm at a fixed price in the event of an unfriendly takeover.
6. *Shark repellent.* A shark repellent is any tactic (a poison pill, for example) designed to discourage unwanted merger offers.
7. *Bear hug.* A bear hug is an unfriendly takeover offer designed to be so attractive that the target firm's management has little choice but to accept it. In August of 2001, two big "bear hug" offers attracted widespread interest. EchoStar Communications (operator of the DISH network) made an unsolicited bid for Hughes Electronics (operator of DirectTV). At about the same time, cable company Comcast Corporation made a surprise $40 billion bid for AT&T's cable unit.
8. *Fair price provision.* A fair price provision is a requirement that all selling shareholders receive the same price from a bidder. The provision prevents a "two-tier" offer. In such a deal, a bidder offers a premium price only for a percentage of the shares large enough to gain control. It offers a lower price for the remaining shares. Such an offer can set off a stampede among shareholders as they rush to get the better price.
9. *Dual class capitalization.* In an earlier chapter, we noted that some firms such as Google have more than one class of common stock and that voting power was typically concentrated in a class of stock not held by the public. Such a capital structure means that an unfriendly bidder will not succeed in gaining control.
10. *Countertender offer.* Better known as the "Pac-man" defense, the target responds to an unfriendly overture by offering to buy the bidder! This tactic is rarely used, in part because target firms are usually too small to realistically purchase the bidder.

Concept Questions

25.7a What can a firm do to make a takeover less likely?

25.7b What is a share rights plan? Explain how the rights work.

25.8 SOME EVIDENCE ON ACQUISITIONS: DOES M&A PAY?

One of the most controversial issues surrounding our subject is whether mergers and acquisitions benefit shareholders. A very large number of studies have attempted to estimate the effect of mergers and takeovers on stock prices of the bidding and target firms. These studies have examined the gains and losses in stock value around the time of merger announcements.

One conclusion that clearly emerges is that M&A pays for target firm shareholders. There is no mystery here. The premium typically paid by bidders represents an immediate, relatively large gain, often on the order of 20 percent or more.

Matters become much more murky when we look at bidders, and different studies reach different conclusions. One thing is clear, however. Shareholders in bidder firms seem to neither win nor lose very much, at least on average. This finding is a bit of a puzzle, and there are a variety of explanations:

1. Anticipated merger gains may not be completely achieved, and shareholders thus experience losses. This can happen if managers of bidding firms tend to overestimate the gains from acquisition.
2. The bidding firms are usually much larger than the target firms. Thus, even though the dollar gains to the bidder may be similar to the dollar gains earned by shareholders of the target firm, the percentage gains will be much lower.
3. Another possible explanation for the low returns to the shareholders of bidding firms in takeovers is simply that management may not be acting in the interest of shareholders when it attempts to acquire other firms. Perhaps it is attempting to increase the size of the firm, even if this reduces its value per share.
4. The market for takeovers may be sufficiently competitive that the NPV of acquiring is zero because the prices paid in acquisitions fully reflect the value of the acquired firms. In other words, the sellers capture all of the gain.
5. Finally, the announcement of a takeover may not convey much new information to the market about the bidding firm. This can occur because firms frequently announce intentions to engage in merger "programs" long before they announce specific acquisitions. In this case, the stock price for the bidding firm may already reflect anticipated gains from mergers.

Concept Questions

25.8a What does the evidence say about the benefits of mergers and acquisitions to target-company shareholders?

25.8b What does the evidence say about the benefits of mergers and acquisitions to acquiring-company shareholders?

25.9 DIVESTITURES AND RESTRUCTURINGS

In contrast to a merger or acquisition, a **divestiture** occurs when a firm sells assets, operations, divisions, and/or segments to a third party. Note that divestitures are an important part of M&A activity. After all, one company's acquisition is usually another's divestiture. Also, following a merger, it is very common for certain assets or divisions to be sold. Such sales may be required by antitrust regulations; they may be needed to raise cash to help pay for a deal; or the divested units may simply be unwanted by the acquirer.

divestiture
The sale of assets, operations, divisions, and/or segments of a business to a third party.

Divestitures also occur when a company decides to sell off a part of itself for reasons unrelated to mergers and acquisitions. This can happen when a particular unit is unprofitable or not a good strategic fit. Or, a firm may decide to cash out of a very profitable operation. Finally, a cash-strapped firm may have to sell assets just to raise capital (this commonly occurs in bankruptcy).

A divestiture usually occurs like any other sale. A company lets it be known that it has assets for sale and seeks offers. If a suitable offer is forthcoming, a sale occurs.

In some cases, particularly when the desired divestiture is a relatively large operating unit, companies will elect to do an **equity carve-out**. To do a carve-out, a parent company first creates a completely separate company of which the parent is the sole shareholder. Next, the parent company arranges an initial public offering (IPO) in which a fraction, perhaps 20 percent or so, of the parent's stock is sold to the public, thus creating a publicly held company.

equity carve-out
The sale of stock in a wholly owned subsidiary via an IPO.

Instead of a carve-out, a company can elect to do a **spin-off**. In a spin-off, the company simply distributes shares in the subsidiary to its existing stockholders on a pro rata basis. Shareholders can keep the shares or sell them as they see fit. Very commonly, a company will first do an equity carve-out to create an active market for the shares and then subsequently do a spin-off of the remaining shares at a later date. Many well-known companies were created by this route. For example, insurance giant Allstate was spun-off by Sears; Palm Computing was a 3Com spin-off; and Conoco was once a part of DuPont.

spin-off
The distribution of shares in a subsidiary to existing parent company stockholders.

In a less common, but more drastic move, a company can elect to do (or be forced to do) a **split-up**. A split-up is just what the name suggests: A company splits itself into two or more new companies. Shareholders have their shares in the old company swapped for shares in the new companies. Probably the most famous split-up occurred in the 1980s. As the result of an antitrust suit by the Justice Department, AT&T was forced to split up through the creation of seven regional phone companies (the so-called Baby Bells). Today, the Baby Bells survive as companies such as BellSouth, SBC Communications, and Verizon.

split-up
The splitting up of a company into two or more companies.

Concept Questions

25.9a What is an equity carve-out? Why might a firm wish to do one?

25.9b What is a split-up? Why might a firm choose to do one?

SUMMARY AND CONCLUSIONS 25.10

This chapter has introduced you to the extensive literature on mergers and acquisitions. We touched on a number of issues, including:

1. Forms of merger. One firm can acquire another in several different ways. The three legal forms of acquisition are merger or consolidation, acquisition of stock, and acquisition of assets.
2. Tax issues. Mergers and acquisitions can be taxable or tax-free transactions. The primary issue is whether the target firm's stockholders sell or exchange their shares. Generally, a cash purchase will be a taxable merger, whereas a stock exchange will not be taxable. In a taxable merger, there are capital gains effects and asset write-up

effects to consider. In a stock exchange, the target firm's shareholders become shareholders in the merged firm.

3. Accounting issues. Accounting for mergers and acquisitions traditionally involved either the purchase method or the pooling of interests method. In 2001, pooling was eliminated as an option. As a result, a merger or acquisition will generally result in the creation of goodwill, but, under the new guidelines, goodwill does not have to be amortized.
4. Merger valuation. If Firm A is acquiring Firm B, the benefits (ΔV) from the acquisition are defined as the value of the combined firm (V_{AB}) less the value of the firms as separate entities (V_A and V_B), or:

   $$\Delta V = V_{AB} - (V_A + V_B)$$

   The gain to Firm A from acquiring Firm B is the increased value of the acquired firm, ΔV, plus the value of B as a separate firm, V_B. The total value of Firm B to Firm A, V_B^*, is thus:

   $$V_B^* = \Delta V + V_B$$

   An acquisition will benefit the shareholders of the acquiring firm if this value is greater than the cost of the acquisition.

   The cost of an acquisition can be defined in general terms as the price paid to the shareholders of the acquired firm. The cost frequently includes a merger premium paid to the shareholders of the acquired firm. Moreover, the cost depends on the form of payment, that is, the choice between paying with cash or paying with common stock.
5. Benefits. The possible benefits of an acquisition come from several sources, including the following:
   a. Revenue enhancement
   b. Cost reductions
   c. Lower taxes
   d. Reductions in capital needs
6. Defensive tactics. Some of the most colorful language of finance comes from defensive tactics used in acquisition battles. *Poison pills, golden parachutes, crown jewels,* and *greenmail* are terms that describe various antitakeover tactics.
7. Effect on shareholders. Mergers and acquisitions have been extensively studied. The basic conclusions are that, on average, the shareholders of target firms do very well, whereas the shareholders of bidding firms do not appear to gain very much.
8. Divestitures. For a variety of reasons, companies often wish to sell assets or operating units. For relatively large divestitures involving operating units, firms sometimes elect to do carve-outs, spin-offs, or split-ups.

Chapter Review and Self-Test Problems

25.1 Merger Value and Cost Consider the following information for two all-equity firms, A and B:

	Firm A	Firm B
Shares outstanding	2,000	6,000
Price per share	$ 40	$ 30

Firm A estimates that the value of the synergistic benefit from acquiring Firm B is \$6,000. Firm B has indicated that it would accept a cash purchase offer of \$35 per share. Should Firm A proceed?

25.2 **Stock Mergers and EPS** Consider the following information for two all-equity firms, A and B:

	Firm A	Firm B
Total earnings	\$3,000	\$1,100
Shares outstanding	600	400
Price per share	\$ 70	\$ 15

Firm A is acquiring Firm B by exchanging 100 of its shares for all the shares in B. What is the cost of the merger if the merged firm is worth \$63,000? What will happen to Firm A's EPS? Its PE ratio?

Answers to Chapter Review and Self-Test Problems

25.1 The total value of Firm B to Firm A is the premerger value of B plus the \$6,000 gain from the merger. The premerger value of B is \$30 × 6,000 = \$180,000, so the total value is \$186,000. At \$35 per share, A is paying \$35 × 6,000 = \$210,000; the merger therefore has a negative NPV of \$186,000 − 210,000 = −\$24,000. At \$35 per share, B is not an attractive merger partner.

25.2 After the merger, the firm will have 700 shares outstanding. Because the total value is \$63,000, the price per share is \$63,000/700 = \$90, up from \$70. Because Firm B's stockholders end up with 100 shares in the merged firm, the cost of the merger is 100 × \$90 = \$9,000, not 100 × \$70 = \$7,000.

Also, the combined firm will have \$3,000 + 1,100 = \$4,100 in earnings, so EPS will be \$4,100/700 = \$5.86, up from \$3,000/600 = \$5. The old PE ratio was \$70/5 = 14.00. The new one is \$90/5.86 = 15.36.

Concepts Review and Critical Thinking Questions

1. **Merger Accounting** Explain the difference between purchase and pooling of interests accounting for mergers. What is the effect on cash flows of the choice of accounting method? On EPS?
2. **Merger Terms** Define each of the following terms:
   - **a.** Greenmail
   - **b.** White knight
   - **c.** Golden parachute
   - **d.** Crown jewels
   - **e.** Shark repellent
   - **f.** Corporate raider
   - **g.** Poison pill
   - **h.** Tender offer
   - **i.** Leveraged buyout, or LBO

3. **Merger Rationale** Explain why diversification *per se* is probably not a good reason for merger.
4. **Corporate Split** In June 2004, Kimberly-Clark, known for its Huggies diapers and Kleenex tissue, announced plans to split into two entities: a consumer products company, and a company that manufactured fine paper, specialty paper, and pulp and managed timber operations. Why might a company do this? Is there a possibility of reverse synergy?
5. **Poison Pills** Are poison pills good or bad for stockholders? How do you think acquiring firms are able to get around poison pills?
6. **Merger and Taxes** Describe the advantages and disadvantages of a taxable merger as opposed to a tax-free exchange. What is the basic determinant of tax status in a merger? Would an LBO be taxable or nontaxable? Explain.
7. **Economies of Scale** What does it mean to say that a proposed merger will take advantage of available economies of scale? Suppose Eastern Power Co. and Western Power Co. are located in different time zones. Both of them operate at 60 percent of capacity except for peak periods, when they operate at 100 percent of capacity. The peak periods begin at 9:00 A.M. and 5:00 P.M. local time and last about 45 minutes. Explain why a merger between Eastern and Western might make sense.
8. **Hostile Takeovers** What types of actions might the management of a firm take to fight a hostile acquisition bid from an unwanted suitor? How do the target-firm shareholders benefit from the defensive tactics of their management team? How are the target-firm shareholders harmed by such actions? Explain.
9. **Merger Offers** Suppose a company in which you own stock has attracted two takeover offers. Would it ever make sense for your company's management to favor the lower offer? Does the form of payment affect your answer at all?
10. **Merger Profit** Acquiring-firm stockholders seem to benefit very little from takeovers. Why is this finding a puzzle? What are some of the reasons offered for it?

Questions and Problems

BASIC
(Questions 1–9)

1. **Calculating Synergy** Pearl Inc. has offered $740 million cash for all of the common stock in Jam Corporation. Based on recent market information, Jam is worth $650 million as an independent operation. If the merger makes economic sense for Pearl, what is the minimum estimated value of the synergistic benefits from the merger?
2. **Balance Sheets for Mergers** Consider the following premerger information about Firm X and Firm Y:

	Firm X	Firm Y
Total earnings	$40,000	$15,000
Shares outstanding	20,000	20,000
Per-share values:		
Market	$ 49	$ 18
Book	$ 20	$ 7

Assume that Firm X acquires Firm Y by paying cash for all the shares outstanding at a merger premium of $5 per share. Assuming that neither firm has any debt before or after the merger, construct the postmerger balance sheet for Firm X assuming the use of (*a*) pooling of interests accounting methods and (*b*) purchase accounting methods.

3. **Balance Sheets for Mergers** Assume that the following balance sheets are stated at book value. Construct a postmerger balance sheet assuming that Meat Co. purchases Loaf, Inc. and the pooling of interests method of accounting is used.

MEAT CO.

Current assets	$10,000	Current liabilities	$ 3,100
Net fixed assets	14,000	Long-term debt	1,900
		Equity	19,000
Total	$24,000	Total	$24,000

LOAF, INC.

Current assets	$3,400	Current liabilities	$1,600
Net fixed assets	5,400	Long-term debt	900
		Equity	6,500
Total	$9,000	Total	$9,000

4. **Incorporating Goodwill** In the previous problem, suppose the fair market value of Loaf's fixed assets is $12,000 versus the $3,400 book value shown. Meat pays $17,000 for Loaf and raises the needed funds through an issue of long-term debt. Construct the postmerger balance sheet now, assuming that the purchase method of accounting is used.
5. **Balance Sheets for Mergers** Silver Enterprises has acquired All Gold Mining in a merger transaction. Construct the balance sheet for the new corporation if the merger is treated as a pooling of interests for accounting purposes. The following balance sheets represent the premerger book values for both firms.

SILVER ENTERPRISES

Current assets	$2,600	Current liabilities	$1,800
Other assets	800	Long-term debt	900
Net fixed assets	3,900	Equity	4,600
Total	$7,300	Total	$7,300

ALL GOLD MINING

Current assets	$1,100	Current liabilities	$900
Other assets	350	Long-term debt	0
Net fixed assets	2,800	Equity	3,350
Total	$4,250	Total	$4,250

6. **Incorporating Goodwill** In the previous problem, construct the balance sheet for the new corporation assuming that the transaction is treated as a purchase for accounting purposes. The market value of All Gold Mining's fixed assets is $2,800; the market values for current and other assets are the same as the book values. Assume that Silver Enterprises issues $8,400 in new long-term debt to finance the acquisition.

7. **Cash versus Stock Payment** Penn Corp. is analyzing the possible acquisition of Teller Company. Both firms have no debt. Penn believes the acquisition will increase its total aftertax annual cash flows by $3.1 million indefinitely. The current market value of Teller is $78 million, and that of Penn is $135 million. The appropriate discount rate for the incremental cash flows is 12 percent. Penn is trying to decide whether it should offer 40 percent of its stock or $94 million in cash to Teller's shareholders.
   a. What is the cost of each alternative?
   b. What is the NPV of each alternative?
   c. Which alternative should Penn choose?
8. **EPS, PE, and Mergers** The shareholders of Aniston Company have voted in favor of a buyout offer from Pitt Corporation. Information about each firm is given here:

	Aniston	Pitt
Price-earnings ratio	5.25	21
Shares outstanding	60,000	180,000
Earnings	$300,000	$675,000

   Aniston's shareholders will receive one share of Pitt stock for every three shares they hold in Aniston.
   a. What will the EPS of Pitt be after the merger? What will the PE ratio be if the NPV of the acquisition is zero?
   b. What must Pitt feel is the value of the synergy between these two firms? Explain how your answer can be reconciled with the decision to go ahead with the takeover.
9. **Cash versus Stock as Payment** Consider the following premerger information about a bidding firm (Firm B) and a target firm (Firm T). Assume that both firms have no debt outstanding.

	Firm B	Firm T
Shares outstanding	1,500	900
Price per share	$34	$24

   Firm B has estimated that the value of the synergistic benefits from acquiring Firm T is $3,000.
   a. If Firm T is willing to be acquired for $27 per share in cash, what is the NPV of the merger?
   b. What will the price per share of the merged firm be assuming the conditions in (*a*)?
   c. In part (*a*), what is the merger premium?
   d. Suppose Firm T is agreeable to a merger by an exchange of stock. If B offers three of its shares for every five of T's shares, what will the price per share of the merged firm be?
   e. What is the NPV of the merger assuming the conditions in (*d*)?

INTERMEDIATE
(Questions 10–12)

10. **Cash versus Stock as Payment** In Problem 9, are the shareholders of Firm T better off with the cash offer or the stock offer? At what exchange ratio of B shares to T shares would the shareholders in T be indifferent between the two offers?

11. **Effects of a Stock Exchange** Consider the following premerger information about Firm A and Firm B:

	Firm A	Firm B
Total earnings	$900	$600
Shares outstanding	550	220
Price per share	$ 40	$ 15

Assume that Firm A acquires Firm B via an exchange of stock at a price of $20 for each share of B's stock. Both A and B have no debt outstanding.

a. What will the earnings per share, EPS, of Firm A be after the merger?

b. What will Firm A's price per share be after the merger if the market incorrectly analyzes this reported earnings growth (that is, the price-earnings ratio does not change)?

c. What will the price-earnings ratio of the postmerger firm be if the market correctly analyzes the transaction?

d. If there are no synergy gains, what will the share price of A be after the merger? What will the price-earnings ratio be? What does your answer for the share price tell you about the amount A bid for B? Was it too high? Too low? Explain.

12. **Merger NPV** Show that the NPV of a merger can be expressed as the value of the synergistic benefits, ΔV, less the merger premium.

CHALLENGE
(Question 13)

13. **Calculating NPV** Foxy News, Inc., is considering making an offer to purchase Pulitzer Publications. The vice president of finance has collected the following information:

	Foxy	Pulitzer
Price-earnings ratio	12.5	9
Shares outstanding	1,000,000	550,000
Earnings	$2,000,000	$580,000
Dividends	600,000	290,000

Foxy also knows that securities analysts expect the earnings and dividends of Pulitzer to grow at a constant rate of 5 percent each year. Foxy management believes that the acquisition of Pulitzer will provide the firm with some economies of scale that will increase this growth rate to 7 percent per year.

a. What is the value of Pulitzer to Foxy?

b. What would Foxy's gain be from this acquisition?

c. If Foxy were to offer $18 in cash for each share of Pulitzer, what would the NPV of the acquisition be?

d. What's the most Foxy should be willing to pay in cash per share for the stock of Pulitzer?

e. If Foxy were to offer 100,000 of its shares in exchange for the outstanding stock of Pulitzer, what would the NPV be?

f. Should the acquisition be attempted, and, if so, should it be as in (*c*) or as in (*e*)?

g. Foxy's outside financial consultants think that the 7 percent growth rate is too optimistic and a 6 percent rate is more realistic. How does this change your previous answers?

26 Leasing

Have you ever flown on GE Airlines? Probably not, but with more than 1,100 planes, GE Commercial Finance, part of General Electric, owns one of the largest aircraft fleets in the world. In fact, the financing arm of GE owns more than $217 billion in assets and generated $3.91 billion in profits during 2003. In addition to airplanes, the company leases ships, drilling rigs, trucks, and real estate. So why is GE Commercial Finance in the business of buying assets, only to lease them out? And why don't the companies that lease from GE Commercial Finance simply purchase the assets themselves? This chapter provides answers to these and other questions associated with leasing.

Leasing is a way businesses finance plant, property, and equipment.[1] Just about any asset that can be purchased can be leased, and there are many good reasons for leasing. For example, when we take vacations or business trips, renting a car for a few days is a convenient thing to do. After all, buying a car and selling it a week later would be a great nuisance. We discuss additional reasons for leasing in the sections that follow.

Up-to-date news and articles on the leasing industry are available at www.monitordaily.com.

Although corporations engage in both short-term leasing and long-term leasing, this chapter is primarily concerned with long-term leasing, where long-term typically means more than five years. As we will discuss in greater detail shortly, leasing an asset on a long-term basis is much like borrowing the needed funds and simply buying the asset. Thus, long-term leasing is a form of financing much like long-term debt. When is leasing preferable to long-term borrowing? This is a question we seek to answer in this chapter.

[1]We are indebted to James Johnson of Northern Illinois University for helpful comments and suggestions on this chapter.

LEASES AND LEASE TYPES 26.1

A *lease* is a contractual agreement between two parties: the **lessee** and the **lessor**. The lessee is the user of the equipment; the lessor is the owner. Thus, in the example we used to open the chapter, GE Commercial Finance is the lessor.

Typically, a company first decides on the asset that it needs. It then negotiates a lease contract with a lessor for use of that asset. The lease agreement establishes that the lessee has the right to use the asset and, in return, must make periodic payments to the lessor, the owner of the asset. The lessor is usually either the asset's manufacturer or an independent leasing company. If the lessor is an independent leasing company, it must buy the asset from a manufacturer. The lessor then delivers the asset to the lessee, and the lease goes into effect.

There are some giant lessors in the United States. For example, IBM Global Financing leases billions in equipment annually. Other major lessors include CitiCapital, International Lease Finance, and Fleet Capital.

lessee
The user of an asset in a leasing agreement. The lessee makes payments to the lessor.

lessor
The owner of an asset in a leasing agreement. The lessor receives payments from the lessee.

Leasing versus Buying

As far as the lessee is concerned, it is the use of the asset that is important, not necessarily who has title to it. One way to obtain the use of an asset is to lease it. Another way is to obtain outside financing and buy it. Thus, the decision to lease or buy amounts to a comparison of alternative financing arrangements for the use of an asset.

Figure 26.1 compares leasing and buying. The lessee, Sass Company, might be a hospital, a law firm, or any other firm that uses computers. The lessor is an independent leasing company that purchased the computer from a manufacturer such as Hewlett-Packard (HP). Leases of this type, in which the leasing company purchases the asset from the manufacturer, are called *direct leases*. Of course, HP might choose to lease its own computers, and many companies, including HP and some of the other companies mentioned previously,

Should you lease or buy that next car? Visit the Charts & Analysis section of www.bloomberg.com for a calculator to help you decide.

FIGURE 26.1 >> **Leasing versus Buying**

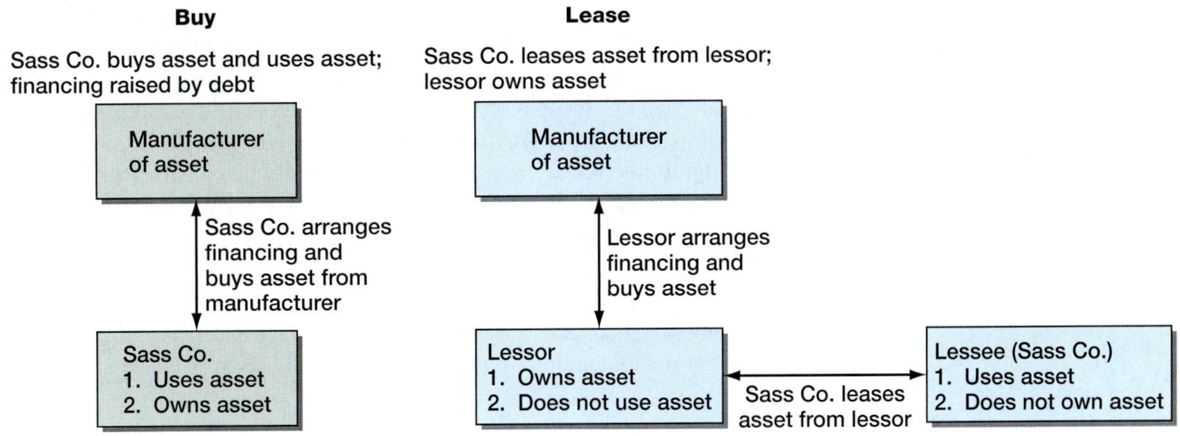

If Sass Co. buys the asset, then it will own the asset and use it. If Sass Co. leases the asset, the lessor will own the asset, but Sass Co. will still use it as the lessee.

have set up wholly owned subsidiaries called *captive finance companies* to lease out their products.[2]

As shown in Figure 26.1, whether it leases or buys, Sass Company ends up using the asset. The key difference is that in one case (buy), Sass arranges the financing, purchases the asset, and holds title to the asset. In the other case (lease), the leasing company arranges the financing, purchases the asset, and holds title to the asset.

Operating Leases

Years ago, a lease in which the lessee received an equipment operator along with the equipment was called an **operating lease**. Today, an operating lease (or *service lease*) is difficult to define precisely, but this form of leasing has several important characteristics.

operating lease
Usually a shorter-term lease under which the lessor is responsible for insurance, taxes, and upkeep. May be cancelable by the lessee on short notice.

First of all, with an operating lease, the payments received by the lessor are usually not enough to allow the lessor to fully recover the cost of the asset. A primary reason is that operating leases are often relatively short-term. Therefore, the life of the lease may be much shorter than the economic life of the asset. For example, if you lease a car for two years, the car will have a substantial residual value at the end of the lease, and the lease payments you make will pay off only a fraction of the original cost of the car. The lessor in an operating lease expects to either lease the asset again or sell it when the lease terminates.

A second characteristic of an operating lease is that it frequently requires that the lessor maintain the asset. The lessor may also be responsible for any taxes or insurance. Of course, these costs will be passed on, at least in part, to the lessee in the form of higher lease payments.

The third, and perhaps most interesting, feature of an operating lease is the cancellation option. This option can give the lessee the right to cancel the lease before the expiration date. If the option to cancel is exercised, the lessee returns the equipment to the lessor and ceases to make payments. The value of a cancellation clause depends on whether technological and/or economic conditions are likely to make the value of the asset to the lessee less than the present value of the future lease payments under the lease.

Web sites for equipment leases include www.keystoneleasing.com and www.assetcapitallease.com.

To leasing practitioners, these three characteristics define an operating lease. However, as we will see shortly, accountants use the term in a somewhat different way.

Financial Leases

financial lease
Typically a longer-term, fully amortized lease under which the lessee is responsible for maintenance, taxes, and insurance. Usually not cancelable by the lessee without penalty.

A **financial lease** is the other major type of lease. In contrast to the situation with an operating lease, the payments made under a financial lease (plus the anticipated residual, or salvage, value) are usually sufficient to fully cover the lessor's cost of purchasing the asset and pay the lessor a return on the investment. For this reason, a financial lease is sometimes said to be a fully amortized or full-payout lease, whereas an operating lease is said to be partially amortized. Financial leases are often called *capital leases* by the accountants.

With a financial lease, the lessee (not the lessor) is usually responsible for insurance, maintenance, and taxes, and, for that reason, financial leases are often called triple net leases. It is also important to note that a financial lease generally cannot be canceled, at least not without a significant penalty. In other words, the lessee must make the lease payments or face possible legal action.

The characteristics of a financial lease, particularly the fact that it is fully amortized, make it very similar to debt financing, so the name is a sensible one. There are three types

[2]In addition to arranging financing for asset users, captive finance companies (or subsidiaries) may purchase their parent company's products and provide debt or lease financing to the users. General Motors Acceptance Corporation (GMAC) and Caterpillar Financial are examples of captive finance companies.

of financial leases that are of particular interest: *tax-oriented leases, leveraged leases,* and *sale and leaseback agreements.* We consider these next.

Tax-Oriented Leases A lease in which the lessor is the owner of the leased asset for tax purposes is called a **tax-oriented lease**. Such leases are also called tax leases or true leases. In contrast, a *conditional sales agreement lease* is not a true lease. Here, the "lessee" is the owner for tax purposes. Conditional sales agreement leases are really just secured loans. The financial leases we discuss in this chapter are all tax leases.

tax-oriented lease
A financial lease in which the lessor is the owner for tax purposes. Also called a true lease or a tax lease.

Tax-oriented leases make the most sense when the lessee is not in a position to efficiently use tax credits or depreciation deductions that come with owning the asset. By arranging for someone else to hold title, a tax lease passes these benefits on. The lessee can benefit because the lessor may return a portion of the tax benefits to the lessee in the form of lower lease payments.

Leveraged Leases A **leveraged lease** is a tax-oriented lease in which the lessor borrows a substantial portion of the purchase price of the leased asset on a *nonrecourse* basis, meaning that if the lessee defaults on the lease payments, the lessor does not have to keep making the loan payments. Instead, the lender must proceed against the lessee to recover its investment. In contrast, with a *single-investor lease,* if the lessor borrows to purchase the asset, the lessor remains responsible for the loan payments regardless of whether or not the lessee makes the lease payments. Leveraged leases can be quite complicated and are primarily used for big ticket transactions.

leveraged lease
A financial lease in which the lessor borrows a substantial fraction of the cost of the leased asset on a nonrecourse basis.

Sale and Leaseback Agreements A **sale and leaseback** occurs when a company sells an asset it owns to another party and simultaneously leases it back. In a sale and leaseback, two things happen:

sale and leaseback
A financial lease in which the lessee sells an asset to the lessor and then leases it back.

1. The lessee receives cash from the sale of the asset.
2. The lessee continues to use the asset.

Often, with a sale and leaseback, the lessee may have the option to repurchase the leased asset at the end of the lease.

An example of a sale and leaseback occurred in April 2004, when EVA Airways Corp., which operates in Taiwan, agreed to sell three new Boeing 777s to GE Commercial Finance under a sale and leaseback agreement. In fact, sale and leaseback agreements are a fairly common method used to finance airplanes.

Concept Questions

26.1a What are the differences between an operating lease and a financial lease?

26.1b What is a tax-oriented lease?

26.1c What is a sale and leaseback agreement?

ACCOUNTING AND LEASING 26.2

Before November 1976, leasing was frequently called *off–balance sheet financing.* As the name implies, a firm could arrange to use an asset through a lease and not necessarily disclose the existence of the lease contract on the balance sheet. Lessees had to report information on leasing activity only in the footnotes to their financial statements.

TABLE 26.1 >>

Leasing and the Balance Sheet

A. Balance Sheet with Purchase (the company finances a $100,000 truck with debt)

Truck	$100,000	Debt	$100,000
Other assets	100,000	Equity	100,000
Total assets	$200,000	Total debt plus equity	$200,000

B. Balance Sheet with Operating Lease (the company finances the truck with an operating lease)

Truck	$ 0	Debt	$ 0
Other assets	100,000	Equity	100,000
Total assets	$100,000	Total debt plus equity	$100,000

C. Balance Sheet with Capital Lease (the company finances the truck with a capital lease)

Assets under capital lease	$100,000	Obligations under capital lease	$100,000
Other assets	100,000	Equity	100,000
Total assets	$200,000	Total debt plus equity	$200,000

In the first case, a $100,000 truck is purchased with debt. In the second case, an operating lease is used; no balance sheet entries are created. In the third case, a capital (financial) lease is used; the lease payments are capitalized as a liability, and the leased truck appears as an asset.

In November 1976, the Financial Accounting Standards Board (FASB) issued its Statement of Financial Accounting Standards No. 13 (FASB 13), "Accounting for Leases." The basic idea of FASB 13 is that certain financial leases must be "capitalized." Essentially, this requirement means that the present value of the lease payments must be calculated and reported along with debt and other liabilities on the right-hand side of the lessee's balance sheet. The same amount must be shown as the capitalized value of leased assets on the left-hand side of the balance sheet. Operating leases are not disclosed on the balance sheet except in the footnotes. Exactly what constitutes a financial or operating lease for accounting purposes will be discussed in just a moment.

The accounting implications of FASB 13 are illustrated in Table 26.1. Imagine a firm that has $100,000 in assets and no debt, which implies that the equity is also $100,000. The firm needs a truck costing $100,000 (it's a big truck) that it can lease or buy. The top of the table shows the balance sheet assuming that the firm borrows the money and buys the truck.

If the firm leases the truck, then one of two things will happen. If the lease is an operating lease, then the balance sheet will look like the one in Part B of the table. In this case, neither the asset (the truck) nor the liability (the present value of the lease payments) appears. If the lease is a capital lease, then the balance sheet will look more like the one in Part C of the table, where the truck is shown as an asset and the present value of the lease payments is shown as a liability.[3]

As we discussed earlier, it is difficult, if not impossible, to give a precise definition of what constitutes a financial lease or an operating lease. For accounting purposes, a lease is

[3]In Part C, we have made the simplifying assumption that the present value of the lease payments under the capital lease is equal to the cost of the truck. In general, the lessee must report the lesser of the present value of the lease payment stream or the cost of the equipment under lease.

declared to be a capital lease, and must therefore be disclosed on the balance sheet, if at least one of the following criteria is met:

1. The lease transfers ownership of the property to the lessee by the end of the term of the lease.
2. The lessee can purchase the asset at a price below fair market value (bargain purchase price option) when the lease expires.
3. The lease term is 75 percent or more of the estimated economic life of the asset.
4. The present value of the lease payments is at least 90 percent of the fair market value of the asset at the start of the lease.

If one or more of the four criteria are met, the lease is a capital lease; otherwise, it is an operating lease for accounting purposes.

A firm might be tempted to try and "cook the books" by taking advantage of the somewhat arbitrary distinction between operating leases and capital leases. Suppose a shipping firm wants to lease a $100,000 barge. The barge is expected to last for 15 years. A (perhaps unethical) financial manager could try to negotiate a lease contract for 10 years with lease payments having a present value of $89,000. These terms would get around Criteria 3 and 4. If Criteria 1 and 2 were similarly circumvented, the arrangement would be an operating lease and would not show up on the balance sheet.

There are several alleged benefits from "hiding" financial leases. One of the advantages of keeping leases off the balance sheet has to do with fooling financial analysts, creditors, and investors. The idea is that if leases are not on the balance sheet, they will not be noticed.

Financial managers who devote substantial effort to keeping leases off the balance sheet are probably wasting time. Of course, if leases are not on the balance sheet, traditional measures of financial leverage, such as the ratio of total debt to total assets, will understate the true degree of financial leverage. As a consequence, the balance sheet will appear "stronger" than it really is. But it seems unlikely that this type of manipulation would mislead many people.

Nonetheless, firms do try to hide leases. For example, a controversial type of lease, known as a synthetic lease, has come to be widely used. The details are a little complex; in essence, a company arranges for a separate entity to purchase an asset (often a building) and then lease that asset back to the company. If the deal is properly structured, the company is considered the owner of the property for tax purposes, but for accounting purposes, the transaction is classified as an operating lease. Faced with investor criticism of this practice, some firms, such as Krispy Kreme Doughnuts, have announced that they will no longer engage in synthetic leasing.

Having said all of this, there are some reasons why a firm might reasonably try to come in under the radar of the accounting lease test. For example, if a firm's managers are told that capital spending is frozen, an operating lease may still be an option. Alternatively, a firm might face a restriction on additional borrowing (a loan covenant, perhaps). A financial lease counts as debt, but an operating lease does not.

Concept Questions

26.2a For accounting purposes, what constitutes a capital lease?

26.2b How are capital leases reported?

26.3 TAXES, THE IRS, AND LEASES

The lessee can deduct lease payments for income tax purposes if the lease is deemed to be a true lease by the Internal Revenue Service. The tax shields associated with lease payments are critical to the economic viability of a lease, so IRS guidelines are an important consideration. Essentially, the IRS requires that a lease be primarily for business purposes and not merely for purposes of tax avoidance.

In broad terms, a lease that is valid from the IRS's perspective will meet the following standards:

1. The term of the lease must be less than 80 percent of the economic life of the asset. If the term is greater than this, the transaction will be regarded as a conditional sale.
2. The lease should not include an option to acquire the asset at the end of the lease term at a price below the asset's projected market value at the end of the lease. This type of bargain option would give the lessee the asset's residual scrap value, implying an equity interest.
3. The lease should not have a schedule of payments that are very high at the start of the lease term and thereafter very low. If the lease requires early "balloon" payments, this will be considered evidence that the lease is being used to avoid taxes and not for a legitimate business purpose. The IRS may require an adjustment in the payments for tax purposes or other modifications in such cases.
4. The lease must survive a profits test, meaning that the lessor must have the reasonable expectation of making a profit without considering income taxes.
5. Renewal options must be reasonable and reflect the fair market value of the asset at the time of renewal. This requirement can be met by, for example, granting the lessee the first option to meet a competing outside offer.

The IRS is concerned about lease contracts because leases sometimes appear to be set up solely to defer taxes. To see how this could happen, suppose that a firm plans to purchase a $1 million bus that has a five-year life for depreciation purposes. Assume that straight-line depreciation to a zero salvage value is used. The depreciation expense would be $200,000 per year. Now suppose the firm can lease the bus for $500,000 per year for two years and buy the bus for $1 at the end of the two-year term. The present value of the tax benefits is clearly less if the bus is bought than if the bus is leased. The speedup of lease payments greatly benefits the firm and basically gives it a form of accelerated depreciation. In this case, the IRS might decide that the primary purpose of the lease was to defer taxes and disallow the tax treatment.

Concept Questions

26.3a Why is the IRS concerned about leasing?

26.3b What are some of the standards the IRS uses in evaluating a lease?

26.4 THE CASH FLOWS FROM LEASING

To begin our analysis of the leasing decision, we need to identify the relevant cash flows. The first part of this section illustrates how this is done. A key point, and one to watch for, is that taxes are a very important consideration in a lease analysis.

<< TABLE 26.2

Incremental Cash Flows for Tasha Corp. from Leasing instead of Buying

Lease versus Buy	Year 0	Year 1	Year 2	Year 3	Year 4	Year 5
Aftertax lease payment		−$1,650	−$1,650	−$1,650	−$1,650	−$1,650
Lost depreciation tax shield		− 680	− 680	− 680	− 680	− 680
Cost of machine	+$10,000					
Total cash flow	+$10,000	−$2,330	−$2,330	−$2,330	−$2,330	−$2,330

The Incremental Cash Flows

Consider the decision confronting the Tasha Corporation, which manufactures pipe. Business has been expanding, and Tasha currently has a five-year backlog of pipe orders for the Trans-Missouri Pipeline.

The International Boring Machine Corporation (IBMC) makes a pipe-boring machine that can be purchased for $10,000. Tasha has determined that it needs a new machine, and the IBMC model will save Tasha $6,000 per year in reduced electricity bills for the next five years.

Tasha has a corporate tax rate of 34 percent. For simplicity, we assume that five-year straight-line depreciation will be used for the pipe-boring machine, and, after five years, the machine will be worthless. Johnson Leasing Corporation has offered to lease the same pipe-boring machine to Tasha for lease payments of $2,500 paid at the end of each of the next five years. With the lease, Tasha would remain responsible for maintenance, insurance, and operating expenses.[4]

Susan Smart has been asked to compare the direct incremental cash flows from leasing the IBMC machine to the cash flows associated with buying it. The first thing she realizes is that, because Tasha will get the machine either way, the $6,000 savings will be realized whether the machine is leased or purchased. Thus, this cost savings, and any other operating costs or revenues, can be ignored in the analysis.

Upon reflection, Ms. Smart concludes that there are only three important cash flow differences between leasing and buying:[5]

1. If the machine is leased, Tasha must make a lease payment of $2,500 each year. However, lease payments are fully tax deductible, so the aftertax lease payment would be $2,500 × (1 − .34) = $1,650. This is a cost of leasing instead of buying.
2. If the machine is leased, Tasha does not own it and cannot depreciate it for tax purposes. The depreciation would be $10,000/5 = $2,000 per year. A $2,000 depreciation deduction generates a tax shield of $2,000 × .34 = $680 per year. Tasha loses this valuable tax shield if it leases, so this is a cost of leasing.
3. If the machine is leased, Tasha does not have to spend $10,000 today to buy it. This is a benefit from leasing.

The cash flows from leasing instead of buying are summarized in Table 26.2. Notice that the cost of the machine shows up with a positive sign in Year 0. This is a reflection of the fact that Tasha *saves* the initial $10,000 equipment cost by leasing instead of buying.

[4]We have assumed that all lease payments are made in arrears, that is, at the end of the year. Actually, many leases require payments to be made at the beginning of the year.

[5]There is a fourth consequence of leasing that we do not discuss here. If the machine has a nontrivial residual value, then, if we lease, we give up that residual value. This is another cost of leasing instead of buying.

A Note on Taxes

Susan Smart has assumed that Tasha can use the tax benefits of the depreciation allowances and the lease payments. This may not always be the case. If Tasha were losing money (or had loss carryforwards), it would not pay taxes and the tax shelters would be worth less (unless they could be shifted to someone else). As we mentioned before, this is one circumstance under which leasing may make a great deal of sense. If this were the case, the relevant lines in Table 26.2 would have to be changed to reflect a zero tax rate. We will return to this point later.

Concept Questions

26.4a What are the cash flow consequences of leasing instead of buying?

26.4b Explain why the $10,000 in Table 26.2 has a positive sign.

26.5 LEASE OR BUY?

Based on our discussion thus far, Ms. Smart's analysis comes down to this: If Tasha Corp. leases instead of buying, it saves $10,000 today because it avoids having to pay for the machine, but it must give up $2,330 per year for the next five years in exchange. We now must decide whether getting $10,000 today and then paying back $2,330 per year is a good idea.

A Preliminary Analysis

Suppose Tasha were to borrow $10,000 today and promise to make aftertax payments of $2,330 per year for the next five years. This is essentially what Tasha will be doing if it leases instead of buying. What interest rate would Tasha be paying on this "loan"? Going back to Chapter 6, note that we need to find the unknown rate for a five-year annuity with payments of $2,330 per year and a present value of $10,000. It is easy to verify that the rate is 5.317 percent.

The cash flows for our hypothetical loan are identical to the cash flows from leasing instead of buying, and what we have illustrated is that when Tasha leases the machine, it effectively arranges financing at an aftertax rate of 5.317 percent. Whether this is a good deal or not depends on what rate Tasha would pay if it simply borrowed the money. For example, suppose Tasha can arrange a five-year loan with its bank at a rate of 7.57575 percent. Should Tasha sign the lease or should it go with the bank?

There's an online lease versus buy calculator at (where else?): www.lease-vs-buy.com.

Because Tasha is in a 34 percent tax bracket, the aftertax interest rate would be $7.57575 \times (1 - .34) = 5$ percent. This is less than the 5.317 percent aftertax rate on the lease. In this particular case, Tasha would be better off borrowing the money because it would get a better rate.

We have seen that Tasha should buy rather than lease. The steps in our analysis can be summarized as follows:

1. Calculate the incremental aftertax cash flows from leasing instead of buying.
2. Use these cash flows to calculate the aftertax interest rate on the lease.
3. Compare this rate to the company's *aftertax* borrowing cost and choose the cheaper source of financing.

The most important thing to note from our discussion thus far is that in evaluating a lease, the relevant rate for the comparison is the company's *aftertax* borrowing rate. The fundamental reason is that the alternative to leasing is long-term borrowing, so the aftertax interest rate on such borrowing is the relevant benchmark.

Three Potential Pitfalls

There are three potential problems with the interest rate that we calculated on the lease. First of all, we can interpret this rate as the internal rate of return, or IRR, on the decision to lease rather than buy, but doing so can be confusing. To see why, notice that the IRR from leasing is 5.317 percent, which is greater than Tasha's aftertax borrowing cost of 5 percent. Normally, the higher the IRR, the better, but we decided that leasing was a bad idea here. The reason is that the cash flows are not conventional; the first cash flow is positive and the rest are negative, which is just the opposite of the conventional case (see Chapter 9 for a discussion). With this cash flow pattern, the IRR represents the rate we pay, not the rate we get, so the *lower* the IRR, the better.

A second, and related, potential pitfall has to do with the fact that we calculated the advantage of leasing instead of buying. We could have done just the opposite and come up with the advantage of buying instead of leasing. If we did this, the cash flows would be the same, but the signs would be reversed. The IRR would be the same. Now, however, the cash flows would be conventional, so we could interpret the 5.317 percent IRR as saying that borrowing and buying is better.

The third potential problem is that our interest rate is based on the net cash flows of leasing instead of buying. There is another rate that is sometimes calculated, which is based solely on the lease payments. If we wanted to, we could note that the lease provides $10,000 in financing and requires five payments of $2,500 each. It would be tempting to then determine a rate based on these numbers, but the resulting rate would not be meaningful for making lease versus buy decisions, and it should not be confused with the return on leasing instead of borrowing and buying.

Perhaps because of these potential sources of confusion, the IRR approach we have outlined thus far is not as widely used as the NPV-based approach that we describe next.

NPV Analysis

Now that we know that the relevant rate for evaluating a lease versus buy decision is the firm's aftertax borrowing cost, an NPV analysis is straightforward. We simply discount the cash flows back to the present at Tasha's aftertax borrowing rate of 5 percent as follows:

$$\begin{aligned} \text{NPV} &= \$10{,}000 - 2{,}330 \times (1 - 1/1.05^5)/.05 \\ &= -\$87.68 \end{aligned}$$

The NPV from leasing instead of buying is −$87.68, verifying our earlier conclusion that leasing is a bad idea. Once again, notice the signs of the cash flows; the first is positive, the rest are negative. The NPV we have computed here is often called the **net advantage to leasing (NAL)**. Surveys indicate that the NAL approach is the most popular means of lease analysis in the real world. Our nearby *Work the Web* box illustrates the use of lease-versus-buy analysis of automobiles.

net advantage to leasing (NAL)
The NPV that is calculated when deciding whether to lease an asset or to buy it.

A Misconception

In our lease versus buy analysis, it looks as though we ignored the fact that if Tasha borrows the $10,000 to buy the machine, it will have to repay the money with interest. In

WORK THE WEB

A major financial decision for many of you will be whether to buy or lease a new car. We went to www.kiplinger.com and looked under the "Tools" link to find a lease-versus-buy calculator. We analyzed a new car purchased for $28,500 on a 60-month loan at 6.9 percent and a $2,000 down payment. To lease the same car for three years requires a $365 monthly payment with a $1,500 upfront payment and a $1,000 security deposit. The savings rate is used to calculate the opportunity cost of the down payment. We assumed that the depreciation on the car would be average. Below is the information we entered.

Purchase			
Purchase price	$	28,500	
Sales tax rate		6.50	%
Vehicle age (years)		0	
Cash rebate	$	0	
Down payment	$	2,000	
Other upfront costs	$	0	
Loan term (months)		60	
Interest rate		6.900	%
Lease			
Lease term (months)		36	
Monthly payment	$	365	
Security deposit	$	1,000	
Cash paid	$	1,500	
Cash rebate	$	0	
Your savings interest rate		1.50	%
Your state & federal tax rates		33.80	%
Future depreciation			
○ Low			
◉ Average			
○ High			

And the results? Here they are:

	If you buy	**If you lease**
Average cost per year	$4,593	$4,823
Total lease payments	N/A	$13,140
Taxes at purchase	$1,852	N/A
Monthly payment	$523	$365
Total interest	$4,908	N/A
Total depreciation	$16,399	N/A

As you can see in this example, the better choice financially is to buy the car because it will cost $4,593 per year compared to the $4,823 annual cost if you lease.

fact, we reasoned that if Tasha leased the machine, it would be better off by $10,000 today because it wouldn't have to pay for the machine. It is tempting to argue that if Tasha borrowed the money, it wouldn't have to come up with the $10,000. Instead, Tasha would make a series of principal and interest payments over the next five years. This observation is true, but not particularly relevant. The reason is that if Tasha borrows $10,000 at an aftertax cost of 5 percent, the present value of the aftertax loan payments is simply $10,000, no matter what the repayment schedule is (assuming that the loan is fully amortized). Thus, we could write down the aftertax loan repayments and work with these, but it would just be extra work for no gain, assuming the lessee is currently paying taxes (see Problem 10 at the end of the chapter for an example).

Lease Evaluation

<< EXAMPLE 26.1

In our Tasha Corp. example, suppose Tasha is able to negotiate a lease payment of $2,000 per year. What would be the NPV of the lease in this case?

With this new lease payment, the aftertax lease payment would be $2,000 × (1 − .34) = $1,320, which is $1,650 − 1,320 = $330 less than before. Referring back to Table 26.2, note that the aftertax cash flows would be −$2,000 instead of −$2,330. At 5 percent, the NPV would be:

$$\begin{aligned} \text{NPV} &= \$10{,}000 - 2{,}000 \times (1 - 1/1.05^5)/.05 \\ &= \$1{,}341.05 \end{aligned}$$

Thus, the lease is very attractive.

Concept Questions

26.5a What is the relevant discount rate for evaluating whether or not to lease an asset? Why?

26.5b Explain how to go about a lease versus buy analysis.

A LEASING PARADOX

26.6

We previously looked at the lease versus buy decision from the perspective of the potential lessee, Tasha. We now turn things around and look at the lease from the perspective of the lessor, Johnson Leasing. The cash flows associated with the lease from Johnson's perspective are shown in Table 26.3. First, Johnson must buy the machine for $10,000, so there is a $10,000 outflow today. Next, Johnson depreciates the machine at a rate of $10,000/5 = $2,000 per year, so the depreciation tax shield is $2,000 × .34 = $680 each year. Finally,

<< TABLE 26.3

Incremental Cash Flows for Johnson Leasing

	Year 0	Year 1	Year 2	Year 3	Year 4	Year 5
Aftertax lease payment		+$1,650	+$1,650	+$1,650	+$1,650	+$1,650
Depreciation tax shield		+ 680	+ 680	+ 680	+ 680	+ 680
Cost of machine	−$10,000					
Total cash flow	−$10,000	+$2,330	+$2,330	+$2,330	+$2,330	+$2,330

Johnson receives a lease payment of $2,500 each year, on which it pays taxes. The aftertax lease payment received is $1,650, and the total cash flow to Johnson is $2,330 per year.

What we see is that the cash flows to Johnson are exactly the opposite of the cash flows to Tasha. This makes perfect sense because Johnson and Tasha are the only parties to the transaction, and the lease is a zero-sum game. In other words, if the lease has a positive NPV to one party, it must have a negative NPV to the other. In our case, Johnson hopes that Tasha will do the deal because the NPV for Johnson would be +$87.68, the amount Tasha would lose.

We seem to have a paradox. In any leasing arrangement, one party must inevitably lose (or both parties exactly break even). Why would leasing take place? We know that leasing is very important in the real world, so the next section describes some factors that we have omitted from our analysis thus far. These factors can make a lease attractive to both parties.

EXAMPLE 26.2 >> It's the Lease We Can Do

In our Tasha example, a lease payment of $2,500 makes the lease unattractive to Tasha, and a lease payment of $2,000 makes the lease very attractive. What payment would leave Tasha indifferent between leasing and not leasing?

Tasha will be indifferent when the NPV from leasing is zero. For this to happen, the present value of the cash flows from leasing instead of buying will have to be −$10,000. From our previous efforts, we know that the lease payment must be somewhere between $2,500 and $2,000. To find the exact payment, we note that there are five payments and the relevant rate is 5 percent per year, so the cash flow from leasing instead of borrowing must be −$2,309.75 per year.

Now that we have the cash flow from leasing instead of borrowing, we have to work backwards to find the lease payment that produces this cash flow. Suppose we let LP stand for the lease payment. Referring back to Table 26.2, we see that we must have that $-\text{LP} \times (1 - .34) - \$680 = -\$2{,}309.75$. With a little algebra, we see that the zero NPV lease payment is $2,469.32.

Concept Questions

26.6a Why do we say that leasing is a zero-sum game?

26.6b What paradox does the previous question create?

26.7 REASONS FOR LEASING

Proponents of leasing make many claims about why firms should lease assets rather than buy them. Some of the reasons given to support leasing are good, and some are not. We discuss here the reasons for leasing that we think are good, and some of the ones that we think aren't so good.

Good Reasons for Leasing

If leasing is a good choice, it will probably be because one or more of the following are true:

1. Taxes may be reduced by leasing.

2. The lease contract may reduce certain types of uncertainty that might otherwise decrease the value of the firm.
3. Transactions costs may be lower for a lease contract than for buying the asset.
4. Leasing may require fewer (if any) restrictive covenants than secured borrowing.
5. Leasing may encumber fewer assets than secured borrowing.

Tax Advantages As we have hinted in various places, by far the most economically justifiable reason for long-term leasing is tax deferral. If the corporate income tax were repealed, long-term leasing would become much less important. The tax advantages of leasing exist because firms are in different tax positions. A potential tax shield that cannot be used as efficiently by one firm can be transferred to another by leasing.

Any tax benefits from leasing can be split between the two firms by setting the lease payments at the appropriate level, and the shareholders of both firms will benefit from this tax transfer arrangement. The loser will be the IRS. A firm in a high tax bracket will want to act as the lessor. Low–tax bracket firms will be lessees, because they will not be able to use the tax advantages of ownership, such as depreciation and debt financing, as efficiently.

Recall the example of Section 26.6 and the situation of Johnson Leasing. The value of the lease it proposed to Tasha was \$87.68. However, the value of the lease to Tasha was exactly the opposite (−\$87.68). Because the lessor's gains came at the expense of the lessee, no mutually beneficial deal could be arranged. However, if Tasha paid no taxes and the lease payments were reduced to \$2,475 from \$2,500, both Johnson and Tasha would find there was positive NPV in leasing.

To see this, we can rework Table 26.2 with a zero tax rate and a \$2,475 lease payment. In this case, notice that the cash flows from leasing are simply the lease payments of \$2,475 because no depreciation tax shield is lost and the lease payment is not tax deductible. The cash flows from leasing are thus:

The biggest lessor by dollar value is www.ilfc.com.

Lease versus Buy	Year 0	Year 1	Year 2	Year 3	Year 4	Year 5
Lease payment		−\$2,475	−\$2,475	−\$2,475	−\$2,475	−\$2,475
Cost of machine	+\$10,000					
Total cash flow	+\$10,000	−\$2,475	−\$2,475	−\$2,475	−\$2,475	−\$2,475

The value of the lease for Tasha is:

$$\begin{aligned} \text{NPV} &= \$10{,}000 - 2{,}475 \times (1 - 1/1.0757575^5)/.0757575 \\ &= \$6.55 \end{aligned}$$

which is positive. Notice that the discount rate here is 7.57575 percent because Tasha pays no taxes; in other words, this is both the pretax and the aftertax rate.

Using Table 26.3, the value of the lease to Johnson can be worked out. With a lease payment of \$2,475, verify that the cash flows to Johnson will be \$2,313.50. The value of the lease to Johnson is therefore:

$$\begin{aligned} \text{NPV} &= -\$10{,}000 + 2{,}313.50 \times (1 - 1/1.05^5)/.05 \\ &= \$16.24 \end{aligned}$$

which is also positive.

As a consequence of different tax rates, the lessee (Tasha) gains \$6.55 and the lessor (Johnson) gains \$16.24. The IRS loses. What this example shows is that the lessor and the lessee can gain if their tax rates are different. The lease contract allows the lessor to take advantage of the depreciation and interest tax shields that cannot be used by the lessee. The

IRS will experience a net loss of tax revenue, and some of the tax gains to the lessor will be passed on to the lessee in the form of lower lease payments.

A Reduction of Uncertainty We have noted that the lessee does not own the property when the lease expires. The value of the property at this time is called the *residual value* (or *salvage value*). At the time the lease contract is signed, there may be substantial uncertainty as to what the residual value of the asset will be. A lease contract is a method of transferring this uncertainty from the lessee to the lessor.

Transferring the uncertainty about the residual value of an asset to the lessor makes sense when the lessor is better able to bear the risk. For example, if the lessor is the manufacturer, then the lessor may be better able to assess and manage the risk associated with the residual value. The transfer of uncertainty to the lessor amounts to a form of insurance for the lessee. A lease therefore provides something besides long-term financing. Of course, the lessee pays for this insurance implicitly, but the lessee may view the insurance as a relative bargain.

Reduction of uncertainty is the motive for leasing most cited by corporations. For example, computers have a way of becoming technologically outdated very quickly, and computers are very commonly leased instead of purchased. In one survey, 82 percent of the responding firms cited the risk of obsolescence as an important reason for leasing, whereas only 57 percent cited the potential for cheaper financing.

Lower Transactions Costs The costs of changing ownership of an asset many times over its useful life will frequently be greater than the costs of writing a lease agreement. Consider the choice that confronts a person who lives in Los Angeles but must do business in New York for two days. It seems obvious that it will be cheaper to rent a hotel room for two nights than it would be to buy a condominium for two days and then sell it. Thus, lower transactions costs may be the major reason for short-term leases (operating leases). However, it is probably not the major reason for long-term leases.

Fewer Restrictions and Security Requirements As we discussed in Chapter 7, with a secured loan, the borrower will generally agree to a set of restrictive covenants, spelled out in the indenture, or loan agreement. Such restrictions are not generally found in lease agreements. Also, with a secured loan, the borrower may have to pledge other assets as security. With a lease, only the leased asset is so encumbered.

Dubious Reasons for Leasing

Leasing and Accounting Income Leasing can have a significant effect on the appearance of the firm's financial statements. If a firm is successful at keeping its leases off the books, the balance sheet and, potentially, the income statement can be made to look better. As a consequence, accounting-based performance measures such as return on assets, or ROA, can appear to be higher.

For example, because an operating lease does not appear on the balance sheet, total assets (and total liabilities) will be lower with an operating lease than they would be if the firm borrowed the money and bought the asset. From Chapter 3, we know that ROA is computed as net income divided by total assets. With an operating lease, the net income is usually bigger and total assets are smaller, so ROA will be larger. In addition, debt covenants often do not consider operating leases as debt, which may allow a firm to obtain debtlike financing without a covenant violation.

As we have discussed, however, the impact that leasing has on a firm's accounting statements is not likely to fool anyone. As always, what matters are the cash flow consequences, and whether or not a lease has a positive NPV has little to do with its effect on a firm's financial statements. However, managerial compensation is sometimes based on accounting numbers, and this creates an incentive to lease assets. This may be an agency problem (see Chapter 1) if leasing is otherwise undesirable.

100 Percent Financing It is often claimed that an advantage to leasing is that it provides 100 percent financing, whereas secured equipment loans require an initial down payment. Of course, a firm can simply borrow the down payment from another source that provides unsecured credit. Moreover, leases do usually involve a down payment in the form of an advance lease payment (or security deposit). Even when they do not, leases may implicitly be secured by assets of the firm other than those being leased (leasing may give the appearance of 100 percent financing, but not the substance).

Having said this, we should add that it may be the case that a firm (particularly a small one) simply cannot obtain debt financing because, for example, additional debt would violate a loan agreement. Operating leases frequently don't count as debt, so they may be the only source of financing available. In such cases, it isn't lease or buy—it's lease or die!

Low Cost Unscrupulous lessors can encourage lessees to base leasing decisions on the "interest rate" implied by the lease payments, which is often called the implicit or effective rate. As we discussed earlier under potential pitfalls, this rate is not meaningful in leasing decisions, and it also has no legal meaning.

Other Reasons for Leasing

There are, of course, many special reasons for some companies to find advantages in leasing. In one celebrated case, the U.S. Navy leased a fleet of tankers instead of asking Congress for appropriations. Thus, leasing may be used to circumvent capital expenditure control systems set up by bureaucratic firms. This is alleged to be a relatively common occurrence in hospitals, for example. Many school districts lease buses and modular classrooms and pay for them out of their operating budgets when they are unable to gain approval for a bond issue to raise funds.

Concept Questions

26.7a Explain why the existence of differential tax rates may be a good reason for leasing.

26.7b If leasing is tax motivated, who will have the higher tax bracket, lessee or lessor?

SUMMARY AND CONCLUSIONS 26.8

A large fraction of America's equipment is leased rather than purchased. This chapter has described different lease types, accounting and tax implications of leasing, and how to evaluate financial leases.

1. Leases can be separated into two types, financial and operating. Financial leases are generally longer-term, fully amortized, and not cancelable without a hefty termination payment. Operating leases are usually shorter-term, partially amortized, and cancelable.

2. The distinction between financial and operating leases is important in financial accounting. Financial (capital) leases must be reported on a firm's balance sheet; operating leases are not. We discussed the specific accounting criteria for classifying leases as capital or operating.
3. Taxes are an important consideration in leasing, and the IRS has some specific rules about what constitutes a valid lease for tax purposes.
4. A long-term financial lease is a source of financing much like long-term borrowing. We showed how to go about an NPV analysis of leasing to decide whether leasing is cheaper than borrowing. A key insight was that the appropriate discount rate is the firm's aftertax borrowing rate.
5. We saw that the existence of differential tax rates can make leasing an attractive proposition for all parties. We also mentioned that a lease decreases the uncertainty surrounding the residual value of the leased asset. This is a primary reason cited by corporations for leasing.

Chapter Review and Self-Test Problems

26.1 Lease or Buy Your company wants to purchase a new network file server for its wide-area computer network. The server costs $75,000. It will be completely obsolete in three years. Your options are to borrow the money at 10 percent or to lease the machine. If you lease, the payments will be $27,000 per year, payable at the end of each of the next three years. If you buy the server, you can depreciate it straight-line to zero over three years. The tax rate is 34 percent. Should you lease or buy?

26.2 NPV of Leasing In the previous question, what is the NPV of the lease to the lessor? At what lease payment will the lessee and the lessor both break even?

Answers to Chapter Review and Self-Test Problems

26.1 If you buy the machine, the depreciation will be $25,000 per year. This generates a tax shield of $25,000 × .34 = $8,500 per year, which is lost if the machine is leased. The aftertax lease payment would be $27,000 × (1 − .34) = $17,820. Looking back at Table 26.2, you can lay out the cash flows from leasing as follows:

Lease versus Buy	Year 0	Year 1	Year 2	Year 3
Aftertax lease payment		−$17,820	−$17,820	−$17,820
Lost depreciation tax shield		− 8,500	− 8,500	− 8,500
Cost of machine	+$75,000			
Total cash flow	+$75,000	−$26,320	−$26,320	−$26,320

The appropriate discount rate is the aftertax borrowing rate of .10 × (1 − .34) = 6.6 percent. The NPV of leasing instead of borrowing and buying is:

$$\begin{aligned} \text{NPV} &= \$75{,}000 - 26{,}320 \times (1 - 1/1.066^3)/.066 \\ &= \$5{,}420.09 \end{aligned}$$

so leasing is cheaper.

26.2 Assuming that the lessor is in the same tax situation as the lessee, the NPV to the lessor is −$5,420.09. In other words, the lessor loses precisely what the lessee makes.

For both parties to break even, the NPV of the lease must be zero. With a 6.6 percent rate for three years, a cash flow of −$28,370.26 per year has a present value of −$75,000. The lost depreciation tax shield is still −$8,500, so the aftertax lease payment must be $19,870.26. The lease payment that produces a zero NPV is therefore $19,870.26/.66 = $30,106.45 per year.

Concepts Review and Critical Thinking Questions

1. **Leasing versus Borrowing** What are the key differences between leasing and borrowing? Are they perfect substitutes?
2. **Leasing and Taxes** Taxes are an important consideration in the leasing decision. Who is more likely to lease, a profitable corporation in a high tax bracket or a less profitable one in a low tax bracket? Why?
3. **Leasing and IRR** What are some of the potential problems with looking at IRRs in evaluating a leasing decision?
4. **Leasing** Comment on the following remarks:
   a. Leasing reduces risk and can reduce a firm's cost of capital.
   b. Leasing provides 100 percent financing.
   c. If the tax advantages of leasing were eliminated, leasing would disappear.
5. **Accounting for Leases** Discuss the accounting criteria for determining whether or not a lease must be reported on the balance sheet. In each case, give a rationale for the criterion.
6. **IRS Criteria** Discuss the IRS criteria for determining whether or not a lease is tax deductible. In each case, give a rationale for the criterion.
7. **Off–Balance Sheet Financing** What is meant by the term *off–balance sheet financing?* When do leases provide such financing, and what are the accounting and economic consequences of such activity?
8. **Sale and Leaseback** Why might a firm choose to engage in a sale and leaseback transaction? Give two reasons.
9. **Leasing Cost** Explain why the aftertax borrowing rate is the appropriate discount rate to use in lease evaluation.

Refer to the following example for Questions 10 through 12:

In June 2004, Skymark Airlines Co. of Japan announced that it would lease a Boeing B767 from Royal Brunei Airlines beginning in July. The lease of the B767 was necessary because Skymark had an existing lease for a B767 with All Nippon Airways that was set to expire in September.

10. **Leasing versus Purchase** Why wouldn't Skymark purchase the plane since it was obviously needed for the company's operations?
11. **Reasons to Lease** Why would Royal Brunei Airlines be willing to buy a plane from Boeing and then lease it to Skymark? How is this different from just loaning money to Skymark to buy the plane?
12. **Leasing** What do you suppose happens to the plane at the end of the lease period?

Questions and Problems

BASIC
(Questions 1–6)

Use the following information to work Problems 1 through 6:

You work for a nuclear research laboratory that is contemplating leasing a diagnostic scanner (leasing is a very common practice with expensive, high-tech equipment). The scanner costs $3,000,000, and it would be depreciated straight-line to zero over four years. Because of radiation contamination, it will actually be completely valueless in four years. You can lease it for $895,000 per year for four years.

1. **Lease or Buy** Assume that the tax rate is 35 percent. You can borrow at 8 percent before taxes. Should you lease or buy?
2. **Leasing Cash Flows** What are the cash flows from the lease from the lessor's viewpoint? Assume a 35 percent tax bracket.
3. **Finding the Break-Even Payment** What would the lease payment have to be for both lessor and lessee to be indifferent about the lease?
4. **Taxes and Leasing Cash Flows** Assume that your company does not contemplate paying taxes for the next several years. What are the cash flows from leasing in this case?
5. **Setting the Lease Payment** In the previous question, over what range of lease payments will the lease be profitable for both parties?
6. **MACRS Depreciation and Leasing** Rework Problem 1 assuming that the scanner will be depreciated as three-year property under MACRS (see Chapter 10 for the depreciation allowances).

Use the following information to work Problems 7 through 9:

INTERMEDIATE
(Questions 7–9)

The Wildcat Oil Company is trying to decide whether to lease or buy a new computer-assisted drilling system for its oil exploration business. Management has decided that it must use the system to stay competitive; it will provide $700,000 in annual pretax cost savings. The system costs $6 million and will be depreciated straight-line to zero over five years. Wildcat's tax rate is 34 percent, and the firm can borrow at 9 percent. Lambert Leasing Company has offered to lease the drilling equipment to Wildcat for payments of $1,400,000 per year. Lambert's policy is to require its lessees to make payments at the start of the year.

7. **Lease or Buy** What is the NAL for Wildcat? What is the maximum lease payment that would be acceptable to the company?
8. **Leasing and Salvage Value** Suppose it is estimated that the equipment will have an aftertax residual value of $500,000 at the end of the lease. What is the maximum lease payment acceptable to Wildcat now?
9. **Deposits in Leasing** Many lessors require a security deposit in the form of a cash payment or other pledged collateral. Suppose Lambert requires Wildcat to pay a $200,000 security deposit at the inception of the lease. If the lease payment is still $1,400,000, is it advantageous for Wildcat to lease the equipment now?

CHALLENGE
(Question 10)

10. **Lease versus Borrow** Return to the case of the diagnostic scanner used in Problems 1 through 6. Suppose the entire $3,000,000 purchase price of the scanner is borrowed. The rate on the loan is 8 percent, and the loan will be repaid in equal installments. Create a lease versus buy analysis that explicitly incorporates the loan payments. Show that the NPV of leasing instead of buying is not changed from what it was in Problem 1. Why is this so?

APPENDIX

A

Mathematical Tables

Table A.1

Future value of \$1 at the end of t periods $= (1 + r)^t$

Table A.2

Present value of \$1 to be received after t periods $= 1/(1 + r)^t$

Table A.3

Present value of an annuity of \$1 per period for t periods $= [1 - 1/(1 + r)^t]/r$

Table A.4

Future value of an annuity of \$1 per period for t periods $= [(1 + r)^t - 1]/r$

Table A.5

Cumulative normal distribution

TABLE A.1 >> Future value of $1 at the end of t periods = $(1 + r)^t$

	Interest Rate								
Period	**1%**	**2%**	**3%**	**4%**	**5%**	**6%**	**7%**	**8%**	**9%**
1	1.0100	1.0200	1.0300	1.0400	1.0500	1.0600	1.0700	1.0800	1.0900
2	1.0201	1.0404	1.0609	1.0816	1.1025	1.1236	1.1449	1.1664	1.1881
3	1.0303	1.0612	1.0927	1.1249	1.1576	1.1910	1.2250	1.2597	1.2950
4	1.0406	1.0824	1.1255	1.1699	1.2155	1.2625	1.3108	1.3605	1.4116
5	1.0510	1.1041	1.1593	1.2167	1.2763	1.3382	1.4026	1.4693	1.5386
6	1.0615	1.1262	1.1941	1.2653	1.3401	1.4185	1.5007	1.5869	1.6771
7	1.0721	1.1487	1.2299	1.3159	1.4071	1.5036	1.6058	1.7138	1.8280
8	1.0829	1.1717	1.2668	1.3686	1.4775	1.5938	1.7182	1.8509	1.9926
9	1.0937	1.1951	1.3048	1.4233	1.5513	1.6895	1.8385	1.9990	2.1719
10	1.1046	1.2190	1.3439	1.4802	1.6289	1.7908	1.9672	2.1589	2.3674
11	1.1157	1.2434	1.3842	1.5395	1.7103	1.8983	2.1049	2.3316	2.5804
12	1.1268	1.2682	1.4258	1.6010	1.7959	2.0122	2.2522	2.5182	2.8127
13	1.1381	1.2936	1.4685	1.6651	1.8856	2.1329	2.4098	2.7196	3.0658
14	1.1495	1.3195	1.5126	1.7317	1.9799	2.2609	2.5785	2.9372	3.3417
15	1.1610	1.3459	1.5580	1.8009	2.0789	2.3966	2.7590	3.1722	3.6425
16	1.1726	1.3728	1.6047	1.8730	2.1829	2.5404	2.9522	3.4259	3.9703
17	1.1843	1.4002	1.6528	1.9479	2.2920	2.6928	3.1588	3.7000	4.3276
18	1.1961	1.4282	1.7024	2.0258	2.4066	2.8543	3.3799	3.9960	4.7171
19	1.2081	1.4568	1.7535	2.1068	2.5270	3.0256	3.6165	4.3157	5.1417
20	1.2202	1.4859	1.8061	2.1911	2.6533	3.2071	3.8697	4.6610	5.6044
21	1.2324	1.5157	1.8603	2.2788	2.7860	3.3996	4.1406	5.0338	6.1088
22	1.2447	1.5460	1.9161	2.3699	2.9253	3.6035	4.4304	5.4365	6.6586
23	1.2572	1.5769	1.9736	2.4647	3.0715	3.8197	4.7405	5.8715	7.2579
24	1.2697	1.6084	2.0328	2.5633	3.2251	4.0489	5.0724	6.3412	7.9111
25	1.2824	1.6406	2.0938	2.6658	3.3864	4.2919	5.4274	6.8485	8.6231
30	1.3478	1.8114	2.4273	3.2434	4.3219	5.7435	7.6123	10.063	13.268
40	1.4889	2.2080	3.2620	4.8010	7.0400	10.286	14.974	21.725	31.409
50	1.6446	2.6916	4.3839	7.1067	11.467	18.420	29.457	46.902	74.358
60	1.8167	3.2810	5.8916	10.520	18.679	32.988	57.946	101.26	176.03

Continued on next page

10%	12%	14%	15%	16%	18%	20%	24%	28%	32%	36%
1.1000	1.1200	1.1400	1.1500	1.1600	1.1800	1.2000	1.2400	1.2800	1.3200	1.3600
1.2100	1.2544	1.2996	1.3225	1.3456	1.3924	1.4400	1.5376	1.6384	1.7424	1.8496
1.3310	1.4049	1.4815	1.5209	1.5609	1.6430	1.7280	1.9066	2.0972	2.3000	2.5155
1.4641	1.5735	1.6890	1.7490	1.8106	1.9388	2.0736	2.3642	2.6844	3.0360	3.4210
1.6105	1.7623	1.9254	2.0114	2.1003	2.2878	2.4883	2.9316	3.4360	4.0075	4.6526
1.7716	1.9738	2.1950	2.3131	2.4364	2.6996	2.9860	3.6352	4.3980	5.2899	6.3275
1.9487	2.2107	2.5023	2.6600	2.8262	3.1855	3.5832	4.5077	5.6295	6.9826	8.6054
2.1436	2.4760	2.8526	3.0590	3.2784	3.7589	4.2998	5.5895	7.2058	9.2170	11.703
2.3579	2.7731	3.2519	3.5179	3.8030	4.4355	5.1598	6.9310	9.2234	12.166	15.917
2.5937	3.1058	3.7072	4.0456	4.4114	5.2338	6.1917	8.5944	11.806	16.060	21.647
2.8531	3.4785	4.2262	4.6524	5.1173	6.1759	7.4301	10.657	15.112	21.199	29.439
3.1384	3.8960	4.8179	5.3503	5.9360	7.2876	8.9161	13.215	19.343	27.983	40.037
3.4523	4.3635	5.4924	6.1528	6.8858	8.5994	10.699	16.386	24.759	36.937	54.451
3.7975	4.8871	6.2613	7.0757	7.9875	10.147	12.839	20.319	31.691	48.757	74.053
4.1772	5.4736	7.1379	8.1371	9.2655	11.974	15.407	25.196	40.565	64.359	100.71
4.5950	6.1304	8.1372	9.3576	10.748	14.129	18.488	31.243	51.923	84.954	136.97
5.0545	6.8660	9.2765	10.761	12.468	16.672	22.186	38.741	66.461	112.14	186.28
5.5599	7.6900	10.575	12.375	14.463	19.673	26.623	48.039	85.071	148.02	253.34
6.1159	8.6128	12.056	14.232	16.777	23.214	31.948	59.568	108.89	195.39	344.54
6.7275	9.6463	13.743	16.367	19.461	27.393	38.338	73.864	139.38	257.92	468.57
7.4002	10.804	15.668	18.822	22.574	32.324	46.005	91.592	178.41	340.45	637.26
8.1403	12.100	17.861	21.645	26.186	38.142	55.206	113.57	228.36	449.39	866.67
8.9543	13.552	20.362	24.891	30.376	45.008	66.247	140.83	292.30	593.20	1178.7
9.8497	15.179	23.212	28.625	35.236	53.109	79.497	174.63	374.14	783.02	1603.0
10.835	17.000	26.462	32.919	40.874	62.669	95.396	216.54	478.90	1033.6	2180.1
17.449	29.960	50.950	66.212	85.850	143.37	237.38	634.82	1645.5	4142.1	10143.
45.259	93.051	188.88	267.86	378.72	750.38	1469.8	5455.9	19427.	66521.	*
117.39	289.00	700.23	1083.7	1670.7	3927.4	9100.4	46890.	*	*	*
304.48	897.60	2595.9	4384.0	7370.2	20555.	56348.	*	*	*	*

*The factor is greater than 99,999.

TABLE A.2 >> Present value of $1 to be received after t periods = $1/(1 + r)^t$

	Interest Rate								
Period	1%	2%	3%	4%	5%	6%	7%	8%	9%
1	0.9901	0.9804	0.9709	0.9615	0.9524	0.9434	0.9346	0.9259	0.9174
2	0.9803	0.9612	0.9426	0.9246	0.9070	0.8900	0.8734	0.8573	0.8417
3	0.9706	0.9423	0.9151	0.8890	0.8638	0.8396	0.8163	0.7938	0.7722
4	0.9610	0.9238	0.8885	0.8548	0.8227	0.7921	0.7629	0.7350	0.7084
5	0.9515	0.9057	0.8626	0.8219	0.7835	0.7473	0.7130	0.6806	0.6499
6	0.9420	0.8880	0.8375	0.7903	0.7462	0.7050	0.6663	0.6302	0.5963
7	0.9327	0.8706	0.8131	0.7599	0.7107	0.6651	0.6227	0.5835	0.5470
8	0.9235	0.8535	0.7894	0.7307	0.6768	0.6274	0.5820	0.5403	0.5019
9	0.9143	0.8368	0.7664	0.7026	0.6446	0.5919	0.5439	0.5002	0.4604
10	0.9053	0.8203	0.7441	0.6756	0.6139	0.5584	0.5083	0.4632	0.4224
11	0.8963	0.8043	0.7224	0.6496	0.5847	0.5268	0.4751	0.4289	0.3875
12	0.8874	0.7885	0.7014	0.6246	0.5568	0.4970	0.4440	0.3971	0.3555
13	0.8787	0.7730	0.6810	0.6006	0.5303	0.4688	0.4150	0.3677	0.3262
14	0.8700	0.7579	0.6611	0.5775	0.5051	0.4423	0.3878	0.3405	0.2992
15	0.8613	0.7430	0.6419	0.5553	0.4810	0.4173	0.3624	0.3152	0.2745
16	0.8528	0.7284	0.6232	0.5339	0.4581	0.3936	0.3387	0.2919	0.2519
17	0.8444	0.7142	0.6050	0.5134	0.4363	0.3714	0.3166	0.2703	0.2311
18	0.8360	0.7002	0.5874	0.4936	0.4155	0.3503	0.2959	0.2502	0.2120
19	0.8277	0.6864	0.5703	0.4746	0.3957	0.3305	0.2765	0.2317	0.1945
20	0.8195	0.6730	0.5537	0.4564	0.3769	0.3118	0.2584	0.2145	0.1784
21	0.8114	0.6598	0.5375	0.4388	0.3589	0.2942	0.2415	0.1987	0.1637
22	0.8034	0.6468	0.5219	0.4220	0.3418	0.2775	0.2257	0.1839	0.1502
23	0.7954	0.6342	0.5067	0.4057	0.3256	0.2618	0.2109	0.1703	0.1378
24	0.7876	0.6217	0.4919	0.3901	0.3101	0.2470	0.1971	0.1577	0.1264
25	0.7798	0.6095	0.4776	0.3751	0.2953	0.2330	0.1842	0.1460	0.1160
30	0.7419	0.5521	0.4120	0.3083	0.2314	0.1741	0.1314	0.0994	0.0754
40	0.6717	0.4529	0.3066	0.2083	0.1420	0.0972	0.0668	0.0460	0.0318
50	0.6080	0.3715	0.2281	0.1407	0.0872	0.0543	0.0339	0.0213	0.0134

Continued on next page

10%	12%	14%	15%	16%	18%	20%	24%	28%	32%	36%
0.9091	0.8929	0.8772	0.8696	0.8621	0.8475	0.8333	0.8065	0.7813	0.7576	0.7353
0.8264	0.7972	0.7695	0.7561	0.7432	0.7182	0.6944	0.6504	0.6104	0.5739	0.5407
0.7513	0.7118	0.6750	0.6575	0.6407	0.6086	0.5787	0.5245	0.4768	0.4348	0.3975
0.6830	0.6355	0.5921	0.5718	0.5523	0.5158	0.4823	0.4230	0.3725	0.3294	0.2923
0.6209	0.5674	0.5194	0.4972	0.4761	0.4371	0.4019	0.3411	0.2910	0.2495	0.2149
0.5645	0.5066	0.4556	0.4323	0.4104	0.3704	0.3349	0.2751	0.2274	0.1890	0.1580
0.5132	0.4523	0.3996	0.3759	0.3538	0.3139	0.2791	0.2218	0.1776	0.1432	0.1162
0.4665	0.4039	0.3506	0.3269	0.3050	0.2660	0.2326	0.1789	0.1388	0.1085	0.0854
0.4241	0.3606	0.3075	0.2843	0.2630	0.2255	0.1938	0.1443	0.1084	0.0822	0.0628
0.3855	0.3220	0.2697	0.2472	0.2267	0.1911	0.1615	0.1164	0.0847	0.0623	0.0462
0.3505	0.2875	0.2366	0.2149	0.1954	0.1619	0.1346	0.0938	0.0662	0.0472	0.0340
0.3186	0.2567	0.2076	0.1869	0.1685	0.1372	0.1122	0.0757	0.0517	0.0357	0.0250
0.2897	0.2292	0.1821	0.1625	0.1452	0.1163	0.0935	0.0610	0.0404	0.0271	0.0184
0.2633	0.2046	0.1597	0.1413	0.1252	0.0985	0.0779	0.0492	0.0316	0.0205	0.0135
0.2394	0.1827	0.1401	0.1229	0.1079	0.0835	0.0649	0.0397	0.0247	0.0155	0.0099
0.2176	0.1631	0.1229	0.1069	0.0930	0.0708	0.0541	0.0320	0.0193	0.0118	0.0073
0.1978	0.1456	0.1078	0.0929	0.0802	0.0600	0.0451	0.0258	0.0150	0.0089	0.0054
0.1799	0.1300	0.0946	0.0808	0.0691	0.0508	0.0376	0.0208	0.0118	0.0068	0.0039
0.1635	0.1161	0.0829	0.0703	0.0596	0.0431	0.0313	0.0168	0.0092	0.0051	0.0029
0.1486	0.1037	0.0728	0.0611	0.0514	0.0365	0.0261	0.0135	0.0072	0.0039	0.0021
0.1351	0.0926	0.0638	0.0531	0.0443	0.0309	0.0217	0.0109	0.0056	0.0029	0.0016
0.1228	0.0826	0.0560	0.0462	0.0382	0.0262	0.0181	0.0088	0.0044	0.0022	0.0012
0.1117	0.0738	0.0491	0.0402	0.0329	0.0222	0.0151	0.0071	0.0034	0.0017	0.0008
0.1015	0.0659	0.0431	0.0349	0.0284	0.0188	0.0126	0.0057	0.0027	0.0013	0.0006
0.0923	0.0588	0.0378	0.0304	0.0245	0.0160	0.0105	0.0046	0.0021	0.0010	0.0005
0.0573	0.0334	0.0196	0.0151	0.0116	0.0070	0.0042	0.0016	0.0006	0.0002	0.0001
0.0221	0.0107	0.0053	0.0037	0.0026	0.0013	0.0007	0.0002	0.0001	*	*
0.0085	0.0035	0.0014	0.0009	0.0006	0.0003	0.0001	*	*	*	*

*The factor is zero to four decimal places.

TABLE A.3 >> **Present value of an annuity of $1 per period for t periods = $[1 - 1/(1 + r)^t]/r$**

Number of Periods	Interest Rate								
	1%	2%	3%	4%	5%	6%	7%	8%	9%
1	0.9901	0.9804	0.9709	0.9615	0.9524	0.9434	0.9346	0.9259	0.9174
2	1.9704	1.9416	1.9135	1.8861	1.8594	1.8334	1.8080	1.7833	1.7591
3	2.9410	2.8839	2.8286	2.7751	2.7232	2.6730	2.6243	2.5771	2.5313
4	3.9020	3.8077	3.7171	3.6299	3.5460	3.4651	3.3872	3.3121	3.2397
5	4.8534	4.7135	4.5797	4.4518	4.3295	4.2124	4.1002	3.9927	3.8897
6	5.7955	5.6014	5.4172	5.2421	5.0757	4.9173	4.7665	4.6229	4.4859
7	6.7282	6.4720	6.2303	6.0021	5.7864	5.5824	5.3893	5.2064	5.0330
8	7.6517	7.3255	7.0197	6.7327	6.4632	6.2098	5.9713	5.7466	5.5348
9	8.5660	8.1622	7.7861	7.4353	7.1078	6.8017	6.5152	6.2469	5.9952
10	9.4713	8.9826	8.5302	8.1109	7.7217	7.3601	7.0236	6.7101	6.4177
11	10.3676	9.7868	9.2526	8.7605	8.3064	7.8869	7.4987	7.1390	6.8052
12	11.2551	10.5753	9.9540	9.3851	8.8633	8.3838	7.9427	7.5361	7.1607
13	12.1337	11.3484	10.6350	9.9856	9.3936	8.8527	8.3577	7.9038	7.4869
14	13.0037	12.1062	11.2961	10.5631	9.8986	9.2950	8.7455	8.2442	7.7862
15	13.8651	12.8493	11.9379	11.1184	10.3797	9.7122	9.1079	8.5595	8.0607
16	14.7179	13.5777	12.5611	11.6523	10.8378	10.1059	9.4466	8.8514	8.3126
17	15.5623	14.2919	13.1661	12.1657	11.2741	10.4773	9.7632	9.1216	8.5436
18	16.3983	14.9920	13.7535	12.6593	11.6896	10.8276	10.0591	9.3719	8.7556
19	17.2260	15.6785	14.3238	13.1339	12.0853	11.1581	10.3356	9.6036	8.9501
20	18.0456	16.3514	14.8775	13.5903	12.4622	11.4699	10.5940	9.8181	9.1285
21	18.8570	17.0112	15.4150	14.0292	12.8212	11.7641	10.8355	10.0168	9.2922
22	19.6604	17.6580	15.9369	14.4511	13.1630	12.0416	11.0612	10.2007	9.4424
23	20.4558	18.2922	16.4436	14.8568	13.4886	12.3034	11.2722	10.3741	9.5802
24	21.2434	18.9139	16.9355	15.2470	13.7986	12.5504	11.4693	10.5288	9.7066
25	22.0232	19.5235	17.4131	15.6221	14.0939	12.7834	11.6536	10.6748	9.8226
30	25.8077	22.3965	19.6004	17.2920	15.3725	13.7648	12.4090	11.2578	10.2737
40	32.8347	27.3555	23.1148	19.7928	17.1591	15.0463	13.3317	11.9246	10.7574
50	39.1961	31.4236	25.7298	21.4822	18.2559	15.7619	13.8007	12.2335	10.9617

Continued on next page

10%	12%	14%	15%	16%	18%	20%	24%	28%	32%	36%
0.9091	0.8929	0.8772	0.8696	0.8621	0.8475	0.8333	0.8065	0.7813	0.7576	0.7353
1.7355	1.6901	1.6467	1.6257	1.6052	1.5656	1.5278	1.4568	1.3916	1.3315	1.2760
2.4869	2.4018	2.3216	2.2832	2.2459	2.1743	2.1065	1.9813	1.8684	1.7663	1.6735
3.1699	3.0373	2.9137	2.8550	2.7982	2.6901	2.5887	2.4043	2.2410	2.0957	1.9658
3.7908	3.6048	3.4331	3.3522	3.2743	3.1272	2.9906	2.7454	2.5320	2.3452	2.1807
4.3553	4.1114	3.8887	3.7845	3.6847	3.4976	3.3255	3.0205	2.7594	2.5342	2.3388
4.8684	4.5638	4.2883	4.1604	4.0386	3.8115	3.6046	3.2423	2.9370	2.6775	2.4550
5.3349	4.9676	4.6389	4.4873	4.3436	4.0776	3.8372	3.4212	3.0758	2.7860	2.5404
5.7590	5.3282	4.9464	4.7716	4.6065	4.3030	4.0310	3.5655	3.1842	2.8681	2.6033
6.1446	5.6502	5.2161	5.0188	4.8332	4.4941	4.1925	3.6819	3.2689	2.9304	2.6495
6.4951	5.9377	5.4527	5.2337	5.0286	4.6560	4.3271	3.7757	3.3351	2.9776	2.6834
6.8137	6.1944	5.6603	5.4206	5.1971	4.7932	4.4392	3.8514	3.3868	3.0133	2.7084
7.1034	6.4235	5.8424	5.5831	5.3423	4.9095	4.5327	3.9124	3.4272	3.0404	2.7268
7.3667	6.6282	6.0021	5.7245	5.4675	5.0081	4.6106	3.9616	3.4587	3.0609	2.7403
7.6061	6.8109	6.1422	5.8474	5.5755	5.0916	4.6755	4.0013	3.4834	3.0764	2.7502
7.8237	6.9740	6.2651	5.9542	5.6685	5.1624	4.7296	4.0333	3.5026	3.0882	2.7575
8.0216	7.1196	6.3729	6.0472	5.7487	5.2223	4.7746	4.0591	3.5177	3.0971	2.7629
8.2014	7.2497	6.4674	6.1280	5.8178	5.2732	4.8122	4.0799	3.5294	3.1039	2.7668
8.3649	7.3658	6.5504	6.1982	5.8775	5.3162	4.8435	4.0967	3.5386	3.1090	2.7697
8.5136	7.4694	6.6231	6.2593	5.9288	5.3527	4.8696	4.1103	3.5458	3.1129	2.7718
8.6487	7.5620	6.6870	6.3125	5.9731	5.3837	4.8913	4.1212	3.5514	3.1158	2.7734
8.7715	7.6446	6.7429	6.3587	6.0113	5.4099	4.9094	4.1300	3.5558	3.1180	2.7746
8.8832	7.7184	6.7921	6.3988	6.0442	5.4321	4.9245	4.1371	3.5592	3.1197	2.7754
8.9847	7.7843	6.8351	6.4338	6.0726	5.4509	4.9371	4.1428	3.5619	3.1210	2.7760
9.0770	7.8431	6.8729	6.4641	6.0971	5.4669	4.9476	4.1474	3.5640	3.1220	2.7765
9.4269	8.0552	7.0027	6.5660	6.1772	5.5168	4.9789	4.1601	3.5693	3.1242	2.7775
9.7791	8.2438	7.1050	6.6418	6.2335	5.5482	4.9966	4.1659	3.5712	3.1250	2.7778
9.9148	8.3045	7.1327	6.6605	6.2463	5.5541	4.9995	4.1666	3.5714	3.1250	2.7778

TABLE A.4 >> **Future value of an annuity of $1 per period for t periods = $[(1 + r)^t - 1]/r$**

Number of Periods	Interest Rate								
	1%	2%	3%	4%	5%	6%	7%	8%	9%
1	1.0000	1.0000	1.0000	1.0000	1.0000	1.0000	1.0000	1.0000	1.0000
2	2.0100	2.0200	2.0300	2.0400	2.0500	2.0600	2.0700	2.0800	2.0900
3	3.0301	3.0604	3.0909	3.1216	3.1525	3.1836	3.2149	3.2464	3.2781
4	4.0604	4.1216	4.1836	4.2465	4.3101	4.3746	4.4399	4.5061	4.5731
5	5.1010	5.2040	5.3091	5.4163	5.5256	5.6371	5.7507	5.8666	5.9847
6	6.1520	6.3081	6.4684	6.6330	6.8019	6.9753	7.1533	7.3359	7.5233
7	7.2135	7.4343	7.6625	7.8983	8.1420	8.3938	8.6540	8.9228	9.2004
8	8.2857	8.5830	8.8932	9.2142	9.5491	9.8975	10.260	10.637	11.028
9	9.3685	9.7546	10.159	10.583	11.027	11.491	11.978	12.488	13.021
10	10.462	10.950	11.464	12.006	12.578	13.181	13.816	14.487	15.193
11	11.567	12.169	12.808	13.486	14.207	14.972	15.784	16.645	17.560
12	12.683	13.412	14.192	15.026	15.917	16.870	17.888	18.977	20.141
13	13.809	14.680	15.618	16.627	17.713	18.882	20.141	21.495	22.953
14	14.947	15.974	17.086	18.292	19.599	21.015	22.550	24.215	26.019
15	16.097	17.293	18.599	20.024	21.579	23.276	25.129	27.152	29.361
16	17.258	18.639	20.157	21.825	23.657	25.673	27.888	30.324	33.003
17	18.430	20.012	21.762	23.698	25.840	28.213	30.840	33.750	36.974
18	19.615	21.412	23.414	25.645	28.132	30.906	33.999	37.450	41.301
19	20.811	22.841	25.117	27.671	30.539	33.760	37.379	41.446	46.018
20	22.019	24.297	26.870	29.778	33.066	36.786	40.995	45.762	51.160
21	23.239	25.783	28.676	31.969	35.719	39.993	44.865	50.423	56.765
22	24.472	27.299	30.537	34.248	38.505	43.392	49.006	55.457	62.873
23	25.716	28.845	32.453	36.618	41.430	46.996	53.436	60.893	69.532
24	26.973	30.422	34.426	39.083	44.502	50.816	58.177	66.765	76.790
25	28.243	32.030	36.459	41.646	47.727	54.865	63.249	73.106	84.701
30	34.785	40.568	47.575	56.085	66.439	79.058	94.461	113.28	136.31
40	48.886	60.402	75.401	95.026	120.80	154.76	199.64	259.06	337.88
50	64.463	84.579	112.80	152.67	209.35	290.34	406.53	573.77	815.08
60	81.670	114.05	163.05	237.99	353.58	533.13	813.52	1253.2	1944.8

Continued on next page

10%	12%	14%	15%	16%	18%	20%	24%	28%	32%	36%
1.0000	1.0000	1.0000	1.0000	1.0000	1.0000	1.0000	1.0000	1.0000	1.0000	1.0000
2.1000	2.1200	2.1400	2.1500	2.1600	2.1800	2.2000	2.2400	2.2800	2.3200	2.3600
3.3100	3.3744	3.4396	3.4725	3.5056	3.5724	3.6400	3.7776	3.9184	4.0624	4.2096
4.6410	4.7793	4.9211	4.9934	5.0665	5.2154	5.3680	5.6842	6.0156	6.3624	6.7251
6.1051	6.3528	6.6101	6.7424	6.8771	7.1542	7.4416	8.0484	8.6999	9.3983	10.146
7.7156	8.1152	8.5355	8.7537	8.9775	9.4420	9.9299	10.980	12.136	13.406	14.799
9.4872	10.089	10.730	11.067	11.414	12.142	12.916	14.615	16.534	18.696	21.126
11.436	12.300	13.233	13.727	14.240	15.327	16.499	19.123	22.163	25.678	29.732
13.579	14.776	16.085	16.786	17.519	19.086	20.799	24.712	29.369	34.895	41.435
15.937	17.549	19.337	20.304	21.321	23.521	25.959	31.643	38.593	47.062	57.352
18.531	20.655	23.045	24.349	25.733	28.755	32.150	40.238	50.398	63.122	78.998
21.384	24.133	27.271	29.002	30.850	34.931	39.581	50.895	65.510	84.320	108.44
24.523	28.029	32.089	34.352	36.786	42.219	48.497	64.110	84.853	112.30	148.47
27.975	32.393	37.581	40.505	43.672	50.818	59.196	80.496	109.61	149.24	202.93
31.772	37.280	43.842	47.580	51.660	60.965	72.035	100.82	141.30	198.00	276.98
35.950	42.753	50.980	55.717	60.925	72.939	87.442	126.01	181.87	262.36	377.69
40.545	48.884	59.118	65.075	71.673	87.068	105.93	157.25	233.79	347.31	514.66
45.599	55.750	68.394	75.836	84.141	103.74	128.12	195.99	300.25	459.45	700.94
51.159	63.440	78.969	88.212	98.603	123.41	154.74	244.03	385.32	607.47	954.28
57.275	72.052	91.025	102.44	115.38	146.63	186.69	303.60	494.21	802.86	1298.8
64.002	81.699	104.77	118.81	134.84	174.02	225.03	377.46	633.59	1060.8	1767.4
71.403	92.503	120.44	137.63	157.41	206.34	271.03	469.06	812.00	1401.2	2404.7
79.543	104.60	138.30	159.28	183.60	244.49	326.24	582.63	1040.4	1850.6	3271.3
88.497	118.16	158.66	184.17	213.98	289.49	392.48	723.46	1332.7	2443.8	4450.0
98.347	133.33	181.87	212.79	249.21	342.60	471.98	898.09	1706.8	3226.8	6053.0
164.49	241.33	356.79	434.75	530.31	790.95	1181.9	2640.9	5873.2	12941.	28172.
442.59	767.09	1342.0	1779.1	2360.8	4163.2	7343.9	22729.	69377.	*	*
1163.9	2400.0	4994.5	7217.7	10436.	21813.	45497.	*	*	*	*
3043.8	7471.6	18535.	29220.	46058.	*	*	*	*	*	*

*The factor is greater than 99,999.

TABLE A.5 >> Cumulative normal distribution

d	N(*d*)	*d*	N(*d*)	*d*	N(*d*)	*d*	N(*d*)	*d*	N(*d*)	*d*	N(*d*)
−3.00	.0013	−1.58	.0571	−0.76	.2236	0.06	.5239	0.86	.8051	1.66	.9515
−2.95	.0016	−1.56	.0594	−0.74	.2297	0.08	.5319	0.88	.8106	1.68	.9535
−2.90	.0019	−1.54	.0618	−0.72	.2358	0.10	.5398	0.90	.8159	1.70	.9554
−2.85	.0022	−1.52	.0643	−0.70	.2420	0.12	.5478	0.92	.8212	1.72	.9573
−2.80	.0026	−1.50	.0668	−0.68	.2483	0.14	.5557	0.94	.8264	1.74	.9591
−2.75	.0030	−1.48	.0694	−0.66	.2546	0.16	.5636	0.96	.8315	1.76	.9608
−2.70	.0035	−1.46	.0721	−0.64	.2611	0.18	.5714	0.98	.8365	1.78	.9625
−2.65	.0040	−1.44	.0749	−0.62	.2676	0.20	.5793	1.00	.8414	1.80	.9641
−2.60	.0047	−1.42	.0778	−0.60	.2743	0.22	.5871	1.02	.8461	1.82	.9656
−2.55	.0054	−1.40	.0808	−0.58	.2810	0.24	.5948	1.04	.8508	1.84	.9671
−2.50	.0062	−1.38	.0838	−0.56	.2877	0.26	.6026	1.06	.8554	1.86	.9686
−2.45	.0071	−1.36	.0869	−0.54	.2946	0.28	.6103	1.08	.8599	1.88	.9699
−2.40	.0082	−1.34	.0901	−0.52	.3015	0.30	.6179	1.10	.8643	1.90	.9713
−2.35	.0094	−1.32	.0934	−0.50	.3085	0.32	.6255	1.12	.8686	1.92	.9726
−2.30	.0107	−1.30	.0968	−0.48	.3156	0.34	.6331	1.14	.8729	1.94	.9738
−2.25	.0122	−1.28	.1003	−0.46	.3228	0.36	.6406	1.16	.8770	1.96	.9750
−2.20	.0139	−1.26	.1038	−0.44	.3300	0.38	.6480	1.18	.8810	1.98	.9761
−2.15	.0158	−1.24	.1075	−0.42	.3373	0.40	.6554	1.20	.8849	2.00	.9772
−2.10	.0179	−1.22	.1112	−0.40	.3446	0.42	.6628	1.22	.8888	2.05	.9798
−2.05	.0202	−1.20	.1151	−0.38	.3520	0.44	.6700	1.24	.8925	2.10	.9821
−2.00	.0228	−1.18	.1190	−0.36	.3594	0.46	.6773	1.26	.8962	2.15	.9842
−1.98	.0239	−1.16	.1230	−0.34	.3669	0.48	.6844	1.28	.8997	2.20	.9861
−1.96	.0250	−1.14	.1271	−0.32	.3745	0.50	.6915	1.30	.9032	2.25	.9878
−1.94	.0262	−1.12	.1314	−0.30	.3821	0.52	.6985	1.32	.9066	2.30	.9893
−1.92	.0274	−1.10	.1357	−0.28	.3897	0.54	.7054	1.34	.9099	2.35	.9906
−1.90	.0287	−1.08	.1401	−0.26	.3974	0.56	.7123	1.36	.9131	2.40	.9918
−1.88	.0301	−1.06	.1446	−0.24	.4052	0.58	.7191	1.38	.9162	2.45	.9929
−1.86	.0314	−1.04	.1492	−0.22	.4129	0.60	.7258	1.40	.9192	2.50	.9938
−1.84	.0329	−1.02	.1539	−0.20	.4207	0.62	.7324	1.42	.9222	2.55	.9946
−1.82	.0344	−1.00	.1587	−0.18	.4286	0.64	.7389	1.44	.9251	2.60	.9953
−1.80	.0359	−0.98	.1635	−0.16	.4365	0.66	.7454	1.46	.9279	2.65	.9960
−1.78	.0375	−0.96	.1685	−0.14	.4443	0.68	.7518	1.48	.9306	2.70	.9965
−1.76	.0392	−0.94	.1736	−0.12	.4523	0.70	.7580	1.50	.9332	2.75	.9970
−1.74	.0409	−0.92	.1788	−0.10	.4602	0.72	.7642	1.52	.9357	2.80	.9974
−1.72	.0427	−0.90	.1841	−0.08	.4681	0.74	.7704	1.54	.9382	2.85	.9978
−1.70	.0446	−0.88	.1894	−0.06	.4761	0.76	.7764	1.56	.9406	2.90	.9981
−1.68	.0465	−0.86	.1949	−0.04	.4841	0.78	.7823	1.58	.9429	2.95	.9984
−1.66	.0485	−0.84	.2005	−0.02	.4920	0.80	.7882	1.60	.9452	3.00	.9986
−1.64	.0505	−0.82	.2061	0.00	.5000	0.82	.7939	1.62	.9474	3.05	.9989
−1.62	.0526	−0.80	.2119	0.02	.5080	0.84	.7996	1.64	.9495		
−1.60	.0548	−0.78	.2177	0.04	.5160						

This table shows the probability [N(*d*)] of observing a value less than or equal to *d*. For example, as illustrated, if *d* is −.24, then N(*d*) is .4052.

APPENDIX B

Key Equations

Chapter 2

1. The balance sheet identity or equation:

$$\text{Assets} = \text{Liabilities} + \text{Shareholders' equity} \quad [2.1]$$

2. The income statement equation:

$$\text{Revenues} - \text{Expenses} = \text{Income} \quad [2.2]$$

3. The cash flow identity:

$$\text{Cash flow from assets} = \text{Cash flow to creditors} + \text{Cash flow to stockholders} \quad [2.3]$$

where

a. Cash flow from assets = Operating cash flow (OCF) − Net capital spending − Change in net working capital (NWC)
   (1) Operating cash flow = Earnings before interest and taxes (EBIT) + Depreciation − Taxes
   (2) Net capital spending = Ending net fixed assets − Beginning net fixed assets + Depreciation
   (3) Change in net working capital = Ending NWC − Beginning NWC

b. Cash flow to creditors = Interest paid − Net new borrowing

c. Cash flow to stockholders = Dividends paid − Net new equity raised

Chapter 3

1. The current ratio:

$$\text{Current ratio} = \frac{\text{Current assets}}{\text{Current liabilities}} \quad [3.1]$$

2. The quick or acid-test ratio:

$$\text{Quick ratio} = \frac{\text{Current assets} - \text{Inventory}}{\text{Current liabilities}} \quad [3.2]$$

3. The cash ratio:

$$\text{Cash ratio} = \frac{\text{Cash}}{\text{Current liabilities}} \quad [3.3]$$

4. The ratio of net working capital to total assets:

$$\text{Net working capital to total assets} = \frac{\text{Net working capital}}{\text{Total assets}} \quad [3.4]$$

5. The interval measure:

$$\text{Interval measure} = \frac{\text{Current assets}}{\text{Average daily operating costs}} \quad [3.5]$$

6. The total debt ratio:

$$\text{Total debt ratio} = \frac{\text{Total assets} - \text{Total equity}}{\text{Total assets}} \quad [3.6]$$

7. The debt-equity ratio:

$$\text{Debt-equity ratio} = \text{Total debt/Total equity} \quad [3.7]$$

8. The equity multiplier:

$$\text{Equity multiplier} = \text{Total assets/Total equity} \quad [3.8]$$

9. The long-term debt ratio:

$$\text{Long-term debt ratio} = \frac{\text{Long-term debt}}{\text{Long-term debt} + \text{Total equity}} \quad [3.9]$$

10. The times interest earned (TIE) ratio:

$$\text{Times interest earned ratio} = \frac{\text{EBIT}}{\text{Interest}} \quad [3.10]$$

11. The cash coverage ratio:

$$\text{Cash coverage ratio} = \frac{\text{EBIT} + \text{Depreciation}}{\text{Interest}} \quad [3.11]$$

12. The inventory turnover ratio:

$$\text{Inventory turnover} = \frac{\text{Cost of goods sold}}{\text{Inventory}} \quad [3.12]$$

13. The average days' sales in inventory:

$$\text{Days' sales in inventory} = \frac{365 \text{ days}}{\text{Inventory turnover}} \quad [3.13]$$

14. The receivables turnover ratio:

$$\text{Receivables turnover} = \frac{\text{Sales}}{\text{Accounts receivable}} \quad [3.14]$$

15. The days' sales in receivables:

$$\text{Days' sales in receivables} = \frac{365 \text{ days}}{\text{Receivables turnover}} \quad [3.15]$$

16. The net working capital (NWC) turnover ratio:

$$\text{NWC turnover} = \frac{\text{Sales}}{\text{NWC}} \quad [3.16]$$

17. The fixed asset turnover ratio:

$$\text{Fixed asset turnover} = \frac{\text{Sales}}{\text{Net fixed assets}} \qquad \textbf{[3.17]}$$

18. The total asset turnover ratio:

$$\text{Total asset turnover} = \frac{\text{Sales}}{\text{Total assets}} \qquad \textbf{[3.18]}$$

19. Profit margin:

$$\text{Profit margin} = \frac{\text{Net income}}{\text{Sales}} \qquad \textbf{[3.19]}$$

20. Return on assets (ROA):

$$\text{Return on assets} = \frac{\text{Net income}}{\text{Total assets}} \qquad \textbf{[3.20]}$$

21. Return on equity (ROE):

$$\text{Return on equity} = \frac{\text{Net income}}{\text{Total equity}} \qquad \textbf{[3.21]}$$

22. The price-earnings (PE) ratio:

$$\text{PE ratio} = \frac{\text{Price per share}}{\text{Earnings per share}} \qquad \textbf{[3.22]}$$

23. The market-to-book ratio:

$$\text{Market-to-book ratio} = \frac{\text{Market value per share}}{\text{Book value per share}} \qquad \textbf{[3.23]}$$

24. The Du Pont identity:

$$\text{ROE} = \underbrace{\frac{\text{Net income}}{\text{Sales}} \times \frac{\text{Sales}}{\text{Assets}}}_{\text{Return on assets}} \times \frac{\text{Assets}}{\text{Equity}} \qquad \textbf{[3.24]}$$

$$\text{ROE} = \text{Profit margin} \times \text{Total asset turnover} \times \text{Equity multiplier}$$

Chapter 4

1. The dividend payout ratio:

$$\text{Dividend payout ratio} = \text{Cash dividends}/\text{Net income} \qquad \textbf{[4.1]}$$

2. The internal growth rate:

$$\text{Internal growth rate} = \frac{\text{ROA} \times b}{1 - \text{ROA} \times b} \qquad \textbf{[4.2]}$$

3. The sustainable growth rate:

$$\text{Sustainable growth rate} = \frac{\text{ROE} \times b}{1 - \text{ROE} \times b} \qquad \textbf{[4.3]}$$

4. The capital intensity ratio:

$$\text{Capital intensity ratio} = \frac{\text{Total assets}}{\text{Sales}} = \frac{1}{\text{Total asset turnover}}$$

Chapter 5

1. The future value of \$1 invested for t periods at rate of r per period:

$$\text{Future value} = \$1 \times (1 + r)^t \qquad \textbf{[5.1]}$$

2. The present value of \$1 to be received t periods in the future at a discount rate of r:

$$\text{PV} = \$1 \times [1/(1 + r)^t] = \$1/(1 + r)^t \qquad \textbf{[5.2]}$$

3. The relationship between future value and present value (the basic present value equation):

$$\text{PV} \times (1 + r)^t = \text{FV}_t$$
$$\text{PV} = \text{FV}_t/(1 + r)^t = \text{FV}_t \times [1/(1 + r)^t] \qquad \textbf{[5.3]}$$

Chapter 6

1. The present value of an annuity of C dollars per period for t periods when the rate of return or interest rate is r:

$$\text{Annuity present value} = C \times \left(\frac{1 - \text{Present value factor}}{r}\right) = C \times \left\{\frac{1 - [1/(1 + r)^t]}{r}\right\} \qquad \textbf{[6.1]}$$

2. The future value factor for an annuity:

$$\text{Annuity FV factor} = (\text{Future value factor} - 1)/r = [(1 + r)^t - 1]/r \qquad \textbf{[6.2]}$$

3. Annuity due value = Ordinary annuity value $\times (1 + r)$ **[6.3]**

4. Present value for a perpetuity:

$$\text{PV for a perpetuity} = C/r = C \times (1/r) \qquad \textbf{[6.4]}$$

5. Effective annual rate (EAR), where m is the number of times the interest is compounded during the year:

$$\text{EAR} = [1 + (\text{Quoted rate}/m)]^m - 1 \qquad \textbf{[6.5]}$$

6. Effective annual rate (EAR), where q stands for the continuously compounded quoted rate:

$$\text{EAR} = e^q - 1 \qquad \textbf{[6.6]}$$

Chapter 7

1. Bond value if bond has (1) a face value of F paid at maturity, (2) a coupon of C paid per period, (3) t periods to maturity, and (4) a yield of r per period:

$$\text{Bond value} = C \times [1 - 1/(1 + r)^t]/r + F/(1 + r)^t \qquad \textbf{[7.1]}$$

$$\text{Bond value} = \text{Present value of the coupons} + \text{Present value of the face amount}$$

2. The Fisher effect:

$$1 + R = (1 + r) \times (1 + h) \qquad \textbf{[7.2]}$$
$$R = r + h + r \times h \qquad \textbf{[7.3]}$$
$$R \approx r + h \qquad \textbf{[7.4]}$$

Chapter 8

1. The dividend growth model:

$$P_0 = \frac{D_0 \times (1 + g)}{R - g} = \frac{D_1}{R - g} \quad [8.3]$$

2. Required return:

$$R = D_1/P_0 + g \quad [8.5]$$

Chapter 9

1. Net present value (NPV):

   NPV = Present value of future cash flows − Investment cost

2. Payback period:

   Payback period = Number of years that pass before the sum of an investment's cash flows equals the cost of the investment

3. Discounted payback period:

   Discounted payback period = Number of years that pass before the sum of an investment's *discounted* cash flows equals the cost of the investment

4. The average accounting return (AAR):

$$\text{AAR} = \frac{\text{Average net income}}{\text{Average book value}}$$

5. Internal rate of return (IRR):

   IRR = Discount rate of required return such that the net present value of an investment is zero

6. Profitability index:

$$\text{Profitability index} = \frac{\text{PV of cash flows}}{\text{Cost of investment}}$$

Chapter 10

1. Bottom-up approach to operating cash flow (OCF):

   OCF = Net income + Depreciation **[10.1]**

2. Top-down approach to operating cash flow (OCF):

   OCF = Sales − Costs − Taxes **[10.2]**

3. Tax shield approach to operating cash flow (OCF):

   OCF = (Sales − Costs) × $(1 - T)$ + Depreciation × T **[10.3]**

Chapter 11

1. Accounting break-even level:

$$Q = (\text{FC} + D)/(P - v) \quad [11.1]$$

2. Relationship between operating cash flow (OCF) and sales volume:

$$Q = (\text{FC} + \text{OCF})/(P - v) \quad [11.3]$$

3. Cash break-even level:

$$Q = \text{FC}/(P - v)$$

4. Financial break-even level:

$$Q = (\text{FC} + \text{OCF*})/(P - v)$$

   where

   OCF* = Zero NPV cash flow

5. Degree of operating leverage (DOL):

   DOL = 1 + FC/OCF **[11.4]**

Chapter 12

1. Variance of returns, Var(R) or σ^2:

$$\text{Var}(R) = \frac{1}{T - 1}[(R_1 - \bar{R})^2 + \cdots + (R_T - \bar{R})^2] \quad [12.3]$$

2. Standard deviation of returns, SD(R) or σ:

$$\text{SD}(R) = \sqrt{\text{Var}(R)}$$

Chapter 13

1. Risk premium:

   Risk premium = Expected return − Risk-free rate **[13.1]**

2. Expected return on a portfolio:

$$E(R_P) = x_1 \times E(R_1) + x_2 \times E(R_2) + \cdots + x_n \times E(R_n) \quad [13.2]$$

3. The reward-to-risk ratio:

$$\text{Reward-to-risk ratio} = \frac{E[R_i] - R_f}{\beta_i}$$

4. The capital asset pricing model (CAPM):

$$E(R_i) = R_f + [E(R_M) - R_f] \times \beta_i \quad [13.7]$$

Chapter 14

1. Value of a call option at maturity:
   a. $C_1 = 0$ if $(S_1 - E) \le 0$ **[14.1]**
   b. $C_1 = S_1 - E$ if $(S_1 - E) > 0$ **[14.2]**

2. Bounds on the value of a call option:
   a. Upper bound:
   $C_0 \le S_0$ **[14.3]**
   b. Lower bound:
   $C_0 \ge 0$ if $S_0 - E < 0$
   $C_0 \ge S_0 - E$ if $S_0 - E \ge 0$ **[14.4]**

3. $S_0 = C_0 + E/(1 + R_f)$
   $C_0 = S_0 - E/(1 + R_f)$ **[14.5]**

4. Value of a call that is certain to finish in-the-money:

   Call option value
   = Stock value
   − Present value of the exercise price

$$C_0 = S_0 - E/(1 + R_f)^t \quad [14.6]$$

Chapter 15

1. Required return on equity, R_E (dividend growth model):

$$R_E = D_1/P_0 + g \quad [15.1]$$

2. Required return on equity, R_E (CAPM):

   $$R_E = R_f + \beta_E \times (R_M - R_f) \quad [15.2]$$

3. Required return on preferred stock, R_P:

   $$R_P = D/P_0 \quad [15.3]$$

4. The weighted average cost of capital (WACC):

   $$\text{WACC} = (E/V) \times R_E + (D/V) \times R_D \times (1 - T_C) \quad [15.6]$$

5. Weighted average flotation cost, f_A:

   $$f_A = \frac{E}{V} \times f_E + \frac{D}{V} \times f_D \quad [15.8]$$

Chapter 16

1. Rights offerings:
   a. Number of new shares:

   $$\text{Number of new shares} = \frac{\text{Funds to be raised}}{\text{Subscription price}} \quad [16.1]$$

   b. Number of rights needed:

   $$\text{Number of rights needed to buy a share of stock} = \frac{\text{Old shares}}{\text{New shares}} \quad [16.2]$$

   c. Value of a right:
   Value of a right = Rights-on price − Ex-rights price

Chapter 17

1. Modigliani-Miller Propositions (no taxes):
   a. Proposition I:
   $V_L = V_U$
   b. Proposition II:
   $$R_E = R_A + (R_A - R_D) \times (D/E) \quad [17.1]$$
2. Modigliani-Miller propositions (with taxes):
   a. Value of the interest tax shield:
   $$\text{Value of the interest tax shield} = (T_C \times R_D \times D)/R_D = T_C \times D \quad [17.2]$$
   b. Proposition I:
   $$V_L = V_U + T_C \times D \quad [17.3]$$
   c. Proposition II:
   $$R_E = R_U + (R_U - R_D) \times (D/E) \times (1 - T_C) \quad [17.4]$$

Chapter 19

1. The operating cycle:

   $$\text{Operating cycle} = \text{Inventory period} + \text{Accounts receivable period} \quad [19.4]$$

2. The cash cycle:

   $$\text{Cash cycle} = \text{Operating cycle} - \text{Accounts payable period} \quad [19.5]$$

Chapter 20

1. Float measurement:
   a. Average daily float:

   $$\text{Average daily float} = \frac{\text{Total float}}{\text{Total days}} \quad [20.1]$$

   b. Average daily float:
   $$\text{Average daily float} = \text{Average daily receipts} \times \text{Weighted average delay} \quad [20.2]$$
2. The Baumol-Allais-Tobin (BAT) model:
   a. Opportunity costs:
   $$\text{Opportunity costs} = (C/2) \times R \quad [20A.1]$$
   b. Trading costs:
   $$\text{Trading costs} = (T/C) \times F \quad [20A.2]$$
   c. Total cost:
   $$\text{Total cost} = \text{Opportunity costs} + \text{Trading costs} \quad [20A.3]$$
   d. The optimal initial cash balance:
   $$C^* = \sqrt{(2T \times F)/R} \quad [20A.4]$$
3. The Miller-Orr model:
   a. The optimal cash balance:
   $$C^* = L + (3/4 \times F \times \sigma^2/R)^{1/3} \quad [20A.5]$$
   b. The upper limit:
   $$U^* = 3 \times C^* - 2 \times L \quad [20A.6]$$

Chapter 21

1. The size of receivables:

   $$\text{Accounts receivable} = \text{Average daily sales} \times \text{ACP} \quad [21.1]$$

2. NPV of switching credit terms:
   a. Present value of switching:
   $$\text{PV} = [(P - v)(Q' - Q)]/R \quad [21.4]$$
   b. Cost of switching:
   $$\text{Cost of switching} = PQ + v(Q' - Q) \quad [21.5]$$
   c. NPV of switching:
   $$\text{NPV of switching} = -[PQ + v(Q' - Q)] + (P - v) \times (Q' - Q)/R \quad [21.6]$$
3. NPV of granting credit:
   a. With no repeat business:
   $$\text{NPV} = -v + (1 - \pi)P/(1 + R) \quad [21.8]$$
   b. With repeat business:
   $$\text{NPV} = -v + (1 - \pi)(P - v)/R \quad [21.9]$$
4. The economic order quantity (EOQ) model:
   a. Total carrying costs:
   $$\text{Total carrying costs} = \text{Average inventory} \times \text{Carrying costs per unit} = (Q/2) \times \text{CC} \quad [21.10]$$
   b. Total restocking costs:
   $$\text{Total restocking costs} = \text{Fixed cost per order} \times \text{Number of orders} = F \times (T/Q) \quad [21.11]$$

c. Total costs:

$$\text{Total costs} = \text{Carrying costs} + \text{Restocking costs} = (Q/2) \times \text{CC} + F \times (T/Q) \quad [21.12]$$

d. The optimal order size Q^*:

$$Q^* = \sqrt{\frac{2T \times F}{\text{CC}}} \quad [21.16]$$

Chapter 22

1. Purchasing power parity (PPP):

$$\text{E}(S_t) = S_0 \times [1 + (h_{FC} - h_{US})]^t \quad [22.3]$$

2. Interest rate parity (IRP):

a. Exact, single period:

$$F_1/S_0 = (1 + R_{FC})/(1 + R_{US}) \quad [22.4]$$

b. Approximate, multiperiod:

$$F_t = S_0 \times [1 + (R_{FC} - R_{US})]^t \quad [22.7]$$

3. Uncovered interest parity (UIP):

$$\text{E}(S_t) = S_0 \times [1 + (R_{FC} - R_{US})]^t \quad [22.9]$$

4. International Fisher effect (IFE):

$$R_{US} - h_{US} = R_{FC} - h_{FC} \quad [22.10]$$

Chapter 24

1. Put-call parity condition:

$$S + P = \text{PV}(E) + C \quad [24.2]$$

2. The Black-Scholes call option formula:

$$\text{C} = S \times \text{N}(d_1) - E \times e^{-Rt} \times \text{N}(d_2) \quad [24.5]$$

where

$$d_1 = [1n(S/E) + (R + \sigma^2/2) \times t]/(\sigma \times \sqrt{t})$$
$$d_2 = d_1 - \sigma \times \sqrt{t} \quad [24.6]$$

3. Value of a risk-free bond:

Value of risky bond + put option **[24.7]**

Chapter 25

1. The NPV of a merger:

$$\text{NPV} = V_B^* - \text{Cost to Firm A of the acquisition} \quad [25.1]$$

APPENDIX

C >>Answers to Selected End-of-Chapter Problems

Chapter 2

2.2 Net income = \$126,100

2.6 Taxes = \$89,720

2.10 Change in NWC = −\$120

2.14 **a.** OCF = \$41,260
b. Cash flow to creditors = \$21,500
c. Cash flow to stockholders = \$2,250
d. Change in NWC = \$5,510

2.18 **a.** Tax_{growth} = \$17,150
Tax_{income} = \$2,890,000
b. \$3,400

2.22 **a.** Owners' equity:
2003 = \$1,785
2004 = \$2,095
b. Change in NWC = \$30
c. Fixed assets sold = \$200
Cash flow from assets = \$1,918
d. Debt retired = \$80
Cash flow to creditors = −\$4

2.26 Cash flow from assets = \$301.12
Cash flow to creditors = −\$867.00
Cash flow to stockholders = \$1,168.12

Chapter 3

3.2 Net income = \$2.61 million
ROA = 7.05%
ROE = 10.88%

3.6 EPS = \$2.61
DPS = \$0.89
BVPS = \$36.11
Market-to-book ratio = 2.16 times
PE ratio = 29.87 times

3.10 82.19 days

3.18 Net income = \$94.80

3.22 Firm A ROE = 50.00%
Firm B ROE = 50.00%

3.26 **a.** 4.33 times; 3.59 times
b. 1.78 times; 1.47 times
c. .45 times; .39 times
d. 1.22 times
e. 3.87 times
f. 13.35 times
g. .29; .26
h. .40; .36
i. 1.40; 1.36
j. 25.82 times
k. 29.90 times
l. 23.41%
m. 28.53%
n. 38.80%

Chapter 4

4.2 EFN = −\$1,035

4.6 Internal growth rate = 5.15%

4.12 Internal growth rate = 8.70%

4.16 Maximum sales growth = 17.65%

4.20 TAT = 1.47 times

4.22 Sustainable growth rate = 22.50%
New borrowing = \$19,125
Internal growth rate = 7.20%

4.28 Maximum sustainable growth rate = 14.33%

Chapter 5

5.2 \$13,761
\$25,320
\$169,152
\$315,796

5.6 10.27%

5.10 \$130,258,959

5.14 \$0.10

5.18 \$145,781
\$56,205

Chapter 6

6.2 @ 5%: PV_x = \$28,431.29
PV_y = \$25,976.86
@ 22%: PV_x = \$15,145.14
PV_y = \$17,181.84

6.6 PV = \$456,262.25

6.10 PV = \$187,500

6.14 1st National: EAR = 12.91%
1st United: EAR = 12.78%

6.18 \$12,405.67

6.22 APR = 1,733.33%
EAR = 313,916,515.69%

6.26 PV = $18,407.91

6.30 7.70% semiannual
3.78% quarterly
1.24% monthly

6.38 G: 11.20%
H: 12.06%

6.42 Balloon payment = $356,387.10

6.46 Profit = $7,700.77
Break-even = 16.89%

6.50 PV = $29,700.29

6.54 $1,361.82

6.58 PV of lease payments = $14,361.31
PV of purchase = $16,893.14
Break-even resale price = $26,216.03

6.60 EAR = 13.64%

6.64 Refundable fee:
APR = 7.58%
EAR = 7.85%
Nonrefundable fee:
APR = 7.50%
EAR = 7.76%

6.70 10.57%

6.74 C = $21,623.50

Chapter 7

7.4 11.09%

7.8 9.16%

7.12 8.52%

7.26 **a.** 15,000 coupon bonds; 114,181 zeroes
b. $16,050,000; $114,181,000

7.28 P: Current yield = 9.26%
Capital gains yield = −1.26%
D: Current yield = 6.52%
Capital gains yield = 1.48%

Chapter 8

8.2 11.46%

8.6 $3.96

8.10 $38.04

8.14 $2.75

8.18 Close = $72.80
Net income = $133,928,571

8.22 $59.51

Chapter 9

9.4 **a.** 1.32 years
b. 2.20 years
c. 3.14 years

9.8 @ 11%: NPV = $7,423.84
@ 30%: NPV = −$1,324.53

9.12 **a.** IRR_A = 16.60%
IRR_B = 15.72%
b. NPV_A = $3,491.88
NPV_B = $4,298.06
c. Crossover rate = 13.75%

9.16 **a.** PI_I = 1.243
PI_{II} = 1.393
b. NPV_I = $7,302.78
NPV_{II} = $1,963.19

9.20 **a.** $C = I/N$
b. $C > I/\text{PVIFA}_{R\%,\,N}$
c. $C = 2.0*I/\text{PVIFA}_{R\%,\,N}$

Chapter 10

10.2 Annual sales = $366.5 million

10.8 $1,927,464

10.12 CF_0 = −$3,000,000
CF_1 = $1,250,968.50
CF_2 = $1,355,958.00
CF_3 = $1,582,573.50
NPV = $153,665.62

10.16 −$97,646.27

10.22 $0.03614

Chapter 11

11.2 Total costs = $5,997,500
Marginal cost = $34.65
Average cost = $39.98
Minimum revenue = $346,500

11.8 D = $612,200
P = $88.22
VC = $56.62

11.12 OCF = $68,750
DOL = 3.18

11.18 DOL = 1.3371
DOL_A = 2.8095

11.22 $\Delta NPV/\Delta P$ = $141,514
$\Delta NPV/\Delta Q$ = $977.73

11.28 DOL = 1.4327
ΔOCF = +3.5817%

Chapter 12

12.2 R_d = +2.73%; R_c = +12.50%

12.6 2.72%; 3.11%

12.16 $R_A = 11.13\%$
$R_G = 10.62\%$

12.20 27.16%

Chapter 13

13.2 $E(R_P) = 14.06\%$

13.6 $E(R_I) = 12.50\%$

13.10 **a.** $E(R_P) = 13.29\%$
b. $\sigma_P^2 = .03171$
$\sigma_P = 17.81\%$

13.14 $\beta_i = 1.67$

13.18 Slope = .0846

13.24 $C = \$343,333$
$R_F = \$206,667$

13.26 $\beta_I = 3.07$
$\sigma_I = 12.15\%$
$\beta_{II} = 0.65$
$\sigma_{II} = 20.39\%$

Chapter 14

14.4 **a.** \$13.96
b. \$2.31

14.8 **a.** $D_0 = \$912.82$
b. $E_0 = \$419.55$

14.12 Warrant price = \$4.09

14.16 **a.** \$1,309,942.84
b. \$1,072,212.80

Chapter 15

15.2 14.25%

15.4 $R_A = 15.14\%$; $R_G = 14.86\%$

15.8 Book value = \$100 million
Market value = \$68 million
Aftertax cost = 5.48%

15.12 **a.** $E/V = 0.2603$
$D/V = 0.7397$
b. $E/V = 0.7978$
$D/V = 0.2022$

15.16 **a.** $D/V = 0.2431$
$P/V = 0.0904$
$E/V = 0.6665$
b. 13.58%

15.20 Break-even cost = \$42,385,321

Chapter 16

16.2 **a.** \$40; anything > 0
b. 1,428,571; 3.64
c. \$39.82; \$1.08

16.6 804,348

16.8 No change;
Declines by \$0.83;
Declines by \$3.33

16.14 \$12,711

Chapter 17

17.2 **a.** EPS = \$1.46; \$3.64; \$4.73
b. EPS = \$1.13; \$4.77; \$6.59

17.6 **a.** EPS = \$7.59, \$8.06, \$7.14
b. EBIT = \$7,700
c. EBIT = \$7,700
d. EBIT = \$7,700

17.10 \$4.55 million

17.12 **a.** 18.30%
b. 15.19%
c. 20.40%, 16.20%, 12.00%

17.16 $V = \$187,000$

Chapter 18

18.4 **a.** \$39.00
b. \$56.52
c. \$45.61
d. \$113.75
e. 250,000; 172,500; 213,750; 85,714

18.8 Shares outstanding = 392,000
Capital surplus = \$2,448,000

18.12 **a.** \$720,000
b. No dividend paid

18.18 **a.** D
b. $.72D$
c. $1.0625D$
d. Price drop = $1.377D$

Chapter 19

19.4 **a.** *I*, *I*
b. *I*, *N*
c. *D*, *D*
d. *D*, *D*
e. *D*, *N*
f. *I*, *I*

19.8 **a.** \$189.00; \$213.00; \$235.50; \$186.30
b. \$162.00; \$189.00; \$213.00; \$235.50
c. \$171.00; \$197.00; \$220.50; \$219.10

19.10 **a.** \$106,666.67
b. \$117,142.86
c. \$136,928.57
\$160,021.43
\$183,200.00

19.16 **a.** 5.523%
b. 5.538%

Chapter 20

20.2 **a.** $100,000
−$80,000
$20,000
b. −$40,000
$60,000

20.6 **a.** $23,083
b. 2.43 days
c. $23,083
d. $4.28
e. $14,250

20.10 NPV = $7.9 million
Net savings = $395,000

Appendix 20A

20A.2 $1,195.23

20A.4 **a.** Opportunity cost = $9.00
Trading cost = $333.33
b. $1,825.74

20A.10 8.68%

Chapter 21

21.2 $8,547,945

21.6 Sales = $322,885
Accounts receivable turnover = 7.019

21.10 NPV = $473,458.33

21.12 Carrying cost = $4,590
Order cost = $7,800
EOQ = 234.65
Orders = 39.89 per year

21.16 2,953.57

Appendix 21A

21A.2 **a.** 2/10, net 30
b. $270,000
d. NPV = −$2,473,200
Break-even price = $101.00
Break-even discount = 10.89%

21A.4 **b.** $58.80
c. NPV = −$353,701.09

Chapter 22

22.6 Great Britain: 4.06%
Japan: 1.54%
Switzerland: 1.90%

22.10 **b.** Krone 6.5257

22.12 **b.** −4.61%

Chapter 23

23.2 Loss = $1,315.00
Profit = $1,635.00

Chapter 24

24.2 $7,633.79

24.6 3.89%

24.10 Call delta = 0.64
Put delta = −0.36

24.14 $3.22

24.16 $5.98

24.20 Equity = $5,930.64
Debt = $16,069.36
Cost of debt = 21.88%

24.22 **a.** $11,876,514.69
b. $10,123,485.31
c. 10.86%
d. $12,481,437.06
e. 10.72%

24.24 **a.** $44,449.09
b. $15,697.93
c. $28,751.16; 14.71%
d. $25,111.66; 17.42%
e. Bondholders lose $3,639.51
Stockholders gain $3,639.51

24.30 One

Chapter 25

25.8 EPS = $4.875
PE = 16.15 times

Chapter 26

26.2 NAL = −$20,187.17

26.6 −$4,787.24

A

B

C

D

E

F

G

H

I

J

K

L

M

O

P

R

S

T

W

Z

A

B

C

D

E

F

G

H

I

L

M

N

O

P

Note: Key terms are in **boldface.**

A

C

D

F

G

K

L

M

P

S

U

V